Handbook of Energy Governance in Europe

Michèle Knodt • Jörg Kemmerzell
Editors

Handbook of Energy Governance in Europe

Volume 2

With 145 Figures and 78 Tables

Editors
Michèle Knodt
Institute of Political Science
Technical University of Darmstadt
Darmstadt, Germany

Jörg Kemmerzell
Institute of Political Science
Technical University of Darmstadt
Darmstadt, Germany

ISBN 978-3-030-43249-2   ISBN 978-3-030-43250-8 (eBook)
https://doi.org/10.1007/978-3-030-43250-8

© Springer Nature Switzerland AG 2022
This work is subject to copyright. All rights are reserved by the Publisher, whether the whole or part of the material is concerned, specifically the rights of translation, reprinting, reuse of illustrations, recitation, broadcasting, reproduction on microfilms or in any other physical way, and transmission or information storage and retrieval, electronic adaptation, computer software, or by similar or dissimilar methodology now known or hereafter developed.
The use of general descriptive names, registered names, trademarks, service marks, etc. in this publication does not imply, even in the absence of a specific statement, that such names are exempt from the relevant protective laws and regulations and therefore free for general use.
The publisher, the authors, and the editors are safe to assume that the advice and information in this book are believed to be true and accurate at the date of publication. Neither the publisher nor the authors or the editors give a warranty, expressed or implied, with respect to the material contained herein or for any errors or omissions that may have been made. The publisher remains neutral with regard to jurisdictional claims in published maps and institutional affiliations.

This Springer imprint is published by the registered company Springer Nature Switzerland AG
The registered company address is: Gewerbestrasse 11, 6330 Cham, Switzerland

Preface

We started working on the *Handbook of Energy Governance in Europe* in a workshop with the first 15 authors in December 2017, began publishing the first chapters online in March 2019, and have continued to do so ever since. As one can imagine, the project did not remain untouched by the global Covid 19 pandemic. Originally, we had planned to complete the work on this handbook by the end of 2020, but unfortunately, this was impossible due to delays in contributions, authors dropping out, and other issues related to the pandemic. Therefore, we could not realize some of the originally planned chapters, for example on the governance of European energy networks or a couple of additional countries. Among them is the chapter on Ukraine that could not be realized due to the dreadful political circumstances.

We finished working on this handbook in February 2022 with the acceptance of the last chapters. Therefore, we were not able to consider the developments in energy governance caused by the Russian war of aggression against Ukraine beginning in late February 2022 after the completion of the handbook, which will have undoubtedly radical consequences for both the European energy architecture and national energy strategies. Several developments are conceivable. Very likely there will be a vast reduction or a cut in energy relations between most European countries and Russia, which will change the geopolitics of energy significantly. Also likely seems a strengthening of the European Union as a strategic actor. Other developments are more in the balance – e.g., the reduction of natural gas supply may cause an at least temporary comeback of coal in the energy mix of some countries. The expansion of renewable energy generation, green hydrogen, and biofuels will gain pace as nuclear power could be strengthened again. However, concrete developments in energy governance and policy will play out differently in different national contexts. And these contexts are shaped to a great deal, independently of external shocks, by the long-term developments and entrenched institutional structures that are presented in this handbook.

That we have been able to complete the handbook is due to the fruitful and instructive cooperation with more than 100 authors, as well as to the understanding and competent supervision of the project by Barbara Wolf and Esther Niederhammer from Springer. Our special thanks go to them. We would like to thank also the German Federal Ministry of Education and Research, which supported the handbook project within the Kopernikus projects ENavi (funding code: 03SFK4P0) and Ariadne (funding code: 03SFK5LO).

SPONSORED BY THE

Darmstadt, Germany
August 2022

Michèle Knodt
Jörg Kemmerzell
Editors

Acknowledgments

We would like to thank the German Federal Ministry of Education and Research for its financial support of this handbook. It has funded two Kopernikus projects in which the editors were involved: ENavi – Energy Transition Navigation System (funding code 03SFK4P0) and Ariadne – Evidence-Based Assessment for the Design of the German Energy System Transformation (funding code 03SFK5LO).

Contents

Volume 1

Part I Introduction 1

1 Energy Governance in Europe: Introduction 3
   Michèle Knodt and Jörg Kemmerzell

Part II Energy Governance Research: Theories, Issues, and Problems 17

2 Transition of Energy Systems: Patterns of
   Stability and Change 19
   Mario Neukirch

3 Energy Democracy and Participation in Energy Transitions 49
   Cornelia Fraune

4 Energy Poverty 67
   Christoph Strünck

5 Monitoring Energy Policy 77
   Jonas J. Schoenefeld and Tim Rayner

6 Extending Energy Policy: The Challenge of Sector Integration ... 101
   Michael Rodi and Michael Kalis

Part III European Governance 119

7 European Union Energy Policy: A Discourse Perspective 121
   Michèle Knodt and Marc Ringel

8 Energy Policies in the EU: A Fiscal Federalism Perspective 143
   Erik Gawel and Sebastian Strunz

9 The EU in Global Energy Governance 163
   Laima Eicke and Franziska Petri

10	EU Energy Cooperation with Emerging Powers: Brazil, India, China, and South Africa	189

Michèle Knodt, Roberto Schaeffer, Madhura Joshi, Lai Suetyi, and Agathe Maupin

11	EU-Russia Energy Relations	237

Marco Siddi

12	EU-US and EU-Canada Energy Relations	263

Petra Dolata

13	Energy Relations in the EU Eastern Partnership	287

Katharina Kleinschnitger, Michèle Knodt, Marie Lortz, and Anna K. Stöckl

14	Energy Relations of the EU and its Southern Neighborhood	315

Britta Daum

15	The Energy Charter Treaty: Old and New Dilemmas in Global Energy Governance	347

Anna Herranz-Surrallés

16	Sustainable Europe: Narrative Potential in the EU's Political Communication	367

Natalia Chaban and Jessica Bain

17	Clean Energy in the European Green Deal: Perspectives of European Stakeholders	383

Nils Bruch, Marc Ringel, and Michèle Knodt

18	Cities in European Energy and Climate Governance	411

Jörg Kemmerzell

Volume 2

Part IV	Country Studies	429

19	Energy Governance in Armenia	431

Shushanik Minasyan

20	Energy Governance in Austria	455

Niclas Wenz

21	Energy Governance in Azerbaijan	483

Murad Nasibov

22	Energy Governance in Belgium	511

Thijs Van de Graaf, Erik Laes, and Aviel Verbruggen

23	Energy Governance in Croatia	533
	Ana-Maria Boromisa	

24	Energy Governance in the Czech Republic	563
	Jan Osička, Veronika Zapletalová, Filip Černoch, and Tomáš Vlček	

25	Energy Governance in Denmark	593
	Helene Dyrhauge	

26	Energy Governance in Finland	619
	Mikael Hildén and Paula Kivimaa	

27	Energy Governance in France	647
	Pierre Bocquillon and Aurélien Evrard	

28	Energy Governance in Germany	667
	Jörg Kemmerzell	

29	Energy Governance in Greece	709
	Marula Tsagkari	

30	Energy Governance in Hungary	737
	John Szabo, Csaba Weiner, and András Deák	

31	Energy Governance in Ireland	769
	Diarmuid Torney	

32	Energy Governance in Italy	791
	Maria Rosaria Di Nucci and Daniele Russolillo	

33	Energy Governance in Latvia	823
	Sigita Urdze	

34	Energy Governance in Lithuania	841
	Šarūnas Liekis	

35	Energy Governance in the Netherlands	863
	Elisabeth Musch	

36	Energy Governance in Norway	897
	Elin Lerum Boasson and Torbjørg Jevnaker	

37	Energy Governance in the Republic of Poland	923
	Maksymilian Zoll	

38	Energy Governance in Portugal	959
	Luís Guerreiro, Helge Jörgens, and Vicente Alves	

39	Energy Governance in Romania	993
	Aron Buzogány and Simona Davidescu	

40	**Energy Governance in Russia: From a Fossil to a Green Giant?** .... 1019 Veli-Pekka Tynkkynen	
41	**Energy Governance in Serbia** .... 1037 Stefan Ćetković	
42	**Energy Governance in Slovakia** .... 1055 Matúš Mišík and Veronika Oravcová	
43	**Energy Governance in Slovenia** .... 1083 Danijel Crnčec	
44	**Energy Governance in Spain** .... 1121 Jose M. Campos-Martín, Laura Crespo, and Rosa M. Fernandez	
45	**Energy Governance in Sweden** .... 1157 Bengt Johansson	
46	**Energy Governance in Switzerland** .... 1187 Andreas Balthasar	
47	**Energy Governance in Turkey** .... 1217 Emre İşeri and Tuğçe Uygurtürk	
48	**Energy Governance in the United Kingdom** .... 1255 Matthew Lockwood, Catherine Mitchell, and Richard Hoggett	

Part V   Comparison and Conclusion **1287**

49	**Energy Governance in Europe: Country Comparison and Conclusion** .... 1289 Jörg Kemmerzell, Nils Bruch, and Michèle Knodt

Index 1319

About the Editors

Michèle Knodt is Professor of Political Science at the Technical University of Darmstadt, Jean Monnet Chair (ad personam) and Director of the Jean Monnet Centre of Excellence "EU in Global Dialogue" (CEDI), Director of the Jean Monnet Centre of Excellence "EU@School," Chair of the COST Network ENTER (EU Foreign Policy Facing New Realities), Co-leader of the Loewe-Excellence Centre "emergenCITY," Co-leader of the DFG Research Training Group "Critical Infrastructures," PI in the Kopernikus Project "Ariadne – Evidence-Based Assessment for the Design of the German Energy System Transformation," and leader of smaller cooperative and interdisciplinary projects. She has published widely on the EU, is especially interested in energy and climate governance, and has received research grants from the German Federal Ministry of Education and Research (BMBF), German Federal Ministry of Economic Affairs and Energy (BMWi), the German Research Council (DFG), the Volkswagen Foundation, and the European Commission.

Jörg Kemmerzell received his Ph.D. in Political Science from the Technical University of Darmstadt, Germany, in 2007. His research interests include energy and climate policy in multilevel systems, comparative politics and methods, and applied theory of democracy. He has published over 50 journal articles, books, and book chapters mostly on energy and climate policy and related topics. After finishing his Ph.D., Jörg Kemmerzell worked as a researcher and lecturer in Political Science at the Technical University of Darmstadt and the University of Hildesheim (Germany). Since 2012, he was a senior researcher in four research projects of the German Research Council (DFG) and the German Federal Ministry of Education and Research (BMBF), focusing on climate policy of cities and the assessment of the German energy transition. He worked also as a consultant for research communication. Since 2021, he is a senior lecturer in Political Science at the Technical University of Darmstadt and a research associate in the Kopernikus project "Ariadne – Evidence-Based Assessment for the Design of the German Energy System Transformation."

Contributors

Vicente Alves CIES_Iscte – Centre for Research and Studies in Sociology, Lisbon, Portugal

Jessica Bain School of Media, Communication and Sociology, University of Leicester, Leicester, UK

Andreas Balthasar University of Lucerne, Lucerne, Switzerland

Elin Lerum Boasson Department of Political Science, Center for International Climate Research, University of Oslo and CICERO, Oslo, Norway

Pierre Bocquillon School of Politics, Philosophy, Language & Communication Studies, University of East Anglia, Norwich, UK

Ana-Maria Boromisa Department for International Economic and Political Relations, Institute for Development and International Relations, Zagreb, Croatia

Nils Bruch Institute of Political Science, Technical University of Darmstadt, Darmstadt, Germany

Aron Buzogány Institute of Forest, Environmental, and Natural Resource Policy (InFER), University of Natural Resources and Life Sciences Vienna (BOKU), Vienna, Austria

Jose M. Campos-Martín Instituto de Catálisis y Petroleoquímica, CSIC, Madrid, Spain

Filip Černoch Center for Energy Studies, Masaryk University, Brno, Czech Republic

Stefan Ćetković Bavarian School of Public Policy, Technical University of Munich, Munich, Germany

Natalia Chaban Department of Media and Communication, University of Canterbury, Christchurch, New Zealand

Laura Crespo Centro de Estudios y Experimentación de Obras Públicas, CEDEX, Madrid, Spain

Danijel Crnčec Faculty of Social Sciences, University of Ljubljana, Ljubljana, Slovenia

Britta Daum Paris, France

Simona Davidescu University of York and ESSCA, Angers, York, UK

András Deák Institute of World Economics, Centre for Economic and Regional Studies, Budapest, Hungary

Institute of Strategic and Security Studies, National University of Public Service, Budapest, Hungary

Maria Rosaria Di Nucci Environmental Policy Research Centre, Freie Universität Berlin, Berlin, Germany

Petra Dolata Department of History, University of Calgary, Calgary, AB, Canada

Helene Dyrhauge Department for Social Sciences & Business, Roskilde University, Roskilde, Denmark

Laima Eicke Energy Systems and Societal Change, Institute for Advanced Sustainability Studies (IASS), Potsdam, Germany

Aurélien Evrard UFR Droit et Sciences Politiques, University of Nantes, Nantes, France

Rosa M. Fernandez Department of Social and Political Science, University of Chester, Chester, UK

Cornelia Fraune Institute of Political Science, Technical University of Darmstadt, Darmstadt, Germany

Erik Gawel Department of Economics, Helmholtz Centre for Environmental Research – UFZ, Leipzig, Germany

Institute for Infrastructure and Resources Management, Leipzig University, Leipzig, Germany

Luís Guerreiro CIES_Iscte – Centre for Research and Studies in Sociology, Lisbon, Portugal

Anna Herranz-Surrallés Faculty of Arts and Social Sciences, Maastricht University, Maastricht, The Netherlands

Mikael Hildén Finnish Environment Institute, SYKE, and the Strategic Research Council, Helsinki, Finland

Richard Hoggett Energy Policy Group, University of Exeter, Penryn, UK

Emre İşeri Department of International Relations, Yaşar University, İzmir, Turkey

Torbjørg Jevnaker Fridtjof Nansen Institute, Lysaker, Akershus, Norway

Bengt Johansson Environmental and Energy Systems Studies, Lund University, Lund, Sweden

Helge Jörgens CIES_Iscte – Centre for Research and Studies in Sociology, Lisbon, Portugal

Department of Political Science and Public Policy, Iscte – Instituto Universitário de Lisboa, Lisbon, Portugal

Madhura Joshi Natural Resources Defense Council, Delhi, India

Michael Kalis Institute for Climate Protection, Energy and Mobility (IKEM), Berlin, Germany

Interdisciplinary Centre for Baltic Sea Region Research, University of Greifswald, Greifswald, Germany

Jörg Kemmerzell Institute of Political Science, Technical University of Darmstadt, Darmstadt, Germany

Paula Kivimaa Finnish Environment Institute, SYKE, Helsinki, Finland

SPRU, University of Sussex, Brighton, UK

Katharina Kleinschnitger Institute of Political Science, Technical University of Darmstadt, Darmstadt, Germany

Michèle Knodt Institute of Political Science, Technical University of Darmstadt, Darmstadt, Germany

Erik Laes Sustainable Energy and Built Environment, VITO/EnergyVille, Genk, Belgium

School of Innovation Sciences, University of Eindhoven, Eindhoven, The Netherlands

Šarūnas Liekis School of Political Science and Diplomacy, Vytautas Magnus University, Kaunas, Lithuania

Matthew Lockwood Science Policy Research Unit, University of Sussex, Brighton, UK

Marie Lortz Institute of Political Science, Technical University of Darmstadt, Darmstadt, Germany

Agathe Maupin SAIIA – South African Institute of International Affairs, University of the Witwatersrand, Johannesburg, South Africa

Shushanik Minasyan Institute of Political Studies and Sociology, University of Bonn, Bonn, Germany

Matúš Mišík Department of Political Science, Comenius University in Bratislava, Bratislava, Slovakia

Catherine Mitchell Energy Policy Group, University of Exeter, Penryn, UK

Elisabeth Musch School of Cultural Studies and Social Sciences, University of Osnabrueck, Osnabrueck, Germany

Murad Nasibov Institute of Political Science, Justus-Liebig University of Giessen, Giessen, Germany

Mario Neukirch Institute for Social Sciences, University of Stuttgart, Stuttgart, Baden-Württemberg, Germany

Veronika Oravcová Department of Political Science, Comenius University in Bratislava, Bratislava, Slovakia

Jan Osička Center for Energy Studies, Masaryk University, Brno, Czech Republic

Franziska Petri Leuven International and European Studies, Faculty of Social Sciences, KU Leuven, Leuven, Belgium

Tim Rayner Tyndall Centre for Climate Change Research, University of East Anglia, Norwich, Norfolk, UK

Marc Ringel Nuertingen Geislingen University, Geislingen, Germany

Michael Rodi Institute for Climate Protection, Energy and Mobility (IKEM), Berlin, Germany

Faculty of Public Law, Finance Law, Environmental and Energy Law, University of Greifswald, Greifswald, Germany

Daniele Russolillo Institute for European Energy and Climate Policies, Amsterdam, The Netherlands

Roberto Schaeffer Energy Planning Program, COPPE, Universidade Federal do Rio de Janeiro, Centro de Technologia, Rio de Janeiro, Brazil

Jonas J. Schoenefeld Institute for Housing and Environment, Darmstadt, Germany

Tyndall Centre for Climate Change Research, University of East Anglia, Norwich, Norfolk, UK

Marco Siddi European Union Research Programme, Finnish Institute of International Affairs, Helsinki, Finland

Anna K. Stöckl Institute of Political Science, Technical University of Darmstadt, Darmstadt, Germany

Christoph Strünck Department of Social Sciences, University of Siegen, Siegen, Germany

Sebastian Strunz Department of Economics, Helmholtz Centre for Environmental Research – UFZ, Leipzig, Germany

Lai Suetyi Centre for European Studies of Guangdong University of Foreign Studies, Guangzhou, China

John Szabo Department of Environmental Sciences and Policy, Central European University, Budapest, Hungary

Institute of World Economics, Centre for Economic and Regional Studies, Budapest, Hungary

Diarmuid Torney School of Law and Government, Dublin City University, Dublin, Ireland

Marula Tsagkari Department of Economics, University of Barcelona, Barcelona, Spain

Veli-Pekka Tynkkynen Aleksanteri Institute, University of Helsinki, Helsinki, Finland

Sigita Urdze Institute of Political Science, Technical University of Darmstadt, Darmstadt, Germany

Tuğçe Uygurtürk Deparment of Economics, Yaşar University, İzmir, Turkey

Thijs Van de Graaf Department of Political Science, Ghent University, Ghent, Belgium

Aviel Verbruggen Department Engineering Management, Antwerp University, Antwerp, Belgium

Tomáš Vlček Center for Energy Studies, Masaryk University, Brno, Czech Republic

Csaba Weiner Institute of World Economics, Centre for Economic and Regional Studies, Budapest, Hungary

Niclas Wenz Institute of Political Science, Technical University of Darmstadt, Darmstadt, Germany

Veronika Zapletalová Center for Energy Studies, Masaryk University, Brno, Czech Republic

Maksymilian Zoll Institute of Political Science, Technical University of Darmstadt, Darmstadt, Germany

Part IV

Country Studies

Energy Governance in Armenia

19

Shushanik Minasyan

Contents

Introduction	432
General Conditions of Energy Governance in Armenia	434
Past Legacies	434
Energy Mix	437
Discourse on Energy Issues and Main Political Actors	439
Coordination, Instruments, and Issues of Armenian Energy Transition	441
Drivers of Energy Transition	441
Renewable Energy/Regulation Framework	442
Wind Energy	443
Solar	445
Hydropower Energy	446
Energy Efficiency	448
Outcomes, Challenges and Prospects for Energy Governance	450
Cross References	451
References	452

Abstract

Armenia's energy policy has seen enormous changes after becoming an independent state in 1991. Being a part of the unified all-union energy system of the then Soviet Union (USSR), the Armenian energy sector was deeply affected by numerous difficulties during political as well as market transition. In the past two decades, the Armenian energy sector has been modernized and deregulated. Several new laws and governmental decisions have been adopted to reorganize and stabilize the sector. Since 2000, the energy sector has undergone a series of reforms, which have significantly improved its performance. They involved unbundling the vertically integrated electricity subsector, and privatizing the

---

S. Minasyan (✉)
Institute of Political Studies and Sociology, University of Bonn, Bonn, Germany
e-mail: Shushanik.minasyan@uni-bonn.de

© Springer Nature Switzerland AG 2022
M. Knodt, J. Kemmerzell (eds.), *Handbook of Energy Governance in Europe*,
https://doi.org/10.1007/978-3-030-43250-8_72

entire power and gas distribution networks and most generating companies. However, the fundamental energy security problems remain problematic.

This chapter examines Armenia's energy sector, focusing on transition process, particularities of the energy system as well as current challenges of energy supply. Taking into consideration Armenia's geopolitical environment, this chapter also aims to illustrate the domestic energy potential and to explore how the energy interdependences affect the energy governance structure.

Keywords

Energy system transition · Energy dependence · Renewable energy · Energy efficiency

Introduction

In the wave of the Soviet Union's collapse, Armenia, like other former Soviet republics, began to struggle with the implications of its newfound independence. Particularly in the electricity sector, the country had to learn how to manage and sustain a system that had never been designed to function as a stand-alone grid. During the Soviet era, Armenia's electricity system had been constructed to operate as part of a much larger, integrated Trans-Caucasus system. The problems of this system became clear at the beginning of the 1990s, particularly after the war over Nagorno Karabakh, which accompanied an economic blockade by Azerbaijan and Turkey. As a result, Armenia's only source of gas and oil for its thermal plants was cut. Supply from a new gas pipeline, engineered in 1993 through neighboring Georgia, was regularly interrupted by conflicts and acts of sabotage. Armenia was left to rely almost entirely on its hydropower resources. In the past two decades, Armenia released its energy sector from Soviet rules and adjusted it to its newfound political surroundings. Armenian government implemented significant reforms and obtained remarkable success. However, the benefits of reform have not been easily won.

The geopolitical environment in the South Caucasus, geography, and history have also a direct impact on Armenia's energy policy. Armenia located in the heartland of the Eurasian continent between the Black Sea and Caspian regions is influenced by political processes in both regions, which are characterized by active geopolitical and economic changes. Unresolved conflicts and closed borders with Azerbaijan and Turkey make Georgia and Armenia natural partners, while the territory of Georgia has great strategic importance for Armenia's energy imports from Russia.

The main sources of energy that are used in Armenia are oil products, natural gas, nuclear energy, hydropower, and coal. Armenia does not have any fossil fuel or coal reserves; therefore, it is highly dependent on the imported fuel for transportation, electricity generation, and heat production. In this context, the promotion of energy efficiency, and introduction of renewable energy technologies, and enhancing the renewable energy capacity are high priorities for the Government of Armenia. Due to the lack of domestic fossil fuel resources, Yerevan meets its demand for fuel through imports. The majority of natural gas supply comes from Russia through Georgia – more than 80% in 2019 (IAEA, 2020). Also, the Islamic Republic of Iran exported a limited volume of gas into Armenia in an electricity-for-gas swap arrangement. Already in 2004 Armenia and Iran signed an agreement which allows Iran to receive electricity from Armenia in exchange for natural gas. In 2019 refined petroleum was the second most imported product in Armenia, which came primarily from Russia, Central Asian Countries, Greece, and Iran (OEC, 2020).

While Armenia imports most of its consumed energy, it has considerable potential for renewable energy. The most advanced renewable energy technology in Armenia is found in the hydropower sector, both in the use of large-scale hydropower and the more recent small run-of-the-river stations throughout the country. The development of small hydropower plants has been a success story in Armenia over the last two decades. Armenian government has adopted several policies to promote renewable energy production. The number of small hydropower plants increased significantly, up to about 184. Renewable energy capacity more than doubled in the last decade (Ministry of Energy Infrastructures and Natural Resources, 2021). The main sources are furthermore thermal power, wind, and biogas. Armenia is characterized also by the significant intensity of solar radiation: the average annual amount of solar energy flow per square meter of horizontal surface is about 1700 kWh and the annual sunshine is 2500 h (Ministry of Nature Protection, 2018). These domestic renewable resources produce roughly 35% of Armenia's electricity enabling the country also to export electricity to Georgia, Iran, and Nagorno-Karabakh.

Nuclear energy remains one of the most important energy sources, but also a serious challenge for Armenia. Medzamor is the only nuclear power plant in the region and contributes significantly to the energy independence of Armenia. The two blocs were built between 1976 and 1980 were temporarily decommissioned after a major earthquake in 1988. To overcome the energy crisis in 1991–1995, the re-opening of the Armenian Nuclear Power Plant was necessary. Nowadays this plant provides about 50% of the energy consumption in Armenia. However, the re-opening of the plant has given rise to critic reaction among the neighboring countries. The objection is primarily based on the argument that the plant is located in the seismically active region, as well as on the presence of numerous conflicts in the region, which could be the cause of sabotage, and Armenia's inability to maintain safety measures of the plant.

The energy sector of Armenia is expected to play a key role in the achievement of the strategic objectives of the government of Armenia in the future. Armenia faces three principal challenges in its energy sector: the need to maintain energy supply reliability; the need to manage the nuclear power policy; and the geopolitical situation with numerous unresolved conflicts and growing tension among countries of the region. The Government's policy was focused on developing specific trials and problem-oriented instruments to overcome the blockade situation of energy sector and enhance energy efficiency. In recent years, economic progress and new technologies have made it possible to further develop strategies as well as legislative frameworks for overcoming the challenges of the energy sector. Strengthening the economic and energy independence, increasing the reliability of the energy system, establishment of industrial infrastructure for the promotion of energy savings, and renewable energy have been defined in all strategies as a key priority of Armenia's energy sector. The recently adopted Energy Development Strategic Plan of January 14, 2021, emphasizes also the basic elements of energy policy for achieving energy security through fuel diversification of primary energy resources and supply routes, promotion of regional integration of the energy system, and development of nuclear energy as well as building up renewable energy sources (Government of Republic of Armenia, 2021a, b).

General Conditions of Energy Governance in Armenia

Past Legacies

Before the collapse of the USSR, Armenia was a Soviet Republic for 70 years. The energy sector of the Soviet Republic of Armenia has been one of the most developed parts of the economy. The country was well connected with its neighbors in the Soviet Union and received its energy supplies, including all its gas and oil needs from Russia, Turkmenistan, and Azerbaijan. Its electricity system was also operated jointly with other South Caucasian countries, and in the 1980s Armenia was a net exporter of electrical power to the region (Ministry of Energy, 1998). After the dissolution of the USSR Armenia went through a serious energy crisis and painfully experienced the loss of its energy security with all consequences, affecting the social, economic, and environmental spheres of the country. The crisis showed how hard is the way of political independence and how vulnerable Armenia is with its energy supply. As an energy importer, Armenia was hit by the abrupt collapse of the Soviet Union. In the early 1990s, Armenia produced less than 1% of its energy demand, which was filled during the Soviet time by imports. In the late Soviet era, Armenia had a share in the Joint Transcaucasian Power System, but the appropriate agreements and short-term supply legal framework ended with armed conflicts in the South Caucasus. The 1988 earthquake in North Armenia destroyed the largest nonnuclear thermoelectric plant and led to the closure of the nuclear power plant Medzamor (Energy Charter Secretary, 2005). In the early 1990s, severe shortages of energy led to blackouts, steady shutdowns of the subway system, and the further decline of the industry. Schools and academic institutions were closed through the winters of 1991–1992 and 1992–1993. In 1993 the delivery of electric power to industrial consumers was cut to one-third of the 1992 level. Under continued blockade conditions because of the Nagorno-Karabakh conflict, the winter of 1993–1994 brought acute shortages of coal, heating oil, and kerosene to heat homes and city apartment buildings and to keep industries running.

In these circumstances, the Armenian government considered the country's energy sector as a driving force in rapidly restoring the whole national economy, and defined the reform process of the sector as one of its policy priorities. As Armenian energy policy has long been determined by the centralist legacy of the Soviet Union, which focused primarily on gas and oil fuels and did not take environmental issues into account, this goal posed a major challenge for the Armenian authorities. The most significant step toward that aim was the establishment of three executive bodies. The Ministry of Energy and Natural Resources established in 1992 became the highest executive authority to elaborate and implement the policies in the energy sector, which includes the reform process. It was responsible for the improvement of management efficiency and commence and leading the way for de-monopolization and reform in the energy sector. The Ministry's objectives also included accommodation of energy efficiency and renewable energy sector policy development, and securing governmental control in the power sector and energy consumption. The second one was the Ministry of Urban Development, which was already established in 1954 as the Construction Ministry of the Soviet Republic of Armenia and reorganized in 1991. The mandate of this ministry was significantly broadened to control construction, building policies, and regulation, as well as the investment process in this sector. The ministry was also responsible for the Social Housing Strategy (Energy Charter Secretary, 2017). The Ministry of Nature Protection was the successor of the former Department for Surface and Underground Water Use and Protection, which was established in 1961. After several restructuring measures it was renamed in 1989 the National Committee of Nature Protection. In 1991 the committee was reorganized into the Ministry of Nature and Environmental Protection by the decree of the Supreme Council of the Republic of Armenia. In 1996, the ministry has been renamed the Ministry of Nature Protection and is responsible environmental sector development and the assessment of renewable energy potential in Armenia (Ministry of Environment, 2021).

Following the end of the energy crisis in 1994, the Government embarked on a series of electricity sector reforms to improve energy security and financial sustainability in the sector. These reforms directed the country out of a period of energy crisis in the mid-1990s into a period of relative stability. Key was the approval of the first Energy Policy Programme, which included a prompt adoption of the Energy Law and fostering the energy sector rehabilitation. The Program was practically implemented in a short time. The first Energy Law was adopted in 1997 (Energy Charta Secretariat, 2005). Regulatory reform was launched by Presidential Order in March 1997 and supported by the Energy Law that formalized the separation of generation, distribution, transmission, and dispatch into separate companies and established an independent sector regulator, the Armenian Energy Regulatory Commission (Sargsyan et al., 2006). An important step in this direction was the unbundling process in the electricity sector, which started in March 1995. Also, key reform was the privatization of electricity distribution and some electricity generating plants as well as the establishment of an independent regulator. The first step of a complete unbundling was the reorganization of the Armenian Electricity Company ARMENERGO, which performed both market and transport functions, as well as other support functions for the daughter enterprises. With this scheme, the Government became the ultimate holder of power sector assets prior to privatization.

In 1997–1998, the Ministry of Energy started a new stabilization policy initiating an institutional development and objectives to overcome the energy crisis. The central tasks of this stage were to rebuild the sector and to create liberal market conditions. The reform policy included above all improvement of the management structure of the Ministry of Energy with the aim to eliminate operational shortcomings and increase the independence of energy companies. Another important objective was to carry out a privatization policy encouraging major investments in the energy sector (IAEA, 2001). While some performance improvements were noted by 2000, the sector remained a duct on budgetary resources and an interenterprise arrear.

Many corrective actions have been undertaken since 2001, including improvements in technical and financial management. The most important measure here was the legislation enhancement in the energy sector. In 2001, the government amended the Energy Law and opened up access of international investors to the energy distribution market. Also, between 2002 and 2003 the government launched a renewed stabilization effort promoting a large privatization process in the electricity sector, which was accomplished in many phases (IMF, 2005). The privatization of the electricity distribution company to foreign investors in the autumn of 2002 marked the first success. In this period the ownership of two of the five main electricity generation companies was transferred to Russia as a repayment of debt.

In 2003, the Government created separate midstream companies for financial settlements, electricity dispatch, and high-voltage distribution, and set up independent boards of directors for the new companies. It was also developed a medium-term strategy for the sector, which envisaged a move away from the single wholesale buyer structure based around ARMENERGO and move toward direct contracting among market participants. In October 2004 ARMENERGO was finally removed from all cash transactions and has been liquidated. Transmission has been unbundled into two separate, state-owned entities – CJSC High Voltage Electricity Networks and CJSC Electricity System Operator. The former is the owner and operator of the transmission assets, while the latter carries responsibility for system operations. There was only one distribution company, the privately-owned CJSC Electric Networks of Armenia, which manages the distribution network and the supply functions such as retail metering, billing, and customer relations (Energy Charter Secretary, 2017). These reforms met with considerable success. This development allowed the country to operate new hydropower plants and to produce a substantial surplus of generation capacity. Armenia's capacity rise allowed it to become a net electricity exporter to its neighbors. During 1991–2004 Armenia reached a significant increase in electricity export from 720 to 813 Gigawatt hours by decreasing the import volume from 2299 to 50 Gigawatt hours (Sargsyan et al., 2006). After the successful implementation of the reform process, the government refined this legislative framework. In 2004 it defined the principles of the national energy efficiency policy in the new Law on Energy Saving and Renewable Energy, which was edited in 2016.

This development has been also promoted by the operation of the nuclear plant in the transition process. The Armenian nuclear power plant was the guarantor of Armenia's energy supply recovery. The government had no choice but to consider the nuclear option as a matter of necessity to gain some degree of energy independence. The situation improved from 1995 when the Medzamor Nuclear Power Plant was reopened after a general rehabilitation and earthquake conditioning. In 1999, it covered approximately 45% of the country's electricity (IAEA, 2004).

Energy Mix

In recent years, Armenia has set specific programs and objectives for the development of its energy sector. These agendas include enhancing energy security, developing renewable and alternative energy resources as well as liberalizing the power market. Other key objectives of the government were maximizing the use of domestic energy resources and replacing obsolete technologies. The authorities took numerous measures to diversify the energy sector and generated clear trends for the rapid development of domestic renewable energy sources. However, it has been a challenging process. Armenia has limited energy resources and can meet only a fraction of the total demand for energy from domestic resources. Its energy needs remain dominated by imported natural gas and oil, which covers 75% of the country's energy demand, followed by electricity (22%) (IEA, 2018). The share of natural gas has almost doubled since 2000. Armenia imports gas and oil products primarily from Russia and Iran. Natural gas imports from Russia account for 80% of total gas imports. Nuclear energy remains one of the most important components of Armenia's energy security. It is responsible for 32.54% (2018) of the Republic of Armenia's total energy production (Armenian Energy Agency, 2021a).

Hydropower and recently developed wind generation facilities are Armenia's mainly existing domestic energy resources. These resources generate approximately 30% of Armenia's electricity (Fig. 1). Electricity is generated by a mix of nuclear, gas, hydro, and thermal power plants; some are privately owned and operated, some are wholly owned by the state. Natural gas comprised over 40% of generational capacity. The available capacity is low when compared to the installed capacity due to the age and poor condition of many generating plants. The baseload capacity is provided by the nuclear power plant. Natural gas-fired thermal power plants and the Medzamor nuclear power plant produce 40% and 30% of Armenia's electricity. Of these, almost all nuclear fuel for the nuclear power plant and almost all of the natural gas for natural-gas thermal power plants are imported from Russia.

Hydropower plants provide daily load regulation while thermal plants operate to support peaks, especially in the winter and when the nuclear power plant goes offline for maintenance. There are three big thermal power plants: Hrazdan-5, Yerevan TPP, and Raz TES (Gazprom Armenia & Hrazdan TPP) are the most significant power plants, which also generate electricity for export under the gas for electricity swap arrangement with Iran (Armenian Energy Agency, 2019). There are two major hydropower plants (Sevan-Hrazdan-Cascade; Vorotan-Cascade), which generate 30% of the electricity production. In recent years, Armenia achieved significant progress in developing small hydropower plants, with about 186 small hydropower stations registered in 2020, which are responsible for 11% of total generated electricity in the country (Armenian Energy Agency, 2021b).

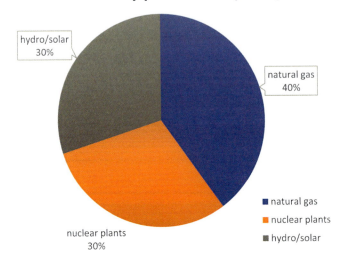

Fig. 1 Electricity production. (Source: International Renewable Energy Agency; IEA)

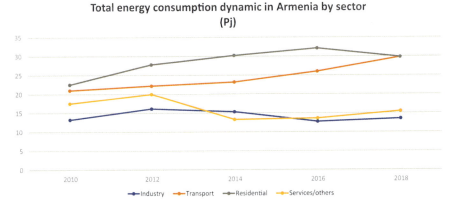

Fig. 2 Total energy consumption dynamic in Armenia by sector (Pj). (Source: International Energy Agency 2021. Note: Pj (One Petajoule))

Armenia relies on electricity and gas to meet the majority of its consumption needs (Fig. 2). The industrial, residential, and transport sectors are the largest energy consumer, responsible for roughly 81% of final energy consumption in Armenia. The industry relies on a combination of electricity and gas to meet its production needs. Industry's share has decreased twofold since 2000, mainly at the expense of the increased share of the transport sector and to some extent of the residential sector. Residential households rely on a mix of electricity and gas for heating, and electricity for lighting and other household appliance. The transport sector relies on oil and gas with 75% of the automobile and truck fleet using compressed natural gas (Statistical Committee of the Republic of Armenia, 2019). The high level of residential energy demand for essential services such as heating and cooking means that energy tariffs are an important economic, political and social issue in Armenia, interlinked with geopolitical concerns related to gas imports and electricity exchanges with third parties. According to Western experts' higher gas and electricity tariffs may be necessary to fund energy infrastructure investments. It could also serve as an incentive for households to invest in energy efficiency. However, they express the fear that without mitigating policies for vulnerable population segments, tariff increases could provoke greater poverty and discomfort for low-income households that cannot afford home efficiency upgrades (IEA and EU4Energy, 2020).

Discourse on Energy Issues and Main Political Actors

The main topics of the Armenian energy discourse focus on ensuring energy independence and developing indigenous energy sources, including through building regulatory incentives for the introduction of modern and high technologies, enhancing the policy development, and energy efficiency measures. The dependence on imported fuels makes Armenia particularly vulnerable to energy price shocks and supply disruptions. It is precisely for this reason that in the past government has endeavored to enhance energy efficiency and to develop renewable domestic energy generation. The Armenian Development Strategy 2014–2025 adopted in March 2014 highlights decidedly the promotion of energy efficiency in all sectors using energy resources among the main directions of the policy to be implemented in the energy sector (Government of the Republic of Armenia, 2014a, b). One year later, Armenia adopted the Least-Cost Plan for Long-Term Development of Armenia's Energy Sector until 2036 which is fully in line with the main strategic document in the energy efficiency sector – the Second National Energy Efficiency Action Plan, adopted in 2017. The program defines an agenda for environmental management, in particular, it outlines as a priority the use of renewable energy. The Government Programme 2019–2024 continued with these objectives once again highlighting the need to enhance the cooperation with international partners and organizations for better promoting appropriate mechanisms enhancing renewable energy potential in the country (European Commission, 2019).

The Armenian energy market is a strictly regulated system of private and state-owned enterprises managed by the Public Services Regulatory Commission (PSRC). While the generation sector is mainly privately owned and the distribution network is operated by a single private entity, transmission networks, market, and system operation and processes are conducted by state-owned enterprises.

The Ministry of Energy Infrastructures and Natural Resources has primary responsibility for the energy policy. According to the RA Law on Energy (the Law), the Ministry:

- Develops strategic plans for the development of the energy sector, as well as relevant legal acts and safety regulations, and presents them for approval by the government.
- Cooperates with the Public Services Regulatory Committee to trigger cross-border sales and expand interstate cooperation.
- Advises the PSRC on the annual limits of licenses to be provided by the PSRC to plants using renewable energy with up to 30 megawatts (MW) installed capacity, taking into consideration the strategic development plans for the sector.
- Approves PSRC decisions to grant licenses to power plants with over 30 MW installed capacity.
- Approves the market rules, indicators of security, and reliability of the energy sector.
- Submits proposals to the government of Armenia about public-private partnerships in the energy sector (Government of Armenia, 2001).

In elaborating and implementing the policies it is supported by the Ministry of Territorial Administration and Infrastructures, which is also involved in determining local energy policy strategy. Other ministries, including Environment, Economy and Finance, also provide implementation or policy support related to energy and energy efficiency.

Regulatory implementation is the responsibility of the PSRC, which was established in 1997. PSRC is an autonomous regulatory agency responsible for electricity, gas, district heating, and telecommunications. According to the Energy Law, the main tasks of the Committee are setting tariff methodology and tariff levels; issuing licenses and authorizations; establishing and controlling service quality standards; examining consumer complaints; and approving *ex-ante* investment plans in the sector under its responsibility. PSRC, in collaboration with the Ministry of Energy Infrastructures and Natural Resources, defines basic market rules. It is also able to impose fines for violations and may issue orders as well as suspend or revoke licenses.

Electro Power System Operator CJSC (EPSO) is also involved in the power generating plants. EPSO is responsible for electric power generation, import and export of electric power, and the supply of electric power based on existing contracts. EPSO owns a subsidiary called Energy Communication, which monitors the operation of the power generating system and dispatch control, and the interaction between the processes (Japan International Cooperation Agency, 2019).

Armenia works also closely with international partners. After joining the Eurasian Economic Union (EEU) Armenia has been forced to conform its energy policy with Russia. In general, Russian companies have a significant influence on Armenia's energy sector. The main power infrastructure is owned or run by Russian corporations, and Armenia's energy sector relies on Russia both in commercial and policy aspects. However, many Western actors operate since the 1990s very successfully in the Armenian energy sector. The European Union has proved especially long-term energy assistance with Armenia in order to strengthen the energy efficiency locally, regionally, and nationally. The cooperation between the EU and Armenia aims to diversify energy resources in the country and reduce import dependency. Over the last years, the EU has been also actively contributing to the development of renewable and sustainable energy sources in Armenia. Under different instruments like INOGATE, Neighbourhood Policy, TACIS, the EU advised Armenia on its energy legislation on rules and charges for reforming the sector based on the EU practice.

Coordination, Instruments, and Issues of Armenian Energy Transition

Drivers of Energy Transition

The main purpose of the Armenian energy transition is to set targets for scaling down energy dependence, foster sustainability of the energy system, and enhancing domestic renewable sources. The development of local resources promises not only to contribute to energy independence of the country but also will offer the prospect of integrating Armenia into the regional energy system.

Armenia demonstrated appreciable progress in the transition process improving its energy efficiency indicators. Since 2005, Armenia reduced around two times the oil equivalent of energy to produce $1000 of its GDP. This tendency was related to achievements and investments toward broad use of energy efficient practices and techniques in the economy and among households, and the expansion of industries with low energy intensity. Around two dozen energy efficiency and renewable energy measures were developed and adopted to support the implementation of sustainable energy practices by business entities as well as households (United Nations, 2018).

Armenia ratified the United Nations Framework Convention on Climate Change in May 1993. In December 2002, Armenia ratified the Kyoto Protocol, and in February 2017, it ratified the Doha Amendment to the Kyoto Protocol and the Paris Agreement. Armenia filed its Intended Nationally Determined Contribution (INDC) to the UNFCCC Secretariat in September 2015. The INDC started with a preparatory period 2015–2019, following with a next phase from 2020, with a horizon to 2050. With the ratification of the Paris Agreement in February 2017, the INDC of Armenia became its nationally determined contribution (NDC) for the period of 2015–2050. In its 2015 INDC, Armenia undertook to pursue economy-wide mitigation measures, striving to achieve per capita net emissions of 2.07 tCO2eq in 2050, subject to adequate international financial, technological and capacity-building support. By 2030, Armenia is going to double its share of renewables in energy generation on the path to achieve climate neutrality in the second half of this century (Government of the Republic of Armenia, 2021a, b). In its updated NDC (2015), Armenia adopted a ten-year NDC implementation period (2021–2030) unlike its INDC, which proposed a timeframe of 2015–2050. Armenia maintains its 2050 mitigation goal of reducing its GHG emissions to at most 2.07 tCO2eq/capita, to be reflected in its Long Term – Low Emission Development Strategy (LT-LEDS). The new mitigation target to be achieved in 2030 equals 40% reduction below 1990 emissions levels (ibid.).

The main provisions of the national energy strategy are to provide for more ambitious development of renewable energy and further lifetime extension of the Armenian Nuclear Power Plant. The measures provided in the new Strategy have been prioritized in the Program of the Government of the Republic of Armenia, adopted in 2019, justifying projections of GHG emissions from the Energy Sector (Government of the Republic of Armenia, 2020). Energy strategy and contributions are also based on the requirement of the UNFCCC Article 2 "Objective," which is to restrain climate change within timeframe sufficient to allow ecosystems to adapt naturally to climate change. Thus, the natural ecosystems adaptation approach in NDC is considered pivotal for Armenia's adaptation strategy and actions (contribution), and a basis for the development of the National Adaptation Plan 2021–2030. General objective of the NAP process is to promote reduction and management of climate risks in Armenia by addressing the impacts of climate change, taking advantage of emerging opportunities, avoiding losses and damages, and building mechanisms enabling adaptation of natural, human, production, and infrastructure systems (Government of the Republic of Armenia, 2021a, b). Armenia seeks also to develop a debt-for-climate innovative financial swap mechanism, which aims at leveraging additional finance into climate action and suggests innovating not only the technical aspects of the debt-for-climate transaction, but the prioritization and value of commitments undertaken by countries across the world on a bilateral and multilateral level (ibid.).

Renewable Energy/Regulation Framework

The strengthening of renewable energy has been an important part of the transition from crisis to stability. For Armenia, it is necessary to develop its renewable source of energy, and there are enough stimuli for this. Initially, it offers numerous benefits as they can not only reduce pollution but also add an economically stable source of energy to the mix of electricity-generation sources in Armenia. Secondly, the country is challenged with difficulties in fuel supply because of political problems in the region and fuel embargo from Azerbaijan and Turkey. Depending on only one external supplier (Russia) makes the country vulnerable to volatile prices and political instrumentation of energy issues. For this reason, the Government has worked for more than a decade to expand the use of renewable energy. Its strategy was driven by the overarching goals of improving energy security, ensuring tariff affordability, and maximizing the use of Armenia's indigenous renewable energy resources.

The Law on Energy Savings and Renewable Energy in 2004 and the establishment of the Renewable Resources and Energy Efficiency Fund (R2E2), a non-governmental agency was the first tangible step to promoting and facilitating renewable energy and energy efficiency in Armenia. R2E2, which was supported by the World Bank and by the Global Environment Facility, implemented a Renewable Energy Program that helped to remove barriers to the development of renewable energy generation and allowed for a better environment for private investment. Development and introduction of financial instruments and mechanisms for the implementation of sustainable energy projects were defined in 2005 as a key priority of the Fund (R2E2, 2019). In cooperation with the World Bank and the European Bank for Reconstruction and Development (EBRD), the Government developed in 2011 the Renewable Energy Roadmap. The most important results of the Roadmap were the establishment of the national targets for renewable energy technologies (R2E2, 2011). A 2013 Decree of the President of Armenia approved an "Energy Security Concept" for the country, which defines the main ways for ensuring energy security for providing affordable and reliable energy supply, considering the lack of significant domestic fossil fuel resources (Government of the Republic of Armenia, 2014a, b). An extensive regulatory framework has been adopted in the last decade. In 2014, the authorities presented the Energy Security Action Plan for 2014–2020 and the Long-Term Development Strategy for 2014–2025, which aimed at ensuring specific actions to be implemented for achieving renewable energy goals. The programs also strived to establish a coordinated post-crises strategic framework for the development of state policies, given the current conditions and global development challenges. Furthermore, the Energy System Long-Term Strategy has been amended in 2015 (up to 2036). The Amendment defines the development strategy to meet the criteria of energy security at the lowest cost based upon nuclear energy and modern gas-fired plants, development, and expansion of economically viable and technically available renewable energy sources, and diversification of fuel supply chains (Ministry of Nature Protection, 2018). The developments and goals in each sector will be presented below.

Wind Energy

Armenia has significant renewable energy resources. According to the World Bank, approximately 740 MW of small hydropower, wind, and geothermal resources have been identified (World Bank, 2006). Due to the huge potential of wind energy in Armenia and the fact that wind energy promises a clean and reliable electricity supply, Armenia has focused since 1999 on the development of the wind energy sector. In the energy transition process, wind energy is one of the fastest-growing sectors. Armenian energy strategy documents highlight wind power as a top priority in the countries' energy sector development. For instance, the Diversification Strategy Document, adopted by the Government in 2005, sets a national target of 500 MW of grid-connected wind-power capacity by 2025 (Government of Armenia, 2005).

Wind energy studies in Armenia began in the late 1980s. In the beginning, most of the wind energy potential studies were premised on synoptic data from meteorological stations (historically since the early 1900s over 80 stations were installed in Armenia that covered most of the area). Most of those stations are defunct now. Unfortunately, the wind data recorded at those stations were and are not reliable due to inaccurate accurate measurement and incomplete data collection. The first wind energy map of Armenia was developed by an Armenian Ecotech scientific association back in 1989–1990. This map, however, highlighted at a macro scale the possible perspective areas for wind energy development (USAID, 2010). As stated in the Armenian Wind Atlas developed in 2002–2003 by the United States National Renewable Energy Laboratory (NREL), the most perspective areas for grid-connected wind power development in Armenia corresponds to the "Good" and "Excellent" classes (R2E2, 2008). The country has many areas with promising wind resources. The most promising areas that have been identified and characterized to date are in the northern and southern regions. Regarding wind-powered electricity generation, in 2003, the National Renewable Energy Laboratory (NREL) drew up a wind condition map which indicates that Armenian wind-power is estimated to have 300–500 MW of developable resource potential (Movsisyan & Danielian, 2016).

In 2005 the Government initiated "Lori 1," the first wind farm project in the South Caucasus with a total installed capacity of 2.64 MW. The wind farm was built with support of a $3.1 million grant from the Government of the Islamic Republic of Iran, which is also working on a natural gas pipeline and hydropower station along the border of the two countries (R2E2, 2008). The project was subsequently expanded in cooperation with the Government of the Netherlands. The Armenian-Italian company Ar Energy has been appointed to monitor on the territory of the Karakhach Pass in the Shirak region and received a license to build the wind farm Karachach-1 with a capacity of up to 20 MW. In the future, Armenia plans to increase total capacity up to 140 MW. The Government worked also within the framework of the European Union's TACIS program "Supporting Armenia's Energy Policy" by monitoring new regions near the lake Sevan. It prepared a preliminary feasibility study for the construction of a wind farm with a total capacity of 35 MW (Ministry of Energy Infrastructures and Natural Resources of the Republic of Armenia, 2021). In recent years, Armenia's large wind potential attracts new international partners. The Emirates company "Access Infra Central Asia Limited" is active in this field and installed 2018 many 80-meter towers to measure wind flows in Gegharkunik region. In March 2017, an agreement was signed between the Emirates company and the Republic of Armenia on leasing land plots in different regions of the country with a total area of 1250 hectares for the construction of wind farms with a total capacity of 150 MW. Also, the Spanish Acciona Energia Global S.L is interested in building wind farms in Armenia. In 2017, the Ministry of Energy Infrastructures and Natural Resources signed with this company a memorandum of understanding on planning of wind farms with a total capacity of 100–150 MW. The company already began assessing the wind potential and installed two monitoring stations with a height of 80 meters each and one "Sodar" system.

Despite very significant efforts in wind power, Armenia needs a series of financial and policy issues to achieve its renewable energy targets for wind. The tariff procedure remains a barrier. The wind tariffs should be fixed so developers can perform project feasibility analyses for a typical project life span of 20–25 years. Second, the initial costs of wind power projects may be reduced by lowering the burden of the value-added tax (VAT) on imported machinery for renewable energy projects, since there is no local manufacturing of modern wind turbines in Armenia. Currently, the cost of wind turbines accounts for about 60–80% of the total acquisition cost of a wind project, and the VAT in Armenia would subject this to a 20% tax (Sonigian, 2010).

Solar

For a country like Armenia, which is situated in the proximity of the subtropical climate zone, the integration of solar sources into the energy supply system is essential. Armenia has a significant advantage in terms of solar energy: most provinces have beneficial climatic conditions that make wide use of solar energy possible. According to the National Energy Strategy, the average annual amount of solar energy flow per square meter of the horizontal surface is about 1720 kWh (the average in Europe is about 1000 kWh/m^2). A quarter of the country's territory has solar energy resources of 1850 kWh/m^2. The surface sunshine on the Lake Sevan basin may be considered a record – 2800 h. The portion of the direct annual radiation upon the entire territory is also significant – 65–70%, which is rather unique for the application of concentration collectors in the European region (Government of the Republic of Armenia, 2005).

Armenian Government has identified two areas for strategic development in the renewable energy sector, namely, solar and hydro-energy, and adopted policies promoting investments in these sectors. The country receives a high amount of solar radiation throughout the year. As the cost of solar power technology has drastically decreased over the past years and with no oil and gas national production, this solution has become very attractive. Currently, the energy strategies of the country are being revised considering more ambitious development of solar sources. A comprehensive set of enabling regulatory documents was adopted to support the effective implementation of appropriate policy on achieving availability, accessibility, and sustainability in solar energy in Armenia, including, inter alia: (i) the National Energy Security Action Plan 2014–2020, and (ii) the National Plan for Energy Efficiency and Renewable Energy (United Nations, 2018). The Energy Law was also in 2016 modified. The Amendment aims at promoting solar energy generation for own needs with a peak capacity of up to 150 kW (inclusive) by stipulating that such plants can be operated without the activity licenses. The net metering for solar energy for autonomous producers has been adopted in the Energy Saving and Renewable Energy Law (2016) stipulating a sales price for net metering for autonomous producers (Vorotnikov, 2016). In 2015, the Armenian government approved the investment program for the construction of solar power plants for a global cost estimated at $129 million. The Government also has applied and received a grant from IBRD for the development of various solar energy technologies, in particular, photovoltaic technology (PV). Also, the improvement of the legal framework was a core objective of this reform process. In recent years, substantial reduction of the cost of the PV-technologies and decline in the volume of capital investments required for the construction of solar power plants made the PV-technology-based power generation more competitive toward the other technologies. The country has achieved, to facilitate a competitive price for the solar-PV plants construction with no negative impact on the end-users. This fact attracts nowadays world-famous leading companies to the energy market of the country (R2E2, 2019).

The Government has been very successful in developing solar energy potential. Together with the Armenian Renewable Resources and Energy Efficiency Fund and with the financial support of EBRD, the Government operated the first solar power plant "Masrik-1" solar power plant (SPP) in Armenia and the Caucasus region. The World Bank helped the government prepare the project and provided transaction advisory support. The bidding process, backstopped by the Scaling-up Renewable Energy Program and the World Bank, was highly competitive. The Masrik-1 PV project is projected to be completed by 2022. The Project will allow producing electricity using solar irradiation, which is comparable with half of the annual electricity consumption of Gyumri, the second-largest city of Armenia. The Masrik-1 SPP will add 1.5% of the annual national electricity generation. It promises to add 2.1% of the annual national internal electricity consumption, and 1.8% of total Armenia's available installed capacity (EBRD, 2019). Successful implementation of the project will increase solar energy's share (up to 10% of total) in the power balance of Armenia allowing the country to partially replace electricity generation from imported fossil fuel (35% of total generation presently).

"Masrik-1" solar PV-plant project has entered into an active phase in 2018, since the Government signed a Government Support Agreement on the organization and implementation of the project. The partner is an international consortium consisting of "Fotowatio Renewable Venture" (Netherlands) and Spanish "FSL-Solar" companies, which won the tender for the construction of a 55 MW Masrik-1 SPP (ArmenPress, 2018). After the owning of the Fotowatio Renewable Ventures business by UAE-based Abdul Latif Jameel Energy in April 2018, the new management board secured the contract to build Masrik-SPP (EBRD, 2019). The company will receive a $35.4 million debt financing package from International Finance Corporation and the EBRD. The project will also receive a EUR 3 million investment grant from the European Union, mobilized by the EBRD.

In 2020 the Armenian Renewable Resources and Energy Efficiency Fund announced the construction of a new project and opened a tender of AYG1, which will generate 200 MW solar power spinning the communities in western Aragatsotn province. It will be 85% owned by the international developer and 15% by R2E2. Various international investors are interested in this project. In 2019, the Abu Dhabi-based clean energy group Masdar entered already into a formal agreement with the Armenian National Interests Fund (ANIF) to develop 400 MW of PV capacity in Armenia, with a projected investment of up to $320 million. The broader agreement also includes the development, construction, operation, and maintenance of ground-mounted PV installations, floating solar arrays, and wind farms (Arka News Agency, 2020).

Hydropower Energy

Among the renewable energy sources, hydropower represents one of the important ways of producing electricity and the development of hydropower energy has been a success story in Armenia over the last two decades. Hydropower was already used in Soviet times for the generation of electricity. Armenia's largest hydropower plant, Sevan-Hrazdan Cascade Hydropower System, which is located along a waterway of many connected rivers, was originally built between 1930 and 1965. The system comprised seven small hydroelectric power plants located on the Hrazdan River and supplied about 10% of the country's electricity (Asian Development Bank, 2020). The second large complex, Vorotan Cascade, was also built during the Soviet period. The complex consists of three power stations, which are situated in the southeast of Armenia.

Armenia must manage its energy crisis after the collapse of the Soviet Union mainly by the deployment of hydropower. Particularly the hydraulic potential of Sevan Lake, which is a unique high mountainous lake, has been very decisive in the economic transition process (Ministry of Energy Infrastructures and Natural Resources, 2021).

In the course of modernization, the Armenian government strived toward the reactivation and widening of hydropower energy generation. In order to improve the sector, several policies have been adopted. The Energy Law adopted in 1996, required that companies receive separate licenses for the generation, transmission, and distribution of electricity, which were issued by the energy regulator in the transition process. It also required legal unbundling between transmission and other activities. In 1997, the government passed a Law on Privatization, defining the hydropower sector companies and assets to be privatized. The adoption of this decision led to a big privatization wave. Between 1997 and 2002, about 25 small hydropower plants have been privatized (Sargsyan et al., 2006).

To support these legal reforms and substantial implementation of renewable energy goals a new licensing system has been developed. To carry out any licensed activity in the energy sector, applicants had to submit to the Public Services Regulatory Commission a business plan that includes an environmental impact assessment and a detailed description of the technical solutions required to meet the environmental impact limits set by law. As a consequence of an amendment passed in April 2001, the Energy Law appointed favorable priority to all electricity produced from small hydropower plants and other renewable energy sources for the 15 years following plant commissioning. As a term of its own license, the privatized distribution system operator had to disburse all small hydropower producers before it can book its own sales. The payments to hydropower plants have been paid fully and on time for the past 10 years. The hydropower plants were paid directly by the privatized distribution operator via a special account administered through an independent Settlement Center and not through any state-controlled agency or middleman. The operator was compelled to enter into a 15-year guaranteed power purchase agreement and to take 100% of all (renewable) production during that period (USAID, 2014). The regulator also established a feed-in tariff system that drives forward hydropower investment, particularly for small plants. The new regulatory regime, including all licensing and permitting requirements, minimized risk and attracted international investors. In 2009, the Armenian government adopted a policy concerning the development of this technology and decided to construct an additional 90 small hydropower plants having a total output of 100 MW. As a result, after 2008, 86 small-scale hydroelectric plants went into operation, and the total output was 169.2 MW (Japan International Cooperation Agency, 2019). In 2016, the legislative framework has been amended by the Hydro Energy Development

Concept of the Republic of Armenia. It aims at promoting the hydropower generation considering public-private partnership options as well as certain legislative guarantees to make the investment environment more attractive (Ministry of Nature Protection, 2018). Currently, the Ministry of Energy Infrastructures and Energy Resources reports about 187 small hydropower plants, with about 370 MW installed capacity. According to the provided licenses, 28 additional small hydropower plants are under construction, with about a projected 59 MW capacity (Ministry of Energy Infrastructures and Natural Resources of the Republic of Armenia, 2021).

Major retrofitting programs have been implemented also at the two biggest hydropower plants Sevan-Hrazdan and Vorotan. Thanks to financial support of the Asian Development Bank, EBRD, and the World Bank, both power system, which generates the bulk of hydro-electricity, has been significantly modernized in recent years. These power systems have a total installed capacity of about 900 MW. Specialists assess the relevance of hydropower in Armenia generally high. It is considered that the latency of sustainable energy due to the existence of domestic water resources for hydroelectric power and other sustainable energy sources is very important. They point out that if Armenia increases the amount of power generated by using sustainable energy, and reduces the cost of electricity, it will be possible to reduce the dependence on natural gas. The development of hydropower would also ease a phaseout of the Medzamor nuclear power plant (IAEA, 2015).

Energy Efficiency

As mentioned above, Armenia's economy almost collapsed after the collapse of the Soviet Union. The slow reconstruction and alteration of the economy from heavy industry to services has decoupled the energy from economic growth and created a relatively low level of energy intensity. Since 2004, Armenia's ratio fell from over 0.25 to below 0.14. It currently enjoys approximately the same ratio as its neighbor Georgia (Energy Charter Secretary, 2017).

Several strategies and action plans are in place to improve energy efficiency. Important for energy efficiency action has been the Law on Energy Saving and Renewable Energy (2004) and the National Programme on Energy Saving and Renewable Energy adopted in 2007. The National Energy Efficiency Action Plan (2010) is the key instrument to provide the high-level energy strategy. The main objective of the action plan was to contribute to the formulation of the future energy framework in order to improve energy efficiency as well as further development of renewable energy sources use. The document presented by the government proposed following measures:

- To adjust the public sector to energy efficiency standards.
- To establish a favorable and stable institutional framework.
- Energy efficiency policies should address all areas with energy savings potentials.
- To develop a well-planned regulation plan for an efficient and cost-effective energy sector.

- To develop adequate pricing, which is a condition for successful energy efficiency policies' implementation to reflect more near-market conditions.
- To promote public/private partnerships to reinforce the effect of public policies.
- To strengthen the quality of energy efficiency services and equipment through certification and testing facilities (Government of Republic Armenia, 2010).

Continuing to work actively on the improvement of energy efficiency regulation, the government adopted in 2013 the National Energy Security Concept. It defined the main ways for ensuring energy security for providing affordable and reliable energy supply, considering the lack of domestic fossil fuel resources. The concept outlined the development and investment in renewable energy and energy efficiency as critical to achieving energy security (Energy Charter Secretary, 2017). These goals were translated into the Second Energy Efficiency Action Plan (2017) by defining concrete policy measures for energy efficiency improvements in all relevant economic sectors (Ministry of Nature Protection, 2018). In the new Energy Sector Development Strategic Program to 2040, which was adopted in 2020, the government repeatedly stressed these goals and determined further promotion, development, and investment in renewable energy technologies as essential to Armenia diversifying its energy supply and gaining energy independence. The program prioritizes energy efficiency as a measure for the country's energy security, increasing economic competitiveness and reducing a negative impact on the environment (Government of the Republic of Armenia, 2020).

Within the framework of the international cooperation, Armenia, by joining the Treaty on "Eurasia Economic Union" in 2013, accepted the technical regulation on "energy efficiency requirements for energy-consuming equipment." Based on the Comprehensive and External Partnership Agreement signed with the EU, Armenia is obligated to adapt about 60 regulations, instructions, and guidelines on energy consumption of buildings and facilities to its legislation in the nearest (Government of the Republic of Armenia, 2020).

An increasing number of donor activities support energy efficiency in Armenia. The World Bank Group had several operations in the energy sector and supported the implantation process of the Energy Efficiency Security Plan (2013) that prioritized energy efficiency measures for various sectors. The International Finance Corporation subsidized the banking sector in developing energy efficiency lending and raising awareness on sustainable energy finance. The EBRD and the US Agency for International Development also supported the banking sector to increase the availability of bank financing for energy efficiency projects. The Global Environment Facility administered by the United Nations Development Programme led the external support for policy improvements in the energy efficiency area, including energy efficiency in buildings, appliances, and equipment (World Bank, 2019).

Many projects and strategies show already successful results and the stakeholders identified the R2E2-Fund, which was the main Armenian contact partner, as a major driver of the fruitful implementation of the strategic goal. The dedicated leadership and strong institutional structure helped to carry out to implement these projects. The Fund had to work around barriers that included a lack of incentives to implement energy efficiency projects, and a lack of capacity of public sector entities and design and construction firms. Potential clients were not interested in energy efficiency investments at the beginning and implementation progress was very slow. The Fund intensified its public awareness campaign, including focused marketing to target clients, lobbying through line ministries, and advertisements on television, radio, and other media channels. With rising awareness about energy efficiency and energy tariffs, the demand for energy efficiency investments expanded (ibid.).

Particularly, in the building sector, which represents the largest energy end-use sector, authorities' measures have been effective. In the early 2000s, the construction of new buildings with less energy consumption began to increase on average by 15–20% annually. With the objective of creating an enabling regulatory environment, skills, and capacity among industry professionals and of introducing the principles of integrated design into Armenian construction practices many projects promoted new energy efficiency directives. As a result of the energy efficiency measures, energy consumption of buildings was reduced from 178 to 74 kWh/m^2 between 2005 and 2016 (Energy Charter Secretary, 2017).

However, several barriers delay the full realization of the defined goals. Significant obstacles are the lack of information about technology options, the weak linkages between research institutes and industry as well as the lack of an enabling policy and regulatory environment. The main barrier to energy efficiency is the weak capacity for building management, project development, and financial planning and management. A lack of financial resources due to low maintenance also hinders the implementation progress. Furthermore, the country needs overall awareness and public understanding of the legal regulatory framework, rights, and responsibilities related to the home owners' associations, and benefits of energy efficiency, in general.

Outcomes, Challenges and Prospects for Energy Governance

Armenia's energy sector experienced a massive transition since the 1990s. During the Soviet Union's collapse, Armenia faced severe implications of its newfound independence. Particularly in the energy sector, the country had to learn how to manage and sustain its own system. The war over Nagorno Karabakh in the 1990s and the economic blockade of Azerbaijan and Turkey worsened the situation considerably. In the past two decades, Armenia released its energy sector from Soviet rules and adjusted it to its newfound political surroundings. The energy sector has moved from a state of severe crisis to relative stability today. Armenian government implemented in recent years numerous significant reforms and obtained remarkable success. The benefits of reform have not been easily won, however, and Armenia's success is a tribute to its ability to learn from mistakes and endure. A combination of policy, legal, regulatory, and institutional reforms has had obvious good results. Various reform measures have helped to create a commercially viable and competitive energy sector.

The geopolitical environment in the South Caucasus has a direct impact on Armenia's energy policy. Due to its high dependence on the imported fuel and the lack of domestic fossil fuel resources promotion of energy efficiency and enhancing renewable energy capacity have been defined as high priorities for the country. Since 2000, the Armenian government has adopted numerous policies and strategies to promote renewable energy production. Thanks to the considerable potential of renewable energy as well as the modernization of the management and regulation system, it was fairly successful. Particularly, in enhancing wind, hydro, and solar, energy governance achieved considerable positive outcomes. Energy efficiency and renewable energy have been defined as a high priority in all sectors and future energy-related policies supported this goal by detailed analysis of energy efficiency potentials in the economy, and the barriers that delay the realization of these potentials.

However, the country faces continuously several challenges in its energy policy. Medzamor nuclear power plant remains a serious problem not only for the country but also for the whole region. The plant is located in the seismically active region, as well as in the presence of numerous conflicts in the region, which could be the cause of sabotage, and Armenia's inability to maintain safety measures of the plant. Nevertheless, it contributes significantly to the energy independence of Armenia. Nowadays, this plant provides 30% of the required energy in Armenia and the country does not have any equivalent sources to replace it.

One of the most important barriers in Armenia's modernization process of energy efficiency is the high cost of investment relative to the currently low-cost electricity generation mix in the country. Tariffs are low because many of the thermal, solar, and hydro plants are fully depreciated and only need to cover variable costs. This will change as new generation plants are brought online and tariffs are raised to reflect their capital costs. In the meantime, however, the low cost of generation makes it difficult for consumers to understand the need for higher-cost renewable energy generation which will satisfy – at least initially – only a small portion of demand.

The obstacles restraining the development are also a policy nature. Many projects suffer from regional political instability. In some regions, developers of hydropower plants assess the political situation as unstable and avoid making large investments. Furthermore, energy legislation in Armenia is still in the phase of development, and some aspects of legislation are still in the development phase.

Cross References

- ▶ Energy Governance in Azerbaijan
- ▶ Energy Governance in Turkey
- ▶ Energy Relations in the EU Eastern Partnership
- ▶ The Energy Charter Treaty: Old and New Dilemmas in Global Energy Governance

References

Arka News Agency. (2020, May 21). *Armenian government to prequalify companies for construction of AYG-1 photovoltaic solar power plant*. https://arka.am/en/news/technology/armenian_government_to_prequalify_companies_for_construction_of_ayg_1_photovoltaic_solar_power_plant/. Accessed 28 Mar 2021.

Armenian Energy Agency. (2019). *Actual measures of electricity production, import, export, delivery, and losses in Armenian energy system*. https://energyagency.am/en/page_pdf/2018t%2D%2Denergetik-balansy-hh-energahamaka. Accessed 22 Mar 2021.

Armenian Energy Agency. (2021a). *Energy system structure*. Nuclear energy. https://energyagency.am/en/page_pdf/atomayin-energetika. Accessed 22 Mar 2021.

Armenian Energy Agency. (2021b). *Energy system structure*. Hydropower. https://energyagency.am/en/page_pdf/hidroenergetika. Accessed 22 Mar 2021.

Armenian Renewable Resources and Energy Efficiency Fund. (2008). *Wind power development in Armenia*. https://r2e2.am/en/r2e2-documents-pdf/. Accessed 26 Mar 2021.

Armenian Renewable Resources and Energy Efficiency Fund. (2011). *Renewable energy roadmap for Armenia*. https://r2e2.am/en/2018/02/27/re/. Accessed 26 Mar 2021.

Armenian Renewable Resources and Energy Efficiency Fund. (2019). *Annual report 2019*. https://r2e2.am/en/r2e2-documents-pdf/. Accessed 25 Mar 2021.

ArmenPress. (2018, April 4). *Masrik-1 project tender winner plans to enhance 55MW capacity*. https://armenpress.am/eng/news/928716.html. Accessed 28 Mar 2021.

Asian Development Bank. (2020). *Extended annual review report*. International Energy Corporation. Sevan-Hrazdan Cascade Hydropower System Rehabilitation Project. No: 46941-014. https://www.adb.org/projects/documents/arm-46941-014-xarr. Accessed 28 Mar 2021.

Energy Charter Secretary. (2005). *Armenia*. Regular review 2005. Trend sin energy and energy efficiency policies, instruments and actors. https://www.energycharter.org/what-we-do/energy-efficiency/energy-efficiency-country-reviews/energy-efficiency-regular-reviews/energy-efficiency-in-armenia-2005/. Accessed 04 Mar 2021.

Energy Charter Secretary. (2017). *In-depth review of the energy efficiency policy of Armenia*. https://www.energycharter.org/what-we-do/energy-efficiency/energy-efficiency-country-reviews/in-depth-review-of-energy-efficiency-policies-and-programmes/in-depth-review-of-the-energy-efficiency-policy-of-armenia-2016/. Accessed 04 Mar 2021.

European Bank of Reconstruction and Development. (2019). *Masrik-1 solar power plant*. https://www.ebrd.com/work-with-us/projects/psd/masrik1-solar-power-plant.html. Accessed 26 Mar 2021.

European Commission. (2019). *Commission implementing decision of 28.11.2019 on the annual action programme in favour of the Republic of Armenia for 2019*. Annex 2. Action Document for EU4 Energy Efficiency and Environment. C (2019) 8734final. Brussels.

Government of Republic of Armenia. (2010, September 13). *National energy efficiency action plan 2010*. Yerevan. https://energyagency.am/en/page_pdf/energakhnayoghoutyoun. Accessed 28 Mar 2021.

Government of Republic of Armenia. (2021a, April 22). Decision of the Government of the Republic of Armenia on Approval of the Nationally Determined Contribution 2021–2030 of the Republic of Armenia to Paris Agreement, N 610-L.

Government of Republic of Armenia. (2021b). *Energy strategy plan of Republic of Armenia until 2040*. https://www.e-draft.am/en/projects/2691/about. Accessed 02 Mar 2021.

Government of the Republic of Armenia. (2001, March 21). *Energy law*. http://www.minenergy.am/legislation/browse/cat_id/1/page/3. Accessed 20 Mar 2021.

Government of the Republic of Armenia. (2005). *Energy sector development strategies in the context of economic development in Armenia*. Adopted by the Government of Armenia. Session Protocol No 24, Resolution No 1.

Government of the Republic of Armenia. (2014a). *Armenia Development Strategy (ADS) for 2014–2025*. https://policy.asiapacificenergy.org/node/1492. Accessed 24 Mar 2021.

Government of the Republic of Armenia. (2014b). *Scaling up Renewable Energy Program (SREP). Investment Plan for Armenia.*

Government of the Republic of Armenia. (2020). *Energy sector development strategic program to 2040.* http://www.mtad.am/en/mtad2020/. Accessed 28 Mar 2021.

International Atomic Energy Agency. (2001). *Armenia: Country report.* https://www-pub.iaea.org/mtcd/publications/pdf/cnpp2003/cnpp_webpage/PDF/2001/Documents/Documents/Armenia%202001.pdf. Accessed 14 Mar 2021.

International Atomic Energy Agency. (2004). *Energy and nuclear power planning study for Armenia.* https://www.iaea.org/publications/7068/energy-and-nuclear-power-planning-study-for-armenia. Accessed 04 Mar 2021.

International Atomic Energy Agency. (2015). *Nuclear power in countries with limited electrical grid capacities: The case of Armenia.* No: TEDCOD-1778. Vienna.

International Atomic Energy Agency. (2020). *Armenia: Country nuclear power profiles.* Updated 2020. https://www-pub.iaea.org/MTCD/publications/PDF/cnpp2020/countryprofiles/Armenia/Armenia.htm. Accessed 02 Mar 2021.

International Energy Agency. (2018). *Country profile. Armenia.* https://www.iea.org/countries/armenia. Accessed 29 Mar 2021.

International Energy Agency & EU4Energy. (2020). *Energy-efficient buildings in Armenia. A roadmap.* https://www.euneighbours.eu/en/east/stay-informed/publications/energy-efficient-buildings-armenia-roadmap. Accessed 23 Mar 2021.

International Monetary Fund. (2005). *Growth and poverty reduction in Armenia.* Achievements and challenges. https://www.elibrary.imf.org/view/IMF058/02948-9781589064515/02948-9781589064515/ch01.xml?language=es&redirect=true. Accessed 22 Mar 2021.

Japan International Cooperation Agency. (2019). *Data collection survey on infrastructure development in Central Asia and the Caucasus.* Final report Armenia.

Ministry of Energy. (1998). *The Armenian energy sector: Development tasks and key issues.* Yerevan.

Ministry of Energy Infrastructures and Natural Resources of the Republic of Armenia. (2021). *Power system. Hydro energy.* http://www.minenergy.am/en/page/448. Accessed 02 Mar 2021.

Ministry of Environment of Republic of Armenia. (2021). *Ministry.* Historical overview. http://www.mnp.am/en/pages/21. Accessed 04 Mar 2021.

Ministry of Nature Protection. (2018). *Republic of Armenia.* Second Biennial National Report on Climate Change. https://unfccc.int/documents/77197. Accessed 02 Mar 2021.

Movsisyan, S., & Danielian, R. R. (2016). *The potential of wind energy in Armenian agricultural sector with modelling and in situ Lidar measurements.* https://www.researchgate.net/publication/309242741. Accessed 26 Mar 2021.

Observatory of Economic Complexity. (2020). *Country profile. Armenia.* https://oec.world/en/profile/country/arm. Accessed 02 Mar 2021.

Sargsyan, G., Balanabyan, A., & Hankinson, D. (2006). *From crisis to stability in the Armenian power sector.* Lesson learned from Armenia's energy reform experience. World Bank Working Paper No. 74. Washington, DC.

Sonigian, J. (2010, February 5). *Listening to the wind of change: Renewable energy in Armenia.* Asbarez. http://asbarez.com/77286/listening-to-the-wind-of-change-renewable-energy-in-armenia/. Accessed 26 Mar 2021.

Statistical Committee of the Republic of Armenia. (2019). *Statistical yearbook of Armenia.* https://www.armstat.am/en/?nid=586&year=2019. Accessed 22 Mar 2021.

United Nations. (2018). *SDG implementation.* Voluntary national review. Armenia. Transformation towards sustainable and resilient societies. Yerevan. https://www.am.undp.org/content/armenia/en/home/library/sdg-implementation-voluntary-national-review%2D%2Dvnr%2D%2Darmenia%2D%2D9%2D%2D1.html. Accessed 26 Mar 2021.

United States Agency for International Development. (2014). *Encouraging renewable energy development. Handbook for international energy regulators.* https://www.naruc.org/international/what-we-do/clean-energy/regulating-clean-energy-handbook/. Accessed 28 Mar 2021.

USAID. (2010). *Wind energy in Armenia: Overview of potential and development perspectives.* Yerevan.
Voroktnikov, V. (2016, January 6). *Legislative reform to promote solar energy in Armenia.* Renewable Energy World. https://www.renewableenergyworld.com/baseload/legislative-reform-to-promote-solar-energy-in-armenia/#gref. Accessed 28 Mar 2021.
World Bank. (2006). *Global environment facility trust fund grant to the Republic of Armenia for a renewable energy project.* Report No: 35352 AM. Washington, DC.
World Bank. (2019). *Energy efficiency project.* Armenia. Project performance assessment report No: 135626. https://ieg.worldbankgroup.org/reports/armenia-energy-efficiency-project-ppar. Accessed 29 Mar 2021.

Energy Governance in Austria

20

Niclas Wenz

Contents

Introduction	456
General Conditions of Energy Governance in Austria	457
Legacies	457
Composition of Austria's Energy Mix	459
Political Institutions and Key Actors	462
Energy Discourse	463
Coordination, Instruments, and Issues of Austria's Energy Transition	464
Drivers of Energy Transition in Austria	465
Strategies and Instruments of Energy Transition	466
Energy Supply	467
Energy Distribution	470
Energy Efficiency and Consumption	472
Outcome, Challenges, and Prospects	476
Cross-References	478
References	479

Abstract

This chapter examines Austria's energy governance system. It concentrates on the institutional coordination of energy policy with particular emphasis on transitional issues. It first introduces historical legacies, which shape both the current energy mix and patterns of energy governance. As hydropower traditionally contributes a considerable share of the energy supply, Austria seems to be comparatively well equipped to achieve a transformation toward a low-carbon energy system. Secondly, the analysis addresses transitional aspects of the energy system, along the topics of energy supply, energy distribution, and energy efficiency and consumption. While energy policy in Austria rests

---

N. Wenz (✉)
Institute of Political Science, Technical University of Darmstadt, Darmstadt, Germany
e-mail: wenz@pg.tu-darmstadt.de

© Springer Nature Switzerland AG 2022
M. Knodt, J. Kemmerzell (eds.), *Handbook of Energy Governance in Europe*,
https://doi.org/10.1007/978-3-030-43250-8_2

upon a long-standing neo-mercantilist tradition, this chapter will show that by means of European influences and the onset of renewables, energy governance underwent a careful modification. It will be shown that Austria's energy transition is characterized by stable governance arrangements that similarly provide the institutional capacities that allow for slow political dynamics. The chapter concludes with an appreciation of these culturally embedded institutional arrangements that forestall rapid political change while obviously granting enough flexibility to manage a long-term transitional development.

Keywords

Austria · Energy and climate policy in Austria · Energy governance · Energy transition · Federalism · Green electricity · Renewables

Introduction

The growing requirement for energy and the associated increase in environmental problems are leading to a great and radical transformation of the energy systems. This calls for a move toward environmental sustainability, a higher proportion of renewables and a flexibility of the grid infrastructure. Modern states are confronted with all of these "wicked problems" (cf. Rittel and Webber 1973) in energy policy today. European States respond strategically to these energy dilemmas in different ways, depending on their institutional and instrumental capacities (Ikenberry 1986; Lehmbruch 1969).

As this chapter demonstrates, Austria has for a long time followed a neo-mercantilist energy strategy, with government-owned power stations and central planning responsibilities held by administrative and political bodies. However, this strategic orientation in energy policy was challenged by national environmental movements in the 1980s (cf. Kok and Schaller 1986), the accession to the European Union in 1995 (cf. Pollak and Riekmann 2017), and a growing pressure from the global climate change regime (cf. Koehane 2015). Since then, Austria has moved from a primarily neo-mercantilist to a more competitive energy strategy. In this respect, the role of the state changes from the self-perception as an energy producer to an embedded negotiator in the specific and peculiar, multi-level pattern of Austria's energy governance system.

This brings the dynamics of energy governance systems into the focus (cf. Benz et al. 2016), which Ikenberry did not address due to his comparative research design (Ikenberry 1986) and which the socio-technical transition literature did not expect due to their attention to key actors without defining more precisely the enabling structures in which they are embedded (Geels and Schot 2007). However, the conditions of governance dynamics are of major interest with respect to the energy transformation, because they shape the capacity of policymaking. For that reason, the analysis emphasizes the governance system along the energy value chain of supply, distribution, and consumption.

20 Energy Governance in Austria

The chapter first outlines Austria's energy legacies, its main actors and its levels of governance, the current energy strategy until 2020, and the new strategy until 2030. It also provides an overview of current policy instruments that are intended to fulfil the strategic ambitions of energy policy. The next section deals with the structures of decision-making processes in energy policy within the Austrian multi-level framework. This analysis captures the different capacities for managing the transition in the fields of energy supply, energy distribution, as well as energy efficiency and consumption. Finally, the conclusion emphasizes political blockades and dynamics in view of the institutional capacities in Austria's governance system.

General Conditions of Energy Governance in Austria

After World War II, the Republic of Austria started to rebuild and construct new power plants with the help of the Marshall Plan. In line with the so-called Second Law of Nationalization (zweites Verstaatlichungsgesetz) in 1947, the Republic of Austria owned every power station with a generating capacity of more than 200 kilowatts. In the following years, especially between 1950 and 1980, Austria generated great electricity capacity from huge run-of-river and pumped-storage plants. This historical tradition of hydropower is still one of the characteristics of Austria's electricity system today (Wagner et al. 2015). While hydropower dominated the landscape in the West and South of Austria, steam power plants dominated in the eastern part of the republic. This regional fragmentation of energy plants is still present today and continues to exist due to the topographical conditions for wind power use (Höltinger et al. 2016, p. 55). Consequently, the electricity mix contains a high proportion of hydropower and thermal power stations. Nuclear energy has never been part of the energy mix because a plebiscite rejected its use in 1978 by a narrow majority (Bayer 2014). In this regard, it is noteworthy that Austria only have limited domestic fossil fuel resource, particularly small mineral oil deposits in the northeastern part of the country. Coal mining reached its peak in the 1950s, but witnessed a sharp decline since then. Domestic mining finally ceased in 2006 (bmwfw 2017).

Legacies

The Austrian energy system is closely linked with the state. During the twentieth century, the energy system was mainly characterized by large power plants owned by the VERBUND (Österreichische Elektrizitätswirtschafts AG), regional electricity utilities (Landesgesellschaften), and special companies (Sondergesellschaften) for large-scale power plants. However, these special companies have now been incorporated into the VERBUND Group, and the local electricity utilities have been merged into nine regional energy providers (Veigl 2004, p. 30f; Stickinger 2004, p. 166f; Winkler-Rieder 2006, p. 678; Lauber 2002; Korom 2012).

Due to the fact that the state-led goals of the energy and electricity industries were widely accepted by the political parties as well as by the political and economic stakeholders, energy policy in Austria has been following a period of "growth consensus" for a long time. The dominant players in the growth paradigm were the two main parties, the Christian Democrats (Österreichische Volkspartei) (ÖVP) and the Social Democrats (Sozialdemokratische Partei Österreichs) (SPÖ), the regional electricity utilities, social partners, construction companies, and banks (Kok 1991).

Until 1958, Austria was one of the net oil-exporting countries, although the administration of oil production was regulated by the Soviet Union in the postwar years (Frank 1982, p. 249). Until the first oil crisis in 1973, Austria pursued the strategy of suppressing the importance of oil as an energy resource (Glatz 1986, p. 76). For this reason, Austria joined the International Energy Agency (IEA) in the year 1974 in order to reduce its dependence on Organization of the Petroleum Exporting Countries (OPEC) oil, just like other industrialized countries (cf. Maull and Mild 1986). After this "critical juncture," the Energy Council was founded, first named "Beirat für Fragen des Energiesparens" and later "Beirat für sinnvolle Energieanwendung," to institutionalize Austria's corporatist interest groups in energy policy (Frank 1982, p. 260). The common goals in the following years were to diversify energy supply, decrease energy dependency, and guarantee low energy prices (Winkler-Rieder 2006, p. 676ff).

The emergence of the environmental movement in the early 1980s and the associated criticism of the traditional large-scale electricity system shifted the prevailing planning paradigm of the postwar period. The rejection of the growth paradigm was supported by national events and external factors. Beginning with the antinuclear protest and environmental movements in the 1980s, environmental and social aspects of energy policy issues were addressed for the first time (Kok and Schaller 1986).

With the limited privatization in 1987, the previously state-run energy industry opened up for new shareholders (Stickinger 2004, p. 172f; Perschy 2012, p. 6). The aim was to refinance the energy companies without losing state influence on the critical energy infrastructure. For this reason, a "50 + 1 principle" to benefit public interests regulates the influence of the growing private economy on energy policy. Against the background of comparatively low electricity prices in Europe, this principle can certainly be regarded as a success to fulfil Austria's strategic targets.

Following the Kyoto Protocol, the Ministry of the Environment passed the first *Climate Protection Strategy* in 2002 as well as a first *Climate Adaptation Strategy* 10 years later (Prutsch et al. 2017; Hackl 2001). The *Climate Protection Strategy* was already evaluated in 2005 and amended 2 years later. Nevertheless, the Austrian states (Bundesländer) did not agree with the *Climate Protection Strategy* after the evaluation because they were not integrated enough into the process, particularly with regard to the building sector (cf. Steurer and Clar 2015). In order to support climate protection, the *Climate-Active* initiative was adopted in 2004. The *Climate-Active* initiative is a network of businesses, politicians, and citizens with the aim of informing, advising, and promoting measures to reduce CO_2 emissions (Komendantova et al. 2018).

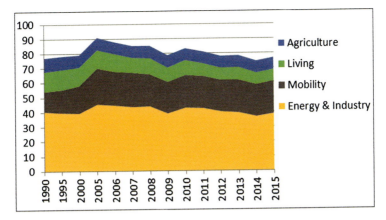

Fig. 1 Greenhouse gas emissions by sector in million tons. (Source: Federal Environmental Agency 2017)

As a result of the Kyoto regime, the EU has implemented the European *Emissions Trading System* (ETS) since 2005 in order to address the international climate problem with regard to the reduction of greenhouse gases for the "collective good" (cf. Ostrom 2010). The European *Emissions Trading System* is a market-based instrument. The relatively poor performance of the reduction of greenhouse gases in Austria can be attributed to the fact that about two-thirds of emissions are produced by companies covered by the ETS, which had suffered from low certificate prices for a long time. The remaining one third are subject to the *National Climate Protection Act* (CPA). The CPA aims for an overall CO_2 reduction of 48.8 million tons by 2020, specified by negotiated sector goals. Nevertheless, in view of the distribution of GHG emissions by sector (Fig. 1), it becomes clear why political strategies and instruments for effectively managing climate change are being applied in the energy and industrial sectors as well as in the mobility sector, in which the biggest opportunities are to be found.

Composition of Austria's Energy Mix

The energy mix in Austria has been based on long-term political planning concepts for a long time. The strong affinity for central planning of energy policy can already be found in both the 1948 *Coal Plan* and the first comprehensive *National Energy Concept* in 1969 which was not adopted due to various conflicts. However, the first *Austrian Energy Plan*, adopted in 1975, largely based on the energy concept. With the *Energy Promotion Act* of 1979, a legal framework for energy planning was passed. It obliged the federal government to submit an annual energy report to the parliament, which contains information on the energy supply for the coming 10 years (Frank 1982, pp. 257–264).

The energy report aimed at the replacement of oil consumption by coal, nuclear, hydropower, and natural gas – mainly in the heating sector. Nuclear energy, for example, was supposed to provide one-third of the energy supply. The second oil crisis in 1979 had comparatively little impact in Austria. To a large extent, energy policy just continued. However, there had been resistance to nuclear energy, which was directed against the launching of the nuclear power plant in Zwentendorf. A referendum held in 1978 abandoned the commissioning of the Zwentendorf plant. From that time on, Austria has been a country without nuclear energy, neither being used nor planned (Bayer 2014). The environmental and anticapitalistic protest against nuclear power soon extended to the increasingly large hydroelectric power plants (Pesendorfer 2007, p. 120). In recent years, criticism of hydropower was extended to small-scale installations due to environmental concerns (Fruhrmann et al. 2018).

By rejecting nuclear power, which increased costs in coal-fired power generation and raised oil prices continually, Austria was forced to realign its energy policy plans in the mid-1980s. The consequences can be seen in the historical longitudinal picture of Austria's energy mix with a growing proportion of renewables and gas (Fig. 2).

Focusing on the energy supply for the electricity system, Fig. 3 indicates why Austria is often described as a "clean energy system." A closer look at the renewable sector shows the central dominance and long history of hydropower. In Austria's electricity system, hydropower is divided into run-of-river power plants, pumping stations, and micro-hydro. This differentiation is not unimportant because both pumped storage power plants and run-of-river power plants are excluded from the promotion of renewable energies. The expansion of "new renewables" wind, solar, and district heating has been growing very slowly in Austria.

The so-called eco-electricity, which excludes hydropower and highlights the new renewables solar, wind, biomass, and micro-hydropower plants, only contributes to a small amount of electricity supply. This correlates with the fact that the Republic of

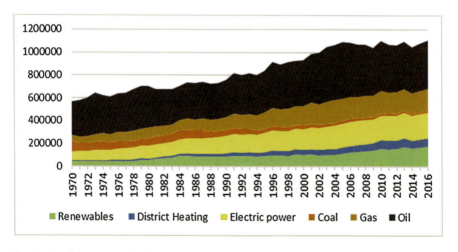

Fig. 2 Austria's energy mix of end use in Pt. (Source: Statistic Austria 2016)

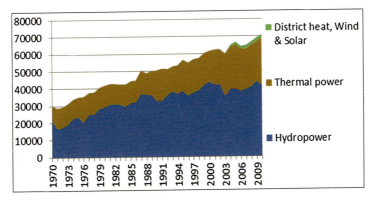

Fig. 3 Electricity supply in Austria in GWh. (Source: Statistic Austria 2016)

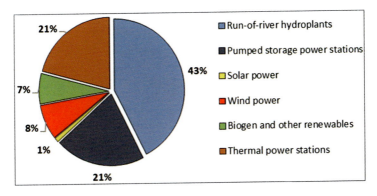

Fig. 4 Electricity generation in 2016. (Source: Statistic Austria 2017)

Austria has no maritime access, which limited especially the use of wind power in comparison to Denmark, Portugal, or the UK. However, studies on the potential of wind power show that there are possibilities for using wind turbines in the eastern federal states of Lower Austria, Upper Austria, and Burgenland (Höltinger et al. 2016, p. 55).

Figure 4 gives a detailed impression of the electricity mix in Austria. The current electricity mix is very flexible because between 1950 and 1980, Austria invested in the expansion of hydropower and pumped storage power plants. In the 1970s, the preference was to build hydropower plants along the Danube, such as the huge power station in Altenwörth near Vienna as well as the construction of pumping stations in the Alps, such as the massive Malta pumped storage power station in Carinthia. In particular, pumped storage power plants allow for flexible energy management. Compared to other EU member states, Austria is ideally situated with regard to the growing importance of storage in the context of the energy transformation.

Political Institutions and Key Actors

The constitution (Bundesverfassungsgesetz B-VG) of the Republic of Austria established a federal political system. In addition, since Austria joined the EU in 1995, the EU had a major influence on national policy. As a result, energy governance in Austria is embedded in a multi-level structure.

Three essential features distinguish the institutional context of policymaking in Austria. Firstly, Austria is characterized by a "semi-federalism" (Niedertscheider et al. 2018, p. 13), a "artificial federalism" (Pelinka 2004, p. 524), or a so-called hierarchical federalism (Pollak and Riekmann 2017, p. 425). It emphasizes the domination of the first chamber of parliament (Nationalrat) over the states chamber (Bundesrat). In general, the Austrian Bundesrat has only a suspensive veto power over the Nationalrat. In cases of conflict and dissent, the first chamber of parliament enforces the decision-making process. However, with regard to energy policy, this general description of federalism in Austria is lacking.

Responsibilities for energy policy in Austria are divided between the federal and the state level. Electricity falls within the jurisdiction of both the federal and state levels. In general, constitutional and general matters are subject to federal legislation, while implementation (executive legislation) is subject to state legislation. However, the federal government is solely responsible for the energy tax, energy meters, and energy supply emergency regulations (IEA 2014, p. 21). But the states also have sole legislative powers that are important in the context of the energy transformation: in construction law and the promotion of housing, regional planning, and nature and landscape conservation. In addition, the states are responsible for all issues that have not been constitutionally assigned to the federal state (Bußjäger 2016a, p. 523).

This applies, for example, to the promotion of green energy and energy efficiency, where delegating law making to the federal government is subject to specific constitutional rules between the federal and states level (Bund- Ländervereinbarungen according to Art. 15a B-VG). Accordingly, in terms of energy policy, Austria can be described as a multi-level governance system confronted by typical challenges between the federal and states level.

Secondly, in Austria there exists a significant culture of corporatism (Armingeon 2017, p. 206). This strong corporatism can be seen in the social partnership principles and their integration in policymaking. In Austria, the central interest groups, the so-called social partners, are closely intertwined with the two major parties, the Christian Democrats and the Social Democrats. The socialists hold majorities in the Chamber of Labor and the Trade Union Confederation. On the other hand, the Christian Democrats hold majorities in both the Economic Chamber and the Chamber of Agriculture (Pelinka 2004, p. 542). That is why Austria is described as an ideal type of corporatism in comparative political science theory (Lehmbruch 1985). Especially in the second half of the 2000s, the influence of the social partners increased again in energy and climate policy (Brand and Pawloff 2014). With regard to energy policy, the two interest groups Federation of Austrian Industries (IV) and Oesterreichs Energie (OE), the latter of which is Austria's association of electricity companies, need to be mentioned. Furthermore, the umbrella associations Renewable Energy Austria (EEÖ) and the "Eco Office" (ÖKOBÜRO) were also involved in the energy policy. All eight interest groups are strongly integrated and constitute the social partnership element in Austria's energy governance system today.

The third feature is the strong party-ruled state system in Austria. The party system is characterized by three main parties, which form the government and build up an ideology-driven party system. These are the ÖVP, the SPÖ, and the right-wing party Freiheitliche Partei Österreichs (FPÖ). Until the 1980s, the Austrian party system was dominated by the two major parties ÖVP and SPÖ and the remarkable smaller FPÖ. The party system was supplemented in the middle of the 1980s by the emergence of the political party Die Grünen (GRÜNE) and once again in the 1990s by the separation of the Liberals (NEOS) from the FPÖ (Pelinka 2004, pp. 534–535). In addition, the Liste Peter Pilz separated from the GRÜNE during the last general election campaign in 2017. As a result of these elections, the GRÜNE failed to meet the four-percent hurdle and is no longer represented in the Nationalrat. Up to this election, the GRÜNE, together with the grand coalition, had commanded a two-thirds majority in energy policy issues. This institutional structure is an important feature of the political system, since it gives opposition parties a lever to block new legislation. Since October 2017 and in the light of the new government between the ÖVP and FPÖ, the ability to block is held by the liberal party, NEOS.

However, the pattern of multi-level policymaking varies considerably depending on the three topics of energy supply, energy distribution, and efficient energy consumption. As I will explain below, energy supply with renewable energies has shifted from decentralized to centralized governance, while both decentralized and centralized governance patterns characterize the topic of energy distribution. Finally, energy efficiency policy is embedded in a governance comparable with "joint decision-making" (cf. Scharpf 1976). The fact that there have been no long-lasting political blockades in the past can be explained by specific mechanisms and processes familiar in Austrian politics for many years (cf. Lehmbruch 1967; cf. Benz 2015). Based on practical experience, political actors had learned and developed heuristic procedures to overcome their tricky institutional structures (Ostrom 1998, p. 8). These processes are embedded in a decision-making culture based on trust and routines, comparable to the game theory strategy called "tit-for-tat" (cf. Axelrod and Hamilton 1981). As a result, those routines of political action allows for dynamical adoptions within Austria's energy governance, despite of the overall institutional rigidity.

Energy Discourse

The energy system, as well as water and air, is generally perceived as clean by the general public in Austria and not as a national problem for the environment or public health. So it is hardly surprising that the energy transformation in Austria is being addressed in particular in the context of the global climate problem and to an increasing extent in terms of energy security. Both aspects shape the energy discourse in Austria today. With regard to climate change challenges, there are little differences between the political parties, since climate change became an issue at all in the late 1980s. Differences exist only in degree. In particular, the GRÜNE in the mid-1990s and mid-2000s addressed the challenges of climate change comparatively above average (Ruß 2014).

The prominence of energy security has increased in the recent past with the expansion of renewables and the gradual establishment of the FPÖ as a governmental party both at the national and the state level.

One dimension of this security discourse addresses the reduction of energy resources such as oil and gas as well as electricity imports from European countries whose supply traced back to coal but mainly nuclear power. In particular, following the reactor disaster in Fukushima, Austria's "freedom from nuclear power" (Atomstromfreies Österreich) was promoted again. As a result, the energy industry introduced voluntary *guarantees of origin* for electricity at the *Nuclear Summit* in 2012 (Rihs 2012, p. 71).

On the other hand, a second dimension of the security discourse address the rising volatility of the electricity grid and their impacts on re-dispatch costs as part of the expansion of new renewables. What both discourses have in common is that they are finally aimed at promoting national energy sources. However, while the first discourse dimension favors the promotion of wind and solar power, the second discourse dimension focuses on baseload power, which is traditionally provided by hydropower in Austria's energy mix. It is worth mentioning in this context that the SPÖ is historical linked to the VERBUND Group, while the ÖVP maintains a traditionally relationship to the former regional electricity utilities (Stickinger 2004, pp. 167–169).

The FPÖ is not homogenous and differs from right-wing parties in Germany or Switzerland with regard to energy issues. This is visible by the fact that the FPÖ is committed to reducing greenhouse gas emissions, promoting the antinuclear consensus from the very beginning and supports the expansion of new renewables in order to reduce the import dependency of Austria's energy system (Forchtner 2013, pp. 130–131). Both the FPÖ and the GRÜNE have no long-term established ties with energy supply companies. This is why both parties are far more critical about large hydroelectric power stations and the operating companies, like the VERBUND AG or the Tyrolean TIWAG. For this reason, it is not surprising that the *Green Electricity Act* (GEA) was adopted by an ÖVP/FPÖ coalition and that in the current government coalition the FPÖ wants to adapt the tendering process for renewable energies in order to put the incumbent companies controlling hydropower into competition with the new renewables wind and solar.

Coordination, Instruments, and Issues of Austria's Energy Transition

As the preceding section demonstrates, energy policy in Austria nowadays is embedded in a federal government system, a culture of corporatism, a plural number of political parties, and a growing network of interest and pressure groups.

The vertical differentiation at political and administrative levels as well as the functional interdependencies for the study of energy transformation in Austria suggest a multi-level perspective. This perspective has its origins in negotiation and game theories and explanations, although today a broad conceptual approach is usually chosen within the framework of a multi-level governance analysis (cf. Benz 2009). Accordingly, the following sections are based on aspects of this broad governance approach.

Due to the cross-sectional nature of the energy policy and the associated complexity of the policy field, it is helpful to divide the governance analysis of energy policy into its three central topics. Thus, the following subsections focus firstly on the supply of renewable energies, secondly on the distribution of electricity, and lastly on energy efficiency and consumption. Initially, the main transitional drivers will be outline, and the current energy strategy of Austria and its targets will be discussed.

Drivers of Energy Transition in Austria

A first rethinking of Austria's energy policy began with the oil crises of the 1970s. Triggered by the first oil crisis, a search for alternative and new energy sources began, while at the same time the antinuclear movement successfully prevents the substitution of oil products by the use of nuclear energy. This means that the use of nuclear energy, which was already favored in 1967 as part of the Enquete *Nuclear Power Austria* (Atomenergie Österreich), failed (Frank 1983, p. 254). In addition to the massive expansion of hydropower and with the rejection of nuclear power, pioneering efforts started to use combined heat and power, solar energy (cf. Mautz et al. 2018), biomass (Madlener 2007), or wind power (Hansch 1998, pp. 84–87). This early development of local initiatives began in the late 1970s and developed in the 1980s. With the unification into the GRÜNE Party in 1986, the isolated movements and decentralized initiatives finally became represented in party politics. Since then green politics is still driving the energy transformation in Austria domestically.

Afterward, the 1990s were dominated by external drivers. On the international scale, from the *Toronto Agreement* in 1988 to the accession to the EU in 1995 and the *Kyoto Protocol* 2 years later, Austria has made far-reaching commitments to reduce national carbon emissions and support the transformation process in the direction of a liberalized energy market (Niedertscheider et al. 2018). Nevertheless, the case of Austria shows the gap between far reaching commitments to cut carbon emission at the international level and national action. In this regard, Austria mostly failed to achieve their climate reduction targets, in the past years. This mismatch is explained by a lack of national measures and instruments (Hackl 2001) and has been widely criticized as opportunistic politics in the recent past (cf. Steurer and Clar 2015). However, the international and in particular the European level is a major driving force for the development of national energy as well as climate strategies. Nevertheless, transition drivers were always mixed between external presser from the international scale and internal factors from the national context.

Strategies and Instruments of Energy Transition

Already in the *White Paper on Renewable Energies* in 1997, the European ambitions to increase the share of renewable energies by 2010 became visible. The common goal was to provide 12% of the energy mix in the EU from renewable energy sources. In addition, energy efficiency should be increased by 1% annually. With the introduction of European legislation in 2001 and 2003 (Directive 2001/77/EG and 2003/30/EG), indicative targets were defined for the member states, which addressed the promotion and improvement of grid access for renewables by 2010 (Zabukovec 2005, p. 25). However, due to the lack of binding targets and sanctions, the Austrian implementation took a slow pace. For this reason, the European Commission has initiated *infringement proceedings* in particular against Italy, Spain, and Austria (KOM 2009, p. 192).

Driven by the weak results of the European benchmarking in the target year 2010 between the member states, Austria has developed a detailed strategy to achieve the next targets in line with the *Europe 2020 Strategy*. This European strategy aims for a reduction of greenhouse gases by 20%, the expansion of renewables by 20%, and an increase in energy efficiency by 20% until 2020. As a result, central directives were adopted to address climate, energy, and efficiency policies (Directive 2009/29/EG, 2009/28/EG and 2012/27EG) which, for the first time, involved binding targets for all member states (Storr 2015, p. 40). In order to achieve these new targets, a national strategy, called *Energy Strategy of Austria 2020*, was drawn up at a very early stage in Austria (bmlfuw and bmwfw 2010; Bergauer-Culver 2012).

The long-term strategy was drafted under the leadership of ministers Reinhold Mitterlehner and Nikolaus Berlakovich in the time of the grand coalition in 2009 (Vones 2011). The strategy was to set out strategic priorities and measures that will enable the transition to a sustainable energy system on the one hand and the implementation of the EU 2020 targets on the other.

The consultation process for drawing up Austria's energy strategy included more than 150 key actors and laid down Austria's four norms of energy policy:

> "The energy strategy follows [...] the energy policy objectives of security of supply, environmental compatibility, social compatibility, competitiveness." (bmlfuw and bmwfw 2010, p. 14)

As part of this strategic planning, three quantifiable targets were formulated: firstly, to increase energy efficiency by 20% by 2020, secondly to raise the share of renewable energies to 34% of gross energy consumption, and finally to reduce greenhouse gases by 21% for sectors covered ETS and 16% for all others, relative to the base year 2005.

In total, 370 proposals were submitted in the consultation process set up by the federal government, the states, social partners, and numerous other interested groups from science and society. These proposals formed the cornerstones of the Austrian energy strategy until 2020, which was presented to the European Commission in July 2010.

The second strategy, called *Austria's Climate and Energy Strategy*, will cover the period from 2020 to 2030. As in the current energy strategy, a consultation process was also established. However, the negotiations were suspended after the sudden resignation of the Minister of Economics and the collapse of the grand coalition in mid-May 2017. Nevertheless, a small amendment to the *Electricity Management and Organization Act* (EMOA) was passed in summer 2017.

In January 2018, the federal government decided to resume the process in climate and energy policy for 2030. The second strategy process was managed by the new right-wing conservative coalition and led by Elisabeth Köstinger and Norbert Hofer. Before that, in 2016, a *Green Paper for an integrated energy and climate strategy* was passed by four ministries during the time of a grand coalition (bmwfw and bmlfuw 2016). In April 2018, the consultation process started under the label *mission2030* (bmnt and bmvit 2018). Compared to the previous energy strategy until 2020, the new climate and energy strategy was adopted by consensus in the council of ministers.

Austria's Climate and Energy Strategy 2030 intends to cut total greenhouse gas emissions by 36% in 2030 compared to 2005 and aims for full decarbonization in 2050. Therefore, the government focuses on cutting fossil fuel use in the mobility and building sectors. To achieve carbon neutrality in the mobility and especially transport sector, the new strategy entails the promotion of rail transport and the increase of energy efficiency in freight logistics. The share of renewables in Austria's energy mix should go up to 45–50% by 2030, according to the new energy strategy. With regard to gross electricity consumption, Austria set a 100% target for renewables by 2030. The government aims to reduce energy intensity by 25–30% compared to 2015. In order to accomplish all these goals, 12 flagship projects have been identified from different ministries, which are to be implemented in the coming years (bmnt and bmvit 2018). Austria has thus once again reacted to the EU's targets up to 2030, as decided by EU leaders and governments at the end of 2014.

Energy Supply

Electricity supply in Austria is part of the *basic and executive legislation* (Art 12 B-VG). This legislative structure is comparable to the former *framework legislation* in Germany or the *basic legislation* in Spain (Bußjäger 2016b, p. 811).

The government started promoting renewable energies in Austria in 1994, when subsidies for them were introduced for the first time. The promotion doubled the market standard tariff for wind power plants in the first 3 years of operation. In addition, the Ministry of Environment supported investments in the construction of wind turbines by up to 30%. However, the increased subsidies for wind power plants were limited until 1996 and no follow-up financing became apparent so that the expansion of wind power declined again in the following years (cf. Fig. 5).

With the reorganization of the structure of the energy market design, in particular in the electricity sector, the *Electricity Management and Organization Act* set targets for

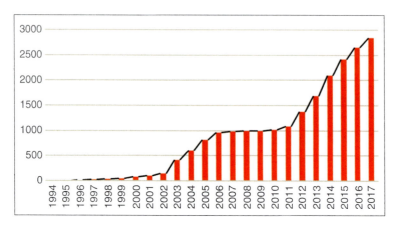

Fig. 5 Wind power expansion in Austria in MW. (Source: IG Windkraft 2018)

new renewables since 1998. In order to manage the expansion of renewables, the federal government again inserted feed-in tariffs within the framework of a *basic and executive legislation act*. However, the amount of the tariffs was not uniformly regulated at the federal level and differed between the states. In the following years and within the framework of the *Energy Liberalisation Act*, the regional governors (Landeshauptleute) were required to calculate the feed-in tariffs for renewable energies on the basis of the average costs of green electricity plants (Junker et al. 2014, p. 8).

With regard to the expansion of renewable energies, the *Green Electricity Act* has been the central instrument since 2002. It is based on a price-oriented incentive scheme. For reasons of cost efficiency, Austria's nine states called for a uniform subsidy for renewables since the turn of the millennium. Furthermore, the states supported the introduction of a regulatory authority and were willing to relocate jurisdiction in energy policy from the regional to the federal level. The responsibilities for the national level in subsidizing renewables are defined by agreements in accordance with Article 15a of the Federal Constitutional Law (B-VG).

Since the states did not want to voluntarily give up their responsibilities in energy policy, the level-shift required a two-thirds majority in the National Council. But to gain a two-thirds majority in Austria's pluralist party system usually requires the involvement of the opposition. Previously in 2004, the federal government had submitted a major amendment to the *Green Electricity Act*. Due to the lack of consent between the SPÖ and ÖVP in the National Council, progress on the amendment was slowed down for 2 years (Stöger 2015, pp. 191–199). Ultimately, the first amendment of the GEA was passed despite regional opposition by consent of the GRÜNE in May 2006. The central modification of the GEA 2006 is the implementation of a green power settlement agency (OeMAG) with an annual funding for the expansion of green electricity (Fig. 6). With the introduction of OeMAG, the unlimited payments for all renewable energy plants stopped. Since then, only renewable installations have been promoted and remunerated which have received a permit within the annual funding volume by the OeMAG.

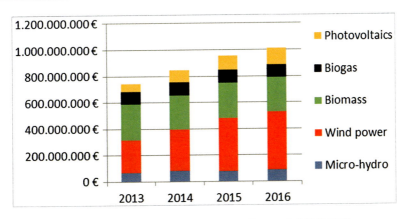

Fig. 6 Funding of green electricity by OeMAG in euros. (Source: OeMAG 2016)

The GEA grants the competence to the OeMAG (under supervision of the Ministry of Economics and the National Audit Office) to assign concessions for renewable energy installations. At the request of the power plant operators, OeMAG enters into contracts as part of the feed-in tariffs. Subsequently, OeMAG sells the generated green electricity to the electricity traders at a fixed price, which was set by the Federal Ministry until 2012. Today, OeMAG sells the green electricity at the market price (day-ahead price) directly to the electricity traders. The additional payments for renewable electricity are financed by the flat-rate renewables charge (Ökostrompauschale) and the renewables contribution (Ökostromförderbeitrag). Both surcharges on the electricity price are paid by the end consumers and are detail listed on consumer bills (Rihs 2012).

The GEA 2012 represents an important revision of the first *Green Electricity Act*. It was adopted in July 2012 in the wake of the *Energy Strategy Austria 2020*. The aim of the amendment was to speed up the expansion of renewable energies, which have seen a significant increase since then, particularly with regard to wind power energy (Fig. 5). With the establishment of the OeMAG in 2008, a long waiting list of power plant operators ensued. In order to reduce the building application for the construction of new eco-power plants, one of the measures was to offer an immediate award of reduced feed-in tariffs in 2012. In addition, the funding of subsidies increased significantly. At the same time, the feed-in tariffs for new plants are being reduced in order to relieve the cost burden for the end customer (cf. Fig. 7).

The amendment of the GEA in 2017 differs only slightly from the fundamental revision of the GEA in 2012, because no modification has been made to the main mechanisms. As a result, the GEA 2017 was referred to as a "small amendment" and was not subject to the notification process of the European Union. In order to reduce the waiting list again, the measures of the small amendment to the *Green Electricity Act* include technology-specific budgets that had already been adopted in the fundamental amendment after the implementation of the energy strategy in 2012.

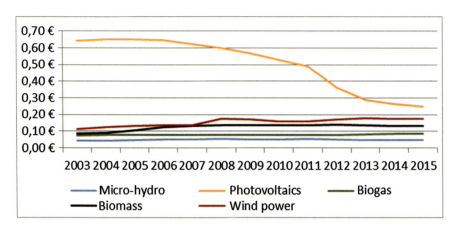

Fig. 7 Feed-in tariffs in Eurocent per KWh. (Source: E-Control 2016a)

Energy Distribution

In contrast to energy supply, the distribution of electricity in Austria remains a monopoly right after the liberalization of the European energy market. The distribution and transmission of power (Wegerecht) are within the responsibility of the federal government if the electrical power lines attach two or more states (Bußjäger 2016a, p. 538f). In this sense, the law on the use of power lines dates back to the 1960s and has remained largely unchanged since then (Hauer 2004, p. 71).

Since February 2016, the central administration department has been the Energy Infrastructure Authority which was established at federal level as part of the scope of the *Infrastructure Act* (E-InfrastrukturG). Nevertheless, the responsibilities of the federal government within the context of new structure are limited, because the approval of the *Environmental Impact Assessment* (EIA-G 2000) is now granted by the states. If power lines or power storage facilities are subject to *EIA audits*, the Energy Infrastructure Authority has only a supporting and coordinating role. The responsibilities for the electricity *Infrastructure Act* and *EIA audits* were supposed to have been centralized in 2017. However, the grand coalition did not have the necessary two-thirds majority to amend the constitution and could not agree on a joint legislative package in negotiations with the GRÜNE party. As a result, responsibilities for energy distribution are fragmented between the levels of government, and the authority of the infrastructure department is usually subject to mediation.

In accordance with Austrian law, the planning of transmission network expansion in both the electricity and gas sectors will be carried out by the Austrian Power Grid (APG). The APG as Austria's transmission system operator (TSO) is managed as a 100% subsidiary company of Austria's VERBUND Group. Although, the VERBUND Group was partially privatized in 1988, the Republic of Austria is still the core shareholder with 51% of the shareholdings. Therefore, the state is significantly involved in its profits and has a comparatively large influence on the organization and policy of the transmission system operator in Austria.

In contrast to the German or UK electricity network with four TSOs, the APG is the only system operator in Austria. The former regional network operators Vorarlberg and Tyrol were incorporated into the nationwide APG Company, following the third so-called European Energy Package. This was made possible by close cooperation agreements with the two regional system operators and the APG. In March 2012, APG has been officially certified as an independent transmission system operator by the EU. Thus, Austria has successfully completed the European requirement to separate the business units of energy distribution and supply in the framework of an independent transmission operator (cf. Schmidt 2011; Storr 2015, pp. 28–29).

Furthermore, the APG is a member of the interest group European Network of Transmission System Operators for Electricity (ENTSO-E), organized at the European level. Together with other European TSOs, ENTSO-E aims to implement a common pan-European transmission network. For this purpose, ENTSO-E prepares a non-binding *Ten Years Network Development Plan* (TYNDP) every 2 years, which also identifies *projects of common interest* (PCI). These projects should have particular priority in the Commission's infrastructure program for cross-border electricity exchange (Fischer and Rosenkranz 2012, pp. 86–88).

The European PCIs are of great importance for the energy transit country Austria. Usually, Austria imports a large share of its electricity from Germany and the Czech Republic and exports electricity to Switzerland, Italy, Slovenia, and Hungary. Due to its flexible energy mix, Austria typically imports electricity during the daytime and exports electricity to its neighbors at night. With the turn of the millennium, Austria changed from an exporter to a net importer in the electricity sector (Fig. 8). In 2016, this resulted in costs of €100 m for Austria. With regard to the total national energy demand, Austria provides 36% of its energy domestically and is clearly above the European average (bmnt 2018, p. 26).

Besides the management of the electricity exchange, APG is responsible for the annual preparation of the *Network Development Plan* (NDP), which is the central

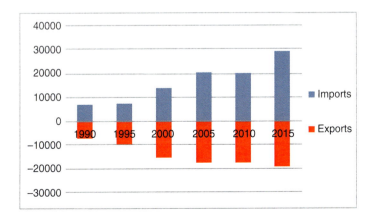

Fig. 8 Electricity imports and exports in GWh. (Source: E-Control 2016b, p. 26)

regulatory instrument for energy distribution. The NDP outlines long-term infrastructure projects for energy transmission. Although the TYNDP is not officially binding, the European pre-planning influences the annual preparation of the legally required NDP. With the renewed amendment to the *Electricity and Organization Act* in 2010, APG was obliged to list upcoming energy infrastructure projects within the regular framework of the NDP. Therefore, APG voluntarily managed the *APG master plan* in 2009 and 2013. These voluntary preparations of a master plan were part of strategic long-term planning. A process that includes universities, research institutes and the civil society with the aim to generate a wider acceptance of future infrastructure projects and a better coordination for the development of the NDP (APG 2013). The regulatory authority E-Control must subsequently authorize all measures proposed in the NDP.

E-Control is Austria's regulatory authority, which was established in 2001 as part of the European liberalization efforts (cf. Haberfellner et al. 2002). As part of the liberalization of the energy market, Austria has adopted the *regulated third-party access* (rTPA). Since then, the regulator sets the grid operation tariffs until they are finally calculated by a benchmarking system between the regional distribution networks. Similar to the ENTSO-E association for the national network operators, the European Agency for Cooperation of Energy Regulators (ACER) is the central European institution for cooperation between the regulatory authorities. ACER monitors and supports the network development plans for free- and cross-border electricity exchange and supports the design of the TYNDP.

Energy Efficiency and Consumption

Energy efficiency, heating systems and energy saving or the reduction of energy consumption in housing and community amenities fall within the key responsibilities of the states, as far as no competence coverage between the federal and regional level shift a unique jurisdiction to the federal state.

Energy efficiency is of great importance in Austria and was addressed for the first time after the oil crisis in the 1970s. Efficiency instruments were drawn up within the framework of international agreements. But it became evident that the Federal Constitutional Law had no regulatory structure for this. It was therefore necessary to find a common policy between the federal and state governments. The initial meetings resulted in a first joint agreement in accordance with Article 15a B-VG on energy saving in the early 1980s (BGBl. No. 351/1980). The agreement between the federal and state governments enabled to pursue a coordinated effort in energy-saving and efficiency policy while retaining the current constitutional jurisdiction. Nevertheless, the agreement had no immediate effect and had to be incorporated into federal and regional laws. While the federal government set basic standards within a basic framework, it was up to the states to expand this in terms of their local requirements. The second agreement in the energy-saving and efficiency policy followed in 1995 in the course of accession to the EU and updated the first contract (BGBl. Nr. 388/1995). Austria's political focus shifted again to energy efficiency in

2006 because energy consumption had almost doubled from 567 PJ to 1,093 PJ since 1970. This renewed attention was supported by the *European directive on energy end-use efficiency* (Directive 2006/32/EC). As before, a jurisdiction agreement with the states was necessary in order to incorporate the supranational requirements into national law. Therefore, the regulatory authority E-Control was commissioned by the Council of Ministers in 2008 to draw up a first Green Paper called *Energy efficiency: proposals for measures to increase energy efficiency*. The aim was to identify the issues where efficiency measures can be taken to keep energy demand at a constant level by 2020 (E-Control 2008).

With regard to the sectoral consumption in Austria, the energy demand in the transport sector has more than tripled since the 1970s. Another striking feature is the contrasting development of final energy consumption between the industrial sector and private households. While the demand for energy in the private building sector tends to decline at the turn of the millennium, the industrial energy demand continues to grow. Only in the context of the economic crisis following the real estate bubble in 2007 energy demand in the industrial sector decreased for a short time. Nevertheless, the European Commission opened treaty violation proceedings against Austria in 2006 because the states failed to implement the minimum energy efficiency standards in the building sector. Subsequently, the federal government passed an *Energy Performance Certificate Act* (EAVG), which provides information on the energy quality of buildings. The states set up the coordination body OIB (Österreichiches Institut für Bautechnik) to develop recommendations for common standards in the building sector (Amann and Huttler 2007, p. 13). The federal and regional governments, in turn, jointly agreed to improve the quality of thermal insulation in the construction of housing (BGBI. II Nr. 19/2006).

Nevertheless, the activities of the states remained limited within the framework of efficient energy policy. However, the unambitious thermal standards of the states in housing subsidies were revised 2 years later (BGBI. II Nr. 251/2009). This could only be managed within the context of the fiscal equalization scheme between the federal and regional governments in 2009, which made a package deal in housing and finance policy possible (Steurer and Clar 2015, p. 338).

Just a few years earlier in 2007, fuel taxes were increased, and the *Climate and Energy Fund* was established. With the establishment of this fund, a financial incentive was created at the national level to promote model regions and local demonstration projects (Komendantova et al. 2018). Austria's long-term ambitions are to expand its European pioneering role in energy efficiency and smart city concepts (Bach 2013, p. 180). Therefore, the Fund works like an instrument of gentle encouragement. In the grand coalition, the management of the fund was traditionally shared between one SPÖ and one ÖVP-led ministry and was accepted by the states. To support local projects and programs, the *Climate and Energy Fund* has an annual budget of about € 6 m (Niedertscheider et al. 2018, p. 12).

In July 2011, the European Commission again filed a proposal for a new directive to achieve the EU-wide 20% efficiency targets (Energy Efficiency Directive 2012/27/EU). In response to the new directive, Austria implemented the *Energy Efficiency Act* (EEffG) in 2014. In order to do this, an agreement defining responsibilities in accordance with Article 15a B-VG between the federal and states was once again necessary. The central tools of the EEffG are, first, the obligation of large companies and energy suppliers to carry out energy audits and, second, to introduce an energy and environmental management system. The results are to be reported annually to the National Energy Efficiency Monitoring Center. These instruments for regulating the industry and the economy are based on voluntary commitments with the industry sector that have already been tried and tested. In addition, modernization quotas in the public building sector have been adopted, and the energy efficiency targets of the energy strategy 2020 have been intensified. In particular, the new and intensified efficiency targets followed the policy of the GRÜNE party, whose approval was necessary to gain the two-thirds majority in parliament.

The transport and mobility sector in Austria has received increased attention as the most important producer of greenhouse gas emissions with a 45% share of the total emissions (bmnt 2018, p. 13; Federal Environmental Agency 2017). Concurrently, the sector has the largest share in final energy consumption reaching 34.6% in the year 2017 (Fig. 9). Due to the growing number of vehicles, the continuous increase in energy consumption and greenhouse gas emissions continues since the 1990s. In general, the vehicle stock almost doubled between 1990 and 2007 (Meyer and Wessely 2009, p. 3780).

Austria's Overall Traffic Plan from 2012 addressed the increasing energy demand of the sector. The plan outlined, similar to the *Austria's Overall Traffic Concept* of 1991 (bmwv 1991), the principles of future transport and mobility policy. It was established in a consensus between federal government, the states, and municipalities (bmvti 2012). In doing so, E-mobility was regarded as a central factor of energy efficiency policy in the *Austria's Overall Traffic Plan* from 2012: "Austria's transport and mobility policy relies above all on electro mobility as a key factor for a modern and efficient transport system" (bmvti 2012, p. 65).

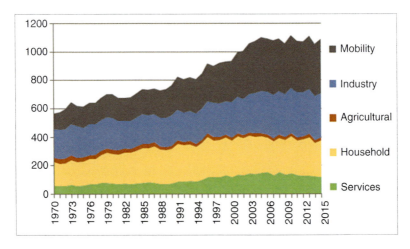

Fig. 9 Sectoral final energy consumption in terajoules. (Source: Statistic Austria 2016)

In this regard, the Environment, Transport, and Economic Ministries adopted by consensus a *Framework for the Support of Electro Mobility* (bmlfuw et al. 2012). Finally, in 2016 the Transport and Environment Ministries, together with the states and the two interest organizations *Austrian Association of Cities and Towns* (Österreichischer Städtebund) and *Austrian Association of Municipalities* (Österreichischer Gemeindebund), proposed the *National Strategic Framework: Clean Energy in Transport*. The close cooperation between the different administrative levels in the transport sector traces back to both the cross-sectoral nature of the sector and the division of competences in mobility issues. While traffic legislation is a domain of national policymaking, regional planning and road law is within the jurisdiction of the states (Bußjäger 2016a, pp. 535–549).

In comparison to other European countries, Austria deserves particular awareness, since renewable energies in the transport sector exceeds the envisaged target of 10%. Together with Sweden, Austria fulfils the European goals defined by the *directive for alternative fuels* (Directive 2014/94/EU). However, even though the annual expansion rate of electric vehicles achieves about 50%, a closer look at the Austrian vehicle stock indicates more registered Porsche cars than electric vehicles (Statistik Austria 2018).

In order to advance electro mobility market and minimize the energy demand and greenhouse gas emissions, the current *Climate and Energy Strategy 2030* highlights three projects. Firstly, it aims at increasing the efficiency of logistics and public transport with the intention to induce a shift of passenger and cargo transport from road to rail. Secondly, the upcoming electro mobility campaign envisages the creation of 34,000 jobs, e.g., in the supply industry for electric vehicles. Thirdly, the campaign aims at a reinforced electrification of rail and bus services and the implementation of a digital logistics system to achieve CO_2 neutrality of the growing urban delivery business (bmnt and bmvit 2018, pp. 56–59).

By the turn of the millennium, particular diesel vehicles benefited from tax reliefs due to their low CO_2 emissions (Meyer and Wessely 2009, p. 3782). Currently, policy shifted from the support of diesel cars to financial incentives for electric vehicles and other alternative engines. For example, the Austrian *Climate and Energy Fund* supports seven E-mobility model regions. These model regions focus on different priorities in the context of E-mobility, like questions of the charging infrastructure or the acceptance for this new technology (cf. Climate and Energy Fund 2015). Moreover, a buyer's premium for fuel cell, hybrid, and electric cars have been adopted in 2019. The *Climate and Energy Strategy 2030* is not constrained to the development of E-mobility. It rather specifies an aspired fuel mix for alternative engine systems, including in particular E-mobility but also hydrogen fuel cells, Bio-CNG and Bio-LNG, as well as bio-fuels (bmnt and bmvit 2018, p. 7).

According to the Ministry of Transport, the growing electrification of mobility in Austria will increase the electricity demand by 14%. Nevertheless, e.g., in contrast to Germany or Poland, E-mobility in Austria, with electricity supply largely based on hydropower and not on coal-fired power stations, may contribute immediately to the overall sustainability of the sector. Accordingly, the allocation of *buyer's premiums for alternative engines* in Austria is strictly linked to the use of renewable energy sources.

Table 1 Austria's key energy policy instruments by topics and type

Long-term strategies		*Mission 2030 (2018)* *Austrian Energy Strategy 2020 (2010)* *APG-Masterplan 2030 (2009; 2013)* *Austrian overall transport plan (2012)* *10-year network development plan (TYNDP 2010)* *EU climate and energy framework 2030 (2014)* *EU package of directives and targets for climate protection and energy (20/20/20 goals)*	
Policy instruments	**Supply**	**Efficiency**	**Distribution**
Regulatory	Electricity Management and Organisation Act (ElMOA)		
		Energy Efficiency Act (EEffA 2014)	National Network Development Plan (NDP 2012) Energy Management Act (EMA 2012) Energy-Control-Act (E-ControlA 2011)
	Climate and Energy Fund (2007)		
	Green Electricity Act (GEA 2002) Environmental Aid Act (EAA 1993)	New Housing Subsidisation Scheme (2009) Climate:Active mobil (2013) Buyer's premiums for alternative engines (2019)	
Quantity driven	EU Emissions Trading System (ETS) special contingents in the GEA (GEA 2012)		
Regulation of prices	Electricity Levy Act (1996, 2014)		

Source: IEA and IRENA 2019

The following table presents the strategies and instruments discussed so far. The columns represent the different areas of action. The rows relate to the policy instruments. On the one hand, the overview emphasizes the diversity and great importance of long-term strategies. On the other hand, it is obvious that regulatory instruments are particularly restricted to energy distribution, whereas particularly incentives characterize the domains of energy supply and efficient energy consumption (Table 1).

Outcome, Challenges, and Prospects

The purpose of this chapter was to provide an overview of Austria's energy governance. This includes the coordination structures, processes, and mechanisms of energy policy regarding the performance of Austria's multi-level governance system. Beyond that, the key instruments and measures of the three energy topics were introduced. In doing so, it has become clear that Austria's current energy strategy is in line with EU 2020 targets and that the second strategy until 2030 goes hand in hand with common European ambitions to fulfil the Paris agreement. Furthermore, it can be assumed that Austria will also be successful in achieving its European targets by 2020 (cf. Garcia-Alvarez et al. 2016, p. 1004).

The positive performance of Austria's energy policy can be explained on the one hand by historical legacies and topographical conditions as well as the involvement of the GRÜNE party in energy reforms. On the other hand, and more elementary, the institutional multi-level governance system opens up capacities for slow dynamics in Austria's energy transition. Because of this dynamic progress, the governance system was complemented by competitive elements. Thus, energy policy is no longer reduced to state-led supply and has been supplemented by new cooperation's and negotiations to manage energy policies. However, the design of Austria's multi-level governance system varies considerably depending on the three topics of energy supply, energy distribution, and energy efficiency.

As I will explain below, the renewable energy supply has shifted from a regional and decentralized pattern to a central governance system. Energy distribution, however, affect both levels with central planning by federal authorities and decentralized responsibility for administrative approval and implementation. Finally, yet importantly, energy efficiency policy is embedded in a governance system comparable with the pattern of "joint-decision-making" (cf. Scharpf 1976). The fact that there have been no long-lasting political blockades and joint decision traps in the past can be explained by various consensual mechanisms that have been the practice in Austria's energy politics for many years. As a result, the Austrian energy governance system is characterized by both stability and dynamics.

The supply of renewable energies is largely regulated by the *Green Electricity Act* and its regular amendments. Since the coordination pattern is centralized, the decision-making processes are less prone to multi-level barriers between the federal and states. However, the analysis showed that especially party-political competition and rivalry could form blockades if the necessary two-thirds majority is not guaranteed in the context of a grand coalition. Nevertheless, long blockades between the parliamentary parties do not occur because those responsible have learned to find a consensus. These solutions are usually made possible by the *lowest common denominator* of their interests.

Energy distribution mainly follows central governance steering in the planning process. The central instrument of the energy distribution is the regulatory *Network Development Plan*. However, the NDP is preceded by so-called soft instrument in form of the TYNDP at the European level. The topic of energy distribution showed that decision-making processes were outsourced from traditional government politics. Instead of parliamentary and party-political influence, the topic of energy distribution is largely independent, organized as a stock company and managed by experts. On the other hand, the tasks in the implementation process are mainly organized by the states and their administrations. These fragmented responsibilities in energy distribution have so far proved to be more difficult than advantageous in managing the energy infrastructure and a flexible grid. If constitutional amendments need two-thirds majorities, but no *compensation payment* between the government and opposition parties can be arranged, reforms might be restricted and dynamics slowed down. This was the case, for example, in the negotiations between the ÖVP, SPÖ, and the GRÜNE parties in the run-up to the *Infrastructure Act*.

A comparatively traditional pattern in multi-level governance challenges can be seen in the area of energy efficiency. Here, the analysis shows that decision-making processes are managed in different ways depending on the sector to be regulated. The industrial sector is largely characterized by regulatory policies that have already been tested in voluntary self-commitments. Instruments in the building and mobility sector are usually embedded in incentive-based and information programs organized at federal level. The states supplement national energy efficiency instruments with own policies within the regulatory limits of their housing policy jurisdiction. Because both levels have veto-power in the joint decision-making process within the framework of 15a B-VG agreements, blockades here are usually avoided by *package deals* between the state and federal levels.

Due to these different institutional capacities in the multi-level governance of energy policy, Austria is characterized by stability and dynamics in the management of the ongoing energy transition. Karl Stöger labeled this coordination pattern as "unwise Austriacum" (Stöger 2015, p. 191, 207, own translation). This is in fact only half the truth, because the notion simplifies the image of the governance system to stable structures without capturing the dynamic processes and mechanisms arranged behind. Nonetheless, it makes a typical phenomenon of conflict regulation in Austria's governance system obvious, which Gerhard Lehmbruch termed *gütliches Einvernehmen* (Lehmbruch 1967). The social mechanism behind this is a strong tradition of mutual trust. This tradition allows consensual decision-making based on solutions on the lowest common denominator as well as compensation payments and package deals. All of this permits "second-best solutions" in Austria's energy governance system, which favors stability and balanced dynamics of policy changes. However, it remains to be seen to what extent the increasing competition in Austria's political party system counteracts and blocks this long practice and culture of common conflict management.

Cross-References

- ▶ Energy Governance in Denmark
- ▶ Energy Governance in Germany
- ▶ Energy Governance in the Czech Republic
- ▶ Energy Governance in the Republic of Poland
- ▶ Energy Governance in the United Kingdom
- ▶ European Union Energy Policy: A Discourse Perspective
- ▶ Monitoring Energy Policy

References

Amann, W., & Huttler, W. (2007). Rahmenbedingungen. In K. Lugger & W. Amann (Eds.), *Ökologisierung der Wohnbauförderung im mehrgeschossigen Wohnbau*. Wien: Institut für Immobilie, Bauen und Wohnen.

APG. (2013). Masterplan 2030: Für die Entwicklung des Übertragungsnetzes in Österreich. Abgerufen von https://www.apg.at/de/netz/netzausbau/masterplan. 22 Jan 2019.

Armingeon, K. (2017). Interessengruppen und Interessenvermittlung: Internationale Gemeinsamkeiten und österreichische Besonderheiten. In L. Helms & D. M. Wineroither (Eds.), *Die Österreichische Demokratie im Vergleich* (pp. 287–315). Baden-Baden: Nomos.

Axelrod, R., & Hamilton, W. (1981). The evolution of cooperation. *Science, 211*, 1390–1396.

Bach, B. (2013). Nachhaltige Energieversorgung für die Zukunft. In *Österreich 2050: Fit für die Zukunft* (pp. 174–182). Holzhausen: Verlag Holzhausen.

Bayer, F. (2014). Die Ablehnung der Kernenergie in Österreich: Ein Anti-Atom-Konsens als Errungenschaft einer sozialen Bewegung? *Zeitschrift für Sozialen Fortschritt, 3*(3), 170–187.

Benz, A. (2009). *Politik in Mehrebenensystemen*. Wiesbaden: Springer VS.

Benz, A. (2015). Lehmbruch versus Lijphart: Comparing democratic governments as multi-dimensional regimes. In V. Schneider & B. Eberlein (Eds.), *Complex democracy: Varieties, crises, and transformations* (pp. 69–82). Heidelberg: Springer.

Benz, A., Detemple, J., & Heinz, D. (2016). *Varianten und Dynamiken der Politikverflechtung im deutschen Bundesstaat*. Baden-Baden: Nomos.

Bergauer-Culver, B. (2012). Die österreichische Energiestrategie als Wegbereiterin für eine innovative, zukunftsfähige Energieversorgung Österreichs. In *12. Symposium Energieinnovation*, 15.-17.2.2012, Graz/Austria.

bmlfuw, & bmwfw. (2010). Energie Strategie Österreich. Abgerufen von https://www.energiestrategie.at. 20 May 2017.

bmlfuw, bmvit, & bmwfj. (2012). Umsetzungsfahrplan: Elektromobilität in und aus Österreich – Der gemeinsame Weg!. Abgerufen von https://www.bmvit.gv.at/verkehr/elektromobilitaet/downloads/emobil_umsetzungsplan.pdf. 22 Jan 2019.

bmnt. (2018). Energie in Österreich 2018: Zahlen, Daten, Fakten. Abgerufen von https://www.bmnt.gv.at/service/publikationen/energie/energie-in-oesterreich-2018.html. 22 Jan 2019.

bmnt, & bmvit. (2018). Mission 2030. Abgerufen von https://mission2030.info/. 01 Aug 2018.

bmvit, et al. (2016). Nationaler Strategierahmen „Saubere Energie im Verkehr". Abgerufen von https://www.bmvit.gv.at/verkehr/elektromobilitaet/downloads/strategierahmen.pdf. 22 Jan 2019.

bmvti. (2012). Gesamtverkehrsplan für Österreich. Abgerufen von https://www.bmvit.gv.at/verkehr/gesamtverkehr/gvp/index.html. 22 Jan 2019.

bmwfw. (2017). Österreichisches Montan-Handbuch: Bergbau Rohstoffe Grundstoffe Energie. Abgerufen von https://www.bmnt.gv.at/energie-bergbau/bergbau/Montanhandbuch.html. 04 Jan 2019.

bmwfw, & bmlfuw. (2016). Green Paper for an integrated energy and climate strategy. Abgerufen von https://www.konsultation-energie-klima.at/. 01 Aug 2018.

bmwv. (1991). Mensch – Umwelt – Verkehr. Das österreichische Gesamtverkehrskonzept. Abgerufen von https://www.parlament.gv.at/PAKT/VHG/XVIII/III/III_00090/imfname_544037.pdf. 22 Jan 2019.

Brand, U., & Pawloff, A. (2014). Selectivities at work: Climate concerns in the midst of corporatist interests. The case of Austria. *Journal of Environmental Protection, 5*(9), 780–795.

Bußjäger, P. (2016a). Die bundesstaatliche Kompetenzverteilung in Österreich. In A. Gamper, P. Bußjäger, F. Karlhofer, G. Pallaver, & W. Obwexer (Eds.), *Föderale Kompetenzverteilung in Europa* (pp. 523–574). Baden-Baden: Nomos.

Bußjäger, P. (2016b). Schlussfolgerungen und Handlungsempfehlungen für die Diskussion über die Reform der bundesstaatlichen Kompetenzordnung in Österreich. In A. Gamper, P. Bußjäger, F. Karlhofer, G. Pallaver, & W. Obwexer (Eds.), *Föderale Kompetenzverteilung in Europa* (pp. 807–820). Baden-Baden: Nomos.

Climate and Energy Fund. (2015). Model regions of electric mobility in Austria. Abgerufen von https://www.klimafonds.gv.at/unsere-themen/mobilitaetswende/modellregionen/. 22 Jan 2019.

E-Control. (2008). *Grünbuch: Energieeffizienz: Maßnahmenvorschläge zur Steigerung der Energieeffizienz.* Abgerufen von https://www.e-control.at/econtrol/projekte/gruenbuch-energieeffizienz. 12 Oct 2017.

E-Control. (2016a). *Entwicklung von Durchschnittsvergütung und Marktpreis 2003–2015, Einspeisetarife 2016.* Abgerufen von https://www.e-control.at/konsumenten/oeko-energie/kosten-und-foerderungen/einspeisetarife-marktpreise. 20 May 2017.

E-Control. (2016b). *Statistikbroschüre 2016: Durchblicken wo immer Zahlen für sich sprechen.* Abgerufen von https://www.e-control.at/publikationen/statistik-bericht. 14 Aug 2017.

Federal Environmental Agency. (2017). *Treibhausgas Bilanz 2015: Daten, Trends und Ausblick.* Abgerufen von http://www.umweltbundesamt.at/news_170117. 01 Aug 2018.

Fischer, K., & Rosenkranz, C. (2012). *Handbuch Energiepolitik Österreich.* Wien: LIT Verlag.

Forchtner, B. (2013). Extrem rechte Parteien im Klimawandel: Ein (kurzer) Blick auf die Schweiz, Österreich und Deutschland. In G. Heinrich, K.-D. Kaiser, & N. Wiersbinski (Eds.), *Naturschutz und Rechtsradikalismus: Gegenwertige Entwicklungen, Probleme, Abgrenzungen und Steuerungsmöglichkeiten.* Bonn: BMU Druckerei. Abgerufen von https://www.bfn.de/naturschutzakademie/tagungsdokumentation/dokumentation/naturschutz-und-rechtsradikalismus-ii.html.

Frank, W. (1982). Zur Geschichte der Energieplanung in Österreich. *Wirtschaft und Gesellschaft, 8*(2), 235–270.

Frank, W. (1983). Expansion, Stagnation und Demokratie – 1982 Heft 2. https://emedien.arbeiterkammer.at/viewer/image/AC08890876_1982_002/97/LOG_0014/

Fruhrmann, C., Tuerk, A., Kulmer, V., & Gubina, A. F. (2018). Balancing environmental benefits and damages of small hydropower generation in policy-making: assessing the implementation of a contradicting EU policy framework in Austria and Slovenia. *International Journal of Sustainable Energy.* doi.org/10.1080/14786451.2018.1452741.

Garcia-Alvarez, M. T., Moreno, B., & Soares, I. (2016). Analyzing the sustainable energy development in the EU-15 by an aggregated synthetic index. *Ecological Indicators, 60*, 996–1007.

Geels, F., & Schot, J. (2007). Typology of sociotechnical transition pathways. *Research Policy, 36*, 399–417.

Glatz, H. (1986). Staatliche Energiepolitik in Österreich. *Österreichische Zeitschrift für Politikwissenschaft, 1*, 72–84.

Haberfellner, M., Hujber, A., & Koch, P. (2002). Liberalisierung und Strompreisentwicklung: Österreich und Deutschland im Vergleich, *Working Paper*, Nr. 4.

Hackl, E. H. (2001). Die österreichischen Reduktionsziele für Treibhausgas-Emissionen von Toronto bis Kyoto. *Wissenschaft & Umwelt, 4*, 19–26.

Hansch, S. (1998). *Wege zum Wind: Das Zustandekommen der politischen Rahmenbedingungen für die Windenergienutzung in Dänemark, mit vergleichenden Perspektiven für Deutschland und Österreich.* University of Vienna (diploma thesis) Abgerufen von https://www.igwindkraft.at/mmedia/download/2005.01.06/1105019989.pdf. 05 Jan 2019.

Hauer, A. (2004). Stand und Entwicklung des Energierechts in der Europäischen Gemeinschaft und in Österreich. In E. Novotny, C. Parak, & R. Scheucher (Eds.), *Handbuch der Österreichischen Energiewirtschaft* (pp. 59–74). Wien: Manz-Verlag.

Höltinger, S., Salak, B., Schauppenlehner, T., Scherhaufera, P., & Schmidt, J. (2016). Austria's wind energy potential: A participatory modeling approach to assess socio-political and market acceptance. *Energy Policy, 98*, 49–61.

IEA. (2014). Energy Policies of IEA Countries – Austria 2014 Review. Abgerufen von http://www.iea.org/publications/freepublications/publication/energy-policies-of-iea-countries%2D%2D-austria-2014-review.html. 23 Oct 2017.

IEA and IRENA. (2019). Joint policies and measures database. Abgerufen von https://www.iea.org/policiesandmeasures/renewableenergy/?country=Austria. 22 Jan 2019.

IG Windkraft. (2018). Windkraft in Österreich – Jahresanfangspressekonferenz. Abgerufen von https://www.igwindkraft.at/mmedia/download/2018.01.09/1515508826794413.pdf. 22 Jan 2019.

Ikenberry, J. (1986). The irony of state strength: Comparative responses to the oil shocks in the 1970s. *International Organization, 40*(1), 105–137.

Junker, J., Schuster, I., & Soteropoulos, A. (2014). *Windige Energie? Ökonomie der Windkraft. Saubere Energie auf Kosten der Landschaft?* Endbericht AG 3 Regulatorisches Umfeld der Windkraft. Masterprojekt an der TU Wien, Österreich.

Koehane, R. (2015). The global politics of climate change: Challenge for political science. *Political Science & Politics, 48*(1), 19–26.

Kok, F. (1991). *Politik der Elektrizitätswirtschaft in Österreich: Vom Wachstumskonsens zur Krise.* Baden-Baden: Nomos.

Kok, F., & Schaller, C. (1986). Restrukturierung der Energiepolitik durch neue soziale bewegungen?: Die Beispiele Zwentendorf und Hainburg. *Österreichische Zeitschrift für Politikwissenschaft, 1,* 61–72.

KOM. (2009). 192: Communication from the commission to the council and the European parliament. The Renewable Energy Progress Report. Abgerufen von https://eur-lex.europa.eu/legal-content/EN/TXT/?uri=COM:2009:0192:FIN. 22 Aug 2018.

Komendantova, N., Riegler, M., & Neumüller, S. (2018). Of transitions and models: Community engagement, democracy, and empowerment in the Austrian energy transition. *Energy Resarch & Social Science, 39,* 141–151.

Korom, P. (2012). Kein Ende der "Österreich AG"? Über die Beständigkeit eines koordinierten Unternehmensnetzwerkes in Zeiten von Privatisierung und Internationalisierung. *Österreichische Zeitschrift für Politikwissenschaft (ÖZP), 41*(2), 141–160.

Lauber, V. (2002). Austria. In D. Reiche (Ed.), *Handbook of renewable energies in the European Union: Case studies of all member states.* Frankfurt am Main: Peter Lang.

Lehmbruch, G. (1967). Proporzdemokratie. Politisches System und politische Kultur in der Schweiz und in Österreich. In *Recht und Staat in Geschichte und Gegenwart 335/336.* Tübingen: J.C.B. Mohr.

Lehmbruch, G. (1969). Konkordanzdemokratie im internationalen System: Ein Paradigma für die Analyse von internen und externen Bedingungen politischer Systeme. In E.-O. Czempiel (Ed.), *Die anachronistische Souveränität: Zum Verhältnis von Innen- und Außenpolitik, PVS Sonderheft* (pp. 139–163). Opladen: Westdeutscher Verlag.

Lehmbruch, G. (1985). Sozialpartnerschaft in der vergleichenden Politikforschung. In P. Gerlich, E. Grande, & W. Müller (Eds.), *Sozialpartnerschaft in der Krise: Leistungen und Grenzen des Neokorporatismus in Österreich* (pp. 85–107). Wien: Böhlau Verlag.

Madlener, R. (2007). Innovation diffusion, public policy and local initiative: The case of wood-fuelled district heating systems in Austria. *Energy Policy, 35,* 2761–2769.

Maull, H., & Mild, E. (1986). Abhängikeit und Verwundbarkeit der westeuropäischen Energieversorgung. *Österreichische Zeitschrift für Politikwissenschaft, 1,* 29–42.

Mautz, R., Fleiß, E., Hatzl, S., Reinsberger, K., & Posch, A. (2018). Bottom-up-Initiativen im Bereich Photovoltaik in Deutschland und Österreich: Rahmenbedingungen und Handlungsressourcen. In L. Holstenkamp & J. Radtke (Eds.), *Handbuch Energiewende und Partizipation* (pp. 599–611). Wiesbaden: Springer VS.

Meyer, I., & Wessely, S. (2009). Fuel efficiency of the Austrian passenger vehicle fleet analysis of trends in the technological profile and related impacts on CO2 emissions. *Energy Policy, 37,* 3779–3789.

Niedertscheider, M., Haas, W., & Görg, C. (2018). Austrian climate policies and GHG-emissions since 1990: What is he role of climate policy integration? *Environmental Science and Policy, 81,* 10–17.

OeMAG. (2016). Ökostromanlagen auf Bundesländerebene. Abgerufen von http://www.oem-ag.at/de/oekostromneu/installierte-leistung/. 20 May 2017.

Ostrom, E. (1998). A behavioral approach to the rational choice theory of collective action: Presidential address, American Political Science Association, 1997. *American Political Science Review, 92*(1), 1–22. https://doi.org/10.2307/2585925.

Ostrom, E. (2010). Polycentric systems for coping with collective action and global environmental change. *Global Environmental Change, 20*(4), 550–557.

Pelinka, A. (2004). Das politische System Österreichs. In W. Ismayr (Ed.), *Die politischen Systeme Westeuropas* (pp. 521–552). Wiesbaden: VS Verlag für Sozialwissenschaften.

Perschy, D. (2012). *Windenergie in Österreich: Ein Vergleich der sozialen Akzeptanz erneuerbarer Energien in der EU*. Saarbrücken: AV Akademikerverlag.

Pesendorfer, D. (2007). *Paradigmenwechsel in der Umweltpolitik: Von den Anfängen der Umwelt- zu einer Nachhaltigkeitspolitik: Modellfall Österreich?* Wiesbaden: VS Verlag für Sozialwissenschaften.

Pollak, J., & Riekmann, S. (2017). Die Europäisierung der demokratischen Institutionen Österreichs im EU-Vergleich. In L. Helms & D. M. Wineroither (Eds.), *Die Österreichische Demokratie im Vergleich* (pp. 423–449). Baden-Baden: Nomos.

Prutsch, A., Steurer, R., & Stickler, T. (2017). Is the participatory formulation of policy strategies worth of effort? The case of climate change adaptation in Austria. *Regional Environmental Change, 18*(1), 271–285.

Rihs, G. (2012). Ökostromgesetz 2012: Rückblende und Schlaglichter. *Recht der Umwelt, 4*, 133–176.

Rittel, H., & Webber, M. (1973). Dilemmas in a general theory of planning. *Policy Sciences, 4*(2), 155–169.

Ruß, D. (2014). Die Entwicklung des Klimawandels als politisches Problem. *Der moderne Staat, 7*(2), 353–373.

Scharpf, F. (1976). Theorie der Politikverflechtung. In F. W. Scharpf, B. Reissert, & F. Schnabel (Eds.), *Politikverflechtung: Theorie und Empirie des kooperativen Föderalismus in der Bundesrepublik* (pp. 13–77). Kronberg/TS: Scriptor-Verlag.

Schmidt, B. (Ed.). (2011). *Stromaufwärts: 10 Jahre Liberalisierung des Strommarkts in Österreich*. Wien: Lit Verlag.

Statistik Austria. (2016). Gesamtenergiebilanz Österreich von 1970 bis 2015: Detailinformation. Abgerufen von http://www.statistik.at/web_de/statistiken/energie_umwelt_innovation_mobilitaet/ energie_und_umwelt/energie/energiebilanzen/index.html. 20 May 2017.

Statistik Austria. (2017). Gesamtenergiebilanz Österreich 1970 bis 2016: Detailinformation. Abgerufen von http://www.statistik.at/web_de/statistiken/energie_umwelt_innovation_mobilitaet/energie_ und_umwelt/energie/energiebilanzen/index.html. 01 Aug 2018.

Statistik Austria. (2018). Fahrzeug-Bestand am 31. Dezember 2018. Abgerufen von https://www. statistik.at/web_de/statistiken/energie_umwelt_innovation_mobilitaet/verkehr/strasse/kraftfahr zeuge_-_bestand/index.html. 22 Jan 2019.

Steurer, R., & Clar, C. (2015). Is decentralisation always good for climate change mitigation? How federalism has complicated the greening of building policies in Austria. *Policy Sciences, 48*(1), 85–107.

Stickinger, H. (2004). Politische Rahmenbedingungen und deren Auswirkungen am Beispiel der Elektrizitätswirtschaft. In E. Novotny, C. Parak, & R. Scheucher (Eds.), *Handbuch der Österreichischen Energiewirtschaft* (pp. 159–178). Wien: Manz-Verlag.

Stöger, K. (2015). Das österreichische Ökostromgesetz: Wege und Irrwege. In T. Rensmann & S. Storr (Eds.), *Die Energiewende im rechtlichen Mehrebenensystem* (pp. 189–207). Stuttgart: Verlag Österreich.

Storr, S. (2015). Der Binnenmarkt für Energie- Wege zur Vollendung. In T. Rensmann & S. Storr (Eds.), *Die Energiewende im rechtlichen Mehrebenensystem* (pp. 25–44). Stuttgart: Verlag Österreich.

Veigl, A. (2004). Der Markt für Elektrizität in Österreich. In E. Novotny, C. Parak, & R. Scheucher (Eds.), *Handbuch der Österreichischen Energiewirtschaft* (pp. 27–42). Wien: Manz-Verlag.

Vones, G. (2011). Energie Strategie Österreich. *Elektrotechnik & Informationstechnik, 128*(9), 299.

Wagner, B., Hauer, C., Schoder, A., & Habersack, H. (2015). A review of hydropower in Austria: Past, present and future development. *Renewable and Sustainable Energy Reviews, 50*, 304–314.

Winkler-Rieder, W. (2006). Energiepolitik. In E. Tàlos, H. Dachs, E. Hanisch, & A. Staudinger (Eds.), *Handbuch des politischen Systems Österreichs* (pp. 619–627). Wien: Manz-Verlag.

Zabukovec, G. (2005). *Ökostromgesetz und Elektrizitätswesen: Europarechtliche Grundlagen und verfassungsrechtliche Fragen*. Wien: Braumüller.

Energy Governance in Azerbaijan

21

Murad Nasibov

Contents

Introduction	484
General Conditions of Energy Governance in Azerbaijan	485
Legacies	485
Composition of the Energy Mix	489
Discourse on Energy Issues	490
Political Institutions and Actors	491
Coordination, Instruments and Issues of Energy Transition Within a Multilevel Context	494
Drivers and Barriers to the Energy Transition	494
Strategies and Instruments of Energy Transitions	499
Coordination Mechanisms and Multilevel Governance	502
Outcomes, Challenges, and Prospects of Energy Governance	503
Cross-References	505
References	505

Abstract

This chapter discusses different aspects of energy governance in Azerbaijan. It looks into the country's Soviet legacies, the path that public institutions in energy governance have gone through, and critical issues in public debates. Consequently, several economic drivers and obstacles to the energy transition path of the country are elaborated within this broader context. Then, it concentrates on strategies and policy instruments in the energy transition path of the country. The final section summarizes the previous discussions and provides a general picture of the energy governance in Azerbaijan and the future of its energy transition path. The energy governance of Azerbaijan is highly centralized, and the state holds a monopoly in the energy market. Patrimonial relations within the elite, which are maintained through widespread corruption, and the authoritarian nature

M. Nasibov (✉)
Institute of Political Science, Justus-Liebig University of Giessen, Giessen, Germany
e-mail: murad.nasibov@sowi.uni-giessen.de

© Springer Nature Switzerland AG 2022
M. Knodt, J. Kemmerzell (eds.), *Handbook of Energy Governance in Europe*,
https://doi.org/10.1007/978-3-030-43250-8_3

of the political regime constitute the main barriers to the liberalization of the energy market. Given the unstable past full of frequent reshuffling, public institutions appear incapable to present strong institutional constraints to corrupt practices and political meddling. However, the rising economic pressure, the abundant potential of alternative and renewable energy sources, and international and European cooperation opportunities, as well as the growing infrastructural upgrading needs, appear as the key drivers for reforms pushing for liberalization and enhancing strategies and policy instruments.

Keywords

Energy in Azerbaijan · EU-Azerbaijan · Market liberalization · Soviet legacy · Institutional instability · Corruption in energy · Energy reforms

Introduction

Since Azerbaijan gained its independence in 1991 with the dissolution of the Soviet Union, the country faced significant challenges in energy governance, not unlike from other sectors of the economy. Leaving the centrally planned economy off and aiming at the market economy, the country had to re-design the governance institutions, as the old Soviet institutions did not fit into the market economy, and to develop new strategies and policies. In parallel, given the economic needs and its political importance, the country started exporting oil and gas resources, which it possesses in abundance. Although the government has been successful in attracting international investment in its oil and gas sector and became a significant oil and gas supplier to the European markets, it has not been able to equally perform in creating good governance in the energy sector in the country. Although the fundamental regulatory framework has been set in the late 1990s and early 2000s, advanced instruments are yet to be developed. Additionally, not all available legal tools are applied necessarily.

Almost three decades after independence, Azerbaijan has not been able to liberalize its energy market. Being monopolist, the government tightly controls the energy market in Azerbaijan. The strict state control is not exclusive in the energy sector but also established to varying degrees in other sectors of the economy as a strategy of political control deployed by the political regime that has become growingly authoritarian after some democratic opening in the early years of independence.

Nonetheless, it is not the only way in which energy governance and the political regime are linked. Revenues from the energy sector, particularly those gained from the export of oil and gas resources, have long been instrumentalized to earn the loyalty of the elite, thus making the survival of the regime dependent on the revenues of the energy sector. Such a linkage with the political regime emerges as one of the most significant obstacles facing energy governance in the country.

However, on the promising side, coupled with the pressures of economic slowdown, growing energy supply demands, and infrastructural upgrading needs, the availability of international cooperation opportunities, in particular with the European Union within, but not limited to, the framework of Eastern Partnership and the abundance of resources, including alternative and renewable energy sources, has brought about some reform initiatives by the government in recent years.

Although, as the legacy of its twentieth century experience, oil and gas remain the primary energy resources of the country, and the country is known to possess some significant potential of alternative and renewable energy sources. The use of renewable and alternative energy sources has entered into the policy discourse only in the last decade. The economic slowdown experienced since 2015 and growing demand for energy in the country have incentivized some efforts toward the development of the alternative and renewable energy sector.

General Conditions of Energy Governance in Azerbaijan

Legacies

The primacy of oil and gas as energy resources and their export in large amounts, centralized management, institutionally unstable past, and the widespread corruption as an instrument of political control are the main legacies that Azerbaijan inherited from its Soviet period that spanned for the most of the twentieth century. These legacies have constituted the major broader factors shaping the energy governance in Azerbaijan since its independence.

The Soviet Legacy of Centralized Management

Energy governance in the Soviet Republic Azerbaijan was conducted in the mode of the centralized planned economy. As a result of the Sovietization of Azerbaijan, the energy sector was nationalized in the 1920s. The nationalization policy was followed by the establishment of centralized command in the energy sector, initially under one umbrella organization, then separating into different organizations responsible for oil, gas, and electricity industries.

From the installment of the Soviet rule until 1954, the oil industry of Azerbaijan was united under an umbrella organization "Azneft" (State Oil Company of the Republic of Azerbaijan [SOCAR] n.d.b). Until 1935, the management of the production and distribution of electricity remained within the responsibility of "Azerneft." In this year, "Azerenerji" Azerbaijan Regional Energy Department has been established, which held the control of all electricity infrastructure in the then Soviet Socialist Republic of Azerbaijan ("Azerenerji" OJSC n.d.b). Similarly, from 1923, when a sub-unit was established within "Azneft" for the production and processing of gas until 1936, the gas industry was managed by "Azneft" but only to spin off in 1936 when "AzQaz" Trust was established on this basis ("Azeriqaz" PU n.d.).

Although the energy sector remained under centralized management during the Soviet time, it went through reshufflings and redefinitions from the 1950s to the 1980s. Even though these institutions were subject to restructuring again in the period of independence, the current institutional infrastructure of the energy sector in

Azerbaijan still reflects the centralized nature of its Soviet past, as discussed in the section on Political Institutions and Actors. Nevertheless, the centralized management institutions did not remain stable either during the Soviet time or afterwards; they were almost in every decade subject to reshuffling and redefinition of legal status from the mid-1950s to the end of 1990s.

An Extended Period of Institutional Instability

The institutional structure of energy governance in Azerbaijan was not very stable, being subject to reshuffling and redefinition of its legal status both during the Soviet period and after the country gained independence. During the Soviet time, the institutional structure of energy governance remained mostly stable until the mid-1950s. However, Nikita Khrushchev, who succeeded Stalin as the leader of the USSR, attempted at reforming the industrial infrastructure and administrative organization, and most of the time clashed with professional bureaucrats (Volkogonov and Shukman 1999). This clash was reflected with institutional instability in the energy governance of Soviet Azerbaijan from the mid-1950s to 1970s, affecting the oil (State Oil Company of the Republic of Azerbaijan n.d.b), gas ("Azeriqaz" PU n.d.), and electricity sectors ("Azerenerji" OJSC n.d.b). In the gas sector, the institutional restructuring continued even through the 1980s ("Azeriqaz" PU n.d.).

Institutional restructuring and redefinition of legal status in the energy sector of Azerbaijan continued throughout the first decade of its independence. The declared transition from the centralized economy to free-market required from the country, as a primary task, to convert its energy producers, transmitters, and distributors from state institutions into privatized companies. In 1991, following the collapse of the Soviet Union, in the institutional basis of "Azneft" – a state institution of the Soviet era, "Azneft" State Group of Companies ("Konsern") was created. In 1991, the State Oil Company of Azerbaijani Republic (SOCAR) was established by presidential order on the institutional basis of "Azneft" State Group of Companies and the oil refinery "Azneftkimya" Production Union (State Oil Company of the Republic of Azerbaijan n.d.b). Following a similar path, "Azerenerji" was converted into a state company in 1993, and open joint-stock company in 1996 ("Azerenerji" OJSC n.d.b).

After the collapse of the Soviets, the gas sector was the one whose institutional infrastructure was most subject to restructuring and redefinition of legal status. In 1992, based on Azerbaijan State Energy Committee, "Azeriqaznagl," and Azerbaijani Scientific Research Project Institute, "Azeriqaz" State Company was established. Shortly afterwards, in 1996, it was redefined as "Azeriqaz" Closed Joint Stock Company ("Azeriqaz" PU n.d.). However, this was not the final legal status of the structure. In 2009, with a presidential order on the improvement of mechanisms in the oil and gas industry, "Azeriqaz" was restructured as Production Union within SOCAR (Azerbaijans.Com n.d.).

Comparatively, the centralized heating system in Azerbaijan developed lately, and therefore, experienced less institutional instability. The centralized governance of the heating systems emerged only when the United Heating Systems Directorship was established in 1965, and it was developed into "Bakiistilikshabaka" unit covering the Baku area. The heating systems in the regions outside the capital Baku remained in the control of the Architecture Committees during the Soviet time. Only in 2005, with a presidential decree, "Azeristiliktechizat" OJSC was established with the full state ownership of its initial shares, covering 51 out of 81 districts of Azerbaijan in total. The development of the heating system took place in the period of 1965–1980s, thus being subject to renovations and additional supply in recent years ("Azeristiliktechizat" OJSC n.d.).

Thus, institutional instability of the energy sector in Azerbaijan in the past more than 60 years, which, as already described above, cannot be restricted only to the change of economic model, appears one of the major limiting factors on the development of energy governance. Restructuring and redefinition of legal status almost every decade from the mid-1950s to the end of 1990s have undermined the profound institutional advancement of the energy sector. However, not less than its legacies of centralized management and institutional instability, the primacy of oil and gas as the main types of energy resources emerges as another important legacy of the Soviet past of Azerbaijan.

Primacy of Oil and Gas as Energy Resources

Oil production in industrial significance in Azerbaijan predates the Sovietization of the country. Around the 1900s, Azerbaijan was the world's leader in oil production, accounting for half of the world's oil production (Balayev 1969). However, the importance that oil and gas have today in the energy sector of Azerbaijan is mostly a legacy of the country's Soviet past. It was during the Soviet time that oil and gas became the primary energy resources of the country. A key development in this path was the construction of "Neft Dashlari" – an industrial settlement in the Caspian Sea, 40 km away from the closest coastline – when oil was discovered in 1949 (Blair 2006). The settlement was then developed further in the late 1950s and 1980s. The 70-year-old oilfields of "Neft Dashları" have produced more than 170 million tons of oil and 15 billion m^3 of associated natural gas (Igorev 2010).

When the Soviet Union dissolved, Azerbaijan inherited a vast oil and gas industry, though burdened with financial and technological needs going far beyond the capacities of the country. Accordingly, the government aimed to attract foreign investment. In 1994, SOCAR signed agreements with numerous transnational, including western, companies to open the route of Azerbaijani oil to European and world markets.

In 2017, the Azeri-Chirag-Gunashli Production Sharing Agreement (signed in 1994) was amended and restated in Baku. The new agreement was extended until 2050 (The Administration of the President of the Republic of Azerbaijan 2019). From the signing of the "Contract of Century" in 1994 to 2017, approximately $33 billion in total were invested in the development of offshore oil reserves in Azerbaijan. In return, 3.2 billion barrels of oil were produced from the Azeri-Chirag-Gunashli fields in this period. In addition to oil, a total of 30 billion cubic meters of associated gas were produced from Azeri–Chirag–Gunashli oil field (ibid.). In 2019, SOCAR's partners in the Azeri-Chirag-Gunashli complex of fields were BP, Chevron, Inpex, Equinor, Exxon Mobil, Turkish TPAO, Itochu, and ONGC. In December 2018, Exxon Mobil and Chevron announced their intention to leave the project (Zhdannikov and Bousso 2018); however, by May 2020, only the latter achieved to do so by selling its shares to Hungarian integrated oil and gas company MOL (Joseph 2020).

After adoption of the "Contract of Century" in 1996, Azerbaijan signed a Production Sharing Agreement with Western companies led by BP on the "ShahDeniz" gas area. In 1999, "ShahDeniz" gas field was found, and since 2006, gas exploited from the ShahDeniz field is exported to Turkey, Georgia, and Greece through Baku-Tbilisi-Erzurum (997 km) pipeline (Budagov 2017). In 2013, a new agreement was signed between Azerbaijan and the "ShahDeniz" consortium for the second phase of the development of "ShahDeniz" field, attracting $28 billion of investment (The Administration of the President of the Republic of Azerbaijan 2019). In 2020, "ShahDeniz" field was operated by BP with a 28.8% share, while other partners included Turkish TPAO (19%), SOCAR (16.7%), Petronas (15.5%), LUKoil (10%), and NIOC (10%). Prior to this, two major companies, namely, TOTAL and Statoil, left the ShahDeniz field. TPAO purchased a 9% share from Total in 2014 (TOTAL 2014). Petronas purchased its shares from Statoil in 2014 (Equinor 2014). In December 2013, Statoil sold 6.7% and 3.3% shares to SOCAR and BP, respectively.

By opening up its oil and gas industry to international investment, Azerbaijan has come to a situation whereby oil and gas provide the largest share of the total export of the country in value terms (The State Statistical Committee of the Republic of Azerbaijan 2019a). Revenues gained from the trading of fossil resources have become the primary source of income (changing between 46% and 49% in the 2015–2018 period) of the public budget (The Auditing Chamber of the Republic of Azerbaijan 2019). Moreover, most of its power plants (94%) are gas-based (Presidential Order No. 1138 Concerning the approval of Strategic Road Maps on the national economy and main sectors of economy 2016).

These three indicators illustrate how the vast oil and gas industry that Azerbaijan inherited from its Soviet past come to play an enormous role in the energy sector and the economy in general. In addition to the economy, the oil and gas revenues play a significant role in the political life of the country as an instrument for buying loyalty within the elite and the society in general, facilitated by the widespread corruption. The distribution of oil income within the elite has become possible thanks to the already established informal patterns inherited from the Soviet past, which is discussed in detail in the next section.

Informal Patterns, Corruption, and Kleptocracy

Independent Azerbaijan inherited not only the Soviet legacy of formal centralized management in the energy sector but also informal patterns such as sharing of bribes through the chain of command and buying of lucrative positions by way of payment to top officials. These patterns found a favorable environment in the early years of independence (Rasizade 2002). Paternalistic mechanisms of controls such as relying on regional groups that once existed in Soviet Azerbaijan in the 1960s–1980s period were reactivated in 1990s (Franke et al. 2009). The energy governance in Azerbaijan has by no means been immune from these re-emerging patterns. Instead, the oil income played a significant role in reinforcing them. Embedding the elite in family, clan, and clientelistic structures has emerged as a way of maintaining power (Franke et al. 2009). The revenues generated from the export of fossil resources also enable the ruling regime to better manipulate the electoral outcomes through pre-election economic policies (Kendall-Taylor 2012).

To achieve all this, first, the Azerbaijani leadership in the 1990s created lucrative conditions for foreign companies investing in the oil sector. The suppression of political parties and interest groups safeguarded the ruling elite from any opposition to investment policies. The isolation of oppositional groups offered foreign investors easy and direct access to the small group of decision-makers. The decision-making structure in the oil industry best depicts the benefits this regime has been able to offer foreign investors so far (Bayulgen 2010). During the reign of Haydar Aliyev, who ruled the country from 1993 to 2003, the system of governance was overwhelmingly tailored to his favor, and he gave personal guarantees to diplomats and investors, while other investors avoiding immediate presidential attention were generally caught in the bureaucratic quagmire (Mehdiyeva 2011).

By distributing the oil revenues in a top-down manner within the elite, the country's leadership maintains political control. As a short-term perspective aimed at safeguarding the continuation of power, this has made the leadership dependent on continuously buying elite loyalty associated with growing costs (Kendall-Taylor 2011). The oil revenues have thus turned into a tool to buy off the potential rivalries. The disproportionally high oil revenues also caused the shrinking share of the economy in private hands and, therefore, precluded the emergence of a business elite autonomous of the regime (Radnitz 2012). The dependence of the political regime on the disperse of oil and gas revenues within the elite, thus, emerges as a critical factor contributing to the continuation of corrupt practices in the state bureaucracy, significantly weakening institutional quality (Öge 2014).

Composition of the Energy Mix

Crude oil and natural gas are the primary energy resources of Azerbaijan. In 2017, the primary production (extraction of energy products from natural resource) of all energy products amounted to 57,036 ton of oil equivalent (TOE). Of this, crude oil, natural gas, and renewables and waste accounted for 69.8%, 29.7%, and 0.5%, respectively (The State Statistical Committee of the Republic of Azerbaijan 2019a).

Between 2005 and 2020, the total primary production of all energy saw the lowest level in 2007 and started increasing again until 2010. However, energy production has been slowly decreasing since its peak in 2010. In parallel, the share of crude oil in the total primary energy production has been gradually diminishing since 2005, thanks to the increase in the percentage of natural gas. The energy produced from renewables and waste has not significantly developed during the 2005–2017 period. During this period, except for the years 2010 and 2011, the energy production from renewables and waste remained stable, with fluctuation in the small range of 240–300 TOE (approx. 1%) (The State Statistical Committee of the Republic of Azerbaijan 2019a).

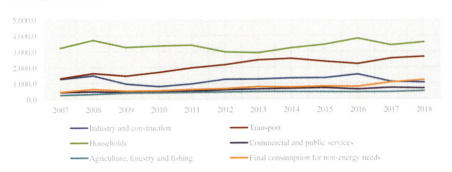

Fig. 1 Final energy consumption by sources, 2007–2018. (Source: State Committee of Statistics of the Republic of Azerbaijan)

A large portion of the primary energy produced in the country is exported, making the country a net exporter of energy. Out of the total primary energy produced in the country, plus the import in the amount of 2,521.6 TOE, only 15,471.9 was directed to supply. The composition of primary energy consumption differs significantly from the composition of primary energy production. Liquid fuels (crude oil-based) constitute 33.4%, while gaseous fuels constitute 64.9% of the total primary energy consumption. In contrast, hydropower accounts for only 1%, biomass and waste less than 0.7%, and other renewables less so. This composition with small changes was the same for the 2007–2017 period (The State Statistical Committee of the Republic of Azerbaijan 2017).

Households and transport had the largest share in the total primary energy consumption – 36.6% and 27.7%, respectively, in 2017 (see Fig. 1). The main types of energy consumed by households are natural gas and electricity, while in the transport sector, mostly oil-based energy products are consumed (The State Statistical Committee of the Republic of Azerbaijan 2017).

Discourse on Energy Issues

Access to energy, the quality of supply, and affordability are the main principles around which the public debates on energy issues revolve. These issues are linked frequently to the liberalization of the energy sector in Azerbaijan and governance reforms, both of which are seen as broad strategies for improving access to electricity, enhancing the quality of supply and making it affordable for all. The economic breakdown caused by the dissolution of the Soviet Union and the Karabakh war that erupted afterwards severely damaged the country's energy supply capacity; the infrastructure, in particular in rural areas, was destroyed and left unused (Ramazanov 2003). Thus, since independence, the key issues prevalent in public debate and the official policy discourse have been the countrywide extension of natural gas and electricity distribution networks, the prevention of power and natural gas outages, affordability of energy prices, the improvement of the registration of natural gas and electricity consumers, and the establishment of fee collection mechanisms.

These objectives were targeted by the government within the State Programme for the Socio-Economic Development of Regions, which accomplished three phases – in 2004–2008, 2009–2013 and 2014–2018 periods. The fourth phase started in 2019 and is envisaged to continue until 2023 (AzerTag 2018; State Programme on Socio-Economic Development of Regions in 2019–2023 2019). Although as a result of the government programs energy supply in the country has significantly improved since the mid of the 2000s, the problems are not entirely eliminated, and still, the country's electricity and natural gas network mostly dates back to Soviet times (Teref.az 2016).

The second broader category of public debates on energy issues concerns the privatization of the state-owned companies such as "Azerienerji," "Azeriqaz," "Azerishiq," and "Azeristiliktechizat." Notably, in the aftermath of the 2015 economic slowdown, the increasing burden of these state companies on the state budget was subject to criticisms by the public, and the government was demanded to privatize the state-owned companies operating in the energy sector (Aslanli 2016; Bunyatli 2017). The issue has also been raised by a range of expert circles in the country, who picture privatization as a way of increasing the quality of services and fighting prevalent corruption within state-owned companies (Vahid 2019). However, the perceived high corruption risks in the privatization process are one of the factors discouraging the public support for the privatization of the state-owned companies in the energy sector. Therefore, the issue of privatization is frequently linked to governance reforms in public discourse (Novator.Az 2016). The unfortunate case of privatization of the electricity distribution of the 2000–2006 period further contributes to the reluctance and contradictory opinions on the issue of privatization in public.

The downward trend in oil production and the diminishing salience of oil in the world markets have triggered discussions about Azerbaijan's alternative and renewable energy industry. The key questions facing the country now is, first, how long this decline of the oil prices will continue, and second, whether the investment should be gradually shifted away from the oil industry to the alternative and renewable energy sector (Vidadili et al. 2017).

Political Institutions and Actors

The current regime in Azerbaijan is characterized by a high degree of power concentration, neo-patrimonial public administration, and the use of patron-client networks as the principal institutional mechanism for wielding political power (Guliyev 2012). The short try of privatization in the early 2000s in the energy sector did not diminish the role of the state in the energy sector. The oil revenues that the country started receiving in large amounts since 2005 further contributed to the concentration of power through patron-client networks, which played a significant role as a factor in disincentivizing privatization in the energy sector that was launched in 1999 amid economic difficulties and guaranteed state dominance.

The key actors in the energy sector include Ministry of Energy, SOCAR and its subunit "Azeriqaz" PU, "Azerenerji" OJSC, "Azerishiq" OJSC, "Azeristiliktechizat" OJSC, as well as the Tariffs Council which gathers together 11 government representatives, namely nine deputy ministers and two deputy head of state committees.

Following the collapse of the Soviet Union, "Azerenerji" Production Union was converted into initially a state company belonging to the cabinet of ministers, and then an open joint-stock company whose full share belongs to the state. "Azerenerji" OJSC operates in the production of electricity, its transmission, and the management of the electric energy systems. It is a centralized body with local offices across the country. The control of the electricity system is operated by the Central Dispatcher Department ("Azerenerji" OJSC n.d.a). The electricity provided by "Azerenerji" OJSC is distributed by another state-owned company, "Azerishiq" OJSC, which is the successor of "Bakielektrikshabaka" OJSC since 2015 (Presidential Order No. 1045 Concerning the "Azerishiq" open joint-stock company 2015).

Similarly, transmission, distribution, and marketing of natural gas inside the country belongs to a single state-owned actor "Azeriqaz" Production Union, which operates under SOCAR. By supplying natural gas to all domestic fossil power plants, "Azeriqaz" is playing a significant role in the development of the country's electrical power industry. Six production divisions and organizations are consolidated in the "Azeriqaz" Production Union. The syndicate supplies gas to 1,312,000 consumers in different parts of Azerbaijan (State Oil Company of the Republic of Azerbaijan [SOCAR] n.d.a). SOCAR not only controls "Azeriqaz" PU but also more than 20 various units including oil and gas exploitation, transportation and processing, and many other types units (State Oil Company of the Republic of Azerbaijan n.d.b). All these make it the most significant player in energy governance in Azerbaijan.

Another critical player in the energy sector is "Azeristiliktechizat" OJSC, which similarly belongs entirely to the state. Compared to the others, it is the latest established state-owned company in the energy sector which was set up in 2005 by a presidential order (Presidential Order No. 847 Concerning the improvement of heat supply in the Republic of Azerbaijan 2005). With this, the process of restructuring and redefinition of the legal status of the Soviet government units into state-owned companies in the energy sector, which was launched in the early years of independence, was mainly finished. It was the first step toward privatization since the old structures of the energy sector, which were part of the state apparatus, were not naturally eligible for privatization. However, as already discussed, the privatization of state-owned companies in the energy sector did not follow further in the succeeding periods.

At the national policy level, the Ministry of Energy is responsible for policy development and regulation of all areas of the fuel and energy sector in Azerbaijan. The area of competence of the ministry is defined as covering all aspects of *activities in the sector of energy*, which is, in turn, set in the Law on Energy as *types of activities for exploration, processing, output, production, development, storage, transportation, distribution, and use of energy resources and materials*. Such a definition provides a wide range of competences to the ministry. The main power of the ministry resides in its function to issue individual permissions and licenses for the sale of oil and gas products, entrepreneurship in the energy sector and use of specific energy equipment, machines, and utilities. It is also responsible for controlling the impact of operations in the energy sector on the environment (Presidential Order No. 149 Concerning the approval of the statute of the Ministry of Energy 2014).

The ministry participates in the regulation of the activities of state-owned enterprises in the energy sector, which also includes "Azerenerji" OJSC, "Azerishiq" OJSC, "Azeristiliktechizat" OJSC, "Azeriqaz" PU, and SOCAR. Also, through its norm and standard-setting and ecological damage control mechanisms, the ministry holds considerable formal power (ibid.). These powers allow the ministry to keep tight control of the state-owned companies. In addition to the Ministry of Energy, the Cabinet of Ministers and the president exercise direct control over the open joint-stock companies.

In December 2017, the Azerbaijan Energy Regulatory Agency was established under the auspices of the Ministry of Energy (Presidential Order No. 1750 Concerning the creation of Azerbaijan Energy Regulatory Agency 2017). The Agency is still at a development stage. The presidential order adopted in July 2018 has identified the areas of duties and responsibilities of the Agency (Presidential Order No. 204 Concerning the approval of "Rules of regulation in the field of electric, heating and gas supply" 2018), which covers mainly the regulation of relations between the consumers and providers of electricity, gas, and heating.

Nevertheless, recent years has seen inconsistency in the government's institutional reforms. The abolishment of governmental structures accompanied the establishment of new ones following the adoption of the so-called strategic road maps. The State Agency on Alternative and Renewable Energy Sources was one of such structures. Initially established in 2009 under the auspices of the Ministry of Energy and then independently in 2013, the Agency was abolished along with some other governmental structures in January 2019 by another presidential order (Virtual Azerbaijan 2019). The abolishment of the Agency after ten years of operation was explained as part of the "optimization" policy of the government given the diminishing scale of public revenues. However, it was also linked to the widespread corruption, which does not contradict the official line of argument about "optimization" of the governance, and intra-elite fights (Cahan.Info 2019; Cumhuriyyet.Info 2019). However, months after the abolishment of the Agency, the Ministry of Energy still was reporting about activities where the Agency had been involved (The Ministry of Energy of the Republic of Azerbaijan 2019b). Uncertainty about the Agency remained almost a year after the presidential order abolishing it. This example illustrates how corrupt practices and inconsistent policies permeate throughout energy governance.

Although the energy sector has gone through significant structural reforms since the early years of independence, the central government remains the single dominant actor, except for the oil and gas production where foreign companies hold their shares. Each subsector is dominated by a single state-owned company with a countrywide presence. This presents a highly centralized governance model which is supervised by the Ministry of Energy, the Cabinet of Ministers, and the president directly. Moreover, as illustrated by the State Agency on Alternative and Renewable Energy Sources, institutional instability remains one of the defining features of energy governance in Azerbaijan. This can be partly explained with the choice of reshuffling of institutional design and personnel as a solution to policy problems (Mehralizade 2019), which emerges as an obstacle to in-depth institutionalization and achieving consistency and deepening in reforms.

Coordination, Instruments and Issues of Energy Transition Within a Multilevel Context

Drivers and Barriers to the Energy Transition

Heavy Dependence on Oil Revenues as an Obstacle to the Energy Transition

Since the mid-2000s, Azerbaijan has started receiving a massive amount of revenues from the export of fossil resources. The oil and gas sectors have much outpaced other sectors of the economy, mainly thanks to foreign investment and transfer of technology. The share of the oil sector in the overall GDP almost doubled during the period 2000–2007. Oil revenues were driven by both the expansion of oil production and higher oil prices, which constituted the major sources of government expenditures (Hasanov 2013). A significant part of these expenditures is oriented toward infrastructural development and social projects through "state programs." These are government action plans of investment, among which four consequent 5-year-long state programs on the socioeconomic development of regions and one on poverty reduction accounted for a large portion of government expenditures. Through these investments, the state has become a driving force of the economy (Hasanov 2013).

However, the effect of the resource abundance is not limited to the growing economic role of the state. As illustrated by Hasanov (2013), the Azerbaijani economy has started showing some symptoms of the *Dutch Disease* from the very early years of the oil revenues. Accordingly, the country did not suffer from "absolute de-industrialization" but from a "relative de-industrialization" in the non-oil tradable sector since 2004, while the non-tradable sector has substantially expanded.

According to the calculations based on official statistics, the share of energy resources, oil and oil products accounted for 91.9% of Azerbaijan's export in 2018. This is 23 percentage point higher than the corresponding figure of 1998 (The State Committee of Statistics of the Republic of Azerbaijan 2019). In other words, Azerbaijan's economy has been increasingly becoming oil-dependent in the last 20 years. Although the country's GDP increased 13 times from 2000 to 2014 in euro terms (The State Statistical Committee of the Republic of Azerbaijan 2019b), this growth can be mostly attributed to the oil sector and the non-tradable sector of the economy.

Such a heavy dependence of Azerbaijan's economy on revenues gained from the export of fossil resources constitutes a significant challenge on the course of energy transition. However, the recent slowdown in the economy due to declining oil prices and oil production has created stronger incentives for diversification of the economy. Accordingly, the exploitation of alternative and renewable energy resources and energy efficiency become more of a focus of government action.

Declining Oil Revenues and Increasing Incentives for Economic Reforms

After 14 years of continued growth, in 2015, Azerbaijan's GDP shrank 15.5% compared to 2014 in euro terms (The State Statistical Committee of the Republic of Azerbaijan 2019b). This resulted from the cut in the oil revenues due to the declining oil prices in international markets. In the same year, without being able to stand the financial pressure, the Azerbaijani manat experienced two times devaluations by the Central Bank of Azerbaijan and lost half of its value (Center for Economic and Social Development [CESD] 2015). Since that the country has not been able to catch its 2014 GDP level in euro terms.

The year of 2015 created a shock effect on both the society and the government. It pushed the government toward considering new developmental perspectives of the non-oil tradable sector and triggered attempts at structural and policy reforms. In 2016, the government adopted a "Strategic Road Map on the National Economy Perspectives" and strategic road maps on 11 different sectors of the economy (Presidential Order No. 1138 Concerning the approval of Strategic Road Maps on the national economy and main sectors of economy 2016). The Road Map presents a new pattern in the government's policy-making – a shift from a previously largely incremental mode of public-policymaking, which was action-based planning, to a rational public policy-making mode, which is output-oriented. The document was followed by structural reforms in the government apparatus in the following years, aimed at increasing efficiency of and achieving effective coordination within the bureaucracy. The whole document presents a stronger emphasis on the development of alternative and renewable energy and energy efficiency.

The declining oil revenues created stronger incentives for economic diversification, for example, by developing alternative and renewable energy resources and enhancing energy efficiency. However, the implementation of the adopted strategic documents requires enormous investment which is calculated to be around 27 billion manats or 14.5 billion euro in current currency rates (Presidential Order No. 1138 Concerning the approval of Strategic Road Maps on the national economy and main sectors of economy 2016). The real amount of investment required for the achievement of the targets set in this document can be much higher than the government's estimations. This transformation of the economy would be a big financial challenge for the government of Azerbaijan. Therefore, it requires international financial support in the form of grants and loans and extensive privatization. Within this context, a strong emphasis is put on the privatization in the energy sector, in particular in the field of alternative and renewable energy. The privatization policy would require extensive and profound reforms in the legal and political system. However, such reforms would find their boundaries in the nature of the political regime, in particular when they put its core mechanism into question.

Growing Demand for Electricity and Aging Infrastructure

Although the economy of Azerbaijan has slowed down significantly in recent years, there is still a growing demand for electricity in the country, at least until 2025 a continuous growth in the market for electricity is forecast (Fitchner 2013). Since 2004, electricity consumption outmatched both GDP growth and electricity production in Azerbaijan. In the 2010–2014 period, GDP growth was 9.2%, and electricity consumption increased by 7.8%, while electricity production had a 2.8% growth rate (Presidential Order No. 1138 Concerning the approval of Strategic Road Maps on the national economy and main sectors of economy 2016). Electricity production has been growing 1% on average annually in recent years, and this trend is expected to continue until 2020. However, peak times electricity demand has been increasing rapidly, too. In result, the reserve capacity decreased from 46% in 2009 to 34% in 2015. The reserve capacity is forecast to fall by 14% in 2020, which is below the internationally accepted 25% security level (ibid. 873). The closure of "Shirvan" power plant, which provided 600 MW electricity or 8.15% of 7,348 MW electricity in total produced in the country in 2014, has further raised electricity provision risks in the country (ibid. 875).

Moreover, the existing power plants and infrastructure is increasingly outdated. The average lifetime by the design of the gas-based power plants is 25 years. Yet, more than 30 years old power plants account for a 56% share of total electricity production in the country. Another 14% of the production is provided by the 10–30-years-old power plant (ibid. 876).

The modernization of electricity generation infrastructure requires a significant amount of investment in the next few years (Fitchner 2013). All these put high pressure on the government of Azerbaijan to develop rapid and active exploitation of alternative and renewable energy resources in parallel to the traditional sector to meet the growing demand. Despite this pressure, the government of Azerbaijan has not explicitly shown any intention to privatize the state-owned companies in the energy sector, although there have been demands for this in public. The government's preference is to direct private investment mainly into alternative and renewable energies rather than the traditional part of the electricity sector. Nonetheless, the need has further been exacerbated by the 42% decline in the amount of investment in the electricity production in the period from 2011 to 2014, which can explain the situation at least partly, constituting a 5.6% share of all the investments in the country (Presidential Order No. 1138 Concerning the approval of Strategic Road Maps on the national economy and main sectors of economy 2016). However, the size of investment made in the development of alternative energy in 2005–2015 has been significant, reaching 987.4 million manats ($613 million). The private sector accounted for a 17% share of this amount (Nazarli 2016).

As illustrated above, the growing demand for electricity and the ageing energy infrastructure requires the government to share the financial burden with private actors, thus opening the doors for privatization in the energy sector. As we will see below, the government favors privatization in the area of alternative and renewable energy more than in the traditional energy sector. These two factors may suggest some perspective for the change of balance between the alternative and renewable energy and the traditional energy sector in favor of the former.

Availability of Natural Resources for the Energy Transition

The economic pressure experienced since 2015 has become a stronger call for the government to consider opportunities beyond the oil and gas sector. As previously discussed, the growing demand for electricity has further accelerated these tendencies in the energy sector. Combined with the government's new efforts for opening up opportunities for developing the national economy and the energy sector, the availability of natural resources emerges as a critical opportunity for the development of the alternative and renewable energy sector.

Azerbaijan has, due to many different climate zones, not only profitable opportunities in agriculture but also in gaining alternative and renewable energy sources with wind, sun, biomass, and hydropower sources. The potential capacity of wind energy and solar energy production is estimated as high as 15,000 MW and 8,000 MW, respectively. However, only 0.4% of each of them is currently exploited. Absheron peninsula, the coasts of the Caspian Sea and its waters, and the territories of the Autonomous Republic of Nakhchivan maintain the significant natural potential for the generation of wind power. The number of sunny hours during a year in Baku varies between 2,000 and 2,800. The solar power generation potential of Kur-Araz lowlands, Absheron peninsula, and the territories of the Autonomous Republic of Nakhchivan is estimated to be around 1,400–1,800 kW solar energy per square meter on average. The close distance of these areas to the main electricity consumption areas further increases the attractiveness of the exploitation of this potential (Presidential Order No. 1138 Concerning the approval of Strategic Road Maps on the national economy and main sectors of economy 2016). The potential capacity of geothermal energy is estimated to be around 800 MW. Potential of renewable energy sources in total exceeds 25,400 MW (Nazarli 2016).

Moreover, the historically developed cotton and wheat agriculture, as well as the government's plans to further expand cotton and wheat production in the country, creates opportunities for the development of bioenergy. Currently, the capacity of bioenergy is 46 MW, and this constitutes only 5.1% of the economically efficient potential of 900 MW (Presidential Order No. 1138 Concerning the approval of Strategic Road Maps on the national economy and main sectors of economy 2016). The potential of bioenergy (a type of renewable energy made available from materials derived from biological sources) is estimated at 900 MW, while the capacity of small hydroelectric power plants is 700 MW (Nazarli 2016).

Despite their abundance, alternative and renewable energy sources remain underexploited. Privatization and liberalization of the energy market can increase the realization of this potential. The abundance of alternative and renewable energy sources also represents one of the attractive areas for international cooperation, in particular with the European Union, which, in turn, could further increase the attractiveness of the sector for private actors.

International Cooperation as a Driving Force of Energy Transition
International cooperation opportunities have become one of the critical drivers of the energy transition in Azerbaijan. Although still limited in scope, there have been several successful cases of international cooperation in the development of alternative and renewable energies. One of the key international actors supporting the energy transition in Azerbaijan has been the European Bank of Reconstruction and Development (EBRD) (European Bank for Reconstruction and Development [EBRD] n.d.). With its support,

Azerbaijan has implemented several projects on modernization and upgrading of existing thermal power plants (Aliyeva et al. 2013). In addition to EBRD, International Finance Corporation (IFC) and Canada Climate Change Program, Green Growth Fund, KFW Bank, Asian Development Bank (ADB) have provided a significant amount of financial support to Azerbaijan in the form of equity and loans (United Nations Development Programme [UNDP] n.d.).

The energy sector of Azerbaijan also benefited a lot within the framework of INOGATE – an energy technical assistance program funded by the European Commission since 1996. Since its launch, Azerbaijan benefited from 33 out of 69 projects of INOGATE (INOGATE n.d.).

In the 2010–2012 period, the EU-funded Energy Reform Support Programme (ERSP) assisted Azerbaijan in reviewing the national energy strategy in order to identify new infrastructural needs and specifying the legislative and institutional reforms to promote energy efficiency, energy savings, and greater use of renewable energy sources (Juan Carrion 2016). In the 2016–2020 period, the EU supported reforms in the energy sector of Azerbaijan within the framework of the EU4Energy program. The program, which has a budget of EUR 21 million, was funded by the European Union (EU) and runs until 2020 (EUNeighbours East 2019). Within the framework of this program, the EU together with the Secretary of Energy Charter supported Azerbaijan in developing an energy strategy document and a draft law on energy efficiency (Ostapenko 2018; The Ministry of Energy of the Republic of Azerbaijan 2018a).

Under the EU4Energy program, the European Commission's Technical Assistance and Information Exchange Instrument (TAIEX) promotes the exchange of best practices between the EU and its partner countries, including approximating the local laws with European legislation in the area of common interest (Ostapenko 2019). Prior to the EU4Energy programs, Azerbaijan and the EU cooperated within the framework of regional cooperation instruments such as the Eastern Europe Energy efficiency and Endowment Partnership (Nabiyeva 2018). Within the latter, four projects were carried out in Azerbaijan, which is significantly a small number compared to other Eastern Partnership countries, save Belarus (Frear et al. 2018).

Paris Agreement – a global agreement on climate change, which Azerbaijan signed on 22 April 2016 along with 195 other countries in New York, is the global level external driver of Azerbaijan's energy transition (UNFCCC 2020). In the Intended Nationally Determined Contribution (INDC), which Azerbaijan submitted to the United Nations Framework Convention on Climate Change (UNFCCC) in September 2015, Azerbaijan targets 35% reduction in greenhouse gas emission by 2030 compared to 1990/base year as its contribution to the global climate change efforts. As part of INDC, Azerbaijan aims to apply new environmentally friendly technologies in the oil and gas sector, more specifically, to modernize its gas pipelines and gas distribution so that the losses are decreased up to 1% by 2020 and ensure the volume of reduction in compliance with international standards by 2050. The document provides general intention of Azerbaijan regarding the measures for energy efficiency in electrical, heat energy, and national gas systems. Equally importantly, the lack of technical and normative documents on the use of alternative and renewable energy sources has been recognized and their development has been set as a target by the government of Azerbaijan. Besides, Azerbaijan has committed itself generally to energy efficiency measures in other sectors such as transport, agriculture, waste, and land use, land-use change, and forestry (Information to the United Nations Framework Convention on Climate Change (UNFCCC) on the Intended Nationally Determined Contribution (INDC) of the Republic of Azerbaijan 2015).

Moreover, in March 2018, Azerbaijan joined the Hague II document of the International Energy Charter as part of the cooperation within the EU4Energy program (Ostapenko 2019; Sultanova 2018). The history of Azerbaijan's cooperation dates as back as 1994 when Azerbaijan signed the European Energy Charter, which later became International Energy Charter and entered into force in 1998 (International Energy Charter Secretariat n.d.).

Overall, as illustrated briefly above, both international cooperation and financial support, particularly by the EU, are emerging as a significant driver for the energy transition in Azerbaijan. A significant increase is observed in the number of projects and the amount of financial support following the establishment of an independent state agency on alternative and renewable energy. All these partnership and cooperation cases, in its turn, have contributed to the growing role and independence of agencies in practice.

Strategies and Instruments of Energy Transitions

Development of Policies and Strategies

By approving the European Energy Charter in 1998, the government of Azerbaijan has shown a growing commitment to the energy transition. In the early 2000s, two key programs were adopted by the government, which wholly or partly concern the issues of the energy transition. These are "National Program on Environmentally Sustainable Socioeconomic Development for the period of 2003–2010" and "State Action Plan for the preservation and sustainable use of biodiversity in the Republic of Azerbaijan for the 2006–2009 period." While the former document set energy efficiency and the use of alternative and renewable energy sources as targets, the latter prioritized, along with other goals, to achieve efficiency in the use of bioenergy (Presidential Order No. 152 Concerning the approval of national programmes on ecology 2003). Although they addressed energy transition in a limited way, the documents were significant in terms of linking energy and ecology in the policy discourse and indicate first steps toward the use of alternative and renewable energy sources and improving energy efficiency. The adoption of these programs constitutes the foundation for the integration of issues concerning the energy transition in future strategic development documents of the government.

At least partly due to the adoption of these two programs, the issues of energy efficiency and the use of alternative and renewable energy made their way into the national development strategies "Azerbaijan 2020: Look Into the Future." Adopted in 2012, the document laid out generally the government's development goals, in which energy efficiency was identified as a quality which the economy needs to gain (Presidential Order No. 800 Concerning the approval of "Azerbaijan 2020: Look into the Future" Concept of Development 2012). The document also affirmed the government's intention to expand opportunities for the development of alternative and reliable energy (ibid., p. 10) and informed about plans "to carry out stimulating measures to speed up the use of alternative (renewable) energy sources." For this, it envisages to develop the institutional environment, strengthen the scientific-technical potential, build the capacity, and raise the awareness of energy consumers. Furthermore, the document emphasizes the importance of involving the private sector in this process for which the quick regulation of alternative energy tariffs was promised (ibid., p. 15).

Policy-making initiatives concerning the issues of energy transition continued in the 2010s. In 2011, an order was signed by the president to establish the "State Strategy on the Use of Alternative and renewable energy for the 2012–2020 period" – a policy document outlining the necessary reform agenda on the development of alternative and renewable energy (Presidential Decree No. 1958 Concerning the development of the State Strategy for the Use of Alternative and Renewable Energy Sources in the Republic of Azerbaijan for 2012–2020 2011). However, 7 years passed after the order, and the document was not adopted yet, although a draft of the document was tabled in 2015 (The Ministry of Ecology and Natural Resources of the Republic of Azerbaijan, IREA, REC Caucasus 2015).

Similarly, the draft of "State Strategy on Energy efficiency" was prepared within the framework of EU4Energy but still was not adopted as of the end of October 2019 (The Ministry of Energy of the Republic of Azerbaijan 2018b). Delay in the adoption of these strategies can partly be explained with gaps in the legal framework and creation of national standards on the use of alternative and renewable energy, which were mainly covered by the "Strategic Plan of the State Agency on Alternative and renewable energy Source for the 2016–2020 period" (State Agency on Alternative and Renewable Energy Sources of the Republic of Azerbaijan [AREA] n.d.).

The strategic development document adopted by the government in the follow-up of the 2015 economic slowdown appears particularly vital as it mainstreams the issues of energy efficiency and, in general, energy transition across all the areas (Presidential Order No. 1138 Concerning the approval of Strategic Road Maps on the national economy and main sectors of economy 2016). The document emphasizes on the reduction of energy use per GDP unit in Azerbaijan and targets to increase the share of renewable energy in the total primary energy production in the post-2025 period (ibid., p. 49). One of these strategy documents, namely "Strategic Road Map on the Development of Utility Services," mainly addresses the energy sector along with other areas of the utility services. Regarding alternative and renewable energy, the government considers it "reasonable" to increase production capacities at the expense of private investment (ibid.). More importantly, the document recognizes the need to separate production, transmission, distribution, and sale of energy resources from one another, though it uses a less concrete language. The green economy has been declared one of the priority areas in the Strategic Road Map on Agriculture (ibid., pp. 221–222). Involving private business actors into the energy sector is also emphasized throughout all sections. Though, privatization appears to be more preferably in the alternative and renewable energy sector. No less importantly, as another significant step toward energy transition, energy efficiency has been declared as an objective in the Strategic Road Map on Heavy Industry and Metallurgy (ibid., p. 404).

All these suggest that Azerbaijan is still at an early stage of an energy transition. Although some specific targets are set in the Strategic Road Maps concrete and measurable overall targets and indicators for energy efficiency and the use of alternative and renewable energy sources are still lacking. Therefore, it is difficult to engage in reasonable measurement of the progress. Such concrete and measurable overall targets and indicators still must be defined, and the energy efficiency strategy and the strategy for alternative and renewable energy sources have yet to be adopted.

Types of Policy Instruments

Policy instruments of the energy transition in Azerbaijan are not advanced, yet. The Law on the Use of Energy resources broadly outlines three approaches: legal, administrative, and economic-financial approaches (Presidential Order No. 94-IQ Concerning the approval of Law on the Use of Energy Resources 1996). It further identifies norm- and standard-setting as a principle of state policy in energy saving and energy efficiency. Also, sanctioning the inefficient use of energy, promoting economically, ecologically and socially advantageous practices, and investment in energy efficient new technologies are identified as central principles for energy usage (ibid.). For achieving this, the state authority of examination is recognized in the Law. Accordingly, any activity related to energy is subject to obligatory state appraisal by experts (ibid. Article 23), and failure to oblige with the set standards and norms is sanctioned (ibid. Article 29). However, specific instruments for ensuring these are not necessarily advanced, and their application remains limited. Although the Law envisages the adoption of state programs on efficient use of energy, such a stand-alone program has never been adopted by the government.

The current state of the energy transition instruments can be described as predominantly regulatory. The Law on the Use of Energy resources establishes obligatory certification on products, technological processes, services, and energy consumption as a regulatory instrument for enhancing energy efficiency (ibid. Article 21). The Law also entitles enterprises over-performing the state-set standards to apply for the state's fund on efficient use of energy. However, at the end of October 2019, such a state fund was still due to be established.

These regulatory instruments apply to all areas of the energy sector. Since the energy sector is dominated by state-owned companies, which are subject to the control of the Ministry of Energy, the application of these standards remains an issue in the relationship between the subordinate and the supervisor in the bureaucratic hierarchy. This raises questions about how seriously the standards are applied. Outside the state-owned companies, the ministry applies these rules and norms only in a few cases, since the number of independent energy producers in the country is limited despite having a relevant legal framework – the Law on Energetics envisages independent energy producers (Presidential Order No. 541IQ Concerning the approval of the Law on Energetics of the Republic of Azerbaijan 1998).

Moreover, the Law requires the creation of a fund for supporting financing energy-saving activities. The responsibility lies with the Ministry of Energy according to its statute (Presidential Order No. 149 Concerning the approval of the statute of the Ministry of Energy 2014). Although the draft of the necessary documents for establishing such a fund has been designed and submitted to the government by the Ministry of Energy as late as 2016, it is still due to be found (Meydan TV 2016).

Nevertheless, incentive-based elements in the energy governance model of Azerbaijan are not absent at all. Through a differentiated tariff policy, the Tariffs Council stimulates the efficient use of energy by individual citizens and business enterprises. The 2016 "Strategic Road Map on Heavy Industry and Machinery" identifies the efficient use of energy and the optimization of demand as important goals (Presidential Order No. 1138 Concerning the approval of Strategic Road Maps on the national economy and main sectors of economy 2016) and provides the Tariffs Council with the task of preparing a new energy balance, identifying a list of strategically important enterprises, equally sharing energy use between peak and non-peak times, and creating a coordinating council between energy producers and energy consumers (ibid., p. 430). Accordingly, the Tariffs Council is required to pursue an incentive-based policy toward the use of energy in non-peak times, and set lower tariff rates for the list of strategically important enterprises. Meanwhile, the Ministry of Energy nudges the industry to energy saving through awareness-raising. In line with it, the Ministry of Energy supports the industry with methodological guidelines on energy efficiency (Ted.Az 2019).

With a stronger emphasis on the importance of involving private actors in the area of alternative and renewable energy, the government provided some incentives for the private sector in this area. The import of equipment for the generation of wind energy was exempted from VAT in 2007. In 2014, the Cabinet of Ministers took another similar decision to exempt 81 types of products used in the area of alternative and renewable energy from VAT. These decisions are intended to incentivize the use of alternative and renewable energy sources and attract private investors.

Coordination Mechanisms and Multilevel Governance

The current energy governance model of Azerbaijan can be characterized as a vertically integrated governance structure. The state holds a monopoly through wholly state-owned companies, and there is a lack of competition. The Ministry of Energy is the main state actor supervising and controlling the energy sector, to which the state-owned companies are subordinated. In addition, the Cabinet of Ministers and the Office of the President have direct influence on these companies.

In 2017, the government of Azerbaijan took a small step toward liberalization of the energy sector by establishing Azerbaijani Energy Regulatory Agency as a public law entity, though under the auspices of the Ministry of Energy, aimed at adjusting the relations between energy producers, transmitters, distributors, and consumers (Presidential Order No. 1750 Concerning the creation of Azerbaijan Energy Regulatory Agency 2017). Nevertheless, the Agency is at its early stage of development and not sufficiently independent from the Ministry of Energy.

At the local level, "Azerenerji" OJSC, "Azerishiq" OJSC, "Azeristiliktechizat" OJSC, and "Azeriqaz" PU hold their district offices. "Shaki SES" OJSC, "Goygol SES" OJSC, and "Mugan SES" OJSC are just three independent local hydropower producers. "Goygol SES" OJSC was privatized in recent years, after being destroyed by a flood in 1997 (Azadlıq.Az 2017). The shares of "Mugan SES" OJSC and "Shaki SES" OJSC were purchased in 2003 by "Messenat" Holding and "General Construction" LLC, respectively ("Shaki SES" OJSC 2014; Messenat Holding n.d.). In addition to these three independent hydropower producers, there are in total five thermal power energy producers (including SOCAR, BP, and a local food giant "Azersun"), two bioenergy producers, seven wind power energy producers, and only two solar power energy producers (The Ministry of Energy of the Republic of Azerbaijan 2019a).

In the area of alternative and renewable energy, Alten Group is the only bigger private actor with divisions throughout the country following the state-owned "Azalternativenerji" LLC. The operation of these private companies is controlled by the Ministry of Energy and until its abolishment by the State Agency on Alternative and Renewable Energy Sources.

Outcomes, Challenges, and Prospects of Energy Governance

This chapter provided a brief sketch of the energy governance in Azerbaijan by, first, looking into a variety of issues ranging from the country's Soviet legacies to prospects of transforming the energy sector that is heavily dominated by fossil fuels. The Soviet heritage of the country overshadows it in many ways. Three broad categories of Soviet legacies were identified and briefly discussed. Firstly, yet, after the collapse of the Soviet Union, Azerbaijan maintains a highly centralized energy governance system. Secondly, Azerbaijan has inherited the unstable institutional past, and the institutional instability continued until the end of the 1990s, preventing in-depth institutionalization in energy governance. Thirdly, informal patrimonial patterns such as sharing of bribes through the chain of command and buying of lucrative positions by way of payment to top officials existed during the Soviet time and found a favorable environment to institutionalize in the early years of independence. Combined, all these erode the formal institutional basis of energy governance in Azerbaijan. Given the unstable past full of frequent reshuffling, public institutions appear incapable to present strong institutional constraints to the incorrupt practices and political meddling.

With the collapse of the Soviet Union, Azerbaijan abandoned the centralized planned economy, yet did not achieve to establish a truly free market. The energy market remains under the monopoly of the state with no real competition. Even though three decades after the dissolution of the Soviet Union, no significant progress was achieved toward the liberalization of the energy market. Only in recent years, under economic pressures, the government has taken a considerable step forward in further clearing its vision in the energy governance through the so-called Strategic Road Maps adopted in the immediate follow-up of the 2015 economic downturn. Although some essential but insufficient legal bases were laid down since the late 1990s, strategies and policy instruments for the energy transition have not been advanced yet. It is mainly the regulatory type of policy instruments that dominates the policy field, supported with very few incentive-based instruments.

Meanwhile, growing demand, aging energy infrastructure, and increasingly shrinking financial capacities of the state raise the pressure on the government to find alternative financial resources and relieve the real burden from its shoulder, or in other words, to open the market to private actors, be they local or international. The government, thus, faces a dilemma of whether to continue its current dominant role or open the energy market to private actors. The former has high financial costs, while the latter bears certain political risks. Given the current political regime, which does not only control the public and political but also the economic sphere, it remains to be seen to what extent the government of Azerbaijan can undertake deep reforms and liberalize the energy sector, which is seen as a crucial strategical area for the state, without compromising the political regime.

Besides growing demand, which pushes the government of Azerbaijan to increase energy efficiency in the country and look for opportunities in the area of alternative and renewable energy, two other factors affect Azerbaijan's energy transition pathway. Firstly, it has committed itself internationally and receives the EU's financial support and guidance. Secondly, it has significant potential for alternative and renewable energy sources waiting to be exploited. The existence of abundant resources can raise private interest in the development of an alternative and renewable energy sector with necessary policy and structural reforms or can create pressure for such changes.

The adoption of two already drafted vital policy documents, namely Energy Efficiency Strategy and Strategy on Alternative and Renewable Energy, carries particular importance. The approval of these strategic documents and clear defined targets and indicators should contribute to a meaningful reform process in the energy sector. Establishing the fund mentioned in the Law on Energy for incentivizing energy efficiency is another significant step that needs to be taken by the government in the short run. Strengthening the institutional capacity and independence of Azerbaijan Energy Regulatory Agency appears another key challenge for the government of Azerbaijan on its energy transition pathway in the short-term.

Meanwhile, the liberalization of its energy market appears only possible to be achieved in the mid-term. Transforming the energy governance model of Azerbaijan could take at least 20 years (Ostapenko 2019). In the long run, the energy transition path of Azerbaijan requires it to decrease the dependence of its economy on the revenues of oil and gas exports. To achieve this, Azerbaijan has to carry out substantial reforms not only in the economic and financial sectors but also in the judiciary, improve its human rights and democracy records, strengthen the capacity of public institutions, and increase their accountability and transparency.

The picture presented above suggests that the energy transition pathway of Azerbaijan faces both severe challenges and opportunities, which is conditioned by economic, physical, and political factors in the country. The country's Soviet legacy and the nature of the current political regime are as strong factors as physical and geographical conditions in shaping the country's energy transition pathway.

Cross-References

▶ Energy Democracy and Participation in Energy Transitions
▶ Energy Relations in the EU Eastern Partnership
▶ European Energy Charter Treaty
▶ Transition of Energy Systems: Patterns of Stability and Change

References

"Azerenerji" OJSC. (n.d.a). Energy systems management. Retrieved from http://azerenerji.gov.az/index/page/15?lang=en
"Azerenerji" OJSC. (n.d.b). General information. Retrieved from http://azerenerji.gov.az/index/page/12?lang=en
"Azeriqaz" PU. (n.d.). About us. Retrieved from http://azeriqaz104.az/az/content/1/1
"Azeristiliktechizat" OJSC. (n.d.). Azəristiliktəchizat ASC. Retrieved from http://azeristilik.gov.az/content/az/10
"Shaki SES" OJSC. (2014). About "Shaki SES" OJSC. Retrieved from https://sheki-ses-1936.io.ua/
Aliyeva, G., Gusev, A., Aboltins, R., Chubyk, A., & Krug, M. (2013). *Eastern partnership prospects on energy efficiency and renewable energy: Workshop*. Luxembourg: EUR-OP.
Aslanli, O. (2016). "Azerishiq", "Azersu", "Azal" should be privatized – Say experts. Baku: ANN. AZ. Retrieved from https://ann.az/az/azerisiqu-azersu-azal-zellesdirilmelidir-ekspertler/
Azadlıq.Az. (2017). "Chichekli" hydroelectric power station is back in use after fundamental reconstruction: Azadlıq.Az. Retrieved from https://www.azadliq.az/xeber/174589/goygolde-cicekli-su-elektrik-stansiyasi-esasli-yenidenqurmadan-sonra-istismara-verilib/
Azerbaijans.Com. (n.d.). Azerigaz CJSC. Retrieved from http://www.azerbaijans.com/content_543_en.html
AzerTag. (2018). A conference dedicated to the fourth year of implementation of the State Programme for the Socio-Economic Development of Regions in the 2014–2018 years was held. The president of Azerbaijan attended the conference – Updated Four Video: AzerTag. Retrieved from https://azertag.az/xeber/Regionlarin_2014_2018_ci_illerde_sosial_iqtisadi_inkisafi_Dovlet_Proqraminin_icrasinin_dorduncu_ilinin_yekunlarina_hesr_olunan_konfrans_kechirilib__Azerbaycan_Prezidenti_Ilham_Aliyev_konfransda_istirak_edib_YENILANIB_4_VIDEO-1132142
Balayev, S. G. (1969). Oil of the country of eternal fire (1st ed.). Baku: Azerneshr Publishing House.
Bayulgen, O. (2010). *Foreign investment and political regimes: The oil sector in Azerbaijan, Russia, and Norway*. Cambridge: Cambridge University Press.
Blair, B. (2006). Oil Rocks in the Caspian, *14*(2), 46–55. Retrieved from http://azer.com/aiweb/categories/magazine/ai142_folder/142_articles/142_salahov_oil_rocks.html
Budagov, N. (2017). 11 years past since the Shah Deniz gas-condensate field was launched. Baku: AzerTag. Retrieved from https://azertag.az/xeber/Sahdeniz_qaz_kondensat_yataginda_hasilata_baslanmasindan_11_il_otur-1121183
Bunyatli, M. (2017). "Azeriqaz" and other state-owned companies should be privatized – The national economy should be built in accordance with the new requirements of time. Baku: Gunun Sesi Info. Retrieved from https://www.gununsesi.org/az%C9%99riqaz-v%C9%99-dig%C9%99r-dovl%C9%99t-sirk%C9%99tl%C9%99ri-oz%C9%99ll%C9%99sdirilm%C9%99lidir/
Cahan.Info. (2019). Akim Badalov is in panic because of the agency abolished by president. Retrieved from http://cahan.info/manset/6145-prezidentin-legv-etdiyi-agentliye-gore-akim-bedelov-tesvisde.html
Center for Economic and Social Development. (2015). *Devaluation of Azerbaijani National Currency; Causes and consequences better research, better policy, better reform devaluation*

of Azerbaijani National Currency: Causes and consequences. Baku. Retrieved from http://cesd. az/new/wp-content/uploads/2015/03/Azerbaijan_National_Currency_Devaluation2.pdf

Cumhuriyyet.Info. (2019). Alternative and renewable incompetence, or? Azerbaijan is losing millions every year...: Cumhuriyyet.Info. Retrieved from https://www.cumhuriyyet.net/manset-2/128085-alternativ-v%C9%99-b%C9%99rpaolunan-s%C9%99rist%C9%99sizlik-yoxsa-az%C9%99rbaycan-h%C9%99r-il-milyonlar-itirir.html

Equinor. (2014). Statoil sells 15.5% share in Shah Deniz to PETRONAS for USD 2.2 billion: Equinor. Retrieved from https://www.equinor.com/en/news/archive/2014/10/13/13OctShahDeniz.html

EUNeighbours East. (2019). EU supports energy reform in Azerbaijan. Retrieved from https://www.euneighbours.eu/en/east/stay-informed/publications/eu-supports-energy-reform-azerbaijan

European Bank for Reconstruction and Development. (n.d.). Azerbaijan project summary documents. Retrieved from https://www.ebrd.com/work-with-us/project-finance/project-summary-documents.html?1=1&filterCountry=Azerbaijan

Fitchner. (2013). *Update of the power sector master plan of Azerbaijan 2013–2025: Final report*. Retrieved from Fitchner website: http://www.inogate.org/documents/3_FICHT-11527706-v2-Final_Report_Azerbaijan.pdf

Franke, A., Gawrich, A., & Alakbarov, G. (2009). Kazakhstan and Azerbaijan as Post-Soviet Rentier states: Resource incomes and autocracy as a double 'curse' in Post-Soviet regimes. *Europe-Asia Studies, 61*(1), 109–140. https://doi.org/10.1080/09668130802532977.

Frear, M., Maniokas, K., Jonavičius, L., & Tabarta, I. (2018). *The EU and Eastern partnership countries – An inside-out analysis and strategic assessment* (EU-STRAT report no. 5). Retrieved from http://eu-strat.eu/wp-content/uploads/2018/07/EU-STRAT-Report-No.-5.pdf

Guliyev, F. (2012). Political elites in Azerbaijan. In A. Heinrich & H. Pleines (Eds.), *Challenges of the Caspian resource boom. Domestic elites and policy-making* (pp. 117–130). Houndmills: Palgrave Macmillan.

Hasanov, F. (2013). Dutch disease and the Azerbaijan economy. *Communist and Post-Communist Studies, 46*(4), 463–480. https://doi.org/10.1016/j.postcomstud.2013.09.001.

Igorev, V. (2010). A man made Island of oil treasures: Azerbaijan's oil rocks: The unique experience of the Caspian shelf pioneers. Retrieved from http://www.oilru.com/or/44/925/

Information to the United Nations Framework Convention on Climate Change (UNFCCC) on the Intended Nationally Determined Contribution (INDC) of the Republic of Azerbaijan (2015).

INNOGATE. (n.d.). INOGATE & Azerbaijan. Retrieved from http://www.inogate.org/countries/2?lang=en

International Energy Charter Secretariate. (n.d.). Signatories/contracting parties to the protocol on energy efficiency and related environmental aspects. Retrieved from https://energycharter.org/process/energy-charter-treaty-1994/energy-efficiency-protocol/

Joseph, M. (2020). Chevron closes sale of Azeri ACG Stake to MOL: Natural Gas World. Retrieved from https://www.naturalgasworld.com/mol-78166

Juan Carrion, C. (2016). *Why Azerbaijan needs a strategic reform of its foreign policy towards the European Union?* (Research paper). Retrieved from Center for Economic and Social Development (CESD) website: http://cesd.az/new/wp-content/uploads/2016/04/CESD-Paper-Why-Azerbaijan-needs-a-Strategic-Reform-of-its-foreign-policy-towards-the-European-Union.pdf

Kendall-Taylor, A. H. (2011). Political insecurity and oil. *Problems of Post-Communism, 58*(1), 44–57. https://doi.org/10.2753/PPC1075-8216580104.

Kendall-Taylor, A. (2012). Purchasing power: Oil, elections and regime durability in Azerbaijan and Kazakhstan. *Europe-Asia Studies, 64*(4), 737–760. https://doi.org/10.1080/09668136.2012.671567.

Mehdiyeva, N. (2011) *Power games in the Caucasus: Azerbaijan's foreign and energy policy towards the West, Russia and the Middle East. Library of International Relations*. London: I. B.Tauris. Retrieved from http://site.ebrary.com/lib/alltitles/docDetail.action?docID=10554327

Mehralizade, F. (2019). Structural reforms in Azerbaijan. Retrieved from https://bakuresearchinstitute.org/az/structural-reforms-in-azerbaijan/

Messenat Holding. (n.d.). "Mugan Suelektrik Stansiyasi" OJSC. Production and Sales of Electricity. Retrieved from http://www.messenat.az/mugan-ses.php

Meydan, T. V. (2016). Natig Aliyev: State fund for efficient use of energy should be established: Meydan TV. Retrieved from https://www.meydan.tv/az/article/natiq-eliyev-dovlet-enerjiden-semereli-istifade-fondu-yaradilmalidir/?/ref=redirect

Nabiyeva, K. (2018). *Energy transition in South East and Eastern Europe, South Caucasus and Central Asia: Challenges, opportunities and best practices on renewable energy and energy efficiency* (Energy Transition). Retrieved from Friedrich Ebert Stiftung website: http://library.fes.de/pdf-files/id-moe/14922.pdf

Nazarli, A. (2016). Azerbaijan seeking much alternative energy in total energy balance. Baku: Azernews. Retrieved from https://www.azernews.az/nation/103870.html

Novator.Az. (2016). From what could a wider privatization campaign start? Baku: Novator.Az. Retrieved from https://novator.az/2016/01/18/genis-oz%C9%99ll%C9%99sdirm%C9%99-haradan-baslana-bil%C9%99r/

Öge, K. (2014). The limits of transparency promotion in Azerbaijan: External remedies to 'reverse the curse'. *Europe-Asia Studies, 66*(9), 1482–1500. https://doi.org/10.1080/09668136.2014.956448.

Ostapenko, Y. (2018). Azerbaijan is developing its energy strategy and law on energy efficiency: But what do they mean for the country? Retrieved from https://www.euneighbours.eu/en/east/eu-in-action/stories/azerbaijan-developing-its-energy-strategy-and-law-energy-efficiency-what

Ostapenko, Y. (2019). Azerbaijan's electric power industry is ready for reforms. Retrieved from https://www.euneighbours.eu/en/east/eu-in-action/stories/azerbaijans-electric-power-industry-ready-reforms

Presidential Decree No. 1958 Concerning the development of the State Strategy for the Use of Alternative and Renewable Energy Sources in the Republic of Azerbaijan for 2012–2020 (2011)

Presidential Order No. 1045 Concerning the "Azerishiq" open joint-stock company (2015).

Presidential Order No. 1138 Concerning the approval of Strategic Road Maps on the national economy and main sectors of economy (2016).

Presidential Order No. 149 Concerning the approval of the statute of the Ministry of Energy (2014).

Presidential Order No. 152 Concerning the approval of national programmes on ecology (2003).

Presidential Order No. 1750 Concerning the creation of Azerbaijan Energy Regulatory Agency (2017).

Presidential Order No. 204 Concerning the approval of "Rules of regulation in the field of electric, heating and gas supply" (2018).

Presidential Order No. 541IQ Concerning the approval of the Law on Energetics of the Republic of Azerbaijan (1998).

Presidential Order No. 800 Concerning the approval of "Azerbaijan 2020: Look into the Future" Concept of Development (2012).

Presidential Order No. 847 Concerning the improvement of heat supply in the Republic of Azerbaijan (2005).

Presidential Order No. 94-IQ Concerning the approval of Law on the Use of Energy Resources (1996).

Radnitz, S. (2012). Oil in the family: Managing presidential succession in Azerbaijan. *Democratization, 19*(1), 60–77. https://doi.org/10.1080/13510347.2012.641300.

Ramazanov, K. N. (2003). Politics of independent Azerbaijan in the power engineering, *2*. Retrieved from http://www.physics.gov.az/PowerEng/2003/v2article/art03.pdf

Rasizade, A. (2002). Azerbaijan after a decade of independence: less oil, more graft and poverty. *Central Asian Survey, 21*(4), 349–370. https://doi.org/10.1080/0263493032000053181.

State Agency on Alternative and Renewable Energy Sources of the Republic of Azerbaijan. (n.d.). Strategic plan of the state agency on alternative and renewable energy source for 2016–2020. Retrieved from http://area.gov.az/page/6

State Oil Company of the Republic of Azerbaijan. (n.d.a). "AzeriGas" production union. Retrieved from http://socar.az/socar/en/company/organization/azerigas-production-union

State Oil Company of the Republic of Azerbaijan. (n.d.b). Azerbaijan Oil Industry Journal. Retrieved from http://socar.az/socar/en/company/organization/azerbaijan-oil-industry-journal

State Programme on Socio-Economic Development of Regions in 2019–2023. (2019).

Sultanova, L. (2018). Azerbaijan Joined Hague II document of International Energy Charter – Updated. Baku: AzerTag. Retrieved from https://azertag.az/xeber/Azerbaycan_Beynelxalq_Enerji_Xartiyasinin_Haaqa_II_senedine_qosuldu_YENILANIB-1145026

Ted.Az. (2019). Methodological guide is prepared for enterprises in the heavy industry and machinery sector. Baku: Ted.Az. Retrieved from http://ted.az/az/view/news/3341/agir-senaye-ve-mashinqayirma-muessiseleri-uchun-enerjiden-semereli-istifade-ile-bagli-metodik-vesait-hazirlanib

Teref.az. (2016). Natig Aliyev: "Still the majority of the electricity and gas infrastructure is the Soviet legacy": Teref.Az. Retrieved from http://teref.az/sosial/37229-natiq-eliyevelektrik-ve-tebii-qaz-xetlerinin-boyuk-ekseriyyeti-sovet-dovrunden-qalib.html

The Administration of the President of the Republic of Azerbaijan. (2019). Oil and gas projects. Retrieved from https://en.president.az/azerbaijan/contract

The Auditing Chamber of the Republic of Azerbaijan. (2019). *Commentary on the Law of the Republic of Azerbaijan on the Implementation of the State Budget of the Republic of Azerbaijan for the year of 2018 and the report on the implementation of the annual state budget*. Baku. Retrieved from The Auditing Chamber of the Republic of Azerbaijan website: http://sai.gov.az/upload/files/ICRA-2018-FINAL(1).pdf

The Ministry of Ecology and Natural Resources of the Republic of Azerbaijan, IREA, REC Caucasus. (2015). *"Strategy on the use of alternative and renewable energy sources for 2015–2020", strategic ecological assessment report project*. Baku. Retrieved from https://www.unece.org/fileadmin/DAM/env/eia/meetings/2015/December_9_Baku_SEA_for_the_National_Strategy/SEA_AZ_Draft_Report_2015.pdf

The Ministry of Energy of the Republic of Azerbaijan. (2018a). *A high-level roundtable was held on the draft Energy Efficiency Law* [Press release]. Baku. Retrieved from http://minenergy.gov.az/index.php/az/news-archive/268-15-03-18

The Ministry of Energy of the Republic of Azerbaijan. (2018b). *The report on the implementation of the strategic road map on development of utility services in 2018 will be completed soon* [Press release]. Retrieved from http://www.minenergy.gov.az/index.php/en/news-archive/138-the-report-on-the-implementation-of-the-strategic-road-map-on-development-of-utility-services-in-2018-will-be-completed-soon

The Ministry of Energy of the Republic of Azerbaijan. (2019a). List of eletricity power stations operatined independently and within Azerbaijan's energy system – 19.01.2019. Retrieved from http://minenergy.gov.az/index.php/az/28-energetika/elektroenergetika

The Ministry of Energy of the Republic of Azerbaijan. (2019b). The Ministry of Energy and the European Bank of Reconstruction and Development discussed "Support to the organization of renewable energy fairs" project. Retrieved from http://www.minenergy.gov.az/index.php/az/news-archive/542-energetika-avropa-yenidenqurma-bank

The State Committee of Statistics of the Republic of Azerbaijan. (2019). Structure of exports by products, in thousands US dollars. Retrieved from https://www.stat.gov.az/source/trade/

The State Statistical Committee of the Republic of Azerbaijan. (2017). Final consumption of energy by types of economic activity. Retrieved from https://www.stat.gov.az/source/balance_fuel/?lang=en

The State Statistical Committee of the Republic of Azerbaijan. (2019a). Energy consumption and share of electricity in energy consumption. Retrieved from https://www.stat.gov.az/source/balance_fuel/?lang=en

The State Statistical Committee of the Republic of Azerbaijan. (2019b). Gross domestic product – Manats, dollars, in euro. Retrieved from https://www.stat.gov.az/source/system_nat_accounts/?lang=en

TOTAL. (2014). Azerbaïdjan: Total vend sa participation de 10% dans Shah Deniz à TPAO: TOTAL. Retrieved from https://www.total.com/media/news/press-releases/azerbaidjan-total-vend-sa-participation-de-10-dans-shah-deniz-tpao

UNFCCC. (2020). Azerbaijan submits its climate action plan ahead of 2015 Paris agreement. Retrieved from https://unfccc.int/news/azerbaijan-submits-its-climate-action-plan-ahead-of-2015-paris-agreement#:~:text=The%20Paris%20agreement%20will%20come,to%20clean%20and%20sustainable%20development

United Nations Development Programme. (n.d.). Renewable energy snapshot Azerbaijan. Retrieved from https://www.undp.org/content/dam/rbec/docs/Azerbaijan.pdf

Vahid, F. (2019). If "Azerishiq", "Azersu", "Azerqaz" and "Azeristilik" is privatized...many would lose "weight". Baku: Redaktor.Az. Retrieved from https://redaktor.az/news/country/65001-azerisiq-azersu-azeriqaz-azeristilik-ozellesdirilse

Vidadili, N., Suleymanov, E., Bulut, C., & Mahmudlu, C. (2017). Transition to renewable energy and sustainable energy development in Azerbaijan. *Renewable and Sustainable Energy Reviews, 80*, 1153–1161. https://doi.org/10.1016/j.rser.2017.05.168.

Virtual Azerbaijan. (2019). President started substantial structural reforms in governance: Virtual Azerbaijan. Retrieved from https://virtualaz.org/bugun/133078

Volkogonov, D. A., & Shukman, H. (1999). *Autopsy for an empire: The seven leaders who built the Soviet regime* (1st Simon & Schuster pbk. ed.). New York: Free Press/Simon & Sxchuster

Zhdannikov, D., & Bousso, R. (2018). Exclusive: Exxon, Chevron seek to exit Azerbaijan's oil after 25 years. London: Reuters. Retrieved from Exclusive: Exxon, Chevron seek to exit Azerbaijan's oil after 25 years

Energy Governance in Belgium

22

Thijs Van de Graaf, Erik Laes, and Aviel Verbruggen

Contents

Introduction	512
General Conditions of Energy Governance in Belgium	513
Path Dependencies	513
Composition of the Energy Mix	516
Discourse on Energy Issues	517
Political Institutions and Actors	520
Coordination, Instruments, and Issues of Belgium's Energy Transition	522
Drivers of Energy Transition	522
Strategies and Instruments of Energy Transitions	522
Coordination Mechanisms and Multilevel Governance	527
Outcomes, Challenges, and Prospects of Energy Governance in Belgium	528
Cross-References	530
References	530

Abstract

This chapter reviews the conditions, policies, and institutions of energy governance in Belgium. Except for coal, Belgium has no indigenous energy sources. Nuclear energy accounts for around half of Belgium's electricity generation but

T. Van de Graaf (✉)
Department of Political Science, Ghent University, Ghent, Belgium
e-mail: thijs.vandegraaf@ugent.be

E. Laes
Sustainable Energy and Built Environment, VITO/EnergyVille, Genk, Belgium

School of Innovation Sciences, University of Eindhoven, Eindhoven, The Netherlands
e-mail: e.j.w.laes@tue.nl

A. Verbruggen
Department Engineering Management, Antwerp University, Antwerp, Belgium
e-mail: aviel.verbruggen@uantwerpen.be

© Springer Nature Switzerland AG 2022
M. Knodt, J. Kemmerzell (eds.), *Handbook of Energy Governance in Europe*,
https://doi.org/10.1007/978-3-030-43250-8_4

all nuclear power plants are scheduled to phase out by 2025. Energy governance in Belgium is characterized by a lack of a strategic and coherent vision. The responsibilities for energy policy in Belgium are shared among the federal government and the three regions (Flanders, Wallonia, and Brussels). The distribution of competences is very heterogeneous and creates coordination problems. The main drivers of policy initiatives are European directives and international agreements. Belgium is currently not on track to meet its 2020 goals for energy efficiency and emission reductions. A major part of the explanation for Belgium's weak performance is the dominant role of energy corporations in the Belgian energy sector.

Keywords

Belgium · Energy policy · Federal state · Nuclear phaseout · Energy governance · Low-carbon transition

Introduction

Belgium is a small, open economy located in the heart of Northwestern Europe. Except for coal, Belgium has no indigenous energy sources. Coal mining in Belgium is unprofitable since the 1960s (Verbruggen 1989) and ended in 1992. Belgium now imports all of the fossil fuels it consumes. While fully dependent on crude oil imports, Belgium is a net exporter of refined products from its large refining complex in the port of Antwerp. With multiple gas interconnections, including a liquefied natural gas (LNG) terminal in the port of Zeebrugge, Belgium has also developed to a significant gas transit hub.

Nuclear energy accounts for around half of Belgium's electricity generation. Belgium has seven nuclear reactors with a combined capacity of about 6000 MW. These reactors were commissioned in the 1970s and 1980s. A law enacted in 2003 prohibited the construction of new nuclear plants and mandated the gradual closure of the existing ones as soon as they reached a lifetime of 40 years (Law of 31 January 2003). Under the 2003 law, the oldest reactors (Doel 1, Tihange 1, and Doel 2) should have been closed in 2015, but a new law in 2015 extended their lifetime to 50 years. All nuclear power plants are now scheduled for closure between 2022 and 2025.

In parallel to the nuclear phaseout, Belgium attempts to pursue a low-carbon transition. Belgium is currently not on track to meet its European Union target for energy efficiency (18% reduction in primary energy consumption by 2020 relative to 2007), while it has also become increasingly doubtful that it will meet its goals for greenhouse gas emissions (15% reduction in 2020 compared to 2005 for sectors not covered in the ETS) (EEA 2016, 2017).

The country performs better with regard to its target for renewable energy (13% by 2020). The share of renewable energy in total energy supply went up from 2.6% in 2004 to 7.6% in 2014 (IEA 2016, pp. 117–118). At the end of 2017, Belgium had the world's third-largest installed solar PV capacity per capita, behind only Germany and Japan (REN21 2018). However, this boom was driven by lavish and ill-designed support schemes, giving rise to financial transfers (Verbruggen 2009; El Kasmioui et al. 2015). In Flanders, part of the financial burden was accumulated on the accounts of the distribution network utilities.

The responsibilities for energy policy in Belgium are shared among the federal government and the three regions (Flanders, Wallonia, and Brussels). This means that a country as small as Belgium has no less than four energy ministers. The federal competence includes broadly all aspects relating to the security of supply of oil and gas, nuclear matters, tariff regulation, electricity transmission (>70 kV), and offshore wind in the North Sea. The regions manage the distribution of electricity and natural gas, energy efficiency, renewables (except offshore wind), and nonnuclear energy research and development (R&D). This heterogeneous distribution of competences creates coordination problems, as illustrated by the protracted negotiations over the allocation of the 2020 EU renewables target. It took no less than 6 years of discussions before an agreement was finally found on 4 December 2015 (NCC 2015), just in time for COP21 in Paris.

General Conditions of Energy Governance in Belgium

Path Dependencies

The structure of Belgium's energy system has been heavily influenced by its once abundant reserves of coal, which were a vital factor in its early industrialization. In the first half of the nineteenth century, Belgium was the largest coal producer on the continent, ahead of Germany and France. The rich coal reserves enabled Belgium to become the first country to industrialize in continental Europe (Hens and Solar 1999, p. 195). Coal extraction itself became uncompetitive in the 1960s, and the last coal pits were closed in 1984 (Wallonia) and 1992 (Flanders). The remaining coal deposits hold a technical potential for coal-bed methane, but the license to explore the Campine Basin, awarded in 2013, expired in 2015 (Van de Graaf and Timmermans 2013). Belgium is now mainly a service-driven economy, but it has maintained a strong manufacturing base with several energy-intensive sectors, such as chemicals, refining, and iron and steel (IEA 2016, p. 17).

The coal and heavy industries were long controlled by the *Société Générale de Belgique* (SGB), founded in 1822 by King William I of the Netherlands. The *Société Générale* developed into a powerful holding with controlling shares in the majority of large companies in nearly every industrial sector. The gas and electricity assets later became one of the crown jewels. In 1988, the French holding company Suez obtained a 55% majority share in the *Société Générale*. The decision center over the Belgian power sector shifted from Brussels to Paris. Suez integrated its Belgian assets slowly but extracted billions from mainly the power sector, i.e., the Belgian low-voltage customers, to finance its industrial expansion. After consecutive restructuration, the multinational company ENGIE emerged in 2015 as a major player in the European power and gas markets.

Beyond coal, Belgium has no indigenous fossil fuel reserves, yet it has developed significant infrastructures and industries around oil and natural gas. In the Antwerp harbor, petroleum refining and lubricant fabrication started before World War II. After the war, large-scale refinery activities were deployed by the Belgian oil company Petrofina and by some oil majors (e.g., Esso and BP in Antwerp, Texaco in Ghent). When crude oil ships became too large to reach Antwerp, in 1971, the RAPL pipeline began to supply crude oil from Rotterdam. In the 1960s, oil substituted coal as the basic fuel for industry, commerce, and heating.

The low price and versatility of oil spurred the decentralization of activities and the sprawling of human settlements (mainly in Flanders). By 1961, urban planning became mandated, but poor practices and indulgent enforcement prevailed. The scattered spatial planning (characterized by suburbanization and ribbon development) thwarts efficient public transport and creates high (commuting) transport needs. Located at the heart of Europe, Belgium has developed into an important logistical hub with a dense network of roads, railways, waterways, airports, and harbors (including Antwerp, the second largest seaport in Europe) (Belgium Federal Government 2017, p. 29). The country also has a relatively old and poorly insulated building stock: 61% of existing buildings were built before 1970 (Statbel 2017), which is one of the reasons why Belgian homes use almost 40% more energy than the European average (calculated with data on total energy consumption per square meter in residential buildings at normal climate, from http://www.entranze.enerdata.eu). These factors go a long way to explaining why Belgium's energy intensity, though decreasing, is above the EU-28 average.

The history of gas in Belgium started with town gas. Already in the nineteenth century, public and office buildings and mansions of the wealthy in the major cities were connected to city gas networks for lighting, cooking, and heating. The gas came from coal gasification in coke plants. In 1966, the import of natural gas took off. The old gas networks and the end-use gas equipment were overhauled. The gas transport company Distrigaz (°1929) revived with participation of Shell and public companies. New transport lines were built. During the 1970s major investments for LNG import from Algeria were made: liquefaction plants, large LNG tankers, and a receiving terminal with storage and decompression. Zeebrugge at the North Sea coast was the receiving harbor and developed to a significant gas hub. Due to the expansion of the gas distribution networks and the higher efficiency of end-use conversion equipment, natural gas substituted for oil in many industrial and building facilities. The EU Directive on gas market liberalization (1997) imposed the unbundling of the gas activities: Distrigaz kept the trade and supply activities, and a new company Fluxys came to own and operate the physical stock (Zeebrugge gas terminal, transport lines, storage facilities). Gas distribution occurs parallel with electricity distribution by the same network companies (1 July 2018, Eandis and Infrax merged to Fluvius).

Belgium has a long industrial history in the nuclear sector. Because the Belgian company Union Minière delivered uranium ore from mines in Congo as well as from stockpiles in Olen (Belgium) to the USA just before World War II for its "Manhattan Project," the country was promised special access to nuclear technology for civil purposes in the postwar era (Groves 1962, p. 170). Without access to Belgium's uranium, the USA would probably not have been able to drop the atomic bombs on Hiroshima and Nagasaki (72% of the uranium used in the bombs originated from Belgian Congo) (Barbé 2005, p. 2). While the USA did not honor the promise to share nuclear know-how with Belgium, the country got a financial compensation for its uranium deliveries. This money was used to finance research into nuclear energy, which would allow Belgium to become one of the pioneers of nuclear research in Europe.

It led in 1952 to the establishment of SCK-CEN (Studiecentrum voor Kernenergie – Centre d'Etude de l'Energie Nucléaire – Belgian Nuclear Research Centre), a study center for nuclear research, in Mol. This center trained the first nuclear scientists, built the first experimental and commercial reactors, and attracted other activities to the region, such as nuclear fuel rod manufacturing (FBFC, Belgonucléaire), reprocessing (Eurochimique), and specialized labs (Govaerts et al. 1994). Following a joint venture with French EDF in the Chooz A nuclear plant, the first commercial nuclear reactor in Belgium, Doel 1, was commissioned in 1974. Six more were connected to the grid in the ensuing decade (Table 2). This resulted in one of the highest nuclear dependencies in Europe and globally, with nuclear accounting for 53% of Belgium's electricity generation in 2016 (IEA 2016).

The construction of a series of new 1300 MW units was proposed in 1976 by a specially installed, experts commission (Commissie van Beraad inzake Kernenergie) and reiterated in the power sector capacity plans of 1981, 1982, and 1983. The state reform law of 1980 imposed 1 month during hearings about submitted plans on power generation expansion. Independent experts enlarged the scope of the planning process and suggested alternatives for the nuclear option. The government did not accept the submitted plans of 1981 and 1982. In February 1985, the plan of 1983 was accepted, i.e., Belgian participation of 25% in two new 1390 MW plants in Chooz B and a later Belgian construction of 1390 MW (N8 = Doel 5), with an announced 50% share for France in it (Verbruggen 1986). Due to nuclear overcapacity, France did not lift this option.

Yet, in the wake of the nuclear accident of Three Mile Island and by the catastrophe of Chernobyl, support for nuclear waned. The 1988 capacity expansion plan, asking the permit to build Doel 5, was rejected by the Belgian government declaring for the first time that priority should be given to nonnuclear scenarios, partly inspired by the overcapacity in take-or-pay contracted gas imports. Doel 5 was shelved indefinitely (Verbruggen et al. 1988). In 1999, the green parties AGALEV and ECOLO participated in a federal coalition government with liberal (VLD and PRL) and socialist (SP and PS) parties. The coalition agreement included the nuclear phaseout, enacted into law on 31 January 2003 (Laes et al. 2007a). This crucial political decision has since dominated the public debate on energy in Belgium.

As a small, rather flat country located in a moderate and rainy climate belt, harnessing Belgium's renewable energy potential is more expensive than in most other European countries. Belgium also has one of the highest population densities in Europe (World Bank 2017). Even so, it is technically possible for Belgium to switch to 100% renewable energy by 2050 (VITO et al. 2013). In the VITO study, offshore wind (with a realistic potential of 8 GW installed in the Belgian exclusive economic zone of the North Sea), onshore wind (with a theoretical potential of 20 GW installed), and PV (with a theoretical potential of 50 GW, assuming 250 km^2 of available rooftop surface) have the highest potentials among renewable energy sources.

Composition of the Energy Mix

Belgium's total primary energy supply (TPES) was 53.3 million tonnes of oil equivalent (Mtoe) in 2015. Energy supply peaked at 60.4 Mtoe in 2010, after consistently growing for over 25 years. From 2010 to 2015, TPES declined by 11.8% (Fig. 1). Fossil fuels accounted for 77.9% of TPES in 2015, including oil (44.6%), natural gas (27.1%), and coal (6.2%). Nuclear power accounted for 13.2% of TPES and renewables for 8.9%. Renewables are mainly made up of biofuels and waste (6.8%), followed at a distance by geothermal, wind and solar (2%), and a negligible share of hydro (0.1%).

In the electricity mix (Fig. 2), nuclear energy is Belgium's primary source. In 1975, Doel 1 and 2 and Tihange 1 started to generate commercial power. Between 1982 and 1985, four additional plants were commissioned. Since 1984, nuclear electricity has covered more than 50% of total production (with a peak of 68% in 1986). From the end of the 1980s, following the de facto moratorium on new investments in nuclear (the initial rejection of the proposed construction of the

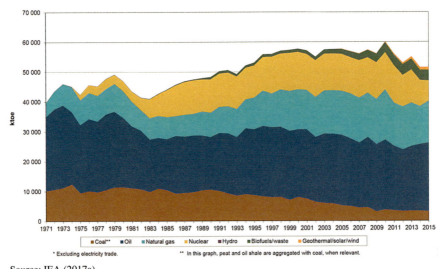

Source: IEA (2017a).

Fig. 1 Belgium's total primary energy supply, 1971–2015. (Source: IEA 2017a)

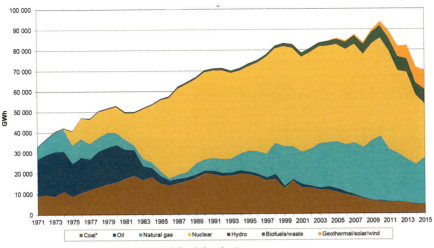

Source: IEA (2017a).

Fig. 2 Belgium's electricity generation by fuel, 1971–2015. (Source: IEA 2017a)

Doel 5 unit in the 1988 capacity plan due to reasons explained earlier was extended by subsequent governments), this proportion has progressively declined, to around 55% during the 2000s.

The share of coal has seen a steady decline, since its final top in 1994 at 27% of the country's electricity generation (IEA 2017a). By closing the last coal-fired plant in Langerlo in April 2016, the once coal-dependent Belgium effectively phased out coal for power generation.

Natural gas was squeezed out of the electricity mix in the 1980s due to the rise of nuclear and European restrictions on gas use in power generation, due to (unfounded) fears about the exhaustion of supplies (EEC 1975). Those restrictions were lifted in 1991 (EEC 1991). Some years before, the Combined Cycle Gas Turbine (CCGT) was introduced with conversion efficiencies beyond 55%. Since then, gas-fired power generation increased to a peak of 31.4 terawatt-hours/year (TWh) in 2010 (33.5% of the total). Afterwards, gas use in electricity generation has fallen to 27.4%, as imports from other countries (partly from new coal power) and wind and solar powers have gained ground (IEA 2016).

Discourse on Energy Issues

Since the early 1970s, Belgium's overall energy policy has focused on security of supply based on diversification of geographical sources and fuels, energy efficiency, transparent and competitive energy prices, and environmental protection (IEA 2001, p. 20). Currently, the federal government has adopted the "triple bottom line" discourse on sustainable development, indicating that it wants to reconcile the three goals of energy security, cost competitiveness, and a low environmental impact. Regarding the latter, Belgium adheres to the EU climate policy agenda of moving toward a low-carbon economy in 2050. However, the inter-federal "energy pact" signed in March 2018 only contains shopping lists of policies and measures (Belgian Federal Government 2018). It however lacks a clear implementation strategy for reaching the ambitious goal of lowering GHG emissions by 80–95% in 2050 compared to 1990 levels. Concerns regarding cost competitiveness are dealt with in a much more concrete way. In particular, the government of Prime Minister Michel, in office since 2014, wants to ensure that Belgian energy prices remain competitive with prices of neighboring countries. Also, the present government pledged that all nuclear power plants would stop running by 2025. Hence, the Michel government seeks to improve the overall energy market investment climate for the construction of baseload capacity and sees demand-side management and interconnections with neighboring countries as clear priorities (Belgian Federal Government 2014b).

Energy security was long the dominant frame in energy policy, with politicians emphasizing and supporting domestic sources of energy. In the immediate aftermath of the World War II, Europe faced a significant shortage of coal that threatened economic recovery. In contrast to the French, German, and Dutch mines, the Belgian coal pits were not severely damaged during World War II. The shortage in mineworkers was relieved by immigration, mostly from Italy – some 75.000 Italians went to work in the Belgian collieries between June 1946 and December 1949 (Leboutte 2005).

In 1962, the Belgian government presented its first energy plan to parliament. The Minister of Economic Affairs emphasized that energy sources had to be selected in consultation with the industry. The plan contained preparatory studies for the construction of four nuclear reactors. In 1962, Westinghouse granted a license to build its pressurized water reactor to the SGB. The view that Belgium should develop a comprehensive nuclear future was largely shared. In the postwar period, nuclear energy captured the lion share of the energy R&D budget in Belgium, typically more than 85% every year (see Fig. 3).

Concerns over competitiveness also informed Belgian energy policy. Low-priced oil (and gas) substituted for coal during the 1960s. Starting from the 1960s, Belgian coal mines were progressively closed down. Initially, this led to heavy contestation and protest by the miners threatened with naked layoffs. For instance, in 1966 a demonstration of miners of the Zwartberg site (in the city of Genk) led to a violent confrontation with the gendarmerie resulting in two deaths and several severe injuries. Over the years, conflicts were progressively pacified. On the one hand, alternative employment plans and favorable dismissal agreements for the employees of the coal mines were developed. On the other, the Belgian government agreed to participate in the management of coal mines (e.g., through the NV Kempense Steenkoolmijnen), compensating for financial losses with taxpayers' money. The 1973 oil price shock affected Belgium harder than its trade partners due to the heavy overall dependence on oil imports and the energy-intensive nature of many Belgian industries. After the crisis year 1975, the government combated the recession by an expansionary budgetary Keynesian policy, causing excessive government deficits, still plaguing subsequent governments to date.

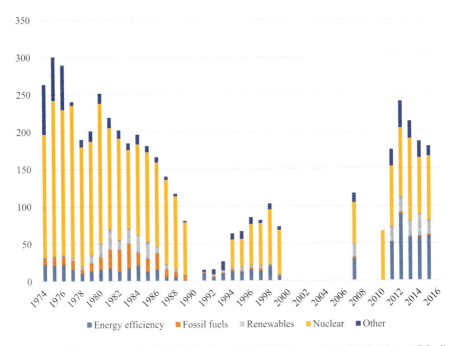

Fig. 3 Belgium's energy-related RD&D budget, 1974–2015. (Source: IEA 2017b. Notes: "Other" includes hydrogen and fuel cells, other power and storage technologies, and cross-cutting technologies. Data are missing for 1990, 2000–2006, and 2008–2009)

The oil price crisis put security of supply on top of the energy agenda. In 1974–1975, the first three nuclear reactors were commissioned. This was important since oil had become the most important source of electricity generation (Fig. 2). In 1974, the industry got approval from the government to build two twins of nuclear reactors (of 900/1000 MW capacity). In the context of the oil crisis, nuclear was touted as a means to diversify away from the OPEC countries. Yet, the 1970s also marked the start of a public debate on nuclear energy. A small but vocal set of antinuclear activist groups began to emerge (REM-U-235, VAKS, and others), opposed to the nuclear plants (Laes et al. 2007b).

The antinuclear movement was strengthened by the Three Mile Island accident (1979) and Chernobyl catastrophe (1986). It took a local scandal with regard to the management of nuclear waste, the 1987 Transnuklear scandal, before the ecological sustainability frame would come to effectively influence the energy debate. The scandal involved illegalities in the transport of radioactive waste to and from West Germany and the reprocessing center at Mol in Belgium. A critical attitude to nuclear gradually spread to political parties other than the Green parties (the Flemish socialist party was the first to follow), and trade unions turned more critical to the nuclear option (Laes et al. 2007b, p. 73). The scandal also made nuclear waste management part and parcel of the energy debate.

Political Institutions and Actors

Belgium is a federal state consisting of three communities (the Flemish, French-speaking, and German-speaking communities) and three regions (Flanders, Wallonia, and Brussels). The current institutional setup is the fruit of successive rounds of state reform since the 1970s, which have transformed Belgium from a unitary into a federal state. These reforms have created a heterogeneous and intricate allocation of competences between the federal government and the three regions. National legislative acts no longer have precedence over regional and community acts. Conflicts have to be decided by the Arbitration Court. EU directives are transposed by the national level or by the regional level, depending on their competences over the directives' substance.

Table 1 depicts the division of energy competences since January 2014, after the sixth phase of state reform. In principle, the federal level is responsible for those matters that require a national approach due to their technical or economical indivisibility (Special Law of 8 August 1980). For example, the federal government is responsible for large infrastructure for energy storage (e.g., the LNG terminal in Zeebrugge or the natural gas storage facility in Loenhout), transport (electricity grid >70 kV, oil and gas transport pipelines), and production (power plants >25 MW, oil refineries) (Vandendriessche 2017). The responsibility for renewable energy was transferred to the regions in 1988 (Law of 8 August 1988), except for offshore wind turbines (the North Sea is federal land), tariffs, and electricity transport, all of which remain federal competences. Since 1993, the regions have been granted residual competences over energy (Special Law of 16 July 1993), which means that all issues that are not formally attributed to the federal authorities fall under the competence of the regions. The result is a very heterogeneous division of competences.

Energy policy is further splintered horizontally. At the federal level, for example, there are separate ministries for energy, environment, and transport. The federal authority over offshore wind energy in the North Sea, in the current administration, is shared between a federal minister (Marie-Christine Marghem, French-speaking

Table 1 Division of competences for energy policy in Belgium

Federal responsibilities	Regional responsibilities
National indicative studies about security of supply	Regulation of gas and electricity retail markets
The nuclear fuel cycle and related research and development (R&D) programs	Distribution of electricity (electricity grid <70 kV) and natural gas, including distribution tariffs
Large infrastructures for the storage, transport, and production of energy	District heating equipment and networks
Transport tariffs and prices	Renewable sources of energy (except offshore wind energy)
Offshore wind energy	Recovery of waste energy from industry or other uses
	Promotion of the efficient use of energy
	Energy R&D (except nuclear)
	Use of coal-bed methane and blast furnace gas

Source: Adapted from IEA (2016, pp. 22–23)

liberals MR) and a state secretary for the North Sea (Philippe De Backer, Flemish liberals Open VLD). There is a federal energy regulator, the Commission for the Regulation of Electricity and Gas (CREG), but the regional governments have set up their own regulatory institutions: in Flanders, the Vlaamse Regulator voor Elektriciteit en Gas (VREG); in Wallonia, the Commission Wallonne pour l'Energie (CWaPE); and, in Brussels-Capital, the Brugel. In addition, municipalities have a legal monopoly on electricity and gas distribution. Nearly all transferred the distribution of electricity and gas to inter-municipal companies, so-called inter-communales (IEA 2016).

The Belgian state has, in general, not chosen to pursue its energy policy through the ownership and control of firms. It did not nationalize its electricity sector in the immediate postwar period, as was done in Italy, France, and the United Kingdom (Hens and Solar 1999). Instead, Belgium chose a corporatist structure: the production of electricity and gas remained mostly in the hands of private companies. In 1955, the Federation of Belgian Enterprises (FBE) and the three official trade unions (Christian, Socialist, and Liberal with their respective links to the three then major political parties) set up in conciliation with the SGB a private regulatory body, the Control Committee for Electricity, in 1966 adding Gas (CCEG). Given the balance of power and know-how, the electricity and gas industry essentially regulated itself. The mission of the CCEG was to increase the productivity of electricity production, transport, and distribution and to allocate the benefits among the participants. SGB and its engineering contractor Tractebel fully succeeded in streamlining the activities in a strategically planned way. In the 1960s, an internally competitive dispatching system was deployed, ahead of most power systems in the world. Gold plating and overemployment were avoided. The large benefits were shared among the participants: industrial companies benefitted from low high-voltage electricity prices, trade unions were satisfied since sector personnel enjoyed some of the best salaries and working conditions in the national economy, while SGB and Tractebel were guaranteed high profit rates. The low-voltage consumers delivered the necessary cash to feed the system. Independent consumer interest organizations were excluded from the CCEG, because trade unions listed their members also as members of their in-house consumer branches. This system survived beyond the Belgian liberalization law of 1999, imposed by the European directives.

The public power generators (joined in SPE since 1978) and public distribution utilities (joined in Interregies) served the market fringe of power generation (about 5%) and distribution (about 20%). Squeezed by the oil price crisis of 1979, SPE avoided bankruptcy by adsorption to the private power sector organizations. Socialist minister Willy Claes negotiated this "Pax Electrica" of 1981. SPE took participations in the Belgian nuclear plants commissioned in the 1980s and in Chooz B1 and B2. The management committee of the electricity sector (BCEO-CGEE) had a private-public membership but clearly dominated by Tractebel. Via BCEO-CGEE the SGB-Tractebel-Electrabel concentration reigned the CCEG: it financed the secretariat of the CCEG, also housed in Electrabel's headquarters (Verbruggen and Vanderstappen 1999).

Coordination, Instruments, and Issues of Belgium's Energy Transition

Drivers of Energy Transition

The drivers for energy policy change in Belgium appear to be mainly external and more specifically related to EU policies. The European directives on the liberalization of electricity (1996) and natural gas (1998) markets led to the first major legislative innovation in energy policy Belgium since the Electricity Act of 1925 and the Natural Gas Act of 1965. The electricity markets were entirely opened in all regions by January 2007. Yet, Electrabel, the historical incumbent, still held 66% of generating capacity in Belgium in 2014, although this share declined from 85% in 2007 (IEA 2016, p. 101).

One of the major drivers which helped to shape (the start of) the low-carbon energy transition in Belgium has been the EU Directive on Electricity Production from Renewable Energy Sources 2001/77/EC, promoting renewable energy use in electricity generation. Directive 2001/77/EC was transposed at the regional levels in Belgium and, from 2002 onwards, it opened the way to government support for renewable energies. The 2001 Renewable Energy Directive was replaced by a new version (directive 2009/28/EC), with more challenging national targets for renewable energy production. Belgium has a binding national target for renewable energy to equal 13% of gross final consumption of energy by 2020, including a separate binding national target for renewable energy to cover 10% of transport fuel demand in 2020. The responsibility for meeting the national 2020 target is shared between the regions and the federal authority. Due to Belgium's institutional structure, it took 6 years to reach a political agreement regarding the federal and regional contributions to the 2020 target (IEA 2016).

The drivers of the nuclear phaseout are both internal and external. The optimistic view on nuclear energy crumbled in the first half of the 1970s, during a conflict on siting the first NPP at the Belgian coast, leading to local protest. Hence, a moratorium was called in 1976 until the issue would be settled by a decision of parliament. This moratorium was in effect for 6 years. No decisions were taken to build new nuclear plants in Belgium. The only nuclear expansion occurred in 1984, when Electrabel and SPE together took a 25% share in the two new 1450 MW NPPs in Chooz, just across the Belgian border in France. In return, the French companies were allowed to take a 50% share in the construction of the proposed new NPP (Doel 5) in Belgium. The Chernobyl disaster in 1986, the abundance of contracted natural gas imports with the introduction of highly efficient CCGT plants and a lower-than-foreseen increase in electricity demand, led again to a moratorium in 1988 for new NPPs in Belgium.

Strategies and Instruments of Energy Transitions

Nuclear Phaseout

The political attitude toward nuclear electricity production changed in the aftermath of the federal elections in June 1999. Even though the environmental grassroots movements of the 1970s and 1980s were rather weak, they were the basis of the

Green parties emerging at the end of the 1980s. Participation of the green parties AGALEV and ECOLO in the Blue-Red-Green coalition Verhofstadt I (1999–2003) was a decisive factor in phasing out nuclear power in Belgium. In January 2003, this component of the coalition agreement was transposed into Belgian law. The law included a "force majeure" clause, which stipulated a conditional invalidity in case unforeseen events beyond the control of Belgian policy-makers (e.g., international crises) threatened the security of electricity supply (Law of 31 January 2003, art. 9). The introduction of this "force majeure" clause effectively implied that upcoming governments would have discretionary power over how to enforce the law. Upcoming governments could extend the lifetime of the NPPs if the energy security of the country was threatened or if the production cost for electricity would become instable. This started a period of prolonged tergiversations on the fate of the nuclear phaseout.

By the end of the 1990s and after enacting the phaseout law in 2003, nuclear proponents deployed many initiatives to bring nuclear back on the agenda. The (media) campaigns by the Nuclear Forum painted gloomy pictures of future energy shortages, and even though the nuclear phaseout agenda was confirmed by the new government agreement of 2004, various political parties (the Flemish Christian-democratic party CD&V and its Francophone counterpart CDH, the Flemish nationalist party N-VA and the extreme right-wing Flemish party Vlaams Belang) continued to argue for postponing the shutdown of the three oldest NPPs. Expert study groups recommended to maintain nuclear power generation (e.g., the GEMIX study of 2009). The Van Rompuy Government (30 December 2008–15 November 2009) signed an agreement with GDF Suez, the parent company of the main Belgian electricity producer Electrabel, under which the three oldest reactors could stay open for a further decade in return for an annual contribution to the federal treasury. The charge was intended to reflect the extra revenue that the company would receive from being allowed to operate the depreciated reactors for longer than planned. The 2009 nuclear deal was tightly linked to the national budget issue, in the context of the banking and economic crisis. However, the agreement never became law because Van Rompuy left Belgian politics for the EU Presidency, and the government was dissolved before the necessary legislation was approved by the federal parliament.

When the next government led by Di Rupo took office in late 2011, the phaseout law of 2003 was still in place. The state secretary for energy, Melchior Wathelet, drew up a new energy plan in June 2012 (the "plan Wathelet"), which involved a compromise. The plan would shut down Doel 1 and Doel 2 in 2015, in accordance with the phaseout law of 2003, and keep Tihange 1 open for an additional 10 years (until 2025). The plan was voted into law in December 2013 (Law of 18 December 2013).

Soon after release of the plan Wathelet, several units experienced unplanned and prolonged shutdowns. In the summer of 2012, Doel 3 and Tihange 2 were taken offline because of widening cracks in their pressure vessels. The fault indications consisted of hydrogen flakes. The two units restarted in June 2013, but shut down again in March 2014 after the operator had performed additional tests requesting more investigations. Finally, after an international peer review by experts, the two units resumed operation in December 2015. In addition, Doel 4 automatically shut

Table 2 Nuclear power plants in Belgium

Unit	Net capacity	Date of commissioning	Projected shutdown			
			2003 phaseout law	2009 agreement	Plan Wathelet (2013)	Law on life extension (2015)
Doel 1	433 MW	15 February 1975	2015	2025	2015	2025
Tihange 1	962 MW	1 October 1975	2015	2025	2025	2025
Doel 2	433 MW	1 December 1975	2015	2025	2015	2025
Doel 3	1.006 MW	1 October 1982	2022	2022	2022	2022
Tihange 2	1.008 MW	1 June 1983	2023	2023	2023	2023
Doel 4	1.033 MW	1 July 1985	2025	2025	2025	2025
Tihange 3	1.038 MW	1 September 1985	2025	2025	2025	2025

Source: Author's compilation based on the website of the Federal Agency for Nuclear Control (FANC), and the respective laws and agreements named in the table

down in August 2014, because release of cooling oil of the turbine axis into an underground storage tank caused wrecking of the steam turbine. By now, a univocal explanation of the accident is missing. Doel 4 was offline until December 2014. Doel 1 was shut down in February 2015, in accordance with the phaseout legislation of 2003, only to be restarted in December 2015. All in all, for almost 5 months in 2014 and most of 2015, around half the nuclear capacity in Belgium had been offline (IEA 2016, p. 131),

The government extended the operational lifetime of Doel 1 and Doel 2 by 10 years in a new law of June 2015 (Law of 28 June 2015). Hence, according to present policy, the nuclear phase out will be implemented in the period 2022–2025 (Table 2). In the context of the "federal energy pact," lobbying for a prolonged nuclear future continues. For example, the federations of electricity-intensive industries (Febeliec), technology companies (Agoria), and chemical industries (Essenscia) insist to keep Doel 4 and Tihange 3 operational for at least 10 years after 2025 (Agoria, Essenscia and Febeliec 2017). This standpoint receives backing from the N-VA, currently the largest political party in Belgium, who pleads on its website for a "realistic exit from nuclear, by 2065 at the latest" (N-VA 2018).

Renewable Electricity

Electricity generation from renewable installations on land is promoted by the three regions and from offshore installations by the federal state. In 2000, Flanders adopted the early (but, ultimately defeated) proposals of the European Commission on market-based instrument (Bollen et al. 2011). For supporting RE a tradable green certificate (TGC) system was set up. Flemish politicians expected lean governance because the market would take over, and they were happy to skip negotiations with the federal government, which were necessary in case a price-based feed-in tariff (FIT) support (like Germany) was installed. TGC is an artificial market creation (comparable to the ETS), with green power quota obligations for electricity suppliers, rewarding one certificate per MWh generated power, classified as green by the EU. All green power sources were treated equally, because of an entrenched belief that "the market should select the technologies, not the government." Hence, the cheap but dubious sources (like domestic refuse incineration, imported bioenergy–palm oil–combustion) prevailed, cashing significant rents and windfall (excess) profits. About 2/3 of the Flemish certificate money flows over the period [2002–2007] were excess profits and rents (Verbruggen 2009). The cost of photovoltaic (PV) power was higher than the certificate ceiling price at €125/MWh. Only few PV was installed with significant investment subsidies and an exceptional €150/MWh premium during 10 years paid by the transmission system operator ELIA.

In 2006, Flanders juxtaposed a premium support for PV at €450/MWh during 20 years (i.e., the German FIT level at that time) alongside the TGC system. Because Belgian policy-makers did not adapt this (already in 2006 too high) premium value in the years after 2007, when PV costs declined continuously and significantly, a rush on PV (mostly by above average income households) quickly accumulated high financial burdens on the electricity bills of all households. Moreover, the occasioned cash drain was charged relatively more on mostly poorer households, subsidizing the richer ones. The €450MWh premium remained until January 1, 2010. Three years too late, the premiums were stepwise reduced, to €350 for 2010, from €330 to €270 in 2011, and from €250 to €90 in 2012, to finish all support for PV < 10 kW in mid-2015. But in the years of excessive premium support, a large financial load until 2030 has been accumulated. In 2016, the new minister introduced a flat €100 tax per low-voltage connection; in 2017, the next new minister reduced it back to about €9, partly because two big biomass projects were cancelled. On all installed small-scale PV units with net metering, a new capacity levy was imposed differing a bit by the area where the unit is sited; in 2018 the capacity levy boils down to about €110/MWh generated solar power levy.

The other regions also set up certificate systems, different from the Flemish one, on quota obligations, granting green certificates, technology-specific support levels, calculation of minimum price levels, and duration of support and tradability. None of the TGC systems delivered in pushing technological development of renewable energy systems. For reaching the quota, too much money was drained from low-voltage consumers to feed rent skimming. More and more certificates were interpreted as direct premium support for particular projects (wind turbines, biomass conversion plants, small hydro). There is no industrial and technological innovation framework to select the most suitable and promising technologies for Belgium or its regions. Flanders has now adopted for the non-small PV renewable power projects a nongeneric regulation. Every new project (also MW-size PV fields) is financially appraised taking into account sector- and company-specific parameters. The support (still under the name of certificate) is adapted per project to make it pass the financial acceptance hurdle typical for the case at hand. This regulation "à la tête du client" contradicts basic principles of sound regulation.

At the federal level, large-scale offshore wind projects are assigned premium support in €/MWh generated. Belgium was generous for the winners of the tenders. At the end of October 2017, some of the earlier promised support for three North Sea wind parks was reduced from €125/MWh to €79/MWh. Although the Belgian ministers touted a benefit of €3.9 billion for the electricity consumers, the remaining support is still excessive compared with practices in other countries bordering the West and North coasts of the European continent.

The many systems have put Belgium on track to achieve its 2020 renewable electricity targets. This likely achievement is paired to high financial flows: the years of running TGC systems according to textbook prescriptions generated significant excess profits for mature and dubiously green technologies (Verbruggen 2009; Bollen et al. 2011). The bills were footed to low-voltage electricity consumers. Along the rents for non-PV technologies, assignment of excessive premiums during 20 years to PV-projects in the period [2008–2010] piled billions of euro transfers across household consumers. The IEA (2016, p. 123) estimates that the support costs for renewable electricity in Belgium in 2013 amounted to EUR 1.7 billion, or EUR 20.8 per MWh of all electricity generated (from renewable energy sources and other sources) (IEA 2016, p. 123). The average level of support was EUR 157.41 per MWh of renewable energy generated, fourth highest in the comparison after the Czech Republic, Italy, and Greece.

Heat Production
Belgium has several types of support policies for renewable heat projects. At the federal level, tax deduction for companies are foreseen concerning investments in solar collector systems and heat pumps. The regions hold legal competences for renewable heat policy and offer tax deductions to households. Especially relevant are the policies for almost energy-neutral buildings which stimulate the uptake of heating technologies using renewable energy. For instance, new buildings in the Flemish region must cover a certain share of their energy use from renewable sources since January 2014. For residential buildings, eligible solutions include thermal solar, solar photovoltaics, biomass boilers or stoves, heat pumps, connection to a district heating, or cooling system using renewable energy.

Other policy instruments include calls for tenders for renewable heating projects. The Flemish region organizes these tenders twice a year for projects that produce renewable heat and for developing district heating from renewable sources or waste heat. Ambitions regarding district heating using renewables or waste are also high. Projects for the equivalent of 50.000 households are planned, and the Flemish distribution network company Fluvius has established "warmte@Vlaanderen" (heating company Flanders). This company is authorized to set up, control, and manage the entire chain of delivery for district heating projects, covering production, distribution, and delivery of heat as well as the construction and management of the infrastructure. Participation of other partners on a project basis is possible. Feasibility appraisals of large-scale district heating networks for the cities of Antwerp, Ghent, Louvain, and Brussels were made between 1976 and 1984, but all were shelved immediately after publication. The surplus in natural gas import contracts, the extended gas networks, and the peculiar scattered urban settlements made and make the feasibility of district heating in Belgium precarious.

Energy Efficiency
Belgium's energy intensity remains above the EU-28 average. Energy efficiency is a regional competence in Belgium, and the regions are responsible for implementing

measures and monitoring progress. Belgium's energy efficiency policy is mostly driven by EU requirements and targets. A review of Belgium's energy efficiency policies in the 1990s found that these policies were "either absent or implemented with large compliance deficits" (Fraunhofer Institute et al. 2003, p. 3). In accordance with EU directives, Belgium has set itself targets for energy savings in sectors not covered in the ETS of −18% by 2020 (Belgian Federal Government 2014a). According to the European Commission, if the trend in primary energy consumption from 2005 to 2013 continues up to 2020, Belgium may not meet its national target for 2020 (European Commission 2015).

According to the National Energy Efficiency Action Plan (NEEAP), submitted to the European Commission in 2014, the regions have, each for its own territory, implemented the "Energy Performance in Buildings" directive (Directive 2010/31/EU); promoted further energy efficiency by households and tertiary buildings through grants, compulsory audit schemes, awareness-raising programs, etc.; fostered energy savings in industry by signing voluntary agreements with industry (Flanders, Wallonia); implemented mobility measures; and promoted renewable energies and cogeneration by setting up green and combined heat and power (CHP) certificates systems (Altdorfer and Baillot 2015).

Transport is one of the main energy-consuming sectors in Belgium and represents about a quarter of the overall energy consumption. Historically, it has been difficult to uncouple strong economic growth and transport demand. With a 23% increase of GHG emissions between 1990 and 2015, together with the commercial sector it has been responsible for a 6.2% rise in Belgian emissions (offset by decreases in other sectors) (National Climate Commission 2017). These trends also demonstrate that new technologies which serve in boosting vehicle fuel efficiency are not being developed fast enough at the moment to offset the rise in energy consumption linked to increased road traffic. E-mobility is still marginal, though on the rise. At the end of 2017, about 6500 fully electric vehicles were registered (representing 0.15% of the total car stock).

Coordination Mechanisms and Multilevel Governance

The fragmentation of authority over the federal and regional levels (section "Political Institutions and Actors") has created the need for coordination. The energy policy coordination platform ENOVER/CONCERE began operating in 1992. It is a consultative body where administrations and cabinets from the regional and federal level meet to strengthen the cooperation on energy matters between the different levels and sort out potential frictions. Plenary sessions are held monthly and working groups by sector have been created. Other relevant federal-regional coordination bodies include the Coordination Committee for International Environmental Policy (CCIEP), which has a working group on climate change, and the National Climate Commission (NCC) (IEA 2016, p. 24).

Belgium does not have a national climate policy. Rather, the federal government and the three regions each develop and implement their own climate policies in accordance with their respective competences. The necessity of dividing the Kyoto targets within Belgium was due to the fact that the regions are competent for industry and thus were responsible for the allocation of GHG emission allowances to industrial companies under the European Emissions Trading System (Happaerts 2015). After the conclusion of the first EU burden sharing agreement (Council of the EU 2002), assigning Belgium a reduction obligation of −7.5% over the period 2008–2012 (compared to 1990), much time and effort was invested in setting up intergovernmental cooperation mechanisms. The negotiations for an intra-Belgian burden sharing agreement first took place within ad hoc administrative and inter-cabinet working groups and eventually within the Interministerial Conference on the Environment (Happaerts 2015). Due to the fact that no government can ever be forced to participate in intergovernmental negotiations in Belgium (a consequence of the "principle of no hierarchy," meaning that the federal government cannot impose anything that falls within the competences of the regions), voluntary cooperation and negotiation are the only leverage for intergovernmental relations in Belgium. Applied to climate policy, this means that the regions negotiate on the GHG reduction targets they want to commit to, while the federal government fills the remaining emission reduction gap with policy measures related to its competences and by applying flexible mechanisms.

The coalition agreement of the Di Rupo Government (December 2011) marked a considerable shift in climate policy negotiation dynamics. The coalition agreement was accompanied by an institutional agreement for a new Belgian state reform, which shifted a number of competences and responsibilities to the subnational level, including some taxation instruments with an impact on climate policy, such as tax breaks for energy-saving investments. Moreover, many of the measures that the federal government had previously undertaken for climate change were abruptly abolished by the coalition agreement due to the need for budget cuts (Happaerts 2015). Belgian climate governance thus became even more dependent on regional decision making, leading to difficult negotiation dynamics between regional governments with often different ideological positions and different economic backgrounds. The protracted negotiations on a post-2012 National Climate Plan, which was only finalized just before the start of the COP21 meeting in Paris in December 2015, serve as an illustration. Overall, Happaerts (2015) concludes that the Belgian context gives each government a set of reasons that motivate why more efforts should actually be done by the other regions, and it entails no leverage to force the subnational governments into a more ambitious role. Belgian climate policy is thus characterized by inertia, both domestically and on the international stage.

Outcomes, Challenges, and Prospects of Energy Governance in Belgium

Belgian energy governance faces multiple challenges in the context of the transition to a low-carbon economy by 2050:

- Switching the electricity production system to an (almost) 100% renewable energy supply

- Decarbonizing the low-temperature heat supply for the built environment, which is currently dominated by fossil fuels, with gas as most used
- Decarbonizing industrial energy use, while Belgium hosts many energy-intensive industrial activities (e.g., iron and steel production, refineries, chemical industry) with a high economic importance for the country, and which are exposed to competition in international markets
- Decarbonizing the transport sector, while Belgium houses several logistic hubs in the dense crossings of European and international transport links

Belgium's performance toward meeting the EU's 2020 goals for renewable energy, energy efficiency, and emissions reductions is weak. The country is unlikely to meet its (non-binding) energy efficiency target, while significant additional efforts are needed for meeting its renewables target (+13%) and its greenhouse gas emissions reduction target (−15%). Ill-designed support programs for renewables through a dysfunctional tradable certificate system (Verbruggen 2009; El Kasmioui et al. 2015) and overly, generous support for solar PV when the investment costs declined fast after 2007 overcompensate the investors. The spending is charged on low-voltage customers (i.e., households and small and medium enterprises), hitting also poor customers. To avoid excessive burdens on the customers, the distribution network utilities were forced to hoard high-priced certificates. When in 2012–2014 the support for PV was adapted to the real cost of the PV technology, the installation pace slowed down, showing the lack of a solid policy for enabling the transition to renewable energy supplies. Since 2017, the PV market is recovering at a slow pace.

Energy governance in Belgium is characterized by a lack of a strategic and coherent vision. The main drivers of policy initiatives are European directives and international agreements. The latest IEA country review report stated plainly: "Belgium does not have a national energy strategy" (IEA 2016, p. 26). The only exception is the nuclear phaseout, first enacted into law in 2003, but this decision has been subject to multiple policy reversals over time (section "Nuclear Phase-Out"). It has also made the quest for a vision on the country's future energy mix much more urgent.

A major part of the explanation for Belgium's weak performance is the dominant role of energy corporates in the Belgian energy sector. Before 1989 it was the SGB holding with Tractebel and its power and gas companies. Since 1989 the strategy of the French corporates ENGIE and EDF prevail. The conflicting interests of private corporates and of public welfare caused splintered competences between the regions and the federal level. This may create deadlocks, as illustrated by the ardent and protracted negotiations on a post-2012 National Climate Plan, which was only finalized just before the start of the COP21 meeting in Paris in December 2015. Clearly, an overarching energy vision could help to overcome the divides between the various authorities while making Belgium fit for a more sustainable future. In 2018, the Belgian federal and regional governments concluded an "Energy Pact" covering the general strategic directions and goals of energy transition policy in the coming decades (Belgian Federal Government 2018). As such, the "Energy Pact" mainly sets out the governments' intentions and does not include any details on the policies and measures to be implemented in light of the ambitious transition goals. One of the most contentious issues in the immediate run-up to the conclusion of the pact was the planned nuclear phaseout. The political party N-VA was in favor of keeping open a nuclear capacity of 2GW after 2025. In the end, the closure dates as foreseen in the law (cf. Table 2) were maintained in the final approved version of the Energy Pact, but political tensions are likely to resurface with federal elections coming up in 2019.

Cross-References

- Energy Governance in France
- Energy Governance in Germany
- Energy Governance in Italy
- Energy Governance in the United Kingdom

References

Agoria, Essenscia & Febeliec. (2017). *Sluit niet alle kerncentrales in 2025*. Press release, November 25, 2017. Available from: http://www.febeliec.be/data/1511860038Kernuitstap%20persbericht_NL.pdf.

Altdorfer, F., & Baillot, Y. (2015). *Energy efficiency trends and policies in Belgium*. November 19, 2015. http://www.odyssee-mure.eu/publications/national-reports/energy-efficiency-belgium.pdf. Accessed April 26, 2019.

Barbé, L. (2005). *Kernenergie in de wetstraat: Dissectie van de deals*. Online book, available from www.lucbarbe.be.

Belgian Federal Government. (2014a). *Belgian energy efficiency action plan*. According to the directives 2006/32/EC and 2012/27/EU article 24.2 Annex XIV part 2. April 2014. https://ec.europa.eu/energy/sites/ener/files/documents/Belgium%20NEEAP.pdf.

Belgian Federal Government. (2014b). *Federal government agreement*, October 9, 2014. http://www.premier.be/sites/default/files/articles/Accord_de_Gouvernement_-_Regeerakkoord.pdf.

Belgian Federal Government. (2017). *Pathways to sustainable development: First Belgian National Voluntary Review on the implementation of the 2030 agenda*. New York: United Nations High Level Political Forum. July 2017. Available at: https://sustainabledevelopment.un.org/content/documents/15721Belgium_English.pdf.

Belgian Federal Government. (2018). *Visienota: Belgisch Interfederaal Energiepact*. Available at: https://emis.vito.be/nl/artikel/visienota-%E2%80%93-belgisch-interfederaal-energiepact.

Bollen, A., Van Humbeeck, P., & Lamote, A. (2011). *Energie voor een groene economie. Hernieuwbare energie: Beleid en evaluatie. Boekdeel 2. SERV.* Gent: Academia Press.

Council of the EU. (2002). *Decision of 25 April 2002 concerning the approval, on behalf of the EC, of the Kyoto protocol to the United Nations framework convention on climate change and the joint fulfilment of commitments thereunder (doc 2002/358/EC)*. Brussels: Council of the European Union.

Directive 2010/31/EU of the European Parliament and of the Council of 19 May 2010 on the energy performance of buildings.

EEA. (2016). *Climate change mitigation: Trends and projections in Europe*. Copenhagen: European Environment Agency.

EEA. (2017). *Climate change mitigation: Trends and projections in Europe*. Copenhagen: European Environment Agency.

EEC. (1975). *Directive 75/404/EEC of 13 February 1975 on the restriction of the use of natural gas in power stations, OJ L 178, 9.7.1975*, pp. 24–25.

EEC. (1991). *Directive 91/148/EEC of 18 March 1991on the restriction of the use of natural gas in power stations. OJ L 75, 21.3.1991*, p. 52.

El Kasmioui, O., Verbruggen, A., & Ceulemans, R. (2015). The 2013 reforms of Flemish renewable electricity support: Missed opportunities. *Renewable Energy, 83*, 905–917.

European Commission. (2015). *Assessment of the progress made by Member States towards the national energy efficiency targets for 2020 and towards the implementation of the energy efficiency directive 2012/27/EU as required by Article 24 (3) of energy efficiency directive 2012/27/EU*. Brussels, November 18, 2015.

Fraunhofer Institute et al. (2003). *Final report: "Beheer van de Energievraag" in het Raam van de door België te leveren inspanningen om de uitstoot van broeikasgassen te verminderen*. Karlsruhe, May 2003.

Govaerts, P., Jaumotte, A., & Vanderlinden, K. (Eds.). (1994). *Un demi-siècle de nucléaire en Belgique. Témoignages*. Bruxelles: Presses Interuniversitaires Européennes.

Groves, L. (1962). *Now it can be told. The story of the Manhattan project*. New York: Harper & Row.

Happaerts, S. (2015). Climate governance in federal Belgium: Modest subnational policies in a complex multi-level setting. *Journal of Integrative Environmental Sciences, 12*(4), 285–301. https://doi.org/10.1080/1943815X.2015.1093508.

Hens, L., & Solar, P. (1999). Belgium: Liberalism by default. In J. Foreman-Peck & G. Federico (Eds.), *European industrial policy: The twentieth century experience* (pp. 194–214). Oxford: Oxford University Press.

IEA. (2001). *Energy policies of IEA countries: Belgium 2001 review*. Paris: OECD/IEA.

IEA. (2016). *Energy policies of IEA countries: Belgium 2016 review*. Paris: OECD/IEA.

IEA. (2017a). *Belgium: Balances for 2015*. https://www.iea.org/statistics/statisticssearch/report/?year=2015&country=BELGIUM&product=Balances. Accessed April 26, 2019.

IEA. (2017b). *Data services: Detailed country RD&D budgets*. http://wds.iea.org/WDS/TableViewer/tableView.aspx. Accessed April 26, 2019.

Laes, E., Chayapathi, L., Meskens, G., & Eggermont, G. (2007a). *Kernenergie (on)besproken*. Leuven: Acco.

Laes, E., Chayapathi, L., Eggermont, G., & Meskens, G. (2007b). Lessen uit het verleden: Een historische analyse van de nucleaire controverse in België. In G. Bombaerts & E. Laes (Eds.), *Burgerparticipatie en energiebeleid voor een duurzame ontwikkeling* (pp. 59–98). Gent: Academia Press.

Law of 18 December 2013 concerning a changes to the law of 31 January 2003 regarding the gradual phase out from nuclear power generation. *Belgian Official Journal*, December 24, 2013.

Law of 28 June 2015 embodying various energy provisions. *Belgium Official Journal*, July 6, 2015.

Law of 31 January 2003 on the phasing out of nuclear energy used for industrial electricity production. *Belgian Official Journal*, February 28, 2003.

Law of 8 August 1988 that modifies the special law of 8 August 1980 on institutional reforms. *Belgian Official Journal*, August 13, 1988.

Leboutte, R. (2005). Coal mining, foreign workers and mine safety: Steps towards European integration, 1946-85. In S. Berger, A. Croll, & N. LaPorte (Eds.), *Towards a comparative history of coalfield societies* (pp. 219–137). Routledge, Abingdon, UK.

National Climate Commission. (2017). *Belgium's seventh national communication and third biennial report on climate change under the United Nations framework convention on climate change*. http://www.klimaat.be/files/4315/1549/8156/NC7_EN_LR.pdf. Accessed April 26, 2019.

NCC. (2015). *Beleidsakkoord over de intrabelgische burden sharing. December 4, 2015*. Brussels: National Climate Commission. http://www.cnc-nkc.be/sites/default/files/content/accord_pol_burden_sharing_nl.pdf. Accessed April 26, 2019.

N-VA. (2018). *Energie: Standpunt*. https://www.n-va.be/standpunten/energie. Accessed February 8, 2018.

REN21. (2018). *Renewables 2018: Global status report* (p. REN21). Paris.

Special Law of 16 July 1993 aiming at completing the federal structure of the state. *Belgian Official Journal*, July 20, 2013.

Special Law of 8 August 1980 related to institutional reforms. *Belgian Official Journal*, August 15, 1980.
Statbel. (2017). *Gebouwenpark*. October 11, 2017. https://statbel.fgov.be/nl/themas/bouwen-wonen/gebouwenpark. Accessed April 26, 2019.
Van de Graaf, T., & Timmermans, D. (2013). Steenkoolgas in Limburg: vloek of zegen? *Samenleving en Politiek, 5*, 73–80.
Vandendriessche, F. (2017). *Energierecht in België en Vlaanderen*. Gent: Larcier.
Verbruggen, A. (1986). De besluitvorming inzake de bouw van kerncentrales in België. In *Liber Amicorum Professor Dr. Pierre-Henri Virenque. Studiecentrum voor Ecnomisch en Sociaal Onderzoek*, UFSIA, pp. 303–326.
Verbruggen, A. (1989). *De betekenis van de KS-steenkoolwinning voor de energie-economie van het Vlaamse Gewest*. Flemish Parliamentary document on demand of the Minister of Energy, May 1989, 48p.
Verbruggen, A. (2009). Performance evaluation of renewable energy support policies, applied on Flanders' tradable certificates system. *Energy Policy, 37*, 1385–1394.
Verbruggen, A., & Vanderstappen, E. (1999). Electricity sector restructuring in Belgium during the 90's. *Utilities Policy, 8*(3), 159–171.
Verbruggen, A., Vanlommel, G., Erreygers, G. (1988). *Een doorlichting van het BCEO-plan 1988-1998. Een andere kijk op Doel 5. Studiecentrum voor Ecnomisch en Sociaal Onderzoek*, UFSIA, 203p.
VITO, Federaal Planbureau, ICEDD. (2013, April). *Towards 100% renewable energy in Belgium by 2050*. https://emis.vito.be/sites/emis.vito.be/files/articles/1125/2013/Rapport_100_procent_Duurzame_Energie.pdf. Accessed April 26, 2019.
World Bank. (2017). *Population density*. Available at: https://data.worldbank.org/indicator/EN.POP.DNST?year_high_desc=true. Accessed April 26, 2019.

Energy Governance in Croatia

23

Ana-Maria Boromisa

Contents

Introduction	534
General Conditions of Energy Governance in Croatia	535
Past Legacies	535
Composition of Energy Mix	539
Discourse on Energy Issues	542
Coordination of the Instruments and Issues of the Croatian Energy Transition	548
Drivers of Energy Transition	548
Strategies and Instruments of Energy Transition	549
Coordination Mechanisms and Multilevel Governance	551
Outcomes, Challenges, and Prospects of Energy Governance	555
Cross-References	558
References	558

Abstract

This chapter outlines the governance of the energy sector transition in the Republic of Croatia since the 1990s. Material basis (available energy sources and infrastructure), historical context, and various internal and external drivers have been shaping energy policy. In this process, decision-makers, public administration, institutions, experts, market participants, and public opinion have influenced the rules and their application.

Croatia is a net importer of energy and relies dominantly on carbon-based fuels. Import dependency is roughly 50%, and the share of fossil fuels in gross available energy is 70%. Material basis provides favorable conditions for the transition toward a low-carbon energy system. There are traditionally high shares of hydropower (roughly one-fourth of the primary energy production), and there is a

---

A.-M. Boromisa (✉)
Department for International Economic and Political Relations, Institute for Development and International Relations, Zagreb, Croatia
e-mail: anamaria@irmo.hr

© Springer Nature Switzerland AG 2022
M. Knodt, J. Kemmerzell (eds.), *Handbook of Energy Governance in Europe*,
https://doi.org/10.1007/978-3-030-43250-8_5

significant potential to increase the use of renewables (solar and wind). Natural gas and LNG are available and can serve as bridging fossil fuels during the transition.

Croatia's national policy documents include EU energy and climate policy goals, but transposition deficiencies are increasing. Weak administrative capacities for energy planning and management, deficiencies in the investment climate, insufficient legal certainty, and corruption slow down the transition of the energy sector.

Thus, these governance patterns are likely to determine the pace and outcomes of energy transition in Croatia.

Keywords

Croatia · Governance · Energy transition · LNG · Renewables · Fossil fuels

Introduction

Croatia declared independence in 1991 and launched an overarching political and economic transformation toward democracy and a market economy. The first decade of transition was turbulent. During the 1991–1995 war, the initial phase of economic reforms, including trade and price liberalization, was launched. Institutional and political reforms that have been more challenging to implement followed (EBRD 2013, 2017).

The beginning of the second decade brought strong growth. Energy-related benchmarks in this period relate to privatization, progress in Socialist Federative Republic Yugoslavia (SFRY) succession negotiations, and adoption of the first package of energy laws.

Croatia became an EU candidate country in 2004, and EU commitments were incorporated into the national energy strategy. Reforms led to gradual deregulation of electricity and gas prices, liberalization of the energy market, vertical unbundling of incumbent gas and power companies, and early stages of decarbonization. New institutions (e.g., regulator, market operator, electricity market, and specialized funds) were established and companies have entered the energy market. By accession to the EU in 2013, Croatia internalized EU policies and adopted goals related to the energy transition. Implementation is slower than planned. There are delays in the adoption of the strategic, legislative, and institutional framework. Transposition deficiencies are increasing (European Commission 2020a).

Investors experience shortcomings regarding establishing and the day-to-day running of their business operations. There is room for rendering administrative procedures speedier, more transparent, and effective, which is documented by Croatia's overall rankings in the World Bank's Doing Business 2020 edition (51st globally, behind most European Union countries) and for improving the overall quality and transparency of public governance (World Bank 2020; OECD 2019). Perception of corruption also remains high and not only by regional standards (Croatia ranked 63rd out of 179 economies in the Transparency International's Corruption Perception Index in 2020).

The global transition to a low-carbon energy economy is expected to have an overall positive impact on the economy, as the costs of a low-carbon energy system are significantly lower than those of a fossil-fuel-based economy (c.f. Nelson et al. 2014). Countries that are net consumers of fossil fuels are more likely to face net benefits to their economies. Croatia could benefit from energy transition as the share of fossil fuels in gross available energy in Croatia is about 70% (Eurostat 2021a).

However, recent evidence shows the complexity of transitioning to a low-carbon energy system that fosters inclusive economic growth and provides affordable and secure supply (WEF 2019). Similarly, the experience from the postcommunist transition shows that despite overall positive impacts, some segments of society have been excluded from the opportunities that a market economy offers and have suffered – rather than benefited – from promarket reforms (EBRD 2013).

The distribution of costs and benefits of energy transition among societal groups depends greatly on demand levels, technology costs, and the timing and shape of policy actions. Insufficient equity considerations, failure to adequately address negative impacts and provide support for individuals and societal groups adversely affected by reforms, can lead to political resistance and social unrest and slow down reforms. This would increase duration and costs of transition.

This chapter presents governance of the energy sector transition in the Republic of Croatia since the 1990s. First, we analyze general conditions, past legacies, energy mix, energy discourse, and political institutions. Next, we discuss the coordination of the instruments and issues of energy transition within a multilevel context. The drivers for reforms and main challenges are also examined. Identification of the strategies and instruments that should be taken into consideration when revising the position of Croatia vis-à-vis the multilevel governance follows. Based on identified changes caused by transition, we argue that the first phase of energy transition was ideologically driven. Currently, Croatia lacks ownership over the process which is mainly driven by EU acquis. Institutional capacity is insufficient for successful implementation. This is documented by the energy transition readiness component of the energy transition index, where Croatia scores low compared to other EU countries (WEF 2020).

The main conclusion is that outcomes, challenges, and prospects of the energy transition are closely linked with deficiencies of governance in Croatia.

General Conditions of Energy Governance in Croatia

Past Legacies

Energy sector legacies are closely connected with the overall development of the Republic of Croatia. These relate to general reform issues and specific energy-sector developments, as presented in Table 1.

The first period, from 1991 to 1995, was characterized by the declaration of independence from the former Socialist Federative Republic Yugoslavia (SFRY), war, and destruction. Infrastructure, including some of the critical energy

Table 1 Chronology of energy sector development in Croatia: general reform framework and specific developments

		General reform framework	Energy-related developments in Croatia
Phase I: independence and war	1990	First parliamentary elections	First step of the transformation of companies – form socially owned to public companies
	1991	Declaration of independence	Destruction of infrastructure
	1992	EU recognized Croatia as a sovereign state	Around 120 MW of diesel and gas power plants installed in Dalmatia
	1993	EU applies general trade preferences toward Croatia Croatia signed European Energy Charter	Second step of the transformation of energy-incumbent companies, from public companies to 100% state-owned limited liability companies Price reform in the electricity sector launched Government's decision to stop using domestic coal
	1995	End of war PHARE application and negotiations on cooperation agreement suspended	
Phase II: Regional approach	1996	EU adopts policy toward Western Balkans Regional approach, Croatia joined Council of Europe	Relaunch of the construction of TPP Plomin B
	1997	Croatia ratified European Energy Charter Treaty	Eastern Slavonia integrated into the Croatian power system
	1998		First energy strategy prepared Deliveries from NPP Krško stopped
	1999	European Commission proposed Stabilization and Association Process, Croatia adopted first action plan for EU integration Croatia signs Kyoto Protocol	Interconnection Tumbri-Hevitz operational
Phase III: toward candidacy	2000	Accession to WTO, beginning of negotiations on Stabilization and Association Agreement (Zagreb Summit)	Package of energy laws adopted Coal-fired TPP Plomin B became operational
	2001	Stabilization and association agreement (SAA)t signed	Plinacro (gas transport) unbundled, 1 part of INA group Agreement on NPP Krško reached with Slovenia Package of energy laws adopted, energy regulator established

(continued)

23 Energy Governance in Croatia

Table 1 (continued)

		General reform framework	Energy-related developments in Croatia
Phase IV: Negotiations	2002	Interim Stabilization and Association Agreement enters into force First Athens memorandum (electricity)	HEP restructured into HEP group, energy strategy formally adopted, Ina Privatization Law adopted, and HEP privatization law adopted
	2003	Croatia applies for EU membership Second Athens memorandum (gas)	First phase of INA privatization Solved issued over TPP Kakanj and TPP Tuzla (B&H)
	2004	European Council confirms Croatia as candidate country	Reconnection of 2 UCTE zones Environmental Protection and Energy Efficiency Fund Established
	2005	SAA enters into force Accession negotiations launched Beginning of the screening process Croatia joins Energy Community	Arbitration on NPP Krško launched
	2006	Screening completed	INA's shares listed on Zagreb stock exchange
	2007	Croatia ratifies Kyoto Protocol; Included in Instrument for Pre-Accession (IPA)	New gas market law adopted Act on the Fund for Financing the Decommissioning of the Krško Nuclear Power Plant and the Disposal of Krško NPP Radioactive Waste and Spent Nuclear Fuel
	2008-	Accession negotiations restrained (border dispute with Slovenia)	Underground gas storage Okoli became an independent legal entity The electricity market has been opened for all customers
	2009	Croatia joins NATO	2009 the Energy Law and the Electricity Market Law have been amended Cogeneration plant Zagreb operational
	2010		HPP Lešće in operation (42 MW) National Renewable Energy Action Plan adopted The first National Energy Efficiency Action Plan adopted LNG Hrvatska Ltd., established by two 100% state-owned companies Plinacro and HEP

(continued)

Table 1 (continued)

		General reform framework	Energy-related developments in Croatia
	2011	Accession Treaty signed	Gas interconnection with Hungary was built Plinacro became an observer of the European Network of Transmission System Operators for Gas (ENTSOG)
Phase V: EU membership and decarbonization	2013, 1 July	Croatia becomes EU member	Croatian system operator unbundled from HEP group, ITO model National action plan for renewables until 2020 adopted Croatia joins EU ETS
	2015	Energy union launched	Peak consumption for the first time in summer New Renewables and High-Efficiency Cogeneration Law, the formal end of feed-in tariff
	2016		Unbundling of supply from the distribution system operator
	2017	Croatia ratifies Paris Agreement	Phase-out of coal-fired thermal power plant Plomin 1 (120 MW)
	2018	Croatia categorized as developed country (World Bank)	
	2019	European Green Deal Accepted	First EV-charging stations installed on motorway Climate change and ozone protection law adopted National Climate and Energy Plan adopted
	2020	Covid 19	New Energy Strategy adopted, climate change adaptation strategy adopted
	2021		LNG terminal becomes operational, low-carbon development strategy adopted

Source: author

infrastructure, was severely damaged. For instance, the hydropower plant Peruća was occupied in 1991. The dam was severely damaged in 1993, threatening to flood the whole downstream flow. Its rehabilitation and renovation were completed in 1995.

Energy assets in other republics, in whose construction Croatia invested, became unavailable. This includes thermal power plants in Serbia (300 MW in thermal power plant Obrenovac) and Bosnia and Herzegovina (60 MW in Kakanj IV,

200 MW in Tuzla IV, and 100 MW in Gacko) and nuclear power plant Krško in Slovenia. Croatia's power system, designed and built to function as part of the system of SFRY started operating independently. War damages at 400 kV substations Ernestinovo and Konjsko (and the substation Mostar in Bosnia and Herzegovina) caused a division of the Union for the Coordination of Transmission for Electricity (UCTE) into two synchronous zones. It was only in 2004 when repair of damages and the creation of political and security preconditions enabled reconnection of two divided UCTE's zones.

In the second phase, investments in the energy sector were focused on the repair of large-scale war damage and construction of infrastructure necessary to increase security of supply, including relaunch of previously planned investments (e.g., Thermal Power Plant Plomin, finalized in 2000) and interconnections. Liberalization was recognized as a basis for the energy sector development and was formally launched by adoption of an energy law package in 2001: Energy Law (2001), Law on Regulation of Energy Activities (2001), Electricity Market law (2001), Gas Market Law (2001), and Oil and Oil Derivatives Law (2001).

Privatization was considered a tool for implementing economic reforms. Special laws for privatization of the incumbent oil and gas company (INA – Industrija nafte d.d.) and the power company (Hrvatska elektroprivreda – HEP d.d.) were adopted in 2002 (INA Privatization Law 2002; HEP Privatization Law 2002).

The EU negotiations phase (2004–2013) was characterized by gradual alignment with the EU acquis (more in Table 1). The most challenging issues related to regional cooperation, decarbonization in line with the Kyoto Protocol, and unbundling of market-based activities from public services in vertically integrated power companies. After two decades of general transition, Croatia met EU membership criteria and finalized EU accession negotiations (Council of the EU 2011).

Accession to the EU 2013 and the launch of the energy union in 2015 set the framework for the next stage of energy transition. By accession to the EU Croatia internalized EU policies and gained the opportunity to participate in policymaking at the EU level. However, energy transition evolves slower than planned. Croatia faces difficulties in transposing EU energy legislation and faces an increasing number of infringement procedures (European Commission 2020b).

Composition of Energy Mix

The following overall features characterize the Croatian energy system:

Croatia is a net importer of energy. It is relying dominantly on (imported) carbon-based fuels. Import dependency is roughly 50%, and the share of fossil fuels in gross available energy accounts for 70% (Eurostat 2021a). The largest sectoral contributors to the final energy consumption are the general consumption sectors: the residential sector, building and construction, tourism, transport, and industry.

Croatia's energy intensity (174.04 kg of oil equivalent per 1000€ GDP in PPP) is higher than the EU28 average (119.36) (Eurostat 2021b). The total available capacities of all power plants in the Republic of Croatia are 4711.8 MW including

1781 MW in thermal power plants, 2199.7 MW in hydropower plants, 646.3 MW in wind power plants, and 84.8 MW in solar power plants (data for 2019). Croatia also owns 50% of the total available capacity of the nuclear unit Krško, Slovenia (348 MW). In terms of share of renewable energy in gross final energy consumption, Croatia is above the EU average (overall share of 28.4% compared to 18.9% EU-29 in 2019 (Eurostat 2021c) and met the 2020 headline target.

An LNG terminal, 50% financed by Connecting Europe Facility as an EU Project of Common Interest and one of the priority projects under the Central and South-Eastern Europe Energy Connectivity (CESEC) initiative, became operational in 2021.

Fossil fuels still dominate the energy mix. Liquid fuels (oil and derivatives) are the largest primary energy source, followed by gas. Consumption of liquid fuels is gradually decreasing (from 188.33 PJ, or 46% of the total primary energy supply in 1990 to 133.21 PJ or 33% in 2019, Table 2). Consumption of gas in the period 1990–2019 ranges between 87 and 105 PJ, 22–27% of the total primary energy supply. Liquid fuel (oil and derivatives), coal, and gas taken together are 63% of total primary energy supply (Table 2). Following the introduction of an incentive system for renewables in 2007, the share of renewables (primarily wind and solar) has been increasing (Table 3). In 2019, intermittent wind and solar capacity accounted for 16% (731 MW) of installed grid-connected power generation capacity in Croatia.

In the structure of primary energy production, the share of fossil fuels is about one-third, and a share of energy produced from large hydropower plants is about ¼ (Fig. 1). Thanks to existing hydropower plants and the recent expansion of wind and solar power generation, Croatia has exceeded the EU renewable energy target of 20% in final energy consumption. In 2019, according to Eurostat, it reached 24.2% and according to the national energy report, Energy in Croatia, 31.5%.

The structure of energy sources used in final energy consumption is dominated by the consumption of liquid fuels (41%, which is 118.4 PJ or 2,828.0 ktoe), followed by electricity (20%, 58.0 PJ or 1,384.4 ktoe), firewood and biomass (16%, 47.6 PJ or 1,136.5 ktoe), natural gas (13%, 37.5 PJ or 896.0 ktoe), thermal energy (7%, 18.7 PJ or 477.0 ktoe), and other renewable energy sources and coal and coke (3%, a total of 8.7 PJ or 207.2 ktoe) (Fig. 2).

In 2019, the total electricity consumption in Croatia amounted to 18,893.3 GWh and production to 12,760.3 GWh. Electricity produced from renewable energy sources accounted for 44.7% of total consumption (66.2% of production). Electricity produced in large hydropower plants accounted for 31.4% of consumption (46.5% of production), while electricity produced from other renewable sources (wind energy, small hydropower plants, biomass, geothermal energy, biogas, and photovoltaic systems) accounted for 13.3% of consumption (19.7% of production). Investments in renewable generation facilities (mostly wind power, and to a lesser extent solar) increased total available generation capacity and contributed to a structural change in electricity production (Table 3).

Roughly 50% of energy is imported. Import is dominated by petroleum products (35%) and crude oil (26%), followed by natural gas (21%), electricity (10%), and coal and coke (7%).

Thus, Croatia is vulnerable to energy prices volatility and the availability of water.

Table 2 Shares of specific energy forms in the total primary energy supply, PJ, %

	1990		2000		2005		2010		2015		2016		2017		2018		2019	
	PJ	%	PJ	%	PJ	%	PJ	%	PJ	%	PJ	%	PJ	%	PJ	%	PJ	%
Coal and coke	34.31	8%	18.65	5%	28.64	7%	30.91	8%	29.86	7%	32.12	8%	21.45	5%	20.36	5%	20.77	5%
Biomass	n/a		n/a		n/a		16.05	4%	52.69	13%	52.47	13%	52.09	13%	53.02	13%	54.18	13%
Liquid fuel	188.33	46%	159.02	44%	186.19	45%	152.54	37%	130.92	33%	130.78	32%	139.83	34%	134.52	33%	133.21	33%
Natural gas	98.22	24%	94.98	26%	101.06	25%	111.37	27%	87.16	22%	91.08	22%	104.67	25%	96.43	24%	101.22	25%
Hydropower	37.48	9%	57.33	16%	62.05	15%	79.71	19%	61.63	15%	65.63	16%	53.81	13%	66.98	16%	51.54	13%
Electricity	25.42	6%	14.4	4%	18.41	4%	17.15	4%	24.44	6%	19.91	5%	25.03	6%	19.4	5%	22.08	5%
Heat	n/a		n/a		n/a		1.76	0%	0.62	0%	0.66	0%	0.67	0%	0.63	0%	0.61	0%
Renewables*	22.68	6%	15.64	4%	14.94	4%	2.24	1%	11.36	3%	12.9	3%	16.11	4%	17.32	4%	22.1	5%
Total	406.33	100%	360.01	100%	411.31	100%	411.73	100%	398.48	100%	405.56	100%	413.86	100%	408.85	100%	405.72	100%

[a]Methodology for calculation changed regarding use of fuel wood, thus the time series are not coherent
Data sources: 2009, Vuk and Šimurina 2009, Ministry of Economy, Labour and Entrepreneurship 2010, Ministry of Economy and Sustainable Development 2019.

Table 3 Installed capacity and produced electric power, 2009 and 2019

	Installed capacity (MW) 2009	2019	Share in total 2009	2019	Produced power, GWh 2009	2019	Share in production 2009	2019
Hydropower plants	2092	2200	50%	47%	6814	5933	44%	46%
Thermal power plants	1686	1781	40%	38%	5908	5277	38%	41%
NPP Krško (50%)	348	348	8%	7%	2730	2767	18%	22%
Solar power plants	0.08	84.8	0%	2%	0,1	83	0%	1%
Wind power plants	70	646	2%	14%	54,2	1467	0%	11%
Total	4197	4712	100%	100%	15,507	12,760	100%	100%

Data sources: 2009, Ministry of Economy and Sustainable Development 2019.

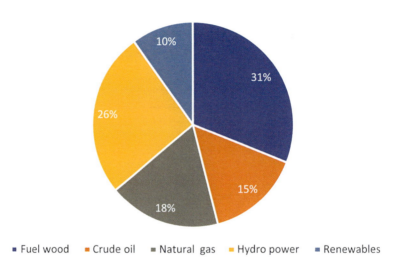

Fig. 1 Primary energy production, 2019. Data source: Ministry of Economy and Sustainable Development 2019

In recent years, shares of renewables have been gradually increasing while the use of coal has been declining. The gas demand is estimated to increase. Improvements in energy efficiency, electrification of transport, and demographic decline are expected to drive changes in the energy mix in the coming years.

Discourse on Energy Issues

The discourse on energy issues has been evolving around specific events (Table 1) and their impact regarding (i) security of supply, (ii) affordability, (iii) sustainability (related to the environment), and (iv) institutional capacity and political will.

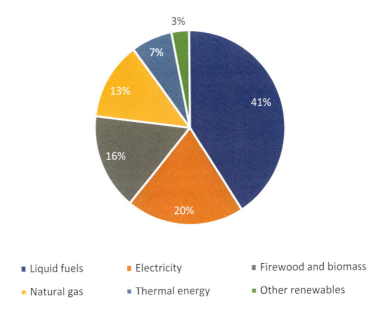

Fig. 2 Structure of energy sources in final energy consumption. Note: other renewables include wind energy, solar energy, biogas, liquid biofuels, and geothermal energy. Data source: Ministry of Economy and Sustainable Development 2019

The discourse on energy issues within the election campaigns is limited, suggesting that energy is not among key political issues (Šimunović 2018). This is coherent with results of the Eurobarometer surveys which show that less than 1% of Croatian respondents consider environmental issues and energy and climate change among the two most important political issues (European Commission 2014, 2020c).

War damages and unavailable generation facilities in neighboring countries highlighted risks related to *security of supply*. The discourse revolved around issues on physical security (availability of resources and possibility of access) and import dependency (in general, and dependence on particular supply source and route). Following the repair of large-scale war damage (rehabilitation of substations) leading to stabilization of the system, establishing new supply routes and sources (new electricity and gas interconnections and an LNG terminal) has been pursued as the main energy security strategy. The importance of this strategy gained more attention at the time of expiration of a long-term gas supply contract with Gazprom in 2010. The construction of a new supply route, interconnection gas pipeline Hungary-Croatia was underway and became operational in 2011. It also fostered preparation of the LNG terminal: Plinacro (100% state-owned gas transport company) and HEP (100% state-owned power company) established LNG Croatia Ltd. with the purpose of speed-up construction of the planned LNG terminal. The LNG terminal Krk was included in the EU's list of projects of common interest and was receiving the support of Connecting Europe Facilities for various stages of project development since 2014 (INEA 2021). The LNG terminal became operational in 2021.

The discourse regarding security of supply and affordability evolved together with negotiations on the protection of investor rights and future supplies from thermal power plants in Bosnia and Herzegovina and Serbia. In 1998, Slovenia disconnected electricity lines from the Krško NPP to Croatia and terminated all electricity deliveries to HEP. The supply from NPP Krško was reestablished in 2002 based on an agreement reached in 2001. Croatia requested arbitrage with the International Centre for the Settlement of Investment Disputes (ICSID) to deal with remaining open issues. The case was decided in 2015 (ICSID 2015).

In 2004, HEP reached an agreement with Elektroprivreda BiH which enabled restoring electricity supply from TPP Tuzla and TPP Kakanj after 11 years. The agreement provided for taking over the total contracted, undelivered electricity (5.22 billion kWh, at EUR 34/MWh) within 6 years (Sušec 2003). Open issues remain regarding TPP Obrenovac (Republic of Serbia) and TPP Gacka (Bosnia and Herzegovina).

The ambitious investment plans included in the Energy Strategy (2002, 2009) and the Government's programs have been mostly driven by security of supply considerations. Progress in implementation opened issues related to affordability and environmental sustainability. For example, in the preparatory and early construction phase of the coal-fired Plomin B project (210 MW unit), the focus was on security of supply. In the operational phase, issues regarding affordability emerged. The construction stopped in 1991 and was relaunched in 1996 based on a build-own-transfer contract between HEP and RWE Energie (Germany). The facility became operational in 2000. HEP and RWE contractually regulated their obligations to ensure business and operation of the thermal power plant, including maintenance services, shared use and supply, and electricity procurement (Purchase Power Agreement – PPA). The PPA was initially regarded as a good example of international cooperation in financing and implementing projects (Sušec 2015). The PPA obliged HEP d.d. to buy all energy produced in Plomin at a guaranteed price. The price formula allowed covering production costs and providing a minimum amount of return on capital at a rate of 14–17% to RWE. HEP did not realize its share in the Plomin project, which opened discussion regarding affordability of the arrangement.

The discourse on *affordability* has been framed from the demand side as an equity issue and from the supply side as a matter of competitiveness. The discourse regarding competitiveness stresses the importance of affordable energy as an economic location factor, the relevance of the market model, the role of the state, ownership issues, and privatization. Decarbonization targets have also been discussed in terms of affordability.

In the first decade of transition, reforms regarding price-liberalization were motivated by security of supply and supply-side affordability. Privatization was regarded as the next stage of reforms, expected to increase the efficiency of the energy industry and to support competitiveness of the economy. Thus, the models and dynamics of privatization gained significant attention. Different models for the privatization of the oil and gas industry (through strategic partners) and the power industry (through initial public offering) were defined in separate privatization laws.

Privatization of INA was expected to be beneficial for the company and the state. For the company, expected benefits from privatization included increased efficiency, capital investment, modernization, and dominance of commercial over political interests in management. State expected income from privatization and, in the long-term, increased revenues from taxes and dividends based on increased efficiency of the company (Cuckovic et al. 2011).

The first phase of privatization of INA was finalized in 2003. Since 2006, the company is listed on Zagreb Stock Exchange. The state was supposed to keep at least 25% +1 share until the accession to the EU. Currently, the state holds about 45% and MOL owns 49% of INA.

Surveys suggest that the privatization of INA has contributed to increased efficiency. The state's influence on decision-making has been reduced. The level of investment is lower than expected, and domestic gas prices are below the level of imported gas. The negative effects are largely due to the weakness of institutions (regulatory, supervisory, and judiciary) and the slow implementation of general reforms.

The power industry had not been privatized, and the HEP Privatization Law was terminated in 2010. Due to the size of the sector, compared to the financial market, privatization of HEP would imply partial or completely foreign ownership.

Affordability of achieving targets (i.e., costs of reducing emissions) was in the focus of the debate on decarbonization launched in the context of ratification Kyoto Protocol. Croatia signed the Kyoto Protocol in 1999 and ratified it in May 2007. Ratification followed the Conference of Parties to the UN Framework Convention on Climate Change (UNFCCC) that allowed Croatia additional 3.5 $MtCO_2$ eq in comparison to 1990 GHG emissions. Croatia required an increase of base year emission for 4.45 Mt. CO_2 eq based on special circumstances. These special circumstances relate to emissions from Croatian power plants situated outside Croatian territory.

Ombudsman's annual reports regularly include the chapter on energy poverty from 2014 onward (Pučki pravobranitelj 2015, 2016, 2017, 2018, 2019, 2020, 2021). Recommendations relate to monitoring energy poverty and developing institutional capacity for defining criteria and support for alleviating energy poverty. Since 2017, a reduced VAT rate (13% compared to the regular rate of 25%) is applied to electricity, as a measure to alleviate the cost of the feed-in system to final customers. The ombudsman proposed extended application of the reduced VAT rate for gas, district heating, and fuelwood in order to reduce energy poverty. However, the proposal was rejected (Pučki pravobranitelj 2018).

Adoption of the legal framework for public participation in environmental decision-making facilitated discussion of *environmental sustainability*. This relates primarily to the ratification of the Aarhus Convention, the Kyoto Protocol, and the adoption of the Environmental Protection Act in 2007. Before adopting the legal framework for public participation, activists' protests and advocacy campaigns were the dominant way of public involvement in decision-making.

Several projects had been put on hold or rejected due to flaws in environmental impact assessments. This also includes projects initially considered strategic, such as the Druzba Adria oil pipeline project, the Ombla hydropower plant, or thermal power plant Plomin C.

The purpose of the Druzba Adria project was to transport Russian oil to the Adriatic coast where it would then be transferred to tankers and further transported internationally. The environmental impact of ballast waters being discharged in the Adriatic from tankers to take up the oil and Croatia's poor ability to deal with environmental accidents in case of major oil discharges or hazards on pipelines and tankers caused a stir among experts, journalists, and the general public. Following an extensive advocacy campaign organized by Croatian environmental NGOs and rising public pressure, in 2003, the Croatian Ministry for Environmental Protection, Physical Planning, and Construction (MEPPPC) required the environmental impact assessment (EIA). The results of the EIA were severely criticized by various actors, including the church, and the project was rejected (Hrvatska biskupska konferencija 2005; Zelena akcija 2005).

The Ombla Hydro Power Project was listed among strategic investment projects in the Energy Strategy. Following the findings of the independent biodiversity study, and considering precautionary principle, EBRD and HEP have agreed to cancel the EBRD loan (HEP 2013; Zelena akcija 2013) and the project had been canceled.

HEP proposed Plomin C (500 MW, coal-fired) as a replacement for Plomin A (120 MW) after its decommissioning. The proposal was based on security of supply considerations. Environmental NGOs have challenged the environmental impact study for Plomin C, but the administrative court rejected the complaint. HEP continued with the preparation of the project, and in 2014 the Japanese company Marubeni was selected as a strategic partner. Finally, the project was abandoned as the European Commission (DG Competition) considered the proposed PPA as prohibited state aid.

The 2020–2024 Program of the Government identifies low-carbon energy transition as one of the priorities. The policies and financial instruments for low-carbon energy transition could have long-term implications on security of supply, affordability, and environmental sustainability. Postponing announced reforms indicates a lack of political will for reforms, deficiency of institutional capacity, and provides opportunities for corruption.

Deficiencies in the planning and/or implementing capacity can be illustrated with the investment plan included in the Energy Strategy (2002, 2009) and application of the Renewables and High-Efficiency Cogeneration Law (2015, 2016, 2017, 2018). According to the 2002 Energy Strategy, three hydropower plants were to be built by 2010 and additional three by 2020. Also, 1000 MW in two coal-fired thermal power plants and 900 MW in gas-fired thermal power plants were planned by 2020 (Energy Strategy 2002).

The 2009 version of the strategy considers 300 MW in HPP, built between 2015 and 2020, and at least 2400 MW in thermal power plants, including 300 MW of cogeneration facilities (Energy Strategy 2009). However, only one hydropower plant was built (Lešće, 42.29 MW), and the progress in the construction of thermal power plants also remained limited.

The lack of *political will and insufficient institutional capacity* for reforms can be illustrated by increasing transposition deficits in general and examples of adoption and implementation of the Renewables and High-Efficiency Co-generation Law (2015, 2016, 2017, 2018) in particular.

There has been a significant deterioration in the transposition of European policies. In 2021, 10% of all infringement cases against Croatia (36 out of 361 cases) and 25% of active cases (18 of 74 active cases) relate to energy (European Commission 2021b). Environment (with eight cases) and energy (with five cases) are the most challenging sectors and make 50% of all pending cases. Conformity deficit has reached 1.9% (last report: 0.9%), which is significantly higher than the EU average of 1.2% and proposed target in the Single Market Act of 0.5%. With 19 directives that have been incorrectly transposed, Croatia now has the second highest conformity deficit in the EU and is one of seven Member States whose conformity deficit is three times or higher than the 0.5% proposed target (European Commission 2021c). Transposition plans are ambitious, with deadlines tighter than in the relevant directives. However, transposition is often postponed, suggesting a poor level of decision-making and a lack of capacity for realistic planning.

Among its key features of the Renewables and High-Efficiency Co-generation Law (2015) was the replacement of feed-in tariff with a market premium model. Implementing regulations were not adopted, so the application of the law was postponed several times (in 2016, 2017, and 2018). It was only in 2020 when the first tender for market premium was launched. The new law that should be aligned with the Renewables Directive is expected to be adopted in 2021.

Thus, it is not surprising that confidence in national institutions is lacking. According to the latest Eurobarometer survey, Croatia is among the countries of the EU whose citizens tend not to trust their national government. The share of people in Croatia who tend not to trust the national government is 73% (European Commission 2021c).

Perception of corruption also remains high and not only by regional standards (Croatia was ranked 63rd out of 179 economies in the Transparency International's Corruption Perception Index in 2020). The cases involving high officials include privatization of INA and 142 MW Krš-Pađene wind park.

In 2009, INA's strategic partner MOL gained management rights, while still having minority ownership. Former Croatian prime minister Ivo Sanader was, after almost a decade of trial, in 2019 convicted of corruption in that case and was sentenced to 6 years jail for accepting a bribe of €10 m from MOL (Hopkins 2019). A previous conviction against Sanader for bribery and illegal profiteering from the INA privatization was overturned by Croatia's constitutional court in 2015 due to procedural errors.

In 2020, the State Attorney's Office initiated an investigation against the Secretary of State in the Ministry of Administration Josipa Rimac for the criminal offenses of trading in influence, abuse of position, and bribery related to procedure and amount of support granted to the biggest wind park in Croatia, Krš Pađene. The investigation includes several high-level officials (e.g., the head of the energy-regulatory agency, several assistant ministers and state secretaries in various ministries, a high-ranking police officer, and a former minister of regional development and EU funds) (Državno odvjetništvo 2021).

Coordination of the Instruments and Issues of the Croatian Energy Transition

Drivers of Energy Transition

Initial phases of reforms (phases I and II as presented in Table 1) have been driven by domestic, mostly ideological reasons. The goal was democracy and a market economy that manages to meet market needs, finance investments, operate efficiently, and embrace new technologies. Within this overall reform process, privatization was launched as part of the process to establish a competitive market.

Since 2000 (phases III and IV according to Table 1), the main strategic goal was European integration. Energy sector reforms have been anchored within this process, and the EU conditionality fostered the reform agenda and its implementation. This primarily relates to regional integration and decarbonization.

Croatia was reluctant to join regional energy initiatives that aimed at establishing a regional market and supporting common infrastructure planning, i.e., the Athens process and the Energy Community. However, faced with strong conditionality, Croatia joined Athens memoranda and supported the Energy Community. Similarly, ratification of the Kyoto Protocol was driven by EU conditionality. This was explicitly recognized as progress regarding the environmental chapter of accession negotiations (European Commission 2007).

Some elements of energy transition have been domestically driven. Privatization of INA was motivated by (i) expected efficiency gains (reduction of costs, increase of quality of supply), (ii) inability to finance new investments and maintenance, (iii) the need to remove subsidies and release funds to finance other public needs, and (iv) the desire to raise funds by selling assets (Čučković et al. 2011). On the other hand, privatization of power company HEP was not implemented, even though special HEP privatization law was adopted.

The energy transition requires long-term investments. Strategic projects had been defined in policy documents. Some of these are eligible for financial support from the EU. System of financial incentives and disincentives (feed-in tariff, emission fees, and emission trading system) and its predictability influence investment decisions and thus the pace of transition.

The success of European integration (phase V) might be evaluated not merely as adherence to EU norms and reducing the differences between old and new countries, but also as active participation in policymaking. The transposition deficit in Croatia is increasing indicating a lack of political will and institutional capacity. Compared to other EU member states, energy transition readiness in Croatia is low. This primarily results from relatively low commitment (in terms of Paris Agreement ambition) and a lack of stability of the regulatory framework (WEF 2020).

Some communities recognized energy transition as a development opportunity and launched bottom-up initiatives. For example, island of Krk adopted a local energy transition strategy in 2012 intending to become the first CO_2 neutral and energy self-sufficient island in the Mediterranean. The perspective of increasing security of supply, decreasing energy costs and air pollution, and creating local employment opportunities is driving the process.

The 2021–2030 phase of transition should be based on the new Croatian energy strategy, the NECP (National Climate and Energy Plan), and the EU Green Deal, and driven by climate change and post-Covid recovery considerations. The regulatory framework in line with Clean Energy for All European package is planned to be adopted in 2021, while financial support is expected from EU funds. State aid is planned to be phased out.

Strategies and Instruments of Energy Transition

Energy transition for the 2021–2030 period is planned within the National development strategy (2021) and several strategic documents dealing with energy and climate change: Energy strategy (2020), Climate Change Adaptation Strategy (2020), and National Energy and Climate Plan (NECP).

The headline targets until 2030 (Table 4) are generally coherent with the EU goals (European Commission 2020a).

As shown in Table 4, Croatia's NECP is ambitious regarding renewables, while the Commission considers ambition regarding energy efficiency low. This is still

Table 4 Objectives and targets according to the NECP 2021–2030

	National targets and contributions	Latest available data	2020	2030	Assessment of 2030 ambition level by the European Commission
GHG	Binding target for greenhouse gas emissions compared to 2005 under the Effort Sharing Regulation (ESR) %	−1%	11%	7%	As in Effort Sharing Regulation
Renewables	Share of energy from renewable sources in gross final consumption of energy (%)	28%	20%	36.4%	Sufficiently ambitious (32% is based on the RES formula)
Energy efficiency	National contribution for energy efficiency:				
	Primary energy consumption	8.2 Mtoe	8.23 Mtoe	10.7 Mtoe	Low
	Final energy consumption (Mtoe)	6.9 Mtoe	7.0 Mtoe	6.85 Mtoe	Low
Interconnectivity			30%	N/A	15%	N/A

Source: European Commission (2020b)

challenging as it is estimated that achievement of 2030 targets will require investment estimated at EUR 19 billion (Ministry of Environment and Energy 2019) or roughly 3.5% of the 2019 BDP annually. Croatia is one of the EU economies most affected by the COVID 19 crisis and is estimated to have contracted by 8.9% in 2020 (European Commission 2021a). This increases energy transition implementation challenges, further complicated by lack of skilled workers, identified by the long-term renovation strategy (2020).

The adoption of several laws in line with the Clean Energy for All Europeans Package is planned for 2021. These laws should facilitate energy efficiency improvements, renewable self-consumption, establishment of renewable energy communities, decarbonization of transport, development of information, and monitoring schemes and provide support for research and innovation (MINGOR, 2021).

The cornerstone of Croatian energy efficiency policy is an energy efficiency obligation scheme. The scheme has been planned for years but experienced delays and should become fully operational in 2021. The scheme targets energy suppliers who supplied more than 50 GWh of energy to the market during the previous year. Suppliers can meet their obligation in one of the following three key ways: investing in and stimulating energy efficiency improvements in final consumption; buying savings from another obligated party; or paying contributions to the Environmental Protection and Energy Efficiency Fund. Expected cumulative savings over the period from 2021 to 2030 are 26.04 PJ or 621.96 ktoe, or 10% of the total target (see Table 4). An Energy management system should be introduced in all public sector buildings. Improvements of the system enabling verification of savings after renovation of the building are also planned.

Several economic instruments (incentives – such as subsidies and disincentives – such as taxes on the CO_2 emission) are also planned. The EU ETS and emission tax for the non-ETS stationary sources are considered key instruments for CO_2 reduction.

Since January 1, 2013, installations from the Republic of Croatia have been integrated into the EU Emissions Trading System (EU ETS) in which 52 facilities from Croatia are included. Through an allocation of emission allowances, Croatia took on an obligation of reducing emissions to contribute to a reduction in emissions by at least 43% by 2030 compared to 2005 levels. The reduction in emissions within the framework of the EU ETS is regulated at the EU level.

According to the Regulation on binding annual greenhouse gas emission reductions by the Member States from 2021 to 2030 for a resilient Energy Union and to meet commitments under the Paris Agreement, the goal of reducing emissions by 7% compared to the 2005 level is determined for Croatia.

The CO_2 emission tax for the non-ETS stationary sources was introduced in 2007 (Government, 2007, 2009, 2018). All stationary sources emitting more than 450 tons of CO_2 per year until first January 2017 are obliged to pay the CO_2 emission tax. Investments in energy efficiency, renewable energy, and other measures to reduce CO_2 emissions and other GHG emissions decrease the tax obligations which are calculated and charged by the Environmental Protection and Energy Efficiency Fund. From 2013 onward, the obligation to pay the CO_2 emission tax has applied only to non-ETS sources.

The system of promoting RES use for the production of electricity and thermal energy was established in 2007 based on feed-in tariffs (FIT). The eligible producers were entitled to a 14-years contract that guaranteed purchase of all the supplied energy at FIT. The FIT depended on the type of technology used and the size of the facility. Feed-in tariff has played a significant role in investment in renewables in the 2007–2015 period. The new support system based on the market premium was planned to be implemented in 2016 but only became operational in 2020. In line with the goals for using renewable energy sources and the planned increase in installed power in all technologies, the Ministry of Economy and Sustainable Development prepares a three-year plan for the increase in RES power by type and technology and at least once a year issues a tender for the construction of facilities using RES.

Various policies concentrate on information, planning, and educational and voluntary measures. These include the establishment and capacity building of regional energy and climate agencies, promoting the use of innovative information and communication technologies (ICTs) to reduce GHG emissions, and vocational training and education programs in the fields of renewable energy installations, energy efficiency, and the establishment of nearly-zero standards in building construction and refurbishment (MINGOR 2021). At the subnational level, the membership of Croatian municipalities in the transnational Covenant of Mayors for Climate and Energy plays an increasing role.

The signatories of the Covenant of Mayors for Climate and Energy in the Republic of Croatia support a joint vision for 2050: accelerating decarbonization of their territories, strengthening capacity to adapt to the inevitable impact of climate change, and allowing citizens to access safe, sustainable, and affordable energy. The signatory cities are committed to action that will support the reduction in greenhouse gases by 40% by 2030 and the adoption of a common approach to mitigating and adapting to climate change. The Covenant encompasses 70 cities and municipalities, i.e., more than two million citizens of the Republic of Croatia (Covenant of Mayors 2021).

Some local governments implement more ambitious initiatives such as carbon-neutral islands and cities or initiatives implemented under the "Mayor's Charter," the concept of "smart cities," and innovative platforms. However, such initiatives are not systematically monitored. There is no knowledge base and examples of good practice that could be used to transfer knowledge and strengthen capacity.

Coordination Mechanisms and Multilevel Governance

Croatia has three governance levels: central government, regional governments (20 counties and city of Zagreb), and local governments (128 cities and 428 municipalities).

The Government has a key role in energy policy formulation and implementation. The Parliament approves long-term energy policy (energy strategy). The President, through a high-level advisory body, Energy Transition Council, promotes the preparation of analytical basis and discussions on particularly important issues in the field of energy transition (the transition to clean and sustainable energy sources, climate protection).

Ministries, state administrative organizations, central government offices, and public agencies operate at the central government level. There is no clear distinction between them. They have similar competencies, including the creation and implementation of public policies, strategic documents, drafting of laws, administrative oversight, etc. (Koprić 2018). Decisions on the number and type of organizations and their classification are mostly political, and the number of central government bodies varies from government to government. Currently, there are 15 ministries, seven state administrative organizations, and five central government offices.

The key document defining energy policy at the national level is the energy strategy. It is adopted by the Parliament upon Government's proposal. The Government and the Parliament are responsible for the establishment of an appropriate framework for the implementation of the Strategy (Energy Law 2012, 2014, 2015a, b, 2018).

The line ministry responsible for energy – in 2021 the Ministry of Economy and Sustainable Development (MESD) – has the key role in formulating and implementing national energy policy.

In addition to Energy Strategy and energy legislation, the MESD is responsible for the National Energy and Climate Plan, Low Carbon Development Strategy, Climate Change Adaptation Strategy, energy efficiency policy, action plans, and implementation of EU legislation in the field of energy efficiency at the national level.

The Ministry of Physical Planning, Construction, and State Assets is currently the most important stakeholder in the formulation of policies and measures for energy efficiency in buildings. The Ministry enacts legislation, strategies, and programs to guide the long-term integral renovation of buildings: family houses, apartment buildings, commercial nonresidential buildings, and public sector buildings.

Other ministries relevant for energy transition include the Ministry of Agriculture, Ministry of Transport and Infrastructure, Ministry of Finance, and Ministry of Regional Development and EU funds. Crosscutting issues are dealt with Ministry of Social Policy and Youth and the Central Office for Digitalization.

Public agencies include various bodies (agencies, regulatory bodies, funds, and legal entities with public powers). They are not subject to uniform rules and operate with great institutional and organizational uncertainty.

National public agencies in the energy sector include the following:

- Fund for Environmental Protection and Energy Efficiency (EPEEF).
- Croatian Energy Regulatory Agency (HERA).
- Hydrocarbons Agency.
- Fund for financing the decommissioning of the Krško Nuclear Power Plant and the disposal of NEK radioactive waste and spent nuclear fuel.
- Agency for Legal Transactions and Real Estate (APN).

The EPEEF, established in 2004, is a central instrument for collecting and investing outside the budget in programs and projects for environmental and nature protection, energy efficiency, and the use of renewable energy sources. The Fund's activities include activities related to financing the preparation, implementation, and development of programs and projects and similar activities in the field of preservation, sustainable use, protection, and improvement of the environment and the field of energy efficiency and use of renewable energy sources.

Croatian Energy Regulatory Agency (HERA) was established by the Energy Regulation Act in 2001. Its work is defined by provisions of the package of energy laws: Energy Regulation Act, Energy Law, Electricity Market Law, Gas Market Law, Oil and oil derivatives market law, Renewables and High-Efficiency Cogeneration Law, Law on Energy Efficiency, and Thermal Energy Law. HERA is an independent and nonprofit legal entity with public authority to regulate energy activities. The founder of HERA is the Republic of Croatia, and the founding rights are exercised by the Government of the Republic of Croatia. HERA is accountable to the Croatian Parliament for its work. Key activities include licensing and defining price methodologies for public service activities in the energy sector.

The Fund for financing the decommissioning of the Krško Nuclear Power Plant and the disposal of NEK radioactive waste and spent nuclear fuel was established in 2008. Its activities relate to the collection, preservation, and increase of the value of assets for financing the preparation, review, and implementation of the Krško Nuclear Power Plant decommissioning. The Fund also should establish a radioactive waste management facility in Croatia.

The Agency for Legal Transactions and Real Estate (APN) implements the program of energy renovation of public sector buildings and the program of systematic energy management of facilities owned by ministries, cities, or counties in terms of reducing financial costs for energy and water, with monitoring through information system for energy management (ISGE) since 2018. In the period 2012–2018, the Center for Monitoring the Energy Sector and Investments (CEI) served as national coordination body for energy efficiency (Zakon o centru za praćenje poslovanja energetskog sektora i investicija 2018, 2012a, 2012b). The CEI was abolished in 2018 (Zakon o centru za praćenje poslovanja energetskog sektora i investicija 2018). The tasks and staff of the CEI were split between the ministry responsible for energy (at the time Ministry of Energy and Environment, currently Ministry for Economy and Sustainable Development) and APN.

Other relevant actors at the national level are market institutions (Croatian Energy Market Operator HROTE; Croatian Power Exchange CROPEX) and market participants. While the energy market is formally liberalized, the power market is still dominated by the 100% state-owned company HEP d.d. and its subsidiaries (100% owned by HEP d.d). In the retail market, HEP holds 91% of the market, and HEP Generation is the largest electricity generation company with an 80% market share (HERA 2020). Incumbent oil and gas company INA, as well as Croatia LNG and Plinacro (gas transport company), has also a significant role.

The system of local and regional authorities in Croatia is characterized by a large number, i.e., 576, of local administrations. Most of the local administrations have less than 3.000 inhabitants and thus quite limited organizational, financial, and human capacities for formulating and implementing regional and local policies and providing services. Local and regional authorities (counties, cities, and municipalities) are in charge of planning their energy needs and energy supply in a manner that is coherent with the national energy development strategy and its implementation plan. Regional energy agencies were established by one or more counties in different legal forms. They develop and implement projects on different scales. For instance, the oldest regional energy agency in Croatia, Regional Energy Agency North-West Croatia (REGEA), was established in 2008 by four counties: City of Zagreb, Zagreb County, Karlovac County, and Krapina-Zagorje as public institutions. Istria County has established the Istrian Regional Energy Agency Labin as limited liability company. Several nongovernmental actors have contributed to energy transition and policy design. The nationwide most visible are Friends of Earth Croatia and DOOR, while a number of organizations are active on the local level.

Public institutions generally suffer from limited capacities (c.f. Security and Intelligence Agency 2014, 2019). Poor coordination and insufficient public policy formulation and implementation capacities harm the socioeconomic development of the Republic of Croatia as well as the exploitation of the full potential of EU funds (Government 2019, p. 39). The distribution of competencies is often vague, and institutions are established and abolished for political reasons. The Council Recommendations within the European Semester regularly stipulate the need to streamline institutional setup, increase institutional capacities, and fight corruption.

There have been several attempts to tackle coordination issues and establish a monitoring system, such as the establishment of CEI in 2012 (Zakon o centru za praćenje poslovanja energetskog sektora i investicija 2012a). Next, in 2014 the Government (2014) established a Committee for inter-sectoral coordination of policies and measures for mitigation and adaptation to climate change. This Committee has been in charge of monitoring and evaluation of the implementation and planning of climate change policies. The composition of the Committee and its activities were determined by government decision. The Committee consists of a Coordination Group (including representatives of various ministries) and two technical working groups: one on low-carbon development, and the other on adaptation to climate change. The members of the coordination group are appointed by the Government, while the members of the technical working groups by the line minister.

In 2017, general institutional framework for strategic planning was established by the Law on the System of Strategic Planning and Development Governance of the Republic of Croatia (2017). It consists of Parliament, Government, central state administration bodies, local and regional self-government units, Office of the Prime Minister of the Republic of Croatia, Coordination Body, coordinators for strategic planning of central state administration bodies, regional and local coordinators, and other public bodies. The coordination body is the Ministry for Regional Development and EU Funds. It is responsible for the coordination of large-scale strategic planning, regular reviews and adaption of planning, the establishment of necessary information systems and registries, organization of public participation, and enabling access to EU funding.

However, the system is not fully operational. Recent strategic documents (e.g., the Climate Change Adaptation Strategy, 2020 the Low Carbon Development Strategy, 2021) provide for the different coordination mechanisms.

Significant coordination challenges persist. The Energy strategy (2020) recognizes that: "In order to create the preconditions for achieving the ambitious goals set by this Strategy, it is necessary to increase the active coordination role of state institutions."

The current situation is characterized by a large number of institutions and actors, whose competencies and responsibilities are not clearly distributed, nor aligned with the capacity needed for implementation (administrative, organizational, and financial). Key planning documents are not harmonized and are sometimes conflicting. There is a lack of coherence between strategic and operational planning. Besides a lack of vertical cooperation, there is an evident lack of horizontal cooperation and coordination (e.g., cooperation between MESD and other line ministries). Regional and local self-government units lack capacities and are not sufficiently involved in policy creation and implementation. A systematic approach, such as reorganization of the territorial structure to reduce fragmentation, could contribute to strengthening local capacities and improve coordination.

Outcomes, Challenges, and Prospects of Energy Governance

The energy transition goals (Table 4) are formally adopted and anchored in European and international (mainly within the UNFCCC) obligations. Sequencing necessary investments require an effective balancing of various interests, problem-solving, and sector integration. Since accession to the EU in 2013, Croatia has gained the opportunity to actively participate in policy-making and the creation of European policies. This opportunity is not adequately exploited. Croatia has insufficient capacity to create policies at the EU, national, or local level. Competencies at various governance levels (central, regional, and local) are not clearly distributed and defined. Cooperation among various institutions and bodies is insufficient. Within the present system, institutions are highly unlikely to implement necessary reforms.

The general weakness of public administration in Croatia relates to organizational, administrative, and professional capacities, overlapping competencies and insufficiently effective coordination (Koprić 2018; Council of the EU 2019). Fulfillment of energy and climate goals requires improvements of the general governance system and tackling the following problems: a) a regulatory system that is inadequate or partially applied, b) an unfavorable investment climate, and c) problems with the judiciary and corruption.

The challenges of the public administration in Croatia are well known: The efficiency is low as well as the capacity to design and implement policies and projects (Council 2019; 2020). Country-specific recommendations within the European Semester regularly relate to efficiency and capacity of public administration, the improvement of corporate governance, the reduction of territorial and sectoral fragmentation, the modernization of strategic planning, or the need to improve vocational training and the labor market. Additionally, there is the need to improve investment-related policies on research and innovation, sustainable urban and railway transport systems, energy efficiency, and renewables and the related infrastructure, and to address regional disparities (Council 2019; 2020). Implementation of these recommendations is necessary for improved energy governance and successful energy transition.

Improved corporate governance in state-owned enterprises and intensification of the sale of such enterprises and nonproductive assets might help to deal with conflicting interests of the state (as policymaker as opposed to incumbent market participant) and balancing short- and long-term perspectives.

The issue of ownership and the role of the state in the market affects priorities and reform readiness. The state, by providing public service, enables affordable prices for customers on the domestic market. Energy industries consider opportunities to participate in profitable projects that enable further investments in research, energy procurement, and infrastructure development. In balancing these interests, the state generally has a short-term perspective. The market participants, due to the size of the necessary investments, need a long-term perspective. The decisions of the management are sometimes guided by political considerations that are not necessarily in the company's best interest. For example, investments in research and innovation, technology, and consumer support might help incumbent companies to increase potential profits in the long term. In the short term, these investments reduce profits and decrease revenues of the state budget, as the government decides on the share of profits that all state-owned companies have to pay into the state budget. In 2020, this share was 60%. The power company HEP contributed HRK 664.4 million (around EUR 88.6 million) to the budget.

Improving corporate governance in state-owned companies and strengthening their managerial independence from the Government could streamline business decisions.

The government often prioritizes short-term benefits over long-term interests. This increases conflict between formally adopted policy goals, which require investment and short-term policy considerations. Limiting the role of the state in the energy market could facilitate the harmonization of mutually opposed goals of energy policy and related policies. The state might be reluctant to implement reforms with negative impact on employment in incumbent energy companies, or on customers who would face higher prices.

Reduction of territorial fragmentation of the public administration and streamlining the functional distribution of competencies could enhance institutional stability. Improving regulatory framework, increasing predictability and reliability of the price-setting mechanisms, could reduce uncertainties and support investments.

Prevention and sanctioning of corruption would attract nonspeculative investments. Investors experience shortcomings regarding establishing and the day-to-day running of their business operations. There is room for rendering administrative procedures speedier, more transparent and effective, which is documented by Croatia's overall rankings in the World Bank's Doing Business 2020 edition (51st globally, behind most European Union countries) and for improving the overall quality and transparency of public governance (World Bank 2020; OECD 2019). Among the biggest corruption cases are those linked with the energy sector: privatization of national oil and gas company, and permitting in the case of wind park Krš Pađene. More transparent and speedier licensing and permitting procedures would contribute to corruption prevention. According to the Security and Intelligence Agency (2019), corruption and economic crime are recognized as issues hindering development and prosperity in Croatia. Not only does corruption in public administration, government institutions and authorities, and state-owned companies have an adverse social impact, but it also poses a significant threat to the economic development of the Republic of Croatia. It hinders the proper functioning of the market and economic growth, curtails public finances, and leads to state budget shortfalls. The same report identifies that major infrastructural projects, including EU-funded projects, are vulnerable to the risks of corruption, given the large financial amounts and complexity of projects (Security and Intelligence Agency 2019. p. 25).

Implementation of the new strategic planning system, together with the National Development Strategy, would facilitate goal setting and monitoring and surveillance of the achievements. An essential prerequisite for the assessment of energy transitions is the application of monitoring mechanisms. The national energy and climate plan only partially complies with data transparency requirements and the use of European statistics (European Commission 2020a). Until now, there are still differences between the national and Eurostat methodologies (e.g., regarding the share of renewables).

Reliable data is necessary for establishing the baseline and realistic targets. Currently, analytical basis and relevant data for energy transition are provided by MESD – which in 2018 absorbed bodies that collected environmental data and energy efficiency data. The Law on the System of Strategic Planning and Development Governance of the Republic of Croatia (2017) is intended to establish an information system that provides tools for the collection, analysis, and storage of data and indicators. These are necessary for the preparation of the strategic planning act as well as monitoring and surveillance of implementation. The system is not operational yet, so Croatia could benefit from considering the Council's recommendations.

Closer monitoring would also facilitate addressing challenges related to sector integration, but it exceeds the current capacities of relevant institutions in Croatia (primarily the Ministry of economy and sustainable development). For instance, social aspects of the energy transition are not adequately addressed. An increase in employment within the construction sector is expected due to planned investment, but the existing strategies and plans do not address the lack of skilled workers. In this respect, Croatia could benefit from implementing recommendations regarding education reform. Also, while measures to address energy poverty are planned, there are no quantitative estimates nor indicators to measure energy poverty.

In addition, Croatia has been facing challenges in the integration of intermittent renewables into the power system. Given the general weaknesses of institutions in Croatia, sector integration, including energy, transport, industrial processes, waste management, agriculture, land use, land-use change and forestry (LULUCF), and other (cross-cutting) policies and measures, represents a significant challenge. Interlinkages and interactions between specific measures are outlined in the NECP, though often in a rather general way. General weaknesses of public administration, together with specific energy and climate-related challenges, and the way they are addressed are likely to determine the pace and outcomes of energy transition in Croatia.

Cross-References

▶ Energy Democracy and Participation in Energy Transitions
▶ Energy Governance in Serbia
▶ Energy Governance in Slovenia
▶ Energy Policies in the EU: A Fiscal Federalism Perspective
▶ European Union Energy Policy: A Discourse Perspective
▶ Extending Energy Policy: The Challenge of Sector Integration
▶ Sustainable Europe: Narrative Potential in the EU's Political Communication

References

Agreement between the Government of the Republic of Croatia and the Government of the Republic of Slovenia on Regulation of Status and Other Legal Issues Regarding Investments in Krško NPP, and its Exploitation and Decommissioning (2002). Official Gazette – International agreements 9/02. Zagreb.

Balkanenergy. (2017). Six months peaceful settlement in TPP Gacko-HEP dispute Bosnia-Herzegovina. http://balkanenergy.com/six-months-peaceful-settlement-tpp-gacko-hep-dispute-bosnia-herzegovina-27-september-2017. Accessed 1 Mar 2021.

Boromisa, A. (2013). *Strateške odluke za energetsku budućnost Hrvatske*. Zagreb: Friedrich Ebert Stiftung.

Boromisa, A. (2020). *Tko će i kako provesti Europski zeleni plan*. Zagreb: Friedrich Ebert Stiftung.

Climate Change Adaptation Strategy of the Republic of Croatia. (2020). Official Gazette 46/20. Zagreb.

Council of the European Union. (2011, December 5). Council conclusions on enlargement and stabilisation and association process. In *3132nd General affairs council meeting Brussels*. https://www.consilium.europa.eu/uedocs/cms_data/docs/pressdata/EN/genaff/126577.pdf. Accessed 1 Mar 2021.

Covenant of Mayors. (2021). Covenant community. Signatories. https://www.covenantofmayors.eu/about/covenant-community/signatories.html

Čučković, N., Jurlin, K., & Vučković, V. (2011). Privatisation of public services sector in Croatia and SEE: Assessment of major gains and pains.

Državno odvjetništvo. (2021). Izvješće Glavnog državnog odvjetnika Republike Hrvatske o radu državnih odvjetništava u 2020. godini. Zagreb, travanj 2021. http://www.dorh.hr/dorh29042021#. Accessed 18 Jul 2021.

EBRD. (2013). *Stuck in transition? Transition report*. London: European Bank for Reconstruction and Development. https://www.ebrd.com/news/publications/transition-report/transition-report-2013.html. Accessed 31 Mar 2021.

EBRD. (2017). Life in transition. Survey III: A decade of measuring transition. European Bank for Reconstruction and Development. London. https://litsonline-ebrd.com/governance-in-the-transition-region/. Accessed 31 Mar 2021.

Electricity Market Law (OG 68/01) (2001), Official Gazette 68/01. Zagreb.

Energy Efficiency Law. (2014). Official Gazette 127/14. Zagreb.

23 Energy Governance in Croatia

Energy Efficiency Law. (2018). Official Gazette 1167/18. Zagreb.
Energy Efficiency Law. (2020). Official Gazette 25/204. Zagreb.
Energy Law. (2001). Official Gazette 68/01. Zagreb.
Energy Law. (2012). Official Gazette 120/12. Zagreb.
Energy Law. (2014). Official Gazette 14/14. Zagreb.
Energy Law. (2015a). Official gazette 102/15. Zagreb.
Energy Law. (2015b). Official Gazette 95/15. Zagreb.
Energy Law. (2018). Official Gazette 68/18. Zagreb.
Energy Strategy. (2002). Official Gazette 38/02. Zagreb.
Energy Strategy. (2009). Official Gazette 130/09. Zagreb.
Energy Strategy. (2020). Official Gazette 25/2020. Zagreb.
European Commission. (2007). Croatia 2007 progress report accompanying the Communication from the Commission to the European Parliament and the Council. Enlargement strategy and main challenges 2007–2008. {COM(2007) 663 final} Commission of the European Communities. Brussels, 6.11.2007, SEC(2007) 1431. https://ec.europa.eu/neighbourhood-enlargement/sites/near/files/pdf/key_documents/2007/nov/croatia_progress_reports_en.pdf. Accessed 1 Mar 2021.
European Commission. (2014). Standard Eurobarometer 82. https://data.europa.eu/euodp/en/data/dataset/S2041_82_3_STD82. Accessed 31 Mar 2021.
European Commission. (2016). Performance by member states. http://ec.europa.eu/internal_market/scoreboard/performance_by_member_state/croatia/index_en.htm. Accessed 28 Mar 2021.
European Commission. (2017). Special Eurobarometer 461. Designing Europe's future: Trust in institutions. Globalization. Support for the euro, opinions about free trade and solidarity.
European Commission. (2018). Commission suspends referral of CROATIA to the Court for failing to amend the law on the privatisation of the energy company INA-Industrija Nafte, d.d. (INA) https://ec.europa.eu/commission/presscorner/detail/en/IP_18_4489. Accessed 28 Mar 2021.
European Commission. (2020a). Commission staff working document assessment of the final national energy and climate plan of Croatia. Brussels, 14.10.2020 SWD(2020) 910 final CORRIGENDUM Brussels.
European Commission. (2020b). Single market scoreboard. Croatia. Croatia – Performance per Member State – The single market scoreboard - European Commission (europa.eu) https://ec.europa.eu/internal_market/scoreboard/performance_by_member_state/hr/index_en.htm. Accessed 28 Mar 2021.
European Commission. (2020c). Standard Eurobarometer 93. 2020. Public opinion in the EU. https://ec.europa.eu/commfrontoffice/publicopinion/index.cfm/Survey/getSurveyDetail/instruments/STANDARD/surveyKy/2262. Accessed 28 Mar 2021.
European Commission. (2021a). Winter 2021 Economic Forecast: A challenging winter, but light at the end of the tunnel. Economic forecast by country. Croatia. https://ec.europa.eu/economy_finance/forecasts/2021/winter/ecfin_forecast_winter_2021_hr_en.pdf. Accessed 28 Mar 2021.
European Commission. (2021b). Infringement decisions. https://ec.europa.eu/atwork/applying-eu-law/infringements-proceedings/infringement_decisions/. Accessed 28 March 2021.
European Commission. (2021c). Single market scoreboard. Croatia. https://ec.europa.eu/internal_market/scoreboard/performance_by_member_state/hr/index_en.htm". Accessed 31 Mar 2021.
Eurostat. (2021a). Share of fossil fuels in gross available energy. https://appsso.eurostat.ec.europa.eu/nui/show.do?dataset=nrg_ind_ffgae&lang=en. Accessed 31 Mar 2021.
Eurostat. (2021b). Energy intensity. Available from Eurostat - Data Explorer (europa.eu), https://appsso.eurostat.ec.europa.eu/nui/show.do?dataset=nrg_ind_ei&lang=en. Accessed 28 Mar 2021.
Eurostat. (2021c). Share of renewable energy in gross final energy consumption. https://ec.europa.eu/eurostat/databrowser/view/t2020_31/default/table?lang=en. Accessed 28 Mar 2021.
Gas Market Law (OG 68/01) (2001). Official Gazette 68/01. Zagreb.
Government of the Republic of Croatia. (2007, 2009, 2018). The Regulation on unit charges, corrective coefficients, and detailed criteria and benchmarks for determining the charge for emissions of carbon dioxide into the environment. Official Gazette 73/07, 48/09, 2/18, Zagreb.

Government of the Republic of Croatia. (2014). Odluka o osnivanju povjerenstva za međusektorsku koordinaciju za politiku i mjere za ublažavanje i prilagodbu klimatskim promjenama. Official Gazette 114/14. Zagreb.

Government of the Republic of Croatia. (2018). Zaključak. https://vlada.gov.hr/UserDocsImages//2016/Sjednice/2018/07%20srpanj/110%20sjednica%20VRH//110%20-%20%20%20%202.pdf. Accessed 28 Mar 2021.

Government of the Republic of Croatia. (2019). National reform program 2019. https://vlada.gov.hr/UserDocsImages/Vijesti/2019/04%20Travanj/30%20travnja/NRP%202019%20i%20Odluka%20Vlade/NRP%202019%20english/National%20reform%20programme%202019.pdf. Accessed 28 Mar 2021.

HEP. (2013, May 28). HEP i EBRD raskidaju ugovor o kreditu za HE Ombla. https://www.hep.hr/novosti/hep-i-ebrd-raskidaju-ugovor-o-kreditu-za-he-ombla/906. Accessed 28 Mar 2021.

HEP. (2021). History. Online. https://www.hep.hr/about-hep-group/history/2523. Accessed 28 Mar 2021.

HEP Privatization Law. (2002). Official Gazette 32/02. Zagreb.

HEP Privatization Law. (2010). Official Gazette 21/20. Zagreb.

HERA. (2017). Annual report 2016. https://www.hera.hr/en/docs/HERA_Annual_Report_2016.pdf. Accessed 28 Mar 2021.

HERA. (2020). HERA annual report for 2019. https://sabor.hr/sites/default/files/uploads/sabor/2020-08-25/155102/IZVJ_HERA_2019.pdf. Accessed 28 Mar 2021.

Hopkins, V. (2019, December 30). Former Croatian PM convicted of corruption in privatisation case. Financial Times. https://www.ft.com/content/caf797ec-2af2-11ea-bc77-65e4aa615551. Accessed 28 Mar 2021.

Hrvatska biskupska konferencija. (2005). Izjava o projektu Družba Adria. https://hbk.hr/izjava-o-projektu-druzba-adria/. Accessed 28 March 2021.

ICSID. (2015). International Centre for settlement of investment disputes. Washington, DC. Award in the matter between Hrvatska Elektroprivreda d.d.(Claimant) and Republic of Slovenia. (Respondent). (ICSID Case No. ARB/05/24). http://icsidfiles.worldbank.org/icsid/ICSIDBLOBS/OnlineAwards/C69/DC7132_En.pdf. Accessed 5 Mar 2021.

INA. (2021). History. https://www.ina.hr/en/home/about-ina/povijest/. Accessed 5 Mar 2021.

INA Privatization Law. (2002). Official Gazette 32/02. Zagreb.

INA Privatization Law. (2019). Official Gazette 21/19. Zagreb.

INEA. (2021). https://ec.europa.eu/inea/en/connecting-europe-facility/cef-energy/projects-by-country/croatia/6.5.1-0018-hr-w-m-16. Accessed 5 Mar 2021.

Jurincic, K. (2020). Wind Park affair. Euractiv. 2 June 2020. https://www.euractiv.com/section/all/short_news/zagreb-wind-park-affair/. Accessed 28 Mar 2021.

Koprić I. (2018). *Public administration characteristics and performance in EU28: Croatia*. Brussels: European Commission. https://op.europa.eu/en/publication-detail/-/publication/97f87f51-9608-11e8-8bc1-01aa75ed71a1/language-en. Accessed 31 Mar 2021.

Law on Regulation of Energy Activities. (2001). Official Gazette 68/01. Zagreb.

Law on the System of Strategic Planning and Development Governance of the Republic of Croatia. (2017). Official Gazette 123/17. Zagreb.

Long Term Renovation Strategy. (2020). Official Gazette 140/2020. Zagreb.

Low Carbon Development Strategy. (2021). Official Gazette 63/2021. Zagreb.

MINGOR. (2021). Policies and measures – Croatia. Ministry of Economy and Sustainable Development. https://mingor.gov.hr/UserDocsImages/UPRAVA%20ZA%20ENERGETIKU/Strategije,%20planovi%20i%20programi/hr%20necp/03_Policies%20and%20Measures%20-%20Croatia%20-%20draft.xlsx. Accessed 28 Mar 2021.

Ministry of Economy and Sustainable Development. (2019). Energy in Croatia. Government of Republic of Croatia. https://mingor.gov.hr/UserDocsImages/UPRAVA%20ZA%20ENERGETIKU/Energija_u_Hrvatskoj/Energija_u_Hrvatskoj_2019-2.pdf. Accessed 31 Mar 2021.

Ministry of Economy, Labour and Entrepreneurship. (2010). Energy in Croatia. Republic of Croatia. Zagreb. https://mingor.gov.hr/UserDocsImages/UPRAVA%20ZA% 20ENERGETIKU/Energija_u_Hrvatskoj/Energija%20u%20Hrvatskoj%202010.pdf. Accessed 31 Mar 2021.

Ministry of Environment and Energy. (2018). Seventh National Communication and Third Biennial Report of the Republic of Croatia under the United Nations Framework Convention on Climate Change (UNFCCC). 2671905483_Croatia-NC7-BR3-2-96481035_Croatia-NC7-BR3-2-7. NC i 3. BR_resubmission_IX_2018_0.pdf (unfccc.int). Accessed 28 March 2021.

Ministry of Environment and Energy. (2019). Integrated national energy and climate plan for the Republic of Croatia for the period 2021–2030. December 2019. Zagreb. https://mingor.gov.hr/ UserDocsImages/UPRAVA%20ZA%20ENERGETIKU/Strategije,%20planovi%20i%20pro grami/hr%20necp/Integrated%20Nacional%20Energy%20and%20Climate%20Plan%20for% 20the%20Republic%20of_Croatia.pdf. Accessed 31 Mar 2021.

MZOE. (2018). Godišnje izvješće o radu za 2017. godinu. Zagreb, svibanj 2018. http://www.mzoip. hr/doc/godisnje_izvjesce_o_radu_za_2017_godinu.pdf. Accessed 28 Mar 2021.

National Development Strategy. (2021). Official Gazette 13/2021. Zagreb.

National Portal for Energy Efficiency. (2021). Glavne institucije zadužene za energetsku politiku u Hrvatskoj. www.enu.hr. Accessed 31 Mar 2021.

Nelson, D., Zuckerman, J., Hervé-Mignucci, M., Goggins, A. S., & Sarah, J. (2014). Moving to a low-carbon economy. The financial impact of the low-carbon transition. Climate Policy Initiative.

OECD. (2019). OECD investment policy reviews: Croatia 2019. https://www.oecd.org/publications/ oecd-investment-policy-reviews-croatia-2019-2bf079ba-en.htm. Accessed 28 Mar 2021.

Oil and Oil Derivatives Law (OG 68/01) (2001). Official Gazette 68/01. Zagreb.

Partnerski sporazum. Online. https://razvoj.gov.hr/UserDocsImages//arhiva/EU%20fondovi/Pro grami%20prekogranicna%202014-2020//GLAVNI%20DOKUMENT_Sporazum_o_ partnerstvu_HR.pdf. Accessed 28 Mar 2021.

Plinacro. (2021). https://www.plinacro.hr/default.aspx?id=584. Accessed 28 Mar 2021.

Poslovni. (2008). Elektroprivreda RS tužit će HEP zbog Gacka. https://www.poslovni.hr/lifestyle/ elektroprivreda-rs-tuzit-ce-hep-zbog-gacka-71009. Accessed 28 Mar 2021.

Pučki pravobranitelj. (2015, March 31). Izvješće pučke pravobraniteljice za 2014. godinu. Zagreb. https://www.ombudsman.hr/hr/download/izvjesce-pucke-pravobraniteljice-za-2014-godinu/? wpdmdl=4739&refresh=6064ca55e497a1617218133 Accessed 28 March 2021.

Pučki pravobranitelj. (2016). Izvješće pučke pravobraniteljice za 2015. godinu (ombudsman.hr). https://www.ombudsman.hr/hr/download/izvjesce-pucke-pravobraniteljice-za-2016-godinu/? wpdmdl=4743&refresh=6064cb7b4916e1617218427. Accessed 28 Mar 2021.

Pučki pravobranitelj. (2017). Izvješće pučke pravobraniteljice za 2016. godinu (ombudsman.hr), Zagreb, ožujak 2017. https://www.ombudsman.hr/hr/download/izvjesce-pucke-pravobra niteljice-za-2016-godinu/?wpdmdl=4743&refresh=6064cd5bd1f5b1617218907. Accessed 28 Mar 2021.

Pučki pravobranitelj. (2018). Izvješće pučke pravobraniteljice za 2017. godinu (ombudsman.hr), Zagreb, ožujak 2018. https://www.ombudsman.hr/hr/download/izvjesce-pucke-pravobra niteljice-za-2017-godinu/?wpdmdl=4745&refresh=6064cc7b3aeff1617218683. Accessed 28 Mar 2021.

Pučki pravobranitelj. (2019). Izvješće pučke pravobraniteljice za 2018. godinu (ombudsman.hr), Zagreb, ožujak 2018. https://www.ombudsman.hr/hr/download/izvjesce-pucke-pravobraniteljice- za-2018-godinu/?wpdmdl=4747&refresh=6064ce5c6376e1617219164. Accessed 28 Mar 2021.

Pučki pravobranitelj. (2020). Izvješće pučke pravobraniteljice za 2019. godinu (ombudsman.hr), Zagreb, ožujak 2020. https://www.ombudsman.hr/hr/download/izvjesce-pucke-pravobra niteljice-za-2019-godinu/?wpdmdl=7580&refresh=6064ce11419271617219089. Accessed 28 Mar 2021.

Pučki pravobranitelj. (2021). Izvješće pučke pravobraniteljice za 2020. godinu (ombudsman.hr), Zagreb, veljača 2021. Accessed 28 March 2021.

Renewables and High Efficiency Co-generation Law. (2015). Official Gazette, 100/15. Zagreb.
Renewables and High Efficiency Co-generation Law. (2016). Official Gazette, 123/16, Zagreb.
Renewables and High Efficiency Co-generation Law. (2017). Official Gazette, 131/17. Zagreb.
Renewables and High Efficiency Co-generation Law. (2018). Official Gazette 111/18. Zagreb.
Security and Intelligence Agency. (2014). Public report 2014. https://www.soa.hr/files/file/Public-Report-2014.pdf. Accessed 28 Mar 2021.
Security and Intelligence Agency. (2019). Public report 2019/2020. https://www.soa.hr/files/file/Public-Report-2019.pdf. Accessed 28 Mar 2021.
Šimunović, L. (2018). Drže li se stranke svoje proklamirane ideologije: analiza predizbornih programa najznačajnijih političkih stranaka u RH. Diplomski rad. Sveučilište u Zagrebu. Filozofski fakultet Odsjek za sociologiju. Zagreb. http://darhiv.ffzg.unizg.hr/id/eprint/11189/1/Diplomski%20rad_Luka%20%C5%A0imunovi%C4%87.pdf. Accessed 28 Mar 2021.
Šoštarić, E. (2008). Rat Za Hrvatske Elektrane: Srbi duguju RH 40 teravatsati struje. Nacional, br. 643, 2008-03-10.
Sušec, Đ. (2003). HEP vratio status. HEP Vjesnik, Zagreb. https://www.hep.hr/UserDocsImages//dokumenti/vjesnik/2003//146.pdf
Sušec, Đ. (2015). Ostvarene nade. HEP Vijesnik 283. Zagreb. https://www.hep.hr/UserDocsImages//dokumenti/vjesnik/2015//283.pdf
Transparency International. (2020). Corruption perception index. https://www.transparency.org/en/cpi/2020/table/nzl. Accessed 31 Mar 2021.
US Department of State. (2019). 019 Investment climate statements: Croatia – United States Department of State.
Vuk, Ministarstvo gospodarstva i održivog razvoja Republike Hrvatske – Energija u Hrvatskoj (gov.hr).
Vuk, B., & Šimurina, I. (2009). Energija u Hrvatskoj 1945–2007. Energetski institut Hrvoje Požar, Zagreb. https://mingor.gov.hr/UserDocsImages/UPRAVA%20ZA%20ENERGETIKU/Energija_u_Hrvatskoj/Energija%20u%20Hrvatskoj%20od%20%201945-2007.pdf
Vuk, B., Vukman, S., Karan, M., Fabek, R., Živković, S., et al. (2009). Energy in Croatia 2009. https://mingor.gov.hr/UserDocsImages/UPRAVA%20ZA%20ENERGETIKU/Energija_u_Hrvatskoj/Energija%20u%20Hrvatskoj%202009.pdf. Accessed 31 Mar 2021.
WEF. (2020, May). Fostering effective energy transition 2020 edition, Geneva. http://www3.weforum.org/docs/WEF_Fostering_Effective_Energy_Transition_2020_Edition.pdf. Accessed 31 Mar 2021.
World Bank. (2020). *Doing business. Comparing business regulation in 190 economies 2020*. Washington, DC: The World Bank. http://documents1.worldbank.org/curated/en/688761571934946384/pdf/Doing-Business-2020-Comparing-Business-Regulation-in-190-Economies.pdf. Accessed 31 Mar 2021.
Zakon o centru za praćenje poslovanja energetskog sektora i investicija. (2012a). Official Gazette 25/12. Zagreb.
Zakon o centru za praćenje poslovanja energetskog sektora i investicija. (2012b). Official Gazette 120/12. Zagreb.
Zakon o centru za praćenje poslovanja energetskog sektora i investicija. (2018). Official Gazette 46/18. Zagreb.
Zelena akcija. (2005, November). Public participation in Croatian environmental impact assessment procedures. Issue No. 2. http://s3-eu-west-1.amazonaws.com/zelena-akcija.production/zelena_akcija/document_translations/400/doc_files/original/casestudyEIAen.pdf?1270310019. Accessed 31 Mar 2021.
Zelena akcija. (2013). EBRD potvrdio odustajanje od HE Ombla. https://zelena-akcija.hr/hr/programi/zastita_prirodnih_resursa/ebrd_potvrdio_odustajanje_od_he_ombla. Accessed 31 Mar 2021.

Energy Governance in the Czech Republic   24

Jan Osička, Veronika Zapletalová, Filip Černoch, and Tomáš Vlček

Contents

Introduction	564
General Conditions of Energy Governance in the Czech Republic	565
Past Legacies	565
Composition of the "Energy Mix"	567
Discourse on Energy Issues	568
Institutions and Actors	570
Coordination, Instruments, and Issues of the Czech Energy Transition	572
Drivers of Energy Transition and Long-Term Strategies	572
Strategies and Instruments of Energy Transitions	575
Coordination Mechanisms and Multilevel Governance	581
Outcomes, Challenges, and Prospects for Energy Governance	583
Cross-References	586
References	586

Abstract

Unlike many of its fellow EU member states, the Czech Republic's vision for its energy future does not include transition to renewable energy. Instead, it embraces the goal of (partial) decarbonization that is to be achieved via technologically neutral tools. Technological neutrality is an important concept for the Czech energy decision-makers since it allows for the pursuit of their preferred decarbonization strategy: further expansion of nuclear energy. Seen from a general perspective, the country's approach towards energy governance has been shaped by the its industrial and engineering tradition, deeply internalized liberalization paradigm, and recently acquired mistrust towards large-scale

J. Osička (✉) · V. Zapletalová · F. Černoch · T. Vlček
Center for Energy Studies, Masaryk University, Brno, Czech Republic
e-mail: osicka@mail.muni.cz; zapletalova@mail.muni.cz; cernoch@mail.muni.cz; tomas.vlcek@mail.muni.cz

© Springer Nature Switzerland AG 2022
M. Knodt, J. Kemmerzell (eds.), *Handbook of Energy Governance in Europe*,
https://doi.org/10.1007/978-3-030-43250-8_6

deployment of renewable energy sources – all of which are driving forces that would be difficult to overcome should a transition towards renewable energy ever take place in the Czech Republic.

The country's energy strategy can be described as an inward-looking, status quo policy. It endeavors to preserve the existing energy system that the decision-makers consider stable, predictable, and secure and that best reflects their preference of an energy-only market on which domestic sources such as coal and domestically sourced engineering solutions such as nuclear compete with one another to deliver reliable and affordable energy to the nation. This strategy is now eroding, mostly as the result of external factors, such as the increased emphasis on environmental sustainability in the European energy policy, rapid development in renewable energy technology, and extensive deployment thereof in neighboring Germany. Altogether, these factors have shaken the established market arrangements and, in turn, traditional energy policy principles. Hence, the future shape of the Czech energy landscape will emerge from the clash between energy transition-promoting external pressures and pro-status quo domestic actors who currently dominate the country's energy politics.

Keywords

Energy governance · Czech Republic · Energy Policy · Energy transition · Institutions · Energy industry · Nuclear energy · Energiewende · Climate skepticism

Introduction

Proud engineering tradition, deeply internalized liberalization paradigm, small decision-making community, ambiguous relations with Russia, powerful corporations and climate skepticism are the main factors to shape the Czech energy governance. This chapter shows how these factors entangle and drive the overall energy strategy of the country as well as the daily routine in the realm of decision-making.

The main result is highly conservative, status quo-oriented energy policy. The most important political and market actors alike prefer large-scale, centralized solutions developed hand in hand with domestic industries. These solutions are viewed as cost-efficient means to achieve what matters the most in energy politics: security and stability of energy supply – terms that are often considered interchangeable with energy self-sufficiency and the use of the proven energy technologies such as coal and nuclear energy.

Competing energy strategies, such as those attempting to improve the industry's environmental footprint, are often viewed as inferior, mostly for relying on technology that is considered inferior (such as renewable energy sources), increasing the country's dependence on international trade with energy or energy technologies, or simply for being proposed by actors who follow different interests, such as environmental NGOs or renewable energy interest groups.

The dominance of the status quo policies has eroded recently, mainly as a consequence of external pressures. They include technological change, which has made renewable energy a more viable alternative to the existing solutions, European energy policy, which strongly promotes renewable energy, and German energy policy, which spills over to the Czech Republic through various channels and makes it increasingly difficult to build the country's energy strategy on nuclear energy.

The results of the ongoing clash between the external pressures and the relatively solidified domestic political and industrial front will be relevant not only for the energy politics in the country itself, but they can also inform our understanding of the concepts of energy transition and energy sovereignty.

General Conditions of Energy Governance in the Czech Republic

Past Legacies

The legacies of the Czech energy system that continue to affect the country's energy policies concern the historical development of the industry, the role of the state in the energy industry, the influence of German energy policy over the regional market, and the structure and culture of the decision-making community.

With regards to historical development, the country's energy industry has been built on biomass, water streams, and coal. Since the 1860s, coal was developed at a rapid pace and by 1895 its production surpassed that of biomass. (Kuskova et al. 2008) The growth in coal production and consumption continued until the start of World War I and another wave of growth in coal production began after World War II. Within four decades, coal production grew fivefold, reaching a yearly production level of 36 million tons of hard coal and 96 million tons of brown coal in the mid-1980s. (Kuskova et al. 2008; Vlček and Černoch 2012, p. 105) Such dynamics were mostly associated with the ever-growing needs of heavy industry, which has traditionally dominated the country's economy. Another reason was the centrally planned stimulation of both coal consumption and production, which stemmed from the high social status coal workers enjoyed during the socialist regime and from the social contract between them and the government. The decline in coal use, which started already in the late 1980s, was significantly accelerated after the fall of the socialist regime. The new government sought to restructure the industry by liberalizing prices, ending state subsidies for industrial operations and privatizing the mines (Pavlínek 2005). It also sought a new approach towards communities inhabiting the mining regions. While until 1989 more than 100 municipalities had been obliterated to expose coal deposits (Glassheim 2007), in 1991 the new government established the "territorial environmental limits on mining," which have, in a legally binding manner, defined the areas where open-pit mining is allowed and where it is not. Ever since, mining coal beyond the limits has been a recurring political question, motivated by social concerns about the cost of centrally supplied heat to households and due to energy dependence concerns (Rečka and Ščasný 2016).

Other traditional energy industries either directly emerged from or were significantly formed by the political, economic, and military ties to the Soviet Union. The Union covered the country's demand for oil and gas, and at the same time both parties closely cooperated on the development of nuclear energy. In the former Czechoslovakia, the nuclear industry was driven by the country's tradition in uranium mining (see, for example, Sivek et al. 2012a) and advanced technological know-how that made the country capable of manufacturing most of its first nuclear plant's components (Jirušek et al. 2015, pp. 116–123; Štubňa et al. 2002). The energy trade with the Soviet Union has therefore effectively shaped the oil, gas, and nuclear industries, including related physical networks, trade arrangements, and governing institutions. The asymmetrical interdependence in energy trade between the country and the Soviet Union/Russia emerged as a major political challenge after the end of the Cold War. Despite successful diversification of both sources and supply routes of oil, gas, and nuclear fuel, many legacies of the past arrangements such as the current long-term natural gas contract remain in place and energy cooperation with Russia continues to be treated as a (geo)politically laden agenda (Jirušek et al. 2015).

Finally, the development of modern renewable energy sources, which was accelerated in 2005 through legislation establishing financial support for renewable energy (Parliament of the Czech Republic 2005), has triggered major controversies that continue to shape the country's energy policy and the related discourse (see section "Discourse on Energy Issues"). In the case of solar energy, the financial incentives introduced by the legal act were set in a manner that did not anticipate the sharp drop in prices of photovoltaic technology in 2010 (Sivek et al. 2012b). One of the results of this policy – a massive rent-seeking response from ad hoc established companies and affluent individuals, including some actively serving politicians and shady characters – has significantly damaged the image of renewable energy in the eyes of the public, contributed to the demise of the Green Party after the 2010 parliamentary elections, and made any policies supporting renewable energy more difficult to establish (Denková 2017b).

As regards the state's role in the industry, its dominant position eroded significantly after the transition to a market economy in the early 1990s. All major state-owned coal, oil, and gas companies, with exception of oil and oil product transportation networks and the "strategically important" electric utility ČEZ, were restructured and completely privatized (Vlček and Černoch 2013). Furthermore, by rigorously adopting the EU's liberalization packages, the country has replaced direct control of the energy industry with indirect oversight and regulation. The state, however, remains very active in ensuring self-sufficiency in electricity production as well as in further development of nuclear power. The former has ranked among the top energy priorities for all Czech governments since the breakup of Czechoslovakia in 1993, while the latter has been the energy source of choice for all past governments, including the one that served between 2006 and 2009 and featured the Greens. Since it has become increasingly difficult to build nuclear power plants without state aid, however, the preference for nuclear energy has begun to clash with the free market paradigm rooted in the energy decision-making culture.

The role of the state in the energy industry has been further challenged by advancing regional market integration. Ties to Germany are especially important in this sense, as high cross-border transmission capacity and high market liquidity allow for nearly 100% price convergence between the two markets (Grossi et al. 2015; Málek et al. 2018). Given their relative sizes, it is clearly the German market which sets the price for the whole region. As a result, Czech decision-makers are left simply to create rules for market participants whose investment decisions are shaped by prices set in Germany as determined by the German market and Germany's energy policy.

Finally, as is common in the CEE region, the Czech energy policy has traditionally been decided upon by a closed community of technicians and (later) economists with very little public discussion about energy issues. At the same time, the central institutions chronically lack personnel and financial resources. Such circumstance regularly forces state officials to seek expertise among market participants, especially the company ČEZ. Altogether, this results in a rather inward-looking, centralized, and technocratic form of decision-making; strong preference for status quo energy policy; a chronic "revolving door" problem (Luechinger and Moser 2014); and periodic manifestations of groupthink (Janis 1972).

Composition of the "Energy Mix"

Since the end of the Cold War, the break-up of Czechoslovakia and the consequent establishment of the Czech Republic in 1993, the country's energy supply has become more diversified. The share of coal declined from 63.4% (in 1993) to 38.5% (2015), while the shares of other sources increased: oil by 3.6 percentage points, gas by 4.4, biofuels and waste by 6.7, and nuclear energy by 12.6 (International Energy Agency 2016).

The structure of electricity generation has not changed considerably since 1993. Coal remains the backbone of electricity supply (see Table 1). Despite the fact that its share in overall production has decreased from 75.8% to 54%, the absolute amount of electricity generated in coal power plants has remained stable. The growth in

Table 1 Energy mix in the Czech Republic (2015)

Fuel	Share on TPES (%)	Share on electricity generation (%)
Coal	39.2	54.0
Oil	20.8	0.1
Nuclear	17.2	32.5
Natural gas	15.9	2.7
Biofuels and waste	8.6	6.3
Solar	0.5	2.7
Wind	0.1	0.7
Hydro	0.2	1

Source: International Energy Agency 2016

demand for electricity and considerable rise in exports (12.5 TWh in 2015, 16.8 TWh per year on average between 2012 and 2014) have been covered by the increase in production in nuclear power plants and in recent years also by renewable energy (Czech Statistical Office 2012; International Energy Agency 2016).

Discourse on Energy Issues

Two discourses on energy policy seem to be relevant in the Czech Republic: media and public discourse and political discourse (Van Dijk 1997). With regards to the political discourse, the main topics that shape its content are energy self-sufficiency, renewable energy, and German energy policy.

Energy self-sufficiency is widely praised by virtually all streams of the discourse. Traceable back to the socialist era when autarky ranked among the core political principles, the concept remained rooted in the decision-making culture even after the end of the Cold War. In the second half of the 2000s, when Russia repeatedly cut off energy supplies to Central and Eastern Europe, it came back to the fore and now nearly all energy policy actors would agree that reliance on imported energy is a direct threat to energy security. This perception mainly concerns electricity and natural gas and persists despite the country having an electricity market deeply integrated with the one in Germany (see section "German Energy Policy") and despite its gas supply being diversified to the extent that it was not affected by the 2006 and 2009 gas crises at all (Jirušek and Kuchyňková 2018) and scores by far the highest in the EU according to the N-1 criterion of security of natural gas supply (European Commission 2014b). Notably, given the importance of energy self-sufficiency in the country's energy discourse, arguments warning against "dependency on Russia" are often used to advocate particular interests in energy politics, typically to promote the use of domestic sources.

The debate on renewable energy seems to have two poles. On the one hand, the negative experience with over-subsidizing solar energy and rather conservative approach towards developing the country's energy system embraced by the leading decision-making institution, the Ministry of Trade and Industry, result in an emphasis on the problems associated with transitions to renewable energy. The key issue being discussed is the integration of renewable energy sources to the transmission system and to the existing market design, while the benefits of renewable energy are superficially acknowledged at best. Renewable energy sources are portrayed as "useful, but (only) under specific circumstances," or "promising, but once the technical issues are solved and business models developed." Furthermore, decarbonization based on renewable energy has long been regarded as "antiarithmetic" (see MacKay 2009), "emotional," or even "ideological" (as opposed to nuclear energy which is "pro-arithmetic," "rational," and definitely "nonideological"). On the other hand, even the most skeptical voices in the debate acknowledge that there are renewable energy targets that the country needs to meet and that small-scale generation facilities such as rooftop solar systems will eventually cut a substantial portion of demand for grid-based electricity supplies. Furthermore, factors such as the difficulties in finding a financing model for new nuclear units, rapid development in renewable energy technologies and their progressive rehabilitation in the eyes of the public, as well as the ongoing generational change at key institutions have all contributed to pro-RES voices being taken more seriously.

Finally, at least since 2011, when the nuclear phase-out decision was made and when large-scale deployment of RES started to affect the regional electricity market, German energy policy has become another important topic in the Czech political discourse. The predominantly negative perception of the government-led diffusion of renewable energy, together with remarkably positive attitudes towards nuclear energy, has contributed to an overall negative portrayal of German energy policy in this discourse. Apart from the common points of criticism of the *Energiewende* project, such as the rise in end-user electricity prices and mediocre achievements with regards to emission targets, the Czech political discourse also focuses on wind energy-induced loop flows that destabilize the transmission networks of Germany's neighbors and the collapse of wholesale prices in the region, which compromises the expected return on investment of the planned nuclear units (see section "German Energy Policy"). Interestingly, the fact that the price collapse means that German electricity consumers, who alone carry the financial burden of the *Energiewende* which contributed to it, effectively subsidize the electricity price for Czech consumers has been completely missing from the discourse.

The media and public discourse on energy is shaped by the fact that people are generally not interested in energy policy. In fact, according to a 2017 poll by the Czech Academy of Science, 33% of respondents claim to be "not at all interested" and 42% "rather uninterested," while only 20% and 4% of respondents regard themselves as "rather interested" or "very interested," respectively (CVVM 2017). As a consequence, the mainstream media are not incentivized to cover energy-related topics in depth and only the major issues such as coal mining beyond the territorial ecological limits or expansion of nuclear power are discussed in a more elaborate manner. In other instances, the role of the media is reduced to reporting the context and content of the major energy policy decisions taken by the policy-makers, with little ambition to stimulate public discussion. Consequently, it is the decision-makers who most shape the mainstream media discourse on energy. The media discourse thus echoes the political discourse and adopts its highly conservative nature, emphasizing domestic sources, domestically sourced engineering solutions, and status quo policies and showing distrust towards potential systemic changes.

The limited interest among the general population in energy policy and the limited coverage thereof in the mainstream media mean that energy issues are largely absent from the public discourse. It appears that energy is not something people talk about when discussing politics and only the most important and/or controversial energy policy issues, such as mining coal beyond the territorial ecological limits, building more nuclear reactors, and subsidizing renewable energy, make it into the public discourse. Public attitudes towards these issues are summarized in Table 2.

Notably, the respondents who consider themselves interested in energy policy and who may consequently act as opinion leaders in shaping the public discourse are, in comparison with the general population, more inclined towards perceiving nuclear

Table 2 Attitudes of the Czech public towards major energy policy issues (2017)

Energy policy issue/attitude	++	+	–	—	?
Domestic coal power plants should be modernized and kept in business for as long as possible	11	34	28	9	18
Coal mining beyond the territorial ecological limits should be allowed	4	23	29	17	27
Nuclear fission is an environmentally sound source of energy	13	39	23	10	15
Renewable energy sources should be subsidized using public money	25	43	16	5	11

Source: CVVM 2017
Note: ++ ... strongly agree, + ... agree, – ... disagree, — ... strongly disagree, ? ... do not know

power as an environmentally sound source of energy and towards modernizing domestic coal power plants and keeping them online for as long as possible. On the other hand, they tend more strongly to oppose the ideas of mining coal beyond the limits and subsidizing renewable energy sources using public money (CVVM 2017). The opinions held by the interested public thus seem to echo the storylines prevalent in the political and media discourses: emphasis on domestic sources, positive attitude towards nuclear energy, and reluctance to subsidize renewable energy.

Institutions and Actors

The Czech energy landscape is shaped mostly by ministries, independent state authorities, large energy corporations, and interest groups. The ministry directly in charge of energy is the Ministry of Trade and Industry, which designs and implements national energy policy, ensures that the country meets its obligations arising from its international agreements and treaties, holds a 100% share in the country's sole electrical grid operator ČEPS, and is ultimately responsible for the security of supply of all energy commodities. The Ministry of Environment seeks to minimize the impact of energy consumption and promote rational energy supply and use and sustainable development (International Energy Agency 2016, p. 22). The Ministry of Finance exercises the state's shareholders' rights in energy companies (co-)owned by the state: the electric utility ČEZ, oil pipeline operator MERO, and ČEPRO, a company operating oil products pipelines and storages (Ministry of Finance 2017).

Other important administrative bodies include the Energy Regulatory Office, which supervises energy markets, awards licenses to aspiring market participants, and determines the levels of regulated prices and energy subsidies (ERO 2018); the State Office for Nuclear Safety, which is responsible for supervision of the use of nuclear energy and for radiation protection; the State Environmental Fund of the Czech Republic, which redistributes financial resources obtained from the EU or collected from polluters among projects that improve the environment; and state-owned companies that facilitate daily operations at energy markets: ČEPS, OTE – the electricity and gas market operator, MERO and ČEPRO.

Table 3 ČEZ and EPH indicators (2016)

	Installed capacity	Electricity supply	Heat supply	EBITDA
ČEZ	15.6 GW	61.1 TWh	24.0 PJ	€2.3bn
EPH	24.4 GW	108.7 TWh	22.7 PJ	€1.7bn

Sources: ČEZ 2016; EPH 2018

Due to their financial resources, personal ties, and expertise often unmatched by that of the state institutions, major energy companies have rather strong influence on Czech energy politics. There are multiple foreign energy corporations active in the country (e.g., E.ON, RWE/Innogy, Dalkia, PKN Orlen, and Shell), but the most influential are the domestic actors: namely, ČEZ and EPH (see Table 3 for the companies' market indicators).

ČEZ ranks among the ten largest energy companies in Europe, both in terms of installed capacity and number of customers. Domestically, it operates 2 nuclear power plants, 11 coal-fired power plants, 35 hydropower plants (including 3 pumped storage plants), 2 locations with wind power plants, 12 solar power plants, and 1 biogas station, which altogether generate nearly 75% of the country's electricity (ČEZ 2018a). The company's shares are owned mostly by the Czech state (nearly 70%); various legal entities, mostly banks and funds (nearly 20%); and private investors (over 10%) (ČEZ 2018b). Since its consolidation in 2003 it has become clear that being a rather large company in a rather small country makes it unusually powerful, even by the standards of former monopolies such as EDF in France (The Economist 2010), and much has been written about ČEZ actively influencing Czech politics (The Economist 2010; Bursík 2013; Zatloukal 2014). Another indication of this could be the fact that ČEZ is the only utility to have its Wikipedia entry feature a chapter titled "Influence on Politics" (Wikipedia 2018).

The company EPH was established in 2009 by the PPF and J&T financial groups as a platform for investment in energy projects. In recent years, its ownership has been consolidated by Daniel Křetínský (the company's chairman and originally a 20% shareholder), who has successfully bought out both groups and now owns 94% of shares. The core of the company's activities lies abroad, mostly in the UK, Germany, Italy, Slovakia, and Hungary, where it provides ancillary services, operates energy networks, and produces electricity and heat. In the Czech Republic, the company is the largest supplier of heat and the second largest producer of electricity. (Vobořil 2015) Within Czech energy politics, EPH may be less visible than ČEZ but, according to insiders, is no less influential. The company's most renowned influencer is Mirek Topolánek, the former Prime Minister and 2018 presidential candidate, who chairs the board of Slovak gas TSO Eustream (49% owned by EPH), the supervisory board of the Czech power plant Opatovice (fully owned by EPH), and the executive board of the Czech Association for the District Heating, an interest group in which EPH plays the most prominent role.

Interest groups, especially those representing traditional energy and engineering industries (e.g., Confederation of Industry, Association for the District Heating, Employers' Association of Mining and Oil Industries, or Mining Union), also enjoy a rather strong position in the country's energy politics. The position of renewable energy interest groups, on the other hand, remains weak, and so too that of environmental NGOs such as Greenpeace, Duha and Calla, which, despite being active at the state level, tend to be more influential at the local level (see "Coordination Mechanisms and Multilevel Governance").

Coordination, Instruments, and Issues of the Czech Energy Transition

Drivers of Energy Transition and Long-Term Strategies

Energy transition, in the sense of intentional, articulated, and managed replacement of the traditional sources of energy supply with renewable energy, is not part of the current Czech energy strategy, which sets out the country's energy policy up to 2040. By that time, the share of renewable energy in electricity production is expected to increase modestly from 10.7% in 2015 to 18–25% in 2040, while the traditional sources (particularly nuclear, but also coal and gas) shall constitute the core of the electricity generation portfolio (see Table 4).

Thus, instead of energy transition, the country seeks (partial) decarbonization in conjunction with further expansion of nuclear energy. Nuclear power is widely praised for being more compatible with the current energy system than are renewable sources and less burdensome for the country's balance of payment. Since the share of the costs of (imported) fuel in total energy costs is very low, nuclear power plants are seen as contributing positively to the country's economic sovereignty (provided the investment costs are not covered via foreign loans) (Krpec and Hodulák 2014; Ramberg 1984, p. 156). Finally, new nuclear units are generally seen as contributing to a revival of the country's fading nuclear energy engineering and bringing qualified jobs to the unemployment-prone regions where the nuclear energy sites are located. Hence, achieving emission targets via expansion of nuclear energy is advocated by politicians, influential interest groups eager to participate in the construction of the new units, as well as the public, which is generally very pro-nuclear (Osička and Černoch 2017).

In sharp contrast to nuclear energy, the expansion of renewable energy has been lacking significant domestic drivers. For the country's executive agencies, the "sustainability" dimension of the energy policy trilemma is generally the least

Table 4 Electricity generation mix in 2015 and the mix envisaged for 2040

Fuel	2015 (%)	2040 (%)
Nuclear fuel	32.5	46–58
Renewable and secondary sources	10.7	18–25
Natural gas	2.7	5–15
Brown and black coal	54.0	11–21

Sources: International Energy Agency 2016, p. 75; Ministry of Industry and Trade 2015c, p. 46

important one, whereas the interests of the established energy and engineering industries, which often use energy security and affordability arguments to push their agenda, often take precedence over environment concerns. Voices representing domestic renewable energy industries are too fragmented to be systematically relevant in the political process (see III.1.1.3). Finally, there is little public demand for such transition. While nearly 70% of Czechs agree that renewable energy should be subsidized (CVVM 2017), only 16% are willing to pay much higher prices (or 21% in the case of taxes) to protect the environment (ISSP Research Group 2012). Thus, out of the 34 countries included in the ISSP research the Czech Republic is among the 5 nations least willing to pay in terms of prices and among the 10 least willing in terms of taxes. Furthermore, Czech society remains highly skeptical about human-induced climate change: just 66% of Czechs would agree that climate change is caused by use of coal, oil, or gas, thus ranking the country 19 out of 19 according to the ISSP study. Consequently, policies supporting renewable energy have been triggered nearly exclusively by external influences, namely, the climate and energy policies of the EU and the spill-over of Germany's *Energiewende*.

European Energy Policy

The Czech Republic joined the EU in May 2004, with the accession process significantly spurring the decarbonization of the country's economy. Both the Accession Treaty and State Energy Policy of 2004 adhered to Directive 2001/77/EC (European Commission 2001a), the pivotal EU legislation in incentivizing RES development in member states at that time. The State Energy Policy called for concerted measures to achieve the pledge of an 8% share of renewable electricity in gross national consumption in the Czech Republic by 2010 (Ministry of Industry and Trade 2004). As a result, Act No. 180/2005 was adopted, strengthening the already existing feed-in tariffs and introducing feed-in premium schemes to boost renewable investments in the country via a predictable subsidy framework (see sections "Past Legacies" and "Strategies and Instruments of Energy Transitions"). In the very same accession process, however, the Czech Republic negotiated a transition period until 31 December 2017 on implementation of Directive 2001/80/ES on the limitation of emissions of certain air pollutants from large combustion plants (European Commission 2001b).

In the following years, the EU renewable energy requirements and targets became increasingly embedded in the Czech energy regulatory framework. The State Environmental Policy of the Czech Republic for the years 2004–2010 and for the years 2011–2020, the National Program to Abate Climate Change Impacts of 2007, the Climate Protection Policy, and the State Energy Policy Updates of 2010 and 2015 all reflected (albeit sometimes hesitantly) the EU consensus regarding the deployment of renewable energy and energy efficiency measures.

As a direct reaction to the EU Biofuels Directive 2003/30/EC (European Commission 2003), the Long-term Strategy for the Use of Biofuels in the Czech Republic was prepared in 2006, providing detailed information about the situation in the country (Ministry of Industry and Trade 2006a). This analysis was followed by the National Program on Energy Management and Use of Renewable Energy

Sources 2006–2009, which set indicative targets of a 5.6% share of biofuels in transportation by 2009 and 10% by 2020 (Ministry of Industry and Trade 2006b). In 2007, an act was passed which set biofuel quotas in a legally binding manner (Parliament of the Czech Republic 2007). After 2014, when Directive 2014/94/EU (European Commission 2014a) came into force, the alternative fuels-promoting National Action Plan for Clean Mobility was prepared (see section "Strategies and Instruments of Energy Transitions") (Ministry of Industry and Trade 2015a).

Directive 2009/28/EC set targets for the Czech Republic of a 13% share of RES in final energy consumption and 10% share of RES in the transport sector by 2020 (European Commission 2009). In response to this Directive, the National Action Plan for Energy from Renewable Sources 2010 was issued, introducing the target of a 13.5% share of renewable energy in gross final energy consumption and 10.8% in transportation. This plan was updated in 2012 and 2016, with the last version updating the targets to 15.3% and 10%, respectively. Based on these plans, specific measures were introduced (see section "Strategies and Instruments of Energy Transitions").

The development of energy efficiency policies has also been stimulated by EU legislation. The efficiency directives 2006/32/EC (on energy end-use efficiency and energy services) and 2012/27/EU (on energy efficiency) obliged member states to prepare national energy efficiency plans and update them regularly (European Commission 2006, 2012), which the Czech Ministry of Industry and Trade did in 2007, 2011, 2014, 2016, and 2017 (Ministry of Industry and Trade 2007, 2011, 2014, 2016a, 2017). The most recent thereof set a target of 51.10 PJ in new energy savings by 2020 and a total cumulative energy saving of 204.39 PJ for the period 2012–2020 (Ministry of Industry and Trade 2017, p. 21). Measures for achieving these targets are introduced in section "Strategies and Instruments of Energy Transitions."

German Energy Policy

With Germany's *Energiewende* ranking among the most comprehensive and ambitious transitions towards renewable energy to date (Quitzow et al. 2016), neighboring Czech Republic is exposed to various influences arising from the changing energy landscape in Germany. Some of them are intense enough to affect the way Czech energy policy is officially intended to develop.

With rapid deployment of renewable energy sources, electricity production in Germany is changing in two ways. First, due to the merit order effect, subsidized RES contribute to a decreasing wholesale price of electricity (Dillig et al. 2016). Second, since the majority of new RES installations are not dispatchable, the volatility of the electricity price is expected gradually to increase (Ballester and Furió 2015; Rintamäki et al. 2017). Since the German and Czech energy markets are integrated to the extent that their price levels fully converge (Grossi et al. 2015; Málek et al. 2018), the German price signals are directly transferred to the Czech Republic.

The impact on the investment climate in the country is noticeable. In recent years, companies and various governmental bodies have repeatedly voiced their concerns about low electricity prices preventing any new investments, except when subsidized (Beneš 2016; Bumba and Čihák 2015; OTE 2018). The sole conventional source built in the last decade, the 2013-commissioned 840 MW CCGT Počerady, confirms this low price conundrum, exhibiting a load factor of 0.25 in 2016 (ČEZ 2017; ERO 2017). Consequently, no company is signaling any plans to invest in conventional sources in the foreseeable future (OTE 2018). Unappealing wholesale electricity prices are also the main reason why the country's energy policy flagship – the expansion of nuclear energy – has not been moving forward as planned (see also section "Outcomes, Challenges and Prospects for Energy Governance.")

Price volatility is also becoming an issue. So far price fluctuations have been muted by the region's generation overcapacity (ACER/CEER 2017). As soon as this situation changes, however, the regional supply system, dominated by non-dispatchable renewable sources, will favor conventional sources with high generation output flexibility. It is expected that such sources will be able to capitalize on price peaks caused by gaps in renewable production and limit losses incurred during periods of negative prices (Alizadeh et al. 2016; Fanone et al. 2013; Kondziella and Bruckner 2016; Lund et al. 2015). As a result, Czech electricity producers will be exposed to a completely new set of price signals. The main beneficiaries will be owners of flexible gas and coal plants and innovative technological solutions, such as demand response and energy storage (Lund et al. 2015). The clear losers will be the operators of base-load sources that require high load factors, in particular nuclear power plants (Cany et al. 2017; Lykidi and Gourdel 2017).

Notably, an ideological spill-over has been considerably less present. Initially, the *Energiewende* was viewed as "emotional," "impulsive," and even "self-destructive" by Czech energy industry insiders, who emphasized the high costs of deployment of RES and their negative impact on regional grid stability (Burket 2014; ČEPS 2012; Lukáč 2014). As it has become clear that the *Energiewende* is here to stay, Czech actors have become more interested in what is actually going on in Germany and how it may affect the Czech energy market. These issues have become widely discussed at conferences (EGÚ Brno 2015; EurActiv.cz 2016) and within executive institutions (Ministry of Industry and Trade 2015e, 2015f; The Office of the Government 2015), and Czech–German experience sharing channels have been opened (Ministry of Foreign Affairs 2014). Nevertheless, the prevailing opinion about the *Energiewende* is critical and voices emphasizing its (potential) benefits to the Czech Republic remain scarce (see also section "Discourse on Energy Issues").

Strategies and Instruments of Energy Transitions

At a general level, the objectives of strengthening the role of renewables (in the field of electricity generation, heat production and transport) and improving energy efficiency are outlined in the State Energy Policy Update of 2015 (Ministry of Industry and Trade 2015c) and developed in more detail in the form of issue-specific national action plans which a system of specific implementing regulations subsequently builds on (see Fig. 1).

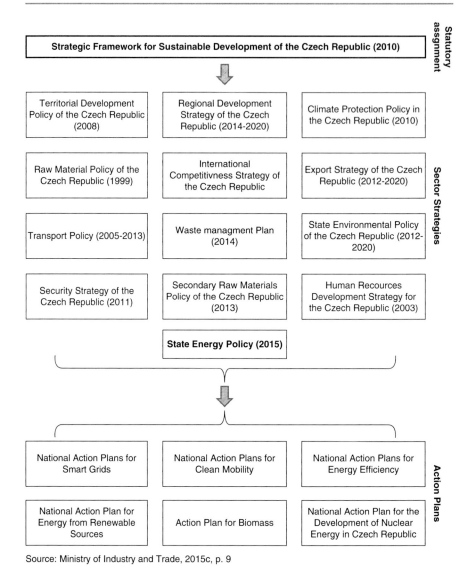

Fig. 1 The Czech Republic's strategic and conceptual energy policy documents. (Source: Ministry of Industry and Trade 2015c, p. 9)

An overview of energy transition instruments in place is presented in Table 5.

Electricity Supply

The gradual shift from coal to nuclear and renewable energy anticipates a reduction in carbon dioxide emissions from combustion processes by 38% in the period 2010–2040 (Ministry of Industry and Trade 2015c, p. 144). A gradual decline in electricity production from coal is expected as a consequence of stricter

Table 5 Key energy transition policy instruments by sector and type in the Czech Republic

	Regulatory instruments	Investment support — EU structural funds	National programs	Operational support	Tax releases	Soft governance
Electricity supply	Priority connection to the grid; Integrated Pollution Prevention and Control; EU ETS	Operational Program Enterprise and Innovation for Competitiveness; Operational Program Environment; Operational Program Rural Development	EFEKT Program; New Green Savings Program	Feed-in tariff; Feed-in premium	Tax depreciation; Exemption from property tax	Energy Consultation and Information Centers
Heat supply	Integrated Pollution Prevention and Control; EU ETS			Feed-in premium		
Energy Efficiency	X	Operational Program Enterprise and Innovation for Competitiveness; Operational Program Environment; The Integrated Regional Operational Program; Operational Program Prague – Growth Pole of the Czech Republic	EFEKT Program; ENERG Program; PANEL 2013+ Program; Nov8 ENERG Program	X	X	
Transport	Biofuels quota	Operational Program Entrepreneurship and Innovation for Competitiveness; Operational Program Transport II; The Integrated Regional Operational Program	National Environment Program	X	Exemption from excise tax; Exemption from road tax	Memorandum of cooperation between stakeholders

Source: authors

environmental standards for power station equipment (the aim of which is to reduce pollution within the framework of so-called Integrated Pollution Prevention and Control) and the EU Emission Trading System (Ministry of Environment 2017). These operations can thus expect to face decreasing profitability, leading to their gradual closure (oenergetice.cz 2017). The issue of taxing emissions outside of the EU ETS scheme by introducing new tools in the form of a carbon tax is currently the subject of negotiations between the state administration (Ministry of Industry and Trade, Ministry of the Environment) and private sector (Denková 2017a).

The Czech government has also endeavored to foster renewable energy production. Dating back to 2002, the original vision was based in particular on the decision to guarantee return on investment for producers of renewable energy for the lifespan of their equipment (EurActiv.com 2010). Such policy was expected to be achieved mainly using regulatory tools in combination with operational support. The system allowed for two options. The first was a feed-in tariff, provision of which was guaranteed for a period of 20 years with a year-on-year reduction of the redemption price by at most 5%. At the same time, the government guaranteed purchase of the produced electricity via regulation. The second option was a feed-in premium (so-called "green bonus"), which was fixed for only one year but, much like the tariff, could not be reduced by more than 5% annually. Producers of renewable energy plants received the premium in an annual mode on top of the regular market price of electricity. Producers generating renewable electricity to cover their own consumption only were also entitled to the payment of a bonus (Parliament of the Czech Republic 2005).

The sharp drop in prices of photovoltaic technology led to a massive increase in installed capacity of solar power plants in the Czech Republic (from 3.4 to 1,959.1 MW between 2007 and 2010) and to a corresponding increase in the costs of the respective subsidies (ERO 2015; Sivek et al. 2012b). In a rather heavy-handed reaction adopted in an atmosphere of negative public discussion, the government effectively halted all support for newly connected solar plants and cut into the profits of existing plants through a series of tax reforms.

As of 2018, support is being awarded almost exclusively to small-scale sources (including households). Producers also have the option of taking advantage of tax depreciation (applicable only to renewable installations with capacity up to 30 kW) and are partially exempt from property tax (amounting to EUR 0.2 per m^2 and applicable to some 9% of installations) (European Commission 2016, pp. 6–10). After the current financial framework of the EU and the current form of the relevant operational programs come to an end in 2020, it is anticipated that these tools will be completely reformed, including the introduction of auction mechanisms intended to revive the deployment of renewable energy (Denková 2017b).

In the field of soft governance, the Czech government has over the long term mainly concentrated on an awareness campaign. Together with an information service for applicants for investment support, this is performed by a network of regional Energy Consultation and Information Centers (Ministry of Industry and Trade 2016b). These centers are grant-funded by the government, and in addition to electricity production from renewable sources they also focus on consultancy in the field of energy efficiency and alternative heat supply.

Heat Supply

Fuel-switching and efficiency measures are the key pathways to reducing the carbon intensity of heat supply. The supply of heat is expected to decrease from approximately 100 PJ in 2010 to approximately 80 PJ in 2040 (Ministry of Industry and Trade 2015c, p. 144). The portfolio of policy instruments used in the heating sector basically copies that of electricity supply. The most notable difference is that the government did not stop the operational support for production of heat from renewable sources after 2010. The support can even be drawn by highly effective equipment for combined production of heat and electricity from nonrenewable sources.

Energy Efficiency

The National Action Plan focused on increasing energy efficiency was formulated in 2007. Since then, it has been updated four times (2011, 2014, 2016, and 2017), in particular as a reaction to EU directives 2006/32/EC and 2012/27/EU (European Commission 2006, 2012) and to the 2015 update of the State Energy Policy. The savings target set forth by the most recent action plan from 2017 is to achieve 51.10 PJ of new energy savings (i.e., a total cumulative energy saving of 204.39 PJ) for the period 2012–2020 (Ministry of Industry and Trade 2017, p. 21).

Domestically funded energy efficiency programs include the EFEKT and PANEL 2013+ programs, which have been in place in different variations since the 1990s. EFEKT focuses on projects performed mainly in the public sector, while PANEL 2013+ concentrates on renovation of apartment blocks (Ministry of Industry and Trade 2017, p. 112). These are complemented by the ENERG program, which incentivizes savings by small and medium-sized entrepreneurs within the territory of the City of Prague. Finally, the New Green Savings program uses financial resources obtained from trading in emission allowances to finance efficiency measures in single-family houses and apartment blocks (Ministry of Environment 2017, pp. 51–52).

As regards EU-funded programs, the Czech Republic, in accordance with EU Directive 2012/27/EU (European Commission 2012), opted for the alternative scheme for achieving the 2020 targets. The government focuses on financing schemes and instruments, as well as training and education, including energy consultancy programs. Thus, almost all measures outlined in the National Energy Efficiency Action Plan utilize financing instruments (mostly direct subsidies) targeted at all types of recipients (households, public administration, and the private sector) to incentivize savings. There are two broad categories of programs according to the source of financing. Operational programs come under the EU structural funds and should ensure savings of roughly 21.68 PJ, while national grant programs are of a smaller scope and aim to ensure support at a level of 11.48 PJ (Ministry of Industry and Trade 2017, p. 76).

So far, the country has faced significant difficulties in absorbing the EU funds and redistributing them among meaningful projects. The demand for efficiency subsidies among target entities as well as the state authorities' ability to prepare, run, and evaluate grant calls now seem to be highly overestimated. The grant scheme of the operational programs copies the EU budgetary period, spanning from 2014 to 2020, but the first calls were not opened until the end of 2015, by which time the EU operational programs should already have been significantly contributing to the 12.1 PJ of new savings envisaged in the 2014 National Action Plan for the 2014–2015 period (Ministry of Industry and Trade 2014, p. 13). The government plans to mitigate the risk of missing the 2020 targets (Supreme Audit Office 2016, pp. 31–32) by increasing the share of the highly absorptive industrial sector in overall energy savings, by speeding up project administration (Denková 2015), and apparently also by creative energy accounting. Unlike its predecessors, the 2017 National Action Plan update newly features the "Strategic Framework for Sustainable Development in the Czech Republic" tool, which refers to a rather general official document outlining the strategy for sustainable development until 2030 (Government of the Czech Republic 2011). Interestingly, despite not being known before 2017, the tool is reported to have achieved 10.6 PJ of savings between 2014 and 2016 and is further expected to achieve another 5.2 PJ of savings by 2020. According to industry insiders, the tool reports increases in energy efficiency that can hardly be regarded as achievements of energy efficiency policies, such as unrelated closures of energy intensive factories and changes in consumer behavior.

Transport

As in the case of electricity and heat production, the country's system of reducing the carbon intensity of the transportation sector has been largely shaped by EU legislation, in particular directives 2003/30/EC, 2009/28/EC, and 2014/94/EU. (European Commission 2003, 2009, 2014a) The system was originally built on regulation and tax allowances for biofuels. In 2007, legislation was passed for the gradual increase in the share of biofuels in conventional fuels up to 3.5% in the case of gasoline and 4.5% in the case of diesel starting from 1 September 2009 (Parliament of the Czech Republic 2007). These quotas were raised to 4.1% and 6%, respectively, in 2015, and a reduction in excise taxes has also been guaranteed until 2020 on so-called high-content biofuels, i.e., biodiesel and bioethanol (Ministry of Agriculture 2014, p. 10).

In response to Directive 2014/94/EU (European Commission 2014a), the Czech government has begun employing other emission reduction tools. Specifically, the government intends to increase the current number of electric cars and plug-in hybrids on Czech roads, of which there were approximately 500 in 2015, to 250,000 by 2030 (Ministry of Industry and Trade 2015b, p. 33). At the same, the share of natural gas in energy used in transportation is envisaged to increase to 10%, corresponding with an increase in the total number of CNG and LNG vehicles to 250,000 and 1,300, respectively (Ministry of Industry and Trade 2015b, pp. 87, 89).

The government plans to achieve these targets primarily via investment support targeted at infrastructure, in particular in the form of the establishment of charging stations (Operational Program Transport II); replacement of technology in public transport (Integrated Regional Operational Program); and actual purchase of electric cars and other equipment (Operational Program Entrepreneurship and Innovation for

Competitiveness and the National Environment Program). The majority of support is for investment into electric cars and plug-in hybrids (approx. 80%), with the target entities being mostly small-scale entrepreneurs and municipalities (Ministry of Environment 2017, pp. 61–62). A complementary tool for supporting alternative fuels takes the form of tax exemptions, whereby alternative fuels are given a preferential standing by means of a significant reduction in excise taxes (e.g., excise on CNG was almost ten times lower than the excise on gasoline in 2018) and the owners of these vehicles are exempt from road tax (Customs Administration of the Czech Republic 2011).

In the case of soft governance, partnership between the government (Ministry of Environment), interest groups (e.g., the Automotive Industry Association), and large corporations such as ČEZ has been reinforced on the basis of memoranda. The partnership focuses mostly on the further popularization of alternative fuels and transport mostly through publications and public lectures (Ministry of Industry and Trade 2017).

Coordination Mechanisms and Multilevel Governance

Following on from four decades of a command economy, postrevolution Czech Republic inherited a highly centralized, hierarchical system of energy governance, with the pivotal position occupied by the Ministry of Industry and Trade (Vlček and Černoch 2013, Chap. 1). Since then, new actors and political alliances have emerged in reaction to EU membership and participation on the common energy market, effectively increasing the complexity of the country's energy politics.

In 2001 the Energy Regulatory Office was established. Having been granted considerable competences, it grew quickly to become a significant counterweight to the Ministry. During the controversial presidency of Alena Vitásková from 2011 to 2017, multiple severe clashes emerged between the two institutions, with the Ministry struggling to enforce its authority over the sector (Dolejší 2016). In 2017, in a far-reaching attempt to limit the volatility of the Office, the government amended the Energy Act (Parliament of the Czech Republic 2000) and replaced the one-person presidency leadership structure with a collective board of five politically nominated directors.

EU membership also emphasized the relationship between energy and environmental and climate issues, thereby gradually strengthening the position of the Ministry of Environment. Especially in the period 2006–2009, during which time the government featured the Green Party and which culminated with the Czech Presidency of the EU Council, the Ministry gained a much stronger voice over the country's energy policy. Climate protection also became more relevant institutionally, as a dedicated ministerial section and a deputy minister position for climate and air protection were established. These changes enabled the Ministry to act as an equal partner to the Deputy Minister for Energy at the Ministry of Industry and Trade in drafting policies that concerned both energy and climate issues. This trend, however, came to an end and, in fact, reversed in 2010, when then Minister of

Environment, Rút Bízková, abolished both the dedicated section and the deputy minister position (Bízková 2010). Bízková, who previously served as a spokesperson for ČEZ's coal power plants (Government of the Czech Republic 2010), was also the first in a series of questionable picks for the position. Her successors, Pavel Drobil and Tomáš Chalupa, were widely criticized for placing the interests of industry before those of the environment. Drobil became famous for his quote "I will breathe for Czech industry" (Procházková 2010), while Chalupa, who once recommended to the municipalities suffering from severe particular matter pollution to "sweep their streets more often" (Ministry of Environment 2011), "attempted to strip the green ideology away from the Ministry" (Šůra 2012). Since 2014, however, when the former CEO of chemical company Lovochemie, Richard Brabec, became Minister, the Ministry has appeared to gradually refocus on the environmental agenda. With the preparation of the National Energy and Climate Plan (European Commission 2017), its influence on the country's energy policy can be expected to increase.

Notably, the regional element of energy governance is very limited in the Czech Republic. Regional and municipal councils do not take part in energy decision-making on a systemic basis. Limited by procedural obstacles and a lack of personnel and financial resources, their participation is chronically reactive. It typically involves opposition pressures against major energy facilities such as open-pit mines, waste incineration plants, or radioactive waste geological repositories (Ďurďovič et al. 2014; Frantál 2016; Frantál and Malý 2017).

NGOs and pro-renewable energy interest groups can be seen as moderately relevant at best. Both are active at the state level, where both participate in ad hoc (renewable) energy-relevant working groups established by the Ministry of Industry and Trade. Also, both use targeted lobbying and achieve moderate successes in amending bills during the legislative process to better reflect the interests of the renewables sector. On the other hand, both lack the resources and political backing that would allow them to substantially influence core energy policies and both are nearly powerless when the interests they promote clash with those of large corporate actors. Furthermore, the aggregation of interests in the renewables sector has not been very successful. The leadership of the renewable energy-promoting associations has been divided by personal disputes and largely fragmented. For example, three associations representing the solar industry now coexist in the country.

In sharp contrast to environmental NGOs and status quo-challenging actors, large energy corporations and interest groups representing the traditional energy industries tend to be very influential. Their expertise, resources, and political backing often enable them to practically dominate the regulatory impact assessment processes for new regulations and policies. They also exert much stronger lobbying pressures than do renewable industries, and, as it is often the case in energy politics, the ties between them and the state authorities are fostered by the revolving door phenomena (for an account from the European environment, see for example Cann 2015). While the literature suggests that the appointment of former politicians and civil servants to corporations and vice versa affects markets (Luechinger and Moser 2014), in the Czech Republic it is not uncommon for individuals to cross that line multiple times.

For example, Pavel Šolc, the former Deputy at the Ministry of Trade and Industry who was mainly responsible for the 2015 State Energy Policy Update, had worked for ČEZ and ČEPS before joining the Ministry in 2012. In 2016, he resigned and joined ČEZ's distribution company (Hospodářské noviny 2016).

Outcomes, Challenges, and Prospects for Energy Governance

The outlook for Czech energy governance will likely be determined by two main challenges that dominate the contemporary Czech energy landscape: the issue of building new nuclear units and the structure and culture of the energy policy-making. The first challenge constitutes a substantive problem associated primarily with the energy supply portfolio but, in a wider context, also with the question of political sovereignty over domestic energy policy in times when national markets are deeply integrated and national policies governing them diverge. The second challenge is more of a structural problem associated with who gets to make decisions on the country's energy policies and how these decisions are made. As such, this challenge is closely related to questions of energy democracy and justice.

With regards to the new nuclear units, the preparatory processes originally envisaged to commence in 2015 (Ministry of Industry and Trade 2015b) are behind schedule. The main issue – establishing a financing model – has not yet been resolved. There are essentially three models identified by the Ministry, and each has at least one significant downside.

If the "vendor financing" model (Barkatullah and Ahmad 2017) is selected, the government would need to accept a politically highly questionable multibillion loan from either Russia or China, likely the only vendors capable of delivering both the technology and financial resources. While Russian financing seems to be out of the question after the 2014 Russian aggression towards Ukraine, the politically more acceptable Chinese option (Turcsanyi 2017) is further hindered by the fact that the Chinese reactor design has not yet been licensed in Europe. The "Generic Design Assessment" process of the HPR-1000 model unit envisaged for the UK started only in early 2017 and is expected to be completed in 2022 (GNS 2018).

The model in which the nuclear units are financed by a private consortium is, given the unfavorable market outlook, unlikely to materialize without some form of state aid, such as the contract-for-difference support scheme used in the UK (Ministry of Industry and Trade 2015b). However, after the painful experience with overly generous financial support to renewable energy, it would be difficult to find political support for such a policy.

Finally, financing the units using domestic resources would entail no-less significant challenges. From the government's perspective, the preferred option is for ČEZ to finance the units itself. Despite the company having enough resources to do so, the minority shareholders have been very clear in rejecting this idea. They simply do not see the new units as a reasonable investment in the current market environment. Hence, the proposal of ČEZ financing the project forces the company's management to choose between following its legal duty to care and fulfilling the expectations of the company's main shareholder. The National Action Plan for Development of Nuclear Energy assumes that this conflict can be overcome by adopting the contract-for-difference financing tool, which would satisfy the minority shareholders but still necessitate significant financial as well as political capital. Another solution appears to be to establish a special purpose company owned by the state, which would benefit from a lower cost of capital (WACC 4–6%) and avoid a clash with the other shareholders. On the other hand, such model would again require public money to be invested and, due to its obvious interference with market competition rules, approval by the European Commission. Finally, the Action Plan is very open about the risk of significant cost overrun due to the limited experience of the existing state institutions in dealing with investment projects like this (Ministry of Industry and Trade 2015b).

The relevance of this issue's further development stretches beyond the question of the appropriate financing model. At a very practical level, the country representatives have not yet formulated any alternate plan to the expansion of nuclear power. The State Energy Policy Update of 2015 only briefly states that if the state institutions fail to facilitate the nuclear option a similar capacity will likely be installed in natural gas (Ministry of Industry and Trade 2015d, p. 35), effectively compromising the country's decarbonization efforts. The future of nuclear energy in the country will also be relevant for the nuclear industry as a whole. Given the Czech sociopolitical environment remains very favorable for its further development, at a time when there are just a few units under construction in Europe (World Nuclear Association 2018) failure to build the envisaged units would certainly undermine nuclear's future prospects in this region (Osička and Černoch 2017). Finally, watching this issue unfold will also be interesting from an energy sovereignty perspective (Kuzemko 2014; McGowan 2008; Padgett 2011). Its development will put the ability of the Czech Republic to resist economic and regulatory pressures coming from abroad to trial and thus reveal the practical limits of EU member states' right to determine their own energy policies.

As regards the structure and culture of energy decision-making, it is notable that throughout recent years the approaches towards energy policy of both relevant Ministries (and to a certain extent also that of the Energy Regulatory Office) seem to be converging. They all appear to embrace the conservative pro-industry approach towards energy policy promoted by the Ministry of Industry and Trade. Such development can be partially attributed to the ongoing energy transition, which increases uncertainty and thus incentivizes the decision-makers to prefer status quo policies. These are viewed as promoting the "much needed stability" of the existing energy systems and the corresponding legal and regulatory frameworks. Another reason seems to be the fast pace of changes introduced at the European level, which claims significant share of the institutions' personnel capacities. The limited personnel resources that remain available are insufficient not only for designing and implementing more ambitious energy policies but every so often also for day-to-day administration. Such circumstance has several far-reaching consequences: First, public officials regularly seek expertise among established market participants, i.e., status quo actors by definition, which further reinforces the conservative and pro-industry nature of the adopted policies. Second, in such an environment it is generally easier for large corporate actors, whose financial and personnel resources are unmatched by those of state institutions, to enforce their particular interests. Third, the close relations between the ministries, regulator, and corporate actors create a positive feedback with the already severe revolving door problem. Fourth, it is generally more difficult for newcomers from non-traditional industries (e.g., renewable energy) to establish themselves in the country's energy landscape. This is due to the status quo actors, whom they are challenging, being stronger than they would be without such influence on the decision-making process. Also, there is not enough demand for non-status quo solutions among the decision-makers. Fifth, the consolidation and domination of the conservative stream in Czech energy politics hinders the emergence of energy transition niches (Geels 2002), which reifies the exogenous and threatening image of the non-status quo industries. The fear of rapid decentralization and subsequent collapse of the centralized electricity supply, which echoes the experience that some regions had with the supply of water or heat, is a frequently used theme in this context.

The recent case of setting the rules for providing ancillary services using battery storage technologies is a telling illustration of the presented line of reasoning. While in Germany and elsewhere in Europe batteries with compliant state-of-charge characteristics are being licensed to provide ancillary services without additional conditions (EUROBAT 2016), thereby allowing small entrepreneurs to participate in the regulation energy business, in its 2018 amendment to the Grid Code Czech TSO ČEPS conditioned the use of batteries with their direct connection to turbo generators with rated power of at least 10 MW (ČEPS 2018). This condition alone prevents the emergence of new market actors such as operators of large battery systems or aggregators of prosumers' available storage capacities, effectively protecting the monopoly of ČEZ and EPH-owned electricity and heat plants over the €220 million ancillary services business (ČEPS 2017, p. 207).

The emphasis on conservative solutions combined with the substantial influence of status quo corporate actors, facing rather weak status quo challengers, creates a self-reinforcing regime that would be difficult to change should a transition towards renewable energy ever take place in the Czech Republic. For the Czech energy landscape, this means that benefits will continue to be distributed mainly among the status quo corporate actors, with citizens participating mostly as consumers and seldom also as prosumers. On the one hand, they may benefit from the absence of energy price spikes that would eventually accompany an environmentally more ambitious energy strategy. On the other hand, they may still face increased energy bills or reduced public services as a result of the financial support the new nuclear units may require. Furthermore, similar to their participation in energy policy-making, citizens and small companies may find opportunities to participate in the development of new segments of the energy industry limited as these would likely be captured by large corporate actors, thus hindering the improvement of energy democracy and justice (Jenkins and McCauley 2015; Sovacool and Blyth 2015; Szulecki 2017) in the country.

Cross-References

▶ Energy Governance in Germany
▶ Energy Governance in Russia: From a Fossil to a Green Giant?
▶ Energy Governance in Slovakia
▶ Energy Governance in the United Kingdom
▶ Energy Relations in the EU Eastern Partnership

References

ACER/CEER. (2017). ACER/CEER annual report on the results of monitoring the internal electricity and gas markets in 2016 electricity wholesale markets volume.

Alizadeh, M. I., Parsa Moghaddam, M., Amjady, N., Siano, P., & Sheikh-El-Eslami, M. K. (2016). Flexibility in future power systems with high renewable penetration: A review. *Renewable and Sustainable Energy Reviews, 57*, 1186–1193. https://doi.org/10.1016/J.RSER.2015.12.200.

Ballester, C., & Furió, D. (2015). Effects of renewables on the stylized facts of electricity prices. *Renewable and Sustainable Energy Reviews, 52*, 1596–1609. https://doi.org/10.1016/j.rser.2015.07.168.

Barkatullah, N., & Ahmad, A. (2017). Current status and emerging trends in financing nuclear power projects. *Energy Strategy Reviews, 18*, 127–140. https://doi.org/10.1016/J.ESR.2017.09.015.

Beneš, D. (2016, March 18). Cena elektřiny padá. Je s podivem, že jsme vůbec v zisku, říká šéf ČEZ Daniel Beneš (interview). *Hospodářské Noviny*. Retrieved from https://archiv.ihned.cz/c1-65212520-dost-se-nadreme

Bízková, R. (2010, April 20). Ozvěny dne 20. dubna 2010 (interview). *Radiožurnál*. Retrieved from http://www.rozhlas.cz/radiozurnal/publicistika/_zprava/723218

Bumba, J., & Čihák, O. (2015). Málo obnovitelných zdrojů, skladování energie i decentralizace, kritizuje vládní energetickou koncepci expert. Retrieved from http://www.rozhlas.cz/plus/ranniplus/_zprava/malo-obnovitelnych-zdroju-skladovani-energie-i-decentralizace-kritizuje-vladni-energetickou-koncepci-expert%2D%2D1491697

Burket, D. (2014, January 14). Zelená revoluce se mění na uhelnou. *Právo*.

Bursík, M. (2013). So there's no critical discourse about energy-related topics (interview). Heinrich Böll Stiftung. Retrieved from https://www.boell.de/en/2013/04/25/so-theres-no-critical-discourse-about-energy-related-topics

Cann, V. (2015, December 7). A heady climate for Brussels' revolving door policy. *EurActiv.Com*. Retrieved from https://www.euractiv.com/section/climate-environment/opinion/a-heady-climate-for-brussels-revolving-door-policy/

Cany, C., Mansilla, C., da Costa, P., & Mathonnière, G. (2017). Adapting the French nuclear fleet to integrate variable renewable energies via the production of hydrogen: Towards massive production of low carbon hydrogen? *International Journal of Hydrogen Energy, 42*(19), 13339–13356. https://doi.org/10.1016/j.ijhydene.2017.01.146.

ČEPS. (2012). Unscheduled power flows across the Czech transmission system. Retrieved from https://www.ceps.cz/en/press-releases/news/unscheduled-power-flows-across-the-czech-transmission-system

ČEPS. (2017). ČEPS, a.s. 2016 annual report. Retrieved from https://www.ceps.cz/en/annual-reports-2

ČEPS. (2018). Kodex přenosové soustavy: Část II. Podpůrné služby (PpS) – Revize 18 XX 2018. Retrieved from https://www.eru.cz/documents/10540/462808/Kodex+PS_revize+ČástII.pdf/134e5ac7-6cd6-4ceb-9054-5476a9d03840

ČEZ. (2016). ČEZ group annual report 2016. Retrieved from https://www.cez.cz/edee/content/file/investori/vz-2016/vz-2016-en.pdf

ČEZ. (2017). CEZ group: The leader in power markets of central and Southeastern Europe. Retrieved from https://www.cez.cz/edee/content/file/investori/2017-05-equity-investors.pdf

ČEZ. (2018a). ČEZ group introduction. Retrieved 4 April 2018, from https://www.cez.cz/en/cez-group/cez-group.html

ČEZ. (2018b). Structure of shareholders. Retrieved 4 April 2018, from https://www.cez.cz/en/cez-group/cez/structure-of-shareholders.html

Customs Administration of the Czech Republic. (2011). Informace ke zdanění zemního plynu (použitého pro pohon motorů) jeho konečným spotřebitelem (provozovatelem plnicího zařízení stlačeného zemního plynu – CNG). Retrieved from http://www.celnisprava.cz/cz/dane/ekologicke-dane/Stranky/default.aspx

CVVM. (2017). Veřejnost o energetické politice a budoucnosti výroby elektrické energie. Czech Academy of Sciences. Retrieved from https://cvvm.soc.cas.cz/media/com_form2content/documents/c2/a4398/f9/oe170818a.pdf

Czech Statistical Office. (2012). Historická ročenka statistiky energetiky. Retrieved 16 November 2017, from https://www.czso.cz/csu/czso/historicka-rocenka-statistiky-energetiky-2012-1cnxjg29ai

Denková, A. (2015, November 5). Česko dohání skluz ve zvyšování energetické účinnosti, má zpoždění dva roky. Retrieved from http://euractiv.cz/clanky/energeticka-ucinnost/cesko-dohani-skluz-ve-zvysovani-energeticke-ucinnosti-ma-zpozdeni-dva-roky-012984/

Denková, A. (2017a, April 18). Emise CO2 v Evropě klesají, problémy ale dělá uhlí nebo doprava. *EurActiv.Cz*. Retrieved from http://euractiv.cz/clanky/klima-a-zivotni-prostredi/emise-co2-v-evrope-klesaji-problemy-ale-dela-uhli-nebo-doprava/

Denková, A. (2017b, September 1). Pre-election Prague says solar power too expensive. *Euractiv*. Retrieved from https://www.euractiv.com/section/energy-environment/news/pre-election-prague-says-solar-power-too-expensive/

Dillig, M., Jung, M., & Karl, J. (2016). The impact of renewables on electricity prices in Germany – An estimation based on historic spot prices in the years 2011–2013. *Renewable and Sustainable Energy Reviews, 57*, 7–15. https://doi.org/10.1016/J.RSER.2015.12.003.

Dolejší, V. (2016, February). Žena, která naštve každého. *Hospodářské Noviny*. (p. 2). Retrieved from https://archiv.ihned.cz/c1-65181460-zena-ktera-nastve-kazdeho-vsichni-tlaci-na-jeji-odchod-ona-presto-zustava

Ďurďovič, M., Vajdová, Z., & Bernardyová, K. (2014). Rozhodování o hlubinném úložišti jaderného odpadu v České republice. *Naše Společnost, 12*(2), 3–14.

EGÚ Brno. (2015, December). Energetika 2015 – Vize, mýty a realita. Retrieved from https://www.egubrno.cz/wp-content/uploads/2016/03/TZ_konferenceEGU2015.pdf

EPH. (2018). Performance indicators. Retrieved from https://www.epholding.cz/en/

ERO. (2015). Yearly report on the operation of the Czech electricity grid 2014. Retrieved from https://www.eru.cz/documents/10540/462820/Annual_report_electricity_2014.pdf/f23d80b5-668a-42c0-9d04-1a19556c9c58

ERO. (2017). Národní zpráva Energetického regulačního úřadu o elektroenergetice a plynárenství v České republice za rok 2016. Retrieved from https://www.eru.cz/documents/10540/462958/NZ_ERU_2016/d5ed924a-f8b8-42c2-b47b-cd71d43dc1b7

ERO. (2018). About ERO.

EurActiv.com. (2010, February 26). EU accession 'boosted' Czech green business. Retrieved from https://www.euractiv.com/section/central-europe/news/eu-accession-boosted-czech-green-business/

EurActiv.cz. (2016). 16. energetický kongres ČR: Transformace energetiky II. *EurActiv.Cz*. Retrieved from http://euractiv.cz/udalost/16-energeticky-kongres-cr-transformace-energetiky-ii-001636/

EUROBAT. (2016). Battery energy storage in the EU: Barriers, opportunities, services and benefits. Retrieved from http://eurobat.org/sites/default/files/eurobat_batteryenergystorage_web_0.pdf

European Commission. (2001a). Directive 2001/77/EC of the European Parliament and of the Council of 27 September 2001 on the promotion of electricity produced from renewable energy sources in the internal electricity market. Retrieved from https://eur-lex.europa.eu/legal-content/EN/TXT/?uri=CELEX%3A32001L0077

European Commission. (2001b). Directive 2001/80/EC of the European Parliament and of the Council of 23 October 2001 on the limitation of emissions of certain pollutants into the air from large combustion plants. Retrieved from https://eur-lex.europa.eu/legal-content/EN/TXT/?uri=celex%3A32001L0080

European Commission. (2003). Directive 2003/30/EC of the European Parliament and of the Council of 8 May 2003 on the promotion of the use of biofuels or other renewable fuels for transport. Retrieved from https://eur-lex.europa.eu/legal-content/EN/ALL/?uri=celex%3A32003L0030

European Commission. (2006). Directive 2006/32/EC of the European Parliament and of the Council of 5 April 2006 on energy end-use efficiency and energy services and repealing Council Directive 93/76/EEC. Retrieved from https://eur-lex.europa.eu/legal-content/EN/TXT/?uri=CELEX%3A32006L0032

European Commission. (2009). Directive 2009/28/EC on the promotion of the use of energy from renewable sources. European Commission.

European Commission. (2012). Directive 2012/27/EU of the European Parliament and of the Council of 25 October 2012 on energy efficiency, amending Directives 2009/125/EC and 2010/30/EU and repealing Directives 2004/8/EC and 2006/32/EC. Retrieved from https://eur-lex.europa.eu/legal-content/EN/TXT/?uri=celex:32012L0027

European Commission. (2014a). Directive 2014/94/EU of the European Parliament and of the council of 22 October 2014 on the deployment of alternative fuels infrastructure text with EEA relevance. Retrieved from https://eur-lex.europa.eu/legal-content/EN/TXT/?qid=1523530561897&uri=CELEX:32014L0094

European Commission. (2014b). Report on the implementation of Regulation (EU) 994/2010 and its contribution to solidarity and preparedness for gas disruptions in the EU. Retrieved from https://ec.europa.eu/energy/sites/ener/files/documents/SWD 2014 325 Implementation of the Gas SoS Regulation en.pdf

European Commission. (2016). State aid SA.40171 (2015/NN). Retrieved from https://ec.europa.eu/competition/state_aid/cases/260911/260911_1866872_294_2.pdf

European Commission. (2017). Third report on the state of the energy union: Annex 3 – State of progress towards the National energy and climate plans. Retrieved from https://ec.europa.eu/commission/sites/beta-political/files/annex-3-progress-national-energy-climate-plans_en.pdf

Fanone, E., Gamba, A., & Prokopczuk, M. (2013). The case of negative day-ahead electricity prices. *Energy Economics, 35*, 22–34. https://doi.org/10.1016/j.eneco.2011.12.006.

Frantál, B. (2016). Living on coal: Mined-out identity, community displacement and forming of anti-coal resistance in the most region, Czech Republic. *Resources Policy, 49*, 385–393. Retrieved from https://www.sciencedirect.com/science/article/pii/S0301420716300733

Frantál, B., & Malý, J. (2017). Close or renew? Factors affecting local community support for rebuilding nuclear power plants in the Czech Republic. *Energy Policy, 104*, 134–143. https://doi.org/10.1016/J.ENPOL.2017.01.048.

Geels, F. W. (2002). Technological transitions as evolutionary reconfiguration processes: A multi-level perspective and a case-study. *Research Policy, 31*(8–9), 1257–1274. https://doi.org/10.1016/S0048-7333(02)00062-8.

Glassheim, E. (2007). Most, the town that moved: Coal, communists and the "Gypsy question" in post-war Czechoslovakia. *Environment and History*. White Horse Press. https://doi.org/10.2307/20723640

GNS. (2018). UK HPR1000 ~ GDA process. Retrieved 3 April 2018, from http://www.ukhpr1000.co.uk/

Government of the Czech Republic. (2010). Rut Bízková Becomes New Environment Minister. Retrieved from https://www.vlada.cz/en/media-centrum/aktualne/rut-bizkova-becomes-new-environment-minister-70734/

Government of the Czech Republic. (2011). The strategic framework for sustainable development in the Czech Republic. Retrieved from https://www.vlada.cz/assets/ppov/udrzitelny-rozvoj/The-Strategic-Framework-for-SD_2011.pdf

Grossi, L., Heim, S., Huschelrath, K., & Waterson, M. (2015). Electricity market integration and the impact of unilateral policy reforms. *SSRN Electronic Journal*. https://doi.org/10.2139/ssrn.2683315

Hospodářské noviny. (2016, March 17). Pavel Šolc, exnáměstek ministra průmyslu, nastoupí do ČEZ Distribuce. Retrieved from https://kariera.ihned.cz/c1-65212380-pavel-solc-exnamestek-ministra-prumyslu-nastoupi-do-cez-distribuce

International Energy Agency. (2016). Energy policies of IEA countries Czech Republic 2016 review. Retrieved from https://www.iea.org/publications/freepublications/publication/Energy_Policies_of_IEA_Countries_Czech_Republic_2016_Review.pdf

ISSP Research Group. (2012, August 27). *International Social Survey Programme: Environment III*. Cologne: GESIS Data Archive. https://doi.org/10.4232/1.11418

Janis, I. L. (1972). *Victims of groupthink; a psychological study of foreign-policy decisions and fiascoes*. Boston: Houghton, Mifflin.

Jenkins, K. E. H., & McCauley, D. (2015). Energy security, equality, and justice. *Energy, 83*. https://doi.org/10.1016/j.energy.2015.02.049.

Jirušek, M., & Kuchyňková, P. (2018). The conduct of Gazprom in central and Eastern Europe: A tool of the Kremlin, or just an adaptable player? *East European Politics and Societies*. https://doi.org/10.1177/0888325417745128.

Jirušek, M., Vlček, T., Koďousková, H., Robinson, R. W., Leshchenko, A., Černoch, F., ... Zapletalová, V. (2015). *Energy security in central and Eastern Europe and the operations of Russian state-owned energy enterprises*. Brno: Masaryk University Press.

Kondziella, H., & Bruckner, T. (2016). Flexibility requirements of renewable energy based electricity systems – A review of research results and methodologies. *Renewable and Sustainable Energy Reviews, 53*, 10–22. https://doi.org/10.1016/j.rser.2015.07.199.

Krpec, O., & Hodulák, V. (2014). *Trade and power: Historical analysis of trade policy*. Brno: Masaryk University.

Kuskova, P., Gingrich, S., & Krausmann, F. (2008). Long term changes in social metabolism and land use in Czechoslovakia, 1830–2000: An energy transition under changing political regimes. *Ecological Economics, 68*(1–2), 394–407. https://doi.org/10.1016/J.ECOLECON.2008.04.006.

Kuzemko, C. (2014). Ideas, power and change: Explaining EU–Russia energy relations. *Journal of European Public Policy, 21*(1), 58–75. https://doi.org/10.1080/13501763.2013.835062.

Luechinger, S., & Moser, C. (2014). The value of the revolving door: Political appointees and the stock market. *Journal of Public Economics, 119*, 93–107. https://doi.org/10.1016/J.JPUBECO.2014.08.001.

Lukáč, P. (2014, December 5). Beneš: EU musí spolupracovat. *Hospodářské Noviny*. Retrieved from https://archiv.ihned.cz/c1-63217260-sef-cez-benes-evropska-unie-musi-spolupracovat

Lund, P. D., Lindgren, J., Mikkola, J., & Salpakari, J. (2015). Review of energy system flexibility measures to enable high levels of variable renewable electricity. *Renewable and Sustainable Energy Reviews, 45*, 785–807. https://doi.org/10.1016/J.RSER.2015.01.057.

Lykidi, M., & Gourdel, P. (2017). Optimal management of flexible nuclear power plants in a decarbonising competitive electricity market: The French case. *Energy, 132*, 171–185. https://doi.org/10.1016/j.energy.2017.05.065.

MacKay, D. (2009). Sustainable energy – Without the hot air. UIT. Retrieved from http://www.withouthotair.com/c24/page_169.shtml

Málek, J., Rečka, L., & Janda, K. (2018). Impact of German Energiewende on transmission lines in the central European region. *Energy Efficiency, 11*(3), 683–700. https://doi.org/10.1007/s12053-017-9594-4.

McGowan, F. (2008). Can the European Union's market liberalism ensure energy security in a time of 'Economic nationalism'? *Journal of Contemporary European Research, 4*(2), 90–106. Retrieved from http://jcer.net/index.php/jcer/article/view/92

Ministry of Agriculture. (2014). Víceletý program podpory dalšího uplatnění udržitelných biopaliv v dopravě na období 2015–2020. Retrieved from http://cappo.i-servis.info/prilohyarchiv/128/POLITIKY-Vicelety_program_biopaliva2015-202.pdf

Ministry of Environment. (2011). Ministr Chalupa navštívil Ostravu i Beskydy. Retrieved from https://www.mzp.cz/cz/news_110404_plan

Ministry of Environment. (2017). Politika ochrany klimatu v ČR. Retrieved from https://www.mzp.cz/C1257458002F0DC7/cz/news_170322_POK/$FILE/POK_v_CR.pdf

Ministry of Finance. (2017). Majetkové účasti Ministerstva financí ke dni 31.7.2017. Retrieved 3 April 2018, from https://www.mfcr.cz/cs/verejny-sektor/majetek-statu/majetkove-ucasti/2017/majetkove-ucasti-ministerstva-financi-ke-29370

Ministry of Foreign Affairs. (2014). Nová energetická koncepce SRN jako šance pro česko-německou spolupráci. Retrieved from https://www.mzv.cz/berlin/cz/aktuality/nova_energeticka_koncepce_srn_jako_sance.html

Ministry of Industry and Trade. (2004). *State energy policy of the Czech Republic*. Prague: Ministry of Industry and Trade.

Ministry of Industry and Trade. (2006a). Long-term strategy for the use of biofuels in the Czech Republic. Retrieved from https://www.mpo.cz/en/energy/gas-and-liquid-fuels/long-term-strategy-for-the-use-of-biofuels-in-the-czech-republic%2D%2D14044/

Ministry of Industry and Trade. (2006b). Národní program hospodárného nakládání s energií a využívání jejích obnovitelných a druhotných zdrojů. MIT CR.

Ministry of Industry and Trade. (2007). *Energy efficiency action plan 2007*. Prague: Ministry of Industry and Trade

Ministry of Industry and Trade. (2011). *2nd national energy efficiency action plan of the Czech Republic*. Prague: Ministry of Industry and Trade

Ministry of Industry and Trade. (2014). *National energy efficiency action plan of the Czech Republic 2014*. Prague: Ministry of Industry and Trade

Ministry of Industry and Trade. (2015a). Národní akční plán čisté mobility. Retrieved from https://www.mpo.cz/assets/dokumenty/54377/62106/640972/priloha001.pdf

Ministry of Industry and Trade. (2015b). National action plan for the development of nuclear energy in the Czech Republic. Retrieved from https://www.mpo.cz/assets/dokumenty/54251/61936/640148/priloha001.pdf

Ministry of Industry and Trade. (2015c). *State energy policy update*. Prague: Ministry of Industry and Trade. Retrieved from http://download.mpo.cz/get/52841/60946/636123/priloha001.pdf

Ministry of Industry and Trade. (2015d). *Supplementary analytical material to the state energy policy update*. Prague: Ministry of Industry and Trade. Retrieved from http://download.mpo.cz/get/52826/60155/632396/priloha003.pdf

Ministry of Industry and Trade. (2015e). Zápis z 18. zasedání Rady vlády pro energetickou a surovinovou strategii České republiky. Retrieved from https://www.mpo.cz/assets/cz/rozcestnik/ministerstvo/kalendar-akci-vse/2017/3/zapis_18-zasedani_05052015.pdf

Ministry of Industry and Trade. (2015f). Zápis z 19. zasedání Rady vlády pro energetickou a surovinovou strategii České republiky. Retrieved from https://www.mpo.cz/assets/cz/rozcestnik/ministerstvo/kalendar-akci-vse/2017/3/zapis_19-zasedani_10092015.pdf

Ministry of Industry and Trade. (2016a). *National Energy Efficiency Action Plan of the Czech Republic 2016*. Prague: Ministry of Industry and Trade

Ministry of Industry and Trade. (2016b). Státní program na podporu úspor energie na období 2017–2021. Retrieved from https://www.mpo.cz/assets/cz/energetika/dotace-na-uspory-energie/program-efekt/2016/12/program_efekt_2017-2021_16_12_2016.pdf

Ministry of Industry and Trade. (2017). Update of the national energy efficiency action plan of the Czech Republic. Retrieved from https://www.mpo.cz/assets/en/energy/energy-efficiency/strategic-documents/2017/11/NEEAP-CZ-2017_en.pdf

oenergetice.cz. (2017, April 19). ČEZ plánuje do roku 2035 odstavit více než polovinu svých českých uhelných elektráren. Retrieved from http://oenergetice.cz/elektrina/cez-planuje-do-roku-2035-odstavit-vice-nez-polovinu-svych-ceskych-uhelnych-elektraren/

Osička, J., & Černoch, F. (2017). Anatomy of a black sheep: The roots of the Czech Republic's pro-nuclear energy policy. *Energy Research & Social Science, 27*, 9–13. https://doi.org/10.1016/j.erss.2017.02.006.

OTE. (2018). The anticipated long-term balance between electricity and gas supply and demand in the Czech Republic. Retrieved from http://www.ote-cr.cz/about-ote/files-annual-reports/Expected_balance_report_2017.pdf

Padgett, S. (2011). Energy co-operation in the Wider Europe: Institutionalizing Interdependence. *Journal of Common Market Studies, 49*(5), 1065–1087. https://doi.org/10.1111/j.1468-5965.2010.02168.x.

Parliament of the Czech Republic. (2000). Zákon o podmínkách podnikání a o výkonu státní správy v energetických odvětvích a o změně některých zákonů (energetický zákon). Retrieved from http://www.zakony.cz/zakon-SB2000458-32

Parliament of the Czech Republic. (2005). Act on promotion of use of renewable sources. Retrieved from https://www.mpo.cz/assets/dokumenty/26665/28468/312170/priloha001.pdf

Parliament of the Czech Republic. (2007). Zákon, kterým se mění zákon č. 86/2002 Sb., o ochraně ovzduší a o změně některých dalších zákonů (zákon o ochraně ovzduší), ve znění pozdějších předpisů – Zákony.cz. Retrieved from http://www.zakony.cz/zakon-SB2007180

Pavlínek, P. (2005). Privatisation and the regional restructuring of coal mining in the Czech Republic after the collapse of state socialism. In J. Pickles, A. Smith (Eds.), *Theorizing transition: The political economy of post-communist transformations* (p. 544). London: Routledge.

Procházková, M. (2010, November). Ministr životního prostředí Drobil: Suďte mě podle práce, ne podle slov – iDNES.cz.

Quitzow, L., Canzler, W., Grundmann, P., Leibenath, M., Moss, T., & Rave, T. (2016). The German Energiewende? What's happening? Introducing the special issue. *Utilities Policy, 41*, 163–171. https://doi.org/10.1016/j.jup.2016.03.002.

Ramberg, B. (1984). *Nuclear power plants as weapons for the enemy: An unrecognized military peril*. Berkeley: University of California Press.

Rečka, L., & Ščasný, M. (2016). Impacts of carbon pricing, brown coal availability and gas cost on Czech energy system up to 2050. *Energy, 108*, 19–33. Retrieved from https://www.sciencedirect.com/science/article/pii/S036054421501645X

Rintamäki, T., Siddiqui, A. S., & Salo, A. (2017). Does renewable energy generation decrease the volatility of electricity prices? An analysis of Denmark and Germany. *Energy Economics, 62*, 270–282. https://doi.org/10.1016/j.eneco.2016.12.019.

Sivek, M., Kavina, P., Jirásek, J., & Malečková, V. (2012a). Factors influencing the selection of the past and future strategies for electricity generation in the Czech Republic. *Energy Policy, 48*, 650–656. https://doi.org/10.1016/j.enpol.2012.05.073.

Sivek, M., Kavina, P., Malečková, V., & Jirásek, J. (2012b). Czech Republic and indicative targets of the European Union for electricity generation from renewable sources. *Energy Policy, 44*, 469–475. https://doi.org/10.1016/J.ENPOL.2012.01.054.

Sovacool, B. K., & Blyth, P. L. (2015). Energy and environmental attitudes in the green state of Denmark: Implications for energy democracy, low carbon transitions, and energy literacy. *Environmental Science & Policy, 54*, 304–315. https://doi.org/10.1016/J.ENVSCI.2015.07.011.

Štubňa, M., Pekár, A., Morávek, J., & Špirko, M. (2002). Decommissioning project of Bohunice A1 NPP. Office of Scientific and Technical Information, US Department of Energy. Retrieved from http://www.wmsym.org/archives/2002/Proceedings/22/141.pdf

Supreme Audit Office. (2016). EU report 2016 – Report on the Financial Management in the Czech Republic. Retrieved from https://www.nku.cz/assets/publications-documents/eu-report/eu-report-2016-en.pdf

Šůra, A. (2012, July). Bez fanatiků a bez peněz. *Respekt*. Retrieved from https://www.respekt.cz/tydenik/2012/31/bez-fanatiku-a-bez-penez

Szulecki, K. (2017). Conceptualizing energy democracy. *Environmental Politics, 27*(1), 21. https://doi.org/10.1080/09644016.2017.1387294.

The Economist. (2010). No, minister. Retrieved from https://www.economist.com/node/15869464

The Office of the Government. (2015). Zápis z 5. jednání Výboru pro udržitelnou energetiku RVUR. Retrieved from https://www.vlada.cz/assets/ppov/udrzitelny-rozvoj/vybory-rvur/Zapis-5%2D%2Djednani-VUE-17-3-2015.pdf

Turcsanyi, R. Q. (2017). Central European attitudes towards Chinese energy investments: The cases of Poland, Slovakia, and the Czech Republic. *Energy Policy, 101*, 711–722. https://doi.org/10.1016/J.ENPOL.2016.09.035.

Van Dijk, T. A. (1997). What is political discourse analysis. *Belgian Journal of Linguistics*, 11–52. Retrieved from http://citeseerx.ist.psu.edu/viewdoc/summary?doi=10.1.1.452.5209

Vlček, T., & Černoch, F. (2012). *Energetický sektor České republiky* (1). Brno: Masarykova univerzita.

Vlček, T., & Černoch, F. (2013). *The energy sector and energy policy of the Czech Republic*. Brno: Masaryk University Press.

Vobořil, D. (2015). Energetický a průmyslový holding (EPH) – profil společnosti. Retrieved 4 April 2018, from http://oenergetice.cz/elektrina/energeticky-a-prumyslovy-holding-eph/

Wikipedia. (2018). ČEZ group. Retrieved 4 April 2018, from https://en.wikipedia.org/wiki/ČEZ_Group

World Nuclear Association. (2018). Plans for new nuclear reactors worldwide. Retrieved 8 April 2018, from http://www.world-nuclear.org/information-library/current-and-future-generation/plans-for-new-reactors-worldwide.aspx

Zatloukal, J. (2014). *Flaws in the Czech political culture*. Oxford: University of Oxford. Retrieved from http://reutersinstitute.politics.ox.ac.uk/sites/default/files/research/files/Flaws%2520in%2520the%2520Czech%2520political%2520culture.pdf

Energy Governance in Denmark

25

Helene Dyrhauge

Contents

Introduction 594
General Conditions of Energy Governance in Denmark 596
    Policy Legacies 596
    The Energy Mix 599
    Discourse on Energy Issues 601
    Political Institutions and Actors 602
Coordination, Instruments, and Issues of Energy Transitions Within a Multilevel Context ... 604
    Drivers of Energy Transition 604
    Instruments of Energy Transition and Coordination Mechanisms 605
Outcomes, Challenges, and Prospect of Energy Governance 610
    Monitoring of Climate Goals and Sector Integration 610
    Energy Conflicts 612
    Multilevel Governance 613
Cross-References 614
References 614

Abstract

Historically, Danish energy governance has been characterized by not-for-profit principles, energy security, and energy efficiency, which have guided individual policy instruments. Moreover, many energy companies are owned by municipalities or by the consumers, for example, through cooperatives. Indeed, the municipalities have a strong role in Danish energy governance. However, national energy agencies are important in this multilevel governance structure, especially with increased focus on liberalization, and where renewable energies are playing a bigger role in energy production. Indeed, the legacy of wind energy and Denmark's forerunner position in renewable energies are crucial for Danish energy policies and politics today, especially in relation to the challenges

H. Dyrhauge (✉)
Department for Social Sciences & Business, Roskilde University, Roskilde, Denmark
e-mail: dyrhauge@ruc.dk

© Springer Nature Switzerland AG 2022
M. Knodt, J. Kemmerzell (eds.), *Handbook of Energy Governance in Europe*,
https://doi.org/10.1007/978-3-030-43250-8_7

Denmark faces in order to achieve a fully decarbonized economy by 2050. Indeed, there is a national climate change consensus across all areas of society from the electorate, businesses, and all political parties, yet there is no consensus on how to reach a low carbon economy by 2050, which is evident in the lack of sector integration in, for example, transport. This chapter brings together the legacy of Danish wind energy and multilevel governance to discuss the current challenges facing Danish energy governance relating to decarbonization of the economy.

Keywords

Denmark · Renewable energy · Energy efficiency · Energy security · Liberalization · Not-for-profit · Multilevel governance

Introduction

The Danish wind energy adventure started in the late 1970s and has left a strong legacy on Danish energy policy today as wind energy has become synonymous with the Danish energy transition. Wind energy together with energy efficiency and energy security have been central principles driving Danish energy governance since the 1970s, where energy security is defined as a self-sufficient domestic energy production independent of imports of fossil fuels, i.e., oil. Crucially, the domestic energy production not only consist of renewable energies but oil production is also important, and North Sea oil remains an important source of revenue for the state. Simultaneously, energy efficiency policies have incentivized industries to develop products that reduce energy consumption in all areas of society. Thus, industrial competitiveness has emerged as a side effect of the policy legacy, and it has become embedded in the domestic energy discourse.

The not-for-profit principle has been another important element in energy governance. Traditionally, Danish energy producers have been owned by municipalities or they have been local not-for-profit energy companies organized in cooperatives and consumer-owned companies, and these companies were also the firsts to invest in wind energy. Overall, energy producers have been grounded in the local community, where municipalities play a central role in energy planning, thereby creating a decentralized energy infrastructure with limited connections between different regions. Nevertheless, liberalization phases out not-for-profit principles instead prioritizing consumer choice. Moreover, investment in big offshore wind parks and integration with neighboring countries' grid are likely to challenge the decentralized energy governance structure.

Simultaneously, climate change has become an important political agenda at all levels from the local to the UN, and energy transition is crucial to this agenda. While Denmark is a forerunner in wind energy and green energy technologies, it also faces several challenges most notably in terms of sector integration and electrification of transport, which are necessary to complete the transition to a low carbon economy by

2050. Different political agreements aim to address transport decarbonization, yet none of the agreement enable the government to meet its targets (the Climate Council 2021). Importantly, the politicians and the societal stakeholders all support the energy transition, thereby creating a national climate change consensus, but they disagree on how to manage the transition and the speed of transition, which have created conflicts. The center-left political parties and some stakeholders, including the green energy sector and green NGOs, want an ambitious climate policy program, for example, through the "green growth" agenda (e.g., the Thorning-Schmidt governments (2011)). Whereas the center-right political parties, who have been in power for most of the twenty-first century, and some industry associations support the "environment worth the money" strategy (e.g., Fogh Rasmussen I (2003), Løkke Rasmussen II (2015) and III (2016)). The Social Democratic Party won the 2019 election and formed a minority government with Mette Frederiksen as prime minister, which has actively pursued an ambitious climate policy. Although Danish climate and energy targets for 2030 are high compared to other European countries, the current political commitment is not sufficient to reach domestic targets for 2030 (the Climate Council 2021).

This debate about the level of climate commitment has shaped the political discourse for much of the century and is likely to continue in the future. The debate is rooted in the Danish pioneership (Andersen 1997; Börzel 2002; Dyrhauge 2021), and it has become a nodal point in the climate and energy discourse today, where Danish leadership is used to discuss the speed of energy transition. Although energy transition in Denmark is well underway, there are still many conflicts and challenges for the country to overcome to become a zero carbon economy by 2050, where the new datacenters and the required decarbonization of transport will increase electricity demand, and that electricity have to come from renewable sources. Thus, more investment in renewable energies is necessary for Denmark to meet its climate obligations. These changes in energy demand challenge Danish leadership, which has already faltered under the Liberal Party coalition governments (2001–2011 and 2015–2019) due to policy instruments often favoring intensive energy consumers and with limited investments in offshore wind. The energy transition by 2050 necessitates radical steps to change energy use (the Climate Council 2018a) thereby making structural changes to energy consumption and production. However, the Danish government and many other governments have been criticized for not taking sufficient steps to meet their mid- to long-term climate and energy targets.

The chapter draws on government documents, legislation, and reports from the Danish Energy Agency and the Climate Council. Additionally, the chapter draws on nine semi-structured interviews with three politicians (former MEP Britta Thomsen (Social Democratic Party); Martin Lidegaard (Social Liberal Party, Minister for Climate, Energy and Buildings (2011–2014)); and Lars Christian Lilleholt (Liberal Party, Minister for Energy, Utilities and Climate 2015–2019)); three environmental NGOs (Concito, NOAH, and the Ecological Council); and three industry organizations (Danish Industry, Danish Chamber of Commerce, and Danish Wind Industry Association). The interviews took place between 2016 and 2017, and bring new insights into Danish climate and energy politics.

The chapter starts by describing the general energy conditions in Denmark and analyzing how the policy legacies of wind energy and North Sea oil influence the energy discourse today. Secondly, the chapter focuses on the drivers of the energy transition and discusses the different policy instruments used to facilitate the shift to renewable energies. Thirdly, the chapter identifies the challenges in Danish energy transition especially in terms of sector integration to enable electrification of all areas of energy consumption. The section also discusses the geopolitical energy conflict caused by Nord Stream II. Finally, the chapter examines the prospects for energy transition and governance by analyzing the UN and EU climate change agenda in relation to the Danish climate and energy political agenda. Overall, the chapter demonstrates that the long-term climate goals – zero carbon economy by 2050 – challenges the Danish forerunner position in renewable energies especially as the next phase of the energy transition requires ambitious political commitment to transform energy consumption in all sectors, where the electrification necessitates investment in more renewable energies to facilitate the projected increase in demand.

General Conditions of Energy Governance in Denmark

Policy Legacies

Denmark relied on imported oil for heating until the 1970s (Sovacool 2013: 28), where the oil crises together with pressure from environmental movements created a new energy paradigm emphasizing two guiding principles – energy security and energy efficiency. Firstly, energy security is understood as a reliable infrastructure and a self-sufficient energy production; here windmills and North Sea oil and gas ensure independence from imported fossil fuels. Secondly, energy efficiency aims to reduce energy consumption of households, buildings, and industries. Later in the 1980s, promotion of renewable energies became a third principle of Danish energy governance.

The principle of energy security initially focused on exploiting resources in the North Sea – oil and natural gas – and only later became associated with wind energy. The exploitation of North Sea oil started in 1962, where the A.P. Møller Group created Danish Underground Consortium and the government granted the company permission to extract oil from the North Sea. In 1972, the state created DONG, a state-owned energy provider, which had priority right to buy oil and gas from the North Sea. The overall operating goal for DONG was to ensure Denmark became independent of imported energy. In the 1990s, DONG started investing in wind energy, and today, DONG, now known as Ørsted, has become the largest energy provider in Denmark, and it is slowly divesting from oil and gas instead focusing on renewable energies. Nevertheless, North Sea oil continue to contribute to the domestic energy mix today (Fig. 1) and the state budget. In 2014, the Thorning-Schmidt government privatized DONG and controversially sold it to Goldman Sachs. The Socialist People's Party was part of the government, but did not support the decision and left the coalition government.

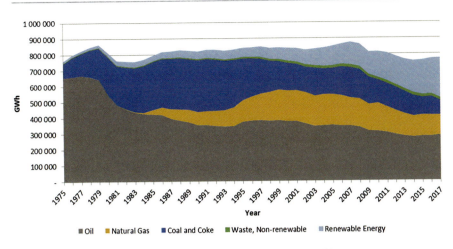

Fig. 1 Gross energy consumption. (Source: The Energy Agency 2018b)

The principle of energy efficiency aims to reduce energy consumption, and governments have used different policy instruments to incentivize both households and businesses to use less energy. Indeed, Danish energy consumption have been stable since 1990 (The Energy Agency 2018b). During the same period, Denmark has experienced economic growth and many see the stable energy consumption as a success (Sovacool 2013; interview with minister Lars Christian Lilleholt 2016), but the figures do not include international shipping, which would show an increase in energy consumption because of the large Danish maritime sector. Indeed, some green NGOs, e.g., NOAH and the Ecological Council (interviews 2016), criticize the governments for not including factors such as changes in industries' energy use and deindustrialization as an explanation for the stable energy consumption.

The legacy of renewable energies is associated with the 1970s environmental grassroots movements that demonstrated against nuclear energy, especially Barsebeck, the Swedish nuclear power plant close to Copenhagen. Simultaneously, entrepreneurs successfully built windmills as an alternative source of electricity. Together these developments created bottom-up pressure against nuclear power, and the government officially abandoned nuclear power in 1980. Moreover, the first wind map in 1981 identified locations for future wind turbines (Meyer 2007). Indeed, 1980s wind energy policies changed Danish energy perspective from energy security to pioneering environmental awareness (Andersen and Nielsen 2016: 84). This pioneership became more important after the 1993 election, where the new coalition government led by the Social Democratic Party with the Social Liberal Party merged the energy ministry and environment ministry into one ministry with Svend Auken (Social Democratic Party) as minister for both environment and energy. Svend Auken was a committed environmentalist and pushed the environmental perspective on energy policy. During his tenure (1993–2001), Denmark became a forerunner, protecting its own higher standards against lower EU and international standards, while Svend Auken defended national environmental standard, he also adopted an activist approach trying to forge alliances with other EU member states and tried to upload domestic policy preference to the EU level (Andersen 1997: 270–283; Börzel 2002). This forerunner position remains important for Danish self-perception and policy discourse today (see next section for detailed discussion).

In 2001, the Liberal Party came back into power in a coalition government with the Conservative Party, and the new Prime Minister Anders Fogh Rasmussen started by dismantling the existing climate and energy policies. However, Fogh Rasmussen later reversed his position on climate change, partly due to the Mohammed cartoon crisis in 2006, which again highlighted the precarious reliance on imported Middle East Oil, and partly due to a visit to the USA, where he heard about Danish export of green energy technology (Meilstrup 2010: 19; Øyen 2018b). These factors contributed to the 2007 policy reversal leading to financial and regulatory commitments to the energy transition.

At the same time, the Minister for Environment, Connie Hedegaard (2004–2007, also Minister for Climate and Energy 2007–2010), wanted Denmark to host COP15 (Meilstrup 2010: 114). Anders Fogh Rasmussen and Connie Hedegaard invested a lot of political capital in the Danish presidency, yet the presidency struggled with coordination between the Prime Minister's office and the Foreign Office (Meilstrup 2010: 117). This was not helped by the change in Prime Minister from Anders Fogh Rasmussen, who, in Spring 2009, became head of NATO, to Lars Løkke Rasmussen, who "throughout his career had focused on domestic politics, did not immediately take a strong interest in the negotiations" (Meilstrup 2010: 124). Nevertheless, the failure of the COP15 cannot be contributed solely to the Danish presidency, conflicts between the delegations attending the conference was another major factor in the lack of a new post-Kyoto agreement (Meilstrup 2010; Park 2016).

Lars Løkke Rasmussen lost the election in 2011 but regained power in 2015, where he reintroduced the "environment worth the money" strategy (The Government 2015). During the interim period, between 2011 and 2015, the Social Democratic Party with Helle Thorning-Schmidt as Prime Minister (Thorning-Schmidt I 2011–2014 and Thorning-Schmidt II 2014–2015) led a coalition government first with the Socialist People's Party and the Social Liberal Party, and between 2014 and 2015 only with the Social Liberal Party. The Thorning-Schmidt I and II governments adopted a "green growth" strategy to kick-start the economy after the crises (The Government 2011), pushing a green agenda both at home with a multiannual energy agreement for 2012–2020 and the 2014 climate law, while it at the EU level used the 2012 Danish presidency to work towards an ambitious energy efficiency directive and later the government pushed for ambitious EU 2030 climate and energy targets. The Social Democratic Party regained power after the 2019 election and formed a minority government with Mette Frederiksen as prime minister. Crucially, the 2019 general election is known as the climate election because climate was the top priority for the electorate (Møller Hansen and Stubager 2021). This gave the Frederiksen government and the political parties in Parliament a mandate to adopt a new climate law and broker political agreements on, for example, transport and agriculture decarbonization thereby pushing a domestic climate agenda.

Overall, the policy legacies have created Danish expertise in wind energy, energy technologies, and energy efficiency. Two factors have influenced the energy governance over the past 30 years; firstly, Svend Auken initiated and pushed the energy transition during the 1990s leaving a legacy of Danish climate leadership, and secondly, the Liberal Party has been in power for most of the twenty-first century, where it predominately has pushed an "environment worth the money" agenda.

The Energy Mix

The Danish energy mix and consumption reflects the above energy principles of energy security, energy efficiency, and renewable energies. Renewable energies have become a dominating energy source as North Sea oil production has peaked, while energy production has remained stable (The Energy Agency 2018b – Fig. 1). The combined picture of Danish energy policy shows a high percentage of renewable energies in electricity production, but the stories behind the figures reveal problems for future energy transition to a low carbon economy.

Figure 2 shows an increase in renewable electricity production, which accounted for 50 percent of electricity production in 2017. Demand for electricity is predicted to increase towards 2030 partly due to increase in household demands for electricity and electrification in general, without further investment Denmark will become a net importer of electricity (The Energy Agency 2021: 25 and 51). Thus, reaching 100 percent renewable electricity target for 2030 requires significant investment in new wind parks, and realization of the planned energy islands in the North Sea and Baltic Sea. Overall, investment in wind power, mostly offshore wind parks, is central for Danish energy transition and self-sufficiency principle.

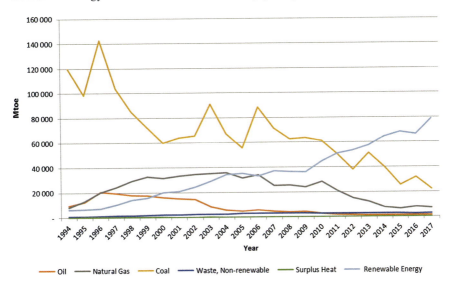

Fig. 2 Electricity production. (Source: The Energy Agency 2018b)

Denmark has been self-sufficient in oil since 1993 and its oil production has exceeded demand for much of the period (The Energy Agency 2017). Moreover, the North Sea oil is an important revenue for the Danish state. In 2015, domestic oil production had accumulated contributed 415 billion kroner (60 billion Euros) to the state budget and the Løkke Rasmussen III government estimated that North Sea oil will contribute another three digit billion kroner over the next 20 years (The Government 2018a: 39). The revenue gone into the general state budget. Yet in 2014, the Thorning-Schmidt I government created "Togfonden," which earmarks revenues from the North Sea Oil to finance future rail infrastructure investment, mainly electrification and high-speed trains (Togfonden 2014). However, oil prices have since dropped leaving a deficit in the program. The Liberal Party, which does not support the program, has argued that the program should be terminated due to the financial deficit. Overall, the oil sector remains important for the Danish economy, and there are no plans to halt domestic oil exploration and production.

Coal continues to be an important fossil fuel in many countries, e.g., Poland or Germany, but it does not have an important role in the Danish energy mix (Fig. 1). The Parliament imposed a moratorium on coal in 1990, which was formalized in 1997 (Sovacool 2013: 28), and coal has to be completely phased out by 2030. Ørsted's two coal powered plants will end operations in 2023, leaving two municipality-owned coal plants, Nordjyllandsværket in Aalborg and Fynsværket in Odense, in operation until 2028 and 2030, respectively (Nielsen 2017). Instead, biomass has replaced coal and has become an important energy source in heating. In 2005, Hvelplund (2005: 86) argued that biomass was reaching saturation point but use of biomass have continued to increase (Fig. 3). Biomass include wood, hay, biodiesel, and waste (The Energy Agency 2017). Forty-three percent of biomass used in Denmark is imported. However, CO_2 emissions from imported biomass is registered in the country of origin; consequently, Denmark does not register its

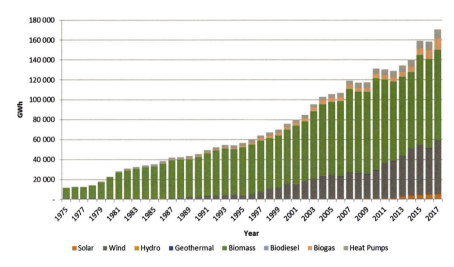

Fig. 3 Production of renewable energy. (Source: The Energy Agency 2018b)

emissions from its imported biomass, and instead, Denmark relies on the country of origin to have a coherent climate strategy (the Climate Council 2018c). Clearly, biomass is not necessarily a sustainable energy source, it depends on the measures taken by the country of origin to mitigate climate change and loss of forests. Waste is another important energy source for many decentralized power plants but increased focus on recycling and circular economy, especially at EU level, have reduced the amount of domestic waste, which lead to more imported biomass. In general, the Danish energy mix is on the path to becoming independent of fossil fuel and the energy security principle remains part of the future renewable energy mix.

Discourse on Energy Issues

Several opinion polls from 2018 show that climate has become more important for the electorate (Holstein and Mølgaard 2018; Holm 2018). One opinion poll from December 2018 shows that climate has jumped from a fifth position in 2017 to first position ahead of health and immigration (Holstein and Mølgaard 2018). Moreover, Møller Hansen and Stubager (2021) shows that climate was a top priority for the electorate in the 2019 general election. Indeed all political parties seized on this and climate change was the main topic in the election pushing concerns about immigration down the list of priorities (ibid). Furthermore, opinion polls reflect the climate change consensus in Denmark, where the political parties agree on energy transition and climate change defined as commitment to ecological modernization (Skovgaard 2017: 361). However, they disagree on the speed and direction of the transition.

The disagreements were evident in the public discourse surrounding the Løkke Rasmussen III government's 2018 Energy Proposal. The proposal was widely criticized by the opposition for being unambitious and ignoring climate dimensions, instead only focusing on the energy sector. As a minority coalition government, the Løkke Rasmussen III government relied on either its support party – the Danish People's Party – or the opposition to adopt legislation. Indeed, broad political agreements are important for domestic policies, because they bind the political parties for the existing and subsequent electoral periods, thereby creating stability in the policy field and for the affected sectors. During spring 2018, the opposition successfully pushed the government towards a more ambitious 2020–2030 energy plan, which was adopted just before the summer holiday. The climate and energy debate continued after the summer holiday into the autumn, where the public debate between the political parties and broader stakeholders focused on the level of investment in new offshore wind parks with the aim of ensuring Denmark remains self-sufficient and that the country will meet its climate commitment in 2030 and 2050. After the Social Democratic Party regained power in 2019, the Frederiksen government continued to focus on the climate agenda and energy transition by brokering political agreements with political parties. The 2020 climate law is one example; the law set a binding target of 70 percent emission reduction (based on 1990) in 2030, and the minister for climate has a legal duty to act and is accountable to the Parliament. Importantly the law prevents backsliding and thus binds future governments to act. The law forms the basis for the subsequent sectoral political agreements on transport and agriculture. Thus, the political prioritization has continued after the election.

The energy discourse is framed within a self-perception of leadership and pioneership (Dyrhauge 2021). The leadership discourse has changed over time, from a defensive forerunner in the 1980s, which was concerned about how EU legislation would negative impact on Denmark's domestic standards, to a pusher position in the 1990s, where Denmark tried to upload its ideas to the EU level (Andersen 1997; Börzel 2002; Andersen and Nielsen 2016). More recently, the Løkke Rasmussen II and III governments understand environmental energy leadership as domestic market conditions for energy technology companies, business start-ups, and high energy security (The Government 2018a: 5). This export-oriented strategy represented symbolic leadership (Dyrhauge 2021). By comparison, the Frederiksen government's focus on both domestic and external policy ambitions again represent a pusher position.

Furthermore, the pioneer position in energy efficiency and renewable energies is closely associated with specific companies specializing in energy technologies, e.g., insulation of pipes (Løgstør rør), insulation (Rockwool), and thermostats (Grundfos and Danfoss), just as Vestas has become synonymous with Danish wind power. Overall, the green energy industry accounts for 11 percent of total export (The Energy Agency 2018c) and has become an important part of Danish foreign policy. The export of green energy technologies started at the beginning of the millennium and has continued as global demand for climate and energy solutions has increased. This demand for Danish green energy solutions has influenced governments' policies, where governments have increasingly focused on exporting green technologies. However, Danish green energy companies want ambitious domestic policy objectives in their home market to facilitate innovation to stay competitive at the global level thereby creating pressure on the government to adopt strong climate and energy objectives. Overall, leadership is central in the domestic energy policy discourse, but the understanding of leadership has changed from domestic policy objectives to include industrial competitiveness and export opportunities.

Political Institutions and Actors

The Ministry of Energy, Utilities and Climate is responsible for the political directions of Danish energy policy and is in close contact with the different energy agencies to prevent political "shit storms" and to discuss implementation of legislation. Climate policy and energy policy have been together in one ministry since 1993, with the exception of Anders Fogh Rasmussen I and II governments (2001–2007) where the two policy fields were separated into different ministries. Integrating climate and energy into one ministry makes it possible to create synergy in decision-making in relation to climate change and energy transition. However, other ministries are also involved in energy policy-making; for example, the Ministry of Finance has become more important in climate and energy policy-making after the 2008 economic crises (Skovgaard 2017), while the Ministry for Foreign Affairs is responsible for the energy technology export strategy, and the Danish Business Authority, under the Ministry of Industry, Business and Financial Affairs, is responsible for the Danish Emission Trading System (ETS). Yet, the main actor in Danish energy governance is the Ministry for Energy, Utilities and Climate, who sets the political directions for the energy sector.

Moreover, there are two energy agencies: the Energy Agency, which administrates energy and supply plus climate initiatives; and Energinet, the state-owned infrastructure manager responsible for the electricity and gas grids. They operate with an arm's length from the Ministry and thus are free from political interference; instead, they are responsible for enforcing national energy laws, thereby playing a central role in energy governance by directly regulating energy producers and suppliers, in addition to interacting with private and public energy stakeholders. Moreover, competences have been transferred from Energinet to the Energy Agency, which is the main regulatory body in energy governance and coordinates policy instruments in a multilevel system with many energy actors, including the municipalities, which are responsible for local energy planning. According to the 1979 district heating law, the municipalities must provide heating to all households, and the law has created decentralized energy grids managed by the municipalities, but today municipalities, who remain responsible for local energy planning, outsource maintenance and development of the local energy grids to private actors.

The heating is regulated on a not-for-profit principle, where profit are reinvested back into the energy-producing companies, which are often consumer-owned cooperatives, or for other companies returned to the consumers. Cooperatives and consumer-owned energy companies continue to dominate the heating sector, whereas the electricity liberalization have consolidated the electricity production, especially as the energy transition require large-scale offshore wind parks. The energy producers are organized in national associations that represent their interests at the central political level, such as Dansk Fjernvarme (Danish District Heating Association), some of its 400 members are also part of the larger energy association, Danish Energy, which represents energy producers, energy distribution, and energy trading. The two associations together with Wind Denmark represent the Danish energy interests in the political discourse. Whereas non-energy industry actors are represented by the two largest business associations: Danish Industry and Danish Chamber of Commerce. All the associations are active in the corporatist political system, where stakeholders are consulted by governments as part of decision-making. "Since 1970s oil crises – a relatives systemic energy policy has been developed and implemented in a dialogue with the important actors, such as grass root organizations, energy companies and the general public" (Hvelplund 2005: 83). However, Læssøe (2007: 236) argues that the 1980s saw a professionalization, which marginalized grassroots movements in favor of industry and academics. More recently, environmental think tanks, i.e., the Ecological Council and Concito, have emerged and are playing a vocal role in the Danish energy debate arguing for a more ambitious climate change agenda. Moreover, Concito works with industry to promote the energy transition, for example, through the "Denmark as a green winner nation" initiative, where Concito collaborates with the

Danish Society of Engineers, Vestas, Grundfos, Danfoss, and Rockwool. These green energy companies are important for Danish export and are increasingly vocal in the energy transition discourse.

The Climate Council, an advisory body to the government, is a new actor. It was established by the 2014 Climate Law and consists of academics from different disciplines and universities. The 2020 climate law gave the Climate Council more competences and resources. The Climate Council is now required to annually comment on the government's climate program, thereby providing a technical assessment of the government's duty to act. The 2021 status report stated that the government only had found measure to reduce emissions by 54 percent. Thus, the Climate Council is often seen as critical of the government of the day and has to strike a balance between analyzing the government's climate policies while not being too critical and risk facing comments about being political.

Coordination, Instruments, and Issues of Energy Transitions Within a Multilevel Context

Drivers of Energy Transition

The bottom-up multilevel perspective on socio-technological changes (Geels and Schot 2007) is useful for understanding the initial developments in the Danish green energy agenda, where the process was driven by entrepreneurs who created new technologies, e.g., windmills and thermostats, just as grassroots movements pushed a nonnuclear policy agenda, both groups influenced the socio-technological regime. However, the multilevel perspective downplays the role of governments as driver or brakeman for energy transition.

During the 1980s, government policies supported investment in windmills, the coalition governments under Prime Minister Poul Schlüter (The Conservative Party) gave financial support to research and development of wind turbines and energy efficiency (Ege 2009: 39) thereby supporting early energy transition. The Schlüter governments also incentivized individuals to install wind turbines by reimbursing 30 percent of the price, yet the policy was phased out by 1989 (Meyer 2007: 359; Auken 2002: 153). The financial support for wind turbines have changed over time, while wind turbines have become bigger and offshore wind parks have emerged, which require bigger investments compared to the early single wind turbine investments.

The 1990s, when Svend Auken was Minister for Environment and Energy, saw a strong top-down approach to environmental protection and energy transition. This top-down approach propelled the Danish energy transition and made Denmark a forerunner (Börzel 2002). Today actors in the energy sectors push for ambitious domestic targets because their home market is important for research and development of new products, especially in an increasing competitive global green energy technology markets (interviews 2016–2017). Thus the energy technology companies need their home market to develop new technologies, which requires government investment in renewable energies and financing of research.

Compared to the other Nordic countries, Denmark lacks a strong heavy industry to lobby for an industrial energy policy (Midttun and Kamfjord 1999: 890). Indeed, the climate change consensus extends to the Danish industry, including energy-intensive companies. For example, Maersk, the world's largest shipping company, has announced a zero-emissions fleet by 2050 (Financial Times 2018). Crucially, Maersk's 36 million tons of CO_2 equivalent in greenhouse gases (Financial Times 2018) do not figure in the Danish emissions statistic because most of the pollution is in international waters. Yet the company is important for the Danish economy and as the biggest maritime company in the world, it is a market leader. The announcement demonstrates the role of industries in facilitating the transition by developing new technologies, just like Vesta's role in developing small land-based windmills and later large offshore windmills is important for both Denmark and renewable energies in general. Unsurprising, the Danish green energy technology sectors support energy transition because it benefit their businesses thereby often pushing for more political commitments because high domestic climate objectives will pull industry towards more technological innovation.

The idea that technologies deliver the transition to a low carbon economy is common among politicians and industry actors. The development of new technologies to mitigate climate change require investment in research and development both in terms of public funding and private funding. The 2018 energy plan allocates 500 million kroner (67 million Euros) to the Program for Development and Demonstration of Energy Technology and 80 million kroner (11 million Euros) to the Innovation Fund in 2020, the amount will increase to one billion kroner (134 million Euros) in 2024 to match the Løkke Rasmussen III government's aim of spending 1 percent of BNP on research (The Government 2018a: 12). Moreover, governments favor a technological neutral policy where industry and universities decide which technologies are most effective. Moreover, "it is important to realize that the present transition from stored fossil fuel and uranium technologies to fluctuating renewable energy represent a fundamental technological change, where technique, organization, knowledge, product and profit streams are all altered" (Hvelplund and Djørup 2017: 1236). In other words, the energy transition requires not only a paradigm shift in use of energy sources, but also in how energy is organized and stored, especially as fluctuations in wind influence the availability of energy and thus energy security. This fluctuation in energy production requires either storages or connectors to neighboring countries to secure supply when there is not sufficient production.

Instruments of Energy Transition and Coordination Mechanisms

The multilevel energy governance system reflects the decentralized energy infrastructure with local energy producers, municipalities, and the central administration, where the Energy Agency plays a central role in coordinating actions and developments. The following sections identify the policy instruments used in regulating electricity and heating sectors and instruments to support energy efficiency and increase uptake in renewable energies.

Regulating the Heating Sector

The regulation on district heating (the consolidated law on heating supply 2018) requires the municipalities to establish a heated water or natural gas grid to supply households and businesses. This has resulted in decentralized heating grids, which the municipalities are responsible for maintaining. The main regulatory tools for heating is the law on heating supply, the planning law, and relevant environmental and building laws (Table 1). Article 3 of the consolidated law on heating supply (2) states that the municipal council, i.e., the mayor and the other local elected politicians, has to

Table 1 Key Danish energy transition policy instruments by sector and type

	Regulations	Incentives based	Taxes and charges/ internationalising external costs	Soft governance
Electricity supply	• Electricity supply law (consolidated 2019)	• Energy savings (2012-2020) • EU renewable energies directive (1992 onwards) • PSO charges, feed-in tariff (phase out by 2022)	• EU ETS (2012-onwards)	
Heat supply	• Heat supply law (consolidated 2019) • Phase out coal by 2030 (1997)	• Energy savings (2012-2020) • EU renewable energies directive		
Household energy users	• EU buildings directive • EU energy efficiency directive • Phase out gas boilers and introduce heat pumps	• Home improvements (2011-onwards)		• Energy savings and efficiency (2012-onwards)
Industrial and commercial energy users		• PSO charges, feed-in tariff (phase out 2022)	• State aid to energy-intensive companies (updated 2017) • EU ETS (2012-onwards)	
Transport	• EU biofuel directive (2012 onwards)	• No registration charges for electrical vehicles (2008–2015)		

Created by the author

cooperate with utility companies, many of these are cooperatives, and other stakeholders to develop and carry out a plan for heating supply in the municipality.

According to Danish District Heating Association, there are around 400 district heating companies, of which 50 companies are owned by municipalities and they supply 50 percent of all district heating, whereas 350 cooperatives supply the last 50 percent and a further 10 private companies supply less than 1 percent. Overall, the ownership structures in the form of public ownership by the municipalities and local cooperatives ensure that the district heating companies are grounded in the local community.

Until now, the not-for profit principle has ensured that the price for heating only reflect production costs, distribution, and administration, where any profits are either reinvested back into the power plant or passed on to the consumers. Only heating originating from renewable sources or surplus heating from industrial companies can incorporate a profit. However, the Løkke Rasmussen III government wanted to liberalize the heating market and remove the not-for-profit principle, whereas the opposition was concerned about how this would affect consumer protection and price for heating. Overall, the ministry can set a maximum price for heating thereby protecting consumers from rising price, and price regulations have resulted in low energy prices. The aim of the heating supply law is to promote the most socioeconomic, including environmental, use of heating of buildings and within this framework reduce reliance on fossil fuels. Unlike other European countries, there is no energy poverty (Pye et al. 2015; Bouzarovski 2014) despite local differences in price of heating.

Regulating the Electricity Sector

The electricity liberalization has phased out the not-for-profit principle (Kooij et al. 2018:56) and replaced it with profit-seeking principles aiming to create a competitive sector benefitting the consumers. The process started in 1998 and was initially influenced by domestic factors (Jakobsen 2010) and was only later driven by EU energy liberalization. The liberalization started by opening the wholesale electricity market and for consumers with an annual consumption above 100 GwH (Midttun 2001: 93). The consumer market was only opened later to give more choice of electricity providers. The universal service obligation for companies to supply electricity and price regulation was removed in April 2016, thereby establishing an open and competitive electricity market. While the wholesale electricity price is one of the lowest in Europe, the charges and taxes are among the highest leading to some of the highest consumer prices in Europe.

Energinet, the state-owned not-for-profit company in charge of the electricity and gas grids, is responsible for investing in renewable energy to enable the energy transition and protect energy security. Moreover, Energinet is responsible for the market conditions in the Danish electricity market, including facilitating electricity sale on the Nord Pool electricity exchange. Nord Pool has been important for "facilitating trade and providing transparent prices for the Nordic system," and the Nord Pool collaboration has led to a "far-reaching integrated liberal market system" (Midttun 2001: 91–92). The electricity exchange has expanded from the original Nordic countries (Norway, Finland, Sweden, and Denmark) to include the Baltic countries, the Benelux countries, Germany, the UK, and Austria. The expansion of Nord Pool is important for the EU energy union, which aims to create more connectivity between the member states' energy grids thereby ensuring security of energy supply throughout the EU. For example, the increased share of wind energy leaves Denmark vulnerable in terms of energy security because surplus supply on windy days and lack of supply on wind still days can interrupt electricity supply if there are no alternative energies, thus, connectivity to neighboring countries have become an important strategy for the transmission of electricity (Hvelplund and Djørup 2017: 1227). Indeed, Denmark has recently won a case at the ECJ against Germany for blocking export of wind energy, which enables Denmark to sell more of its surplus wind energy.

The liberalization of the electricity sector and the investment in wind energy have increased the number of actors, especially in terms of companies that supply electricity through the open market to consumers. Moreover, big companies like Vattenfall and Ørsted, have won public tenders to build the political decided offshore wind parks (Hvelplund and Djørup 2017: 1224). Importantly, no power plants have been built since 2000; instead, the big power companies build offshore wind parks (Kooij et al. 2018: 56). Despite these changes electricity production remains in the hands of 25 cooperatives and consumer-owned companies that produce 70 percent of Danish electricity, while 10 municipality companies represent 5 percent of electricity production and Ørsted is responsible for 25 percent of electricity production (Danish Energi 2018: 3). Thus, the cooperative movement continues to be an important form of ownership in electricity production, where some local cooperatives have grown into national and European actors. SEAS-NVE, e.g., produces and distributes electricity mainly on Zealand, but it also runs charging stations for electrical vehicles throughout the Nordic countries.

Support for Renewable Energies

Renewable energies have been a key priority in Danish electricity policy since the 1980s, where governments have used "planning policies, feed-in-tariffs, purchasing obligations and support for technological developments" to promote investment in renewable energies (Andersen and Nielsen 2016: 88). The policy approach to wind parks started with an open door policy, both on land and offshore. In 2004, the approach to offshore wind parks changed to single site tenders. Support for investment in offshore wind parks has been centralized through a one-stop-shop governing by the Danish Energy Agency that is responsible for the tender process (Fitch-Roy 2016: 595). The project owner is responsible for connecting the offshore wind park to the electricity grid (Fitch-Roy 2016: 589), which is managed by Energinet, and the owner of the offshore wind park liaises with Energinet regarding connectivity to the grid and sell the energy either on the wholesale market or directly to the consumers. The 2012 and 2018 political energy agreements identified specific offshore wind park locations and set dates for their complexion. However, a change in government and majority in Parliament can delay or cancel planned offshore wind projects, as happened in 2001 when Fogh Rasmussen I government cancelled all planned wind parks, and later Løkke Rasmussen II government delayed investments. Thus, the top-down centralized support for expansion of renewable energies depend on political commitment and financing. The centralization of the expansion of renewable energies do not extend to onshore wind parks or private windmills, where a bottom-up approach allows private individuals/companies or municipality-owned energy companies to apply to the local municipality to build onshore windmills.

All types of renewable energies receive some form of financial support to facilitate the expansion of renewable energies. The public service obligations (PSO) was an important policy instrument placed on the price of energy for both private and industrial consumers. The PSO was a feed-in-tariff and was introduced in 1998 to support new renewable energy technologies that were not able to compete in an open market. The PSO charge is determined by the market, where a high market price lead to a low PSO charge and vice-versa (Energinet.dk n.d.). The price for renewable electricity has declined due to expansion of renewable energies thereby increasing availability of renewable energies in the overall energy mix, yet the price guarantee for the renewable energy producers has resulted in a higher PSO charge for both private consumers and industries. In 2015, Apple was considering where to build its new datacenter and it informed the government about its concern about the PSO charge, which was reduced shortly before Apple decided to build its datacenter in Denmark (Svaneborg 2015). Yet, the PSO was already contested by many actors, and there had been discussions to reduce the PSO charge, thus Apple's concern was shared by others, who had already lobbied the government. In November 2016, the Løkke Rasmussen II government decided to remove it from the electricity bill. The phaseout of the PSO charge will be complete in 2022, and the money to renewable energy expansion will be moved to the annual budget.

Energy Efficiency

Energy efficiency has been an important policy objective; it not only aims to reduce consumption of fossil fuels, it also aims to reduce pollution from industries, buildings, and private households. Simultanously, the expansion of renewable energies alleviate the problem with pollution. Emission trading is a central market-based instrument that internalizes externalities through a quota system that aims to change companies' energy consumption behavior (Table 1). Denmark was an early supporter of the emission trading system (ETS). It started to implement a domestic system shortly after Kyoto, even before the European Commission had published its green paper on an EU ETS, and later, the Commission explicitly mentioned the Danish ETS as a national model (Skjærseth and Wettestad 2008: 90). The ETS has been problematic from the start because the high number of permits have flooded the market leading to low prices. In 2013, the Thorning-Schmidt I government supported the Commission's proposal to back load permits on the condition that the Commission would introduce a plan for a structural reform of the ETS (Skovgaard 2017: 359). The domestic intra-government discussion included the Ministry of Finance and Ministry of Climate and Energy, where "both ministries agreed that back loading in itself would have little impact on climate change, as the allowance would later be reintroduced into the market" (Skovgaard 2017: 359). Furthermore, the discussion focused on the impact on the allowance price and the

Ministry of Finance wanted to maintain the integrity of the market and emphasized a structural reform instead of one-off back loading as a solution to preserving the ETS (Skovgaard 2017: 359). This position on the ETS reform follows previous governments' view of ETS as a good instrument for changing industries energy consumption. The Løkke Rasmussen III government's Climate and Air Plan, published in November 2018, wants to annul eight million quotas until 2030, which will be deducted from Denmark's 2030 EU climate commitment and it expects the reduction in quotas will increase the price (The Government 2018b: 39). Compared to other countries with heavy industry, the Danish service orientated industry has not had major objections towards the ETS (Skovgaard 2017), which has made it easier for the government to propose the annulment and reform.

While the ETS focuses on industry and businesses, there are other policy instruments, which aim to reduce private energy consumption, such as the 1980s information campaign about lightbulbs and campaigns to get people to switch off the light. Measures to reduce buildings' energy consumption have been important since the 1970s oil crises and several Danish companies specializes in energy performance of buildings, e.g., thermostats and insulations. Moreover, private households can get tax-deductible renovation of their homes. The initiative has existed in different forms since the 1980s. The tax-deduction is an incentive-based policy instrument where private persons can deduct the workers' wages from the overall renovation bill. The aim of the current version is twofold, it aims to create work for the construction sector while updating buildings to become more energy efficient and it was part of the Thorning-Schmidt I and II governments' green growth strategy, yet the scheme has been continued by the Løkke Rasmussen II and III governments.

Denmark has actively supported the EU energy efficiency directive by trying to upload the Danish approach to the EU level (2017 Interview with Martin Lidegaard, Social Liberal Party, and Minister for Climate, Energy and Buildings (2011–2014)). Martin Lidegaard said, he pushed for an ambitious directive during the 2012 Danish EU presidency and gained support from some East European countries, who have to renovate their building stock and needed new standards. The Danish MEP Britta Thomsen (Social Democratic Party) was rapporteur for the proposal and she received support from the government (interview with Britta Thomsen 2017). Thus, there was a Danish footprint on the final directive. Simultaneously, the Thorning-Schmidt I government had agreed to reduce the final energy consumption by 7 percent between 2010 and 2020.

Outcomes, Challenges, and Prospect of Energy Governance

Monitoring of Climate Goals and Sector Integration

The Danish Energy Agency as the regulatory agency not only monitors implementation of energy legislation, it also carries out energy analyses, including the annual energy and climate outlook (based on a frozen policy scenario and existing measures). The outlooks generate both ex ante and ex post data, assessing the impact of adopted policy instruments as well as their future impact. The annual outlooks focus on the overall climate and energy policy objectives, i.e., the multiannual energy agreements, individual energy legislation, Danish commitment to EU targets, and other international climate commitments. Denmark exceeded its renewable energy target for 2020, which is 30 percent but the country reached 40 percent (The Energy Agency 2021: 12). According to the Climate Council (2021: 13), the 2021 climate plan has a positive impact on Denmark's climate commitment but is not sufficient to meet its international commitment by 2030: 39 percent reduction in GHG remissions in non-ETS sectors from 2005 to 2030 and 7 percent share of renewable energy in the transport sector. Like other EU member states, the transition curve from 2030 to 2050 is very steep and many countries put their faith in new technologies to facilitate the energy transition. The policy objectives require the EU and its member states to reduce their fossil fuel use from 50 to 95 percent over 20 years, this is a shorter period compared to the period until 2030, and this begs the question if the current level of ambition, at national, EU, and global level, will deliver the full transition to a zero carbon society. This debate is not exclusive to Denmark; instead, it is part of a wider debate based on the IPCCC reports and other monitoring data.

A central element in the energy transition debate, especially after 2020, is sector integration, and Denmark has agreed to reduce CO_2 emissions from non-ETS sectors by 39 percent in 2030 compared to 2005 levels (Ministry for Energy, Utilities and Climate 2016: 8–9). Nevertheless, reports (Climate Council 2018b: 4; The Energy Agency 2018a) show that the forerunner position in renewable energies does not include non-ETS sectors, i.e., transport, housing, and agriculture. The Frederiksen government under the Climate Law's duty to act has started to look at decarbonization of industry, transport, and agriculture, but the current agreements are not sufficient for the sectors to meet their 2030 target especially as the government relies on niche technologies like carbon capture storage and power-to-X to meet these goals.

Transport decarbonization has been a problem for several governments. Although the Løkke Rasmussen II-III governments were hesitant to support the switch from fossil fuel vehicles to low emissions vehicles, i.e., hybrid, electrical, and biofuels vehicles, the government together with the Danish People's Party, the Social Democratic Party, and the Social Liberal Party agreed to phase in registration charges for low emission cars, e.g., electrical and hydrogen vehicles (The Government 2015). The agreement led to a "panic buy" in the last quarter of 2015 and sharp reduction in registration of new electrical vehicles in 2016 and 2017 (Climate Council 2018a: 7). The government recognized the impact had been too severe, and in Spring 2017 with support from the Social Democratic Party and Social Liberal Party made adjustments to the phase-in period in the hope that it would facilitate more sales of electrical vehicles (The Government 2017a). Yet later in 2017, the government and the Danish People's Party agreed to reduce the registration charges for fossil fuel cars (The Government 2017b) thereby making fossil fuel vehicles attractive compared to electric cars. The continued tinkering with the registration charges, according to the Electrical Vehicles Alliance, created uncertainty and keep people from buying electrical vehicles (interview 2016). Nevertheless, private companies have invested in charging facilities and there are now more charging facilities than needed for the current electrical vehicle fleet (Altman 2018). In other words, the infrastructure is ready for more electrical vehicles. Simultaneously, the battery technologies have become more mature, just as many car manufacturers have pledged to phase out production of fossil fuel cars over the next 10 years.

From a broader perspective, electrification creates vulnerability because more sectors will depend on the digitalized electricity grid, which make the electricity system vulnerable to cybersecurity attacks that will affect the rest of society. As such, the Ministry for Energy, Utilities and Climate (2019) has published a strategy to protect the energy grids from cyberattacks. The strategy is part of a wider priority to coordinate efforts in all the critical infrastructures, e.g., energy, transport, finance, health, and maritime. This strategy involves partners from public authorities, including the defense and security services, and industry.

Energy Conflicts

The climate change consensus in Danish energy politics has prevented large-scale conflicts. However, the use of Danish territory for international infrastructure projects, i.e., Nord Stream 1 and 2 pipelines in the Baltic Sea have been controversial because Gazprom, the Russian state energy company, owns the pipelines. The Nord Stream pipelines run through the Baltic Sea from Russia to Germany, and "have since the mid-2000s provoked a deep conflict between Russia with Germany on the one hand, and Sweden, Denmark, Poland and the Baltic states, on the other" (Schmidt-Felzmann and Engelbrekt 2018: 10). Nord Stream 1 was finished in 2011 but Nord Steam 2 is still in the planning phase. The EU and its member states' energy relations with Russia is problematic due to security of supply, member states' dependence on imported Russian gas, and concerns over Russia's aggressive behavior in the gas markets and militarily (Schmidt-Felzmann 2011; Schmidt-Felzmann and Engelbrekt 2018). Nevertheless, Sweden has given permission for the Nord Stream 2 to run through its territory (Gotev 2018), which leaves Denmark, as the last country, to make a final decision about whether the pipeline can run south of Bornholm, a Danish island in the Baltic Sea, which the Soviet Union occupied between 1945 and 1946.

The Danish Parliament has moved the final decision from the Energy Agency to the Ministry for Foreign Affairs. The change in decision-maker clearly indicate the controversial nature of the pipeline and the Danish concerns over an aggressive Russia in the Baltic region. Indeed, Polish civil servants participated in a public hearing about the pipeline on Bornholm in 2017 and gave multiple environmental and fisheries objections to the pipeline (Arnfred 2017). Instead, Poland prefers the Baltic Pipe between Norway and Poland with Denmark as transit country. This will, according to the Polish ambassador to Denmark Henryka Mościcka-Dendys (2018), create a greener Europe and improve energy security especially in Central and Eastern Europe. Poland's relationship with Russia has historically been difficult and the complexities of geopolitics of energy security has not helped the relationship (Bouzarovski and Konieczny 2011: 8). Denmark and Poland share concerns about

Russia's behavior in the Baltic region and Denmark has approved the Baltic Pipe (Øyen 2018). Normally, the two member states oppose each other at EU level on issues concerning climate and energy, but their apprehensions over Russia's presence in the Baltic Sea brings them together, especially, as Nord Stream 2 will increase the EU's dependency on Russian imported gas and increase Russia's geo-economic powers in the gas markets.

Domestically, most political parties oppose Nord Stream 2 except for the Danish People's Party. The left-wing parties are concerned about the environmental impact of the pipelines and believe building fossil fuel infrastructure is misplaced given the energy transition's focus on renewable energies. Due to the stalled Danish decision-making, Nord Stream 2 has decided on an alternative route north of Bornholm, which moves the pipeline out of Danish territory, and prevent the government from using national security as an argument and only leaves it with environmental or fisheries objections (Redder 2018).

Multilevel Governance

Danish energy governance does not exist in a vacuum, it is part of a broader global political agenda on climate change and energy. Most of the interactions occur between Denmark and the EU, where Denmark, as mentioned earlier, tries to influence EU policy-making by uploading its policy preferences and governance practices (Andersen 1997: Dyrhauge 2017). Simultaneously, the forerunner position has enabled Denmark to implement EU energy and climate change legislation without administrative problems, which are often difficult in a multilevel governance system (Schoenefeld et al. 2018). This creates a multilevel governance framework with interactions between local municipality, companies, and national central agencies, who communicate with EU actors, in addition to cooperation between countries such as the Nordic electricity markets, not to mention UN cooperation, such as the COP.

The chapter has shown that energy security and energy efficiency have been crucial for Danish energy policy agenda, where the early shift from fossil fuels to renewable energies gave Denmark a forerunner position and enabled the country to pick the low-hanging fruits, but successful energy transition to a zero CO_2 emission society requires sector integration. The transition to complete the energy transition by 2050 necessitate major paradigm shift in energy due to electrification of society (Szulecki 2016: 54). This paradigm shift requires climate policy integration (Adelle and Russel 2013) and increased policy coordination at all levels. Both Bürgin (2015) and Skovgaard (2) demonstrate how the differences within the European Commission makes climate and energy policy coordination difficult due to conflicting values and interests. While Denmark pushed for ambitious EU 2030 climate and energy targets (European Commission 2014: 207), other member states, e.g., Poland, pushed for less ambitious targets without mandatory national targets. In the end, the climate leaders lost and the 2030 EU climate and energy targets do not include national mandatory targets.

The merger of climate and energy into one ministry aims to facilitate climate policy integration. This worked during Svend Auken's tenure in the 1990s because of his ideological focus on the environment above energy. However, later governments, most notably Fogh Rasmussen I, Løkke Rasmussen II and III, have prioritized energy above climate, and this is evident in Løkke Rasmussen III's decision to divide the 2018 energy plan and the 2018 climate plan into two different plans. Nevertheless, increased policy coordination and sector integration is important for successful energy transition especially in the Danish multilevel governance framework with many private and public actors. Indeed, coordination between policies increase policy coherence and enable Denmark to achieve full decarbonization in all areas of society and the economy, yet the energy transition depends on political commitment and legislation. Thus, interaction between all actors in the multilevel energy governance system and the government is important for achieving the 70 percent reduction in emissions in 2030 as set out in the 2020 climate law.

Cross-References

► Energy Governance in Germany
► Energy Governance in Norway
► Energy Governance in the Republic of Poland
► European Union Energy Policy: A Discourse Perspective
► EU-Russia Energy Relations
► Transition of Energy Systems: Patterns of Stability and Change

Acknowledgments I would like to thank Barbara Hofmann for help with the figures and Jörg Kemmerzell for thorough comments on earlier draft.

References

Adelle, C., & Russel, D. (2013). Climate policy integration: A case of Déjà Vu? *Environmental Policy and Governance, 23*, 1–12.
Altman, L. (2018, December 13). Debat: Ladestanderne har vi. Nu mangler vi bare elbilerne. *Altinget.dk*. https://www.altinget.dk/transport/artikel/groen-transport-lad-os-prioriterer-rigtigt-og-skaffe-flere-elbiler-paa-de-danske-veje. Accessed 13 Dec 2018.
Andersen, M. S. (1997). Denmark: The shadow of the 'green' majority. In M. S. Andersen & D. Liefferink (Eds.), *European environmental policy: The pioneers*. Manchester: Manchester University Press.
Andersen, M. S., & Nielsen, H. Ø. (2016). Denmark: Small state with a big voice and bigger dilemmas. In K. K. W. Würzel, J. Connelly, & D. Liefferink (Eds.), *The European Union in international climate change politics: Still taking a lead?* London: Routledge.
Arnfred, C. E. (2017, September 2). Polakker tog livtag med russisk gasledning på Bornholm. *Politiken*. https://politiken.dk/indland/art6091963/Polakker-tog-livtag-med-russisk-gasledning-p%C3%A5-Bornholm. Accessed 3 January 2019.
Auken, S. (2002). Answers in the wind: How Denmark became a world pioneer in wind power. *The Flecher Forum of World Affairs, 26*(1, winter/spring), 149–157.

Börzel, T. A. (2002). Pace-setting, foot-dragging, and fence-sitting: Member state responses to Europeanization. *Journal of Common Market Studies, 40*(2), 193–214.

Bouzarovski, S. (2014). Energy poverty in the European Union: Landscapes of vulnerability. *WIREs Energy and Environment, 2014*(3), 276–289.

Bouzarovski, S., & Konieczny, M. (2011). Landscapes of paradox: Public discourses and policies in Poland's relationship with the Nord Stream pipeline. *Geopolitics, 15*(1), 1–21.

Bürgin, A. (2015). National binding renewable energy targets for 2020, but not for 2030 anymore: Why the European Commission developed from a supporter to a brakeman. *Journal of European Public Policy, 22*(5), 690–707.

Climate Council. (2018a, September 26). *Flere elbiler på de danske veje Forslag til pejlemærker og virkemidler til elektrificering af personbilerne.*

Climate Council. (2018b, November 23). *Status for Danmarks klimamålsætninger og –forpligtelser 2018.*

Climate Council. (2018c, May). *Biomassens betydning for grøn omstilling: Klimaperspektiver og anbefalinger til regulering af fast biomasse til energiformål.*

Climate Council. (2021). *Status Outlook 2021. Denmark's national and global climate efforts.* English summary, February 2021.

Danish Energy. (2018). *5 punkterede myter om energikoncerner.* https://www.danskenergi.dk/sites/danskenergi.dk/files/media/dokumenter/2018-06/5_punkterede_myter_om_energikoncerner.pdf. Accessed 28 Dec 2018.

Dyrhauge, H. (2017). Denmark: A wind powered forerunner. In I. Solorio & H. Jörgens (Eds.), *A guide to EU renewable energy policy: Comparing Europeanization and domestic policy change in EU member states.* Cheltenham: Edward Elgar.

Dyrhauge, H. (2021). Political myths in climate leadership: The case of Danish climate and energy pioneership. *Scandinavian Political Studies, 44*(1), 13–33.

Ege, C. (2009). Er Danmark foregangsland? In I. Sohn (Ed.), *Dansk klima politik, et globalt udsyn?* Rødovre: Sohn.

Energinet. (n.d.). *Spørgsmål og svar om PSO.* https://energinet.dk/El/Tariffer/PSO#Hvorfor%20forekommer%20der%20store%20udsving%20i%20PSO-tariffen. Accessed 30 Dec 2018.

European Commission. (2014). COMMISSION STAFF WORKING DOCUMENT *IMPACT ASSESSMENT Accompanying the document Communication from the Commission to the European Parliament, the Council, the European Economic and Social Committee and the Committee of the Regions A policy framework for climate and energy in the period from 2020 up to 2030.* SWD(2014) 15 final.

Financial Times. (2018, December 4). Maersk pledges to cut carbon emissions to zero by 2050. *Ft. com.* https://www.ft.com/content/44b8ba50-f7cf-11e8-af46-2022a0b02a6c?desktop=true&segmentId=d8d3e364-5197-20eb-17cf-2437841d178a. Accessed 6 Dec 2018.

Fitch-Roy, O. (2016). An offshore wind union? Diversity and convergence in European offshore wind governance. *Climate Policy, 16*(5), 586–605.

Geels, F., & Schot, J. (2007). Typology of sociotechnical transition pathways. *Research Policy, 36*, 399–417.

Gotev, G. (2018, June 11). All eyes on Denmark after Sweden awards Nord Stream 2 permit. *Euractiv.com.* https://www.euractiv.com/section/energy/news/all-eyes-on-denmark-after-sweden-awards-nord-stream-2-permit/. Accessed 3 Jan 2019.

Holm, T. A. (2018, June 14). En splinterny måling afslører danskernes vigtigste dagsorden: Det er formentlig den mulighed, Socialdemokratiet har for at vinde næste valg. *Berlingske Tidende.* https://www.berlingske.dk/politisk-morgenpost/en-splinterny-maaling-afsloerer-danskernes-vigtigste-dagsorden-det-er. Accessed 18 Dec 2018.

Holstein, E., & Mølgaard, C. J. (2018, December 17). Miljø og Klima har erobret toppen af vælgernes dagsorden. *Altinget.dk.* https://www.altinget.dk/christiansborg/artikel/miljoe-og-klima-stormer-op-ad-dagsordenen. Accessed 18 Dec 2018.

Hvelplund, F. (2005). Denmark. In *Handbook of renewable energies in the European Union: Case studies of the EU-15 states.* Frankfurt a.M.: Peter Lang AG.

Hvelplund, F., & Djørup, S. (2017). Multilevel policies for radical transition: Governance for a 100% renewable energy system. *Environment and Planning C: Politics and Space, 35*(7), 1218–1241.

Jakobsen, M. L. F. (2010). Untangling the impact of Europeanization and globalization on national utility liberalization: A systematic process analysis of two Danish reforms. *Journal of European Public Policy, 17*(6), 891–908.

Kooij, H. K., Oteman, M., Veenman, S., Sperling, K., Magnusson, D., Palm, J., & Hvelplund, F. (2018). Between grassroots and treetops: Community power and institutional dependence in the renewable energy sector in Denmark, Sweden and the Netherlands. *Energy Research & Social Science, 37*, 52–64.

Læssøe, J. (2007). Participation and sustainable development: The post-ecologist transformation of citizen involvement in Denmark. *Environmental Politics, 16*(2), 231–250.

Meilstrup, P. (2010). The runaway summit: The background story of the Danish Presidency of COP15, the UN Climate Change Conference. In N. Hvidt & H. Mouritzen (Eds.), *Danish foreign Policy annual yearbook 2010*. DIIS: Danish Institute for International Studies.

Meyer, N. I. (2007). Learning from wind energy policy in the EU: Lessons from Denmark, Sweden and Spain. *European Environment, 17*, 347–362.

Midttun, A. (2001). Deregulated energy markets and the environment. The Nordic experience. *Environmental Politics, 10*(2), 90–114.

Midttun, A., & Kamfjord, S. (1999). Energy and environmental governance under ecological modernization: A comparative analysis of Nordic countries. *Public Administration, 77*(4), 873–895.

Ministry for Energy, Utilities and Climate. (2016, October 26). *Klimapolitisk redegørelse 2016: - Energi-, forsynings- og klimaministerens redegørelse til Folketinget om klimapolitikken*.

Ministry for Energy, Utilities and Climate. (2019, January 7) *Cyber- og informationssikkerhedsstrategi for energisektorerne*.

Møller Hansen, K., & Stubager, R. (2021). *Klimavalget*. Copenhagen: Djoef.

Mościcka-Dendys, H. (2018, November 25). Polens ambassadør i Danmark: Baltic Pipe gør Europa grønnere. *Altinget.dk*. https://www.altinget.dk/forsyning/artikel/polens-ambassadoer-i-danmark-baltic-pipe-goer-europa-groennere. Accessed 3 Jan 2019.

Nielsen, M. K. (2017, February 4). Danmark bliver kulfrit i 2030. *Berlingske.dk*. https://www.berlingske.dk/virksomheder/danmark-bliver-kulfrit-i-2030. Accessed 23 Nov 2018.

Øyen, M. (2018a, January 11). Fra atommarch og uldsweatre til konsensus om grøn vækst. *Altinget*. https://www.altinget.dk/energi/artikel/fra-atommarch-og-uldsweatre-til-konsensus-om-groen-vaekst

Øyen, M. (2018b, December 3). Grønt lys til omstridt gasledning. *Altinget.dk*. https://www.altinget.dk/forsyning/artikel/groent-lys-til-omstridt-gasledning. Accessed 3 Jan 2019.

Park, S. (2016). The power of presidency in UN climate change negotiations: Comparison between Denmark and Mexico. *International Environmental Agreements, 16*, 781–795.

Pye, S., Baffert, C., Brajković, J., Grgurev, I., De Miglio, R. and P. Deane (2015, May). Energy poverty and vulnerable consumers in the energy sector across the EU: Analysis of policies and measures, Policy report 2. *Insights_E*.

Redder, A. (2018, November 25). Konflikt om russisk gasledning nærmer sig en afslutning – var det kampen værd? *Altinget.dk*. https://www.altinget.dk/artikel/176831-konflikt-om-russisk-gasledning-naermer-sig-en-afslutning-var-det-kampen-vaerd. Accessed 3 January 2019.

Schmidt-Felzmann, A. (2011). EU member states' energy relations with Russia: Conflicting approaches to securing natural gas supplies. *Geopolitics, 16*(3), 574–599.

Schmidt-Felzmann, A., & Engelbrekt, K. (2018). Challenges in the Baltic Sea region: Geopolitics, insecurity and identity. *Global Affairs, 4*(4–5), 445–466.

Schoenefeld, J. J., Hildén, M., & Jordan, A. J. (2018). The challenges of monitoring national climate policy: Learning lessons from the EU. *Climate Policy, 18*(1), 118–128.

Skjærseth, J. B., & Wettestad, J. (2008). *EU emissions trading initiation, decision-making and implementation*. Farnham: Ashgate.

Skovgaard, J. (2017). The role of Finance Ministries in Environmental Policy Making. The case of European Union emission trading system reform in Denmark, Germany and the Netherlands. *Environmental Policy and Governance, 27*, 351–364.

Skovgaard, J. (2018). Policy coherence and organisational cultures: Energy efficiency and greenhouse gas reduction targets. *Environmental Policy and Governance, 28*, 350–358.

Sovacool, B. K. (2013). *Energy and ethics: Justice and the global energy challenge.* Basingstoke: Palgrave Macmillan.

Svaneborg, T. (2015, August 14). Mogens Jensen: Apple har ikke fået særaftale. *DR Nyhederne.* https://www.dr.dk/nyheder/indland/mogens-jensen-apple-har-ikke-faaet-saeraftale. Accessed 3 Jan 2019.

Szulecki, K. (2016). European energy governance and decarbonization policy: Learning from the 2020 strategy. *Climate Policy, 16*(5), 543–547.

The Energy Agency. (2017, November 21). *Energistatistik 2016.*

The Energy Agency. (2018a, April). *Basisfremskrivning 2018: Energi- og klimafremskriving til 2030 under fravær af nye tiltag.*

The Energy Agency. (2018b, November). *Energistatistik 2017.*

The Energy Agency. (2018c). *Eksport af energiteknologi og –service 2017.* https://ens.dk/sites/ens.dk/files/Statistik/analyse_-_energiteknologi_eksporten_2018.pdf. Accessed 21 January 2019.

The Energy Agency. (2021, April). *Klimastatus- og Fremskrivning 2021.*

The Government (Fogh Rasmussen I). (2003, April). *Grøn markedsøkonomi – mere miljø for pengene.*

The Government (Lars Løkke Rasmussen II). (2015, June 25). *Regeringsgrundlag: sammen for fremtiden.*

The Government (Løkke Rasmussen III). (2015, October 9). *Aftale mellem regeringen (V) og Socialdemokratiet, Dansk Folkeparti og Radikale Venstre om de fremtidige afgiftsvilkår for elbiler og brændselscelle biler.*

The Government (Løkke Rasmussen III) (2016, November 27). *Regeringsgrundlag: Marienborgaftalen 2016: for et friere, rigere og mere trygt Danmark.*

The Government (Løkke Rasmussen III). (2017a, April 18). *Aftale mellem regeringen (V, LA, K), Socialdemokratiet og Radikale Venstre om justering af aftalen om de fremtidige afgiftsvilkår for elbiler og brændselscellebiler af 9. oktober 2015 (nye lempelser for elbiler).*

The Government (Løkke Rasmussen III). (2017b, September 21). *Omlægning af bilagifterne.* https://www.regeringen.dk/media/4044/aftaletekst-omlaegning-af-bilafgifterne-ny.pdf. Accessed 9 Jan 2019.

The Government (Løkke Rasmussen III). (2018a, April). *Energi – til et grønt Danmark.* Energi, Forsynings- og Klimaministeriet.

The Government (Løkke Rasmussen III). (2018b, October). *Sammen om en grønnere fremtid: klima- og luftudspil*, published by the Ministry for Energy, Utilities and Climate. Accessed 13 Dec 2018.

The Government (Thorning-Schmidt). (2011, October). *Regeringsgrundlag: Et Danmark der står sammen.*

Togfonden. (2014, January 14). *Regeringen har sammen med EL og DF indgået aftale om "En moderne jernbane – udmøntning af Togfonden DK".* https://www.trm.dk/da/politiske-aftaler/2014/aftale-om-togfond

Energy Governance in Finland

26

Mikael Hildén and Paula Kivimaa

Contents

Introduction	620
General Conditions of Energy Governance in Finland	621
Patterns of Energy Consumption	621
The Energy Mix	623
Discourses on Energy	624
Political Institutions and Actors	625
Coordination of the Instruments and Issues of Energy Transitions within a Multilevel Context	626
Drivers of Energy Transition	626
Strategies and Instruments of Energy Transitions	629
Coordination Mechanisms and Multilevel Governance	633
Outcomes, Challenges, and Prospects of Energy Governance	636
The Forestry Problem in Energy Governance	637
Overall Energy Transitions	638
Monitoring and Surveillance	640
Cross-References	641
References	642

Abstract

Finland has a diverse energy mix with a large share of bioenergy. The share of renewables is high (32%) and the Government that begun its term in June 2019 has declared that Finland will become carbon neutral by 2035. To reach this goal major socio-technical transitions are required. The country will need to change energy

M. Hildén (✉)
Finnish Environment Institute, SYKE, and the Strategic Research Council, Helsinki, Finland
e-mail: mikael.hilden@ymparisto.fi

P. Kivimaa
Finnish Environment Institute, SYKE, Helsinki, Finland

SPRU, University of Sussex, Brighton, UK
e-mail: paula.kivimaa@ymparisto.fi

© Springer Nature Switzerland AG 2022
M. Knodt, J. Kemmerzell (eds.), *Handbook of Energy Governance in Europe*,
https://doi.org/10.1007/978-3-030-43250-8_9

production and the use of energy in industry, heating, and transport, and develop energy storage further. For achieving carbon neutrality carbon sinks are also crucial. This chapter shows that some of the transitions are progressing, backed by ambitious energy and climate strategies. At the same time, there is a strong path dependency that emerges from the central role of the forest industry and bioenergy, and heavy industries more generally in Finland. Major tasks for the future governance of the energy system include continuous improvement in energy efficiency, increasing the share of low carbon energy production that does not depend on biomass, and strengthening demand side management. The energy transition needs support from an ambitious policy mix in which policy coherence is ensured.

Keywords

Socio-technical transitions · Carbon neutrality · Bioenergy · Energy policy · Renewable energy

Introduction

Finland is a heavy consumer of energy. In 2017, it ranked 15th in the global statistics of energy consumption per capita, with only Luxembourg and Iceland ahead in Europe (IEA 2019). The standard explanation for the high energy consumption is Finland's industrial structure, cold climate, and long distances (Valkila and Saari 2013). The share of industry in the total consumption has varied between 45% and 50% since the 1970s. The share of energy used for space heating has declined from a third to less than a fourth of the total energy consumption. The share of transport has increased from 13–14% to 16–17%. Total energy consumption increased almost continuously from 1970 until 2010, after which it declined by about 10% by 2015, only to rise again close to the peak level in 2018 (Official Statistics of Finland 2019).

The energy intensity of the economy puts Finland in somewhat an odd club. Most of the other global top energy intensive economies, such as Qatar, Bahrain, Kuwait, the United States, and Canada, are producers of fossil energy, although Iceland and Norway with large renewable sources are also in the top list. Finland is, in contrast, a net importer of energy, with imports accounting for more than half of the total energy supply. The high-energy intensity and the dependence on imported energy have made energy issues politically very important. All governments, since the early 2000s, have delivered an energy and climate strategy (Hildén 2011). The latest in the series was agreed upon in 2016 (Government of Finland 2017a). Major concerns since the 1970s have been energy prices, energy security, self-sufficiency, and regional issues, and, since the 1990s, also environment and the reduction of greenhouse gases (Kivimaa and Mickwitz 2011).

In contrast with many other energy-intensive economies, Finland has a high (32%) share of renewables in the total primary energy supply. The share of solid biofuels is particularly high. More than 75% of renewable energy is largely a "side product" of the intensive forest-based industry that is a significant player in the Finnish economy. For example, Sweden and Austria, which also have large forest resources, are somewhat less dependent on forest-based energy with comparable figures around 50% (IEA 2019). The importance of forest-based bioenergy has put Finland in league of its own in the European policy discussions concerning the regulation of greenhouse gas emissions from land use and forestry, and Finland made numerous attempts to influence the emerging Land Use, Land Use Change and Forestry (LULUCF) Regulation (EU) 2018/841 (Ministry of the Environment 2017).

The high-energy intensity, a large heavy industry sector, and the importance of wood biomass both for the economy and the energy supply have framed energy governance in Finland for decades. Climate and energy policies have strengthened existing technological options rather than introduced new ones (Kivimaa and Mickwitz 2011). The EU targets for emission reduction have been met, but the aim has been to achieve the targets through gradual change that challenges existing patterns of consumption as little as possible. A basic view that Finland should develop a diverse set of energy sources and reduce its dependence on Russian energy is shared by citizens and the energy elite, which is dominated by large energy producers (Ruostetsaari 2017). However, there are also clear differences in the preferences of the energy elite and the citizenry. The elite believes in the emergence of market-based solutions, whereas the citizenry sees a greater role for state interventions, including R&D for renewables (Ruostetsaari 2017, p. 97).

The need for a transition in the energy system is generally recognized by all key actors, but unsurprisingly there is less agreement on the required pace of the transition and the specific actions that can make it happen. This chapter explores how specific conditions affect the potential for an energy transition and its possible evolution in Finland.

General Conditions of Energy Governance in Finland

Patterns of Energy Consumption

Forests were the base for industrialization in Finland and have remained important ever since. In 1980, the forest industry's share of Finnish exports was still above 40%, but it has fallen to around 20% (2018) (Statistics Finland 2019c). Yet, the forest industry continues to be an important political actor. Other important energy users are the chemical industry (19% share of exports), metal and metal product industry (15%). The machinery and equipment industry (13%) and the electric and electronics industry (12%) are important from an energy point of view as their products influence the consumption of energy and energy efficiency in many other sectors.

The investments of the heavy industry are long-term, and the energy intensive industry has had a strong position in formulating the Finnish energy policies. Consequently, a long-standing explicit goal of the energy policies has been to ensure an abundant supply of cheap energy. Statistics reveal that the energy intensity of the Finnish economy is well above average in EU-28 and the decrease in energy intensity between 2007 and 2017 has been relatively modest (−10%), with the EU average reduction in energy intensity being about 17% for the same time period (Eurostat 2019a).

The electrification of the Finnish society has been a clear trend, also reflecting path dependency in investments, policies, and technologies. However, a trend break can be seen after 2008 with electricity consumption leveling off (Fig. 1). This break has been driven by structural change in the forest industry, in which the consumption of electricity declined from peak consumption in 2006 by 32% until 2015, and a slight increase thereafter. In all other sectors, the electrification is still a trend, but it has partly leveled off since 2010.

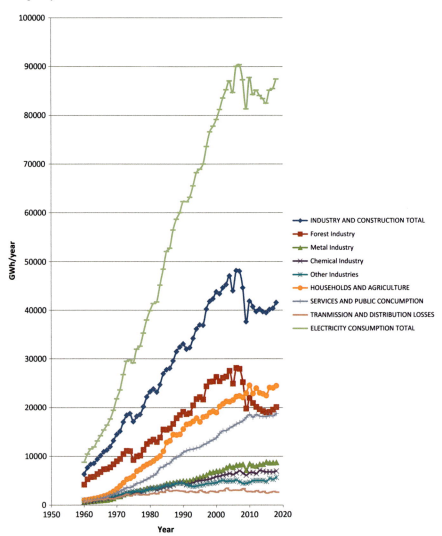

Fig. 1 Consumption of electricity in key industries, households, and agriculture 1970–2015 (Statistics Finland 2019a)

The Energy Mix

The Finnish energy mix is diverse, and it has been a conscious policy to maintain diversity. Oil, nuclear energy, and wood fuels are the most important in terms of volume, but hydropower, natural gas, peat and coal also play a role (Fig. 2). Maintaining a high degree of diversity has been seen to be important as the diversity helps to create resilience against external shocks.

Finland has no fossil fuel resources except peat. About 50% of the total domestic energy consumption is based on imports, which is close to the EU-average. Oil and natural gas are currently mainly imported from Russia, coal from Russia and Poland, but also from North America. Finland is furthermore a net importer of electricity, mainly from Sweden, Russia, and Norway (Finnish Customs 2020). The large role of Russia in the import of energy has motivated initiatives to increase self-sufficiency and to reduce imports of fossil fuels.

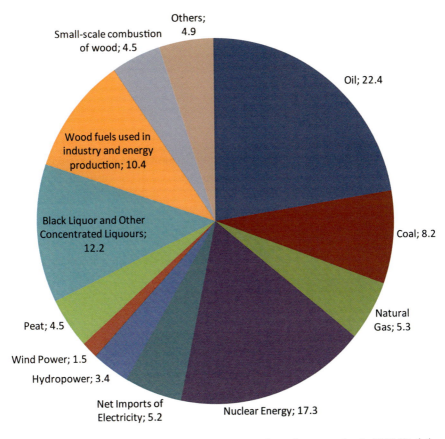

Fig. 2 The percentage share of different energy sources in total consumption in 2018 (Statistics Finland 2019b)

Discourses on Energy

As in many Western countries, systematic discourses on energy were initiated by the government in the 1970s in response to the volatility of energy prices. Energy was first explicitly mentioned in a Government Program in 1972 (Government of Finland 1972). A specific program for energy policy was approved in 1979. The intention was to "promote domestic energy – first and foremost, the production and use of wood and peat" (Ministry of Trade and Industry 1979, p. 7). It was followed by a new program in 1982 (Council on Energy Policy 1982) and energy strategies in 1992 and 1997 (Government of Finland 1997). Since the late 1990s, every government has prepared or revised a national energy and climate strategy.

Energy security has been a dominant concern in Finland, and it has also been noted in international reviews (e.g., IEA 2013). The early programs focused on ways to reduce oil dependence, but they also addressed security of supply and self-reliance. Furthermore, competitiveness played an important role in the energy discourse. Attention to competitiveness has been framed as a necessity determined by geography, climatic conditions, and the energy-intensive industries (Valkila and Saari 2013).

Energy saving was a key topic from the very first programs, and a relative decoupling of energy consumption from economic growth has been an explicit target (Council on Energy Policy 1982). Since the 1990s, climate change and the need to reduce emissions of greenhouse gases have been included in the energy discourse. For example, in 1997, the government presented a national energy strategy, which underlined the importance of reducing emissions of greenhouse gases (Government of Finland 1997). Climate change mitigation has become a key driver in all energy and climate strategies since the turn of the century (Hildén 2011).

Since the 1970s, there has been a broad consensus in the energy debate on the need to reduce dependency on imported fossil energy and on the merits of improving energy efficiency. Initially, the focus was on reducing dependency on imported crude oil, but the discourse has evolved to deal with fossil fuels generally, and also import of electricity, in particular from Russia. Tensions in the discourse have arisen in relation to nuclear energy and the use of peat. In Finland, the antinuclear movement has not succeeded in halting the development of the nuclear industry. This may reflect the observation that Finland is a strong administrative state in which key administrative players have sided with major users of energy (Säynässalo 2009). However, the Eurobarometer survey of 2009 also reveals that Finland has had, among all the EU countries, one of the highest proportion of public views that nuclear energy should be maintained at current levels or even increased (76%) (Eurobarometer 2010).

The nuclear energy discourse in Finland has been strongly geared toward emphasizing the role of nuclear energy as a way to maintain energy security, reduce oil dependency, and imports of electricity from Russia (where it would have been produced by "more unreliable nuclear plants"). Somewhat ironically the approval (Decision-in-Principle) for a new nuclear plant in 2010 was granted to Fennovoima of which the Russian Rosatom's subsidiary RAOS Voima Oy owns 34%

(Fennovoima 2019). This has somewhat reduced the confidence in nuclear energy as a solution for Finland's energy policy. Soaring costs and the fact that the Russian Rosatom is involved have not improved ratings. Thus, the proportion of the energy elite and the citizenry who expressed a preference for increasing (substantially or somewhat) the use of nuclear energy in the future fell drastically between 2007 and 2016. The elite responses indicated a fall from 84% to 43% and the citizen survey a fall from 43% to 22% (Ruostetsaari 2017).

Another particularly Finnish discourse has centered on the use of peat as an energy source. Finland has abundant peat resources and in the early energy strategies peat was considered to be one of the important substitutes for coal (Leinonen 2010). Thus, the strategy of 1997 still stated that the use of peat should be continued, especially for combined heat and power production (Government of Finland 1997, p. 12). Those producing and using peat have insisted that peat is a renewable energy source.

In the year 2000, the Ministry of Trade and Industry ordered a study that concluded that peat should be regarded as a slowly renewable energy source (Crill et al. 2000). The purpose of the study was to influence both the domestic and the international debate in order to ensure the energy use of peat, without accounting for the resulting greenhouse gas emissions. The government program 2007–2010 set this as a target (Government of Finland 2007, p. 40), but the attempt largely failed. Although peat is currently recognized as a particular form of fuel, emissions from using peat in energy production are still counted as emissions from fossil fuels. In the latest energy and climate strategy, peat is recognized as a fuel that will be used to some extent but the discourse has changed, and its nature as a fossil fuel is accepted (Government of Finland 2017a). The case of peat shows how a domestic policy issue can lead to willful blindness of impacts and loss of international credibility by fighting for lost causes.

Political Institutions and Actors

In Finland, the Cabinet in power has a central role in forming energy policies. The process of drafting energy and climate strategies has thus become an important institution in the energy sector. The policy is drafted by civil servants in relevant ministries, but under political guidance of key Ministers and the politically guiding Government Program. In 2015, the Climate Act (609/2015) introduced a new institutional structure by formalizing the state-led climate (and energy) planning by making long-term and intermediate term climate plans mandatory.

The key policy decisions on energy and climate are taken by the government, but they are also debated in Parliament through the submission of the energy and climate strategies and plans as government reports to the Parliament that gives feedback on them. Any legislative changes that are needed to implement the policies will obviously also have to be politically approved by the Parliament. In addition, the Parliament has the formal last word concerning permission allowing the building of nuclear reactors (Act on Nuclear Energy 990/1987).

Municipalities are important local actors in energy policy. Several municipalities own energy utilities or have shares in energy producing companies and can thereby influence choices concerning energy production. Municipalities also maintain a significant building stock and other infrastructure, making them major consumers of energy.

Ilkka Ruostetsaari has in a series of studies (Ruostetsaari 2006, 2010a, b, 2017) explored actors and elites in Finnish energy policy. The long list of actors he has identified makes it possible to explore the different institutional roles they have in forming energy policies (Table 1). The main policy institutions are those related to the drafting of national policies and strategies. These institutions bring together leading civil servants from key ministries (Economic Affairs and Employment, Agriculture and Forestry, Finance, Environment, and Transport and Communication) and the politically appointed ministers and their staff. The processes are also open to stakeholder input and the results are debated in the Parliament. Relevant parliamentary committees organize hearings to which experts and interest organizations are invited.

The actors have since 2010 basically remained the same as those identified by Ruostetsaari (2010a), but the processes have become more participatory and open. Participation is explicitly demanded by the Climate Act (2015). The importance of some of the actors has partly changed and there are also some actors that were not recognized in the survey. Thus, the Ministry of the Environment currently has a larger role in being the coordinator of the medium-term climate plan that focuses on the sector outside the emission trading scheme.

The increasing role of bioenergy in heating and also as a source of liquid fuels has strengthened the roles of the Ministry of Agriculture and Forestry and the Ministry of Transport and Communication in energy-related questions. The increasing share of intermittent energy and the growing importance of electricity trade between the neighboring countries have strengthened the role of the national transmission system operator Fingrid as an energy player. The Energy Authority plays an important operative role but is also a provider of information that feeds into policy processes. It's goal is to "promote cost efficient achievement of climate goals and efficient operation of the energy market"(Energy Authority 2019a). For RDI activities, Business Finland (previously Tekes) has been an important funder of energy-related innovations. Finland has had one of the greatest shares of RD expenditures on energy in relation to GDP among the OECD countries and more than 90% has been used on renewables (OECD 2016). Policy-oriented energy research has recently also been funded by the Strategic Research Council that focuses directly on transformative changes in the system. The interest in and emergence of small-scale energy production has opened a role for specialized niche actors especially in the field of renewable energy.

Coordination of the Instruments and Issues of Energy Transitions within a Multilevel Context

Drivers of Energy Transition

Finland is, as noted in the introduction, a somewhat peculiar player on the European energy scene. The high-energy intensity of the economy suggests that there is an urgent need for an energy transition. However, with more than 40% renewable

Table 1 Important domestic actors in energy policy based on two separate surveys (Ruostetsaari 2010a) and the relevant institutions and channels through which they can influence energy policies. The table is based on Ruostetsaari (2010a), but categories have been compressed and regrouped to reflect specific actor organizations

Actor group	Relevant institutions and/or channels of influence and their role in shaping energy policy
Government - Ministry of Economic Affairs and Employment. - Ministry of Finance. - Ministry of the Environment. - Ministry of Agriculture and Forestry. - Ministry of Transport and communications. - Ministry of the Interior. - Ministry for Foreign Affairs.	The government shapes domestic, EU, and international energy policy The Ministry for Economic Affairs and Employment is the lead ministry in drafting national energy and climate strategies and long-term climate plans in accordance with the Climate Act (609(2015) The Ministry of Finance leads fiscal and budget policy and examines all subsidies and other economic policy instruments The Ministry of the Environment leads international climate negotiations, and is responsible for coordination of intermediate term climate plans as defined by the Climate Act The Ministry for Agriculture and Forestry drafts plans for biomass use and bioenergy The Ministry of Transport and Communications has become an important energy actor through climate policies and transport issues The Ministry of the Interior leads in matters of energy security The Ministry for Foreign Affairs is involved in international climate and energy policy and politics, being the lead ministry for development co-operation
Parliament	The Parliament shapes policies through legislative processes and by guiding the governments in commenting on reports on energy and climate strategies, and in the national positions on emerging EU policies
Municipal administration	Many municipalities own energy companies fully or partly and are involved in choice of energy production. Municipalities are also major consumers of energy
Energy producers; major consumers such as the forest, metal, and chemical industries; other large firms	Energy producers and major consumers are involved in working groups shaping policy and make expert statements in formal hearings at the level of government and parliament. Activities also in European level policy processes. The major consumers of energy (see Fig. 1) are recognized in all institutional processes concerning energy and energy policy. The IT sector may have an interest to influence, e.g., energy efficiency

(continued)

Table 1 (continued)

Actor group	Relevant institutions and/or channels of influence and their role in shaping energy policy
Civil society: Civic associations, consumers/citizens, employee organizations	Involvement in processes concerning energy and energy policy (hearings, submission of statements, debates on policies). Focused activism and debate on specific topics such as nuclear energy, small-scale energy production, greenhouse gas reduction, use of forest resources
Governmental and private research institutes, universities and polytechnics	Research institutes are commissioned to carry out specific studies on climate and energy policies. Government research institutes also provide input needed for reporting on energy and carry out research often jointly with universities, polytechnics, and private research institutes on policies and policy change
Mass media	Public debate on energy issues, affecting the policy processes

energy, the second highest in the EU after Sweden (54%), and 17% nuclear energy, Finland appears to be a forerunner in reducing dependency on fossil fuels (Eurostat 2019b). In particular, the large share of forest-based bioenergy (Fig. 2) makes Finland a special case in the energy transition.

In the spring of 2019, a new government led by the Social Democrats, and including both the Green Party and the Center Party, formulated its program with a very strong agenda for climate change mitigation. A key objective is to *"put Finland on a path towards achieving carbon neutrality by 2035"* (Government of Finland 2019, p. 12). The previous government stressed the replacement of imported fossil fuel-based energy even at the risk of continuing the use of peat: *"The use of emission-free, renewable energy will be increased in a sustainable way so that its share will rise to more than 50% during the 2020s and the self-sufficiency in renewable energy to more than 55%, **also including peat**"* (Emphasis added) (Government of Finland 2015a, p. 24). The quote shows the long-standing effort by especially the Center Party to maintain the use of peat, even if the overall aim was to move toward carbon-free, clean, and renewable energy cost-efficiently. The current government plans to slowly phase out peat: *"We will decrease the use of peat for energy by at least half by 2030"* (Government of Finland 2019, p. 35).

Another major driver and potential cause of tension in the current domestic energy transition are the efforts to build up a forest-based bioeconomy. When the Finnish electronics industry was at its peak in 2007–2008, it appeared that the role of the forest industry would diminish further in the Finnish economy. More profitable high-tech industries would become the backbone of the economy. With that energy consumption would diminish. However, although paper and board production have decreased, chemical pulp and sawn wood have increased since 2009. This led the previous government to state in its program that the 10-year objective is to make Finland "*a pioneer in the bioeconomy, a circular economy and cleantech*" (Government of Finland 2015a, p. 24). The current government is also a believer in the bioeconomy, but has added that the aim is to achieve a "*transition to a low-carbon bioeconomy and circular economy*" (Government of Finland 2019, p. 105).

In the past, political support for other renewable sources has at times emerged but after a while wood-based bioenergy has been seen to be the best option (Kivimaa 2008; Kivimaa and Mickwitz 2011). This was largely the approach also taken in the national forestry strategy that encourages a significant increase of cuttings in forests to build up the bioeconomy and, as a side product, the production of wood-based renewable energy (Government of Finland 2015b). Tensions now arise because the planned increase would potentially decrease the forest carbon sink to levels that may violate the so-called no debit rule of the Land Use, Land Use Change, and Forestry (LULUCF) Regulation (EU) 2018/841. The rule implies that a country is not free to reduce its sink below a reference level that will be set individually for each member state in a process specified by the regulation. A significant increase in the cuttings would require Finland to identify ways to either increase the forest carbon sinks through other means, for example, by accelerating forest growth, or to reduce emissions from land use by changing the use of organic soils that currently cause significant emissions.

Strategies and Instruments of Energy Transitions

The need for an energy transition was expressed explicitly in the energy and climate strategy (Government of Finland 2017a) and in the medium-term climate change plan under the Finnish Climate Change Act (Government of Finland 2017b), which aimed to fulfil Finland's EU targets (i.e., a 39% reduction in emissions from the effort sharing sector by 2030 compared to 2005). The current government has increased the stakes. Hence, the strategy of 2016 and the medium-term plan need an update. The strategies and plans in force are characterized by path dependency with respect to the choice of actions. Although they reflect the increasing ambitions of the EU from 2020 to 2030 in the choice of instruments, they fall short of the carbon neutrality target for 2035.

The increasing ambition will potentially lead to greater complexity in policy making. Kern et al. (2017) have observed that, in the building sector, there is an increasing variety of goals and instruments and that different instrument types are combined to influence energy consumption. The same development can also be seen in other areas (Table 2). Thus, it is necessary to examine policy goal and instrument mixes rather than individual instruments. This will make it challenging to monitor and evaluate the energy and climate strategy (2016) and the medium-term climate plan (2017) in order to determine which additional actions should be taken. With numerous instruments expected to jointly contribute to a transition toward a low carbon society, it is difficult to examine the effectiveness of any particular instrument. As such, this is in line with findings suggesting that a multiplicity of

Table 2 Categories of recent instruments potently affecting the energy transition in key areas of energy production and use

Sector of energy consumption/ production	Regulatory	Incentive-based instruments	Internalizing instruments	Soft governance
Large-scale energy production	The prohibition against the use of coal in energy production enters into force May 1 2029 (Act 416/2019)	Investment subsidies for major energy production investments (transport fuels or innovative renewable production) (Council of State Regulation 145/2016)	Carbon emission-based taxation of liquid fuel (Act 1472/1994); Act on production taxes on electricity and some fuels (1260/1996). The European ETS internalises emission costs	The regularly updated energy and climate strategies represent independently of the specific measures they identify, "soft" governance toward low carbon transitions
Energy production based on renewables (bioenergy, wind, and solar)	Act on energy markets 588/2013 ensuring access to electricity grid also for small-scale production	Energy subsidies to companies and communities for energy efficiency and renewables (Council of State, Regulation 1063/2012, Act on production subsidies for electricity generated with renewables 1396/2010)	-.	Same as for large-scale energy production. Advisory services for, e.g., wood chip use
Industrial consumption	-	Act on state guarantees for environmental and energy investments 609/1973	Carbon emission-based taxation of liquid fuel (Act 1472/1994); Act on production taxes on electricity and some fuels (1260/1996). The European ETS	Energy efficiency agreements and energy audits (Motiva ltd)
Buildings	Regulations on energy efficiency in buildings	Subsidies in 2013–2014 to	Carbon emission based	Act on energy certificates for

(continued)

Table 2 (continued)

Sector of energy consumption/ production	Regulatory	Incentive-based instruments	Internalizing instruments	Soft governance
	(collection of building regulations D3, D7); Land use and building act (132/1999)	municipalities for repair and energy efficiency; act on subsidies for repairs, energy efficiency and health improvement of dwellings, 1184/2005 (discontinued 1.1.2017); Tax reduction based on home renovation (act on income tax 1535/1992); Support for experimental low energy buildings	taxation of liquid fuels (Act 1472/1994) raises costs of oil heated buildings	buildings 50/2013 Information dissemination and campaigns targeted to residents and other users of buildings. Energy advice architecture
Transport	Act on the promotion of biofuels in transport 446/2007: Mandatory share of biofuel. The transport service act 320/2017 (allowing new mobility services aiming to reduce private car use)	Planned subsidies for purchase of electric vehicles (Energy and Climate Strategy 2016). Innovation funding for electric vehicle infra development and mobility as a service	Carbon emission-based taxation of liquid fuels (Act 1472/1994) Act on vehicle taxation (1281/2003) higher tax for vehicles with high-emission levels	Energy efficiency agreements for the transport sector (Motiva ltd). Experimental initiatives to support low-carbon transport as part of intelligent transport systems, e.g., the traffic lab
Agriculture	-.	Support for energy efficiency and renewables through regional development funds.	The internalizing of carbon costs in fuel and electricity affects energy costs in agriculture	Farm energy program and energy advice to the farms

instrument mixes are needed to foster low-carbon transitions (Rogge et al. 2017), but it clearly complicates policy learning.

In Finland, all types of policy instruments have been used to foster energy transitions, but the instruments are not evenly spread across sectors and activities (Table 2). Not surprisingly, there is a preference for incentive-based instruments and soft governance. The transport and buildings sectors have also important regulatory instruments and all sectors are in principle affected by the internalizing instruments that raise the price of fossil energy. However, political decisions have drastically reduced the internalizing effect.

The transport sector is one of the more challenging areas for reducing emissions. Three alternative scenarios for eliminating transport-caused emissions have been elaborated (Särkijärvi et al. 2018), but there is no unequivocal support for any solution. A significant increase in electric vehicles is likely to be one element but other instruments such as extending a form of emissions trading to transport fuels (Liski et al. 2019) have been proposed. There is significant policy development (both regulations and soft governance) supporting a transition to intelligent transport systems. These may be significant in the low-carbon transition, if climate change mitigation is properly integrated into these developments. A special working group has also been appointed to examine the long-term future of transport-related taxation (Ministry of Finance 2019b).

Tax authorities estimate that there are 13 different categories of energy tax subsidies, many directed to support fossil fuels or energy intensive sectors. In 2018, they were estimated to amount to more than 2,500 Million euro, with an increase from 2016 by approximately 200 Million euro. Important tax subsidies include a lowered tax rate for diesel fuel (nearly 800 M€), lower tax rate for light oil that replaces diesel in machinery (460 M€), lower tax rate for peat (130 M€), lower tax rate for industry and greenhouses (625 M€), and lower tax rate for combined heat and power plants (around 100 M€). In addition, major energy consumers receive a direct repayment of energy taxes amounting to more than 200 M€. These figures can be compared with the actual fiscal income from energy taxation which, for 2020, has been estimated to be 4 666 Million euro (Ministry of Finance 2019a, p. 07. Taxation).

The tax deductions and repayments demonstrate a concern for heavy energy users and a political choice to reduce the transformative power of the internalizing instruments in use. The tax subsidies also reveal the political strength of the energy intensive industry. The repayment of taxes to energy intensive companies has been shown to be noneffective in a meticulous evaluation carried out by the Government Economics Research Institute VATT for the Council of State (Harju et al. 2016). However, this "anti-transitional" instrument has remained in the state budget. There is also a recent Act to compensate for the indirect effects of the European Emission Trading Scheme (138/2017) and specified by a regulation of the Council of State (311/2017). The subsidy (up to 78 M€ in the budget proposal for 2020) (Ministry of Finance 2019a, p. 32.60.46) aims at compensating industries that may be subject to the risk of a carbon leak. In practice, the list of activities has been made broad enough to reduce the internalizing effect of the emission trading system.

The main incentives for a transition toward renewables are an energy investments subsidy (110 M€ in the budget proposal for 2020) and the production subsidies for renewable energy (233 M€ in the budget proposal for 2020), distributed on feed in tariffs for wind energy (229 M€), wood chip and wood burning (310,000 €), and biogas (2.7 M€). Increasing attention is being put on energy efficiency, and part of the 110 M€ investment subsides in the state budget for 2020 can be used for promoting energy efficiency. The Energy Authority has dedicated activity to energy efficiency (Energy Authority 2019b).

The high costs of the production subsidies have drawn extensive criticism from the energy producers who claim that they have disrupted the energy market. Consumers have, however, benefited. Liski and Vehviläinen (2016) have shown that a relatively small-scale entry of renewables leads to a large-scale transfer of surplus from the incumbent producers to the consumers. *"With 10 % market share for wind, consumers" expenditures decline by one-half*" (Liski and Vehviläinen 2016, p. 2). From a consumer point of view, the partial transition has thus been a blessing and the money well spent. This view is obviously not shared by the incumbents. The Finnish energy producers' organization argues that subsidies should be directed to *"new, higher-risk technologies or investments that promote energy efficiency and clean solutions instead of spending the resources on already tested technology in the form of production subsidies*" (Finnish Energy n.d.).

Coordination Mechanisms and Multilevel Governance

The previous sections have demonstrated that Finland has aimed for a political consensus that safeguards the position of the energy intensive industry and that provides as much development space for the bio-based industry as possible. The coordination mechanisms that have been used to this end build on three main pillars. The overall political pillar is that of the government program agreed upon by the governing coalition and issued in the beginning of the government's term. The next level of coordination is that achieved by national energy and climate strategies that are prepared jointly by key ministries. The Ministry of Economic Affairs and Employment has coordinated the work. The resulting strategies have been approved by the government. As of 2015, the planning according to the Climate Act constitutes the third key mechanism for coordination. The planning, according to the Climate Act, is closely connected with the preparation of the Energy and Climate Strategy, e.g., in applying the same basic scenarios. As most of the significant energy-related policies emerge at or have links with the EU policies, the government's positions on EU policies are coordinated both internally within the government and also reported to the Parliament that provides statements on the Finnish positions.

Since 2007, all government programs have dealt extensively with energy issues (Table 3). The programs have been reflected in subsequent strategies that the governments have submitted as reports to Parliament and in the governments' position on EU policies. The general logic has been to safeguard the Finnish

Table 3 Key points in relation to energy and energy transition in Finnish Government Programs from 2007

Coalition	Key positions on energy and climate issues
Matti Vanhanen's II cabinet 19.4.2007 coalition: Centre party, National Coalition Party, greens, Swedish People's party. PM: Centre party; minister of economic affairs: Centre party; minister of the environment: Centre party	Strong focus on bio-based renewable energy, including the emphasis of regulatory instruments to increase bio-based fuels in transport. Energy saving underlined Long-term plan for energy and climate futures (2050)
Mari Kiviniemi's cabinet 22.6.2010 coalition a continuation of Matti Vanhanen's II cabinet	Continuation of previous program. Explicit statement to implement regulatory instruments for renewable energy
Jyrki Katainen's cabinet 22.6.2011, National Coalition Party, social democratic party, left Alliance, greens, Swedish party, and Christian democrats. PM: National Coalition Party, minister of economic affairs: Conservatives, minister of the environment: Greens The left Alliance left 4.4.2014	Emphasis on need for energy transition to renewables, while simultaneously underlying the lowering of taxation for energy intensive activities. Gradual increase in taxation of peat Strong emphasis on possibilities for clean tech exports Aim to proactively influence European energy and climate policies in such a way that Finland's special features are duly acknowledged in the EU Recognition of increasing integration of energy markets and smart grid development, also taking increasing share of renewables into account
Alexander Stubb's cabinet 24.6.2014. Continuation of Jyrki Katainen's cabinet, but the greens left 26.9.2014 and the minister of the environment was taken over by the National Coalition Party	Continuation of the previous program Basic acceptance of the EU 2030 energy and climate package with a 40% emission reduction target on the condition that the burden sharing is fair An energy and climate road map for the 2050 is to be developed and the climate Act is to be approved An analysis of options for the energy sector based on the parliamentary work Special emphasis on renewable energy and distributed energy production competitiveness and self-sufficiency in energy are underlined
Juha Sipilä's Cabinet 29.5.2015, Centre Party, National Coalition Party, True Finns, split in June 2017 into the Blue Future that continued in government PM: Centre party; minister of economic affairs: Centre party, minister of the environment: Center party	Adoption of low-emission energy sources will be encouraged through taxation. The EU 2020 goals are to be achieved ahead of schedule Imported fossil fuel-based energy to be replaced by clean and renewable domestic energy A key project is "towards carbon-free, clean and renewable energy cost-efficiently." renewable energy will be increased in a sustainable way so that its share will rise to

(continued)

Table 3 (continued)

Coalition	Key positions on energy and climate issues
	more than 50% during the 2020s and the self-sufficiency in renewable energy to more than 55%, also including peat A compensation system for the indirect impacts of emissions trading on electricity prices will be introduced, financed by means of the revenue from emissions trading. Disruptive statements include the aim that coal should no longer be used in energy production, and the use of imported oil for the domestic needs will be cut by half during the 2020s The share of renewable transport fuels will be raised to 40% by 2030 All climate policies must take account of the competitiveness of Finnish export industries and ensure fair burden sharing
Antti Rinne's cabinet 6. 6. 2019, social democratic party, Centre party, greens, Swedish People's party and left Alliance PM: Social democratic party Minister of finance: Centre party; minister of economic affairs: Centre party, minister of the environment and climate: Greens. Reconfigured as Sanna Marin's cabinet 10.12. 2019 without change of program	A promise to work toward making Finland carbon neutral by 2035 Carbon neutrality is combined with the protection of biodiversity Climate action is linked to the wider sustainable development goals Tax reforms to speed up transitions Strengthening the role of the climate act Emphasis on a fair transition and extensive societal dialogues Active phase out of coal by 2029 to be followed by phase out of fossil oil In cooperation with industry operators, sector-specific low-carbon roadmaps Strengthen carbon sinks and stocks in the short- and long-term Diversification of forest management Reduction of the carbon footprint of construction and housing Climate friendly food policy

positions, which in practice has meant searching for ways to fulfil EU-obligations in a way that minimizes structural changes in the Finnish industries. The statement that *"all climate policies must take account of the competitiveness of Finnish export industries and ensure fair burden sharing"* (Government of Finland 2015a) illustrates the thinking. The challenge of becoming carbon neutral by 2035 has changed the argumentation somewhat. Competitiveness is still emphasized, but in a more inclusive form *"The Government's objectives are to safeguard real competitiveness and cost-competitiveness, to ensure the stability and predictability of decision-making, to broaden the export base to include new enterprises, sectors and markets, and to boost added value."* (Government of Finland 2019, p. 13). It remains to be seen, if this inclusive approach is retained, or if the government will be forced by the industry to revert to the exclusive approach that focuses on the immediate interests of the domestic industries.

The governments' positions can be understood against a backdrop of strong influence from major energy utilities, the heavy industry and the grid operators and their organizations (see Table 1). These actors have had direct access to key processes in the governments and Ministries through personal contacts and through deep involvement in strategy processes and more detailed legislative process of specific instruments. Their influence is likely to remain strong. However, the processes have become increasingly open and also less influential actors are given a say. For example, the draft renewal of the Energy Subsidies Regulation (1063/2012) was opened for public hearing in a letter to 20 named actors, including small-scale operators and their organizations (letter TEM/2096/03.03.01/2017). In addition, the proposal was posted on the internet, and anybody could comment on it. In the end, only one unsolicited statement was obtained (Lausuntopalvelu 2017).

The coordination within the energy and climate policies has been achieved through the energy and climate strategies. As revealed by the most recent Government Program, the coordination between energy, climate, and forest policies has been strengthened. The national forest strategy (Government of Finland 2015b) and the associated process has, therefore, also become an important element of the energy policy coordination. It has influenced the statements and goals in the energy policies and given forestry actors a strong say also in energy issues.

Municipalities have in the past not been ranked as influential actors in the energy sector (Ruostetsaari 2010a), but the increasing attention paid to energy consumption may change the situation. Collectively, municipalities can be influential in energy policy. They can also act as sites for "transition experiments" (Heiskanen and Matschoss 2016; Matschoss and Heiskanen 2017). Municipalities have been recognized as relevant actors in the recent energy and climate strategies and the medium-term climate change plan. The latter makes explicit reference to the experimental work that is ongoing in the Carbon Neutral Municipalities' "Hinku"-network (Carbon neutral Finland 2019). Furthermore, twelve Finnish municipalities or regions participate in the European Covenant of Mayors initiative, representing in total about 40% of the Finnish population. The diversity of the municipalities have until recently largely hindered them from having a strong say in energy policy development. The need to find new solutions for the upscaling of the use of renewables, for mobility and land use planning may open up new routes of influence. So far, municipalities have been ordinary stakeholders in the processes leading to energy and climate strategies and the medium-term plan.

Outcomes, Challenges, and Prospects of Energy Governance

Finland has so far achieved EU targets, and is likely to be able to fulfill also the 2020 targets (Government of Finland 2015a). The 2030 EU targets are more demanding, but Finland expects to be able to achieve them (Government of Finland 2017a, b). Finland has decided to phase out coal and cut oil use by a quarter by 2030 by relying heavily on nuclear power and bioenergy. Under the current government, Finland seeks a path toward carbon neutrality by 2035 (Table 3), which is truly challenging. It will require rethinking the energy production to avoid long-term risks (Lund 2017). Such risks can be identified in interaction between plans for forest use and bioenergy and the emerging rules for setting objectives in the land use, land use change and forest sector (LULUCF). Demands to preserve biodiversity may also become an obstacle to increased intensity in the forestry. Criteria for renewable energy, in particular, those that apply to forest-based energy sources are also likely to limit the opportunities to replace fossil fuels by forests biomass.

The Forestry Problem in Energy Governance

The challenges of heavy reliance on forest bioenergy arise because an increase in forest use, which provides a side stream of raw material that can be converted to biofuels and chips for forest bioenergy, reduces the carbon sinks of forests. This reduction is potentially so large that Finland's net emissions, taking into account both sources and sinks, will not diminish by 2030 relative to current levels (Koljonen et al. 2017). If the reference level for the forest sink in Finland is calculated based on the average intensity of exploitation in 2000–2009, and the actual exploitation develops as foreseen in the current national Finnish Forest Strategy, Finland may find itself in a position where it is necessary to achieve additional reductions (i.e., reduction beyond those currently planned) of emissions in the sector subject to the EU effort sharing decision or, alternatively, obtain additional sinks for the LULUCF-sector by buying them from countries with surpluses.

The possibility that Finland will have to take into account the climate consequences of an increasing exploitation of forests has caused strong national reactions. A Finnish MEP was instrumental in turning the view of the European Parliament on the LULUCF regulation in such a way that forest use could expand with minimal restrictions due to diminishing sinks. This was hailed as an important achievement in Finland by the Minister of Agriculture and Forestry, with the argument that "*Finnish forests will be a significant carbon sink also in the future, even if their use is to be increased.*" (Ministry of Agriculture and Forestry 2017). This standpoint was also reflected in Finland's position in advance of the meeting of the Council of Environment Ministers "*The aim for Finland is that the proposal would allow to increase harvesting for the needs of sustainable forestry and to adopt a longer-term perspective on the accumulation of carbon sinks*" (Ministry of the Environment and Ministry of Agriculture and Forestry 2017).

The outcome of the negotiations in the Council of Ministers did not, contrary to the vote in the European Parliament, please Finland. Finland felt that the reference period for forest sinks proposed by the Council (2000–2009) is unfair as it includes a period of economic recession and slow or no increase in cuttings, while forest growth increased substantially. The period resulted in an accumulation of sinks that Finland plans to exploit 2020–2030, in order to meet the targets for renewable energy and reduction of fossil fuel use by 2030. Thus, the agreed LULUCF regulation granted Finland an additional compensation of ten million tons of CO_2 equivalent for the period 2021–2030 (Regulation (EU) 2018/841, Article 13.4). This did, however, not satisfy the Finnish government nor, for example, the Finnish forest industry. The Minister of Energy and Climate repeated the argument that, if Finland is not allowed to increase the exploitation of forests as planned, without compensating for the reduction in sinks, Finland would have to reduce emissions more than 40% by 2030, which would be against the principle agreed upon in 2014 in the EU. According to this principle, no member state would have to reduce its emissions by more than 40% by 2030. The current government has, however, made this argumentation redundant with its objective to become carbon neutral by 2035.

The strong reaction against the drafted LULUCF regulation, and the efforts to change it, was already at the time in conflict with the bold statement that Finland aims to be climate neutral by 2045, and a forerunner in climate action (Government of Finland 2017b). This conflicting message can be understood as the expression of a reluctance to recognize any obligations concerning the maintenance of carbon sinks, beyond ensuring that Finnish forests are "a significant carbon sink also in the future." In other words, the logic is that the forests and the forest sinks are Finland's own and nobody, especially not the EU, is allowed to put any conditions on their use, because Finland has successfully managed forests in a sustainable way for decades. Ultimately, this reflects an unwillingness to accept that the maintenance of current carbon sinks, not just a sink level determined independently at the discretion of individual countries, is an important part of any serious effort to reach the Paris Agreement. The Finnish policy and governance was dictated by a dominant pathway that aimed to safeguard increased timber production, reflecting a productivist forest policy described as "forest bioeconomy" (Kröger and Raitio 2017). It reflected the Centre party's strong position holding key positions in drafting the governments' energy and climate policies (Table 3), but also more generally the historically important position of the forest industry both for the country's wealth and for energy consumption (see Fig. 1). A major challenge of the current government, in which the Centre Party also is a member, will be to reconsider some of the fundamental long-term assumptions in Finnish energy, forest, and industrial policies.

Overall Energy Transitions

The Finnish positions in the EU's energy and climate policy represented for a long time a rather tightly coordinated approach that was conservative and cautious. A growing number of activities and dedicated research challenged this regime and the current government seeks to achieve a transition (Table 3). Partly, the situation can be seen to resemble that of a socio-technical transition (cf. Geels 2002; Geels and Schot 2007). There are, however, multiple transitions that progress with different speed and toward different solutions.

Apart from the painful processes related to the role of forests, there are several ongoing transition debates. On a general level, Kivimaa and Mickwitz (2011) argued that if *"public policies are to enhance the shift toward low-carbon, sustainable energy systems, they would need to be more comprehensive, be more consistent over time, and emphasize energy use more."* Some debates have progressed in this direction with discussion on, for example, grassroots action and energy use (Majuri 2016), and experiments (Matschoss and Heiskanen 2017). The role of consumers and consumption has been explicitly flagged in the medium-term energy plan (Government of Finland 2017b) but without very clear targets. The Program of the Marin Cabinet (Government of Finland 2019) suggests that the efforts to change the situation have been successful, at least at the level of political rhetoric.

Another discussion concerns the links to industrial policy (Johnstone and Kivimaa 2017), the role of policy mixes (Kivimaa and Kern 2016) and their specific application in sectors such as housing (Kivimaa et al. 2017). There is also a recognition of the importance of demand-side management that is becoming increasingly important with the increased share of intermittent energy production (Kopsakangas-Savolainen and Svento 2013; Olkkonen et al. 2017; Huuki et al. 2017). The discussion on demand side management differs radically from the debate on forest energy in that there is a broad consensus on the need for it. An ad hoc working group appointed by the Ministry of Economic Affairs and Employment published its report on smart grids (Pahkala et al. 2018). The working group emphasized novel business models, including owning and operating storages that the working group saw as a task of market players, not monopolies.

The partly separate and parallel discussions may pave the way for somewhat different transitions (Hyysalo et al. 2019a, b). Toivanen et al. (2017) have explored expert views on electricity futures and found three central views with respect to the main thrusts in the expected transition. One view emphasizes international competition and smart solutions, another has a strong belief in active consumers, and a third stresses national competitiveness and maximizing the use of local energy sources. The differences between the views pertain to the extent to which they support international or national electricity markets, and the role they prefer to assign to for state-level governance (Toivanen et al. 2017, p. 155). Toivanen et al. (2017) are basically optimistic concerning possibilities to reshape the energy system and break existing path-dependencies. In the corporatist Finnish system, this may, however, not come about through innovative niche activities but through a reorientation of the incumbents. The reorientation toward carbon neutrality has already been achieved with the Finnish Energy, i.e., the producers' advocacy organization, explicitly stating *"Our goal is a carbon-neutral Finland, a country with a Nordic climate where energy demand and energy production meet in a sustainable way. We will achieve this goal through smart energy solutions aimed for the long-term."* (Finnish Energy 2019)

One of the struggles will be that over electricity supply. Currently, nuclear energy is still a planned energy resource to play an important role but, as noted above (section "Discourses on Energy"), the confidence in the technology has declined rather drastically. The future of the subsidies for renewable energy is also an issue. In the Nordic case, the subsidies to technologies that, once installed, operate with zero marginal costs – such as wind and solar power – have led to reduced final prices for outputs, and hence *"the electricity producers, rather than the consumers, end up paying a major part of the final cost of the new technologies*" (Liski and Vehviläinen 2016, p. 29). This partly explains the often aggressive campaign of energy incumbents against subsidies for renewables.

The transport sector is one of the difficult areas in Finnish energy and climate policy. The fuel base of the transport sector appeared to be secured with the use of side streams from the booming forest industry, but now the prospects look bleaker. There is also the global debate on the future of the internal combustion engine versus electric vehicles. Finland's transport sector, being a small market and practically devoid of any automobile industry, will depend on global developments. However, large-scale investments in the exclusive production of biofuels for private cars may turn out to be highly risky as they can create a costly lock-ins. Investments in biorefineries that can flexibly switch between products are likely to be a more robust strategy. Recent, globally innovative developments in Finland in intelligent transport systems and mobility as a service hold some promise for low-carbon transport systems. If climate change is taken seriously in this context, these developments can contain significant potential to transform transport systems away from fossil fuels and private car ownership.

Monitoring and Surveillance

The regular updating of the energy and climate strategies has provided a regular feedback and policy learning process within the responsible Ministries. They have also given the Parliament regular insights into the evolution of the energy policy. The Climate Act formalizes the monitoring requirement (Section 12, 'Monitoring the implementation of the climate policy plans'). The role of the Parliament is also specified in detail as the government is obliged to provide an annual report on the emissions of greenhouse gases. A biannual report should provide information evaluating the specific measures that have been included in the medium-term climate plan (Section 14, 'The annual climate report').

The requirements concerning the domestic monitoring of greenhouse gas emissions and policies and measures match those of the EU Monitoring Mechanism Regulation 525/2013. The combination of national and EU (and UNFCCC) reporting obligations has minimized the administrative burden associated with reporting, which has often been used to oppose reporting obligations (Schoenefeld et al. 2018). There is little doubt that reporting and learning is needed, but the current system of monitoring of policies faces serious challenges (Schoenefeld et al. 2019). It is nevertheless possible to document progress and the perception of what is achievable in terms of greenhouse gas emission by 2020 has changed significantly (Fig. 3). The most recent "with measures" projection (2016) is clearly below the previous projections based on policies "with additional measures." The development goes in the right direction, but it is of interest to explore why the aggregated measures appear to have been more effective than originally anticipated. As noted above, the multitude of instruments (Table 2) significantly complicates evaluation and policy learning.

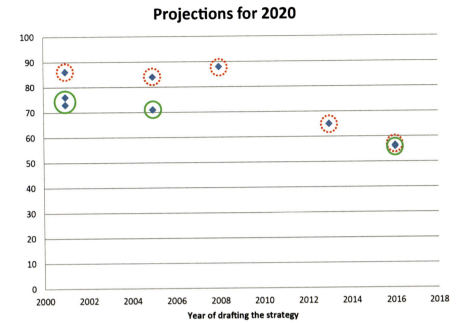

Fig. 3 The greenhouse gas emission projections for 2020 in consecutive energy and climate strategies. Symbols marked with a red-dotted circle indicate some variant of the business as usual or "with measures" policy option whereas the symbols marked with a green circle indicate projections based on additional measures. (Data from the published energy and climate strategies 2001–2016)

The monitoring indicates initial steps in a transition, and the changes in the energy production and consumption are important drivers. For example, in 2016, the total consumption of electricity was projected to be approximately 88 TWh, whereas the policy scenarios in 2001 projected a 10% higher consumption for 2020. Projections for total energy consumption in 2020 were similarly nearly 10% higher when projected in 2001 than when projected in 2016. This indicates an ongoing decoupling. Whether this ongoing process results is a full-scale transition toward genuine carbon neutrality as opposed to the rhetoric statement in the latest medium-term energy plan (Government of Finland 2017b), remains to be seen.

Cross-References

- Cities in European Energy and Climate Governance
- Energy Governance in Europe: Country Comparison and Conclusion
- Energy Governance in Europe: Introduction
- Energy Governance in Denmark
- Energy Governance in Norway

- Energy Governance in Russia: From a Fossil to a Green Giant?
- Energy Governance in Sweden
- European Union Energy Policy: A Discourse Perspective
- EU-Russia Energy Relations
- Extending Energy Policy: The Challenge of Sector Integration
- Monitoring Energy Policy
- The EU in Global Energy Governance
- Transition of Energy Systems: Patterns of Stability and Change

Acknowledgment We acknowledge the support of the Strategic Research Council at the Academy of Finland (Grants 314325 and 314350), project Smart Energy Transition and program coordination.

References

Carbon neutral Finland. (2019). *Hinku Network—Towards Carbon Neutral municipalities*. http://www.hiilineutraalisuomi.fi/en-US/Hinku.

Council on Energy Policy. (1982). *Programme on Energy Policy (in Finnish)* (1982:76; Komiteanmietintö).

Crill, P., Hargreaves, K., & Korhola, A. (2000). *Turpeen asema Suomen kasvihuonekaasutaseissa* (20/2000; Kauppa- Ja Teollisuusministeriön Tutkimuksia Ja Raportteja). Ministry of Trade and Industry.

Energy Authority. (2019a). *Energy authority: About us*. Energiavirasto. https://energiavirasto.fi/en/energy-authority.

Energy Authority. (2019b). *Energy efficiency*. Energiavirasto. https://energiavirasto.fi/en/energy-efficiency.

Eurobarometer. (2010). *Europeans and nuclear safety* (No. 324; special Eurobarometer). European Commission. https://ec.europa.eu/commfrontoffice/publicopinion/index.cfm/Survey/getSurveyDetail/instruments/SPECIAL/surveyKy/769.

Eurostat. (2019a). *Energy statistics—An overview—Statistics explained*. https://ec.europa.eu/eurostat/statistics-explained/index.php?title=Energy_statistics_-_an_overview#Energy_intensity.

Eurostat. (2019b). *Eurostat—Data explorer: Share of energy from renewable sources*. http://appsso.eurostat.ec.europa.eu/nui/setupDownloads.do.

Fennovoima. (2019). *Board of Director's Report 2018* (Annual Reports). Fennovoima. https://www.fennovoima.fi/en/media/publications/annual-reports.

Finnish Customs. (2020). *Finnish import statistics* [Statistical tables]. Uljas Database. https://uljas.tulli.fi/v3rti/db/0/views/dc8723a215f149388d074740db1ffb08.

Finnish Energy. (2019). *Finnish energy is creating a sustainable society*. https://energia.fi/en.

Finnish Energy. (n.d.). *The greatest challenge is the emissions reduction target for the burden-sharing sector*. Retrieved October 30, 2019, from https://energia.fi/en/advocacy/energy_policy/energy_and_climate_strategy.

Geels, F. W. (2002). Technological transitions as evolutionary reconfiguration processes: A multi-level perspective and a case-study. *Research Policy, 31*(8–9), 1257–1274. https://doi.org/10.1016/S0048-7333(02)00062-8.

Geels, F. W., & Schot, J. (2007). Typology of sociotechnical transition pathways. *Research Policy, 36*(3), 399–417. https://doi.org/10.1016/j.respol.2007.01.003.

Government of Finland. (1972). *The programme of Prime Minister Rafael Paasio's II government 23.2.1972 (in Finnish)* (Government Programme). Government of Finland. https://valtioneuvosto.fi/hallitusohjelmat/-/asset_publisher/55-paaministeri-rafael-paasion-ii-hallituksen-ohjelma.

Government of Finland. (1997). *Finland's energystrategy—The Government's report on energy policy to the Parliament (in Finnish)* (VNS 5/1997vp; Valtioneuvoston Selonteko Eduskunnalle). Council of State.

Government of Finland. (2007). *Government programme of prime minister Matti Vanhanen's second Cabinet*. Prime Minister's Office.

Government of Finland. (2015a). *Finland, a land of solutions Strategic Programme of Prime Minister Juha Sipilä's Government 29 May 2015* (12/2015; The Government Publications). Prime Minister's Office.

Government of Finland. (2015b). *National Forest Strategy 2025 Government Resolution of 12 February 2015* (6b/2015; Publications of the Ministry of Agriculture and Forestry). Ministry of Agriculture and Forestry.

Government of Finland. (2017a). *Government report on the National Energy and Climate Strategy for 2030* (12/2017; Publications of the Ministry of Economic Affairs and Employment). Ministry of Economic Affairs and Employment.

Government of Finland. (2017b). *Kohti ilmastoviisasta arkea—Valtioneuvoston selonteko keskipitkän aikavälin ilmastopolitiikan suunnitelmasta vuoteen 2030* (Government Report to the Parliament). Ministry of the Environment.

Government of Finland. (2019). *Programme of Prime Minister Antti Rinne's (and Sanna Marin's) Government 6 June 2019 INCLUSIVE AND COMPETENT FINLAND – A socially, economically and ecologically sustainable society* (Government Programme). http://urn.fi/URN:ISBN:978-952-287-760-4.

Harju, J., Hokkanen, T., Laukkanen, M., Ollikka, K., & Tamminen, S. (2016). *Vuoden 2011 energiaverouudistuksen arviointia* (61/2016; Valtioneuvoston Selvitysja Tutkimustoiminnan Julkaisusarja). VATT Institute for Economic Research. http://vatt.fi/documents/2956369/3243686/Vuoden%202011%20energiaverouudistuksen%20arviointia%20VNK/86970bfe-3656-4756-88ef-06d941aa4e80.

Heiskanen, E., & Matschoss, K. (2016). *Experiments for identifying necessary and missing competences for a smart and sustainable energy system*. European conferences on the human dimensions of global environmental change, Berlin, Germany, 23/05/2016, Berlin. http://hdl.handle.net/10138/176455.

Hildén, M. (2011). The evolution of climate policies – The role of learning and evaluations. *Journal of Cleaner Production, 19*(16), 1798–1811. https://doi.org/10.1016/j.jclepro.2011.05.004.

Huuki, H., Karhinen, S., Kopsakangas-Savolainen, M., & Svento, R. (2017). Flexible demand and flexible supply as enablers of variable energy integration. *SSRN Electronic Journal*. https://doi.org/10.2139/ssrn.2966053.

Hyysalo, S., Lukkarinen, J., Kivimaa, P., Lovio, R., Temmes, A., Hildén, M., Marttila, T., Auvinen, K., Perikangas, S., Pyhälammi, A., Peljo, J., Savolainen, K., Hakkarainen, L., Rask, M., Matschoss, K., Huomo, T., Berg, A., & Pantsar, M. (2019a). Developing policy pathways: Redesigning transition arenas for mid-range planning. *Sustainability, 11*(3), 603. https://doi.org/10.3390/su11030603.

Hyysalo, S., Marttila, T., Perikangas, S., & Auvinen, K. (2019b). Codesign for transitions governance: A mid-range pathway creation toolset for accelerating sociotechnical change. *Design Studies, 63*, 181–203. https://doi.org/10.1016/j.destud.2019.05.002.

IEA. (2013). *Energy policies of IEA countries 2013 review Finland*. IEA. Paris, France.

IEA. (2019). *IEA Energy Atlas*. http://energyatlas.iea.org/#!/tellmap/-297203538/4.

Johnstone, P., & Kivimaa, P. (2017). Multiple dimensions of disruption, energy transitions and industrial policy. *Energy Research & Social Science*. https://doi.org/10.1016/j.erss.2017.10.027.

Kern, F., Kivimaa, P., & Martiskainen, M. (2017). Policy packaging or policy patching? The development of complex energy efficiency policy mixes. *Energy Research & Social Science, 23*, 11–25. https://doi.org/10.1016/j.erss.2016.11.002.

Kivimaa, P. (2008). Finland: Big is beautiful—Promoting bioenergy in regional-industrial contexts. In W. Lafferty & A. Ruud (Eds.), *Promoting sustainable electricity in Europe: Challenging the path dependence of dominant energy systems.* (pp. 159–188). Edgar Elgar, Cheltenham, UK & Northampton, MA, USA.

Kivimaa, P., & Kern, F. (2016). Creative destruction or mere niche support? Innovation policy mixes for sustainability transitions. *Research Policy, 45*(1), 205–217. https://doi.org/10.1016/j.respol.2015.09.008.

Kivimaa, P., & Mickwitz, P. (2011). Public policy as a part of transforming energy systems: Framing bioenergy in Finnish energy policy. *Journal of Cleaner Production, 19*(16), 1812–1821. https://doi.org/10.1016/j.jclepro.2011.02.004.

Kivimaa, P., Kangas, H.-L., & Lazarevic, D. (2017). Client-oriented evaluation of 'creative destruction' in policy mixes: Finnish policies on building energy efficiency transition. *Energy Research & Social Science*. https://doi.org/10.1016/j.erss.2017.09.002.

Koljonen, T., Soimakallio, S., Asikainen, A., Lanki, T., Anttila, P., Hildén, M., Honkatukia, J., Karvosenoja, N., Lehtilä, A., Lindroos, T. J., Regina, K., Salminen, O., Savolahti, M., Siljander, R., & Tiittanen, P. (2017). *Energia- ja ilmastostrategian vaikutusarviot: Yhteenvetoraportti* (21/2017; Valtioneuvoston Selvitysja Tutkimustoiminnan Julkaisusarja). Valtioneuvoston kanslia.

Kopsakangas-Savolainen, M., & Svento, R. (2013). Promotion of market access for renewable energy in the Nordic power markets. *Environmental and Resource Economics, 54*(4), 549–569. https://doi.org/10.1007/s10640-012-9605-z.

Kröger, M., & Raitio, K. (2017). Finnish forest policy in the era of bioeconomy: A pathway to sustainability? *Forest Policy and Economics, 77*, 6–15. https://doi.org/10.1016/j.forpol.2016.12.003.

Lausuntopalvelu. (2017). *Luonnos valtioneuvoston asetukseksi energiatuen myöntämisen yleisistä ehdoista. Lausuntopyynnön diaarinumero: Tem/2096/03.03.01/2017*. Lausuntopalvelu.fi. https://www.lausuntopalvelu.fi/FI/Proposal/Participation?proposalId=05d9f489-aefe-4368-891f-d07c278b636f.

Leinonen, A. (Ed.). (2010). *Turpeen tuotanto ja käyttö Yhteenveto selvityksistä*. VTT Technical Research Centre of Finland. Espoo, Finland.

Liski, M., & Vehviläinen, I. (2016). Gone with the wind? An empirical analysis of the renewable energy rent transfer. *CESifo Working Paper Series, 6250*, 1–70.

Liski, M., Nokso-Koivisto, O., Nurmi, E., & Vehviläinen, I. (2019). *Towards carbon free transport: A proposal for a mechanism (in Finnish)* (p. 20). Aalto University, School of Economics. https://www.dropbox.com/s/j4r511z64ndjlav/AaltoEI_LVM-raportti_Final.pdf?dl=0.

Lund, P. D. (2017). Implications of Finland's plan to ban coal and cutting oil use. *Energy Policy, 108*, 78–80. https://doi.org/10.1016/j.enpol.2017.05.043.

Majuri, P. (2016). Ground source heat pumps and environmental policy – The Finnish practitioner's point of view. *Journal of Cleaner Production, 139*, 740–749. https://doi.org/10.1016/j.jclepro.2016.08.017.

Matschoss, K., & Heiskanen, E. (2017). Making it experimental in several ways: The work of intermediaries in raising the ambition level in local climate initiatives. *Journal of Cleaner Production*. https://doi.org/10.1016/j.jclepro.2017.03.037.

Ministry of Agriculture and Forestry. (2017, September 13). *European Parliament voted on the LULUCF Regulation – Important step for forestry*. https://mmm.fi/en/article/-/asset_publisher/euroopan-parlamentti-aanesti-lulucf-asetuksesta-tarkea-askel-metsataloudelle.

Ministry of Finance. (2019a). *The Finnish State Budget 2020 [in Finnish]* (State Budget).

Ministry of Finance. (2019b, August 30). *Working Group appointed to assess long-term development of transport taxation (in Finnish)*. Valtiovarainministeriö. https://vm.fi/artikkeli/-/asset_publisher/tyoryhma-selvittamaan-liikenteen-verotuksen-kehittamista-pitkalla-aikavalilla.

Ministry of the Environment. (2017). *Ministeri Tiilikainen: Ympäristöneuvoston LULUCF-päätös Suomelle pettymys*. Valtioneuvosto. https://valtioneuvosto.fi/artikkeli/-/asset_publisher/ministeri-tiilikainen-ymparistoneuvoston-lulucf-paatos-suomelle-pettymys.

Ministry of the Environment, & Ministry of Agriculture and Forestry. (2017, October 12). *Environment Ministers to agree on the LULUCF regulation*. Https://Www.Ymparisto.Fi/En-US/Climate_and_air/Environment_Ministers_to_agree_on_the_LU(44766). https://www.ymparisto.fi/en-US/Climate_and_air/Environment_Ministers_to_agree_on_the_LU(44766).

Ministry of Trade and Industry. (1979). *Programme for energy policy, approved by the Govenmnet 15.3.1979 [in Finnish]* (p. 30).

OECD. (2016). *OECD economic surveys FINLAND* (January 2016; OECD Economic Surveys). OECD.

Official Statistics of Finland. (2019). *Statistics Finland—Statistics by topic—Energy supply and consumption.* http://www.stat.fi/til/ehk/tau_en.html.

Olkkonen, V., Rinne, S., Hast, A., & Syri, S. (2017). Benefits of DSM measures in the future Finnish energy system. *Energy, 137,* 729–738. https://doi.org/10.1016/j.energy.2017.05.186.

Pahkala, T., Uimonen, H., & Väre, V. (2018). *Flexible and customer-centred electricity system Final report of the Smart Grid Working Group* (33/2018; Publications of the Ministry of Economic Affairs and Employment). Ministry of Economic Affairs and Employment. http://julkaisut.valtioneuvosto.fi/handle/10024/161119.

Rogge, K. S., Kern, F., & Howlett, M. (2017). Conceptual and empirical advances in analysing policy mixes for energy transitions. *Energy Research & Social Science.* https://doi.org/10.1016/j.erss.2017.09.025.

Ruostetsaari, I. (2006). Social upheaval and transformation of elite structures: The case of Finland. *Political Studies, 54*(1), 23–42. https://doi.org/10.1111/j.1467-9248.2006.00564.x.

Ruostetsaari, I. (2010a). Changing regulation and governance of Finnish energy policy making: New rules but old elites?: Changing regulation and governance of Finnish energy policy making. *Review of Policy Research, 27*(3), 273–297. https://doi.org/10.1111/j.1541-1338.2010.00442.x.

Ruostetsaari, I. (2010b). Citizens, politicians and experts in energy policy-making: The case of Finland. *Energy & Environment, 21*(3), 203–222. https://doi.org/10.1260/0958-305X.21.3.203.

Ruostetsaari, I. (2017). Stealth democracy, elitism, and citizenship in Finnish energy policy. *Energy Research & Social Science, 34,* 93–103. https://doi.org/10.1016/j.erss.2017.06.022.

Särkijärvi, J., Jääskeläinen, S., & Lohko-Soner, K. (Eds.). (2018). *Carbon-free transport by 2045 – Paths to an emission-free future interim report by the transport climate policy working group.* Ministry of Transport and Communications. http://urn.fi/URN:ISBN:978-952-243-555-2.

Säynässalo, E. (2009). Nuclear energy policy processes in Finland in a comparative perspective: Complex mechanisms of a strong administrative state. In M. Kojo & T. Litmanen (Eds.), *The renewal of nuclear power in Finland* (pp. 126–158). London: Palgrave Macmillan.

Schoenefeld, J. J., Hildén, M., & Jordan, A. J. (2018). The challenges of monitoring national climate policy: Learning lessons from the EU. *Climate Policy, 18*(1), 118–128. https://doi.org/10.1080/14693062.2016.1248887.

Schoenefeld, J. J., Schulze, K., Hildén, M., & Jordan, A. J. (2019). Policy monitoring in the EU: The impact of institutions, implementation, and quality. *Politische Vierteljahresschrift, 60*(4), 719–741. https://doi.org/10.1007/s11615-019-00209-2.

Statistics Finland. (2019a). *Electricity consumption by sector, year and data. PxWeb.* http://pxnet2.stat.fi/PXWeb/pxweb/en/StatFin/StatFin__ene__ehk/statfin_ehk_pxt_013_en.px/table/tableViewLayout1/.

Statistics Finland. (2019b). *Total energy consumption by source and CO2 Emissions by Energy source, Year, Season and Data. PxWeb.* http://pxnet2.stat.fi/PXWeb/pxweb/en/StatFin/StatFin__ene__ehk/statfin_ehk_pxt_001_en.px/table/tableViewLayout1/?rxid=8d24da60-f00f-4aca-b7a9-a27f980bcdf4.

Statistics Finland. (2019c). *Trade.* https://www.tilastokeskus.fi/tup/suoluk/suoluk_kotimaankauppa_en.html.

Toivanen, P., Lehtonen, P., Aalto, P., Björkqvist, T., Järventausta, P., Kilpeläinen, S., Kojo, M., & Mylläri, F. (2017). Finland's energy system for 2030 as envisaged by expert stakeholders. *Energy Strategy Reviews, 18,* 150–156. https://doi.org/10.1016/j.esr.2017.09.007.

Valkila, N., & Saari, A. (2013). Experts' view on Finland's energy policy. *Renewable and Sustainable Energy Reviews, 17,* 283–290. https://doi.org/10.1016/j.rser.2012.09.036.

Energy Governance in France

A Nuclearized Socio-technical Regime "in transition"?

Pierre Bocquillon and Aurélien Evrard

Contents

Introduction	648
General Conditions of Energy Governance in France: Legacies of a Centralized and Nuclearized Energy System	649
Historical Legacies: The Path Toward an "all nuclear, all electric" System	649
The French Energy Mix: Stability and the Slow Growth of Renewables	651
Institutions and Actors: Incumbent Resilience and Evolutions	652
Energy Discourses: From State Modernization to Climate Leadership?	654
Coordination of the Instruments and Issues of the French Energy Transition	655
Drivers of the Energy Transition Narrative: The Green Coalition, the EU, and Fukushima	655
Strategies and Instruments of the Energy Transition	657
Horizontal and Vertical Coordination in an Increasingly Multilevel Context	660
Outcomes, Challenges, and Prospects: French Energy Governance at the Crossroads	662
Cross-References	664
References	664

Abstract

French energy governance is the embodiment of a stable and closed policy subsystem. It is characterized by large-scale centralized infrastructures, the singular dominance of nuclear energy, and historically controlled by a technocratic network of bureaucratic and economic elites. Yet, under the umbrella of the "energy transition," the country has adopted a series of new targets, strategies, and legislation to increase the share of renewables, energy savings,

---

P. Bocquillon (✉)
School of Politics, Philosophy, Language & Communication Studies, University of East Anglia, Norwich, UK
e-mail: p.bocquillon@uea.ac.uk

A. Evrard
UFR Droit et Sciences Politiques, University of Nantes, Nantes, France
e-mail: aurelien.evrard@univ-nantes.fr

© Springer Nature Switzerland AG 2022
M. Knodt, J. Kemmerzell (eds.), *Handbook of Energy Governance in Europe*,
https://doi.org/10.1007/978-3-030-43250-8_10

and reduce GHG emissions. In addition, it has engaged in the twin endeavours of "democratizing" the decision-making process and "decentralizing" energy and climate action. Yet, despite ambitious rhetoric and noticeable new initiatives, French energy governance remains at a crossroad. While emerging dynamics, from the consolidation of a coalition of green actors, to the politicization of energy debates, and to the activism of local authorities, points to incremental change, powerful veto players and sources of path dependence remain.

Keywords

Climate change · Energy · Energy transition · Nuclear · France · Governance · Public participation · Policies · Policy-making

Introduction

French energy policy is at a turning point. The embodiment of a stable and closed policy subsystem, it is increasingly presented as undergoing a process of "transition." New legislation has been adopted to steer the transition – from the Grenelle I and II laws on the environment in 2008–2009 to the Law on the Energy Transition and Green Growth in 2015 – one of the first pieces of legislation in the world to include the objective of "energy transition" in its name – and to the 2021 Climate and Resilience Law. According to the narrative promoted by the French government, it is not only the goals and policy instruments that are undergoing profound change, but also the policy-making process itself, with greater involvement of policy stakeholders and citizens, through local and national consultation processes and, most recently, a deliberative Assembly, the Citizens' Climate Convention. The sector has become the focus of institutionalized debates on its future, as well as on the measures required to accelerate the "transition."

In international comparisons of national energy sectors, some key characteristics of the French system stand out (Lucas and Papaconstantinou 1985; Kitschelt 1986; Finon 1996): its "all-electric, all-nuclear" energy mix; the concentration and vertical integration of its energy industries; and its traditionally centralized and technocratic governance structures. It is also often pointed that, due to the predominance of nuclear energy in electricity generation, the French energy system is less carbon-intensive than most of its European neighbors. Indeed, France has the second lowest GHG emission intensity in electricity generation in the EU (56 g CO_2e/kWh) and the eighth lowest GHG emissions per capita (6.8 tons of CO_2e/capita).

Among French governmental elites, the view that implicitly dominates is that thanks to the low-carbon dividend of nuclear electricity production, the clean energy transition is less pressing an issue than for European neighbors. In the electricity sector, the most heated debates about the "transition" focus on the possible reduction of the share of nuclear energy in the electricity mix and appropriate support to the development of renewable energy sources. The clean energy transition remains particularly challenging in transport, heating, and other sectors that are more heavily reliant on fossil fuels, oil and gas in particular.

In this context, two questions emerge: (1) What are the drivers and dominant narratives underpinning the debate on the energy transition in France? (2) How is the French energy model being transformed, if at all? This chapter argues that despite a now well-institutionalized transition narrative and the emergence of new governance structures and processes, the French energy policy remains in fact at a turning point. While some developments have undeniably been initiated and are already perceptible, sources of path dependence and inertia are still at work and considerably limit the scope for change. In the first section, we present the historical legacies that have shaped French energy governance, emphasizing the collective representations, institutional arrangements, and centralized infrastructures on which it has been built. Then, we discuss how the transition has emerged on the political agenda, showing how the ambiguity of the concept makes it possible to aggregate competing and sometimes contradictory logics, both at the levels of visions and instruments. Finally, we conclude by presenting prospects and the most pressing challenges for energy governance in France in the mid- to long term.

General Conditions of Energy Governance in France: Legacies of a Centralized and Nuclearized Energy System

The French energy system is particularly prone to inertia, or stability to say the least. Strong state control over policy formulation and implementation constitutes one of the principal characteristics of the policy regime. To characterize and explain how a highly centralized and interventionist state has promoted a modernizing paradigm in the energy sector, scholars have usually invoked the tradition of "Colbertism" – referring to the longstanding French preference for large-scale state-led projects (Finon 1996); the institutions of the Jacobin state (Finon 1991); or the Napoleonic legacy (Lucas and Papaconstantinou 1985). However, these *ex post* reconstructions of intellectual legacies hide the fact that this paradigm only emerged and was institutionalized after World War II.

Historical Legacies: The Path Toward an "all nuclear, all electric" System

Energy production and distribution were originally dominated by private actors (for coal and oil) or by highly dispersed public local actors for electricity supply and distribution (Poupeau 2014). The first major inroad of the state in energy was justified by World War I. Managing coal shortages became a crucial challenge, and the government had to set up a rationing policy for electricity. The economic crisis in the 1930s further reinforced this trend, while municipal and regional electricity networks were progressively developed and unified. The state took the responsibility of making important decisions in relation to energy tariffs – in particular the equalization of tariffs throughout the national territory – in order to alleviate the effects of the crisis. In this period, the French state also aimed to increase its influence in the growing and strategic oil sector with the creation of the *Companie Française des Pétroles* (1924), which became an oil major later renamed *Total*. At the end of the decade, it also created other oil companies, which were merged to form ERAP (*Entreprise de Recherches et d'Activités Pétrolières*) later renamed *Elf Aquitaine*.

After World War II, state control over the energy sector was solidified through mergers and nationalizations for electricity, gas, and coal, leading to the creation of three large public utilities with quasi-monopolistic positions: *Électricité de France* (EDF), *Gaz de France* (GDF), and *Charbonnages de France*. This centralization, enshrined in the nationalization legislation of 1946, was however not complete. As shown by Poupeau (2014), preexistent local actors were not kept completely out of production, distribution, and regulatory activities. Through the nationalization process, utilities were entrusted with a public service mission, giving them the ability to define the public interest, while also being directly subject to the regulatory limits set by the government (Bauby 1998). The nationalization process has been thoroughly examined in the case of the electricity sector. EDF's leaders saw themselves as agents of progress for the benefit of the whole national community. In the words of Wieviorka and Trinh (1991: 40): "they [were] confident that they further[ed] the general interest and, in their eyes, the collective optimum and that of EDF [were] only one." Often referred to as a "state within the state" (de Gravelaine and O'Dy 1978), EDF also played a crucial role in the energy policy-making process, sharing power with the powerful Directorate General for Energy and Raw Materials (*Direction Générale de l'Energie et des Matières Premières, DGEMP*) within the Ministry of Industry.

French energy policy was traditionally dominated by a relatively closed policy network, which controlled the decision-making process. Technical elites constituted of engineer-economists from the so-called *Grands corps techniques d'Etat* – specifically the *Corps des Mines* in the energy sector – who held top positions at the highest levels of the state (e.g., heads of central administration, ministerial cabinets) and national energy companies (e.g., top executives) (Bauby 1998; Kessler 1994). Under the intellectual influence of these technocratic elites, the French approach to energy policy was – in the name of the general interest – productivist (i.e., supply driven) and centralized (i.e., top-down and large scale).

French energy policy was driven by three main objectives. The first pillar was social and territorial cohesion. To contribute to the reconstruction and then the modernization of the country, rising energy demand needed to be met at the lowest possible price. The second key objective was to gain national independence vis-à-vis oil-producing countries, an objective that became even more pressing as oil progressively replaced coal in the national energy mix. Finally, the French governments aimed to develop domestic industries and aspired to technological leadership and prestige. Although France was relegated to second-class status on the international stage after WWII, the Gaullist vision that "France cannot be France without greatness" motivated the development of military and then civil nuclear energy (Hecht 1998).

The 1973 oil crisis was a turning point. France had already developed civil nuclear energy (the first reactor was launched in 1956 in Marcoule), and the decision in 1969 to allow EDF to use the more efficient American technology of Pressurized Water Reactors for civil purposes, despite military concerns, was key to its mass deployment (Hecht 1998). However, it is the oil crisis that decided Pierre Messmer's government to launch a massive electronuclear program as an alternative to oil supplies in 1974. The slogan "all-electric, all-nuclear," put forward by EDF in the early 1970s, summarizes the strategy that dominated French energy policy for decades. The objective was the construction of 13 nuclear reactors by 1980, then followed by the construction of four reactors per year. This massive increase in nuclear energy production capacities fitted with the preferences of the technical and economic elites that dominated the sector, whose expertise and vision underpinned the design and implementation of the "Messmer Plan" (Bess 2003). Estimates of future energy needs, on which the plan was based, were upbeat and led to overcapacity in the 1980s when the economic crisis triggered a drop in energy consumption. Under these new conditions, EDF's main objective became to make the investments more profitable, the public monopoly advocating the continuity of the "all-electric, all-nuclear" strategy (Jasper 1990).

The French Energy Mix: Stability and the Slow Growth of Renewables

The French energy mix has remained relatively stable since the 1990s. The share of nuclear power increased rapidly following the start of the electronuclear program in the 1980s, before stabilizing in the early 2000s. In 2019, nuclear represented 40% of French primary energy consumption (see Fig. 1), compared with 29% for oil, 15%

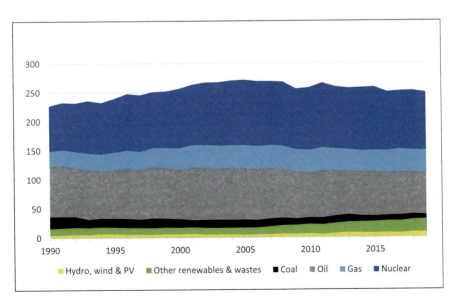

Fig. 1 French primary energy consumption in Mtoe 1990–2019. (Source: Key energy data 2020 Edition – Ministry of the Energy Transition)

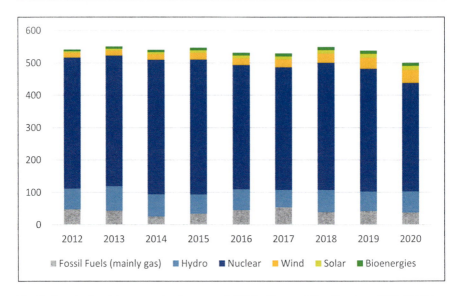

Fig. 2 French electricity generation by source in TWh. (Source: Bilan électrique, RTE (2020))

for natural gas, and only 3% for coal. In contrast, all renewable energy sources (including large hydroelectricity, wood-burning, biofuels, and wastes) represented just 12% of the energy mix. Renewables have been slowly growing over the past decade but without fundamentally transforming the energy mix and at a lower rate than other European neighbors.

The French "all nuclear" strategy appears particularly clearly in the electricity mix of the country (see Fig. 2). In 2020, 67.1% of the country's total electricity production was coming from nuclear energy, while renewable energy sources (RES) represented a quarter (25.3%) – coming mainly from hydropower (13%) and wind power (7.9%) (RTE 2020). Overall, the share of renewable electricity has remained relatively stable for the past 25 years and dominated by large hydroelectricity production developed largely before the electronuclear program. With limited growth potential, the decline of the share of hydroelectricity has been offset by the development of new renewable energy sources. The growth of solar and wind remains slow, however, given the country's very favorable geographical conditions and potential.

Institutions and Actors: Incumbent Resilience and Evolutions

The dominant energy coalition combines public and private actors. While the state-owned electricity company EDF has been in charge of the construction and operation of electricity plants, Orano (formerly FRAMATOM, then Areva) has dealt with the supply, transport, and management of nuclear fuel. GDF (now ENGIE) has been in charge of gas supplies and distribution. For the state, energy was traditionally the remit of the powerful Directorate General for Energy and Raw Materials (*Direction*

27 Energy Governance in France

Générale de l'Energie et des Matières Premières, DGEMP) within the Ministry of Industry, while the Ministry of Economy and Finance also took a strong interest due to the importance of the sector for public coffers (Poupeau 2020). Closely connected to the former energy monopolies through elite expert networks and a shared vision of the sector, the Directorate played a central role in the definition of French energy policies. In addition, other public institutions have played an important role in policy formulation. The Centre for Atomic Energy (*Centre d'Energie Atomique – CEA*) has been a key hub for research and development, which took strong positions on technology choices during the development of the electronuclear program (Hecht 1998). The Authority for Nuclear Safety (*Autorité de Sûreté Nucléaire – ASN; formerly the DSIN*) monitors safety and authorizes decisions. Since it was made an independent authority in 2006, it has regularly flexed its muscles against EDF's commercial interests to enforce stronger safety standards, especially post-Fukushima.

The critical juncture of the energy markets liberalization engaged reluctantly at the turn of the century following the adoption of European Union directives on electricity (1996) and gas (1998) has led to a partial restructuring of the sector and challenged the cozy relationship between energy monopolies and state actors. As mandated by European directives, the 2000 "Law on the Modernization and Development of the Public Service in Electricity" created an independent regulatory authority, the Energy Regulatory Commission (*Commission de Regulation de l'Energie – CRE*), and introduced unbundling of supply/generation, transmission, and distribution activities. This eventually led to the creation of *Réseau de Transport de l'Electricité* (RTE) and GRTgaz for transmission, and ERDF (electricity, now ENEDIS) and GRDF (gas) for distribution, which are subsidiaries of their parent companies but operationally independent and regulated as requested by EU legislation (2003 Directives). Despite several waves of liberalization directives, competition has remained relatively limited in practice as public monopolies, EDF and GDF/ENGIE, have resisted it domestically (Glachant and Finon 2005). Stability is particularly evident in the electricity sector, with only 15% of residential sites supplied by EDF's competitors. The liberalization process has been accompanied by the partial privatization of the former public energy monopolies, which have also embarked on a strategy of aggressive expansion abroad, notably on EU markets.

Liberalization, however partial, has contributed to the fragmentation of state and economic actors' interests and reshaped the structures of power in the energy sector. Paradoxically, it has empowered economic actors vis-à-vis the State, which has increasing difficulties to impose its energy policy preferences. It has also opened a window of opportunity for a greater (re-) involvement of local authorities and actors (Poupeau 2020; see below). However, this fragmentation is partly counterbalanced by the fact that the same network of political and administrative elites remains in key positions of power in the energy governance system (Bauby and Varone 2007).

The other important group of actors is the "green coalition" of supporters of renewable energy and decentralization (Evrard 2013; Poupeau 2020). On the government's side, it has traditionally centered around ADEME, a state agency attached jointly to the three Ministries of Ecology, Research, and Higher Education, which focuses on renewable energy and efficiency. From 2007 onward, following large-scale administrative reforms and in the context of heightened attention to climate issues, the DGEMP (energy directorate) became the Directorate General for Energy and Climate (Direction Générale de l'Energie et du Climat, DGEC) and was moved to the Ministry of Ecology – currently the Ministry for the Ecological and Just Transition. This reorganization has contributed to influencing its positioning, at the interface between the two coalitions. Other private actors that are part of the "green coalition" include interest groups representing the renewable energy sector (e.g., *Syndicat des Energie Renouvelables, France Energie Eolienne*) as well as environmental NGOs (e.g., *France Nature Environment, Climate Action Network*), and the Green Party. As renewable energies have developed, both in terms of installed capacities and prominence on the political agenda, the coalition has grown in numbers and influence, using European and international developments to advance their positions nationally.

Energy Discourses: From State Modernization to Climate Leadership?

The dominant energy discourse has traditionally centered on the security of energy supplies, social equity, and domestic and international competitiveness. A central element of the French energy policy discourse after World War II relates to "public service obligations," not precisely defined yet widely accepted and traditionally performed by state-owned monopolies for the benefits of French consumers and citizens (Bauby and Varone 2007). Energy supplies were central to the reconstruction and modernization of the country, and energy access was a key objective, with territorial and social cohesion being paramount. According to the postwar consensus, energy provision needed to respect the principle of citizen's equality for public service access. This objective notably motivated the creation of the pricing adjustment mechanism called "*péréquation tarifaire*," which requires pricing rules to be the same independently of the location or production and transmission costs. Another example was the social energy tariffs for low-income households, recently replaced by the so-called "energy cheque" in 2018. The liberalization process has enshrined competitiveness as a core issue, with significant consequences, not only on how energy issues are discussed but also on the choice of policy instruments (see the section on instruments).

Nuclear energy has played a central role in relation to security of energy supplies and domestic and international competitiveness. Since the launch of the electronuclear program following the first oil shock, nuclear energy has been presented as a key to ensuring the energy autonomy of the country, limiting the dependence on foreign oil and gas, in particular from Russia and the Middle East. That nuclear fuel is imported from a limited number of countries (Canada, Kazakhstan, and Niger) has rarely registered in the public debate. In addition, civil nuclear is promoted as a high-tech national industry with multiple benefits for the country: creation and maintenance of skilled jobs; source of revenues for the state through its ownership of EDF and Orano; relatively cheap electricity for consumers; and exports of technologies and know-how that contributes to redressing the trade balance. The French nuclear industry has positioned itself as a leader on international markets, vying for contracts with state support, from Europe (Finland, UK) to the Middle East and China (Szarka 2013). Civil nuclear has therefore been hailed as contributing not only to the national economy but also to the international "radiance of France" (Hecht 1998).

Since the late 1990s, environmental and especially climate issues have risen on the international, European, and national agenda, becoming increasingly prominent in the national energy discourse. A major step in that respect was the "Grenelle de l'environnement," a national consultation initiated by the newly elected President Sarkozy at a time of heightened attention for European and international climate negotiations (Boy et al. 2012; Whiteside et al. 2010). The "greening" of nuclear energy has become a key feature of the dominant policy narrative (Mühlenhover 2003; Topçu 2013). Nuclear, an energy source that compares favorably to fossil fuel in terms of Green House Gas (GHG) emissions, is no longer only presented as an essential element of France's security of supply strategy and industrial policy, but also as a central touchstone of its climate policy.

Coordination of the Instruments and Issues of the French Energy Transition

Drivers of the Energy Transition Narrative: The Green Coalition, the EU, and Fukushima

Despite its overall stability, endogenous and exogenous pressures for change have opened spaces for potentially more transformative future shifts of the energy system. The first driver is domestic, as a result of the growth and strengthening of the green coalition. The second, external factor, is the growing involvement of the European Union in energy policy from the mid-1990s onward. In conjunction, they have contributed to destabilizing – but not overturning – existing institutional arrangements while influencing the framing of energy policy, increasingly presented as a response to climate change. The third factor is the intense debate on the future of nuclear energy after Fukushima.

Due to the strategic decision to develop large-scale civil nuclear, France has been a slow mover in terms of deployment of renewable energy sources. A turning point was the united left coalition government ("Gauche plurielle") of Prime Minster Jospin including the dominant Socialist Party, the Communists, and a junior Green partner (Evrard 2013). During this period, the first Feed-in-Tariff (FIT) was adopted on the model of the German EEG, as part of the 2000 energy bill, mainly designed to liberalize energy markets. The presence of the Green Party in government, and also as part of local executives, has contributed to bolstering the influence of the broader green coalition, in particular the network of renewable energy interest groups.

These internal dynamics have converged with external pressures for change, in particular from the EU level. With the adoption of the 2000 European Climate Change Programme, followed by a raft of legislation to implement the EU's Kyoto commitments, including the first renewable electricity directive in 2001, the energy efficiency directive of 2003, the burden-sharing agreement, and the Emission Trading Scheme (2003) – which was revised multiple times since then – France has been under increasing pressure to live up to its European commitments. This context has been used by the green coalition to put pressure on the government, especially since France has repeatedly lagged behind its European targets, on renewable energy developments in particular.

Only recently, however, the energy transition narrative has become mainstream. The term had initially been promoted by militant civil society organizations such as the association NegaWatt with its zero-carbon scenario, advocating sobriety, efficiency, and renewable energy to achieve a nuclear phaseout and limited use of fossil fuels by 2050 (NegaWatt 2003). The eruption of the objective of "energy transition" on the domestic political agenda dates from the early 2010s. The spread of the notion of transition in political and media circles internationally coincided with a domestic context of crisis and public controversies about civil nuclear power, caused by a combination of factors: the Fukushima disaster in Spring 2011; setbacks in the construction of the European Pressurised Reactor (EPR) in Flamanville; and financial difficulties for Areva. As these controversies were brewing at the time of the 2012 presidential election, and in particular during the primary election of the Socialist Party, the candidate and future President, François Hollande, adopted the transition rhetoric, proposing to "diversify supply sources" and to "promote a low-energy society" through the move away from oil dependence for transport and nuclear dependence for electricity – including the flagship commitment to reducing to 50% the share of nuclear power in the electricity mix. More specifically, he committed to closing the oldest nuclear power plant in Fessenheim, while modernizing the nuclear industry and finishing the construction of the EPR in Flamanville. This sequence gave energy issues unprecedented political attention in a Presidential campaign (Brouard et al. 2013). The candidate Hollande also announced the organization of a major national debate on the energy transition, to prepare legislative work.

Over the years, two competing visions of the transition have been advocated: on the one hand, a more militant, "bottom-up," and decentralized approach, carried by the outsider green coalition; on the other, a more "top-down" and centralized approach, carried by the insiders, i.e., dominant actors in the existing energy regime. The second coalition has gradually succeeded in imposing its conception (Aykut and Evrard 2017; Poupeau 2020). The energy transition has been redefined as a transition to a "decarbonized" or "low-carbon" economy (e.g., Percebois and Mandil 2012), rather than toward decentralized renewable energy sources, preserving the future role of nuclear energy as the primary low-carbon source. From Hollande's Presidency onward, the transition has increasingly become state-initiated and controlled. Yet, fundamental ambiguities remain. Given the relatively low-carbon nature of the electricity mix, should the transition move the country away from nuclear and toward a larger share of renewables, or maintain the share of nuclear energy, with renewable energy in a complementary role? Another ambiguity is that if other sectors than electricity have been progressively enlisted in the transition

27 Energy Governance in France

narrative – agriculture and transport – at least nominally, a major blind spot remains concerning the use – and subsidies – for fossil fuels.

Strategies and Instruments of the Energy Transition

A "millefeuille" of Public Participation Initiatives, Legislation, Strategies, and Targets

Over the past decade, to foster and guide the energy transition, comprehensive national strategies and objectives have been adopted relatively swiftly, albeit in a top-down fashion, and new institutions and processes established, notably to monitor progress and embed citizens' participation in the transition.

Upon its entry into office, the Hollande government followed up on one of its campaign promises and launched a large-scale, multilevel National Energy Transition Debate (DNTE, 2012–2013). President Hollande also established in 2013 the National Council for the Energy Transition, a consultative body charged with issuing recommendations and opinions on new initiatives. The DNTE symbolized the government's ambition to substantively transform not only French energy policy but also the policy-making process itself. A debate on energy policy was not an innovation in and of itself, however, as the DNTE was in fact the continuation of a process of gradual opening of energy issues to public debate, initiated from the 1990s and characterized by the multiplication of fora (national, local, and Internet), diversification of actors involved (local authorities, economic actors, trade unions, and associations), as well as the recognition of the principle of contradictory expertise (Brugidou and Jobert 2015). At the national level, the "Grenelle de l'environnement" set a prominent precedent and template of public consultation (Whiteside et al. 2010). The DNTE was initially framed as a radical rupture with the existing energy regime, aiming to prioritize energy efficiency and sobriety as well as renewables, and opening for debate contested aspects such as scenarios on the evolution of the energy mix, industrial development strategies, and financing. It provided political recognition to challenger actors such as the NegaWatt association, whose scenarios played an important role in the deliberations. However, through the DNTE, the nuclear issue quickly shifted back to the center of controversy. Moreover, the complexity of the debate's organizational structure was a source of confusion, exacerbated by the lack of continuity in the Ministry of Ecology in charge of its implementation, contributing to fuel mistrust in the articulation of the debate with government announcements and decisions (Tsuchiya 2016). In the end, the DNTE did not contribute to clarifying the directions of the energy transition, as constructive ambiguity helped aggregate different visions and enabled each actor to develop their own acceptable interpretations (Aykut and Evrard 2017). The deliberative and decision-making functions of this policy instrument were also partly overshadowed by its role as a tool for communication and legitimation purposes.

The debate paved the way for the Law on the Energy Transition and Green Growth (LTECV) finally promulgated in August 2015, after being postponed several times. There was, however, a relative disconnect between the deliberative spaces set up as part of the debate and the decision-making process, with NGOs noting that some of the key conclusions had been left out and pointing that central administration, in particular the Directorate-General for Energy and Climate, had taken over the matter (Lindgaard 2014). The LTECV deployed a transition narrative through a set of ambitious targets: a 40% GHG emissions reduction target by 2030; a reiteration of the objective of dividing emission by a "Factor Four" by 2050; a target of 32% renewables in energy consumption (40% in electricity); and a 50% reduction in final energy consumption by 2030. The broad objectives enshrined in the law were further specified in the newly instituted National Low Carbon Strategy (SNBC) – a broad strategic document which sets from 2015 onward multiannual carbon budgets to reach France's domestic and international commitments. Concerning nuclear, the LTECV also translated President Holland's two main commitments into law: a reduction to 50% of the nuclear share in electricity production by 2025 and the closure of the Fessenheim power station before the end of his mandate. The law and SNBC were characterized by a major tension between the affirmation of ambitious objectives suggesting a path-shifting strategy, and continuity in terms of policy instruments and implementation. Implementation relied on complementary regulatory texts, notably the Pluri-annual Plan on Energy (Programmation Pluriannuelle de l'Energie, PPE), a technical document in the tradition of French indicative planning which contains detailed energy targets and investment priorities, notably for infrastructure development. However, after being repeatedly postponed, the publication of this text in July 2016 did not dispel existing doubts (Greenpeace 2016; RAC-F 2016). The document did not address the evolution of the nuclear fleet, even though 17 to 20 reactors need to be shut down to meet the 50% target (Cour des Comptes 2016).

Since his election in 2017, President Emmanuel Macron has rhetorically claimed the mantel of leader on climate issues and the energy transition. The first legislative initiative to embody these commitments came in the form of the Climate-Energy Law subsequently adopted in 2019. Of limited ambitions, this law reiterates existing commitments while notably including a 40% reduction in the use of fossil fuels by 2030 (compared to 2012), the phaseout of the last four coal power plants by 2022, assorted with various measures to speed up the deployment of renewable energy, and the renovation of energy-inefficient housing. While this law was still under discussion and contested, the government's agenda was shaken by a mass protest movement, the "Yellow vests," triggered by a rise in the carbon tax on fuel contents (see instrument section below) and lasting for over a year across 2018–2019. This led the government to innovate at the institutional level and to open further the decision-making process. Two new institutions have been created. First, the High Climate Council (Haut Conseil pour le Climat) was established, as an independent expert body responsible for issuing opinions and recommendations on the implementation of French climate policy. Second, the government proposed a Citizen's Climate Convention (Convention Citoyenne pour le Climat). This deliberative assembly was set up in October 2019, bringing regularly together 150 citizens chosen by lot and assisted by experts over 9 months to formulate concrete policy proposals to fight global warming (for an overview, see Gougou and Persico 2020; and Giraudet et al. 2021). The President promised that 146 (of the 149) proposals – generally considered ambitious but relatively incremental rather than transformative – would be passed on to Parliament with "no filter." The political and legal translation of the proposals by the government and Parliament, in the form of the "Climate and Resilience Law," formally adopted in August 2021, has been subject to widespread criticisms for failing to meet the country's ambitions and leaving behind some of the most ambitious proposals of the Convention (Actu Environment 2021; Mediapart 2021). Once again, this episode illustrates the tension between state-sponsored efforts to open the decision-making process and institutional path dependence. At the same time, it is undeniable that the process has contributed to politicizing the energy transition and setting it up permanently in the public agenda.

Contested Instruments

French environmental and climate policy-making was characterized by a tradition of "meso-corporatism" which saw powerful public and private sectoral interests working in close collaboration and under the supervision of specialized central administrations (Szarka 2006). Voluntary agreements and top-down regulation were therefore dominant, until the mid-1990s when the government started embracing economic incentive-based "new policy instruments" (Szarka 2003).

In 2000, the first Feed-in-Tariffs were introduced on the model of Germany as part of the Electricity bill. Initially set at a low level, they were raised and proved relatively effective. Yet they suffered from a stop-and-go approach, were marred in controversy about costs when solar PV costs collapsed (Cointe 2015), and were contested by an antiwind coalition called "Wind of Anger." FITs have eventually been progressively replaced by Feed-in-Premiums from 2015 onward, under the influence of the European Commission, as more compatible with market competition, while tenders have become the norm for large projects (Bocquillon and Evrard 2017). Wind energy is facing significant challenges, which have hindered its development. Onshore wind power already accounts for 17.6 GW in 2020 but is fiercely contested in the name of landscape protection and has become increasingly politicized in recent election campaigns. As for offshore wind energy, it is still in the starting blocks, as the first wind farms, under construction following a series of calls for tenders (the first two of which were in 2011 and 2013), will not be connected to the grid before 2022. The conditions of implementation of these policies – in particular the complex relations between the state and territorial actors – are a key explanation of this long and chaotic policy process (Evrard and Pasquier 2018).

Another flagship policy instrument has proved especially controversial: the carbon tax. The Parliament adopted the first carbon tax in 2000, which was eventually rejected by the Constitutional Court for its incompatibility with the principle of equality, because of exemptions for large companies (Deroubaix and Lévèque 2006). From then on, successive right-wing governments have avoided taxation and favored fiscal incentives and informational instruments – including incentives for low-carbon vehicles, energy labels, efficiency certificates for buildings, tax credits for efficient appliances, and biofuels (Bocquillon and Evrard 2016). Similarly, a Heavy Vehicle Transit Tax (Ecotaxe) planned as part of the Grenelle laws was postponed. When the new socialist government of Hollande tried to implement it following its election, strong controversy arose, and it was finally abandoned in autumn 2014. A domestic carbon tax was eventually reintroduced by the Hollande government in 2013 but initially set at a low level and presented as a "carbon component" of existing energy taxation on fossil fuels. Its increase (from 7€/ton of CO2 in 2014 to 30€ in 2017) went initially relatively unnoticed because it was offset by the sharp decline in world oil prices. The rise in oil prices, coupled with a tax increase in 2018 made it more visible, triggering the mass social movement of the "yellow vests" targeted at rising costs of living and disconnected political elites. In reaction, President Macron decided to freeze its increase for 2019. The conditions of implementation of the carbon tax (Ollivier-Trigalo 2019) have largely contributed to undermining the legitimacy of this instrument, which is perceived more like a fiscal than an ecological policy tool. More positively, however, it has made it unavoidable to consider the socioeconomic dimension of the energy transition, which for too long had been side-lined in the dominant technocratic approach.

Horizontal and Vertical Coordination in an Increasingly Multilevel Context

Horizontal coordination of the energy transition sits within the remit of the Ministry of the Ecological & Just Transition (*Ministère de la Transition Ecologique et Solidaire*). In the past, energy was part of the Ministry of Industry – with strong oversight from the Finance Ministry for all decisions with budgetary implications – while the environment had a dedicated department and Minister, created in 1971. The Ministry of Environment was originally a weak administration, whose remit was far broader than its competencies and resources (Lascoumes 2010), while environmental considerations barely registered in energy decisions. Since the wide-ranging administrative reorganization of 2007, four departments – the environment, energy, transport, housing and planning – have become part of a single superentity. Its name, remit, and internal organization have varied, but the Ministry of Ecology is under the authority of a single Minister, and this restructuring has partly rebalanced inter-ministerial relations toward the environment. Energy and climate have become tightly integrated as part of the Directorate General for Energy and Climate (DGEC). The Ministry has authority over various environmental agencies, as well as on territorialized state services at regional and departmental levels, in charge of energy, environment, and planning – the so-called DREAL. This organization facilitates in principle the integration of climate and energy transition concerns in other related sectors, such as housing, transport, and infrastructure planning, as well as across France's territory. Yet in practice, each policy sector is driven by different policy concerns, constituencies, and objectives, which limits the scope of policy integration. Examples abound of decisions that contradict energy transition objectives, for instance, on road traffic and air transports or infrastructure developments.

Vertical coordination has become increasingly complex. Despite the decentralization laws of 1982–1984, the energy sector remained largely state-dominated and centralized until the mid-2000s. Climate change has shifted the emphasis away from industrial competitiveness and energy security, associated with centralization and national sovereignty, and toward renewable energy development, GHG emission reduction, and energy efficiency, contributing to relegitimize the action of local authorities in energy (Bertrand and Richard 2014). The empowerment of local authorities has been encouraged by the state itself to facilitate the achievement of national objectives, notably through the establishment of local energy and climate-planning documents. The first national Climate Action Plan of 2004 invited local authorities to establish voluntary plans with local actors, while the 2005 energy bill endowed them with new competencies. The Grenelle laws of 2009 and 2010 represented a turning point. They required regions, as well as large cities and urban areas, to establish Local Climate-Energy Plans (PCET, subsequently renamed PCAE after the inclusion of air quality in 2016), as well as of Regional Plans on Climate, Air Pollution and Energy (SCRAE). Although nonprescriptive, these plans closely associating territorialized states services and local authorities have strengthened and integrated local and regional planning on energy, climate, and air quality. The 2015 law of decentralization has endowed regions with new competences on environment and energy and created an integrated and binding planning framework for regional and sustainable development – the Schéma Régional d'Aménagement, de Développement Durable et d'Egalité des Territoires (SRADDET). Regions and cities have seized the climate and energy transition momentum and become increasingly proactive in developing new initiatives leading to a flurry of local projects branded as "green." Yet, even though local authorities have become more visibly active in energy governance, most key levers of action remain outside of their control, such as market regulation (price setting, choice of supplier) or support schemes for renewable energy or energy efficiency (FIT, calls for tender for large wind projects, and support for building renovation). As a result, their capacity for action has remained limited while the centrality of the state has endured (Poupeau 2014). If the multiplication of overlapping planning documents has helped raise awareness, integrate energy and climate concerns in local planning, and mobilize local stakeholders, questions remain as to their coherence, implementation, and effectiveness (Yalçın and Lefèvre 2012). In fact, it has been argued that local plans have served as an opportunity for the state to reassert itself and tame the ambitions of local authorities through the steering and influence of its territorialized services, the DREAL (Poupeau 2013).

The European level of governance has also become increasingly influential in driving French commitments and policies. Since the 2000s, national energy and climate legislation and policies have been justified in relation to the EU targets and the necessity to "catch up" both with European objectives and more advanced neighbors (Bocquillon and Evrard 2017). Keen to demonstrate international climate leadership, France has often sided with those countries asking ambitious climate targets. During its 2008 EU Presidency, it steered the adoption for the EU's Climate and Energy Package – including nationally binding GHG emission reductions and renewable energy targets for 2020 (Bocquillon and Evrard 2016). The country played an instrumental role as the host of COP-21, where the ground-breaking Paris agreement was brokered and was again among the EU members pushing for a 40% EU GHG emission target in 2030 as part of the EU pledge to implement the 2015 Paris agreement. Most recently, it actively supported the EU objective of reducing EU GHG emissions by 55% in 2030 and reaching net-zero in 2050 (Bocquillon and Maltby 2020). At the same time, it has taken a more cautious or ambiguous attitude to renewable energy (and energy efficiency), endorsing a modest EU target while rejecting binding national targets, reflecting its slow domestic progress.

Outcomes, Challenges, and Prospects: French Energy Governance at the Crossroads

The energy transition "à la française" is full of contradictions. While its energy sector is prone to inertia, it is one of the countries whose government has discursively mobilized the most explicitly and aggressively the transition narrative to support recent sectoral reforms. From the National Debate on the Energy Transition (2012) and Law on the Energy Transition and Green Growth (2015) to the recent adoption (in summer 2021) of the "Climate and Resilience" Law, successive governments have kept proclaiming their determination to steer the transition, and more generally to ensure a certain leadership in climate policy (Bocquillon and Evrard 2016). Beyond such buoyant rhetoric and branding, continuity and incremental change still largely prevail in French energy policy.

First, there is still a large gap between proactive stances, both domestically and at the European and international levels, and uneven and partial implementation. France's progress against its 2020 EU objectives is mixed at best. Although it has already overshot its GHG target as part of the EU's Effort Sharing Decision, it is lagging behind on renewables and energy efficiency. RES accounted for 17.3% of France's final energy consumption in 2019, falling way short of its 23% target. For energy efficiency, the European Environmental Agency also noted that the country had not reduced its final energy consumption enough to stay below its linear trajectory toward meeting its self-defined indicative target for 2020 (EEA 2020). Domestically, the picture is similar. In February 2021, the French government was condemned by the Paris Administrative Court, following an appeal filed by a coalition of the third sector organizations, for its failure to adequately implement the 2015–2019 National Low Carbon Strategy (SNBC). France overshot its first carbon budget for the period 2015–2018 as defined in the SNBC. The High Council for the Climate, the independent expert body set up by President Macron, considers that France is lagging behind its trajectory of reducing greenhouse gas emissions and that its European and international commitments will be difficult to meet. While emissions have fallen by 1.2% per year on average over the past 5 years, to meet its target of 40% GHG emission reductions by 2030 as agreed at the European level and enshrined in the LTECV, emissions are required to decrease by 1.5% per year between 2019 and 2023 (second carbon budget), and then by 3.2% per year from 2024 (third carbon budget).

The adoption of the 2021 Climate and Resilience Act casts doubts as to the ability of the country to close this gap without additional measures. Reviewing the draft law, the HCC suggests that, compared to the ambitions of the 149 proposals of the Citizens' Assembly, a large number of measures included in this new law have been "reduced in scope by a limited, or even ad hoc, scope of application, extended implementation deadlines and numerous conditions associated with their application" (Haut Conseil pour le Climat 2021). The regulation of advertising, the construction sector, and air traffic are notably flagged as watered-down and insufficient. In the meantime, the new climate law adopted at the EU level in July 2021 commits the EU as a whole to 55% net GHG emission reduction by 2030 (instead of 40%) and net-zero by 2050, with the implication that France will have to take up more ambitious targets and adopt new measures to implement them.

Second, the energy transition remains to a large extent dominated and overshadowed by debates on the future of nuclear energy. While President Macron has endorsed the goal of the previous government of reducing the share of nuclear power in the French electricity mix from 75% to 50%, the implementation of this commitment remains controversial. The protracted case of the closure of the Fessenheim power plant, the oldest in activity, finally achieved in June 2020 during Emmanuel Macron's term, highlights the powers of institutional "lock-ins" (Deront et al. 2018). The forthcoming major challenge is the decommissioning and renewal or replacement of an aging nuclear fleet, temporarily delayed since the life span of the plants has been extended to 50 years (instead of the originally planned 40 years). The new generation Flamanville EPR is only expected to start at the end of 2022, a decade behind schedule following multiple delays, technical problems, and escalating costs (which have been multiplied by three from inception to completion). This fiasco raises questions as to the ability to replace the nuclear fleet in time, in the absence of a rapid scaling up of other sources.

In this context, the slow development of renewable energy sources remains an outstanding issue. As has been the case for several decades (Evrard 2013), renewable energy promotion is intermingled with debates and policy on the future of nuclear electricity. In March 2021, the Ecology Minister for the Ecological Transition, Barbara Pompili, asked: "What choice do we make concerning our electricity production after 2035? Do we relaunch nuclear power by creating new plants or do we decide to let the current nuclear fleet expire and replace it with renewable energy?" (Pompili 2021). Such uncertainty about the strategic direction of national energy policy contrasts with the ambitious commitments made by France at the European level and enshrined domestically in legislation and strategies. By 2030, renewable energies should account for 32% of final energy consumption and 40% of electricity production. Yet, the country remains far away from meeting these objectives.

Overall, the crux of the challenge for the French energy transition seems to reside in its decision-making process and governance. Two emerging dynamics have the potential to become major drivers: participation and territorialization. With regard to the former, several major state-impulsed initiatives have been launched, from the Grenelle de l'Environment (2007) – a national multistakeholder forum on environmental issues – to the National Debate on the Energy Transition (2015) – a national multilevel consultation on the energy transition – and the Citizens' Climate Convention (2020) – a national deliberative assembly tasked with making policy proposals to be translated into legislation. Each of these institutional innovations contributed to foster debate, to politicize energy transitions issues, and produced tangible policy outcomes, legitimized by the participants, energy stakeholders, and more generally by public opinion. They also fed into the legislative processes, namely and respectively the Grenelle Laws (2008–2009), the Energy Transition law (2015), and Climate and Resilience law (2021). The ex post takeover, co-option, and watering down of ambitions by governmental actors and politicians has limited the impact of these processes on public policies and contributed to fuel distrust and disillusions among participants and citizens. The process of territorialization of the energy transition also remains largely incomplete. In a historically centralized sector, cooperative projects are still confined to acting within niches (Wokuri 2019), and local actors within the scope granted by state actors (Chailleux and Hourcade 2021). This shows that in France, just like elsewhere, the energy transition cannot be reduced to the replacement of carbon-intensive energy sources by other less carbon-intensive ones and represents a major challenge for democratic governance itself.

Cross-References

▶ Energy Governance in Germany
▶ Energy Democracy and Participation in Energy Transitions
▶ European Union Energy Policy: A Discourse Perspective
▶ Transition of Energy Systems: Patterns of Stability and Change

References

Actu Environment. (2021). *Projet de loi climat: bataille d'expertises sur l'ambition du texte*, 10/02/21. Available at: https://www.actu-environnement.com/ae/news/projet-loi-climat-resilience-conseil-ministres-presentation-ambition-37027.php4.
Association négaWatt, Couturier, C., Jedliczka, M., & Salomon, T. (2003). *Manifeste négaWatt pour un avenir énergétique sobre, efficace et renouvelable*. Available at www.négawatt.org.
Aykut, S. C., & Evrard, A. (2017). Une transition pour que rien ne change? Changement institutionnel et dépendance au sentier dans les 'transitions énergétiques' en Allemagne et en France. *Revue Internationale de Politique Comparée, 24*(1), 17–49.
Bauby, P. (1998). Service public: de la tutelle à la régulation. *Flux, 14*(31), 25–34.
Bauby, P., & Varone, F. (2007). Europeanization of the French electricity policy: Four paradoxes. *Journal of European Public Policy, 14*(7), 1048–1060.
Bertrand, F., & Richard, E. (2014). L'action des collectivités territoriales face au 'problème climat' en France: une caractérisation par les politiques environnementales. *Natures Sciences Sociétés, 22*(3), 195–203.
Bess, M. (2003). *The light-green society. Ecology and technological modernity in France, 1960–2000*. University of Chicago Press.

Bocquillon, P., & Evrard, A. (2016). French climate policy: Diplomacy in the service of symbolic leadership. In R. Wurzel & J. Connelly (Eds.), *The European Union in international climate change politics* (pp. 122–137). Routledge.

Bocquillon, P., & Evrard, A. (2017). Complying with, resisting or using Europe? Explaining the uneven and diffuse Europeanization of French renewable electricity and biofuels policies. In I. Solorio, M. Bechberger, & H. Jörgens (Eds.), *A guide to renewable energy policy in the EU* (pp. 162–182). Edward Elgar.

Bocquillon, P., & Maltby, T. (2020). EU energy policy integration as embedded intergovernmentalism: The case of Energy Union governance. *Journal of European Integration, 42*(1), 39–57.

Boy, D., Brugidou, M., Halpern, C., & Lascoumes, P. (2012). *Le Grenelle de l'environnement. Acteurs, discours, effets*. Armand Colin.

Brouard, S., Gougou, F., Guinaudeau, I., & Persico, S. (2013). Un effet de campagne. *Revue Française de Science Politique, 63*(6), 1051–1079.

Brugidou, M., & Jobert, A. (2015). Le débat sur l'énergie a-t-il lieu(x) ? Une perspective topologique. In J. Cihuelo, C. Grandclément, & A. Jobert (Eds.), *Energie et transformations sociales. Enquête sur les interfaces énergétiques* (pp. 141–164). Lavoisier.

Chailleux, S., & Hourcade, R. (2021). Introduction. Politiques locales de l'énergie: un renouveau sous contraintes. *Natures Sciences Sociétés, 29*(1), 3–12.

Cointe, B. (2015). From a promise to a problem: The political economy of solar photovoltaics in France. *Energy Research & Social Science, 8*, 151–161.

Cour des Comptes (2016). *La maintenance des centrales nucléaire: une politique remise à niveau, des incertitudes à lever*, Rapport public annuel 2016.

de Gravelaine, F., & O'Dy, S. (1978). *L'État EDF*. Alain Morceau.

Deront, E., Evrard, A., & Persico, S. (2018). Tenir une promesse électorale sans la mettre en œuvre. Le cas de la fermeture de Fessenheim. *Revue Française de Science Politique, 68*(2), 265–289.

Deroubaix, J. F., & Lévèque, F. (2006). The rise and fall of French Ecological Tax Reform: Social acceptability versus political feasibility in the energy tax implementation process. *Energy Policy, 34*(8), 940–949.

European Environmental Agency (2020). *Trends and projections in Europe 2020: Tracking progress towards Europe's climate and energy targets*. EEA Report N° 13/2020.

Evrard, A. (2013). *Contre vents et marées*. Presses de Sciences Po.

Evrard, A., & Pasquier, R. (2018). Territorializing offshore wind energy policy in France. *Gouvernement et action publique, 7*(4), 63–91.

Finon, D. (1991). Les Etats et le nucléaire civil depuis 1955 : l'empreinte des structures étatiques et des styles politiques. In B. Edith, D. Finon, & P. Muller (Eds.), *La grande technologie entre l'Etat et le marché. Politiques publiques comparées* (pp. 29–66). CERAT.

Finon, D. (1996). French energy policy: The effectiveness and limitations of Colbertism. In F. McGowan (Ed.), *European energy policies in a changing environment* (pp. 21–56). Physica-Verlag.

Giraudet, L.G., Apouey, B., Arab, H., Baeckelandt, S., Begout, P., Berghmans, N., ... & Tournus, S. (2021). *Deliberating on climate action: Insights from the French citizens' convention for climate*. Working paper hal-03119539.

Glachant, J. M., & Finon, D. (2005). A competitive fringe in the shadow of a state owned incumbent: The case of France. *The Energy Journal, 26*, 181–204.

Gougou, F., & Persico, S. (2020) *Deciding together: The Citizens' convention on climate and the democratic challenge*. Books & Ideas.net, 16.07.20. Available at: https://booksandideas.net/Deciding-Together.html.

Greenpeace. (2016). *Transition énergétique: le gouvernement démissionne*, 28.10.16. Available at: https://www.greenpeace.fr/transition-energetique-le-gouvernement-demissionne

Haut Conseil pour le Climat. (2021). *Avis portant sur le projet de loi Climat et Résilience*, 23/02/2021. Available at https://www.hautconseilclimat.fr/wp-content/uploads/2021/02/hcc-avis-pjl-climat-resilience-1.pdf

Hecht, G. (1998). *The radiance of France: Nuclear power and national identity after World War II*. MIT Press.

Jasper, J. (1990). *Nuclear politics: Energy and the state in the United States, Sweden, and France*. Princeton University Press.

Kessler, M.-C. (1994). *Les grands corps de l'État*. Presses Universitaires de France.

Kitschelt, H. P. (1986). Political opportunity structures and political protest: Anti-nuclear movements in four democracies. *British Journal of Political Science, 16*(1), 57–85.

Lascoumes, P. (2010). *L'Éco-pouvoir: environnements et politiques*. La Découverte.

Lindgaard J., Transition énergétique: le gouvernement patauge, *Mediapart*, 26.01.2014.

Lucas, N., & Papaconstantinou, D. (1985). *Western European energy policies: A comparative study of the influence of institutional structure on technical change*. Oxford University Press.

Mediapart, Loi climat: les pauvres et la planète attendront, 22/04/2021. Available at: https://www.mediapart.fr/journal/france/220421/loi-climat-les-pauvres-et-la-planete-attendront

Mühlenhover, E. (2003). *L'environnement en politique étrangère*. L'Harmattan.

Ollivier-Trigalo, M. (2019). Écologie et fiscalité: convergence des luttes? Cas de l'introduction d'une assiette carbone dans la TICPE en France. *VertigO: la revue électronique en sciences de l'environnement, 19*(2).

Percebois, J., & Mandil, C. (2012). Rapport énergies 2050. *Ministère de l'industrie, de l'énergie et de l'économie numérique*, p 532.

Pompili, B. (2021). *Nucléaire ou renouvelables, nous devons avoir plusieurs options*, Le Monde, 27/01/2021.

Poupeau, F. M. (2013). Quand l'État territorialise la politique énergétique. L'expérience des schémas régionaux du climat, de l'air et de l'énergie. *Politiques et Management Public, 30*(4), 443–472.

Poupeau, F. (2014). Central-local relations in French energy policy-making: Towards a new pattern of territorial governance. *Environmental Policy & Governance, 24*(3), 155–168.

Poupeau, F. M. (2020). Everything must change in order to stay as it is. The impossible decentralization of the electricity sector in France. *Renewable & Sustainable Energy Reviews, 120*, 109597.

RAC-F (2016). *Transition énergétique: le gouvernement fait l'autruche sur le nucléaire*, 28.10.16. Available at: http://www.rac-f.org/Transition-energetique-le-gouvernement-fait-l-autruche-sur-le-nucleaire

RTE (2020) *Bilan électrique 2020*. RTE, Direction innovation et données, p. 175. Available at: https://www.rte-france.com/sites/default/files/be_pdf_2018v3.pdf

Szarka, J. (2003). The politics of bounded innovation: "new" environmental policy instruments in France. *Environmental Politics, 12*(1), 93–114.

Szarka, J. (2006). From inadvertent to reluctant pioneer? Climate strategies and policy style in France. *Climate Policies, 5*(6), 627–638.

Szarka, J. (2013). From exception to norm–and back again? France, the nuclear revival, and the post-Fukushima landscape. *Environmental Politics, 22*(4), 646–663.

Topçu, S. (2013). *La France nucléaire. L'art de gouverner une technologie contestée*. Seuil.

Tsuchiya, M. (2016). *Gouverner l'énergie : la dynamique de changement des politiques publiques de l'électricité d'origine nucléaire et renouvelable. Une comparaison entre la France et le Japon*. PhD Dissertation. Université Panthéon-Assas, Paris.

Whiteside, K. H., Boy, D., & Bourg, D. (2010). France's 'Grenelle de l'environnement': openings and closures in ecological democracy. *Environmental Politics, 19*(3), 449–467.

Wieviorka, M., & Trinh, S. (1991). *Le modèle EDF: essai de sociologie des organisations*. La Découverte.

Wokuri, P. (2019). Participation citoyenne et régimes de politiques publiques: nouvelle donne ou donne inchangée? Le cas des projets coopératifs d'énergie renouvelable au Danemark et en France. *Lien social et Politiques, 82*, 158–180.

Yalçın, M., & Lefèvre, B. (2012). Local climate action plans in France: Emergence, limitations and conditions for success. *Environmental Policy and Governance, 22*(2), 104–115.

Energy Governance in Germany

28

Jörg Kemmerzell

Contents

Introduction	668
General Conditions of Energy Governance in Germany	669
Legacies	669
Composition of the Energy Mix	672
Discourse on Energy Issues	673
Institutions and Actors	678
Coordination, Instruments, and Issues of the German Energy Transition	681
Drivers of Energy Transition	681
Strategies and Instruments of the Energy Transition	683
Coordination and Multilevel Governance	695
Lock-In and Entrenchment of the Feed-In Tariffs	697
Centralization Through Uneven Development in the Energy Sector	698
External Influence from Above and Below	699
Post-Corporatism and Delegation	700
Challenges of German Energy Governance	700
Cross-References	702
References	703

Abstract

Germany has cultivated an image as the country of the *Energiewende*. Beginning in the early 1990s, it has adopted several strategies and legislation to increase the share of renewables, improve energy efficiency, and reduce GHG emissions. By 2021, the German government has declared the will to become climate-neutral by 2045. A major step to climate neutrality of the energy system is the coal phase-out that is set to be completed between 2030 and 2038. However, not only the phase-out of nuclear energy by 2022 increases the pressure to expand renewable energies more quickly. Indeed, the federal government's energy policy goals call for a

J. Kemmerzell (✉)
Institute of Political Science, Technical University of Darmstadt, Darmstadt, Germany
e-mail: kemmerzell@pg.tu-darmstadt.de

© Springer Nature Switzerland AG 2022
M. Knodt, J. Kemmerzell (eds.), *Handbook of Energy Governance in Europe*,
https://doi.org/10.1007/978-3-030-43250-8_11

doubling of renewable capacity by 2030 from 2020 levels. In addition, building a hydrogen economy and making progress on energy consumption, particularly in the fields of housing and mobility, will also require significant effort and resilient governance structures among the various levels of government.

Keywords

Climate policy · Coal · Energiewende · Energy · Energy policy · Energy transition · Germany · Governance · Renewable energy · Nuclear

Introduction

Germany has cultivated a self-understanding as the *country of the Energiewende*, literally *energy turnaround*, and understood as a long-term exhaustive transition to an energy system dominated by renewable energy (Lauber 2017). And the longstanding German Chancellor Angela Merkel, in office from 2005–2021, had cultivated an image as *climate chancellor* who strongly advocates climate protection in global politics (Frehse et al. 2017). This may seem hardly expectable, since the country still has the largest industrial sector in Europe, commands significant reserves of fossil fuels (hard coal and lignite), and established its wealth particularly on fossil technologies (e.g., the automotive sector). Furthermore, traditions of the political economy privilege long-established actors dependent on fossil and nuclear technologies through structures of corporatist policymaking.

Nevertheless, the expansion of renewable energy generation became a success story despite the entrenched power structures of the economy. This chapter particularly concentrates on the drivers, instruments, and governance that shape the transition of the German energy sector. However, over the last few years, it became obvious that the transition to an energy system characterized predominantly by renewable energy supply has various consequences for power transmission, network stability, and consumption. Additionally, the positive effects of renewable energy expansion for the achievement of the German climate goals developed toward a saturation range, as monitoring of the *Energiewende* shows a growing implementation deficit, e.g., indicated by a sharp decline in newly installed wind power since 2017 (BMWi 2021a). At the same time, the German parliament, the *Bundestag*, adopted a climate change law that introduced ambitious climate mitigation goals, greenhouse gas (GHG) emission reduction of 65% by 2030 compared to 1990, and climate neutrality by 2045 (BMU 2021). Particularly, the climate neutrality target compels a rapid extension of the *Energiewende* to sectors where GHG abatement is much harder to achieve than in the power sector. Climate neutrality is particularly challenging for heavy and primary industries, but also transportation and the building sector. In addition to the concerned sectors themselves, the governance of such an extended transformation will also face major difficulties. First, the challenge of sector coupling requires the integration of energy and climate policy as a cross-sectoral governance issue. Secondly, new applications of direct (e.g., charging infrastructure for battery electric vehicles) and indirect electrification (e.g., electrolyzers for the production of green hydrogen) increase the demand for green electricity. According to the coalition agreement of the center-left German government that came into office in December 2021, electricity from renewable sources should cover 80% of the gross electricity supply. Consequently, renewable energy generation must at least be doubled by 2030 from 2020 levels.

This chapter first presents general conditions and legacies that shaped the German energy system. Secondly, it discusses the governance of the energy transition in a narrower sense. Therefore, it addresses the drivers of the transition, long-term policy programs, crucial political decisions, policy instruments, and general governance patterns. Finally, this chapter is concluded by reviewing the main challenges and prospects for German energy governance, which are particularly triggered by the long-term goal of climate neutrality.

General Conditions of Energy Governance in Germany

Three crucial features characterized the development of the German energy sector during the twentieth century. First, the energy sector relied predominantly on fossil fuels supplemented by nuclear power since the commissioning of the first commercial nuclear power plant in June 1961 (Trapmann 2001). Secondly, there has been an ongoing concentration process of electricity companies, which were eventually reduced to the number of four. Thirdly, the energy sector exhibited a distinctly neo-corporatist governance regime, which was based on the close cooperation of federal and state (*Bundesländer*) governments with the regional monopolies of coal companies, the oligopolistic utilities, and the influential trade union of the energy industry and mining (IGBE/IGBCE), which organized a remarkable share of the employees in the sector. Moreover, the public sector became a significant shareholder of the large utilities (Mautz 2012), which resulted in a pattern of a mixed economy in the energy sector.

Legacies

The German economy is characterized by an important industrial sector (including the construction industry) that contributes about 30% of the GDP and employs about 30% of the workforce. This high share of industry causes a significant dependence on fossil fuels, which can only partially be satisfied by domestic sources. The only viable domestic sources are lignite and hard coal; all other fossil fuels need to be imported. Four legacies that unfolded during the twentieth century characterize the German energy sector: first, the long- dominance of the combustion of domestic coal; secondly, the invention of nuclear power that was massively supported by public funding; thirdly, a highly concentrated energy industry depending on legally protected regional monopolies; and finally, a growing pluralization of the sector, induced significantly by European integration and the politically supported ascent of renewable energies.

Particularly hard coal served as the backbone of industrial development in Germany. The rise of the country to a leading position in heavy industries and technological innovations in the nineteenth and early twentieth century would have not been thinkable without exploitation of the vast hard coal resources, especially in the Ruhr area. Production reached its highest level in the late 1950s with about 170 coal mines, which produced nearly 150 million tons per year and employed over 500,000 people. However, in 1959, the first *coal crisis* hit the mining sector and initiated organizational restructuring that led to the establishment of the *Ruhrkohle AG (RAG)* in 1968 (Abelshauser 2011). However, since the 1970s, German hard coal never again became competitive on the world market and required heavy subsidies. From 1975 to 1996, a surcharge on the electricity consumers bill (the *coal penny*) supported domestic coal production, and from 1996, subsidies were directly paid from the overall tax revenue. In 2007, the federal government, the *coal states* North Rhine-Westphalia and Saarland, the RAG, and the mining union IGBE negotiated the complete phase-out of German hard coal mining by 2018, despite available resources amounting to about 80,000 Mto (BMWi 2021b). Nevertheless, hard coal still contributes a significant share to primary energy consumption now particularly imported from Russia, Colombia, and South Africa (SRU 2017, p. 19). Germany is still the world's largest lignite producer and has the third largest lignite reserves (BGR 2019). The exploitation of lignite takes place within three main areas, the Rhineland district, the Central German district, and the Lusatia district in Eastern Germany along the Polish border. In comparison to hard coal, lignite mining is less expensive and still competitive in world market terms. Germany's significant lignite reserves and resources amount to 72,400 Mto, with an annual production of 166 Mto in 2018 (BMWi 2021b). Lignite and hard coal together still make for about 20% of primary energy consumption, so it is still valid to label Germany a *coal nation* (Rosenkranz 2014; Osička et al. 2020). Particularly, lignite came under pressure by the strong German environmental movement, first only on a local scale, where open-pit mining implies significant environmental damages. After the definitive decision on the nuclear phase-out in 2011, the impact of fossil fuels on climate change became an even more pressing national issue (Leipprand and Flachsland 2018). Eventually, in 2019, a governmental *Special Commission on Growth, Structural Economic Change, and Employment* (colloquial the *Coal Commission*) proposed a plan for a coal phase-out latest by 2038 (Kemmerzell and Knodt 2021).

A second trajectory is based on the unsteady fate of nuclear power. Germany turned early to nuclear power, with the first research reactor installed in 1957 (Becker 2011). In its heydays nuclear power became the second pillar of energy supply and contributed to nearly 30% of German electricity generation (Lauber 2017, p. 162). Until the end of the 1970s, all relevant political parties supported nuclear energy, however, since the 1970s a growing suspicion against nuclear power generation emerged (Hake et al. 2015). After the Chernobyl disaster in 1986 opponents to nuclear power gradually gained the upper hand in the public discourse, as the Social Democrats adopted a critical position on nuclear power (Renn and Marshall 2016, p. 228).

After years of high contestation on the nuclear issue, a phase-out was negotiated in 2000 by the SPD-Green coalition government, which was then partly rejected in 2009 by a new CDU-Liberal coalition government, only to be relaunched in a tougher version after the Fukushima disaster in 2011 (Benz 2019). The accelerated phase-out had a vitalizing effect on the coal industry, which saw a consolidation of the production quotas since 2011 and just a slight decline after 2017 (BMWi 2021b).

An economic legacy relates to the highly concentrated energy sector. Since the 1920s, vertically integrated regional monopolies acquired a growing share of the energy/electricity sector, covering the whole chain from electricity generation to electricity supply. The 1935 Energy Sector Law (*Energiewirtschaftsgesetz*) fostered the regional monopolies and left remarkable competencies to the industry to coordinate its affairs by self-regulation within the cartel. The large utilities concentrated on the combustion of fossil fuels (particularly domestic coal) and expanded their portfolios, supported by massive public subsidies, with a growing share of nuclear power since the 1960s (Meyer and Küchler 2010). By that time, further diversification was not on the agenda at all (Lauber 2017). Based on those early developments a stable pattern of energy governance emerged and remained dominant until the 1990s. Detlef Sack (2018) identified four main characteristics of the old energy regime: the dominance of fossil fuels, supplemented by nuclear power; the dominance of national regulation and centralized infrastructure; a strong neo-corporatist decision-making structure, established by the regional integrated utilities, associations, and the state, i.e., the Federal and State Ministries of Economic Affairs; and an effective oligopoly of the electricity corporations (with municipalities as important shareholders), politically represented by vertical and sectoral differentiated associations. At the end of the twentieth century, the *big four* utilities (Eon, RWE, Vattenfall, and EnBW) controlled the German electricity market.

European integration created a fourth legacy of the German energy system. European regulations brought on the liberalization of the energy market, unbundling of energy generation and distribution, and an incremental retreat of the public sector from the business (Sack 2018). Moreover, the public sector reduced its investments, resulting in de facto privatization of the power utilities. While the characteristics of the *mixed economy* vanished due to the retreat of the state, liberalization does not mean pluralization, since the *big four* managed to create and maintain an oligopolistic market structure in the fossil and nuclear sector. However, the growing importance of renewable energies has weakened the position of the *big four*. While renewables contributed in 1990 to less than 2% of the primary energy consumption, the figure nearly increased tenfold by 2020 (BMWi 2021b). This development would not have happened without the establishment of feed-in tariffs for renewable energies. The *Stromeinspeisegesetz* (grid feed-in law) from 1991 and the succeeding *Erneuerbare Energien Gesetz* (Renewable Energy Law *EEG*) from 2000 have been described as the cornerstone of the *Energiewende* and a "major policy innovation" within German energy and environmental law (Lauber 2017, p. 164). At least in the electricity sector, the development has been accompanied by a new structure of interest mediation and policymaking. The old regime, dominated by the large electricity incumbents controlling electricity generation from fossil and nuclear fuels, came under pressure from a more pluralistic system of renewable energy producers. However, also the incumbents became active in the renewable business, and even dominate some subsectors like offshore wind power. Nevertheless, the neo-corporatist structures that shaped the old regime were gradually supplemented and replaced by a more networked style of governance (Mautz 2012).

Composition of the Energy Mix

The German energy mix experienced significant changes since 1990. While there was a clear shift from conventional fossil fuels to renewables, coal production and usage remain at a high level, particularly in comparison to other Western European countries. Primary energy consumption is still dominated by fossil fuels, even though their share decreased from 87% in 1990 to less than 80% in 2019. Mineral oil, which is mainly important in the transport sector, remained roughly at the same level (about 35%) in 2019 as in 1990. Renewable energy has increased from 1.3% in 1990 to 17.8% in 2019. The most important renewable source is biomass with a share of around 55% of the renewable energy supply. It is mainly used in the cogeneration of heat and power (CHP), while wind power and photovoltaic are still nearly exclusively used for electricity generation (BMWi 2021a). Primary energy consumption scored highest in 1979 with 371 Mtoe (BP 2020) and declined moderately during the 1990s due to processes of deindustrialization and modernization of the economy after German reunification (Fig. 1). After another moderate decline since 2008, it increased again to 335 Mtoe in 2017 (BP 2020).

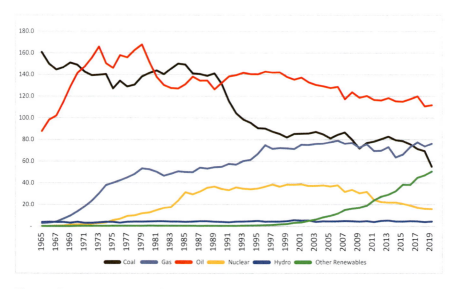

Fig. 1 Primary energy consumption (million tons oil equivalent). Data Source: BP (2020)

Germany is largely dependent on energy imports for covering its energy requirements. The share of net imports for the total demand in fossil energy carriers has risen from 57–70% between 1990 and 1995. The most important foreign energy supplier is Russia. The increased use of renewables thus contributed to a consolidation of the high share of energy imports, but not to a substitution.

Since domestic energy production has declined in all energy sources, the import share has stabilized around 70% since 2010. The import share of mineral oil is especially high at about 97.4%. The domestic share of natural gases decreased further in 2016 and now stands at around 8.2% (approximately 9.8% own share in 2015). The import share of hard coal has risen to 100% due to the closing of domestic mines in 2018. The highest share of the domestic generation was recorded in renewable energies, which were again ahead of lignite in 2016.

Breaking Germany's energy consumption down by sector, in 2020 transport represented 27.5% of final energy consumption. Industry accounted for 28.3%, services for 15.3%, and private households for 28.9% (BMWi 2021b). While industry and services slightly reduced energy demand over time, the transport sector is characterized by a steady if moderate surge, both by absolute and proportional numbers.

If we consider gross electricity generation exclusively, overall transformations and the growth of renewables are more significant. While renewables were nearly negligible in 1990 (contributing to 3.5% of gross electricity generation), they have become the most important source since 2010, with a share of 43% reached in 2015 (BMWi 2021b). However, this success of renewables only led to a partial reduction of greenhouse gas emissions, as overall electricity consumption rose between 1995 and 2017 from about 550–650 TWh. The decline to 570 TWh in 2020 particularly owes to the global pandemic. A remarkable effect was born by the decline of nuclear power, which started in 2006 due to agreements of the first nuclear phase-out. After the Fukushima disaster, the phase-out has accelerated as a result of the immediate shutdown of the eight oldest nuclear power plants. While nuclear power provided about 30% of electricity generation in 2000, its share declined to 11.2% in 2020. The decline in nuclear power caused, under the boundary conditions of constant electricity demand and low production costs for coal-generated power, a renaissance of lignite and hard coal, which provided 42% of the electricity supply in 2015, but afterward declined to 24% in 2020 (Figs. 2 and 3).

The development of the energy mix shows that the Energiewende particularly concentrates on the electricity sector, while it only took partially root in other domains. Particularly, the heating and transport sectors depend nearly completely on fossil fuels. Strengthening renewable energy within those sectors requires the large-scale adoption of *sector coupling* in the future (Wietschel et al. 2018).

Discourse on Energy Issues

Energy discourses usually revolve around three *Leitbilder* (guiding principles), energy security, affordability, and ecological sustainability. Energy security is

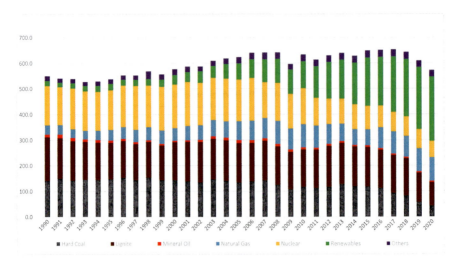

Fig. 2 Gross electricity generation by source (TWh). Data Source: BMWi (2021b)

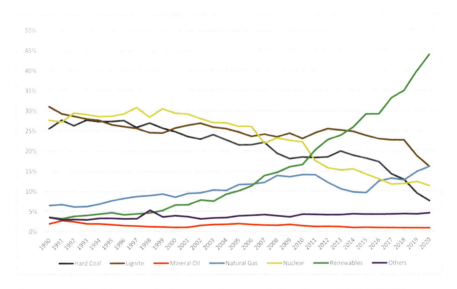

Fig. 3 Gross electricity generation by source (percentage). Data Source: BMWi (2021b)

concerned with stable energy supply both from domestic and foreign sources. In a chronological analysis of German energy discourses, Hake et al. (2015) draw on both the dominant political discourse and arguments raised by its main contenders. They show that contestation long concentrated on the civil use of nuclear energy and the surrounding infrastructure, like the disposal of radioactive waste.

By the time of the foundation of the Federal Republic of Germany (1949), energy policy concentrated primarily on the reconstruction of the energy infrastructure and the prevention of shortages. While domestic coal was the main pillar of supply at this time, the government launched the first nuclear program based on the German membership in the European organization for the development of nuclear energy EURATOM to establish a second pillar of energy supply. The third pillar of imported mineral oil and natural gas was ensured by an active energy foreign policy. After post-World War II energy shortages had been managed, energy security played only a limited role in German energy politics. Access to oil was guaranteed by the alliance with the USA and supply of gas by the "energy détente" with the Soviet Union, as part of the "new Eastern policy" under the center-left government in the 1970s (Lauber 2017, p. 157). During the 1960s, gas quickly replaced coal as the main energy source for household applications like heating and cooking. Today, it is the most important energy source in the residential heating market, with a current share of around 44% (BMWi 2021c).

However, particularly oil crises and the growing instability of the global oil market underlined the importance of domestic energy resources. Besides the combustion of hard coal and the development of nuclear power, particularly in the 1970s, the lignite industry expanded in North Rhine-Westphalia (Renn and Marshall 2016, p. 228) where large-scale open-pit mining took place and huge power plants like *Neurath* or *Niederaußem* were commissioned. Western Germany followed in this regard a pattern already familiar in the German Democratic Republic where the lignite industry, particularly located in Eastern Saxony, long served as the backbone of energy supply. All relevant political parties represented in the German Bundestag during the 1960s and 1970s, the Christian Democrats CDU/CSU, the Social Democrats SPD, and the Liberals FDP, shared a positive attitude toward coal and nuclear energy. Political conflicts within the dominant discourse related to specific policies, like subsidies for the coal industry, but did not question the overall orientation of the fossil-nuclear regime. Discontent with the regime was raised in the extra-parliamentary opposition, which became, besides already existing organizations for nature conservation, one cornerstone of the forceful environmental movement that took root in the 1970s. Local protests against planned nuclear power plants in the Southwest of Germany (*Breisach* and *Whyl*) have been considered as starting points of a nationwide antinuclear movement (Morris and Jungjohann 2016) that dominated German environmentalism in the following decades.

In the wake of the nuclear incidents of Harrisburg 1979 and particularly Chernobyl 1986, nuclear power lost its promise to be the advantageous energy technology of the future and a new and more realistic assessment as "quite dangerous, but absolutely necessary part of German energy supply" (Hake et al. 2015, p. 535) became dominant. However, it was not until the Chernobyl disaster that the nuclear consensus broke up. The Social Democrats turned to the antinuclear camp already represented by the Green Party, which held seats in the Bundestag as of 1983. CDU/CSU and FDP continued their support for nuclear power and did not call for a phase-out. However, although those parties defended the status quo and did not plan new nuclear projects, some projects, like the fast breeder reactor in *Kalkar* and the reprocessing plant in *Wackersdorf*, were canceled, due to both public protests and technological and financial problems.

During the 1980s, sustainability as the third *Leitbild* of the energy discourse entered the stage. A select committee of the German Bundestag on *Preventive Measures to Protect the Earth's Atmosphere* tabled its final report in late 1990 and proposed specific goals for the reduction of energy-related GHG emissions. In the energy sector, the expansion of renewable energy, particularly wind, photovoltaic, and biomass, was considered a promising action to tackle global warming. However, while climate change has been considered a serious problem in the energy discourse, the parties still were divided by the nuclear question. CDU/CSU and FDP considered nuclear power to be a climate-friendly technology, while the SPD, the Greens, and the radical left PDS called for a nuclear phase-out.

The change in government to an SPD and Green coalition in 1998 constitutes a critical juncture in German energy governance, as the former oppositional view on nuclear power reached a political majority at the general elections. The new coalition concentrated on the expansion of renewables and the nuclear phase-out of the government reached an agreement with the power utilities in 2000. The rise of renewable energy expressed a growing concern for sustainability issues and had been backed by the new EEG that introduced fixed feed-in tariffs for electricity from renewable sources. Lauber and Jacobsson (2016, p. 150) quote from an explanatory statement of the EEG issued at its introduction in 2000 by the Federal Ministry for the Environment of the then Red-Green coalition:

> ... the overwhelming share of the external costs associated with the generation of electricity from conventional energy sources is not reflected in the price. (...) Another reason for the higher costs [of renewable energy generation] is the structural discrimination of new technologies. Their lower market share does not allow economies of scale to become effective. (...) the purpose of this Act is (...) to break this vicious circle and to stimulate a dynamic development in all fields of electricity generation from renewable energy sources.

After the takeoff of renewable energy generation in the mid-2000s with the help of the EEG as the cornerstone of the Energiewende (Mangels-Voegt 2004), the debate shifted toward issues of affordability and competitiveness. Particularly, the Liberal Party FDP, backed by powerful business interests and concerns raised by the European Commission against the feed-in tariffs, complained about costs for feed-in tariffs getting out of hand. The shift to auctions in the support of renewables can be seen as a, at least partial, success of the criticism against the original EEG (Leiren and Reimer 2018).

In this context, Buschmann and Oels (2019) analyze the emergence of two equally strong energy discourses, the "energy transition discourse" and the "energy mix discourse." The first stems from the former oppositional alternative energy discourse, which entered the political mainstream in the late 1990s at the latest. The latter can be described as some kind of enlightened discourse of the fossil-nuclear coalition. While it did not reject the energy transition altogether, it is less optimistic about the potential to transform the whole energy system to renewable sources. The main topics of the energy transition discourse are the quick phase-out of nuclear power and all fossil energy sources, as well as the promotion of a decentralized system of energy supply with the *prosumer* of energy as a central figure (Buschmann and Oels 2019, p. 7). On the other hand, the energy mix discourse highlights the deficits of renewables with regard to energy security and the problematic price dynamic of support schemes. The idea of bridging technology became particularly prominent in this discourse. By the time of drafting the German Energy Concept of 2009, nuclear power was declared by the then CDU/CSU-FDP coalition as a bridging technology, and the running time of the operating nuclear power plants was extended by an average of 12 years compared to the phase-out agreement of the SPD-Green government. However, after the Fukushima incident, the lifetime extension for nuclear power plants was canceled and the government decided to phase out nuclear energy by 2022. Other topics of the energy mix discourse are the necessity of modern fossil power plants, the maintenance of a fossil capacity reserve (Leipprand and Flachsland 2018), the superiority of carbon pricing compared with subsidies and regulations, and the use of natural gas as a bridging technology.

Particularly since the climate neutrality target was set, the use of *green gases* like hydrogen became a new topic in the energy discourse (Kemmerzell et al. 2021; Ueckerdt et al. 2021). The two discourses identified by Buschmann and Oels are still present even if it comes to those new topics. While the energy transition discourse claims for a concentration exclusively on *green* hydrogen (SRU 2021), the energy mix discourse highlights technology openness and the production and import of *blue* and *turquoise* hydrogen, that bases on natural gas and the storage of carbon dioxide that originates in the production process (Nationaler Wasserstoffrat 2021).

The energy transition has been accepted by all parties of the German Bundestag, except for the right-wing populist AfD, which overtly rejects the *Energiewende*, however to a large extent for tactical reasons (Selk and Kemmerzell 2021). Among the Bundestag parties, the CDU/CSU and the FDP belong more to the energy mix discourse while the Greens and the Left are aligned with the energy transition discourse. In the SPD, the two discourses are rather balanced. On the one hand, the party has strong ties with the climate movement and environmental organizations, and on the other hand, it is aligned to the unions of the energy sector and industries and has a strong faction attached to municipal utilities, which are particularly engaged in the gas business. Therefore, it is no surprise that we can detect elements of both discourses in the coalition agreement of the SPD-Green-FDP coalition that took office in December 2021. On the one hand, very ambitious targets for the expansion of renewable energies and the accelerated reduction of fossil fuels (80% of electricity production in 2030 should be from renewables, 2% of the German land surface should be suitable for wind power, and the coal phase-out should be brought forward from 2035/2038 to 2030) find their justification in the energy transition discourse. On the other hand, the commitment to technology openness, modern gas power plants, and carbon pricing as the major instrument of all climate and energy transition policies are rooted in the energy mix discourse (Coalition Agreement 2021). Natural gas will remain a conflict issue both domestically and internationally since it will be a necessary bridge to an exclusively renewable future in the face of both nuclear and coal phase-out. Particularly the pipeline Nordstream 2 that increases the capacity of direct natural gas supply from

Russia to Germany became a disputed issue between Germany and partner countries like Poland, the Baltic countries, or the USA. Although within the current coalition, views on Nordstream 2 diverge. Chancellor Olaf Scholz and the SPD, which has many prominent members like the former chancellor Schröder or the prime minister of the Bundesland Mecklenburg-Western Pomerania Schwesig, who are deeply involved in the project and maintain long-time ties with Russian state-led companies, classified the pipeline as a "purely business project." The FDP is more critical about it and points to the perils of becoming even more dependent on Russia, while the Greens are skeptical both for geostrategic and climate protection reasons (Tagesspiegel 2021). In February 2022, in the light of the Russian assault on Ukraine, the pipeline project has been stopped.

Institutions and Actors

The implementation of energy policy in Germany is divided between the federal government and the *Länder* (states). The federal parliament, the *Bundestag*, is responsible for all legislation on the federal scale. The state governments participate in many legislative processes through the second chamber of parliament, the *Bundesrat*, establishing a need for joint decision-making in various policy fields.

Besides the ministries, several agencies, both on the federal and the states level, share responsibilities in energy matters. At the national level, the primary responsibility rests with the Federal Ministry for Economic Affairs and Climate Action (until 2021 Federal Ministry of Economic Affairs and Energy). It controls regulations for the supply of electricity, gas, and oil. The ministry organizes five platforms (*Energiewendeplattformen*) on different issues of energy transition: power grids, electricity market, energy efficiency, buildings, and research and development. Within these five platforms, members of the federal government and various stakeholders should facilitate "the development of solutions and strategies for key action fields in the energy transition" (BMWi 2021c).

From 2002 to 2013, the Federal Ministry for the Environment, Nature Conservation, and Nuclear Safety controlled the competencies for the market adoption of renewable energies and the supervision of nuclear power plants. Due to a cabinet reorganization under the grand coalition of CDU/CSU and SPD in 2013, responsibilities for renewables have been shifted to the Ministry of Economic Affairs and Energy, while the Ministry for Environment maintained competencies in European and international climate protection as well as the authority over the nuclear phase-out and the building sector. However, in 2017 as well as 2021, the Ministry for the Environment lost many competencies. In 2017, responsibility for buildings transferred to the Ministry of the Interior, and in 2021, all responsibilities related to climate protection were transferred to the Ministry of Economic Affairs, which is now the most important ministry in overall energy and climate policy.

Since sector integration/sector coupling becomes a pivotal topic in energy policy, the Federal Ministry of Transport and Digital Infrastructure has gained in importance in energy matters. Together with the Ministry of Economic Affairs and Energy, it established the *Nationale Plattform Zukunft der Mobilität* (National Platform for the Future of Mobility NPM) in 2018. While the overall focus of the platform is on the technically informed debate on a largely carbon-neutral as well as socially and economically sustainable mobility, it particularly deals with tighter integration of the energy and the transport sector. Within the federal government, also the Federal Ministry of Food and Agriculture, the Federal Ministry of Finance, and a unit of the Federal Chancellery (akin to a prime minister's office) have competencies in energy policy.

An institutional innovation has been established in 2019, the *Klimakabinett* (climate cabinet), that brings together relevant ministers while its meetings are prepared by the state secretaries and interministerial coordination by senior civil servants. The climate cabinet has been understood as an answer to the cross-sectoral nature of climate policy and the growing need for coordinated governance (Kemmerzell and Knodt 2019) and policy integration (Flachsland and Levi 2021). The climate cabinet prepared the adoption of the *Climate Protection Package 2030* and the *Climate Change Act* (Flachsland and Levi 2021, p. 129).

While we detect a similar structure on the subnational Länder level, it is important to emphasize federal offices, public agencies, and expert bodies. Most prominent appears the Federal Network Agency (Bundesnetzagentur) of the Ministry of Economic Affairs and Climate Action, which oversees the electricity and gas markets, the expansion of the grid under consideration of European requirements, and the future development of renewable energies. The National Federal Cartel Office (Bundeskartellamt), the Monopolies Commission, the competition authorities of the Länder, the German Emissions Trading Authority, as well as the German Energy Agency (DENA) and the National Organization Hydrogen and Fuel Cell Technology (NOW) likewise play significant roles in energy policy. Furthermore, the aforementioned advisory boards (German Advisory Council on the Environment, German Council of Economic Experts, and German Advisory Council on Global Change, to name just a few) play a distinct role in agenda setting, policy formulation, and evaluation (see Flachsland et al. 2021 p. 10 for an overview of the most important advisory bodies). Three of those bodies seem particularly important: first, the expert committee established to monitor the *Energy of the Future* process, a yearly published progress report on the German Energy Concept (see below). The expert commission evaluates the progress report, points to critical issues of the Energiewende, and suggests appropriate policy instruments (Löschel et al. 2021). Secondly, the *Climate Change Act* adopted in 2019 introduced an obligatory monitoring mechanism that reviews the sectoral emissions on an annual basis. An *Expert Advisory Council* has been established to evaluate the progress of emission reductions in a biannual report. If the Advisory Council identifies sectoral shortcomings with regard to GHG emission reduction, the responsible ministries are obliged to propose instant programs within 3 months. The adequacy of these programs will be reviewed by the Advisory Council. If the review finds the proposed measures insufficient to achieve sectoral targets, the federal government should adjust the concerned policies (Flachsland and Levi 2021, p. 130). And thirdly, the adoption of the *National Hydrogen Strategy* in 2020 established a *National Hydrogen Council* that should propose concrete measures to implement the goals of the hydrogen strategy. The Council consists of 26 high-ranking experts from business, science, and civil society who are not part of the public administration. The mission of the National Hydrogen Council is to advise and support the federal government by making proposals and recommendations for action in the implementation and further development of the hydrogen strategy (BMWi 2020a). In July 2021, the National Hydrogen Council published a Hydrogen Action Plan for the years 2021–2025 that recommends 81 policies for the implementation of the strategy (Nationaler Wasserstoffrat 2021).

Energy policy is embedded in the wider European context in general and the European Union in particular, which is relevant in two ways. First, with regard to legislative action (e.g., EU Directives on Energy Efficiency or Renewable Energy Promotion) and in setting long-term strategies (Climate & Energy Package for 2020, Climate & Energy Framework for 2030, European Green Deal). Secondly, the European Commission acts as a political entrepreneur that has not only promoted the liberalization of energy markets but also constantly opposed the German feed-in tariff scheme (Lauber 2017, p. 165).

In the field of long-term strategies and planning (see below), extraordinary *summits* or *consensus rounds* including the significant stakeholders are responsible for crucial decisions. Notably, if redistributive policies or issues that affect the core competencies of stakeholders are in question, consensual committees solve problems. At last, governmental commissions are often pivotal in preparing political decisions. The most recent examples are first the *Ethics Commission for a Safe Energy Supply*, which had been handpicked by the federal government to legitimate ex post the nuclear phase-out decision of 2011 (Hake et al. 2015, p. 542). Secondly, the *Commission for the Decommissioning of Plants and the Storage of Nuclear Waste* started in October 2015 on behalf of the federal government and proposed recommendations in April 2016. Its members (politicians, representatives of business associations, unions, and civil society) belonged to a broad range of organizations, representing a great variety of interests and alignments, which was a prerequisite for a widely accepted final report (Delsa et al. 2019). The most recent example is, thirdly, the *Coal Commission* that has been established to prepare a viable path for a German coal exit. The commission, made up of representatives of the industry, unions, environmental groups, and scientists, proposed a plan for a coal phase-out latest by 2038, which has been transferred into applicable federal law in 2020 (Kemmerzell and Knodt 2021).

As noted above, in the German federal system many competencies are not explicitly distributed between the levels but belong to the category of joint decision-making (Scharpf 1985). Therefore, it seems appropriate to underscore functional differentiation that applies to energy matters. The federal government is primarily responsible for legislation, though not autonomously since about 55% of the bills fall into the category of *Zustimmungsgesetze* (consent laws, i.e., federal law proposals that are subject to consent by representatives of Länder governments, who are represented in the Bundesrat), while Länder competencies concentrate on implementation and administration of federal law. Power supply is subject to federal and

European legislation. Under those regulations (energy industry law EnWg, Renewable Energy Law EEG, or the European ETS), the Länder and municipalities decide on the location of power plants autonomously. Since 2011, the Länder report their expansion plans for energy installations to the Federal Network Agency (Bundesnetzagentur). This procedure became necessary, as the federal government identified a mismatch between the development paths of the Länder and the targets of the Federal Energy Concept (BMWi & BMU 2010). However, the still poor coordination of the Energiewende raised criticism both by public authorities like the Federal Audit Office (Bundesrechnungshof 2018) and scientific experts (Benz 2019). In the 2021 revision of the EEG, the federal government eventually reacted to the shortcomings and established the *Bund-Länder-Kooperationsausschuss*. This Cooperation Council tabled its first report on the state of renewable energies in October 2021 and concluded that although the expansion of wind energy is slowly recovering, the current land use designations in the Länder are not sufficient to achieve the renewable energy targets. The Cooperation Council, which brings together the responsible state secretaries (senior officers in ministerial administration) of the federal and state governments, aims to improve coordination, particularly in land use planning and approval procedures for wind power plants.

Coordination, Instruments, and Issues of the German Energy Transition

Germany is keen to sustain its self-image as the country of the *Energiewende*, which has come to stand for a policy of a thorough transformation of energy supply through a shift to renewables, particularly with regard to electricity generation. This chapter introduces the drivers and long-term strategies of the energy transition. Then it gives an overview of the phase-out policies for nuclear power and coal that become decisive for the course of the transition. Finally, it describes the major policy instruments in the fields of energy supply, transmission, energy efficiency, and mobility, and outlines general patterns of the multilevel governance of the energy transition.

Drivers of Energy Transition

Since the heights of industrialization in the early twentieth century, domestic coal played a dominant role in German power generation. The importance of coal (and steel) fostered the development of large corporations in the energy sector, which served both as the foundation of the German "war economy" during and as an essential source for industrial reconstruction after World War II (Becker 2011). During the 1960s, the energy incumbents included nuclear power into their portfolios and pursued an ambitious nuclear energy program as a consequence of the oil crisis of 1973 (Berlo and Wagner 2015; Lauber 2017). However, in the mid-1970s, social change and technological development challenged the fossil-nuclear "socio-technic regime" (Geels 2002, 2014; Strunz 2014). While an optimistic framing of technological progress still dominated, several crises of the incumbent fossil-nuclear regime prevailed and forced the upcoming claim for a transition of the energy system, the *Energiewende* (Bossel et al. 1980). Nevertheless, the significant power concentration in the energy sector provoked the emergence of effective regime resistance against a more flexible supply and distribution of energy and the inclusion of renewables *within* the existing regime. Therefore, the impulse for innovations toward renewable energy generation came from outside the regime. It was located within a network of research and consulting institutions, administrative bodies like the *Umweltbundesamt* (Federal Environmental Agency), and some dedicated politicians who were rather marginalized in their parties.

On a societal level, in the 1970s and 1980s, the growing environmental movement exerted pressure from below, establishing a new force in energy policy that rejected the dominant centralist structure and promoted renewable energy generation in a far more decentralized fashion. Twenty years after its onset in the 1970s, the environmental movement gained significant impact as its adherents were the main shareholders of the emerging energy cooperatives and the Green Party. Socio-ecological viewpoints entered the political mainstream, particularly as the Greens became meanwhile a coalition partner of all other mainstream parties in the states and twice in the federal government (1998–2005 and since 2021).

General support of renewable energies was introduced in 1990 with the passage of the first feed-in tariff law (*Stromeinspeisegesetz*) by the Bundestag, promoted by an unlikely coalition of backbenchers from various parties (Stefes 2014). The feed-in tariffs belong to the category of distributive policy, whose introduction does not disadvantage significant groups, at least at first glance. This might be a reason for the significant success of this instrument. A combination of institutionalized incentives and beliefs established a new infrastructure and network of energy producers (Mautz and Rosenbaum 2012), which became the main domestic driving force of the energy transition.

In addition to global and UN-led environmental protection and climate change negotiations in the 1990s (e.g., Kyoto Protocol), the climate and energy policy of the European Union became the main external driver of the German energy transition, albeit to a different extent in different sectors. Germany adopted ambitious GHG reduction targets and development goals for renewable energies before the launch of a cohesive European program, the *Climate and Energy Package* of 2008. Regarding the issues of energy efficiency and transport and mobility, the package of agreements and the related EU *Directives* constitute challenges for the German government that has not been sufficiently accomplished so far. Eikeland (2016) particularly emphasizes that Germany correctly transposed the Renewable Energy Directive (and the Energy Efficiency Directive), but faces problems in adopting proper policies for transport and building stock issues. Particularly, it failed to meet the 10% renewable transport-fuel target and to adhere to the 3% refurbishment rate for buildings. European regulations may thus become a driver for policy innovations that are necessary to meet the agreed goals. Another example of clear European effect pertains to emissions trading. Emissions trading is to some extent at odds with the

German major instrument of the *Energiewende*, the feed-in tariffs that were challenged by the EU Commission several times. In fear of the negative effects of the emissions trading instrument for the export industry, Germany has been reluctant to support this EU policy (Eikeland 2016, p. 105). During the negotiation of the *ETS Directive*, the federal government argued for specific regulations on free allowances or source-related standards privileging coal-based energy generation (Ziesing 2009). Implementation of ETS affected the Länder, which means the *German Emissions Trading Act* (TEHG) and the National Allocation Plans are subject to consent by the Federal Council. As the Länder together with the affected industry successfully lobbied for various derogation rules, in its initial phase the German ETS almost collapsed by the excess supply of allowance certificates (Monstadt and Scheiner 2014, p. 391). However, carbon pricing first introduced by the European ETS (particularly in the energy sector and heavy industries) had a diffusion effect, as Germany introduced a national carbon pricing system *nEHS* for sectors not covered by the European ETS, heat generation and transport in particular.

Strategies and Instruments of the Energy Transition

This section addresses the implementation of the energy transition. It analyzes long-term strategies that set the agenda and formulate general political goals, phase-out policies, and sector-specific policy instruments. Instruments refer to different fields of activity, namely energy supply, with a specific focus on electricity, energy distribution, and energy consumption. The inclusion of mobility in energy policy is discussed as an energy consumption issue with a particular focus on sector coupling.

Long-Term Strategies

The federal government laid down the long-term targets of energy governance in two strategic documents: the *Energiekonzept für eine umweltschonende, zuverlässige und bezahlbare Energieversorgung* (Energy Concept for environmentally friendly, dependable, and affordable supply of energy) of 2010 (BMWi & BMU 2010) and the *Klimaschutzplan 2050* (Climate Action Plan) of 2016 (BMUB 2016) that laid the base for the *Climate Change Act* and the accompanying *Climate Protection Program 2030*, both adopted in 2019 (Bundesregierung 2019). The Energy Concept, issued by the center-right coalition of CDU/CSU and FDP, should serve as a compass for steering the development of the energy system and sets out a strategic approach for the switch to renewables and energy efficiency for a secure, environmentally compatible, and competitive supply of energy. Therefore, it establishes specific targets through the year 2050, implementation measures, and a plan for financing (the Energy and Climate Fund). Climate protection targets agreed under the Energy Concept are: to achieve a 40% cut in GHG emissions by 2020, 55% by 2030, 70% by 2040, and between 80 and 95% in 2050 from 1990 levels. In this context, renewables should account for the main share of the energy supply. The *Energy of the Future* process, moreover, includes yearly monitoring reports (the eighth monitoring report has been released in February 2021) and progress reports (every 3 years, starting in 2013).

The Climate Action Plan of the federal government was issued by the grand coalition of CDU/CSU and SPD in 2016. While the Ministry of Economic Affairs mainly carried out the Energy Concept, responsibility for the Climate Action Plan lay with the Ministry of the Environment. The latter tried to set out concrete measures for climate protection with a global focus but had to compromise on many issues during internal governmental consultations (Frehse et al. 2017). The most important innovation of the Climate Action Plan is the detailed sector-specific GHG reduction targets and milestones.

The Climate Action Plan substantiates the targets with measures and milestones for 2030. It emphasizes the governance dimension, as it frequently refers to other jurisdictions (states and municipalities), the industry, and R&D. However, while it portrays technical measures and development options in detail, it failed to propose governance institutions or commitment mechanisms that push the process forward in a significant manner.

Nevertheless, despite its original flaws (Deutsche Umwelthilfe 2016), the Climate Action Plan set the stage for the adoption of a German *Climate Change Act* passed in 2019 and accompanied by the *Climate Protection Program 2030*. The Climate Protection Program outlines 63 concrete activities and a financial budget. The most important innovation is the introduction of a CO_2 levy for the non-ETS sector. It differs from the ETS in two ways. First, it sets fixed prices for CO_2 emissions until 2025, starting with €25 per ton (p. t.) CO_2 in 2021, and upgrades the price to €55 p. t. by 2025. Beginning in 2026, within a corridor between €55 and €65 p. t., the amount of the levy should be transferred into an auctioning system or integrated into an extended ETS. Secondly, it establishes *upstream* pricing, where fuel distributors buy pollution rights in the form of certificates and therefore pay for the emissions that result from the subsequent burning of the fuels. In contrast, the ETS follows a *downstream* logic, as the operators of an installation must acquire certificates (DEHSt 2020).

The *Climate Change Act* backed the measures of the program with legislative authority. The *Climate Change Act* legislates a net GHG emission reduction target of 65% by 2030 from 1990 levels. It specifies several institutional reforms, like the invention of an independent *Expert Advisory Council* and a policy adjustment mechanism. Most importantly, it determines a net-zero GHG emission target for 2050 (in 2021 uplifted to 2045 in response to a decision of the constitutional court) and introduces sectoral goals for GHG reduction (Table 1). Depending on these targets, the government is determined to set up sectoral *instant programs*, if a sector fails to reach its reduction targets (Flachsland and Levi 2021).

Phase-Out Policies

As energy transition is not only about the expansion of new but also the removal of old technologies, phase-out policies are of particular importance. Germany decided to phase out both nuclear power by 2022 and coal latest by 2038. This section outlines both decisions and gives an overview of both processes.

Table 1 Sector-specific GHG reduction goals of the Climate Change Act (yearly emissions in million tons of CO_2 equivalents)

Sector	1990	2020	2030	2030 (reduction from 1990 levels)
Energy	466	280	108	76%
Buildings	209	118	67	68%
Transport	163	150	85	48%
Industry	283	186	118	59%
Agriculture	88	70	56	36%
Other	39	9	4	90%
Total	**1248**	**781**	**438**	**65%**

Data Source: BMU (2021)

Nuclear Phase-Out

Nuclear power became the main target of the German environmental movement as of the 1970s, while coal combustion remained a minor issue. Particularly the political Left that united on the antinuclear policy remained incoherent and divided on the question of coal consumption (Renn and Marshall 2016, p. 228). Therefore, it is not surprising that phasing-out nuclear power was a top priority of the SPD-Green coalition that gained office in 1998. The government and the power utilities negotiated the nuclear phase-out in 2000. It set no specific dates for the shutdown of single plants but granted a "quasi-quota for nuclear energy which the German nuclear operators have been granted" (Mez 2009, p. 264). Every power plant was granted a residual electricity volume, as a reference quantity a total of 161 TWh per year had been set. Furthermore, the *Act for the Orderly Termination of the Use of Nuclear Energy for the Commercial Use of Electricity* prohibited the construction of new nuclear power plants and tightened regulation on nuclear waste disposal (Hake et al. 2015, p. 539). Even though the nuclear phase-out was a broad-based negotiated law (in the shadow of hierarchical decision-making as a possible alternative), the then oppositional parties CDU/CSU (that had, however, some opponents to nuclear power in its ranks) and FDP and some industrial sectors never agreed to the compromise reached in 2000, which set the stage for the *stop and go* character of the nuclear phase-out (Benz 2019).

In the context of the *Energy Concept* of 2010, nuclear power saw a limited comeback as a bridging technology on the track to an energy system predominated by renewables, as the lifetime of existing power plants was extended by an average of 12 years. While this decision by no means was an *exit from the nuclear energy exit*, as exaggerated in the public discourse, it increased the total amount of residual electricity in a way that the last reactor would have been commissioned until about 2036. The general phase-out decision as well as the ban on new nuclear power plants remained untouched (Hake et al. 2015).

However, the lifetime extension was only short-lived, as the Fukushima incident on March 11, 2011 changed power relations within the federal government. Additionally, the CDU was at risk of losing its majority in an important state election in Baden-Württemberg, which actually did happen. In fact, the Fukushima disaster caused a power shift within the governing coalition, as a minority within the CDU led by the then Minister of the Environment Norbert Röttgen seized the opportunity to cancel the lifetime extension that was included in the coalition agreement of 2009. With the support of Chancellor Merkel, Röttgen pushed through his position within the CDU/CSU and against the coalition partner FDP. Whereas the decision to gradually shut down the nuclear power plants of the Red-Green government was based on an agreement with the companies concerned, the second nuclear phase-out was the result of a unilateral decision by the German government (Benz 2019). The decision, moreover, was reached swiftly. After a consultation with the prime ministers of the Länder, Chancellor Angela Merkel announced a *moratorium* on nuclear power. The seven oldest reactors were shut down immediately and the lifetime extension was suspended. Finally, the decommissioning of all nuclear power plants by 2022 has been passed via an amendment of the *Atomic Act*. The second phase-out decision was accompanied by an *Ethics Commission for a Safe Energy Supply* that provided ex post justification for the unilateral government decision. The phase-out decision of 2011 was supplemented by the commitment to speed up the energy transition, partly through the centralization of competencies. This whole *Energiewendepaket* (package) of measures has been coined "German energy consensus" (Hake et al. 2015, p. 542). However, as policy analyses demonstrate, this consensus was largely confined to the goals of the Energiewende, while policy instruments and measures largely remain contested among political parties and between the federal states (Fischer et al. 2016; Chemnitz 2019).

The nuclear phase-out was completed by the *Commission for the Decommissioning of Plants and the Storage of Nuclear Waste*. The commission had 19 members from political parties, industry and unions, science, and civil society. It was appointed to decide how to apportion the costs for the decommissioning of plants and the storage of nuclear waste. It submitted its final report in April 2016, and its recommendations were passed into law in 2017. They obligate Germany's four nuclear power plant operators to pay a basic amount totaling €17.4 billion as well as an additional risk surcharge of 35.5% (or €6.2 billion). However, after payment, all responsibilities for nuclear waste storage are passed to the state.

Coal Phase-Out

To achieve the stricter national and European energy and climate policy goals, it seems essential to decarbonize the energy supply to a large extent. A key element is the phase-out of coal production and combustion. Unintentionally, the nuclear phase-out had helped coal in Germany to make a temporary comeback, rendering it necessary to take immediate action to ensure that the climate targets were met in the long term (Kemmerzell and Knodt 2021).

In contrast to the nuclear phase-out, the German coal phase-out was immediately established by law. The *Gesetz zur Reduzierung und zur Beendigung der Kohleverstromung und zur Änderung weiterer Gesetze* (Coal Phase-Out Act) passed parliament on August 14, 2020. The legislation was preceded by the report of the so-called *Coal Commission*, in which the basic outlines of the subsequent law were drawn up

(BMWi 2019). As announced in the coalition agreement of the then reining grand coalition of CDU/CSU and SPD, the Coal Commission started its work in 2018. Its task was to propose an exit path from coal-fired power generation and accompanying structural and growth policy measures. The commission had 28 voting members representing a broad spectrum of societal interests and the regions particularly affected by a coal phase-out (Lusatia, Upper Rhine, and Central German lignite mining regions). After controversial discussions, the final report was presented in January 2019, with 27 of the 28 commission members voting in favor. The Commission's proposals were largely, but not fully, adopted in the legislation. In particular, controversy flared up over the commissioning of an already approved new hard coal-fired power plant. Another issue in public debate was the design of the exit path. While the Coal Commission advocated a linear phase-out path that would have led to lower emissions, the law for lignite-fired power plants provides for a stage model, with final shutdown dates at which a larger number of power plants would be decommissioned at the same time.

The coal phase-out was made possible by a debate about the slow reduction of GHG emissions that has intensified since 2010. Stakeholder and media analyses identified a slow discursive destabilization of the fossil-fuel-dominated energy regime and a growing negative framing of coal (Leipprand and Flachsland 2018; Osička et al. 2020). Coal was often interpreted either as the dirtiest form of power generation or as a technology of the past in the two narratives identified as dominant: environmental sustainability and technological change (Osička et al. 2020, p. 6). The increasingly critical view of coal can certainly explain why the coal phase-out in Germany has met with broad acceptance despite coal's high importance in the energy mix.

The Coal Phase-Out Act regulates the phase-out of lignite and hard coal (Wettengel 2020). It must be taken into account that hard coal production in Germany already ended in 2018, which is why the effects of the lignite phase-out on employment and the economic structure of the affected regions are stronger. In its phase-out report, the Coal Commission estimates around 20,000 employees directly employed in the lignite industry, with a further 60,000 jobs also depending on lignite. The most important legal provision affects the phase-out path: first, the net power plant capacity of 22.8 GW of hard coal and 21.1 GW of lignite in operation in 2019 is to be reduced to 15 GW each by the end of 2022; secondly, by 2030, there should be a reduction to a maximum of 8 GW of hard coal and 9 GW of lignite; and thirdly, the phase-out is to be completed by 2038 at the latest, although 2035 may be adopted if binding reviews in 2026, 2029, and 2032 determine the consistency of an earlier phase-out with the security of power supply (Kemmerzell and Knodt 2021). However, the 2021 elected government of SPD, Greens, and FDP announced to start earlier with the reviews to enable a speedier coal exit, soonest in 2030 (Coalition Agreement 2021).

Other important provisions of the coal phase-out law are compensation payments to power plant operators and the opportunity for the German government to cancel free certificates in the European ETS. This is intended to prevent the CO_2 certificates released by the coal phase-out from causing a price drop and simply being used elsewhere in Europe. In this way, the statutory implementation of the coal phase-out responded to one of the most important points of criticism, namely that the climate effect of the regulatory coal phase-out would be neutralized by the *waterbed effect* of emissions trading (Pahle et al. 2019). Compensation for power plant closures has a differentiated arrangement. For hard coal–fired power plants as well as small lignite-fired plants (less than 150 megawatts nominal capacity), decommissioning premiums are tendered and auctioned. The first auction round took place in the fall of 2020, and the federal government will pay €317 million in decommissioning premiums for 4.8 GW of decommissioned power plant capacity. Operators of lignite-fired power plants, on the other hand, are compensated according to a legally defined scheme, with the total volume of compensation amounting to €4.35 billion (Kemmerzell and Knodt 2021, p. 63).

The German coal phase-out is fundamentally regulatory in design and sets fixed dates for reducing power plant capacity. No reliance was placed on the effect of incentives, i.e., an increase in certificate prices in the ETS or, to counter the associated uncertainty, the introduction of floor prices. The example of the UK shows that such an instrument can be used quite successfully. However, the coalition agreement of the SPD-Green-FDP coalition announces the introduction of floor prices for CO_2 emissions, if prices in the emission trading systems fall below a certain barrier (Coalition Agreement 2021).

Energy Supply

The main instrument of the Energiewende is the Renewable Energy Law EEG, which specifies the priority of renewables on the grid, and regulates the feed-in tariffs that are paid to every producer of renewable electricity (Müller 2012). The EEG succeeded the *Stromeinspeisegesetz* in 2000 and has been praised as the cornerstone of the Energiewende and a "major policy innovation" within the German energy and environmental law (Lauber 2017: 164). Against the background of negative experiences with direct technology support – that failed in the case of wind power development (Bruns et al. 2009; Kriener 2012) – SPD-Green coalition elected in 1998 established an incentive-based price-driven model. The instrumental design of the original EEG and its revisions – at least until 2012 – was the unlimited purchasing obligation for utilities and the payment of fixed tariffs for 20 years. The tariffs differed between the different energy sources and a *degression factor* had been established to reduce possible *windfall profits*. The logic of the Act proved particularly appealing for small producers, citizen investors, farmers, and municipal utilities, which experienced a minor renaissance as electricity suppliers (Mautz and Rosenbaum 2012). Before the major EEG revision with the amendments of 2012 and 2014, the EEG had four crucial characteristics that made it an archetypical price-driven instrument. First, the priority of EEG power; secondly, payment of fixed tariffs independent of real provision costs and the overall growth of renewables; thirdly, the degression factor; and fourth, an apportionment of the costs for fixed tariffs (surcharge) at the expense of consumers. The design of the feed-in tariffs ensured a significant expansion of renewable energy generation and the renewable technologies quickly developed from niche to market competitiveness. Successful

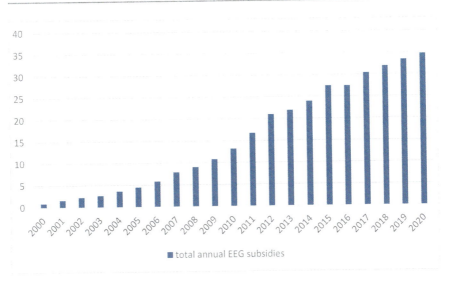

Fig. 4 EEG (Renewable Energy Law) subsidies (annually in billion €). Data Source: BMWi (2020b)

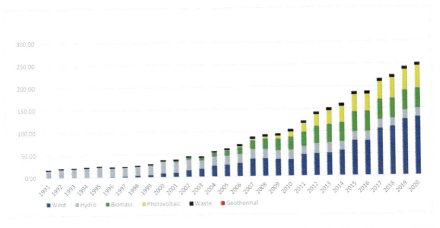

Fig. 5 Gross electricity production from renewables by source (TWh). Data Source: BMWi (2021b)

expansion also led to a steep increase in annual payments to renewable electricity producers, totaling €330 billion by 2020 (Fig. 4).

On the one hand, the EEG effectively supported the goal of a rapid expansion of renewable energy generation (Fig. 5). On the other, it raised growing criticism about inefficient location choices, which partly depend on state policies (Monstadt and Scheiner 2014; Wurster and Köhler 2016), and an unfavorable cost dynamic for end consumers. Particularly the last aspect does not only depend on inefficiencies of the

EEG but also price decline at the electricity exchange (Morris 2016). High levels of electricity supply from coal-driven power plants cut prices, which caused an increase in EEG surcharges that reached an all-time high of 6.88 cents/kWh in 2017 (BMWi 2020b).

The revision of 2012 introduced caps for the installation of new PV and the opportunity for direct purchasers to receive a market premium instead of feed-in tariffs. The newly elected grand coalition undertook a thorough revision in 2014 and altered distinct features of the EEG. Caps were extended to wind power and biomass, resulting in lower payments if the caps were exceeded (BMWi 2014). The most important revision was the introduction of pilot projects with a quantity-driven tender system. Under the new system, contingents for new installations were auctioned, for which bidders offer fixed surcharges (Wenz 2021).

The 2014 reform laid the foundation for tendering subsidies from 2017 onward. The 2017 amendment introduced an auction system for nearly all renewable energy sources with an exemption clause for small-scale installations (below 750 kW installed capacity) and extended the existing auction scheme for ground-mounted photovoltaic systems to rooftop plants. Additionally, it extended permitted areas for PV installations and established targets for the auctioning of onshore and offshore wind (Schomerus and Maly 2018). However, since the introduction of the auction scheme for all major installations, there has been a decrease in the EEG surcharge but also in the expansion rate of renewables. Particularly wind power suffered a significant decline after 2017 (Fig. 6). This might be caused by those bidders who win the bid but do not necessarily build the plant if the investment conditions change. Here, the time horizon for project implementation must be considered, which is set at

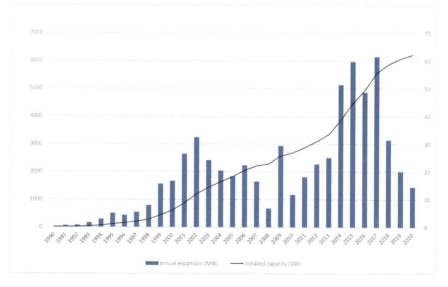

Fig. 6 Annual expansion (megawatt) and total installed wind power capacity (gigawatt). Data Source: BWE (2021)

36 months for commercial investors or 54 months for citizen cooperatives (Schomerus and Maly 2018, p. 1127). If bidders withdraw from the project within these time frames, the respective plant or installation will not be built. Additional reasons are growing protests and lengthy lawsuits against wind turbines (Langer et al. 2018). In 2020, out of about 620,000 acres of designated areas for wind energy, about 175,000 acres were subject to complaints (EEG Kooperationsausschuss 2021).

The latest reform of the EEG in 2021 curtailed the EEG surcharge to be paid directly by the consumers to 6.5 cents per kWh electricity. Deficits will be paid from the general federal budget. Beyond that, the newly elected federal government announced in its coalition agreement to expire the EEG surcharge from 2023 onward and switch to full budget financing (Coalition Agreement 2021). The second important update is the increase of the auctioning tenders to overcome the problems in the development of wind power but also photovoltaic, while the system of auctioning largely remained. Thirdly, to tackle the ongoing coordination deficits, the *EEG Kooperationsausschuss* (Cooperation Council) of the federal and the state governments has been established to provide for better coordination especially of wind power installations and nationwide planning of renewables, e.g., the designation of land usable for wind power or large-scale ground-mounted photovoltaics.

Transmission Grid

The transition of energy supply requires the adaption of the network infrastructure. This becomes important for all energy sources, particularly for the electricity sector, where the transition has advanced furthest. The effects of the expansion of renewable energies differ from energy supply to energy distribution. While energy supply became more pluralist and polycentric (Berlo and Wagner 2015), stability of the still unified transmission network needs a higher level of harmonization. Electricity generation from renewables is mainly concentrated in Northern Germany, while electricity demand, especially from industry, is high in the south and west. The governance of the extra-high voltage transmission network falls under the responsibility of the Federal Network Agency (FNetA), which has been assigned by the federal government by consent of the Federal Council (Münch 2013; Heimann 2015). The compromise on the centralization of grid planning was achieved by an extraordinary *Energy Summit* in 2013, where the federal government exchanged concessions for maintaining support schemes for existing renewable installations for the transfer of planning competencies to the federal level (Benz 2019).

The FNetA is responsible for those projects spanning borders of the Bundesländer (states) or national borders, e.g., those that are included in the European Ten Years Network Development Plan (TYNDP). The rationale behind the concentration of competencies is to enable an accelerated extra-high voltage network expansion. The *Power Grid Expansion Act* of 2009 (EnLAG) and the *Grid Expansion Acceleration Act* of 2011 (NABEG) provided the legislative basis for the transfer of the competencies. Due to intractable implementation deficits, the federal government supplemented the two laws with an *Electricity Grid Action Plan* in 2018. This Action Plan pursues two general purposes: first, optimizing existing grids using new technologies and operating strategies, and secondly, accelerating grid expansion by simplifying planning procedures and applying forward-looking controlling (BMWi 2018). The governance of the transmission network refers to four major instruments:

1. The biannually (until 2015 annually) updated *Joint Scenario Framework* for grid expansion is developed by the four regional network operators (50Hertz, Amprion, TenneT, and TransNet BW) and approved by the FNetA. The Joint Scenario Framework is explicitly linked to renewable energy installations since it matches forecasts of the network operators and Länder announcements on the envisaged expansion of installations (Heimann 2015; Fink and Koch 2016). Furthermore, it takes into account the results of public consultation.
2. After a consultation process including different stakeholders and environmental monitoring, the FNetA drafts a *Network Development Plan* every 2 years (until 2015 annually). Following an obligatory environmental impact assessment, the plan serves as the basis for the *Network Development Act* which must be adopted by the federal parliament at least every 4 years and in which the role of the Bundesrat is limited to a suspensive veto that can be overruled by the governmental absolute majority in the Bundestag.
3. The implementation of the extra-high-voltage network became a competence of the FNetA as well. It includes both spatial planning (*Bundesfachplanung*) and land use planning (*Raumordnungsverfahren*). This is a remarkable innovation since spatial and land use planning usually belongs to the core competencies of the states.
4. *Plan approval*, which usually also falls under state jurisdiction, and specifies the exact routes of the projects, has also been transferred to the FNetA.

At least administrative planning responsibilities interfere with primary Länder competencies, as decisions about the expansion of renewable energy installations, land use planning, and plan approval procedures are concerned. Even though an extraordinary Energy Summit in 2013 removed the most obvious obstacles, important questions remained: First, it is still under debate to what extent the FNetA can effectively coordinate the expansion of renewable energies as a trustee of the Energiewende goals (Fink and Koch 2016, p. 293). Secondly, there is some indication that the Länder governments, now free from the constraints of joint decision-making, adopted a new role: that of the people's tribune that contests certain federal decisions. The territorialized conflict about the extra-high-voltage powerlines and demands for underground cables might be an indicator for those new relations. Likewise, protests against wind turbines, particularly the planning for the *Suedlink* route, the transmission line connecting Northern and Southern Germany, triggered protests by citizen groups in the concerned regions (Neukirch 2020). Of the expansion projects decided under the ENLAG and NABEG from 2009 to 2015 comprising 7,656 kilometers of lines, 950 kilometers have been put into operation by 2020, and a further 1,060 kilometers are under construction. This means that the majority of the approved lines are still in the stage of spatial or land use planning (BMWi 2020c).

Energy Consumption

Despite the *success story* of renewable energy expansion, Germany hardly reaches its climate targets. The newly appointed Minister for Economic Affairs and Climate Action, Robert Habeck, conceded in an interview with the weekly *Die Zeit* that Germany will most likely miss its reduction targets in 2022 and 2023 (Die Zeit 2022), particularly due to problems in the building and transport sectors. Traditionally, the improvement of energy efficiency depends on state subsidies for private investments in real estate (*KfW Loans*), regulative demands for the best available technologies, and specific regulations for energetic buildings standards. The most important national instruments in this regard were the *Energy Saving Act* EnEG, the *Energy Saving Ordinance* EnEV, and the *Renewable Energies Heat Act* EEWärmeG. In 2020, the *Energy Act for Buildings* GEG, which was adopted after a nearly 10-year debate about details of the new law, integrated the EnEG, the ENEV, and the EEWärmeG. The new law became particularly necessary to implement the *European Directives* on *Efficiency* and *Energy Performance of Buildings*.

The federal government reacted to the shortcomings already in the 2010s with the adoption of a *National Action Plan* in 2014 and the *Green Paper on Energy Efficiency* in 2016. The government emphasizes that to achieve the Energiewende goals, the "existing potential for raising energy efficiency will have to be exploited even more" (BMWi 2016).

In 2020, these papers eventually resulted in a *National Efficiency Strategy* that covers housing, industry, mobility, and agriculture (BMWi 2020d). The *Efficiency Strategy*, as the *Climate Protection Program 2030*, became necessary as part of the *German National Energy and Climate Plan* (NECP) that has been submitted to the European Commission according to the *Governance Directive* (Knodt et al. 2020). In the remainder of this section, focus is placed on buildings and mobility as the most crucial sectors since the building sector is the only sector that, despite the COVID-19 pandemic, has already failed to meet the 2020 sector target. The mobility sector is somewhat like the *problem child* of energy policy since it is the only sector with a steady increase in total energy consumption since 1990.

Energy Consumption in Buildings

The regulatory framework for energy consumption is set by the *GEG*, while funding and soft governance tools are found in the *Efficiency Strategy*.

The GEG aims to use energy in buildings as efficiently as possible, including increasing the share of renewable energies to generate heat, cooling, and electricity. The public sector is supposed to serve as a role model in this respect (Leymann 2020). The GEG has three main sections. The first contains regulations for new buildings. These may have a final energy demand of no more than 45–60 kWh/m^2 per year. The exact limit is determined by the extent to which electricity generated from renewable energies near the building is included in the building's annual primary energy demand. The second main section deals with existing buildings. In the case of renovation, the energy quality of the building must not deteriorate, the top floor ceiling must be insulated, and certain minimum standards must be considered when replacing windows or the exteriors. The third main section prohibits the installation of oil-fired heating systems after 2026 unless the main heat demand is covered by renewable heat. The coalition agreement of the SPD-Green-FDP coalition is committed to the GEG but announces an incremental improvement. This includes tighter minimum energy standards for new buildings, concrete efficiency standards for the renovation of existing buildings for the first time, and preference for energy-efficient heating systems, e.g., heat pumps (Coalition Agreement 2021).

While the GEG provides the regulatory framework, concrete measures can be found in the Efficiency Strategy and corresponding programs of the states and municipalities, so that energy efficiency still represents a fragmented governance structure (Wenz 2021). The Efficiency Strategy lists 17 general measures in the building sector (covering several detailed instruments and programs; for further detail, see BMWi 2020d, p. 37). They include financial support as well as advisory services and information for building owners. Important instruments are in particular tax incentives for energy-efficient refurbishment, replacement premiums for oil heating systems, and the promotion of energy consulting. This summary shows the problem of energy governance in the building sector, namely a multitude of programs and offers which are difficult, if not impossible in some parts, for the addressees, i.e., the building and real estate owners, to keep track of.

Energy Consumption in Mobility

A great deal of the *Green Paper* centers on the chapter on *sector coupling*. It portrays sector coupling as "necessary to drive further decarbonization in all sectors as effectively and economically as possible" (BMWi 2016, p. 25). Sector coupling should be approached through a bundle of instruments (including storage and *power-to-X* technologies) that expand the *Energiewende* more effectively from the electricity sector to other sectors, e.g., mobility (BMWi 2016, p. 27).

Mobility seems to be the laggard of the Energiewende, particularly on account of the dominant automotive sector (Canzler and Knie 2020) and the high importance of individual traffic (Gössling and Metzler 2017). The sector-specific goals of transport and mobility are far removed from being accomplished. The gross energy consumption in the transport sector increased by 7%, a stark contrast indeed to the envisaged reduction of 10% by 2020 (compared to 2008 levels). The goal of one million electric vehicles (EV) by 2020 was not achieved, since only 309,000 EVs were registered by 1 January 2021. However, by the end of 2021, one million EVs have been registered, including plug-in hybrid vehicles (BMWi 2021d).

The major policy incentive for shifting from fossil fuel driven to electric vehicles is a buyer's premium ranging from €5,625–€9,000 according to the type of vehicle. Another instrument involves the establishment of a public charging infrastructure, which is still underdeveloped in comparison to private charging points (Kemmerzell and Knodt 2020, p. 364). The governance of (electro-)mobility amounts to a cross-sectoral governance problem, as regularly both the Ministry for Economic Affairs and the Ministry for Transport share responsibility. The two ministries have long cooperated and established both the *National Platform Electromobility* (2010–2018) and its successor the *National Platform Future of Mobility* (since 2018). The *NPM* as a broad umbrella organization brings together industry, civil society, and scientific expertise, about 100 persons that are organized in six working groups. The NPM published its first *result report* by the end of 2021 that gives a good overview of achievements in the transition of the mobility sector but also mirrors the problems of integrating different policy arenas representing different actors, institutions, and guiding principles (BMVI 2020).

As with buildings, concrete action programs in the mobility sector can be found in the Efficiency Strategy. Here, too, measures are added at the state and municipal levels. The 12 measures (each comprising several individual instruments) relate on the one hand to a modal shift from individual to public modes of transport. These include comprehensive funding of €86 billion for the renewal and expansion of the rail network and an increase in federal funding to support local public transport. On the other hand, particularly the change in drive train technologies for cars and trucks will be supported. In addition to the aforementioned purchase premiums and efforts to expand the charging infrastructure (*Masterplan Charging Infrastructure*), there also includes tax incentives for electric vehicles and the establishment of a network of hydrogen filling stations, which will be particularly important for low-CO_2 freight transport (BMWi 2020d). For the latter, the option of direct electrification, which seems to be gaining acceptance for passenger cars, can only be used to a limited extent (Kemmerzell and Knodt 2020, p. 375).

However, this set of measures increases electricity demand, requires flexibility of the distribution grids, and calls for new infrastructural interfaces between the sectors with the involvement of the responsible political levels. In the case of the necessary expansion of renewables, this concerns the states and municipalities or, in the case of the distribution grids, the consultation and cooperation of the often municipal-owned operators.

Key Policy Instruments of the Energy Transition

Table 2 summarizes the key policy instruments of the German energy transition. As a consequence of the manifold instruments provided on different levels, it concentrates on a selection of the most important instruments on the federal scale. We can distinguish four major types: regulations that set standards or exclude particular practices; subsidies and incentive-based instruments; internalizing instruments that apply negative incentives to support change; and instruments of soft governing.

Coordination and Multilevel Governance

Germany has been categorized as *compound polity* (Schmidt 2006) and *consensus democracy* (Lijphart 1999), even though Arend Lijphart acknowledges a shift toward a more majoritarian style of policymaking (Lijphart 2012). In terms of the *varieties of capitalism approach* (Hall and Soskice 2001; Hoffmann 2003; Cetkovic and Buzogany 2016) Germany corresponds to the type of a coordinated market economy. However, many authors emphasize a shift of governance within the energy

Table 2 Key German policy instruments of energy transition by sector and type

	Regulation	Incentives			Internalizing	Soft governance
		Price driven	Quantity driven			
Electricity supply	Centralized land use planning for expansion of the transmission grid (NABEG); Nuclear phase-out by 2022, coal phase-out by 2035/2038	Fixed feed-in tariff for renewables (since 2000); Fixed feed-in tariffs for small plants (since 2017) (EEG); Market premium for direct purchase of renewable electricity	Auctioning of renewable quotas for large plants (since 2017) (EEG)			
Energy consumption in buildings	Standards for energy efficiency and heating in new buildings (GEG)	Loans and subsidies for the renovation of existing buildings			National carbon pricing scheme for non-ETS sectors (nEHS)	Energy consulting in the public and private sector; Knowledge transfer in construction
Mobility	Charging infrastructure and alternative fuel infrastructure planning (Masterplan Charging Infrastructure)	Buyer's premium for electric and plug-in hybrid vehicles; Subsidies for private charging points			National carbon pricing scheme for non-ETS sectors (nEHS); Tax exemptions for electric vehicles	
Industry	Minimum efficiency standards of production technologies	Investment program for renewable process heat			Exemptions for energy-intensive industries in the European ETS	Consulting for improvement of energy audits

sector from the dominance of neo-corporatism to a more networked style of governing (Mautz 2012). The need to find consensus also applies to the vertical arena, which is characterized by a particular kind of *cooperative federalism* (Kisker 1971). German cooperative federalism emphasizes joint decision-making and a functional division of competencies instead of assigning exclusive jurisdiction to the governmental levels. The energy policy of the federal government significantly depends on the cooperation of the Länder. Wurster and Köhler (2016) emphasize that Länder pursue independent renewable energy policies and issue own climate protection programs/laws leading to particular territorial interests. It can be shown that GHG emissions remarkably differ between "high-carbon" and "low-carbon" Länder. Additionally, Monstadt and Scheiner (2014, p. 385) estimate that the states provide more than half of direct public investment for business-related infrastructure and R&D activities. Particularly in the fields of energy efficiency and mobility, municipalities are of utmost importance since they control a significant share of real estate, supervise building regulation, and hold significant shares of public transport utilities and power distribution networks.

Due to the basic features of the political system, it is alleged that policymaking slants heavily toward continuity, generating strong path dependencies and occasionally stalemate. Moreover, cooperative federalism privileges distributive policies over redistributive policies, which might provoke conflict within the federal system on the reallocation of costs and benefits. However, we can identify four governance patterns of the German Energiewende that partly maintain and partly change these characteristics. The first pertains to the path dependency of renewables. After the *lock-in* of the feed-in tariffs as an, at first sight, distributive instrument, the energy transition became entrenched by their growing importance for regional economies. A second governance pattern is the centralization of decisions, which face manifold problems of implementation. Thirdly, even though the Energiewende started as a domestic project, external influence from above (e.g., European regulations) and below (e.g., social and protest movements) have influenced decision-making and the adoption of policy instruments. Fourthly, the energy transition may foster broad developments in the political economy, namely a rise of post-corporatist decision-making and tendencies of delegation to expert boards.

Lock-In and Entrenchment of the Feed-In Tariffs

The first feed-in tariff law passed parliament in 1990. It was promoted by an unusual coalition of backbenchers in parliament from both the then governing CSU and the oppositional parties Greens and SPD. This case is a good example of a small event that had significant effects (Stefes 2014). The policy innovation took place below the political radar, while the governing apparatus and the energy incumbents were occupied with the management of the great challenges of German unification (Lauber 2017, p. 162). Additionally, feed-in tariffs belonged seemingly to the category of distributional policies, whose introduction does not disadvantage significant groups at first sight.

The passing of the EEG, which has been labeled the "prestige project of the energy transition" (Mangels-Voegt 2004), was not that likely in 2000, since the two chambers of the federal parliament were dominated by different majorities, the SPD-Green governing coalition in the Bundestag and a CDU majority in the Bundesrat. However, the state of Thuringia, led by a CDU government, was in favor of the EEG draft in the Bundesrat to support the emerging regional biomass production (Monstadt and Scheiner 2014, p. 387). The exemption of the energy-extensive industries from paying the EEG surcharge followed also a territorial logic, even though the *deal* took place within the federal government. The then Minister for Economic Affairs, Wolfgang Clement, was the former prime minister of North Rhine-Westphalia, which generates about one-third of total German GHG emissions due to its energy-extensive industry and large coal-fired power plants. The *hardship clause* of the EEG excluded over 500 industrial consumers from paying the surcharge (Jacobsson and Lauber 2006). Territorial stakes defended the feed-in tariff scheme in the first EEG revision in 2004, despite the theoretical assumption that countervailing majorities in Bundestag and Bundesrat cause political stalemate and gridlock, an assumption that traces back to Gerhard Lehmbruch's incompatibility thesis of the dominance of party competition over territorial interest representation in the Bundesrat (Lehmbruch 2000). Many states led by the then oppositional CDU did not confirm this assumption and instead supported the federal government since renewables gained significant economic importance. Entrenchment came from an interest in maintaining the stable expectations for investment provided by the fixed feed-in tariffs.

Centralization Through Uneven Development in the Energy Sector

The growing share of installed renewable energy caused an increase in regional disparities, as we consider variation in the expansion of energy generation from renewable sources since the onset of the EEG (Wurster and Köhler 2016; Wurster and Hagemann 2018). The EEG distributed the costs for renewable energy installations nationwide through the consumer surcharge, while it induced a growing competition between the Länder to benefit as much as possible from the fixed tariffs. For instance, in Schleswig-Holstein, Mecklenburg-Western Pomerania, or Rhineland-Palatine, the renewable energy industry has developed into one of the most important industries, since it creates a large number of jobs around the construction and operation of renewable energy installations. The rise of a rather polycentric structure of energy supply triggered concerns about energy security and thus calls for stronger coordination (Ohlhorst et al. 2013).

The uneven development of renewable energy installations has also raised growing concerns about appropriate rules for the development of the transmission network. The existing planning law has been criticized as ineffective for the demands of an energy system that depends mainly on renewables (Faßbender and Leidinger 2013). Since land use planning usually belongs to their competencies, it was necessary that the Länder consent to a transfer. A compromise was achieved at the *Energy Summit* in 2013, as the states agreed upon the transfer of planning competencies to the Federal Network Agency. On the one hand, the compromise surely was driven by federal and states concerns about the future of renewable energies. On the other hand, the federal government made concessions to the Länder concerning the support scheme for existing installations. Some observers furthermore suspected that informal agreements for future revisions of the EEG had been made (Krohn 2013). However, the establishment of the EEG Cooperation Council may indicate that both the federal and the state governments recognized the limits of centralization and a limited return to cooperative federalism.

External Influence from Above and Below

In the terminology of the multilevel approach to transitions, influence from above can be understood as "landscape developments," while influence from below may be understood as a "contestation" of the "socio-technical regime" (Geels and Schot 2007, p. 401). Influence from above is mostly exerted by the European Union, particularly in carbon pricing but also with regard to biofuels, renewable energy support schemes, and energy efficiency. The implementation of the German Emissions Trading Act was an immediate consequence of the European ETS, as explained above. The establishment of the national emission pricing scheme nEHS can be seen as a case of diffusion of carbon pricing. Furthermore, the nEHS has been indirectly triggered by European regulations. As Germany was in danger of missing its reduction commitments under the *European Effort Sharing Regulation*, the introduction of a national pricing system, especially for the transport and building sectors, was increasingly discussed (ESYS 2019). If Germany did not meet its effort sharing targets, it would either have to acquire emission rights from other countries or even face an infringement proceeding.

The European Commission acted as a policy entrepreneur as it regularly resumed its general criticism of the German feed-in tariffs and publicly asked the German Government to stop the electricity price increase (Lauber and Jacobsson 2016, p. 153). The European Commission pursued a rather linear view of innovation policy under the principle of *technology neutrality* and rejected the idea of surcharges on principle (Lauber 2017). The goal of a unified European energy market with streamlined instruments reinforced the suspicion of the Commission about national peculiarities. So, the switch to auctioning in renewables was partly triggered by the Commission. In both renewable energy and energy efficiency, European regulations and the NECP process significantly affected German policies. The adoption of the *Climate Protection Program 2030* and the *Climate Change Act* in 2019 as well as its revision was influenced by commitments made on the international scale as well as domestic protest. The emission reductions and instruments are part of the long-term climate change strategy which is required both by European Law and the Paris Agreement (Flachsland and Levi 2021, p. 130), or rather the *National Determined Contributions* NDC, which are at the heart of the agreement. The climate movement, in turn, exerted a great deal of influence from below as

Fridays for Future has a particularly strong backing in Germany (Neuber et al. 2020). Additionally, in some instances of the regular opinion polls of the *Forschungsgruppe Wahlen*, for the first time, a majority of the respondents considered climate change the most important policy issue in 2019 (Flachsland and Levi 2021, p. 128). Therefore, and in the face of the expected success of the Green Party in opinion polls, the then governing grand coalition of CDU/CSU and SPD decided to pursue a more active climate agenda.

Post-Corporatism and Delegation

A final governance pattern relates to a specific form of consensus-oriented policymaking that nonetheless deviates from the structures of neo-corporatism. Post-corporatist institutions lack fundamental characteristics of the older neo-corporatist institutions (Czada 2015) such as long-term durability of institutions, weak publicity, a small circle of participants, and the development of mutual trust between the participants. Such features are largely missing in specific and timely restricted commissions like the *Coal Commission* that represents manifold but hand-picked stakeholders. Critical observers describe those commissions as *government-friendly expert rounds*, with energy policy as the most significant area where this kind of extra-parliamentary consensus mobilization took place (Czada 2019, p. 405). While some authors describe the new mode of interest mediation as pluralistic (Mautz 2012), others are more skeptical, e.g., Roland Czada who criticizes interest mediation in the changing energy regime as a "multitude of initiatives taking place in hyperactivity mode in an uncoordinated manner" (Czada 2019, p. 405, own translation). This is a difference to other countries with a stronger consensual-democratic tradition, where corporatist structures were adopted to manage the transitional project, e.g., Austria or the Netherlands.

A similar pattern of extra-parliamentary politics emerges with the growing importance of expert bodies, like the Expert Advisory Council established by the Climate Change Act (Flachsland and Levi 2021). In addition to its monitoring role, the council can request the adaptation of policy programs if any sectoral GHG reduction targets will be missed. Delegation of policy formulation to such bodies can foster a higher quality of evidence-based policymaking. However, the effects seem double-edged, as delegation of *political competencies* to experts bears the risk of blurring the lines between science and politics, so that the impartiality of expertise becomes politically disputed (Selk et al. 2019; Bogner 2021).

Challenges of German Energy Governance

The climate goals of the Climate Change Act, reducing GHG emissions by 65% by 2030 and becoming climate-neutral by 2045, put unparalleled pressure on the German energy system and the governance of the transition. In this context, three challenges stand out: firstly, a significantly growing electricity demand, which must be increasingly covered by renewable sources; secondly, the need for large-scale use of hydrogen, which currently appears to be the only realistic alternative to fossil fuels in many hard-to-abate applications; and thirdly, a significant reduction in overall energy consumption shall be achieved in particular through a transformation of the heating sector (Prognos et al. 2021).

According to various scenarios of the energy system, electricity demand will increase by 20–34% from 2020 levels by 2030 and by 70–170%, depending on technological developments and political decisions, by 2045 (Luderer et al. 2021, p. 6). As electricity demand was about 570 TWh in 2020, it will approach about 700 TWh in 2030. The increasing demand coincides with the political goal of generating 80% of electricity in 2030 from renewable sources (Coalition Agreement 2021), which corresponds to a doubling within 10 years. The German Think Tank Agora Energiewende predicts an unexpected expansion of photovoltaics (10 GW p.a. compared to 5 GW in 2020), and a renaissance of wind power with an annual expansion of 7 GW (compared to 1.4 GW in 2020) (Prognos et al. 2021, p. 31). To reach these ambitious goals, the federal government plans to designate 2% of the territory for wind power installations, which may run the risk of coming into conflict with nature conservation. This increases the need for consensus building and coordination between the federal and state governments, also given the already widespread opposition to wind power. The extent to which the EEG Cooperation Council can achieve this has already been questioned. Likewise, the demand for a Wind Power Commission modeled on the Coal Commission has been raised by the wind power lobby (Zaremba 2022). Due to the phase-out of nuclear energy and the incremental reduction of coal combustion, in coincidence with the still sluggish expansion of renewables and the uncertain future of natural gas due to sanctions on Russia, Germany is likely to turn from a net exporter into a net importer of electricity (Prognos et al. 2021, p. 17). This could have the adverse effect that Germany will have to import nuclear power from its European neighbors.

The second major challenge is the need to develop a large-scale hydrogen economy. A recent scenario study of the energy system assumes a hydrogen demand of 69 TWh in 2030 and 265 TWh in 2045 (Prognos et al. 2021). Two-thirds of the demand will be imported. In the industry, hydrogen is mainly used for the direct reduction of iron ore for CO_2-free steel production, as a raw material in basic chemicals, and to generate process steam. In transport, hydrogen is required for heavy goods traffic. Synthetic fuels are also based on hydrogen, which in the future will contribute to climate-neutral aviation and shipping (Prognos et al. 2021, pp. 103–109). Even though the National Hydrogen Strategy has been released in 2020 (BMWi 2020a), the targets are not ambitious enough to meet the transitory demands of climate neutrality. While an upgrade of the production goals seems quite easy, the implementation of the strategy requires extensive coordination between the federal levels, particularly about infrastructure, and within the European Union about a common hydrogen foreign policy that establishes reliable relations with hydrogen export countries. Decisions also have to be made about the *color* of the hydrogen. Should hydrogen always be green, i.e., carbon-free, or is low-carbon blue hydrogen also acceptable? If blue hydrogen is produced from natural gas with

CO_2 storage, a new debate on carbon capture and storage looms. The implementation of the hydrogen strategy also involves conflicts between various industrial interests. While the electricity sector might take a restrictive line on hydrogen usage and focus on domestic production and direct electrification, the gas industry has an interest in a broad application spectrum and extensive import relationships. Related to this is the issue to which extent hydrogen creates new path dependency in gas and up to what point direct electrification is an alternative to the use of hydrogen (Ueckerdt et al. 2021).

Finally, primary energy consumption must be cut by 30% in 2030 from 2020 levels, if Germany is to stay on track for GHG emission reduction (Prognos et al. 2021). Accordingly, both the housing and the mobility sector might undergo significant transitions. Other than in the energy industry, which relates to renewables and hydrogen, energy governance must address the end consumer immediately. When it comes to building and housing renovations or the choice of vehicles and modes of transportation, investment decisions of private actors are key to the transition. Therefore, it will depend on political decisions to build up trust in new technologies and to stabilize expectations. However, decisions on preferential technologies in heating have systemic repercussions on the energy system, e.g., if a broad application of heat pumps accelerates electricity demand (Höfling 2021). Therefore, transitional energy governance must be aware of those systemic effects of sector coupling and will need to improve its capacities for both political coordination and evidence-based policymaking.

Cross-References

- ▶ Energy Governance in Austria
- ▶ Energy Governance in Europe: Country Comparison and Conclusion
- ▶ Energy Governance in Europe: Introduction
- ▶ Energy Governance in the Netherlands
- ▶ Energy Governance in the United Kingdom
- ▶ Energy Governance in the Republic of Poland
- ▶ European Union Energy Policy: A Discourse Perspective
- ▶ EU-Russia Energy Relations
- ▶ EU-US and EU-Canada Energy Relations
- ▶ Extending Energy Policy: The Challenge of Sector Integration
- ▶ Monitoring Energy Policy
- ▶ Transition of Energy Systems: Patterns of Stability and Change

Acknowledgments Funding from the Kopernikus-Projekt ENavi (FKZ 03SFK4P0) and the Kopernikus-Projekt Ariadne (FKZ 03SFK5LO) by the German Federal Ministry of Education and Research is gratefully acknowledged. I would like to thank Michèle Knodt, Nils Bruch, and Lucas Flath for their thorough review of the chapter and helpful comments. Jared Sonnicksen deserves special thanks for his indispensable help with language editing.

References

Abelshauser, W. (2011). *Deutsche Wirtschaftsgeschichte. Von 1945 bis zur Gegenwart* (2nd ed.). Munich: C. H. Beck.

Becker, P. (2011). *Aufstieg und Krise der deutschen Stromkonzerne.* Bochum: Ponte Press.

Benz, A. (2019). Koordination der Energiepolitik im deutschen Bundesstaat. *dms – der moderne staat – Zeitschrift für Public Policy, Recht und Management, 12*(2), 299–312.

Berlo, K., & Wagner, O. (2015). Strukturkonservierende Regime-Elemente der Stromwirtschaft als Hemmnis einer kommunal getragenen Energiewende. Eine Akteursanalyse aus der Multi-Level-Perspektive der Transitionsforschung. *Momentum Quarterly, 4*(4), 233–253.

BGR (Bundesanstalt für Geowissenschaften und Rohstoffe). (2019). BGR Energiestudie 2018 – Daten und Entwicklungen der deutschen und globalen Energieversorgung (22). Hannover.

BMU (Bundesministerium für Umwelt, Naturschutz, und Reaktorsicherheit). (2021). Klimaschutzgesetz. Berlin.

BMUB (Bundesministerium für Umwelt, Naturschutz, Bau und Reaktorsicherheit). (2016). *Klimaschutzplan 2050.* Berlin: Klimapolitische Grundsätze und Ziele der Bundesregierung.

BMVI (Bundesministerium für Verkehr und digitale Infrastruktur). (2020). Fortschrittsbericht der Nationalen Plattform Zukunft der Mobilität. Berlin.

BMWi (Bundesministerium für Wirtschaft und Energie). (2014). Die Reform des EEG im Jahr 2014: Wichtiger Schritt für den Neustart der Energiewende. http://www.erneuerbare-energien.de/EE/Redaktion/DE/Dossier/eeg.html;jsessionid=E4541C4615D67B8DBB4FF44118FD6B20?cms_docId=73930.

BMWi (Bundesministerium für Wirtschaft und Energie). (2016). *Green Paper on Energy Efficiency.* Berlin: Evaluation report on the public consultation.

BMWi (Bundesministerium für Wirtschaft und Energie). (2018). Aktionsplan Stromnetz. Berlin.

BMWi (Bundesministerium für Wirtschaft und Energie). (2019). Abschlussbericht der Kommission "Wachstum, Strukturwandel und Beschäftigung". Berlin.

BMWi (Bundesministerium für Wirtschaft und Energie). (2020a). Die Nationale Wasserstoffstrategie. Berlin.

BMWi (Bundesministerium für Wirtschaft und Energie). (2020b). EEG in Zahlen. Vergütungen, Differenzkosten und EEG-Umlage 2000–2021. Berlin.

BMWi (Bundesministerium für Wirtschaft und Energie). (2020c). Der Netzausbau schreitet voran. https://www.bmwi.de/Redaktion/DE/Downloads/M-O/netzausbau-schreitet-voran.pdf?__blob=publicationFile&v=8.

BMWi (Bundesministerium für Wirtschaft und Energie). (2020d). Energieeffizienzstrategie 2050. Berlin.

BMWi (Bundesministerium für Wirtschaft und Energie). (2021a). Die Energie der Zukunft. Achter Monitoring-Bericht zur Energiewende. Berichtsjahre 2018 und 2019. Berlin.

BMWi (Bundesministerium für Wirtschaft und Energie). (2021b). Energiedaten: Gesamtausgabe. Berlin.

BMWi (Bundesministerium für Wirtschaft und Energie). (2021c). Erdgasversorgung in Deutschland. https://www.bmwi.de/Redaktion/DE/Artikel/Energie/gas-erdgasversorgung-in-deutschland.html.

BMWi (Bundesministerium für Wirtschaft und Energie). (2021d). Gemeinsame Pressemitteilung: Erstmals rollen eine Million Elektrofahrzeuge auf deutschen Straßen. https://www.bmwi.de/Redaktion/DE/Pressemitteilungen/2021/08/20210802-erstmals-rollen-eine-million-elektrofahrzeuge-auf-deutschen-strassen.html.

BMWi (Bundesministerium für Wirtschaft) & BMU (Bundesministerium für Umwelt, Naturschutz und Reaktorsicherheit). (2010). Energiekonzept für eine umweltschonende, zuverlässige und bezahlbare Energieversorgung, Berlin.

Bogner, A. (2021). *Die Epistemisierung des Politischen. Wie die Macht des Wissens die Demokratie gefährdet.* Ditzingen: Reclam.

Bossel, H., Krause, F., & Müller-Reißmann, K.-F. (1980). *Energie-Wende. Wachstum und Wohlstand ohne Erdöl und Uran*. Ein Bericht des Freiburger Öko-Instituts.

BP (British Petroleum). (2020). Statistical review of world energy. https://www.bp.com/en/global/corporate/energy-economics/statistical-review-of-world-energy.html.

Bruns, D., et al. (2009). *Erneuerbare Energien In Deutschland. Eine Biographie des Innovationsgeschehens*. Berlin: Universitätsverlag der TU Berlin.

Bundesrechnungshof. (2018). Bericht nach § 99 BHO über die Koordination und Steuerung zur Umsetzung der Energiewende durch das Bundesministerium für Wirtschaft und Energie. Bonn.

Bundesregierung. (2019). Klimaschutzprogramm 2030 der Bundesregierung zur Umsetzung des Klimaschutzplans 2050, Berlin.

Buschmann, P., & Oels, A. (2019). The overlooked role of discourse in breaking carbon lock-in: The case of the German energy transition. *WIREs Climate Change, 10*, 1–14.

BWE (Bundesverband Wind Energie). (2021). Windenergieanlagen in Deutschland. https://www.wind-energie.de/themen/zahlen-und-fakten/deutschland/

Canzler, W., & Knie, A. (2020). Neues Spiel, neues Glück? Mobilität im Wandel. In A. Brunngräber & T. Haas (Eds.), *Baustelle Elektromobilität* (pp. 139–160). Bielefeld: Transcript.

Cetkovic, S., & Buzogany, A. (2016). Varieties of capitalism and clean energy transitions in the European Union: When renewable energy hits different economic logics. *Climate Policy, 16*(5), 642–657.

Chemnitz, C. (2019). Die Umsetzung der Energiewende im Föderalismus – Koordination und Steuerung durch mehr Politikverflechtung. *dms – der moderne staat – Zeitschrift für Public Policy Recht und Management, 12*(1), 116–144.

Coalition Agreement. (2021). *Koalitionsvertrag 2021–2025 zwischen der Sozialdemokratischen Partei Deutschlands (SPD), BÜNDNIS 90 / DIE GRÜNEN und den Freien Demokraten (FDP) (2021): Mehr Fortschritt wagen*. Berlin: Bündnis für Freiheit, Gerechtigkeit und Nachhaltigkeit.

Czada, R. (2015). Post-democracy and the public sphere: Informality and transparency in negotiated decision-making. In V. Schneider & B. Eberlein (Eds.), *Complex democracy: Varieties, crises, and transformations* (pp. 231–246). Cham: Springer.

Czada, R. (2019). Politikwenden und transformative Politik in Deutschland. *dms – der moderne staat, 12*(2), 400–417.

DEHSt (Deutsche Emissionshandelsstelle). (2020). *Nationales Emissionshandelssystem. Hintergrundpapier*. Berlin: Deutsche Emissionshandelsstelle (DEHSt) im Umweltbundesamt.

Delsa, L., Fahl, U., Fydrich, M., Ganal, H., Kemmerzell, J., Krause, E., Pahle, M., & Reckinger, I. (2019). *Germany country report*. Potsdam: ENavi-Report.

Deutsche Umwelthilfe. (2016). Stellungnahme der Deutschen Umwelthilfe zum Klimaschutzplan 2050. http://www.duh.de/fileadmin/user_upload/download/Projektinformation/Klimaschutz/Stellungnahme_DUH_zum_KSP_2050.pdf.

EEG Kooperationsausschuss. (2021). *Bericht des Bund-Länder-Kooperationsausschusses zum Stand des Ausbaus der erneuerbaren Energien sowie zu Flächen*. Berlin: Planungen und Genehmigungen für die Windenergienutzung an Land.

Eikeland, P. O. (2016). Implementation in Germany. In J. B. Skjarseth, P. O. Eikeland, L. H. Gulbrandsen, & T. Jevnaker (Eds.), *Linking EU climate and energy policies decision-making, implementation and reform* (pp. 91–119). Cheltenham: Edward Elgar.

ESYS (Energiesysteme der Zukunft). (2019). Über eine CO_2-Bepreisung zur Sektorenkopplung: Ein neues Marktdesign für die Energiewende. Berlin.

Faßbender, K., & Leidinger, T. (2013). Praxishandbuch Netzausbau und Netzplanung. In H. Posser & F. Faßbender (Eds.), *Einführung und Rechtsquellen* (pp. 1–26). Berlin/Boston: De Gruyter.

Fink, S., & Koch, J. (2016). Agiert die Bundesnetzagentur beim Netzausbau als Agent oder als Treuhänder? *dms – der moderne staat – Zeitschrift für Public Policy, Recht und Management, 9*(2), 277–297.

Fischer, W., Hake, J.-F., Kuckshinrichs, W., Schröder, T., & Venghaus, S. (2016). German energy policy and the way to sustainability: Five controversial issues in the debate on the "Energiewende". *Energy, 115*(3), 1580–1591. https://doi.org/10.1016/j.energy.2016.05.069.

Flachsland, C., & Levi, S. (2021). Germany's federal climate change act. *Environmental Politics, 30*(1), 118–140.

Flachsland, C., aus dem Moore, N., Müller, T., Kemmerzell, J., Edmondson, D., Görlach, B., Kalkuhl, M., Knodt, M., Knopf, B., Levi, S., Luderer, G., & Pahle, M. (2021). *Wie die Governance der deutschen Klimapolitik gestärkt werden kann. Ariadne Kurzdossier.* Potsdam: Kopernikus-Projekt Ariadne.

Frehse, L., et al. (2017). Das Naturschauspiel. *Die Zeit, 45*, 13–15.

Geels, F. W. (2002). Technological transitions as evolutionary reconfiguration processes: A multi-level perspective and a case-study. *Research Policy, 31*, 1257–1274.

Geels, F. W. (2014). Regime resistance against low-carbon transitions: Introducing politics and power into the multi-level perspective. *Theory, Culture & Society, 31*, 21–40.

Geels, F. W., & Schot, J. (2007). Typology of sociotechnical transition pathways. *Research Policy, 36*, 399–417.

Gössling, S., & Metzler, D. (2017). Germany's climate policy: Facing an automobile dilemma. *Energy Policy, 105*, 418–428.

Hake, J.-F., Fischer, W., Venghaus, S., & Weckenbrock, C. (2015). The German Energiewende. History and status quo. *Energy, 92*(3), 532–546.

Hall, P. A., & Soskice, D. W. (2001). *Varieties of capitalism. The institutional foundations of comparative advantage.* Oxford: Oxford University Press.

Heimann, U. (2015). Der Rechtsrahmen der Bedarfs- und Netzplanung im Föderalismus. In T. Müller & H. Kahl (Eds.), *Energiewende im Föderalismus* (pp. 219–250). Baden-Baden: Nomos.

Hoffmann, J. (2003). Der kleine Unterschied: Varieties of capitalism. *WSI Mitteilungen, 2*(2003), 124–130.

Höfling, M. (2021). Die Wärmepumpe für alle naht – und die wahren Folgen macht sich keiner klar. Welt Online, 19 December 2021. https://www.welt.de/wirtschaft/plus235720436/Die-Waermepumpe-fuer-alle-naht-und-die-wahren-Folgen-macht-sich-keiner-klar.html.

Jacobsson, S., & Lauber, V. (2006). The politics and policy of energy system transformation. Explaining the German diffusion of renewable energy technology. *Energy Policy, 34*(3), 256–276.

Kemmerzell, J., & Knodt, M. (2019). Das "Klimakabinett" – wie es erfolgreich sein könnte und wie nicht. Tagesspiegel Background Energie & Klima, 08 May 2019.

Kemmerzell, J., & Knodt, M. (2020). Governanceprobleme der Sektorkopplung. Über die Verknüpfung der Energie- mit der Verkehrswende (mit M. Knodt). In A. Brunngräber & T. Haas (Eds.), *Baustelle Elektromobilität* (pp. 355–381). Bielefeld: Transcript.

Kemmerzell, J., & Knodt, M. (2021). Dekarbonisierung der Energieversorgung Der deutsche Kohleausstieg im europäischen Kontext. In Bundeszentrale für politische Bildung (Ed.), *Abschied von der Kohle. Struktur- und Kulturwandel im Ruhrgebiet und in der Lausitz* (pp. 58–73). Bonn: Bundeszentrale für politische Bildung.

Kemmerzell, J., Flath, L., & Knodt, M. (2021). *"Champagner" oder "Tafelwasser" der Energiewende: Wie weiter mit dem Wasserstoff in der nächsten Bundesregierung? Ariadne Hintergrund.* Potsdam: Kopernikus-Projekt Ariadne.

Kisker, G. (1971). *Kooperation im Bundesstaat. Eine Untersuchung zum kooperativen Föderalismus in der Bundesrepublik Deutschland.* Tübingen: Mohr (Siebeck).

Knodt, M., Ringel, M., & Müller, R. (2020). Harder soft governance in the European Energy Union. *Journal of Environmental Policy & Planning, 22*(6), 787–800.

Kriener, M. (2012). Die Kraft aus der Luft. *Die Zeit* 06/2012. https://www.zeit.de/zustimmung?url=https%3A%2F%2Fwww.zeit.de%2F2012%2F06%2FWindkraft.

Krohn, P. (2013). Bund koordiniert den Netzausbau. FAZ.net. https://www.faz.net/aktuell/wirtschaft/energiegipfel-bund-koordiniert-den-netzausbau-12123675.html.

Langer, K., Decker, T., Roosen, J., & Menrad, K. (2018). Factors influencing citizens' acceptance and non-acceptance of wind energy in Germany. *Journal of Cleaner Production, 175*, 133–144.

Lauber, V. (2017). Germany's transition to renewable energy. In T. C. Lehmann (Ed.), *The geopolitics of global energy. The new cost of plenty* (pp. 153–182). Boulder/London: Lynne Rienner.

Lauber, V., & Jacobsson, S. (2016). The politics and economics of constructing, contesting and restricting socio-political space for renewables – The German Renewable Energy Act. *Environmental Lee Innovation and Societal Transitions, 18*(2016), 147–163.

Lehmbruch, G. (2000). *Parteienwettbewerb im Bundesstaat*. Wiesbaden: Westdeutscher Verlag.

Leipprand, A., & Flachsland, C. (2018). Regime destabilization in energy transitions: The German debate on the future of coal. *Energy Research & Social Science, 40*, 190–204.

Leiren, M. D., & Reimer, I. (2018). Historical institutionalist perspective on the shift from feed-in tariffs towards auctioning in German renewable energy policy. *Energy Research & Social Science, 43*, 33–40.

Leymann, M. (2020). Das neue Gebäudeenergiegesetz und seine Bedeutung im Recht der Wärmewende. *Zeitschrift für Umweltrecht, 12*(2020), 666–673.

Lijphart, A. (1999). *Patterns of democracy: Government forms and performance in thirty-six countries*. New Haven: Yale University Press.

Lijphart, A. (2012). *Patterns of democracy: Government forms and performance in thirty-six countries* (2nd ed.). New Haven: Yale University Press.

Löschel, A., Grimm, V., Lenz, B., & Staiß, F. (2021). *Stellungnahme zum achten Monitoring-Bericht der Bundesregierung für die Berichtsjahre 2018 und 2019*. Berlin/Münster/Nürnberg/Stuttgart: Expertenkommission zum Monitoring-Prozess "Energie der Zukunft".

Luderer, G., Kost, C., & Sörgel, D. (Eds.). (2021). *Deutschland auf dem Weg zur Klimaneutralität 2045. Szenarien und Pfade im Modellvergleich. Ariadne report*. Potsdam: Kopernikus-Projekt Ariadne.

Mangels-Voegt, B. (2004). Erneuerbare Energien – Erfolgsgaranten einer nachhaltigen Politik? Die Novelle des EEG im Zeichen der Nachhaltigkeit. *APuZ, 37*(2004), 12–17.

Mautz, R. (2012). Atomausstieg und was dann? Probleme staatlicher Steuerung der Energiewende. *dms – der moderne staat – Zeitschrift für Public Policy, Recht und Management, 3*(1), 149–168.

Mautz, R., & Rosenbaum, W. (2012). Der deutsche Stromsektor im Spannungsfeld energiewirtschaftlicher Umbaumodelle. *WSI Mitteilungen, 2*(2012), 85–93.

Meyer, B., & Küchler, S. (2010). *Staatliche Förderungen der Atomenergie (Studie vom Forum Ökologisch-Soziale Marktwirtschaft im Auftrag von Greenpeace)*. Berlin: Forum Ökologisch-Soziale Marktwirtschaft.

Mez, L. (2009). Expansion and phasing-out nuclear power in Germany. In L. Mez, M. Schneider, & S. Thomas (Eds.), *International perspectives on energy policy and the role of nuclear power* (pp. 263–277). Bentwood, Essex: Multi-Science Publication.

Monstadt, J., & Scheiner, S. (2014). Allocating greenhouse gas emissions in the German federal system: Regional interests and federal climate governance. *Energy Policy, 74*, 383–394.

Morris, C. (2016). German renewable power surcharge increases by 8%. https://energytransition.org/2016/10/german-renewable-power-surcharge-increases-by-8/.

Morris, C., & Jungjohann, A. (2016). *Energy democracy. Germany's Energiewende to renewables*. Basingstoke: Palgrave.

Müller, T. (2012). Vom Kartell- zum Umwelt(energie)recht. In T. Müller (Ed.), *20 Jahre Recht der Erneuerbaren Energien* (pp. 129–161). Baden-Baden: Nomos.

Münch, U. (2013). Energiewende im föderalen Staat. in Europäisches Zentrum für Föderalismus-Forschung Tübingen (EZFF) (Ed.): *Jahrbuch des Föderalismus 2013* (pp. 31–47). Baden-Baden: Nomos.

Nationaler Wasserstoffrat. (2021). Wasserstoff Aktionsplan Deutschland 2021–2025. Berlin.

Neuber, M., Kocyba, P., Gardner, B. G. (2020): The same, only different. Die Fridays for Future-Demonstrierenden im europäischen Vergleich. In: S. Haunss, & M. Sommer (Eds.), Fridays for Future – Die Jugend gegen den Klimawandel. Konturen der weltweiten Protestbewegung (pp. 67–93). Bielefeld: Transcript.

Neukirch, M. (2020). Grinding the grid: Contextualizing protest networks against energy transmission projects in Southern Germany. *Energy Research & Social Science, 69*(2020), 101585.

Ohlhorst, D., Tews, K., & Schreurs, M. (2013). Energiewende als Herausforderung der Koordination im Mehrebenensystem. *Technikfolgenabschätzung – Theorie und Praxis, 22*(2), 48–55.

Osička, J., Kemmerzell, J., Zoll, M., Lehotský, L., Černoch, F., & Knodt, M. (2020). What's next for the European coal heartland? Exploring the future of coal as presented in German, Polish and Czech press. *Energy Research & Social Science, 61*. https://doi.org/10.1016/j.erss.2019.101316.

Pahle, M., Edenhofer, O., Pietzcker, R., Tietjen, O., Osorio, S., & Flachsland, C. (2019). Die unterschätzten Risiken des Kohleausstiegs. *Energiewirtschaftliche Tagesfragen, 6*(2019), 31–34.

Prognos, Öko-Institut, & Wuppertal-Institut. (2021). *Klimaneutrales Deutschland 2045. Wie Deutschland seine Klimaziele schon vor 2050 erreichen kann*. Studie im Auftrag von Stiftung Klimaneutralität, Agora Energiewende und Agora Verkehrswende. Berlin.

Renn, O., & Marshall, J. P. (2016). Coal, nuclear and renewable energy policies in Germany: From the 1950s to the "Energiewende". *Energy Policy, 99*(2016), 224–232.

Rosenkranz, G. (2014). Deutschland ewig Kohleland: Energiewende in der Sackgasse? *Blätter für deutsche und internationale Politik, 5*(2014), 101–111.

Sack, D. (2018). Zwischen europäischer Liberalisierung und Energiewende – Der Wandel der Governanceregime im Energiesektor (1990–2016). In L. Holstenkamp & J. Radtke (Eds.), *Handbuch Energiewende und Partizipation* (pp. 81–99). Wiesbaden: Springer VS. https://doi.org/10.1007/978-3-658-09416-4_6.

Scharpf, F. W. (1985). Die Politikverflechtungs-Falle: Europäische Integration und deutscher Föderalismus im Vergleich. *Politische Vierteljahresschrift, 26*(4), 323–356.

Schmidt, V. (2006). *Democracy in Europe. The EU and national polities*. Oxford: Oxford University Press.

Schomerus, T., & Maly, C. (2018). Zur Vergangenheit und Zukunft des Erneuerbare-Energien-Gesetzes. In L. Holstenkamp & J. Radtke (Eds.), *Handbuch Energiewende und Partizipation* (pp. 1117–1133). Wiesbaden: Springer VS. https://doi.org/10.1007/978-3-658-09416-4_6.

Selk, V., & Kemmerzell, J. (2021). Retrogradism in context. Varieties of right-wing populist climate politics. *Environmental Politics*. https://doi.org/10.1080/09644016.2021.1999150.

Selk, V., Kemmerzell, J., & Radtke, J. (2019). In der Demokratiefalle? Probleme der Energiewende zwischen Expertokratie, partizipativer Governance und populistischer Reaktion. In J. Radtke, W. Canzler, M. Schreurs, & S. Wurster (Eds.), *Energiewende in Zeiten des Populismus* (pp. 31–66). Wiesbaden: Springer VS.

SRU (Sachverständigenrat für Umweltfragen). (2017). *Kohleausstieg jetzt einleiten*. Berlin: Stellungnahme.

SRU (Sachverständigenrat für Umweltfragen). (2021). *Wasserstoff im Klimaschutz: Klasse statt Masse*. Berlin: Stellungnahme.

Stefes, C. H. (2014). Energiewende: Critical Junctures and Path Dependencies since 1990. *Zeitschrift für Politik* (Sonderheft 6: Rapide Politikwechsel in der Bundesrepublik), 45–68.

Strunz, S. (2014). The German energy transition as a regime shift. *Ecological Economics, 100*, 150–158.

Tagesspiegel Online. (2021). Scharfe Kritik von Grünen an Scholz-Aussagen zu Nord Stream 2. https://www.tagesspiegel.de/politik/es-ist-belaemmernd-scharfe-kritik-von-gruenen-an-scholz-aussagen-zu-nord-stream-2/27903720.html

Trapmann, D. (2001). Atomkraftwerk Kahl wird abgebaut. Die Welt. https://www.welt.de/print-welt/article461083/Atomkraftwerk-Kahl-wird-abgebaut.html.

Ueckerdt, F., Pfluger, B., Odenweller, A., Günther, C., Knodt, M., Kemmerzell, J., Rehfeld, M., Bauer, C., Verpoort, P., Gils, H.-C., & Luderer, G. (2021). *Eckpunkte einer adaptiven Wasserstoffstrategie. Tragfähige Wasserstoffpfade im Lichte technologischer Unsicherheit. Ariadne Kurzdossier*. Potsdam: Kopernikus-Projekt Ariadne.

Wenz, N. (2021). *Die Governance der Energietransformation von Deutschland und Österreich im Vergleich*. Darmstadt: Technische Universität. https://doi.org/10.26083/tuprints-00011674.

Wettengel, J. (2020). Spelling out the coal exit – Germany's phase-out plan. www.cleanenergywire.org/factsheets/spelling-out-coal-phase-out-germanys-exit-law-draft.

Wietschel, M., Plötz, P., Pfluger, B., Klobasa, M., Eßer, A., Haendel, M., Müller-Kirchenbauer, J., Kochems, J., Hermann, L., Grosse, B., Nacken, L., Küster, M., Pacem, J., Naumann, D., Kost,

C., Kohrs, R., Fahl, U., Schäfer-Stradowsky, S., Timmermann, D., & Albert D. (2018). Sektorkopplung – Definition, Chancen und Herausforderungen, Fraunhofer ISI Working Paper Sustainability and Innovation No. S 01/2018, Karlsruhe.

Wurster, S., & Hagemann, C. (2018). Two ways to success: Expansion of renewable energies in comparison between Germany's Federal States. *Energy Policy, 119*, 610–619. https://doi.org/10.1016/j.enpol.2018.04.059.

Wurster, S., & Köhler, C. (2016). Die Energiepolitik der Bundesländer. Scheitert die Energiewende am deutschen Föderalismus? In A. Hildebrandt & F. Wolf (Eds.), *Die Politik der Bundesländer. Zwischen Föderalismusreform und Schuldenbremse* (pp. 283–314). Wiesbaden: Springer VS.

Zaremba, N. M. (2022). Ruf nach Windkraft-Kommission wird laut. *Tagesspiegel Background Energie & Klima*, 07 January 2022.

Zeit. (2022). Es wird vielleicht auch Zorn geben. *Die Zeit*, 1 (2022).

Ziesing, H.-J. (2009). EU emission trading and national allocations plans 2005–2007: The case of Germany. In B. Eberlein & B. G. Doern (Eds.), *Governing the energy challenge. Canada and Germany in a multi-level regional and global context* (pp. 344–372). Toronto: University of Toronto Press.

Energy Governance in Greece

29

Marula Tsagkari

Contents

Introduction	710
General Conditions of Energy Governance in Greece	711
Path Dependencies	711
Composition of the Energy Mix	712
Discourses on Energy	713
Political Institutions and Actors	717
Coordination, Instruments, and Issues of Energy Transitions Within a Multilevel Context	719
Drivers of Energy Transition	719
Strategies and Instruments	720
Coordination Mechanisms and Multilevel Governance	727
Outcomes, Challenges, and Prospects	728
Cross-References	730
References	731

Abstract

Greece has made a significant development in the energy sector; however, the decarbonization process still lags behind. In the awaking of the economic crisis, in 2009, the country was highly dependent on lignite for electricity production, and the energy market was controlled by a monopoly of the public power corporation. In order to comply with the EU regulation, and the imposed memorandum of understanding, Greece tried to reform the energy sector by liberating the energy market through market initiatives and more concretely through privatization and liberalization. At the same time, a number of mostly incentive-based instruments have managed to reduce emissions by increasing energy efficiency and the penetration of the renewable energy sources. Nonetheless, the highly bureaucratic and complex administrative system controlled by a

M. Tsagkari (✉)
Department of Economics, University of Barcelona, Barcelona, Spain
e-mail: marouko.tsagkari@mespom.eu; marou.tsagari@gmail.com

© Springer Nature Switzerland AG 2022
M. Knodt, J. Kemmerzell (eds.), *Handbook of Energy Governance in Europe*,
https://doi.org/10.1007/978-3-030-43250-8_12

centralized state and the presence of strong lobbies often overshadow these efforts. In order to increase energy security, Greece is currently building two new lignite plants prolonging that way its reliance on coal. With the entrance of the country in a period of economic stability, it is important to revaluate the energy planning, design a coherent long-term climate policy, reform the energy sector, and try to overcome the various barriers in the way to energy transition.

Keywords

Greece · Energy governance · Energy transition · Recession · Energy policy · Energy reforms

Introduction

Greece is a service-based economy, and the three main pillars, tourism, shipping, and the public sector account for 80% of the gross domestic product (GDP). In 2017, it had a GDP of €16,600 and ranked 20th among the European Union countries. With the entrance in the Monetary Union of Europe, the country experienced rapid economic development and a significant increase in GDP. From 2002 to 2008, Greece was among the fastest-growing economies in Europe, with an annual growth rate of about 4% (Neubäumer 2015). This rapid growth was powered by a lignite-based system, which has been the backbone of the country's economy.

However, during this prosperous period, there were not structural changes to increase the productive capacity and competitiveness nor to impugn the large shadow economy, the tax evasion, and the corruption (Kouretas and Vlamis 2010; Arghyrou and Tsoukalas 2011; Karagiannis and Kondeas 2012). As a result, the global economic crisis of 2008 left the country's economy decimated, and, in 2009, Greek debt peaked in 310.4 billion Euros. Since then, Greece has been trapped in a vicious circle of bailout programs and austerity measures imposed by the International Monetary Fund (IMF). The austerity plans included strict public measures (health and education cuts), increased taxes, and reduced pensions.

The crisis and the austerity measures affected all the facets of the economy, and the energy sector was not an exception. One of the many prerequisites that accompanied the bailout programs was a reform program in the energy sector. This program resulted in the opening of the electricity market, the reduction of subsidies on renewable energy sources (RES) that led to the substitution of feed-in tariffs (FiT) with feed-in premium (FiP), and an increase in the price of heating fuel in an effort to increase the state revenues. In addition to the structural reforms, the country initiated a privatization program as an effort to attract foreign investments and to increase capital flow. The privatization of the Public Power Company (PPC) is currently in the forefront of the Greek energy planning despite the significant obstacles and delays.

The energy transition in Greece has been slow, and the primary energy mix used in the country is still lignite followed by imported oil and gas, which makes the country highly dependent on foreign suppliers. The PPC and the Greek authorities try to prolong the life of many old lignite plants in the country, standing against the EU regulations. Additionally, the lack of a coherent energy policy, the heavily bureaucratic and centralized administrative system, and the public opposition delay further the transition. Despite that, the country has a high potential for transition to a more sustainable model based on renewable energy. Over the past few years, the Greek government has put significant attention on the renewable energy sector trying to augment the investments, increase the public acceptance, and promote a more decentralized system. Although the fruits of this effort remain unclear, these initiatives point to the right direction in order to achieve a successful transition to the post-lignite era for Greece.

In the light of the aforementioned, this chapter aims to examine the present situation and the trends in the Greek energy sector and to analyze the paths for the energy transition in the upcoming years.

General Conditions of Energy Governance in Greece

Path Dependencies

It is estimated that Greece has about 5 million tons of lignite, of which, about 3.2 million tons are considered exploitable. The basic sources of lignite can be found in Ptolemaida (total production 4.6 tons in 2009) and in Megalopoli (total production 13.2 tons in 2009). The majority of these deposits (78%) where formed during the Neocene age but remained unexploited until 1873 where the first extraction site opened in Aliveri. However, it was only after 1950 that intensive exploitation started in order to cover the increased demand.

Before the economic crisis, Greece was heavily dependent on lignite, which is the only domestically produced fuel. Lignite accounted for more than half of the country's electricity production, and as such, Greece was the second-largest lignite producer in EU and fourth worldwide in 2008 (Kavouridis 2008), while in 2017 it still ranked in the fourth place among all the European countries, according to Eurostat (2018b). However, despite its importance for the local economy, the domestic lignite is characterized by low calorific value, making it costly. A study commissioned by the Public Power Corporation and the consultancy Booz & Co. in 2014 highlighted that the lignite production in Greece is the costliest in Europe. Since the beginning of the economic crisis, and in line with the EU targets, the use of lignite has been reduced from 63% in 2004 to 45% in 2014 and 32% in 2016. Nonetheless, this didn't change the pre-crisis plans of the government to install two new lignite plants (Ptolemais V and Melitis II). Currently, the local lignite deposits cover 23% of the total inland energy consumption. The reasons for these reductions are the strict EU directives, the penetration of Renewable Energy Systems (RES), and the increased gas imports through new pipes. Nevertheless, lignite remains an important source for heat and electricity generation, and the PPC is the only owner of the eight lignite stations in the country.

In Greece, energy is mainly produced or imported from the North, despite higher demand occurring in the South around the urban center of Athens; presenting a problem with transportation of the energy. Another challenge regarding the distribution of energy in Greece is the plethora of islands that make up the country. Greece has more than 200 islands, many of which are not yet connected to the mainland grid. In order to meet their needs, these islands use costly, polluting methods like diesel combustion. To date, 32 independent island stations exist, of which, 19 are small stations (up to 10 kw), 11 are medium-sized stations (10–100 kw), and 2 big systems can be found in Crete and Rhodes (more than 100 kw) (Petrakopoulou 2015). The operating and environmental costs of these stations burden the whole country as everybody pays higher prices through a unified system. According to the data published from RAE (2014), the total cost is more than 800 m€/year. Additionally, the CO_2 emissions from these islands are responsible for a large proportion of Greece's total emissions.

Composition of the Energy Mix

Based on the national energy mix of 2016, depicted in Fig. 1, the petroleum products still dominate the total gross inland consumption, while the renewables represent almost 11% of it. This percentage is significant lower compared to other Mediterranean countries with similar weather conditions like Spain (see Chap. 44, ▶ "Energy Governance in Spain"), Portugal (see Chap. 38, ▶ "Energy Governance in Portugal"), and Italy (see Chap. 32, ▶ "Energy Governance in Italy"). Regarding the final energy consumption (Fig. 2), there has been a significant reduction since 2007, mainly due to the recession and the increased taxes on oil products. The share of

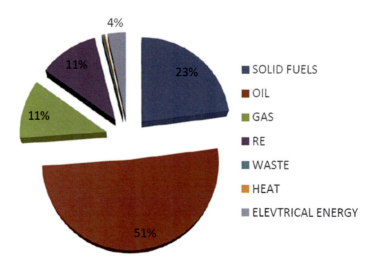

Fig. 1 National share of fuels in gross inland energy consumption in Greece, 2016. (Data source: Eurostat (2018b), Simplified energy balances – annual data)

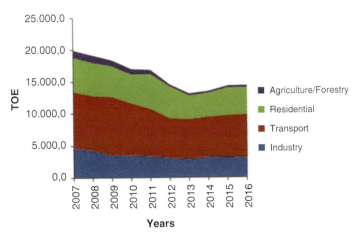

Fig. 2 Final energy consumption by fuel type 2000–2016, primary energy equivalents. (Data source: Eurostat (2018b), Simplified energy balances – annual data)

natural gas in the energy mix has been increased around 5% since 2000, while the renewable increased about 6%.

Local lignite production has long been unable to cover the continuously increased demand, mainly in the domestic sector and in transportation. Thus, currently Greece's energy market is highly dependent on imports of petroleum products (99.6% dependency rate) and natural gas (99.2% dependency rate) (Fig. 3). In 2016, the total energy dependency rate of the country was 73.6%, which is 4.5% higher compared to 2010. The imports of oil products reached an all-time high in 2016 when 32.77 thousand tones where imported. Despite higher imports, the overall gross inland consumption significantly decreased since 2009, mainly due to the recession and the increased taxes on oil products (Fig. 3).

Nowadays, Greece imports 100% of the natural gas and 98% of the oil needed to cover the remained of its energy needs. Oil is the dominant fuel source and is imported mainly from Iraq and Russia. In the years since the beginning of the recession, oil consumption has been reduced as well, due in part to the increased oil price. As a result, 58% of the Greek households experienced energy poverty, and people have turned to wood-burning stoves and open fires to keep warm during the winter months. This has been reported to have severe effect on the atmosphere, especially above the big cities which are often covered with smog (Papada and Kaliampakos 2016).

Discourses on Energy

Greece's first electrical grid came in 1889, and it soon expanded to cover much of the country, including the second bigger city, Thessaloniki, that was part of the Ottoman Empire during this time. However, it was only after 10 years that the first

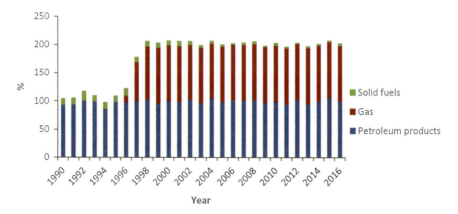

Fig. 3 Energy dependency rate by product (1990–2016). (Data source: Eurostat (2018b), Energy dependence)

multinational electricity companies began appearing in Greece. By 1950, a costly system of numerous autonomous stations, operating with imports, was created. As a result of the high costs, only a small part of the population had access to electricity. The situation changed with the creation of the Public Power Corporation (PPC in August 1950). From this point the PPC is the main generator and distributor of electricity in the country. The PPC initiated the extraction of the lignite that continues to today and integrated the local autonomous systems into a bigger unified system.

This allowed PPC to achieve a monopoly in the energy market in Greece that lasted until 2001. The introduction of Law 2773/1999 liberalized the energy market in an effort to comply with the EU regulations (92/96 EU Directive). Later, in 2003, Law 3175/2003 established the Day-Ahead Market based on the system of marginal prices. The same Law, in article 24, paved the way for further market liberalization as it allowed the power generators to choose their gas supplier. When the law went into effect in 2003, 15% of the PPC's shares were sold in an effort to initiate the privatization process; however, prior to the economic crisis, the privatization of the PPC was low on the political agenda, and any effort was fragmented.

During the crisis, another decisive step was taken with the Law 4001/2011, which incorporated the Directive 2009/72/EC of the European Parliament. According to this law, the PPC is now divided into two affiliated companies: one responsible for energy transport and one for supply. Under this law, the independent regulatory authority (RAE) took over regulatory and monitoring responsibilities. The purpose of this was to protect the consumers, to ensure a fair licensing system, and to create a favorable environment for new players to enter the market (RAE 2018).

The privatization of PPC found strong opposition among the workers and in public opinion. Many claimed that the PPC was a unique part of the country's history and a symbol of the development of the postmodern Greece (Malouhos 2014). Additionally, the fear of job losses increased the public resentment. Despite continued protests from employees and the worker's unions, a new big privatization step is under discussion for 2018, in an effort to comply with the demands of the European Union.

In 2016, the first NOMA (Nouvelle Organisation du Marché de l'Electricité) auction took place in accordance with the Law 4389/2016. According to this model, the PPC is committed until 2020 to sell a part of the electricity produced below the initial price in order to enable other actors to participate in the market. Three additional auctions took place in 2017, with prices lower than those in the mandatory pool; however the target to reduce the shares of PPC in 75% was not achieved. Currently, PPC is still the dominant player in the market with a share of 85%. This was expected to drop in 49% by 2019. However, the target does not appear to be achievable at present. According to the CEO of PPC "The reduction of PPC's share to below 50% by the end of 2019 is not feasible. To achieve that we would have to lose 4.8 million clients in 2 years" (Energyworld 2017). Four more auctions are scheduled for 2018 in an effort to approach the targets. The total amount of 1711 Mw/h has been expected to be auctioned during 2018. Nonetheless, the strong presence of PPC in the electricity market, in combination with the lack of structural reforms and the high cost of capital and the market uncertainties are still significant barriers for the potential competitors (Fafaliou and Polemis 2010).

The liberalization of the gas market is also a priority for the Greek government in line with the requisites of the memorandum of understanding (MoU). In 2015, the Law 4336/2015 separated the retail from the wholesale market opening the way for new companies. Although the public company (DEPA) is still the main actor, the liberalization of both the retail and the wholesale market is quick. Currently two companies, the M&M and Prometheus, operate as distributors breaking the monopoly of DEPA. In 2016, in an attempt to boost further the liberalization of the market DEPA committed to share in auctions 16% in 2017, 17% in 2018, 18% in 2019, and 20% in 2020.

One of the most important energy discourses concerns gas pipelines, as Greece has become an important player in the gas market. In 1996, the first Russian gas pipeline was constructed in Greece and to date remains the main entry point for gas in the country. In 2016, the construction of the Trans Adriatic Pipeline (TAP) that will start in Turkey, pass through Greece and Albania, and end in Italy was announced. This will increase significantly the country's energy security. Another important gas pipe, the East Med, will transfer gas from Israel to Italy and is also expected to pass through Greece. Recently Greece, Italy, and Russia agreed also on the construction of the new pipe "Poseidon."

All the aforementioned examples highlight the important role of Greece in the gas market. Despite the potential benefits, the plans met strong opposition from the local communities. For example, the municipality of Kavala objected to the development of TAP in its area. According to the association of the municipality, more than 70% of the people whose land will be crossed by the pipeline refused to sign the contract with TAP AG. So far, the company has had to redesign 16% of the initial plans (88.5 km) for similar reasons (Energypress 2017). This has led to significant delay in the project's timeline.

Finally, the newly discovered oil reservoirs in Greece have raised hopes and concerns. For a long time, there was evidence that oil reservoirs exist in the territory. Recently it is estimated that only in the area southwest of Crete, in Southern Greece, more than ten billion barrels exist. In 2014, the Greek government gave to private entities the rights for research and extract oil in 20 areas in the Aegean and Ionian Sea, while in 2018 US Exxon Mobil, France's Total, and Hellenic Petroleum were selected to explore for oil and gas in Crete. Rich oil reserves are currently considered to be in at least in six more areas (Prinos, Katakolo, Patraikos, Corfu, Kyparissia, Preveza-Arta). Of course, this discovery raised opposition from environmental organizations especially around Natura 2000 areas. In contrast, a study carried out in the Katakolo region showed that citizens were in favor of extraction because they saw the potential for economic improvement (Vergoulis and Damigos 2013).

The transition to the post-lignite era in Greece is slow and complicated, as lignite has been traditionally considered one of the main pillars of the country's electricity system. However, this system of production has been declining, and many of the old plants have been shut down to comply with the Industrial Emissions Directive, leaving Greece with only four operating plants by 2020, two of which are currently under construction. The government and the PPC put forward the arguments that lignite can reduce energy dependency from gas imports, can increase energy security, augment the economic benefits for the surrounding areas, and open new jobs. Thus, the PPC proposes that lignite comprises 35% of the country's energy mix in the next 15 years.

In line with this thought, the government approved the construction of two new lignite plants: "Ptolemaida V" and "Meliti II." The construction of Ptolemaida V will cost a total of 1.4 billion Euros, and it is expected to produce 660 MW by 2020 and to create 300 new jobs. The construction of the plant is supported by a €739 million loan from a KfW-Ipex, the German export bank, under the guarantee of the German Export Credit Agency Euler Hermes (PPC 2013). The new plant will be "tailor-made" to the lignite of the area and is expected to offer lignite in the price of 25–35 Euro/MWh (WWF Hellas 2012). The yet-to-be lignite plant at Meliti will have a capacity of 350–450 MW and is due to 2021. Given those plans, it comes as no surprise that Greece was one of the two countries (with the other one being Poland) that refused to sign the Eurelectric agreement not to build new coal power plants beyond 2020 (Hall 2017).

The construction of new plants caused significant resistance from environmental organizations and the local communities due to the environmental and health impacts (WWF 2018; Power Engineering International 2012). In four villages in the area of Ptolemaida, people were forced to evacuate their houses, and two more villages are expected to be evacuated after the completion of the construction of Ptolemaida V. According to the silent killers report, more than 1200 deaths occur per year due to coal pollution, and 260,000 days of work are lost due to pollution-related diseases in Greece (Greenpeace 2017).

Political Institutions and Actors

As discussed, the energy sector in Greece is highly politicized and has been at the forefront of national and international political discourse. Many of the decisions in recent years have been driven by the need to comply with EU and IMF regulations. However, every piece of proposed energy legislation must pass through the Greek parliament. There are a number of different actors and governmental organizations working to implement the legislation. The Hellenic Ministry of Environment and Energy is responsible for enforcing any new laws and the Ministry of Finance is responsible for energy taxation and subsidies. The Special Secretariat for the Environment and Energy Inspectorate (SSEEI) founded under the Law 3818/2010 is the monitoring entity of the Ministry, responsible for the implementation of the Directives. The Hellenic Energy Inspectorate is the committee under SSEEI tasked with monitoring national energy policy, in particular when it comes to energy saving and efficiency (Ypeka 2018). The Centre for Renewable Energy Sources and Saving (CRES), founded in September 1987, is responsible for the promotion of RES, the sustainable energy planning, and the energy efficiency programs. It also operates under the supervision of the Ministry of Environment and Energy.

The regional authorities and the municipalities are, since 2008, eligible to participate in the Covenant of Mayors, a network that aims to bring closer local and regional authorities, which strive to achieve ambitious targets for the climate and energy. By the end of 2018, 110 municipalities participate in the network representing one third of the municipalities of Greece. The regions (peripheries) regulate the participation of the municipalities in the Convent, and they provide the local authorities with technical and economic assistance. The role of the regional authorities, however, does not go beyond the coordination and support of the local and national initiatives. The recent data of LAGIE (2018) show an unequal distribution of renewable energy installations among the peripheries and inside the same periphery. According to the report, the region of Sterea Ellada had the preeminence in the wind sector (612.53 MW), while the region of Attica produced 6.86 MW from biomass followed by Central Macedonia with 14.91 MW. Inside the region of Sterea Ellada that currently produces 45% of the exploitable potential of the country, the regional unit of Evoia produces mostly wind and geothermal energy, while Evritania and Fokida have high hydroelectric production. Trikkalioti (2018) emphasized that the different peripheries have different priorities and targets according to their needs and potentials.

The local authorities play minor roles in the energy sector decisions. Nonetheless, they are often key actors when it comes to the actual implementation of renewable energy projects and particularly to public acceptance. Despite a generally inconsequential role in national energy policymaking, a number of initiatives arose during the past years from various municipalities. A recent example occurred in the municipality of Kampos in Thessaly. The city installed five photovoltaic parks with a capacity of 20 kW/h each. This resulted a 60,000–65,000 Euros profit per year of which 50% is invested in other environmental projects and the rest in cultural activities. Another good example is the small island of Tilos, in the Southeast Aegean. The inhabitants of the island, with the support of the municipality, received 11 million Euros from the Horizon 2020 program aiming to become the "green island" in the Mediterranean (European Commission 2018).

A new Law, 4513/2018, is expected to further empower local authorities in the renewable energy sector. This regulation recognizes the importance of energy communities as an active part in the promotion of RES and provides favorable a framework for their operation and development. In this context, seven municipalities of Athens are designing the "Prodesa" project, which focuses on renewable energy generated from photovoltaic cells installed on 74 public buildings (Prodesa 2018). These photovoltaic systems are expected to produce 4.8 GWh/year. Under this regulation, the Orthodox Church also aims to enter the renewable energy market with the installation of PVs in monasteries.

Despite these municipality level initiatives, the PPC dominates the Greek electricity market. While PPC owns power supply, the Hellenic Transmission System Operator (HTSO) regulates operation and development of the transmission system. The HTSO is responsible to meet the electricity demand and to operate the system effectively. It provides access to the grid and manages long-term contracts and sales. Working with the HTSO to ensure efficient and continued operation is the Regulatory Authority for Energy (RAE). The RAE is the independent regulatory entity for the energy market whose responsibility is to manage and police the numerous actors. The organization is responsible for handling complaints that arise and imposing fines. It also calculates and approves the unit charges, supervises the function of the energy market, and organizes auctions (RAE 2018). The foundation of RAE, with Law 2773/1999, was necessary in order to achieve a progressive liberalization and privatization of the energy sector based on transparency and fair competition. After the opening of the Greek market, a number of private companies created an energy lobby in Greece. Among them Protergia, Elpedison, Watt & Volt, Iron, and Green were some of the companies that pushed for the liberalization of the market. Despite the efforts, changes in market shares have been slow. All the independent energy providers in the country have reported to share a share of 19.2% in 2017 (LAGIE 2017).

Similarly to the energy market, the gas market in Greece is dominated by the Public Gas Corporation and its subsidiary company, the Hellenic Gas Transmission Systems Operator (DESFA). The Public Gas Corporation (PGC) supervises the importation of gas products and is the main actor in the wholesale gas market with a share of 90.4% in the total gas imports in 2016 (DEPA 2016). The rest is mainly distributed among two other private companies, Prometheus Gas and M&M Gas, who report significant increase in their market share since 2016. The subsidiary company of the PGC, the Hellenic Gas Transmission System Operator (DESFA) was founded in 2007 and is responsible for the function of the National Natural Gas System. Currently DESFA is also going through privatization and through 2018, 66% of the company is expected to be sold. In the oil market, two big players (Hellenic Petroleum SA and Motor Oil Hellas SA) have created a strong lobby and control four refineries with a total capacity of refining 25 million tons. These two companies control over 70% of the wholesale market.

The environmental movement is not as strong in Greece as in other European countries, despite the significant empowerment of the movement after 1990 (Botetzagias 2001). The economic crisis reported to have a severe effect on the environmental attitudes and organizations. Environmental organizations lost members, had decreased access to funding, and faced increased public dissent (Simiti 2017). Despite the barriers, there are still flagship NGOs that are actively involved in the energy transition, including Greenpeace and WWF. Among others, these two organizations have coordinated movements mainly against coal, for example, the protests against the new lignite power stations and the oil-plant in Keratsini (Rootes 2003). However, these initiatives often lack broad support outside the activist groups and have low impact (Koussis 2013).

The 22 public universities are leaders in the research and development area, including research on energy transitions. Along with the public research centers, they absorb 70% of the total R&D funding annually (not only energy-related). The main public research providers that work on energy-related issues are the Centre for Research and Technology-Hellas (CERTH), the Centre for Research and Technology-Hellas (CERTH), and the Institute for Solid Fuels Technology and Applications (ISFTA). The private sector receives only 30% of the R&D budget, a share significantly lower than the EU average. The main source of funding is the Community Support Framework (CSF) and other EU structural funds.

Coordination, Instruments, and Issues of Energy Transitions Within a Multilevel Context

Drivers of Energy Transition

After the economic crisis, the energy sector has been acknowledged as having significant potential to assist in the economic recovery of the country. The wind resources in Greece are some of the most attractive in Europe for the installation of windmills. Additionally the country experiences more than 250 days of sunshine annually making it suitable for installation of PVs as well. Additionally, the average of solar irradiation and the force of the winds is expected to increase by the end of the century (Bank of Greece 2011). RES can also provide a basis for a better economic environment as they can contribute to the GDP growth and create new employment opportunities. According to the European Wind Energy Association (2012), 8.6–11 billion Euro of GDP can be gained from the RES, enough to lead the country out of the severe economic crisis.

The Syriza government, in office until July 2019, emphasized renewable energy can create new jobs, attract investments, and help Greece to achieve the 2020 targets set by the EU. The government is trying to achieve this using market initiatives and more concretely through privatization and liberalization (as presented in the section "Discourses on Energy"). Political games and lobbying have also influenced the energy transition of the country. With the economic crisis and the crises in Ukraine and Syria, energy security has become a priority issue for the EU. Greece's strategic geopolitical location has uniquely positioned the country to act as a "transit hub" for energy to the rest of the EU. The TAP and the Vertical Corridor are expected to increase the energy security for the whole EU.

Energy security in Greece is still very low. The country is extremely dependent on energy imports from many neighboring countries. This lack of energy autonomy became evident in 2016, when the major electricity, oil, and gas companies had severe difficulties in meeting the demand, as they couldn't afford to pay for the required imports. Similarly, it was reported that "the Greek energy system faced significant problems in January 2017 when the country's electricity network nearly collapsed on two occasions and blackouts were averted only at the last minute" (European Commission 2017, p. 5). The problem of energy security is even bigger on the islands of the Aegean where the summer demand often exceeds the winter demand by 500% (Kaldellis and Zafirakis 2007). For this reason, energy security is of high importance for covering the tourist's needs on these areas. A balanced energy mix, with an increased focus on RES, seems to be the best way to achieve energy security and to avoid future blackouts.

Finally, tourism as one of the main pillars of the economy has proven to play an important role in the energy transition. Energy savings associated with tourist activities like cooking and air conditioning can lead to significant cost reduction and increased competitiveness. Additionally, many local communities have realized the potential of sustainable tourism that targets tourists who are willing to spend more for sustainable tourism experiences (IRENA 2014). The survey of Tsagarakis et al. (2011) in Crete confirmed this as 87% of the respondents claimed that they prefer to stay in hotels with RES.

Strategies and Instruments

Energy is at the top of the present government's agenda, and the three specific targets are to find and manage energy resources in order to ensure the country's energy security, to create an energy stock and alliances and alternatives in order to prevent an energy crisis, and to achieve a sustainable development of the energy sector. Short before the economic recession, in an attempt to comply with the EU targets, the Ministry of Environment announced the Law 3851/2010 "Accelerating the development of Renewable Energy Sources to deal with climate change and other regulations addressing issues" (Governmental Gazette 85/4-6-2010) with a focus on renewable energy production and energy efficiency. Greece set the target of 20% share of renewable energy resources by 2020 (penetration level: 40% electricity, 20% heat and 10% transport) (Ypeka 2010). It remains uncertain if Greece will achieve those targets on time. Despite the reassurance from the government, various organizations like WWF Hellas (2017) have expressed concerns that Greece is running out of time to reach the targets.

More recently, the ambitious 2030 framework for climate and energy, adopted by the EU, aims to promote sustainable transition and to ensure that the EU will meet its long-term 2050 greenhouse gas reductions targets. These targets include a 40% cut in greenhouse gas emissions compared to 1990 levels, at least a 27% share of renewable energy consumption and at least 27% energy savings compared with the business-as-usual scenario by 2030. Greece incorporated these targets in the national planning and set the target of 30% for the share of renewable energy consumption. The total investment needed in the energy sector in order to achieve the national targets was estimated at 22.2 billion Euro for the 2010–2020 timeframe. From these, 16.5 billion will be allocated to new RES capacity, nearly 7 billion to wind, 5.5 billion to PV, 1.6 billion to pump storage for supporting the variable RES production, 1.1 billion to solar heating and cooling, and 0.5 billion to biomass and biogas projects (Chaviaropoulos 2010). Apart from the operational programs, energy efficiency projects in Greece have received significant financial support from the EU. For instance, the EU SAVE, THERMIE, and ENERGIE, implemented between 1997 and 2000, were covered almost by 40% from EU contributions (Patlitzianas and Christos 2011). In order to achieve its national targets, the country has designed a strategy built upon a number of instruments that vary among the different energy sectors (Table 1).

Renewable Energy Sector
The history of the renewable energy policies in Greece starts in 1997 with the ministerial Law 2244 (see Fig. 4). Following the German (see Chap. 28, ▶ "Energy Governance in Germany") example, Greece introduced the feed-in tariffs (FiT) scheme with the long-term purpose to increase the investment incentive. Worldwide, the FiTs have proven to be effective and are generally the preferred policy by the investors (Bürer and Wüstenhagen 2009) even in times of crisis (Hofman and Huisman 2012). The program started with high FiT, similar to the ones implemented in Germany. However, as a response to the high demand and reduced price, the tariffs for RE installments, mainly solar PV, witnessed a considerable decrease. The new RES Law (L.4414/2016), adopted by the Greek Parliament in 2016, was an effort to increase the integration of RES in the market through a feed-in premium (FiP) mechanism.

This change was part of the new adjustment program that was imposed in the country from the EU, according to the third memorandum of understanding and was in line with the general plan of the EU agenda to move from guaranteed RE support to market-based instruments. Especially in the case of Greece, this transition was considered necessary, as the investments on the renewable energy sector have stagnated since 2013.

According to the new scheme, the premium will be calculated as the difference between the marginal price and a fixed price decided via a competitive tender. The old FiT support scheme will be continued to be valid for all new RE projects with maximum installed capacity of 3 MW for onshore wind parks and 0.5 MW for solar PVs. The initial competitive tenders were completed successfully in 2016 and were divided into two categories: PV projects up to 1.0 MW and PV projects between 1.0 and 10.0 MW. The lower offers for the first category was in 94.97 €/MWh and 79.97 €/MWh for the second category. In the recent auction in 2018, the price was 75.87 €/MWh for the category 1 projects and 62.97 €/MWh for the category 2 projects, highlighting a significant drop in the prices.

Table 1 Key Greek energy transition policy instruments by sector and type

	Regulatory	Incentive based	Internalizing	Soft governance
Electricity	Electricity consumption taxation (ΕΦΚ) (1980–present)	Feed-in tariff (2006–2015)	EU emissions trading system (EU ETS)	Promotion of renewable energy communities (2018 onward)
		Feed-in premium (2016–present)		
Energy efficiency in buildings	Regulation of Building's Thermal Insulation (TIR) (1979 onward)	Saving at Home (2011–present)		EPBD (2002)
	Compulsory energy performance certificate (2011–present)			
	Regulation for the building energy performance (REPB) (2011–present)	Green roofs on public buildings (2013–2017)		
	Tackling illegal building – Environmental Balance and other provisions (2013–present)			
Energy efficiency in transport	Phase out of old diesel cars from Athens (2021 onward)	Vehicle withdraw program (2009–2016)		Improve road infrastructure
				Increase of EV charging points
		Tax relief for EV		Upgrade of public transport (third community support framework 2000–2008)
				Requirement for CO_2 labeling in new vehicles
Energy efficiency in agriculture and industry	Excise tax refund for fuels used in the production of energy products for intra-EU use	Incentives for the implementation of environmental management systems	EU greenhouse gas emissions trading scheme (2003 onward)	Climate change agreements (2001)
		"Green business" incentives (2009 onward)	Lignite levy	Voluntary agreements

(continued)

Table 1 (continued)

	Regulatory	Incentive based	Internalizing	Soft governance
		Promoting environmental industry (2017 onward)		Ecolabels (1991, 2008)
Energy poverty	Social electricity tariff			
	Subsidies for heating oil			

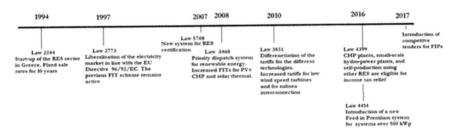

Fig. 4 An overview of the evolution of the policy and regulatory framework for the RES sector in Greece. (Data source: Ministry of Environment and Energy (YPEN))

Despite the clear regulation and the significant efforts, the administrative practice remains still complex especially due to the inherent bureaucracy of the Greek system. One of the major barriers is the overall authorization procedure. According to Boemi et al. (2010), the approval process duration for a PV park is about 2 years and for a wind farm 4 years. Often, the public opposition delays the process even more. Although some studies have highlighted that the economic crisis increased the public acceptance of renewable energy sources, there are still various examples of strong opposition like in the case of Chios and Thessaly (Argenti and Knight 2015).

The new regulation for the operation of Energy Efficiency Obligation Scheme (National Gazette 1242B/11-4-2017) was published in April 2017. It aims to regulate the energy efficiency sector and to set specific 2020 targets for energy retailers and sales. Complementary, the program Energy Performance Contracting (EPC) will apply to low-income households, old vehicles, and polluting industries. The program's actions will vary from providing information to technical interventions and is expected to help the country achieve the 2020 targets of 24.7 Mtoe in primary energy consumption or 18.4 Mtoe of final energy consumption.

The economic crisis led to significant economic adjustments in the country, including major reforms in the taxation system as part of the 2010–2011 bailout program. Part of this agreement was the increase of the motor fuel tax followed by an increase in the heating oil tax in 2012 (Petmesidou 2013). In Greece, the share of environmental tax revenues from total tax revenues was 9.09% in 2016. Of this, the energy tax corresponds to 7.19% and the remaining 1.9% is a transport tax, as Greece does not have a pollution tax. These taxes are above the EU average and Greece ranks among the EU countries with the higher taxes. Currently, there is an energy tax on oil products, natural gas, coal, and coke. According to IEA World Energy Prices database, Greece has the fourth highest price in gasoline, the 2/3 of which is taxes. These taxes increased by almost 3% since 2011. Additionally, Greece witnessed the biggest increase in the prices of electricity (12.8) in the first trimester of 2018. Of this, 41% is taxes. This is above the EU average, which is 37%. On the contrary, the taxes for natural gas are only 16% of the total price, way below the EU average.

Energy Saving in Buildings
The building sector consumes the 37% of the final energy in Greece mainly because the buildings are old and lack appropriate insulation. More particularly 69% of the buildings in Greece were constructed before 1980. Those buildings are estimated to consume 45% more energy compared to the newer buildings. The European Directive on the energy performance of buildings EPBD was transposed to Greek law with a significant delay in 2008, only after the European Court of Justice sentenced Greece for failing to comply with EPBD. The law "Measures for the reduction of energy consumption in buildings and other provisions" sets the EPBD framework in Greece including mandatory Energy Performance Certificates (EPC) and mandatory energy design in new buildings which cannot be below class B (Dascalaki et al. 2012). Additionally, Law 3851/2010 determines that in order to get a new building permit, it is obligatory to have an annual solar fraction of 60% for sanitary hot water (SHW) production from solar thermal systems (Balaras et al. 2018).

The program "energy savings in households" started in 2011 in an effort to increase the energy efficiency in the buildings especially in those built before 1980. The second phase of the program was announced in 2018 and will continue until 2023. The program includes incentives that can be used to replace window frames, to upgrade the insulation, the production of hot water from RES, and automation in electricity systems. The total budget of 350 million Euros will be distributed among 30–40,000 beneficiaries.

Another program related with the building sector is the "green roofs on public buildings" program that aims to upgrade the environmental standards of public buildings and to promote initiatives like the creation of rooftop-gardens to reduce energy consumption and emissions of greenhouse gases. The "Intelligent Nearly Zero Energy Theme Museums" is a pilot program implemented in Greece with finance from the European Union aiming mainly to improve capacity in order to achieve high-energy efficiency.

Energy Efficiency in Transport
Emissions from transport increased significantly in the two decades from 1990 to 2010 as a result of the economic development and then decreased with the beginning of the economic crisis in 2010. The Greek transport sector is highly energy demanding and almost totally dependent on oil (98% in 2017). According to data from the

European Environment Agency, 18,000 premature deaths a year in Greece are attributed to poor air quality. An analysis by Nanaki and Koroneos (2013) highlighted hybrid and electric vehicles can cause significantly lower emissions than the conventional vehicles and relief the heavily polluted area of Athens. However, biodiesel is the dominant fuel, and electric and hybrid vehicles are not as prevalent as in other countries. According to data from 2017, only 199 hybrid and 161 electric cars were sold in Greece that year. Although there is a reported increase since 2016, the share of the Greek market is rather small compared to the 115,405 electric vehicles, and 216,566 hybrid vehicles sold in Europe the same year (Kathimerini 2018). Due to this lack of available alternatives in the local market, the country still lacks behinds in energy efficiency in the transport sector, which accounts for 40% of the total final energy consumption.

According to the current legislation (N. 4439/2016 p. 1) by the end of the year 2020, there must be a secure number of charging positions available for the country's emerging fleet of EVs, which must be accessible to the public in order to facilitate the circulation of EVs in the road network. Currently, 45 charging stations provide in total 64 charging positions (Perellis et al. 2018).

A study by Ecorys (2006) highlighted that despite the fact that Greece is highly dependent on road transport (95%), the road accessibility is below the EU average, and the road infrastructure is insufficient and lacks interconnections. Additionally, the vehicle fleet is outdated, with an average of 14 years (European Environment Agency 2016). In recent years, the government has taken steps to change this and adopted a number of high impact measures like the improvement of road infrastructure and the upgrading of public transport. A number of medium impact measures such as the replacement of old cars and technical inspections on vehicles and low impact measures like the requirement for CO_2 labeling in new vehicles are also being implemented (Tsita and Pilavachi 2017). The most successful among these initiatives was the vehicle withdraw program that provided incentives for the replacement of old cars. From 2011 to 2015, more vehicles were recycled than pursued leading to a decrease in the overall number of registered vehicles. In 2016 the vehicle withdraw program was completed, and since then the number of old vehicles has risen.

Greece imposes taxes for acquisition and ownership of diesel cars. The annual tax calculation bases on the year of the acquisition of the car, the CO_2 emissions per km, and the engine capacity of the vehicle. Moreover, cars with a price exceeding €20,000 or more than 1929 cc engine capacity are subject to an extra tax known as the luxury tax (ACEA 2017). On the contrary, incentives in the form of tax relief are awarded to owners of electric or hybrid vehicles. According to a review by OECD (2018), the mobility sector is the more heavily taxed in Greece, and within this sector, gasoline has the higher tax rate.

Energy Efficiency in Industry and Agriculture

In the industry sector, the main policy framework is the "Operational Program for Competitiveness 2000–2006 (OPC)" that aims in improvement of the energy efficiency. The "Private Incentives for Economic Development and Regional Convergence" development law includes special grants up to 60% in order to improve energy efficiency and install RES in industries. Additionally, the Emissions Trading System (ETS) that started in 2005 is still the main pillar of the country's efforts to improve the energy efficiency in industry.

Fossil fuels used in agriculture are taxed, but gasoline consumed for agriculture activities remains free of tax. Despite that, during the period of the economic crisis, the CO_2 emissions in the agricultural sector sharply decreased. A rapid decrease was observed in the period 2003–2008 (-84%) due to a decrease in energy intensity as a result of the use of cleaner technologies. The period 2008–2017 was characterized by further decrease on the CO_2 due to further modernization of the technology but mainly because of the economic contraction. For instance, during this period biomass use increased from 6 ktoe in 2003 to 25.7 ktoe in 2013 (Roinioti and Koroneos 2017).

Energy crops are not of major interest in Greece despite the fact that the country has high potential as the agriculture sector accounts for more than 5% of the gross domestic product (Panoutsou 2007). The binding commitment to replace 10% of transport fuels with sustainable biofuels by 2020 is a motivating factor, and already the topic has gained a lot of attention. Many industries like the Greek sugar industry already use fuels from energy crops which are subject of tax relief. However, Greece lacks a complete comprehensive planning and specific instruments for the promotion of energy crops.

Energy Poverty

During the years after the start of the economic crisis, energy poverty in Greece reached to severe levels. A similar phenomenon was observed also in other European countries in recession like Ireland (see Chap. 31, ▶ "Energy Governance in Ireland") and Portugal (see Chap. 38, ▶ "Energy Governance in Portugal") since 2010, and shortly thereafter, the issue was brought to the attention of the EU. In 2017 according to Eurostat (2018a), 29.1% of the population was unable to keep their homes' adequately heated. The share is more than twice as high (73.5%) in the mountainous areas due to the lower incomes and the higher energy prices (Papada and Kalampakos 2016). Additionally, more than 40% of Greek households are in debt to their electricity providers as they are unable to pay regularly the monthly bills. In an effort to fight energy poverty, the Greek government offered financial support for the vulnerable households (Tagaris and Kountatou 2018). A budget of 650,000,000 Euros was allocated to 580,000 beneficiaries in 2014 and 330,000 in 2016, in order to subsidize the heating oil price. However, in 2017 the government announced a 50% reduction in the budget leading many households to suffer energy poverty. Low prices of electricity the days with smog and reconnection of electricity for households that paid back part of their debt were others proposed measures that did not flourish.

Because of the increased energy poverty, there was a significant increase in the demand for wood and pallet used in fireplaces and woodstoves. This led to an augment in illegal logging in the mountainous areas of the country and in illegal import of wood, mainly from Bulgaria and the Republic of North Macedonia. An increase in the fuel smuggling has also been observed the past years. A common practice is to smuggle oil in the country with ships as they have a privileged tax rate. The fuels are then smuggled to gas stations and sold as legal. Adulteration of fuels is another common practice (Kalligeros et al. 2003; National Technical University of Athens 2008; Bitzenis and Kontakos 2014). According to Mardas (2014) up to 20% of fuel sold in regular gas stations in Greece is illegal, while the IMF reported that fuel smuggling costs Greece about one billion Euros annually (Karakasis 2014). The authorities have been unable to control these phenomena despite some efforts, e.g., equalize the price of heating oil with petrol pump prices, installation of systems that control inflows and outflows of the fuels' volume, and increased controls. However, fuel smuggling is still a plague for the Greek energy market and a limiting factor toward a successful policy that will push for energy transition.

Coordination Mechanisms and Multilevel Governance

Many authors (e.g., Mirakyan and De Guio 2013; Melica et al. 2018) have highlighted the importance of a multilevel energy governance model in the past years. In Greece, however, central government still dominates energy policy through the Ministry of Environment and Climate change. Local and regional authorities had played a minor role the past years, and there are few intermediate bodies with limited power like the Hellenic Agency for Local Development and Local Government (E.E.T.A.A.).

Lack of communication among the various municipalities involved in energy projects and the local authorities is another barrier. On the one hand, the government lacks a clear plan for the support and management of energy communities, and, on the other hand, there is limited communication and exchange of information among the various projects. According to a report by the Expert Steering Committee on Social Economy and Social Entrepreneurship (2013, p. 12): "The public image of social economy actors (NGOs and cooperatives) has suffered from bad examples that lack a social mission, a business model independent of public funding, democratic governance, and an entrepreneurial approach." In the same report, the need for transfer of experience and expertise among projects was also highlighted. Similarly, in the more recent report of the European Committee of Regions (2018), the cooperation between local energy communities and local authorities is seen as an important factor that can define the success of these initiatives. Often, innovative projects remain in the shadows, and best practices, approaches, and tools are not transferred. Useful tools like platforms and institutions can play the role of intermediates in this process.

Carney and Shackley (2009) put forward the idea that in several policy fields' excessive centralization has led to the failure of many sustainable energy policies. Indeed, the Greek state is highly centralized, party-oriented, and deeply bureaucratic. In this hierarchical system, the local governments are weak and have limited power and responsibilities (Spanou 2001, p. 67; Demetropoulou et al. 2006). Additionally, there is also limited space for democratic actions that can enforce the participation of nongovernmental actors in policymaking (Blavoukos and Pagoulatos 2003). Despite the existence of a Ministry of Environment and Energy, environmental responsibilities are often divided among many Ministries (e.g., Ministry of Finance, Education, etc.), leading to fragmented policies due to lack of effective coordination mechanisms. This absence of independent bodies adds further difficulties in the implementation and monitoring of the environmental policies.

Outcomes, Challenges, and Prospects

Greece is traditionally seen as a "laggard" in the European environmental policy arena as it is often among the member states that set for the lower limit of requirements (Holmes 2005). Börzel (2003) points to the gap between the policies pursued by the EU as a whole and the needs of its southern member states. It is true that despite the efforts of the EU to achieve harmonization, there are different levels of national response and environmentalism across Europe (Börzel 2000, 2009) that divide Europe in leaders and laggards (Ward et al. 1996). The EU legislation has served as a guide for Greek legislators and has put pressure on the governments, especially in the case of the RES. Due to these pressures from the EU, Greece has made a significant effort in decarbonizing the energy system. However, most of these efforts are overshadowed by the present economic crisis and political instability. The lack of a well-designed and long-term planning is obvious, and in many cases, new governments come with a new portfolio and abolish previous efforts resulting in a stop-and-go style of policymaking. For instance, the Ministry of Environment and Energy and Climate Change founded in 2009 was replaced by the Ministry for Productive Reconstruction, Environment and Energy in 2015, and soon after that by the Ministry of Environment and Energy. Many of the energy-related policies were abandoned or are continually replaced (e.g., car replacement, subsidies for household energy savings, etc.).

A stable political environment can create a safe market environment for investments, while a well-functioning administrative system along with a comprehensive policy can make energy investments more attractive and reduce the risk (Masini and Menichetti 2011). Manolopoulos et al. (2016) highlight also the need for a more active role from the local and regional authorities. Increase of knowledge among the local communities and higher incentives can be drivers for higher levels of social acceptance (Kaldellis et al. 2012; Ntanos et al. 2018).

In many cases, the copy of legislation from other EU countries fails to respond to the specific needs of the country. For instance, the effort to equalize carbon tax for vehicles and heating use in 2017 led to an increase in energy poverty. The decrease demand for oil reduced the tax incomes for the government (1,199,550 tons in 2016 instead of 2,908,247 tons in 2010) and increased the smog over the cities due to the burning of wood fuel and the illegal oil imports. As Weale et al. (2000, p. 160) put it "while the EU has been by far the most significant factor behind Greek environmental policy in the past decade and more, its impact on policy principles has been largely superficial and that on policy style minimum."

When it comes to incentives, lack of information and the extensive bureaucracy are the main challenges for Greece. To illustrate this point, briefly consider that the installation of PVs requires more than ten different permits and there is lack of information on how to obtain these permits. Similarly, Manolopoulos et al. (2016) reported that there are more than 25 different report authorities involved in the licensing process. These factors often extend approval processes and increase risks on the part of possible investors (Boemi and Papadopoulos 2013). In this context, the need to simplify the complex licensing and permitting system still remains a challenge.

Despite the aforementioned, Greece the country has achieved a good share of renewable energy generation even in times of economic crisis. However, the future of the sector remains unclear, and some scholars predict a decrease of the RES penetration in the next years due to the lack of regulatory and budgetary support (Worrall and van der Burg 2017; Roadmap 2050 2017).

Private renewable energy projects also meet the increased dissatisfaction of many local populations who believe that privatizations and foreign investments have a corrosive effect on their national identity and sovereignty. Already community activists contested the construction of a wind park on the island of Chios and of a photovoltaic park in the area of Thessaly (Argenti and Knight 2015). This is deeper related with the lack of information regarding the social and economic benefits that can be obtained from the implementation of local RES projects. For instance, these projects can affect the tourist sector positively as they will increase energy security and allow the arrival of more tourists while ending the need to use portable generator units (Tsakiris 2010). Increased participation from the local authorities can also enhance the social acceptance. The new Law 4513/2018 about the energy communities is expected to lead in this direction if properly implemented.

The interconnection of the Aegean islands should be another top priority for the Greek government. Numerous studies (e.g., Kaldellis et al. 2012; Kougias et al. 2018) have indicated the potential of these islands to achieve high levels of RES penetration and to become energy autonomous. In the beginning of 2018, the first phase of the interconnection program that started in 1995 was completed and eight of the Cycladic islands are now connected to the main grid. This resulted in the shutdown of two of the polluting autonomous stations in Paros and Syros and is expected to reduce the cost of electricity by 80 million Euros annually (IBNA 2018) However, there is still a long way until the majority of the big islands connect to the main grid.

The transport sector, which is currently one of the more polluting, needs severe reforms, combined with improvements in the infrastructure. According to Tsita and Pilavachi (2017) "Future challenges can only be overcome if green vehicle development and the relevant infrastructure, go ahead hand in hand." The creation of the new pedestrian zones and the construction of the new metro line in the city of Athens are some of the plans that are expected to contribute to a reduction in emissions. These measures if combined with the continuation of the subsidies program for the retirement of old cars and the stricter implementation of the vehicle inspection program can improve significantly the transport sector.

Despite the claims that the worst years of the financial crisis have passed, energy poverty remains a major problem. In order to face this issue, it is essential to pursue a coherent policy including social, economic, and environmental aspects. This can be depicted in a roadmap to combat energy poverty that will be part of the National Action Plan and implemented in connection with other policies like the RES policies. Other important pillars of this map are the information, education, awareness, and monitoring processes. Education campaigns can change the everyday practices of people, leading to higher energy savings. For instance, a research by WWF Hellas (2012) indicated that only by adjusting the thermostatic valve 1 °C lower can lead to a reduction in energy waste by 10% or in other words in 50 Euro. The privatization of the energy sector and the liberalization of the energy market have proved to be slow and less effective than expected (Michalopoulos 2018; Gotev and Michalopoulos 2018). However, this will change in the next years, and already many providers, including PPC, are planning to offer combined packages of electricity and gas at competitive prices. Along with the energy communities that already pop up, this development can create a new era of energy transition in Greece.

It has often been emphasized that the policy decisions of countries in crisis will define their future environmental and economic performance, and thus, times of crisis are also times of opportunity (e.g., Siddiqi 2000; Lekakis and Kousis 2013). Any of the environmental benefits countries face in times of crisis will be of short term if the country returns to business as usual. For instance, in the case of the Asian crisis, the governments focused on recompensing for the lost ground rather than investing on sustainability, and thus, they turned to coal, gold, diamond, and nickel mining with catastrophic consequences, which are still evident (Elliott 2011). In this line, Greece is currently witnessing a number of environmental benefits like a reduction in GHG emissions. This reduction however is expected to be short term as the country invests in coal mining (Lekakis and Kousis 2013; Nantsou 2015), and it seems likely that fossil fuels will continue to play an important role in the country's energy supply.

Cross-References

- ▶ Energy Governance in Germany
- ▶ Energy Governance in Ireland
- ▶ Energy Governance in Italy
- ▶ Energy Governance in Portugal
- ▶ Energy Governance in Spain

Acknowledgments The author would like to thank Jordi Roca Jusmet and Brayton Noll for the useful comments and Jörg Kemmerzell and Michèle Knodt for the useful feedback throughout the process.

References

ACEA. (2017). *ACEA tax guide* (pp. 109–118). Brussels: ACEA. https://www.acea.be/uploads/news_documents/ACEA_Tax_Guide_2018.pdf. Accessed 29 Oct 2018.

Argenti, N., & Knight, D. (2015). Sun, wind, and the rebirth of extractive economies: Renewable energy investment and metanarratives of crisis in Greece. *Journal of the Royal Anthropological Institute, 21*(4), 781–802. https://doi.org/10.1111/1467-9655.12287.

Arghyrou, M., & Tsoukalas, J. (2011). The Greek debt crisis: Likely causes, mechanics and outcomes. *The World Economy, 34*(2), 173–191. https://doi.org/10.1111/j.1467-9701.2011.01328.x.

Balaras, C., Dascalaki, E., Gaglia, A., Droutsa, P., & Kontoyiannidis, S. (2018). An overview of the new Hellenic regulation on the energy performance of buildings (KENAK). In *3rd international conference on renewable energy sources & energy efficiency*, pp. 420–430.

Bank of Greece. (2011). The environmental, economic and social impacts of climate change in Greece. Climate change impacts study committee. http://www.bankofgreece.gr/BoGEkdoseis/ClimateChange_FullReport_bm.pdf. Accessed 22 Oct 2018.

Bitzenis, A., & Kontakos, P. (2014). Energy Trade and Tax Evasion in Greece. *Proceedings of the 7th Annual Conference of the EuroMed Academy of Business*, September, Kristiansand, Norway.

Blavoukos, S., & Pagoulatos, G. (2003). A medium country's middle-of-the-road success: The 2003 Greek Presidency of the European Union. *South European Society and Politics, 8*(3), 147–164. https://doi.org/10.1080/13608740808539660.

Boemi, S. P., & Papadopoulos, A. M. (2013). Times of recession: Three different renewable energy stories from the Mediterranean region. In E. H. Michalena & J. M. Hills (Eds.), *Renewable energy governance* (pp. 263–275). London/Heidelberg/New York/Dordrecht: Springer.

Boemi, S., Papadopoulos, A., Karagiannidis, A., & Kontogianni, S. (2010). Barriers on the propagation of renewable energy sources and sustainable solid waste management practices in Greece. *Waste Management & Research, 28*(11), 967–976. https://doi.org/10.1177/0734242x10375867.

Booz & Co. (2014). Understanding lignite generation costs in Europe. https://www.dei.gr/Documents2/INVESTORS/MELETH%20BOOZ/Understanding%20Lignite%20Generation%20Costs%20in%20Europe.pdf. Accessed 22 Oct 2018.

Börzel, T. (2000). Why there is no "southern problem." On environmental leaders and laggards in the European Union. *Journal of European Public Policy, 7*(1), 141–162. https://doi.org/10.1080/135017600343313.

Börzel, T. (2003). *Environmental leaders and laggards in Europe*. Aldershot: Ashgate.

Börzel, T. (2009). *Coping with accession to the European Union* (1st ed.). Basingstoke: Palgrave Macmillan.

Botetzagias, I. (2001). *The environmental movement in Greece, 1973 to the present; an illusory social movement in a semi-peripheral country* (Doctor of philosophy). Keele University.

Bürer, M., & Wüstenhagen, R. (2009). Which renewable energy policy is a venture capitalist's best friend? Empirical evidence from a survey of international cleantech investors. *Energy Policy, 37*(12), 4997–5006. https://doi.org/10.1016/j.enpol.2009.06.071.

Carney, S., & Shackley, S. (2009). The greenhouse gas regional inventory project (GRIP): Designing and employing a regional greenhouse gas measurement tool for stakeholder use. *Energy Policy, 37*(11), 4293–4302. https://doi.org/10.1016/j.enpol.2009.05.028.

Chaviaropoulos, P. (2010). Renewable energy programs of Greece. http://www.academyofathens.gr/sites/default/files/Renewable%20Energy%20Programs%20of%20Greece.pdf. Accessed 22 Oct 2018.

Dascalaki, E., Balaras, C., Gaglia, A., Droutsa, K., & Kontoyiannidis, S. (2012). Energy performance of buildings – EPBD in Greece. *Energy Policy, 45*, 469–477. https://doi.org/10.1016/j.enpol.2012.02.058.

Demetropoulou, L., Getimis, P., & Markantonis, V. (2006). Multilevel governance versus state centralization in Greece. In C. Paraskevopoulos, P. Getimis, & N. Rees (Eds.), *Adapting to EU multi-level governance: Regional and environmental policies in cohesion and CEE countries*. London: Ashgate.

DEPA. (2016). Annual financial statements for the year from 1 January 2016 to 31 December 2016 in accordance with International Financial Reporting Standards. http://www.depa.gr/uploads/files/26072017/DEPA%20FINANCIAL%20STATEMENT%2031-12-2016.pdf. Accessed 22 Oct 2018.

Ecorys. (2006). *Study on strategic evaluation on transport investment priorities under structural and cohesion funds for the programming period 2007–2013. Country report Greece*. Rotterdam: Ecorys. http://ec.europa.eu/regional_policy/sources/docgener/evaluation/pdf/evasltrat_tran/greece.pdf

Elliott, L. (2011). Shades of green in East Asia: The impact of financial crises on the environment. *Contemporary Politics, 17*(2), 167–183. https://doi.org/10.1080/13569775.2011.565985.

Energypress. (2017). *TAP project obstructed by local resistance in Kavala area*. Athens: Energypress. https://energypress.eu/tap-project-obstructed-local-resistance-kavala-area. Accessed 28 Oct 2018.

Energyworld. (2017). Greece to miss target to cut share of retail power market by 2019. https://energy.economictimes.indiatimes.com/news/power/greece-to-miss-target-to-cut-share-of-retail-power-market-by-2019-press/58557224

European Commission. (2017). *Energy Union factsheet Greece*. Brussels: European Commission. https://ec.europa.eu/commission/sites/beta-political/files/energy-union-factsheet-greece_en.pdf. Accessed 22 Oct 2018.

European Commission. (2018). TILOS – Innovation and Networks Executive Agency – European Commission. *Innovation and Networks Executive Agency*. https://ec.europa.eu/inea/en/horizon-2020/projects/h2020-energy/storage/tilos. Accessed 28 Oct 2018.

European Committee of the Regions. (2018). Models of local energy ownership and the role of local energy communities in energy transition in Europe. *Commission for the Environment, Climate Change and Energy*. https://cor.europa.eu/en/engage/studies/Documents/local-energy-ownership.pdf. Accessed 28 Oct 2018.

European Environment Agency. (2016). Average age of road vehicles per country. https://www.eea.europa.eu/data-and-maps/daviz/average-age-of-road-vehicles-6#tab-chart_1. Accessed 28 Oct 2018.

European Wind Energy Association. (2012). Green growth: The impact of wind energy on jobs and the economy. http://eletaen.gr/wp-content/uploads/2018/05/2012-04-01-green-growth.pdf. Accessed 22 Oct 2018.

Eurostat. (2018a). Population unable to keep home adequately warm by poverty status. https://ec.europa.eu/eurostat/tgm/table.do?tab=table&init=1&language=en&pcode=sdg_07_60&plugin=1. Accessed 20 Oct 2018.

Eurostat. (2018b). Gross inland consumption of brown coal by Member State. https://appsso.eurostat.ec.europa.eu/nui/show.do?dataset=nrg_cb_sff&lang=en. Accessed 25 Oct 2019.

Expert Steering Committee on Social Economy and Social Entrepreneurship. (2013). Outline strategy and priorities for action to develop the social economy and social entrepreneurship in Greece, Athens. http://www.neetsonboard.gr/wp-content/uploads/2017/09. Accessed 29 Oct 2018.

Fafaliou, I., & Polemis, M. (2010). Trends in the European electricity markets: The case of Greece. *International Journal of Economics and Business Research, 2*(5), 369. https://doi.org/10.1504/ijebr.2010.035006.

Gotev, G., & Michalopoulos, S. (2018). The energy conundrum in Bulgaria and Greece. *euractiv.com*. https://www.euractiv.com/section/energy/linksdossier/the-energy-conundrum-in-bulgaria-and-greece. Accessed 29 Oct 2018.

Greenpeace. (2017). *Silent killers: Why Europe must replace coal power with green energy.* Amsterdam: Greenpeace International.

Hall, S. (2017). Poland, Greece reject Eurelectric's no new coal plant after 2020 plan | S&P Global Platts. *Spglobal.com.* https://www.spglobal.com/platts/en/market-insights/latest-news/coal/040517-poland-greece-reject-eurelectrics-no-new-coal-plant-after-2020-plan. Accessed 22 Oct 2018.

Hofman, D., & Huisman, R. (2012). Did the financial crisis lead to changes in private equity investor preferences regarding renewable energy and climate policies? *Energy Policy, 47,* 111–116. https://doi.org/10.1016/j.enpol.2012.04.029.

Holmes, M. (2005). *Ireland and the European Union.* Manchester: University Press.

IBNA. (2018). 4 Cycladic islands to be linked with the power grid on the mainland. *Balkaneu.com.* http://www.balkaneu.com/4-cycladic-islands-to-be-linked-with-the-power-grid-on-the-mainland. Accessed 22 Oct 2018.

IRENA. (2014). Renewable Energy Opportunities for island Tourism. https://www.irena.org/-/media/Files/IRENA/Agency/Publication/2014/IRENA_RE_Island_Tourism_report_2014.pdf. Accessed 5 Jan 2020.

Kaldellis, J., & Zafirakis, D. (2007). Optimum energy storage techniques for the improvement of renewable energy sources-based electricity generation economic efficiency. *Energy, 32*(12), 2295–2305. https://doi.org/10.1016/j.energy.2007.07.009.

Kaldellis, J., Kapsali, M., & Katsanou, E. (2012). Renewable energy applications in Greece – What is the public attitude? *Energy Policy, 42,* 37–48. https://doi.org/10.1016/j.enpol.2011.11.017.

Kalligeros, S., Zannikos, F., Stournas, S., & Lois, E. (2003). Fuel adulteration issues in Greece. *Energy, 28*(1), 15–26. https://doi.org/10.1016/s0360-5442(02)00091-9.

Karagiannis, N., & Kondeas, A. (2012). The Greek financial crisis and a developmental path to recovery: Lessons and options. *Real-World Economics Review, 60,* 54–73.

Karakasis, V. (2014). *Oil smuggling as a variable in the Greek crisis' equation.* Athens: Bridging Europe.

Kathimerini. (2018). Sales of electric vehicles and hybrids soar in Greece. http://www.ekathimerini.com/225582/article/ekathimerini/business/sales-of-electric-vehicles-and-hybrids-soar-in-greece. Accessed 29 Oct 2018.

Kavouridis, K. (2008). Lignite industry in Greece within a world context: Mining, energy supply and environment. *Energy Policy, 36*(4), 1257–1272. https://doi.org/10.1016/j.enpol.2007.11.017.

Kougias, I., Szabó, S., Nikitas, A., & Theodossiou, N. (2018). Sustainable energy modelling of non-interconnected Mediterranean islands. *Renewable Energy.* https://doi.org/10.1016/j.renene.2018.10.090.

Kouretas, G., & Vlamis, P. (2010). The Greek crisis: Causes and implications. *Panoeconomicus, 57*(4), 391–404. https://doi.org/10.2298/pan1004391k.

Koussis, M. (2013). The Greek protest campaign against troika memoranda and austerity policies' (in Greek). *Greek Sociological Review, 1,* 33–40.

LAGIE. (2017). Monthly wholesale and retail penetration and market share report, May 2017. http://www.lagie.gr/fileadmin/groups/EDSHE/FEP/MonthlyReports/FEPAS_MonthlyReport_201705_EN_pv01.pdf. Accessed 22 Oct 2018.

LAGIE. (2018). Energy MIix of 2018. http://www.lagie.gr/fileadmin/groups/EDSHE/2018_YPOLEIPOMENO_ENERGEIAKO_MEIGMA.pdf. Accessed 5 Jan 2020.

Lekakis, J., & Kousis, M. (2013). Economic crisis, troika and the environment in Greece. *South European Society and Politics, 18*(3), 305–331. https://doi.org/10.1080/13608746.2013.799731.

Malouhos, G. (2014). Η ιστορία της ΔΕΗ ως ιστορία της χώρας -. Το Βήμα Online. https://www.tovima.gr/2014/03/11/opinions/i-istoria-tis-dei-ws-istoria-tis-xwras. Accessed 22 Oct 2018.

Manolopoulos, D., Kitsopoulos, K., Kaldellis, J., & Bitzenis, A. (2016). The evolution of renewable energy sources in the electricity sector of Greece. *International Journal of Hydrogen Energy, 41*(29), 12659–12671. https://doi.org/10.1016/j.ijhydene.2016.02.115.

Mardas, D. (2014). Research on the oil adulteration and oil smuggling. Federation of Merchants and Craftsmen and the Hellenic Federation of Traders and Owners of petrol stations. https://www.popek.gr/index.php/el/meletes. Accessed 29 Oct 2018.

Masini, A., & Menichetti, E. (2011). The impact of behavioral factors in the renewable energy investment decision making process: Conceptual framework and empirical findings. *SSRN Electronic Journal*. https://doi.org/10.2139/ssrn.2246759.

Melica, G., Bertoldi, P., Kona, A., Iancu, A., Rivas, S., & Zancanella, P. (2018). Multilevel governance of sustainable energy policies: The role of regions and provinces to support the participation of small local authorities in the Covenant of Mayors. *Sustainable Cities and Society, 39*, 729–739. https://doi.org/10.1016/j.scs.2018.01.013.

Michalopoulos, S. (2018). Greek energy market hindered by lack of competition. *euractiv.com*. https://www.euractiv.com/section/energy/news/greek-energy-market-hindered-by-lack-of-competition. Accessed 22 Oct 2018.

Mirakyan, A., & De Guio, R. (2013). Integrated energy planning in cities and territories: A review of methods and tools. *Renewable and Sustainable Energy Reviews, 22*, 289–297. https://doi.org/10.1016/j.rser.2013.01.033.

Nanaki, E., & Koroneos, C. (2013). Comparative economic and environmental analysis of conventional, hybrid and electric vehicles – The case study of Greece. *Journal of Cleaner Production, 53*, 261–266. https://doi.org/10.1016/j.jclepro.2013.04.010.

Nantsou, T. (2015). Will Greece ignore the economic omens and go for new coal? – WWF CrisisWatch. *wwf.gr*. https://www.wwf.gr/crisis-watch/crisis-watch/energy-climate/10-energy-climate/will-greece-ignore-the-economic-omens-and-go-for-new-coal. Accessed 22 Oct 2018.

National Technical University of Athens. (2008). Έρευνα Σχετικά με την Διακίνηση Νοθευμένων Καυσίμων.

Neubäumer, R. (2015). The prologue to the Greek crisis. *Vierteljahrshefte zur Wirtschaftsforschung, 84*(3), 9–28. https://doi.org/10.3790/vjh.84.3.9.

Ntanos, S., Kyriakopoulos, G., Chalikias, M., Arabatzis, G., & Skordoulis, M. (2018). Public perceptions and willingness to pay for renewable energy: A case study from Greece. *Sustainability, 10*(3), 687. https://doi.org/10.3390/su10030687.

OECD. (2018). *Taxing energy use: Companion to the taxing energy use database*. Paris: OECD Publishing. https://doi.org/10.1787/9789264289635-en. Accessed 22 Oct 2018.

Panoutsou, C. (2007). Socio-economic impacts of energy crops for heat generation in Northern Greece. *Energy Policy, 35*(12), 6046–6059. https://doi.org/10.1016/j.enpol.2007.08.032.

Papada, L., & Kaliampakos, D. (2016). Measuring energy poverty in Greece. *Energy Policy, 94*, 157–165. https://doi.org/10.1016/j.enpol.2016.04.004.

Patlitzianas, K., & Christos, K. (2011). Sustainable energy investments in Hellenic urban areas: Examining modern financial mechanisms. *Renewable and Sustainable Energy Reviews, 15*(9), 5186–5193. https://doi.org/10.1016/j.rser.2011.03.006.

Perellis, A., Mezartasoglou, D., & Stambolis, C. (2018). Anticipated penetration rate of electric vehicles in Greece's motor vehicle market. In *3rd HAEE energy conference: Energy transition: European and global perspectives*, Institute of Energy for SE Europe (IENE). https://www.haee.gr/media/3956/a-perellis-d-mezartasoglou-c-stambolis-anticipated-penetration-rate-of-electric-vehicles-in-greeces-motor-vehicle-market.pdf. Accessed 22 Oct 2018.

Petmesidou, M. (2013). Is social protection in Greece at a crossroads?. *European Societies, 15*(4), 597–616. https://doi.org/10.1080/14616696.2013.836407.

Petrakopoulou, I. (2015). Energy statistics and renewable energy potential of greece. GENERSIS – Green Energy for Islands. http://www.genergis.eu/wordpress01/wpcontent/uploads/2015/06/StatisticsOfGreece1.pdf. Accessed 22 Oct 2018.

Power Engineering International. (2012). Greece to sell coal power fleet as debt reality bites. http://www.powerengineeringint.com/articles/2012/08/greece-to-sell-coal-powerfleet-as-debt-reality-bites.html. Accessed 5 Jan 2020.

PPC. (2013). Clarifications on the item of the extraordinary General Meeting of shareholders on 29.3.2013 Approval for materialization of the investment for the construction of the Plant Ptolemais V and the pertinent contract. https://www.dei.gr/Documents2/%CE%95%CE%93%CE%A3% 2029032013/Ptolemais%20V%20EGM%20-%20FINAL%20EN.pdf. Accessed 22 Oct 2018.

Prodesa. (2018). Energy efficiency project development for South Attica. https://www.prodesa.eu/?lang=en. Accessed 28 Oct 2018.

RAE. (2014). Approval of the consideration to cover the costs of public service for the years 2012 and 2013 – No. of decision 356/2014. http://www.rae.gr/site/file/categories_new/global_regulation/global_national/global_national_laws/2014/FEK1873_100714?p=file&i=0. Accessed 27 Oct 2018.

RAE. (2018). Regulatory authority for energy. http://www.rae.gr/site/en_US/categories_new/about_rae/intro.csp. Accessed 28 Oct 2018.

Roadmap 2050. (2017). *Roadmap 2050*. Brussels: European Commission. http://www.roadmap2050.eu/project/roadmap-2050. Accessed 22 Oct 2018.

Roinioti, A., & Koroneos, C. (2017). The decomposition of CO_2 emissions from energy use in Greece before and during the economic crisis and their decoupling from economic growth. *Renewable and Sustainable Energy Reviews, 76*, 448–459. https://doi.org/10.1016/j.rser.2017.03.026.

Rootes, C. (2003). *Environmental protest in western Europe*. Oxford: Oxford University Press.

Siddiqi, T. (2000). The Asian Financial Crisis – Is it good for the global environment? *Global Environmental Change, 10*(1), 1–7. https://doi.org/10.1016/s0959-3780(00)00003-0.

Simiti, M. (2017). Civil society and the economy: Greek civil society during the economic crisis. *Journal of Civil Society, 13*(4), 357–373. https://doi.org/10.1080/17448689.2017.1355033.

Spanou, K. (2001). *Ελληνική Διοίκηση και Ευρωπαϊκή Ολοκλήρωση (Greek administration and European integration)* (p. 92). Athens: Papazisi.

Tagaris, K., & Kountatou, A. (2018). Greece's dark age: How austerity turned off the lights. *Reuters*. https://www.reuters.com/article/us-eurozone-greece-poverty-electricity/greeces-dark-age-how-austerity-turned-off-the-lights-idUSKBN1781IQ. Accessed 22 Oct 2018.

Trikkalioti, S. (2018). Η *ανάπτυξη των ΑΠΕ στην Ελλάδα: Υφιστάμενη κατάσταση και προοπτικές ανάπτυξης σύμφωνα με τα μέτρα και τους στόχους της Ευρώπης 2020* (Undergraduate). Polytechnic School, Aristotelous University of Thessaloniki.

Tsagarakis, K., Bounialetou, F., Gillas, K., Profylienou, M., Pollaki, A., & Zografakis, N. (2011). Tourists' attitudes for selecting accommodation with investments in renewable energy and energy saving systems. *Renewable and Sustainable Energy Reviews, 15*(2), 1335–1342. https://doi.org/10.1016/j.rser.2010.10.009.

Tsakiris, F. (2010). *Energy development in the non-connected islands of the Aegean Sea*. Reykjavík: Orkustofnun.

Tsita, K., & Pilavachi, P. (2017). Decarbonizing the Greek road transport sector using alternative technologies and fuels. *Thermal Science and Engineering Progress, 1*, 15–24. https://doi.org/10.1016/j.tsep.2017.02.003.

Vergoulis, P., & Damigos, D. (2013). Oil development and social acceptance in Greece: The Katakolo field case. In *6th international conference on sustainable development in the minerals industry*.

Ward, N., Buller, H., & Lowe, P. (1996). The Europeanisation of local environmental politics: Bathing water pollution in south-west England. *Local Environment, 1*(1), 21–32. https://doi.org/10.1080/13549839608725478.

Weale, A., Pridham, G., Cini, M., Konstadakopolos, D., Porter, M., & Flynn, B. (2000). *Environmental governance in Europe*. Oxford: Oxford University Press.

Worrall, L., & van der Burg, L. (2017). *Cutting Europe's lifelines to coal: Tracking subsidies in 10 countries: Greece, Briefing Paper*. London: ODI. https://www.odi.org/sites/odi.org.uk/files/resource-documents/11501.pdf. Accessed 19 Oct 2018.

WWF. (2018). Οχι στην Πτολεμαιδα V. *WWF*. http://www.wwf.gr/campaigns/ptolemaida5. Accessed 22 Oct 2018.
WWF Hellas. (2012). Οδηγός εξοικονόμησης ενέργειας. Όλα όσα μπορείτε να κάνετε για να εξοικονομήσετε ενέργεια και χρήμα. https://www.wwf.gr/images/pdfs/wwf_odigos%20ex_energeias.pdf. Accessed 22 Oct 2018.
WWF Hellas. (2017). Νόμος και Περιβάλλον στην Ελλαδα. https://www.wwf.gr/images/pdfs/WWF-NOMO-2017-Sinopsi.pdf. Accessed 22 Oct 2018.
Ypeka. (2010). Accelerating the development of Renewable Energy Sources to deal with climate change and other regulations addressing issues under the authority of the Ministry of Environment, Energy and Climate Change. http://www.ypeka.gr/LinkClick.aspx?fileticket=qtiW90JJLYs%3d&tabid=37. Accessed 29 Oct 2018.
Ypeka. (2018). Special Secretariat for the Environment and Energy Inspectorate. *Ypeka.gr*. http://www.ypeka.gr/Default.aspx?tabid=348&locale=en-US. Accessed 22 Oct 2018.

Energy Governance in Hungary

30

John Szabo, Csaba Weiner, and András Deák

Contents

Introduction	738
General Conditions of Energy Governance	740
Energy Legacies	740
Composition of the Energy Mix	742
Political Institutions and Actors	746
Discourse on Energy Issues	749
Coordination of the Instruments and Issues of Energy Transitions Within a Multilevel Context	751
Drivers of Energy Transition	751
Strategies and Instruments of Energy Transition	753
Coordination Mechanisms and Multilevel Governance	757
Outcomes, Challenges, and Prospects of Energy Governance	760
Cross-References	763
References	763

J. Szabo (✉)
Department of Environmental Sciences and Policy, Central European University, Budapest, Hungary

Institute of World Economics, Centre for Economic and Regional Studies, Budapest, Hungary
e-mail: szabo_john@phd.ceu.edu

C. Weiner
Institute of World Economics, Centre for Economic and Regional Studies, Budapest, Hungary
e-mail: weiner.csaba@krtk.mta.hu

A. Deák
Institute of World Economics, Centre for Economic and Regional Studies, Budapest, Hungary

Institute of Strategic and Security Studies, National University of Public Service, Budapest, Hungary
e-mail: deak.andras@krtk.mta.hu

© Springer Nature Switzerland AG 2022
M. Knodt, J. Kemmerzell (eds.), *Handbook of Energy Governance in Europe*,
https://doi.org/10.1007/978-3-030-43250-8_13

Abstract

Hungarian energy governance conveys a unique disposition, filled with contradictions, lacking clarity, but reflecting centralized control at the highest echelons of politics. Like many of its Central and Eastern European (CEE) neighbors, it is still entrenched in preexisting producer-consumer relations that shape its amicable relations with Russia, while its accession to the European Union has led it to take on disruptive climate and energy policy targets. The country's energy transition has been unfolding slowly, as the government maintains a moderate pace of action. The diffusion of renewables continues to unfold in the shadow of other historical legacies, most prominently Russia-sourced nuclear power technology, natural gas, and oil. Power and control over energy corporations is concentrated in the hands of those closely aligned with the government, and multilevel governance is subordinated to anticipate or execute the objectives dictated by political leaders. Challenges mount in the Hungarian sector as we move towards the 2030 and 2050 EU decarbonization targets, which will pressure the government to implement much more disruptive measures, severing and rewriting historical energy based ties.

Keywords

Energy governance · Hungary · Lock-in · Government control · Centralization · Energy transition

Introduction

Hungary's energy system reflects the imprint of an energy system conveying typical Central and Eastern European (CEE) patterns combined with Prime Minister Viktor Orbán's general approach to political economics. The energy scene is shaped by powerful path dependencies: reliance on Russian hydrocarbons and nuclear technology as well as relatively low GDP per capita leading energy bills to constitute a higher share in total household expenditure. Motorization has been in full swing and GDP growth is higher than the EU average, both driving a rise in energy and especially electricity consumption. Reducing greenhouse gas (GHG) emissions has not been a prominent issue until very recently, due to deindustrialization and a related fall in emissions after the regime change in 1989. EU targets concerning renewable energy and emissions from sectors not included in the EU Emissions Trading System (EU ETS) pose a growing challenge for the country, leading Hungary to engage in tug-of-war over how the energy transition's costs should be split between CEE and other Western EU states. Amidst these, PM Orbán's approach to energy governance has continued to primarily focus on exploiting utility price controls for political gain, the nationalization of energy assets, and centralizing control over the sector. Overall, Hungary shows few signs of being the exception among the EU's energy governance models. It shares a multitude of similarities with CEE countries, while perhaps being a bit louder, more intractable, and intrusive than its regional counterparts.

The current form of Hungary's energy system has co-evolved with the political economics of the Orbán regime. Fidesz reshaped the fundamentals of the Hungarian constitutional order and cemented its extensive rule over the country after it gained a supermajority in the 2010 elections. The set of these all-encompassing changes ushered in what some have referred to as "Orbánism," despite its lack of a coherent ideology and multiplicity of interpretations (Müller 2014). PM Orbán often positions himself in defiance of the declining Western liberal order, lamenting the withering away of traditional values and offering to restore those. Orbán (2014) claimed that he aimed to establish an illiberal democracy, incorporating the convergence of nationalism and capitalism. His governance has also been assessed as a "hybrid regime" (Filippov 2018), implying a competitive market coupled with authoritarian rule, or a "postcommunist Mafia state" (Magyar 2016), a crony capitalist entity. Scheiring (2018) describes this Hungarian regime as an authoritarian accumulative state in a dependent market economy environment, which simultaneously incentivizes the formation of a strong national capitalist class and multinational investment. The "developmental state" arguments within the world-systems theory highlight the later features and present Hungary as a country serving international capital and striving to upgrade its standing in the global division of labor (Wilkin 2016).

Characterizing Hungary's political economics as well as its embeddedness in European and global relations of production are essential to understand the country's approach to energy governance. The aforementioned interpretations and approaches of the Orbán regime treat local energy trends and developments differently. The hybrid regime approach proposes that energy is a linchpin connecting Hungary to other illiberal states, most notably Russia (Filippov 2018). The crony capitalist narrative suggests that nationalization within the sector serves as a mode of politically motivated sectoral rent redistribution, while the related neo-utilitarian interpretation describes the strong focus on reducing utility prices as an indelible mark of excessive politicization of the matter (Magyar 2016). The accumulative state approach argues that the sector was a target of the revolting national bourgeoisie (Scheiring 2018). Dependency and world-systems theories focus on Hungary's reliance on importing hydrocarbons to ensure its competitive role in global supply chains, leading it to shape intricate linkages with resource exporting countries, such as Russia. This approach also suggests that Hungarian laggardness in climate policies can be understood as an effort to maintain inexpensive inputs for multinational companies. While all these features are true for Orbán's Hungary, they also indicate the complexity of local energy governance and its intractability within a single existing theory.

The following chapter attempts to provide an overview of the focal mechanisms shaping energy governance in Hungary. In section "Energy Legacies," it explores the historical legacies shaping the energy system in place today, by introducing the country's reliance on Russian hydrocarbon imports and nuclear technology. It then turns to the composition of the country's energy mix (section "Composition of the Energy Mix"), providing an overview of the *status quo*, which indicates the potential extent of an energy transition. Subsequently, it discusses the main actors in Hungary's energy scene and prevalent discursive themes (section "Political

Institutions and Actors"). In section "Drivers of Energy Tranition," the chapter explores the drivers of an energy transition, where energy security will be a crucial factor that the authors flesh out in more detail. After this, the chapter turns to the specific strategies the government and the energy sector have adopted to meet energy transition goals (section "Strategies and Instruments of Energy Transition"), pertaining to both energy security and decarbonization, before discussing the characteristics of Hungary's multilevel governance in the sector (section "Coordination Mechanisms and Multilevel Governance"). Finally, in section "Outcomes, Challenges, and Prospects of Energy Governance" we draw conclusions and discuss what our findings imply for the energy sector's governance in light of the need to undertake an energy transition.

General Conditions of Energy Governance

Energy Legacies

Hungary was the third most energy dependent country of the 11 Eastern EU member states in 2018 with an import ratio of 58.1% (Eurostat 2020a). By reclassifying nuclear energy from domestic to imported fuel, warranted by Hungary's importation of the technology and source fuel (BP 2019a), the country's dependency rate would be over 73%. It would approach Lithuania's 77.2%, the most dependent former Eastern bloc state. Resource scarcity and declining production levels became well-established trends after the early 1970s, resulting in a steep increase of Soviet imports of electricity as well as fossil and nuclear fuels. Hungary established an energy resource trade regime and constructed the physical infrastructure with the Soviet Union between the 1960s and the1980s that resembled general Comecon patterns (Szabo and Deak 2020). Basic patterns of energy relations still preserve the imprints of the Socialist era. The first connection between the Soviet and Hungarian oil networks was the Friendship (Druzhba) pipeline in 1962, still functioning as the main route for imports. First gas deliveries from the Soviet Union arrived in 1975 through the Brotherhood (Bratstvo) pipeline. Between 1982 and 1987 four Soviet VVER-440 nuclear blocs were constructed in Paks, still providing the bigger half of domestic electricity supply. The rest of the electricity generation fleet consists of different, primarily Soviet-era natural gas power plants and the lignite-based Mátra Power Plant at Visonta, built between 1969 and 1972.

Energy dependency remained a recurring concern of Hungarian energy policy, especially after the 1989 dissolution of the Soviet bloc, but policy-makers made limited effort to change the situation. Affordability considerations – cheap and convenient energy supplies for households in particular – constituted the top political priority following the country's regime change. In the early 1990s, this manifested in excessive and politically supported gasification programs, while after the turn of the millennium discourses on low utility prices became a distinguished field of domestic political competition (Szabo and Fabok 2020). Affordability issues are considered a legacy from the communist era. After the 1956 failed revolution, the initially unpopular Kádár regime achieved social consolidation by making welfare concessions to the masses. Trade-offs between political loyalty and economic benefits, "Gulash communism" became a systematic feature of Hungary for the next 30 years, creating an increasingly paternalistic-populistic embeddedness for upcoming governments (Benczes 2016). The major expectation from regime change in the 1990s was not necessarily related to political freedoms, but to higher living standards, preserving broad social guarantees (a sort of "Gulash capitalism"). Consequently, increased estrangement from emerging market institutions and democratic competition as well as nostalgia toward the Kádár regime developed amongst the populace (Pap 2017).

Attitude towards Russia also remained relatively friendly following the system change. Until 2010, Hungary had a quasi-bipolar political system, dominated by the Russia-pragmatist leftist communist successor party and Russia-skeptical conservative forces. Since 2010, Viktor Orbán has transformed from a fierce Moscow-opponent to a proponent, driving the positive views of Russia at both party and societal level. Even the far-right nationalist party, Jobbik, has become pro-Russia and only tiny green and liberal formations in the parliament maintain Russia-skeptic positions. According to opinion polls conducted after the Russian–Ukraine conflict in 2016, 58% of the respondents supported closer economic ties with Russia, 28% opposed those, while one-third of the population could have even imagined political rapprochement (35% for and 40% against) (Szvák 2016). Consequently, Hungary's perception and relations with Russia is a relatively weak driver to change the existing energy *status quo*.

Ownership relations comprised another focal point of Hungarian energy policies. Due to the government's high indebtedness and austerity measures following the regime change, it sold a significant part of the natural gas and electricity industry to foreign multinationals in 1995. This early privatization and the accompanied establishment of an independent regulator to secure the 8% profit rate for new incomers became a major cleavage between the political left and right (Mocsáry 2001; Báger and Kovács 2004). Early privatization led to a colorful ownership pattern for the next 15 years. The nuclear energy generation and the electricity transmission system operator (TSO) remained in the hands of a state-owned enterprise (SOE), MVM (Hungarian Electricity Works). The oil industry and various parts of the gas sector (most notably the gas TSO) came to be owned by domestic private actor, MOL. Meanwhile, all other assets including electricity and gas distribution and a number of power plants were sold to foreign, predominantly European, multinational corporations. After 2010, PM Viktor Orbán enlisted the energy sector as a strategically important branch of the economy, where Hungarian ownership shall prevail. By the end of his second term in office, foreign companies were mostly squeezed out by regulatory means and/or purchased by local and state entities. Investments into the electricity sector, for example, were major victims of the Orbán governments' reforms (Eurostat 2020a, b). Investment intensity per consumption practically halved after 2011, a decline that can be only partly explained by the financial crisis and higher electricity imports. Initially this was due to voracious nationalization efforts, but low sectoral profitability sustains due to utility rate setting. The outcome of these changes is that the Hungarian energy landscape became subject to strong political control through formal and informal means, with little autonomy for the regulator and increased statist attitudes in management and planning.

The government of Hungary welcomed EU policies and common governance in a restrained manner and applied these initiatives selectively. Hungary was an early mover to enhance natural gas interconnections and implement supply security policies, leading EU efforts and taking advantage of supranational support following the 2009 Russian–Ukrainian gas disputes. The European Commission's bids to further market coupling and unbundling had a more selective reception and required longer adaptation. Common climate policy objectives, especially regarding renewables and non-ETS administrative measures, comprise the biggest emerging point of conflict between the government of Hungary and its Western counterparts. The former has been foot-dragging, accepting new targets only conditionally and under external pressure. 2017 GHG emissions may have been 31.9% lower, at 63.8 million tons of CO_2 equivalent (MtCO_2eq), than 1990 figures of 93.8 MtCO_2eq, but most of the decrease is due to the deindustrialization during transition years following the collapse of the communist regime. The trajectory of GHG emission declines have, however, reversed since 2015, steadily rising in subsequent years (ITM 2020b). Meanwhile, few domestic drivers for a more ambitious climate stance have been visible, and the Orbán government views the matter through a lens of short-term cost-benefit calculations. Climate policy and energy transition commitments largely rely on external, mainly Western and the European Commission's pressure as well as domestic industrial policy.

Hungarian energy policy has maintained its Russia-focus by renewing natural gas and nuclear contractual relations, the preeminence of sovereignty and affordability of energy policy, restored formal and informal statism, while firmly maintaining its position among climate laggards. Policy attitudes seem to be fairly stable under the Orbán government, but institutions lack any solid fundamentals and have been subservient to political objectives. Until 2010, policy controls over the industry were relatively weak, usually set under the Ministry of Economy with rare interferences from the Prime Minister's side in issues such as Russia or hostile acquisition attempts from foreign companies. After 2010, energy became a sector closely and actively managed at the highest political level. PM Viktor Orbán takes an active decision-making role in a set of major issues, while policy supervision became increasingly fragmented between various entities whose roles were regularly reshuffled by the PM.

Composition of the Energy Mix

Hungary features a heavily import-dependent hydrocarbon-based energy system, predicated on its legacies and shaping its approach to the sector's governance. The country used hydrocarbons to meet 69.2% of its gross inland consumption in 2018, dominated by natural gas (31.0%) and closely followed by oil and petroleum products (30.3%). Nuclear energy held a 15.0% share, exceeding both renewables and biofuels (10.5%) as well as solid fossil fuels (7.9%) in gross demand (Table 1) (MEKH 2020f). In 2017, the country's GHG emissions amounted to 63.8 MtCO_2eq not including land use, land use

Table 1 Hungary's energy consumption, by fuel, 2018 (%)

	Total	Natural gas	Oil and petroleum products	Nuclear heat	Renewables and biofuels	Solid fossil fuels	Electricity	Nonrenewable waste
Gross available energy	100.0	31.0	30.3	15.0	10.5	7.9	4.6	0.7
Gross inland consumption	100.0	31.0	30.3	15.0	10.5	7.9	4.6	0.7
Total energy supply	100.0	31.3	29.6	15.2	10.6	8.0	4.7	0.7

Source: Own calculations based on MEKH (2020f)

change, and forestry (LULUCF), with the energy sector accounting for 72% of emissions (ITM 2020c). Hungary imports the bulk of its primary energy supply, apart from domestically produced lignite. Regarding natural gas, the production-to-consumption ratio has fallen below 20%. Hungarian gas production declined rapidly until 2015; since then, it has grown slightly (MEKH 2020c). There were significant hopes for unconventional gas, but this has proven to be an illusion. Approved in January 2020, Hungary's National Energy and Climate Plan (NECP) states that natural gas production may continue to grow through 2030, to which unconventional gas will only make a very small contribution (ITM 2020c, 202–203). Oil production is growing much more rapidly (MEKH 2020d), but despite a large oil field discovery, recently announced, it will still be limited. According to the NECP, in 2030 oil production will be lower than the current level, but increases will be seen in the mid-2020s. Currently, oil imports account for around 90% of consumption (ITM 2020c, 31, 202).

Hungary's final energy consumption has been quite fluctuant since the fall of the communist regime with natural gas playing a key role in meeting demand. Between 2014 and 2017, total final energy consumption grew at a rate well above the EU average, in-part reflecting wastefulness, but this trend stopped in 2018, and residential consumption declined (the latter is mainly because of the mild winter weather, though) (Eurostat 2020a; MEHI 2019; MEKH 2020f). The residential sector has the largest share in final energy demand (32.6% in 2018), followed by the transport (26.9%) and the industrial sector (24.9%) (MEKH 2020f). The residential sector primarily relies on gas (48.6% in 2018), followed by renewables (23.6%), electricity (16.8%), derived heat (8.0%), coal and coal products (1.6%), as well as oil and petroleum products (1.3%) (Table 2) (MEKH 2020e). Hungary's transportation sector, on the other hand, consumes petroleum products to meet rapidly growing demand. In 2018, 62.2% of consumption was diesel (MEKH 2020f) leading Hungary's Russian crude-based oil refiner to optimize for diesel production.

The share of renewables in gross final energy consumption only reached 12.5% in 2018, most of which is in the heating sector (Fig. 1) (ITM 2018; MEKH 2020h). Solid biomass is the dominant renewable energy source, amounting to 77.3% of renewable consumption in 2018 (MEKH 2020g). This is almost exclusively constituted of firewood, with straw playing a measurable, but relatively minuscule role. The majority of this biomass is consumed by the household sector, also entailing that Hungary's ability to meet its EU renewable energy target heavily relies on household biomass consumption.

The relative role of nuclear, coal, natural gas as primary fuels, and that of electricity imports have been volatile in Hungary's electricity supply in past years, changing with market and policy conditions (Fig. 1). Electricity consumption increased until 2007 to 43.9 TWh, followed by a fall in 2009. The years 2010–2014 brought stagnation (42–43 TWh), but consumption has been growing since 2015 and climbing to over 46 TWh in 2018 (Eurostat 2020c). Hungary's domestic generation is heavily reliant on the Paks Nuclear Power Plant and the Mátra Power Plant. Gas comprised the largest share in 2007 and 2008, followed by nuclear, and coal was a distant third. Market shares were reshuffled by the mid-2010s, when nuclear's role increased to over 50%, while coal overtook natural gas in relative

Table 2 Residential final energy consumption by type of end-use and the share of fuels used for space, water heating and cooking in Hungary, 2018 (%)

Type of end-use	Share of fuels						
Space heating	71.7	Gas	Renewables and wastes	Derived heat	Solid fuels	Electricity	Total petroleum products	Total
		56.3	32.0	8.3	2.3	0.8	0.2	100.0
Water heating	12.8	Electricity	Gas	Derived heat	Renewables and wastes	Total petroleum products	Solid fuels	Total
		39.5	38.4	16.1	4.5	1.4	0.0	100.0
Lighting and appliances	10.4							
Cooking	4.9	Gas	Total petroleum products	Electricity	Renewables and wastes	Solid fuels	Derived heat	Total
		67.9	19.5	12.4	0.2	0.0	0.0	100.0
Space cooling	0.1							
Total	100.0							

Source: MEKH (2020e)

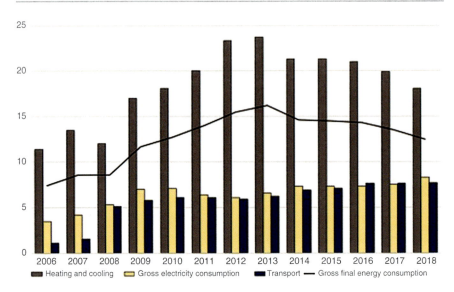

Fig. 1 Share of energy from renewable sources in Hungary, by sector, 2006–2018 (%). (Source: MEKH 2020h)

importance. These developments were paired with a surge of electricity imports to more than 30% of demand in 2014 and 2015, compared to around 9% in 2007 and 2008 (Eurostat 2018a, 2020c; MEKH 2020a). Shifts have been the result of (1) natural gas' competitive disadvantage, (2) low carbon prices, and (3) low electricity prices (Stern 2017; KWK-Index n.d.; Sandbag n.d.).

As climate consideration came to play a growing role, coal lost its relative competitiveness vis-a-vis natural gas, in part due to the rise of carbon prices since 2015 (BP 2019b; KWK-Index n.d.; Sandbag n.d.). Coal's role in Hungary's electricity generation dwindled and natural gas' increased. Nuclear's and electricity imports' roles have slightly decreased, while renewables' relative role has climbed, reaching 11.6% in 2018 (Fig. 2). However, biomass continues to play the role of the largest source of renewable electricity generation, the sustainability of which is still disputed by various stakeholders (EASAC 2019). Hydro energy was the second most important source of renewable electricity until 2008, but wind energy took its place between 2009 and 2017 (Fig. 2). Due to the government's failure to grant new wind permits and the subsequent de facto ban on new wind projects, emerging solar PV overtook wind in 2018. Despite some changes, the nuclear–gas–coal–biomass electricity generation composition has continued to dominate the sector.

Political Institutions and Actors

Energy governance is highly fragmented in Hungary, with influence over policy and market developments divided between multiple ministries and private actors. In theory, the Ministry of Innovation and Technology is at the center of energy policy, but competences are split with other ministries, while PM Orbán and his office have

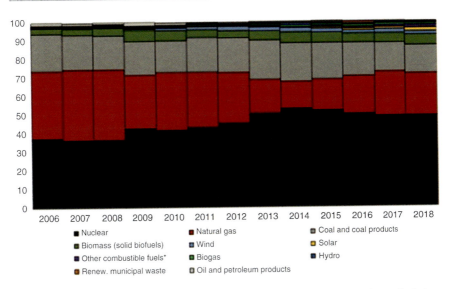

Fig. 2 Gross electricity production in Hungary, by fuel, 2006–2018 (%) (Source: Own calculations based on Eurostat (2018a, b) for the years 2006–2013, and MEKH (2020a, b) for the years 2014–2018) [*Other combustible fuels = industrial waste + nonrenewable municipal waste + other sources]

the last say in prominent issues. The Ministry of Innovation and Technology has held the responsibility for planning activities and developing a strategy for energy and climate issues since 2018. However, according to the organization and operational rules of the ministry, the state secretary in charge is only responsible for climate policy related issues and "establishing the strategic conditions for energy business" (ITM 2019). The state secretary has been particularly active in fields of renewables, designing and managing related subsidies and auctions, as well as streaming investments into efficiency and environmental projects.

Natural gas issues and their links to foreign affairs are managed by the Ministry of Foreign Affairs and Trade. Since 2014, when the Orbán-confidant Péter Szijjártó was nominated to foreign minister, negotiations about gas pipelines, long-term supply contracts and import prices, regional and interconnectivity projects firmly belong to this unit of the government. While it is officially mandated to only coordinate energy and climate diplomacy (KKM 2019), it has a more active role in natural gas and some oil-related issues. The ministry's elevated status largely stems from strong personal ties between Minister Szijjártó and PM Orbán and their bid to closely control all gas-related issues.

In principle, the nuclear industry and the management of the new nuclear blocs' construction exclusively belong to the "Minister without Portfolio for maintaining the capacity of the Paks nuclear power plant." Despite the existence of such a portfolio, related issues are also regularly discussed at Putin–Orbán summits and the Prime Minister's Office has also been involved since the onset of the project – represented at ministerial level since 2018. The separation of the project can be justified by its complexity, its magnitude (EUR 12.5 billion, roughly 9% of the 2019 Hungarian

GDP), its sensitivity with respect to domestic policy and obvious delays in its completion. Besides low utility prices for households, the Paks II project constitutes the other fixed points of any governmental thinking on the future energy landscape.

While these players remain relatively visible, the Minister without Portfolio in charge of National Assets also takes on an important role in the domestic energy scene. Ministries often controlled SOEs in their respective fields in the past; but ownership control has been separated from policy supervision under Orbán's governments and state ownership has dramatically increased. The controlling ministry shall allocate investment funds for respective development projects within SOEs, can veto any major decision, as well as approve all nominations in the management and board. Theoretically, this should not be a problem, as long as the government can preserve its unity, but the separation between corporate and political control certainly represent a potential point of conflict. This affects the energy scene primarily through its say in the governance of Hungarian Electrical Works Plc. (MVM), the country's utility behemoth.

A further key actor is the Hungarian Energy and Public Utility Regulatory Authority (MEKH), established by the National Assembly of Hungary in its current form in 2013. In doing so, its scope of competences was broadened with the waste, water, and district heating sectors, but its price setting and controlling authority vis-a-vis the government were weakened. MEKH pursues conventional regulatory activities such as licensing, supervision, and statistical data collection. Nevertheless, its most important duty is tariff-setting and keeping the administratively managed pricing system in the household sector under the government's firm control.

Despite high levels of foreign ownership in the past, national private and state companies have always enjoyed a good deal of legal and financial support from the government. MOL was defended from hostile takeover attempts by Russian (2001, 2011) and Austrian (2009) companies. The close links between the government and MOL led the latter to cooperate in strategy-design and implementation. These included the creation of the strategic gas storage after 2009 and the development of the country's energy interconnections. Alongside MOL, a number of private entities play focal roles in the domestic energy scene. German E.ON's purchase of MOL's natural gas wholesale and storage firms drove foreign ownership in the sector to a peak. Due to their multinational corporate strategies, foreign companies became less involved in Hungarian policymaking and tensions at the regulatory level were always relatively high between private and public actors. The issue's relevance has declined since the mid-2010s due to extensive (re-)nationalization.

At the heart of this multiactor energy system is PM Viktor Orbán and the parliamentary majority his party has held since 2010. This horizontally fragmented and vertically integrated decision-making system relies on his political interests, circumstances, and room for maneuver regarding energy policy. He uses selected issues from the energy field for political purposes, including control over utility prices, as well as Russia-policy and nuclear developments. Simultaneously, growing climate consciousness offers increasing gains for various opposition parties. Fidesz followed a climate-neutral, mildly climate skeptical conservative line, putting the government into the defensive, against a mix of green and liberal parties. Changes in this approach are only beginning to surface.

A final cluster of actors active in Hungary's energy sector is composed of those which are neither government entities nor private corporations involved in the energy supply chain. This includes independent nongovernmental organizations, such as Energiaklub, National Society of Conservationists – Friends of the Earth Hungary, or Greenpeace Hungary, which have had a limited capacity to shape policy and have frequently faced hostility from Orbán governments.

Discourse on Energy Issues

The themes of energy prices, energy security, ownership of energy assets, and nuclear power have been at the center of energy discourses in Hungary, with climate changes' importance only recently rising. The most pervasive energy discourse in Hungary pertains to price, which has been a key political issue for decades (Szabo and Fabok 2020). The Hungarian government has traditionally taken a paternalist role in society dating back to the communist era. Governments have been vocal about subsidizing prices, building political capital from this undertaking. Ensuring low prices has also been intertwined with a dominant discourse of energy security, entailing the government's and companies' ability to secure access to inexpensive energy resources. This has also warranted the state's objective to consolidate domestic ownership of energy assets that underpinned low prices and secure supplies. The Paks nuclear power plant's role at the heart of Hungary's energy system has made it a key constituent of domestic energy discourse, especially since MVM launched the planning and construction of its successor, Paks II. These four interlinked discourses have dominated the Hungarian energy scene essentially for decades, but have recently been expanded with climate change primarily in light of European and global developments.

Hungarian governments have a long-standing history in controlling energy prices, by developing domestic deposits or negotiating favorable import terms. Hungary has long produced and consumed fossil fuels, but this was especially accelerated when governments of the communist era accelerated industrialization (KBM 2008; VGF and HKL 2013). Demand for energy quickly outpaced supply and the country became reliant on inexpensive soviet hydrocarbon imports during the second half of the twentieth century (Hoffman and Dienes 1985). These factors laid the foundation to a discourse emanating from essentially all cabinets of the government and the party that focused on sustaining access to imports and low costs, which continued following the regime change. Energy prices remained a pervasive political issue that political parties heatedly debated, while Hungary's oil and natural gas major, MOL, provided energy to consumers at subdued prices, incurring the associated losses. Meanwhile, broader society expected the state to find a way to sustain low end-user prices. The need for the state to take action to secure access to inexpensive energy sources was especially pertinent given the technological and infrastructural lock-ins (e.g., an extensive natural gas network) that also drove a proliferating energy poverty throughout the country (Bouzarovski et al. 2016).

Political parties in Hungary have avoided raising energy prices by all means possible after being voted into office by the populace. The confluence of liberalization and high global energy prices led to climbing prices in the 2000s, culminating under the rule of the Hungarian Socialist Party (MSZP) (Ürge-Vorsatz et al. 2006). By this time, EU-backed liberalization efforts had been implemented by the government and E.ON had acquired a large part of the Hungarian energy sector, but these actors' discursive emphasis on a competitive market benefitting the consumers did not materialize. PM Orbán-led Fidesz launched a campaign for the need to maintain low energy prices and reclaim energy assets, contributing to their win at the polls in 2010, 2014, and 2018. In the run up to the 2014 election, "utility [price] reductions" [*rezsicsökkentés*] was the dominant discursive theme of the campaign and after winning office. Fidesz widely publicized its overhead price reductions and launched an era of the "fight for utility prices" [*rezsiharc*] (Böcskei 2015; Horváth 2016). The "fight for utility prices" included a bid to shape prices and to allow the state to nationalize energy assets, concentrating ownership in public companies (Mihályi 2018). Fidesz reversed MSZP-led governments' actions to open the Hungarian energy sector for foreign investors, which it already began in 2011 with a large stock-purchase share in the national oil company MOL and followed with further acts of sectoral consolidation after its 2014 re-election. The guiding rhetoric the government has deployed claims that energy assets are strategic and therefore should be Hungarian-owned, while this form of ownership also ensures energy security.

The nationalization of energy assets in Hungary is embedded in the wider discourse of supply security, given the import dependence that the country has built in past decades (see section "Composition of the Energy Mix"). This is predicated on the country's need to exploit domestically available resources, maintain amicable relations with Russia, and diversify import routes. The Hungarian energy system is set up in a manner where actors throughout the supply chain rely on good relations with Russia, ensuring a secure supply of energy resources at subdued prices. Consequently, there is a strong Russia-friendly element of the government's foreign policy, which has become especially pronounced and discursively emphasized in recent years under Fidesz governments. This has been accompanied with government-backed initiatives to diversify energy import sources and routes, ushering in a strong focus on natural gas pipeline politics especially following the 2006 and 2009 natural gas crises (Weiner 2017). Decision-makers from the public and private sector extensively discussed large infrastructure projects including the Nord Stream, Nabucco pipeline, South Stream, the Trans-Adriatic Pipeline, the Azerbaijan–Georgia–Romania–Hungary LNG project (AGRI), Krk LNG, Turkish Stream, Nord Stream 2, the Bulgaria–Romania–Hungary–Austria pipeline (BRUA), and interconnectors to neighboring countries (e.g., Slovakia and Croatia). Representatives of the EU and the USA have continuously articulated their support for undertakings delivering non-Russian natural gas. Many of these projects were heatedly debated for years, but few have come to fruition given the preexisting lock-ins of the energy system and Hungary's unwillingness to pay the surplus price for non-Russian hydrocarbons.

Hungary's focus has also been targeted to address supply security and price issues by leveraging domestic sources of energy, which includes the exploitation of lignite, oil, and natural gas, as well as continuing domestic nuclear power-based electricity generation. The need to sustain domestic fossil fuel production has been a key point of discourse emphasized by government officials and the upstream industry at large.

However, lignite deposits are of weak quality and hydrocarbon reserves are rapidly being depleted by producers, leaving the future of these energy sources in question. Moreover, they may enhance supply security and energy autonomy, but their production is not economically competitive. Nuclear power, however, continues to be a staple of Hungary's energy and broader political discourse, given its intimate linkages to the country's foreign policy towards Russia. The government and state-owned firms (e.g., MVM) have continuously emphasized the need for Paks to be expanded, since the current reactors will have to be retired in the 2030s and are a key source of domestically produced energy. Surveys show that 61% of society is generally against the construction of an additional Russian-financed nuclear power station (Greenpeace Hungary 2018). Fidesz supporters have been slightly in favor of the project, which has also fused with their positive perception of Russia (Hargitai 2018; Magyari 2018). The populace favors renewables over nuclear, which are seen as tools to mitigating exposure to Russian influence, thereby enhancing energy security.

Climate change has only become a recent addition to prominent energy discourses in Hungary. There had been a wave of focus on renewable energy in the early-2000s that led to the expansion of wind generation capacities, but this came to an abrupt halt, when the government decided to suspend support for wind and essentially ban the technology. The founding of Hungary's green party, Politics Can Be Different (LMP), in 2009 provided some impetus for a more environmentally conscious dialogue in the Parliament and in wider society. Meanwhile, Hungarian media's reporting of the *Energiewende* and the potential of renewables remained subdued (Antal and Karhunmaa 2018). Integration into the European Union (Kerényi and Szabó 2006), the Paris Agreement, and the European Commission's (2016) introduction of the Clean Energy Package began to shift the prominence of environmental and climate discourse. However, this only rose in prominence in 2019, when the Fidesz-led government lost key cities in municipal elections, where climate and environmental action was an important factor that mobilized voters. Fidesz went from snubbing EU 2050 climate goals, to a proponent of climate action (Jávor 2020). Carbon lock-ins still dominate the climate discourse, since the government has continuously emphasized the need for prudent action in phasing out emitting sources of energy and underscoring that nuclear is a carbon-neutral technology – thus, Hungary should support Paks II on climate grounds as well – but as the costs of renewables decline their potential is increasingly incorporated into societal discourses and future planning.

Coordination of the Instruments and Issues of Energy Transitions Within a Multilevel Context

Drivers of Energy Transition

Energy security and pressure from Western institutions to enact change are the prime drivers of Hungary's energy transition. The former has been a continuous concern for the country with governments, the private sector, and society seeking to ensure the accessibility and affordability of imported energy, since domestic fossil fuel resources are insufficient to meet demand. In principle, an energy transition provides an opportunity for Hungary to reduce its import reliance and meet its energy needs through domestic production. This should entail a shift away from imported fossil fuels towards domestically sourced energy, primarily via renewables. Domestically produced renewable-based electricity offers an opportunity to reduce the import-reliance of the country – approximately one third of demand (see section "Composition of the Energy Mix"). The forthcoming need to retire the Mátra Power Plant further pressures the government to take action and deploy renewables to avoid a hike in import reliance. The state has also accepted nuclear as a source of domestic energy that maintains supply security reliant on low-carbon technologies. These ambitions generally impede an energy transition (Antal 2019), but the government has been adamant as framing the project as an integral part of a transition to a low-carbon energy system, despite Paks' and Paks II's reliance on foreign technology and source-fuel. Energy security is thus a driver of Hungary's energy transition to renewables, but renewable penetration is impeded by nuclear which the government has also supported on inter alia energy security grounds.

A strong push of EU climate goals and obligations as well as the rising competitiveness of renewables have complemented energy security considerations driving Hungary's energy transition. The European Union has been a self-proclaimed leader in climate action, which has led the European Commission to set binding goals (e.g., renewable deployment targets) and introducing mechanisms (e.g., EU ETS) to decarbonize its economy (Maltby 2013). The European Commission (2008, 2011, 2014) pushed for an energy transition in its 2020, 2030, and 2050 goals, which Western European countries came to support (Sattich 2018). Hungary, like most European countries, took little action prior to the 2010s, apart from a wave of investment in wind power generation between 2000 and 2010, leading to the 325 MW of capacity still online (MAVIR 2019). Many Western European countries accelerated their energy transitions in the early-2010s, but initially this had little influence on Hungarian policy-makers. Fossil fuel and nuclear lock-ins sustained. Simultaneously, the government was able to claim that it was *en route* to meeting emission targets, since its targets were unambitious (see section "Strategies and Instruments of Energy Transition"). The composition of the energy mix saw little change, apart from an abrupt rise in the share of biomass (see section "Strategies and Instruments of Energy Transition") – a result of a shift in statistical accounting as opposed to substantial change (Hvg.hu 2017). Drivers of the energy transition remained insufficient to effectuate any substantial change in Hungary until the mid-2010s, but allowed the country to move towards its 2020 EU targets. The forthcoming decade through 2030 is what seems to pose a much greater challenge and induce wide-ranging change.

The acceleration of Western Europe's energy transition increasingly pressured Central and Eastern Europe's EU members to take action (Szabo and Deak 2020). Lock-ins of energy consumption patterns sustained and renewables could not yet challenge the price of fossil fuels. The government-supported lock-in of nuclear technology also formed an impediment to the diffusion of renewables, as policy-makers' ambitions to construct Paks II overshadowed most other energy policy objectives in Hungary (Antal 2019). However, it has become clear that Hungary has to facilitate the diffusion of renewables, its technology of choice is solar PV, to meet 2020 and 2030 EU targets. To facilitate the transition, the Commission has applied carrot and stick approach to push EU member states to meet obligations, by providing some funding for renewables and increasing energy efficiency. This has been a lure that has driven Hungary's energy transition. Simultaneously, the EU ETS penalizes the consumption of high emission fuels and has recently become a policy vehicle with teeth, as allowance prices rose to the EUR 20–25 band (see section "Composition of the Energy Mix"). In the short term, energy companies have had to rely on imports, but these factors can lead investment into renewables. The Commission's other *stick* is the measures it can take against member states who do not meet renewable energy targets they set for 2020 and 2030. *If* and *how* the Commission will take action in these cases is unclear for now.

The political imposition of renewable penetration by EU-level institutions is complemented by the rising competitiveness of renewables. Technological advancements and economies of scale have led wind turbines and solar photovoltaics to become competitive with their fossil fuel counterparts (Lazard 2018). Hungary also has a generally favorable setting that allows producers to harness wind and solar energy and relatively high utilization rates (Pálfy 2017). This, paired with the urgent need to invest in domestic electricity generation capacities given the forecasted gap in demand and supply, has led investors to show heightened interest in the Hungarian market (MAVIR 2018). The government has also provided ample support for the diffusion of renewables (see section "Strategies and Instruments of Energy Transition"). As the relative competitiveness of solar PV continues to rapidly increase, market forces are taking over political obligations in driving the energy transitions. Projects may still rely on some state support, but developers expect that the market will move away from this reliance and solar PV will gradually outcompete other modes of electricity generation, provided that a favorable environment (both legal-regulatory and socio-technical) is maintained. Enmeshed in these drivers is a sliver of industrial policy that began to adapt the Hungarian economy for a decarbonized world, by backing lithium-ion battery, solar PV, and electric bus production. Overall, drivers for Hungary's energy transition are thus political and primarily externally imposed, with some impetus provided by energy security considerations.

Strategies and Instruments of Energy Transition

Hungary's energy transition strategy has relied on it being embedded in the EU's climate and energy governance structures. This sets some targets and the broad framework, within which the country can navigate and develop its strategies to meet its goals. The EU imposed a legally binding obligation on Hungary to include a 13% minimum share of renewables in gross final energy consumption by 2020, while the government set an even more ambitious target of 14.65% (European Parliament and Council 2009b; NFM 2010). Subsequently, Hungary adopted a 21% target for 2030 (ITM 2020c). Due to a 2017 change in the EU's accounting methodology of biomass, it seemed that Hungary would swiftly meet its 2020 renewable targets, with renewables' relative share climbing to a peak of 16.2% in 2013, heavily predicated on biomass (Fig. 1). However, despite this boost, the relative role of renewables has been going downhill since then. The temporary optimism has deferred focus on the diffusion of nonbiomass renewables and may have hindered an even quicker deployment of solar PV (HVG 2017). The government recently reversed this course of action, heavily promoting the diffusion of solar PV to enable the country in meeting 2020 EU targets (ITM 2020a, c).

The heating and cooling sector will continue to be responsible for highest share of the renewable consumption, where the share of renewables may increase from 18.1% in 2018 to 28.7% in 2030 (Table 1) (ITM 2020a, c; MEKH 2020h). The NECP aims to decrease gas consumption and the role of gas both in residential individual household- and in district heating by the combination of energy efficiency measures and fuel mix diversification. However, according to the NECP, Hungary will also reduce residential firewood use. The NECP supports further heat pump installations and efficient biomass-heating solutions. The role of gas is set to be substituted in district heating through the introduction of more renewables, such as biomass and geothermal energy. In addition, the NECP places emphasis on recovering energy from nonrecyclable waste and the use of biogas from sewage, landfills, and agricultural waste materials for district heating. The NECP states that the replacement of natural gas-based district heating with renewable-based heat production will not be carried out on a market basis; rather, it requires substantial investment support through instruments such as the Green District Heating Program (ITM 2020c). Therefore, in the 2014–2020 programming period, investment is provided for the construction of renewable-based heat generation, which may facilitate significant growth in biomass-based and geothermal energy.

The low-carbon electricity sector envisioned in the NECP will continue to be based mainly on nuclear energy, partly preserving the old model with baseload power and a centralized structure provided by a large and inflexible power plant, but complemented with renewables. The role of renewables in gross electricity consumption will increase from 8.3% in 2018 to 21.3% in 2030 and 29.3% in 2040 per the so-called WAM ("with additional measures") scenario, reflecting additional measures to be taken, as compared to the WEM ("with existing measures") scenario (Fig. 1) (ITM 2020a; MEKH 2020h). On the generation side in the WAM scenario, the share of renewables is projected to grow from 11.6% in 2018 to 19.7% in 2030 and 44.1% in 2040. The combined share of renewables and nuclear in the electricity mix is planned to be 78.6% in 2030 and 90.7% in 2040 from 60.8% in 2018 (Fig. 2) (ITM 2020a; MEKH 2020a). The four Soviet-designed units (500 MW each) at the Paks power station in operation will be phased out in the 2030s, after the end of their 20-year lifetime extension program. Although uncertainties are large, the two new units are planned to be commissioned until 2030, with a slightly higher combined capacity (two units of 1200 MW each) than that of the four old units. Therefore, the share of nuclear power will surge by 2030 and then decline. In 2030, Hungary plans to be almost self-sufficient in electricity on a yearly basis (ITM 2020c).

The government's centralized and nuclear-centric approach to the energy transition in inter alia the NECP reflects its skepticism towards the reliability of intermittent renewables, weighing on their expansion. However, external, mainly EU, pressure and the rising competitiveness of solar PV have changed this situation. The government has chosen solar PV as *the* renewable of the future, providing it ample backwind. According to the NECP's WAM scenario, the technology's share in output will increase from 1.9% in 2018 to 3.9% in 2020, 11.5% in 2030, and 29.3% in 2040 (Fig. 2) (ITM 2020a; MEKH 2020a). The anticipated rapid spread of solar PV across Hungary will strengthen decentralized energy system structures. Biomass can also continue to expand and may provide an easy way to increase the role of renewables in electricity. On the other hand, the Hungarian government does not intend to exploit the remaining wind potential. It introduced a de facto ban on new wind power plant projects in 2016, with no new permits issued since 2006. There are multiple theories as to why this executive decision was taken, a plausible one of which is that the technology was overly linked to the Socialist government's scandalous distribution of construction quotas in 2006 – an act that the Fidesz government had looked to distance itself from (Weiner 2019). We also see this ban linked to the government's energy policy priorities that focused on Paks II. Lastly, hydro potential is also not likely to be utilized (ITM 2020a).

The government has driven renewable electricity generation through various support schemes. The first of these was KÁP in place between 2003 and 2007, followed by the KÁT between 2008 and 2016. The third generation of support schemes (METÁR) was launched in 2017 (Haffner 2018). Not only does METÁR provide operating aid for electricity generation, but it also facilitates market integration of renewable energy production. According to the original plans, power plants with a capacity of less than 0.5 MW or pilot technologies and projects were to be eligible for support (METÁR-KÁT), while METÁR's green premium was to be granted without a tender for installations with a capacity of between 0.5 MW and 1 MW, and through a tender for facilities with a capacity of at least 1 MW. Ultimately, projects with a capacity of under 0.5 MW were also included in the premium scheme, and the fixed-rate feed-in tariff option ceased to exist. In addition to supporting the building of new units, the METÁR system also supports the preservation of existing renewable energy capacities through METÁR's brown premium system. Hungary will distribute a maximum annual amount of HUF 45 billion (EUR 130 million) within the framework of METÁR through 2026 (ITM 2020c).

The maturity of solar PV technology and the safe investment it provided prompted developers to submit over 1 GW of project proposals before the KÁT system was set to expire at the end of 2016 (Kulcsár 2019). Developers are still realizing projects from this wave of proposals, which have contributed to total solar PV capacities increasing to 1144 MW in mid-2019 from 321 MW at the end of 2017 (MEKH 2019a). Subsequently, the government waited until 2019 to launch a tender under the METÁR scheme, as its foot-dragging to introduce further change continues. Nonetheless, investors still see Hungary's geography as favorable for solar PV, but issues such as grid connection and instability in the regulatory environment weigh on the diffusion of the technology as the government continues to hesitate to take action that would accelerate the energy transition. Hungary also encourages the installation of solar PV systems, partially replacing household electricity consumption drawn from the grid. There is an interest-free energy-efficiency loan in the Hungarian market that has been offered to households since 2017, but the Hungarian regulation on the energy characteristics of buildings is the one which is expected to drive further exponential growth of production units currently defined as small-scale household power plants, since it requires that at least 25% of the energy needs of new public and residential buildings should be covered by renewables post-2018 and post-2020, respectively. The 2030 target of the NECP is to have at least 200,000 households with roof-mounted solar panels averaging 4 kW each from 29,593 small-scale household solar PV power plants at end-2017 (ITM 2020c; MEKH 2019b).

Despite strategies to expand renewable-based power generation, nuclear, natural gas, and coal still dominate the country's domestic electricity scene. Lignite still enjoys a solid position in Hungary, but its NECP established 2030 as the year for achieving a lignite-free power sector (ITM 2020c). Since then, the respective minister has fast-tracked this objective to 2025 (Marczisovszky 2020). Internalizing instruments are strongly affecting the future of the lignite-fired Mátra Power Plant which buys 100% of its CO_2 quotas (Mert.hu n.d.). The power plant's profitability thus depends primarily on electricity and carbon prices, and consequently under the current market conditions, it is a loss-making operation. The NECP expects the role of gas in electricity generation will increase until significant PV capacity enters the grid and Paks II starts operating (ITM 2020a). However, after that time, gas-based generation will decrease both in absolute and relative terms, but gas will continue to play an important role in electricity generation as a flexible peaking resource or a standby reserve in the electricity system.

Growth in renewable energy consumption in the transport sector has primarily been attributable to the use of biodiesel produced from first generation (food and feed crops-based) biofuels and used cooking oil. In 2020, the government increased the mandatory blending ratio to 8.2% of biofuels, driving a 6.1% blending percentage of bioethanol in gasoline (ITM 2020c). Despite some action, Hungary is unlikely to meet its relevant 2020 EU target requiring a 10% share of renewables in the transport sector by 2020, which stood at 7.7% in 2018 (Fig. 1) (MEKH 2020h; ITM 2020a). According to the NECP's WAM scenario, the share of energy from renewable sources used for transport could increase to 16.9% in 2030 and 28.8% in 2040 (Fig. 2) (ITM 2020a), compared to the minimum binding target of 14% in 2030 (European Parliament and Council 2018a). In order to achieve at least the latter goal, the government plans to raise the proportion of first-generation biofuels to nearly 7%, while the share of second generation biofuels and biogas should be raised to 3.5%. The remainder will hinge on transportation's electrification. Hungary supports the spread of electric vehicles with financial instruments, including direct subsidies for individuals seeking to purchase these vehicles and tax breaks. It is also implementing programs that encourage the spread of electromobility through the development of charging infrastructure. Moreover, the country is also expected to put nearly 1300 environmentally friendly buses into operation by 2029 through the

Green Bus Program. In addition to public transport, natural gas and biogas can play a greater role in freight transport (ITM 2020c).

Hungary has taken on modest energy efficiency targets in comparison to the EU's overall goals, but even so, it may face difficulties in meeting its 2030 final energy consumption target. Primary and final energy consumption reached 1025 PJ and 776 PJ in 2018 (MEKH 2020f), respectively, with 2020 targets of 1009 PJ and 693 PJ (Government Decree 1160/2015 [III. 20.]). Residential final energy consumption was 244 PJ in 2018 (MEKH 2020f), despite the government's former goal set at 207 PJ for 2020 (NFM 2015, 18). Hungary is far from this goal. Meanwhile, the government aims to keep Hungary's final energy consumption below 2005 levels in 2030 (Government Decree 1772/2018 [XII. 21.]). This represents a modest commitment in light of the fact that the EU decided to reduce final energy consumption by 20% compared to the 2005 levels (European Parliament and Council 2018b). In its WEM scenario, the NECP assumes an 18.7% increase in the final energy consumption between 2015 and 2030. And even if the WAM scenario materializes, final energy consumption will still increase by 7.6% in this period. There is only a 9.4% difference between the 2030 final energy consumption data based on WEM and WAM. In contrast, the NECP expects final household energy consumption to decrease by either 0.8% or 31.7% depending on existing or additional policy measures (ITM 2020a), indicating that Hungary's total final energy consumption target depends on the exploitation of the residential energy savings potential, which, however, would require further proactive intervention (Table 3).

Hungary has to take vastly larger efforts to increase energy efficiency and renewable penetration rates in comparison to meeting its GHG targets. The NECP suggests that with existing measures GHG emissions would rise to 62.8 MtCO$_2$q by 2030, beyond the 40% reduction in emissions compared to 1990 level Hungary has committed to. With additional measures, Hungary will be able to reduce them to 56.2 MtCO2$_2$q by 2030, slightly below its target of 56.3 MtCO$_2$q. Since the Mátra Power Plant is responsible for around six million tons of annual CO$_2$ emissions (Napi.hu. 2016), the majority of the target can be met by eliminating lignite use. While GHG emissions under the ETS must fall significantly, the situation is much better in sectors outside the ETS. As part of the EU's 2009 Effort Sharing Decision, Hungary can increase its emissions by 10% between 2013 and 2020, relative to 2005 emissions levels (European Parliament and Council 2009a). It is unlikely to do so. In contrast, as part of the 2018 Effort Sharing Regulation, emissions for sectors outside the ETS should be reduced in Hungary by 7% between 2021 and 2030, in relation to its 2005 levels (European Parliament and Council 2018c), ushering a disruptive force into Hungary's energy system.

Coordination Mechanisms and Multilevel Governance

Hungary's energy governance features a horizontally fragmented and vertically integrated decision-making system that heavily relies on the goals and ambitions of PM Orbán, although shaped by the historical legacies of the country and its

Table 3 Key Hungarian energy transition policy instruments, by sector and type

	Regulatory instruments	Incentive-based instruments	Internalizing instruments	Information-based instruments (soft governance)
Electricity supply	Hungarian Government Decree 277/2016 (IX. 15.) on the de facto ban on new wind projects	METÁR support scheme for renewable electricity	EU ETS affecting the future of the lignite-fired Mátra Power Plant	Prioritizing the focus on Paks II
Heat supply		Support for high-efficiency renewable cogeneration, but discontinued support for cogeneration using nonrenewables Green District Heating Program	EU ETS affecting the future of the lignite-fired Mátra Power Plant	
Household energy users	The 31/31/EU Directive and Hungary's TNM Regulation 7/2006 (V. 24.) on nearly zero energy and at least 25% renewable requirements for new residential buildings from 2021 Post-2012 utility cost reduction program	Warm Home Program for thermal insulation; replacement of old doors, windows, heating systems, boilers and large domestic appliances; district-heating related investments; and renewable energy installation Interest-free energy-efficiency loan for thermal insulation; replacement of old doors, windows and heating systems; and renewable energy installation		Maintaining low utility prices irrespective of the energy transition
Industrial and commercial energy users	European Parliament and Council (2010) and Hungary's TNM Regulation 7/2006 (V. 24.) on nearly zero energy and at least 25% renewable requirements for nonpublic buildings from 2021 Setting up a network of energy engineers helping SMEs and local self-governments Large companies must employ energy engineers and conduct energy audits every 4 years	Government support scheme for SME investment into renewables and energy efficiency Tax advantages for corporate energy investments	EU ETS forcing those included to invest in low carbon technologies	

Transport	Biofuel blending obligation based on European Parliament and Council (2009b) and Hungary's Government Regulation 279/2017 (IX. 22.)	Subsidy to individuals and businesses for the purchase of an electric car and a light truck under 3.5 tons
Programs encouraging the spread of electric mobility using the sources of the green economy financing system
All-electric cars, plug-in hybrids, extended-range hybrids and zero-emission cars are exempt from vehicle tax, company car tax and registration tax
Vehicle tax on buses and trucks, company car tax and registration tax based on the environmental rating of the vehicle
Tax relief for trucks when using combined transport
Green Bus Program to put nearly 1300 environmentally friendly buses into operation by 2029

Source: Own compilation

dialogue with the EU. Coordination mechanisms, including strategy design, are shaped by the dialogue between the Prime Minister's office, as well as decision-makers in the EU and Russia. The Hungarian government has continuously engaged with EU policy-makers in an attempt to lower climate action-related targets. This has become especially evident in European Council meetings, where the country was continuously seen as a laggard and one that sought to obstruct the acceptance of targets, primarily since it sought to ensure that the EU provides it with ample funding to finance its transition. On the other hand, Hungary has maintained strong ties to Russia, which are heavily based on its energy system. The government's continued goal to ensure access to ample natural gas supplies at favorable prices and its bid to construct Paks II were coordinated at the highest levels of government with essentially no input from other actors.

Coordination in Hungary's energy scene primarily takes place between the highest levels of government, from where implementation is managed through a top-down approach. Various branches of the ministry possess competences over decision-making, but their positions are subjugated to the goals of the PM's office, as is the role of MEKH. The increasing state ownership of energy firms has also limited their ability to challenge government policy, instead, taking orders or shaping policy in close coordination with political decision-makers. Lastly, the Orbán regime has systematically sought to curtail the voices of NGOs, limiting their ability to become involved in energy governance as well. Meanwhile, a portion of the populace may be developing into prosumers over the past few years, but this has only had a minor impact on the overall landscape of energy governance.

Outcomes, Challenges, and Prospects of Energy Governance

This chapter has shown that the future of Hungary's energy governance relies on two basic factors: the Orbán regime's objectives and the broader energy trends impacting CEE countries. The objectives of PM Orbán's regime-building have clearly materialized. Fidesz governments have fortified the current setup since 2010, where governance-design reflects objectives of subduing prices, maintaining national ownership and pervasive institutional fragmentation, as well as hands-on control from the highest echelons of politics – all of which have become key descriptors of the country's illiberal energy governance regime. These objectives have been nested in the broader setting of a Russian energy dependent CEE country, where the lock-ins of existing consumption patterns are extremely powerful as is the disruption executed by the EU. Regional market, technology, and industrial developments, as well as international security considerations are set to continue to shape energy policies. Even if Hungarian political and policy designs are not fully congruent with those of its neighbors, we postulate that limitations posed by national self-rule will continue to be a basic policy benchmark. These two sets of factors provide an overarching framework, within which Hungary's energy system has shown some flexibility and adaptability, primarily in response to external pressure from the European Union.

Hungary's low-carbon energy transition is particularly interesting and challenging, since the country will implement this in a unique, in some regards, archaic policy setup. Its policy objectives frequently contradict one another, but leave space for a high number of variegated configurations. Hungarian energy policy should keep household prices low in a time when price intensity of energy and its networks have been on the rise. It also needs to limit price hikes for industrial consumers to maintain economic competitiveness, while raising domestic investments from current untenably low levels. Energy policy shall simultaneously maintain the government's control over the sector, capture its rents, while forging new coalitions with emerging constituencies, companies, and institutions of the ongoing energy transition. It also has to transform the country's industrial policy, shifting its heavy reliance on combustion car manufacturing to meet the demands of e-mobility, while its capabilities as a high-value added host country have been fading away. In meeting these contradicting goals, key actors of Hungarian energy governance will have to carefully maneuver between its legacies that closely link it to Russia and the commitments the country has taken on by joining the EU, without surrendering the government's bid to enhance energy security.

Investment into electricity infrastructure (including power generation, transmission, and distribution) plummeted in recent years, which stands in sharp contrast with the need for investment into the sector to meet demand and increase self-sufficiency per the government's rhetoric. Where will the investments come from? Meanwhile, projects launched reflect the Orbán government's preference towards equity subsidization through budgetary means from taxpayers' money, as is the case with the Paks II nuclear deal and solar capacity expansion. The former is entirely financed from the central budget without being reflected in consumer prices during its construction. The government's solar power expansion goal has to be met amid tight-fisted subsidies reliant on government support and EU funds. Other segments, like gas power plants and transmission networks, almost exclusively belong to domestic private- and state-owned companies, opening up the way for extensive bargaining with the government. This unfolds as actors understand the prospects of the sector, including the urgent need to expand their capacities and alter their business models to an age with high capacity demand but low utilization rates.

The prospects of Hungary's energy transition rely on its ability and willingness to overcome historical lock-ins. The Paks II case is particularly relevant in this regard. Opponents criticize the project, characterizing it as an old-fashioned, expensive investment, providing incremental exposure to Russian influence, and opening up excessive corruption opportunities through state financing. Undeniably, the government decision to develop the project can be described as a classic case of sectoral lock-in, when not only the choice of fuel, but also the decision-making process and major characteristics of the deal reflect the previous agreement from the 1970s. Paks II can be a major barrier to energy transition, since it saps the government's attention and resources away from renewables, capping their expansion. Even though the two sources of energy could work alongside one-another: nuclear providing baseload electricity generation and renewables an intermittent source of electricity. Moreover, the government's narrative suggests that nuclear is a low-carbon technology, which will provide cheap energy – pending the operating company will not repay capital costs – and contributing to low utility prices. From this angle, maintaining the current nuclear capacity beyond 2040 is an indispensable step to successful energy transition. On the other hand, potential delays of the project, high capital expenditure, sustainment of path dependencies, and its inhibition of renewable diffusion despite their plummeting costs all hinder Hungary's move to renewables. Nonetheless, Paks II continues to be at the heart of the government's energy policy agenda, shaping the prospects of the energy sector, while overriding essentially all other considerations.

After having extensively relied on biomass, solar PV has become the Hungarian government's main tool to meet EU-imposed climate targets and enhance energy security. In doing so, however, it has disrupted the energy system, corroding lock-ins, and shaping future energy prospects. The competitiveness of the technology would allow for a thriving market, but its full potential remains to be realized. State plans and strategies show growing support for solar PV, but simultaneously representatives urge caution and a moderate pace, to avoid the rapid disruption of energy producer-consumer relations. The scaling-up of solar PV would primarily impact electricity imports and substitute the lignite-based Mátra Power Plant's generation – the latter of which has to be retired in forthcoming years. This substitution would only have a moderate impact on the country's energy security, leaving the hydrocarbon and nuclear-based Russia-centric geopolitical relations of Hungary in-tact for the foreseeable future. It is set to continue to rely on imported natural gas and oil for heating and industrial consumption as well as transportation, respectively. Biofuels and electric vehicles have been playing an increasing but still moderate role in the transportation sector, leaving their diffusion to be a task of the future. Meanwhile, district heating based on the rising consumption of biomass and the utilization of the country's geothermal potential remains untapped. As the government proposes its EU-mandated climate and energy plans, observers can attain a rough understanding of the country's planned trajectory. Specifics may be lacking, but it seems clear that the transition will be moderately paced and centrally controlled.

Hungarian energy governance conveys a unique disposition, filled with contradictions and lacking clarity. Much like many of its CEE neighbors, it is still entrenched in preexisting producer-consumer relations that shape its amicable relations with Russia. This, like most of the country's energy policy, is shaped at the highest political level. Multilevel governance is subordinated to anticipate or execute the objectives dictated by policy-makers in the highest echelons of government. Other actors have very limited powers to question, contradict, or substantially shape the government objectives. Power and control over public and private entities is concentrated in the hands of a few, who have continuously undertaken a balancing act between the forces and requirements posed by the EU upon Hungary and the relations that tie it to Russia. Solar PV has had some, but still limited impact on the country's energy scene. It decarbonizes the energy system, but carries limited ramifications in shaping the governance structures of the country, while continuing to exist in the shadow of nuclear power. In the nonelectricity sectors, natural gas continues to be dominant, entrenched by infrastructural path dependencies and through its role as the backbone of Hungary-Russia relations. Oil takes on a similar role as well. The real challenges in the Hungarian energy sector are set to increase as we move closer to 2030 and 2050 EU decarbonization and renewable energy targets, but it remains unclear how Hungary will enact the radical change necessary to meet these goals.

Cross-References

- Energy Governance in Austria
- Energy Governance in Croatia
- Energy Governance in Russia: From a Fossil to a Green Giant?
- European Union Energy Policy: A Discourse Perspective
- EU-Russia Energy Relations
- Transition of Energy Systems: Patterns of Stability and Change

Acknowledgments *Csaba Weiner*'s research was supported by the János Bolyai Research Scholarship of the Hungarian Academy of Sciences. We would like to thank the editors, Jörg Kemmerzell and Michèle Knodt, for their work on the volume, as well as Áron Buzogány for his helpful comments on this chapter.

References

Antal, M. (2019). How the regime hampered a transition to renewable electricity in Hungary. *Environmental Innovation and Societal Transitions, 33*, 162–182. https://doi.org/10.1016/j.eist.2019.04.004.

Antal, M., & Karhunmaa, K. (2018). The German energy transition in the British, Finnish and Hungarian news media. *Nature Energy, 3*(11), 994–1001. https://doi.org/10.1038/s41560-018-0248-3.

Báger, G., & Kovács, Á. (2004). *Privatizáció Magyarországon I. kötet [Privatisation in Hungary, Vol. I]*. Budapest: Állami Számvevőszék. https://www.asz.hu/storage/files/files/Publikaciok/Archiv_tanulmanyok/privatizacio.pdf?download=true. Accessed 5 Mar 2020.

Benczes, I. (2016). From goulash communism to goulash populism: The unwanted legacy of Hungarian reform socialism. *Post-Communist Economies, 28*(2), 146–166. https://doi.org/10.1080/14631377.2015.1124557.

Böcskei, B. (2015). Rezsicsökkentés: a közpolitikai változás mint politikai innováció [Utility price reduction: Public policy change as political innovation]. *Politikatudományi Szemle, 24*(4), 94–114. https://www.ceeol.com/search/article-detail?id=366236. Accessed 10 Feb 2020.

Bouzarovski, S., Herrero, S. T., Petrova, S., & Ürge-Vorsatz, D. (2016). Unpacking the spaces and politics of energy poverty: Path-dependencies, deprivation and fuel switching in post-communist Hungary. *Local Environment, 21*(9), 1151–1170. https://doi.org/10.1080/13549839.2015.1075480.

BP. (2019a). Statistical review of world energy – All data, 1965–2017. *BP – Definitions and explanatory notes*. https://www.bp.com/en/global/corporate/energy-economics/statistical-review-of-world-energy.html. Accessed 2 Apr 2019.

BP. (2019b). BP statistical review of world energy 2019. https://www.bp.com/content/dam/bp/business-sites/en/global/corporate/xlsx/energy-economics/statistical-review/bp-stats-review-2019-all-data.xlsx. Accessed 4 Oct 2019.

EASAC (European Academies' Science Advisory Council). (2019). Leading scientists warn: Wood pellets threat to climate: "No silver pellet". European. https://www.ria.ie/news/policy-and-international-relations-international-activities/leading-scientists-warn-wood. Accessed 14 Feb 2020.

European Commission. (2008). Communication from the Commission to the European Parliament, the Council, the European Economic and Social Committee and the Committee of the Regions: 20 20 by 2020 – Europe's climate change opportunity. COM(2008) 30 final. https://eur-lex.europa.eu/legal-content/EN/TXT/?uri=CELEX:52008DC0030. Accessed 7 Aug 2019.

European Commission. (2011). Communication from the Commission to the European Parliament, the Council, the European Economic and Social Committee and the Committee of the Regions: A Roadmap for moving to a competitive low carbon economy in 2050. COM(2011) 112 final. http://eur-lex.europa.eu/legal-content/EN/TXT/?uri=CELEX:52011DC0112. Accessed 21 Nov 2017.

European Commission. (2014). Communication from the Commission to the European Parliament, the Council, the European Economic and Social Committee and the Committee of the Regions: A policy framework for climate and energy in the period from 2020 to 2030. COM(2014) 15 final. https://eur-lex.europa.eu/legal-content/EN/TXT/?uri=CELEX:52014DC0015. Accessed 11 Feb 2020.

European Commission. (2016). Communication from the Commission to the European Parliament, the Council, the European Economic and Social Committee, the Committee of the Regions and the European Investment Bank: Clean energy for all Europeans. COM(2016) 860 final. https://eur-lex.europa.eu/resource.html?uri=cellar:fa6ea15b-b7b0-11e6-9e3c-01aa75ed71a1.0001.02/DOC_1&format=PDF. Accessed 17 Aug 2018.

European Parliament and Council. (2009a). Decision No 406/2009/EC of the European Parliament and of the Council of 23 April 2009 on the effort of Member States to reduce their greenhouse gas emissions to meet the Community's greenhouse gas emission reduction commitments up to 2020. https://eur-lex.europa.eu/legal-content/EN/TXT/?uri=CELEX%3A32009D0406. Accessed 9 Dec 2019.

European Parliament and Council. (2009b). Consolidated text: Directive 2009/28/EC of the European Parliament and of the Council of 23 April 2009 on the promotion of the use of energy from renewable sources and amending and subsequently repealing Directives 2001/77/EC and 2003/30/EC (Text with EEA relevance). https://eur-lex.europa.eu/legal-content/EN/TXT/?uri¼CELEX:02009L0028-20151005. Accessed 29 Mar 2020.

European Parliament and Council. (2010). Consolidated text: Directive 2010/31/EU of the European Parliament and of the Council of 19 May 2010 on the energy performance of buildings (recast). https://eur-lex.europa.eu/legal-content/EN/TXT/?uri=CELEX:02010L0031-20181224. Accessed 29 Mar 2020.

European Parliament and Council. (2018a). Directive (EU) 2018/2001 of the European Parliament and of the Council of 11 December 2018 on the promotion of the use of energy from renewable sources (Text with EEA relevance). https://eur-lex.europa.eu/legal-content/EN/TXT/?uri=CELEX:32018L2001. Accessed 9 Dec 2019.

European Parliament and Council. (2018b). Directive (EU) 2018/2002 of the European Parliament and of the Council of 11 December 2018 amending Directive 2012/27/EU on energy efficiency (Text with EEA relevance). https://eur-lex.europa.eu/legal-content/EN/TXT/PDF/?uri=CELEX:32018L2002&from=EN. Accessed 9 Dec 2019.

European Parliament and Council. (2018c). Regulation (EU) 2018/842 of the European Parliament and of the Council of 30 May 2018 on binding annual greenhouse gas emission reductions by Member States from 2021 to 2030 contributing to climate action to meet commitments under the Paris Agreement and amending Regulation (EU) No 525/2013 (Text with EEA relevance). https://eur-lex.europa.eu/legal-content/EN/TXT/?uri=celex:32018R0842. Accessed 9 Dec 2019.

Eurostat. (2018a). Supply, transformation and consumption of electricity: Annual data [nrg_105a]. (Last update: 04-06-2018). http://appsso.eurostat.ec.europa.eu/nui/show.do?dataset=nrg_105a&lang=en. Accessed 30 Oct 2018. (This link does not exist anymore.)

Eurostat. (2018b). Supply, transformation and consumption of heat: Annual data [nrg_106a]. (Last update: 04-06-2018). http://appsso.eurostat.ec.europa.eu/nui/show.do?dataset=nrg_106a&lang=en. Accessed 30 Oct 2018. (This link does not exist anymore.)

Eurostat. (2020a). Complete energy balances [nrg_bal_c]. (Last update: 13-01-2020). https://appsso.eurostat.ec.europa.eu/nui/show.do?dataset=nrg_bal_c&lang=en. Accessed 5 Feb 2020.

Eurostat. (2020b). Gross capital formation by industry [NACE A*64]. (Last update: 31-01-2020). https://ec.europa.eu/eurostat/data/database. Accessed 5 Feb 2020.

Eurostat. (2020c). Supply, transformation and consumption of electricity [nrg_cb_e]. (Last update: 31-01-2020). https://appsso.eurostat.ec.europa.eu/nui/show.do?dataset=nrg_cb_e&lang=en. Accessed 5 Feb 2020.

Filippov, G. (2018, 31 July). A hibrid ellenforradalom kora [The age of the hybrid counterrevolution]. *24.hu*. https://24.hu/belfold/2018/07/31/filippov-gabor-a-hibrid-ellenforradalom-kora/. Accessed 28 Feb 2020.

Government Decree 1160/2015 (III. 20.). http://www.kozlonyok.hu/nkonline/MKPDF/hiteles/MK15036.pdf. Accessed 20 Dec 2019.

Government Decree 277/2016 (IX. 15.). https://net.jogtar.hu/jogszabaly?docid=A1600277.KOR&timeshift=20160923&txtreferer=00000001.txt. Accessed 31 Mar 2019.

Government Decree 1772/2018 (XII. 21.). https://magyarkozlony.hu/dokumentumok/dd82ad295f630940ab7308cb468a715d71acb540/letoltes. Accessed 20 Dec 2019.

Government Regulation 279/2017 (IX. 22.). https://net.jogtar.hu/jogszabaly?docid=A1700279.KOR. Accessed 31 Mar 2019.

Greenpeace Hungary. (2018, 19 January). A magyarok túlnyomó többsége ellenzi Paks II-t, főként a projekt veszélyessége miatt [The majority of Hungarians oppose Paks II, mainly because of the project's dangers]. https://www.greenpeace.org/hungary/sajtokozlemeny/2317/a-magyarok-tulnyomo-tobbsege-ellenzi-paks-ii-t-fokent-a-projekt-veszelyessege-miatt/. Accessed 10 Feb 2020.

Haffner, T. (2018). A megújuló energia termelés támogatásának intézményi változásai – a Megújuló Energia Támogatási Rendszer bevezetése [Institutional changes in support of renewable energy production: Introduction of renewable energy support scheme]. *Közép-Európai Közlemények, 11*(2), 17–29. http://vikek.eu/wp-content/uploads/2018/05/KEKNo412018.2.sz%C3%A1m.pdf#page=17. Accessed 19 Nov 2018.

Hargitai, M. (2018, 23 July). Hatástalan a propaganda: nem akarjuk Paks 2-t [Ineffective propaganda: We do not want Paks 2]. *Népszava*. https://nepszava.hu/3002452_hatastalan-a-propaganda-nem-akarjuk-paks-2-t. Accessed 15 Feb 2020.

Hoffman, G. W., & Dienes, L. (1985). *The European energy challenge: East and west*. Durham: Duke University Press. https://trove.nla.gov.au/version/21773416. Accessed 27 Jun 2019.

Horváth, M. T. (2016). A fáraó varázsol. A rezsicsökkentés beágyazottsága [The magic of the pharaoh: The embeddedness of the utility price reductions]. *Politikatudományi Szemle, 25*(3), 135–146. http://real-j.mtak.hu/6520/26/Nyomdai%20Poltud_Szemle_2016-03%20bel%C3%ADv.pdf. Accessed 10 Feb 2020.

Hvg.hu. (2017, 3 April). Energia: zöldebbek lettünk, de ez nem sok jót jelent [Energy: We have become greener, but this does not mean much good]. https://hvg.hu/gazdasag/20170403_Energia_zoldebbek_lettunk_de_ez_nem_sok_jot_jelent. Accessed 11 Feb 2020.

ITM. (2019). Az innovációért és technológiáért felelős miniszter 4/2019. (II. 28.) ITM utasítása az Innovációs és Technológiai Minisztérium Szervezeti és Működési Szabályzatáról [The Ministry of Innovation and Technology's decree on its organisational and operational rules]. https://www.kormany.hu/download/8/02/91000/Innov%C3%A1ci%C3%B3s%20%C3%A9s%20Technol%C3%B3giai%20Miniszt%C3%A9rium%20Szervezeti%20%C3%A9s%20M%C5%B1k%C3%B6d%C3%A9si%20Szab%C3%A1lyzata.pdf. Accessed 2 Mar 2020.

ITM. (2020a). *Magyarország Nemzeti Energia- és Klímaterve – 2–3. melléklet [Hungary's National Energy and Climate Plan – Annexes 2–3]*. Budapest: ITM. https://www.kormany.hu/hu/dok?source=11&type=402#!DocumentBrowse. Accessed 2 Feb 2020.

ITM. (2020b). *Magyarország Nemzeti Energia- és Klímaterve – 4. melléklet [Hungary's National Energy and climate plan – Annex 4]*. Budapest: ITM. https://www.kormany.hu/hu/dok?source=11&type=402#!DocumentBrowse. Accessed 2 Feb 2020.

ITM. (2020c). *Magyarország Nemzeti Energia- és Klímaterve [Hungary's National Energy and Climate Plan]*. Budapest: ITM. https://www.kormany.hu/hu/dok?source=11&type=402#!DocumentBrowse. Accessed 2 Feb 2020.

ITM (Ministry for Innovation and Technology). (2018). *National Energy and climate plan of Hungary (draft)*. Budapest: Ministry for Innovation and Technology (ITM). https://ec.europa.eu/energy/sites/ener/files/documents/ec_courtesy_translation_hu_necp.pdf. Accessed 25 May 2019.

Jávor, B. (2020, 15 January). Jávor Benedek: Új magyar klímapolitika – A fordulat éve? [Jávor Benedek: New Hungarian climate politics, the year of the turn?]. *Mérce*. https://merce.hu/2020/01/15/javor-benedek-uj-magyar-klimapolitika-a-fordulat-eve/. Accessed 10 Feb 2020.

KBM. (2008). A magyar bányászati termelés története [The history of Hungary's mining]. Központi Bányászati Múzeum (KBM). http://www.kbm.hu/hu/node/6. Accessed 10 Feb 2020.

Kerényi, S., & Szabó, M. (2006). Transnational influences on patterns of mobilisation within environmental movements in Hungary. *Environmental Politics, 15*(5), 803–820. https://doi.org/10.1080/09644010600937249.

KKM. (2019). A külgazdasági és külügyminiszter 4/2019 (III. 13.) KKM utasítása a Külgazdasági és Külügyminisztérium Szervezeti és Működési Szabályzatáról [The Ministry of Foreign Affairs and Trade's directive on its organisational and operational rules]. https://www.kormany.hu/download/d/64/91000/A%20K%C3%BClgazdas%C3%A1gi%20%C3%A9s%20K%C3%BCl%C3%BCgyminiszt%C3%A9rium%20SZMSZ-e.pdf. Accessed 2 Mar 2020.

Kulcsár, B. (2019). Kötelező átvételi rendszerben benyújtott naperőmű létesítési igények, megvalósulásának hatása a magyarországi településállomány villamosenergia ellátására [The impact of realisation of solar power plant installation requests in Mandatory Purchase (KÁT) system on the electricity supply of Hungarian settlements]. *International Journal of Engineering and Management Sciences (IJEMS), 4*(2), 54–60. https://doi.org/10.21791/IJEMS.2019.2.6.

KWK-Index. (n.d.). Quarterly prices according to CHP law. European Energy Exchange. https://www.eex.com/en/market-data/power/power-indices/kwk-index. Accessed 16 Jan 2020.

Lazard. (2018). Levelized cost of energy and levelized cost of storage 2018. *Insights*, 8 November. https://www.lazard.com/perspective/levelized-cost-of-energy-and-levelized-cost-of-storage-2018/. Accessed 13 Sept 2019.

Magyar, B. (Ed.) (2016). *Post-communist mafia state: The case of Hungary*. Budapest: CEU Press.

Magyari, P. (2018, 14 March). A fideszesek nagyon megszerették Putyint és Oroszországot [Fidesz supporters have really come to love Putin and Russia]. 444. https://444.hu/2018/03/14/a-fideszesek-nagyon-megszerettek-putyint-es-oroszorszagot. Accessed 15 Feb 2020.

Maltby, T. (2013). European Union energy policy integration: A case of European Commission policy entrepreneurship and increasing supranationalism. *Energy Policy, 55*, 435–444. https://doi.org/10.1016/j.enpol.2012.12.031.

Marczisovszky, M. (2020, 19 February). Palkovics: 2025-től földgáz alapú lesz a Mátrai Erőmű [Palkovics: The Mátra Power Plant will be natural gas-based beginning in 2025]. Index.hu. https://index.hu/gazdasag/2020/02/19/matrai_eromu_palkovics_bejelentette_foldgaz_alapu/. Accessed 19 Feb 2020.

MAVIR. (2018). *A magyar villamosenergia-rendszer közép- és hosszú távú forrásoldali kapacitásfejlesztése [The Hungarian electricity system's mid- and long-term supply side capacity expansions]*. Budapest: MAVIR. https://www.mavir.hu/documents/10258/15461/Forr%C3%A1selemz%C3%A9s_2018_IG.pdf/fc043982-a8ea-e49f-6061-418b254a6391. Accessed 11 Feb 2020.

MAVIR. (2019). *Data of the Hungarian electricity system, 2018*. Budapest: MAVIR. http://mavir.hu/documents/10258/45985073/MAVIR_VER_2018.pdf/292fd722-ec62-2826-6e8d-1bcd6c86c49c. Accessed 11 Feb 2020.

MEHI. (2019, 7 February). 2017-ben immár harmadik éve nőtt az EU energiafogyasztása [EU energy consumption increases in 2017 for the third year]. https://mehi.hu/hir/2017-ben-immar-harmadik-eve-nott-az-eu-energiafogyasztasa. Accessed 7 July 2019.

MEKH (Hungarian Energy and Public Utility Regulatory Authority). (2019a, 3 October). 1,1 GW összteljesítményt értek el a napelemek 2019 közepére [Solar PVs have reached 1.1 GW total generation by mid-2019]. http://www.mekh.hu/1-1-gw-osszteljesitmenyt-ertek-el-a-napelemek-2019-kozepere. Accessed 11 Feb 2020.

MEKH. (2019b). Összefoglaló a nem engedélyköteles – ezen belül a háztartási méretű – kiserőművek adatairól (2008–2017) [A summary about small power plants that do not have to be permitted – including household sized installations]. http://www.mekh.hu/download/3/28/60000/nem_engedelykoteles_es_hmke_beszamolo_2008_2017.xlsx. Accessed 10 Jan 2020.

MEKH. (2020a). Annual data on gross electricity production, 2014–2018. (Date of the last update: in January 31, 2020). http://www.mekh.hu/download/4/c2/c0000/4_2_gross_electricity_production_2014_2018.xlsx. Accessed 22 Feb 2020.

MEKH. (2020b). Annual data on heat production, 2014–2018. (Date of the last update: in January 31, 2020). http://www.mekh.hu/download/5/c2/c0000/5_1_thermal_energy_production_2014_2018.xlsx. Accessed 22 Feb 2020.

MEKH. (2020c). Annual natural gas balance 2014–2018. (Date of the last update: in January 31, 2020). http://www.mekh.hu/download/3/c2/c0000/3_2_annual_natural_gas_balance_2014_2018.xlsx. Accessed 22 Feb 2020.

MEKH. (2020d). Annual supply of crude oil, other primary oil and secondary petroleum products 2014–2018. (Date of the last update: in January 31, 2020). http://www.mekh.hu/download/1/80/c0000/2_2_annual_supply_of_petroleum_and_petroleum_products_annual_2018.xlsx. Accessed 22 Feb 2020.

MEKH. (2020e). Final energy consumption of households, 2015–2018. (Date of the last update: in January 31, 2020). http://www.mekh.hu/download/9/c2/c0000/8_1_annual_energy_consumption_of_households.xlsx. Accessed 22 Feb 2020.

MEKH. (2020f). National detailed energy balance – Eurostat format – (annual) 2014–2018. (Date of the last update: in January 31, 2020). http://www.mekh.hu/download/e/b2/c0000/7_4_orszagos_eves_%20Eurostat_%20tipusu_%20reszletes_%20energiamerleg_2014_2018.xlsx. Accessed 22 Feb 2020.

MEKH. (2020g). Production and consumption of primary renewable energy sources, 2014–2018. (Date of the last update: in January 31, 2020). http://www.mekh.hu/download/7/c2/c0000/6_2_primary_renewable_en_sources_2014_2018.xlsx. Accessed 22 Feb 2020.

MEKH. (2020h). Share of renewable sources in gross final energy consumption, 2005–2018. (Date of the last update: in January 31, 2020). http://www.mekh.hu/download/6/c2/c0000/6_1_share_of_renewable_en_sources_2005_2018.xlsx. Accessed 22 Feb 2020.

Mert.hu. (n.d.). Mátrai Erőmű. Köszöntő [Mátra Power Plant: Greetings]. http://www.mert.hu/hu/elnoki-koszonto. Accessed 9 Nov 2018.

Mihályi, P. (2018). *A privatizált vagyon visszaállamosítása [The re-nationalisation of privatized wealth]*. Manuscript. Budapest: MTA KRTK. https://www.mtakti.hu/wp-content/uploads/2018/04/10_Visszaallamositas_KTRK_eloadashoz.pdf. Accessed 15 Feb 2020.

Mocsáry, J. (2001). Visszapillantás a privatizációra [Taking a look back on privatisation]. *Eszmélet, 49.* http://www.eszmelet.hu/mocsary_jozsef-visszapillantas-a-privatizaciora/. Accessed 27 Mar 2020.

Müller, J-W. (2014). Putinism, Orbanism... But is there an "ism"? IWM. https://www.iwm.at/transit-online/putinism-orbanism-ism/. Accessed 28 Feb 2020.

Napi.hu. (2016, 7 July). Az EU legszennyezőbb szénerőművei között a Mátrai Erőmű [Mátra Power Plant is one of the most polluting coal power plants in the EU]. https://www.napi.hu/magyar_vallalatok/az_eu_legszennyezobb_szeneromuvei_kozott_a_matrai_eromu.617386.html. Accessed 4 May 2017.

NFM. (2015). *Hungary's National Energy Efficiency Action Plan until 2020*. Budapest: NFM. https://ec.europa.eu/energy/sites/ener/files/documents/hungaryActionPlan2014_en.pdf. Accessed 1 June 2019.

NFM (Ministry of National Development). (2010). *National renewable energy action plan 2010–2020*. Budapest: NFM. http://2010-2014.kormany.hu/download/6/b9/30000/RENEWABLE%20ENERGY_REPUBLIC%20OF%20HUNGARY%20NATIONAL%20RENEWABLE%20ENERGY%20ACTION%20PLAN%202010_2020.pdf. Accessed 1 June 2019.

Orbán, V. (2014). *A munkaalapú állam korszaka következik [The age of a work-based system is next]*. Tusnádfürdő: Speech at the XXV. Bálványosi Summer University and Student Camp. https://www.kormany.hu/a-miniszterelnok/beszedek-publikaciok-interjuk/a-munkaalapu-allam-korszaka-kovetkezik. Accessed 28 Feb 2020.

Pálfy, M. (2017). A napenergia fotovillamos hasznosítása [Solar power's PV utilisation]. *Magyar Tudomány, 178*(5), 532–539. http://epa.oszk.hu/00600/00691/00164/pdf/EPA00691_mtud_2017_05_532-539.pdf. Accessed 11 Feb 2020.

Pap, I. S. (2017, 3 November). A Kádár-rendszerről álmodoznak a magyarok [Hungarians reminisce of the Kádár system]. *Mérce*. https://merce.hu/2017/11/03/a-kadar-rendszerrol-almodoznak-a-magyarok/. Accessed 2 Mar 2020.

Sandbag. (n.d.). EUA price. https://sandbag.org.uk/carbon-price-viewer/. Accessed 7 Jan 2020.

Sattich, T. (2018). The international reverberations of Germany's Energiewende: Geoeconomics in the EU's geo-energy space. In D. Scholten (Ed.), *The geopolitics of renewables* (pp. 163–185). New York: Springer.

Scheiring, G. (2018). *Lessons from the political economy of authoritarian capitalism in Hungary*. Challenging Authoritarianism Series, no. 1. Amsterdam: Transnational Institute. https://www.tni.org/files/publication-downloads/tni-authoritarian-capitalism-in-hungary.pdf. Accessed 28 Feb 2020.

Stern, J. (2017). *The future of gas in decarbonising European energy markets: The need for a new approach*. OIES paper, NG 116. Oxford: Oxford Institute for Energy Studies. https://www.oxfordenergy.org/wpcms/wp-content/uploads/2017/01/The-Future-of-Gas-in-Decarbonising-European-Energy-Markets-the-need-for-a-new-approach-NG-116.pdf. Accessed 15 May 2018.

Szabo, J., & Deak, A. (2020). The CEE energy transition: Recurring 50 year old dynamics? In M. Matúš & V. Oravcová (Eds.), *From economic to energy transition – Three decades of transitions in Central and Eastern Europe*. London: Palgrave Macmillan.

Szabo, J., & Fabok, M. (2020). Infrastructures and state-building: Comparing the energy politics of the European Commission with the governments of Hungary and Poland. *Energy Policy, 138*, 111253. https://doi.org/10.1016/j.enpol.2020.111253.

Szvák, G. (Ed.) (2016). *A magyarok orosz-képe (2006–2016) [Hungarians' image of Russians (2006–2016)]*. Budapest: Russica Pannonica. https://www.russianstudies.hu/docs/Poszt.szovjet.f%C3%BCzetek.22..pdf Accessed 2 Mar 2020.

TNM Regulation 7/2006 (V. 24.). https://net.jogtar.hu/jogszabaly?docid=a0600007.tnm. Accessed 20 Dec 2019.

Ürge-Vorsatz, D., Miladinova, G., & Paizs, L. (2006). Energy in transition: From the iron curtain to the European Union. *Energy Policy, 34*(15), 2279–2297. https://doi.org/10.1016/j.enpol.2005.03.007.

VGF & HKL. (2013). A magyar olaj és földgáz története VI [The history of Hungary's oil and natural gas]. *Víz, Gáz, Fűtéstechnika és Hűtő, Klíma, Légtechnika szaklap, 14*(9). https://www.vgfszaklap.hu/lapszamok/2013/szeptember/3000-a-magyar-olaj-es-foldgaz-tortenete-vi. Accessed 10 Feb 2020.

Weiner, C. (2017). *Managing energy supply security and gas diversification in Hungary: Putting theory into practice*. IWE working papers, no. 238. Budapest: Institute of World Economics, MTA KRTK. http://real.mtak.hu/73435/1/WP_238_Weiner.pdf. Accessed 10 Feb 2020.

Weiner, C. (2019). *Revisiting the management of stationary fuel supply security and gas diversification in Hungary*. IWE working papers, no. 254. Budapest: Institute of World Economics, MTA KRTK. http://real.mtak.hu/94539/1/WP254_Weiner_Fuel_supply_security.pdf. Accessed 1 Oct 2019.

Wilkin, P. (2016). *Hungary's crisis of democracy: The road to serfdom*. Lanham/Maryland: Lexington Books.

Energy Governance in Ireland

31

Diarmuid Torney

Contents

Introduction	770
General Conditions of Energy Governance in Ireland	771
Ireland's Economy and Energy System	771
Ireland's Overall Approach to Energy Policy	775
Institutions of Energy Governance	776
Coordination, Instruments, and Issues of the Irish Energy Transition	779
Electricity Generation	780
Heating	781
Transport	782
Outcomes, Challenges, and Prospects of Energy Governance in Ireland	785
Cross-References	786
References	787

Abstract

Ireland is committed to significant decarbonization of the energy system by mid-century, including an aggregate reduction in CO_2 emissions from electricity generation, the built environment, and transport of at least 80% by 2050 relative to 1990 levels. There has been limited consideration to date of the governance of Ireland's energy transition in the literature. This chapter attempts to fill this gap. It introduces the characteristics of Ireland's economy and energy system. Ireland's economy has been characterized by late industrialization, a very pronounced pattern of boom and bust over the past two decades, relative lack of heavy industry, low population density, and dispersed spatial development. In terms of energy, Ireland is heavily dependent on imported fossil fuels, though renewables have grown significantly as a share of electricity generation in the past decade.

D. Torney (✉)
School of Law and Government, Dublin City University, Dublin, Ireland
e-mail: diarmuid.torney@dcu.ie

© Springer Nature Switzerland AG 2022
M. Knodt, J. Kemmerzell (eds.), *Handbook of Energy Governance in Europe*,
https://doi.org/10.1007/978-3-030-43250-8_14

The chapter maps Ireland's governance institutions as they pertain to the energy system, draws attention to the fragmented governance landscape, and outlines Ireland's principal policy approaches. In the electricity generation sector, the principal type policy instrument that has been used to date is incentive-based instruments. In the heating and transport sectors, by contrast, policy has been more varied, comprising a mix of incentive-based instruments, regulatory policy-making, and soft governance. The chapter concludes with prospects for the future, highlighting significant challenges facing Ireland's future energy transition pathway.

Keywords

Ireland · Energy governance · Electricity generation · Heat · Transport · Decarbonization

Introduction

Ireland is committed to significant decarbonization of the energy system by mid-century. In 2014, the government agreed a National Policy Position on Climate Action and Low Carbon Development that commits to a long-term vision of low-carbon transition based on an aggregate reduction in CO_2 emissions across the electricity generation, built environment, and transport sectors of at least 80% by 2050 relative to 1990 levels (Government of Ireland 2014). A 2015 Energy White Paper committed to transforming Ireland's energy sector into a clean, low-carbon system by 2050, stating that "eventually, we will have to generate 100% of all our energy needs – not just electricity – from clean sources" (DCENR 2015).

Appropriate policies and governance institutions are key to facilitating the sustainable transition of energy systems. Research on the institutional underpinnings of sustainable energy transitions emphasizes in particular how institutions can often constrain transitions to sustainability. Research on "carbon lock-in," for example, emphasizes how "techno-institutional complexes" create inter-locking path dependencies in both technologies and governance systems that are resistant to change (Unruh 2000, 2002). Other perspectives, meanwhile, emphasize the ability of government to steer economy and society towards sustainability. For example, the literature on transition management suggests that governments can do so by providing a long-term vision for the direction of transition. However, this approach underestimates the need for political legitimacy for transition and the role of politics (Andrews-Speed 2016, p. 218). It also downplays the power of incumbent interests and veto players (Kuzemko et al. 2016). Furthermore, it paints a picture of energy as a technical system that is detached from society. By contrast, the idea of a "socio-technical regime" captures the notion that technology and society are not separate spheres of activity but rather are highly interdependent (Andrews-Speed 2016, p. 218).

The literature on governance of energy in Ireland has been limited. Existing research has examined the feasibility and potential cost of low carbon transition pathways to 2050 in Ireland (e.g., Chiodi et al. 2013; Ó Gallachóir et al. 2012). However, this analysis looked at the technical feasibility of transition and did not consider the policies and institutions that would be necessary to translate these transition pathways into reality. An exception to this general trend was a report by the National Economic and Social Council, *Ireland and the Climate Change Challenge*, which identified the importance of an effective enabling institutional and policy framework to drive and measure progress on addressing climate change challenges at a national level (NESC 2012). As the First Report of Ireland's Climate Change Advisory Council noted, transitioning to a carbon neutral economy and society represents a more difficult task than any other area of public policy (CCAC 2017, p. i).

This chapter attempts to fill a gap in the literature by developing our understanding of the energy governance system in Ireland. It introduces the characteristics of Ireland's economy and energy system. Key features of Ireland's economy include late industrialization, a pattern of boom and bust over the past two decades, relative lack of heavy industry, low population density, and dispersed spatial development. In terms of the energy system, the chapter emphasizes Ireland's heavy dependence on fossil fuels in the energy mix. This, combined with few indigenous fuel sources, means that Ireland is very heavily dependent on imported fossil fuels, though renewables have grown significantly as a share of electricity generation in the past decade.

The chapter proceeds to map Ireland's governance institutions as they pertain to the energy system, draws attention to a fragmented governance landscape, and outlines Ireland's principal policy approaches. In the electricity generation sector, the principal type policy instrument that has been used to date is incentive-based instruments. In the heating and transport sectors, by contrast, policy has been more varied, comprising a mix of incentive-based instruments, regulatory policy-making, and soft governance. The chapter concludes by outlining prospects for the future, highlighting significant challenges facing Ireland's future energy transition pathway.

General Conditions of Energy Governance in Ireland

Ireland's Economy and Energy System

Ireland's economic development occurred relatively late by comparative European standards. A relatively poor economy for much of the period since independence in the 1920s, Ireland caught up with European average standards of living only in the 1990s (Barry et al. 1999). After experiencing rapid economic growth through much of the 1990s and 2000s, Ireland was hit by profound economic crisis in the late 2000s driven by the bursting of a property bubble and subsequent severe banking crisis. From 2007 to 2009, Irish GNP fell by over 11%, and in November 2010, the government was forced into requesting a bailout of EUR 85 billion from the

European Union (EU) and the International Monetary Fund. Although exacerbated by the global financial crisis, the Irish banking and economic crisis was predominantly a home-grown phenomenon, caused by inadequate risk management practices in Irish banks and regulatory failure (O'Sullivan and Kennedy 2010). Just as unexpected as the severity of the economic crash has been the speed and strength of the recovery since the early 2010s, with Ireland registering the fastest economic growth rate in the EU for several years running in the mid-2010s.

The structure of Ireland's economy is dominated by services, which accounted for nearly 60% of gross value added in 2016. Industry accounted for just under 40%, while the primary sector accounted for just 1% of gross value added (OECD 2018). This is striking for a country the economy of which was historically dominated by agriculture. However, the broader agri-food sector accounted for 7% of gross value added in 2016 (Teagasc 2018). Because of its late industrialization, Ireland does not have the same legacy of heavy industry that characterizes many other industrialized countries. Ireland's industrial production is concentrated in a small number of sectors, the largest of these being the pharmaceutical industry. In fact, pharmaceutical products accounted for 43.7% of total net selling value in 2016. Ireland is a significant outlier in EU terms in this respect, with pharmaceutical products accounting for just 3.8% in the EU28. The next largest sectors are: food (16.1%); chemical products (12%); and computer, electronic, optical, and electrical equipment (11%) (CSO 2017).

Ireland has a comparatively low population density and a dispersed pattern of spatial development by comparison with other industrialized countries. Ireland's population density was 69.3 persons per square kilometre, compared with an EU28 average of 117.5 persons per square kilometre (Eurostat 2018b). This includes significant development of "one-off housing" – houses built in rural areas in recent decades that are not in close proximity to existing houses. This characteristic has reduced the viability of public transport and increased car dependency. A more dispersed rural population has perhaps also led to greater objections to wind farm developments, which became increasingly prevalent in the 2010s (NESC 2014). Moreover, a very significant construction boom in the 2000s combined with lax enforcement of building regulations to leave a legacy of relatively poor quality housing stock (Baker 2011).

Gross energy consumption in Ireland has tracked economic growth trends closely. Figure 1 illustrates the trend in overall gross energy consumption as well as by fuel between 1990 and 2016. The total trend can be seen to correspond very closely with economic growth. Over this period, gross energy consumption increased by 51.8%. As discussed above, Ireland experienced strong economic growth in the 1990s and 2000s, giving rise to a significant increase in gross energy consumption. The economic crash at the end of the 2000s resulted in a sharp decline in gross energy consumption, but the recovery since the early 2010s has led to a return to strong growth in energy consumption.

In terms of fuel composition, Fig. 1 illustrates that fossil fuels remain the predominant fuel source in Ireland's energy mix. Despite the growth of renewable sources, fossil fuels still accounted for 90.2% of gross energy consumption in 2017. Of this, oil was by far the largest individual fuel source, at 48.0%, with natural gas

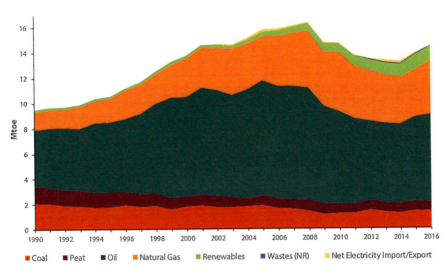

Fig. 1 Gross energy consumption, 1990–2016. (Source: SEAI 2017, p. 12)

accounting for 29.8%, coal 7.6%, and peat 4.8% (SEAI 2018a, p. 14). Renewables accounted for 9.3% of gross energy consumption, of which nearly half (4.4%) consisted of wind. Comparing 2017 with 1990 figures, fossil fuels declined as a share of total energy use from 98.2% to 90.2%. Within this category, coal declined significantly in percentage terms from 22% to 7.6%, while natural gas nearly doubled as a share from 15.2% to 29.8%. Total renewables increased very significantly as a share from 1.8% to 9.3% (SEAI 2016a, p. 12; 2018, p. 14).

Breaking Ireland's gross energy consumption down by sector, in 2017 transport represented 35% of gross energy consumption. Electricity accounted for 33%. Heat meanwhile accounted for 32%. This contrasts markedly with the breakdown in 1990, when transport accounted for 21% while thermal uses accounted for 46% (SEAI 2016a, p. 14; 2018a, pp. 16–17).

The fuel mix for electricity generation has also changed significantly since 1990. Figure 2 illustrates relevant trends. It can be seen that oil declined significantly since 1990, while coal declined relatively marginally. Natural gas increased significantly, both displacing oil and coal but also accounting for much of the increase in total electricity generation over this period. In 2017, fossil fuels accounted for 80.4% of the fuel mix for electricity generation, composed of gas at 51.0%, coal at 18.3%, peat at 10.3%, and oil at 0.8%. Renewables consisted of 15.6%, of which 11% was wind and 1.2% was hydro (SEAI 2018a, p. 23). Under the Electricity Act 1999, there is a legal prohibition on the domestic generation of electricity from nuclear fission, though in practice nuclear-generated electricity is imported through the electricity interconnectors between the all island Single Electricity Market and Great Britain. 44.9% of electricity generation inputs are accounted for by transformation losses. In terms of gross electricity consumption, in 2017 natural gas accounted for 51.1% of

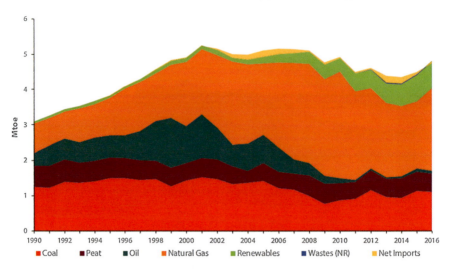

Fig. 2 Primary fuel mix for electricity generation, 1990–2016. (Source: SEAI 2017, p. 25)

gross consumption while renewable sources accounted for 30.1% of consumption (normalized) (SEAI 2018a, p. 23).

Because of a lack of indigenous supplies, Ireland is heavily dependent on imported fossil fuels. Ireland's energy import dependency increased significantly over the course of the 1990s as a result of increasing energy consumption, a decline in peat use, and a decline in production from the Kinsale Head gas field off the south coast, which was discovered in 1973 and is expected to be exhausted completely by 2021. Import dependency reached a peak of 90% in 2006 and remained between 85% and 90% from then until 2015. It fell to 69% in 2016 and declined further to 66% in 2017, principally as a result of the coming on stream of production from the Corrib gas field (SEAI 2018a, p. 44). However, from 2017 to 2018 onwards, production from the Corrib gas field is expected to decline (DCCAE 2018c).

All of Ireland's imported natural gas comes from the UK. This raises challenges for two reasons. First, the UK has been net importer of natural gas since 2011. Second, Brexit casts uncertainty over the future of gas flows from the UK to Ireland. In July 2017, the Port of Cork (in southwest Ireland) signed a memorandum of understanding with Texas-based LNG company NextDecade to "advance a joint development opportunity in Ireland for a new floating storage and regasification unit and associated LNG-import terminal infrastructure" (Hamilton 2017). As of 2018, there are no LNG import terminals in Ireland. Ireland has a relatively abundant indigenous supply of peat. This is used for electricity generation and domestic heating. Peat-fired electricity generation supported has been provided through a Public Service Obligation (PSO) for three peat-fired stations in the midlands. Support for one of these, the Edenderry power station, ended in 2015. This plant is now in receipt of PSO support for biomass co-firing with peat (see below). Support for the two remaining power stations, West Offaly and Lough Ree, will expire at the end of 2019. A state-owned company, Bord na Móna, is responsible for industrial scale harvesting of peat for both electricity generation and sale to residential customers. Bord na Móna has committed to ending peat harvesting for power generation by 2030 and, in October 2018, it announced it would bring this date forward to 2028 (DCCAE 2018a).

Ireland's Overall Approach to Energy Policy

Ireland's policy approach to energy has been framed for the past decade by the three pillars of security, sustainability, and competitiveness. The government's Energy Policy Framework 2007–2020, entitled "Delivering a Sustainable Energy Future for Ireland," framed Ireland's response to energy challenges in terms of broader European and global trends and approaches, noting a "global and European context which has put energy security and climate change among the most urgent international challenges" (DCMNR 2007, p. 5).

The next government white paper on energy, published 8 years later in 2015, took a markedly different approach. It framed the discourse around energy policy more explicitly in terms of sustainability and decarbonization. Entitled "Ireland's Transition to a Low Carbon Energy Future, 2015–2030," it put climate change and the transition to a decarbonized energy system much more front and center, with the themes of energy security and energy costs not appearing until Chaps. 6 and 8 respectively (DCENR 2015). Although sustainability and decarbonization have grown in prominence in energy policy discourse in Ireland over recent years, media attention to climate change for a long time remained low in Ireland. Extreme weather events such as the winter 2013–2014 storms and flooding have raised risk perceptions, and an upswing in public concern to climate change was witnessed in 2018 and 2019, driven by a variety of factors including the IPCC Special Report on Global Warming of 1.5°C and Greta Thunberg (Cullinane and Watson 2014; Fox and Rau 2016; Robbins 2019).

Another notable evolution between the 2007 and 2015 government energy white papers was the prominence given in the latter to the concept of the "energy citizen" (DCENR 2015). The 2015 Energy White Paper sought to give greater prominence to the role of citizens and participation, at least in part in response to a perception that concerns of local communities had not adequately been taken into account in the siting of large scale wind farms and other energy infrastructure such as electricity pylons. Of late, the distributional impact of energy policy, including proposals for a "just transition" away from fossil fuels, has grown in prominence in energy policy debates (FitzGerald and Valeri 2014; Curtin 2017).

Public engagement on the energy transition has also been evident in other policy developments. In autumn 2017, the Citizens' Assembly – a deliberative forum established by and reporting to parliament consisting of 99 members of the public selected to be representative of the wider population – was tasked with considering the question of "How the state can make Ireland a leader in tackling climate change." Over two weekends in September and November 2017, the assembly received testimony from a variety of experts and were given time to deliberate on the evidence they had received. At the end of the two weekends, the citizens were asked to vote on 13 questions relating to the role that Ireland should play in responding to climate change. The results were striking, with strong support (80% or higher in all cases) for all proposed actions, including paying higher taxes on carbon intensive activities (Citizens' Assembly 2018). On foot of these recommendations, a special parliamentary committee was established in summer 2018 to consider how to take the recommendations forward. It published a landmark report in March 2019 (Houses of the Oireachtas 2019), which in turn shaped to a significant degree an all-of-government Climate Action Plan published in June 2019 (DCCAE 2019).

Separately, the Minister for Communications, Climate Action, and Environment established a "National Dialogue on Climate Action" in 2017, the aim of which was "to ensure an inclusive process of engagement and consensus building across society towards enabling the transformation to a low carbon and climate-resilient future" (DCCAE 2017b). This subsumed the National Energy Forum that was envisaged under the 2015 Energy White Paper. The National Dialogue on Climate Action held its first public event in the midlands town of Athlone in June 2018.

Institutions of Energy Governance

The Irish political and administrative system is heavily centralized, with very limited powers devolved to subnational level. There has also been a progressive "agencification" of the Irish state over recent decades. Comparative research has found that, across sectors, regulatory agencies overall in Ireland enjoy the highest level of formal independence across 17 West European countries (Gilardi 2005). The array of institutions responsible for governance of the energy sector – and thus charged with decarbonizing electricity generation – includes aspects of the regulatory state, the developmental state, and the adjudicatory state. MacCarthaigh (2011) argues that agencies have been created in Ireland in a relatively ad hoc fashion, with a wide variety of accountability and reporting relationships with central government.

The creation of the Irish regulatory state – through delegation to arm's length regulators – has been a relatively recent development in comparison with other countries, with many regulatory agencies created in a short space of time (Hardiman and Scott 2010, p. 182; MacCarthaigh 2011). Where powers are delegated to independent regulators, this effectively introduces new veto players over which central government has relatively little control (Lockwood et al. 2017). However, other research suggests that, contrary to expectations of unaccountable regulators acting contrary to the wishes of central government, oftentimes the relationship between central government and regulatory agencies is characterized by "principal drift," where agencies in fact seek greater rather than less guidance from their line ministries (Schillemans and Busuioc 2014).

The main central government ministry responsible for energy policy is the Department of Communications, Climate Action and Environment (DCCAE), which was formed in July 2016 by the transfer of functions relating to climate action and environment from the (then) Department of Environment, Community and

Local Government to the Department of Communications, Energy and Natural Resources. The department has separate divisions for Climate Action & Environment, and Energy. It also has a Natural Resources division, a significant focus of which is domestic hydrocarbons resources and extraction. The Department is responsible for formulation of policies related to the electricity sector, including renewables support and the PSO. DCCAE is also responsible for the National Dialogue on Climate Action. This subsumed a planned National Energy Forum proposed under the 2015 Energy White Paper, linking to the focus in the White Paper on the energy citizen and citizen engagement (DCENR 2015).

Other energy-related functions are located in other departments, in particular transport policy which is the responsibility of the Department of Transport, and housing and built environment matters which are the responsibility of the Department of Housing, Planning and Local Government. However, DCCAE has overall responsibility for energy transition and climate change mitigation policy, including responsibility under the 2015 Climate Action and Low Carbon Development Act for preparation of the National Mitigation Plan (NMP). It is also the department responsible for the electricity generation sector within that process. The department also participates in cross-government coordination bodies relevant to decarbonization, including the Cabinet Committee on Infrastructure, Environment and Climate Action and its related Senior Officials Group, which are chaired by the Taoiseach (Prime Minister) and Department of the Taoiseach, respectively.

The independent regulator for the energy sector is the Commission for Regulation of Utilities (CRU), previously the Commission for Energy Regulation, which was established under the Electricity Regulation Act 1999 as the independent economic regulator for the electricity sector. Since then, its functions have been expanded significantly to include regulation of the gas sector, safety, regulation of the Single Electricity Market, and regulation of public water and waste water services. Harrington (2016) advocates narrowing and hierarchically ordering its wide-ranging existing set of 17 objectives. Its approach to decarbonization – as well as ensuring security of supply – is to deliver these goals at least cost to consumers.

Ireland and Northern Ireland share a single electricity transmission system and a single, all-island wholesale electricity market called the Single Electricity Market (SEM). CRU is jointly responsible for designing and regulating the SEM along with the Northern Ireland Utility Regulator through the SEM Committee. The design of the SEM was changed considerably to take account of the requirements of the European Network Codes and the Target Model. The new design became operational in October 2018 and is referred to as I-SEM (Integrated–Single Electricity Market).

In regulating the SEM, CRU does not have regard to the carbon content of fossil fuels. It ensures that the full marginal cost of carbon (via the EU ETS) is included in electricity prices, but does not intervene to ensure a particular balance between coal, peat, and gas. CRU does, however, play an active role in relation to promoting integration of renewable energy generation into the electricity system through grid connection policies and priority dispatch for renewable generation. It also seeks to enable higher levels of renewable generation on the system and lower levels of renewables curtailment by providing incentives to conventional generators to be more flexible, stimulating demand-side participation, and efficient use of interconnectors (CER 2014, p. 24). CRU's regulation of the electricity retail prices to domestic consumers ended in 2011, and electricity prices in the retail electricity market are fully deregulated for all consumers.

CRU is responsible for calculating the annual level of the Public Service Obligation, the support mechanism for peat generation, for certain conventional generation constructed for security of supply purposes, and for the development of renewable electricity. However, CRU has no discretion in this role and is mandated solely to calculate the level of the PSO in accordance with government policy. It also has a role in funding research and pilot projects such as electric vehicle (EV) charging infrastructure and use of compressed natural gas in vehicles.

EirGrid is the Transmission System Operator (TSO) and Market Operator for the electricity system in Ireland and is licenced by CRU. With the establishment of the Single Electricity Market in 2007, EirGrid together with SONI, the Market Operator in Northern Ireland, operate the wholesale electricity market in Ireland through the Single Electricity Market Operator (SEMO), a joint venture between EirGrid and SONI. EirGrid is a state-owned company. Since 2009, EirGrid Group, the parent company of EirGrid, also owns SONI. In Ireland, the Electricity Transmission System is operated by EirGrid but owned by Electricity Supply Board (ESB), a 95% state-owned vertically integrated utility. ESB Networks is responsible for maintenance, repairs, and construction on the grid while EirGrid is responsible for future planning and development of the grid. The Electricity Distribution System is owned by ESB and operated by ESB Networks.

In 2008, EirGrid published its Grid25 strategy which was premised on pre-crash projections for growth in electricity demand. It subsequently revised its plans for grid development, against a backdrop of increased opposition from local communities. EirGrid's revised Grid Development Strategy published in 2017 is committed to using new and emerging technologies to enhance the capacity of existing grid infrastructure (EirGrid 2017). EirGrid's DS3 Program, "Delivering a Secure, Sustainable Electricity System," aims to address the challenges associated with managing a grid with increasing levels of non-synchronous renewable electricity, in the context of meeting Ireland's EU 2020 renewable electricity target of 40%.

The Sustainable Energy Authority of Ireland (SEAI) is the national energy authority, with associated statutory functions across energy efficiency, energy technology and innovation, and decarbonization of energy supply including renewables. It is an autonomous agency established under the Sustainable Energy Act 2002. SEAI allocates in excess of EUR 100 million of capital funding annually to support energy efficiency and renewable energy. SEAI has a lead role in compiling and publishing statistics on energy production and consumption as well as future projections related to EU energy targets. It supports research, development, and deployment of sustainable energy technologies including bioenergy and CHP, ocean energy, and EVs. It is also responsible for delivery of large scale public programs. Several of these include significant community engagement, including the Better Energy Communities and Sustainable Energy Communities programs. These focus on both energy efficiency and renewable energy at community level.

Governance of the transport sector is similarly fragmented (Devaney and Torney 2019). The central ministry responsible is the Department of Transport, Tourism and Sport (DTTAS), which has responsibility for all aspects of transport policy, including public and sustainable transport. DTTAS is responsible for the transport sector within the climate change planning process under the Climate Action and Low Carbon Development Act. The National Transport Authority (NTA) is a statutory noncommercial body operating under the aegis of DTTAS. Originally conceived as a transport authority for the greater Dublin area and established under the Dublin Transport Authority Act 2008, it was renamed the National Transport Authority in 2009 under the Public Transport Regulation Act 2009. The NTA has a variety of statutory functions, including procurement of public transport services, developing the public transport network, licensing certain public transport services, and regulating the taxi sector (NTA 2018). Transport Infrastructure Ireland is responsible for providing an integrated approach to the future development and operation of the national roads network and light rail infrastructure throughout Ireland. It was created under the Roads Act 2015 through the merging of the National Roads Authority and the Railway Procurement Agency. The Commission for Railway Regulation was established under the Railway Safety Act 2005. It has responsibility for railway safety on passenger, freight, and industrial railways. All of Ireland's railways and much of Ireland's bus services remain in public ownership.

Coordination, Instruments, and Issues of the Irish Energy Transition

The drivers of Ireland's energy transition have been principally external. EU membership in particular provides a crucial policy context. The EU's 2020 climate and energy package set for Ireland a binding renewable energy target of 16% by 2020. This is broken down into component targets for electricity (40%), heat (12%), and transport (10%) (Government of Ireland 2010). This has been a strong motivator of national policy responses. Nonetheless, despite significant increases in deployment of renewables particularly for electricity generation, Ireland's 2020 renewable energy targets remain challenging. The contribution of renewables to gross final consumption was 10.6% in 2017, compared to the 16% target by 2020 (SEAI 2018a, p. 32).

Although Ireland is heavily dependent on imported fossil fuels, dependence on energy imports has been a less prominent driver of energy policy. As noted above, energy security became less prominent in the 2015 Energy White Paper compared with the previous 2007 Energy White Paper. However, the UK's decision to leave the EU raised the profile once again of energy security, since all of Ireland's imported gas is delivered though pipelines from the UK.

In December 2015, Ireland enacted a climate change law, the Climate Action and Low Carbon Development Act. This was very loosely modelled on the UK Climate Change Act, but was different in key respects – including that it does not contain a 2050 target or shorter term carbon budgets (Torney 2017). The Irish climate law established a planning and reporting framework for climate change policy. Under the climate law, the government is required to publish a National Mitigation Plan (NMP) and a National Adaptation Framework once every 5 years. The Minister is required under the Act to make an "Annual Transition Statement" to both houses of parliament each year. The Act also established an independent Climate Change Advisory Council with a remit to provide advice to Government and to assess progress in achieving national policy goals. The Council has not shied away from critical commentary on the government's response to climate change (CCAC 2016, 2017, 2018).

The first NMP under the climate law was published by the government in July 2017 (DCCAE 2017c). It details a range of existing and planned measures across the electricity generation, built environment, and transport sectors to reduce greenhouse gas emissions. When publishing the Plan, the government described it as a "living document" and acknowledged that it "does not provide a complete roadmap to achieve the 2050 objective, but begins the process of development of medium to long term mitigation choices for the next and future decades" (DCCAE 2017c). In January 2019, the High Court heard a legal challenge to the adequacy of the NMP brought by environmental NGO Friends of the Irish Environment.

The NMP provides an overview of existing and planned policy measures to achieve the national transition objective of "progressively pursuing a low carbon, climate resilient and environmentally sustainable economy by 2050" (DCCAE 2017c, p. 14). In the category of internalizing instruments, Ireland introduced a carbon tax in 2010. It applies to carbon dioxide emissions outside the ETS sector associated with both liquid and solid fossil fuels including petrol and diesel, coal, peat briquettes, heating oil, and gas and is applied at the point of sale. Originally set at €15 per tonne of CO2 for liquid fossil fuels only, it was increased to €20 in 2012. A rate of €10 per tonne on solid fuel, introduced in May 2013, increased to €20 per tonne in 2014. As an EU member state, Ireland is also covered by the EU-ETS, which is the other principal internalizing policy instrument in the energy field.

In February 2018, the government unveiled a new National Planning Framework with a 2040 time horizon as well as a 10-year capital expenditure program, combined under the heading "Project Ireland 2040" (see http://www.gov.ie/en/project-ireland-2040). The capital plan included €22 billion climate change program over the period 2018–2027 as well as a new €500 million Climate Action Fund intended to spur technological innovation.

Electricity Generation

In the electricity generation sector, the principal type policy instrument that has been used to date is incentive-based. The Alternative Energy Requirement (AER) program was introduced in 1996. Six AER competitions were held in the period 1995–2003. Under this scheme, winning bidders were entitled to a 15 year power purchase agreement whereby the ESB bought the electricity output of the winning facility at the bid price. The AER program was superseded by three subsequent incentive-based schemes in the form of feed-in tariffs. The first of these, REFIT 1, opened in 2005 and provided long-term feed-in tariffs to encourage new capacity development of proven technologies and short-term feed-in tariffs to support the development of emerging ocean energy technologies. REFIT 1 closed for new projects at the end of 2009.

In 2012, the REFIT 2 and REFIT 3 schemes were launched. REFIT 2 provided for up to 4,000 MW of renewable generation. The technologies covered are small wind (< 5 MW), large wind (>5 MW), hydroelectricity, and biomass/landfill gas. REFIT 3 was designed to incentivize the addition of 310 MW of renewable electricity capacity to the Irish grid composed of high efficiency combined heat and power (using both anaerobic digestion and the thermochemical conversion of solid biomass), biomass combustion, and biomass co-firing. Both schemes closed for new projects at the end of 2015. These schemes are funded by a charge on electricity consumer bills through the Public Service Obligation (PSO) levy. Section 39 of the Electricity Act 1999 provides the legal basis for the PSO, which has been in existence since 2001.

A high level design paper for a new Renewable Electricity Support Scheme (RESS) was approved by government in July 2018 (DCCAE 2018d). The RESS scheme aims to help deliver Ireland's contribution to the EU RES target of 32% and, through a first auction in 2019, to contribute to meeting Ireland's 2020 RES-E target of 40%. The RESS scheme will operate on the basis of competitive auctions, which will be technology neutral rather than technology specific. It places an emphasis on community participation through financial support for community-led projects, mandatory community benefit fund and register, mandatory investment opportunities for communities, and a separate community category in RESS auctions.

As well as supporting deployment of renewable energy sources, government has also committed to phase out of coal and peat in electricity generation. The 900 MW Moneypoint coal-fired power plant is the only coal fired power plant in the Republic of Ireland (though not the only one operating within the all-island electricity market). In 2016, government pledged that "the National Dialogue on Climate Change will identify, as soon as possible, the most suitable replacement low-carbon generation technology" (Government of Ireland 2016, p. 125). The 2017 NMP committed to undertaking "a study to identify the most suitable replacement low carbon technology for the Moneypoint generation plant" (DCCAE 2017c). With respect to peat, as discussed above Bord na Móna has committed to ceasing peat harvesting for power generation by 2030, which was subsequently brought forward to 2028.

Heating

Under Ireland's energy and climate planning process, heat is subsumed within the "built environment" category. In the built environment sector, Irish energy policy has been more varied, comprising a mix of different types of policy instrument.

In terms of regulation, "Nearly Zero Energy Buildings" standards apply to all new buildings occupied after 31st December 2020. For public sector bodies, the standard applies to all new buildings owned or occupied after 31st December 2018. The Building Energy Rating (BER) program, which is managed by SEAI, became mandatory in 2013 for all housing that is being sold or rented. The BER is a scale ranging from A1 (most efficient) to G (least efficient) that indicates the energy performance of a building. All BERs are available to view through a public registry administered by SEAI. There is some evidence that the BER rating affects the property values, with the effect stronger for property sales compared to property rentals (Hyland et al. 2013; Stanley et al. 2016).

The Efficiency Obligation Scheme, commenced in 2014, obliges energy suppliers and distributors to deliver energy savings across all energy types, including electricity, gas, and solid fuel. The Energy Auditing Scheme requires companies that either employ 250 people or more or have an annual turnover in excess of €50 million and an annual balance sheet total in excess of €43 million to undertake an energy audit every 4 years.

SEAI administers a number of incentive-based schemes that provides supports for homeowners to improve the energy performance of their homes. The Better Energy Homes scheme provides grant aid to individual homeowners for measures such as insulation, heating system upgrades, and solar thermal panels. The Better Energy Warmer Homes scheme provides funds for energy efficiency of the homes of those in energy poverty. The Better Energy Communities scheme focuses on the community level and seeks to improve the energy efficiency of clusters of buildings. In December 2017, the government announced a new incentive mechanism for renewable heat targeting large heat demand non-domestic users, called the Support Scheme for Renewable Heat, to be which is administered by SEAI. The scheme consists of two types of support: first, an ongoing operational support of 15 years duration for new renewable heat installations or conversion of fossil fuel heating systems to biomass or anaerobic digestion; and second, a grant of up to 30% for renewable heating systems that use heat pumps. The maximum tariffs will be are 5.66 cents per kilowatt hour for biomass heating systems and 2.95 cents per kilowatt hour for anaerobic digestion heating systems (SEAI 2018b).

The carbon tax, discussed above, is the principal internalizing policy instrument in the built environment sector. There are also a range of soft governance approaches in the built environment sector, including education and training to boost relevant skills in the construction sector, support from SEAI to public bodies to improve energy efficiency, and measures to increase public understanding of energy efficiency. SEAI also supports a number of relevant networks, including the Large Industry Energy Network and the Support Network for Delivery of Public Sector Energy Efficiency Targets.

Transport

In the transport sector, the suite of policy instruments includes a mix of regulation, incentive-based measures, as well as direct provision of, e.g., public transport. The principal regulatory measures employed in the transport sector include EU regulations that govern average emission performance of vehicles and the Biofuels Obligation Scheme (BOS). EU Regulation 443/2009 set CO_2 emission performance standards for new passenger cars. Under EU Regulation 510/2011, standards have also been put in place for new light commercial vehicle fleets. The BOS aims to progressively increase the share of biofuels in the fuel mix over time. Under Article 3 of the Renewable Energy Directive (2009/28/EC), member states are required to "ensure that the share of energy from renewable sources in all forms of transport in 2020 is at least 10% of the final consumption of energy in transport." The BOS requires that road transport fuel suppliers must ensure that biofuels represent a certain percentage of the motor fuel they place on the market. The obligation was increased on 1 January 2017 from 6.383% to 8.695% by volume. A policy statement published by DCCAE in April 2018 signaled the Government's intention to continue the BOS until at least 2030, with progressive increases in the level of obligation (DCCAE 2018b).

A range of incentive-based instruments are employed in the transport sector. As well as the carbon tax discussed above that is applied to petrol and diesel, these include preferential treatment of lower emission vehicles through the Vehicle Registration Tax (VRT) and motor tax regimes, and supports for EVs. The VRT and motor tax regimes were reconfigured in 2008 to support reducing CO_2 emissions. The VRT rate applicable to new cars registered on or after 1 July 2008 was changed from engine capacity to CO_2 emissions. A seven-band system – A to G – was introduced. In 2013, this banding system was revised, splitting A (1–120 g CO_2/km) into four bands and B (121–140 g CO_2/km) into two bands (DCCAE 2017a, p. 50). Since 2008, Motor Tax is also charged according to CO_2 emissions rather than engine capacity.

Consumers are incentivized in the purchase of EVs through grants as well as favorable treatment through the VRT and Motor Tax regimes. The EV Grant Scheme, administered by SEAI, provides consumers with a grant of up to €5000 towards purchase of a new EV. EVs also qualify for €5000 relief from VRT. Additionally, ESB committed to installing free home charge points for the purchasers of new EVs that qualified for the SEAI grant for EVs. This scheme involved the installation of 2,300 home chargers, and concluded at the end of 2017. Since the beginning of 2018, SEAI is responsible for administering a grant of up to €600 available to home owners to install a home charging point. There are also financial incentives for businesses to purchase lower emission vehicles, including the Accelerated Capital Allowance (ACA) scheme that promotes investment in energy efficient products and equipment. The Finance Act 2013 added natural gas vehicles and associated equipment and natural gas vehicle conversions to the ACA Scheme for Energy Efficient Equipment (DCCAE 2018, p. 21).

A range of soft governance programs has been established to promote low carbon and sustainable travel through education programs. These include the Green School Travel program, the Smarter Travel Workplaces Program, and the Smarter Travel Campus program. Other initiatives such as the Smarter Travel Areas pilot program include an education/behavior change component as part of the overall program, though most of the funding was targeted at infrastructure investment (Aecom 2015).

Table 1 Classification of policy instruments across sectors

	Regulatory	Incentive based	Internalizing	Soft governance
Electricity generation	• Pledge to phase out coal by 2025 • Pledge to phase-out peat by 2028	• Alternative Energy Requirement scheme (1996) • Renewable Energy Feed-in Tariff 1 scheme (2005) • Renewable Energy Feed-in Tariff 2 scheme (2012) • Renewable Energy Feed-in Tariff 3 scheme (2012)		
Built environment, including heat	• Nearly Zero Energy Buildings standards (2018) • Energy Efficiency Obligation scheme (2014) • Energy Audits for Large Energy Users (2014)	• Better Energy Homes scheme (2009) • Better Energy Warmer Homes scheme (2013) • Better Energy Communities scheme (2013) • Support Scheme for Renewable Heat (2017)	• Carbon tax (2010)	• Large Industry Energy Network • Support Network for Delivery of Public Sector Energy Efficiency Targets
Transport	• Biofuels Obligation Scheme (2010)	• Grants for purchase of EVs and plug-in hybrids (various) • Reduced Vehicle Registration Tax for low-emissions vehicles (2008) • Motor Tax incentives for low-emissions vehicles (2008) • Accelerated Capital Allowance for low-emission vehicles (2013)	• Carbon tax (2010)	• Smarter Travel Initiative • Smarter Travel Areas pilot program • Smarter Travel Workplaces Program Smarter Travel Campus program • Green Schools Travel Program

Source: Author's compilation

The government has also invested directly in public transport provision, including construction of a new tram line in Dublin city. Nonetheless, spending on road infrastructure remains higher than spending on public transport infrastructure. Between 2002 and 2013, roads expenditure accounted for an average of 64% of DTTAS expenditure on land transport, with public and sustainable transport accounting for 36%. This gap narrowed in recent years, but this took place in a context of a sharp decline in overall expenditure on land transport (DTTAS 2018) (Classification of policy instruments across sectors is captured in Table. 1).

Outcomes, Challenges, and Prospects of Energy Governance in Ireland

Ireland has set out a national transition objective of significantly decarbonizing the energy system by 2050. This is emphasized in the 2015 Energy White Paper, which placed significantly greater emphasis on decarbonization and long-term transition than its 2007 predecessor. The 2014 National Policy Position on Climate Action and Low Carbon Development foresees significant decarbonization across electricity, the built environment, and transport by 2050, and the 2015 Climate Action and Low Carbon Development Act put in place a more robust planning and reporting process for climate mitigation and adaptation across these sectors. Ireland's energy transition has been motivated in large part by external impetus from the EU. Indeed, Ireland's short-term domestic policies are aimed at achievement of EU targets for greenhouse gas (GHG) emissions reductions in the non-ETS sector and renewable energy targets in the electricity, heating, and transport sectors.

However, Ireland will miss by a wide margin its EU GHG emissions target for 2020 of a 20% reduction on 2005 levels for the non-Emissions Trading sector. According to projections from the EPA, in the best-case scenario – that is, "with additional measures" – Ireland's GHG emissions in the non-Emissions Trading sector will decline by just 1% (EPA 2018). At 13.5 tons of CO_2 equivalent per capita in 2016, Ireland's per capita emissions are third highest in the EU and significantly higher than the EU-28 average of 8.7 tons (Eurostat 2018a). Ireland is likely to miss its target for renewable energy development (European Environment Agency 2018). At the end of 2018, the Germanwatch/Climate Action Network Climate Change Performance Index gave Ireland a "very low" rating on climate policy for the fifth year in a row, ranking it 48th out of 60 countries, the lowest ranking of any EU state (Burck et al. 2018).

The longer-term outlook is challenging as well. Projections from the EPA for CO_2 emissions out to 2035 show Ireland's emissions essentially flat over that time horizon, as Fig. 3 illustrates. The estimates shown in these projections to 2035 are based on the "with additional measures" scenario.

The challenge of decarbonizing energy in Ireland, along with the broader transition to a low carbon economy and society, is partly technical, but it is also a profoundly societal and political challenge. It is important to put in place an appropriate enabling institutional architecture, but focusing solely on institutional questions would risk missing critical pieces of the jigsaw (Torney 2018).

A more positive economic and social narrative is required that highlights not only the challenges but also opportunities of the transition. The business sector could play a stronger role, as the Confederation of British Industry has done in the UK (CBI 2017). The transition narrative ought to be about more than compliance with externally-imposed targets, and it must take seriously the need to protect those who will lose as a result of the transition. The challenge of decarbonization should also be connected with the need to address other pressing societal challenges including strengthening the social model and the democratic system.

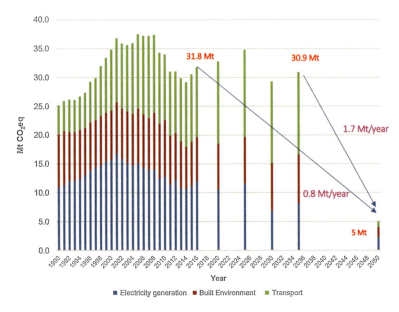

Fig. 3 Historic and projected CO_2 emissions from the electricity generation, built environment, and transport sectors. (Source: EPA 2018, p. 9)

Despite some positive developments as a result of the merging of energy and climate within one centralized department, policymaking remains significantly fragmented. At present, there is ad hoc contact between governance agencies. More joined-up governance is needed to facilitate decarbonization, including a feedback loop from governance agencies to central government. Publication of an all-of-government Climate Action Plan in June 2019 represents an important development in this regard, in particular the creation of a Climate Action Delivery Board within the Department of the Taoiseach (Prime Minister).

Community engagement remains a key challenge. Future decarbonization of the energy system, including in time through deployment of greater amounts of offshore wind and, eventually, ocean energy, will inevitably require construction of new grid infrastructure. Further engagement, including building a new narrative around energy transition, will be required in order to achieve this. Without these and other crucial enablers, it is unlikely that Ireland will be able to achieve the laudable vision set out in the 2015 Energy White Paper and the National Policy Position on Climate Action and Low Carbon Development.

Cross-References

- ▶ Energy Democracy and Participation in Energy Transitions
- ▶ Energy Governance in the United Kingdom
- ▶ Transition of Energy Systems: Patterns of Stability and Change

Acknowledgments I am grateful to Michèle Knodt and Jörg Kemmerzell as well as to the participants in the authors' workshop in Darmstadt in November 2017 for helpful comments on an earlier version of this chapter. Some of the research underpinning this chapter was supported by a small-scale study grant from the Irish Environmental Protection Agency (2016-CCRP-SS.15).

References

Aecom. (2015). *Ex-post evaluation of smarter travel areas: Interim report 2015*. Dublin: Aecom. http://www.dttas.ie/sites/default/files/publications/corporate/english/sta-interim-evaluation-report/sta-interim-evaluation-report.pdf. Accessed 7 Oct 2018.

Andrews-Speed, P. (2016). Applying institutional theory to the low-carbon energy transition. *Energy Research & Social Science, 13*, 216–225.

Baker, N. (2011, November 30). Many boom buildings do not meet standards. *Irish Examiner*. https://www.irishexaminer.com/ireland/many-boom-buildings-do-not-meet-standards-175507.html. Accessed 20 July 2018.

Barry, F., Hannan, A., & Strobl, E. A. (1999). The real convergence of the Irish economy and the sectoral distribution of employment growth. In F. Barry (Ed.), *Understanding Ireland's economic growth*. Basingstoke: Macmillan.

Burck, J., Marten, F., Bals, C., & Höhne, N. (2018). *The climate change performance index: Results 2018*. Berlin: Germanwatch.

CBI. (2017). *Stepping up to the challenge: Creating a globally competitive low-carbon economy in 2030*. London: Confederation of British Industry.

CCAC. (2016). *First report of the climate change advisory council*. Dublin: Climate Change Advisory Council.

CCAC. (2017). *Annual review 2017*. Dublin: Climate Change Advisory Council.

CCAC. (2018). *Annual review 2018*. Dublin: Climate Change Advisory Council.

CER. (2014). *Strategic plan 2014–18*. Dublin: Commission for Energy Regulation.

Chiodi, A., Gargiulo, M., Rogan, F., Deane, J. P., Lavigne, D., Rout, U. K., et al. (2013). Modelling the impacts of challenging 2050 European climate mitigation targets on Ireland's energy system. *Energy Policy, 53*, 169–189.

Citizens' Assembly. (2018). *Third report and recommendations of the citizens' assembly: How the state can make Ireland a leader in tackling climate change*. Dublin: Citizens' Assembly.

CSO. (2017). Irish industrial production by sector: CSO statistcal release, 27 July. https://www.cso.ie/en/releasesandpublications/er/iips/irishindustrialproductionbysector2016/. Accessed 18 July 2018.

Cullinane, M., & Watson, C. (2014). *Irish public service broadcasting and the climate change challenge: Summary of research findings*. Dublin: RTÉ Audience Council.

Curtin, J. (2017). *A just transition to a low-carbon economy: Implications for IMPACT and its members*. Dublin: IMPACT.

DCCAE. (2017a). *National energy efficiency action plan for Ireland # 4, 2017–2020*. Dublin: Department of Communications, Climate Action and Environment.

DCCAE. (2017b). Minister Naughten appoints new Chair of National Dialogue on Climate Action Advisory Group. https://www.dccae.gov.ie/en-ie/news-and-media/press-releases/Pages/Press-Release-Minister-Denis-Naughten-appoints-new-Chair-of-National-Dialogue-on-Climate-Action-Advisory-Group.aspx. Accessed 19 July 2018.

DCCAE. (2017c). *National mitigation plan*. Dublin: Department of Communications, Climate Action and Environment.

DCCAE. (2018a). *Annual transition statement 2018*. Dublin: Department of Communications, Climate Action and Environment.

DCCAE. (2018b). *Biofuels obligation scheme policy statement April 2018*. Dublin: Department of Communications, Climate Action and Environment.

DCCAE. (2018c). Gas. https://www.dccae.gov.ie/en-ie/energy/topics/gas/Pages/default.aspx. Accessed 20 July 2018.

DCCAE. (2018d). *Renewable electricity support scheme (RESS): High level design*. Dublin: Department of Communications, Climate Action and Environment.

DCCAE. (2019). *Climate action plan 2019 to tackle climate breakdown*. Dublin: Department of Communications, Climate Action and Environment.

DCENR. (2015). *Ireland's transition to a low carbon energy future, 2015–2030*. Dublin: Department of Communications, Energy and Natural Resources.

DCMNR. (2007). *Delivering a sustainable energy future for Ireland*. Dublin: Department of Communications, Marine and Natural Resources.

Devaney, L., & Torney, D. (2019). Advancing the low-carbon transition in Irish transport. NESC Research Series Paper No. 13. Dublin: National Economic and Social Council.

DTTAS (2018). Transport trends: An overview of Ireland's transport sector 2018. Dublin: Department of Transport, Tourism and Sport. http://www.dttas.ie/sites/default/files/publications/corporate/english/transport-trends/transport-trends-2018.pdf. Accessed 7 Oct 2018.

EirGrid. (2017). *Ireland's grid development strategy: Your grid, your tomorrow*. Dublin: EirGrid.

EPA. (2018). Ireland's greenhouse gas emissions projections, 2017–2035. http://www.epa.ie/pubs/reports/air/airemissions/ghgprojections2017-2035/EPA_2018_GHG_Emissions_Projections_Summary_Report.pdf. Accessed 19 July 2018.

European Environment Agency. (2018). *Trends and projections in Europe 2018: Tracking progress towards Europe's climate and energy targets*. Copenhagen: European Environment Agency.

Eurostat. (2018a). Greenhouse gas emissions per capita. http://ec.europa.eu/eurostat/tgm/table.do?tab=table&init=1&language=en&pcode=t2020_rd300&plugin=1. Accessed 19 July 2018.

Eurostat. (2018b). Population density. http://ec.europa.eu/eurostat/tgm/table.do?tab=table&init=1&language=en&pcode=tps00003&plugin=1. Accessed 18 July 2018.

FitzGerald, J., & Valeri, L. M. (2014). *Irish energy policy: An analysis of current issues*. Dublin: Economic and Social Research Institute.

Fox, E., & Rau, H. (2016). Climate change communication in Ireland. *Oxford Research Encyclopedia of Climate Science*. https://doi.org/10.1093/acrefore/9780190228620.013.459.

Gilardi, F. (2005). The formal independence of regulators: A comparison of 17 countries and 7 sectors. *Swiss Political Science Review, 11*(4), 139–167.

Government of Ireland. (2010). National Renewable Energy Action Plan – Ireland. http://www.dccae.gov.ie/documents/The%20National%20Renewable%20Energy%20Action%20Plan%20(PDF).pdf. Accessed 20 July 2018.

Government of Ireland. (2014). *Climate action and low-carbon development: National Policy Position Ireland*. Dublin: Department of Communications, Climate Action and Environment.

Government of Ireland. (2016). Programme for a partnership government. https://www.merrionstreet.ie/MerrionStreet/en/ImageLibrary/Programme_for_Partnership_Government.pdf. Accessed 3 Dec 2018.

Hamilton, P. (2017, July 20). Texan gas company NextDecade signs deal with Port of Cork. *Irish Times*. https://www.irishtimes.com/business/energy-and-resources/texan-gas-company-nextdecade-signs-deal-with-port-of-cork-1.3161212. Accessed 20 July 2018.

Hardiman, N., & Scott, C. (2010). Governance as polity: An institutional approach to the evolution of state functions in Ireland. *Public Administration, 88*(1), 170–189.

Harrington, T. (2016). Accountability and regulatory governance in a cross-jurisdictional market: A case study of the all-island energy market (Ireland). Doctorate in Governance (DGov) thesis, Queens University Belfast.

Houses of the Oireachtas. (2019). *Report of the Joint Committee on Climate Action: Climate change - a cross-party consensus for action*. Dublin: Houses of the Oireachtas.

Hyland, M., Lyons, R. C., & Lyons, S. (2013). The value of domestic building energy efficiency: Evidence from Ireland. *Energy Economics, 40*, 943–952.

IPCC. (2018). Global Warming of 1.5°C. Geneva: Intergovernmental Panel on Climate Change.

Kuzemko, C., Lockwood, M., Mitchell, C., & Hoggett, R. (2016). Governing for sustainable energy system change: Politics, contexts and contingency. *Energy Research & Social Science, 12*, 96–105.

Lockwood, M., Kuzemko, C., Mitchell, C., & Hoggett, R. (2017). Historical institutionalism and the politics of sustainable energy transitions: A research agenda. *Environment and Planning C: Politics and Space, 35*(2), 312–333.

MacCarthaigh, M. (2011). Politics, policy preferences and the evolution of Irish bureaucracy: A framework for analysis. *Irish Political Studies, 27*(1), 23–47.

NESC. (2012). *Ireland and the climate change challenge: Connecting 'how much' with 'how to'*. Dublin: National Economic and Social Council.

NESC. (2014). *Wind energy in Ireland: Building community engagement and social support*. Dublin: National Economic and Social Council.

NTA. (2018). About the authority. https://www.nationaltransport.ie/about-us/. Accessed 19 July 2018.

Ó Gallachóir, B. P., Chiodi, A., Gargiulo, M., Deane, P., Lavigne, D., & Rout, U. K. (2012). *Irish TIMES Energy Systems Model* (EPA climate change research program report CCRP 2008 3.1). Wexford: Environmental Protection Agency.

O'Sullivan, K. P. V., & Kennedy, T. (2010). What caused the Irish banking crisis? *Journal of Financial Regulation and Compliance, 18*(3), 224–242.

OECD. (2018). *OECD economic surveys: Ireland*. Paris: Organisation for Economic Co-operation and Development.

Robbins, D. (2019). *Climate change, politics and the press in Ireland*. Abingdon: Routledge.

Schillemans, T., & Busuioc, M. (2014). Predicting public sector accountability: From agency drift to forum drift. *Journal of Public Administration Research and Theory, 25*, 191–215.

SEAI. (2016a). *Energy in Ireland 1990–2015*. Dublin: Sustainable Energy Authority of Ireland.

SEAI. (2016b). *Energy security in Ireland: A statistical overview*. Dublin: Sustainable Energy Authority of Ireland.

SEAI. (2017). *Energy in Ireland 1990–2016*. Dublin: Sustainable Energy Authority of Ireland.

SEAI. (2018a). *Energy in Ireland: 2018 report*. Dublin: Sustainable Energy Authority of Ireland.

SEAI. (2018b). Support scheme for renewable heat. https://www.seai.ie/sustainable-solutions/support-scheme-renewable-/. Accessed 20 July 2018.

Stanley, S., Lyons, R. C., & Lyons, S. (2016). The price effect of building energy ratings in the Dublin residential market. *Energy Efficiency, 9*(4), 875–885.

Teagasc. (2018). Agriculture in Ireland. https://www.teagasc.ie/rural-economy/rural-economy/agri-food-business/agriculture-in-ireland/. Accessed 18 July 2018.

Torney, D. (2017). If at first you don't succeed: The development of climate change legislation in Ireland. *Irish Political Studies, 32*(2), 247–267.

Torney, D. (2018). *Enabling decarbonisation: A study of energy sector governance in Ireland* (Climate change research program report 246). Wexford: Environmental Protection Agency.

Unruh, G. C. (2000). Understanding carbon lock-in. *Energy Policy, 28*(12), 817–830.

Unruh, G. C. (2002). Escaping carbon lock-in. *Energy Policy, 30*, 317–325.

Energy Governance in Italy

Path Dependence, Policy Adjustments and New Challenges for Sustainability

32

Maria Rosaria Di Nucci and Daniele Russolillo

Contents

Introduction	792
General Conditions of Energy Governance in Italy	793
Path Dependencies	793
Composition of the "Energy" Mix	795
Discourse on Energy Issues	797
Political Institutions and Actors	802
Coordination, Instruments, and Issues of the Italian Energy Transition	805
Drivers of Energy Transition	806
Instruments of the Energy Transitions	808
Coordination Mechanisms and Multilevel Governance	813
Outcomes, Challenges, and Prospects	816
Cross-References	820
References	820

Abstract

The chapter analyzes the structural constraints that influenced the decision-making processes and organization of the Italian energy sector. Although renewables account for over 17.5% of gross final energy consumption, the current energy system is still quite centralized, path-dependent, and hampered by discontinuous research, energy, and industrial policies.

Firstly, external and domestic drivers as well as coordination mechanisms and instruments for the energy transition are analyzed from a multilevel governance

---

M. R. Di Nucci (✉)
Environmental Policy Research Centre, Freie Universität Berlin, Berlin, Germany
e-mail: dinucci@zedat.fu-berlin.de

D. Russolillo
Institute for European Energy and Climate Policies, Amsterdam, The Netherlands
e-mail: daniele@ieecp.org

© Springer Nature Switzerland AG 2022
M. Knodt, J. Kemmerzell (eds.), *Handbook of Energy Governance in Europe*,
https://doi.org/10.1007/978-3-030-43250-8_16

perspective. The chapter then reflects on the role the Italian incumbents played for the success of low carbon technologies, energy policies, and digitalization of the power sector. We claim that European policies will still provide a suitable model for Italian policy makers, but also that coherent measures are needed to keep fostering distributed generation or high-efficiency co-generation. Moreover, placing energy communities and prosumers at the center of the new energy model seems necessary to ensure a sustainable transition.

Keywords

Energy · Energy governance · Path dependence · Sustainability · Policy · Discourse · Transition

Introduction

According to the latest International Monetary Fund figures, Italy is the world's eighth biggest economy with a GDP of $2.18 trillion (WEF 2018). Its economic structure relies mainly on services and manufacturing, with the tertiary sector accounting for almost three quarters of total GDP. Italy has a limited amount of domestic energy resources and is a net electricity importer (50.8TWh imported; 4.5 TWh exported in 2016) (IEA 2016b). In 2015, the ratio between primary energy import/export was 76% (MSE 2017). Within the UN Framework Convention on Climate Change (UNFCCC), Italy is committed by 2020 to achieve a 18% decrease in global greenhouse gas (GHG) emissions, with a 21% reduction in Emissions Trading System (ETS) sectors and a 13% reduction in non-ETS sectors, compared to 2005 levels. This should be attained through an enlarged use of natural gas in combined heat and power plants (CHP), RES, as well as through the enhancement of energy efficiency. The National Energy Strategy (Strategia Energetica Nazionale – SEN) is more ambitious than the European goals for Italy and contains targets – with respect to 1990 emissions – of a 39% reduction to be achieved by 2030 and 63% by 2050 (MSE 2017).

Over the past decades, Italy has witnessed an extraordinary growth of renewable energy sources (RES) and has reached some EU energy goals (e.g., 17% share of RES in percentage of the national gross final energy consumption) before the deadline. However, some observers consider the achievement of some of the 2020 European targets to be due to the effects of the economic crisis, rather than to the implementation of coherent policies for the promotion of renewable energy and energy efficiency (Deloitte 2015; Di Nucci and Russolillo 2017; Galgóczi 2015). Whereas the EU-renewables directive set a goal of 25% by 2010, in the future plans of the EU, the goal for Italy is 32% by 2030. This goal is within reach, as the share of RES to the gross-electricity-generation amounted in 2015 to approximately 32% (TERNA 2016b).

Although Italy is on a transition path from fossil energy to a low-carbon energy system, oil and natural gas are still the dominant energy carriers. The country has a well-developed natural gas sector, in all its upstream, midstream, and downstream segments and represents the third greatest natural gas market in Europe after the UK and Germany (Eurostat 2017a).

Final energy use has been declining in recent years. If it is true that part of this result can be ascribed to the economic crisis, it is also true that part of this decrease can be traced back to improvements in electric generation performance, as well as the active adoption of numerous energy efficiency measures (i.e., white certificates, fiscal measures, etc.). Indeed, energy efficiency is key to achieving the SEN energy policy objectives. However, it should be noted that in comparison with other EU countries, Italy is one of the Member States with the lowest energy intensity level of about 100 kg of oil equivalent (kgoe) per 1000 EUR of GDP in 2015 against almost 110 kgoe per 1000 EUR of GDP of the average for the EU-28 group (Eurostat 2017b). The relatively low energy intensity in Italy can in part also be attributed to the tariffs structure for energy. Energy prices in Italy are among the highest in the EU, especially for electricity in the industrial sector. Italian prices are the second highest after Liechtenstein, because of the role of taxes and levies besides value added tax (VAT) (Eurostat 2016). In Italy, tariffs have traditionally been a powerful energy policy instrument; however, the liberalization of the energy market somehow restricted the potential impact of this instrument. Incentives for renewables also have a significant impact on electricity prices together with regulatory costs, including tariffs (to dismantle nuclear plants, conduct system research and support special regimes) and other subsidies topping all together at least 20% of the energy bill for final uses in the residential sector. In 2016, the national energy authority calculated that the incentives to RES reached €13.6 billion, up 8.8% from the year prior (AEEGSI 2017).

The industry sector no longer accounts for the largest energy consumer. While the energy consumption of the residential sector has almost remained constant in the last 30 years, the transport sector has increased steadily along the same timeframe (IEA 2016a). This trend is expected to continue into the next decade.

The chapter, starting with an overview on path dependence, will analyze external and domestic drivers as well as coordination mechanisms and tools for the energy transition from a multilevel governance perspective. Peculiar elements, such as the discourse on the energy issues and the role of the Italian incumbents for the success of low carbon policy and technologies, will also be assessed. The concluding remarks will underline some new trends such as the digitalization in the power sector and electro-mobility.

General Conditions of Energy Governance in Italy

Path Dependencies

Path dependence is a useful concept to illustrate the historical but also structural continuities that influenced the decision processes and structural organization of the Italian energy sector. The Italian energy system was/is subject to a path dependence, especially because of technological (hydrocarbons also used in power plants for electricity generation), infrastructural (large projects), institutional (centralization), and instrumental (subsidies) lock-ins. These lock-ins have proved to be strong barriers to affect changes in the energy system towards more sustainable paths and had serious implications for sustainable and timely policy responses.

The present energy system is burdened by the legacy of over 60 years of discontinuous and incoherent research, energy, and industrial policy (Di Nucci 2007; Di Nucci and Russolillo 2017). Contradictory political decisions aimed largely at strengthening the role of one or another industrial group or state-owned enterprises (mostly supported by various political parties) in research and development (R&D) and technology as well as industrial policy. These steered the development of the energy sector in a particular direction and provoked a strong dependence on hydrocarbons. Thus, in the case of Italy, it can be claimed that not only "history matters," but also that "energy incumbents matter." The two national champions in the electricity, oil, and gas field ENEL (Ente Nazionale Energia Elettrica) and ENI (Ente Nazionale Idrocarburi) played a pivotal role to set the direction of energy policy and ENEL is now playing an even larger role to set the future direction.

As elsewhere in Europe – and more because of a lack of domestic resources – in the post-World War II period, energy issues were constrained and ruled by energy security concerns and the need for a sufficient supply of fuels to enhance the "economic miracle." For this reason, energy became a subject of international policy and geopolitics. This matter has to be brought together with the surge and consolidation of the national champion in oil and gas, ENI. For over a decade, a daunting concentration of domestic and external interests developed that attributed Italy to the role of the refinery of Europe. Indeed, fossil energy carriers in particular oil – and later gas – played a pivotal role in the Italian energy mix and set the frame for long-run equilibria of a process that still shows its legacies today in the power relations present in the energy system. In the last 50 years, ENI has been a significant player in the development of the energy sector in Italy. The state-owned enterprise was transformed into a joint stock company in 1992 and today is still controlled by the Italian Ministry of Economics and Finance, and for a very small (<1%) by the Treasury, with a 30.11% stake (ENI 2017).

A relevant milestone along the Italian development path was achieved in 1962, as the nationalization of the electricity sector was completed and the national electricity monopolist ENEL was established. By that time, hydropower, predominantly located in the Alpine regions, had still the lion's share in the generation of electricity. Due to the growing political and economic power of ENI, political forces pushed for an energy policy that gave priority to the exploitation and the massive use of oil also for power generation. Thus in the early 1960s, hydroelectric plants were substituted by oil-fired power plants. Following the first oil crisis in 1973, the vulnerability of this system became evident and a new path was pursued in order to diversify the energy balance. However, this mainly occurred through the substitution of oil with natural gas and via the diversification of foreign producers. The existence of this path dependence is somehow proved by the fact that in 1975, as the first oil crisis showed the vulnerability of Italy's energy system and the price of crude oil had already more than quadrupled; the largest order in Europe for oil-fired power plants was placed in Italy (Di Nucci 2006).

Nuclear power played a marginal role but has a turbulent history (characterized by stop-and-go policy decisions), which has left strong legacies and whose fortunes depended on the goodwill of the oil lobby and the parties supporting it (see section "Discourse on Energy Issues").

Composition of the "Energy" Mix

The energy balance of Italy is characterized by a relevant quota of imports (see Fig. 1) that account for almost 94% of the gross inland consumption. The energy mix of such imports is illustrated in Fig. 2 where it can be noted that coal is still being used and in 2016 accounted for 15% of primary energy for electricity generation. The last National Energy Strategy (MSE 2017) foresees the political commitment in 2025 to stop thermoelectric generation with coal. In terms of final uses, the civil sector tops 38% of the national final energy consumption (see Fig. 1). The energy production by source is illustrated in Fig. 3 where the recent growth of wind, solar, biogas and waste, with a relevant role of the last two sources, is evident.

Italy makes use of renewable energy sources (RES) mainly to generate electricity and to a lesser extent for heating and cooling and to produce bio-fuels. At the end of 2016, RES had a very important role within the national electricity system. It contributed to around 44.5% of the totally installed gross power in Italy (TERNA 2016b) and to 33% of the total gross electricity production (see Fig. 4).

The overall Italian installed gross electricity at the end of 2016 reached 117.1 GW (more than double the average daily maximum power load). This increase is mostly due to the installation of PV systems, wind parks, hydropower, and also small-size thermoelectric plants that has compensated for the halt of large traditional thermoelectric power stations. Against the background of such an over-dimensioned

ID	National Energy Balance 2016 (Mtoe)	Solid	Gas	Oil	Renewables	Electricity (*)	Total
1	Primary production	0,3	4,74	3,75	31,57	-	40,35
2	Imports	11,64	53,47	82,07	1,91	9,5	158,59
3	Exports	0,24	0,17	28,82	0,22	1,35	30,81
4	Stock Changes	-0,08	-0,05	-0,82	0,04	0	-0,9
5	Gross inland consumption (1+2-3-4)	11,78	58,08	57,81	33,21	8,15	169,03
6	Consumi e perdite del settore energetico	-0,14	-1,65	-3,88	-0,01	-38,18	-43,87
7	Trasformazione in energia elettrica	-9,33	-18,3	-1,96	-24,67	54,27	-
8	Final Energy consumption (5+6+7)	2,31	38,13	51,97	8,53	24,23	125,17
	- industry	2,24	12,31	2,97	0,11	9,04	26,67
	- transport	-	0,89	35,82	1,28	0,9	38,9
	- civil uses	0	24,14	3,11	7,11	13,84	48,19
	- agriculture	-	0,13	2,2	0,03	0,46	2,81
	- final non-energy consumption	0,07	0,66	4,95	-	-	5,67
	- bunkering	-	-	2,93	-	-	2,93

(*) Primary (hydro, geothermal, wind); import/export; losses

Fig. 1 Italy's energy balance 2016. (Source: Official national energy agency data (www.arera.it/it/dati/bilancio_en.htm) with further elaboration (and translation) by the authors)

Energy Vector	Quantity	Import/Export Country
Crude Oil		
Imports	67.2 Mt	Iraq (17.8%)
Exports	1.8 Mt	France (15.4%)
Oil Products		
Imports	14.4 Mt	Algeria (13.4%)
Exports	27.8 Mt	Spain (12.5%)
Natural Gas		
Imports	65.3 bcm	Russian Federation (41.3%)
Exports	0.2 bcm	Switwerland (40.6%)
Coal		
Imports	16.8 Mt	Russia (26.8%)
Exports	0.1 Mt	Spain (61.4%)
Electricity		
Imports	50.8 TWh	Switwerland (51.5%)
Exports	4.5 TWh	Greece (37.4%)

Fig. 2 Italy's import/export of energy in 2016. (Source: IEA World Energy Balances 2017)

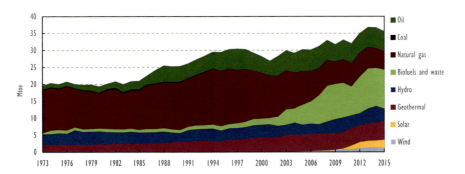

Fig. 3 Energy production by source, 1973–2015. (Source: IEA 2016a)

Italy's gross power production in 2016 (GWh)	Production	Self-production	Total
Thermo-electric (fossil)	181,524.1	17,905.6	199,429.7
Hydro	43,695.3	561.7	44,257.0
Wind	17,688.7		17,688.7
PV	22,104.3		22,104.3
Geothermal	6,288.6		6,288.6
Total gross production	**271,300.9**	**18,467.3**	**289,768.2**

Fig. 4 Electricity gross generation in 2016. (Source: TERNA (2016a) and further elaboration by the authors)

capacity, a decrease in final consumptions and in wholesale energy prices as well as a strong decrease of working hours of natural gas fired plants (e.g., 4.120 h/year in 2007 as opposed to 2.633 h/year in 2011), and following a disruptive audition at the

Senate in 2014, ENEL announced in 2016 the closure of 23 power stations for a total of almost 23GW (Agostinelli 2016). This decision, albeit disliked by the trade unions, was considered a strong opportunity for the whole country to steer the domestic energy system towards sustainability. Moreover, ENEL announced a zero-carbon company balance to be achieved by 2050. These decisions by ENEL are helpful to clarify the large role the incumbent plays to set directions in energy policy. The national regulatory framework matched the trend with the definition of a national capacity market that was finally approved by the EU Antitrust Directorate at the beginning of 2018 after a 7 years legislative and regulatory process (ARERA 2018).

Due to its natural potential, Italy together with France and Hungary has also a leading position in the European geothermal production (EC 2017).

Discourse on Energy Issues

While the legacies we treated above refer to the "material" basis of energy governance, there are discursive aspects of energy governance that also played an important role. As elsewhere in the EU, in Italy debates related to energy policy also concentrated on various general principles and frames. The most relevant ones are:

(a) Energy security and the role that nuclear power could have in reinforcing it (this was a recurrent argument for over three decades).
(b) Competitiveness, stressing the importance of affordable energy as an economic location factor and liberalization as a means to achieve it (this was initiated in the 1990s).
(c) Ecologic sustainability, emphasizing a "clean" energy supply that relies on RES (this discourse started in the 1980s and is still ongoing). Centralization versus decentralization paths.

The sequence of these principles corresponds also to the temporal succession of framing these issues and their anchorage in the societal debate.

The Security of Supply and the Nuclear Discourse

The rigidity created by the use of large thermal oil-fired power plants and the strong industrial interests related to them represented a serious legacy for the modernization of the energy sector in Italy. In the 1960s, the age of such power plants, the high cost of oil following the Suez crisis, and the ensuing shortage of power encouraged a rapid construction of nuclear power plants (NPP). Political and economic interests facilitated the engagement in the development of nuclear energy as a means to acquire energy and technological autonomy (see Di Nucci 2006; Baracca et al. 2017). The Comitato Nazionale per le Ricerche Nucleari (CNRN), established in 1952, was restructured and the National Nuclear Energy Agency (CNEN) was created in 1960. Plans were made to install 6000 MW by 1965, the technology to be chosen from the British gas-graphite (Magnox) reactor and the US Light Water Reactor (LWR) technology. Three power plants of various technologies were ordered. As a result of the bilateral agreement signed with the UK, a Magnox plant to be located at Latina, near Rome, was followed by the purchase from General Electric of a 165 MW Boiling Water Reactor (BWR) ordered by SENN (a 75% state-owned utility) to be located near the Garigliano River, between Rome and Naples. Edison Volta, a major electric utility went for a larger size and, through its subsidiary SELNI, ordered a 270 MW Pressurized Water Reactor (PWR) – to be located at Trino-Vercellese (Di Nucci 2006, 2009). The interest the electric utilities showed in nuclear power was also shared by the private manufacturing industry, eager to enter a new field and to gain capabilities in a technology just in its infancy stage, with prospects for large economic opportunities. However, the interests of the oil lobby spoilt the "nuclear ambitions." In particular, the pro-USA social democratic party headed by Giuseppe Saragat later elected third President of Italy organized in 1963, 1 year after the entering on line of the first NPP, a scandal-mongering campaign, resulting first in the suspension and then incarceration of the president of the Secretary of the Italian Commission for Nuclear Energy (CNEN) Felice Ippolito for administrative irregularities (see Baracca et al. 2017). By 1965, when the first three power stations were all operating, Italy covered 13.8% of the world's installed nuclear power capacity (excluding the socialist block) as against 3% of France and 0.5% of Germany, and represented an attractive market for both the American and British nuclear industries. With the nationalization of the electricity sector, ENEL's creation in 1962 and the drop in oil prices, the interests of the former electric utilities shifted to expanding sectors such as petro-chemicals. From 1964 to 1966, the ownership of the nuclear power plants at Latina, Garigliano, and Trino was transferred to ENEL (Di Nucci 2006). The last commercial order for the construction of a NPP in Italy (at Caorso) was placed in 1966. Further plans for nuclear power development were abandoned (Di Nucci 2006). The nuclear option, which was discarded rather quickly in the 1960s, was reanimated following the first oil crisis in 1973. A national energy plan to cope with the problems provoked by the first oil shock was only worked out in 1975 (Piano Energetico Nazionale – PEN 1975) and remained largely ineffectual. Following the second oil crisis of 1979, an entirely new plan was prepared in 1980 and revised in 1981. This foresaw a reduction in consumption through energy saving measures, coal, nuclear power, and also RES. Against this background, in 1974–1975, an intensive nuclear program was announced, envisaging 20 GW by 1985 and 40 GW by 1990. Such an initiative, taken at a time of a harsh economic crisis, although provoking objections from some of the left-wing political parties and some trade unions, was welcomed by a large majority. Regardless of which particular technology might be adopted, any project was viewed as a source of industrial growth and employment opportunities. These massive nuclear development programs were never realized (Di Nucci 2009).

Following the Chernobyl disaster in 1986, the public debate on the implications of nuclear energy became a highly political issue. In November 1987, three referenda promoted by environmental associations blocked any further activity in the nuclear field. Soon afterwards, the Italian government put a 5-year moratorium on all nuclear activities, including research reactors and extended it there since. Following the results of the referendum, in December 1987, the Parliament passed a motion calling for the final shut down of the Latina and Garigliano NPPs and to stop any construction work (Di Nucci 2009). The phase-out of all four NPPs started in 1991. However, the debate on the need for nuclear power in the Italian energy system continued for two decades and was justified also on the grounds of CO_2 reduction, security of supply, and vague technological advantage arguments. The media accompanied this debate and announced in regular intervals of time the renaissance of nuclear power. In 2008, a change of government revived the debate on the nuclear option and a feasibility study investigated the construction of three to four NPPs to be located for the most part on already existing sites. The pro-nuclear Berlusconi government introduced a package of nuclear rulings and by-laws, which included measures to simplify the licensing of siting and construction. The new legislation was passed in July 2009 and envisaged 6 months to select sites for new NPPs (Di Nucci 2015). It was not until the Fukushima accident that Italy, by a second national referendum in 2011, definitively abandoned the nuclear option. In the meantime, the decommissioning of four reactors and the disposal of nuclear waste remain unsolved with pernicious environmental and health hazards implications (Baracca et al. 2017; Di Nucci 2015).

The current discourse on security of supply focuses on the electricity and natural gas systems. For the former, the capacity market, and the digitalization of the energy infrastructure – also to ensure resilience and the correct management of peaks – storage and energy efficiency in final uses are indeed the most relevant issues to debate. These were fully acknowledged by the government after large consultations (MSE 2017). For the latter, the most important issue is related to new transport systems for natural gas especially to spread the import risk.

Liberalization and Competitiveness. Challenging the Old Paradigms and Creating a New Path

In spite of decades of state intervention in energy and industrial matters and public ownership of industrial groups, Italy took in the middle of the 1990s a neo-liberal stand concerning its energy market and embarked on a far-reaching liberalization and deregulation reform (see Di Nucci 2004; Polo and Scarpa 2003).

Designing and implementing policies inspired by privatization and liberalization processes started very early based on logics such as competition and market opening, factors that were incongruent with preexistent Italian culture and policy characterized by a strong state intervention and dirigisme. The liberalization of the sectors was triggered not only by the need to transpose EU directives but especially by the belief that this represented an opportunity to start a reform and put an end to direct state participation (Di Nucci and Russolillo 2017). In a way, we could talk about a "new path creation." At the same time, the crisis of the party system that had shaped the policy of the national energy utilities in the previous decade "*disadvantaged the traditional players in electricity policy making and provoked a change in the structure of relationships in the policy field*" (Prontera 2010).

At the end of the 1990s, Italy's energy sector experienced a deep structural transformation. The change was, in a way, institutionally driven. The "material" engines of these changes were three decrees in the late 1990s, which laid the groundwork for change, and also enabled to enlarge the spectrum of actors in the energy policy arena. The Bassanini decree of 1998 (Legislative Decree 112/1998) about decentralization of administration and the Bersani decree (Legislative Decree 79/1999) on the liberalization of the electricity sector paved the way for a new hierarchical reorganization of the multilevel governance and interaction of the renewable energy sector and set out a new incentive system for RES. The Bersani Decree was passed in 1999, to liberalize the electrical sector and to foster competition in the national electricity system. The Letta Decree of 2000 transposed the EU Directive 98/30 into national policy and forced a gradual opening and a modernization of the natural gas sector. The reform implied the "unbundling" of the former energy monopolies with separation between production, transport, and distribution and mandated divestments in power generation (Polo and Scarpa 2003; Di Nucci 2004).

The internal debate on liberalization had been already strongly influenced in 1994–1995 by the ongoing debate in the EU – especially in the UK – before the EU set up a new legal framework with the Directive 96/92/EC. The Italian reform took place in a political context characterized by great instability and loss of influence of traditional state actors. In this case, one can paraphrase Radaelli (2004) and claim that Europe represented the "solution" to legitimatize the willingness to reform and change paradigm (from state intervention to competition). Subsequent to sectoral EU directives (96/92/EC and 2003/54/EC), Italy's electricity market underwent a steady process of liberalization with a restructuring process that lasted many years and witnessed adjustments and novel developments regarding market rules, new market actors, and new institutions. The debate on the reform in Parliament and in wider circles has been characterized by an "anomalous" actors' cohesion on the necessity to transpose the EU directive into domestic legislation embracing conservative parties as well as the leftist parties and the trade unions opposing the reform. Both the technocratic Dini government and the center-leftist Prodi government (with his Industry Minister Bersani) became part of an "implicit" coalition of interest that achieved in relatively short time a radical unbundling of the national electricity monopolist ENEL (Di Nucci and Russolillo 2017). In 1999, the so-called Bersani Decree changed the situation both on the supply and demand side. The Decree was issued to transpose the European Union's Directive 96/92/EC but actually acted as a "framework law" for restructuring the Italian electricity sector and brought about the most radical changes also for the development of renewables.

Another momentous event was the enactment of Law N.112/98, which transferred competencies on local energy planning and RES exploitation to regional governments. It is not coincidental that the first stage of sustained diffusion of wind power in Italy occurred in a time in which the transfer of powers from the central state to the regions took place, especially in matters concerning government of the territory and energy planning. Regions started to grant capital cost subsidies to promote the setting up of competitive RES-E plants, in addition to the available incentive mechanisms. However, the Regions did not seem to be sufficiently prepared and played a minor role and in a way, the involved municipalities were left alone to manage a complex and delicate phase, which for some aspects is still ongoing.

Sustainability, RES, and "Clean" Energy Paths: Centralization Versus Decentralization

From the beginning of 1997, a general political consensus emerged on the need for enhancing renewable energy paths and reorganizing the whole incentives system and to identify new mechanisms promoting the RES sector (Di Nucci 2007). Even though the societal debate in Italy has not been as pervasive as in Germany with the "Energiewende" (energy transition), the public discourse on sustainable energy paths indicated a bias towards clean energy, anticipating the results of the referendum following the Fukushima disaster in 2011 and banning any further nuclear development. This discourse could also be interpreted as a systemic struggle between centralized and decentralized energy solutions. Brondi et al. (2014, p. 46) assumed that Italy's energy transition is exemplified by a hard link to a technocentric perspective and a soft – even weak – link to societal goals such as citizens' awareness and participation that pushes for technical and societal transformations. They point out that discourses in the parliamentary debates and the national press issues about centralization are more present than decentralized governance, suggesting a "traditional" approach to energy issues. If one considers the parliamentary debates, centralized governance is indeed the prevalent form in almost half the cases. Overall, it can be claimed that there is a very low coordination between centralized and decentralized energy policies.

The energy-policy goals of the two middle-leftist-governments in the years 1997–2000 were based on a duplication of the production-share of hydropower and other RES until 2012 and on an overall RES-E generation of 7 GW. Parallel to this, the "Guidelines for national policies and measures for reduction of GHG emissions" (approved by CIPE in October 1998) specified objectives and actions to achieve Italy's Kyoto commitment for reducing CO_2 emissions by 6.5% versus 1990 data.

A milestone of the energy policy of this period was marked in 1998 by the "National energy and environment conference," a consultative process consisting of a hundred national and a few international hearings and workshops with all relevant stakeholders dealing with institutional, legal, economic, technical, and social aspects of the national energy structure. The outcome of this process culminated in the signing of agreements by all relevant stakeholders and institutional actors ranging from financial institutions to NGOs (Di Nucci 2007; Di Nucci and Russolillo 2017). The way to reach this objective and the RES potential was illustrated in the White Book of 1999. The great merit of the White Book was to provide a survey of RES technologies, indicate their potential, and set intermediate targets for 2002 and 2006. It was planned to increase the RES share from 2.7 GW to 3.3 GW representing a growth from approximately 17.5% to roughly 25% of the electricity generated in Italy. RES-E was to be increased from about 11.7 to 20.3 Mtoe. The White Book also specified policies, strategies, and targets and stressed the importance of the regions by regional and local initiatives and in supporting the national policies. In order to integrate RES at the local level, the White Paper envisaged the initiation of regional and local guidelines and of so-called Renewable Energy Action Plans.

Technological success is feasible when priority is given to the transition, as demonstrated by the German *Energiewende*. In Italy there has not been a pervasive societal debate as in Germany and the energy transformation came only recently. However, there has been a pervasive debate about the incentive system for renewables, and in both politics and society, there have been contrasting arguments concerning the costs and affordability of a sustainable and secure energy system.

Lauber and Schenner (2011, p. 508) referring to the European situation argue that "the coalition ..[.around the feed-in tariff schemes] was able to build a discourse around subsidiarity, good governance and flexibility . . ." This interpretation can be borrowed to describe the development in Italy.

Within 25 years (in 1992 the so-called CIP6 incentive system was introduced), Italy "experimented" with a shift of the incentive systems for renewables (see section "Instruments of the Energy Transitions" below) moving from an initial feed-in system to quota and certificates and back again to various forms of FIT differentiated according to technologies and energy sources.

In order to understand the reasons why there has been a continuous change in support schemes, it is important to consider how the major stakeholders framed the issue and – to put it as Lauber and Schenner (2011, p. 512) *"discussed the topic into discursive issue networks,"* which are *"kept together by a common 'argumentative strategy' or 'interpretative scheme and frame."*

The green economy set into motion by the RES boom is still developing slowly, but steadily. The Italian green economy companies make up for 27% of all Italian companies and are responsible for almost 40% of new jobs created in Italy in 2017 (Brizzo 2018). The activation of the capacity payments in 2018 (ARERA 2018) will surely trigger the emergence of new actors, such as energy aggregators and other service providers exploiting the digitalization trend of the sector. This should benefit the final users and enhance distributed generation.

Political Institutions and Actors

In the first half of the last century, the Italian energy policy arena was dominated by only a few actors: the two state-owned energy enterprises for natural gas and electricity ENI and ENEL, the Ministry of Industry (changing its name regularly), later in 1986 joined by the Ministry of Environment and the national nuclear Energy Agency CNEN, later in 1994 transformed into an agency for alternative energy and sustainable development (ENEA). The implementation of planning efforts was regularly hampered by a plethora of regulations, often contradicting each other, by the absence of a statutory power to enforce the various plans, by technical weaknesses of the political and ministerial bureaucracy, and by representatives of the political parties serving as presidents or CEOs in state enterprises.

Today Italy has a rather complex decision-making system, exemplified in some cases by a large number of entities and by a high level of fragmentation both vertically at the government level and horizontally at the sector level. Energy policy is characterized by an entangled system of interactions among the most important institutional actors and a rather complex subdivision of responsibilities. The key competencies for energy policy remain within the Ministry of Economic Development (MSE, Ministero dello Sviluppo Economico). Its department for energy and mining is also in charge of renewable energy policy. The Environment Ministry coordinates the activities concerning greenhouse gas emissions, the transposition of the EC-directives for emission trading, and the solar-programs and is also the co-signer of policy measures promoting renewable energy and energy efficiency within the responsibility of the MSE. The responsibility for biomass lies within the Ministry of Agriculture that promotes the utilization of RES in agriculture sector and provides financial backing for the cultivation of energy crops. Beside these institutions, some responsibilities also rest within the Ministries of Transport, Finance, Culture and National Heritage, 19 Regions and two autonomous Provinces. Additionally, there are a number of governmental organizations like the National Research Council (CNR) and the National Agency for New Technologies, Energy and Environment (ENEA). The latter deals with R&D of technologies in the field of energy-efficiency, renewables, and their dissemination. Furthermore, CIPE (Interministerial Committee for Economic Planning) chaired by the President of the Council of Ministers is responsible for the co-ordination and horizontal integration of national policies. Its competencies, among many others, include climate change. The committee approves national GHG emissions reduction programs. In addition, there is also the Inter-Ministerial Technical Committee for Emissions of GHGs (CTE) established in 2012 to support the CIPE's climate-related work.

New actors were made necessary through the liberalization process. Law 481/95 (also known as "Authority Law") laid out the rules for competition and for the regulation of public utilities, in line with the European reform. It created a new regulatory authority, at the time named AEEG, only involved in electricity and natural gas regulation. Later its mission (including the setting of tariffs, service quality standards, and the technical and economic conditions for access and interconnections to the networks) was enlarged to include also water and the regulator was renamed in AEEGSI. This is a strong, independent, and capable watch-dog and can be considered as the most robust motor of the energy system transformation in Italy. The commissioners (one president and four members) in charge for 7 years are nominated by a decree of the President of Italy. Currently the Authority is named Authority for Energy, Networks and the Environment – ARERA.

The decentralization of the public administration brought about by the so-called Bassanini-Decree (Nr.112/98), and an amendment of the Constitution have strengthened the role of the "Regioni." A shift of responsibilities for energy policy has taken place from the central ministries to the regional administrations. However, there is a blurred distribution of competencies between State and Regions, which has often resulted in differing energy policies. Feliziani (2013) speaks of fragmented regulatory frameworks. Italian regions have competencies for economic development, but their capacity for policy action remains limited, and central government still plays an important role in regional development issues. The role of the regions in policy matters has been strengthened especially as a result of progressive devolution and of the EU regional policy. Against this background, it is not surprising that the first stage of sustained expansion of renewables occurred in a time in which the transfer of powers from the central state to the regions took place, especially in matters concerning governance of the territory and energy planning. Regions started to grant capital cost subsidies promoting the setting-up of competitive RES-E plant, in addition to the available incentive mechanisms. The Regions, however, have no responsibility for fundamental policy decisions that are still in the jurisdiction of the national state. The amendment of the national law on Environmental Impact Assessment 104/2017 establishing uniform rules has for example affected a sort of "re-centralization" of procedures on infrastructure and energy projects and has affected changes in the distribution of administrative tasks between State and Regions and in regulatory competencies. Another example showing a "re-centralization" tendency was the failed attempt to establish the supremacy of "strategic national interest" for the case of "production, transport, and distribution of energy" (by amending via a referendum in December 2016 an article of the Constitution).

Within the government, energy policy is supervised by the inter-ministry committee for economic planning (CIPE) that is responsible for guidelines on a national level.

The Competition Authority (AGCM, Autorità Garante della Concorrenza e del Mercato,) is the independent antitrust body, established by Law in of 1990. The AGCM enforces rules against anticompetitive behavior also in the electricity and natural gas sectors, and recently even in the district heating sector.

The liberalization of the energy market enlarged the spectrum of the relevant actors and established an independent transmission system operator, TERNA, responsible for managing electricity transmission and dispatching, as well as issuing technical rules for planning and operating connections to the grid. The Gestore dei Sistemi Energetici (GSE) is the state-owned company in charge with fostering RES. GSE is also the parent company of:

- Acquirente Unico (AU) is in charge of serving as a national wholesaler to protect energy consumers.
- Gestore dei Mercati Energetici (GME) in charge of the electronic platform to exchange power, natural gas and energy tradable certificates (e.g., white certificates for energy efficiency).
- Ricerca sul Sistema Energetico (RSE) in charge of R&D.

Additionally, there are over 30 regional and local energy-agencies, established in the framework of the SAVE-Programs of the EC, dealing mostly with energy-efficiency, renewables, information, and counselling at local level. The complexity of the current governance is illustrated in Fig. 5.

In the electricity market, the major actor continues to be the ex-monopolist ENEL, which was privatized in 1992 and transformed into a joint stock company. Through the reform, ENEL was mandated to reduce its vertical integration in electricity transmission and to divest about a third of its total 56,000 MW of generation capacity and some distribution networks. Today, the Italian power market is fairly dispersed, but power generation is still dominated ENEL and the power

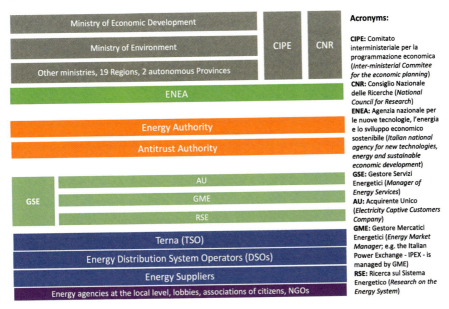

Fig. 5 Energy governance in Italy – The current stakeholders' ecosystem (elaboration by the authors)

distribution market is concentrated with ENEL Distribuzione operating almost 80% of the network despite the existence of more than 130 local operators.

In the gas sector, ENI controls primary distribution, storage facilities, and gas imports, while Snam Rete Gas (ENI holds 50.07% of the shares) still dominates the transport network. The existing barriers to access appear to prevent the full development of competition. The market is strongly integrated and the former monopolists still enjoys a dominant position in the whole value chain.

Coordination, Instruments, and Issues of the Italian Energy Transition

The analysis of the coordination among different scales has been a rather neglected subject. Coordinated actions are a prerequisite for low-carbon paths. Following Sarrica et al. (2018), we can claim that there is a coexistence of top-down and bottom-up processes of translation connecting supranational regulations and targets with policies and discourses implemented at the national and even local level. In fact, there is a strong integration of EU, Italian (national state level) and regional/local policy and energy and environmental issues. The case of Italy allows us to underline that a European policy can provide a model around which to redesign a domestic policy, but for this to take place, the actors able to exploit adaptational pressures are indispensable (Di Nucci and Russolillo 2017).

On the one hand, there is an ongoing process of decentralization of energy policy and planning procedures; on the other hand, there has been a tendency in the last few years for a re-centralization of legislative and administrative competences in the energy field. Thus, although the various governance levels in matters of energy coexist, there is now a sort of renaissance of positions supporting the supremacy of the national governance level which has been reinforced in the last few years. A part for the examples of a failed amendment of the Constitution and of changes in the Environmental Impact Assessment regulations mentioned above in section "Political Institutions and Actor," another example for a shifting of competences at the national level is the so-called Sblocca Italia (Unlock Italy) law (Legge 164/2014). This enhances and streamlines permitting for infrastructure projects of national interest such as transmission lines for natural gas and electricity, onshore and offshore oil, GNL conversion systems.

A number of programs and initiatives have paved the way for the transition to a low carbon future, which evolved at both central and regional/local level and acted as drivers. In the following, we discuss briefly these external and domestic drivers and describe the instruments mix.

Drivers of Energy Transition

We can distinguish between external and domestic drivers for energy transition. European policy has been a major driving force for initiating the energy transition in line with other European countries. Amongst the domestic drivers, the most notable ones are regulatory drivers and eventually the propulsive role of some "change agents." In this respect, a key question is to what extent the Italian incumbents played important influences, negative or positive, for the success of low carbon technologies and policies.

We can claim that in Italy, external (EU) as well as internal dynamics (political parties, NGOs, regional political actors and economic interests) determined new priorities (e.g., in RES) and drove a change towards low carbon development paths and enhanced the transition. These have taken place at a central as well as a regional level. In some policy areas, which are also relevant for renewable energy policy such as regional and cohesion policy, cooperation and coordination mechanisms at EU levels set through more deeply. In this case, the pressure of the EU was exerted through the allocation and administration of the cohesion and structural funds. The case of competition policy is even more significant, since the realization of the internal market for energy and the subsequent liberalization of the energy markets has transported EU influence and mechanisms into the Italian energy arena.

It is important to point out that participation in EU programs, especially in EFRE and cohesion programs, pushed participating regions to adapt to the changing institutional environment. The case of RES-T and bio-methane, however, shows that where the EU-induced policy practices were conflicting with the actors' interests, they tended to adjust only "formally" without changing their preferences or internalizing the new requirements. By contrast, when EU-imported practices were compatible with the actors' goals and preferences, mechanisms of Europeanization through learning and horizontal diffusion of what is considered a "good practice" could also be initiated and entangled with the motivation for adjustment (e.g., RES-E incentives) (Di Nucci and Russolillo 2017).

From the institutional and regulatory point of view, the decentralization of administration (the Bassanini Decree) and the already mentioned Bersani Decree (liberalization of the electricity sector) – both released in the late 1990s – can be considered as the major institutional/regulatory drivers and as the landmarks for change. They paved the way for a new hierarchical reorganization of the multilevel governance and interaction of the (renewable) energy sector. Thus in the late 1990s, there was a concomitant adaption of polity and policy, and the radical changes through the Bassanini Law and Bersani Law have represented the point of departure for a Europeanization of politics, policy, as well as of polity (a good example is the creation of the energy regulator) in line with the creation of European regulators (Di Nucci and Russolillo 2017).

The Bassanini Law of 1998 (Legislative Decree 112/1998) about administrative decentralization transferred several RES policy tasks and competencies on local energy planning to regional administrations whereby regions were empowered to establish funds to promote RES in an autonomous way. The Bersani Decree (Legislative Decree 79/1999) about the liberalization of the electricity sector set in motion the liberalization of the electricity market and established a new incentive system for RES. A major driver for energy transition is certainly the sustained deployment of RES. The current development has taken place in a context where domestic and European policies evolved together. The adjustment to European policy implied a continuous calibration between national differences, various pressures to adapt, and different processes of mediation and responses. An example is the changing choice of instruments to support renewables that moving from a sort of FIT regime opted for quota and certificates and then following the European trend returned to a FIT scheme. However, the actors in the RES arena presented evolving strategies over a time horizon of 20 years. For this reason, it is difficult to separate the net effect and role of the EU and the domestic mechanisms through which changes were set into motion.

In that respect, it should be underlined that the Italian regulation of the power market could not *"promote a coherent strategy for the transition towards a decentralized paradigm, in spite of the unquestionable economic and environmental benefits related to the deployment of distributed energy resources"* (Gaspari and Lorenzoni 2018). An open question remains whether in Italy there is a dominance of the technocentric perspective with regard to energy transition and whether developments of smart grids and distributed generation has acted/can act as a driver towards a sustainable transition. In the case of the Italian electricity incumbents, the realization and exploitation of the smart grid (primarily for a better load management and future capacity market management) has helped avoid lock-in situations. Starting in 2001, Italy was among the first European countries to deploy smart meters, and now the DSOs are preparing the second wave of rollouts (Di Nucci 2014). The DSO of the ENEL group alone is planning to install almost 40 million second generation meters (enabled to provide innovative services for the final users) by 2030, with a first milestone of 13 million by 2019 (Ryberg 2017).

Instruments of the Energy Transitions

Flanagan et al. (2011) pointed out that analyzing a policy mix means more than a combination of policy instruments; it also includes the processes by which such instruments emerge and interact and the continuous adjustment between actors and systems. This observation is useful while analyzing the Italian "instrument mix." In particular, the Europeanization in Italian RES policies shows a continuous calibration between national distinctness, various pressures to adapt, and processes of mediation and response (Di Nucci and Russolillo 2017). Amongst the instruments that determined changes, we can find regulatory instruments, incentive-based instruments, GHG emission reduction goals, and elements of soft governance. The wealth of these instruments, especially those supporting RES, seems to suggest that with each of them there has been an attempt to meet different policy objectives and that different stakeholder groups might have been actively taking part in designing policies.

Long-Term Strategies and Programs
At a national level, there are a number of specific support plans. The most important ones are: the National Energy Efficiency Action Plan; the National Renewable Energy Action Plan; the National Energy Strategy (NES); and the National Reform Program.

The 10-year plan released in November 2017 by the Italian government (MSE 2017) represents a milestone for addressing the adjustment of the national energy system towards sustainability at the same time guaranteeing security of supply and industrial competitiveness. The National Energy Strategy is more ambitious than the European goals for Italy and contains a target of a 21% decrease in global GHG emissions. This strategy defined four main objectives to improve the competitiveness and sustainability of the Italian energy sector by 2020: reducing energy costs by aligning prices to European average prices; meeting and going beyond European targets set out in the 2020 European Climate-energy package and Italy's National Action Plan of June 2010 (NAP); improving security of supply, with a reduction in foreign dependency from 84% to 67% of total energy needs; enhancing growth and employment by mobilizing investments in the "green economy" (MSE 2017). The novelty of this document is that it is the outcome of a participation process in which the Italian Parliament, the Regions, and approximately 250 stakeholders were involved. Another novelty is that the strategy for the long-term energy transition is no longer based on setting sectoral targets but also indicated measures and fields for coordination. In general, the NES is aligned with the content of the Clean Energy for All Europeans Package, confirming our analysis of Europeanization driven changes.

Regulatory Instruments

For a long time, despite favorable support conditions, the Italian green energy sector witnessed a stalemate-situation. In spite of promising market prospects, the sector, in a state of insecurity for years, suffered from a sort of paralysis of the national market, characterized by many announced measures that, however, failed to materialize or were implemented with delay. Moreover, the different positions of the political parties on energy strategies, but especially the influence of local politicians "[..] *transformed the procedure of localization for new power plants* [including renewables] *into an exhausting negotiation between central and local government*" (Prontera 2010, p. 498). Overall, the major obstacles for RES expansion have been the plentiful bureaucratic and institutional barriers.

One of the most important regulatory instruments is the so-called single authorization" (Autorizzazione Unica) for large installations (Legislative Decree No. 387/2003). This helped with streamlining and accelerating authorization procedures and halving the time for issuing the single authorization (AU) (Legislative Decree No. 28/2011). Additionally, in 2012 there were introduced administrative simplifications concerning strategic infrastructures and plants for the supply of key services (including biofuel production) (Law No. 35). From 2014 onwards, there were bureaucratic and procedural simplifications for the so-called Thermal Account" (Law No. 164/2014).

The National Energy Strategy (adopted in March 2013 in its first version) comprised measures for energy planning which included further upgrading of the governance system, to improve and simplify national-level horizontal coordination. These measures concern mainly the interaction between the energy matters under the remit of the different Ministries and relations between the Government and the ARERA in the regulated sectors, and interaction with network and service operators. The energy strategy stresses the need for better coordination between the national government and the regions regarding legislative functions and between the national government, the Regions, and the local authorities regarding administrative functions, in order to generate reliable rules and to render authorization procedures simpler and faster.

RES Support Instruments and Incentives

The support of RES-E in Italy has been characterized by a contradictory, discontinuous development and there is still a controversial debate on the instruments and the "best mix" of instruments to promote RES. It is commonplace that one of the grounds for the steady growth of renewables is the rather generous incentive policy.

The present system of incentives is very complex and differentiates according to size and technologies. Depending on the renewable energy source and the size of the plants, RES-E plant operators may be obliged to opt for a certain system or may have more options. In the last 25 years, there has been a transition from a sort of FIT (so-called CIP 92) to quota and certificates and back to a FIT (feed-in tariff) premium regime and back again to market-based instruments. The Italian government adopted in March 2011 a legislative decree implementing the EU Directive 2009/28/EC.

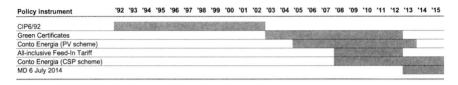

Fig. 6 Overview of RES support systems in Italy 1992–2015. (Source: IEA 2016: 83)

The new ruling covered issues such as administrative permits, grid improvements, incentives, control and penalties. The law – as the Government declared in a statement – aimed to *"strengthen and rationalize the renewable energy subsidy system and to reach the double objective of increasing renewable energy production in line with European objectives and reducing the linked subsidies which are ultimately passed-through to the consumer"* (LOC 2011). In 2005, the Italian government introduced the first "Conto Energia" scheme, a specific feed-in tariff system for PV generated electricity (and also CSP, i.e., concentrated solar power). The payments were designed to be made over a 20-year period and to encourage both smaller and larger producers to invest in the installation of photovoltaic systems. Between 2005 and 2013, five different "Conto Energia" schemes were introduced by ministerial decree. Each scheme had differing terms and conditions and tariffs provided to prosumers and industrial operators. The evolution of the RES support schemes is illustrated in Fig. 6.

Instruments to Support Energy Efficiency

In 2014, Legislative Decree No. 102/2014 transposed the Energy Efficiency Directive 2012/27/EU into national legislation, with the aim of achieving the 2020 energy saving objective of 20 Mtoe of primary energy, equivalent to 15.5 Mtoe of final energy. A plan is devoted to the energy upgrading of the national stock of buildings in order to activate investments and the National Plan for Nearly Zero Energy Buildings. The Italian policy package also contains the definition of minimum energy performance standards and energy performance certificates. With respect to residential housing, fiscal and financial schemes such as tax allowances and low interest loans are main elements in the Italian energy efficiency instruments in the building sector. Italy has implemented various measures to increase the energy efficiency of appliances.

Legislative Decree No. 102/2014 that transposed the Directive 2012/27/EU on energy efficiency also establishes the National Energy Efficiency Fund at the Ministry of Economic Development to foster energy efficiency projects implemented by public authorities, ESCOs and businesses to increase the energy efficiency of the buildings, industrial installations and production processes. This Fund is endowed with €490 million in the period 2014–2020 (Trotta et al. 2015).

White Certificates

A number of EU Member States are implementing energy efficiency policy portfolios that consist of energy saving obligations imposed on some category of energy market operators, in some cases coupled with a trading system for energy efficiency certificates (known as white certificates, often shortened in WhCs). The energy efficiency market opening has relied on White Certificates with some positive results, surely they *"help internalize energy-use externalities and address information gaps, organizational inefficiencies and liquidity constraints that hamper energy efficiency investments"* (Giraudet and Finon 2014, p. 24).

White certificates were introduced in Italy in 2005 and trading them is justified in the case of energy market operators that fall short of their predefined target. They are allowed to buy certificates from operators that exceeded theirs or from other subjects, such as ESCOs, whose market growth has always been a goal of the White Certificates scheme. This has often been confirmed publicly by the current public system operator (GSE). In Italy, the system imposed the obligation on to energy distributors (power and natural gas). Albeit some governance and regulatory changes that saw, among other things, the leading role being shifted from the national energy authority (that remains in charge of regulatory issues) to GSE (in charge of the evaluation), the system has remained substantially the same so far. In 2016, GSE issued a total of 5.5 million WhCs, equivalent to almost 1.7 Mtoe of primary energy savings, with a growing trend with respect to previous year (GSE 2016).

Economic and Fiscal Incentives

For RES, there are also *fiscal regulation mechanisms* which act as incentives to invest in RES-E facilities. Renewables are supported at a national level as well as by regions, provinces, and local authorities. Furthermore, RES promotion in southern regions benefit from additional fiscal support. Tax deductions (topping 55%) for the energy upgrading of buildings were introduced in Italy by the Budget Law 2007 and are still in force. These fiscal deductions have been key drivers of energy efficiency improvements in the housing sector. Nevertheless there are some flaws, as *"the main drawback of income tax incentives is that the taxpayer must pay the efficient equipment's up-front cost and recoup a part of that cost later through tax deductions or credits"* (de la Rue du Can and Leventis 2014).

The total number of actions implemented have been decisive to achieve the energy saving goals. Tax deductions (for both residential and commercial buildings) consist of reductions of IRPEF (personal income tax) and IRES (corporate income tax) in respect of actions to improve the energy efficiency of existing buildings, in particular for expenses for reducing heating demand by upgrading of the building's energy performance; improving the building's thermal insulation (replacement of windows, including blinds or shutters, and insulation of roofs, walls and floors); installing solar thermal panels; replacing heating systems (with condensing boilers or heat pumps); replacing electrical water heaters with heat pump water heaters.

The key policy instruments analyzed are summarized in Table 1, using three macro categories: regulatory, economic, and fiscal instruments.

Soft Governance

Soft forms of governance including the diffusion of best practice and information campaigns may also have played a role in driving the transition. If one takes into

Table 1 Sample of key policy instruments in Italy for the energy sector

Sector	Regulatory instruments	Economic incentives	Fiscal incentives
Electricity supply	Reform of the electricity market and liberalization (Legislative Decree No. 79 of 16 March 1999) Smart meter and smart grids deployment (2001-onwards) Open-up of the wholesale market (2004-onwards) Liberalization of the retail market (2007-onwards) Single authorization decree streamlining and accelerating authorization procedures (Legislative Decree No. 28/2011). Yearly National Energy Strategy (2013-onwards) National capacity market (2018)	CIP6/92 for renewables and so-called assimilated energy sources Green certificate scheme (2003–2012) PV incentives (2005–2013) All inclusive Feed-in Tariff (2008–2012) Ministerial Decree 6.7.2014 and 23.6.2016 introducing new schemes for FIT and the use of auctioning systems	Lower VAT (10%) for PV systems (2007-onwards)
Heat supply	Inclusion of District Heating and Cooling sector amongst the target of the national energy agency (2014-onwards)	Thermal energy production from RES (2012-onwards)	Fiscal credits for district heating systems with biomass (2001-onwards)
Energy efficiency (industry, households, buildings	White certificates scheme (2005–2013) Building regulations Nearly zero energy buildings (Law no.90/2013) from 2018 – onwards (for new public buildings) and 2021-onwards (private buildings)	Legislative Decree 102/2014° (ref. 2012/27/ EU and national Energy Efficiency Fund) White certificates scheme (2013-onwards) Bureaucratic and procedural simplifications for the so-called Thermal Account (Law No. 164/2014). National Energy Efficiency Fund (Ministry of Economic Development) to foster energy efficiency projects implemented by public authorities	Fiscal incentives for energy efficiency retrofitting (Ecobonus, 2014-onwards) Reductions of IRPEF (personal income tax) and IRES (corporate income tax) for activities improving the energy efficiency of existing buildings, in particular for investments aimed at reducing heating demand by upgrading of the building's energy performance

(continued)

Table 1 (continued)

Sector	Regulatory instruments	Economic incentives	Fiscal incentives
Transport	Energy Authority decisions (ARG/elt 56/10 and RG/elt 242/10) to jump start the EVs recharging stations (2010-onwards) Legislative Decree no. 257, 2016 (EVs charging stations for new buildings) Interministerial decree 2 March 2018 (promotion of biomethane for transport)		Fiscal incentives for VAT account owners with regards to LPG, Hybrid and EVs (2018)

consideration the number of cooperative EU projects in which Italian institutions and economic actors participate(d) and the levels of funding received, the beneficial role of dissemination activities and coordinating actions are apparent. Active participation in such programs facilitated policy transfer from the EU to domestic level and meant that policy learning was a continual and reflexive process. EU Programs (Framework Program, Intelligent Energy Europe, INTERREG, EFRE) and projects as well as approaches to policy and the transfer of best practices were key and were positively endorsed by the broadest range of actors in a wide variety of institutions.

Coordination Mechanisms and Multilevel Governance

As Florini and Sovacool (2009: 5239) remarked "...*international energy markets suffer from lack of appropriate governance. Price signals in these markets are distorted by national government policies on both the supply and the demand side. Investment in future energy supply is often inadequate and fails to serve the public interest, leading to extreme price volatility. Because national governments see energy services as crucial to national security and national power, they intervene in the sector to promote energy "independence" or at least to assure supplies. Yet governments largely fail to regulate energy in other key international aspects, such as climate change...*" In order to accomplish a transition to a low carbon economy at a political level, new paradigms are needed. Energy transition is a multi-level task. From the multilevel perspective (MLP), government and firms, as well as other stakeholders, have a central role to play in a system's change and in the diffusion of low carbon technologies (Foxon 2011). It has been advocated that in complex adaptive systems, policy-makers should manage the dynamics of possible transitions and avoid early lock-ins (van den Bergh et al. 2011). Rogge and Reichardt (2016) purport that policy mixes are embedded in multilevel governance systems spanning supranational, national and sub-national levels of governance.

Smith et al. (2010, p. 446) noted that *"the MLP provides a useful heuristic for considering the temporal aspects of transitions. It does this by considering multi-level processes of socio-technical structuration constituting specific functional spaces (e.g. mobility, energy, housing)."* Moreover, coordination mechanisms imply a discussion of the struggle/balancing of centralization and decentralization within multilevel governance. However, it appears that in Italy centralized and decentralized energy systems do not necessarily exclude each other. At different levels, technological, organizational and regulatory governance and social mechanisms are involved in both systems and a transitional, sustainable energy system might combine centralized elements – such as large-scale technological infrastructures – together with community-owned generation plants and microgeneration (Brondi et al. 2014). Sarrica et al. (2018, p. 444) analyzed political debates and newspaper reports and carried out interviews to elicit how "alternative views associated with energy sustainability are translated, supported or resisted, across different scales." They discovered both coherence, but also inconsistencies between discourses on energy sustainability taking place at different governance levels. They concluded that there is a need to consider bottom-up inputs in national and regional strategies by enhancing participation and public engagement in energy governance. Participation issues have been taken adequately into consideration in the National Energy Strategy 2017. Consultations included 40 meetings with the stakeholders and one online consultation. In the online consultation, 14% of the total contributions received (251) came from citizens while 10% from academic institutions and research centers (MSE 2017).

The Supranational Level

We argued that European directives offered the "solution" to legitimatize the willingness to reform and change energy paradigm and challenge some path dependence (strong centralism and dirigisme) (Di Nucci and Russolillo 2017). We did not find evidence that the transformation of the energy system induced by the Europeanization acted as a driver for changing the balance between interest groups. There are signs for the existence of mediation factors such as actors and institutions (e.g., new actors such as regulators; "reformed" political parties, etc.) who can facilitate adaptive pressures at the national level.

For example, in the late 1990s, there has been a concomitant adaption of polity, policy, and politics. A good example is the creation of the regulatory Agency for Electricity and Gas AEEG, in line with the creation of European regulators.

The National Level

The governance at the national level is very complex and two key ministries, i.e., the MSE and the Ministry for the Environment, Land and Sea (MATTM) oversee the energy policy arena in Italy and hence most of the EU directives' reception. The competency of each ministry is clear but often various institutions belong to such ministries and interact in the energy field. This appears to result in coordination difficulties and higher transaction costs than may otherwise be the case. In the past, overlapping measures evolved, which have also changed several times in the recent years. This has contributed to unnecessary complexity and regulatory uncertainty for sector stakeholders (IEA 2016a).

The Regional Level
In the past, regional policy has mostly concentrated on north-south disparities and promoted industrial subsidies, investment in infrastructure, and state-owned industrial activities under the coordination of a special agency (Cassa per il Mezzogiorno). Later this agency was abolished and the institutional infrastructure for regional policy was reorganized. Europeanization of the Italian regional policies has promoted an increased participation of Italy in EU decision-making processes in this area, especially due to a stronger engagement of regions in Brussels. Thus the participation of Italian regional actors in the programs and definition of the EU cohesion and structural policy constitutes an interesting case (also for the RES field) showing a timid shift from a top-down to a bottom–up approach, or – to put as Brunazzo (2010) – from the role of a "policy-taker" to that of a "policy-shaper." Up to the end of 2012, investment co-financed by the European Regional Development Fund (ERDF) in the period 2007–2012 resulted in a cumulative RES-E capacity of 625.8 MW, of which 250.8 MW in the period 2011–2012. Moreover, if we look at the Italian participation in typical EU dissemination and near-to market RES project such as ALTENER within the Intelligent Energy Europe program, we can see that in the period 2005–2014 the regional participation in these projects increased notably with a peak in Lombardy, Latium and Tuscany. On the other hand, projects in energy within the INTERREG program regions, such as Abruzzi, Liguria, etc., were also very active.

Following Graziano (2010) we can consider the EU cohesion policy to have *"[..] reinforced the 'politicization of the regional territory' and further legitimized the regions as political arenas due to the development and support of regional interests in connection with the availability of EU resources for development."* In fact, in the period 2000–2006, an exceptional amount of financial resources corresponding to 70% of the total Structural Funds available for Italy was allocated to the various Italian regional administrations that were involved in projects and regional programs in the RES field. It is important to point out that for example participation in EU programs, especially in EFRE and cohesion programs pushed participating regions to adapt to the changing institutional environment. Renewable energy generation has a positive impact on economic growth at the regional level (Magnani and Vaona 2013). This is somehow also confirmed by Corsatea (2014). By identifying the key drivers of renewable energy patenting activity, he analyzed data from 1998 to 2007 in 20 Italian regions and discovered not only that local researchers and regional public research subsidies contributed enormously to the development of innovation activities but also that regional characteristics, such as regional energy dependence and political orientation of regional councils, have played an important role.

Recent research is showing some interesting issues related to spending efficiency of regions (Meleddu and Pulina 2018). In fact, special statute regions and southern ones are performing best in term of technical efficiency. Nevertheless, the review of the first regional Energy Plans required by the Law 112/1998 (Art. 30) and issued between 2003 and 2010 is still considered a matter of national energy governance.

Municipal Level

Affiliation to European and international or national climate/energy networks is a good indicator for the role played by municipal actors in this policy field. City alliance networks (Energy Cities, Climate Alliance, Cities for Climate Protection, etc.) play an important role to engage local decision makers in initiating sustainable energy paths at the municipal level and provide some technical support, especially tools.

The Covenant of Mayors (CoM), launched in 2008, can be considered an interesting example of multi-level governance in which local and regional authorities take the lead in increasing energy efficiency and the deployment of RES and try to meet the EU 2020 targets in their territories through Sustainable Energy Action Plans (SEAP). With the help of SEAPs, cities implement sustainable measures in a structured way and monitor their effects. "A SEAP is also an instrument for cities to communicate to stakeholders – both locally and beyond – the importance of energy and climate protection and to encourage citizens and other relevant actors to take a part in the city's ambitions" (ICLEI 2011).

Italy is the country with the highest share of cities integrated in the CoM. New signatories pledge to reduce CO_2 emissions by at least 40% by 2030 and to adopt an integrated approach to tackling mitigation and adaptation to climate change. As of November 2017, according to the CoM website (http://www.covenantofmayors.eu/about/covenant-in-figures_en.html) out of 7755 signatories, 3981 Italian signatories representing 71% of the Italian population joined the network. Of these, 3775 (95%) have submitted SEAPs and 106 (3%) monitor them. These data indicate the responsiveness of the Italian local governments to the issues of energy efficiency and renewable energy.

Outcomes, Challenges, and Prospects

Italy has already achieved its RES targets for 2020, with a 17.5% RES share of total energy consumption in 2015 vis-a-vis a 17% target to be reached by 2020. The target of a 28% RES share of total energy consumption by 2030 is ambitious but feasible. In fact, the challenge of decarbonizing the energy system and especially the electricity sector together with the ambition to drive the transition to a low carbon economy and society is at least partly mirrored in the National Energy Strategy (NSE) of 2017. Long-term policy signals are key for new investment in energy. The NSE was originated from a novel participation process, which involved all the public and private stakeholders of the sector in both its preliminary stage and during the public consultation. In line with the EU long-term targets, there is a clear recognition for the need to render the Italian energy system sustainable in the long run. The document provides an overview on how the domestic energy market should look by

2030, and therefore proposes recommendations and indicates the conditions necessary to succeed. Beyond the rhetoric of such documents, the NES is characterized by ambition and multifaceted targets, which call for coherent and coordinated energy, environmental, regional, and industrial policies. The challenges for policy makers are not trivial; they are technical, political, and societal and imply a balanced approach to combine the security of supply, sustainability, and competitiveness and may also involve institutional changes.

While, on the one side, it is reassuring that the Italian strategy is also concerned with societal aspects and the role that citizens can play through a sustainable energy use, on the other side, community engagement remains a key challenge. Citizens-as-prosumers, large initiatives, and sizing the opportunity for the flexibility of the electricity system offered by smart energy communities are still practically in their infancy. Moreover, the NSE long-term strategy is not legally binding and it is unclear whether following the change of Government in June 2018 all the measures contained in the strategy will have a chance to become law. On top of that, it remains unclear how Italy will meet the ambitious targets indicated in the NES.

The EU Clean Energy Package, including a recast of the Directive on the Promotion of RES (EC 2016), also addresses renewable energy communities (REC). The EC acknowledges that REC can bring about added value in terms of local acceptance of RES and private investment capital. Article 22 of the proposed Recast Directive, which includes definitions, criteria, and guidance for their realization, also contains new provisions to empower REC to participate in the market and to become market actors. It defines REC as entities through which citizens and/or local authorities own or participate in the production and/or use of renewable energy. A REC can be an SME or a nonprofit organization of which the shareholders or members cooperate in the generation, distribution, storage, or supply of energy from RES, fulfilling a set of criteria. The proposal also stipulates that Member States shall take into account the specificities of REC when designing support schemes. These bottom-up initiatives and energy democracy set free the entrepreneurial potential of citizens.

We identified some past energy trajectories and features of the energy system that may be useful for understanding the ongoing transition. However, it remains an open question how the political and institutional legacies we analyzed will influence this transformation.

The process of Europeanization has been without doubt key to jump starting the energy transition in Italy. The Italian RES policies show a continuous calibration between (i) national distinctness, (ii) various pressures to adapt, and (iii) processes of mediation and response. Some policy areas have played a more important role than others have, for example, the regional and cohesion policy, cooperation and coordination mechanisms at the EU level, and the latter also in relationship with the governance of the energy sector.

Among the domestic drivers, decentralization and the role attributed by the devolution to the regional governments have played an important role in enhancing the deployment of renewables and set forth more sustainable paths.

On top of the issues stated above, a number of additional open questions remain:

- Is there a predominant technocentric perspective about energy transition concerning distributed generation, smart grids and ultimately the digitalization of the sector and is this acting as a driver towards a sustainable path?
- What is the role of electro mobility in particular?
- What kind of role will the incumbents play?

The topic of the digitalization process of the power sector (and of the smart technology and practices associated to it in the framework of smart cities, such as smart grids and the connected new solutions, including "Internet of things") might rapidly add new layers and actors to the governance system analyzed in our work and also act upon the regulatory framework. Surely, the recent full start of the capacity market is a good example and is fully in line with the foreseen stronger role of intermittent RES-E in the country. The national energy strategy of 2017 seems to confirm that a technocentric perspective on energy transition can act as a driver for sustainability, also because starting from 2020 the supporting mechanisms for RES-E might evolve towards the market parity (MSE 2017), i.e., policies that will trigger more investment on renewables and hopefully a simplified regulatory framework for decarbonization.

Concerning the broad and long-term societal debate, an open question remains whether future public support may shift the focus from renewables to energy efficiency. This support regime has been heavily criticized, and Italy's incentives system is said to introduce distortions with respect to the cost of public resources allocated for each unit of CO_2 avoided. As part of the country's energy saving incentives, the public cost of energy per MWh is now 25 times lower than the public cost to support renewables. As remarked by Deloitte (2015), this has contributed to the adoption of not-yet-mature renewable technologies. In the long term, this may not result in the most capable system for reducing emissions and may provoke a diminishing societal acceptance for certain development paths.

In Europe, Italy showed in 2017 the highest motorization index: 62.4 cars per 100 inhabitants, even higher than Germany (55.7 cars per 100 inhabitants). This record is, on the one side, responsible for congestion in traffic that costs around 1% of GDP, and on the other side, it pinpoints that a third of the Italian energy consumption derives from the transport sector. Against this background, sustainable mobility can play an important role in the national energy transition and help realizing the ambitious plan aiming at carbon reduction of 80–95% from the 1990 level by 2050. The goals are expected to be met through a reinforcement of the mechanisms put in place for the 20-20-20 energy package. Electric vehicles (EVs) are expected to contribute to CO_2 abatement strategies (Perujo and Ciuffo 2010) as well as to provide a suitable solution to urban air quality, a highly sensitive topic for local administrators and policy makers in northern Italy. Although in Italy the presence of EVs and recharging stations is still negligible and both public awareness and acceptance by the final user are still underdeveloped, in 2016 the Legislative Decree No. 257 set the obligation for new buildings – excluding public real estate – larger than 500 square meters to foresee the presence and the necessary systems of charging stations for EVs. Such a focused policy might help kick-start the process as an integral element for a sustainable transition.

Some strategic energy targets have already been met also thanks to the impact of the economic crisis on the country. Deloitte (2015) warned from a competitive and economic growth point of view that the transition should not penalize the Italian economy in sectors exposed to international competition. It is, however, legitimate to question to what extent a positive economic reversal could spoil Italy's ability to reach its efficiency objectives, especially from the starting position of good performance of the national energy efficiency as opposed to other EU countries. The 2050 Energy Roadmap could represent an important drive for structural changes on incumbents and in general on Italy's energy markets. Incumbent energy companies are forced to invest in paths that gauge between the external pressure of accomplishing sound environmental goals (e.g., GHG reduction) and conforming to existing technology paths and especially sunk costs in infrastructures. Problems for the incumbent can emerge if such a path is broken or changed due to a change of policy (for example, affected through a change in the incentive/subsidy policy).

The most relevant role to foster a sustainable transition, considering what has been mentioned in our analysis about the incumbents, is to be expected from ENEL. For the time being, ENEL could be considered as a sort of change agent on two main directions: digitalization and electro-mobility. The establishment in 2018 of a new brand in the group, ENELX, supports this standpoint, as this is entirely focused on the design of innovative (digital) solutions for cities and households and on the promotion of electro-mobility.

Concluding, the case of Italy seems to underline that European policies can provide a model around which to redesign and adapt a domestic policy, but that for this to take place, actors or better change agents able to exploit adaptational pressures are indispensable. Coherent streamlining procedures for supporting self-generation of electricity from RES or high-efficiency co-generation, and to put the new energy communities and prosumers at the center of the new energy model for the transition are necessary. This means opening the energy market to new actors, a wide participation of prosumers either as municipally owned companies, cooperatives, or as citizens. An increasing participation of prosumers in the energy system is also a milestone for a democratization of a (ecologically and socially) sustainable energy system.

Whether the present government will be willing to continue with the new narrative around the energy transition initiated with the NSE and consequently enhance the necessary steps to such a transition is questionable. But it is also a question of whether the "change agents" necessary to drive the transition are at work and whether it is the incumbents' or "citizens' energy" that can take up this role. The road to be taken for the energy transition calls for improving transparency and public accountability in the energy sector. The aimed solutions and the path to be followed are going to enormously affect the process of democratization of the energy landscape as they imply also access of data to the public, involvement of the public in the allocation of benefits and in key decisions. And this may also imply new modes of governance.

Cross-References

▶ Energy Governance in Germany
▶ Energy Governance in the United Kingdom

References

AEEGSI – Autorità per l'energia il gas ed il servizio idrico integrato. (2017). Relazione annuale sullo stato dei servizi e l'attività svolta, 31 marzo 2017. https://www.autorita.energia.it/allegati/relaz_ann/17/RAVolumeI_2017.pdf. Accessed 4 Apr 2017.

Agostinelli, M. (2016, September 19). Enel spegne 23 centrali, i sindacati protestano ma l'occasione è irripetibile. *Il fatto quotidiano*. https://www.ilfattoquotidiano.it/2016/09/19/enel-spegne-23-centrali-i-sindacati-protestano-ma-loccasione-e-irripetibile/3042014/. Accessed 10 July 2018.

ARERA – Autorità di Regolazione per Energia reti e Ambiente. (2018). Comunicato stampa, 7 febbraio 2018. https://www.arera.it/it/com_stampa/18/180207c.htm. Accessed 10 July 2018.

Baracca, A., Ferrari, G., & Renzetti, R. (2017). The "go-stop-go" of Italian civil nuclear programs, beset by lack of strategic planning, exploitation for personal gain and unscrupulous political conspiracies: 1946–1987. http://arxiv.org/abs/1709.05195. Accessed 4 June 2018.

Brizzo, F. (2018, June 13). Sempre più imprese italiane scommettono sulla green economy. *La Stampa*. http://www.lastampa.it/2018/06/13/scienza/sempre-pi-aziende-italiane-scommettono-sulla-green-economy-xitRmNjd3gABwOncOCUJqM/pagina.html

Brondi, S., Armenti, A., Cottone, P., Mazzara, P., & Sarrica, M. (2014). Parliamentary and press discourses on sustainable energy in Italy: No more hard paths, not yet soft paths. *Energy Research & Social Science, 2*, 38–48.

Brunazzo, M. (2010). From policy-taker to policy-shaper: The Europeanization of Italian cohesion policy. *World Political Science Review, 6*. https://doi.org/10.2202/1935-6226.1074.

Corsatea, T. D. (2014). Localised knowledge, local policies and regional innovation activity for renewable energy technologies: Evidence from Italy. *Papers in Regional Science, 95*(3), 443–466.

de la Rue du Can, S., & Leventis, G. (2014). Design of incentive programs for accelerating penetration of energy-efficient appliances. *Energy Policy, 72*, 56–66. https://doi.org/10.1016/j.enpol.2014.04.035.

Deloitte. (2015). European energy market reform Country profile: Italy. https://www2.deloitte.com/content/dam/Deloitte/global/Documents/Energy-and-Resources/gx-er-market-reform-italy.pdf. Accessed 30 Oct 2017.

Di Nucci, M. R. (2004). The liberalisation of the Italian energy market: Part I: The structure and framework of the electricity system. *Energiewirtschaftliche Tagesfragen, 1*(2), 101–108.

Di Nucci, M. R. (2006). The nuclear power option in the Italian energy policy. *Energy & Environment, 17*(3), 341–357.

Di Nucci, M. R. (2007). The role of renewables in the Italian energy policy: The development of green power. In L. Mez (Ed.), *Green power markets* (pp. 311–314). Brentwood: Multi-Science Publishing Ltd.

Di Nucci, M. R. (2009). Between myth and reality: Development, problems and perspectives of nuclear power in Italy. In L. Mez, M. Schneider, & S. Thomas (Eds.), *International perspectives on energy policy and the role of nuclear power* (pp. 279–300). Brentwood: Multi-Science Publishing Ltd.

Di Nucci, M. R. (2014). The roll-out of smart metering between discording interests and institutional inertia. In A. Brunnergräber & M. R. Di Nucci (Eds.), *Im Hürdenlauf zur Energiewende. Von Transformationen, Reformen und Innovationen* (pp. 265–287). Wiesbaden: Springer Fachmedien.

Di Nucci, M. R. (2015). Breaking the stalemate. The challenge of nuclear waste governance in Italy. In A. Brunnengräber, M. R. Di Nucci, A. M. Isidoro Losada, L. Mez, & M. Schreurs (Eds.), *Nuclear waste governance. An international comparison* (pp. 299–322). Wiesbaden: Springer VS.
Di Nucci, M. R., & Russolillo, D. (2017). The fuzzy Europeanization of the Italian RES policies: The paradox of meeting targets without strategic capacity. In I. Solorio & H. Jörgens (Eds.), *A guide to EU renewable energy policy. Comparing Europeanization and domestic policy change in EU member states* (pp. 121–140). Cheltenham: Edward Elgar.
ENI. (2017). Shareholders' guide 2017. https://www.eni.com/docs/en_IT/enicom/company/governance/shareholders-meeting/2017/shareholders-guide-2017.pdf. Accessed 24 Oct 2017.
European Commission. (2016). Proposal for a Directive of the European Parliament and of the Council on the promotion of the use of energy from renewable sources (recast). COM/2016/0767 final.
European Commission. (2017). Report from the Commission to the European Parliament, the Council, the European economic and social committee and the Committee of the regions. Renewable energy progress report. Brussels, 1.2.2017 COM(2017) 57 final. https://ec.europa.eu/transparency/regdoc/rep/1/2017/EN/COM-2017-57-F1-EN-MAIN-PART-1.PDF. Accessed 18 July 2018.
EUROSTAT. (2016). Electricity prices for industrial consumers, second half 2015 (EUR per kWh). http://ec.europa.eu/eurostat/statistics-explained/index.php/File:Electricity_prices_for_industrial_consumers,_second_half_2015_(%C2%B9)_(EUR_per_kWh)_YB16.png. Accessed 25 Oct 2017.
EUROSTAT. (2017a). Natural gas consumption statistics (data from July 2017). http://ec.europa.eu/eurostat/statistics-explained/index.php/Natural_gas_consumption_statistics. Accessed 11 Nov 2017.
EUROSTAT. (2017b). Consumption of energy (data from June 2017). http://ec.europa.eu/eurostat/statistics-explained/index.php/Consumption_of_energy. Accessed 21 Oct 2017.
Feliziani, C. (2013). The impact of the EU energy policy on member states' legal orders: State of art and perspectives of renewable energy in Italy and Great Britain. *Review of European Studies, 5*(2), 67.
Flanagan, K., Uyarra, E., & Laranja, M. (2011). Reconceptualising the policy mix for innovation. *Research Policy, 40*(5), 702–713.
Florini, A., & Sovacool, B. K. (2009). Who governs energy? The challenges facing global energy governance. *Energy Policy, 37*(12), 5239–5248.
Foxon, T. J. (2011). A coevolutionary framework for analysing a transition to a sustainable low carbon economy. *Ecological Economics, 70*(12), 2258–2267.
Galgóczi, B. (2015). *Europe's energy transformation in the austerity trap*. Brussels: ETUI.
Gaspari, M., & Lorenzoni, A. (2018). The governance for distributed energy resources in the Italian electricity market: A driver for innovation? *Renewable and Sustainable Energy Review, 82*(3), 3623–3632.
Giraudet, G., & Finon, D. (2014). European experiences with white certificate obligations: A critical review of existing evaluations. https://hal.archives-ouvertes.fr/hal-01016110. Accessed 7 Nov 2017.
Graziano, P. (2010). From local partnerships to regional spaces for politics? Europeanization and EU cohesion policy in Southern Italy. *Regional and Federal Studies, 20*(3), 315–333.
GSE. (2016). Rapporto annuale certificate bianchi. https://www.gse.it/documenti_site/Documenti%20GSE/Rapporti%20Certificati%20Bianchi/_RAPPORTO+ANNUALE+CB+2016_EXECUTIVE+SUMMARY.PDF. Accessed 18 July 2018.
ICLEI. (2011). Europe Sustainabke now. Ways to successful sustainable energy action planning in Cities. http://www.iclei-europe.org/fileadmin/templates/iclei-europe/files/content/ICLEI_IS/Publications/SustainableNOW_Final-Brochure_www_SKO.pdf. Accessed 10 Nov 2017.
IEA. (2016a). Energy policy of IEA countries. 2016 review. https://www.iea.org/publications/freepublications/publication/EnergiePoliciesofIEACountriesItaly2016Review.pdf. Accessed 30 Oct 2017.

IEA. (2016b). Energy balances of OECD countries 2016. http://www.oecd.org/publications/world-energy-balances-2016-9789264263116-en.htm Accessed 9 Nov 2017.

IEA. (2017). World Energy Balances.

Lauber, V., & Schenner, E. (2011). The struggle over support schemes for renewable electricity in the European Union: A discursive-institutionalist analysis. *Environmental Politics, 20*(4), 508–527.

LOC, Library of Congress, Global Legal Monitor of the 25th of March 2011. http://www.loc.gov/law/foreign-news/article/italy-renewable-energy-law-adopted/. Last accessed 1 Oct 2018.

Magnani, N., & Vaona, A. (2013). Regional spillover effects of renewable energy generation in Italy. *Energy Policy, 56*(C), 663–671.

Meleddu, M., & Pulina, M. (2018). Public spending on renewable energy in Italian regions. *Renewable Energy, 115*, 1086–1098.

MSE. (2017). Italian energy strategy. http://www.sviluppoeconomico.gov.it/images/stories/documenti/testo_della_StrategiaEnergeticaNazionale_2017.pdf. Accessed 10 Nov 2017.

Perujo, A., & Ciuffo, B. (2010). The introduction of electric vehicles in the private fleet: Potential impact on the electric supply system and on the environment. A case study for the Province of Milan, Italy. *Energy Policy, 38*(10), 4549–4561. https://doi.org/10.1016/j.enpol.2010.04.010.

Polo, M., & Scarpa, C. (2003). The liberalization of energy markets in Europe and Italy. Working paper 2003 No 230, IGIER (Innocenzo Gasparini Institute for Economic Research), Bocconi University.

Prontera, A. (2010). Europeanization, institutionalization and policy change in French and Italian electricity policy. *Journal of Comparative Policy Analysis: Research and Practice, 12*(5), 491–507.

Radaelli, C. (2004). Europeanization: Solution or problem? *European Integration Online Papers (EIoP), 8*(16). http://eiop.or.at/eiop/texte/2004-016a.html. Accessed 22 Oct 2017.

Rogge, K., & Reichardt, K. (2016). Policy mixes for sustainability transitions: An extended concept and framework for analysis. *Research Policy, 45*(8), 1620–1635.

Ryberg, T. (2017). The second wave of smart meters rollouts begin in Italy and Sweden. https://www.metering.com/regional-news/europe-uk/second-wave-smart-meter-rollouts-begins-italy-sweden/. Accessed 18 July 2018.

Sarrica, M., Biddau, F., Brondi, S., Cottone, P., & Mazzara, B. (2018). A multi-scale examination of public discourse on energy sustainability in Italy: Empirical evidence and policy implications. *Energy Policy, 114*, 444–454.

Smith, A., Voß, J. P., & Grin, J. (2010). Innovation studies and sustainability transitions: The allure of the multi-level perspective and its challenges. *Research Policy, 39*(4), 435–448.

TERNA. (2016a). National power balance, 2016. http://download.terna.it/terna/0000/1007/09.PDF. Accessed 22 Oct 2017.

TERNA. (2016b). National power production, 2016. http://download.terna.it/terna/0000/0964/25.PDF. Accessed 23 Oct 2017.

Trotta, G., Ripa, M., & Lorek, S. (2015). Consumers and energy efficiency – Country report Italy. An inventory of policies, business and civil society initiatives, focusing on heating, hot water and the use of electricity. EUFORIE – European Futures for Energy Efficiency. http://www.utu.fi/en/units/euforie/Pages/home.aspx. Accessed 18 July 2018.

van den Bergh, J. C. J. M., Truffer, B., & Kallis, G. (2011). Environmental innovation and societal transitions. Introduction and overview. *Environmental Innovation and Societal Transitions, 1*(1), 1–23.

World Economic Forum- WEF. (2018). The world's 10 biggest economies in 2018. https://www.weforum.org/agenda/2018/04/the-worlds-biggest-economies-in-2018/. Accessed 3 Sept 2018.

Energy Governance in Latvia

33

Sigita Urdze

Contents

Introduction	824
General Conditions of Energy Governance	824
Legacies/Path Dependencies	824
Composition of the "Energy Mix"	826
Discourse on Energy Issues	829
Political Institutions and Actors	830
Coordination of the Instruments and Issues of Energy Issues Within a Multilevel Context	832
Drivers of Energy Transition	832
Strategies and Instruments of Energy Transition	834
Coordination Mechanisms and Multilevel Governance	836
Outcomes, Challenges, and Prospects of Energy Governance	838
Cross-References	838
References	839

Abstract

This chapter provides an overview of energy governance in Latvia. The most important narrative in the context of energy governance is energy security and thus independence from energy imports, especially from Russia. The chapter illustrates the strategies that have been used to pursue this goal so far and the approaches that are available for future developments. It becomes clear why Latvia, which has had a high share of renewable energies in comparison with other European countries, now needs to catch up in this area.

Keywords

Energy security · Hydropower · Energy island · Russia

S. Urdze (✉)
Institute of Political Science, Technical University of Darmstadt, Darmstadt, Germany
e-mail: urdze@pg.tu-darmstadt.de

© Springer Nature Switzerland AG 2022
M. Knodt, J. Kemmerzell (eds.), *Handbook of Energy Governance in Europe*,
https://doi.org/10.1007/978-3-030-43250-8_17

Introduction

Latvia is the middle one of the three Baltic States. When the Baltic States Estonia, Latvia, and Lithuania are viewed from the outside, the first things striking often are the commonalities. Differences are frequently less noticed or not considered at all. There are certainly issues where the three Baltic States have more similarities with each other than they do with other states, although even with these issues it is still important to look at the detailed differences.

The issue of energy governance, however, is one where the three Baltic States differ significantly, both in terms of their starting positions and in terms of the current focus of developments. With a 41.0 % share of renewable energy in gross final energy consumption, Latvia had the third highest value in this field in the EU in 2019. With 31.9% in the case of Estonia and 25.5% in the case of Lithuania, these states also have high shares of renewables in an EU comparison (EU28 average: 18.9%) but are still well behind Latvia (Eurostat, 2021f). Looking at the GHG emissions per capita, the difference between the three states also becomes clear: In Latvia, the per capita emissions in 2019 were 6.1 tons, in Lithuania 7.4 tons, and Estonia 11.2 tons (EU28 average: 8.2 tons) (Eurostat, 2021a). The difference in GHG emissions should also be seen in the context of energy governance.

After this brief introduction, which is intended to encourage us to consider the three Baltic States individually, we will now leave the Baltic perspective and deal directly with Latvia's energy governance.

General Conditions of Energy Governance

To understand energy policy in Latvia, it is crucial to understand the country's legacies. The country's past as part of the Soviet Union not only has a major impact on the more technical aspects of energy policy, such as the energy mix, energy transportation options, etc. It is also important for understanding political decisions in this context. On almost all key issues of energy policy, Russia is the elephant in the room whose presence cannot be ignored. This will become clear in the next four sections.

Legacies/Path Dependencies

Latvia reappeared on the political map in 1990/1991. Before that, Latvia, which first gained independence in 1918 and lost it in 1939 as a result of the Hitler-Stalin Pact, had belonged to the Soviet Union for more than 50 years. During the Soviet period, the entire economy, as well as the energy networks of Latvia and its Baltic neighbors Estonia and Lithuania, were built with a strong orientation toward the Soviet center. More than 90% of the Baltic countries' trade was oriented toward other Soviet republics. In terms of energy, dependence was even stronger. This dependence not only left Latvia heavily dependent on its neighbor Russia for energy. It also strongly influences the whole discourse on energy issues in Latvia until today.

To spell out this energetic legacy of the Soviet Union in Latvia in more detail:

Latvia is a country with limited natural resources. There are no fossil resources on its territory. Available resources are hydropower, peat, and wood. In 1990, 83% of energy was imported from other republics of the Soviet Union (Salay et al., 1993:183). Energy consumption was cheap in Soviet times and high consumption was not uncommon. Power systems in all three Baltic States were well developed and strongly interconnected. Other connections existed with the neighboring Soviet republics of Russia and Belarus, but no connections existed with countries beyond the Soviet Union (Miskinis et al., n.d.:3954). As a result, after regaining independence, Latvia, as well as Estonia and Lithuania, was perceived as an energy island from a Western European perspective.

Gas was imported 100% from Russia via the "Northern Lights" pipeline. The heavy dependence on Russia was mitigated to a certain extent in the case of Latvia, as one of the largest underground gas storage facilities in Europe is located and still in operation in northern Latvia, in Inčukalns, and is also used for gas distribution to Estonia and Lithuania (Miskinis et al., n.d.:3954). The gas stored there would be sufficient to supply Latvia with enough gas for an entire winter if it was cut off from further supplies from Russia. However, since Gazprom is one of the owners of this underground storage facility, access to the gas stored there would also be made difficult in the event of a gas dispute. To reduce dependence on Russian gas imports, an LNG terminal has been built in Lithuania at the port of Klaipėda, which could also provide relief for Latvia in the event of an energy conflict (Keating, 2015).

Latvia has also inherited a strong dependence on Russian oil supplies from Soviet times. In Soviet times and to this day, the port of Ventspils in Latvia, which is ice-free in winter, is important for oil exports from Russia. The oil is transported there by rail and via pipelines (Salay et al., 1993: 182ff).

Both oil and gas together accounted for 76% of total energy supply in 1990. Considering that Latvia is a country without significant mountains, it had a somewhat surprisingly high share of hydropower. Five percent of total energy supply came from this source, mainly generated by run-of-river power plants (International Energy Agency, 2020b). If we look at primary energy consumption, the importance of hydropower becomes even more obvious – 22% of primary energy consumption was covered by this source in 1990 (Salay et al., 1993:181). Hydropower is an energy source with a long tradition. The first hydroelectric power plant on the Daugava River was built as early as 1939, and after its destruction during the Second World War, it was rebuilt in 1945. The next hydroelectric power plants were built in the 1960s and 1970s, respectively. At the end of the 1970s, the construction of another hydroelectric power plant was started and in the beginning of the 1980s, it was accompanied by a wide public discussion, including in newspapers, about ecological and economic issues. These discussions were later accompanied by signature collections, which finally led to a stop of the project in 1986 (Muižnieks, 1987). In the context of path dependencies and legacies of energy policy in Latvia, it is important to keep in mind these events surrounding the construction of hydropower plants. The described protests were later perceived as one of the starting points for Latvia's regaining independence. Hydroelectric power plants were perceived as ecologically problematic, as large areas had to be flooded for their construction and thus negatively connotated.

Other domestic energy sources used in Latvia are peat and wood. In the early 1990s, energy from these sources accounted for 7% of primary energy consumption. Especially in rural areas, these sources were important for heating, as they were available for free or at very low prices. Unlike in other countries of Eastern Europe, however, coal never played a major role as an energy source in Latvia (Salay et al., 1993:181).

When Latvia regained independence, the country was heavily dependent on fossil fuel imports from Russia. Additionally, the country had a notable share of hydropower in primary energy consumption. However, this very energy source, which is counted among the green energy sources in energy discourse, was perceived as an environmentally destructive source in the public discourse in Latvia and had a negative connotation.

Another legacy of Latvia after regaining its independence was an energy system that was in itself very inefficient. Because energy was cheap, there were hardly any incentives for engineers or other relevant groups such as homeowners to save energy. For example, district heating was common, and to lower the temperature in an apartment, the only option was often to open a window. After regaining independence and the resulting disruptions in access to cheap Russian energy, Latvia was confronted with rising energy prices, which suddenly created great incentives not only for finding new energy sources but also for efforts to increase energy efficiency (Makijenko et al. 2016; Miskinis et al., 2019; Salay et al., 1993). We will return to this topic when we discuss the discourse on energy issues below.

Composition of the "Energy Mix"

Since 1990, Latvia's total final energy consumption has decreased from 6420 ktoe in 1990 to 4120 ktoe in 2018 – in other words, it has decreased by more than one-third. Final energy consumption reached a low in 2000 with 3299 ktoe. After 2000, there was no stable increase in energy consumption. However, the last years seem to show a slight upward trend (International Energy Agency, 2020d). In the same period, CO2 emissions have decreased by an even larger proportion, from 19 Mt in 1990 to 7 Mt in 2018. In this regard, since early 2000s no trend of either increase or decrease can be seen; rather, the level seems to remain about the same (International Energy Agency, 2020a). Part of this decrease in total energy consumption can be attributed to the decrease in population from 2.7 million in 1990 to 1.9 million in 2019 (Eurostat, 2021e). At the same time, however, there is also a decline in total energy supply per capita from 3.0 toe in 1990 to a low point in 2000, when total energy supply per capita was 1.6 toe. The value then rose almost continuously to 2.3 toe by 2019 (International Energy Agency, 2020c).

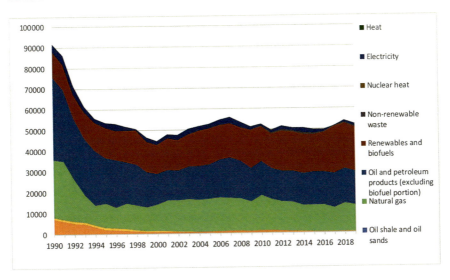

Fig. 1 Total energy supply by source in Gigawatt-hours (Eurostat, 2021g)

Some changes can also be observed in the energy mix. As Fig. 1 shows in both 1990 and 2019, oil and natural gas were the main sources of total energy supply in Latvia. However, while oil had a share of 44% in 1990, this share has decreased to 30.89% in 2019. The share of gas decreased from 30.20% to 25.19% in the same period. Looking at the absolute figures, the loss of importance of these two fossil fuels becomes even more evident: oil provided 39,979 GWh in 1990 and 16,142 GWh in 2019. Gas provided 27,681 GWh in 1990 and 12,832 GWh in 2019. Thus, its use has more than halved. An even sharper decline can be seen in solid fossil fuels. While they accounted for 8.01% of total energy supply in 1990, they have become almost insignificant, accounting for only 0.97% of total energy supply in 2019. Given the overall decline in total energy supply from 1990 to 2019, it is obvious that the use of coal declined even more in absolute terms (Eurostat, 2021g).

On the other hand, renewable energy sources have gained significantly in importance in Latvia since 1990. The largest share is accounted for by biofuels and waste, which accounted for 8.69% of the total energy supply in 1990 and whose share has increased to 38.55% by 2019 – making them now the most important source of energy in Latvia, ahead of the originally very important contributions of oil and gas. Other renewable energy sources are far less important in Latvia. This is also true for hydropower, whose importance in Latvia's energy mix has already been mentioned. The shares of both hydropower and wind, solar, etc. have decreased since 1990. In 2019, hydropower contributed to 4.14% of the total energy supply, while wind, solar, etc. contributed to only 3.2% of the energy supply (International Energy Agency, 2020b). A detailed overview of the developments in the supply of renewable natural energy inputs in Latvia is provided in Fig. 2.

Before we turn to the discourse on energy issues in the next section, let us now take a brief look at the origin of energy sources – this is important in order to

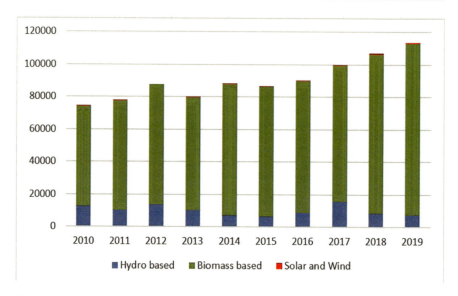

Fig. 2 Supply of renewable natural energy inputs in TJ (Centrālā statistikas pārvalde, 2021)

understand the discourse in Latvia. In terms of fossil fuels, of which Latvia has no deposits of its own – we will ignore coal in this context from now on, as it plays only a minor role in Latvia's energy supply – Russia has been the most important trading partner to date. Natural gas comes 100% from Russia (Eurostat, 2021c). In terms of oil imports, Lithuania is Latvia's most important trading partner (in 2019 with 43.02%), Russia is only the second most important trading partner (18.93%). However, Lithuania has no natural oil resources itself and imports 74.40% of its oil from Russia so this means dependence on Russian sources as well. Belarus is another important trading partner for Latvia in importing oil – and Belarus also has Russia as an important trading partner (9.15%) (Eurostat, 2021d).

Russia is also an important trading partner for Latvia for raw materials that form the basis for biofuels. In 2019, for example, 22.60% of imported wood pellets came from Russia (Eurostat, 2021b). However, as these are resources that are also naturally available in Latvia – in fact, in 2017 Latvia was highlighted as the top exporter of wood pellets in the European Union (Eurostat, 2017) – there is no dependence on trading partners in this area. Hydropower in Latvia is generated by hydroelectric plants on the Daugava River, as discussed earlier. Currently, there are no plans to build additional large-scale power plants. If anything, small hydropower plants are planned. However, such plans are confronted with environmental legislation, which according to Kasiulis et al. is one of the strictest in the EU (Kasiulis et al., n.d.:3). Regarding solar energy, conditions for this source in Latvia are not the best. Nevertheless, they are similar to, e.g., Denmark or Germany, where solar energy is used much more widely than in Latvia. Therefore, this is identified as an energy source with significant potential (Sakipova et al., 2016; Valancius et al., 2020). Wind energy is also identified as having growth potential. Due to Latvia's location on the

Baltic Sea and hilly areas in other parts of the country, there are some favorable areas. In their estimates of the potential of these sources, Sakipova et al. conclude that the decrease in solar energy in winter could be offset by an increase in wind energy due to higher wind speeds at that time of the year (Aniskevich et al., 2017; Sakipova et al., 2016).

Discourse on Energy Issues

The discourse on energy issues in Latvia is dominated by one major topic – achieving the greatest possible independence from imports from Russia. Unlike Western European countries, which only experienced the risks of heavy dependence on gas from Russia in 2009 in connection with the conflicts between Russia and Ukraine and the so-called gas crisis, the three Baltic States had the experience of being cut off from energy supplies by Russia much earlier. After Lithuania declared its independence from the Soviet Union in March 1990, the country experienced a 2-month blockade of gas and oil supplies from Russia in April 1990. These events were closely followed in neighboring Latvia, whose movement to restore independence was closely linked to those in Lithuania and Estonia. Even after regaining independence, gas supplies were frequently interrupted (Collins, 2017). Thus, by the early 1990s, Latvia had already experienced Russia's willingness to use energy sources to exert pressure on other countries.

Against this background, Latvia's energy policy objective has always been a strong orientation toward diversification to reduce dependence on Russian supplies, and it is supported in this policy by the European Union. Given the strong interconnectedness of the Baltic energy systems, any progress in this regard in Estonia and Lithuania is also of great importance for Latvia. Within the framework of the Baltic Energy Market Interconnection Plan, whose main objective is "is to achieve an open and integrated regional electricity and gas market between EU countries in the Baltic Sea region" (European Commission, 2020b), various projects have now been launched or even completed. Among other issues, the electricity grid is being synchronized with the continental European grid and gas pipelines are being built to Poland and Finland (European Commission, 2020b; Miskinis et al., 2020). A comparative study of the development of gas supply security in the EU-27 member states after the 2006 and 2009 gas crises shows that Latvia has made the greatest progress in increasing gas security of all the states studied. However, this increased security is not the result of new efforts. It is a result of previously used underground gas storage facilities as well as hydropower (Rodriguez-Fernandez et al., 2020). Thus, with respect to the dominant theme in the energy discourse – namely, reducing dependence on Russian energy sources – much remains to be done in Latvia.

To reduce energy dependence, Latvia had three main options: (1) diversify its energy suppliers, (2) develop new energy sources, (3) increase energy efficiency, and thus indirectly reduce the need for additional energy imports. The first option has already been described and has produced remarkable results by connecting to Western European energy networks. The development of new energy sources – due to the lack of natural resources in Latvia, these can only be renewable energy sources – is slow. As described above, hydropower has a long tradition in Latvia. However, since a significant surface area has to be flooded, this technology is very controversial in Latvia from an environmental point of view. Wind and solar energy are also not very popular in the country. In recent years, an increasingly critical attitude can be observed; especially in connection with wind energy, the negative effects are strong in the public discourse. In politics, the already high share of energy from renewable sources compared to other European countries is emphasized, which seems to lower the pressure for additional activities (Green Liberty, 2020; Zalāne, 2021). This leaves bioenergy as the main source, which is widely accepted and therefore used to increase the share of renewable energy in Latvia. However, even in this area, legislation is perceived as restrictive in comparison to other countries (Miskinis et al., n.d.). Thus, even though there is widespread agreement in Latvia that energy dependence on Russia should be reduced, and that sustainable development is seen as one of the main ideologies in Latvia (Miskinis et al., 2019:20), progress in increasing the share of renewable energy is overall very slow.

The third of the options described above, increasing energy efficiency and thus indirectly reducing the need for additional energy imports, was a path that was much more important. The energy system inherited from the Soviet past was highly inefficient, so this was an area where great success was possible with limited resources. It was also noted that given Latvia's economic problems, the resources used for this goal would have a more rapid impact on the economy in terms of growth (Streimikiene, 2016:1033).

Overall, then, the discourse on energy issues in Latvia is strongly dominated by the issue of reducing dependence on Russia. And this goal is pursued both by diversifying external energy suppliers and by increasing energy efficiency and thus reducing the need for energy imports. In contrast, a possible expansion of renewable energy sources beyond biofuels is viewed critically and no important issue in the public debate at all.

Political Institutions and Actors

Within the Latvian government, there are two main actors related to energy policy. One is the Ministry of Economy, the other is the Ministry of Environmental Protection and Regional Development. The Ministry of Economy lists energy policy as one of its main tasks and is more influential in the field of energy policy (Ekonomikas ministrija, 2020a). In this policy field, it is the main actor for the preparation of the country's long-term energy strategies and the national energy and climate plan, which are then approved by the Cabinet of Ministers (Ekonomikas ministrija, 2013). Key issues in the energy context addressed by the Ministry of Economy include both fossil and renewable energy sources, energy security and energy efficiency issues, and the national energy research program. The last research program call had four focus areas: (1) analytical framework for national long-term energy policy planning, (2) energy efficiency, (3) sustainable energy infrastructure and markets, (4) renewable and local energy resources. In this context, aspects of Latvia's climate goals are important and the Ministry of Economy contributes to the relevant aspects in Latvia's long-term climate plans (Ekonomikas ministrija, 2020a).

Responsibility for climate policy lies with the Ministry of Environmental Protection and Regional Development. This area deals, among other things, with monitoring, emissions trading, climate adaptation, and the preparation of legislative acts for accession to international agreements and the definition of monitoring standards (Vides aizsardzības un reģionālās attīstības ministrija, 2020a, 2020b). Basically, this shows that the topic of energy governance is perceived as a separate issue, which is of course linked to climate issues but has more economic than environmental aspects.

Another important player in the field of energy policy is the Investment and Development Agency of Latvia, which mentions environmental technology, i.e., the development of further potential for renewable energy production, as one of the key sectors for investment in Latvia. While there are several projects financed that include energy aspects, there is no single funding program focused on this topic (Latvijas Investīciju un attīstības aģentūra, 2020a, 2020b). Another actor for financing projects is the state financial institution ALTUM, which offers various financial instruments, including loans and loan guarantees. It has several fields of activity, including increasing the energy efficiency of buildings and allocating Renewable energy funds that focus on small investments. However, the focus is on energy efficiency rather than renewable energy, as Latvia is already quite advanced in the latter compared to other EU member states (ALTUM, 2021; European Commission, 2020a).

Latvia does not have a national-level energy agency, and Latvia is not a member of the International Energy Agency. The largest energy agency is that of the capital, Rīga, which has been established as a non-profit municipal agency established in 2007. Sustainable energy supply, energy efficiency, and renewable energy sources are among the issues this agency deals with. However, looking at the action plans in detail, it once again becomes clear that the focus is mainly on energy efficiency and much less on increasing the shares of renewable energy (Rīgas pašvaldības aģentūra "Rīgas enerģētikas aģentūra", 2020).

Finally, for renewable energy, there are various energy associations, the largest of which is LATbio, which is active in the field of bioenergy. Far more important is the largest electricity supplier, state-owned Latvenergo. Sixty percent of the energy generated by Latvenergo comes from renewable sources, mostly hydropower, as Latvenergo is the owner of the large hydropower plants in Latvia. While the development of renewable energy projects is included in Latvenergo's activity plans, a closer look reveals that this is more about consolidating existing hydropower projects than developing additional ones (Latvenergo, 2021). Last but not least, the gas company Latvijas Gāze must also be mentioned in this section. Thirty-four percent of the shares in Latvijas Gāze are owned by Gazprom. Other major shareholders are Luxembourg-based Marguerite Gas II with 28.97% of all shares and Germany-based Uniper Ruhrgas International with 18.26% of all shares (Latvijas Gāze, 2021). While energy efficiency is mentioned as one of Latvijas Gāze's fields of activity, the development of renewable energy sources is, as can be expected, not an issue for this company, whose core business is fossil energy.

Summarizing the overview of the actors in the field of energy policy in Latvia, a picture emerges which shows that the development of renewable energies is not a central issue for the main actors, while efforts of increasing energy efficiency are much more important. A picture that also emerged in the previous sections.

Coordination of the Instruments and Issues of Energy Issues Within a Multilevel Context

In the previous sections, we have dealt with the foundations of energy policy in Latvia, especially with regard to renewable energy. In the following, we will concentrate on how this policy is shaped in concrete terms, which coordination mechanisms can be found, and which influences can be observed in the multilevel context.

Drivers of Energy Transition

As discussed in detail in the previous sections, the main driving force in Latvia in the field of energy is to become as independent as possible from fossil fuels imported from Russia. There is a widespread fear, based on historical experience, that energy could be used as a means to exert pressure in political affairs. Energy independence is therefore also a means of securing political independence (Aniskevich et al., 2017:10).

Another important reason for the energy transition is European integration. First, it was in the context of EU accession and then in the context of regulations for EU members. As Klevas et al. put it, "The requirements for the EU integration are the key driver for the implementation of climate change mitigation policies and measures in the Baltic States. Climate Change mitigation was only a secondary benefit of these implemented measures" (Klevas et al., 2007:81). However, since Latvia already had a high share of renewable energy in its energy mix in the pre-EU accession period due to the high share of electricity from hydropower plants, this driver was less influential in the Latvian case than in the cases of Estonia and Latvia. In 1999, Latvia already had a 42.4% share of renewables in electricity consumption, and the target for 2010 was set at 49.3% (Klevas et al., 2007:78).

However, while Latvia has been successful in implementing its energy regulation goals, these goals have largely been treated as necessary outcomes, not as something with value in its own right. To summarize this in the words of Klevas et al., "Institutions in the Baltic States have successfully implemented the EU directives targeting sustainable energy development issues (promotion of renewables and energy efficiency improvements), however, the decision-makers are not aware that the main aim of directives, policies, and measures is not the distortion of market equilibrium, but overcoming of market failures seeking to create the opportunities for the sustainable energy development. The main guide and criteria for the evaluation of energy policies is sustainable development strategy because market forces fail to solve the problems of sustainable energy development strategies, state policies, financing measures from the EU SF and implementing bodies are needed" (Klevas et al., 2007:79).

After Latvia acceded to the EU, the energy transition was supported by the availability of funds, especially European development funds. Among other things, it was possible to conduct research on the feasibility of wind and solar energy to identify suitable sites for the construction of power plants. The goal was to attract investors for commercial projects in this area (Aniskevich et al., 2017; Sakipova et al., 2016). However, despite the financial support and efforts to create favorable conditions for potential investors, it is evident that little has changed in the basic attitude toward renewable energy after EU accession. In Latvia, the switch from fossil fuels to renewable energy is still seen less as an end in itself that contributes to climate goals, which would also be important from a national perspective than as a necessity within the framework of international agreements, both directly through EU agreements and indirectly such as the Paris Agreement. Thus, it is still primarily external pressure that is the key driver in the area of energy governance (Miskinis et al., 2019:3f). However, it should be noted again that, in general, the potential for CO_2 savings in Latvia in the area of energy efficiency is very high – also with regard to a large number of residential buildings. Moreover, both in terms of the geographical framework, i.e., the natural potential for renewable energy in Latvia, and in terms of the scale of investment required, this is the area where CO_2 savings are easier to achieve compared to switching to renewable energy. It should also be mentioned, even if this is not a central argument in the energy discourse in Latvia, that also from a climate policy perspective, energy-saving is usually viewed more positively compared to alternative energy sources. Alternative energy sources also interfere with nature and consume resources such as production materials for wind turbines, while energy savings do not require these aspects.

The rather hesitant attitude of politicians in Latvia regarding the energy transition is also reflected in social surveys. In a Eurobarometer survey on climate change, only 11 % of respondents said they considered it "the single most serious problem facing the world as a whole"; the EU average was 23 %. International terrorism and armed conflict were perceived as the most serious problems by 20% and 18% of respondents, respectively. The focus is thus on security policy aspects (European Commission, 2019:T1ff). Interestingly, however, only 61% of respondents agree or strongly agree with the statement that "reducing fossil fuel imports from outside the EU can increase energy security and benefit the EU economically" – this is a surprisingly low figure compared to 71% for the EU average (European Commission, 2019: T10ff). Other questions in the Eurobarometer survey also show a rather reserved attitude toward climate policy issues. For example, fewer respondents in Latvia than the EU average are in favor of increasing public subsidies for renewable energies, even at the expense of fossil energies if necessary. Similarly, fewer respondents than the EU average expect positive effects of climate protection measures for the population as a whole (European Commission, 2019). Other surveys also show that popular attitudes are not among the important drivers of the transition from fossil to renewable energies. In a survey on the acceptance of wind energy among the population, comparatively low results are obtained in Latvia (Leiren et al., 2020:8).

Summarizing the overview of the drivers of the energy transition, it is clear that the most important drivers are external. There is no strong intrinsic motivation for the energy transition in Latvia, neither from a political nor from a societal perspective. As for the external drivers, they are not so many incentives of a financial nature, but rather obligations arising from international agreements. First, it was EU accession, now there are the targets to which the EU has committed itself and which thus also become effective for Latvia. These are supported by Latvia, but they are not an end in themselves. In terms of CO2 savings, energy efficiency also plays a much greater role than the expansion of renewables.

Strategies and Instruments of Energy Transition

The framework for the energy transition in Latvia is set by the two documents "National Energy and Climate Plan 2021–2030" (Ministru Kabinets, 2020) and "Strategy towards Climate-Neutrality 2050" (Latvijas Republikas Ministru kabinets, 2020), both of which were approved by the Cabinet of Ministers in February 2020.

The "National Energy and Climate Plan 2021–2030" is the main document for long-term climate and energy policy planning, setting out fundamental principles, objectives, and directions for action. The basis for this document is the EU Regulation 2018/1999 of December 11, 2018 "on the Governance of the Energy Union and Climate Action" (European Parliament and Council of the European Union, 2018) which requires the preparation of such a plan. The "National Energy and Climate Plan 2021–2030" establishes the main vision and a central objective, both of which are in the economic sphere. The main vision is to develop sustainable development competitively and securely, and the main objective is to promote climate-neutral development of the economy by improving energy security and the welfare of society in a sustainable, competitive, cost-effective, secure, and market-based manner. Despite this economically oriented focus of the National Energy and Climate Plan's goals, the climate targets defined in this document are quite ambitious in some areas compared to the EU level, if we focus only on the targets. For example, in terms of greenhouse gas emissions, Latvia has set a target to reduce them by 65% by 2030 compared to 1990 levels, while the EU reduction target at the time when the plan was written was 40%. On the one hand, it should be kept in mind that Latvia has already reduced 57% from 1990 levels in 2017, while the EU has only reached 20% in 2020. On the other hand, this target is nevertheless more ambitious than it may seem when just looking at these figures, as the main reduction already took place in the early 1990s when it was comparatively easy to achieve a lot with rather a little effort. In the field of renewable energy, the targets are even more ambitious, especially considering the rather cautious attitude toward this issue both in politics and in society in Latvia. At the EU level, an increase from 20% in 2020 to 32% in 2030 is envisaged, while in Latvia the share is to rise from 39% in 2017 to 50% in

2020. In the transport sector, no increase in the share of renewable energy is envisaged in principle. The aspect of energy security is also reflected in the National Energy and Climate Plan. According to the plan, 44.1% of gross energy consumption was imported in 2020, and this figure is expected to drop to 30–40% by 2030. As the plan also gives a concrete figure of how much energy should be saved by 2030 – 1.76 Mtoe – the decrease in the share of imported energy underlines the need to increase national energy production, which in the case of Latvia, without significant natural resources, automatically means increasing the share of energy from renewable sources (Ministru Kabinets, 2020).

To implement the goals, the "National Energy and Climate Plan 2021–2030" provides for 13 action priorities. The first three are (1) energy efficiency, (2) research and innovation, and (3) public information, education, and awareness. So while we find technical aspects of climate and energy policy at the very beginning, the next two already target other fields of action – the creation of further knowledge and the need for cooperation with society in general. Increasing the share of renewable energy is not explicitly listed in the action areas; it is included in the topic of energy security, among others. Thus, the plan once again underlines the finding described above that Latvia focuses more on energy efficiency than on increasing the share of renewable energy – which is surprising given the objectives of the plan described above, where quite ambitious targets are also set for this area. One of the keys to increasing the share of renewable energy is the construction of new wind farms. To encourage this increase, both research in this area is supported and the benefits of wind energy for the economy and society as a whole are demonstrated. Among other things, a conference with high-ranking speakers such as the Latvian President, the EU Commissioner for Energy, and others on the topic of "Prospects for wind energy in Latvia" was held in early 2021 (Windworks, n.d.; Ministru Kabinets, 2020).

The other key document mentioned above in the context of the energy transition in Latvia is the "Strategy towards Climate Neutrality 2050". Here, too, we find a strong focus on energy efficiency to achieve climate goals. Two general approaches are described there: (1) technological solutions, (2) lifestyle change. The targets and sub-targets under technological solutions have a focus on energy efficiency. However, renewable energy is also included. For the prioritization of the principles outlined in the document, the most cost-effective principles must be realized first. Furthermore, not only short-term but also long-term perspectives should be included, they should be based on national resources, economic development must not be based on intensive energy use, social justice must be taken into account and developments must not contradict goals related to biodiversity and environmental protection. The remainder of the document emphasizes that although awareness of climate change in Latvia is still quite low, it is increasing. However, there is still a need for education. The strategy as a whole also corresponds to this: on the one hand, concrete climate targets are set and the need for research and development is emphasized. At the same time, however, there is also a need to intensify climate education, so that new technologies can find acceptance (Latvijas Republikas Ministru kabinets, 2020).

The main financial instruments supporting the energy transition in Latvia are, on the one hand, the corresponding subsidies from the European Union's Structural

Funds and, on the other hand, the state support program Climate Change Financial Instrument and its successor, the Emission Quota Tendering Instrument. The Ministry of Finance coordinates the allocation of funding within the framework of the structural funds. Looking at the last three planning periods, there has been a significant increase in the share of funding for renewable energies and energy efficiency. In the current period, 22% of the funding is earmarked for the area of Greener Europe (, 2021a; Kalna et al., 2020; Latvijas Republikas Finanšu ministrija, 2021b). The details of renewable energies and energy efficiency are regulated in the National Energy and Climate Plan 2021–2030, which has already been presented above, and in the long-term strategy for building renovation. The long-term strategy for building renovation envisages climate neutrality by 2050 and is itself integrated into the National Energy and Climate Plan 2021–2030, with EU funding being supplemented by national funding (Ekonomikas ministrija, 2020b). The Climate Change Financial Instrument was managed by the Latvian Environmental Investment Fund and aims to reduce greenhouse gas emissions and promote adaptation to climate change. The Climate Change Financial Instrument was financed from Assigned Amount Units (AAUs) that Latvia is entitled to receive under the Kyoto Protocol's international emissions trading scheme (Kalna et al., 2020; Vides aizsardzības un reģionālās attīstības ministrija, 2020d). The Emission Quota Tendering Instrument also aims to reduce climate change impacts and promote climate adaptation. Funding is provided for projects to increase the energy efficiency of buildings, for the wider use of renewable energies, and for technologies to increase energy efficiency, among other things (Vides aizsardzības un reģionālās attīstības ministrija, 2020c).

Overall the approach to the energy transition in Latvia can be well summarized with a quote from the opening speech of the President of Latvia to the above-mentioned conference on the prospects of wind energy in Latvia: "Throughout history Latvians have been living in close synergy with nature, and our traditions have coexisted in harmony with nature.[...] However, I am afraid that lately we have become complacent and take for granted what nature has given to us. [...] With plenty of windy days per year, Latvia has a great potential to harvest its own, completely renewable, secure, and cost-efficient energy from the wind. However, when it comes to the development of wind energy projects our progress is slow. I am afraid that the reason is the general lack of knowledge" (Levits, 2021).

Coordination Mechanisms and Multilevel Governance

Within Latvia, multi-level governance in the areas of energy and climate policy only rudimentary takes place. This is because Latvia has a centralized political system. There is no regional level. At the local level, Latvia is divided into 9 cities and 110 municipalities, which have very limited influence on the general lines of energy policy.

So, in the context of multilevel governance in the case of Latvia, the gaze must go outward, toward the European Union. Much has already been said on this influence in the above sections, so it remains here to tie up the loose ends.

After Latvia regained its independence, the country went through a severe economic crisis in the 1990s. Issues of climate protection in general and the development of renewable energies were of secondary importance. If they played a role, it was first and foremost with a view to energy independence from Russia. These issues were only addressed as a separate topic due to the need for adjustments or corresponding progress that arose in the course of the EU accession negotiations (Klevas et al., 2007:81). Recently, Latvia has been making independent efforts to develop renewable energy, independent of external energy supplies, but the main driving force is still the integration into the multilevel governance of the European Union. But also in the area of energy efficiency, the EU was originally the main driver of the effort. One reason for Latvia's reluctance in this area is that energy efficiency has been given little consideration in the pricing of housing so that owners have little incentive to take action in this area. Efforts in this area are often triggered by the possibility of financial support at the European level (Streimikiene, 2016:1033).

It is interesting to note that the strong focus on the issue of energy efficiency, compared to the significantly lower attention paid to the development of renewable energy in Latvia, is at least partly due to the financial support provided by the European Union. Streimikiene emphasizes that for the National Strategic Reference Framework document 2007–2013, both topics were important. However, against the backdrop of the economic crisis in 2008, there was a shift in emphasis toward the topic of energy efficiency, as faster economic policy results and employment effects were expected in this area. In 2008 and 2009, these shifts in focus were then realized in actual activities. Another indirect aspect resulting from the integration into the EU system and increasing the focus on the promotion of renewable energy is the fact that Latvia already has a very high share of renewable energy compared to the other EU Member States. The urgency for activities in this area seems to be lower in Latvia than in other countries of the European Union (Streimikiene, 2016:1033).

With regard to multilevel governance, it is clear that the central objectives of Latvia have been taken over from the European level. So far, there has been no significant resistance to the European targets in this area at the national level, which is certainly since the issues of renewable energies and energy efficiency are of outstanding importance for Latvia given the political goal of achieving energy independence. However, the issue of climate neutrality itself do not represent a central narrative in Latvia. Accordingly, Latvia is also less concerned with seeking innovative opportunities in this area than with achieving progress in the area of energy security that is as well adapted as possible to the Latvian context – which in this sense happens to coincide with the European Union's climate policy goals – with the support of available funding.

With regard to the coordination mechanisms of energy governance at the national level, namely, the "National Energy and Climate Plan 2021–2030," the coordinating body is the "National Energy and Climate Council" led by the prime minister. Further members are 8 ministers and 24 heads of departments. Among the ministries, the Ministry of Economy is in charge of the bulk of responsibilities. Inter alia it is the responsibility of this ministry to coordinate the plan with European regulations together with the Ministry of Environmental Protection and Regional Development. Other ministries involved are the Ministry of Transport, the Ministry of Agriculture, the Ministry of Finance, the Ministry of Welfare, the Foreign Ministry, and the Education and Science Ministry. Their task is to adapt the legal acts within their jurisdiction or to develop corresponding legal acts in the first place. Another important actor emphasized by the "National Energy and Climate Plan 2021–2030" is the Cross-Sectoral Coordination Centre whose responsibility is inter alia to involve civil society actors in planning processes (Ministru Kabinets, 2020; Pārresoru koordinācijas centrs, 2021).

Outcomes, Challenges, and Prospects of Energy Governance

Energy governance issues have played a central role in Latvia since the early 1990s. The focus is less on climate protection than on energy security. Regardless of the objective, however, Latvia is one of the countries in Europe that has already made particularly good progress with the share of renewable energies. It should be emphasized that this strong share of renewable energies has been reached even though in the field of energy governance, the development of renewable energies – except for renewable energy from biomass – still stands in the shade of energy efficiency. In Latvia, the focus is much more on energy efficiency. Renewable energies, especially hydropower, which played a major role in Latvia even before the country regained its independence, are not perceived positively by society as a whole; instead, the associated interference with nature is emphasized. However, a first rethinking in the field of renewable energies has recently become apparent in Latvia. There are increasing efforts on the part of politicians to emphasize the necessity of creating appropriate energy sources and to communicate this to society.

Thus, Latvia's comparatively advanced development in the field of renewable energy also represents the country's greatest challenge in this area. Approaches and strategies for further development are only in their initial stages, and there is an only limited experience to date beyond the area of biomass and the rather unpopular hydropower. Energy-saving potentials will be exhausted at some point, so energy governance will be increasingly dependent on the expansion of renewable energies to achieve CO2 reduction targets. Given this situation, Latvia runs into danger to lose its status as a pioneer of the energy transition in Europe, but will instead fall behind.

A particular challenge is posed by the reticent attitude of large parts of the population toward the expansion of renewable energies. It is also precisely the self-perception of living in harmony with nature described above among many of the country's inhabitants that leads to wind turbines in particular being perceived as interventions in nature rather than as long-term protection of nature.

The natural framework conditions for the expansion of renewable energies, e.g., the number of hours of sunshine and preferential wind levels, are available in the country. Ultimately, the switch from fossil fuels to renewable energy sources in Latvia will depend on how successful information and education work is in this case.

Cross-References

▶ Energy Governance in Lithuania
▶ EU-Russia Energy Relations
▶ The EU in Global Energy Governance

References

Altum. (2021). Kas Mēs Esam.
Aniskevich, S., Bezrukovs, V., Zandovskis, U., & Bezrukovs, D. (2017). Modelling the spatial distribution of wind energy resources in Latvia. *Latvian Journal of Physics and Technical Sciences, 54*(6), 10–20.
Centrālā statistikas pārvalde. (2021). *ENB180. Physical energy flow accounts (TJ) by supply, use, energy resources, indicator and time period.*
Collins, G. (2017). Russia's use of the 'energy weapon' in Europe. *Energy Today.* https://doi.org/10.1515/energytoday-2017-1927
Ekonomikas ministrija. (2013). Informatīvais Ziņojums. Latvijas Enerģētikas Ilgtermiņa Stratēģija 2030 – Konkurētspējīga Enerģētika Sabiedrībai.
Ekonomikas ministrija. (2020a). Enerģētika.
Ekonomikas ministrija. (2020b). Informatīvais Ziņojums 'Ēku Atjaunošanas Ilgtermiņa Stratēģija.'
European Commission. (2019). Special eurobarometer 490. climate change.
European Commission. (2020a). Altum and EIB join forces for energy efficiency investments in Latvia.
European Commission. (2020b). Baltic energy market interconnection plan.
European Parliament, and Council of the European Union. (2018). Regulation (EU) 2018/1999 of the European Parliament and of the Council of 11 December 2018 on the Governance of the Energy Union and Climate Action, Amending Regulations (EC) No 663/2009 and (EC) No 715/2009 of the European Parliament and of the Council, Directives 94/22/EC, 98/70/EC, 2009/31/EC, 2009/73/EC, 2010/31/EU, 2012/27/EU and 2013/30/EU of the European Parliament and of the Council, Council Directives 2009/119/EC and (EU) 2015/652 and Repealing Regulation (EU) No 525/2013 of the European Parliament and of the Council (Text with EEA Relevance.).
Eurostat. (2017). Eurostat celebrates Latvia.
Eurostat. (2021a). Greenhouse gas emissions per Capita [T2020_RD300].
Eurostat. (2021b). Imports of biofuels by partner country.
Eurostat. (2021c). Imports of natural gas by partner country.
Eurostat. (2021d). Imports of oil and petroleum products by partner country.
Eurostat. (2021e). Population on 1 January by age and sex.
Eurostat. (2021f). Share of energy from renewable sources [Nrg_ind_ren].
Eurostat. (2021g). Simplified energy balances [NRG_BAL_S__custom_1149388].
Green Liberty. (2020). A breath of fresh air: How Latvia can increase wind power capacity tenfold by 2030.
International Energy Agency. (2020a). CO2 emissions by energy source, Latvia 1990–2018.
International Energy Agency. (2020b). Total Energy Supply (TES) by Source, Latvia 1990–2019.
International Energy Agency. (2020c). Total Energy Supply (TES) per Capita, Latvia 1990–2019.
International Energy Agency. (2020d). Total Final Consumption (TFC) by Sector, Latvia 1990–2018.
Jevgenija, M., Burlakovs, J., Brizga, J., & Klavins, M. (2016). Energy efficiency and behavioral patterns in Latvia. *Management of Environmental Quality, 27*(6, SI), 695–707.
Kalna, S., Lauka, D., Vaiskunaite, R., & Blumberga, D. (2020). Blind spots of energy transition policy – case study of Latvia. *Environmental and Climate Technologies, 24*(2, SI), 325–336.
Kasiulis, E., Punys, P., Kvaraciejus, A., Dumbrauskas, A., & Jurevičius, L. (n.d.). Small hydropower in the baltic states—current status and potential for future development. *Energies, 13.* https://doi.org/10.3390/en13246731
Keating, D. (2015). *Energy Legacy of the Baltic States. Politico.*
Klevas, V., Streimikiene, D., & Grikstaite, R. (2007). Sustainable energy in baltic states. *Energy Policy, 35*(1), 76–90. https://doi.org/10.1016/j.enpol.2005.10.009
Latvenergo. (2021). Korporatīvās Pārvaldības Modelis.
Latvijas Gāze. (2021). Akcionāru Sastāvs.
Latvijas Investīciju un attīstības aģentūra. (2020a). Key sectors.
Latvijas Investīciju un attīstības aģentūra. (2020b). Programmas.

Latvijas Republikas Finanšu ministrija. (2021a). ES Fondu 2014. – 2020.Gada Plānošanas Perioda Ieviešanas Progress Un 2021. – 2027.Gada Plānošanas Perioda Uzsākšanas Aktualitātes.

Latvijas Republikas Finanšu ministrija. (2021b). Plānošana.

Latvijas Republikas Ministru kabinets. (2020). Informatīvais Ziņojums 'Latvijas Stratēģija Klimatneitralitātes Sasniegšanai Līdz 2050. Gadam.'

Leiren, M. D., Aakre, S., Linnerud, K., Julsrud, T. E., Di Nucci, M.-R., & Krug, M. (2020). Community acceptance of wind energy developments: Experience from wind energy scarce regions in Europe. *Sustainability, 12*(5).

Levits, E. (2021). Address of the president of Latvia, Egils Levits, at the conference 'WindWorks. Powering Latvia's energy future.'

Makijenko, J., Burlakovs, J., Brizga, J., & Klavins, M. (2016). Energy efficiency and behavioral patterns in Latvia. *Management of Environmental Quality, 27*(6), 695–707. https://doi.org/10.1108/MEQ-05-2015-0103

Ministru Kabinets. (2020). Latvijas nacionālais enerģētikas un klimata plāns 2021–2030. GADAM.

Miskinis, V., Galinis, A., Konstantinaviciute, I., Lekavicius, V., & Neniskis, E. (2019). Comparative analysis of the energy sector development trends and forecast of final energy demand in the baltic states. *Sustainability, 11*(2).

Miskinis, V., Galinis, A., Konstantinaviciute, I., Lekavicius, V., & Neniskis, E. (2020). Comparative analysis of energy efficiency trends and driving factors in the baltic states. *Energy Strategy Reviews, 30*, 100514. https://doi.org/10.1016/j.esr.2020.100514

Miskinis, V., Slihta, G., & Rudi, Y. (n.d.). Bio-energy in the baltic states: Current policy and future development. *Energy Policy, 34*, 3953–3964. https://doi.org/10.1016/j.enpol.2005.09.021

Muižnieks, N. (1987). The daugavpils hydro station and 'Glasnost' in Latvia. *Journal of Baltic Studies, 18*(1), 63–70.

Pārresoru koordinācijas centrs. 2021. Par PKC.

Rīgas pašvaldības aģentūra "Rīgas enerģētikas aģentūra." (2020). Darba Plāns 2020. Gadam.

Rodriguez-Fernandez, L., Carvajal, A. B. F., & Ruiz-Gomez, L. M. (2020). Evolution of european union's energy security in gas supply during Russia-Ukraine Gas Crises (2006–2009). *Energy Strategy Reviews, 30*.

Sakipova, S., Jakovics, A., Gendelis, S., & Buketov, E. A. (2016). The potential of renewable energy sources in Latvia. *Latvian Journal of Physics and Technical Sciences, 53*(1), 3–13.

Salay, J., Fenhann, J., Jaanimägi, K., & Kristofersen, L. (1993). Energy and environment in the baltic states. *Annual Review of Environment and Resources, 18*, 169–216.

Streimikiene, D. (2016). Review of financial support from EU structural funds to sustainable energy in baltic states. *Renewable & Sustainable Energy Reviews, 58*, 1027–1038.

Valancius, R., Jurelionis, A., Jonynas, R., Borodinecs, A., Kalamees, T., & Fokaides, P. (2020). Growth rate of solar thermal systems in baltic states: Slow but steady wins the race? *Energy Sources Part B-Economics Planning and Policy, 15*(7–9), 423–435.

Vides aizsardzības un reģionālās attīstības ministrija. (2020a). Klimata Pārmaiņas.

Vides aizsardzības un reģionālās attīstības ministrija. (2020b). Normatīvie Akti Klimata Politikas Ieviešanai.

Vides aizsardzības un reģionālās attīstības ministrija. (2020c). Par EKII.

Vides aizsardzības un reģionālās attīstības ministrija. (2020d). Par KPFI.

Windworks. (n.d.) Powering Latvia's Energy Future. 29 April 2021, 10h00 – 15h00 EEST, Hybrid Conference.

Zalāne, L.. (2021). Why does Latvia use so little wind and solar energy?

Energy Governance in Lithuania

34

Šarūnas Liekis

Contents

Introduction	842
General Conditions of Energy Governance in Lithuania	843
Development of Energy Policy	843
Composition of the Energy Mix	845
Discourse on Energy Issues	845
Nuclear Power	845
Perception of Threats to Energy Governance	847
Policies Regarding the Baltic (Russian Federation) and Ostrovets Nuclear Power Plant in the Republic of Belarus	849
Coordination, Instruments, and Issues of the Lithuanian Energy Transition	850
Oil and Gas Infrastructure	851
The LNG Terminal	853
Nord Stream 2	854
Green Energy in Lithuania	855
Synchronization of the Electricity Network with EU Networks	857
Outcomes, Challenges, and Prospects	858
Cross-References	860
References	860

Abstract

Historically, Lithuanian energy governance has been characterized firstly by the private ownership of energy production. State-owned energy production started with the state's plans for electrification in 1938. The Soviet period from 1940 was marked by a state-owned structure of energy production and distribution infrastructure. After regaining independence, from 1991 the market economy found its way into energy production. Apart from the privatization of distribution networks, diversification of ownership in line with not-for-profit principles, energy

---

Š. Liekis (✉)
School of Political Science and Diplomacy, Vytautas Magnus University, Kaunas, Lithuania
e-mail: sarunas.liekis@vdu.lt

© Springer Nature Switzerland AG 2022
M. Knodt, J. Kemmerzell (eds.), *Handbook of Energy Governance in Europe*,
https://doi.org/10.1007/978-3-030-43250-8_18

security, and energy efficiency, an emphasis on non-nuclear energy has guided Lithuania's policy instruments. The national energy system for the provision of energy is important in this multilevel governance structure, especially with its focus on the liberalization of supplies. On the other hand, the recent emphasis on the development of renewable energy is crucial for Lithuanian energy policies. There is consensus regarding a green agenda within the political establishment to achieve the sustainable generation of predominantly green energy by 2050.

Keywords

Lithuania · Energy governance · Green energy · Belarus · Baltic States · Ostrovets Nuclear Power Plant · Ignalina Nuclear Power Plant

Introduction

Lithuania's energy sector can be divided into five areas of activity: natural gas, oil, electricity, heating, and renewable energy sources. The energy sector is an important part of the Lithuanian economy. A substantial part of Lithuanian enterprises and equipment is perceived as having strategic importance to national security for ensuring a reliable supply of energy and possibilities for the development of the energy market. State control and participation in the market were meant to ensure the implementation of these aims. Security of the energy sector had to be ensured based on the following principles: physical and cybersecurity of energy infrastructure supported by a risk assessment; assured compliance of investment into the energy sector according to national security criteria; security of the enterprises and its personnel. Resilience to cyber threats is used to manage risks. Planning continuity in information infrastructure, regarding planning, regulation, and testing of the plans in training and exercises is also important, as is trying to ensure transparency of the governance of the enterprises and their activities, the effectiveness of their activities, and level of professionalism. Therefore, the major topics of energy governance are resilience against corruption; transparency of activities; professionalism, technological training of the needed specialists and raising the competence of personnel; effective governance and implementation of innovative technologies; and society's participation in monitoring the services of the companies providing public services.

The management of state-owned companies has to be assured by establishing common principles in corporate management based on good practice and transparency. The necessary competencies have to be assured to attract and maintain the highest level of professionals in enterprises (Lietuvos Respublikos Seimas 2018). There is evidence that small countries like Lithuania can band together to develop a common EU interest while aligning themselves with the policy formation of the major European states (Thorhallsson and Steinsson 2017). Vaičiūnas discussed Lithuania's national interests in the framework of the EU common energy policy (Vaičiūnas 2009). Molis and Vaišnoras (2015) demonstrated that active measures in the EU and NATO help implement Lithuanian interests in the field of energy security. Grøn and Wivel (2011) maintain that apart from lobbying and acting as intermediaries, small states, like Lithuania, support ideological norm formation but not specific policies.

General Conditions of Energy Governance in Lithuania

Development of Energy Policy

Lithuanian energy governance developed gradually with the development of EU regulations. EU energy policies were followed and consistently supported. Apart from normative and ideological support of the EU, it participated in the founding of regulatory institutions and informal cooperation between states and continued to back the dominant trends for the liberalization of the energy market.

Lithuania also identifies with the ambitious goals of seeing an increase in effectiveness and energy diversification. The EU regulative model may differ by the degree of commitment to implement certain political decisions and possible intervention in case of inaction or deviation from the established policies. Despite the declared support of the Lithuanian state for renewable energy, actual implementation still suffers from administrative obstacles, especially concerning land allocation for renewable energy projects. Changing the legal status of land from agricultural to commercial is usually only implemented after numerous obstacles are overcome. Very often, municipalities do not support their pronounced strategy of support for renewable energy by any practical steps at the national level. Therefore, state priorities are not matched up with real actions and remain only as rhetorical declarations without necessarily being effective (Mažylis and Pikšrytė 2013).

Nonetheless, Lithuanian energy governance appeared on the integration agenda of EU energy policy only recently, almost in parallel with the country's accession – the main principles of EU energy policy were laid down in 2005 and 2006. Due to this timing, Lithuania has had a unique opportunity to participate in the formation of EU energy policy from the beginning.

Lithuanian governments view EU energy policy as the key instrument for increasing its energy security. As a country having a negligible influence on general political processes internationally, it views itself as vulnerable to international instability as it does not have enough resources to eliminate its exposed points. Therefore, the Lithuanian political establishment tends to securitize most of the aspects of their foreign policy interactions, including energy governance and supply, because they are not able to distinguish actions threatening their sovereignty from the actions of any third countries acting in their own interests.

Consequently, Lithuania was interested in the adoption of an EU energy policy in line with its priorities, clearly prioritizing issues relating to energy supply and widening the EU energy policy agenda by including supply security principles. EU energy policy is developing in a favorable direction that meets Lithuania's interests. The country's strategy documents are more practically applicable while ensuring the energy security of Lithuania, compared to previous documents that were mostly orientated toward the identification of energy security problems without offering any solutions as to how they could be overcome.

The energy security problems of the Baltic States, identified in 2006 in the European Commission's Energy Green Paper, were transformed in 2009 into specific plans on how these problems could be solved. One of the recent EU energy policy documents –the Baltic Energy Market Interconnection Plan – has binding content. For the first time in the history of EU energy policy, these developments demonstrate that the EU has already drawn the trajectory of its energy policy and is currently moving toward the implementation stage in the main energy policy options.

Four main achievements can be identified, which show that EU energy policy is developing according to Lithuania's main energy policy interests: (1) deepening and widening consideration for the external dimension of EU energy policy; (2) a comprehensive attitude toward the phenomenon of the energy isolation of the Baltic States; (3) the integration of the EU energy policy into other areas of EU integration; (4) increasing significance for the principle of security of supply.

The Lithuanian National Energy Independence Strategy foresaw an advanced energy industry that uses non-polluting energy sources. It should create added value, be resilient to cyber threats and climate changes, and ensure a reliable supply of energy at a competitive price. The Lithuanian energy sector plans to produce 80% of its energy from non-polluting sources (Ministry of Energy 2018). There are plans to supply energy to consumers safely and at a competitive price, and it will contribute to the country's modern economy, competitiveness, and attraction of investments. The implementation of the Lithuanian energy sector's vision by 2020 is estimated to require up to EUR 2.4 billion, and in 2021–2030 – up to EUR 10 billion in public, including EU, and private funds for the development and modernization of the energy sector and the restoration of run-down facilities. The vision of the Lithuanian energy sector is based on the Paris Agreement adopted under the UN Framework Convention on Climate Change, the strategic provisions for the EU's 2030 energy and climate change policy targets, and the energy legislation of the EU and the Energy Union. The mandatory joint target for the EU (reducing GHG emissions by at least 40% by 2030, as compared to 1990) defined in the EU 2030 Climate and Energy Framework is aligned with its target to reduce GHG emissions by 80–95% by 2050 in Lithuania as well (Ministry of Energy 2018).

Implementation of the governance aims, the EU energy policy objectives for 2030, and the concept of the Energy Union are to be ensured through a common European Energy Governance System, based on the drawing up of National Integrated Energy and Climate Action Plans, which in the future, in Lithuania, could replace strategic planning documents related to the Strategy insofar as it does not conflict with strategic interests and national safety. The vision of the updated Strategy and the main strategic objectives, directions, and tasks of the development of the country's energy sectors are substantially in line with the EU's energy and climate change policy and the objectives of the Energy Union to achieve all this (Lietuvos Respublikos Seimas 2018).

Composition of the Energy Mix

Lithuanian gross inland energy consumption amounted to the equivalent of 7.69 million tonnes of oil and, compared to 2017, grew by 0.2% in 2018. The fuel and energy consumption was made up of crude oil and petroleum products (39.6%). Natural gas accounted for 23.1%, renewable energy sources, and electricity – 19.8 and 10.8% respectively; the rest – 6.7% – included coal, peat, etc. Among final consumers, the transport and household sectors predominate, respectively consuming 39.8 and 26.6% of energy in 2018.

Renewable energy in Lithuania is dominated by solid biofuel. In 2018, the largest amount of biofuel was used for the production of electricity and centralized heat supply (51.8%) and in households (37.3%).

In 2018, 23 wind farms operated in Lithuania. Electricity production by these wind farms together with small wind power plants was the highest in the energy history of the country. Electricity production exceeded 1.3 TWh and made up a third of total electricity production in the country, or over 8.7% of electricity consumed in the country. In the same year, hydropower plants produced 431 million kWh of electricity – 28.5% less than in 2017. In 2018, electricity produced by solar power plants reached 86.6 million kWh, actually, 27.3% more than in 2017. On the other hand, electricity demand in Lithuania increased by 2.2% and amounted to 13.1 TWh in 2018. To satisfy the country's needs, almost 75% of electricity consumption was imported and just 3.5 TWh of electricity was produced in Lithuania. In 2018, electricity produced from biogas amounted to almost 139.9 million kWh, i.e., 10% more than in 2017. Biofuel in 2018, and biodiesel and bioethanol for transportation amounted to 79 thousand and 12.4 thousand tonnes, respectively. Fuel consumption in road transport was 1.9 million tonnes in 2018, of which road diesel accounted for 82.8%, motor gasoline – 12.1%, and liquefied gas – 5.1% (Statistical Yearbook of Lithuania 2019).

Discourse on Energy Issues

Nuclear Power

The most fundamental issues in policy debates concerned turning around the future of nuclear power energy in the country. The Lithuanian Ignalina Nuclear Power Plant contained two Soviet-designed RBMK-1500 water-cooled graphite-moderated channel-type power reactors. After the Chernobyl disaster of April 1986, the reactor was de-rated to 1,360 MW. Each unit of the power plant was equipped with two K-750-65/3000 turbines with 800 MW generators. The INPP had two power-generating units, both with two turbines of 750 MW capacity each (Ignalina Nuclear Power Plant 2020). Lithuania decommissioned the Second Ignalina Power Plant reactor on December 31, 2009, thereby stopping its nuclear energy production.

The consequence was the unintended result of the 1999 commitment to close down its nuclear power station by 2010, conditional for its accession to the EU in

2004. Lithuania agreed early on in 1999 to close the existing units of the station, citing the Ignalina Plant's lack of a containment building as a high risk. The first unit was closed in December 2004; the second unit, which made up 25% of Lithuania's electricity generating capacity, supplied about 70% of Lithuania's electricity demands (Švedas and Vilpišauskas 2015). Energy production was a rather noticeable indicator of the energy balance by 2009, but as was mentioned earlier, energy production in 2010 dropped by 65% with the closure of the Ignalina Nuclear Power Plant. Growth of GDP in 2005–2015 saw a 7% increase in energy production. As with GDP growth rates, the growth rate of consumption of energy products declined significantly. However, unlike GDP growth in the post-crisis years, consumption of energy products does not have a significant growth trend. Based on data provided by the Department of Statistics of the Republic of Lithuania, the consumption of energy products did not reach 2006–2008 levels (Mačerinskienė and Kremer-Matyškevič 2017).

Thus, over a few years, Lithuania underwent a transition from an energy exporting to an energy importing country. For example, Lithuania imports around 75% of its electricity needs, as domestic electricity generation is fairly small, following a 78% decrease since the end of 2009, when the country shut down its second (and last) nuclear reactor. Electricity imports and natural gas use in electricity generation have compensated and filled the gap left by the shut-down of nuclear energy production. Natural gas quickly became the main source of electricity generation, increasing from 14% in 2009 to 63% in 2010 (around 2 TWh). The country became dependent on energy supply sources outside of the EU. Since the closure of the Ignalina Nuclear Power Plant, Lithuania has been importing electricity from Belarus, Latvia, Russia, and Sweden (International Energy Agency 2021). The development occurred in parallel with an absence of efforts to diversify energy sources. The natural gas market came under the partial control of the Russian monopolist Gazprom because of the sale of 34% of stocks in the Lithuanian gas supply monopolist Lietuvos Dujos (Lithuanian Gas). Dependency on Russian sources reached its climax by 2009.

The decision to build a new nuclear power plant in Visaginas drew a great deal of policy work and attention from state institutions. The LEO LT company was built on the principles of a public-private partnership in 2008. However, the policy for supporting the extended life of a nuclear plant did not receive public backing during the advisory referendum on 12 October 2008. The referendum did not gather the necessary 50% quorum, with only 48.43% supporting the motion (Lietuvos Respublikos Seimas 2008). This advisory referendum freed the government's hands, despite the Nuclear Power Law of the Republic of Lithuania and the 2007 and 2012 National Energy Strategies, which outlined a clear prioritization of nuclear energy (Lietuvos Respublikos Seimas 2007a, b, 2012a). A new consultative referendum was held together with parliamentary elections on 14 October 2012. The population had a chance to express its attitude toward the construction of a new nuclear power plant instead of the old Soviet one. One-third of the electorate (34.09%) supported the idea, but it was dismissed by a much larger proportion – 62.68%. The referendum did not go through and left the government free to choose whether to build or to have an excuse for not building a new nuclear power plant (Lietuvos Respublikos Seimas 2012d).

Prioritization of nuclear energy ended with the new 2016 strategy prepared by the Ministry of Energy, where nuclear energy expansion was no longer mentioned. Then Minister of Energy Žygimantas Vaičiūnas stressed that nuclear energy did not have any political prospects (Samkus 2017). As a result of the announced strategy, it soon became clear that Lithuania was not planning to proceed with the construction of a new nuclear power plant. Hitachi Europe Limited terminated its activities in Lithuania on 12 October 2017, and the Hitachi Visaginas Project Investment office abandoned its activities altogether (Samkus 2017).

The Lithuanian approach was to overcome infrastructural barriers in order to change its geostrategic position of dependence on particular types of energy supplies, to find possibilities to supplement energy sources, and to search for energy import alternatives. Lithuania started to challenge the Russian monopoly on energy resources rather late. It took some time to comprehend that infrastructural barriers depend on the geo-energetical positions of the states involved, and its possibilities to find alternatives for the supply of energy resources. For example, Lithuania's neighbor, the Republic of Belarus, did not have an effective infrastructural barrier to diminish Russian influence. The existing transit of Russian energy resources and infrastructure was sufficient not to change the *status quo*. To build such a barrier, one needs to have a perception of the threats questioning the existing infrastructural dependencies. Infrastructural barriers can only be built by having barriers of a social and political character (Česnakas 2014).

Perception of Threats to Energy Governance

Lithuania is not fully integrated into international energy and fuel markets. The country is dependent on Russia – its main energy supplier. The existing Lithuanian systems of energy production, supply, and distribution are outdated. Therefore, virtually all kinds of threats are relevant to the Lithuanian energy system.

Threats caused by infrastructure reliability issues within the energy sector are unlikely to materialize in Lithuania. Equipment in electricity, gas, heat and other sectors is not new and recent investments have been minimal. However, because equipment for the generation, transmission, and distribution of energy was planned for much larger loading capacities than exist at present, there are considerable excess capabilities and qualified personnel. This allows the prevention of larger accidents.

Nevertheless, technical threats remain, and reducing their consequences demands constant investment. In addition, it is necessary to renew equipment and technologies, which can only be done after extensive scientific research (Energy Security Research Centre 2013).

The perception is that being dependent on a single gas supplier and electricity import from a sole country places Lithuania at great risk. The country is affected by high fuel and energy prices when compared to other member states of the European Union. Abuse of dominance by monopolies is a contributing factor to the rising prices. The uneven development of the global economy, political instability, and economic crises lead to a destabilized supply of resources and their prices. It also makes it more difficult to ensure steady supplies and to implement necessary energy projects (Energy Security Research Centre 2013).

Three conditions of (in)security can be distinguished in energy security research – critical, pre-critical, and normal.

- The critical condition is when the energy security level is below 33%. This means that the security level is unacceptable and actions must be taken to eliminate the causes of such a condition because it is a threat to energy security.
- The pre-critical condition is when the energy security level is between 33 and 66%. This means that the security level is tolerable, however, it is likely that security threats might emerge. In due time, appropriate actions should be taken.
- The normal condition is when the energy security level is above 66%. This means that the security level is acceptable, security is ensured. In this case, actions should only be aimed at maintaining the present level of security (Energy Security Research Centre 2013).

Lithuanian energy security has been under assessment since 2007. Then, the Lithuanian energy security level reached 52.8%. Over the last 5 years, the highest security level was reached in 2008 (54.1%), and the lowest security level – in 2010 (51.2%), immediately after the closure of the Ignalina Nuclear Power Plant. Since its closure, the situation in the energy sector changed in 2010 due to a different dominant source of electricity generation. Baseload electricity generation was taken over by gas-powered plants. Gas supply is the most sensitive to economic and geopolitical factors. Therefore, domination of this type of fuel in energy production decreases energy security.

The slight increase in the energy security level in 2011 is related to the emergence of an electricity market and the accretion of biomass-biofuel in energy production. The import of more electricity as a result of the closure of the Ignalina Nuclear Power Plant has threatened energy security, although the situation is softened by the fact that purchasing electricity in the market is cheaper than producing it in Lithuania (Energy Security Research Centre 2013). Seven years after nuclear was phased out, in 2016, Lithuania produced a total of 3.97 TWh of electricity. Half of all electricity produced in the country was generated by power plants using renewable energy sources. About 0.45 TWh of electricity was generated by hydropower plants (excluding Kruonis PSPP), 1.13 TWh – by wind turbines, and about 0.44 TWh was produced by solar, biomass and biogas fired power plants. The remaining amount of electricity was produced by conventional fuel-fired power plants. The largest share of electricity consumed in the country (about 72% of total electricity consumption or 68% of total electricity demand) was imported in Lithuania during 2016. Most of it (37%) was imported from Latvia and Estonia, 27% – via the NordBalt interconnection with Sweden, 5% – via the LitPol Link interconnection with Poland, and the rest (31%) – from third countries. Lithuania will continue to be dependent on imports in the coming decades (Ministry of Energy 2018).

The results showed that the Lithuanian energy security level would increase the most (compared to the level in 2011) with the completion of the LNG Terminal project. The LNG Terminal would increase the security level by 5.8%. Successful realization of the LNG Terminal project should see the Lithuanian energy security level reach 57.3%.

One of the issues of greatest concern to society is the affordability of energy resources. A public survey of Lithuanians in 2013 (Augutis et al. 2014) indicated that this aspect of energy security was the most important for the absolute majority of the respondents (89.7% indicated important or very important). In this sense, Lithuanian energy policy aims to obtain energy resources at the lowest prices, complying with the interests of the majority. Two representative public surveys were conducted in 2013 and 2014. Although most of the Lithuanian population understands that energy independence from Russia is important (71.8% marked important or very important), 68.7% noted that the "state has to care more about the low price of energy resources rather than energy security," and only 30.8% asserted that the "state has to care more about energy independence, irrespective of the need for higher financial gains" (Augutis et al. 2014).

When the issue regarding the high price of energy independence arises, two-thirds of society did not support energy independence. It is evident then that the perception of security and energy policy affect the polarization of society. Some would like Lithuania to be less dependent on Russian energy supplies, but at the same time, they do not intend to support this purpose at the expense of their well-being. Nevertheless, energy independence is an important part of energy security – it remains of secondary importance in comparison to prices for energy resources for Lithuanian citizens (Energy Security Research Centre 2015).

Security concerns over energy supplies seem to play a much more important role in guiding policy than is approved by a majority of the public. The fundamental concerns expressed by consumers over prices are not reflected in policy choices made by governments.

Policies Regarding the Baltic (Russian Federation) and Ostrovets Nuclear Power Plant in the Republic of Belarus

On 26 June 2012, the Lithuanian parliament (Seimas) approved a strategy for Lithuanian energy independence and national security. The nuclear power plants being planned for construction in neighboring Ostrovets in Belarus, and the so-called Baltic Nuclear Power Plant in the Kaliningrad Oblast of the Russian Federation were named as a challenge to Lithuanian national security. The National Security Strategy identified the development of nuclear energy in the region as a threat to Lithuanian national security if international safety standards were not being followed. Plans to construct the Baltic and Ostrovets nuclear power plants were deemed as electric power plants of doubtful security in third countries (Lietuvos Respublikos Seimas 2012b). Yet, these formulations did not articulate any clear aims for how they would be implemented. The government program that was approved in 2012 did not mention nuclear power plants at all (Lietuvos Respublikos Seimas 2012c). The Lithuanian position later concentrated predominantly on nuclear safety and the international laws related to both nuclear power plants in progress (Juozaitis 2020).

Lithuania was backing its stance based on predominantly expert and normative arguments, with political arguments largely absent (Juozaitis 2020). In June 2013, the construction of the Baltic Nuclear Power Plant was stopped temporarily, while the project was to be allegedly redesigned.

From 12 May 2016, Lithuania started to put more stress on its demands to suspend construction, demonstrating the connection of the Ostrovets Power Plant with Russian technologies and interests. Lithuania pursued a contradictory campaign, on the one hand, attempting to promote claims that the plant did comply with international safety requirements. On the other hand, however, Lithuania emphasized Russian geopolitical interests and attempted to stop its activities (Juozaitis 2020). The Lithuanian government attempted to bring into the EU agenda the Ostrovets and Baltic nuclear power plants as a bilateral issue at the EU level. Efforts were also made to question the safety of Russian-built nuclear power plants. Moreover, it attempted to impose the same ecological criteria on nuclear power plants built in the EU and outside of the Union. Additionally, the Lithuanian government suggested imposing restrictions on all "unsafe" nuclear power plants in these countries and urged halting construction of the Ostrovets Nuclear Power Plant at the EU level (Juozaitis 2020). Despite these efforts and campaigns, the stance of the EU remains abstract – there are demands to assure the safety of the nuclear power plant, but there is no mention of incidents or non-compliance with international law.

The Lithuanian government's stance and international campaign at the UN, OSCE, Council of Europe, EU, and TATENA did not win the support of the international community, nor did it create any legal consequences, or obstruct construction or the launch of the Ostrovets Nuclear Power Plant in 2020 (Juozaitis 2020).

Coordination, Instruments, and Issues of the Lithuanian Energy Transition

Energy policies should serve the interests of a country's energy security, competitiveness, sustainability, and innovation. Important institutional reforms have taken place in the Lithuanian energy sector since the creation of the Ministry of Energy in January 2009. As a result of the reforms, independent system operators for gas and electricity, unbundled from supply activities, were created. Lithuania has made progress in gradually opening up its electricity and gas markets. However, amid security concerns, it has increased the level of state ownership in its energy sector in recent years. Lithuania maintains high market concentration in the residential gas market with price regulation measures. Amid rising geopolitical tensions in the Baltic region, energy security remains as important as ever before.

In response to this, the Lithuania 2030 Strategy promotes a smart society, smart governance and smart economy to place Lithuania among the top ten in Europe on sustainable growth, openness, inclusiveness and well-being, and having a strong renewables strategy based on bioenergy and wind power. Lithuania's energy and climate targets are set by EU and national policies. By 2030, Lithuania wants to reduce its electricity imports by half and produce 70% of its electricity needs from domestic renewable sources, and to complete synchronization with the continental European power system by 2025. By 2050, total electricity consumption in the country should be supplied domestically.

The country needs to complete the liberalization of electricity and gas markets, reform energy and environmental taxes and levies, and promote energy technology innovation particularly in clean energy technologies.

Oil and Gas Infrastructure

At the infrastructural level, Lithuania is the only Baltic State with an oil refinery in Mažeikiai with an annual capacity of 10–11 million tonnes of refined products. Lithuania has an export and import terminal in Būtingė, which has a 12 million tonnes import capacity and 14 million tonnes export capacity. The country also has a reverse terminal for oil products in Klaipėda with an annual capacity of 7.1 million tonnes, with all the accompanying technical infrastructure to import oil and its products and to ensure safety procedures are in place.

Politics and perceptions have been an important factor in pursuing energy policies in general, not just in the case of developments in the nuclear power energy sector. The capacity to import and export oil products to overcome dependency on the traditional Soviet-built "Druzhba" pipeline was a step ahead of its time. The terminal in Būtingė started to be planned in 1993. The Būtingės Nafta Company was established in 1995 and became part of the Mažeikiai Nafta Group (now part of AB ORLEN Lietuva) in 1998. The terminal was constructed by the US company Flour Daniel and the German company Preussag Wasser & Rohrtechnik and started to operate in 1999. The Mažeikiai Refinery in Lithuania and the Ventspils Oil Terminal in Latvia are connected to the main pipeline by a branch pipeline from the Unecha junction in Bryansk Oblast. This branch ceased operation in 2006 and is not likely to become operational again any time soon. When the Russian Federation stopped delivering oil via the "Druzhba" pipeline in 2006, the Būtingė terminal started to function as an oil import terminal.

Another political issue – dependency on gas supplies from Russia – assumed a top position on the national agenda. Reforms started in 2008 when the newly-elected majority from the Conservative Party (*Tėvynės sąjunga – Lietuvos krikščionys demokratai, TS–LKD*) formed the ruling majority and a government coalition. The new government used EU energy policy tools, such as the EU Third Energy Package of 2009, and the Security of Supply Regulation of 2010, to reform the domestic gas sector. They also employed general EU antitrust policy tools. Application of EU tools and changes in domestic opportunity structures became possible when they coincided with and/or were adopted in Brussels. The spirit of the Third Energy Package harbors the aim to provide choice for consumers and establish a competitive gas market. Lithuanian ruling parties mainly used the Third Energy Package for exclusively prioritizing their single aim of security of supply.

Amid rising Russian gas import prices, the closure of the Ignalina Nuclear Power Plant was the issue that brought the focus of Lithuanians onto the organization of the gas sector. However, the start of the reform was marked by even further increases in gas prices, which coincided with the country's slow recovery from its largest economic crisis to date. Lithuania continued to pay more for gas than the other two Baltic States until the end of 2014, but since then, the price has fallen. Along with the planned opening of the Independence LNG regasification terminal in Lithuania, Gazprom reportedly proposed a 20% discount for natural gas sold to the Lithuanian gas utility Lietuvos Dujos "retroactively," starting from January 2013. Even though some energy researchers foresee the possibility of Gazprom involving itself in a gas *price war* to protect its market share against US LNG, the decrease in gas prices to Lithuania could have also been motivated by the arbitration proceedings of Lietuvos Dujos against Gazprom in 2014, to demand a contractual price adjustment for natural gas supplies (Pakalkaitė 2016). At the same time, in March 2012, the state-owned company Klaipėdos Nafta signed an agreement with the Norwegian company Höegh LNG to build a floating liquefied natural gas storage and regasification unit (FSRU), which was later named Independence. The 10-year lease agreement has a purchase option. The maximum technical regasification capacity is up to 4 bcm/year (approximately 11mmcm/day). The FSRU Independence had to be operational by 3 December 2014; the total value of the contract in 10 years could amount very roughly to EUR 500 million (the proposed rental price of the FSRU was $189,000 / day). In order to save time on construction, the Klaipėda LNG terminal was considered a national terminal and it did not apply for the status of a Project of Common Interest (PCI).

In May 2014, under the Social Democratic government, E.ON sold its shares in Lietuvos Dujos and Amber Grid, and also 11.76% of shares of the electricity distribution network operator LESTO to the Lithuanian State for EUR 147.3 million. Following E.ON, in June 2014 Gazprom sold its 37% interests in associates, Lietuvos Dujos and Amber Grid, to companies controlled by the Republic of Lithuania for EUR 121 million. Amber Grid was certified as a gas transmission system operator according to the ownership unbundling rules in 2015. Companies engaged in transmission and other infrastructure activities are placed under the Ministry of Energy of Lithuania, some of them via a holding company EPSO-G that was established in 2013. On the other hand, the state-owned electricity company group Lietuvos Energija, owned by the Ministry of Finance of Lithuania, controls gas trade, distribution, and supply companies.

Amber Grid owns and operates the entire gas transmission system of Lithuania. Currently, 96.58% of the shares in Amber Grid are held by the Lithuanian State via the Ministry of Energy, via EPSO-G, with the remainder being free-floated on the stock exchange. Amber Grid also holds 66% of natural gas exchange GET Baltic. The Finnish group Gasum Oy holds the other 34% of Klaipėdos Nafta, also controlled by the Ministry of Energy. It manages the LNG FSRU Independence, and Liga's is the designated supplier via the terminal. On 1 January 2016, Lietuvos Dujos was merged with LESTO, and the new juridical person, active in electricity and gas distribution, was called Energijos Skirstymo Operatorius. Lietuvos Dujos ceased existing as a juridical person and was de-registered from the registry. Lietuvos Duju Tiekimas, established in 2014 following the unbundling requirements, is currently responsible for natural gas supply to (mostly) residential, business and other customers. This company is also owned by Lietuvos Energija: it took over the supply business of Lietuvos Dujos. Energijos Tiekimas, which was already previously owned by Lietuvos Energija, also acquired a gas supply license in addition to its electricity supply license. Thus, the gas industry has moved from being largely privately-owned to being largely state-owned.

However, several new private energy companies have entered the wholesale and retail level of the Lithuanian gas sector by acquiring gas supply licenses since 2013, and several of them became active in the market. At the end of 2014, natural gas supply licenses were held by 32 companies, 11 of these were performing supply operations (Pakalkaitė 2016). As of June 2019 one company, Amber Grid, had a license for gas transmission, five companies had licenses to distribute gas, and 30 companies had a license to supply gas (National Energy Regulatory Council 2020b). On the other hand, in 2019 the State Energy Regulation Service issued 506 permits to produce electric energy, 800 permits to develop energy production capacity, and six permits to import electric energy from non-EU countries (National Energy Regulatory Council 2020a).

The LNG Terminal

FSRU Independence, an LNG carrier built by Hyundai Heavy Industries, is designed as a floating LNG storage and regasification unit for the terminal. It is leased from Höegh LNG for 10 years with a buyout option. It has a maximum capacity to handle almost 4 billion cubic meters per annum (140 billion cubic feet per annum) of natural gas (2.2 million tonnes of LNG) and has four storage tanks with a total capacity of 170,000 cubic meters (6,000,000 cu ft). However, until the end of 2015, the maximum capacity was lowered to 2 billion cubic meters per annum (71 billion cubic feet per annum) due to limited pipeline capacity between Lithuania and underground storage in Latvia, and due to a closed gas market in Latvia.

The Klaipėda liquefied natural gas floating storage and regasification unit terminal, or Klaipėda LNG FSRU, is an LNG terminal in the port of Klaipėda, Lithuania. It cost $128 million to construct. The project operator is Klaipėdos Nafta.

Even though the Klaipėda LNG terminal was considered as a national terminal and did not apply for the status of a project of common interest in the EU, Lithuania has been promoting the idea of using the LNG Terminal in Klaipėda as the Regional Baltic LNG Terminal in their public communication and presentations. The aggregate gas demand in the Baltic States in 2015 was around 4.5 bcm, and the Lithuanian LNG terminal could, at full capacity, cover nearly 90% of total demand in the

Baltics. If the Lithuanian government acquires the LNG vessel Independence before its lease runs out in 2024, it is likely to remain in Klaipėda Port after 2024.

Despite the failure to transform this LNG project into an EU-supported regional energy security project from the very beginning, it was the first project that made it possible for Lithuania no longer to depend on a single Russian natural gas supplier. As a result, the price of natural gas supplied by Gazprom to Lithuania had been reduced by one-fifth before the outset of the terminal's exploitation. The terminal got a chance to operate not only in the gas market of the Baltic States but also to work in the Polish and Ukrainian gas supply systems (Energy Security Research Centre 2015).

The FSRU Independence would be even more likely to remain in Klaipėda Port after 2024 if the European Commission grants it the status of a regional terminal. This kind of status could mean that no more LNG terminals of a regional scale would be built in Latvia or Estonia, or that at least no potential competitors of FSRU Independence would receive EU funding. Unlike in 2013, neither Finland nor Latvia have placed LNG projects on their shores on the second PCI list published by the European Commission in the autumn of 2015. Both the Estonian LNG terminal proposals – Paldiski LNG and Tallinn LNG – have remained on the PCI list. Should Finland, Latvia, or Estonia still plan to build a regional LNG terminal for which they would receive EU funding, the European Commission would likely take into account the funding decision if these projects do not gain a commercial advantage over the LNG Terminal in Klaipėda. The EU LNG and Storage Strategy of 2016 highlights that "EU funds can help to make up for the weak commercial viability of terminals that are particularly important for security of supply." Having the Klaipėda LNG in place, it is more difficult to argue that additional LNG terminals are as important to the security of supply in the Baltics as would have been the case before FSRU Independence arrived. If the Klaipėda LNG gets regional terminal status and if Lithuania acquires rather than leases the terminal, Lithuanian energy sector officials may attempt to receive EU support for the Klaipėda LNGT and calculate the acquisition of the ship as a new investment (Šeputytė 2014). Lithuania intends to organize a public procurement process in the second half of 2021 for selecting the most advantageous offer. State guarantees are necessary to obtain a loan that cannot exceed EUR 160 million from a private financial institution, as this amount should cover the costs of FSRU. The Commission found that the measure remains compatible with the Internal Market and, therefore, approved the additional state guarantee under EU State aid rules. Thus, the project has moved from being a national project to prioritizing security of supply, turning into a project of EU importance in line with European practices (European Commission 2020).

Nord Stream 2

Lithuania has been the most active in advocating against Nord Stream 2 and expressed the highest concerns over the implementation of the Russian-dominated gas pipeline, arguing that the project would compromise EU energy security and general safety. The approval of Nord Stream 2 was perceived as a betrayal on both economic matters and European values, as the aforementioned East European states have experienced violence and hostilities from Russia and previously, the Soviet Union, in the past. Inconsistency with EU policies would also mean a failure of the Lithuanian strategy for energy governance, which was based on its fear about the indirect political repercussions of Nord Stream 2 (Bros et al. 2017). After the signing of the second Nord Stream 2 agreement, resistance toward German-Russian energy plans intensified. During a meeting with German Foreign Relations Minister Heiko Maas in May 2018, the leaders of the Baltic States stated that the project does not comply with European energy market policies and priorities. Lithuanian Minister of Foreign Affairs Linas Linkevičius said that Nord Stream 2 is threatening European common energy policy and its consistency, therefore, the project is simply disrespectful of those states that are trying to diversify their energy sources and follow EU energy market rules (ELTA 2019). In September 2019, Polish Prime Minister Mateusz Morawiecki publicly said that both Lithuania and Poland consider Nord Stream 2 as "a threat to security in Central and Eastern Europe" (Barteczko 2019). Lithuania invested in an LNG terminal in Klaipėda, Latvia is willing to follow in its steps. Therefore, countries are actively seeking to become less dependent on Russia and promote an example of route and supplier diversification, which was in line with Lithuanian policies of securitization regarding any projects coming from the Russian sphere of influence.

Green Energy in Lithuania

Lithuania has very limited domestic energy resources. The main source of electricity production in Lithuania was the closed Ignalina Nuclear Power Plant, which generated 80–85% of total electricity production. However, Lithuania does not have an overwhelming potential for renewable energy, with only biofuel, hydro, and wind power considered as potential renewable sources. The share of renewable energy sources in the Lithuanian primary energy supply is the lowest among the three Baltic States (Estonia, Latvia, and Lithuania), though the trends of development are positive. The Lithuanian National Energy Strategy adopted in 2002 set the strategic priorities for Lithuanian energy sector development. One of the main strategic priorities was to achieve a 12% share of renewable energy sources in primary energy supply by 2010. The development strategy on domestic renewable and waste energy resources accounted for a 9% share of these resources in the year 2000. The target was to ensure that approximately two million tonnes of oil equivalent of the above resources are used per year by 2010 (Streimikienė et al. 2005). The Renewable Energy Directive (2009/28/EC) of the European Parliament established an overall policy for the production and promotion of energy from renewable energy sources in the EU. It requires the EU to fulfill at least 20% of its total energy needs with renewables by 2020. This target is to be achieved through the attainment of individual national targets.

The National Strategy for the Development of Renewable Energy Sources of 2010 in Lithuania followed the EU lead, and for the first time, put significant emphasis on the development of renewable energy sources. The idea behind the strategy was to ensure an attractive alternative to traditional energy because the combustion of fossil energy sources substantially increases environmental pollution and accelerates climate warming. In Lithuania, the use of local fossil resources (oil, peat) has limits of growth (Varnagirytė-Kabašinskienė et al. 2019). Therefore, the target is to increase the share of renewable energy sources to at least 23% of the country's final gross energy consumption by 2020. The development of renewable energy sources had to ensure sustainable energy supplies to consumers. Additionally, further development of heating and electricity production from renewable energy sources; implementation and development of production and user technologies in the transport sector; reduction of amounts of pollutants (including greenhouse gases); saving fossil energy sources; reduction of the dependence on fossil energy sources and their imports; diversification of energy sources; and improving national energy security (National Renewable Energy Action Plan, 2010). From 2017, legal acts were adopted and/or amended to remove regulatory and non-regulatory barriers for the expansion of the development of energy from renewable sources. Plans were made to increase renewable sources to at least 38% of Lithuania's gross final energy consumption by 2025. By adopting the latest and most efficient technologies for the use of renewable energy sources and promoting energy efficiency, the share of electricity produced from renewable energy sources in the country's gross final consumption of electricity should reach at least 38% in 2025. The legislation also provides for an increase in the share of district heating produced from renewable energy sources in the heat balance to at least 70% in 2020. A new and detailed regulation has been established for the development of the use of renewable energy sources for electricity production, recognized as one of the strategic goals of national energy policy, along with the promotion of their use and allocation of the costs of connecting power plants to the electricity grid. Moreover, a new regulation has been established for auctioning the allocation of promotion quotas between the Republic of Lithuania and the other Member States, announced and organized by the National Control Commission for Prices and Energy. There is a consensus in the country that energy markets alone cannot deliver the desired level of renewable energy in the EU; Lithuania offers the ability for energy producers to strengthen their positions in the energy markets in different ways. It promotes the activities of renewable energy electricity self-consumers, who will now be able to receive support for renewable energy installations up to 10 kW. In September of 2019, a new technology-neutral support scheme for electricity production from renewable energy sources was launched (2019 Progress Report of the Republic of Lithuania on the Promotion and Use of Renewable Energy Sources, 2019). Additionally, the Climate Change Program under the Environmental Project Management Agency supports household renovation projects, energy efficiency measures and subsidizes renewable energy installations in existing buildings.

Synchronization of the Electricity Network with EU Networks

Lithuania, Latvia, and Estonia are the only EU members whose energy electric systems are synchronized with an IPS/UPS (Integrated Power System/Unified Power System) controlled de facto by Russia, which includes the electricity network of the Russian Federation, the Republic of Belarus, and the Baltic States. According to the BRELL Agreement between Belarus, Russia, Estonia, Latvia, and Lithuania, the management and regulation of frequency is assured centrally from Moscow. National network operators have to coordinate their expansion with the other BRELL countries (Kadisa et al. 2016; Molis and Juozaitis 2017). Synchronization with continental European networks is the longest-lasting project in EU energy integration. In theory, it should be finished by 2025, which is longer than it took to prepare to join the EU and NATO. 2017 became a turning-point because an essential element joined the process – Poland supported the synchronization through its electrical networks. The EU Commission urged the Baltic States to settle on an agreement as soon as possible. The discussions were primarily financial – the extended period of the substantial cost of synchronization for the three Baltic States. Then Estonia decided to retreat from the synchronization scenario via the Nordic countries, due to the greater costs to be incurred there compared to the Polish-Lithuanian cross-border option. Latvia and Estonia agreed to discuss different synchronization scenarios via Poland (Janeliūnas and Maskoliūnaitė 2019). Nevertheless, synchronization as a solution still depends on many circumstances. There is still no guarantee that synchronization will take place by 2025. There are many potential obstacles to implementing synchronization that make the political goal of attaining energy supply independence (synonymous to energy supply without Russian participation) difficult to attain. The most troublesome aspects are the procedural, cost/benefit, and political aspects of synchronization. Procedure-wise, the so-called catalog of measures means each country has to comply with 409 requirements. Lithuania only complied with 169 in 2019. The total cost for all the Baltic countries would reach over EUR 1 billion. However, the most problematic issues are the political aspects of synchronization.

The Kaliningrad Oblast of the Russian Federation, which is isolated from Belarus by Lithuania might become a focal point for disagreements stemming from Russia or Belarus on whether to allow synchronization or to ensure it is obstructed. They have the option of disconnecting Lithuania or all the Baltic States earlier than they are ready to disconnect from BRELL. Latvia and Estonia indefinitely postponed trials on how they would function if isolated from the BRELL regime. In 2020–2025, the Baltic States and Poland will undergo political changes because of elections, and commitment to synchronization may also wane on account of pressure from Russia and the increasing number of technical demands (Janeliūnas and Maskoliūnaitė 2019).

Outcomes, Challenges, and Prospects

The chapter has analyzed the structures and major problems of Lithuanian energy governance, which likewise constitute its future challenges. The process of integration into the single EU market and regulation, ensuring transparent, non-discriminatory, and predictable operating conditions within the energy sector and the protection of consumer rights and interests became a dominant feature of Lithuanian energy policy. Infrastructural developments, namely, the synchronization of Baltic electricity networks with continental Europe, borne by the electricity transmission system operator (TSO) AB Litgrid, went ahead, and a joint agreement between all regulators – Lithuania, Latvia, Estonia, and Poland – on cross-border cost allocation was also signed. This was an important step that enabled the TSOs of the four countries to submit requests for funding to the European Commission under the Connecting Europe Facility (CEF). The total costs of the second stage of synchronization incurred by Lithuania, Latvia, Estonia, and Poland amount to more than EUR 1.22 billion, while the costs incurred by Lithuania alone amount to EUR 474 million. EU funds can be used to finance up to 75% of the total value of second-stage synchronization projects: this is the maximum possible support granted to projects concerning energy infrastructure. The amendments to the Law on Electricity adopted in May 2020 will allow Lithuania to join the majority of EU countries whose consumers can choose an electricity supplier best suited to their individual needs. From 1 January 2021 to 1 January 2023, the monopoly services of the public supplier will be consistently terminated and conditions will be created to facilitate the active engagement of electricity suppliers.

Taking into account the requirements of European Commission Regulation No. 2017/2195, which establishes electricity balancing guidelines, in 2019, the National Energy Regulatory Council (NERC) approved the Standard Terms and Conditions for the Imbalance Sales Contract drawn up by AB Litgrid, which apply to entities operating in Lithuania and ensure uniform and non-discriminatory operating conditions for all system users by providing clear regulations regarding the mutual obligations of market participants and TSOs, the conditions for the submission, amendment, and adjustment of balance sheet schedules, and the payment procedure. The NERC also approved the Standard Terms and Conditions for the Balancing Service Sales Contract prepared by AB Litgrid, which are mandatory for the suppliers of balancing services operating in Lithuania.

Within the natural gas sector, cooperation in the Regional Gas Market Coordination Group (RGMCG) continued to create a common natural gas market of the three Baltic States and Finland. On 1 January 2020, the common natural gas tariff zone of Finland, Estonia, and Latvia (FINESTLAT) was launched. In 2020, the Lithuanian transmission system is considered a separate tariff zone. However, to efficiently develop the regional gas market in the Baltic-Finnish countries and to seek further integration of these countries, the entry point prices approved for 2020 were harmonized with other prices set by FINESTLAT, i.e., the entry price is the same at all entry points of the Baltic-Finnish region. It is important to note that in April 2020, the road map for the integration of regional markets between Estonia, Finland,

Latvia, and Lithuania, which provides for a common zone of the prices of the four countries starting from 2022, was approved in the High-Level Group on the Baltic Energy Market Interconnection Plan (BEMIP) (National Energy Regulatory Council 2020a). Security of supply continues to be the dominant topic in national energy governance. The National Strategy for Energetic Independence, prepared by the Lithuanian Ministry of Energy in 2018, emphasizes independence from old channels of supply in non-EU countries and new renewable sources of energy (Lietuvos Respublikos Seimas 2018). The Strategy underlines the importance of competitiveness, reliability, reducing the impact on climate change and air pollution (saving energy and green energy), and the participation of private enterprises in promoting progressive trends in the energy industry. In 2020, this Strategy is aimed at achieving safety of energy supplies; by 2030, the Strategy aspires to make Lithuania competitive and sustainable on the energy front before 2050. The plan to raise domestically produced energy from 35% to 100% in 30 years seems ambitious. It demonstrates very clearly how a country that, for political-symbolic gains, voluntarily stopped producing nuclear power energy and became dependent on imported electricity, has had to plan to reverse the trend of importing energy with the help of different technologies within almost 50 years. And this is only a plan, which is itself dependent on many variables, for example, the success of pan-EU transformations, technological progress, and sustainability of the green and recyclables economy overall. Moreover, for a small country like Lithuania, an important element is the creation and integration of the EU energy market, achievement of EU climate change goals, and implementation of energy policy aims. No less important is EU financial assistance. The political aspect continues to be significant, especially because the economic effect of these policies is not yet certain. The analysis of the Lithuanian energy sector's indicators for 2005–2015 (such as the change in energy sector participants, energy balance indicators, changes in energy sector prices, value-added and other taxes, and net profitability of the energy sector) has produced findings that indicators such as GDP, number of participants, energy products import and export, final consumption of energy products, values added generated by the energy sector, key taxes, and net profit margins in the post-crisis years tended to increase. However, only the dynamics of GDP and gross energy consumption variation coincide. Energy production and general internal expenditure decreased over the analyzed period. Studies of the influence of the energy sector on the growth of Lithuanian GDP showed that the ratio of correlation between total energy consumption and GDP was weak (Mačerinskienė and Kremer-Matyškevič 2017).

The policies and priorities will be sustained unless further integration into the EU energy market is assured as well as financial EU assistance is guaranteed. To finance the energy transition, Lithuania estimates EUR 14 billion of investments coming from the public sector and the EU. The decarbonization of the economy will absorb over 70% of total investments, which is expected to be leveraged largely by public funds (International Energy Agency 2021). Sustainability of the policy will be a challenge for the economy and the state in the foreseeable future, keeping in mind the limited success of public-private partnerships. The government needs to identify private sector investment and create more domestic resources, as it is largely relying on EU funding for most of its energy sector public spending. However, Lithuanian energy policy dependency on the EU framework offers opportunities for energy policy innovations. If Lithuanian energy policy had remained without these external influences, it would have had to make do with poorer infrastructure and would not have had access to any innovation resources.

Cross-References

▶ Energy Governance in Latvia
▶ Energy Governance in Russia: From a Fossil to a Green Giant?
▶ Energy Governance in the Republic of Poland
▶ Energy Policies in the EU: A Fiscal Federalism Perspective
▶ EU-Russia Energy Relations
▶ Monitoring Energy Policy

References

2019 Progress Report of the Republic of Lithuania on the Promotion and Use of Renewable Energy Sources. (2019). https://www.ec.europa.eu/energy/sites/ener/files/documents/lt_-_tr_into_eng_-_5th_progress_report_red_for_2017_and_2018.pdf. Accessed 13 September 2021.

Augutis, J., Leonavičius, V., Genys, D., Česnakas G., Martišauskas, L., Krikštolaitis, R., & Pečiulytė, S. (2014). Lietuvos energetinis saugumas ir visuomenės vertinimai. *Delfi.lt*. 3 March 2014. https://www.delfi.lt/verslas/energetika/lietuvos-energetinis-saugumas-ir-visuomenes-vertinimai.d?id=64172002. Accessed 29 January 2021.

Barteczko, A. (2019). Poland and Lithuania see Nord Stream 2 as threat to energy security. *Reuters*. 17 September 2019. https://www.reuters.com/article/us-poland-lithuania-nordstream2/poland-and-lithuania-see-nord-stream-2-as-threat-toenergy-security-idUSKBN1W20TQ. Accessed 29 January 2021.

Bros, A., Mitrova, T. & Westphal, K. (2017). *German-Russian gas relations*. https://www.swp-berlin.org/fileadmin/contents/products/research_papers/2017RP13_wep_EtAl.pdf. Accessed 28 January 2021.

Česnakas, G. (2014). *Energijos ištekliai Rusijos užsienio politikoje Baltarusijos ir Ukrainos atžvilgiu (2000–2012 metais)*. Doctoral dissertation. Vytautas Magnus University, Kaunas.

ELTA. (2019). Linkevičius užsienio žiniasklaidai: Rusijos grėsmė yra reali ir turi būti vertinama rimtai, *LRT*, 20 June 2019. https://www.lrt.lt/naujienos/lietuvoje/2/1071381/linkevicius-uzsienio-ziniasklaidai-rusijos-gresme-yra-reali-ir-turi-butivertinama-rimtai. Accessed 3 February 2021.

Energy Security Research Centre. (2013). *Lithuanian energy security annual review 2011–2012*. Kaunas: Vytautas Magnus University.

Energy Security Research Centre. (2015). *Lithuanian energy security annual review 2013–2014*. Kaunas: Vytautas Magnus University.

European Commission. (2020). *State aid: Commission approves an additional state guarantee for Klaipėda LNG terminal in Lithuania*. https://www.ec.europa.eu/info/news/state-aid-commission-approves-additional-state-guarantee-klaipeda-lng-terminal-lithuania-2020-nov-20_en. Accessed 19 February 2021.

Grøn, C. H., & Wivel, A. (2011). Maximizing influence in the European Union after the Lisbon treaty: From small state policy to smart state strategy. *Journal of European Integration, 5*(33), 523–539.

Ignalina Nuclear Power Plant. (2020). https://www.iae.lt/en/about-us/technical-data/138. Accessed 24 January 2021.

International Energy Agency. (2021). *Lithuanian energy policy review.* https://iea.blob.core. windows.net/assets/4d014034-0f94-409d-bb8f193e17a81d77/Lithuania_2021_Energy_Pol icy_Review.pdf. Accessed 15 September 2021.

Janeliūnas, T. & Maskoliūnaitė, E. (2019). *Elektros tinklų sinchronizacija su kontinentine Europa: politinis procesas 1999–2019 m. Analitinė Studija.* Vilnius: ETI.

Juozaitis, J. (2020). *Mažųjų valstybių nacionalinių interesų įgyvendinimas tarpvyriausybinėse organizacijose: Lietuvos pasipriešinimas Astravo ir Baltijos elektrinių statyboms.* Doctoral dissertation. Vytautas Magnus University, Kaunas.

Kadisa, S., Radziukynas, V., Klementavičius, A., & Radziukyniene, N. (2016). Challenges for the Baltic power system connecting synchronously to European continental network. *Electric Power Systems Research, 140,* 54–64.

Lietuvos Respublikos Seimas. (2007a). *Nutarimas dėl nacionalinės energetikos strategijos patvirtinimo, 2007 01 18, Nr. X-1046, Valstybės žinios, Nr. 11-430,* Vilnius.

Lietuvos Respublikos Seimas. (2007b). *Lietuvos Respublikos atominės elektrinės įstatymas. 2007 m. birželio 28 d. Nr. X-1231,* Vilnius. https://e-seimas.lrs.lt/portal/legalAct/lt/TAD/TAIS. 301267?jfwid=-n126u3scv.

Lietuvos Respublikos Seimas. (2008). *Nutarimas dėl referendumo dėl Ignalinos atominės elektrinės darbo pratęsimo paskelbimo, Nr. X-1693, Valstybės žinios, Nr. 81-3194,* Vilnius. *Lietuvos Respublikos vyriausiosios rinkimų komisijos sprendimas dėl patariamojo referendmo dėl Ignalinos atominės elektrinės darbo pratęsimo galutinių resultatų, 2008 m. spalio 17 d. Nr. 167,* Vilnius. https://e-seimas.lrs.lt/portal/legalAct/lt/TAD/TAIS.329224. Accessed 1 January 2021.

Lietuvos Respublikos Seimas. (2012a). *Nutarimas dėl nacionalinės energetinės nepriklausomybės strategijos patvirtinimo, 2012 06 26, Nr. XI-2133, Valstybės žinios, Nr. 80-4149,* Vilnius.

Lietuvos Respublikos Seimas. (2012b). *Dėl Lietuvos Respublikos Seimo nutarimo „Dėl Nacionalinio saugumo strategijos patvirtinimo" pakeitimo Str. 35.4.*

Lietuvos Respublikos Seimas. (2012c). *Dėl Lietuvos Respublikos Vyriausybės programos.* https:// eseimas.lrs.lt/portal/legalAct/lt/TAD/TAIS.439761. Review: 2020-12-25. Accessed 18 January 2021.

Lietuvos Respublikos Seimas. (2012d). *Nutarimas dėl Referendumo Dėl Atominės Elektrinės Statybos Lietuvos Respublikoje paskelbimo.* http://www3.lrs.lt/pls/inter3/dokpaieska. showdoc_l?p_id=430183&p_query=refere*&p_tr2=2. Accessed 16 January 2021.

Lietuvos Respublikos Seimas. (2018). *Nacionalinė energetinės nepriklausomybės strategija-energija Lietuvos ateičiai, Lietuvos Republikos Seimas nutarimas dėl Lietuvos Respublikos Seimo 2012 m. birželio 26 d. Nutarimo Nr.XI-2133 "Dėl Nacionalinės Energetinės Nepriklausomybės Strategijos patvirtinimo,, pakeitimo birželio 21 d. Nr. XIII-1288,* Vilnius.

Mačerinskienė, I., & Kremer-Matyškevič, I. (2017). Assessment of Lithuanian energy sector influence on GDP. *Montenegrin Journal of Economics, 13*(4), 43–59.

Mažylis, L., & Pikšrytė, A. (2013). Europos Sąjungos reguliavimo politikos modelių taikymas atsinaujinančių išteklių energetikos srityje. *Public Policy and Administration, 12*(1), 120–132.

Ministry of Energy. (2018). *National energy independence strategy executive summary-energy for competitive Lithuania.* https://enmin.lrv.lt/uploads/enmin/documents/files/National_energy_ independence_strategy_2018.pdf. Accessed 14 January 2021.

Molis, A., & Juozaitis, J. (2017). Baltic plug into European electricity network: Perspectives of success. *Humanities and Social Sciences: Latvia, 25*(1), 20–44.

Molis, A., & Vaišnoras, T. (2015). Energy security through membership in NATO and the EU: Interests and achievements of Lithuania. *Lithuanian Foreign Policy Review, 32,* 13–32.

National Energy Regulatory Council (2020a). Annual report on electricity and natural gas markets of the Republic of Lithuania to the European Commission. Vilnius. https://www.vert.lt/ SiteAssets/naujienu-medziaga/2020/2020-09/20200922_Ataskaita_EK_2019.pdf. Accessed 12 January 2021.

National Energy Regulatory Council (2020b). https://www.vert.lt/dujos/Puslapiai/default.aspx. Accessed 20 December 2020.

National Renewable Energy Action Plan. (2010). https://www.ena.lt/uploads/PDF-AEI/KITI-doc/ EN/6a-national-renewable-energy-action-plan-lithuania-en.pdf. Accessed 13 September 2021.

Pakalkaitė, V. (2016). *Lithuania's strategic use of EU energy policy tools: A transformation of gas dynamics*. Oxford: Oxford Institute for Energy Studies. https://doi.org/10.26889/9781784670658. Accessed 25 January 2021.

Samkus, M. (2017). Hitachi uždaro atstovybę Lietuvoje. 15Min.lt. 9 November 2017. https://www.15min.lt/verslas/naujiena/bendroves/hitachi-uzdaro-atstovybe-lietuvoje. Accessed 24 January 2020.

Šeputytė, M. (2014). Lithuania grabs LNG in effort to curb Russian dominance, *Bloomberg News*, 27 October 2014. https://web.archive.org/web/20141027171638/http://www.businessweek.com/news/2014-10-27/lithuania-grabs-lng-in-effort-to-curb-russian-dominance. Accessed 21 January 2021.

Statistical Yearbook of Lithuania. (2019). https://www.osp.stat.gov.lt/en/lietuvos-statistikos-metrastis/lsm-2019/aplinka-ir-energetika/energetika. Accessed 13 September 2021.

Streimikiene, D., Burneikis, J., & Punys, P. (2005). Review of renewable energy use in Lithuania. *Renewable and Sustainable Energy Reviews, 9*, 29–49.

Švedas, R., & Vilpišauskas, R. (2015). Kada reformos virsta pokyčiais? In V. Nakrošis, E. Barcevčius, & R. Vilpišauskas (Eds.), *Kodėl Visagino atominės elektrinės projektas patyrė politinę nesėkmę?* (pp. 326–390). Vilnius: VUL.

Thorhallsson, B., & Steinsson, S. (2017). *Small state foreign policy*. Oxford: Oxford University Press.

Vaičiūnas, Ž. (2009). Europos Sąjungos bendros energetikos politikos formavimas ir Lietuvos interesai. *Politologija, 3*(55), 89–120.

Varnagirytė-Kabašinskienė, I., Lukminė, D., Mizaras, S., Beniušienė, L., & Armolaitis, K. (2019). Lithuanian forest biomass resources: Legal, economic and ecological aspects of their use and potential. *Energy, Sustainability and Society, 9*(41), 1–19.

Energy Governance in the Netherlands

35

Elisabeth Musch

Contents

Introduction	864
General Conditions of Energy Governance in the Netherlands	865
Legacies	865
The Energy Mix	867
Narratives on Energy	869
Political Institutions and Actors	872
Coordination, Instruments, and Issues of Energy Transitions in the Netherlands	875
Drivers of Energy Transition	875
Strategies and Instruments	877
Coordination Mechanisms	882
Outcomes, Challenges, and Prospects of the Energy Transition	885
Annotation	887
Cross-References	887
References	888

Abstract

The Dutch energy transition governance is marked by distinct approaches of policy coordination, expert involvement and strategic planning, consensus building, and mutual self-commitments. These patterns of negotiation democracy with their roots in the period of pillarization (1890 until 1960s) have already been successfully applied by the Dutch government in the past. In the 1980s and 1990s, the government negotiated a consensus on socioeconomic policy reforms with the social partners, the so-called polder model. State actors also referred to this governance approach in the fields of immigrant integration and religious governance. In the field of energy, led by the Social and Economic Council (SER) in 2013, the Dutch government negotiated a comprehensive energy accord with

E. Musch (✉)
School of Cultural Studies and Social Sciences, University of Osnabrueck, Osnabrueck, Germany
e-mail: elisabeth.musch@uos.de

© Springer Nature Switzerland AG 2022
M. Knodt, J. Kemmerzell (eds.), *Handbook of Energy Governance in Europe*,
https://doi.org/10.1007/978-3-030-43250-8_20

employers' federations, trade unions, energy suppliers, environmental and conservationist organizations, and other interest groups. However, path dependence went along with institutional adaptations. These changes are manifest in the inclusion of lower administrations, new forms of citizen participation, and improved monitoring and evaluation systems.

Keywords

Energy governance · The Netherlands · Negotiation democracy · Neo-corporatism · Path dependence · Institutional change

Introduction

Gas, oil, coal, uranium, wind, water, biomass, and sunlight are the energy sources from which the Netherlands draws its energy (de Jong et al. 2005, 11). At present, fossil fuels (gas, oil, and coal) still make up a major part of the energy supply, while the share of renewable energies is relatively modest. The country's energy mix is mainly based on large gas reserves of the Groningen field that ensure gas supply security until 2030. Recently, however, in March 2018, the government announced that it will stop gas extraction from the Groningen field by 2030. The decision was made for safety reasons concerning the increase of earthquakes caused by gas extraction (Boffey 2018; Government of the Netherlands 2018a). The phasing out implies a significant turn in Dutch energy supply policy.

In 2013, energy transition policies were adopted by amicable agreement laid down in the *Energieakkoord voor duurzame groei* (Energy Agreement for Sustainable Growth). Renewable energy policies have been launched by the government since the early 1990s. But as discovered by van Rooijen and van Wees (2006, 60), the policies have not been stable, and policy objectives have often been partly ambiguous. Attempts to institutionalize negotiations on environmental matters at the national level in the 1990s failed. In its 2001 published Fourth National Environmental Policy Plan (NMP4), the government adopted a transition management approach aiming at system innovation in vital economic sectors like energy. The Ministry of Economic Affairs (Ministerie van Economische Zaken, EZ) implemented the approach in energy transition policies (Kern and Howlett 2009, 396). However, the implementation did not have the expected success, both on the policy level and on the organizational level. In 2013, by means of the Energy Agreement, the government reached a decision on energy targets up until 2020 and in some cases until 2023 and 2030. The *Energieakkoord* is based on negotiations between public and private stakeholders in the field of energy policy and beyond, namely, employers' and employees' associations and government appointees. The process dragged on through 2012 and 2013 under the leadership of the advisory body of the Social and Economic Council (Sociaal-Economische Raad, SER) to whom the government had delegated the task. On the basis of the overarching objectives on energy efficiency savings, an increase in renewable energies, and the creation of jobs, the participating actors of the agreement committed themselves to implement various measures. The third cabinet under Prime Minister Mark Rutte (People's Party for Freedom and Democracy VVD), established by the VVD, the Christian Democratic Alliance (CDA), Democrats 66 (D66), and the Christian Union (CU) and in office since October 2017, has strengthened the climate protection energy link in its policy program (Coalition Agreement 2017–2021). In February 2018 it initiated negotiations with representatives of lower administrations, industry, and interest groups on a *Klimaatakkoord* (Climate Change Agreement). The participants are supposed to agree on measures to achieve the government's goal to reduce CO_2 emissions by 49% in 2030 compared to 1990 levels (Government of the Netherlands 2017a, 2018b).

This chapter aims to give insight into the governance of the energy transition in the Netherlands. It will be shown that government actors referred to the traditional patterns of negotiation democracy in order to cope with the climate change and energy challenges. The advisory body of the Social and Economic Council (SER) was given a decisive role in this process. But path dependency went along with institutional adaptations. First, they related to organizational and operational efficiencies. Secondly, new forms of participatory governance have been introduced.

General Conditions of Energy Governance in the Netherlands

Legacies

As a low-lying country, the Netherlands has a long history of struggle against water through dike building and land reclamation through water drainage. Twenty-six percent of the country is under sea level, and 29% is susceptible to river flooding. Thus, 55% of the Netherlands is at risk of flooding (PBL 2018a). The country has a vast system of windmills, canals, ditches, dikes, dams, and dunes for the protection from flooding and land maintenance (Babe 2016). Windmills, once used to pump out surplus water, today no longer play a role in the system of water management. But the dikes and drainage systems must be maintained also in the future in order to protect the country from water incursion (Andeweg and Irwin 2014, 4–5; Netherlands Water Partnership (NWP) 2018). Due to the long-lasting experience, the country has developed strong and worldwide respected expertise in water management and water technologies (Ministry BZ 2018a, b; Netherlands Water Partnership (NWP) 2018). In the thirteenth century, waterboards (waterschappen), or cooperatives to manage water flows, were established, which represent first examples of democratic institutions (Rijkswaterstaat 2011; van Koningsveld et al. 2008, 367). Today, the *waterschappen* are responsible for the regional and local water systems. The *Rijkswaterstaat*, established in the eighteenth century, is the central organization of water management. It administers the national road network (3,260 km), the national waterways network (1,686 km), and the water system (65,250 km^2), including the Dutch part of the North Sea (Dutch Water Authorities 2018; Rijkswaterstaat 2011, 18).

The gas discoveries in Groningen in the Northern Netherlands in 1959 have had a crucial impact on the energy system structure. As a result, a shift from coal to gas took place starting at the beginning of the 1970s. Previously, coal as an energy source had lost shares to oil in the Dutch electricity market. In consequence of the structural change toward gas, the then Minister of Economic Affairs Joop den Uyl (Social Democrats PvdA) declared to gradually close down the coal-fired power stations (Correljé et al. 2003, 9; Kok 2004; Reiche 2002, p. 23 ff., p. 31 ff.; Verbong et al. 2001, 57). But when closing the coal mines, imported coal as an energy source became again relevant. This was due to the first oil crisis in 1973–1974. In addition, as social protests against nuclear energy increased, coal became more accepted as an alternative resource. Further supporting factors were technological innovations in coal combustion and comparatively favorable purchase options for coal (Reiche 2002, 33; Verbong et al. 2001, 64, 114, 361). Consequently, operation in new power plants was started again from the mid-1990s onward (Reiche 2002, 33; Verbong et al. 2001, 114). In 2004, the Ministers of Economic Affairs and Environment signed an agreement with the owners of the coal-fired power plants which aimed to increase the use of biomass (Roggenkamp 2016, 765).

Nuclear energy plays a small but steady part in the energy supply (OECD/IEA 2014, 119). In the early 1950s, the Netherlands had started cooperation on nuclear research with Norway. In 1955 the government installed the Reactor Centrum Nederland (RCN) for nuclear energy research in Petten. With the shift toward research on alternative forms of energy such as biomass, wind, solar, and geothermal energy as well as on energy saving, in 1976 the RCN was changed into the Energy Research Center of the Netherlands (ECN 2018a; Reiche 2002, 36). The only nuclear power plant in operation is located in Borssele, which started to operate in 1973 (OECD/IEA 2014, 119; Roos 2011). Previously in 1965, the government had built a first nuclear power plant in Doodewaard in order to gain experience in the construction and operation of nuclear installations (OECD/IEA 2014, 120; Roos 2011). This nuclear power plant was shut down in 1997, whereas the license for operation of the Borssele power plant has been steadily prolonged. In 2006, the government once again reached an agreement with the owner and operator EPZ (Elektriciteits-Produktiemaatschappij Zuid-Nederland, EPZ N.V.) and the two shareholders Delta and Essent to extend its operation time until 2033 (OECD/IEA 2014, 119; Roos 2011).

From 1996 onward, European legislation increasingly has influenced Dutch government policy. With the implementation of the electricity directive and natural gas directive, the country gradually but completely opened up its electricity market, and the energy companies were legally unbundled (Roggenkamp 2016, 764). Since 2004, the Dutch market for supply of gas and electricity has been fully liberalized (de Vlam and Oosterhuis 2015, 307).

Regarding the governance structure, the Ministry of Economic Affairs has had the overall responsibility for energy policy since the postwar period (Janssen et al. 2009, 150; OECD/IEA 2014, 22). It is the central government which provides guidance on energy-related decisions. The provinces and municipalities have been involved in the implementation of energy and climate policies (Government of the Netherlands

2018c, d). The regional water authorities, as explained above, manage the water systems and are responsible for the protection against flooding (Dutch Water Authorities 2018; Government of the Netherlands 2018e; Rijkswaterstaat 2011; regarding the public responsibilities, see section "Political Institutions and Actors").

The government controls the energy sector through legislation and/or direct ownership. Until the beginning of the liberalization process, local, regional, or central governments entirely or partly owned the electricity sector and the downstream gas sector. At present, the government still fully owns the electricity and gas transmission system operators (TSOs) TenneT and Gasunie Transport Services B.V. (GTS). The regional distribution system operators Cogas, Enduris, Enexis, Liander, Rendo Netwerken, Stedin, and Westland Infra are independent organizations in the hands of the provinces and municipalities (de Keijzer et al. 2016, 486; Janssen et al. 2009, 150; Roggenkamp 2016, 730–31, 766; van Heumen 2014, 10, 25–26). Looking at the governance mode, we see that the Dutch government refers to its repertoire of negotiation democracy in order to manage the energy transition. The policy patterns are rooted in the pillarization period (1890 until 1960) during which the social peace politics (pacificatie-politiek) were established. These politics resulted from the *pacificatie* of 1917, when the political elites of the protestant-calvinist pillar, the catholic pillar, and the secular pillar (the latter was further divided in a social democratic and a liberal pillar) reached consensus on universal suffrage, the proportional representation of the pillars, and equal treatment between private religious schools and public schools (Daalder 1996, 3; Lijphart 1968, p. 122 ff.; Musch 2011, 96–98). Later on, state actors repeatedly referred to these consociational and corporatist patterns in order to negotiate consensus on policy reforms. In the 1980s and 1990s, the government negotiated with the social partners a consensus on socioeconomic policy reforms, known as the polder model (see Visser and Hemerijck 1997). The neo-corporatist pattern could also be detected in the fields of immigrant integration and religious governance (see Musch 2011).

The Energy Mix

The Netherlands still relies largely on fossil fuels, which are gas, fuel oil, and coal. As of 2016, natural gas made up 1243.6 Petajoule (40%) of total energy consumption; in 2017 it was 1281.6 Petajoule. The share of crude and petroleum products in 2016 was 1225.8 Petajoule (40%) (2017: 1221.9 PJ), and the share of coal and coal products was 427.3 Petajoule (14%) (2017: 383 PJ) (see Fig. 1). Thus, gas still builds the major source of consumption in the domestic market. The country also remains Europe's second-largest gas producer and a major gas supplier to the Northwest European markets (OECD/IEA 2014, 129, 159). According to estimations, natural gas supply security can be ensured for approximately another 30 years (DNHK 2018, 12; OECD/IEA 2014, 20). On the ground of safety risks, the government decided in March 2018 to terminate gas extraction by 2030. Consequently, changes in the energy system are to be expected. The share of renewables has risen rather gradually. In 2016, biomass made up 119 Petajoule (3.8%) (2017: 123.1 PJ) of total

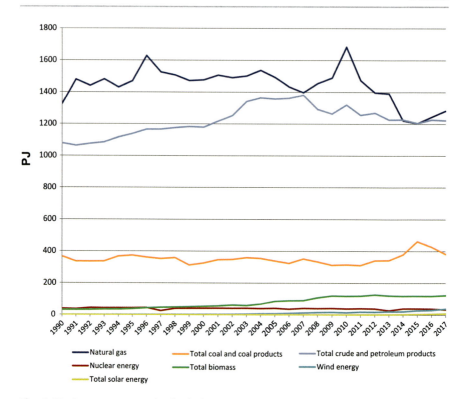

Fig. 1 Total energy consumption by fuel type 1990–2017. (Source: CBS StatLine 2018a. [Total energy consumption = total net energy transformation + total own use energy sector + distribution losses + total final consumption]. 2016: Revised provisional figures. 2017: Revised provisional figures)

energy consumption, wind energy was 29.4 Petajoule (1%) (2017: 38 PJ), and solar energy had a share of 6.8 Petajoule (0.2%) (2017: 8.9 PJ) (see Fig. 1).

Over the years, imports of energy commodities have been higher than exports. While the ratio declined from 2006 onward, it raised again in 2014. Since then, imports have increased more compared to exports of energy commodities (see Fig. 2).

The figures on the electricity production by energy source in Fig. 3 show again that fossil fuels still make up a large part in the energy mix. In 2016, natural gas generated 45.6% (2017: 49.2%) of the country's electricity and hard coal 31.9% (2017: 26.7%). The shares of biomass and wind energy are modest (2016: 4.3% and 7.1%; 2017: 4% and 9,1%) but have increased steadily since the year 2000 (see Fig. 3).

Due to the continuing large shares of fossil fuels in industry and power generation sectors, the energy sector is significantly responsible for the CO_2-intensive economy. Under the Kyoto Protocol, the Dutch government made the commitment to reduce greenhouse gas emissions by an average of 6% in the period 2008–2012

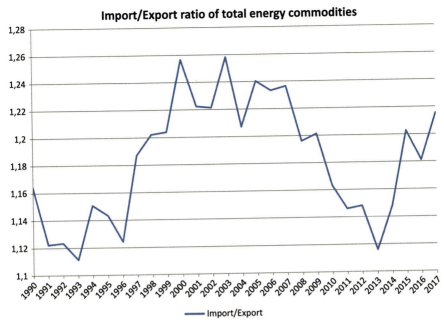

Fig. 2 Import/export ratio. (Source: CBS StatLine 2018a. 2016: Revised provisional figures. 2017: Revised provisional figures)

compared to 1990s base year emissions (PBL 2013). The country was successful in reducing the emissions in the years 2008–2012 by 6.4% (CBS et al. 2017; Nederland voldoet aan Kyoto-doelstellingen 2014). In the second Kyoto commitment period from 2013 to 2020, the EU countries (together with Iceland) agreed to reduce emissions by 20% compared to 1990. This is consistent with the EU's target to reduce GHG emissions by 20% in 2020 from 1990 levels (European Commission 2017a; Government of the Netherlands 2018e). The third Rutte cabinet pursues the ambitious goal of reducing greenhouse gas emissions by 49% in 2030, which goes beyond the EU's target of 40% as agreed upon in the Paris Agreement (Coalition Agreement 2017–2021, 11; Regeerakkoord 2017–2021, p. 37 ff.). Though, as we can see from the figures on CO2 emissions by sector for the period 1990–2017, CO2 emissions decrease on a rather slow pace in the different sectors – the household sector being the most advanced (see Fig. 4).

Narratives on Energy

Until the 1970s, energy policy was primarily part of industrial policy. The focus of concern was on the diversification and regulation of energy supply, rather than on security and reliability issues (de Jong et al. 2005, 69). The gas discoveries in Groningen led to the first significant transformation of the energy system. During

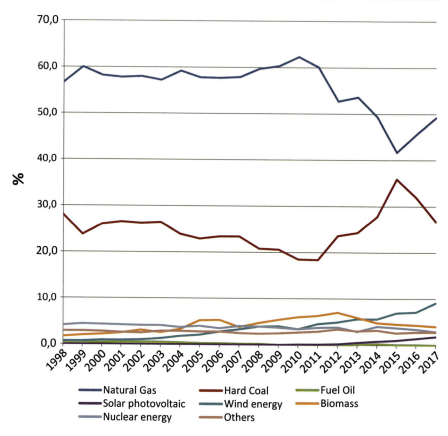

Fig. 3 Electricity production by source 1998–2017, in %. (Source: CBS StatLine 2018b. 2016: Adjusted provisional figures. 2017: Provisional figures)

the 1950s the Netherlands also began to explore the potential of nuclear energy as an energy source. Then, in the 1970s, the report of the Club of Rome of 1972 and the first oil crisis of 1973 triggered policy discussions and shifts in energy strategies (van der Loo and Loorbach 2012, 222). In its first Energy policy paper (Energienota) published in 1974, the Ministry of Economic Affairs intended to pursue a more strategic energy policy approach. The previous aims of an affordable and reliable energy supply were supplemented by the objective to diversify the energy sources (Verbong et al. 2001, 361). Internationally and with the IEA, an oil crisis management was established. On the national level, the Dutch government aimed to reduce dependencies by spreading risks. This policy strategy comprised of a reduction in oil imports, more coal use, an eventual use of nuclear energy, and more domestic production (such as gas) (de Jong et al. 2005, 220; OECD/IEA 2018). In the early 1980s, the Minister of Economic Affairs organized the so-called broad societal debate on energy policy. By means of this debate, the government intended to have broad discussions on energy issues, particularly regarding the use of nuclear

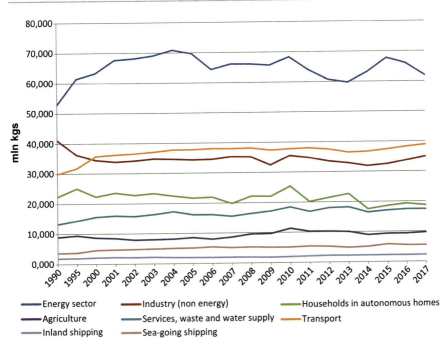

Fig. 4 CO2 emissions by sector 1990–2017. (Source: CBS StatLine 2018c. 2017: Provisional figures)

power (van der Loo and Loorbach 2012, 222; Verbong et al. 2001, 105). In consequence of the nuclear accidents at Three Mile Island in 1979 and the Chernobyl nuclear accident of 1986, social resistance to nuclear energy increased. The government subsequently withdrew its plans on nuclear energy (de Jong et al. 2005, 220; Roggenkamp 2016, 788; van der Loo and Loorbach 2012, 222). The same year, 1986, the first subsidy scheme for the implementation of wind energy was opened. In its third energy policy paper (1995), the Ministry of Economic Affairs generally aimed to promote renewable energies, energy savings, and to liberalize electricity markets (van der Loo and Loorbach 2012, 222; Verbong et al. 2001, 164, 190). From the 1990s onward, research on innovative and sustainable technological solutions was and has been increasingly funded. This science-policy interaction had an effect on policy-makers' views on innovation. It was no longer regarded as a purely technological process. The ecological and societal effects of growth and innovation were newly taken into consideration (van der Loo and Loorbach 2012, 222). Since the mid-1990s with the implementation of EU Directives, the liberalization of the energy markets preoccupied politics. The focus shifted to market mechanisms and their adequate regulation (de Jong et al. 2005, 13–14).

In its fourth National Environmental Policy Plan (NMP4) of 2001, the government presented a concept of transition management as a new strategy for system innovation. The concept derives from a research group led by Jan Rotmans, which introduced it in preparation for the NMP4 (Ministry VROM 2001; Rotmans 2011; van der Loo and Loorbach 2012, 223). The Ministry of Economic Affairs used the approach to undertake various activities furthering the energy transition (van der Loo and Loorbach 2012, 223). As the study of Kern and Howlett shows, however, the layering of transition management reforms made the already complex energy policy more complicated instead of bringing in more coherence and consistency (Kern and Howlett 2009, p. 403 ff.). Also Rotmans (2011, p. 1 ff.) determines deficiencies in the coordination between targets, transition paths, and experiments. He states that governmental actors put too much emphasis on technological innovations and neglected social and institutional aspects. With regard to the process level, he notices that the intention to strongly involve new niche players was not achieved, but the established stakeholders and traditional administrative patterns prevailed.

In 2011, the transition management approach was replaced by the energy top sector approach as part of the government's innovation policy strategy. By means of the top sector policy (topsectorenbeleid), the government promotes different economic sectors in order to increase their national and international competitiveness (DNHK 2016, 11). Besides energy, further dedicated sectors are agriculture and food, the chemical industry, the creative industry, high technologies, life science and healthcare, logistics, the horticulture sector, and raw materials as well as water management (DNHK 2016, 28; OECD/IEA 2014, p. 170 ff.). In the energy sector, the government aims to reach a competitive and low or zero carbon energy system (OECD/IEA 2014, 171–172). The second and the third Rutte cabinets have continued this policy strategy (Regeerakkoord 2012–2017 VVD – PvdA, Regeerakkoord 2017–2021 VVD, CDA, D66 en ChristenUnie). The *Energieakkoord* of 2013 has been based on the overall aims of sustainable energy supply and green growth (Tweede Kamer 2013). The underlying goal of the negotiations of the *Klimaatakkoord* is to reduce CO2 emissions by 49% in 2030 compared to 1990 levels.

Political Institutions and Actors

The Ministry of Economic Affairs and Climate Policy (Ministerie van Economische Zaken en Klimaat, EZK) holds the overall responsibility on energy policy. The third coalition government headed by Prime Minister Rutte put energy and climate change issues together under one department. Consequently, the Ministry EZK is responsible for climate change issues, sustainable economy and circular economy, renewable energy and energy efficiency, gas extraction in Groningen, air quality, and economic innovation (Ministry EZK 2018a). In the previous years, the then Ministry of Economic Affairs (Ministerie van Economische Zaken, EZ) was in charge of renewable energy, energy transition and bio-based economy, research, development and demonstration (RD&D), energy efficiency questions, and measures in agriculture (Ministry EZ 2016a; OECD/IEA 2014, 22). The responsible administrative unit within the ministry is the Directorate General for Energy, Telecommunications and Competition. The State Supervision of Mines (Staatstoezicht op de Mijnen, SodM) is a separate division of the Ministry charged with the supervision of the upstream petroleum industry (Roggenkamp 2016, 734). In February 2018, the SodM advised the government to reduce gas extraction from the Groningen gas field to 12 billion cubic meters per year. The Cabinet intends to go beyond this advice in order to reduce seismic risks as much as possible (Government of the Netherlands 2018a; Pieters 2018; van Santen and van der Walle 2018a).

Due to its responsibilities, the Ministry of Economic Affairs also has a leading role in the negotiations and implementation of the Energy Agreement and the Climate Change Agreement. While in the case of the Energy Agreement, the Ministry delegated the tasks to negotiate and later on to coordinate the implementation to the Social and Economic Council (SER), the Ministry conducts the negotiations of the Climate Agreement with the support of the SER.

In addition to the Economics Ministry, further ministries hold responsibilities on energy and climate change issues. The Ministry of Finance and the Ministry of Infrastructure and Water Management (Ministerie van Infrastructuur en Waterstaat, IenW, formerly the Ministry of Infrastructure and Environment (Ministerie van Infrastructuur en Milieu, I&M)) are particularly relevant (Roggenkamp 2016, 734). Apart from infrastructure and mobility, environmental questions, and water management, the Ministry IenW is involved in matters of sustainable economy and circular economy, renewable energies, air quality, and energy efficiency in transport (Ministry IenW 2018). The responsibility for energy efficiency in buildings, water management, and spatial planning is covered by the Ministry of the Interior and Kingdom Relations (Ministerie van Binnenlandse Zaken en Koninkrijksrelaties, BZK) (Ministry BZK 2018; OECD/IEA 2014, 22). The Ministry of Education, Culture and Science (Ministerie van Onderwijs, Cultuur en Wetenschap, OCW) is another relevant department for energy research and science issues (Ministry OCW 2018).

Several advisory boards give advice on energy and sustainability issues. One of them is the Mining Council (Mijnraad), first established in 1903. The present Mining Council, established by act in 2002, reports on matters concerning the exploration for and production of mineral resources (Roggenkamp 2016, 734). Following the oil crisis of 1973–1974, the General Energy Council (Algemene Energieraad, AER) was set up by law in 1976. Its tasks were to give advice to the government on energy issues, provide information for public discussions, and monitor the advisory process. The AER was abolished in 2014, and its tasks were delegated to the newly established Council of Environment and Infrastructure (Raad voor de leefomgeving en infrastructuur, Rli). Around this time another council was established, the Advisory Council on Research, Technology and Innovation (Adviesraad voor Wetenschap, technologie en innovatie, AWTI), which accordingly advises on research questions, technology, and innovation (AWTI 2018; Europa Nu 2016; FluxEnergie 2015a; Rli 2018; Verbong et al. 2001, 60; Wet RLI, Wet AWTI).

Over time, the Social and Economic Council (SER) has become an important actor in the field of energy and climate protection policies. The government established the SER in 1950 as the central advisory body on social and economic questions. The Social and Economic Council Act (until 2015 the Industrial

Organization Act) builds its legal basis. Its members are employers' and workers' representatives and independent experts – so-called Crown members (Kroonleden) (SER 2017a, b). Over the years, the Social and Economic Council has broadened the range of issues on which it gives advice. This included the integration of consumer associations as well as nature conservation and environmental associations in relevant SER committees (Peet 2010, 241–243; Schrijvers 2012, 162; SER 2016a). The SER published its first reports on environmental and sustainability policies in the 1970s. By the end of the 1980s, the government asked the council to give advice both on the Brundtland report and the first environmental policy plan (NMP). From the 1990s onward, it has increasingly advised the government on climate and energy policies. In 1999, when discussions on the establishment of a green polder model came up, the SER decided to include nature conservation and environmental organizations in its committees dealing with spatial and sustainable development (Touwen 2014, 187–188; van Zanden 2010, 182–183). At present the SER bases its mission on a broad understanding of welfare, which seeks to balance economic, ecological, and social dimensions. Since energy and climate policies affect all sectors, different levels and stakeholders, the council supports cooperative policy-making by government, the social partners, and further interest groups (SER 2017c, 8).

Another important expert institution is the Netherlands Environmental Assessment Agency (Planbureau voor de Leefomgeving, PBL). The PBL works out cost calculations and projections on energy and climate policy measures, CO2 emission developments, and energy efficiency measures. The PBL is organizationally assigned to the Ministry of Infrastructure and Water Management (IenW) (PBL 2018b). Together with the Energy Research Centre of the Netherlands (ECN), the PBL has been involved in the negotiations and implementation of the *Energieakkoord* in order to check the feasibility of the agreed targets. The PBL also participates in the negotiations on the *Klimaatakkoord*. The expert institution of ECN, which was accountable to the Ministry of Economic Affairs, was integrated into the TNO, the Netherlands Organization, for applied scientific research, in spring 2018 (ECN 2018a, b; de Thouars 2018). The task of TNO as an independent research organization regulated by public law is to make knowledge on applied sciences and technology together with social science knowledge available for general interests. On that basis it aims to interconnect actors and to further international cooperation (Art. 4 TNO-wet; TNO 2018).

The Netherlands Authority for Consumers and Markets (Autoriteit Consument & Markt, ACM) under the responsibility of the Ministry of Economic Affairs and Climate Policy (EZK) supervises the electricity, gas, and district heating markets (ACM 2018; OECD/IEA 2014, 22–23). In accordance with the 2013 enacted Establishment Act of the Netherlands Authority for Consumers and Markets, the ACM is responsible for overseeing competition, the sector-specific regulation of several sectors, and the enforcement of consumer protection laws (ACM 2018). Consequently, the ACM is charged with the regulation of the transmission system operators (TSOs) and distribution system operators (DSOs) of the electricity and natural gas networks (ACM 2017). The state-owned companies TenneT and Gasunie Transport Services (GTS) are the designated TSOs of the national high-voltage electricity grid and the gas transport system, respectively (Roggenkamp 2016, 766). Both TenneT and Gasunie also operate in Germany. The regional grid operators Cogas, Enduris, Enexis, Liander, Rendo Netwerken, Stedin, and Westland Infra (added by Zebra for gas) manage the lower-voltage networks (ACM 2017; de Keijzer et al. 2016, 470; Gasunie 2018; Roggenkamp 2016, 766, 767). The Netherlands Enterprise Agency (RVO) and the Authority for Nuclear Safety and Radiation Protection (Autoriteit Nucleaire Veiligheid en Stralingsbescherming, ANVS) are further relevant agencies. The RVO implements the energy efficiency programs and gives advice on energy efficiency solutions (OECD/IEA 2014, 23, 53–54). The ANVS ensures that the highest standards of nuclear safety and radiation protection are met in the Netherlands (ANVS 2018). The agency organizationally belongs to the Ministry of Infrastructure and Environment, but it is independent in its task performance (ANVS 2018; OECD/IEA 2014, 23).

The central government also involved the provinces and municipalities in the negotiations of the Energy agreement via their umbrella organizations, the Association of the Provinces of the Netherlands (IPO) (Interprovinciaal Overleg) and the Association of Netherlands Municipalities (VNG) (Vereniging van Nederlandse Gemeenten). According to their statutory role in the fields of spatial planning, regional economy, licensing procedures, and mobility, the provinces undertake various implementation tasks (Government of the Netherlands 2018c, d; IPO 2015, 4, 2018). Likewise, local authorities are included in the implementation. Besides the provinces and the municipalities, the regional government bodies of the Dutch Water Authorities (waterschappen) have been involved. They are united in the Association of Dutch Water Authorities (Unie van Waterschappen) and are charged with managing water barriers, waterways, and water quality in their respective regions (see above section "Legacies"; Government of the Netherlands 2018e; Roggenkamp 2016, 729; Sloover and Klootwijk 2014; Smit 2004).

The implementation of the targets of the Energy Agreement is surveilled by a monitoring commission, the Monitoring Commission Energy Agreement (Borgingscommissie Energieakkoord, BEA). It consists of representatives of all 47 signatories of the Energy Agreement, which are representatives of the government, trade unions and employers' associations, energy companies, natural conservation and environmental organizations, and further interest groups. The commission is headed by an independent chairman. The expert institution PBL is again involved to assess consequential costs (SER 2016b).

Coordination, Instruments, and Issues of Energy Transitions in the Netherlands

Drivers of Energy Transition

Since the postwar period, the Ministry of Economic Affairs has always been charged with energy supply policy. Consequently, it is also the central driving force behind the energy transition management. The first energy policy program (Energienota) was published in 1974 as a consequence of the first oil shock in 1973–1974 (de Jong et al. 2005, 12, 46–51; Verbong et al. 2001, 59). In this policy outline, an integrated approach was promoted, and emphasis was laid on energy saving and diversification of energy sources (Verbong et al. 2001, 59). In the period 1974–1986, energy policy focused primarily on supply security (de Jong et al. 2005). In consequence of the Chernobyl nuclear accident of 1986, this changed to clean energy. In the first years, clean energy was considered from a supply perspective. Later on, environmental protection issues became more relevant. From the beginning of the 1990s onward, the focus was laid on the affordability of energy. Since 1995, influenced by European policies, the Ministry emphasized market mechanisms (de Jong et al. 2005, 13–14, p. 161 ff.). Since the 1990s the EU and the UN increasingly have acted as drivers of Dutch energy transition and climate policies. The Netherlands advocates the EU and international commitments on greenhouse gas reductions, the expansion of renewable energies, and the development of an internal EU energy market. This is shown by the government's engagement in fulfilling the country's obligations within these frameworks (Government of the Netherlands 2018f). In historical retrospect, the implementation of the first EU electricity and gas directives (1996, 1998) led to the liberalization of the country's gas and electricity markets and the unbundling of energy companies (Roggenkamp 2016, p. 756 ff., p. 762 ff.). The Electricity Act (1998) and the Gas Act (2000) have been amended several times, inter alia, to implement the Electricity and Gas Directives of 2003 and 2009 (Roggenkamp 2016, 756, 764). With regard to the reduction of greenhouse gas emissions, the Netherlands achieved to reduce emissions by 6.4% during the first commitment period of the Kyoto Protocol (2008–2012) (CBS et al. 2017). In the second period (2013–2020), the parties committed themselves to reduce emissions by 20% below 1990 levels. This corresponds with the 20-20-20 targets set by EU leaders in 2007 that besides a 20% reduction of CO_2 emissions includes 20% increase in energy efficiency and 20% renewable energies by 2020 (European Commission 2017a, 2018a; Government of the Netherlands 2018f). Since a need for improvement of the existing EU emissions trading system (EU ETS) is identified, the participants of the *Energieakkoord* promote to introduce appropriate measures (SER 2013a, p. 20 ff.). The participants of the *Klimaatakkoord* negotiations have worked out measures to realize the government's goal to reduce emissions by 49% in 2030. This national reduction goal exceeds the EU's intended nationally determined contribution to the Paris Agreement to achieve an at least 40% domestic reduction in greenhouse gas emissions compared to 1990 levels by 2030 (see European Commission 2018b). EU law also influences the production of renewable energies. While the RES Directive of 2001 required the Netherlands to reach a share of at least 9% renewables in the electricity consumption in 2010, the RES Directive of 2009 has increased the target to 14% in 2020. The Dutch government has voluntarily set a goal to increase the share of renewables to 16% in 2023 (Roggenkamp 2016, 788–789). The participants of the *Energieakkoord* agreed on a range of measures to increase the development of renewable energy sources (Roggenkamp 2016, 789; SER 2013a, b).

Back from European and international levels to the national level, over time the Social and Economic Council (SER) has become a driver in energy transition and climate change policies. By the end of the 1990s, the SER firstly strengthened its role in the field of energy by involving environmental organizations in its committee on spatial development and accessibility (Commissie Ruimtelijke Inrichting en Bereikbaarheid, RIB, closed in 1999) and the committee on sustainable development (Commissie Duurzame Ontwikkeling, DUO). Since the 1970s, the SER regularly has published reports on energy and climate issues. During the negotiations of the Energy Agreement, the SER's position strengthened further as it acted as a facilitator to create social consensus on energy transition policies. On the basis of the council's 2012 advice, the Ministry of Economic Affairs charged it with the task of conducting negotiations with various stakeholders. In the negotiations on a Climate Change Agreement launched in spring 2018, the Ministry, however, leads the negotiations together with the SER. The expert institution of the Environmental Assessment Agency (PBL) can be seen as another relevant actor since it provides specialized information on energy and climate issues and regularly assesses the effects and costs of the energy transition.

Strategies and Instruments

Strategies and Goals

The energy sector has been involved in the innovation policy approach, the so-called top sector policy introduced by the government in 2011 (see section "Narratives on Energy"). The policy runs for three periods, from 2011–2012 and 2013–2016 to 2017–2025. In the field of energy, seven priority areas are chosen, among them natural and bio-based gas, offshore wind, solar photovoltaics, energy savings in industry, energy use in buildings, smart grids, and bio-based resources (OECD/IEA 2014, p. 171 ff.). The *Energieakkoord*, which sets targets until 2020 (2023 and 2030), integrates the top sector policy aims in its framework. In order to fulfill the country's obligations arising out of the EU's 20-20-20 goals, the signatories agreed on the following objectives:

- Savings in the final energy consumption of 1.5% annually, which is 100 Petajoule (PJ) saving of the country's final energy consumption by 2020,
- An increase in the share of renewable energies of total final consumption (TFC) from 4.4% in 2013 to 14% in 2020 and a further increase to 16% in 2023,
- At least 15,000 full-time jobs related to the energy transition (OECD/IEA 2014, 25; SER 2013a, 3).

On that ground, supply reliability and security shall be guaranteed. Further aims are the investment in sustainable economic growth and the strengthening of the Dutch market position in international energy markets. Special attention is given to the level of energy costs, which shall be significantly reduced for consumers and energy companies (SER 2013a, 3, b, 31, 68, 71). In order to reach these goals, the signatories agreed to measures on energy savings and energy efficiency in the built environment and industry, agriculture, and the rest of the commercial sector. They also agreed to scaling up renewable energy generation, decentralized energy generation, the preparation of the energy transmission network, minimizing energy generation from fossil fuels and the closing down of old coal-fired power stations, mobility and transport measures, the production of employment opportunities, energy innovation and energy export, as well as funding programs for investments in energy saving and renewable energy. In terms of Europe, they promote a properly functioning EU emissions trading system (SER 2013a).

In its Energy Report (Energierapport), published in 2016, the Ministry of Economic Affairs focuses on the time frame beyond 2023. In order to achieve a CO2 neutral energy supply system by 2050, the government wants to focus on three main principles: CO2 reduction, using the economic potentials, and integrating energy matters in spatial planning policy (Ministry EZ 2017a, 3). The *Energieakkoord* (2013), together with the Cabinet's Energy Agenda (2016) consisting of the Energy Report, the results of the Energy Dialogue (Energiedialoog), and the Energy Agenda, formed the government's energy transition agenda (SER 2017d, 4). The third Rutte cabinet strongly links climate issues with energy policies. In its Coalition Agreement of October 2017, the government announces to conclude an agreement on climate and energy policies that would provide more security for long-term goals. It is based on the overall objective to reduce emissions by 49% by 2030. This goal goes beyond the EU's intended contribution to the UN Paris Agreement of March 2015, which is a national contribution of at least 40% domestic reduction in greenhouse gas emissions by 2030 compared to 1990 levels (European Commission 2017b, c; Interview NL1). In the case of the top sector policy approach, the future focus will be placed on economic opportunities in the domains of energy transition and sustainability, agriculture, and water as well as on food and quantum, high-tech, nano, and photonics. The government also aims to adopt a climate law, which should include the priorities of energy and climate change policies (Coalition Agreement 2017–2021, 11; Regeerakkoord 2017–2021, 33, p. 37 ff.).

Policy Instruments

The Electricity Act of 1998 (Elektriciteitswet, E-Act), which implemented the first EU Electricity Directive (96/92/EC), regulates the production, transportation, and supply of electricity. The production, transportation, and supply of natural gas are regulated by the 2000 enacted Gas Act, which implemented the European Gas Directive (98/30/EC). Both the Electricity Act and the Gas Act have been amended numerous times (Janssen et al. 2009, 147; Roggenkamp 2016, 764, 756–757; Wildeboer and van der Weijden 2015). A 2015 introduced proposal for fundamental revisions of the two acts, the STROOM bill, was rejected by the Senate of Parliament (de Keijzer et al. 2016, 469). On 1 January 2014, the Heat Act (Warmtewet) entered into force, which regulates heat distribution to small-scale consumers (de Vlam and Oosterhuis 2015, 307). The Environmental Management Act (Wet Milieubeheer), revised in 2017, contains environmental protection regulations. These encompass environmental plans and programs, environmental quality standards, compensation, and handling as well as financial instruments such as taxes, premiums, and compensations (Rijkswaterstaat 2018).

On the basis of the Environmental Taxes Act of 1994, several taxes are imposed on consumers, producers, and/or suppliers based on the "polluter pays" principle (Roggenkamp 2016, 766). The Dutch government imposes a coal tax for the use of coal and coal imports (Government of the Netherlands 2018g). In January 2016, an exemption for electricity production from coal tax was reintroduced. An energy tax is imposed on the combustion of natural gas and the consumption of electricity and mineral oils (other than motor fuel). There are tax exemptions for energy products and fuels used to generate electricity (Government of the Netherlands 2018g; OECD/IEA 2014, 27, 166–167; PBL 2014, 19, 24).

The SDE+ scheme (Stimulering Duurzame Energieproductie) is the central instrument for stimulating the production and consumption of renewable energies. The SDE+ was introduced in 2011 on a proposal of the Ministry of Economic Affairs and replaced the previous SDE scheme which had fixed tariffs per technology (Der Energieblog 2015). The SDE+ is financed by households as a surcharge on the energy tax (OECD/IEA 2014, 28). The government allocates the budget of the SDE+ subsidies on a yearly basis and connects it to the market-relevant energy prices (DNHK 2016, 33; IEA 2016; IHK Munich and Upper Bavaria 2016, 23, 29–30). Thus, the subsidy is comprised of the gap between the market price of the energy produced and the cost price of the technology. If the market price increases, the subsidy declines and vice versa (Frontier Economics 2015). In 2016, the budget made available was 9 Bn. Euros. For the year 2017, 6 Bn. Euros were provided on a half-yearly basis, totaling 12 Bn. Euros (Ministry EZ 2016b, 2). Also for 2018 the government has provided a budget of 6 Bn. Euros on a half-yearly basis (12 Bn. Euros in total) (RVO 2018a, b). The yearly budget is split in allocation rounds. All eligible technologies compete for the same budget, which is distributed on a "first-come, first served" basis prioritizing low-cost technologies through a phase-in process (IEA 2016).

Several other schemes supporting the sustainable use of resources add up to the SDE+ scheme (IHK Munich and Upper Bavaria 2016, 23, 29–30; OECD/IEA 2014, 27). For instance, steering instruments support companies and small-scale users in investments in energy efficiency and renewable technologies (European Commission 2012). First, tax deductions for the use of energy efficient resources are possible (Energie Investeringsaftrek, EIA). Second, companies that invest more than 2500 Euros in environmentally friendly utilities can profit from a reduction of VAT (Milieu Investeringsaftrek, MIA). And third, companies can be granted liquidity and interest advantages. Then, house and flat owners can apply for green loans (groene beleggingen) to finance energy efficient measures (DNHK 2016; IHK Munich and Upper Bavaria 2016, 30). Further instruments promoting energy-saving measures for homeowners are the 2013 introduced *Nationaal Energiebespaarfonds* (NEF) and the *Subsidie Energiebesparing Eigen Huis* (SEEH) introduced in 2016 (SER-BEA 2017, 10). With the ISDE premium feed-in scheme (Investeringssubsidie Duurzame Energie (ISDE), sustainable energy investment subsidy scheme) and net metering, small installations for the use of renewable energies are supported (European Commission 2012; IHK Munich and Upper Bavaria 2016, 30; Wilming 2014). In 2011, the government initiated Green Deals as a policy instrument for energy efficiency. By means of the Green Deals, governmental actors support energy efficiency initiatives by removing administrative barriers. The deals involve businesses, provinces, municipalities, and nongovernmental organizations (OECD/IEA 2014, 60; Tweede Kamer 2015).

Measures of the *Energieakkoord* 2013–2020 (2023, 2030)

The *Energieakkoord* comprises ten thematic components, which again contain various measures the signatories agreed upon (SER 2013a, p. 4 ff., b, p. 12 ff.). The measures build upon the energy legislation, previous policy instruments, and financial instruments. The signatories strive for an improved implementation of the *Wet milieubeheer*, and they consider the SDE+ scheme to be the central instrument to further the transformation of the energy system. The participants had been supportive of the revision proposals of the STROOM bill, which later on was rejected by the Senate of Parliament (SER 2013b, 19). The formerly agreed upon multi-annual covenants (meerjarenafspraken, MJA) on *energy efficiency* measures (first component) are integrated in the Energy Agreement. This also applies for other covenants. In previous years the government concluded the MJA/MEE-covenants with industrial companies. The covenants include self-commitments of companies to undertake energy efficiency measures. In return they are compensated by tax incentives or by means of the EU ETS. The government has covenants with companies that are subject to the EU ETS (meerjarenafspraak energie-efficiëntie 2008–2020 MJA3) and with those that do not fall under the EU ETS (meerjarenafspraak energie-efficiëntie MEE) (OECD/IEA 2014, 56; SER 2013b, 56). In 2018, 1062 companies from 37 sectors including the service sector, the industrial sector, the food manufacturing industry, and the transport sector participate in these schemes (RVO 2018c). In the framework of the *Energieakkoord*, governmental actors and energy-intensive companies intended to conclude additional contracts in order to increase energy efficiency and the economic competitiveness. In general, measures on energy savings concern the built environment and the industry and agriculture sectors as well as further enterprises. Additional government funds are made available (SER 2013b, 12–16). With respect to the second component, the *expansion of renewables*, participants agreed on support measures for onshore and offshore wind energy, diverse forms of local renewable energy production, and biomass. Decentralized generation of renewable energies (third component) by people themselves and by cooperative initiatives is supported by a tax relief introduced in 2014 (SER 2013a, 8, b, 19). The participants further agreed on measures to prepare the energy transport network for a sustainable future (fourth component, SER 2013a, 8). In the case of the fifth component, the participants commit themselves to contribute to improvements of the ETS system (SER 2013a, 9). Regarding the *coal-fired power plants* (sixth component) in the country, they agreed to phase out the capacity of the five oldest ones in order to improve the carbon balance (OECD/IEA 2014, 166). Environmental organizations have had particular interest in the decision. In exchange for the phaseout, the government granted the affected energy companies a tax discount for the remaining power plants. The resulting tax loss should be compensated by an increase of the energy tax payed by industrial companies and households at 50% each (OECD/IEA 2014, 166–167; SER 2013b, 21; Zuidervaart and Redactie Politiek

2014). However, the Dutch Authority for Consumers and Markets (ACM) considered the deal to be a restriction of competition (FluxEnergie 2015b; OECD/IEA 2014, 167). After renegotiations, the then Minister of Economic Affairs Henk Kamp agreed with the energy companies and environmental organizations on a legal solution, which enabled to shut down three of the five coal-fired power plants in 2016 and the two others in 2017 (FluxEnergie 2015b; OECD/IEA 2014, p. 167; Zuidervaart/Redactie Politiek 2014). The tax exemption should become effective by 1 January 2016 (SER 2013b, 21). The third Rutte cabinet plans to close all remaining coal-fired plants in 2030. The subsidization of biomass as a supplementary fuel shall be stopped in 2024 (Regeerakkoord 2017–2021, 38). In May 2018 the cabinet decided that the two older power plants should stop power generation from coal by 2024 and the three newer ones by 2029 (Government of the Netherlands 2018i). The use of CCS technology is generally supported.

The seventh component consists of *mobility and transport measures*. In order to make traffic and transport more efficient and mobility more sustainable, the participants agreed on a 60% reduction in CO2 emissions by 2050 compared to 1990 (SER 2013a, 10, b, 22). In terms of the objective to produce job opportunities in the installation and construction sectors as well as in the renewable energy sector (eighth component), measures are undertaken to create an average of at least 15,000 additional full-time jobs (SER 2013a, 11, b, 22–23). Ninth, the parties aim to invest in *energy innovation and export*. In order to achieve these goals, they focus on financing, domestic market development, international market development, the establishment of legislation and regulations, connecting up with the SME sector, and human capital (SER 2013a, 11, b, 23–24). Finally, the tenth component consists of a funding program to encourage investments in energy savings and projects on renewable energies (SER 2013a, 12, b, 24–25). The implementation of the agreed measures is regularly monitored by the Monitoring Commission Energy Agreement (BEA).

Soft governance instruments can be found in elements of participatory governance. Governmental actors and the SER organized meetings on energy-related issues for citizens, meetings with experts, and online consultations during the negotiations on the Energy Agreement. Then, throughout the implementation process, during spring and summer 2016, the Ministry of Economic Affairs organized an Energy Dialogue (Energiedialoog) about the future energy supply in the country (Government of the Netherlands 2016; Ministry EZ 2016c, d; see section "Narratives on Energy").

Energy Storage

There is no specific legislation for energy storage. The envisaged STROOM bill, which was rejected, would have provided more possibilities for research and development on energy storage (van der Weijden 2016). In 2015, the international certification body and consultancy DNV GL, the Technical University of Delft, and the consultancy firm Berenschot released the Energy Storage Roadmap (Routekaart energieopslag 2030), which they developed on behalf of the Ministry of Economic Affairs. The Roadmap contains an action plan for energy storage with a focus on electricity. Recent developments and solutions in the field of energy storage are in line with this Roadmap (DNV GL et al. 2015; Energy Storage NL 2015; van der Weijden 2016). In its Energy Agenda of 2016, the government states that electricity storage systems are seen as one important source of flexibility in the trading and supply of energy, for maintaining balance and for efficient grid use. Accordingly, it strives for investments in research, innovation, and the application of technologies (Ministry EZ 2017b, 46). The government thinks about introducing an incentive scheme for electricity storage comparable to the one applied for natural gas. Natural gas (input) consumed by gas-fired power stations and CHP (cogeneration of power and heat) installations are subject to tax exemption. This exemption prevents double taxation because the electricity generated (the output) is already taxed (Ministry EZ 2017b, 46–47). The present government declares to continue and expand the SDE+ scheme and the associated storage of sustainable energy (Coalition Agreement 2017–2021, 39). In the future, the state-owned TSO TenneT responsible for balancing supply and demand for electricity increasingly will have to consider issues of energy storage (van der Weijden 2016) (Table 1).

Coordination Mechanisms

Against the background of the polder model, which was the successfully negotiated consensus between government actors and the social partners on social and economic reforms in the 1980s and 1990s, attempts were made to establish similar polder model processes on environmental issues. However, in the field of sustainability, the government opted for negotiations on an ad hoc basis. In the 1990s, the government tested green polder negotiations in projects on the expansion of Schiphol Airport and the port expansion in Rotterdam as well as in the spatial planning sector. But only in the Rotterdam case the participants reached a satisfying consensus. And yet, in all three cases, the participants judged the negotiations positively (Touwen 2014, 187–188; van Zanden 2010, 181–186; Weggeman 2003, 223, 185, 297–298). Besides these project and sector-based polder debates, the Social and Economic Council (SER) integrated environmental and nature conservation associations in the work of its committees (Touwen 2014, 187–188; van Zanden 2010, 181–186; Weggeman 2003, 223, 185, 297–298).

In 2012, the Ministry of Economic Affairs made another effort to establish an overall polder model process by initiating negotiations on the *Energieakkoord* (Musch 2018). The negotiations were preceded by an advice of the SER on behalf of the Ministry of Economic Affairs (SER 2012). In consequence of this advice, representatives of the central government and subnational authorities negotiated the Energy Agreement with trade unions, employers' associations, energy companies, nature conservation, and environmental organizations and other civil society organizations under the leadership of the SER. Energy savings, the increase of renewable energies, and the costs of the energy transition were central questions that had to be balanced out during the negotiations. In 2013, 47 actors signed the agreement on a comprehensive package of measures. The signatories committed themselves to

Table 1 Energy transition policy instruments by sector and type

Type of policy instrument/ energy sector	Regulatory	Incentive-based instruments	Internalizing instruments	Soft governance
Electricity supply	Electricity Act (1998)	SDE+ subsidy scheme	EU ETS (2005)	Information meetings and online consultation
	Gas Act (2000)			Energy Dialogue (April–July 2016)
	Environmental Taxes Act (1994)			
Heat supply	Heat Act (2014)	SDE+ subsidy scheme		Information meetings and online consultation
				Energy Dialogue (April–July 2016)
Built environment energy efficiency	Environmental Management Act ([2014] 2017)	Covenants energy saving/efficiency (Convenant Energiebesparing Gebouwde Omgeving)		Information meetings and online consultation
	Covenants energy saving/efficiency (Convenant Energiebesparing Huursector)			Energy Dialogue (April–July 2016)
Industrial and commercial energy efficiency	Environmental Management Act ([2014] 2017)	Green Deals	Agreement between Dutch government and owners of coal-fired power plants on an increase in the use of biomass with the objective to reduce CO2 emissions (2004)	Information meetings and online consultation
	Covenants energy saving/efficiency (MJA, MEE)	Energie Investeringsaftrek, EIA		Energy Dialogue (April–July 2016)
		Milieu Investeringsaftrek, MIA		
		ISDE premium feed-in scheme		
		Net metering		
		Covenants energy saving/efficiency (MJA, MEE)		
Household energy efficiency	Covenants energy saving/efficiency	Subsidie energiebesparing eigen huis (SEEH)		Information meetings and online consultation

(continued)

Table 1 (continued)

Type of policy instrument/ energy sector	Regulatory	Incentive-based instruments	Internalizing instruments	Soft governance
	Convenant Energiebesparing Huursector	National Energy Savings Fonds (Nationaal Energiebespaarfonds)		Energy Dialogue (April–July 2016)
		Green loans (groenfonds, Groene beleggingen)		
		Green Deals		
		ISDE premium feed-in scheme		
		Covenants energy saving/efficiency (Convenant Energiebesparing Huursector)		
Transport	Environmental Management Act ([2014] 2017)	Covenants energy saving/efficiency (MJA, MEE)		Information meetings and online consultation
	Covenants energy saving/efficiency (MJA, MEE)			Energy Dialogue (April–July 2016)

See Chaps. II.1, III. 2., and III. 3., SER (2013b, 13, 38, 42, 46–48, p. 50 ff.); Stimuleringsfonds Volkshuisvesting Nederlandse gemeenten (SVn) (2018); and SER-BEA (2017)

implement the measures agreed upon. The monitoring commission BEA set up in the SER has regularly reported about the status of implementation and has developed future implementation agendas (SER 2016b). In addition to the regular meetings of the commission members, a small group consisting of SER senior officers, governmental actors, trade unions, and employers' associations as well as environmental organizations regularly meets informally (so-called high-level negotiations, KWINK Groep 2016, 18).

Parallel to the implementation process of the Energy Agreement, from April to July 2016, the Ministry of Economic Affairs organized the Energy Dialogue. During this period, governmental actors discussed the future of energy supply in the Netherlands with companies, researchers, citizens, and others in discussion groups and online forums. The government took the results of the dialogue into account when it worked out its future Energy Agenda. The agenda was published in December 2016 and contains long-term targets for reaching a low CO_2-emitting energy system (Government of the Netherlands 2016; Ministry EZ 2016d, e). In March 2017, the SER published an advisory note in which it sets out its visions on the governance of energy and climate change policies (SER 2017c, p. 7 ff.). The SER recommends extending the Energy Agreement which ends in 2020 (in some cases in 2023 and 2030). To improve the governance process, the authors consider it necessary to differentiate between transition paths in buildings, the industry, the mobility and transport sector, agro-food products, and the energy system (SER 2017c, 13). While the third Rutte cabinet has continued the implementation of the *Energieakkoord*, in spring 2018 the government and the SER started negotiations with companies, societal groups, and the provinces and municipalities on climate policy measures. This shows that the government strengthens the climate protection energy link of its program. In July 2018 the Climate Board (Klimaatberaad), the monitoring commission of the negotiations, published a first outline over the priority actions reached in the *Klimaatakkoord* negotiations (SER 2018). PBL and the Netherlands Bureau for Economic Policy Analysis (CPB) (Centraal Planbureau) generally approved the proposals, but asked for more specification (PBL 2018c, d; CPB 2018). In December 2018 the Climate Board presented its draft report on the planned actions. Though, environmental organizations and the FNV trade union refused to accept it at the current stage. PBL and CPB again have the task of assessing the proposed measures (Government of the Netherlands 2018h; van Santen and van der Walle 2018b). Both, in the *Energieakkoord* and the *Klimaatakkoord*, the central governments have involved representatives of the lower administrations. According to the assigned responsibilities, the provinces and municipalities assume implementation tasks, and the waterboards are charged with water management. But, in general, despite decentralization since the early 1980s, the Netherlands is still a highly centralized country (see Andeweg and Irwin 2014, p. 212 ff.). Over time the EU level has gained in importance. Since the end of the 1990s, EU politics of energy and climate change increasingly have had an impact on Dutch policy-making (see section "Drivers of Energy Transition").

Outcomes, Challenges, and Prospects of the Energy Transition

The Netherlands still largely relies on fossil fuels in its energy mix, while the share of renewable energies is comparatively small. Biomass and wind energy build the predominant renewable sources. With 21,500 jobs in 2016, the Netherlands ranks among the leading European countries in respect to wind power employment. The country is also very strong in offshore wind energy, following the United Kingdom, Germany, and Denmark (IRENA 2018, 19). The building of onshore wind energy plants however triggered discussions and opposition. Those affected protested against visual intrusion, noise, and the loss of value of their houses (de Groene Rekenkamer 2014; Rengers 2014).

The signatories of the *Energieakkoord* decided to expand renewable energies at a rather moderate pace. At the same time, the participating actors aim to invest in innovative technologies. In turn, this will allow for savings in the subsidy regime SDE+. By means of these savings together with an increase in the energy taxation and the abolition of the coal tax, the total financial burden shall be reduced.

Consequently, energy costs are expected to decrease for private households and businesses.

The modest increase of renewables can be associated with the country's gas reserves. The Netherlands can assure gas supply for the estimated national demand for approximately another 30 years. However, in March 2018, the government declared that it will terminate gas extraction from the gas field in Groningen by 2030, which will have consequences for the Dutch energy system structures. The main consideration for the decision is that of safety. As the Cabinet states, "safety perception as well as actual safety can only be guaranteed for the near future in Groningen by fully eliminating the source of the earthquake risk" (Boffey 2018; Government of the Netherlands 2018a). Since mid-2012, social and political concerns about the growing number and severity of earthquakes induced from the gas extraction have increased (Vlek 2018, 5). In order to achieve the "phasing out" of Groningen gas (Boffey 2018), the government envisages various measures. The government intends to increase gas imports, including those from Norway and Russia. It also intends to increase its gas supply from the smaller gas fields in the North Sea (van Santen 2018). This requires more nitrogen production capacity in the country. Therefore, a new nitrogen plant will be built in Zuiderbroek, which will convert high-calorific gas to low-calorific gas. The costs are estimated at 500 million Euros, which the consumers will have to bear. Furthermore, all large industrial users of Groningen gas must switch to using high-calorific gas or renewable sources by 2022. In addition, the government will decrease export of low-calorific gas to Germany, France, and Belgium in the coming years (Ministry EZK 2018b; Pieters 2018). Precise measures should be specified during the ongoing negotiations of the Climate Change Agreement (Ministry EZK 2018b).

The management of the energy transition by the government reveals the pattern of negotiation democracy in many respects. The action repertoire is marked by delegation, administrative interest intermediation, and mutual self-commitment (see Czada 1991; Lehmbruch 1987; Czada and Musch 2017). On the base of the SER's advice, the Ministry of Economic Affairs invited various stakeholders to negotiate on energy politics and delegated the task of conducting the negotiations to the SER. By signing the agreement, the participating actors committed themselves to a package of measures to be implemented. The Ministry of Economic Affairs and the SER have acted as advocates of the energy transition. Conflicts of interest were solved by means of these consensus-building strategies (Interview NL1). The "coal deal," which entails the closure of coal-fired power stations and compensations for the operating companies, is one example.

When it became apparent during the implementation process that there will be difficulties in achieving the energy goals regarding renewables, energy savings, and the reduction of GHG emissions, the Ministry of Economic Affairs announced to take compulsory measures in case that the energy companies fail to undertake voluntary action (ECN 2016; Ministry EZ 2016c; Postma 2016). In the shadow of hierarchy, the relevant energy-intensive companies committed themselves to additional saving measures in order to fulfill their savings obligations of the *Energieakkoord* (Government of the Netherlands 2017b, Ministry EZ 2017c).

With regard to the reduction of GHG emissions, they could be successfully reduced from 2008 onward, but in 2015 emissions increased again (CBS et al. 2017). According to the National Energy Outlook 2017 (Nationale Energieverkenning 2017, ECN 2017), it is estimated that in the period from 1990 to 2020, GHG emissions will be reduced by 23%. This figure is not sufficient to comply with the legal obligation of a 25% reduction in 2020, which resulted from the Urgenda Climate Case. In 2015, the District Court of The Hague ruled that the government is obliged to reduce its emissions by 25% in 2020 compared to 1990 levels (Government of the Netherlands 2015; Neslen 2015; Saurer and Purnhagen 2016). The case was brought by an environmental group, the Urgenda Foundation. The Dutch government appealed against the judgment. However, in its judgment of 9 October 2018, the court of appeal in The Hague upheld the ruling of 2015. The court declares that climate change poses a concrete threat against which the Dutch state must protect its citizens. Consequently, the Dutch government has to make sure for reducing CO2 emissions by 25% in 2020 (Gericht zwingt Niederlande zu Klimaschutz 2018; Niederlande müssen Bürger vor Klimawandel schützen 2018; Neslen 2018; van Santen and Luttikhuis 2018).

The third Rutte cabinet has set ambitious targets with its aim to reduce GHG emissions by 49% in 2030. This target setting indicates that the government makes ambitious efforts to accomplish the country's commitments in the frameworks of international and EU agreements on climate and energy policy.

To conclude, the Dutch government opted for its historically established pattern of negotiation democracy in order to reach a consensus on long-term energy transition policies. Path dependency in policy-making, however, was accompanied by institutional adaptations. These relate to the inclusion of the provinces, the municipalities and the water authorities, new participatory governance mechanisms, more output transparency and refined methods of formal monitoring, and supervision instruments of the implementation process. With the launch of negotiations on a Climate Change Agreement (Klimaatakkoord) in February 2018 by the Ministry of Economic Affairs and Climate Policy (EZK) together with the Social and Economic Council (SER), the path is continued.

Annotation

In 2018 the Dutch government initiated negotiations on the *Klimaatakkoord*. The negotiations are mentioned in the chapter, but not further discussed in detail. The time frame of the analysis is 2016 and 2017 respectively.

Cross-References

▶ Energy Governance in Austria
▶ Energy Governance in Belgium
▶ Energy Governance in Denmark

- Energy Governance in Europe: Introduction
- Energy Governance in France
- Energy Governance in Germany
- Energy Governance in Ireland
- Energy Governance in Norway
- Energy Governance in Sweden
- Energy Governance in the United Kingdom
- European Union Energy Policy: A Discourse Perspective
- Transition of Energy Systems: Patterns of Stability and Change

Acknowledgements I would like to thank the editors, Jörg Kemmerzell and Michèle Knodt, as well as Roland Czada for helpful comments and proofreading. Thanks also to the participants of the workshop on the handbook held at the Schader Foundation in Darmstadt in November 2017. I myself am responsible for any remaining errors.

References

ACM (Authority for Consumers and Markets, Autoriteit Consument & Markt). (2017). *Incentive regulation of the gas and electricity networks in the Netherlands. General information about the method of regulation of the system operators of natural gas and electricity in the Netherlands by the Netherlands Authority for Consumers and Markets*. The Hague: ACM.

ACM. (2018). De ACM als werkgever. https://www.acm.nl/nl/organisatie/werken-bij/acm-als-werkgever. Accessed 18 Dec 2018.

Andeweg, R. B., & Irwin, G. A. (2014). *Governance and politics of the Netherlands*. Basingstoke/New York: Palgrave Macmillan.

ANVS (Authority for Nuclear Safety and Radiation Protection, Autoriteit Nucleaire Veiligheid en Stralingsbescherming). (2018). Home. ANVS. https://english.autoriteitnvs.nl/anvs. Accessed 18 Dec 2018.

AWTI (Advisory Council for science, technology and innovation, Adviesraad voor wetenschap, technologie en innovatie). (2018). Over ons. https://www.awti.nl/over-ons. Accessed 19 Apr 2018.

Babe, A. (2016). One country's endless war against water. http://www.bbc.com/travel/story/20160126-the-dutch-war-against-water. Accessed 30 Sep 2018.

Boffey, D. (2018, January 23). Gas field earthquakes put Netherlands' biggest firms on extraction notice. *The Guardian*.

CBS, PBL, Wageningen UR. (2017). *Emissies broeikasgassen, 1990–2015 [23]* (indicator 0165, versie 30, 25 april 2017). www.compendiumvoordeleefomgeving.nl. CBS, Den Haag; Planbureau voor de Leefomgeving, Den Haag/Bilthoven en Wageningen UR, Wageningen.

CBS StatLine. (2018a). Energy balance sheet; supply, transformation and consumption. https://opendata.cbs.nl/statline/#/CBS/en/dataset/83140ENG/table?ts=1525112893632. Accessed 18 Dec 2018.

CBS StatLine. (2018b). Electricity and heat; production and input by energy commodity. https://opendata.cbs.nl/statline/#/CBS/en/dataset/80030eng/table?ts=1525182142634. Accessed 18 Dec 2018.

CBS StatLine. (2018c). Emissions to air on Dutch territory; totals. https://opendata.cbs.nl/statline/#/CBS/en/dataset/37221eng/table?ts=1525184005028. Accessed 18 Dec 2018.

Coalition Agreement. (2017–2021). Confidence in the future. 2017–2021 Coalition Agreement. People's Party for Freedom and Democracy (VVD), Christian Democratic Alliance (CDA), Democrats '66 (D66) and Christian Union (CU). The Hague.

Correljé, A., van der Linde, C., & Westerwoudt, T. (2003). *Natural gas in the Netherlands. From cooperation to competition?* Amsterdam-Zuidoost: Oranje Nassau Groep B.V.

CPB (Centraal Planbureau). (2018). *Beoordeling Voorstel voor hoofdlijnen van het Klimaatakkoord.* CPB Notitie 13 September 2018.

Czada, R. (1991). Regierung und Verwaltung als Organisatoren gesellschaftlicher Interessen. In H.-H. Hartwich & G. Wewer (Eds.), *Regieren in der Bundesrepublik 3: Systemsteuerung und Staatskunst* (pp. 151–173). Wiesbaden: Springer Fachmedien [Opladen: Leske Verlag + Budrich GmbH].

Czada, R., & Musch, E. (2017). National and temporal patterns of policymaking. Energy transformation in the Netherlands and Germany compared. Paper presented at the ECPR General Conference, Oslo, 6–9 September 2017.

Daalder, H. (1996). The Netherlands: Still a consociational democracy? Reihe *Politikwissenschaft/Political Science Series* 33, April 1996.

De Groene Rekenkamer. (2014). Protesten tegen windmolens bedreigen energieakkoord. 26 January 2014. http://www.groenerekenkamer.nl/2190/protesten-tegen-windmolens-bedreigen-energieakkoord/. Accessed 11 Feb 2018.

de Jong, J. J., Weeda, E. O., Westerwoudt, T., & Correljé, A. F. (2005). *Dertig Jaar Nederlands Energiebeleid. Van Bonzen, Polders en Markten naar Brussel zonder Koolstof.* The Hague: Clingendael International Energy Programme.

de Keijzer, J., Kleinhout, A., van der Hoeven, C., & Di Bella, L. (2016). The Netherlands. In P. D. Cameron & R. J. Heffron (Eds.), *Legal aspects of EU energy regulation: The consolidation of energy law across Europe* (pp. 467–487). Oxford: Oxford University Press.

de Thouars, J. (2018). ECN en TNO samen verder vanaf april. https://www.duurzaambedrijfsleven.nl/industrie/27411/ecn-en-tno-samen-verder-vanaf-april. Accessed 18 Dec 2018.

de Vlam, R., & Oosterhuis, M. (2015). Chapter 23. Netherlands. In D. L. Schwartz (Ed.), *The energy regulation and markets review* (4th ed., pp. 306–540). London: Law Business Research Ltd.

Der Energieblog. (2015). Niederländisches Ausschreibungssystem für Erneuerbare Energien darf in die nächste Runde. 22 April 2015. http://www.derenergieblog.de/. Accessed 30 Sep 2018.

DNHK (German Dutch Chamber of Commerce, Deutsch-Niederländische Handelskammer). (2016). *Zielmarktanalyse Smart Grids Niederlande 2016* (Mit Profilen der Marktakteure). The Hague: DNHK.

DNHK. (2018). *Niederlande – Intelligente Lösungen für die Wärmewende und Energieinfrastruktur* (Zielmarktanalyse mit Profilen der Marktakteure). The Hague: DNHK.

DNV GL, TU Delft, Berenschot, Topsector Energie. (2015). *Energy storage roadmap NL 2030. System integration and the role of energy storage.* Arnhem: DNV GL.

Dutch Water Authorities. (2018). About us. https://dutchwaterauthorities.com/about-us/. Accessed 19 Apr 2018.

ECN (Energy Research Centre of the Netherlands, Energieonderzoek Centrum Nederland). (2016). Nationale Energieverkenning 2016. Amsterdam/Petten: ECN.

ECN. (2017). *Nationale Energieverkenning 2017.* Amsterdam/Petten: ECN.

ECN. (2018a). History. https://www.ecn.nl/about-ecn/history/. Accessed 18 Dec 2018.

ECN. (2018b). Joining of forces between ECN and TNO. https://www.ecn.nl/about-ecn/krachtenbundeling-ecn-tno/. Accessed 18 Dec 2018.

Energy Storage NL. (2015). Topsector presenteert Routekaart Energieopslag 2030. https://www.energystoragenl.nl/topsector-presenteert-routekaart-energieopslag-2030/389. Accessed 13 May 2018.

Europa Nu. (2016). Energieraad opgeheven (AER). https://www.europa-nu.nl/.

European Commission. (2012). Legal sources on renewable energy. Netherlands: Overall Summary. http://www.res-legal.eu/search-by-country/netherlands/. Accessed 26 Apr 2018.

European Commission. (2017a). Climate action. Kyoto 2nd commitment period (2013–20). https://ec.europa.eu/clima/policies/strategies/progress/kyoto_2_en. Accessed 13 Aug 2017.

European Commission. (2017b). Paris agreement. https://ec.europa.eu/clima/policies/international/negotiations/paris_en. Accessed 10 Nov 2017.

European Commission. (2017c). Environment council approves the EU's intended nationally determined contribution to the new global climate agreement, 3 June 2015. https://ec.europa.eu/clima/news/articles/news_2015030601_en. Accessed 10 Nov 2017.

European Commission. (2018a). Climate action. 2020 climate and energy package. https://ec.europa.eu/clima/policies/strategies/2020_en. Accessed 8 Oct 2018.

European Commission. (2018b). Climate action. Environment council approves the EU's intended nationally determined contribution to the new global climate agreement. https://ec.europa.eu/clima/news/articles/news_2015030601_en. Accessed 8 Oct 2018.

FluxEnergie. (2015a). Energieraad in stilte opgeheven. 21 July 2015. https://www.fluxenergie.nl/energieraad-in-stilte-opgeheven/. Accessed 14 Aug 2017.

FluxEnergie. (2015b). D66 wil kolenparagraaf Energieakkoord herzien. 18 March 2015. https://www.fluxenergie.nl/d66-wil-kolenparagraaf-energieakkoord-herzien/. Accessed 14 Aug 2017.

Frontier Economics. (2015). Scenarios for the Dutch electricity supply system. A report prepared for the Dutch Ministry of Economic Affairs (Ministerie van Economische Zaken). Frontier Economics.

Gasunie. (2018). All Dutch distribution network operators. https://www.gasunietransportservices.nl/en/connected-party/system-operators/distribution-network-operators-ldc/all-distribution-network-operators. Accessed 14 May 2018.

Gericht zwingt Niederlande zu Klimaschutz. (2018, October 10). *Frankfurter Allgemeine Zeitung* (FAZ) (Politik) (p. 1).

Government of the Netherlands (Rijksoverheid). (2015). Nieuwsbericht 1 September 2015. Kabinet begint met uitvoering Urgenda-vonnis en gaat in hoger beroep. https://www.rijksoverheid.nl/actueel/nieuws/2015/09/01/kabinet-begint-met-uitvoering-urgenda-vonnis-en-gaat-in-hoger-beroep. Accessed 14 Nov 2017.

Government of the Netherlands. (2016). Kamp en Kuipers starten energiedialoog. Nieuwsbericht 31 March 2016. https://www.rijksoverheid.nl/actueel/nieuws/2016/03/31/kamp-en-kuipers-starten-energiedialoog. Accessed 3 Oct 2016.

Government of the Netherlands. (2017a). Rutte III government sworn in. News item of 26 October 2017. https://www.government.nl/latest/news/2017/10/26/rutte-iii-government-sworn-in. Accessed 3 Nov 2017.

Government of the Netherlands. (2017b). Kamp verheugd over besparingsakkoord energie-intensieve industrie. Nieuwsbericht 6 April 2017. https://www.rijksoverheid.nl/actueel/nieuws/2017/04/06/kamp-verheugd-over-besparingsakkoord-energie-intensieve-industrie. Accessed 14 Nov 2017.

Government of the Netherlands. (2018a). Dutch cabinet: Termination of natural gas extraction in Groningen. News item 29 March 2018. https://www.government.nl/latest/news/2018/03/29/dutch-cabinet-termination-of-natural-gas-extraction-in-groningen. Accessed 17 May 2018.

Government of the Netherlands. (2018b). Kabinet geeft startschot voor Klimaatakkoord. Nieuwsbericht 23 February 2018.

Government of the Netherlands. (2018c). Taken van een provincie. https://www.rijksoverheid.nl/onderwerpen/provincies/taken-provincie. Accessed 27 Sept 2018.

Government of the Netherlands. (2018d). Taken van een gemeente. https://www.rijksoverheid.nl/onderwerpen/gemeenten/taken-gemeente. Accessed 27 Sept 2018.

Government of the Netherlands. (2018e). Provinces, municipalities and water authorities. https://www.government.nl/topics/public-administration/provinces-municipalities-and-water-authorities. Accessed 27 Sept 2018.

Government of the Netherlands. (2018f). Dutch goals within the EU. https://www.government.nl/topics/climate-change/eu-policy. Accessed 18 Dec 2018.

Government of the Netherlands. (2018g). Environmental taxes. https://www.government.nl/topics/taxation-and-businesses/environmental-taxes. Accessed 17 May 2018.

Government of the Netherlands. (2018h). Klimaatbeleid. https://www.rijksoverheid.nl/onderwerpen/klimaatverandering/klimaatbeleid. Accessed 30 Dec 2018.

Government of the Netherlands. (2018i). Kabinet verbiedt elektriciteitsproductie met kolen. Nieuwsbericht 18 May 2018. https://www.rijksoverheid.nl/actueel/nieuws/2018/05/18/kabinet-verbiedt-elektriciteitsproductie-met-kolen. Accessed 10 Jan 2019.

IEA (International Energy Agency). (2016). Feed-in premium programme SDE + (Stimulering Duurzame Energie +). https://www.iea.org/policiesandmeasures/pams/netherlands/name-24872-en.php. Accessed 21 Aug 2017.

IHK Munich and Upper Bavaria (Chamber of Commerce and Industry). (2016). Finanzierung der Erneuerbaren Energien in EU-Strommärkten. IHK Studie, January 2016.

Interview NL1. Interview with senior policy officer of the SER held in November 2017.

IPO (Interprovinciaal Overleg). (2015). Provincies investeren in Energietransitie. The Hague.

IPO. (2018). De zeven kerntaken van de provincies. http://www.ipo.nl/over-de-provincies/de-zeven-kerntaken-van-de-provincies#Milieu. Accessed 27 Sept 2018.

IRENA. (2018). *Renewable energy and jobs* (Annual review 2018). Abu Dhabi: IRENA.

Janssen, J. E., Pigmans, M., & Brinkman, M. (2009). Netherlands. In E. H. O'Donnell (Ed.), *Electricity regulation in 34 jurisdictions worldwide 2009* (pp. 147–153). London: Getting The Deal Through.

Kern, F., & Howlett, M. (2009). Implementing transition management as policy reforms: A case study of the Dutch energy sector. *Policy Sciences, 42*, 391–408.

Kok, W. C. (2004). De nieuwe energietransitie in het licht van de vorige. http://www.double-energy.eu/publicat/Kema_Kok_Eenrgitransitie_okt_2004.doc. Accessed 5 June 2016.

KWINK Groep. (2016). *Evaluatie Energieakkoord voor duurzame groei*. Onderzoek naar de werking van de aanpak van het Energieakkoord voor duurzame groei. The Hague: KWINK Groep.

Lehmbruch, G. (1987). Administrative Interessenvermittlung. In A. Windhoff-Héritier (Ed.), *Verwaltung und ihre Umwelt. Festschrift für Thomas Ellwein* (pp. 11–43). Opladen: Westdeutscher Verlag.

Lijphart, A. (1968). *The politics of accommodation. Pluralism and democracy in the Netherlands*. Berkeley: University of California Press.

Ministry BuZa (Ministry of Foreign Affairs, Ministerie van Buitenlandse Zaken). (2018a). Hollandtradeandinvest.com. Water technology. https://www.hollandtradeandinvest.com/key-sectors/water/water-technology. Accessed 30 Sept 2018.

Ministry BuZa. (2018b). Hollandtradeandinvest.com. Water. https://www.hollandtradeandinvest.com/key-sectors/water. Accessed 30 Sept 2018.

Ministry BZK (Ministry of the Interior and Kingdom Relations, Ministerie van Binnenlandse Zaken en Koninkrijksrelaties). (2018). Onderwerpen. https://www.rijksoverheid.nl/ministeries/ministerie-van-binnenlandse-zaken-en-koninkrijksrelaties/onderwerpen. Accessed 18 Dec 2018.

Ministry EZ (Ministry of Economic Affairs, Ministerie van Economische Zaken). (2016a). Onderwerpen – Ministerie van Economische Zaken.

Ministry EZ. (2016b). Report to the Second Chamber. Openstelling van de SDE+ in 2017. 30 November 2016. The Hague.

Ministry EZ. (2016c). Report to the Second Chamber. Evaluatie Energieakkoord en Nationale Energieverkenning 2016. 14 October 2016. The Hague.

Ministry EZ. (2016d). Report to the Second Chamber. Energiedialoog. 31 March 2016. The Hague.

Ministry EZ. (2016e). Report to the second chamber. Energieagenda. 7 December 2016. The Hague.

Ministry EZ. (2017a). *Energy report. Transition to sustainable energy*. The Hague.

Ministry EZ. (2017b). *Energy agenda. Towards a low-carbon energy supply*. The Hague.

Ministry EZ. (2017c). Report to the Second Chamber. Uitvoeringsagenda Energieakkoord 2017. 6 April 2017. The Hague.

Ministry EZK (Ministry of Economic Affairs and Climate Policy, Ministerie van Economische Zaken en Klimaat). (2018a). Onderwerpen. https://www.rijksoverheid.nl/ministeries/ministerie-van-economische-zaken-en-klimaat/onderwerpen. Accessed 12 Mar 2018.

Ministry EZK. (2018b). Report to the second chamber. Gaswinning Groningen. 29 March 2018. The Hague.

Ministry IenW (Ministry of Infrastructure and Water Management, Ministerie van Infrastructuur en Waterstaat). (2018). Onderwerpen. https://www.rijksoverheid.nl/ministeries/ministerie-van-infrastructuur-en-waterstaat/onderwerpen. Accessed 19 Apr 2018.

Ministry OCW (Ministry of Education, Culture and Science, Ministerie van Onderwijs, Cultuur en Wetenschap). (2018). Onderwerpen. https://www.rijksoverheid.nl/ministeries/ministerie-van-onderwijs-cultuur-en-wetenschap/onderwerpen. Accessed 19 Apr 2018.

Ministry VROM (Ministry of Housing, Spatial Planning and the Environment, Ministerie van Volkshuisvesting, Ruimtelijke Ordening en Milieubeheer). (2001). Een wereld en een wil. Werken aan duurzaamheid. Nationaal Milieubeleidsplan 4. The Hague.

Musch, E. (2011). *Integration durch Konsultation. Konsensbildung in der Migrations- und Integrationspolitik in Deutschland und den Niederlanden*. Münster: Waxmann.

Musch, E. (2018). Der Energiepakt (Energieakkoord) in den Niederlanden: "grünes" Poldermodell? In J. Radtke & N. Kersting (Eds.), *Energiewende. Politikwissenschaftliche Perspektiven. Schriftenreihe Energietransformation* (pp. 131–153). Wiesbaden: Springer VS.

Nederland voldoet aan Kyoto-doelstellingen. Maar vraag niet hoe. (2014, November 8). *HP/De Tijd*. http://www.hpdetijd.nl/2014-11-08/nederland-voldoet-aan-kyoto-doelstellingen-maar-vraag-niet-hoe/. Accessed 14 Aug 2017.

Neslen, A. (2015, June 24). Dutch government ordered to cut carbon emissions in landmark ruling. *The Guardian*. https://www.theguardian.com/environment/2015/jun/24/dutch-government-ordered-cut-carbon-emissions-landmark-ruling. Accessed 11 Nov 2017.

Neslen, A. (2018, October 9). Dutch appeals court upholds landmark climate change ruling. *The Guardian*. https://www.theguardian.com/environment/2018/oct/09/dutch-appeals-court-upholds-landmark-climate-change-ruling. Accessed 9 Oct 2018.

Netherlands Water Partnership (NWP). (2018). Dutchwatersector.com. Our history. https://www.dutchwatersector.com/our-history/. Accessed 30 Sept 2018.

Niederlande müssen Bürger vor Klimawandel schützen. (2018, October 10). *Frankfurter Allgemeine Zeitung* (FAZ) (Wirtschaft), p. 15.

OECD/IEA. (2018). Oil security. https://www.iea.org/topics/energysecurity/oilsecurity/. Accessed 5 Mar 2018.

OECD/IEA (Ed.). (2014). *Energy policies of IEA countries. The Netherlands* (2014 review). Paris: OECD.

PBL (Netherlands Environmental Assessment Agency, Planbureau voor de Leefomgeving). (2013). Nieuwsberichten. Nederland voldoet aan de Kyoto verplichting uitstoot broeikasgassen. 8 September 2013. http://www.pbl.nl/nieuws/nieuwsberichten/2013/nederland-voldoet-aan-de-kyoto-verplichting-uitstoot-broeikasgassen. Accessed 13 Aug 2017.

PBL. (2014). *Green tax reform: Energy tax challenges for the Netherlands* (PBL Policy Brief). The Hague: PBL.

PBL. (2018a). Correction wording flood risks for the Netherlands in IPCC report. http://www.pbl.nl/en/dossiers/Climatechange/content/correction-wording-flood-risks. Accessed 17 May 2018.

PBL. (2018b). About PBL. http://www.pbl.nl/en/aboutpbl. Accessed 19 Apr 2018.

PBL. (2018c). PBL en CPB presenteren analyse van het Voorstel voor Hoofdlijnen van het Klimaatakkoord. Nieuwsbericht 24 September 2018.

PBL. (2018d). Voorstel Klimaatakkoord: genoeg potentieel voor doel 2030, maar succes hangt af van keuzes. Nieuwsbericht 28 September 2018. http://www.pbl.nl/nieuws/nieuwsberichten/2018/voorstel-klimaatakkoord-genoeg-potentieel-voor-doel-2030-maar-succes-hangt-af-van-keuzes. Accessed 11 Oct 2018.

Peet, J. (2010). Zelfbeeld en zelfinzicht – De SER over de SER en de overlegeconomie. In T. Jaspers, B. van Bavel, & J. Peet (Eds.), *SER 1950–2010. Zestig jaar denkwerk voor draagvlak. Advies voor economie en samenleving* (pp. 225–247). Amsterdam: Boom.

Pieters, J. (2018, March 29). Politics. Gas extraction in Groningen to be reduced to zero. *NL Times*. https://nltimes.nl/2018/03/29/gas-extraction-groningen-reduced-zero. Accessed 17 May 2018.

Postma, R. (2016, May 18). Boete op komst voor wie zich niet aan Energieakkoord houdt. *NRC Handelsblad*.

Regeerakkoord. (2012–2017). *Bruggen slaan. Regeerakkoord VVD – PvdA. 29 October 2012*. The Hague.
Regeerakkoord. (2017–2021). *Vertrouwen in de toekomst. Regeerakkoord 2017–2012. VVD, CDA, D66 en ChristenUnie. 10 October 2017*. The Hague.
Reiche, D. (2002). *Erneuerbare Energien in den Niederlanden. Pfadabhängigkeiten, Akteure, Belief Systeme und Restriktionen*. Frankfurt a.M.: Peter Lang GmbH.
Rengers, M. (2014, April 24). Steeds meer weerstand tegen windmolens. *De Volkskrant*. https://www.volkskrant.nl/politiek/steeds-meer-weerstand-tegen-windmolens~a3640525/. Accessed 8 Feb 2018.
Rijkswaterstaat. (2011). *Water management in the Netherlands*. The Hague.
Rijkswaterstaat. (2018). Wet milieubeheer. https://www.rijkswaterstaat.nl/water/wetten-regels-en-vergunningen/natuur-en-milieuwetten/wet-milieubeheer.aspx. Accessed 26 Apr 2018.
Rli (Council for the Environment and Infrastructure, Raad voor de leefomgeving en infrastructuur). (2018). Over de raad. http://rli.nl/over-de-raad. Accessed 16 May 2018.
Roggenkamp, M. (2016). Energy law in the Netherlands. In M. Roggenkamp, C. Redgwell, A. Rønne, & I. del Guayo (Eds.), *Energy law in Europe. National, EU and international regulation* (pp. 725–806). Oxford: Oxford University Press.
Roos, M. (2011). Energiewirtschaft in den Niederlanden. IV. Niederländischer Atomstrom. (NiederlandeNet). https://www.uni-muenster.de/NiederlandeNet/nl-wissen/umwelt/vertiefung/energiewirtschaft/atomstrom.html. Accessed 14 May 2018.
Rotmans, J. (2011). Staat van de Energietransitie in Nederland. Concept-versie. DRIFT, Erasmus University Rotterdam. http://janrotmans.blogspot.de/2011/08/staat-van-de-energietransitie-in.html. Accessed 4 Mar 2018.
RVO (Netherlands Enterprise Agency, Rijksdienst voor Ondernemend Nederland). (2018a). 3.899 beschikte projecten SDE+ voorjaar 2018. https://www.rvo.nl/actueel/nieuws/3899-beschikte-projecten-sde-voorjaar-2018. Accessed 2 Oct 2018.
RVO. (2018b). SDE+ najaarsronde 2018 opent op 2 oktober. https://www.rvo.nl/actueel/nieuws/sde-najaarsronde-2018-opent-op-2-oktober. Accessed 2 Oct 2018.
RVO. (2018c). Deelnemers MJA3/MEE. https://www.rvo.nl/onderwerpen/duurzaam-ondernemen/energie-besparen/meerjarenafspraken-energie-effici%C3%ABntie/deelnemers. Accessed 16 May 2018.
Saurer, J., & Purnhagen, K. (2016). Klimawandel vor Gericht – Der Rechtsstreit der Nichtregierungsorganisation "Urgenda" gegen die Niederlande und seine Bedeutung für Deutschland. *ZUR, 1*, 16–23.
Schrijvers, E. K. (2012). *Ongekozen bestuur. Opkomst en ondergang van het stelsel van adviescolleges en bedrijfsorganen (1945–1995)*. Doctoral dissertation, University of Utrecht, Utrecht.
SER (Social and Economic Council, Sociaal-Economische Raad). (2012). *Naar een Energieakkoord voor duurzame groei. Advies 12/07. November 2012*. Uitgebracht aan de Minister van Economische Zaken en de Staatssecretaris van Infrastructuur en Milieu. The Hague: SER.
SER. (2013a). *Summary of energy agreement for sustainable growth*. The Hague.
SER. (2013b). *Energieakkoord voor duurzame groei. Rapport. September 2013*. The Hague.
SER. (2016a). Werkwijze. https://www.ser.nl/nl/raad/ser_kort/werkwijzeser.aspx. Accessed 5 June 2016.
SER. (2016b). Commissie Borging Energieakkoord (BEA). https://www.ser.nl/nl/raad/commissies/borging-energieakkoord.aspx. Accessed 17 Aug 2017.
SER. (2017a). The SER's responsibilities. https://www.ser.nl/en/about_the_ser/responsibilities.aspx. Accessed 15 Aug 2017.
SER. (2017b). Members of the SER. https://www.ser.nl/en/about_the_ser/members.aspx. Accessed 15 Aug 2017.
SER. (2017c). *Briefadvies Governance van het energie- en klimaatbeleid*. The Hague: SER.
SER. (2017d). *Uitvoeringsagenda Energieakkoord 2017*. The Hague: SER.
SER. (2018). *Voorstel voor hoofdlijnen van het Klimaatakkoord*. The Hague: SER.

SER-BEA (Commissie Borging Energieakkoord). (2017). *Energieakkoord voor duurzame groei.* Voortgangsrapportage 2017. The Hague.

Sloover, I. S., & Klootwijk, K. (2014). *Juridische handreiking Duurzame Energie en Grondstoffen Waterschappen.* In opdracht van de Unie van Waterschappen en STOWA. Utrecht: Berenschot Groep B.V.

Smit, J. (2004). Geographie der Niederlande. VI. Politische Ebenen. (updated in September 2014 by Keim, D.; NiederlandeNet). https://www.uni-muenster.de/NiederlandeNet/nl-wissen/geographie/vertiefung/geographie/regionen.html. Accessed 18 Dec 2018.

Stimuleringsfonds Volkshuisvesting Nederlandse gemeenten (SVn). (2018). Over ons. Het Nationaal Energiebespaarfonds. https://www.energiebespaarlening.nl/over-ons/. Accessed 17 May 2018.

TNO (de Nederlandse Organisatie voor toegepast-natuurwetenschappelijk onderzoek). (2018). Mission and strategy. Organisation. https://www.tno.nl/en/about-tno/. Accessed 1 Oct 2018.

Touwen, J. (2014). *Coordination in transition. The Netherlands and the world economy 1950–2010.* Leiden: Brill.

Tweede Kamer der Staten Generaal TK. (2013). Duurzame ontwikkeling en beleid. Brief van de Minister van Economische Zaken. Vergaderjaar 2012-2013, 30196, Nr. 189.

Tweede Kamer der Staten Generaal TK. (2015). Groene economische groei in Nederland (Green Deal). Brief van de Minister van Economische Zaken en Staatssecretaris Infrastructuur en Milieu. Vergaderjaar 2014–2015, 33043, Nr. 42.

van der Loo, F., & Loorbach, D. (2012). The Dutch energy transition project (2000–2009). In G. Verbong & D. Loorbach (Eds.), *Governing the energy transition. Reality, illusion and necessity?* (pp. 220–250). New York: Routledge.

van der Weijden, C. (2016). Lexology. CMS guide to energy storage: The Netherlands. https://www.lexology.com/library/detail.aspx?g=5a326284-f6aa-4439-b733-05d4eecc70f5. Accessed 13 May 2018.

van Heumen, J. (2014). *Energy cooperatives, the distribution system operator and energy transition.* Master's thesis, TU/e Eindhoven University of Technology, Eindhoven.

van Koningsveld, M., Mulder, J. P. M., Stive, M. J. F., van der Valk, L., & van der Weck, A. W. (2008). Living with sea-level rise and climate change: A case study of the Netherlands. *Journal of Coastal Research, 24*(2), 367–379.

van Rooijen, S. N. M., & van Wees, M. T. (2006). Green electricity policies in the Netherlands: An analysis of policy decisions. *Energy Policy, 34*, 60–71.

van Santen, H. (2018, March 10). Geen gas? Dan bedenken we iets anders. NRC.NL. https://www.nrc.nl/nieuws/2018/03/10/geen-gas-dan-bedenken-we-iets-anders-a1595175. Accessed 25 May 2018.

van Santen, H., & Luttikhuis, P. (2018, October 9). Hof: Staat moet burger behoeden voor klimaatverandering. NRC.NL. https://www.nrc.nl/nieuws/2018/10/09/gerechtshof-staat-moet-co2-reductie-verminderen-a2417254. Accessed 9 Oct 2018.

van Santen, H., & van der Walle, E. (2018a, March 29). Uiterlijk 2030 geen gas meer uit Groningen. Gaswinning. Het kabinet wil de gaswinning in Groningen zo snel mogelijk terugschroeven en uiterlijk in 2030 geheel stoppen. NRC.NL. https://www.nrc.nl/nieuws/2018/03/29/uiterlijk-2030-geen-gas-meer-uit-groningen-a1597604. Accessed 18 Dec 2018.

van Santen, H., & van der Walle, E. (2018b). Pas politieke steun voor klimaatakkoord – ontwerp als de cijfers kloppen. NRC.NL. https://www.nrc.nl/nieuws/2018/12/21/pas-politieke-steun-als-cijfers-kloppen-a3126827. Accessed 30 Dec 2018.

van Zanden, J. L. (2010). Economische groei en duurzaamheid – over de doelstellingen van het sociaal-economisch beleid. In T. Jaspers, B. van Bavel, & J. Peet (Eds.), *SER 1950–2010. Zestig jaar denkwerk voor draagvlak. Advies voor economie en samenleving* (pp. 171–186). Amsterdam: Boom.

Verbong, G., van Selm, A., Knoppers, R., & Raven, R. (2001). *Een kwestie van lange adem. De geschiedenis van duurzame energie in Nederland.* Boxtel: Aeneas.

Visser, J., & Hemerijck, A. (1997). *A Dutch miracle. Job growth, welfare reform and corporatism in the Netherlands*. Amsterdam: Amsterdam University Press.

Vlek, C. (2018). Induced earthquakes from long-term gas extraction in Groningen, the Netherlands: Statistical analysis and prognosis for acceptable-risk regulation. *Risk Analysis, 38*(7), 1455–1473. https://doi.org/10.1111/risa.12967.

Weggeman, J. (2003). *Controversiële besluitvorming: opkomst en functioneren van groen polderoverleg*. Utrecht: Lemma.

Wet Adviesraad voor wetenschap, technologie en innovatie. Wet AWTI.

Wet houdende regeling van de Nederlandse Organisatie voor toegepast-natuurwetenschappelijk onderzoek TNO, TNO-wet.

Wet Raad voor de leefomgeving en infrastructuur. Wet RLI.

Wildeboer, L., & van der Weijden, C. (2015). STROOM; the new electricity and gas act in the Netherlands. https://www.lexology.com/library/detail.aspx?g=550baa67-409a-4d0f-9032-ca65 85977dc5. Accessed 25 May 2018.

Wilming, W. (2014). "SDE+" ersetzt bisherige Förderung Erneuerbarer Energien in den Niederlanden, Sonne, Wind und Wärme. http://www.sonnewindwaerme.de/photovoltaik/sde-ersetzt-bisherige-foerderungerneuerbarer-energien-den-niederlanden. Accessed 21 Aug 2017.

Zuidervaart, B., & Redactie Politiek (2014, June 20). Kolencentrales toch dicht. *Trouw.* https://www.trouw.nl/home/kolencentrales-toch-dicht~a4d06ccd/. Accessed 14 Aug 2017.

Energy Governance in Norway

Too Much of a Good Thing?

Elin Lerum Boasson and Torbjørg Jevnaker

Contents

Introduction	898
General Conditions of Energy Governance in Norway	899
Material Endowments	899
Composition of the Energy Mix	900
Norwegian Energy and Climate Discourses	901
Political Institutions and Actors	906
Coordination, Instruments, and Issues of the Norwegian Energy Transition	909
Strategies and Instruments of Energy Transitions	909
Drivers of the Energy Transition and Multilevel Governance	915
Outcomes, Challenges, and Prospects	916
Cross-References	918
References	918

Abstract

Norway faces energy and climate transition challenges very different from those of most other European countries: power production is already decarbonized, but domestic emissions are rising due to increased emissions from oil and gas exploration and transport. A "global cost-efficiency" discourse has dominated Norwegian climate politics, and yet the country has adopted a wide range of domestic climate and energy transition measures across sectors. This chapter reviews the climate and energy governance literature, focusing on the transition of the Norwegian stationary electricity system (production, transmission, and use

E. L. Boasson (✉)
Department of Political Science, Center for International Climate Research, University of Oslo and CICERO, Oslo, Norway
e-mail: e.l.boasson@stv.uio.no

T. Jevnaker
Fridtjof Nansen Institute, Lysaker, Akershus, Norway
e-mail: tjevnaker@fni.no

© Springer Nature Switzerland AG 2022
M. Knodt, J. Kemmerzell (eds.), *Handbook of Energy Governance in Europe*,
https://doi.org/10.1007/978-3-030-43250-8_21

of electricity) but also the overarching energy transition challenges relating to offshore petroleum production and energy use in transportation. The emergence of a green electricity surplus and sinking power prices have triggered discussion of whether Norway should build more interconnectors or use cheap, clean power to attract new domestic industry. With the electricity system transition, the political discourse has centered on the dilemmas related to having too much of a good thing: plentiful and steadily increasing renewable power production from large-scale hydropower. Norwegian authorities must walk the fine line between power-producers and energy-intensives, discontinuing the renewable support scheme after 2020 while aiming at modest expansion of interconnectors.

Keywords

Norwegian politics · Energy policy · Climate policy · Petroleum policy · Green certificates · Carbon capture and storage · Electric vehicles · Electricity surplus · Hydropower · Global cost-efficiency

Introduction

Norway produces ten times more energy annually than it consumes, and over 90% of produced energy stems from fossil fuels (NVE 2018). It also produces more renewable electricity every year than needed to cover domestic demand. Hence, the country faces very different energy and climate transition challenges than most other European Union (EU) and European Economic Agreement (EEA) members. Unlike its European peers, national emissions are increasing, while domestic power production is already decarbonized. The main energy transition challenges concern to oil/gas production and transportation, not electricity production. Climate mitigation became a salient political issue in Norway very early, with disagreement over climate policy triggering a shift of government back in 2000. This chapter questions: How has Norwegian climate and energy governance developed over time? To what extent and how are the key energy transition dilemmas covered in the literature on Norwegian climate governance?

There is little agreement about what constitute the burning issues relating to Norwegian climate and energy transition. While some argue that it is crucial to replace current use of fossil fuels within the two sectors that rely primarily on fossil fuels – offshore petroleum production and the transport sector – others hold that reducing domestic emissions has little relevance. Rather than enacting costly carbon emission reductions domestically, Norway should finance carbon emission reductions elsewhere while ensuring that its plentiful domestic energy resources continue to drive national economic growth. As a result of three decades of political compromises, Norway has adopted an encompassing climate and energy policy portfolio that represents a combination of these two positions: some measures are aimed at global cost-efficient climate mitigation; others aim at reducing national emissions.

Concerning the electricity system transition, the political discourse in Norway has centered on the dilemmas entailed in having too much of a good thing: plentiful and steadily increasing power production from large hydropower. Climate change is expected to lead to more precipitation, enabling even greater hydropower production. Due to record-high power production and decreased consumption, Norway has experienced historically low electricity prices after 2000, reducing the profits of electricity producers. Hence, it is widely felt that Norway has too much "green" electricity production and that major new investments in renewables are not needed. However, and despite an already decarbonized power sector, Norway has promoted renewables and energy efficiency in the electricity sector. The emergence of a green electricity surplus has put power-producers and energy-intensives at loggerheads, with the former pushing for more interconnectors to export electricity and the latter wanting to avoid further interconnection and instead use cheap, clean power to attract new domestic industry. The authorities must toe the fine line between two powerful sectors, discontinuing the renewable support scheme after 2020 while seeking a modest expansion of interconnectors.

The chapter draws primarily on official governmental reports, figures from Statistics Norway, and research on Norwegian climate and energy governance.

General Conditions of Energy Governance in Norway

Material Endowments

Norway is blessed with natural resources that have enabled it to develop major hydropower production, a significant energy-intensive industry, and larger oil and gas production than any other EU/EEA countries. Many decades before climate change came on the agenda, plentiful waterways in mountainous regions had enabled Norway to develop large-scale hydropower. With numerous waterways and advantageous topography, natural conditions in Norway favored the development of an electricity system based on hydropower, and dams were often constructed to supply electricity to local industry (Wicken 2011). Access to cheap electricity from large hydro has been important for Norway's energy-intensive industries (Wicken 2011). Norway has a relatively large energy-intensive industry and has become Europe's largest aluminum producer (NOU 2012, p. 550). The abundance of hydropower contributed to the rejection of nuclear plants in Norway already in the 1970s (Hofstad 2018).

Norwegian electricity (144 TWh in 2015) is predominantly produced from hydro (96%) complemented by some thermal power from waste or gas (2.5%) and wind (1.7%). Climate change has contributed to higher precipitation; this, together with modest development of small hydro- and wind power, has ensured steadily increased electricity production (SSB 2018). Vast uninhabited areas with much wind hold excellent potential for wind power development, but this has not been much exploited thus far. Since the mid-1990s, Norway's electricity sector has been closely integrated with those of the other Nordic countries. Further, an interconnector between Norway and the Netherlands was built in 2008, and new interconnectors to the UK and Germany will be operational by 2021 (Statnett 2017). Already today, Norway is a net exporter of electricity, in most years exporting as much as 15% of its electricity production (SSB 2018).

After the discovery of sizeable petroleum resources offshore in the late 1960s, Norway became a major producer of oil and gas, and is today the second-largest gas supplier to the EU (Norsk petroleum 2018). Norway has marginal petroleum resources compared to countries like Saudi Arabia and Russia, and production costs are high. However, high oil and gas prices after the turn of the millennium allowed Norway to expand extraction from fields previously deemed unprofitable. Petroleum is central to Norwegian export, representing more than half of export value (Norsk Petroleum 2018), although overall energy production decreased slightly from 2431 TWh in 2010 to 2428 TWh in 2016 (SSB 2018f). While oil remains important, the production of natural gas has risen to match that of oil. Due to low oil prices after 2014, more revenues have come from gas than oil (Hall 2018, p.2), although rising oil prices would change this picture in the short term.

In terms of primary energy production, petroleum production stands for a far larger share than hydro. Norway produced 2428 TWh in 2016, of which 94% came from fossil fuels (mostly natural gas and crude oil) and 6% from hydro and wind (SSB 2018e). Roughly 90% of all energy produced in Norway is exported – nearly seven times its own consumption (SSB 2018e). Major buyers of Norwegian oil and gas are the UK, Germany, the Netherlands, and France, receiving 75% (1644 TWh) of Norwegian energy exports (SSB 2018e). Norway's position as an exporter of energy sets it apart from most other European countries.

Petroleum production relies primarily on on-site gas-power production. Even after the climate issue emerged in the early 1999s, Norway continued to develop all new offshore oil and gas fields that the industry deemed commercially viable. As many oil and gas reservoirs are aging and approaching the last stage of production, more energy is needed to pump the fossil fuels out of the ground. Very few offshore installations have been connected to the onshore electricity grid. All in all, the GHG emissions from the petroleum sector have almost doubled since 1990 (SSB 2018b). Despite its significant oil and gas production, Norway is responsible for only 1/1000 of global GHG emissions. (Emissions from combustion of oil and gas produced in Norway are not included in this figure.) However, due to increased emissions from petroleum exploration and transport, domestic emissions in 2015 were slightly higher than in 1990 (Miljøstatus 2015).

Composition of the Energy Mix

Norwegian energy consumption grew until the late 1990s but has since stabilized. It even fell slightly between 2010 and 2016, although falling less in transport. Norwegian energy consumption is highly electrified – this goes for energy-intensive industry as well as buildings. The country is also in the forefront in electrifying the car fleet. The transport sector still relies primarily on fossil fuels, although the number of electric vehicles has increased steadily. By 2018, Norway had almost 600 passenger cars per 1000 persons, well above the EU average (Eurostat 2018; SSB 2018c); 5.1% of these cars were electric vehicles, a 40% increase from the previous year (SSB 2018d).

In 2016, Norwegians consumed 215 TWh, of which electricity was the largest carrier (53%), followed by oil (33%), biofuels (6%), coal (4%), district heating (3%), gas (2%), and waste (1%) (SSB 2017). Sector-wise (Fig. 1), stationary energy consumption is highly electrified: 65% of industrial energy use and 75% of energy use in households and other sectors (e.g., services). In contrast, transport has a much smaller share of electricity in its energy use (1%), being based predominantly on oil (89%) with some biofuels (7%) and gas (2%) (SSB 2017).

Norwegian Energy and Climate Discourses

The scholarly literature on Norwegian energy and climate governance discourses has labeled the dominant discourse in various ways, like "cost-efficiency" (Andresen and Butenschøn 2001; Gullberg and Skodvin 2011), "thinking globally" (Hovden and Lindseth 2004: 63), "a quota discourse" (Tellmann 2012), and "green growth" (Eckersley 2016). Several authors note how Norwegian politicians have applied various rhetorical ploys to "manage and minimize the tensions between Norway's role as an ambitious climate leader and its economic role as a major petroleum and gas producer" (Eckersley 2016: 191; see also Boasson 2015; Roettereng 2016), also by seeking international cooperation on climate issues within the UN (Boasson and Lahn 2017) and the EU (Boasson 2015; Jevnaker 2016; Christensen 2018).

The "global cost-efficiency" approach has become increasingly dominant in Norway (Boasson and Lahn 2017). This is a discourse that seeks to reconcile the increasing domestic emissions with global leadership ambitions, but it also serves as an institutional logic that portrays certain climate targets and measures as more appropriate. A key element has been the development of a binding global regime, based on flexible national commitments and emissions trading, and the adoption of national neutrality targets that can be met through emission reductions elsewhere (Gullberg 2009: 5; Lahn 2013; Boasson 2015). Norway's approach is explicitly based on the view that a country does not necessarily have to achieve domestic GHG emission reductions in order to be a global leader – the important thing is to promote solutions that can work well on a global scale. In that sense, Norway's international climate policy leadership has remained remarkably consistent over time.

Eckersley (2016:192) shows that Norwegian politicians have framed "Norway's role as a climate pioneer, example-setter, front runner, and leader." However, this frame primarily concerns the development of carbon capture and storage (CCS), Norway's international forest initiative REDD+ and carbon taxation – not measures relating to energy system transition (Tellmann 2012; Boasson 2015). Eckersley (2016) notes that the petroleum industry is part of this leadership story: it is seen as more environmentally friendly than its counterparts elsewhere; moreover, it is argued that gas sold to the European electricity market replaces dirtier sources like

Fig. 1 Distribution of energy consumption by sector in 2016. (Compiled by authors based on data from SSB (2017). *Households and others also include agriculture, forestry, fisheries, and services)

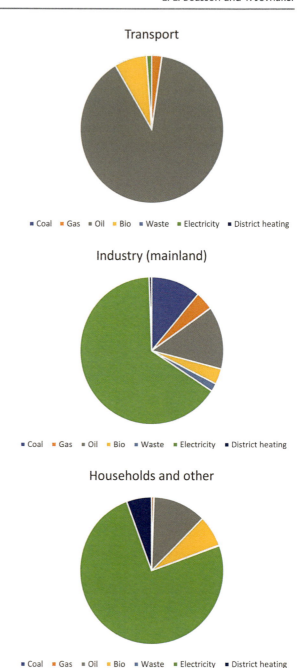

coal. The industry itself also propagates this image (Equinor undated). Interestingly, the export of clean, stationary electricity is not highlighted in the same way.

Value creation has been the overarching objective of Norwegian energy policy. Policy-makers have emphasized public ownership, strict regulations, and high tax levels for the country's two major energy sectors (petroleum and hydro) (Jevnaker et al. 2015). This is in accordance with the heavy emphasis on allocating the resource rent to the public (NOU 2012: 548–50). As Norway has ample energy resources, security of supply has mainly been a matter of ensuring adequate transmission, although occasional periods of high electricity prices have triggered attention to electricity supply. This was framed as "generation adequacy" around 2000; in recent years, attention to supply and energy prices has been linked more to interconnectors (see below).

While not a member, Norway cooperates extensively with the EU. Norway is not bound by overarching EU political climate and energy targets but must implement most EU climate and energy legislation (Jevnaker 2016). Still, the EU has attracted relatively little attention in Norwegian climate, petroleum, and electricity discourses. With respect to climate, Norwegian ambitions have always been to influence global emission developments, with Europe in focus mainly in relation to Norway's export of national gas. Until 2010, EU climate policy was rather soft. Boasson (2015) has shown how Norwegian actors have creatively altered and adjusted EU climate policies to Norway's traditional approaches. This also applies to EU energy policy, with successive Oslo governments employing flexibility to uphold domestic practices—for instance, reinforcing public ownership when EU legislation banned differential treatment of public and private ownership in licensing contracts on energy (Austvik and Claes 2011). Although Norwegian energy players engage within EU-wide industry associations to lobby early in EU decisionmaking processes, Norwegian stakeholders lobby mainly in Norway, also to influence EU legislation (Gullberg 2015).

In 2015, Norway accepted the EU's political target for emission reduction in non-ETS sectors by 2030, thereby moving the Norwegian climate target from global to European cost-efficiency (Christensen 2018). This shift does not imply that it has become commonplace to hold that Norway – with its abundant renewable resources – should work in tandem with the rest of Europe to ensure energy transition in the whole region. The prevalence of national political concerns is brought out in Anne Therese Gullberg's (2013) assessment of the political feasibility of Norway serving as a "green battery" for Europe. Norway has great technical potential for producing pumped-storage hydropower, thereby contributing to the European transition by providing some of the balancing power needed to increase the share of renewable energy. However, this idea has encountered resistance from energy-intensive industry, labor unions, and environmental organizations. Electricity industry and environmental groups have tried to establish a discourse of Norway as part of the Europe-wide energy transition, but concern for the local environment, and in particular local industrial employment and value creation, has prevailed.

Norway is part of the EU Emissions Trading System (EU ETS); and as this is a EU-level instrument, there is less room for adjustment than with other EU policies that set objectives but leave the development of instruments to the member states. Although carbon taxation, with CO_2 taxes and EU ETS as the key measures, is central to the dominant global cost-efficiency discourse, few scholars have assessed Norwegian political deliberations in relation to these issues. However, Anne Therese Gullberg and Tora Skodvin (2011) show how the energy-intensives used information strategically in order to obtain exceptions from the carbon taxation regime, but this was no longer possible after Norway was included in EU ETS. Further, Ingvild Sæverud and Jørgen Wettestad (2006) show that because the EU ETS fit with overall Norwegian climate policy, Norway was willing to link up to the system long before it became clear that Norway would be formally required to do so by its EEA membership. Subsequent reform of the allocation system in the EU ETS saw the introduction of free allocation for the petroleum sector under EU carbon leakage rules. The Norwegian authorities did not welcome this, as they wanted the Norwegian petroleum industry to pay for the ETS allowances instead. Nonetheless, Norway had to comply with the new EU rules. To compensate for this, Norway increased the CO_2 levy for the petroleum sector (Jevnaker 2016).

Ever since the early 1990s, the overarching global cost-efficiency approach has been challenged by actors who are calling for national action, portraying national emission reductions and sector-specific targets as crucial (Hovden and Lindseth 2004: 63). This national action discourse has been mixed with a strong "technology discourse" (Tellmann 2012: 747) heavily influenced by the German *Energiewende*. The argument goes that Norway should help solve the climate challenge by developing and refining various technologies, specifically CCS and electric vehicles (Boasson and Lahn 2017). Renewable energy technologies (like offshore wind power) have been linked to this debate only to a minor extent (Normann 2017).

A significant literature surveys the overarching themes and discourses in Norwegian climate policy (Tellmann 2012; Eckersley 2016:192; Jevnaker 2016; Boasson and Lahn 2017; Christensen 2018). There are, however, few attempts at covering the whole range of Norwegian climate policies and measures and explaining specific changes in targets, timetables, and instruments over time.

The issue that has gained the most attention among climate and energy governance researchers is the conflict over gas-power plants and later CCS, which began in the late 1990s and lasted for more than a decade (Hovden and Lindseth 2004; Boasson 2015; Normann 2017). In the two first decades after the power sector was liberalized in Norway, energy consumption was expected to grow. There were widespread fears that this, combined with the political constraints imposed on the development of large-scale hydro, would make Norway reliant on import of electricity. Hence, energy security played a certain role in energy policy in general, and gas-power in particular, in discussions during this period (Boasson 2015). Since the 1990s, plans have been mooted for building new gas-fired power plants. If built, they would significantly increase emissions from electricity production. If gas-power plants were to be constructed, this would result in "carbonization" of a sector that was renewable at outset. This quickly became the most heated issue in the emerging climate policy debate in Norway (Tjernshaugen 2011).

In the 2000s, CCS from gas-power plants emerged as a grand compromise that enabled political parties with diverging views on gas-power to join in coalition governments (Langhelle and Ishii 2011; Tjernshaugen 2011; Boasson 2015; Roettereng 2016). CCS is a suite of technological processes that involve capturing carbon dioxide from the gases discarded by industry and transporting and injecting it into geological formations. To make controversial plans for facilitating onshore consumption of natural gas acceptable, the Norwegian government started working with industry, to develop CCS technology for application to gas-fired power plants (Tjernshaugen and Langhelle 2011: 180). However, falling electricity prices after 2010 made gas-power unprofitable – with repercussions for development of CCS technology which was closely linked to gas-power. The Norwegian CCS initiative was also struggling due to poor project management and unexpected difficulties in implementing the EU's CO_2 storage directive (Jevnaker 2016).

After 2010, petroleum production in the High North replaced gas-power as the most contested climate policy issue in Norway (Boasson and Lahn 2017). The climate discourse related to the petroleum sector has generally focused on cost-efficiency and "cleaner" extraction, rather than targeting production itself (Boasson 2015; Eckersley 2016). Moreover, it was only after 2010 that climate issues became strongly linked to Norwegian petroleum activity (Boasson and Lahn 2017). While some studies have explored the political impact of Norway's petroleum industry on climate policy (Gullberg and Skodvin 2011; Boasson 2015), to our knowledge, there have been few studies of the climate mitigation aspects of the political decisionmaking concerning petroleum production in the High North after 2010.

There is a rather scattered literature on renewable energy support and energy efficiency, the issues that have dominated the energy transition in many other European countries. Political attention has been low; and the "global cost-efficiency" discourse was for many years an obstacle to the development of active Norwegian polices in these areas (Boasson 2015). Eventually, however, entrepreneurship from the largest Norwegian utility Statkraft and environmental organizations ensured that Norway joined the Swedish electricity certificate scheme, offering additional support for all new renewable plants. Sweden was an important model for Norwegian policy-makers in this debate (Gullberg and Bang 2014). However, in 2016, Norway decided to stop including *new* Norwegian renewable projects after 2021, primarily because Statkraft now opposed the scheme that led to reduced electricity prices, in turn leading to less income from its hydropower plants. Concerning energy efficiency, Norway has adopted a broad array of measures in buildings and in the industry. Boasson (2015) shows that this was hardly politicized but happened primarily because of implementation of EU policies and initiatives from various governmental agencies. We are not aware of any scholarly assessments of Norwegian energy-efficiency measures targeting industry.

Although transport is responsible for a major share of Norwegian emissions, it has not been central in Norwegian climate policy. There are a few contributions that focus on policy developments regarding electric vehicles, but most research in this field employs economic and engineering perspectives, not those of political science. Generally, Norwegian transport policy is demand-driven, with measures aimed at meeting – not restricting – growth in transport (Osland 2015). However, improving road capacity entails growth in passenger car traffic, which in turn increases emissions (Strand et al. 2009). Some measures like the CO_2 tax on fuels and technology standards have helped improve energy efficiency and thus lower emissions, but this has been neutralized by the overall growth in the transport sector (Aamaas and Fridstrøm 2014; Osland 2015). Electric vehicles have become central in Norwegian climate politics. Initially, the plan was to stimulate the emergence of a domestic automobile industry (Figenbaum et al. 2015). That failed, but the policy measures survived. In 2007, the government introduced a CO_2 component to the sales tax for cars. Electric vehicles have been exempt from this sales tax since 2001, with other privileges added over time, including locally (Figenbaum 2017; Fridstrøm and Østli 2017).

In addition, the Norwegian climate discourse has focused on Norway's international contributions to fighting climate change, like as its international forest initiative REDD+. However, we do not review this literature here, as our focus is on energy governance.

Political Institutions and Actors

Here we present the key institutions and actors in Norwegian discussions on climate and energy policy and politics. However, research on how and to what extent various actors have influenced Norway's energy transition is limited. As Norwegian energy and climate governance research is directed primarily toward exploring policy outcomes in specific issue areas, we know less about the overall importance of the various actors. Here we begin by discussing the role of politicians and political institutions and then move on to the national governmental apparatus, various business actors, and the environmental movement. Lastly, we briefly review the literature on the electorate.

Climate issues have been high on the agenda of most political parties in Norway for quite some time (Andresen and Butenschøn 2001; Boasson and Lahn 2017). Norway is a parliamentary democracy with a proportional representation electoral system. This gives it a multiparty system where coalition governments have been the rule, as the government needs a supportive majority in parliament. The two largest political parties, the Labor Party and the Conservatives, form coalition governments which usually include or rely on support from smaller parties that tend to have a stronger emphasis on climate policy.

While the two largest parties are opponents on other major issues, they are remarkably similar as regards climate change. Both parties support the global cost-efficiency approach (Gullberg 2009: 5; Lahn 2013; Boasson 2015). By contrast, a grouping of smaller parties – the Christian Democrats, Liberal Party, Center Party (former Agrarian Party), and Socialist Left Party – has opposed global cost-efficiency and favored more national action, likewise with the Green Party, which won its first seat in the Storting (Norwegian parliament) in the 2013 elections.

Since 2001, government formation in Norway has relied on the ability of either Labor or the Conservatives to create stable agreements with the smaller parties in the Storting (Boasson and Lahn 2017). This need for alliances with parties that promote domestic-level measures for mitigating climate change has resulted in greater national action on the issue. The Labor Party, the Center Party, and the Socialist Left Party formed a majority coalition government from 2005 to 2013. The right-wing Progress Party is the only party to doubt or deny that climate change is human-induced and was the only parliamentary party that did not support the 2008 climate settlement (see also section "Strategies and Instruments of Energy Transitions"). The climate-skeptical stance of the Progress Party has become muted but continues to surface occasionally. However, the party has supported the global cost-efficiency approach. In October 2013, the Conservatives and the Progress Party formed a coalition government, where the latter supported a government platform that subscribed to the 2008 climate settlement (Jevnaker 2014). However, as the parties in the government coalition represented a minority in the Storting, the government still required support from the Christian Democrats and the Liberal Party. Norwegian climate policy has therefore continued along much the same path as before.

The literature consistently highlights how one politician in particular – Jens Stoltenberg (Labor) – has played a key role in Norwegian climate and energy policy, not only because he was prime minister for 8 years (Andresen and Butenschøn 2001:348; Gullberg and Skodvin 2011:130; Boasson 2015). Stoltenberg was a keen promoter of the global cost-effectiveness approach, but as prime minister of a coalition government he had to accept direct funding of CCS as well as the renewable electricity certificate scheme (Boasson 2015). Already before Stoltenberg became prime minister, Steinar Andresen and Siri Butenschøn wrote (2001):

> Jens Stoltenberg was the main architect behind the Norwegian climate policy during most of the post-Rio interval (Skjærseth Nielsen 1998). He was first the State Secretary in the Ministry of Environment (1990–93) and later the Minister of Energy (1993–1997). His shift of position and strong role may have contributed to the strengthened energy (and economic) dimension of Norwegian climate policy.

A Ministry of Environment was created already in 1972 but has remained small and rather weak (Boasson 2005). It administers emissions trading, but all other climate measures that target production and transmission of energy are administered by the Ministry of Petroleum and Energy. The Ministry of Climate and Environment has had little power to steer national climate policy development ever since the early 1990s (Andresen and Butenschøn 2001:348). In contrast, the Ministry of Finance has a very strong position in the central government; already in the late 1980s, it started to worry that climate politics would reduce Norway's oil revenues. Kristin Asdal (2014:2110) describes how in the late 1980s and the 1990s the Norwegian Ministry of Finance depicted the macroeconomy, and not the environment, as an "object" endangered by climate change. It rapidly succeeded in keeping Norwegian petroleum policy isolated from climate policy debates (see also Andresen and Butenschøn 2001). The Ministry of Finance continues to have a key position in Norwegian climate policy discussions, often teaming up with the Ministry of Petroleum and Energy (e.g., Boasson 2015). This contributes to explain the dominance of the global cost-efficiency approach.

Production and transmission of electricity and petroleum fall within the competence of the Ministry of Petroleum and Energy. Although gathered inside a single ministry, petroleum and electricity are internally organized into separate departments

(Ministry of Petroleum and Energy undated). This division is also reflected in the government agencies that are subsumed under the ministry, with two petroleum agencies and an energy agency. The energy agency (NVE, the Water Resources and Energy Directorate) is responsible for managing Norway's water and energy resources in power production and is the licensing body with regard to construction of new power generation and transmission lines. It also regulates system operation and adopts income regulation for grid companies such as Statnett. As the Norwegian transmission system operator (TSO), Statnett is responsible for building and maintaining the transmission grid; it is a state-owned enterprise subsumed under the ministry. Enova, another state-owned enterprise subsumed under the Ministry of Petroleum and Energy, allocates funding for climate and energy R&D. Enova provides financial support to projects that can reduce GHG emissions, develop energy and climate technology, and strengthen security of supply. For the petroleum sector, a parallel structure exists, with a petroleum agency (Petroleum Directorate), a gas TSO (Gassco), and an R&D enterprise (Gassnova). Gassnova funds petroleum-related projects, such as CCS projects in petroleum and, recently, also carbon capture from industrial processes (Ministry of Petroleum and Energy 2018).

Energy-consuming sectors are regulated by the Ministry of Transport and Communications and by the Ministry of Trade, Industry and Fisheries. These sectors are rarely discussed when energy policy is determined: for instance, they were hardly mentioned in the 2016 white paper on energy policy (Meld. St. 25 2015–2016). Moreover, when Norway reported to the EU on its national target on renewables, the policy measures for increasing the share of renewable energy in consumption concentrated solely on power production, with no measures included from the ministries in charge of energy-consuming sectors (Jevnaker 2016).

Concerning business organizations, differing industry groups have to varying degrees aimed at and succeeded in influencing policy development. Several business organizations engage in climate issues – most prominently, oil and gas, energy-intensive industry, and electricity industry associations. Business primarily supports global cost-efficiency, but the considerable internal conflicts of interest within this grouping rarely surface in political discussions (see Boasson 2015). From 2000 to 2010, energy-intensive industries managed to ensure exemption from CO_2 taxation but were later included in the EU ETS (Gullberg and Skodvin 2011).

Norwegian energy production is dominated by state-owned corporations. The upstream petroleum producer Equinor (formerly known as Statoil), 70% state-owned, dominates petroleum activities (MPE 2015). In the power sector, the transmission network is in state hands, which also applies to roughly 90% of production capacity, at the national and local level. The ten biggest electricity producers together have about 70% of installed capacity in Norway. The largest of them is Statkraft (36% of installed capacity in 2014, with the other nine having less than 10% each), a state-owned company. Public regulations ensure that hydropower will be in public hands, so Norway has not experienced the inflow of foreign utilities seen in most EU countries after the liberalization of the energy sector (Regjeringen 2018).

While Statkraft is subsumed under the Ministry of Trade, Industry and Fisheries to separate regulation from ownership interests, such separation does not exist for

Equinor, where both regulation and ownership are handled by the Ministry of Petroleum and Energy (MPE 2015). That ministry also owns Petoro, a fully state-owned company, which manages the state's substantial direct financial interest (SDFI) on the continental shelf (Petoro 2017) and seeks to ensure the highest possible value creation for the Norwegian state.

Generally, business organizations report having good access to the policy-makers responsible for climate policy, both civil servants in the ministries and the parliament (Gullberg 2011). Environmental groups report good access to politicians, but less access to the ministries. Norway has a broad range of national environmental NGOs, ranging from traditional nature protection organizations to newer groups focusing on climate change (Tjernshaugen 2007; Boasson 2015). The major international environmental group, WWF, gained a foothold in Norway after 2000. Environmentalists in Norway challenge the global cost-efficiency approach but are more positively disposed to market measures than are similar groups in other European countries (Boasson and Lahn 2017). Trade unions have campaigned for greater use of gas domestically, low electricity prices, and continued high investment in petroleum exploration, but have not been deeply engaged in discussions on renewables and energy efficiency.

What then about the *electorate*? In 1989, 40% of polled voters stated that they were "very concerned" about climate change (Tjernshaugen et al. 2011: 334–335; Austgulen and Stø 2013: 144). Concern dropped markedly during the 1990s and early 2000s but increased again toward the end of the decade. Since 2009, some 20% to 30% of those surveyed have consistently ranked climate change among the top challenges facing Norway, rising to 34% in 2015 (TNS Gallup 2015). Survey- and focus group-based research indicates that climate change denial is uncommon in Norway, but there has been increasing polarization over climate concerns: people with less individualistic values and those holding egalitarian values are increasingly concerned about climate change, whereas persons with individualistic and less egalitarian values show less and less concern (Ryghaug et al. 2011; Aasen 2017).

Coordination, Instruments, and Issues of the Norwegian Energy Transition

Strategies and Instruments of Energy Transitions

Together with the USA, Norway was an early champion of ideas such as cost-efficiency and emissions trading. These approaches had a significant imprint on the Kyoto Protocol and later gained prominence in EU policymaking. In 2008, Norway became the first country to declare that it aimed for carbon neutrality: "Norway will reduce global GHGE by an equivalent of 100 per cent of its own emissions by 2050" (Innst. S. nr. 1,45 2007–2008: 2, our translation; see also Gullberg 2009; Boasson 2013). Offsetting Norwegian emissions by paying for emission reductions in other countries was hailed as the key to achieving carbon neutrality.

Except for the initial controversy over introducing gas-power in the electricity system, Norwegian electricity policy discussions and climate policy discussions have not been closely interlinked (Boasson 2015). Climate policy has centered on Norway's role in the global climate negotiations, the development of gas-power plants, CCS technology, and whether to allow petroleum exploration in Arctic waters. Regulation of electricity transmission and production has generally remained depoliticized after the gas-power conflict, with one exception: 2006/2007 discussions on introducing a green certificate scheme (Boasson 2015).

Overarching Targets and Timetables

Norway has adopted overarching climate neutrality targets that reduce the need for transformation at the national level. It has a 2020 carbon neutrality target of reducing emissions by 30% compared to 1990 levels (Jevnaker 2014: 17; Meld. St. 13 2014–2015: 18; Boasson and Lahn 2017). Official documents repeatedly declare that Norway is to become a low-carbon society through the "green transition" (*det grønne skiftet*). A search on the site of the Norwegian parliament shows that this was key term in white papers on many topics: energy policy, research, fishery, forestry, and foreign policy (Stortinget 2018). The term seems influenced by the German energy transition (*Energiewende*), but the exact meaning in the Norwegian context remains unclear. While the German *Energiewende* focuses on national transformation, Norway intends to meet its 2020 neutrality target through extensive procurement of international carbon credits (primarily CDM).

When it became increasingly clear that an agreement establishing a global price on CO_2 would not be adopted soon, the Norwegian government sought instead to ensure international cost-efficiency through closer cooperation with the EU. In February 2015, the government presented the commitment that Norway would deliver to the Paris climate summit in December 2015 (Meld. St. 13 2014–2015). The government declared that Norway intended to be included in the EU effort-sharing decision, not least because this would allow Norway to participate in the flexible mechanisms to be developed for sectors outside the EU ETS. If, however, a common solution with the EU could not be achieved, the EU's 40% reduction target for 2030 compared with 1990 would be Norway's indicative commitment (Christensen 2018). The government did not adopt any national objectives or strategy beyond requesting the EU to include Norway in its effort-sharing agreement.

CO_2 Taxation and the ETS

A few studies from the early 2000s indicate that the introduction of a CO_2 tax in the early 1990s may initially have helped to accelerate technological changes that caused emissions to grow somewhat more slowly than they would have otherwise (Christiansen 2001; Bruvoll and Larsen 2004; Christiansen and Skjærseth 2005). Eventually, the tax was supplemented with the ETS, but the total level of carbon taxation did not change much. There has been a radical increase in emissions from petroleum production after 1990, showing that the economic measures have generally had very limited effect on emission developments.

The EU ETS is central to Norway's climate strategy. It perfectly matches the discourse on cost-efficiency, without threatening growth in the petroleum sector. Norway adopted a CO_2 tax early on and had intended to set up an emissions trading system for sectors not covered by that tax (like steel, cement, and refining). However, the benefits of cooperating with the EU soon became clear. As a result, in 2005 Norway set up a system to prepare for joining the EU ETS, which it did in 2009 (NOU 2012, p. 98). Following expansion of the EU ETS in 2013, almost half of Norway's emissions are covered, which in turn means that in total 80% are included in the ETS and/or covered by a carbon tax (St. meld. 21 2011–2012). Norwegian petroleum activity is covered by a CO_2 tax in addition to the ETS. Compared with other European countries, Norway has a high carbon tax (with some sectoral variations), but the energy taxation level is relatively low (Boasson 2013: 26–27). Beyond the ETS, Norway's onshore energy-intensive industries have been shielded from costly climate policy (Environment Agency 2014a).

In contrast to the dominant global cost-efficiency rhetoric, Norway has adopted a significant number of supplementary measures. For example, it now has direct regulations requiring new onshore gas-power plants to install CCS (St. meld. St. 21 2011–2012).

Renewable Support Schemes

Together with Sweden, Norway has a green certificate scheme for renewable electricity, aimed at increasing renewable electricity production by 26 TWh by 2020 (Boasson 2015). The scheme is planned to run until 2035, but no plants will be included in Norway after year 2020. The scheme is technology-neutral and includes all renewable energy plants, also hydropower.

Various governmental regulations determine the functioning of the market, the key factor being the size of the quota that renewable energy producers are obliged to produce or purchase (Boasson 2015). What the purchaser of a green certificate buys is not the actual energy but a security confirming its economic contribution to the operation of green electricity somewhere within the area where the scheme applies. Such schemes provide operational support, not investment support; and the extra cost is paid by the consumers, not by state funds. Green certificate schemes will yield sizeable profits for companies that can produce renewable energy efficiently and will favor actors large enough to deal with considerable financial risks.

The following actors are required to purchase green certificates: all those that deliver electricity to end users and all those who consume electricity they have produced themselves/bought on the Nordic electricity exchange/required through a bilateral deal (Lov om elsertifikater 2016: §16). Energy-intensive industry may apply for exemptions (Jevnaker 2016). The size of quota that the actors are required to purchase varies according to a predetermined ratio (Lov om elsertifikater 2016: § 17). Quota prices are decided by market forces and have fluctuated significantly over time.

Norway offers modest investment support to individuals who install small-scale renewable plants on their homes, primarily PV and solar heating. Neither commercial nor public buildings are included, only residential buildings (Enova 2016).

A 2020 target for a 20% biofuel share in fuels used in road transport was adopted in 2016. This was connected to the EU's target for 10% renewables in transport, which was included in the 2009 Renewable Energy Directive. However, the choice of biofuels also resulted from pressures from the forestry business and government coalition partners: the right-wing government in power from 2013 needed the support of smaller parties that negotiated for concessions on climate policy (Riksrevisjonen 2018). Norwegian consumption of biofuels has grown strongly, increasing by 140% from 2010 to 2016, with 3.9 TWh in 2016. Consumption doubled from 2015 to 2016. All This is almost entirely reliant on imports, which in 2016 provided roughly 93% of consumption (SSB 2017b).

Energy Consumption

Considerable energy-efficiency measures have been adopted over the years (Boasson 2013: 42–43). There is a state aid scheme for energy-efficiency measures in industry which is not directly related to carbon emissions (Enova 2018), and Norway has developed a series of measures directed at reducing energy consumption in buildings. Enova has developed a cost-minimizing state funding scheme for buildings (Boasson 2015). The energy requirements of the Norwegian building code regulate which techniques and technologies may be applied in building construction. The energy requirements for new and renovated buildings are tightened approximately every 5 years, aimed at achieving a passive house standard (or other demanding holistic standard) in all new buildings from 2020. Energy certification is required of all large nonresidential buildings and other buildings that are rented or sold (NVE 2010; Ot. prp. nr. 24 2008–2009).

In the transport sector, Norway has used exemptions from high tax rates to incentivize consumers to purchase less carbon-intensive automobiles, including electric vehicles (Meld. St. 34 2006–2007: 68). Zero-emission vehicles have been granted various tax exemptions and other benefits, including free parking in all public inner-city parking zones and permission to use priority lanes (TØI 2013). Since 2010, the Norwegian electric vehicle market has become among the largest in Europe – comparable to or even bigger than those of France, Germany, or the UK (TØI 2013). Electric vehicles (28%) and hybrid cars (18%) made up almost half of all new car sales, according to preliminary figures for 2018 (Norsk elbilforening 2018).

The absence of a car manufacturing industry in Norway and the high taxation on car sales may explain some of the policy entrepreneurship in this area. Due to a sharp rise in overall care sales over the past two decades, however, electric vehicles and hybrid plug-ins still comprise only a small share of the overall number of cars (roughly 5% each) (SSB 2018d). Although supporting EVs has been established as a relatively firm path, it was long contested because it ran against the cost-efficiency principle. Although more and more voices have been critical of the benefits accorded to electric vehicles, the benefits have remained unchanged as yet.

Research and Development

Norway has adopted a range of research and development (R&D) programs aimed at unlocking technological change that could resolve the tension between economic growth and increases in emissions. R&D has been promoted through government-owned companies like Enova, which has allocated funding to projects on renewable energy and energy efficiency. R&D programs have sought to bring about technological change that could resolve the tension between economic growth and increases in emissions. Particular research emphasis has been given to carbon capture and storage (CCS), with Norway launching a national project for developing CCS technology that the government compared to a "moon landing." With CCS, gas plants could be built in Norway without adding emissions to the power sector. The government allocated almost €1 billion in funding between 2007 and 2012 and partnered up with major Norwegian petroleum companies like Equinor to establish a CCS test center at Mongstad in 2012. The ambition, supported by parliament, was to have a full-scale facility in place by 2020 (Meld. St. 21 2011–2012: 112–116).

Preparations for full-scale CO_2 capture at the Mongstad gas-fired power plant and refinery were conducted in parallel with the development of the test facility (MoE 2012: 116). A major target has been to realize full-scale CCS by 2020 (MoE 2012). However, the CCS test center experienced problems and repeated delays, and the government's project management was heavily criticized (Office of the Auditor General 2013). In 2014, the conservative government announced a more flexible approach to CCS, opening up the possibility of funding projects abroad. Lack of projects for CO_2 capture in Europe indicated limited demand for storage sites in Norway, so it was decided to postpone large-scale storage projects on the continental shelf until the situation changed (MPE 2014f). Norwegian business interests supported the new approach (see Federation of Norwegian Industries 2014). Having struggled with provisions for extensive private liability under the EU's CO_2 storage directive, interest for CCS in the petroleum sector had reached a nadir for government and business alike (Jevnaker 2016).

CCS in industrial processes emerged as an alternative, and subsequent years saw piloting, with the announcement of three test projects. Following evaluation, all three projects got support for a second phase of tests. The plan was to realize full-scale capture on one installation by 2022 *(Teknisk Ukeblad* 2017a). In 2017, Gassnova provided funding for a project for offshore storage of CO_2 captured via such industrial processes *(Teknisk Ukeblad* 2017b). Following pilots, one project got continued government funding for a feasibility study of CCS in cement. However, the government repeatedly postponed the investment decision on a full-scale installation, and realization remained unclear at the time of this writing *(Teknisk Ukeblad* 2018).

Regarding the phaseout of the use of fossils, the main strategy for decarbonizing fossil fuel-based sectors has been R&D funding. This was announced in a 2016 white paper that outlined Norway's energy strategy (Meld. St. 25 2015–2016; see also below). For instance, the state-owned enterprise Enova should increase its support to climate and energy projects. Projects that would reduce emissions were now to be given priority. Enova's mandate had been extended to transport in 2015. Enova has contributed to funding charging stations for electric vehicles, aiming for continuous availability of speed charging alongside important transit corridors. It would also support projects for electrifying shipping, particularly charging stations for ships in ports (Meld. St. 25 2015–2016, chap. 16).

Energy Exports

Norwegian authorities and petroleum companies alike have been deeply concerned about future demand for Norwegian gas. They have highlighted how Norway needs "security of demand" (in contrast to security of supply): signals of long-term demand from European countries when investing in new petroleum fields (*Teknisk Ukeblad* 2011; Lien 2015).

In theory, Norway's surplus of electricity from large-scale hydro could be exported to underpin energy transformation in other European countries. Despite the expansion of electricity interconnection, this remains a highly contentious topic in Norway – including the idea of Norwegian hydropower as a "green battery" for Europe (Gullberg 2013). At the root of the controversy have been energy-intensive industry keen on cheap electricity and industrial trade unions concerned with employment. The argument has been that electricity trade would lead to higher (European) electricity prices to Norway. Because electricity export is related to expanding electricity production, the nature protection segment of the environmental movement has also been critical to electricity export. The energy-intensives also share a concern for higher production and interconnector construction, as both increase the grid tariffs. On the other hand, electricity producers have been eager to expand export capacity, to avoid price drops triggered by an expansion of renewables (Jevnaker 2016).

In 2016, the Norwegian government released a white paper on energy, the first in 17 years (Meld. St. 25 2015–2016). Some had hoped that the document would outline a broad energy strategy, also on replacing fossil fuel use with renewable energy. However, the primary focus was on electricity production and how to expand its use by sectors already using electricity – with few tangible targets and timetables. On the production side, ensuring security of electricity supply through grid reinforcements was central, as was facilitating *profitable* (non-subsidized) expansions of renewable electricity production. The government also highlighted the commercial opportunities for electricity export (demand abroad), including the potential to exploit hydropower's flexibility to offer balancing services. However, this was balanced against an emphasis on the continuation of attracting (and keeping) new energy-intensive industry demand via access to cheap electricity (Meld. St. 25 2015–2016). Thus, the Norwegian government was essentially caught between the demands of its energy-intensive industries and those of the power-producing industries and sought a compromise approach by exiting the green certificates scheme after 2020 and taking a gradual approach to expanding trade via new interconnectors.

Drivers of the Energy Transition and Multilevel Governance

Climate governance research on the Norwegian energy transition has been patchy, so we lack a basis for robust conclusions as to which actors and factors have promoted or obstructed the adoption and implementation of various policies and measures. Deep disagreement over what an ambitious climate and energy transition should entail, and the wide use of the ambiguous term *det grønne skiftet* (the green transition), makes explanations difficult. In the following, we discuss the role of the EU and how various coalition governments have had to offer green concessions to smaller parties in order to secure a parliamentary majority.

Although not an EU member, Norway cooperates closely through the Agreement on the European Economic Area (EEA Agreement). The EU and Norway face diverging energy transformation challenges – the former with imported fossil fuels dominating the power and heating sectors and the latter as a major petroleum exporter with a hydro-based power system covering most of its heating needs. EU climate and energy policy tailored to the EU situation does not necessarily assist Norway: while the EU sought a transition in which sustainability could be combined with energy security, such a link could not be made in Norway, thereby reducing the scope for synergies envisaged in Brussels (Jevnaker 2016). There is more common ground on transport, but Norway has been more ambitious than the EU (Gulbrandsen and Christensen 2014). The EU has struggled to tighten its climate stringency in transport policy and has thus not been a driver for Norwegian developments (Jevnaker 2016).

EU policies have promoted the Norwegian energy transition in some instances while obstructing it in other areas. Boasson (2015) finds that, between 2000 and 2010, Norway implemented EU policies relating to renewables and EU energy policy for buildings and carbon capture and storage – but these policies had little direct influence on a Norwegian transition. However, EU climate and energy policy gained importance with the 2009 EU climate and energy package, notably with revamped emissions trading and national renewable targets (Jevnaker 2016). Although emissions trading was well-aligned with Norway's emphasis on cost-efficiency and cross-sectoral climate regulation, the EU's decision to shield the petroleum sector from carbon pricing from 2013 onward challenged Norwegian practice. Norway managed to counter this by increasing the CO_2 levy (Jevnaker 2016). The EU-mandated national renewable target did little for Norway's already decarbonized power and heating sectors. Nevertheless, because of how the renewable share is calculated, Norway could achieve the target by expanding its capacity for renewable electricity production (Statistics Norway 2014: 8; Boasson 2015; Jevnaker 2016). Here, EU state aid regulations significantly constrained the development of support schemes for renewables as well as the energy performance of buildings (Boasson 2015).

However, growth in electricity production without sufficient interconnector capacity for exporting surplus electricity entails the risk of a drop in domestic prices, which is why Norway eventually decided to leave the green certificates scheme with Sweden. While Norway might increase its renewable share by decarbonizing transport, no measures have been reported to the EU (Jevnaker 2016). Finally, the renewable target did not contribute to replacing fossils with renewables in energy consumption within the petroleum sector, because energy used in connection with energy production is not included in the Renewable Energy Directive's calculation of a country's renewable share (Statistics Norway 2014: 8). Overall, then, neither climate nor energy policies from the EU have driven emission reduction in Norway's main emitting sectors (Jevnaker 2016).

National factors differ substantially from one issue area to another (Boasson 2015). CCS stands out, due to the massive amounts of time and energy that elected politicians have spent on the issue (Boasson 2015). And yet, no large-scale CCS facility has been constructed in Norway, and it is uncertain whether that will ever occur. Most other issue areas have experienced brief instances of politicization, whereas initiatives have generally been propelled by governmental experts, environmental groups or business organizations, or a combination of the three (Boasson 2015).

For several decades, Norway's small left-leaning or centrist political parties whose support has been needed to form a government have been clear drivers of policy change, although perhaps not truly transformative change (Jevnaker 2014, 2016; Boasson 2015). While the smaller parties have not been able to change the overall course of Norwegian climate and energy policy, they have managed to score smaller, symbolic victories on climate issues and occasionally more important ones. However, these concessions have not brought about a change in course, like preventing the opening of new licensing rounds for new petroleum fields or halting the rising emissions from transport in general. An important exception is the favorable regulatory framework for electric vehicles, and partly CCS, which was pushed also by the major parties.

Examples of political concessions that junior coalition parties were able to secure include the compromise on the distribution of emission reductions, where the Socialist Left Party managed to secure that two-thirds would be reduced domestically, not through international flexible mechanisms. In practice, however, this was watered down and hidden behind a forest of nitty-gritty formulations on baselines and how to calculate them (Jevnaker 2014: 17).

Outcomes, Challenges, and Prospects

How has Norwegian climate and energy governance developed over time? To what extent and how are the key energy transition dilemmas covered in the Norwegian climate governance literature? Here we have paid particular attention to the transition of the stationary electricity system (production, transmission, and use of electricity) while also noting overarching energy transition challenges related to offshore petroleum production and energy use in transportation. Moreover, we have highlighted the debate – among academics and practitioners alike – on whether the key challenge is to reduce emissions domestically or to contribute to global climate mitigation.

The global cost-efficiency discourse has dominated for several decades. But despite the focus on carbon pricing and financing low-cost emission reductions abroad, Norway has adopted an array of sector-specific climate measures. It has become increasingly common to label policies and measures across various sectors as part of the larger "green transition" (*det grønne skiftet*), but fundamental unclarity persists as to what this entails and what the overarching objectives are. Part of the confusion stems from the unique climate challenges facing Norway, with increasing emissions from oil and gas and hardly any emissions from electricity production. The abundant, and growing, electricity production from large hydro and other renewable energy sources is regarded as problematic, since it leads to low electricity prices. Hence, Norway is in a very different situation than many other European countries.

The EU has clearly, and increasingly, contributed to Norwegian climate and energy policy via the EEA Agreement, but its policies have not triggered significant transition in Norway so far. Domestic politics play an important role, although the two major political parties have long focused on the traditional global cost-efficiency approach. The separation between different strands of policies relevant to a green transition is made sharper by the decentralized ministerial structure, with weak means of enforcing cross-sectoral coordination. The Ministry of Finance is perhaps the only ministry that could push for greater coordination: but, deeply immersed in the cost-efficiency discourse, its efforts serve mainly to uphold the status quo. The separation continues all the way down, throughout the public administration. At the political level, Norwegian politicians face cross-pressure from the country's petroleum, energy-intensive, and power-producing industries. This too contributes to a status quo orientation.

The Norwegian electoral system has created a multiparty system where governments depend on the support of minor parties; and such junior coalition partners tend to be more "green" in orientation. As a result, green concessions emerge from government negotiations, although specific choices and instruments may often be traced back to interest groups. Measures in transport stem from government coalition deals, trumping the cost-efficiency logic.

Behind politics lie business interests. The absence of a domestic fossil fuel-based car industry made it easier to introduce measures promoting electric vehicles. The opposite was the case with biofuels, which was pushed by the forestry industry. Despite "green" tweaks to government platforms, coalition deals have not entailed a change of overall course in Norway's energy and climate policy.

There exists a significant literature on climate and energy governance, but it is too scattered and incoherent to enable solid conclusions to be drawn concerning the relative importance of the various actors and factors that shape Norwegian policy development. In particular, more systematic and comparative literature across issue areas is needed, and larger projects that aim to conceptualize and explain shifts and turns in the Norwegian energy transition policy portfolio over time. Comparisons with other countries could also enable clearer specification of the drivers and hurdles that are especially salient in the case of Norway.

Cross-References

▶ Energy Governance in Germany
▶ Energy Governance in Sweden

References

Aamaas, B., & Fridstrøm, L. (2014). Klimagassutslipp fra norsk transport. In L. Fridstrøm & K. H. Alfsen (Eds.), *Vegen mot klimavennlig transport* (TØI-rapport 1321/2014). Oslo: Transportøkonomisk Institutt.
Aasen, M. (2017). The polarization of public concern about climate change in Norway. *Climate Policy, 17*(2), 213–230.
Andresen, S., & Butenschøn, S. H. (2001). Norwegian climate policy: From pusher to laggard? *International Environmental Agreements, 1*, 337–356.
Asdal, K. (2014). From climate issue to oil issue. *Environment and Planning A, 46*, 2110–2124.
Austgulen, M. H. & Stø, E. (2013). Norsk skepsis og usikkerhet om klimaendringer. *Tidsskrift for samfunnsforskning, 54*, 124–150.
Austvik, O. G., & Claes, D. H. (2011). *EØS-avtalen og norsk energipolitikk*. Oslo: Europautredningen.
Boasson, E. L. (2005). *Klimaskapte beslutningsendringer?[a new climate for decision-making?]* (FNI report 13/2005). Lysaker: Fridtjof Nansen Institute.
Boasson, E. L. (2013). *National climate policy ambitiousness* (CICERO report 2013:02). Oslo: CICERO.
Boasson, E. L. (2015). *National Climate Policy*. London: Routledge.
Boasson, E. L., & Lahn, B. (2017). Norway: A dissonant cognitive leader? In R. K. W. Wurzel, J. Connelly, & D. Liefferink (Eds.), *Still taking a lead? The European Union in international climate change politics* (pp. 189–203). London: Routledge.
Bruvoll, A., & Larsen, B. M. (2004). Greenhouse gas emissions in Norway: Do carbon taxes work? *Energy Policy, 32*, 493–505.
Christensen, L. (2018). Norges klimamål for 2030. Fra global til europeisk kostnadseffektivitet. *Norsk statsvitenskapelig tidsskrift, 34*. 02-03/2018 (no page numbers on electronic version).
Christiansen, A. C. (2001). Climate policy and dynamic efficiency gains: A case study on Norwegian CO2-taxes and technological innovation in the petroleum sector. *Climate Policy, 1*(4), 499–515.
Christiansen, A. C., & Skjærseth, J. B. (2005). Climate change politics in Norway and the Netherlands: Different instruments, similar outcome? *Energy & Environment, 16*(1), 1–25.
Eckersley, R. (2016). National identities, international roles, and the legitimation of climate leadership: Germany and Norway compared. *Environmental Politics, 25*(1), 180–201.
Enova. (2016). *Solenergi: El-produksjon*. https://www.enova.no/privat/alle-energitiltak/solenergi/el-produksjon-/ Published 27 December 2016, Accessed December 16, 2018.
Enova. (2018). *Industri og anlegg*. https://www.enova.no/bedrift/industri-og-anlegg/. Accessed December 16, 2018.
Equinor. (undated). *Natural gas*. https://www.equinor.com/en/what-we-do/natural-gas.html. Accessed December 17, 2018.
Eurostat. (2018). *Passenger cars in the EU*. https://ec.europa.eu/eurostat/statistics-explained/index.php/Passenger_cars_in_the_EU. Data extracted in April 2018, Accessed December 11, 2018.
Federation of Norwegian Industries. (2014). Brev til SMK - Regjeringens arbeid knyttet til CO2-fangst, transport og lagring (CCS) – anbefalinger. On file with author.

Figenbaum, E. (2017). Perspectives on Norway's supercharged electric vehicle policy. *Environmental Innovation and Societal Transitions, 25*, 14–34.

Figenbaum, E., Assum, T., & Kolbeinstveit, M. (2015). Electromobility in Norway: Experiences and opportunities. *Research in Transportation Economics, 50*, 29–38.

Fridstrøm, L., & Østli, V. (2017). The vehicle purchase tax as a climate policy instrument. *Transportation Research Part A: Policy and Practice, 96*, 168–189.

Gulbrandsen, L. H., & Christensen, A. R. (2014). EU legislation to reduce Car emissions. *Review of Policy Research, 31*, 503–528.

Gullberg, A. T. (2009). *Norsk klimapolitisk debatt og klimaforliket fra 2008 [Norwegian climate policy and the 2008 climate agreement]* (CICERO Working Paper 2009:3). Oslo: CICERO.

Gullberg, A. T. (2011). Access to climate policy-making in the European Union and in Norway. *Environmental Politics, 20*(4), 464–484.

Gullberg, A. T. (2013). The political feasibility of Norway as the "green battery" of Europe. *Energy Policy, 57*, 615–623.

Gullberg, A. T. (2015). Lobbying in Oslo or in Brussels? The case of a European economic area country. *Journal of European Public Policy, 22*(10), 1531–1550.

Gullberg, A. T., & Bang, G. (2014). Look to Sweden: The making of a new renewable energy support scheme in Norway. *Scandinavian Political Studies, 38*(1), 95–114.

Gullberg, A. T., & Skodvin, T. (2011). Cost effectiveness and target group influence in Norwegian climate policy. *Scandinavian Political Studies, 34*(2), 123–142.

Hall, M. (2018). *Norwegian gas exports: Assessment of resources and supply to 2035* (OIES Paper NG 127). Oxford: Oxford Institute for Energy Studies.

Hofstad, K. (2018). Kjernekraft i Norge. *Store Norske Leksikon*. https://snl.no/kjernekraft_i_Norge

Hovden, E. & Lindseth, G. (2004). Discourses in Norwegian Climate Policy: National Action or Thinking Globally? *Political Studies, 52*(1), 63–81

Innst. S. nr. 145. (2007–2008). *Innstilling fra energi- og miljøkomiteen om norsk klimapolitikk [recommendation from the standing committee on energy and environment on Norwegian climate policy]*. Oslo: The Storting.

Jevnaker, T. (2014). *Norway's implementation of the EU climate and energy package: Europeanization or cherry-picking?* (FNI report 7). Lysaker: Fridtjof Nansen Institute.

Jevnaker, T. (2016). Implementation in Norway. In J. B. Skjærseth, P. O. Eikeland, L. H. Gulbrandsen, & T. Jevnaker (Eds.), *Linking EU climate and energy policies: Decision-making, implementation and reform* (pp. 175–203). Cheltenham: Edward Elgar.

Jevnaker, T., Lunde, L., & Skjærseth, J. B. (2015). EU–Norway energy relations towards 2050: From fossil fuels to low-carbon opportunities. In C. Dupont & S. Oberthür (Eds.), *Decarbonization in the European Union: Internal policies and external strategies* (pp. 222–243). Palgrave Macmillan. isbn:ISBN 9781137406828.

Lahn, B. (2013). *Klimaspillet* [The climate game], Oslo: Flamme.

Langhelle, O., & Ishii, A. (2011). Toward policy integration: Assessing carbon capture and storage policies in Japan and Norway. *Global Environmental Change, 21*, 358–367.

Lien, T. (2015). Role of gas in EU energy policy must be recognised. *Euractiv*, November 30. https://www.euractiv.com/section/energy/opinion/role-of-gas-in-eu-energy-policy-must-be-recognised/. Accessed December 18, 2018.

Lov om el-sertifikater. (2016). https://lovdata.no/dokument/NL/lov/2011-06-24-39, https://www.regjeringen.no/contentassets/f6a0df1f2c244c35b95818dfe7a2dbb3/energinorge.pdf

Meld. St. 13. (2014–2015). *Ny utslippsforpliktelse for 2030—En felles løsning med EU [white paper: New emissions requirements for 2030—Common solution with the EU]*. February 2015. Oslo: Ministry of Climate and Environment.

Meld. St. 21. (2011–2012). *Norsk klimapolitikk [white paper: Norwegian climate policy]*. April 2012. Oslo: Ministry of Environment.

Meld. St. 25. (2015–2016). *Kraft til endring. Energipolitikken mot 2030*. Oslo: Olje- og energidepartementet.

Meld. St. 34. (2006–2007). *Norsk klimapolitikk [white paper: Norwegian climate policy]*. June 2007. Oslo: Ministry of Environment.

Miljøstatus. (2015). *Globale utslipp av klimagasser [Global emissions of climate gases]*. http://www.miljostatus.no/tema/klima/globale-utslipp-klimagasser/. Published October 30, 2015, Accessed January 12, 2016.

Ministry of Climate and Environment (2012). Norsk klimapolitikk (Meld.St.21 (2011–2012)) Oslo: Ministry of Climate and Environment.

Ministry of Climate and Environment. (2015). *The background of Norwegian Carbon Credit Program*. https://www.regjeringen.no/no/tema/klima-og-miljo/klima/innsiktsartikler-klima/norwegian-carbon-credit-procurement-program/the-background-of-norwegian-carbon-credit-program/id2415679/. Accessed January 6, 2016.

Ministry of Petroleum and Energy. (2014). *Fakta 2014: Norsk petroleumsverksemd [fact sheet 2014: Norwegian petroleum activity]*. Oslo: Ministry of Petroleum and Energy.

Ministry of Petroleum and Energy. (2015). https://www.regjeringen.no/contentassets/fd89d9e2c39a4ac2b9c9a95bf156089a/1108774830_897155_fakta_energi-vannressurser_2015_nett.pdf

Ministry of Petroleum and Energy. (2018). *Etater og virksomheter under Olje- og energidepartementet [Subordinated agencies and affiliated enterprises under the Ministry of Petroleum and Energy]*. https://www.regjeringen.no/no/dep/oed/org/etater-og-virksomheter-under-olje–og-energidepartementet/id2409321/ Updated July 2 2018, accessed July 1, 2018.

Ministry of Petroleum and Energy. (undated) *Organisation* https://www.regjeringen.no/en/dep/oed/organisation/id774/. Accessed December 17, 2018.

Normann, H. E. (2017). Policy networks in energy transitions: The cases of carbon capture and storage and offshore wind in Norway. *Technological Forecasting and Social Change, 11*, 80–93.

Norsk elbilforening. (2018). *Statistikk elbil*. https://elbil.no/elbilstatistikk/ Updated September 30, 2018. Accessed December 18, 2018.

Norsk petroleum. (2018). http://www.norskpetroleum.no/en/production-and-exports/exports-of-oil-and-gas/ Updated 21 December. Accessed December 18, 2018.

NOU. (2012). *Innenfor og utenfor: Norges avtaler med EU (NOU 2012 (2))*. Oslo: Norges offentlige utredninger.

NVE. (2010). *Forskrift om energimerking av bygninger og energivurdering av tekniske anlegg. Forslag til endringer i forskrift av 18.12.2009 nr.* 1665. Oslo: Norwegian Water Resources and Energy Directorate.

NVE. (2018). *Energibruk i Norge*. Issued June 11, 2015, updated September 17, 2018. https://www.nve.no/energibruk-og-effektivisering/energibruk-i-norge/

Osland, O. (2015). Økologisk modernisering i transportsektoren. *Norsk statsvitenskapelig tidsskrift, 31*, 221–245.

Petoro. (2017). *A driving force offshore Norway*. https://www.petoro.no/home. Accessed November 10, 2017.

Regjeringen. (2018). *Organisering og eierskap i kraftsektoren*. https://www.regjeringen.no/globalassets/upload/oed/pdf_filer/faktaheftet/evfakta08/evfakta08_kap05_no.pdf. Accessed December 18, 2018.

Riksrevisjonen. (2018). *Undersøkelse av myndighetenes satsing på bioenergi for å redusere utslipp av klimagasser [Auditor General's investigation of bioenergy measures to reduce GHG emissions]*. Oslo: Riksrevisjonen [Office of the Auditor General].

Roettereng, J. S. (2016). How the global and national levels interrelate in climate policymaking: Foreign policy analysis and the case of carbon capture storage in Norway's foreign policy. *Energy Policy, 97*, 475–484.

Ryghaug, M., Sørensen, K. H., & Næss, R. (2011). Making sense of global warming: Norwegians appropriating knowledge of anthropogenic climate change. *Public Understanding of Science, 20*, 778–795.

Sæverud, I. A., & Wettestad, J. (2006). Norway and emissions trading. *International Environmental Agreements, 6*, 91–108.

SSB. (2017a). *Netto innenlands forbruk eksl råstoff.* https://www.ssb.no/energi-og-industri/statistikker/energibalanse/aar-forelopige. Updated June 28, 2017, Accessed December 17, 2018.

SSB. (2017b). *Bruk av biodrivstoff i transport.* https://www.ssb.no/natur-og-miljo/artikler-og-publikasjoner/bruk-av-biodrivstoff-i-transport. Updated August 9, Accessed December 18, 2018.

SSB. (2018a). *Elektrisitet.* https://www.ssb.no/energi-og-industri/statistikker/elektrisitet/aar. Updated November 29, 2018, Accessed December 12, 2018.

SSB. (2018b). *Utslipp til luft.* https://www.ssb.no/klimagassn. Updated and accessed December 11, 2018.

SSB. (2018c). *Registrerte kjøretøy.* https://www.ssb.no/transport-og-reiseliv/statistikker/bilreg/aar. Updated March 22, 2018, Accessed December 11, 2018.

SSB. (2018d). *Over 140 000 Elbiler i Norge.* https://www.ssb.no/transport-og-reiseliv/artikler-og-publikasjoner/over-140-000-elbiler-i-norge. Updated March 22, 2018, Accessed December 11, 2018.

SSB. (2018e). *Produksjon og forbruk av energi, energibalanse.* https://www.ssb.no/energibalanse. Updated November 28, 2018; Accessed December 13, 2018.

SSB. (2018f). *StatBank Norway. Statistical Database.* https://www.ssb.no/en/statbank

Statistics Norway. (2014). Fornybar energibruk i EU og Norge: Høye mål for fornybar energi. Samfunnsspeilet no. 3. https://www.ssb.no/energi-og-industri/artikler-og-publikasjoner/_attachment/183137?_ts=146a4801d30. Accessed November 2, 2017.

Statnett. (2017). *Pågående prosjekter.* http://www.statnett.no/Nettutvikling/. Accessed November 10, 2017.

Stortinget. (2018). *Stortinget.* https://stortinget.no/no/# Accessed December 18, 2018.

Strand, A., Næss, P., Tennøy, A., & Steinsland, C. (2009). *Gir bedre veier mindre klimautslipp? TØI-rapport 1027.* Oslo: Transportøkonomisk Institutt.

Teknisk Ukeblad. (2011). *Risikerer stort fall i gassforsyningen,* September 29. https://www.tu.no/artikler/risikerer-stort-fall-i-gassforsyningen/246949. Accessed December 17, 2018.

Teknisk Ukeblad. (2017a). *Mer CO2-fangst ved Norcem, Yara og på Klemetsrud,* April 19. https://www.tu.no/artikler/mer-co2-fangst-ved-norcem-yara-og-pa-klemetsrud/380257. Accessed December 18, 2018.

Teknisk Ukeblad. (2017b). *Shell, Total og Statoil går sammen for å lagre CO2 på norsk sokkel,* October 2. https://www.tu.no/artikler/shell-og-total-skal-hjelpe-statoil-lagre-co2-fra-industrien-pa-norsk-sokkel/408687. Accessed December 17, 2018.

Teknisk Ukeblad. (2018). *Regjeringen dropper Yara, og utsetter CO2-rensing på nytt,* May 14, 2018. https://www.tu.no/artikler/dropper-yara-og-utsetter-co2-rensing-pa-nytt/437452. Accessed December 17, 2018.

Tellmann, S. T. (2012). The constrained influence of discourses: The case of Norwegian climate policy. *Environmental Politics, 21,* 734–752.

Tjernshaugen, A. (2007). *Gasskraft [Gas power].* Oslo: Pax.

Tjernshaugen, A. (2011). The growth of political support for CO2 capture and storage in Norway. *Environmental Politics, 20,* 227–245.

Tjernshaugen, A., & Langhelle, O. (2011). CCS som politisk lim. In J. Hanson, S. Kasa & O. Wicken (Eds.), *Energirikdommens paradokser: Innovasjon som klimapolitikk og næringsutvikling* (pp. 172–194). Oslo: Universitetsforlaget.

Tjernshaugen, A., Aardal, B., & Gullberg, A. T. (2011). Det første klimavalget? [the first climate election? Environmental and climate issues in the 2009 elections]. In B. Aardal (Ed.), *Det politiske landskap.* Oslo: Cappelen Damm Akademisk.

TNS Gallup. (2015). *TNS Gallup Klimabarometer 2015,* http://www.tns-gallup.no/documentfile1906?pid=Native-ContentFile-File. Accessed January 20, 2016.

TØI. (2013). 85g CO2 per kilometer i 2020, *TØI report* 1264/2013. Oslo: Institute of Transport Economics. Available at https://www.toi.no/getfile.php?mmfileid=33029, Accessed January 20, 16.

Wicken, O. (2011). Kraft frå infrastruktur til marked. In J. Hanson, S. Kasa, & O. Wicken (Eds.), *Energirikdommens paradokser: Innovasjon som klimapolitikk og næringsutvikling* (pp. 126–144). Oslo: Universitetsforlaget.

Energy Governance in the Republic of Poland

Maksymilian Zoll

Contents

Introduction	924
General Conditions of Energy Governance	925
Past Legacies	925
Composition of the "Energy Mix"	930
Discourse on Energy Issues	932
Political Institutions and Actors	934
Coordination of Polish Instruments and Issues of Energy Transitions Within the Multilevel Context	937
Drivers of Energy Transition	938
Strategies and Instruments of Energy Transitions	940
Coordination Mechanisms and Multilevel Governance	943
Outcomes, Challenges, and Prospects of Polish Energy Governance	945
Monitoring and Surveillance	945
Sector Integration	946
Prospects of Polish Energy Governance	948
Cross-References	950
References	950

Abstract

Governance of energy transitions has become an issue of growing prominence in the social sciences and in political practice. Examining the understudied case of the "least climate ambitious" European Union Member State, Poland, the investigation demonstrates that it has a highly centralized energy system in decision-making. Employing a state-led governance approach, which includes an overlap between political and administrative actors in terms of personal and organizational capacity, the analysis highlights the government to act as the primary actor

M. Zoll (✉)
Institute of Political Science, Technical University of Darmstadt, Darmstadt, Germany
e-mail: zoll@pg.tu-darmstadt.de

© Springer Nature Switzerland AG 2022
M. Knodt, J. Kemmerzell (eds.), *Handbook of Energy Governance in Europe*,
https://doi.org/10.1007/978-3-030-43250-8_22

within the energy sector. As such, it is involved not only in regulating market conditions but also in exercising substantial influence and control over the market participants. While the country's key resource coal increasingly faces challenges, e.g., increasing lack of social acceptance due to environmental problems, high cost to maintain the level of production, and looming power generation gap, the government remains committed to "stand on coal." The development of renewable energy sources has been actively hindered by substantial changes in the legal framework. Public discourse about energy issues is strongly economized and is favoring opinions and attitudes of experts, politicians, and government actors, while the perspective of sustainable development is marginalized. External support, particular from the EU, plays a decisive role for the future directions of the energy transition. It is largely occurring on the regional and local level where municipalities are developing a progressive agenda on climate and renewable energy issues.

Keywords

Energy policy · Climate policy · Coal · Renewables · Electricity · Energy transition · Energy Governance · Poland

Introduction

The Republic of Poland is often termed a "laggard" (Jänicke and Quitzow 2017) and "least climate ambitious" (Climate Action Network Europe 2018) with regard to energy and climate policy when compared with the EU's Member States (Agora Energiewende and Sandbag 2018). Apparent nonexistent progress and constraints of energy transition were explained by past research related to norm diffusion and Europeanization (cf. Jankowska 2011, 2017; Ancygier 2013; Ceglarz and Ancygier 2015; Wedel 2016; Jankowska and Ancygier 2017; Skjærseth 2018) while "ignoring domestic political and organizational fields and the material and structural constraints of the energy system and resource endowment" (Szulecki 2017). While institutional and instrumental capacities of energy policy are relevant factors of energy transition (Ikenberry 1986), much literature pays attention to key actors without defining more precisely the enabling structures in which they are embedded (Geels and Schot 2007). Accordingly, conditions of Poland's energy transition governance dynamics are of major interest in this chapter since existing literature found that, e.g., external shocks, green parties, and the resource endowment or topographical conditions of country all to be driving energy paths of this process (cf. Geels et al. 2016).

National energy transitions in the European Union are, however, embedded not only in domestic governance structures but also in international agreements, most recently the Paris Agreement on Climate Change of 2015 as well as the European Energy Union. Accordingly, Poland's energy policy is embedded in a comprehensive multilevel governance architecture, entailing commitments to renewable energy,

energy efficiency, and climate policy, which, following Kemmerzell and Hofmeister (2019), is understood in terms of climate protection and measures aimed at avoiding or mitigating climate change by reducing greenhouse gas (GHG) emissions. Reflecting earlier research, energy security (Judge and Maltby 2017) and economic progress (Szulecka and Szulecki 2013) have been prioritized over the environmental and climate dimension in the past. Mirrored in the public and political debate, which is characterized by a wide lack of awareness on climate issues (Jankowska 2011; Marcinkiewicz and Tosun 2015; Kundzewicz et al. 2017), interest groups and energy representatives often voice strong doubts about both the form of and the need for global climate protection efforts (Cianciara 2017; Szulecki 2018). Likewise, none of the nation's political parties within parliament has ever fully supported the EU's long-term decarbonization vision or made a clear statement on the limitation of coal (i.e., hard coal and lignite) in the economy (Karaczun et al. 2013:191ff; Fuksiewicz and Klein 2014) with coal-biomass-based co-firing, in line with EU regulations, having a significant share in the renewable energy mix. Particularly the current Prawo i Sprawiedliwość (PiS) government, which is highly climate-skeptical, has been visibly slow with implementing the law on renewable energy sources (Ciepiela 2018), instead continuing to defend clean coal technologies and technological neutrality (Skjærseth 2018). The commitment to "stand on coal" (*Polska węglem stoi*) as the backbone of the economy despite shortcomings, e.g., high CO_2 content, local air pollutants, and negative health impacts (Interview 2017a, b, c, d, e; Vasev 2017), is reimaging the historical slogan in connection with the strategic importance of guaranteeing energy security and national sovereignty (Kuchler and Bridge 2018; Herold et al. 2017). Building in its argumentation on government documents, legislation and reports from public energy actors, previous conducted third-party research, as well as semi-structured expert interviews that took place between 2017 and 2018, this chapter will demonstrate that this process is largely driven by the political and organizational fields (Szulecki 2017), as well as a glamorized vision of the coal industry in terms of social, electoral, and economic policy considerations (Kuchler and Bridge 2018).

General Conditions of Energy Governance

Past Legacies

The energy system of the socialist Polish People's Republic founded after WWII focused upon coal-powered heavy industry, with production and consumption of energy growing rapidly as nationalization and central planning were adopted to all financial activities and industrial sectors (Kuchler and Bridge 2018, pp. 138–141). The democratic transition of 1989–1990 coincided with an economic "shock therapy" (Balcerowicz plan) initiated by the new government that altered the state socialist planned economy to a capitalist free-market economy (Sachs 1992, 1994; Gomułka 2016). Together with globalization and Europeanization pressures of the early 1990s, a variety of transformations and liberalizations unfolded, including the energy sector which was "inefficient, centralized, highly polluting and dependent on Russia" (Bradshaw 2014, pp. 84–119 as cited in Wagner et al. 2016, p. 160).

Consuming 77 million tons of coal per year, Poland is the 12th largest coal consumer in the world and the 2nd largest in the European Union (EU), after Germany (World Energy Council 2014). In 2016, hard coal production stood at 70.7 million tons and lignite production at 60.2 million tons (Central Statistical Office 2017). The majority of these reserves are processed in large hard coal or lignite power plants like Bełchatów, suppling 20% of electricity to the national system and the largest lignite power plant in Europe, or Kozienice, the country's largest hard coal plant, providing 8% of the country's electricity alone (World Energy Council 2014; International Energy Agency 2016). Except for a power plant near Szczecin in the North-West, all major plants are situated either in the Center or South/South-West of the country, leaving the North and East to face energy poverty and vulnerability in terms of energetic resources. This dominance is expected to change drastically in the upcoming years as the coal industry is increasingly pressured by various environmental, social, and economic restraints (Baran et al. 2018).

Key restraint is the struggle with profitability of mines due to higher extraction costs as the best and lowest coal deposits have long been depleted (Jonek Kowalska 2015, pp. 144–145; Barteczko and Koper 2017). As high as 80% coal mines are declared unprofitable, and, despite government subsidies, the coal mining industry has a reported loss of PLN 4.5 billion (= EUR 1.05 billion) back in 2015. This is largely due to the high level of coal production costs, coupled with a steady decrease in the revenues from coal sales and growing debt (Herold et al. 2017). A second issue concerns high environmental damages. The aforementioned lignite plant Bełchatów is the EU's most polluting power plant with CO_2 emissions 25% higher than the second most polluting (Euractiv 2018). Likewise, the lack of coal standards results in many households burning low-quality coal in stoves for heating, exacerbating the smog problem (Nabrdalik and Santora 2018). Unsurprisingly with 33 of the EU's 50 most polluted cities, Poland exhibits the worst air quality in Europe (cf. Rylukowski 2016). Smog is the most noticeable sign for this (Huber 2016; Berendt 2017; Interview 2017e, 2018a; Simon 2017), with drastic health implications for the population (Interview 2017e; Vasev 2017; Włodarski and Martyniuk-Pęczek 2017). The fight against air pollution slowly becomes a government policy with potential countermeasures being discussed in light of national legislation originating from the European regulations (e.g., Adamczyk et al. 2017). Nevertheless, on 22 February 2018, the European Court of Justice (ECJ) ruled that Poland had excessively high concentrations of fine dust that causes lung diseases (ECJ Case C-336/16). This increases the lack of local acceptance and protests against the opening of new mines (cf.; Badera 2014, p. 29; Badera and Kocoń 2014; Simon 2017).

Lastly, there is the issue of labor force as coal extraction is labor intensive. In the early 1990s, there were 400,000 miners; today the number is around 82,000 to 100,000 people directly employed in the sector, representing a decline of approximately 80% to nearly 10% of the coal workforce. These 82,000 are equal to 0.7% of the country's total (Bukowski et al. 2015, pp. 9–11; Herold et al. 2017; Gawlik 2018) with further downscaling foreseeable (Witajewski-Baltvilks et al. 2018). The establishment of strong trade unions with significant interests in maintaining the coal industry and coal-supportive policies plays a decisive role in the country's overall employment sector (Manowska et al. 2017; Baran et al. 2018). The sector employs a high-skilled workforce with expertise not easily transferable to other sectors (Witajewski-Baltvilks et al. 2018). Thus, the mining sector is among the most important economic sectors but lacks profitability and faces environmental problems, falling prices on global markets, as well as increasing pressure from the EU to reduce CO2 emissions. This has affected governments since 1989 to avoid the politically and socially awkward debate about the future of the mining industry (Popkiewicz 2015, pp. 78–79); cf. also Kuchler and Bridge 2018).

Although overall energy dependency rate increased over time due to the changes in the energy market after the breakdown of the Eastern Bloc, the high share of indigenous coal helps to make Poland among the least energy-dependent Member States in the EU-28 (Fig. 1). The heavy industry sector began to experience problems as it was exposed to a global market with increased competition. Consequently, natural gas was seen as the best and cheapest alternative to satisfy energy needs, but domestic reserves of gas are scarce, making it necessary to increase its imports in Poland (cf. World Energy Council 2014).

The dependency on Russia as the dominant distributor of gas supply is reflected in the circumstance that it is the source of 55% of Poland's natural gas consumption in 2015 and 72% of its imports (International Energy Agency 2016, p. 140). This puts Poland in relation to gas from Russia in what Keohane and Nye (1989 [2012])

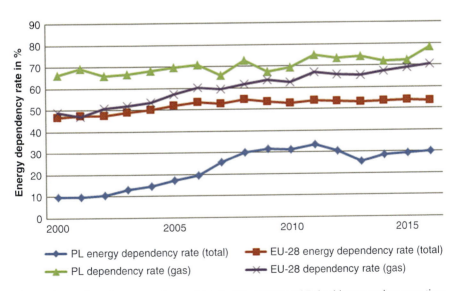

Fig. 1 Energy dependency rates (gas and total) of the EU-28 and Poland in comparison over time (2000–2016, %). (Source: Eurostat 2018a, b)

call an "asymmetrical interdependence" and jeopardy in terms of its domestic energy security (cf. Rosicki 2016; Kłaczyński 2017). For Gazprom, this has been a profitable market, especially when compared to its domestic market that is dominated by low government-regulated natural gas prices (Boussena and Locatelli 2013). Due to historical-rooted skepticism, Poland has always approached the energy business with Russia with great distrust and looked for alternative exporters of gas (Rosicki 2016; Kłaczyński 2017). This was highlighted during the Ukrainian gas crises of 2006 and 2009, as well as the since 2014 ongoing pro-Russian unrest in eastern Ukraine, which shows the entire EU's vulnerability toward Russian gas imports. Poland has opposed current projects discussed for new transport routes for Russian natural gas such as Nord Stream 2 and already vocal with regard to its predecessor Nord Stream 1 (Śliwiński and Pourzitakis 2018) as it does not alleviate the problem of the gas dependency. As such, former Prime Minister and current President of the European Council Donald Tusk emphasized that the EU should "confront Russia's monopolistic position with a single European body charged with buying gas" in a wider effort of "breaking up the Russian gas monopoly and restoring free market competition" (Tusk 2014). Ultimately, this vision for an "Energy Union" was taken up by Jean-Claude Juncker as part of his Commission tenure. He instructed Vice-Commissioner Maroš Šefčovič (responsible for the Energy Union) and Commissioner for Climate Action and Energy Miguel Arias Cañete to draft a framework (Fischer and Geden 2015). Yet, the concepts of Juncker and Tusk for an Energy Union differ significantly (cf. Szulecki et al. 2016).

The reliance on gas and the increasingly unproductive extraction of coal have prompted calls to diversify the country's energy mix. Already in the 1970s, the socialist government began exploring the possibility of nuclear energy as way to reduce domestic dependency on coal. The construction of the Żarnowiec Nuclear Power Plant, based on Soviet technology, began in the early 1980s, but in the aftermath of the Chernobyl accident in 1986, the public outcry resulting in continuous pressures from civil society led to an abandonment of construction site. Accordingly, a moratorium on nuclear energy became one of the first decisions of the new democratic government in 1990 (Szulecka and Szulecki 2013; Szulecki et al. 2015; Wagner et al. 2016). In 2009 nuclear energy regained some momentum, when the PO-led government issued the "Polish Energy Policy until 2030" strategy, which specified, as part of the future policy directions for the development of the energy sector, a diversification of electricity generation by introducing nuclear energy (Ministry of Economy 2009, pp. 15–17). Consequently, a series of ordinances and resolutions aiming for the introduction and promotion of nuclear energy were adopted but ultimately never surpassed the planning phase. The topic seemed off the table but regained attention in November 2018 with the long-awaited draft long-term energy planning strategy "Energy Policy of Poland until 2040" where it is sought to replace lignite (Ministerstwo Energii 2018). Yet, nuclear power is accompanied with a similar set of problems that characterize the energy dependence on natural gas, as nuclear power would make Poland also dependent on foreign suppliers and expertise (Adamus and Florkowski 2016, p. 176; Szczerbowski 2013, pp. 41–42). Hence, the apparent appeal of nuclear lies predominately in the "conviction that coal needs to be replaced with a similar source of energy that can run more than 7000 hours per year" (Simon 2017).

Furthermore, shale gas, which is a technique combining deep-rock fracturing with horizontal drilling techniques and hence sometimes also called as fracking, has gained attraction for harnessing unconventional shale gas deposits (Goldthau and LaBelle 2016, p. 603; Goldthau 2018, p. 1). It has been coined a "game changer" for Polish energy security (Gény 2010) for geopolitical concerns, e.g., independence from Russia (Bilgin 2009; Myers Jaffe and O'Sullivan 2012), as well as lowering overall energy prices in the European market (European Commission 2011). Debates in academic, political, media, and public spheres emerged on the potential of shale gas for a self-sufficient and energy-independent Poland, resulting in a "shale gas euphoria" (e.g., Adamus and Florkowski 2016; Goldthau and LaBelle 2016; Godzimirski 2016). When first exploratory diggings were, however, less successful than anticipated, the enthusiasm declined. This led the companies to minimize further exploration, leaving no single well that produces commercially shale gas (cf. Goldthau 2018 for comprehensive analysis on the politics of shale gas in Poland).

Renewable energy sources (RES) were first explored in the early 1990s. The first (commercial) wind power plant had a capacity of 150 kilowatt (kW), installed in 1991 and financed mostly by the Danish government. Consequently external pressures, particularly through the European environment, have been crucial in promoting RES support policies throughout the past (Szulecki 2017). However, it was "only after Poland joined the EU [in 2004] and introduced a support mechanism for renewables did these sources of energy start to play an increasingly important role in the Polish energy sector" (Szulecki 2017, p. 7). This development of RES was not as straightforward as Szulecki (2017) highlighted, as the highly instable domestic political field has triggered a "domestic soap opera" of RES legislation. The partisan complexion of governments has generated (an often far-reaching) repeated pattern, which sees each new government starting new drafts, plans, and amendments in RES, resulting into legal instability in this field. The country's most important RES biomass benefits from a 2004 EU regulation that allows co-firing coal plants to be treated as renewable energy source (Ericsson 2007; Paska et al. 2009; Nilsson et al. 2006; Szulecki 2017, p. 13). As such, it has been labeled the country's "pet renewable" (Szulecki 2017, p. 13) with its flexibility as an energy carrier for different applications and varying end-use sectors making it quite popular. It is particularly deployed in cogeneration vis-à-vis co-firing plants with lignite, as well as for household space and water heating and for solid fuel stoves and boilers (cf. Dzikuć and Piwowar 2016; Jezierska-Thöle et al. 2016; Piaskowska-Silarska et al. 2017). In 2007, Deputy Prime Minister and Minister of Economy Waldemar Pawlak proposed the initiative "a biogas plant in every commune (*gmina*)." The aim was to gain a 0.7–3 MW biogas power and/or heat production plant in every commune by 2020, thus increasing energy independence at the local level and ultimately contributing to the country's climate policy obligations and grassroot economic development. While local governments were favorable to the project (Ancygier and Szulecki 2014), it, however, was impeded by a lack of strategic thinking, weak commitment by the national government, and unfavorable support mechanisms. By late 2015, there were only 57 biogas plants (Golonko 2015). Hence, a big potential was unused as according to the International Renewable Energy Agency (IRENA)'s REmap 2030 (2015), with calculations indicating up to 5.2 GW, total power generation capacity in 2030 could have come from biomass (including solid biomass and biogas). The other promising RES is onshore wind energy (Michalak and Zimny 2011; Brzezińska-Rawa and Goździewicz-Biechońska 2014; Wagner 2017). As of late 2015, total installed onshore wind capacity was 5,100 megawatts (MW) (EurObserv'ER 2017) that provided 10,858 gigawatt-hours (GWh) (ibid.), or approximately 6.22% of the electricity consumed in the country. By the end of 2016, the total installed capacity had risen to 5,782 MW (EurObserv'ER 2017), yet this development has been haltered by politically motivated legal challenges as outlined below.

Composition of the "Energy Mix"

As outlined above, raw material deposits of domestic coal have dominated Poland's energy sector throughout its (recent) history (cf. Kamiński and Kudełko 2010; Gawlik et al. 2016; Bento et al. 2017; Manowska et al. 2017; Gawlik 2018; Suwala 2018). This aligns with the "Energy Law Act of 10 April 1997," which states the primary Polish energy policy goal is to ensure the energy security. This is understood as the independence from foreign energy sources and supplies. Figures 2 and 3 reflect upon this dominance of coal in the composition of the "energy mix" of electricity supply and consumption.

With 31.1 GW out of the total 44.2 GW (equal to 70%) in installed capacity in the Polish energy mix still provided by coal-fired power units, the energy sector is poorly diversified (Fig. 2). As such, coal-fired power plant restoration investments in recent years have not resulted in increased generation capacity (Forum Energii 2019a, p. 13) with 129.9 terawatt hours (TWh) of the total 169.9 TWh electricity still being produced in coal-based power plants (Fig. 3). The RES share in electricity production decreased to 12.7%, which is the lowest production and share of RES in the energy mix after 2014 (Forum Energii 2019a).

While the share (and role) of different fossil fuels has changed over time, coal remains the dominant resource. Accordingly, the 2018 official energy strategy planning document "Energy Policy of Poland until 2040" (EPP 2040) emphasizes that strategic direction number one should be an "optimal use of domestic energy resources" (Ministerstwo Energii 2018, p. 3) with coal expected to have a 60% share in the generation of electricity by 2030. Hence, the strategy forecasts that by 2020 Poland will need 165 TWh of electricity of which 128.8 TWh will be generated from lignite and bituminous coal, or approximately 78% of the total share. As early as 2035, the strategy anticipates the demand for energy to increase to 215.6 TWh of which then 46% would be generated from hard coal and approximately 10% from nuclear sources, which is so far not harvested for energy production within the country. Finally, in 2040 it is estimated that the demand for energy will reach 231.8

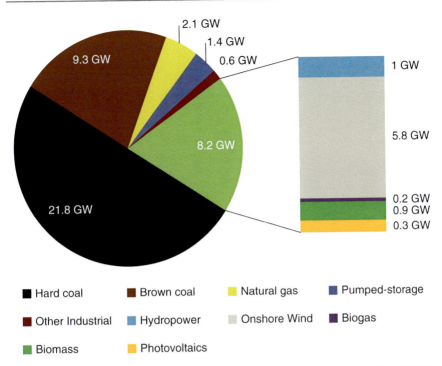

Fig. 2 Installed capacity within the Polish system in 2018 (GW). (Source: Forum Energii 2019a, p. 8)

TWh of which 32% would be generated from hard coal and approximately 18% from nuclear sources (Ministerstwo Energii 2018). To achieve this goal, the strategy explains that the current government seeks a reduction in dependency on coal (virtually by 50%) and aims to replace lignite with nuclear energy after 2030 (Ministerstwo Energii 2018). At the same time, however, an increased need for electricity is suspected, and also since the 2017 "Electromobility Development Plan" (Ministerstwo Energi 2017; cf. "Sector integration") assumes one million electric vehicles will be driving on Polish roads by 2025. Coal is thereby projected to serve as the main fuel behind the plan source behind the needed electricity (Ministerstwo Energi 2017). Thus, increased electricity consumption may maintain rather than reduce the current quantities of coal in the energy mix if nuclear energy is not developed as proposed by the EPP 2040. This puts the drafted strategy as well as energy and climate policy planning at odds with the EU Energy and Climate 2030 policy as well as the Paris Agreement of 2015.

In addition, the increased number of outdated (older than 30 years) power plants is now over half of the installed capacity of conventional power plants (including cogeneration from heat and power plants (CHP) (Świerzewski and Gładysz, 2017, p. 97)), challenging the aforementioned projections further. As such, a 2016 study by the transmission system operator Polskie Sieci Elektroenergetyczne (PSE) exposed that in the next 15 years, power equivalent to roughly 20–30 GW needs to be

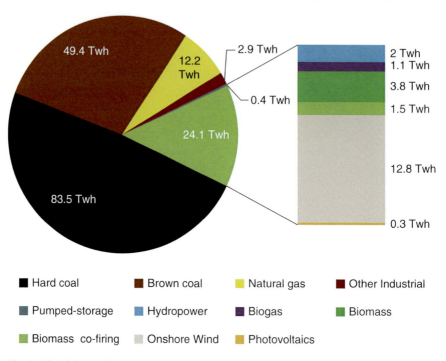

Fig. 3 Electricity production in 2018 (TWh). (Source: Forum Energii 2019a, p. 13)

switched off in the future because Polish power plants are not economically efficient and/or will not meet current or future environmental standards (PSE: w 2020 r. może wystąpić 2016; Simon 2017). Additional obstacles are the comparably low efficiency of energy transmission and distribution and the overall electricity loss in transmission and distribution that stood at 7.3% in 2011 (Biuro Bezpieczeństwa Narodowego 2012). In order to address these troubles, however, in the past decade, only a total of 500 megawatts (MW) of new (net) capacity has been added mainly via coal resources to the system with only some or little replacement and modernization of the power generation fleet (Simon 2017). Hence, the majority of power plants will operate until 2030, but afterward the energy production will fall sharply. This creates an existing artificial oversupply of energy within the system, which with the unfolding crisis in the coal sector will leave Poland with a looming power generation gap. This will force decision-makers to reconsider the country's energy mix by overcoming resistance related to past negative experiences with coal sector restructuring programs (Gawlik et al. 2015; Kamola-Cieślik 2018; Simon 2017).

Discourse on Energy Issues

While the material basis of energy governance is an important dimension for understanding the energetic foundation of a country and its energy transition, the discursive dimension should not be underestimated. Wagner et al. (2016, p. 158) in that respect point out that "[e]nergy transition refers not only to technological-economic transformation, but also to the sphere of social thinking about energy and individual practices." Previous research indicates that Polish dialogue on energy issues – despite many public consultation processes – has been mainly linked to the elitist model (Stankiewicz 2014; Wagner et al. 2016; Świątkiewicz-Mośny and Wagner 2012) favoring positions of experts, politicians, and the government. Studies on (mainstream) media in the country focus largely on these views as well as economic and political elites (Świątkiewicz-Mośny and Wagner 2012; Adamus and Florkowski 2016; Wagner et al. 2016; Kundzewicz et al. 2017). In other words, in Poland there is a tendency in (media) discourse of favoring opinions and attitudes of particular "elites," while those of civil society and NGOs are rather marginalized and not able to challenge status quo of the main discourse (Osička et al. forthcoming). Despite calls for more public involvement in the decision-making processes (particularly during the "shale gas euphoria"), there is more persuasion than deliberation to be found in Polish energy governance. This supports the argument made by Świątkiewicz-Mośny and Wagner (2012) asserting a lack of readiness among decision-makers to move from an elitist to a participative model of interest formation in energy policy.

With Poland prioritizing security of energy supply (Judge and Maltby 2017), and economic development (Szulecka and Szulecki 2013) over environmental and climate protection, this thinking is mirrored in the country's public and political debate that is characterized by a lack of awareness on climate issues (Jankowska 2011; Marcinkiewicz and Tosun 2015; Kundzewicz et al. 2017). Interest groups (Cianciara 2017) and representatives across different media and news outlets often voice strong doubts about both the form of and the need for global climate protection efforts. This mirrors the political debate that has developed a climate-skeptical stance by all parties unanimously, regardless of the political orientation of the governments in office (Marcinkiewicz and Tosun 2015; Hess and Renner 2019). This shapes how principles and frames of energy are perceived by the public vis-à-vis the wider EU climate and energy policy, and thus the debate surrounding it, which is generally perceived as a serious challenge for the economy. International opinion polls show that Poland is exceptional for its lower level of concern about climate change in comparison to other European countries (Kundzewicz and Matczak 2012), which implies that Poles are generally aware of climate change, but on average do not consider it a top priority. Indeed, evidence suggests that many Poles view the cure (climate mitigation) as worse than the disease (climate change) (Kundzewicz et al. 2015). Instead, common arguments include that Poland is "too poor" to afford "clean technologies," "renewables are too expensive," and a successful transition from the low cost of production based on cheap coal toward a low emission economy would require more time and financial support (by the EU) (Interview 2017e; Świątkiewicz-Mośny and Wagner 2012, p. 389). In that vein, Poland has (and is likely to continue) opposed concrete EU policy measures that limit the use of coal, instead defending clean coal technologies as well as technological neutrality

(Skjærseth 2016, 2018) that would allow the country to continue its coal program (Interview 2017a, b, c, d, e).

Political Institutions and Actors

The 1997 adopted constitution stipulates that Poland is a parliamentary democracy and is organized as a unitary, but decentralized state with the municipality being the basic unit of local self-government (Polish Const. art. 3, Polish Const. art. 15, and Polish Const. art. 164). The Parliament is bicameral, composed of an upper house, Senate, and a lower house, Sejm, with neither chamber directly representing local and regional authorities. This means that the foundations of all public authority agencies (or even all public authorities themselves) are regulations adopted by the central institutions of the state where the Nation as the sovereign is represented within the decision-making process.

While the numerous alterations in the partisan complexion of the government have regularly triggered a radical change in energy and climate policy – at times even in complete reversals (Szulecki 2017, p. 8) – since 2005 the political competition in party politics is "fought" between the two dominating parties, conservative PO (2007–2015) and right-wing PiS (2005–2007; 2015–on going). The restriction toward these two can be explained mainly by several changes in the political landscape that took place as of the 2005 elections (Markowski 2006). PiS – which is a member of the Alliance of Conservatives and Reformists in Europe in the European Parliament – has largely promoted nationalistic and conservative social policies combined with EU and climate skepticism, while PO, a member of the European People's Party in the EP, has always represented a more conservative-liberal and Christian democratic position combined with strong pro-Europeanism (Markowski 2006; Stępińska et al. 2017; Szczerbiak 2007, 2008). However, in the parliamentary debate, both parties were uniform in criticizing the 2030 climate and energy framework, as well as the Decarbonization Roadmap for 2050 (Marcinkiewicz and Tosun 2015, pp. 187–200). Regarding the latter, Poland vetoed it, which met with widespread public approval (Marcinkiewicz and Tosun 2015, p. 199). Likewise, the transition of power from PO to PiS after the 2015 elections did not entail a dramatic shift in energy policy. Like PO, PiS highlighted the need for energy security, support for natural gas infrastructure development, and continued reliance on the country's coal industry (Hess and Renner 2019). PO holds a more pragmatic position and adhered to the European energy and climate frameworks, commensurate with its pro-European attitude, leading the party to subordinate particular policies to a broad European raison d'être, which PiS by contrast does not seem willing to do.

Next to party politics, Poland's energy governance architecture and its implementation of energy policy is inherently embedded in its national administrative and territorial division. A number of institutions, actors, and authorities are involved in the governance process, but with none of the territorial divisions enjoying notable autonomy and with all sublevels having specified administrative tasks, objectives, and competencies that are outlined by legislative acts and/or are vested in them by the constitution. Table 1 illustrates the key governmental actors in energy governance with their distribution of competences along the different governmental levels. The supranational, i.e., EU, level has been omitted as it will be dealt with exclusively in another other segment below.

The key level of the decision-making process of energy matters is entrusted at the central level, where the resolution of all relevant dimensions of energy policy is executed by the Ministry of Energy, established in December 2015 as part of the broader reorganization of government ministries by the new government "due to the strategic nature of the subject of its operation and an enormous number of issues to be tackled in this field" (Szydło 2016). The ministry sets the legal framework and is responsible for the development and implementation of energy policy, covers the mining sector and its development, as well as represents the government as the asset owner with regard to the transferred management of the state-owned and state-controlled energy and power-producing companies (Bałtowski and Kozarzewski 2016; RAP 2018). In addition, there is the Urząd Regulacji Energetyki (URE, Energy Regulatory Office) that – as an independent regulatory authority – is responsible for the regulation of the electricity, gas, and heating markets. Its responsibilities are set forth in the "Energy Law Act of 10 April 1997" with its president appointed by the Prime Minister for a term of 5 years. The office responsibilities include licensing, setting tariffs, approving investment plans by regulated companies, deregulation of electricity and gas markets, and oversight of supply quality and customer service. The URE also supervises compliance of energy company obligations under the country's (former) colored certificate schemes. Finally, Urząd Ochrony Konkurencji i Konsumentów (UOKiK, Office of Competition and Consumer Protection) serves as the competition authority, shaping antitrust and consumer protection policies. Yet, URE also plays a role in antitrust and competition issues as it has directed cases to UOKiK in the past based on customer complaints about company activities related to customer switching. As outlined further below, these close state-economic ties render the national level a vital actor in the steering and regulation process of the overall energy policy, exercising a high level of control over the decision-making process (Tomjałojc 2008) that leads to state-led governance approach toward the industry structure and its ownership.

Poland has unbundled electric transmission from distribution. The transmission system operator PSE is the owner and operator of the national transmission grid. PSE is in turn wholly owned by the state. There are five vertically integrated main distribution companies which, while legally unbundled, are in fact part of larger parent companies with significant generation and distribution assets, as well as a significant share of the retail market. Exceptions to this are Energa, which has less generation assets than the other companies, and Innogy that primarily focusses on retail supply and network operation in the capital city Warsaw. The consolidation of the power companies into four vertically integrated companies, with three of them being majority state-owned (PGE, Energa, and Enea), the fourth with a state-owned controlling share (Tauron), and the fifth (Innogy) operating solely in the capital city, is the result of the 2006 policy "Program for the Electric Power Sector" (RAP 2018, p. 12)

Table 1 Governmental actors and their competences and tasks in Polish energy governance alienated by national sublevels. (Source: own depiction)

Governance level	Governmental actors and their competences and tasks in energy governance
Central level	In leading role, the Ministry of Energy is responsible for:
	Coordinating the overall energy policy and managing the mineral deposits
	National energy policy and participation in shaping the EU's energy (and climate) policy
	Energy markets, energy and fuels, energy efficiency, the development and use of renewable energy sources and nuclear energy for socioeconomic needs
	The country's energy security, including security of energy supply, energy, and fuel
	Energy infrastructure, including the operation of energy systems, taking into account the principles of rational economy and the country's energy security needs
	Coordinating and supervising international cooperation in the field of energy, raw materials, energy and fuel, and participation in the work of bodies of the European Union
	Exercising control over the public (state-controlled and state-owned energy companies)
	The Ministry of Environment is also in charge of:
	Creating inventories of greenhouse gas emissions, particular carbon dioxide, and sinks
	Reporting and verification of their levels
	Approving the licenses for exploration and extraction of raw materials
	The Ministry of Investment and Economic Development is:
	Responsible for economy and regional development with regard to energy matters
Regional level (*Województwa*): Voivodships or provinces	Regional authorities are responsible for:
	Testing compliance of energy and fuel supply with the state energy policy
	Promoting and disseminating knowledge about the future direction of energy policy in the region
Intermediate level (*Powiat*): Ccounties or districts	County authorities are responsible for local issues which cannot be granted to the municipalities:
	Nothing in direct reference to energy but issuing building permits for all infrastructure (e.g., important with regard to wind power)
Local level (*Gmina*): Ccommunes or municipalities	Local authorities are responsible for:
	Providing electricity, gas, and heat supply
	Planning and organizing activities aimed at achieving energy efficiency, as well as promoting the reduction of energy consumption

Table 2 Proprietorship structure of Polish energy companies. (Source: RAP 2018, p. 13 as based upon the annual reports for 2015)

Company name	Ownership of the energy company (divided share)
Polskie Sieci Elektroenergetyczne (PSE) Operator	100% owned by the state
Polska Grupa Energetyczna (PGE)	57.39% Ministry of Energy; 42.61% other stakeholders
Tauron Polska Energia	30.06% Ministry of Energy; 10.39% KGHM Polska Miedź; 5.06% ING Retirement Fund; 54.49% other individual and institutional investors
Energa	51.52% Ministry of Energy; 48.48% remaining stakeholders
Enea	51.50% Ministry of Energy; 9.96% PZU Investment Fund (PZU TFI); 38.54% other stakeholders
Innogy Polska (former RWE Polska)	innogy Polska (former, RWE Polska) is wholly owned by RWE East, which in turn is owned by RWE AG that is 86% owned by institutional investors, 13% by private shareholders, and 1% by employees

that laid the path for the future development of the electricity market. Three out of four of the largest distribution companies remain majority state-owned (Table 2).

The relevance of state enterprises in the energy economy is thus extensive (Bałtowski and Kozarzewski 2016). Since 2016, the PiS government attempted to change the statutes of the four major energy companies with a more active control in their steering process. The intent was announced by declaring energy companies an "instrument of national energy security," implicating that not just economic, market-logic but rather "national security" interests (though left unspecified) would take priority (Szulecki 2018). PiS-loyal company leadership introduced these changes in the statutes of three of the four energy companies; the move was not accepted by Tauron's board when the issue became public. These developments confirm a state-led governance approach, subjecting "markets to the political objectives of the state" and with governments as "the primary actors, not only involved in regulating market conditions, but also exercising substantial influence and control over the actions of market participants" (Judge and Maltby 2017: 184f).

Coordination of Polish Instruments and Issues of Energy Transitions Within the Multilevel Context

The previous section highlighted that Polish energy governance is largely shaped by past legacies, (political and administrative) institutional structures, as well as the (public and private) actors in the field. With European (Energy Union) and international obligations (Paris Agreement), Poland's energy transition and policy are embedded in comprehensive multilevel governance architecture. This section moves away from previous research that has focused particularly on questions related to norm diffusion and Europeanization, but instead looks at the (external) stimulation of energy transitions and the internal/domestic involvement of the different levels of government.

Drivers of Energy Transition

Poland's energy sector faces numerous internal/domestic challenges. These are, namely, diminishing national resources of fossil fuel in the medium-term perspective (e.g., up to 40 years for hard coal) (Olkuski 2014; Simon 2017), outdated power plants with over half of the installed capacity in CHP units, and conventional power plants being older than 30 years. This represents an equivalent power of 30 GW to soon face shutdown due to their lack of meeting future environmental standards, while only 500 MW have been built in new (net) power capacity to close this power gap (Szczerbowski 2013; Simon 2017), and finally a low efficiency of energy transmission and distribution (Biuro Bezpieczeństwa Narodowego 2012). In addition, governmental prioritization of coal, general opposition to climate policy, and privileged access by coal actors to decision-making shows that domestic politics has a pivotal role in influencing the country's energy transition.

While there is external pressure on the Polish energy regime, the country appears increasingly resistant to long-term policies from EU level. For example, Marcinkiewicz and Tosun (2015, pp. 187–200) found parliamentary members in the early 2010s were "almost uniformly" critical of EU climate policy, particularly the 2030 Climate and Energy Package and the (decarbonization) Roadmap for 2050. Moreover Poland has become perhaps the most prominent advocate of less ambitious climate policy within the EU (Bocquillon and Maltby 2017; Skjærseth 2018). It also serves as informal leader in the "Visegrád Group/Four" (also including the Czech Republic, Hungary, and Slovakia), whose members are largely united in opposing EU climate and energy policy by insisting on national sovereignty concerning their national energy mix. This preference for a limited EU and the priority of energy supply security (Fischer 2014; Knodt 2018) have been particular promoted by Poland including the original introduction of renewable and efficiency targets. Thus, from a long-term perspective on RES support and against the background of its domestic changes, Szulecki (2017, pp. 10–18) identified four phases, to which a fifth (present) phase has been added by the author, illustrating the patterns of European influence regarding policy instrument(s) for supporting Poland's renewable energy policy (Table 3).

In turn, cities like Bielsko-Biała, which established its Energy Management Office as early as 1997 and was the first Polish municipal government to formulate a Sustainable Energy Action Plan within the Covenant of Mayors, demonstrate that "municipalities in Poland are showing signs of developing a progressive agenda on climate and renewable energy issues" (Jänicke and Quitzow 2017, p. 133). They are interested in energy projects as a form of investment and local development as well as for diversifying energy sources. In that regard, Liebe et al. (2017) show that, in

Table 3 Five phases of RES support instruments over time. (Source: Own depiction on the basis of phases I–IV as identified by Szulecki (2017), V added by author)

Phases (time frame)	Role of the European level	Policy instrument(s) for supporting RES
Phase I (1991–1999)	Emulating European modernity	Feed in tariff, since 1993
		Quota system, since 1999
Phase II (2000–2004)	Pre-accession conditionality	Quote system maintained but reformed in light of EU membership with mandatory goals, since 2000
Phase III (2005–2009)	Navigating EU waters	Quota mechanism combined with tradable "green certificates," since 2005
Phase IV (2010–2016)	Domestic struggle and EU assertiveness	EUETS, since 2010
Phase V (2017 and on-going)	Confrontation against EU actions	Capacity market, since 2018
		Auctioning system, since 2017

order to gain acceptance for renewable energy production sites, it is not sufficient to only develop the appropriate technology but also to consider the social context and fairness concerns. They conclude that people would be willing to accept, e.g., new turbines in their neighborhood, if they can, firstly, participate in decision-making, secondly, if the turbines are owned by a group of citizens, and, most importantly, if the generated electricity is consumed in the region instead of being exported. This discovery is vital when considering that particularly the North and the East of the country face energy poverty and vulnerability (in terms of lacking resources), while at the same time the Baltic Sea region in the North and East offers substantial potential for wind energy. This puts the municipal level, however, at odds with the central interests, which is rather focused on building new lignite power plants. As such, in 2009 when several municipalities held local referenda in which citizens voted against the construction of new coal-based power plants and thus against the construction of mines, the national government still adopted plans beginning their construction (Skorupska 2015). Here, the involvement of the local levels in vertical energy governance to oppose governmental plans, however, is uneven throughout the country due to their limited legal guaranteed rights and provisions (Interview 2017e). The current PiS government has tried to undercut the growth of onshore wind power with legal changes hindering its further expansion as part of the 2016 "Act on Investments in Wind Power Plants," e.g., with increased property taxes imposed on the owners of the plants as well as a minimum distance ("buffer zone") required between wind farms and residential buildings, forests, or national parks at ten times the height of a wind turbine. This "buffer zone" of H10 or 10 × the height of the pole on which the turbine is mounted, in practice, approximates between 1.5 and 2 km. This eliminates several investment opportunities in terms of land for wind turbines and their construction (cf. Dawid 2017; Hajto et al. 2017; Liebe et al. 2017; Sokołowski 2017). By April 2018 the Ministry of Energy announced intents to repeal current taxation rules and distance obligations and restore the law to its previous version. The regulation has blocked any new growth in the onshore wind energy sector in the country slowing down and interrupting the development of RES capacity at the turn of 2016/2017 (International Energy Agency 2018, p. 24). In addition, the ongoing drafted EPP 2040 by the Ministry of Energy predicts an end of onshore wind power within the current energy mix by 2040 (Ministerstwo Energii 2018; Forum Energii 2019b).

Strategies and Instruments of Energy Transitions

Research has shown that a wide spectrum of instruments can contribute to promoting the transition toward a greater share of renewable energy sources in the primary energy supply (e.g., Verbruggen and Lauber 2012, Gawel et al. 2017; Bayer et al. 2018). Within the academic debate, however, the adoption of specific instruments and their "best mix" is controversial as some adhere to incentive-based instruments; others prefer regulatory policies or concentrate on soft governance approaches. Thus, the development of the national energy systems, particularly the deliberate energy transformation strategy, can be best described in relation to four types of policy instruments: direct regulation, internalizing instruments (e.g., carbon pricing), incentive-based instruments (e.g., subsidies for low-carbon energy production), and soft governance (e.g., information schemes and voluntary agreements). Table 4 sketches the main policy instruments used in the Polish energy transition by instruments and energy sector (electricity, heating and cooling, as well as transport). Central to this is the earlier outlined "Energy Law Act of 10 April of 1997" as it is the most comprehensive centerpiece of Polish energy legislation. Since its introduction, it has been revised 60 times (on average every 4 months) and grown tenfold in length (Derski 2017). Even the 2015 adopted (and subsequently amended) "Renewable Energy Act" is, though the name suggests otherwise, only a codified amendment of the "Energy Law Act" of the 2001 "Environmental Protection Law."

Table 4 demonstrated that there is a distort picture in the instruments used in the energy sector to promote RES development. The electricity sector is stimulated from renewable sources predominantly through (national) tenders for the definition of a support level of a feed-in tariff or premium, tax relief and subsidy and loan schemes, as well as a quota system for some older power plants. The recent introduced capacity market must, compared with other Member States (Leiren et al. 2019), be therefore seen as an countermeasure due to the risk of future power shortages due to decommissioning of fossil power plants. Heat generated from renewable energy sources is supported through subsidy and loan schemes as well as priority purchase obligation, whereas renewable energy in the transport sector is promoted only through a biofuel quota obligation. Understanding the nature of these support mechanisms can be attained with the help of the concept of vertical and horizontal Europeanization (Szulecki 2017, pp. 10–18). The EU is thereby determining the "menu" of available support schemes by putting pressure on the Polish authorities. When, for example, the original quotas/green certificates were perceived as the optimal and preferred support scheme in many Member States, also Poland adopted this policy approach. But once the green certificate mechanism became under crises in 2012 (Wędzik et al. 2017), and cost-efficiency discussions dominated the political

Table 4 Polish policy instruments aligned by category and their sector. (Source: Own depiction on the basis of res-legal.eu (2016))

Category of policy-making instruments	Branch of energy sector			
		Electricity	Heating and cooling	Transport
Regulatory policy making		Law: General energy law (Energy Law Act, 1997) Law: General environmental protection (Environmental Protection Act, 2001)	Law: General environmental protection (Environmental Protection Act, 2001)	Biofuel quota (Regulation on the National Indicative Targets, 2013)
Incentive-based instruments	Price drive	Subsidy: Capacity Market (2017) Tenders: Auctions (Renewable Energy Law Act, 2015) Quota system: Renewable portfolio standards Renewable (Energy Law Act, 2015)[a] Support scheme: Financing for purchase and installation of micro-installations of renewable energy sources (Priority Programme "Prosumer," 2014)[b] Loan: The National Fund for Environmental Protection and Water Management (NFOSiGW) grants low interest loans to support the purchase and installation of RES installations. (RES Priority Programme "Stork," 2014) Subsidy: The National Fund for Environmental Protection and Water Management (NFOSiGW) grants low interest loans together with subsidies to support the purchase and installation of small and micro-RES installations for the needs of residential single-family or multi-family houses	Loan (National Fund for Environmental Protection and Water Management – "Efficient Heating and Cooling," 2016) Loan (National Fund for Environmental Protection and Water Management – Stork, 2015) Loan: Financing for purchase and installation of micro-installations of renewable energy sources (Priority Programme "Prosumer," 2014)[b] Priority program: Improvement of energetic efficiency – thermo-modernization of single-family buildings (Priority Programme "Lynx," 2014)[b] Subsidy: Thermal rehabilitation grants (Act on thermo-modernization, 2009)	

(continued)

Table 4 (continued)

Category of policy-making instruments		Branch of energy sector		
		Electricity	Heating and cooling	Transport
Internalizing instruments	Quantity driven	EU Emissions Trading System (2005) Quota system: renewable portfolio standards (Renewable Energy Law Act, 2015)		
	Regulation of prices	Tax incentives: Producers of electricity from renewable sources are exempt from the tax on the sale and consumption of electricity (Excise Tax Act 2009)		
	Regulation of quantities			
Soft governance		Public information campaigns		

Clarification:
[a] Until 2016, the main support scheme was a quota system in terms of a quota obligation, which was combined with a certificate trading scheme. Currently, only the installations that started to produce energy before the new law (i.e., auctions) came into force can choose between the two different support systems
[b] Discontinued for new applications

agenda (with Poland's significant input) and state aid rules limited the "available choice" on the "menu," auctioning became the new policy adopted in 2015.

Coordination Mechanisms and Multilevel Governance

The successful governance of energy transition is a multilevel task that is to say that political institutions and actors in the sector have not only distributed competences, but they are also scattered between different governmental levels (i.e., supranational, national, subnational/regional, and local), which need to be coordinated along (an imaginary) horizontal and vertical governance dimension. While the horizontal dimension refers to the responsibility of departments and ministries for energy issues, the vertical refers to distribution of competences between different levels of government.

Under its 1997 adopted constitution, Poland is organized as a unitary state on a decentralized basis (Polish Const. art. 3 and Polish Const. art. 15) with parliamentary democracy based upon a majoritarian style of policy-making (Lijphart 2012). Neither the upper house nor the lower house of the bicameral parliament is directly representing local and regional authorities. In terms of the "varieties of capitalism approach" (Hall and Soskice 2001; Ćetković and Buzogány 2016 with emphasis on RES), Poland classifies as the added "dependent market economy." The category was added to the original dichotomous classification of "coordinated market economy" and "liberal market economy," given that many CEEC did not fit this original classification. Central is also the repeatedly mentioned "Energy Law Act of 10 April of 1997" that defines the bodies in charge of national energy and oversight, including their responsibilities. As such, after the 2015 elections, established Ministry of Energy aimed for a streamlining of policies and competences that previously have being scattered across different departments and ministries. This has resulted energy policy in Poland to be now less fragmented between the different branches of government as it was before (Smyrgała 2016, p. 38).

Coordination of energy governance in terms of administrative bodies in the horizontal dimension is shaped by close state-market ties with the national governmental level and its largely state-controlled public energy actors being predominately in charge of the national governance system. This original influence of state intervention in the energy sector was originally justified by the argument that government would be able to represent the best solution to ensure energy and national security (Judge and Maltby 2017, p. 198). These close state-economic ties result in the actors at the national level being particularly vital as they are responsible for state-led governance steering and regulation process of the overall energy policy by exercising a high level of paternalism in the decision-making process (Tomjałojc 2008). That is to say "the subservience of markets to the political objectives of the state. Governments are the primary actors, not only involved in regulating market conditions, but also exercising substantial influence and control over the actions of market participants" (Judge and Maltby 2017: 184f). When looking at the supranational level and its influence on the country's energy and climate policy, particular

RES support schemes (Szulecki 2017), it can be clearly seen that the support schemes only exist (albeit largely national dysfunctional) fundamentally due to external (i.e., EU) influences. Due the strategic dominance of domestic coal, however, the country has opposed the far-reaching EU climate and energy policies like the EU 2020 framework and 2030 framework packages (Skjærseth 2018, p. 12).

At the same time, there seems to be the issue that "municipalities in Poland are showing signs of developing a progressive agenda on climate and renewable energy issues [particular] in the face of strong national-level resistance" (Jänicke and Quitzow 2017, p. 133). A survey conducted among the authorities of municipalities concludes that the opposition expressed against the government is related to their opposition of governmental plans for the building of new lignite power plants (Ancygier and Szulecki 2014). This raises conflict lines along the regional and local level versus the national level that effects further coordination questions with regard to the country's energy transition. Hence the energy transition toward more RES utilization is an opportunity for the supranational level (i.e., EU) to focus on additional causes, which, besides the energy sector, stimulate the development of economic activities with a significant role being attributed to the instruments of EU cohesion policy (i.e., European Structural and Investment Funds) (e.g., Streimikiene et al. 2007, and with explicit focus on Poland; see also Chodkowska-Miszczuk et al. 2016; Włodarski and Martyniuk-Pęczek 2017). The previous funding period (2007–2013) saw a record in the largest support for all investments in renewable energy sources with the total value of the co-financed projects amounting to 2 billion euro (Chodkowska-Miszczuk et al. 2016). Expert opinion thereby emphasized that this financial independence in funding from the national budgets was a crucial factor in the past RES development and increased territorial cohesion of regions in Poland (Interview 2017d). Although Poland has acquired yet again vast amounts (a total of €82.5 billion across all categories of support projects) for the new funding period (2014–2020) (Formuszewicz and Gawlikowska-Fyk 2014, p. 2), the future usage of these financial resources is left ambiguous due to recent political and legal changes regarding the legal framework of particular renewable energy sources (e.g., Sokołowski 2017) and the overall regulations of NGO funding as "[i]nvestments in renewable energy projects can receive subsidies from [. . .] EU funds, as well as Polish national funds" (Osiecka-Brzeska 2016, p. 321). Receiving this funding is, however, bound to the condition to receive funding from the national government through the "Narodowy Instytut Wolności – Centrum Rozwoju Społeczeństwa Obywatelskiego" (National Freedom Institute – Center for the Development of Civil Society). This in autumn 2017 by the PiS government through law issued executive agency is responsible for centralized distribution of public funds for NGOs. It is attached to the Prime Minister's office as the Institute's Director, and the majority of the Director's Council are appointed by another new institution – the "Komitet do spraw Pożytku Publicznego" (Committee for Public Benefit Activity) – which is chaired by a member of the Council of Ministers, which is the collective executive decision-making body of the Polish government. The council consists of the Prime Minister; the Deputy Prime Minister, who acts as a vice-president of the council; and other ministers. This means the government has the de facto broad powers to influence and control the work of the National Institute and, in turn, ultimately the distribution of funding across NGOs, including those supporting, developing, and researching RES use (Ciobanu and Kość 2017).

Outcomes, Challenges, and Prospects of Polish Energy Governance

Monitoring and Surveillance

As demonstrated earlier, previous governments have been outspoken pro-coal and rather hostile toward renewable energy, as well as wider climate policy (Fuksiewicz and Klein 2014). Since PiS came to power in 2015, the current government has done much to maintain some form of renewable energy policy under EU pressure while inheriting an already dysfunctional program from previous governments (Szulecki 2017). This results in the country to be lacking behind for the EU 2020 framework goals on different dimensions, e.g., development of renewable energy, improvement of energy efficiency, as well as the reduction of GHG emissions.

As evident from Table 5, GHG emissions decreased strongly by 37% in the period 1990–2002, but after 2002 emissions grew by 3% until 2015. While Poland has a growth target of 14% for the 2005–2020 period under the Effort Sharing Decision (ESD), it is currently on track to reach this target because the actual emission

Table 5 Poland's progress toward the EU 2020 framework goals. (Source: Eurostat 2018c)

Topic	Indicator, unit	2016, EU-28 values	2020, EU target value	2016, PL value	2020, PL target value
GHG emissions	GHG emissions, Index 1990 = 100, for Poland 1988	77.88[a]	80[a]	82.76[a]	80[a]
Renewable energy	Share of renewable energy in gross final energy consumption, %	17.0	20	11.3	15
	Share of renewable energy in transport(RES-T), %	29.6	/	13.4	/
	Share of renewable energy in electricity (RES-E), %	7.1	10	3.9	10
	Share of renewable energy in heating and cooling (RES-H&C), %	19.1	/	14.7	/
Energy consumption	Primary energy consumption, million tonnes of oil equivalent	1,542.7	1,483	94.3	96.4
	Final energy consumption, million tonnes of oil equivalent	1,107.7	1,086	66.7	71.6

Clarification:
[a]2015 data instead of 2016, and GHG emissions, Index 1990 = 100, for Poland 1988

increase is lower than expected in the ESD target. Other comparative indicators such as emission intensity indicate that Poland performs worse than most other Eastern European countries and average EU-28 Member States in terms of emission reductions and decarbonization in the energy sector due its strong reliance on coal. Likewise the earlier brought up decisions and revised legislation will lead to an increased role of coal in energy supply compared to the past, and therefore a much slower expansion of renewable energies than in recent years, in particular of wind power, is expected. This leads to the deduction that achieving the 2020 goals (and even more so the follow-up 2030 and even tighter 2050 goals) will be an overwhelming task to do for Polish energy governance.

Considering the way renewable energy support policies are designed, redesigned, changed, and revoked – erasing any meaningful investment stability – one has to conclude that the development of Polish renewables is actually happening against all rational odds (Szulecki 2017). In addition, frequent changes in the partisan complexion of government generate (radical) reforms and increase uncertainty, policy U-turns and "stop-go policies or policy changes which take the form of two steps forward and two steps back" (Schmidt 2002, p. 151). The European environment has been crucial in leading to the establishment of RES support as it should be not forgotten that this target is, however, met with very conservative means as it is mostly with the help of the biomass and is widespread utilized through the co-firing method in CHP plants (e.g., Paska and Surma 2014; Dzikuć and Piwowar 2016; Świerzewski and Gładysz 2017). Options like nuclear energy or clean coal technologies and legal framework changes hinder development of certain RES, leaving questions of the future energy mix to be open. Hence, a reduced share of 25% coal in the power mix by 2050 is only realistic if alternative energy carriers are further developed and not blocked in their development (Simon 2017). The unstable political climate and (often) changing energy decisions, however, seem most likely to highlight that the vital role of domestic coal in the energy mix will remain; thus the country will not follow a decarbonization sensu stricto with regard to its future energy system (Interview 2017e, 2018a, b, c). Thus, Polish plans in the energy sector will not contribute to significant further emission reductions in the future as it is the fifth largest EU emitter, which may slow down the overall progress of the EU in emission reductions (Herold et al. 2017).

Sector Integration

The topic of sector integration of renewable energies (i.e., the coupling of electricity, heat/cold, and mobility) has increasingly become a research topic (International Energy Agency 2016). In Poland, CHP and electromobility represent two distinct types of sector integration with the former being a rather "old topic," while the latter is a "new one" for the Polish energy sector one.

Central planning of cogeneration had experienced a steady grow in industrial and power plants in place since the 1970s and 1980s (Matuszewska et al. 2017) and was most often applied in Polish district heating. With the internal (economic, social, and political) and external (globalization and Europeanization) transition pressures of the 1990s, however, a decrease in the amount of heat generated in industrial CHP plants occurred, while simultaneously the professional CHP plants growth had been maintained (Matuszewska et al. 2017). The years 1970–1995 were characterized by the highest growth rates, but it was not until the "Energy Law Act of 10 April 1997" that (financial) support mechanisms for energy generation from CHP plants as a possibility of sector integration were discussed. Consequently, the CHP certificate support system was introduced in 2007 (Muras 2011) and remained operational till the end of 2017. The system then required electricity suppliers and certain entities to purchase from the beneficiaries a specific number of CHP certificates, in proportion to the amount of power supplied to end users or purchased (Muras 2011). It was based on the so-called certificates of origin from cogeneration (former Energy Law Article 9 l). There were three categories of beneficiaries, eligible to receive different types of certificates. The certificates were color-coded (yellow, purple, or red) and allocated to the beneficiaries depending on the source of fuel and the capacity of the CHP plant. The system then required electricity suppliers and certain entities to purchase from the beneficiaries a specific number of CHP certificates, in proportion to the amount of power supplied to end users or purchased (Muras 2011). While throughout the years 2006–2012, heat production from cogeneration experienced a minimal decline, the electricity production cogeneration grew steadily and in 2012 amounted to almost 17% of total electricity production (Jožef Stefan Institute 2014). Thus, the system was based on the amount of electricity produced from cogeneration sources in contrast to price-oriented systems (i.e., feed-in tariff mechanism). Now, in 2018, all existent cogeneration installations are allowed to benefit from a new introduced support system. It is based on a premium paid extra in the electricity price. For new units, an auction mechanism will be introduced. A feed-in premium mechanism provides for those installations with total installed capacity lower than 1 MW. The amount of premium directed toward existent installations of high-efficient cogeneration would be annually set by the Minister of Energy. The support for the new installations will be based on a "pay-as-bid" auction system, where the premium is the object in auction. Each of the investors is to present one offer – the winning offer would be those with the lowest prices offered. The system is supposed to promote solely the most effective technologies and locations, simultaneously minimalizing expenses of the system's functioning (noerr.com 2017; dentons.com 2017).

On the other side, a recent interest has emerged within the EU on the coupling of electricity and mobility vis-à-vis the usage electric vehicles. As such, Member States have established incentives to increase demand with the measures, however, being scattered (cf. Cansino et al. 2018). In Poland attention is given to electromobility's possible CO_2 reduction (Skwierz 2017; Zawieska and Pieriegud 2018). On 5 February 2018, the Polish President signed the "Act on Electromobility and Alternative Fuels" (Ministerstwo Energii 2017), which not only transposes European directives but is seen as the new key guideline on the all new electro-mobility strategy that plans to put one million electric vehicles on the road by 2025 (Simon 2018). It since then has been hailed the country's "constitution for electromobility" as it aims to challenge the current infrastructure for electromobility, which is largely not in place (in 2016 only 324 public charging stations were available) (Wasik 2017). It defines basic terms such as charging point, charging station, electric vehicle, and alternative fuels. Most importantly, it establishes a framework for building a basic alternative fuel infrastructure and vital administrative benefits for the development of such infrastructure. For instance, the new legislation foresees that a building permit will not be required for charging stations or charging points. Also will the charging of electric vehicles not be regarded as a sale of electric energy under existing legislation, and consequently, electricity supplier licenses will not be required. Albeit some experts (Interview 2017e) are skeptic with regard to these developments, others (Simon 2018) have expressed their openness in view of the opportunities. With coal being set to become the driving fuel behind this plan, the objective of reducing urban air pollution from the vehicle fleet is lead ad absurdum. Policy-makers reportedly admitted that the plan will have the added benefits of boosting demand for coal in electrical power generation (and thus intensifying pollution generated from here) and instead focous on reducing imports of crude oil (Świderek 2017). Thus, the key challenge will be to promote the measures and incentives to convince people to use electric cars as laid down in the act. From a political science perspective of these two dimensions of sector coupling, the challenge is that "electricity and heat belong to the same policy field constituting a policy arena constituted by similar actors and discourses, mobility and traffic represents a different arena established by different actors, institutions and logics" (Knodt and Kenmerzell 2017, p. 10). For cogeneration this can be observed as the policy arena (electricity and heat) remained within the same key actor (Ministry of Energy) at joined territorial dimension (national level). Yet, with regard to electromobility, challenges, e.g., departmental coordination problems, can unfold. The key regulator (and advocate of the act) is the Ministry of Energy, while the Ministry of Infrastructure is the traditional one in charge with transport.

Prospects of Polish Energy Governance

As outlined earlier, Polish climate and RES policy developed largely due to the external influences with "municipalities in Poland [...] showing signs of developing a progressive agenda on climate and renewable energy issues [particularly] in the face of strong national-level resistance" (Jänicke and Quitzow 2017, p. 133). This transition toward more RES utilization is largely attributed to stimulated economic development through the instruments of EU cohesion policy (Streimikiene et al. 2007; Chodkowska-Miszczuk et al. 2016; Włodarski and Martyniuk-Pęczek 2017). The last funding periods (2007–2013; 2014–2020) saw a record in the largest support for all investments in renewable energy sources. Thus, as argued above, the supranational plays a decisive role for the country's energy transition occurring at the regional and local level. As such, a "cleavage line between the center versus periphery" (Lipset and Stein 1967) can be overserved, which in Poland is reflected in the regional versus central level in the development of RES. Research of Ancygier and Szulecki (2014), Skorupska (2015), as well as Jänicke and Quitzow (2017) have all established the progressiveness of cities and municipalities, as their responsibility for the supply of electric, thermal, and gas energy on the local level provides additional support for the hypothesis that RES policy in Poland develops in a dynamic and uncoordinated fashion at the local level. Basically, municipal authorities show greater enthusiasm for a progressive agenda on climate and renewable energy issues, particularly expansion of renewables, due to its contribution in promoting spatial development, territorial cohesion, and even the reduction of energy poverty (Bouzarovski and Tirado Herrero 2016).

At the same time, political parties and their MPs seem to show a uniform opposition toward wider EU energy and climate policy, independent of their left/right adherence or their membership in the government (Marcinkiewicz and Tosun 2015). Thus none of the parties in the current Polish parliament has supported long-term EU climate policy or even clear position on limiting the role of coal in the economy (Karaczun et al. 2013: 191ff; Fuksiewicz and Klein 2014). These circumstances may also derive from completely different assumptions and visions of European integration (Cianciara 2017, p. 240), which is particularly noticeable in what Braun (2014: 445 f.) argues to be in Poland two "categories" of interest groups. While norm entrepreneurs are often to be found among environmental NGOs, "norm opponents are found primarily within the energy producing sector" (Braun 2014, p. 455). The "norm opponent" interest groups foster mobilizing the national/local perspective, defending economic interests, favoring the energy-intensive industry and fossil fuel energy producers, and opposing potentially costly climate regulations, while the "norm entrepreneurs" interest groups that largely support international organizations rather promote supranational solutions including EU policies toward climate change. This strong power is supported by the fact that Poland's electricity producers and energy-intensive industry were united in opposing the EU climate and energy package, with the four (majority) state-owned electric power groups forming a pivotal bloc with considerable political influence – particularly in their protection of coal, opposition to carbon pricing, and reluctance to utilize renewables other than biomass co-firing. These groups' key resource – coal – enjoys not only wide political support, but also popular opinion on the whole does not support the vision of leaving coal underground and paying much more for energy (Kundzewicz 2013), resulting in energy carriers having a strong societal backup particularly from the mining industry. Similarly, Edwin Bendyk (2015, p. 13) notes that during the early 2015 miners' strike, Poland's green party used the slogan "We support the miners but fight against the coal lobby." Such polarization is based on the belief that the decarbonization of the country's economy is inevitable and necessary. However, this could not be done at the expense of workers and their rights. Later that year during the electoral campaign for the parliamentary elections, a particular focus of PO and PiS concerned the situation and future of miners. PiS were able to gain an absolute majority after making a pledge to coal miners not to close a single mine (Olszewski 2017). Likewise, both parties claimed that the EU directives were inappropriate for the Polish energy sector, yet differed on how to respond (Hess and Renner 2019). Yet, little research so far addresses the possible influence of these interest groups on national (or even European) climate and energy legislation. In addition, discourse on energy issues has been based mainly on the elitist model (e.g., Stankiewicz 2014; Świątkiewicz-Mośny and Wagner 2012; Wagner et al. 2016) with favoring opinions and attitudes of experts, politicians, and government whose discourse is strongly economized and the perspective of sustainable development being marginalized. At the same time, miners' unions, utilities, as well as mining companies are much more involved in the decision-making than, e.g., local authorities or farmers (Vasev 2017, p. 1151). This is additionally reinforced through the ease which individuals cross the frontier between political posts (e.g., parliamentarians, political ministerial officials) and organizational roles (e.g., leadership and supervisory positions in state-owned and private companies), without raising alerts about a conflict of interests (Szulecki 2018). Yet, besides their small numbers and geographical concentration in specific Polish regions (i.e., Upper Silesia and Lublin), the miners still have strong power to exercise influence in the energy governance process. Hence, the opportunities for a successful energy transition (however this will unfold) will remain strongly linked to the situation in the coal-mining industry.

Cross-References

- ▸ Energy Governance in the Czech Republic
- ▸ Energy Governance in Germany
- ▸ Energy Governance in Hungary
- ▸ Energy Governance in Russia: From a Fossil to a Green Giant?
- ▸ Energy Governance in Slovakia
- ▸ European Union Energy Policy: A Discourse Perspective

Acknowledgments The author would like to thank all colleagues for comments, feedback, and suggestions given throughout the writing process of this chapter. The findings here draw upon research conducted with the financial support of the German Federal Ministry of Education and Research (Reference: 03SFK4P0, Consortium ENavi, Kopernikus).

References

Adamczyk, J., Piwowar, A., & Dzikuć, M. (2017). Air protection programmes in Poland in the context of the low emission. *Environmental Science and Pollution Research International, 24*(19), 16316–16327.
Adamus, W., & Florkowski, W. J. (2016). The evolution of shale gas development and energy security in Poland: Presenting a hierarchical choice of priorities. *Energy Research & Social Science, 20*, 168–178.
Agora Energiewende and Sandbag. (2018). *The European Power Sector in 2017*. State of Affairs and Review of Current Developments. London and Berlin.
Ancygier, A. (2013). *Misfit of interests instead of the 'Goodness of fit'? Implementation of European*. Directives 2001/77/EC and 2009/28/EC in Poland. Hamburg: Verlag Dr. Kovac.

Ancygier, A., & Szulecki, K. (2014). Does local energy mean renewable? Report from a survey on the acceptance for the development of renewable energy sources among Polish Local Authorities. In *ESPRi Report* (1).

Badera, J. (2014). Problems of the social non-acceptance of mining projects with particular emphasis on the European Union – A literature review. *Environmental & Socio-Economic Studies, 2*(1), 27–34.

Badera, J., & Kocoń, P. (2014). Local community opinions regarding the socio-environmental aspects of lignite surface mining: Experiences from central Poland. *Energy Policy, 66*, 507–516.

Bałtowski, M., & Kozarzewski, P. (2016). Formal and real ownership structure of the Polish economy: State-owned versus state-controlled enterprises. *Post-Communist Economies, 28*(3), 405–419.

Baran, J., Lewandowski, P., Szpor, A., & Witajewski-Baltvilks, J. (2018). *Coal transitions in Poland – Options for a fair and feasible transition for the Polish coal sector*. IDDRI & Climate Strategies.

Barteczko, A., & Koper, A. (2017, September 26). Polish coal miner struggles to meet demand after investment cut. *Reuters*. Retrieved from https://www.reuters.com/article/us-poland-coal/polish-coal-miner-struggles-to-meet-demand-after-investment-cut-idUSKCN1C11T0

Bayer, B., Schäuble, D., & Ferrari, M. (2018). International experiences with tender procedures for renewable energy – A comparison of current developments in Brazil, France, Italy and South Africa. *Renewable and Sustainable Energy Reviews, 95*, 305–327.

Bendyk, E. (2015). Świat bez węgla. In E. Bendyk, U. Papajak, M. Popkiewicz, & M. Sutowski (Eds.), *Polski węgiel* (pp. 7–70). Warsaw: Wydawnictwo Krytyki Politycznej.

Bento, J. P. C., Szczygiel, N., & Moutinho, V. (2017). Fossil fuel power generation and economic growth in Poland. *Energy Sources, Part B: Economics, Planning, and Policy, 10*, 1–6.

Berendt, J. (2017, January 14). Warsaw grapples with gloomy, Gray Smog. *The New York Times*. Retrieved from https://www.nytimes.com/2017/01/14/world/europe/warsaw-air-pollution-smog.html

Bilgin, M. (2009). Geopolitics of European natural gas demand: Supplies from Russia, Caspian and the Middle East. *Energy Policy, 37*(11), 4482–4492.

Biuro Bezpieczeństwa Narodowego. (2012). *Analiza nt. wielkości strat w przesyle energii elektrycznej w Polsce*. Warsaw: Biuro Bezpieczeństwa Narodowego.

Bocquillon, P., & Maltby, T. (2017). The more the merrier? Assessing the impact of enlargement on EU performance in energy and climate change policies. *East European Politics, 33*(1), 88–105.

Boussena, S., & Locatelli, C. (2013). Energy institutional and organisational changes in EU and Russia: Revisiting gas relations. *Energy Policy, 55*, 180–189.

Bouzarovski, S., & Tirado Herrero, S. (2016). Geographies of injustice: The socio-spatial determinants of energy poverty in Poland, the Czech Republic and Hungary. *Post-Communist Economies, 29*(1), 27–50.

Bradshaw, M. J. (2014). *Global energy dilemmas: Energy security, globalization, and climate change*. Cambridge, UK: Polity.

Braun, M. (2014). EU climate norms in East-Central Europe. *JCMS: Journal of Common Market Studies, 52*(3), 445–460.

Brzezińska-Rawa, A., & Goździewicz-Biechońska, J. (2014). Recent developments in the wind energy sector in Poland. *Renewable and Sustainable Energy Reviews, 38*, 79–87.

Bukowski, M., Maśnicki, J., Śniegocki, A., & Trzeciakowski, R. (2015). *Polski węgiel: quo vadis? Perspektywy rozwoju górnictwa węgla kamiennego w Polsce*. Warsaw: Warszawski Instytut Studiów Ekonomicznych.

Cansino, J., Sánchez-Braza, A., & Sanz-Díaz, T. (2018). Policy instruments to promote electro-mobility in the EU28: A comprehensive review. *Sustainability, 10*(7), 2507.

Ceglarz, A., & Ancygier, A. (2015). Chapter 6: The Polish renewable energy and climate policies under the impact of the EU. In I. P. Karolewski & M. Sus (Eds.), *The transformative power of Europe: The case of Poland* (pp. 137–168). Baden-Baden: Nomos.

Central Statistical Office. (2017). Statistical Yearbook of the Republic of Poland 2017.

Ćetković, S., & Buzogány, A. (2016). Varieties of capitalism and clean energy transitions in the European Union: When renewable energy hits different economic logics. *Climate Policy, 16*(5), 642–657.

Chodkowska-Miszczuk, J., Biegańska, J., Środa-Murawska, S., Grzelak-Kostulska, E., & Rogatka, K. (2016). European Union funds in the development of renewable energy sources in Poland in the context of the cohesion policy. *Energy & Environment, 27*(6–7), 713–725.

Cianciara, A. K. (2017). Contestation of EU climate policy in Poland: Civil society and politics of national interest. *Prakseologia, 159*, 237–264.

Ciepiela, D. (2018, March 6). Rząd przyjął nowelizację ustawy o OZE. *wnp.pl.* Retrieved from https://energetyka.wnp.pl/rzad-przyjal-nowelizacje-ustawy-o-oze,318927_1_0_0.html

Ciobanu, C., & Kość, W. (2017, August 12). Warsaw grabs purse strings of Polish NGOs. *politico.eu.* Retrieved from https://www.politico.eu/article/pis-polish-ngos-fear-the-governments-embrace/

Climate Action Network Europe. (2018). *Off target. Ranking of EU countries' ambition and progress in fighting climate change.* Brussels: Climate Action Network Europe.

Dawid, L. (2017). German support systems for onshore wind farms in the context of Polish acts limiting wind energy development. *Journal of Water and Land Development, 34*(1), 109–115.

dentons.com. (2017). Changes to RES Act in Poland. Retrieved from https://www.dentons.com/en/insights/alerts/2017/july/27/changes-to-res-act-in-poland

Derski, B. (2017, April 20). 20 lat Prawa energetycznego. wysokienapiecie.pl. Retrieved from http://wysokienapiecie.pl/prawo-energetyczne/2203-20-lat-prawa-energetycznego

Dzikuć, M., & Piwowar, A. (2016). Ecological and economic aspects of electric energy production using the biomass co-firing method: The case of Poland. *Renewable and Sustainable Energy Reviews, 55*, 856–862.

Ericsson, K. (2007). Co-firing – A strategy for bioenergy in Poland? *Energy, 32*(10), 1838–1847.

Euractiv. (2018, April 4). EU carbon market emissions rise for first time in 7 years in 2017. Retrieved from https://www.euractiv.com/section/emissions-trading-scheme/news/eu-carbon-market-emissions-rise-for-first-time-in-7-years-in-2017/

EurObserv'ER. (2017). The state of renewable energies in Europe. 2017 Edition. Retrieved from https://www.eurobserv-er.org/category/barometer-2017

Eurostat. (2018a). Energy dependence (Code: t2020_rd320). Retrieved 1 February, 2018, from http://ec.europa.eu/eurostat/tgm/table.do?tab=table&init=1&language=en&pcode=t2020_rd320&plugin=1

Eurostat. (2018b). Energy dependence by product (Code: sdg_07_50). Retrieved 1 February, 2018, from http://ec.europa.eu/eurostat/tgm/refreshTableAction.do?tab=table&plugin=1&pcode=sdg_07_50&language=en

Eurostat. (2018c). Europe 2020 indicators. Climate change and energy (t2020_hc). Retrieved 1 February, 2018, from http://ec.europa.eu/eurostat/web/europe-2020-indicators/europe-2020-strategy/main-tables

Fischer, S. (2014). The EU's new energy and climate policy framework for 2030, SWP Comments, 55, December 2014, Berlin.

Fischer, S., & Geden, O. (2015). Die Grenzen der Energieunion, SWP SWP-Aktuell, 2015/A 36, April 2015. Retrieved from https://www.swp-berlin.org/fileadmin/contents/products/aktuell/2015A36_fis_gdn.pdf

Formuszewicz, R., & Gawlikowska-Fyk, A. (2014). New EU energy and climate framework: Challenges for Poland and Germany (PISM policy paper, Vol. 6, No. 89, pp. 1–6). Warsaw: Polish Institute of International Affairs (Polski Instytut Spraw Międzynarodowych, PISM) in cooperation with the Konrad Adenauer Foundation.

Forum Energii. (2019a). Energy transition in Poland 2018. Retrieved from https://forum-energii.eu/en/analizy/transformacja-2019

Forum Energii. (2019b). PEP2040 scrutinized by Forum Energii. Comments and recommendations on Poland's Energy Policy until 2040.

Fuksiewicz, A., & Klein, J. (2014). *Euroscepticism in the Polish and German 2014 European Election Campaign*. Warsaw: Instytut Spraw Publicznych.

Gawel, E., Strunz, S., & Lehmann, P. (2017). Support policies for renewables – instrument choice and instrument change from a public choice perspective. In D. Arent, C. Arndt, M. Miller, F. Tarp, O. Zinaman, & D. Arent (Eds.), *The political economy of clean energy transitions* (pp. 80–99). Oxford: Oxford University Press.

Gawlik, L. (2018). The Polish power industry in energy transformation process. *Mineral Economics, 31*(1–2), 229–237.

Gawlik, L., Szurlej, A., & Wyrwa, A. (2015). The impact of the long-term EU target for renewables on the structure of electricity production in Poland. *Energy, 92*, 172–178.

Gawlik, L., Kaliski, M., Kamiński, J., Sikora, A. P., & Szurlej, A. (2016). Hard coal in the fuel-mix of Poland: The long-term perspective. *Archives of Mining Sciences, 61*(2), 301.

Geels, F. W., & Schot, J. (2007). Typology of sociotechnical transition pathways. *Research Policy, 36*(3), 399–417.

Geels, F. W., Berkhout, F., & van Vuuren, D. P. (2016). Bridging analytical approaches for low-carbon transitions. *Nature Climate Change, 6*(6), 1–8.

Gény, F. (2010). Can Unconventional Gas be a Game Changer in European Gas Markets? Oxford: Oxford Institute for Energy Studies. Retrieved from https://www.oxfordenergy.org/publications/can-unconventional-gas-be-a-game-changer-in-european-gas-markets/?v=3a52f3c22ed6

Godzimirski, J. M. (2016). Can the Polish shale gas dog still bark? Politics and policy of unconventional hydrocarbons in Poland. *Energy Research & Social Science, 20*, 158–167.

Goldthau, A. (2018). *The politics of shale gas in Eastern Europe: Energy security, contested technologies and the social license to frack* (Cambridge studies in comparative public policy). Cambridge, UK/New York: Cambridge University Press.

Goldthau, A., & LaBelle, M. (2016). The power of policy regimes: Explaining shale gas policy divergence in Bulgaria and Poland. *Review of Policy Research, 33*(6), 603–622.

Golonko, J. (2015, September 23). Plan budowy biogazowni w każdej gminie spalił na panewce. *Polskie Radio*. Retrieved from https://www.polskieradio.pl/42/3167/Artykul/1509433,Plan-budowy-biogazowni-w-kazdej-gminie-spalil-na-panewce

Gomułka, S. (2016). Poland's economic and social transformation 1989–2014 and contemporary challenges. *Central Bank Review, 16*(1), 19–23.

Hajto, M., Cichocki, Z., Bidłasik, M., Borzyszkowski, J., & Kuśmierz, A. (2017). Constraints on development of wind energy in Poland due to environmental objectives. Is there space in Poland for wind farm siting? *Environmental Management, 59*(2), 204–217.

Hall, P. A., & Soskice, D. W. (2001). *Varieties of capitalism: The institutional foundations of comparative advantage*. Oxford: Oxford University Press.

Herold, A., Siemons, A., & Wojtal, L. (2017). Climate and Energy policies in Poland. Retrieved from http://www.europarl.europa.eu/thinktank/en/document.html?reference=IPOL_BRI%282017%29607335

Hess, D. J., & Renner, M. (2019). Conservative political parties and energy transitions in Europe: Opposition to climate mitigation policies. *Renewable and Sustainable Energy Reviews, 104*, 419–428.

Huber, E. (2016, December 31). Polish city more polluted than Beijing. *Financial Times*. Retrieved from https://www.ft.com/content/6712dd66-c91d-11e6-8f29-9445cac8966f

Ikenberry, G. J. (1986). The irony of state strength: Comparative responses to the oil shocks in the 1970s. *International Organization, 40*(1), 105–137.

International Energy Agency. (2016). Energy policies of IEA countries – Poland – 2016 Review.

International Energy Agency. (2018). Poland is working on amending its Renewable Energy Law, 26 April 2018 Renewable Energy Policy Update, 19.

International Renewable Energy Agency. (2015). *REmap 2030: Renewable energy prospects for Poland*. Abu Dhabi: IRENA.

Jänicke, M., & Quitzow, R. (2017). Multi-level reinforcement in European climate and energy governance: Mobilizing economic interests at the sub-national levels. *Environmental Policy and Governance, 27*(2), 122–136.

Jankowska, K. (2011). Poland's climate change policy struggle: Greening the East? In R. Wurzel & J. Connelly (Eds.), *The European Union as a leader in international climate change politics* (pp. 163–178). London: Routledge.

Jankowska, K. (2017). Poland's clash over energy and climate policy. Green economy or grey status quo? In R. K. W. Wurzel, J. Connelly, & D. Liefferink (Eds.), *The European Union in international climate change politics. Still taking a lead?* (pp. 145–158). New York: Routledge.

Jankowska, K., & Ancygier, A. (2017). Poland at the renewable energy policy crossroads: An incongruent Europeanization? In I. Solorio & H. Jörgens (Eds.), *A guide to EU renewable energy policy* (pp. 183–203). Cheltenham: Edward Elgar.

Jezierska-Thöle, A., Rudnicki, R., & Kluba, M. (2016). Development of energy crops cultivation for biomass production in Poland. *Renewable and Sustainable Energy Reviews, 62*, 534–545.

Jonek Kowalska, I. (2015). Challenges for long-term industry restructuring in the Upper Silesian Coal Basin: What has Polish coal mining achieved and failed from a twenty-year perspective? *Resources Policy, 44*, 135–149.

Jožef Stefan Institute. (2014). CODE2 Cogeneration Observatory and Dissemination Europe D5.1 Final Cogeneration roadmap for Poland.

Judge, A., & Maltby, T. (2017). European energy union? Caught between securitisation and 'riskification'. *European Journal of International Security, 2*(2), 179–202.

Kamiński, J., & Kudełko, M. (2010). The prospects for hard coal as a fuel for the Polish power sector. *Energy Policy, 38*(12), 7939–7950.

Kamola-Cieślik, M. (2018). The Government's policy in the field of hard coal mining restructuration as an element of Poland's energy security. *Polish Political Science Yearbook, 46*(2), 247–261.

Karaczun, Z., Kassenberg, A., Szpor, A., & Śpionek, A. (2013). Część V: Klimat dla polityki klimatycznej [Part V: The climate for climate policy]. In M. Bukowski (Ed.), *2050.pl – podróż do niskoemisyjnej przyszłości* [Report 2050.pl – the journey to the low-emission future] (pp. 187–214). Warsaw: Instytut Badań Strukturalnych/Instytut na rzecz Ekorozwoju.

Kemmerzell, J., & Hofmeister, A. (2019). Innovationen in der Klimaschutzpolitik deutscher Großstädte. *Politische Vierteljahresschrift, 60*(1), 1–32. C:\Users\enie\AppData\Local\Temp \0134-4.

Keohane, R. O., & Nye, J. S. (1989 [2012]). *Power and interdependence* (4th ed.). Boston: Longman.

Kłaczyński, R. (2017). Polsko-rosyjska współpraca w sektorze energetycznym: stan obecny, perspektywy. *Nowa Polityka Wschodnia, 2*(13), 44–59.

Knodt, M. (2018). Energy policy. In H. Heinelt & S. Münch (Eds.), *Handbooks of research on public policy. Handbook of European policies: Interpretive approaches to the EU* (pp. 224–240). Cheltenham: Edward Elgar.

Knodt, M., & Kenmerzell, J. (2017). *European energy transitions compared. Building blocks of a framework for analysis.* Paper presented at the ECPR general conference, Oslo, September 6–9, 2017.

Kuchler, M., & Bridge, G. (2018). Down the black hole: Sustaining national socio-technical imaginaries of coal in Poland. *Energy Research & Social Science, 41*, 136–147.

Kundzewicz, Z. W. (2013). *Cieplejszy świat: Rzecz o zmianach klimatu.* Warsaw: Wydawnictwo Naukowe PWN.

Kundzewicz, Z. W., & Matczak, P. (2012). Climate change regional review: Poland. *Wiley Interdisciplinary Reviews: Climate Change, 3*(4), 297–311.

Kundzewicz, Z. W., Masson-Delmotte, V., Cubasch, U., Skea, J., & Kleiber, M. (2015). Climate change – Is it worse than expected? *Papers on Global Change IGBP, 22*(1), 9–18.

Kundzewicz, Z. W., Painter, J., & Kundzewicz, W. J. (2017). Climate change in the media: Poland's exceptionalism. *Environmental Communication, 3*, 1–15.

Leiren, M. D., Szulecki, K., Rayner, T., & Banet, C. (2019). Energy security concerns versus market harmony: The Europeanisation of capacity mechanisms. *Politics and Governance, 7*(1), 92–104.

Liebe, U., Bartczak, A., & Meyerhoff, J. (2017). A turbine is not only a turbine: The role of social context and fairness characteristics for the local acceptance of wind power. *Energy Policy, 107*, 300–308.

Lijphart, A. (2012). *Patterns of democracy: Government forms and performance in thirty-six countries* (2nd ed.). New Haven: Yale University Press.

Lipset, S. M., & Stein, R. (Eds.). (1967). *Party systems and voter alignments: Cross-national perspectives*. New York: The Free Press.

Manowska, A., Osadnik, K. T., & Wyganowska, M. (2017). Economic and social aspects of restructuring Polish coal mining: Focusing on Poland and the EU. *Resources Policy, 52*, 192–200.

Marcinkiewicz, K., & Tosun, J. (2015). Contesting climate change: Mapping the political debate in Poland. *East European Politics, 31*(2), 187–207.

Markowski, R. (2006). The polish elections of 2005: Pure chaos or a restructuring of the party system? *West European Politics, 29*(4), 814–832.

Matuszewska, D., Kuta, M., Górski, J., Suwała, W., Dudek, M., Leszczyński, J., & Łopata, S. (2017). Cogeneration – Development and prospect in Polish energy sector. *E3S Web of Conferences, 14*, 1021.

Michalak, P., & Zimny, J. (2011). Wind energy development in the world, Europe and Poland from 1995 to 2009; current status and future perspectives. *Renewable and Sustainable Energy Reviews, 15*(5), 2330–2341.

Ministerstwo Energii. (2017). Plan Rozwoju. Elektromobilności w Polsce. "Energia do przyszłości".

Ministerstwo Energii. (2018). *Energetyczna Polski do 2040 roku (PEP2040)*. Warsaw: Ministerstwo Energi.

Ministry of Economy. (2009). *Energy policy of Poland until 2030*. Warsaw.

Muras, Z. (2011). *'Rainbow Vertigo' – Or a description of Polish support schemes for renewable and cogeneration sources*. Warsaw: Energy Regulatory Office, Department of Energy Enterprises of Energy Regulatory Office.

Myers Jaffe, A., & O'Sullivan, M. L. (2012). *The geopolitics of natural gas*. Report of Scenarios Workshop of Harvard University's Belfer Center and Rice University's Baker Institute Energy Forum. Retrieved from https://www.belfercenter.org/publication/geopolitics-natural-gas

Nabrdalik, M., & Santora, M. (2018, April 22). Smothered by smog, Polish Cities Rank among Europe's Dirtiest. *New York Times*. Retrieved from https://www.nytimes.com/2018/04/22/world/europe/poland-pollution.html

Nilsson, L. J., Pisarek, M., Buriak, J., Oniszk-Popławska, A., Bućko, P., Ericsson, K., & Jaworski, L. (2006). Energy policy and the role of bioenergy in Poland. *Energy Policy, 34*(15), 2263–2278.

noerr.com (2017). Poland: New support scheme for cogeneration. Retrieved from https://www.noerr.com/en/newsroom/News/poland-new-support-scheme-for-cogeneration.aspx

Olkuski, T. (2014). Analiza krajowej struktury wytwarzania energii elektrycznej z węgla kamiennego. *Zeszyty Naukowe Instytutu Gospodarki Surowcami Mineralnymi I Energią PAN, 87*, 37–47.

Olszewski, M. (2017). Walk away from coal? Poland and European climate policy. Energy Transition. The Global Energiewende. Retrieved from https://energytransition.org/2017/04/walk-away-from-coal-or-not-poland-and-eu-climate-policy/

Osička, J., Kemmerzell, J., Zoll, M., Lehotský, L., Černoch, F., & Knodt, M. (forthcoming). What's next for the European coal heartland? Exploring the future of coal in German, Polish and Czech press. *Energy Research & Social Science* (Manuscript accepted for publication).

Osiecka-Brzeska, K. (2016). Conditions for development of renewable energy in Poland. In A. Batisha, M. M. Erdoğdu, T. Arun, & I. H. Ahmad (Eds.), *Practice, progress, and proficiency in sustainability. Handbook of research on green economic development initiatives and strategies*. Hershey: IGI Global.

Paska, J., & Surma, T. (2014). Electricity generation from renewable energy sources in Poland. *Renewable Energy, 71*, 286–294.

Paska, J., Sałek, M., & Surma, T. (2009). Current status and perspectives of renewable energy sources in Poland. *Renewable and Sustainable Energy Reviews, 13*(1), 142–154.

Piaskowska-Silarska, M., Gumuła, S., Pytel, K., & Migo, P. (2017). Technical and economic analysis of using biomass energy. *E3S Web Conferences*, 14.

Popkiewicz, M. (2015). Polska bez węgla. In E. Bendyk, U. Papajak, M. Popkiewicz, & M. Sutowski (Eds.), *Polski węgiel* (1st ed., pp. 71–172). Warsaw: Wydawnictwo Krytyki Politycznej.

PSE: w 2020 r. może wystąpić niedobór mocy w systemie energetycznym. (2016, May 23). Retrieved from http://biznes.onet.pl/wiadomosci/kraj/pse-w-2020-r-moze-wystapic-niedobor-mocy-w-systemie-energetycznym/2ze35l

RAP. (2018). Report on the Polish Power System. Version 2.0 Study commissioned by Agora Energiewende.

res-legal.eu. (2016). Legal sources on renewable energy: Poland. Retrieved from http://www.res-legal.eu/search-by-country/poland/

Rosicki, R. (2016). Poland's gas security. *Przegląd Politologiczny, 1*, 159–172.

Rylukowski, W. (2016, May 16). Poland's Żywiec is the most polluted city in EU. wbj.pl. Retrieved from http://wbj.pl/polands-zywiec-is-the-most-polluted-city-in-eu/

Sachs, J. (1992). The economic transformation of Eastern Europe: The case of Poland. *The American Economist, 36*(2), 3–11.

Sachs, J. D. (1994). *Shock therapy in Poland: Perspectives of five years*. The Tanner Lectures on Human Values, University of Utah, 6–7 April 1994.

Schmidt, M. G. (2002). Political performance and types of democracy: Findings from comparative studies. *European Journal of Political Research, 41*(1), 147–163.

Simon, F. (2017, November 15). Think tank: Coal crisis, not climate policy, is forcing Polish energy overhaul. Retrieved from https://www.euractiv.com/section/electricity/interview/15-nov-think-tank-coal-crisis-not-climate-policy-is-forcing-polish-energy-overhaul

Simon, F. (2018, February 9). Polish exec: Electro-Mobility Act creates whole ecosystem for EVs. Retrieved from https://www.euractiv.com/section/energy/interview/polish-exec-electro-mobility-act-creates-whole-ecosystem-for-evs/

Skjærseth, J. B. (2016). Implementation in Poland. In J. B. Skjærseth, P. O. Eikeland, L. H. Gulbrandsen, T. Jevnaker, & J. B. Skjræseth (Eds.), New horizons in environmental politics. Linking EU climate and energy policies: Decision-making, implementation and reform (pp. 120–146). Cheltenham, UK: Edward Elgar.

Skjærseth, J. B. (2018). Implementing EU climate and energy policies in Poland: Policy feedback and reform. *Environmental Politics, 27*(3), 1–21.

Skorupska, A. (2015). *Polish local government support for green energy and climate project*. Bulletin no. 60(792). The Polish Institute of International Affairs.

Skwierz, S. (2017). The role of transport sector in CO2 reduction in Poland. *E3S web conferences*, 14.

Śliwiński, K., & Pourzitakis, S. (2018). European energy security through foreign policy analysis: Nord stream 1 and its consequences. *Asia-Pacific Journal of EU Studies, 15*(2), 41–65.

Smyrgała, D. (2016). Energy governance and compliance with the EU regulations in Poland prior to the adoption of the 2030 energy and climate framework. *Securitologia, 23*(1), 33–45.

Sokołowski, M. M. (2017). Discovering the new renewable legal order in Poland: With or without wind? *Energy Policy, 106*, 68–74.

Stankiewicz, P. (2014). Zbudujemy wam elektrownię (atomową!): Praktyka oceny technologii przy rozwoju energetyki jądrowej w Polsce. *Studia Socjologiczne, 1*(212), 77–107.

Stępińska, A., Lipiński, A., Hess, A., & Piontek, D. (2017). A fourth wave of populism? In T. Aalberg, F. Esser, C. Reinemann, J. Stromback, & C. De Vreese (Eds.), *Populist political communication in Europe* (pp. 311–325). London: Routledge.

Streimikiene, D., Klevas, V., & Bubeliene, J. (2007). Use of EU structural funds for sustainable energy development in new EU member states. *Renewable and Sustainable Energy Reviews, 11*(6), 1167–1187.

Suwala, W. (2018). Coal sector in Poland, light in the tunnel or dimming candle? *Mineral Economics, 31*(1–2), 263–268.

Świątkiewicz-Mośny, M., & Wagner, A. (2012). How much energy in energy policy? The media on energy problems in developing countries (with the example of Poland). *Energy Policy, 50*, 383–390.

Świderek, T. (2017, July 11). Auta elektryczne napędzą popyt na prąd. Wysokie Napięcie. Retrieved from http://wysokienapiecie.pl/technologie/2406-auta-elektryczne-napedza-popyt-na-prad

Świerzewski, M., & Gładysz, P. (2017). Environmental and economic assessment of a biomass-based cogeneration plant: Polish case study. *MAZOWSZE Studia Regionalne*, (22), 97–114.

Szczerbiak, A. (2007). 'Social Poland' defeats 'liberal Poland'?: The September–October 2005 Polish parliamentary and presidential elections. *Journal of Communist Studies and Transition Politics, 23*(2), 203–232.

Szczerbiak, A. (2008). The birth of a bi-polar party system or a referendum on a polarising government?: The October 2007 Polish parliamentary election. *Journal of Communist Studies and Transition Politics, 24*(3), 415–443.

Szczerbowski, R. (2013). Bezpieczeństwo energetyczne Polski – mix energetyczny i efektywnooeæ energetyczna. *Polityka Energetyczna, 16*(4), 35–47.

Szulecka, J., & Szulecki, K. (2013). Analysing the Rospuda River controversy in Poland: Rhetoric, environmental activism, and the influence of the European Union. *East European Politics, 29*(4), 397–419.

Szulecki, K. (2017). *Poland's renewable energy policy mix: European influence and domestic soap opera*. CICERO working papers 1/2017. Available at SSRN: https://ssrn.com/abstract=2964866

Szulecki, K. (2018). Poland. The revolving door between politics and dirty energy in Poland: A governmental-industrial complex. In *Revolving doors and the fossil fuel industry: Time to tackle conflicts of interest in climate policy-making* (pp. 96–107). Report commissioned by The Greens/EFA Group in the European Parliament, Brussels.

Szulecki, K., Ancygier, A., & Szwed, D. (2015). *Energy democratization? Societal aspects of decarbonization in the German and Polish energy sectors*. In ESPRi working papers 5.

Szulecki, K., Fischer, S., Gullberg, A. T., & Sartor, O. (2016). Shaping the 'Energy Union': Between national positions and governance innovation in EU energy and climate policy. *Climate Policy, 16*(5), 548–567.

Szydło, B. (2016). Likwidacja Ministerstwa Skarbu Państwa. Retrieved from https://www.premier.gov.pl/mobile/wydarzenia/aktualnosci/likwidacja-ministerstwa-skarbu-panstwa.html

Tomjałojc, L. (2008). Energetyka obywtaelska czyli od kopałł do wiatru i sćołca. *Czysta Energia, 6*(80), 20–23.

Tusk, D. (2014, April 21). A united Europe can end Russia's energy stranglehold. *Financial Times*. Retrieved from https://www.ft.com/content/91508464-c661-11e3-ba0e-00144feabdc0

Vasev, N. (2017). Governing energy while neglecting health – The case of Poland. *Health Policy, 121*(11), 1147–1153.

Verbruggen, A., & Lauber, V. (2012). Assessing the performance of renewable electricity support instruments. *Energy Policy, 45*, 635–644. https://doi.org/10.1016/j.enpol.2012.03.014.

Wagner, A. (Ed.). (2017). *Visible and invisible: Nuclear energy, shale gas and wind power, in the Polish media discourse* (1st ed.). Krakow: Jagiellonian University Press.

Wagner, A., Grobelski, T., & Harembski, M. (2016). Is energy policy a public issue? Nuclear power in Poland and implications for energy transitions in Central and East Europe. *Energy Research & Social Science, 13*, 158–169.

Wasik, Z. (2017, September 14). Poland pins hopes on electric-vehicle future. *Financial Times*. Retrieved from https://www.ft.com/content/1c1f982c-5823-11e7-80b6-9bfa4c1f83d2

Wedel, M. (2016). *The European integration of RES-E promotion: The case of Germany and Poland. Energiepolitik und Klimaschutz. Energy policy and climate protection*. Wiesbaden: Springer.

Wędzik, A., Siewierski, T., & Szypowski, M. (2017). Green certificates market in Poland – The sources of crisis. *Renewable and Sustainable Energy Reviews, 75*, 490–503.

Witajewski-Baltvilks, J., Lewandowski, P., Szpor, A., Baran, J., & Antosiewicz, M. (2018). Managing coal sector transition under the ambitious emission reduction scenario in Poland. Focus on labour. IBS Research Report 04/2018.

Włodarski, M., & Martyniuk-Pęczek, J. (2017). Relevance of the EU structural funds' allocation to the needs of combating air pollution in Poland. Analysis of the operational programmes of regions threatened with critical air pollution from distributed energy sources. *IOP conference series: Materials Science and Engineering, 245*, 82060.

World Energy Council 2014. (2014). *Energy sector of the world and Poland: Beginnings, development, present state*. Warsaw.

Zawieska, J., & Pieriegud, J. (2018). Smart city as a tool for sustainable mobility and transport decarbonisation. *Transport Policy, 63*, 39–50.

Energy Governance in Portugal

38

Luís Guerreiro, Helge Jörgens, and Vicente Alves

Contents

Introduction	960
General Conditions of Energy Governance in Portugal	961
Legacies of Energy Governance	961
Composition of the Energy Mix	963
Discourse on Energy Issues	966
Political Institutions and Actors	967
Coordination, Instruments, and Issues of the Portuguese Energy Transition	970
Drivers of the Energy Transition	970
Strategies and Instruments	974
Coordination Mechanisms and Multilevel Governance	978
Outcomes, Challenges, and Prospects of Energy Governance in Portugal	979
Cross-References	983
References	983

Abstract

Portugal is in the middle of a major transformation of its energy supply, which has been shaped by internal resource constraints, growing environmental concerns, and the dynamics of European integration. Portugal's past choices – the investment in hydropower and the refusal of nuclear energy – and the lack of an endowment of resources have constrained the Portuguese energy policy. With the accession to the European Union in 1986, environmental concerns moved up

---

L. Guerreiro · V. Alves
CIES_Iscte – Centre for Research and Studies in Sociology, Lisbon, Portugal
e-mail: luis.a.c.guerreiro@gmail.com; Vicente_Silva_Alves@iscte-iul.pt

H. Jörgens (✉)
CIES_Iscte – Centre for Research and Studies in Sociology, Lisbon, Portugal

Department of Political Science and Public Policy, Iscte – Instituto Universitário de Lisboa, Lisbon, Portugal
e-mail: helge.jorgens@iscte-iul.pt

© Springer Nature Switzerland AG 2022
M. Knodt, J. Kemmerzell (eds.), *Handbook of Energy Governance in Europe*,
https://doi.org/10.1007/978-3-030-43250-8_23

the Portuguese policy agenda. The EU's push for a common electricity market influenced a set of policies oriented toward the liberalization of the energy market, which was centralized, monopolistic, and public owned. The investment in renewable energy gained momentum in the 2000s, led by the Portuguese government and EDP, the (then) publicly owned energy company, supported by a public discourse on climate change and energy policy imbued with economic rationality. The financial crisis that hit Portugal in 2010 led to a temporary stall in the promotion of the use of energy from renewable energy sources (RES), but new market-based support schemes, such as photovoltaic solar auctions, have fostered the recent new investment in renewables.

Keywords

Portugal · Energy governance · Renewable energy · Energy transition · Energy policy · Climate policy · Feed-in tariffs · Solar auctions

Introduction

Portugal is in the middle of a major transformation of its energy supply. The Portuguese Energy and Climate Plan projects a significant shift toward renewable energy combined with a decommissioning of coal power plants, improved energy efficiency, investment in technologies that substitute oil in the transportation sector, and better interconnections with Spain (and, indirectly, with France and Europe) to achieve the goals of the European Energy Union (European Commission 2020a). The commitment to ratify the Paris Agreement is a key driver, and a National Plan for turning the economy carbon neutral by 2050 was approved in 2019 (República Portuguesa 2019a). In 2018, Portugal's gross inland energy consumption of renewables reached 30.3%, while the EU average stood at 18.9% (Eurostat 2020).

This chapter maps the evolution of the Portuguese energy governance, focuses on the development of renewable energy that has been at the core of the Portuguese energy transition, and identifies the drivers and major actors that have been relevant in shaping this policy. The Portuguese transition has been driven by internal resource constraints, growing environmental concerns, and European integration. Early Portuguese energy policies took a pragmatic approach to energy efficiency and independence with an investment in coal and oil, as well as hydropower (Madureira and Baptista 2002), which was the most accessible endogenous energy resource in the country, but refrained from including nuclear energy in the national energy mix (Barca and Delicado 2016, p. 504). These choices shaped the Portuguese investment in renewable energy and the evolution of the Portuguese energy mix in the 1990s and 2000s.

With the accession to the European Union in 1986, environmental concerns moved up the Portuguese policy agenda, and more coherent environmental policies were developed (Araújo and Coelho 2013, pp. 147–148). Since then, successive governments have prioritized energy security, energy efficiency, and sustainable development. The European Union's push for a common electricity market and the recommendations and directives aimed at the liberalization of national energy markets influenced the Portuguese policies. In the late 1990s, Portugal initiated the liberalization of its energy market which previously was centralized, monopolistic, and public owned. Since then, all public companies – including the transportation and the distribution companies that have high stakes in energy supply and security – have been privatized, the retail markets have been deregulated for industrial and household consumers, and an Iberian energy market has been created, which facilitated the import and export of energy (although limited by network capacity).

In the 2000s, investment in renewable energy gained momentum. The main actors were the Portuguese government, pushing forward the renewable agenda in tandem with the EU, and EDP, the (then) publicly owned energy company. The energy mix changed as the share of renewable energy sources (RES) in electricity generation increased and fossil fuel consumption declined. By 2010, the economy had significantly reduced its energy intensity (Guevara and Domingos 2017) and Portugal had become a forerunner in RES deployment. The Portuguese energy transition became palpable.

Public discourses on climate and energy policy were strongly influenced by notions of economic rationality (Carvalho et al. 2014). The media and government emphasized the idea of ecological modernization, explaining the need for climate change mitigation and the benefits of a green economy. However, despite high levels of environmental concern, centralized processes of decision-making hindered civic participation in the definition of environmental and renewable energy policies (Delicado 2015b). This has changed more recently, as both policy makers and private actors seek to include other stakeholders in policy debates.

The financial crisis that hit Portugal in 2010 led to a temporary stall in RES promotion. However, unlike its neighbor Spain, Portugal never abandoned its commitment to renewable energy support. Instead, renewable energy support schemes were revised to become more cost-efficient and the push for energy market liberalization increased (see below). New market-based support schemes, such as photovoltaic solar auctions, were introduced (Jörgens 2020) and investment in renewables resumed with less public incentives and more private commitment. The Portuguese milestones for 2030 are ambitious: The rate of electrification shall rise in all sectors, and the overall penetration of renewables shall reach 47%, with 80% in the final consumption of electricity, 38% in heating and cooling, and 20% in transports (República Portuguesa 2019b).

General Conditions of Energy Governance in Portugal

Legacies of Energy Governance

In the first half of the twentieth century, agriculture was the most important pillar of the Portuguese economy (Araújo and Coelho 2013). While coal was the main source of energy, hydropower constituted the most accessible endogenous energy resource (Law 2002 of 1944), and the need to electrify energy consumption led to a significant investment in hydroelectricity. By the end of the 1960s, hydropower was responsible for more than 90% of total electricity production (Madureira and Baptista 2002). Together with coal, these were the two main energy sources up to the 1970s. Oil became increasingly used in industry and transportation in the 1970s and exposed the Portuguese economy to the oil shocks of 1973 and 1979 (Araújo and Coelho 2013).

After the revolution of 1974, the Portuguese power sector was nationalized. All existing public and private electricity producers were merged into the new energy company Electricidade de Portugal (EDP) (Decree Law 502/76), which became responsible for the production, transmission, distribution, and retailing of electricity. A first feed-in tariff scheme was approved already in 1981 (Decree Law 20/81) with the goal of reducing oil imports, and in 1984 the National Energy Plan (Plano Energético Nacional) diagnosed that Portugal needed to increase energy efficiency and develop alternative energy sources. The plan triggered a national debate about the adoption of nuclear power (Araújo and Coelho 2013), an option that was never realized and was ultimately abandoned in 1986 (Barca and Delicado 2016, p. 504). This renunciation of nuclear energy differentiated Portugal from its two closest neighbors – Spain (the first nuclear power plants were installed in the 1970s, and nuclear energy has developed since then) and France (nuclear power plants were installed in the 1960s and have dominated French electricity production since the 1980s) – and aligned Portugal with smaller EU countries which had similarly rejected the nuclear option (e.g., Denmark and Ireland).

After Portugal's adhesion to the EU, the country stabilized politically and economically. In the next 10 years, the Portuguese economy averaged an annual growth rate of 3.81% (PORDATA), and the increase in energy consumption was matched with investments in coal and gas power plants. This reduced the Portuguese oil dependence in electricity generation, but not its overall dependence, as oil consumption increased from 6 Mtoe in 1990 to more than 10 Mtoe in the early 2000s (European Commission 2020b). In 1987, already within the EU context, environmental concerns became part of the Portuguese policy agenda (Araújo and Coelho 2013) and general environmental laws were approved (Lei de Bases do Ambiente, Lei das Associações de Defesa do Ambiente). The government plan of 1987–1991 referred explicitly to the use of endogenous, renewable energy sources for electricity generation. Since then, all governments have included this point on their policy agenda (Araújo and Coelho 2013). Despite the existence of domestic coal reserves, coal mining had not been competitive since the 1970s. Environmental groups, which perceived coal mining as degrading the natural landscape and the environment, together with weak stakeholders in this industry (Caetano 1998), led to the decay of coal mining in the early 1990s (Miguel et al. 2018, p. 6). Portugal now depends on imported coal (Miguel et al. 2018; Pinho and Hunter 2019), with national coal production having ceased in 1994.

In 1988, the year when the first small-scale pilots for wind energy production were installed in the Azores (Santa Maria) and Madeira, the regulatory framework that governed the energy sector since 1977 changed. Private business activity in the energy sector (Decree Law 449/88) was explicitly allowed in all stages of the value chain – production, transportation, distribution, and retailing. Energy producers and energy distributers could apply for operation licenses to the National Electricity Transmission Grid (RNT), a public company created in 1991 (Decree Law 99/91) to manage the electricity transportation network for high voltages. And in 1993, the integration of natural gas in the Portuguese market was regulated (Decree Law 274-C/93).

The 1994 Energy Program (Decree Law 195/94) established as a priority the replacement of fossil fuel consumption. Within this program, investments in the development or installation of technology that used either natural gas or renewable energy sources would be eligible for public subsidies leveraged by European funds. In 1995, the Portuguese electrical system was divided into two interdependent systems (Decree Law 182/95) – the public system (SEP) and the independent system (SEI), subject to different regulations. Both cogeneration plants and RES became part of the SEI, and a RES-specific incentive, which guaranteed support for up to 50% of the investment needed to develop or install a RES technology, was approved (Legislative order 11-B/95). Compensation contracts were given to incumbent energy producers guaranteeing returns for the next 15 years. A Regulatory Authority for Energy Services – Entidade Reguladora dos Serviços Energéticos (ERSE) – was also created.

By 1995, all the institutions required for further liberalization of the sector were in place. Hydropower had been the renewable energy most consistently promoted, while oil and coal dominated the primary energy sources. In the 1990s, Portuguese energy import dependency averaged 83.7% – which rose to 84.3% in the 2000s and declined to 75.3% in the 2010s (European Commission 2020b).

Composition of the Energy Mix

In the first half of the twentieth century, coal was the main source of energy, followed by hydropower. Only from the 1960s did petrol use increase in Portugal's energy mix. While in 1995 residential and industrial energy needs were covered almost completely by oil and coal, in 2010 renewables produced the largest share of electricity available to consumers (Guevara and Domingos 2017, p. 134).

Oil still is the primary energy supply in Portugal (see Fig. 1). Portugal imports its oil from a range of suppliers to cover about 50% of its energy needs (IEA 2016). However, after peaking in the 2000s, the importance of oil in the Portuguese energy mix is declining.

Coal has been a relevant primary energy supply in the 1980s and 1990s. Since the 2000s, its consumption is declining, with natural gas partially replacing coal (see Fig. 1; note: In Figs. 1 and 2, coal is included in the category "solid fossil fuels"). Coal is used for electricity generation in the two coal-fired power plants in Sines (1250 MW) and Pego (620 MW) that serve as a backup system for periods of low renewable energy production, or in drought periods when hydropower output is lowest (Miguel et al. 2018). Currently, the coal power plants are being phased out and should be fully decommissioned by 2023 (PNEC 2019b, p. 36). Biofuels have been used in industrial production processes and residential and commercial heating. Since the 2000s, a small but increasing fraction of transportation runs on biofuels.

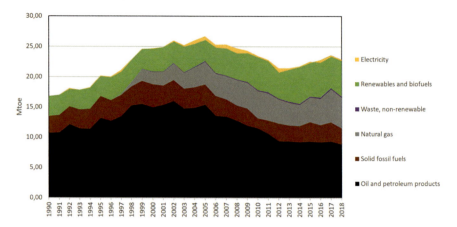

Fig. 1 Total energy supply. (Source: EU Commission (2020))

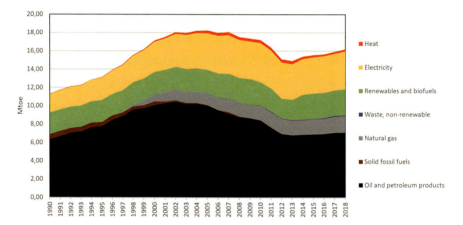

Fig. 2 Final energy consumption. (Source: EU Commission (2020))

The share of renewables in final energy consumption is increasing (see Fig. 2). Solar thermal is used mainly for warm water, and biofuels are used for heating (the green stripe in the graphic). 50% of the final consumption of electricity (the yellow stripe in Fig. 2) is also made from renewables, and the share of renewables in electricity generation is continuously increasing (see Fig. 4). The overall increase in electricity consumption – observed in the industry, the residential, and the commercial segments – further consolidates the role renewables have in final consumption. On the other hand, the final consumption of oil, mostly used in transportation, is declining.

The boom of wind and, to a lesser extent, solar power has been the main driver of the increasing domestic energy production in Portugal (IEA 2016, p. 16) – wind generation now accounts for about one-fifth of energy production (see Fig. 3). Portugal produces only renewable energy: The largest share belongs to solid

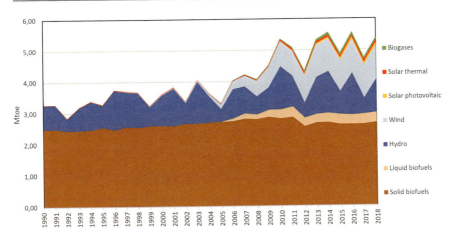

Fig. 3 National energy production. (Source: EU Commission (2020))

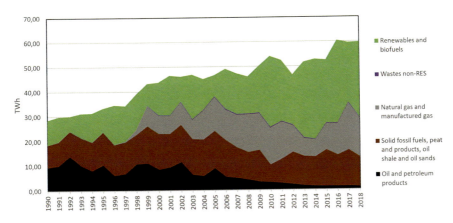

Fig. 4 Gross electricity generation, by fuel. (Source: EU Commission (2020))

biofuels, followed by wind and hydro. These account for more than 90% of national energy production.

The Portuguese energy transition becomes most visible with regard to electricity generation (see Fig. 4). Renewables are now responsible for generating about 50% of Portugal's electricity needs. This success in greening electricity generation has turned the further electrification of industry, transport, and household consumption into one of the primary goals of the Portuguese energy transition. Overall, electricity and biofuels today account for about 40% of final energy consumption, and this share is continuously increasing, while fossil fuel consumption is declining.

In 2019, renewable energy sources were responsible for 51% of electricity consumption (slightly below the 52% of the previous year). Wind turbines produced 26% of the overall consumption, followed by hydro (17%) and solar power (2.1%). Coal was responsible for 10% of consumption and natural gas for 32% (REN 2019).

Discourse on Energy Issues

Media discourse analyses suggest that the social construction of climate change in Portugal has been strongly influenced by policymakers, with the media often reproducing official discourses of administrative and economic rationality, and rarely adopting critical stances. Mitigation of climate change is regarded as solvable by state and expert-led policies, and ecological modernization – that is, policies that promote technological solutions to increase the eco-efficiency of products, production processes, and services (Jänicke 2009) – can be a driver of economic growth (Carvalho et al. 2014; Delicado 2015b; Horta and Carvalho 2017). While the media focuses mainly on economic issues, citizens are concerned with environmental degradation and global warming and consider the investment in renewable energies an adequate response to the risks associated with climate change (Delicado 2015b, p. 136).

Overall, the Portuguese show high levels of concern regarding the environment, viewing climate change as a serious personal and global threat (Carvalho et al. 2014). According to the 2019 Parlemeter (European Parliament 2019), climate change and the environment rank fifth after social exclusion and poverty, employment, health, and economic growth. Portuguese citizens view climate change as the most pressing environmental concern, followed by pollution, water, and forest-related concerns, and only then energy issues (eighth position). However, a 2009 Eurobarometer survey shows that the Portuguese feel poorly informed not only about the causes but also about the consequences and ways to combat climate change. Thus, the high levels of concern among Portuguese citizens go along with relatively low levels of knowledge about climate change (Carvalho et al. 2014, p. 208).

According to a survey led by Ribeiro et al. (2014), solar and wind power lead the preferences of the Portuguese toward renewable energy, with hydropower ranking last (but still with a 77% acceptance rate). Moreover, the economic outcomes of renewable energy projects rather than their positive environmental impact are the fundamental drivers for the population's acceptance of renewable energy (Ribeiro et al. 2014, p. 48).

Levels of civic participation are quite low, as the Portuguese tend to have limited trust in public officials (Carvalho et al. 2014). Government initiatives engaging civil society have been scarce, with a preference for top-down approaches and centralized forms of decision-making, with no real fora for active participation or feedback from civil society representatives (Carvalho et al. 2014; Delicado et al. 2014; Jörgens 2020). Companies from the energy sector tend to organize themselves to lobby for greater investment in renewables, but the state is seen as unavailable to listen to other stakeholders (Delicado 2015a). Environmental nongovernmental organizations (ENGOs), on the other hand, tend to have an ambivalent discourse, due to the "green on green" dilemma: They tend to support the development of renewable energies, while also showing concerns for its negative social and territorial impacts. Overall, Portuguese ENGOs support energy generation on a smaller scale, with less local environmental impacts, criticize incoherent planning in renewable energy deployment, and accuse the government of favoring the big energy companies (Delicado 2015a, p. 91).

Due to the weak tradition of environmental politics and values, Portugal's governmental climate change policies have been shaped and applied under a strong influence of the EU (Carvalho et al. 2014, p. 199). Until the first decade of the twenty-first century, renewable energy policy was relatively unaffected by changes of government. The main political parties – the social democrats on the center-right and the socialists on the center-left – have had divergences that resulted in complementary policies: The center-right pushed for liberalization, while the center-left pushed for state incentives for renewables.

However, after the strong investment by the governments led by socialist prime minister José Sócrates (2005–2011), and in the context of the financial crisis, the center-right government elected in 2011 adopted a more reluctant stance toward investments in renewable energy, giving greater priority to financial stability (Araújo and Coelho 2013; Boemi and Papadopoulos 2013; Delicado 2015a; Andreas et al. 2019). Ecological arguments lost importance, and economic factors became more dominant in the political discourse (Soares and Silva 2014; Delicado 2015a). Parties on the center-right criticized the feed-in tariffs that created additional costs for domestic and industrial consumers while opposition parties on the left criticized government policies for favoring big companies instead of consumers (Delicado 2015a).

Even though the Portuguese show a strong concern for the environment, this has not affected the emphasis given by mainstream political parties during elections (Volkens et al. 2020). Aside from the two green parties – PEV and PAN – environmental concerns are not given particular attention by most Portuguese parties in their political manifestos. Nonetheless, there was an increase in party attention after Portugal joined the EU. By contrast, during the 2008 economic crisis, all parties lowered the emphasis given to environmental topics.

Political Institutions and Actors

Government
The Ministry of Industry and Energy was created in 1980 and existed until 1995 (with a brief interruption from 1985 to 1987). From 1995 to 2013, energy policies were conducted by secretaries of state under the Ministry of the Economy. However, from 2005 to 2009, prime minister José Socrates – who previously had been Minister of the Environment from 1999 to 2002 – assumed the responsibility for energy policy, focusing on the promotion of renewable energy (Resolution of the Council of Ministers 169/2005). In 2013, the Ministry of Environment, Territory and Energy was created and existed until 2015. In 2018, the Ministry of Environment and Energy Transition was created, which is responsible for climate policy and for achieving a competitive, resilient, and low-carbon economy. In 2019, its name was changed to Ministry of Environment and Climate Action.

Administrative Actors
Within the Ministry for Environment and Climate Action, the Directorate-General for Energy and Geology (DGEG) is responsible for the development and

implementation of policies related to energy sources. The competencies relating to energy efficiency at the local or regional levels rest with municipal authorities. Local actors are supported by regional energy agencies, whose main role is to identify local needs and to find solutions to reduce energy consumption (IEA 2016).

The Energy Services Regulatory Authority (ERSE) is the national regulatory authority for natural gas and electricity. It is a financially autonomous public corporate body whose purpose is to oversee the natural gas and electricity sectors, protecting the rights and interests of consumers in relation to prices, service quality, information access, and security of supply, while also regulating transmission, distribution, and supply infrastructures. The Agency for Energy (ADENE) is responsible for managing and certifying the energy efficiency sector and related areas (IEA 2016). Finally, the Portuguese Environmental Agency (APA) is a public institute under the authority of the environmental ministry. Its mission is to propose, develop, and monitor environmental and sustainable development policies, in close cooperation with other public and private entities. APA also manages the Portuguese Carbon Fund, which provides financial support to the transition to a low-carbon economy (IEA 2016).

Green Parties and the Environmental Movement

Despite their impact on politics and policy, a strong Green party supported by the main environmentalist organizations is still missing from the political landscape (Queirós 2016, p. 64). There are two small environmentalist parties in Portugal – Ecologist Party "The Greens" (PEV) and People-Animals-Nature (PAN). Founded in 1972, PEV has always been in an electoral coalition with the Portuguese Communist Party (PCP) and is seen as an attempt by the PCP to take hold of the environmental electorate (Biorcio 2016, p. 191; Silveira et al. 2019, p. 15). PAN, which gained its first seat in parliament in 2015, was founded in 2009 by a small and diverse group of activists who advocated for a strengthening of animal rights and environmental protection and who reject a right-left-positioning (Silveira et al. 2019, p. 85). In the 2019 elections, PAN received 3.3% of the vote and gained four parliament seats. Since its foundation, the party has gradually moved from a single-issue animal rights party to a more broadly positioned green party. In the European Parliament, it has joined the Greens while the PEV together with PCP is part of the Left in the European Parliament.

PEV presents itself as an alternative to the "economic environmentalism" of the two main Portuguese parties – the Socialist Party (PS) and the Social Democrat Party (PSD) – defending a decentralized and participative environmental strategy (Silveira et al. 2019). Despite close coordination of its program and activities with the coalition partner PCP, the two parties sometimes diverge on energy matters. While PCP is in favor of nuclear energy and the strategic use of fossil fuels, PEV rejects it completely, defending renewable energies and the closure of nuclear plants in neighboring Spain (Carius and Jörgens 1993; Biorcio 2016; PCP 2019; PEV 2019). PAN, on the other hand, defends an energy transition based principally on wind and solar power, and greater democratization and decentralization of energy production, with greater investment in new RES, such as tidal, hydrogen, and geothermal power (PAN 2019).

Despite their rather small membership, Portuguese ENGOs have gained increasing influence on the national environmental agenda since the 1990s. This has mainly been due to the high level of professional skills of their members and representatives. Taking a technocratic approach, they ground their positions on scientific knowledge, allying with private and public actors to pursue ecological objectives (Franco 2015, p. 99; Sardo and Weitkamp 2012). According to Queirós (2016), the environmental movement has transformed into a form of "professional environmentalism," focusing its activity on influencing policy-making, rather than changing the populations' beliefs (Queirós 2016, pp. 63–65; see also Carius and Jörgens 1993). Nonetheless, environmental groups still engage in localized strategies, mobilizing popular support for causes that are physically closer to citizens (Guimarães and Fernandes 2016). The most relevant environmentalist organizations, by size and influence, are LPN (League for Nature Protection), founded in 1948, Quercus (1984), Geota (1986), and Zero, created in 2015. LPN is a conservationist organization that focuses on species protection, responsible for the creation of the main protected areas in Portugal (Queirós 2016, p. 62). Quercus was founded by academics and skilled professionals who aimed to become agenda-setters in environment-related policies in Portugal. It has strong connections with public bodies and environmental authorities (Queirós 2016, p. 63). Two years after Quercus, Geota (Environmental and Land Use Planning Study Group) was founded, working as a think tank dedicated to environmental education (Queirós 2016, p. 63). Zero was created by Quercus dissidents. Inspired by the 2015 Paris Agreement, it focuses on achieving "zero waste, zero unsustainable consumption and zero ecosystem destruction" (Neves 2016).

Transmission and Distribution Companies
The management of natural gas and high voltage electricity distribution networks is under the responsibility of National Electric Network (REN), which has the concession to explore the Portuguese transmission network in a public service regime (IEA 2016; Torres et al. 2016). The medium to low voltage distribution network is managed by EDP Distribuição, a company that was created when EDP was split into different companies in 2005 (Lourenço 2010, p. 23).

Energy Generation and Retailing Companies
The energy transition brought new players into the energy market, although incumbents also seized the opportunity to grow in the market for renewable energies. Considering wind energy – the fastest-growing energy market in Portugal in the late 2000s and 2010s – EDP Renováveis (23.5%), Iberwind (13.6%), Finerge (12.7%), Trustwind (9.2%), and Generg (8.2%) accounted for more than two-thirds of the installed capacity in 2016 (https://www.iberwind.pt/pt/o-poder-do-vento/mercado-portugues/). The retail electricity market is dominated by EDP Comercial, with over 77% of the liberalized market. The natural gas market is dominated by two main distributors: GALP Energy and EDP Comercial (IEA 2016). GALP Energy is also the most significant player in the Portuguese oil market, operating both refineries and maintaining a strong position in the downstream oil market (IEA 2016).

Horizontal concentration in the Portuguese energy generation and retailing markets is high, and new entrants are often incumbents in other domestic markets (Teixeira and Salavisa 2016, p. 232), such as Endesa and Iberdrola – both are Spanish companies with a leading role in the Iberian energy generation and retailing market (EDP 2018, p. 20). The importance of energy companies in the Portuguese economy is significant: The two leading companies in the national stock market are EDP and Galp, and more than 40% of the national stock market belongs to four energy companies: EDP, GALP, EDPR (EDP Renewables), and REN (Moreira 2020).

Associations

In the renewable energy market, the Portuguese Association for Renewable Energies (APREN) represents the companies from the sector, lobbying for greater investment in renewable energies and a greater influence in the European energy market through policy advice, monitoring, and development of studies and statistics (Delicado 2015a). The Portuguese Energy Association (APE) is a nonprofit, nongovernmental public service institution whose mission is to promote public debate on the development of the energy sector (IEA 2016).

Coordination, Instruments, and Issues of the Portuguese Energy Transition

Drivers of the Energy Transition

In the 1990s, the Portuguese energy policy stood at a crossroads: Hydropower potential was not fully explored (less than 50% (PNBEPH 2007, p. 9), yet one of the highest rates in Europe), coal reserves were not productive (Miguel et al. 2018; Fidalgo et al. 2019), nuclear power was not a viable option (Pereira et al. 2018, p. 522), and energy dependence from imports was close to 90% (European Commission 2020). The prospect of growing energy demand – in a period of consistent growth – led Portugal to make a shift in its energy policy and invest in renewable energy, coupled with more investment in hydro- and in combined-cycle power plants fired by natural gas (more energy efficient and less pollutant than coal) to balance the renewables' intermittency problem. While many of these constraints had been present in the 1980s already, additional drivers of the Portuguese turn toward renewables were growing environmental concerns, which were prominent on the EU agenda and subsequently gained influence in national energy policymaking (Araújo and Coelho 2013), and the liberalization of the energy market, which Portugal pushed forward in tandem with the EU. These two drivers were embraced by Portuguese political actors to transform the energy sector in Portugal.

Liberalization Process

The 1996 Electricity Directive (96/92/EC) was one of the first initiatives of the European Commission to liberalize the European energy market. All energy market players should have access to the grid, and vertically integrated energy companies should be split into smaller companies operating in their market segment activity. In Portugal, the first steps toward liberalization had been taken in the 1990s (see section "Legacies of Energy Governance"). However, in 1997, the planned privatization of the public electricity company (EDP) was reconsidered and only a minority percentage of the company was to be privatized (Decree Law 56/97). In 1999, the legislation that allowed the participation of new companies in the energy distribution segment (high and medium voltage) was revoked so that only EDP could operate as an energy distribution company (Decree Law 24/99). Finally, in 2000, new legislation guaranteed that the national electricity transmission grid RNT would remain under public control and that its operations would be independent of medium-to-low voltage distributers (Decree Law 198/2000).

The 2001 energy program (E4 – energy efficiency and endogenous energy) (Resolution of the Council of Ministers 154/2001) defined five main energy guidelines, two of which were related to the liberalization of the energy market: the implementation of an internal energy market in line with European recommendations and the establishment of an Iberian energy market (the other three were the reduction of energy intensity and energy dependence, the promotion of energy efficiency in both supply and demand, and the development of RES, in line with the 2001 EU directive). New guidelines for the implementation of a free and competitive electricity market (Decree Law 185/2003) in line with EU recommendations were laid down, and the vertically integrated energy market was broken down: Producers, distributors, and retailers were to operate as independent entities. The 2003 Internal Market in Electricity Directive (2003/54/EC) turned some of the 1996 directive's guidelines mandatory and demanded member state compliance. In Portugal and Spain, this was followed by the creation of an Iberian electricity market (OMIP and MIBEL) in early 2004 (Resolution of the Assembly of the Republic 33-A/2004), to complement (and eventually replace) the traditional over-the-counter market and enable competitive energy trading.

In the following years, liberalization of the energy sector accelerated. Regulatory changes were introduced in the energy markets – market agents could now operate in either the gas market, the electricity market, or both – and the EU's 2003 liberalization directive was transposed into national law in early 2006 (Decree Law 29/2006). MIBEL was created in 2007, although interconnection capacity developed more slowly than expected and has impeded a true common market until today (Cardoso 2011).

In 2009, a new national renewable energy plan (Resolution of the Council of Ministers 29/2010) proposed the liberalization of the energy market for small consumers, which was formally approved in 2011 (Decree Law 104/2010) and scheduled to happen until 2012. In the Memorandum of Understanding, signed with the European Financial Stability Facility in May 2011, Portugal committed to conclude the liberalization of the electricity and gas markets, reduce its energy dependence, reduce the costs with electricity production, review fiscal incentives in the energy sector, and conclude the Iberian integration of the energy market (Araújo and Coelho 2013). In June 2011, the 2009 Internal Market in Electricity Directive 2009/72/EC was transposed into national legislation (Decree Law 78/2011).

During the financial crisis, the government's main policy goal was to push forward the liberalization of the energy market along the lines of the EU directive (Decree Laws 215-A/2012, 178/2015). In 2012, a new law determined that all residential consumers should participate in the liberalized consumption market, and that regulated consumption tariffs were to end. However, this law was updated every year to postpone its implementation (Decree Laws 75/2012, 256/2012, 13/2014, 15/2015, ordinance 39/2017, ordinance 364-A/2017). Only since 2017, consumers are allowed to choose between market-based tariffs and the regulated tariff (Law 105/2017). The electricity VAT was also increased from 6% to 23% (Law 51-A/2011).

Liberalization also included the privatization of EDP (in 2011) and REN (in 2012), which became powerful private stakeholders. Both were acquired by Chinese companies (themselves owned by the Chinese state) in one of the major Chinese investments in Europe (Pareja-Alcaraz 2017), which shows the relevance of finance in the liberalization of the energy market and the promotion of renewables (Mazzucato and Semieniuk 2018).

Renewable Energy Policy

The Single European Act, approved in 1987, defined three goals for future energy policies: positive environmental impact, energy security, and a single energy market. In 1992, environmental problems were further discussed and acknowledged in the Rio Conference, which led to the signing of the Kyoto protocol in 1997, a revision of the energy policies in place, and an emphasis on renewable energy. In the 1990s, the European Commission started defining a Renewable Energy Policy (de Lovinfosse 2008, pp. 63–75; Solorio and Bocquillon 2017).

With Portugal's accession to the EU in 1986, the EU's focus on ecological issues was at least partially transferred to the national level, leading to an increased salience of environmental issues (Araújo and Coelho 2013), the creation of a Ministry of Environment and Natural Resources and a National Council of the Environment and Sustainable Development (CNADS) in 1990, and an increased use of European funds to design and implement pilot projects of innovative RES. The European Commission's 1996 Green Paper on RES (COM (96) 576 final) described the status of renewable energy in Europe and suggested approaches for its future development. One year later, the White Paper "Energy for the Future" (COM (97) 599 final) detailed the advantages of renewable energy for Europe and suggested the adoption of a target for renewable energy production. These recommendations were included in the 2001 Renewable Electricity Directive (2001/77/EC), which established renewable energy targets for all member countries (Solorio and Bocquillon 2017). In 2000 and 2007, Portugal held the presidency of the Council of the EU. The first coincided with the negotiation of the 2001 EU directive, where Portugal joined the countries that defended (with success) that large hydropower should be considered RES (de Lovinfosse 2008, p. 74). José Sócrates, the future Prime Minister who would become a main political actor pushing RES forward, was then Minister of the Environment.

The 2001 national energy plan prioritized the security of supply and sustainable development, without risking national competitiveness (Resolution of the Council of Ministers 63/2003), and ambitious goals for RES deployment were set. By 2010, the amount of electricity generated from RES was planned to more than double – from 4603 to 9680 MW. With more than 3600 MW, onshore wind power was assigned the largest share. In 2007, the Lisbon treaty was approved under the Portuguese EU presidency. Alignment with EU goals was crucial in three dimensions: access to funds, circulation of ideas, and political support. During the preparation of the Lisbon treaty, Portugal was generally perceived as being at the forefront of RES development due to its significant investment in renewables. The Portuguese government tried to rebrand Portugal as technologically developed and environmentally committed. Portugal had also successfully sidelined with advocates of feed-in-tariffs as the main support scheme for electricity from renewables, such as Spain and Germany, against supporters of a system based on RES quotas and tradeable certificates (Solorio and Jörgens 2017). Also in 2007, a new plan for hydropower was approved to explore the remaining hydro potential (PNBEPH 2007) and RES technology bonus factors were reviewed to increase RES operational returns (Decree Law 225/2007).

In 2009, the EU Renewable Energy Directive, which revised and updated the 2001 directive, consolidated the 20% average renewable production target for the EU in 2020. The 2010 Portuguese renewable energy plan – Plano Nacional de Acção para as Energias Renováveis – revised the guidelines for RES policies (Resolution of the Council of Ministers 29/2010): Existing feed-in tariffs should be less costly (to reduce the costs passed on to end consumers), investment funds would be created to develop innovative RES technologies with export potential (solar thermal energy was then seen as a promising technology), the Iberian Center for Renewable Energy and Energy Efficiency was to be created (it was never implemented), wind repowering procedures were simplified (Decree Law 51/2010), and a smart city pilot concept, with smart metering technologies, electrical vehicles, and demand-side management, was to be launched. In the period from 1995 to 2010, installed renewable energy sources increased dramatically, e.g., installed wind power jumped from 8 MW in 1995 to almost 4000 MW by 2010 (PORDATA).

By the end of the 2000s, the continued strengthening of Portuguese RES policy became increasingly affected by the financial crisis. In 2012, the new government canceled all future electricity power contracts (Decree Law 25/2012) (including RES contracts) as the recession led to a decline in energy consumption. In 2013, energy selling price incentives for microproduction and miniproduction were canceled (Decree Law 25/2013): Local power production had to be below 50% of local power consumption and used for self-consumption. Although the government kept committed to the global RES targets set by the previous government, technology-specific targets were reviewed, with priority given to mature RES technologies (Resolution of the Council of Ministers 20/2013).

Overall, the past three decades saw a continued strengthening of renewable energy policies which was slowed down, but not dismantled, by the financial crisis. During this period, renewable energy – the core of the Portuguese energy transition – was promoted primarily because of its positive environmental impact and as a strategy to reduce the Portuguese external energy dependence. However, during this period, energy costs rose substantially for end consumers (Peña et al. 2017).

Strategies and Instruments

The Portuguese energy transition's main goal is to increase the endogenous supply of clean energy for final consumption at competitive prices (República Portuguesa 2019b). This includes the following strategies:

1. Increase the share of renewable production.
2. Liberalize the energy market by enforcing competition in all segments of the energy value chain and by extending the market to Iberia.
3. Promote energy efficiency in buildings and transportation.
4. Electrify final consumption.
5. Replace fossil fuels used in transportation with biofuels, electricity, and other clean fuels (such as hydrogen).

The key instrument for increasing the share of electricity from renewable energy sources were the feed-in tariffs. Feed-in tariff incentives for wind and solar energy were progressively revised upward, which led to a surge in RES projects. While for solar energy there were feed-in tariffs for small production, most RES incentives favored large-scale electricity production. The major operator in Portugal was EDP; it became the most important investor and operator in wind power. Feed-in tariffs were replaced in the 2010s by premium feed-in tariffs and, more recently, complemented by auctions. These changes coincided with the financial crisis in Portugal and with decreasing trends in the levelized cost of wind and solar energy. The simplification of licensing procedures and public tenders for renewable energy has also accelerated the deployment of RES (Heer and Langniß 2007). Grid connection rules were simplified in 2001 (Decree Law 312/2001) and 2004; in 2007, new legislation was approved to simplify the repowering process of existing wind parks; and in 2014 (Decree Law 94/2014), ownership rules of repowered wind turbines changed. Direct subsidies were used in early RES deployment but became less relevant over time. In 1986, the government created an investment line that used EU funds to subsidize the deployment of fully researched and innovative energy production technologies (Decree Law 250/86, enacted by ordinance 464/86) open only to companies in the energy industry or with meaningful energy production operations. Direct subsidies were also used in targeted low-scale applications. In 1988, investment subsidies were available for any private company engaged in technologies or processes that would reduce its oil dependency (Decree Law 188/88).

To achieve the goal of market liberalization, regulatory instruments were used in combination with privatizations with regulations imposing the unbundling of the energy market and the creation of specific markets for each stage of the value chain – production, transportation, distribution, and retailing. Production and retailing were deregulated, and energy companies in the public sphere were privatized. The redefinition of the electricity market structure also demanded the revision of long-term energy supply contracts: The previous schemes (named CAEs) were replaced by new schemes (the CMECs) (Decree Law 240/2004).

A third dimension of the Portuguese strategy is energy efficiency. Incentives were given to companies, households, and public institutions to reduce their energy consumption (Resolution of the Council of Ministers 2/2011). These policies, together with the shift of the economy to the service sector, were partially responsible for reducing the energy intensity of the Portuguese economy (Guevara and Rodrigues 2016; Guevara and Domingos 2017).

The goal of electrification of consumption has not been fully embraced in the Portuguese strategy until recently, as in the 2000s the plan was to use natural gas in combined cycle power plants and in supplying households. In late 2010, the incentives for microproduction were reviewed (Decree Law 118-A/2010) to promote widespread solar microproduction, up to an aggregate maximum power of 25 MW. The revision mandated microproducers to adopt energy efficiency measures and utilities to buy microproduced electricity, while it lowered the premium on the price paid for microproduced energy. A new bonification system to incentivize public institutions to become microproducers was also created. RES targets were also updated according to the 2009 Renewable Energy Directive (Decree Law 141/2010): By 2020, Portugal should reach 31% of RES on final consumption. In 2011, the procedures to become a solar miniproducer (up to 250 kW) were simplified and third parties could conclude energy service contracts to establish miniproduction units (Decree Law 34/2011). New self-consumption incentives for using RES in buildings (Decree Law 162/2019) are now creating energy communities – and virtual power plants in the future – which push for the electrification of households. Electric vehicles are also a part of this strategy. The purchase of electric vehicles has been incentivized through subsidies and no public charging costs since 2010 (Decree Law 39/2010).

Finally, the Portuguese transition in the transportation sector has not been successful. The percentage of vehicles running on diesel (the most pollutant fuel) is high due to tax incentives that were only revised in 2017 (Resolution of the Council of Ministers 88/2017), and the use of biofuels in transportation has remained relatively low in Portugal (Ferreira et al. 2009). The production of clean hydrogen to fuel heavy-duty vehicles (buses and trains) has recently emerged as a potential future policy strategy (República Portuguesa 2020).

In the following, we present in more detail two mechanisms of the Portuguese energy transition: the feed-in tariffs, which have been the core mechanism, up to the crisis, in the promotion of RES, and solar energy auctions, which have been used recently to select new photovoltaic energy plants.

Feed-In Tariffs

Portugal has been an early adopter of feed-in tariffs, the first of which was approved in 1981. Compensation was given to independent producers (which produced their own electricity) for dispatching excess electricity to the grid with the price per kWh being set by the grid operator (Decree Law 149/86). In 1988, a new version of the feed-in tariff was approved (Decree Law 189/88). Entities were recognized as being independent energy producers if the installed power was below 10,000 kW (an exception was made for combined heat and power installations) and became eligible for a compensation subsidy equal to the compensation subsidy given to thermal power plants – 1 kWh was equivalent to 300 g of fuel oil – which was added to the grid selling price of the voltage level above the interconnection and paid for by government funds. The compensation was guaranteed to cover at least 90% of the price negotiated between the grid operator and the energy supplier (during the first 8 years of operation).

In 1995, the feed-in tariff was updated (Decree Law 313/95). The guaranteed price was matched with the average tariff applicable to the voltage level of the interconnection (which meant a higher price), and only installations of less than 10 MW were eligible. The price of the feed-in tariff was further changed in 1999 to include three components (Decree Law 168/99): a component proportional to the power installed (about 1090 PTE/kW), a variable component proportional to the energy produced (about 5.00 PTE/kWh), and another variable component related to the positive environmental impact also proportional to the energy produced (5.55 PTE/kWh). The length of the feed-in contracts was extended to 12 years (instead of 8). RES electricity was given grid priority. Incentives to combined heat and power plants were also reviewed along these lines (Decree Law 538/99). A technology modulation factor was introduced in the calculation of the environmental incentive in 2001 (Decree Law 339-C/2001): Wind power plants were given a bonus factor of 1.70 for the first 2000 h of operation, which was gradually reduced to 0.40 for operations above 2600 h, while photovoltaic power plants from 5 kW to 50 MW received a bonus factor of 6.55 and those below 5 kW were given a bonus factor of 12.

In 2005, the feed-in contracts were extended to last 15 years (instead of twelve), and the variable components of the feed-in tariff were changed (Decree Law 33-A/2005): The energy supply component was set to €3.6ct/kWh, and the environmental component was set to €2ct/kg CO_2. The technology bonus factors, which differentiate the tariff according to the technologies used, were also reviewed: The wind power bonus factor was reduced to 4.6; the solar power bonus factor was increased to 35 for installations above 5 kW, and 52 for installations below 5 kW (up to a maximum of 150 MW installed nationally); the biomass bonus factors were set to 8.2 and 7.5, for forest residues and animal residues, respectively; and other technologies, such as wave energy, received no bonification. Wind power was the only technology for which the technology bonus factor remains unaffected. For solar microproduction (up to 150 kW), a premium price was added to excess local production that was not used for self-consumption, so that instead it could be sold to the grid at a profitable rate (Decree Law 363/2007).

In 2013, the feed-in tariff changed to a premium feed-in tariff. When the feed-in contract ended (or before it ended), wind energy producers had to contribute €5000 to €5800 per MW installed to continue to operate and adhere to a premium tariff for the next 5–7 years (respectively), with two options (Decree Law 35/2013): either a doubly bounded market-based payment price, with a minimum guaranteed of €74/MWh and an upper limit of €98/MWh, or a lower bounded market-based payment price with a minimum guarantee of €60/MWh. This last option was compulsory for the cases of wind turbine repowering.

Renewable Energy Auctions (For Solar)

More recently, auctions have become an important complementary policy instrument to promote the production of electricity from renewable energy sources in a more cost-efficient way. While in 2005 only 6 countries used auctions of renewable energy sources, by 2017 at least 84 countries had adopted this instrument (Kitzing et al. 2019). Portugal was one of the first European countries to use such renewable energy auctions. In the first-generation auctions, electricity producers were still subsidized. The government set a reference tariff for electricity produced from renewable energy sources above the market price, which could be undercut by participants in the auction. In this way, the volume of subsidies was significantly reduced (del Río 2016).

In 2019, the Portuguese government modified the instrument of renewable energy auctions with the new photovoltaic solar auction. The maximum price producers now obtain is below the market price (del Río et al. 2019), and what is auctioned is the access to the electricity grid. The first auction of this new generation was launched in June 2019 to increase installed capacity for renewable energy production. Competitors could choose between two remuneration systems: (1) a guaranteed tariff for 15 years where competitors offered a discount on a reference price set by the government, and (2) a general tariff corresponding to the market value where competitors offered a fixed contribution to the National Electric System. The tariff that served as the basis for bidding was around €45/MWh, which at the time was slightly below the market value. The auction covered a total of 1400 megawatts (MW) divided into 24 lots in four regions of the country (Centro, Lisboa e Vale do Tejo, Alentejo, and Algarve). The auction was considered a success (del Río et al. 2019): Of the 24 lots (1400 MW), 23 were awarded (1292 MW). The demand articulated by the 64 bidders was nine times higher than the auctioned network capacity. The average tariff for the lots awarded was €20/MWh, which corresponds to less than half of the reference price. The most competitive of the bids was only €14.76/MWh, which at the time was the lowest ever feed-in tariff worldwide for electricity from renewable sources.

A second auction, scheduled for March 2020, but postponed because of the Covid-19 pandemic, started in June 2020. A total of 670 MW of capacity in the Alentejo and Algarve regions was auctioned. In addition to the fixed tariff and the fixed contribution to the National Electric System, bidders could bid through a third modality based on the creation of storage capacities for at least 20% of the granted network capacity (Bellini 2020). With a total allocation of 483 MW, this storage modality turned out the biggest of the three. The lowest bid for a fixed feed-in tariff was set at €11.14/MWh, which corresponds to a 73.3% discount from the reference tariff established by the government and which once again set a new world record (SEAE 2020). But a comparison of the 14 successful bids based on their net present value – a measure developed by the Portuguese government to make offers in the different modalities comparable and calculate each project's net benefit to the National Electric System – shows that four projects based on fixed contributions and/or storage capacities were even more compatible than the one based on the fixed tariff of €11.14/MWh (Antuko 2020). Overall, the Portuguese photovoltaic auctions show that solar energy has become competitive, even if combined with requirements to build the storage capacities necessary for more efficient distribution and greater grid stability. In 2021, the government considers to extend renewable energy auctioning to green hydrogen, and wind energy auctions are being discussed, albeit without concrete plans.

Coordination Mechanisms and Multilevel Governance

Over the past decades, energy governance in Portugal has become a matter involving a broad range of public and private organizations, the participation of nonstate actors, both from business and the environmental movement, and spanning different levels of government from the global and EU level to the national and subnational. Early RES policy in Portugal was partially not only a product of the EU's renewable energy directives and the EU's financial support, but also horizontal policy transfer between member states. Incentive framing and incentive schemes observable in other EU countries led to the early adoption of a FIT scheme. In the early 2000s, Portugal was a policy-taker rather than a policy-shaper in EU environmental policy (Börzel 2002; Fernández and Font 2009, p. 72). The liberalization of the energy market, which culminated with the creation of an Iberian energy market (MIBEL), strengthened policy cooperation between Portugal and Spain. RES promotion relied on similar schemes, and both committed to develop the interconnection grid – which developed at a slower pace than predicted. European support declined with the financial crisis of 2008, but incentives to liberalization persisted. While in Spain, RES policies were suspended – or even revoked – in Portugal RES policies were only temporarily put on hold and then reconfigured.

Despite high levels of environmental concern, civic participation in environmental decision-making is still low in Portugal. A centralized administrative tradition undermines the chance of participation of civil society actors in decision-making (Carvalho et al. 2014; Delicado et al. 2014), the population lacks technical and environmental knowledge, and public officials do not disclose information transparently. RES development in Portugal remains a product of predetermined political decisions taken from above (Delicado 2015c). The process of liberalization and administrative reforms, together with EU compliance and growing societal mobilization, led to an increasing interdependence of state and nonstate actors. In 2008, a Climate Change Forum was created to promote interactions between government officials and civil society representatives but evolved toward a top-down structure where there was limited space for active participation and feedback (Carvalho et al. 2014).

The national institutional setup within which energy policy takes place has been characterized by a continuous strengthening and differentiation of the responsible government departments. At the same time, responsibilities for energy governance have gradually moved from the economic to the environmental policy domain. Since 2018, matters related to energy are of the responsibility of the Ministry of Environment and Energy Transition (since 2019 Ministry of Environment and Climate

Action) (República Portuguesa 2018). The Directorate General for Energy and Geology (DGEG) within the Ministry of Environment is responsible for the design, promotion, and assessment of energy policies. The Portuguese Environment Agency (APA), also under the tutelage of the Ministry of Environment, is responsible for the design, implementation, and monitoring of environmental policies that combat climate change. The National Policies and Measures System (SPeM), created in 2015, assesses the implementation of mitigation policies and reinforces the accountability of different sectors regarding climate change (República Portuguesa 2018, 2019b). An Interministerial Climate Change and Air Commission (CIAAC) was created in 2015 to monitor policies for air and climate change. Recently renamed Interministerial Air, Climate Change and Circular Economy Commission (CA2), it oversees the promotion and supervision of policies related to the circular economy, monitors the Portuguese compliance with international commitments, and validates the Portuguese position in international negotiations. The Commission is coordinated by the Minister of Environment and composed of representatives from the remaining ministries (República Portuguesa 2018, 2019b).

The autonomous regional authorities of Madeira and Azores enjoy a certain degree of independence and autonomy in energy policymaking as they develop their own strategies and plans within the established national and European frameworks (República Portuguesa 2019). Local authorities (i.e., municipalities), on the other hand, share competencies related to energy efficiency and adopt municipal climate change mitigation plans (IEA 2016; Campos et al. 2017). However, according to a recent survey, municipal actors do not find climate change to be an important issue, and the absence of appropriate organizational structures – mostly in inland small municipalities – compromises effective policy-making processes (Campos et al. 2017).

Outcomes, Challenges, and Prospects of Energy Governance in Portugal

Outcomes

Four outcomes of the Portuguese energy transition stand out as most important: the increase of energy costs, the decline in energy dependence, the creation of powerful national stakeholders, and a competitive energy market. Higher electricity costs are in part related to the promotion of RES, as grid costs and subsidized production are passed on as taxes that add to the tariffs of end consumers. If, as Fidalgo et al. (2019) show, it is possible to have a system entirely based on renewable sources by 2050, it is important to consider what the costs of that system will be for Portuguese consumers and for the Portuguese economy. On the other hand, the Portuguese energy dependence has been declining steadily and in 2019 stood at 75.1% (DGEG 2019), 13.7% less than in 2005 (Observatório da Energia et al. 2020). The investment in RES technologies also led to the creation of a new industrial cluster within the energy sector and to the investment in RES project development and operation. In the second half of the 2000s, several solar companies were founded and a wind power consortium, ENEOP, was founded in Viana do Castelo, backed by EDP, to manufacture wind turbines. With increasing competition from Asia, the solar cell manufacturers have disappeared, while the wind turbine consortium in Viana do Castelo dissolved in 2019, but its former members will continue their commercial activities individually.

Investment in RES project development and operation was early on led by EDP, backed mostly by foreign capital. A myriad of market players – large international funds, banks, established Iberian companies, construction companies, and new startups – have come to populate the energy market, seizing the financial and market opportunities (Bento and Fontes 2015). Nonetheless, EDP was the company that benefited most from the Portuguese energy transition. Before the liberalization of the energy market, EDP had the monopoly of the electricity market and invested in RES technology, becoming the national leader in wind energy production, and later aiming at the internationalization of its operations. In 2007, EDP created a new company that concentrated on RES – EDP Renováveis – which is one of the largest RES companies in the world (Wehrhahn et al. 2011). The stability of the Portuguese energy transition, which was only temporarily affected by the financial crisis – especially if we compare the Portuguese RES policies in this period with Spain's RES policies – can only be understood if the importance of these actors is taken into account. The strong and enduring power alliance between the (former) monopolist utilities – which were privatized during the energy transition – and the state guaranteed that these companies reaped a great share of the economic benefits of the Portuguese energy transition and supported it even in times of financial austerity.

Finally, the Portuguese energy market has become increasingly competitive. Portuguese companies entered the Spanish market – most prominently, EDP – and all large Spanish companies entered the Portuguese market – Endesa, Iberdrola, and Unión Fenosa as energy retailers and some, notably Iberdrola, also as RES producers. The former electricity monopolists EDP and GALP, the oil and gas monopolists, compete now in the same markets. Although EDP's market share in the electricity market is still above 77%, EDP has recently been losing market share (ERSE 2020a).

Challenges

Portugal's location in the European continent is peripheric (as is its economy (Santos et al. 2017)), with land borders only with Spain, which in turn is separated from continental Europe by the Pyrenees. As electrical interconnections are land-based, Portuguese access to the European energy markets is technically more difficult and economically more costly, especially since the interconnection between Portugal and the rest of Europe must go through Spain. Therefore, one of the main challenges that hinders the consolidation of an Iberian market is the interconnection between Portugal and Spain (and also the interconnection between Spain and France). These interconnections remain underdeveloped, below the capacity needed to have equal wholesale energy prices for both markets, and the energy market price in Portugal is generally higher than in Spain (MIBEL 2019). However, the development of the interconnection between Portugal and Spain is more interesting for

Portugal than for Spain, due to relative national market sizes (Cardoso 2011). The development of the French interconnection is also relevant for Portugal because it would enable energy exports when both Portugal and Spain are saturated by RES production, which already drives prices down in certain periods of excess production. With increasing RES penetration – and if current market rules are maintained – zero cost energy may endanger other energy producers that are responsible for balancing electricity needs, while the viability of some RES projects may also be threatened.

Energy poverty is another challenge that Portugal must overcome. With 15–23% of households living in energy poverty in 2013 (Horta et al. 2019), Portugal is one of the countries in the EU most vulnerable to energy poverty. Until very recently, the problem has been overlooked by national decision-makers. The price of electricity has increased in the last decade and is above the EU28 average since 2012. In 2010 and 2011, the government established social tariffs for electricity and natural gas to assist vulnerable households. However, this has been insufficient, as low incomes and high energy prices result in an increasing vulnerability to energy poverty (Horta et al. 2019). In addition, many low-income households had been deterred by the bureaucratic requirements of applying to the social tariff, but this obstacle was removed in 2016 when social security data was used to identify eligible households and automatically switch them to the social tariff (Observatório de Energia 2019). While the social tariffs help those in poverty, stronger consumer protection policies, which are notoriously weak in Portugal, and additional forms of financial aid would help low-income households (Kyprianou et al. 2019, pp. 52–53). Energy poverty is often associated with low-quality housing, as 70% of the building stock was built before any energy performance regulations were implemented in the country (Horta et al. 2019; Vaquero 2020, p. 541). Since 2017, there is a loan-based investment program (IFRRU 2020) for the renovation of buildings (Horta et al. 2019), which was added to other funds directed at home improvements in vulnerable households. These funds are coordinated at both national and municipal levels (Kyprianou et al. 2019, p. 51). However, these programs have proved to be ineffective, with limited application and implementation. As of 2018, only 256 applications had been submitted to IFRRU, and only 71 contracts had been signed, mainly due to poor information and complex application procedures (Horta et al. 2019).

Finally, the Portuguese energy transition has yet to reach the transportation sector. In 2014, the Portuguese transport sector accounted for 41% of the final energy consumption and 35% of fuel combustion emissions. Road transportation dominates 80% of transportation energy consumption with fossil fuels accounting for 95% of its supply and renewable fuels for the remaining 5% (Lorenzi and Baptista 2018, p. 920). Electricity use is negligible in the transport sector, despite efforts to incentivize electric mobility, and fossil fuels are expected to continue to dominate the transport sector in the next 15 years (Lorenzi and Baptista 2018). Nonetheless, there is a trend of decreasing consumption of fossil fuels (Pinho and Hunter 2019, p. 285) that can be further incentivized by market-based policies to promote cleaner vehicles (Nunes et al. 2019, p. 438).

Prospects

The future of the Portuguese energy transition depends on increasing the RES share in the energy mix and electrifying end consumption. The Portuguese goal is to transition to a carbon-neutral economy by 2050 and to implement the 2015 Paris Agreement (Republica Portuguesa 2019a). The new solar auctions are seen by the government as the optimal tool to balance the strong demand for generation permits with the scarcity of grid capacity as auctions speed up investment in new capacity, give priority to projects with lower costs and greater guarantees of execution, and allow for better articulation between the permitting process and investments in new grid capacity (https://leiloes-renovaveis.gov.pt/). The Portuguese solar energy auctions have received great international recognition and are regarded as a successful approach to a cost-effective increase of the share of renewable electricity. Del Río et al. (2019, p. 18) consider the design of the auctions as "one of the most innovative in Europe (...) which provided the participants with flexibility with respect to their project risk profile." However, despite the surprisingly low-price guarantees achieved at the auctions in 2019 and 2020, it is still early to assess their success in terms of photovoltaic capacity creation. One of the biggest risks associated with renewable capacity auctions is the uncertainty of project implementation. The winners of the auction can only apply for photovoltaic power plant licenses – which include obtaining land rights, the production license, the license or admission of prior notice to carry out urban planning operations, and the operating license – after the rights to feed solar energy into the grid have been auctioned and granted. So far, the winners of the 2019 auction have completed the first phase of their contractual obligations relating to the presentation of the relevant documents attesting their land rights.

Another key strategy is the development of virtual power plants which is leveraged in three vectors: decentralized energy production, real-time energy monitoring, and new market mechanisms and agents (aggregators). Regarding the first vector, the Portuguese government recently approved new legislation that incentivizes local self-consumption and shared consumption of small RES production (Decree Law 162/2019). Regarding the second, the digitalization of energy monitoring is being pursued through widespread installation of digital meters that allow for measuring real-time production and consumption of energy, which also poses new challenges to the regulator (Crispim et al. 2014). Regarding the third, it is expected that future market regulations and more flexible tariffs will open the door to new market players.

Last, but not least, Portugal is considering investing in renewable energy to produce hydrogen, which can be used to store renewable energy and as an alternative to fossil fuels in transportation. A National Hydrogen Strategy that sets out some general guidelines was adopted in 2020. However, investment in hydrogen generation is not consensual. The largest opposition party PSD claims that Portugal is betting on an uncertain technology that may not pay off (Marques 2020), whereas the energy regulator warned that infrastructure costs could endanger the prices of natural gas paid by end consumers (ERSE 2020b).

Cross-References

▶ Energy Governance in Europe: Country Comparison and Conclusion
▶ Energy Governance in Europe: Introduction
▶ Energy Governance in Spain
▶ Energy Poverty
▶ European Union Energy Policy: A Discourse Perspective

References

Andreas, J. J., Burns, C., & Touza, J. (2019). Portugal under austerity: From financial to renewable crisis? *Environmental Research Communications, 1*(9), 91005. https://doi.org/10.1088/2515-7620/ab3cb0.
Antuko. (2020). *Full 2020 Portuguese solar auction results*. Antuko. https://antuko.com/full-2020-portuguese-solar-auction-results/ Accessed 30 Oct 2020.
Araújo, L., & Coelho, M. J. (2013). Políticas públicas de energia e ambiente: rumo a um país sustentável? *Sociologia, Problemas E Práticas, 72*, 145–158. https://doi.org/10.7458/SPP2013722622.
Barca, S., & Delicado, A. (2016). Anti-nuclear mobilisation and environmentalism in europe: A view from Portugal (1976–1986). *Environment and History, 22*(4), 497–520. https://doi.org/10.3197/096734016X14727286515736.
Bellini, E. (2020). Analysis: Initial results of Portugal's solar+storage auction. *Pv Magazine*. https://www.pv-magazine.com/2020/09/02/analysis-initial-results-of-portugals-solarstorage-auction/. Accessed 30 Oct 2020.
Bento, N., & Fontes, M. (2015). The construction of a new technological innovation system in a follower country: Wind energy in Portugal. *Technological Forecasting and Social Change, 99*, 197–210. https://doi.org/10.1016/j.techfore.2015.06.037.
Biorcio, R. (2016). Green parties in Southern Europe (Italy, Spain, Portugal, and Greece). In E. van Haute (Ed.), *Green parties in Europe* (pp. 177–195). London: Routledge.
Boemi, S. N., & Papadopoulos, A. M. (2013). Times of recession: Three different renewable energy stories from the Mediterranean region. In E. Michalena & J. M. Hills (Eds.), *Renewable energy governance: Complexities and challenges* (pp. 263–275). London: Springer. https://doi.org/10.1007/978-1-4471-5595-9_16.
Börzel, T. (2002). Pace-setting, foot-dragging and fence-sitting: Member states responses to europeanization. *Journal of Common Market Studies, 40*(2), 193–214.
Caetano, L. (1998). A Dinâmica da produção carbonífera em Portugal: Impactes sócio-económicos e ambientais. *Cadernos de Geografia, 17*, 247–257.
Campos, I., Guerra, J., Gomes, J. F., Schmidt, L., Alves, F., Vizinho, A., & Lopes, G. P. (2017). Understanding climate change policy and action in Portuguese municipalities: A survey. *Land Use Policy, 62*, 68–78. https://doi.org/10.1016/j.landusepol.2016.12.015.
Cardoso, C. F. M. (2011). *The electrical interconnection between Portugal and Spain*. Manuscript. University of Lisbon. https://fenix.tecnico.ulisboa.pt/downloadFile/395143439017/artigo-resumo-alargado.pdf. Accessed 1 Nov 2020.
Carius, A., & Jörgens, H. (1993). Bürgerinitiativen und Parteien im Umweltschutz in Portugal. *Forschungsjournal Neue Soziale Bewegungen, 6*(1), 76–87.
Carvalho, A., Schmidt, L., Santos, F. D., & Delicado, A. (2014). Climate change research and policy in Portugal. *Wiley Interdisciplinary Reviews: Climate Change, 5*(2), 199–217. https://doi.org/10.1002/wcc.258.

Crispim, J., Braz, J., Castro, R., & Esteves, J. (2014). Smart grids in the EU with smart regulation: Experiences from the UK, Italy and Portugal. *Utilities Policy, 31,* 85–93. https://doi.org/10.1016/j.jup.2014.09.006. Elsevier.

de Lovinfosse, I. (2008). *How and why do policies change? A comparison of renewable electricity policies in Belgium, Denmark, Germany, the Netherlands and the UK.* Brussels: P.I.E. Peter Lang.

del Río, P. (2016). *Auctions for Renewable Support in Portugal: Instruments and Lessons Learnt.* Karlsruhe: AURES Report D.4.1-PT.

del Río, P., Lucas, H., Dézsi, B., & Diallo, A. (2019). *Auctions for the Support of Renewable Energy in Portugal: Main Results and Lessons Learnt. Deliverable D2.1-PT of the AURES II Project.* Budapest: Regional Centre for Energy Policy Research (REKK).

Delicado, A. (2015a). Ações e discursos políticos sobre as energias renováveis. In A. Delicado (Ed.), *Terras de sol e de vento: Dinâmicas sociotécnicas e aceitação social das energias renováveis em Portugal* (pp. 49–96). Lisbon: Imprensa de Ciências Sociais.

Delicado, A. (2015b). As energias renováveis nos media e na opinião pública. In A. Delicado (Ed.), *Terras de sol e de vento: Dinâmicas sociotécnicas e aceitação social das energias renováveis em Portugal* (pp. 97–137). Lisbon: Imprensa de Ciências Sociais.

Delicado, A. (2015c). Participação Pública nos processos de decisão sobre energias renováveis. In A. Delicado (Ed.), *Terras de sol e de vento: Dinâmicas sociotécnicas e aceitação social das energias renováveis em Portugal* (pp. 223–262). Lisbon: Imprensa de Ciências Sociais.

Delicado, A., Junqueira, L., Fonseca, S., Silva, L., Horta, A., & Figueiredo, E. (2014). Not in anyone's backyard? Civil society attitudes towards wind power at the national and local levels in Portugal. *Science & Technology Studies, 27*(2), 49–71.

DGEG. (2019). *Balanço Energético 2019 – Sintético.* DGEG. https://www.dgeg.gov.pt/media/11inpxds/balan%C3%A7o-sintetico-2019.pdf. Accessed 18 Apr 2021.

EDP. (2018). *Dados Ibéricos 2018.* Lisbon: EDP.

ERSE. (2020a). *Boletim ERSE: Mercado Liberalizado Eletricidade.* ERSE. https://www.erse.pt/media/2fhpqtwt/ml-ele-mai-2020.pdf Accessed 16 Dec 2020.

ERSE. (2020b). Parecer: projeto de diploma que estabelece a organização e o funcionamento do Sistema Nacional de Gás (SNG), permitindo a injeção de outros gases na Rede Nacional de Gás – Diploma que revoga os Decretos-Lei n.°s 30/2006 e 140/2006. Lisboa. https://www.erse.pt/media/rusdcomb/parecererse_projdl_sng.pdf. Accessed 31 Oct 2020.

European Commission. (2020a). 2020 report on the state of the Energy Union pursuant to regulation (EU) 2018/1999 on governance of the Energy Union and climate action. Brussels: European Commission (COM (2020) 950 final). https://ec.europa.eu/energy/sites/ener/files/report_on_the_state_of_the_energy_union_com2020950.pdf. Accessed 31 Oct 2020.

European Commission. (2020b). *Energy statistics: Energy datasheets: EU countries – Portugal. EU Commission, DG Energy, Unit A4. 15 june 2020 update.* Brussels: European Commission.

European Parliament. (2019). *Parlemeter 2019: Portugal factsheet.* Brussels: European Parliament.

Eurostat. (2020). *Renewable energy statistics.* Eurostat. https://ec.europa.eu/eurostat/statistics-explained/index.php/Renewable_energy_statistics. Accessed 31 Oct 2020.

Fernández, A. M., & Font, N. (2009). Portugal: The challenges of environmental governance and the realities of government. In T. A. Börzel (Ed.), *Coping with accession to the European Union* (pp. 70–94). London: Palgrave Macmillan UK. https://doi.org/10.1057/9780230245358_5.

Ferreira, S., Moreira, N. A., & Monteiro, E. (2009). Bioenergy overview for Portugal. *Biomass and Bioenergy, 33*(11), 1567–1576. https://doi.org/10.1016/j.biombioe.2009.07.020.

Fidalgo, J. N., de São Jose, D., & Silva, C. (2019). Impact of climate changes on the Portuguese energy generation mix. In *16th international conference on the European energy market,* pp. 1–6. https://doi.org/10.1109/EEM.2019.8916539.

Franco, R. C. (Ed.). (2015). *Diagnóstico das ONG em Portugal.* Lisbon: Fundação Calouste Gulbenkian.

Guevara, Z., & Domingos, T. (2017). Three-level decoupling of energy use in Portugal 1995–2010. *Energy Policy, 108,* 134–142. https://doi.org/10.1016/j.enpol.2017.05.050.

Guevara, Z., & Rodrigues, J. F. D. (2016). Structural transitions and energy use: A decomposition analysis of Portugal 1995–2010. *Economic Systems Research, 28*(2), 202–223. https://doi.org/10.1080/09535314.2016.1157456.

Guimarães, P., & Fernandes, F. (2016). Os conflitos ambientais em Portugal (1974-2015): uma breve retrospetiva. In P. Guimarães & J. Cebada (Eds.), *Conflitos Ambientais na Indústria Mineira e Metalúrgica: o passado e o presente* (pp. 19–63). Évora: Centro de Investigação em Ciência Política.

Heer, K., & Langniß, O. (2007). *Promoting renewable energy sources in Portugal: Possible implications for China.* Centre for Solar Energy and Hydrogen Research Baden-Württemberg. Stuttgart: ZSW. https://resource-solutions.org/document/promoting-renewable-energy-sources-in-portugal-possible-implications-for-china/. Last accessed 1 Nov 2020.

Horta, A., & Carvalho, A. (2017). Climate change communication in Portugal. In *Oxford research encyclopedia of climate science* (Vol. 1). Oxford: Oxford University Press. https://doi.org/10.1093/acrefore/9780190228620.013.599.

Horta, A., Gouveia, J. P., Schmidt, L., Sousa, J. C., Palma, P., & Simões, S. (2019). Energy poverty in Portugal: Combining vulnerability mapping with household interviews. *Energy and Buildings, 203.* https://doi.org/10.1016/j.enbuild.2019.109423.

IEA. (2016). *Portugal: 2016 review (Energy policies of IEA countries).* Paris: International Energy Agency.

Jänicke, M. (2009). On ecological and political modernization. In A. P. J. Mol, D. A. Sonnenfeld, & G. Spaargaren (Eds.), *The ecological modernisation reader: Environmental reform in theory and practice* (pp. 28–41). London: Routledge.

Jörgens, H. (2020). Ambiente. In R. P. Mamede & P. A. e. Silva (Eds.), *O Estado da Nação e as Políticas Públicas 2020 – Valorizar as Políticas Públicas* (pp. 43–48). Lisbon: IPPS.

Kitzing, L., Anatolitsis, V., Fitch-Roy, O., Klessmann, C., Kreiss, J., del Río, P., Wigand, F., & Woodman, B. (2019). Auctions for renewable energy support: Lessons learned in the aures project. IAEE Energy Forum (Third Quarter 2019), 11–14.

Kyprianou, I., Serghides, D. K., Varo, A., Gouveia, J. P., Kopeva, D., & Murauskaite, L. (2019). Energy poverty policies and measures in 5 EU countries: A comparative study. *Energy and Buildings, 196,* 46–60. https://doi.org/10.1016/j.enbuild.2019.05.003.

Lorenzi, G., & Baptista, P. (2018). Promotion of renewable energy sources in the Portuguese transport sector: A scenario analysis. *Journal of Cleaner Production, 186,* 918–932. https://doi.org/10.1016/j.jclepro.2018.03.057.

Lourenço, M. I. D. (2010). *O sector da electricidade em Portugal – o papel da EDP Soluções Comerciais. Mestrado em Economia Industrial – Relatório de Estágio.* Coimbra: Faculdade de Economia da Universidade de Coimbra.

Madureira, C., & Baptista, V. (2002). *Hidroelectricidade em Portugal – memória e desafio.* Lisbon: REN – Rede Eléctrica Nacional.

Marques, B. (2020). Rui Rio classifica projeto de Governo para o hidrogénio como "extremamente perigoso". *Jornal Económico.* https://jornaleconomico.sapo.pt/noticias/rui-rio-classifica-projeto-de-governo-para-o-hidrogenio-como-extremamente-perigoso-617430. Accessed 16 Apr 2021.

Mazzucato, M., & Semieniuk, G. (2018). Financing renewable energy: Who is financing what and why it matters. *Technological Forecasting and Social Change, 127,* 8–22. https://doi.org/10.1016/j.techfore.2017.05.021.

MIBEL. (2019). Estudo sobre comparação dos preços MIBEL (à vista e a prazo) com outros mercados Europeus e a sua relação com o mercado único. https://www.mibel.com/wp-content/uploads/2019/07/20190705E_PT.pdf. Accessed 31 Oct 2020.

Miguel, C., Mendes, A., & Madeira, L. (2018). An overview of the Portuguese energy sector and perspectives for power-to-gas implementation. *Energies, 11*(12), 3259. https://doi.org/10.3390/en11123259.

Moreira, A. V. (2020). PSI-20 caiu no último mês 12% face a agosto de 2019. Energéticas continuam a ser os "pesos pesados". *Jornal Económico.* https://jornaleconomico.sapo.pt/noticias/psi-20-caiu-no-ultimo-mes-12-face-a-agosto-de-2019-energeticas-continuam-a-ser-os-pesos-pesados-631725. Accessed 16 Apr 2021.

Neves, F. (2016). Chama-se Zero. É uma nova ONG de ambiente portuguesa. *Diário De Notícias*, January 23. https://www.dn.pt/sociedade/chamase-zero-e-uma-nova-ong-de-ambiente-portuguesa-4995767.html. Accessed 31 Oct 2020.

Nunes, P., Pinheiro, F., & Brito, M. C. (2019). The effects of environmental transport policies on the environment, economy and employment in Portugal. *Journal of Cleaner Production, 213*, 428–439. https://doi.org/10.1016/j.jclepro.2018.12.166.

Observatório da Energia. (2019). *Estudo sobre a aplicação da tarifa social de energia em Portugal*. Coimbra: Universidade de Coimbra.

Observatório da Energia, DGEG, & ADENE. (2020). *Energia em Números – Edição 2020*. ADENE. ISBN: 978-972-8521-26-4 https://www.dgeg.gov.pt/media/43zf5nvd/energia-em-n%C3%BAmeros-edi%C3%A7%C3%A3o-2020.pdf. Accessed 18 Apr 2021.

PAN. (2019). *Da diferença à emergência ainda vamos a tempo: Programa Eleitoral do PAN – Legislativas 2019*. Lisbon: PAN.

Pareja-Alcaraz, P. (2017). Chinese investments in Southern Europe's energy sectors: Similarities and divergences in China's strategies in Greece, Italy, Portugal and Spain. *Energy Policy, 101*, 700–710. https://doi.org/10.1016/j.enpol.2016.09.034. Elsevier.

PCP. (2019). Política patriótica e de esquerda - Soluções para um Portugal com futuro. In *Programa eleitoral do PCP – Legislativas 2019*. Lisboa: PCP.

Peña, I., Azevedo, I. L., & Ferreira, L. A. F. M. (2017). Lessons from wind policy in Portugal. *Energy Policy, 103*, 193–202. https://doi.org/10.1016/j.enpol.2016.11.033.

Pereira, T. S., Fonseca, P. F. C., & Carvalho, A. (2018). Carnation atoms? A history of nuclear energy in Portugal. *Minerva, 56*, 505–528. https://doi.org/10.1007/s11024-018-9354-4.

PEV. (2019). *Compromissos do PEV: 12 Compromissos do Partido Ecologista Os Verdes*. Lisbon: PEV.

Pinho, A., & Hunter, R. (2019). The Portuguese energy sector: Its multiple aspects and challenges – A country study. *Journal of Sustainable Development Studies, 12*(2), 281–304. https://doi.org/10.28924/ip/jsds.1905.

PNBEPH. (2007). Plano Nacional de Barragens com Elevado Potencial Hidroelétrico.

PORDATA. (n.d.). *Base de Dados Portugal Contemporâneo*. Fundação Francisco Manuel dos Santos (FFMS). https://www.pordata.pt/. Accessed 14 Dec 2020.

Queirós, M. (2016). *Environmental knowledge and environmental politics in Portugal: From resistance to incorporation*. Munich: Rachel Carson Center for Environment and Society. https://doi.org/10.5282/RCC/7701.

REN. (2019). *Dados técnicos 2019*. Lisbon: REN.

República Portuguesa. (2018). *Integrated national energy and climate plan 2021–2030*. Lisbon: República Portuguesa.

República Portuguesa. (2019a). Roteiro para a Neutralidade Carbónica 2050.

República Portuguesa. (2019b). *Plano Nacional Energia e Clima 2021–2030 (PNEC 2030)*. Lisbon: República Portuguesa.

República Portuguesa. (2020). *EN-H2 – Estratégia Nacional para o Hidrogénio. Versão Draft*. Ministério do Ambiente e Ação Climática.

Ribeiro, F., Ferreira, P., Araújo, M., & Braga, A. C. (2014). Public opinion on renewable energy technologies in Portugal. *Energy, 69*, 39–50. https://doi.org/10.1016/j.energy.2013.10.074.

Santos, A. C., Rodrigues, J., & Teles, N. (2017). Semi-peripheral financialisation and social reproduction: The case of Portugal. *New Political Economy, 23*(4), 475–494. https://doi.org/10.1080/13563467.2017.1371126.

Sardo, A. M., & Weitkamp, E. (2012). Exploring the ways environmental science is used and valued by policy-makers in Portugal: A case study. *Journal of Science Communication, 11*(03). https://doi.org/10.22323/2.11030305.

SEAE. (2020). *Procedimento concorrencial, sob a forma de leilão eletrónico, para atribuição de reserva de capacidade de injeção na rede elétrica de serviço público para eletricidade a partir da conversão de energia solar (Despacho SEAE n° 5921/2020, de 29 de Maio)*. Secretary of State for Energy. https://leiloes-renovaveis.gov.pt/EnmTipoFicheiro/Download/229. Accessed 30 Oct 2020.

Silveira, P., Rogeiro Nina, S., & Humberto Teixeira, L. (2019). *Breve história do Partido Ecologista "Os Verdes" e do Pessoas-Animais-Natureza*. Lisbon: Público.
Soares, C. D., & Silva, S. T. d. (2014). *Direito das energias renováveis. Manuais universitários*. Lisbon: Almedina.
Solorio, I., & Bocquillon, P. (2017). EU renewable energy policy: A brief overview of its history and evolution. In I. Solorio & H. Jörgens (Eds.), *A guide to EU renewable energy policy: Comparing Europeanization and domestic policy change in EU member states* (pp. 23–42). Cheltenham: Edward Elgar.
Solorio, I., & Jörgens, H. (Eds.). (2017). *A Guide to EU Renewable Energy Policy: Comparing Europeanization and Domestic Policy Change in EU Member States*. Cheltenham: Edward Elgar. https://doi.org/10.4337/9781783471560
Teixeira, E., & Salavisa, I. (2016). Energy, innovation and competition: How public policies coordination may contribute to a new energy model. In A. Figueiredo & P. Oliveira (Eds.), *A regulação energética em Portugal 2007–2017* (pp. 213–235). Lisbon: ERSE.
Torres, P. J. F., Ekonomou, L., & Karampelas, P. (2016). The correlation between renewable generation and electricity demand: A case study of Portugal. In P. Karampelas & L. Ekonomou (Eds.), *Energy systems. Electricity distribution* (pp. 119–151). Berlin: Springer. https://doi.org/10.1007/978-3-662-49434-9_5.
Vaquero, P. (2020). Buildings energy certification system in Portugal: Ten years later. *Energy Reports, 6*, 541–547. https://doi.org/10.1016/j.egyr.2019.09.023.
Volkens, A., Burst, T., Krause, W., Lehmann, P., Matthieß, T., Merz, N., Regel, S., Weßels, B., & Zehnter, L. (2020). *The Manifesto data collection. Manifesto project (MRG/CMP/MARPOR). Version 2020*. Berlin: Wissenschaftszentrum Berlin für Sozialforschung (WZB). https://doi.org/10.25522/manifesto.mpds.2020a.
Wehrhahn, R., Saint-Aubyn, J., & Casas, J. (2011). Iberia – Giants and windmills. In R. Berger (Ed.), *Green growth, green profit. How green transformation boosts business* (pp. 127–138). London: Palgrave Macmillan. https://doi.org/10.1057/9780230303874_9.

Legislation

Decree Law 104/2010. Establishes the procedure applicable to the extinction of regulated tariffs. Ministério da Economia, da Inovação e do Desenvolvimento, Diário da República n.° 190/2010, Série I de 2010-09-29, pp. 4327–4329. https://data.dre.pt/eli/dec-lei/104/2010/09/29/p/dre/pt/html
Decree Law 118-A/2010. Simplifies the regime applicable to the production of electricity with micro production units. Ministério da Economia, da Inovação e do Desenvolvimento, Diário da República n.° 207/2010, 1° Suplemento, Série I de 2010-10-25, pp. 4834-(2)-4834-(15). https://data.dre.pt/eli/dec-lei/118-a/2010/10/25/p/dre/pt/html
Decree Law 13/2014. Changes Decree Law 104/2010 and sets new rules for transitory tariffs in the electricity sold to final consumers. Ministério do Ambiente, Ordenamento do Território e Energia, Diário da República n.° 15/2014, Série I de 2014-01-22, pp. 469–469. https://data.dre.pt/eli/dec-lei/13/2014/01/22/p/dre/pt/html
Decree Law 141/2010. Considering the Estratégia Nacional da Energia 2020, defines the targets of renewable energy in final consumption and partially transposes Directive 2009/28/CE, of the European Parliament and the Council. Diário da República n.° 253/2010, Série I de 2010-12-31. https://data.dre.pt/eli/dec-lei/141/2010/p/cons/20200817/pt/html
Decree Law 15/2015. Changes Decree Laws 74/2012, 75/2012, 66/2010, 104/2010, and changes the transitory tariffs applicable to the supply of natural gas and electricity to final consumers with low gas volume consumption and/or low voltage. Ministério do Ambiente, Ordenamento do Território e Energia, Diário da República n.° 21/2015, Série I de 2015-01-30, pp. 628–631. https://data.dre.pt/eli/dec-lei/15/2015/01/30/p/dre/pt/html

Decree Law 162/2019. Approves the applicable legal framework to the self-consumption of renewable energy, by partial transposition of Directive 2018/2001. Ambiente e Transição Energética -Presidência do Conselho de Ministros. Diário da República n.° 206/2019, Série I de 2019-10-25, pp. 45–62. https://data.dre.pt/eli/dec-lei/162/2019/10/25/p/dre

Decree Law 168/99. *Reviews the applicable regulatory regime for the production of electric energy in the Independent Electric System, with utilizes renewable resources or industrial, agricultural, or urban residues*. Ministério da Economia, Diário da República n.° 115/1999, Série I-A de 1999-05-18, pp. 2619–2628. https://data.dre.pt/eli/dec-lei/168/1999/05/18/p/dre/pt/html

Decree Law 178/2015. Changes Decree Law 29/2006, which establishes common rules for the internal energy market. Ministério do Ambiente, Ordenamento do Território e Energia, Diário da República n.° 167/2015, Série I de 2015-08-27, pp. 6428–6429. https://data.dre.pt/eli/dec-lei/178/2015/08/27/p/dre/pt/html

Decree Law 182/95. *Establishes the organization of the National Electric System (SEN)*. Ministério da Indústria e Energia, Diário da República n.° 172/1995, Série I-A de 1995-07-27, pp. 4772–4783. https://data.dre.pt/eli/dec-lei/182/1995/07/27/p/dre/pt/html

Decree Law 185/2003. Establishes the rules for the creation of a free and competitive electric market. Ministério da Economia, Diário da República n.° 191/2003, Série I-A de 2003-08-20, pp. 5196–5199. https://data.dre.pt/eli/dec-lei/185/2003/08/20/p/dre/pt/html

Decree Law 188/88. *Creates the incentive system for the rational utilization of energy (SIURE)*, Diário da República n.° 123/1988, Série I de 1988-05-27, Ministério da Indústria e Energia, pp. 2284–2289.

Decree Law 189/88. *Establishes norms related to the production of electric energy by singular persons or collective persons of public or private right*, Diário da República n.° 123/1988, Série I de 1988-05-27, Ministério da Indústria e Energia, pp. 2289–2296.

Decree Law 195/94. *Creates the Energy Program*. Ministério da Indústria e Energia, Diário da República n.° 165/1994, Série I-A de 1994-07-19, pp. 3906–3910. https://data.dre.pt/eli/dec-lei/195/1994/07/19/p/dre/pt/html

Decree Law 198/2000. *Reviews the legislation of the electric sector (changes several decree laws)*. Ministério da Economia, Diário da República n.° 195/2000, Série I-A de 2000-08-24, pp. 4297–4299. https://data.dre.pt/eli/dec-lei/198/2000/08/24/p/dre/pt/html

Decree Law 20/81. *Establishes incentives for the self-production of electric energy*, Ministério da Indústria e Energia, Diário da República n.° 23/1981, Série I de 1981-01-28, pp. 242-244

Decree Law 149/86, *New redaction of DL 20/81*, Ministério da Indústria e Comércio, Diário da República n.° 137/1986, Série I de 1986-06-18, pp. 1436–1437.

Decree Law 215-A/2012. Changes Decree Law 29/2006. Ministério da Economia e do Emprego, Diário da República n.° 194/2012, 1° Suplemento, Série I de 2012-10-08, pp. 5588-(2)-5588-(45). https://data.dre.pt/eli/dec-lei/215-a/2012/10/08/p/dre/pt/html

Decree Law 215-B/2012. Changes Decree Law 172/2006 and completes the transposition of Directive 2009/72/CE of the European Parliament and the Council, that establishes the common rules for the internal electricity market. Ministério da Economia e do Emprego, Diário da República n.° 194/2012, 1° Suplemento, Série I de 2012-10-08, pp. 5588-(45)-5588-(133). https://data.dre.pt/eli/dec-lei/215-b/2012/10/08/p/dre/pt/html

Decree Law 225/2007. Implements the renewable energy measures of the national energy strategy established in the Resolution of the Council of Ministers 169/2005. Ministério da Economia e da Inovação, Diário da República n.° 105/2007, Série I de 2007-05-31, pp. 3630–3638. https://data.dre.pt/eli/dec-lei/225/2007/05/31/p/dre/pt/html

Decree Law 24/99. *Reviews Decree Law 182/95, which had established the organization of the National Electric System*. Ministério da Economia, Diário da República n.° 23/1999, Série I-A de 1999-01-28, pp. 551–552. https://data.dre.pt/eli/dec-lei/24/1999/01/28/p/dre/pt/html

Decree Law 240/2004. Defines the cessation conditions for the energy acquisition contracts (CAE) and defines compensations. Ministério das Actividades Económicas e do Trabalho, Diário da República n.° 301/2004, Série I-A de 2004-12-27, pp. 7330–7345. https://data.dre.pt/eli/dec-lei/240/2004/12/27/p/dre/pt/html

Decree Law 25/2012. Suspends the tenders for new power injections in the national electric grid (Rede Elétrica de Serviço Público). Ministério da Economia e do Emprego, Diário da República n.° 26/2012, Série I de 2012-02-06, pp. 589–590. https://data.dre.pt/eli/dec-lei/25/2012/02/06/p/dre/pt/html

Decree Law 25/2013. Changes Decree Law 363/2007, which establishes the regime applicable to the production of electricity with micro production units, and Decree Law 34/2011, which establishes the regime applicable to the production of electricity with mini production units. Ministério da Economia e do Emprego, Diário da República n.° 35/2013, Série I de 2013-02-19, pp. 1037–1058. https://data.dre.pt/eli/dec-lei/25/2013/02/19/p/dre/pt/html

Decree Law 250/86. *Creates the incentive system for the rational utilization of energy and the development of new forms of energy*, Diário da República n.° 194/1986, Série I de 1986-08-25, Ministério da Indústria e Comércio, pp. 2162–2166.

Decree Law 256/2012. Establishes conditions to ensure tariff stability. Ministério da Economia e do Emprego, Diário da República n.° 231/2012, Série I de 2012-11-29, pp. 6827–6829. https://data.dre.pt/eli/dec-lei/256/2012/11/29/p/dre/pt/html

Decree Law 274-C/93. *Regulates the public service concession of natural gas importation, transportation, and supply through the high pressure network*, Ministério da Indústria e Energia, Diário da República n.° 181/1993, 2° Suplemento, Série I-A de 1993-08-04, pp. 4184-(6) a 4184-(13). https://data.dre.pt/eli/dec-lei/274-c/1993/08/04/p/dre/pt/html

Decree Law 29/2006. Establishes the general principles for the organization and operation of the national electric system, as well as the production, transportation, distribution, and commercialization of electricity, and for the organization of electricity markets. Diário da República n.° 33/2006, Série I-A de 2006-02-1. https://data.dre.pt/eli/dec-lei/29/2006/p/cons/20201001/pt/html

Decree Law 312/2001. *Defines the system that manages the reception capacity of the network of the Electric System of Public Service of the electric energy originating in the electroproduction centres of the Independent Electric System.* Ministério da Economia, Diário da República n.° 284/2001, Série I-A de 2001-12-10, pp. 8016–8024. https://data.dre.pt/eli/dec-lei/312/2001/12/10/p/dre/pt/html

Decree Law 313/95. *Updates Decree Law 189/88, of May 27 (establishes measures related to the production of electric energy by individuals and legal persons covered by public or private law).* Ministério da Indústria e Energia, Diário da República n.° 272/1995, Série I-A de 1995-11-24, pp. 7273–7276. https://data.dre.pt/eli/dec-lei/313/1995/11/24/p/dre/pt/html

Decree Law 324/2011. Establishes the regime applicable to the production of electricity by mini production units. Ministério da Economia, da Inovação e do Desenvolvimento, Diário da República n.° 47/2011, Série I de 2011-03-08, pp. 1316–1325. https://data.dre.pt/eli/dec-lei/34/2011/03/08/p/dre/pt/html

Decree Law 339-C/2001. Changes Decree Law 168/99, which reviews the regime applicable to the production of electricity in the independent electric system. Ministérios da Economia e do Ambiente e do Ordenamento do Território, Diário da República n.° 300/2001, 1° Suplemento, Série I-A de 2001-12-29, pp. 8520-(2)-8520-(3). https://data.dre.pt/eli/dec-lei/339-c/2001/12/29/p/dre/pt/html

Decree Law 33-A/2005. Changes Decree Law 189/88, by reviewing the remuneration of renewable power plants that deliver energy to the Portuguese Electric System, and defines procedures for assigning available power and deadlines for obtaining renewable power plant permits. Diário da República n.° 33/2005, 1° Suplemento, Série I-A de 2005-02-16, pp. 1180-(2) a 1180-(9). https://data.dre.pt/eli/dec-lei/33-a/2005/02/16/p/dre/pt/html

Decree Law 35/2013. Changes the compensation given to electricity producers covered by Decree Law 189/88. Ministério da Economia e do Emprego, Diário da República n.° 42/2013, Série I de 2013-02-28, pp. 1154–1165. https://data.dre.pt/eli/dec-lei/35/2013/02/28/p/dre/pt/html

Decree Law 363/2007. Establishes the regime applicable to the production of electricity in units of micro-production. Ministério da Economia e da Inovação, Diário da República n.° 211/2007, Série I de 2007-11-02, pp. 7978–7984. https://data.dre.pt/eli/dec-lei/363/2007/11/02/p/dre/pt/html

Decree Law 39/2010. Establishes the electric mobility regime, applicable to the organization, access, and implementation of electric mobility, as well as the rules for the creation of a pilot network of electric mobility. Ministério da Economia, da Inovação e do Desenvolvimento, Diário da República n.° 80/2010, Série I de 2010-04-26, pp. 1371–1386. https://data.dre.pt/eli/dec-lei/39/2010/04/26/p/dre/pt/html

Decree Law 449/88. *Changes some dispositions of law 46/77, of 8 July, related to the delimitation of sectors (including the energy sector)*. Diário da República n.° 284/1988, Série I de 1988-12-10, Presidência do Conselho de Ministros, pp. 4886–4887.

Decree Law 502/76. *Creates the Eletricidade de Portugal – Empresa Pública – EDP*, Ministério da Indústria e Tecnologia, Diário da República n.° 151/1976, Série I de 1976-06-30, pp. 1438–1447.

Decree Law 538/99. *Establishes the legal framework of the co-generation activity.* Ministério da Economia. Diário da República n.° 288/1999, Série I-A de 1999-12-13, pp. 8801–8809. https://data.dre.pt/eli/dec-lei/538/1999/12/13/p/dre/pt/html

Decree Law 56/97. *Reviews the legislation of the national electric sector (changes several decree laws)*. Ministério da Economia, Diário da República n.° 62/1997, Série I-A de 1997-03-14, pp. 1162–1207. https://data.dre.pt/eli/dec-lei/56/1997/03/14/p/dre/pt/html

Decree Law 75/2012. Establishes the regime for the extinction of regulated tariffs in electricity contracts for clients in low tension and safeguards clients who are economically vulnerable. Ministério da Economia e do Emprego, Diário da República n.° 61/2012, Série I de 2012-03-26, pp. 1442–1445. https://data.dre.pt/eli/dec-lei/75/2012/03/26/p/dre/pt/html

Decree Law 78/2011. Establishes common rules for the internal electricity market, transposing the Directive 2009/72 of the European Parliament and the Council. Ministério da Economia, da Inovação e do Desenvolvimento, Diário da República n.° 117/2011, Série I de 2011-06-20. pp. 3352–3381 https://data.dre.pt/eli/dec-lei/78/2011/06/20/p/dre/pt/html

Decree Law 94/2014. Establishes the regime applicable to the additional power or the repowering of existing equipment of electricity producers under a guaranteed remuneration regime. Ministério do Ambiente, Ordenamento do Território e Energia, Diário da República n.° 119/2014, Série I de 2014-06-24, pp. 3352–3356. https://data.dre.pt/eli/dec-lei/94/2014/06/24/p/dre/pt/html

Decree Law 99/91. *Establishes the legal framework for the production, transportation, and distribution of electric energy.* Ministério da Indústria e Energia, Diário da República n.° 51/1991, Série I-A de 1991-03-02, pp. 1076–1080. https://data.dre.pt/eli/dec-lei/99/1991/03/02/p/dre/pt/html

Law 105/2017. Establishes that household consumers can choose to remain in the regulated tariff regime. Assembleia da República. Diário da República n.° 167/2017, Série I de 2017-08-30, pp. 5212–5212. https://data.dre.pt/eli/lei/105/2017/08/30/p/dre/pt/html

Law 19/2014. Guidelines for the environmental policy. Diário da República n.° 73/2014, Série I de 2014-04-14. https://data.dre.pt/eli/lei/19/2014/p/cons/20140414/pt/html

Law 2002 of 1944. *'Electric energy production should come from hydraulics'*, Ministério das Obras Públicas e Comunicações, Diário do Govêrno n.° 285/1944, Série I de 1944-12-26, pp. 1311–1314.

Law 51/2010. Simplifies the procedure for the repowering of wind power stations, reviews the price regimes and mandates the installation of equipment to protect from voltage dips. Ministério da Economia, da Inovação e do Desenvolvimento, Diário da República n.° 98/2010, Série I de 2010-05-20, pp. 1740–1742. https://data.dre.pt/eli/dec-lei/51/2010/05/20/p/dre/pt/html

Law 51-A/2011. Eliminates the reduced VAT tax for electricity and natural gas. Assembleia da República, Diário da República n.° 189/2011, 1° Suplemento, Série I de 2011-09-30, pp. 4566-(2)-4566-(2). https://data.dre.pt/eli/lei/51-a/2011/09/30/p/dre/pt/html

Legislative order 11-B/95. *Regulates how endogenous renewable energy resources can be exploited.* Ministério da Indústria e Energia, Diário da República n.° 55/1995, 1° Suplemento, Série I-B de 1995-03-06, pp. 1228-(5) a 1228-(9). https://data.dre.pt/eli/despnorm/11-b/1995/03/06/p/dre/pt/html

Ordinance 364-A/2017. Changes several Decree Laws related to the extinction of transitory tariffs. Economia, Diário da República n.° 232/2017, 1° Suplemento, Série I de 2017-12-04, pp. 6510-(2)-6510-(2). https://data.dre.pt/eli/port/364-a/2017/12/04/p/dre/pt/html

Ordinance 39/2017. Changes the deadline for the extinction of transitory tariffs for the electricity supplied to low voltage clients. Economia, Diário da República n.° 19/2017, Série I de 2017-01-26, pp. 519–520. https://data.dre.pt/eli/port/39/2017/01/26/p/dre/pt/html

Resolution of the Assembly of the Republic 33-A/2004. Approves the Agreement, between the Portuguese Republic and the Kingdom of Spain for the creation of an Iberian Electricity Market, signed in Lisbon in 20 January 2004. Assembleia da República, Diário da República n.° 93/2004, 1° Suplemento, Série I-A de 2004-04-20, pp. 2386-(2)-2386-(10). https://data.dre.pt/eli/resolassrep/33-a/2004/04/20/p/dre/pt/html

Resolution of the Council of Ministers 154/2001. *Approves the E4 Program, Energy Efficiency and Endogenous Energies*. Presidência do Conselho de Ministros, Diário da República n.° 243/2001, Série I-B de 2001-10-19, pp. 6648–6649. https://data.dre.pt/eli/resolconsmin/154/2001/10/19/p/dre/pt/html

Resolution of the Council of Ministers 169/2005. Approves the energy national strategy, Presidência do Conselho de Ministros, Diário da República n.° 204/2005, Série I-B de 2005-10-24, pp. 6168–6176. https://data.dre.pt/eli/resolconsmin/169/2005/10/24/p/dre/pt/html

Resolution of the Council of Ministers 2/2011. Launches ECO.AP (the energy efficiency program for the public administration) to reach 20% energy efficiency until 2020. Presidência do Conselho de Ministros, Diário da República n.° 8/2011, Série I de 2011-01-12, pp. 270–271. https://data.dre.pt/eli/resolconsmin/2/2011/01/12/p/dre/pt/html

Resolution of the Council of Ministers 20/2013. Approves the national action plan for energy efficiency in the period 2013–2016 and the national action plan for renewable energy for the period 2013–2020. Presidência do Conselho de Ministros, Diário da República n.° 70/2013, Série I de 2013-04-10, pp. 2022–2091. https://data.dre.pt/eli/resolconsmin/20/2013/04/10/p/dre/pt/html

Resolution of the Council of Ministers 29/2010. Approves the national energy strategy for 2020 (Estratégia Nacional para a Energia 2020). Presidência do Conselho de Ministros, Diário da República n.° 73/2010, Série I de 2010-04-15, pp. 1289–1296. https://data.dre.pt/eli/resolconsmin/29/2010/04/15/p/dre/pt/htmlDecree

Resolution of the Council of Ministers 63/2003. Approves the guidelines of the Portuguese energy policy and revokes the Resolution of the Council of Ministers 154/2001. Presidência do Conselho de Ministros, Diário da República n.° 98/2003, Série I-B de 2003-04-28, pp. 2722–2731. https://data.dre.pt/eli/resolconsmin/63/2003/04/28/p/dre/pt/html

Resolution of the Council of Ministers 88/2017. Approves the national action framework for the development of an alternative fuel market in the transportation sector. Presidência do Conselho de Ministros, Diário da República n.° 121/2017, Série I de 2017-06-26, pp. 3190–3228. https://data.dre.pt/eli/resolconsmin/88/2017/06/26/p/dre/pt/html

Energy Governance in Romania

39

Aron Buzogány and Simona Davidescu

Contents

Introduction	994
General Conditions of Energy Governance in Romania	995
Past Legacies	995
Composition of the Energy Mix	997
Energy Discourses	999
Coordination, Instruments, and Issues of Romanian Energy Transition	1001
Drivers of Energy Transition	1001
The Lasting Appeal of Hydro Power	1002
The Boom and Bust of Renewables	1004
High Expectations and the Nuclear Sector	1007
Outcomes, Challenges, and Prospects for Energy Governance	1010
Cross-References	1012
References	1013

Abstract

This chapter examines the governance structures of energy policy in Romania and current challenges. We provide an overview of the characteristics of Romania's energy system that includes a historical perspective that reaches beyond the last decade and explains developments such as privatization, Europeanization and energy transition before the background of physical, political, and societal structures. Romania is Central and Eastern Europe's largest producer of hydrocarbons and has an evenly distributed energy mix, which includes domestic coal, gas,

---

A. Buzogány (✉)
Institute of Forest, Environmental, and Natural Resource Policy (InFER), University of Natural Resources and Life Sciences Vienna (BOKU), Vienna, Austria
e-mail: aron.buzogany@boku.ac.at

S. Davidescu
University of York and ESSCA, Angers, York, UK
e-mail: simona.davidescu@york.ac.uk

hydro, and nuclear energy, as well as high potential for renewables such as wind and solar energy. At the same time the Romanian energy sector is confronted with underinvestment in faltering infrastructures, a legacy of low energy prices that hinder far-reaching investments, heavy bureaucratization, and endemic corruption. The promotion of renewable energy sources is contested due to increasing energy prices and political turf wars. Instead of domestic forces supporting sustainability transitions, EU pressure to keep up with higher standards has been a main force driving changes throughout the last two decades.

Keywords

Romania · Energy transitions · Europeanisation · Underinvestment · Corruption · Politicization · Climate change

Introduction

This chapter examines the governance structures of energy policy in Romania, its main characteristics, and current challenges. We aim to provide an overview of the characteristics of Romania's energy system that includes a historical perspective that reaches beyond the last decade and explain developments such as privatization, Europeanization, and energy transition before the background of physical, political, and societal structures. Given the complexity of energy issues this also means reaching out in an interdisciplinary manner to multiple disciplines, including energy economics, political economy, energy social science, science and technology studies, and energy humanities (Ćetković and Buzogány 2016; Jasanoff and Kim 2013; Roberts et al. 2018; Szeman and Boyer 2017). Building on insights from these literatures we offer an assessment of Romania's energy governance that focuses on three interconnected levels of analysis: the geophysical and technical preconditions related to Romania's energy mix, the systemic characteristics of Romania's politico-economic regime, as well as the external arena, which is mainly influenced by the European Union (EU).

The overall picture that we draw of Romania's energy governance using this framework is an ambivalent one. On the one hand, it is the Central and Eastern European country with the highest share of renewable energy and the lowest CO^2 per capita amounts. At the same time, Romania is far less dependent on energy imports than other countries of the region. It is also Central and Eastern Europe's largest producer of hydrocarbons and has a quite evenly distributed energy mix, which includes domestic coal, gas, hydro and nuclear energy. Romania holds over 60% of the region's oil reserves and 80% of its gas. Compared to the peak in the late 1970s, oil production has fallen back by three quarters. Romanian gas reserves have in the meantime strongly decreased from 713 billion cubic meters in 1980 to below 100 cubic meters in 2017. At the same time, renewable energies – wind, solar, and biomass – are becoming an increasingly important part of Romania's mixed energy portfolio while the days of coal are counted.

On the other hand, and despite (or perhaps because) of this enviable geological legacy, the Romanian energy sector is confronted with underinvestment in faltering infrastructures, a legacy of low energy prices that hinder far-reaching investments, heavy bureaucratization, and endemic corruption. Even though Romania reached its renewable energy 2020 target 6 years in advance, this makes a sustainable energy transition pathway difficult to reach (Cîrstea et al. 2018). The promotion of renewable energy sources (RES) is contested due to increasing energy prices and political turf wars (Davidescu 2017). Instead of domestic forces supporting sustainability transitions, EU pressure to keep up with higher standards has been a main force driving changes throughout the last two decades.

The next section provides the background to understand the complexities of Romanian energy governance by highlighting its historical legacies, the development of the energy mix over time, and the energy discourses that shape the field. We then outline the governance structures in the Romanian energy sector and discuss instruments and policies with special attention given to controversies around non-fossil sources such as hydropower, wind and solar energy as well as nuclear power. The final section provides an outlook on future challenges.

General Conditions of Energy Governance in Romania

Past Legacies

Coal, gas, and oil exploitation have a significant history on the territory of contemporary Romania. Coal deposits were documented from the late sixteenth century in the Jiu Valley in Transylvania and the Banat region, then part of the Habsburg empire. Exploitation started already in 1790 in Anina and Doman in Banat, with large-scale industrial exploitation taking off in the 1840s in the Jiu Valley supported by Habsburg mercantilist policies. First mentions of oil extraction on the historical territory of Romania date back to the sixteenth century, when wells and ditches were dug in the Wallachian principality in what is now Southern Romania to collect oil spilling freely from the soil. Industrial exploitation started in the second half of the nineteenth century, when a first refinery was installed in Ploiesti in 1858. This was also the beginning of the golden age of oil (and later natural gas) exploitation in Romania. Following the adoption of the 1895 mining law which allowed for foreign investments, large-scale foreign investments from British, French, Belgian, and German companies including Standard Oil or Royal Dutch Shell have played an important role in developing the oil industry, owning about 95% of the production (Gerali and Gregory 2017). By the early twentieth century, Romania was the second largest oil producer in Europe, however, during WWI a large part of the installations were destroyed at the request of Great Britain, to prevent Germany from gaining access to much needed energy resources (Tulucan et al. 2018). It took almost a decade until production reached pre-war levels in the interwar years. During this period new oil fields were opened in Moldova at Moinești and natural gas fields were explored in Bazna and Sărmășel in Transylvania. Forced takeovers of foreign assets in the oil industry increased Romanian presence in the industry but the emphasis remained on quick primary exhaustion and export of crude oil as domestic refinery capacities were limited (Turnock 1970, p. 545). During WWII, Romania became Nazi Germany's main energy supplier which was increasingly dependent on Romanian oil after its war offensive to gain access to the Baku oil fields failed. Being a German ally made Romania, the target of massive allied bombing campaigns that destroyed a large part of the oil and gas infrastructure even though they did not manage to fully cut off energy supplies to Germany before Romania switched to the side of the Allies following the coup d'état in August 1944 (Craig et al. 2018). After WWII, Romania was forced to make reparation payments to the Soviet Union, which resulted in seizing much of the equipment of the oil and gas industry. In 1948 the industry was nationalized and Western companies forced to leave the country with the Soviet–Romanian joint venture Sovrompetrol taking over the commanding heights in the oil and gas industry.

Romania gained back control of the energy industry in the 1950s which saw a rapid development in the following decades with oil production peaking at 313 thousand barrels a day in 1977. Developing domestic energy exploitation and infrastructures to support forced industrialization became a central aspect during the whole state socialist period. During this period, Romania witnessed massive developments not only in the previously existing coal, oil, and gas industry but developed hydro and nuclear energy to be part of the domestic energy mix. Particularly under the long leadership of Communist dictator Nicolae Ceaușescu (1965–1989) Romania has managed to distance herself from the Soviet Union, including in energy affairs (Balmaceda 2017). The main tenets of Romania's energy policy included developing extensive domestic oil refining capacities, establishing friendly relations and importing cheap oil from Libya, Iraq, and Iran and seeking Western technology to develop domestic capacities for nuclear energy technology (Gheorghe 2013, 2014).

As we will detail further below, hydropower has reached maturity during this period, with 115 hydropower stations being built between 1950 and 1990 (Štanzel 2017), including major dams on the Danube in collaboration with neighboring Yugoslavia and Bulgaria (Costea et al. 2021; Crețan and Vesalon 2017; Năstase et al. 2017; Șerban 2020). At the same time, communist industrial policy in Romania, which emphasized autarchy even more than the other states of the Eastern Bloc, was far from being efficient or taking environmental considerations into account. Energy production often relied on domestic low-quality fossil-fuels (Turnock 2007) and coal mining. Hydropower development and nuclear energy became important propagandistic elements of creating a new, socialist Romania based on autochthonous industrial development (Kideckel 2004, 2019; Štanzel 2017). The availability of inexpensive energy supported the growth of energy-intensive industrial sectors without much attention to the proliferation of wasteful practices. Results of forced industrialization, including some of the highest pollution levels in Europe at some hot spot areas such as Copșa Mică or the social and the environmental consequences of hydropower development became an uneasy heritage after 1989 when Romania transitioned toward democracy and market economy (Buzogány 2015; Dragomirescu et al. 1998).

Compared to other states of the region, Romania followed a more gradualist economic transition strategy which had several implications also for the energy sector. Restructuring the energy sector became a highly contentious political issue that was accompanied by violent protests of miners raiding Bucharest in five so-called Mineriade during the 1990s (Gledhill 2005. Restructuring the energy industry was not only opposed by veto players, but investments into less polluting installations posed the danger of triggering an increase in energy prices, which were deemed of having negative effects on entire industrial sectors and the population. At the same time, EU accession became an important, but ambivalent, driver of developments in the field. This meant opening the Romanian energy market and making it part of a competitive European market structure envisioned by the European Commission, but also massive investments into compliance with the EU's environmental requirements, which came as part of the acquis communautaire that Romania needed to adopt in order to become an EU member. For instance, the costs of fulfilling the requirements of the EU's large combustion plants directive targeting most of the coal-firing installations, were estimated to be around € 2.6 billion (DANCEE 2003). While the Romanian government repeatedly considered the privatization of the energy sector in order to obtain the financial resources necessary to comply with EU air pollution standards, sectoral veto players remained strong, politically well-connected and ultimately successful in stopping restructuring and privatization in the energy field (Capital 2007). Trade unions in energy-related sectors also opposed reforms fearing that privatization or the transfer of power plants under the jurisdiction of local authorities would make their jobs more vulnerable to lay-offs (Buzogány 2011; Pilat 2007). Private companies appeared on the energy market during the years immediately preceding Romania's EU accession in 2007. International investors, such as German and French energy companies (E.ON, RWE and Gas de France) acquired shares in the Romanian energy sector but their influence remained for a longer period limited as the envisioned opening of the energy market was affected by non-transparent insider trading (Diaconu et al. 2009).

Composition of the Energy Mix

Romania has an energy mix that is diverse and balanced. Coal, natural gas, oil, and uranium are available domestically in different parts of the country. Hydropower and nuclear energy play an important role in the energy mix and the country has a good potential both for wind and solar energy, which can be further exploited. Even though import dependency slightly increased over the last decade, Romania is ranked second in the EU after Estonia concerning energy independence, having a dependency ratio of 28% in 2020 (2010: 21.2%) (Eurostat 2020). This means that despite strong fluctuations in energy demand over the past decades, the energy system remained independent of imports and could adjust well to changes by exporting the surplus.

The longitudinal patterns of Romania's electricity production are illustrated in Fig. 1. Coal, oil, natural gas, and hydro energy have been dominating Romania's

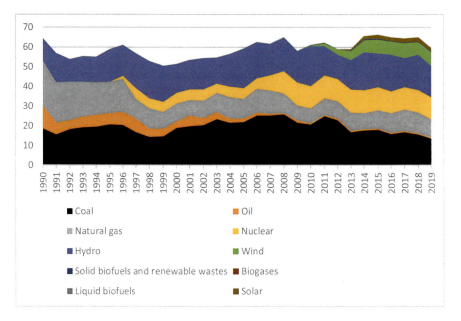

Fig. 1 Gross Electricity Generation, by Fuel [TWh], Eurostat 2020

electricity landscape. The most important trends have been the decline of oil production and the increase, since the opening of the Cernavodă Plant in the mid-1990s, of nuclear energy's role. Wind and solar energy production started to become significant around 2010, matching the slow decline of coal as a source of electricity generation. Renewable energy sources, including hydro energy, wind solar, and biofuels, have accounted for 42% of Romania's electricity generation in 2019.

Figure 2 illustrates that over the last decades Romania's energy consumption patterns have changed significantly. It can be seen that natural gas has declined from 50% to 30% in 2019, while oil remained relatively constant at around 30%. Coal has started to decline steeply in particular after 2010 but it still accounts for ca. 15% of the energy consumption. The continuous rise of hydropower can be witnessed over the last decades and seems to have stabilized at around 10%. The same is true for nuclear energy, which in 2019 accounts for 6% of the energy consumption. Wind and solar energy started to rapidly rise around 2010 but plateaued soon after.

While the Romanian energy mix is relatively balanced and can rely to a large extent on domestically available sources, including uranium for the nuclear sector, an important vulnerability is the age of assets particularly in the coal, gas, hydro, and oil sectors. With coal phase-out announced in 2021 for 2032, Romania is set to finalize the already long-lasting process of closing the remaining mines of the Jiu Valley. While decreasing in importance, oil and natural gas will remain an essential part of the energy mix as they are essential for transportation, heating, and the country's petrochemical industry.

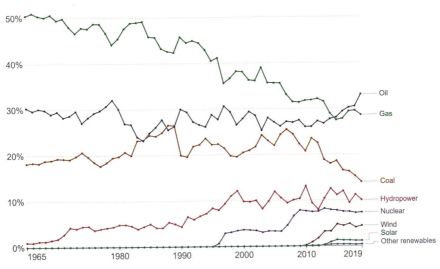

Fig. 2 Energy consumption by source, 1965–2019, Source: BP, Statistical Review of World Energy, Our World in Data

Energy Discourses

Romania's diverse and relatively balanced energy mix, its energy history, but also, and in particular, the (lack of) developments of the last three decades in the energy sector provide the background for contemporary energy discourses. A first level is constituted by deeply seeded narratives going back to imaginaries of sociotechnical development (Jasanoff and Kim 2013). Historically, in Romania, this was based on the abundance of autochthonous natural resources exploited under the state socialist regime. Communist sociotechnical imaginaries were full of references to hard-working men (and sometimes women), producing the energy resources needed to modernize the country industrially and secure its independence, also in terms of energy. The coal miners of the Jiu Valley, or the construction workers building dams to tame the wild rivers of the Carpathians became emblematic figures of this period. As a recent analysis of communist era textbooks argues, "dams and hydropower production emphasize socialist progress and production and, therefore, play an essential role in the depiction of the socialist world order." (Ilovan et al. 2018) A related aspect present in the collective imagination is the collective ownership of energy resources and the nature-blind perspective on economic development.

Many of these historical energy narratives have been seriously challenged after 1989, albeit to a different extent. First of all, the idea of economic autarchy and energy independence became soon criticized as isolationism and (resource) nationalism. This was partly related to the need to integrate into international transport and distribution systems, but also to open up the domestic market for foreign investors. Echoing discussions at the end of the nineteenth century and the 1920s about the role of foreign capital in Romanian energy industry, the discourse about integration into the EU market and opening up for strategic foreign investment was carried by the hope of technological modernization but with lasting undertones of protecting national champions (Haar and Marinescu 2011). The recent discovery of gas reserves in the Black Sea, estimated at 100 billion cubic meters, boosted the energy independence narrative and is delayed only by the adoption of legislation on offshore investments, with a projected extraction start by 2026 (Neagu 2021). The power of energy independence narrative has also informed Romania's stance within the EU as one of the member states pushing for the recognition of gas and nuclear energy as transition investments in the EU's green finance taxonomy. The current Romanian energy minister, Virgil Popescu, considers that "even a negative decision will not change Romania's plans to invest in natural gas" (Neagu 2021).

The other side of the coin has been the discourse about energy security with a focus on Russia, which continues to play an important role in the energy discourse despite the comparatively privileged situation of Romania. Russia is generally regarded to have strong energy interests and influence in the CEE region (Balmaceda 2013). This often leads to an emphasis on energy self-sufficiency and diversification of energy-mixes to counteract Russia's "energy imperialism" (Michalache 2018). In term of energy relations with Russia, Nosko and Mišík (2017) differentiate between a group of *"Russia skeptics"* which includes Estonia, Lithuania, Poland, and Romania, *"Russia advocates,"* such as Cyprus, Greece, Hungary, and Slovakia and countries which are ambivalent or change positions typically with the onset of new governments (Czech Republic, Bulgaria, and Latvia). Polish and Romanian governments have been most consistent in their anti-Russian attitude when it comes to resisting closer political and economic ties (Ćetković and Buzogány 2019; Michalache 2018; Ostrowski 2018). Particularly, President Băsescu has been a vehement supporter of reducing Romanian dependence on Russian natural gas imports and finalizing the construction of the Cernavodă nuclear plant based on Canadian assistance (Tudoroiu 2008).

At the same time, the discourses of isolationism and energy independence have been successfully employed by the emerging Romanian capitalist class to block both Russian and Western capital from entering the energy market (Michalache 2018). As a result, the Romanian energy market became only partially liberalized with only about 1/6 of the energy being traded on the competitive stock market. For most of the last two decades, the largest part of the energy market remained controlled by interim companies with political connections. Based on political relations, these have been able to buy energy at low and sell at high prices, often from state-owned companies to state-owned companies. At the same time, energy production remained dependent on state subsidies. Political scandals concerning the activities of the well-connected "smart boys" network in the energy sector erupted regularly (Consiliul Concurenței, Societatea Academică din România,, and CEROPE 2010; Pirvoiu 2010).

Second, these developments in the energy sector have obviously challenged the inherited *collective ownership* narrative. The perhaps most obvious ramification of this narrative regards consumer energy prices which were traditionally low in all socialist states. The restructuring of the energy sector and of heavy industry involved high social costs and affected consumers directly through energy prices and also indirectly through negative effects on economic competitiveness through increasing production costs (Manoleli et al. 2002). However, increasing household energy prices were rejected regularly by all political parties (Mulas-Granados et al. 2008). In particular, the discourse on RES support has been linked to socially and politically unacceptable costs and skepticism over the future of renewable energy in the following decades (Davidescu 2021).

Third, nature-blind energy imaginaries have been challenged in recent years by a discourse connected to decarbonization and climate issues. At the same time, these changes are rather cosmetic at the elite level and seem to result from strategic isomorphism with global discourses than convictions or domestic pressures. While survey data shows that only 6% of Romanians think that climate change is not a serious problem, climate change-related discourses remain rare in Romania and mobilization around these issues is weak and limited to some prominent NGOs (Vulpe 2020). While explicit climate skepticism remains rare (Raileanu 2015), political elites, including the former President Băsescu or former Prime Minister Ludovic Orban, often voice skepticism toward the EU's common climate policies or the European Green Deal based on considerations of national interests (Vulpe 2020).

Coordination, Instruments, and Issues of Romanian Energy Transition

Drivers of Energy Transition

Romania is in an enviable position among the countries in Central and Eastern Europe, as it has historically benefited from important domestic fossil fuel reserves of oil and coal, and to some extent gas, while also being able to diversify its energy mix early on, starting from the communist period and in the early transition period, due to investments in hydropower and nuclear power. The developments of these sectors were framed in terms of addressing energy security and exploiting the wealth of domestic natural resources for the benefit of the country, under strong "statist control and centralized planning" (Dudău 2019) that survived as a key legacy from the communist period. Liberalization, privatization, and restructuring of the energy sector were almost absent in the first decade of the post-communist transition, following a view that "utilities in the energy sector should remain integrated and property of the state" (Constantinescu 2013).

State capture features prominently in the energy sector in Romania (Popescu and Gavris 2020). This has only been challenged over the last decade, with the addition of other renewable energy sources to the energy mix, primarily wind, and the slow liberalization of the energy system, starting with distribution, as a result of EU policies, targets, and Romania's accession into the European Union in 2007. The main impetus toward an energy transition is coming primarily from the EU via the energy and climate change targets for 2020 and 2030. Romania's level of ambition on these has been generally low, despite the great potential in most energy sectors and a healthy energy mix. Within the 2020 energy and climate package, Romania has committed to the goal of a 24% share of renewable sources within the country's gross final energy consumption, which was achieved much earlier, in 2014, as an unexpected consequence of a generous incentive package, as will be detailed in the following sections. However, the Romanian National and Energy Climate Plan for 2030, has been criticized by the Commission as going below EU level targets on both non-ETS greenhouse gas (GHG) emissions and renewable energy, failing to include sufficient information on other interrelated areas, such as air quality and very low ambition on final energy consumption targets (European Commission 2020). This lack of ambition on the sustainability of its energy policy is rooted both in the legacies of the communist period and the lack (and ability) of long-term planning, significant levels of political and legislative instability and a chronic lack of investment in infrastructure. In the following sections of this chapter, we describe a range of potential drivers of the energy transition and the key actors and institutions related to these, including the hydropower sector, renewable energy sources, as well as the nuclear sector.

The Lasting Appeal of Hydro Power

Hydro power was hailed as a significant success during both the communist and post-communist periods. Its historical development and governance system was separate from other types of renewable energy, which started to develop in Romania much later, largely after 2008, driven by EU targets. Hydro energy was considered one of the most competitive energy sectors and a key contributor to the decarbonization of the energy sector in Romania. However, the details surrounding its development offer a more nuanced story and challenge some of the sustainability credentials of a sector that benefited from consistent political and societal support.

The origins of hydropower in Romania during the communist period involved "the fusion of industrial development, social policies, international relations and, not least, of ideology and political discourses in the construction of hydro-power systems in the communist space" (Crețan and Vesalon 2017). This signaled the Ceaușescu regime's prioritization of "big installations," such as the largest dam, the "Iron Gates" (jointly built on the Danube with Yugoslavia), under the communist model of industrialization, electrification, urbanization and its "cult of scale" and "gigantomania" (Kornai 1992, p. 176, cited in Crețan and Vesalon 2017). Hydropower was included, as all sectors of the economy, into the 5-year economic plans of the Communist Party, and helped accomplish energy production targets (Štanzel 2017). The system was heavily reliant on water supplies for agriculture and electricity (Crețan and Vesalon 2017) and this proved particularly problematic at times of drought. Furthermore, its construction phase involved significant displacement of people and used forced labor for its completion (ibid.).

After 1990, in the transition period, the number of installed hydropower plants decreased, by 2010 totaling an installed capacity of only 838 MW, which means less than 14% of what was done before 1990 (Costea et al. 2021). The post-communist period saw a change in emphasis from large to micro-hydro projects, but funding was sparse in the early 1990s and small hydro plants under construction or in need of refurbishment were being abandoned or slowly privatized (Pencea 1993). These took off significantly only after the 2008 changes to the incentive system for renewable energy investments, which we look at in the next section.

Currently, hydroelectric energy in Romania is close to 30% of the total installed energy capacity, of which more than one-third is produced by two large hydro power plants, Iron Gate 1 and 2, on the Danube (Costea et al. 2021). The proliferation of micro-hydro in the last decade contributed significantly to the fact that "49% of the documented 545 hydropower plants in Romania are located in Natura 2000 or other protected areas, while only 5% are located in water bodies with 'very good' ecological status, and another 12% in water bodies with 'good' ecological status and 'very good' hydromorphological status, according to the EU's Water Framework Directive" (Costea et al. 2021). The lack of concern over the environmental impact of these projects, coupled with corrupt practices in issuing construction permits, has led the European Commission to start infringement procedures against Romania in 2015 on small hydropower. This was the result of repeated complaints from environmental NGOs and a public petition requesting urgent action for the protection of river ecosystems heavily affected by uncontrolled and destructive development (WWF 2015).

The main actor in the hydropower sector is Hidroelectrica, the state-owned company operating more than 200 hydro power plants that emerged from the unbundling of the energy sector in 2000, in which the Romanian Government retained 100% of shares in the newly created five independent companies: Transelectrica, Electrica, Termoelectrica, Nuclearelectrica, and Hidroelectrica, according to HG nr. 627/2000. Despite Hidroelectrica being considered the most profitable energy company in the Romanian energy sector, its fortunes have varied in the last decades due to a combination of environmental factors such as severe droughts in 2003, and economic (mis-)fortunes that made the company shift from Romania's "investor of the year" from 2005 to 20,077, to insolvency procedure in 2012–3, followed by a return to the highest profits in the history of the company in 2014. The shock of the insolvency period was explained by the company as the result of interrelated factors, including an overstretch in investments and high maintenance and repair costs, unprofitable contracts with other electricity producers, losses from electricity sales, high labor costs, the effects of a draught on profits and dysfunctional management (Hidroelectrica 2020). More recently, Hidroelectrica has been in direct conflict with the energy regulator ANRE with regards to restrictions imposed by the latter on electricity exports and legal requirements to sell all electricity produced on the domestic power market operator OPCOM. The case made it to the European Court of Justice, which in September 2020 adjudicated in favor of Hidroelectrica. The ruling also carries implications for other energy sectors, as any electricity producer with the Romanian state as the main shareholder is now able to conclude direct contracts for energy exports on the EU market.

Overall, the appeal of hydro power persists on the Romanian energy policy agenda, with the Romanian energy strategy and Hidroelectrica's investment plans including the potential strategic development of another large dam on the Danube, the hydro-power complex at Turnu Măgurele-Nicopole, on the border with Bulgaria. The ideological appeal of hydro did not diminish and successive governments have embraced this as a key part of the main priority of addressing energy security by having a balanced energy mix and ensuring energy consumption needs at low prices. For critics, this means an overstretched focus on "white elephants" such as the hydro-power complexes Tarnița-Lăpuștești or Turnu Măgurele (Dudău 2019). Furthermore, critics also highlight the lack of discussion and analysis of the potentially environmentally harmful effects of hydro power, and the emphasis on unnecessary projects that move away attention from more pressing and potentially more useful ways of addressing decarbonization by investing in "network development, digitalization, renewables, storage, and energy efficiency" (Dudău 2019; Pirvoiu 2021). In what follows, we turn to the development of other renewable energy sources and their wavering fortunes, as a case of unexpected, but ultimately short-lived success.

The Boom and Bust of Renewables

In contrast to the lasting political support for large hydro throughout the transition period, other renewable energy sources in Romania have been negligible in terms of energy production until 2008, due to "no incentive for private investment" (United Nations 2001: 185) coupled with high technology prices and lack of state support (Davidescu et al. 2018). The sector has been described as one of great economic potential, with renewable energy sources plentifully available, but insufficiently and unequally exploited (Zamfir et al. 2016). However, in a short period, an extensive incentive system and supportive legislation, coupled with relatively ambitious targets negotiated with the European Commission have led to a surprising level of success (Davidescu 2017). By 2013, Romania was considered one of the most attractive countries for investors in renewable energy, leading to investments above 8 billion Euros (Davidescu 2021).

Domestic legislation supporting renewables (Law 220/2008) anticipated the EU's 2009 Renewable Energy Directive (RED) and was promoted by a cross-party coalition of parliamentarians with strong business backing aimed at stimulating investment and creating jobs (Davidescu 2017). The extensive support measures included:

- Guaranteed connection to the grid.
- Green certificates (GCs) (equivalent to 1 MWh of electrical energy from RES) differentiated on the type of technology.
- Minimum and maximum values of the GCs set by the national regulator ANRE.
- Variation in the duration of the scheme according to how new the equipment was.
- Tax exemptions and mandatory annual quotas of green energy (Davidescu 2021).

Tax exemptions involved a guarantee of maximum 50% of the value of the medium, long-term loans or tax and fee exemptions or discounts for reinvested profit, for 3 years from the adoption of the Law 220/2008. The legislation obliged distributors to acquire GCs up to a set annual quota and passed on the costs to final consumers (Davidescu et al. 2018). Investment soared, mainly on wind and also some solar capacity, allowing Romania to reach its 2020 RED target of 24% renewable electricity in the energy mix as early as 2014 (Davidescu 2017). OPCOM (the Green Certificates Market Operator) was going to ensure the setting of prices on the centralized market where green certificates were sold independently from the electricity market. The value of GCs depended on bilateral contracts negotiated between generators and suppliers and the centralized market organized and administered by OPCOM. The market regulation was the remit of the Romanian Regulatory Authority for Energy (ANRE), which established an annual quota of renewable electricity that suppliers must buy (Zamfir et al. 2016).

However, soon after the boom caused by this policy, the sun was setting and the wind stopped blowing for renewable energy support in Romania. The first generation of investors in the sector were large international energy companies, some of which were already active in the energy distribution market, such as CEZ, Enel, RWE Innogy, Iberdrola, Verbund, Energias de Portugal; while a second wave of smaller domestic investors started to emerge when the dismantling of the support scheme from 2013 onwards took effect. The process of policy dismantling was protracted and involved a large number of amendments to the legislation within a few years, ranging from delay tactics (not connecting new capacity due to saturation of the electricity grid, or not notifying the EC about the potential conflicts with state aid rules), to suspension of GCs, lowering annual quotas and several exemptions granted to large industrial consumers (Davidescu 2018). The issue of costs has been central to the backlash on RES due to significant distortions to the GCs market and unintended consequences stemming from the gradual dismantling of the scheme that resulted in uncertainty for investors leading to large fluctuations in the value of GCs, a backlog of unused certificates and corrupt practices in concluding "preferential" contracts for some of the big RES producers (Davidescu et al. 2018).

The Romanian government intervened heavily in the electricity market, reassessed policy regulations to "redirect consumption patterns in favor of renewable energy producers," widening the gap between the coal and renewable sectors and raising the EU's concerns about distortions in competition (Popescu and Gavris 2020. p. 13). Market distortions have affected both businesses and domestic consumers. One-third of the renewable energy projects was facing bankruptcy in 2016, while the GCs quota remained extremely small. Estimates at the end of 2016 predicted that "the market will be flooded with about 22-23 million GCs, and the set quota, of about 12%, approved by the national regulatory body ANRE, allowed buyers to get only about 12 million" (Tudorache 2016). The RES business lobby was concerned that the Government's support for large industrial consumers meant that none of their suggestions for reform of the system were heard (ibid.). Furthermore, domestic consumers have also seen an increase in their bills, but this was due more to distortions in the market since the real price of RES cannot be fully ascertained by distributors: "power distributors did not know how to calculate the price and distribution of GCs, since some of their customers have been exempted and the other clients, including the regulated (the subsidized household segment) small consumers and larger companies alike, will have to be surcharged with an unknown amount to balance the situation" (Tudorache 2016). The position of the Energy Ministry on the issue of costs was linked to the nature of the technology as well as policy dismantling: "Their intermittent nature caused technical difficulties and costs of integration into the National Electricity System (SEN), as well as had an impact on the bill for final consumers. The support scheme for RES technologies through Green Certificates has suffered repeated modifications in a short period, which in turn created serious problems of predictability and functionality in this industry" (Ministry of Energy 2016: 29).

Overall, the early compliance with the 2020 RES targets and increase in production capacity on wind and solar did not translate into either sustainable practices or concern about climate change and a long-term plan for an energy transition. In terms of sustainability and green economy links, the RES growth was not matched by technological innovation and investment in smart grids and interconnectors (Davidescu et al. 2018). This, in turn, produced imbalances and questions of long-term sustainability of the energy system, with overproduction in the summer that could not be stored or exported and a surge in demand in the winter, which is addressed by a return to the use of coal-powered power plants (Davidescu 2021). Furthermore, this also did not engage with emissions reduction, as the government granted exemptions from the acquisition of green certificates to the most polluting industries (such as steel), (Davidescu 2018). Thus, subsidies for renewable energy facilities worked directly against the business model of the state-owned power utilities, mainly those operating nuclear plants, by depressing market prices and affecting the utilities' revenues negatively (The Diplomat 2017).

While the wind and solar renewable energy capacity has increased, for biomass, the most promising renewable sector according to government strategies, the focus remained its use for heating and RES-E (particularly co-generation), rather than transport (RES-T) (Ministry of Economy 2010). While at a declaratory level, there was widespread political support for biofuels, with biomass being named a top priority for the Energy Strategy of Romania (2015–2035) (Matei 2014), the sector faced a wide range of barriers to implementation, coupled with the availability of external solutions, mainly cheap imports (Davidescu 2017).

The main legislation related to RES-T, GD 456/2007, placed the burden of implementation on economic operators to introduce the fuel mix on the market. There was deliberate non-compliance from the main domestic fuel producers (Petrom and OMV), which were waiting for financial incentives and legislative clarifications before making any investments (Chiriac and Vasilache 2006). This was addressed by the government with a new fiscal code that eliminated taxes for biofuels (ibid.). Significant regulatory uncertainty followed in 2008 and again in 2011, as the Ministry of Finance engaged in blame-shifting to the EU for increases in the price of fuel (Budusan 2011). The 2009 RED set targets at 10% biofuels for the transport sector, but this was negotiated hard by the Tariceanu government in exchange for EU financial aid and making the Romanian automobile industry eligible for European Investment Bank loans (Financiarul 2008).

The main barriers for the use of domestic grown crops for biofuels were related to infrastructure, such as the small size of farms, the differing amounts of feedstock, and the poor quality of the roads in rural areas (*Diplomat*, 2011); coupled with financial barriers to securing funding for projects (Ministry of Economy 2010, p. 5) due to much larger start-up investments and higher production costs in the short-run (Budusan 2011). Further administrative barriers included a protracted and complex permitting system and approvals from too many institutions (Miron 2014). In addition, practical obstacles to the consumption of biofuels were linked to difficulties in changing consumer behavior and a large pool of older vehicles that could not use biofuels (Budusan 2011).

Overall, even there has been some success in reaching set targets on RES-E, these were short-lived, easily dismantled, and had unintended consequences in terms of costs due to market distortions, while on RES-T widespread non-compliance by private actors was coupled with a wide range of barriers that made the targets almost unattainable under the current incentives system (Davidescu 2017). The costs of the RES-E support scheme reflected in the final bills of consumers have made this sector unpopular with politicians and the public alike, leading to a highly visible, albeit gradual policy dismantling of the support scheme (Davidescu 2018), in line with similar developments in other EU countries.

High Expectations and the Nuclear Sector

The wavering fortunes of the renewable energy sector have been matched by a similar trajectory of nuclear energy, despite its significant level of popularity in Romania. Successive Romanian governments on all sides of the political spectrum have been highly supportive of the nuclear sector, while opposition has been sparse and mainly limited to some prominent environmental NGOs. The share of nuclear power in Romania's energy mix has been 15–20% since the opening of its two nuclear reactors at Cernavodă in 1996 and 2007, respectively, so this alone would not constitute a significant step toward an energy transition. But there has been a long-standing commitment from various Romanian governments over the last decades to increase this capacity with two additional reactors, already partially developed during the communist period, which would double the nuclear power supply within one decade (World Nuclear News 05/10/2021). Nevertheless, the development of nuclear power capacity in Romania has followed a rather unexpected trajectory both during and after the end of the communist period, and despite the strong political support and elaborated future projects, further developments have proven elusive for economic, geopolitical, and energy security reasons.

Romania started developing nuclear power in the communist period, but followed a very different path than neighboring countries, with a surprising and "maverick" option that "turned an otherwise minor power into an international actor" (Gheorghe 2013, p. 373). Romania secured the Canadian Candu technology at the height of the Cold War "based on technology transfer from Canada (Atomic Energy Canada

Limited, AECL), Italy and the USA" (World Nuclear Association 2021), playing "occasionally the role of intermediary in international conflicts" (Gheorghe 2013, p. 375), including the Vietnam War. The construction started in the late 1970s, for a five-unit nuclear power plant at Cernavodă, on the Danube River. The first unit started in July 1982, unit 2 in July 1983, and units 3–5 over the following 4 years (World Nuclear Association 2021), but out of these only unit 1 could be finalized during the first post-communist decade.

The enviable position of having Western technology for its nuclear sector meant that Romania was able to avoid much of the conditionality related to nuclear safety that led to the closure of some of the neighboring countries' nuclear reactors before the EU accession (Ivanov 2008). Moreover, Romania benefited from significant EU financial help for its nuclear sector. The completion of unit 2 at Cernavodă was going to prove very expensive and required a range of successive investments, initially from the Romanian Government (€60 million in 2000, followed by a €382.5 million package by 2003, including €218 million from Canada) and became finalized with a €223.5 million Euratom loan (World Nuclear Association 2021).

The Cernavodă nuclear plant is operated by the state-owned nuclear power corporation Nuclearelectrica, established in 1998 to oversee the entire sector, encompassing the nuclear fuel factory FCN Pitesti. In response to calls from the International Monetary Fund (IMF) and the EU to start a privatization process for Nuclearelectrica, the Romanian government sold a 10% share for $85 million (ibid.) in 2013 and listed the company on the stock market. The company is directly subordinated to the Ministry of Energy, which de facto appoints its director general and administration council, as the main shareholder. This has been the object of criticism and speculation regarding the politicization of this process (Pirvoiu 2013). The safety oversight was allocated to the National Commission for Nuclear Activity Control (CNCAN), which had much earlier origins, at the start of the construction process in the mid-1950s, and from 1990 was renamed and functions as the main body for control and authorization in the nuclear sector, including a working group on nuclear emergencies and risk evaluation (Romanian Government 2021). Continuing with the work on reactors 3–5 was going to prove a lot more difficult, despite the consistent political support, due to the repeated failure of funding projects.

A large consortium was set up in 2008 to fund reactors 3 and 4, which included Nuclearelectrica and a range of companies with a wider interest in the Romanian energy sector, such as ArcelorMittal, CEZ, GDF SUEZ, Enel, Iberdrola, and RWE. One by one the partners have withdrawn citing costs and infeasibility of the project (World Nuclear Association 2021). After years of delays, a single partner was announced in August 2011, the China Nuclear Power Engineering Co. (CNPEC, a subsidiary of China General Nuclear Power Group). CNPEC was able to provide the entire financing through Exim-Bank and ICBC, which promised to simplify and speed up the process (World Nuclear News 2013). Four investment memoranda were signed with CGN in 2013 by the Ponta government: the nuclear reactors 3 and 4 at Cernavodă Nuclear Plant, the Tarnița-Lăpuștești Hydropower Plant, the Rovinari Thermal Power Plant, and the Mintia-Deva Thermal Power Plant (Popescu and Brinza 2018, p. 31). Following the positive signals sent by the Romanian

Government, CNPEC signed a "binding and exclusive" cooperation agreement with Candu Energy for the "development, construction, operation and decommissioning of units 3 and 4 of the Cernavodă plant" in 2015 (World Nuclear News 2016).

During this decade, many Chinese companies were interested in investing in Romania in infrastructure projects, but both sides complained that things were moving very slowly, blaming delays on bureaucracy, corruption, non-transparent negotiations, and frequent policy reversals. This was coupled with political instability in Romania, as in a "period of two and a half years, five prime ministers have led the Romanian Government and the negotiations at Cernavodă" (Popescu and Brinza 2018: 32). The political support for the CGN investment at Cernavodă was fairly uncontested at the top of the political establishment within the left-wing Social Democratic Party (PSD) Governments of the last decade and Nuclearelectrica, and the project was part of the main energy agenda (World Nuclear News 2016). There has been little contestation in Parliament of this project, even though the details of the memorandum of understanding with CGN were never made public (ibid.). Only environmental groups opposed the expansion of nuclear power in general on environmental grounds, citing the danger for human health caused by heating the Danube river and tritium liquid discharges (Fairlie 2007).

Given the lack of domestic opposition, it came as a surprise when the Romanian Government announced a sudden change of plans. By June 2020 a new center-right coalition government (PNL, UDMR, USL-PLUS) suspended abruptly negotiations with CGN, blaming tensions between China and the USA, and stating that Romania needs to find investment partners from the EU or USA, to strengthen its strategic partnership with the USA and NATO alliance (World Nuclear News 2020). A few months later, in October 2020, Romania and the USA have signed an intergovernmental agreement of cooperation in key sectors, including the Cernavodă nuclear reactors 3&4, modernization of Cernavodă 1 and cooperation in other areas of civil nuclear power (ibid.).

The agreement between Romania and the US Government on the Cernavodă 3&4 reactors seemed to silence domestic critics and despite the change in the US administration in the meantime, the process has been going ahead with a joint strategy with the US Department of Energy (DOE) (World Nuclear News 2021). Romania's Ministry of Economy, Energy and Business Climate also signed a memorandum of understanding with the Export-Import Bank of the USA covering the energy and infrastructure industries and on 26 October 2020, Romania and France signed a declaration of intent on cooperation in the civil nuclear field (ibid). Despite all these agreements, there is widespread skepticism among energy experts that this costly and lengthy project will have any significant impact on Romania's energy transition (Pirvoiu 2021).

The global context of an ongoing crisis since 2008 seemed to be highly beneficial to Chinese investments in the nuclear energy sector, as China emerged as the sole investor willing and able to play the long game in a sector that requires state guarantees. However, even though successive Romanian Governments have been framing Chinese investments in nuclear power as an economic opportunity, the subsequent political framing as a security issue caused the reversal of this project, coupled with the emergence of credible Western-backed alternatives in the context of the US-China trade conflict. The recent developments in this sector have highlighted a significant shift toward energy security as a dominant discourse that is now used as a counterbalance to an energy transition fueled by renewable energy.

Outcomes, Challenges, and Prospects for Energy Governance

This chapter has presented a picture of a "healthy" energy mix in the case of Romania, some degree of change particularly in the restructuring of the coal sector, and more recent growth of renewable energy and continuity in sectors such as gas, hydro, and nuclear. At the same time, the last years of political instability have been reflected in policy-making stasis, as Romania's "Energy Strategy 2019–2030 with a perspective on 2050" has been under debate, subject to environmental assessment and constant redrafting since 2016, until it was finally adopted in 2020 by emergency procedure (Pirvoiu 2020). During this period different governments have shifted priorities and the overall approach to energy transition, leading to uncertainty for businesses. This went together with difficulties to access EU funds needed for investments in the energy sector and infringement procedures launched by the EC regarding the approval of micro-hydro power plants in protected natural areas and the level of emissions from the Oltenia Energetic Complex (ibid.).

Overall, Romania's energy governance is lacking ambition in its energy transition in terms of targets and quality of planning (European Commission 2020; Greenpeace 2020), although at a declaratory level the current energy strategy emphasizes the shift from solid fossil fuels to electricity production based on low carbon emissions technologies (natural gas, nuclear and renewable energy) (Energy Ministry 2018). Adding to this, areas of progress toward energy transition, such as renewable energy, have been marred by active policy dismantling (Davidescu 2018) and reversals of decisions regarding investment plans in the case of nuclear development (World Nuclear News 2020), running alongside a sustained period of political crisis and political parties infighting and coupled more recently with disastrous management of the Covid-19 crisis and the parallel gas crisis (Dunai 2021).

Our assessment of Romania's energy governance has focused on three interconnected levels of analysis: the geophysical and technical preconditions related to Romania's energy mix, the systemic characteristics of Romania's politico-economic regime, as well as the external arena, which is mainly influenced by the European Union. On all these levels, we find important constraints that hamper clean energy transitions in the country.

Concerning the geophysical and technical preconditions, Romania's balanced energy mix, which relies to a large extent on domestic energy sources that secures one of the highest energy independence levels in the EU, fails to offer strong incentives for developing a more sustainability-oriented pathway. New discoveries of gas in the Black Sea are likely to support this development. Despite the economic pressure that coal mining is facing, the social consequences of closing coal mines and coal-firing installations made politicians cautious of tackling this question before

2021 when coal exit was finally announced. At the same time, the rapid replacement of fossil energies seems unlikely. When the renewables market share expanded due to regulatory support, supporters of incumbent fossil, hydro, and nuclear energy made sure that this will not negatively affect their interests.

Geophysical preconditions play an important role in shaping Romania's politico-economic energy regime. With a capitalist growth model geared toward dependent integration into Western European production cycles (Ban 2019), over the last three decades, Romania was characterized by weak state capacities and frequent crisis-driven restructuration. The country's energy infrastructure provided manifold opportunities for making profit through asset stripping, with the emerging domestic capitalist class preventing market opening for foreign investors both from Russia or Western Europe alike until it could make sure its interests were meaningfully protected (Michalache 2018). Discourses of energy poverty and energy security provided the background for political and economic struggles over reforming the energy landscape. Most political parties, and in particular the social-democratic PSD which maintained close clientelistic ties to coal-producing regions, have avoided taking far-reaching steps toward a clean energy transition. Adding to this, political volatility of the frequent coalition governments as well as the rapidly changing competencies over the energy sector made policy implementation cumbersome. Examples from Western Europe suggest that without support from political parties chances of energy transitions remain bleak (Ćetković and Hagemann 2020). This matters also in Romania, as the country's political landscape does not look promising for pushing such large-scale changes forward. The same applies to civil society which is vibrant and well-organized, but lacks a focus on climate change-related issues and is far away from the commanding heights of decision-making (Davidescu and Buzogány 2021).

The third level of analysis concerns the external arena, in our case mainly the EU, which plays an important role in setting the standards and influencing developments. Romania has a long and winding history of EU-triggered development over the last two decades, including in the energy sector (Buzogány 2021; Davidescu 2017; Davidescu et al. 2018). After becoming an EU member, Romania joined other states of the region in going for the bare minimum in climate change targets at the prize of the highest financial support possible (Braun 2014a, 2014b; Buzogány and Ćetković 2021; Sinea 2020; Volintiru et al. 2021). At the same time, and in contrast to the much more vocal Poland and Hungary, Romania adopts a "fence-sitting" approach which rarely clashes openly with the EU on climate and energy matters or the European Green Deal (Maris and Flouros 2021). This attitude is moderated by the necessity to invest in the energy sector and gain access to EU coffers, such as the Just Transition Fund or the Modernisation Fund. Nevertheless, even if based on a rather pragmatic view, the examples in this chapter show that the pace and content of the Romanian clean energy transition have been strongly influenced by the EU (Davidescu 2017; Leal-Arcas et al. 2020).

While our assessment mainly highlights the stability of the status quo in the Romanian energy sector, the conceptual approach we used provides hints regarding potential breakout points. There is considerable space for increasing energy efficiency both in the housing and the district heating sector which would in the long-term reduce energy demand. Re-gaining the lost momentum in the RES sector would also be imperative. As above, what matters is an adequate regulatory framework, the availability of financing, and the domestic capacities to acquire them. In this regard, the decision by the European Commission to include gas and nuclear energy under its "sustainable finance taxonomy" (Simon and Taylor 2022) could prove particularly beneficial to countries like Romania, given the priorities of its last Energy Strategy 2019–2030, as well as Romania's National Plan for Recovery and Resilience (NPRR) (2021). The € 29.2 billion recovery plan received initial negative feedback from the EC in June 2021 and was finally endorsed after revisions in September 2021. For the energy sector, the revisions included a deadline and concrete measures for "phasing out coal and lignite power production by 2032, (...) decarbonization of road transport, green taxation, incentives for zero-emissions vehicles (...) and a strong focus on improving the energy efficiency of private and public buildings" (European Commission 2021). However, there has been significant criticism that the coal phase-out is based on a switch from coal to fossil gas, as Romania wants to start extracting gas from the Black Sea by 2026 (Neagu 2021). The Romanian Government's optimism on future investments in gas, nuclear, and more recently hydrogen, do not seem to match existing practices and the unfulfilled expectations in terms of costs and jobs in the renewable energy sector (Davidescu 2021), the lack of strategic planning and funding of energy infrastructure, as well as an imbalance between future planning and long-term vision across sectors, such as energy, transport, and industrial development (Pirvoiu 2021).

Overall, the Romanian energy sector exhibits remarkable continuity in being inward-looking, status-quo preserving, and maintaining state control and centralized decision-making. Domestic decision-makers have favored throughout the transition period stable, predictable, and secure domestic sources such as gas, nuclear, and hydro, in a bid to become energy independent and a regional energy hub. The unexpected growth of the renewable energy sector showed what could happen when the state is no longer the dominant actor and investment opportunities are created for new business actors, while policy priorities are driven by EU targets. However, the short-lived success of the incentives scheme for renewable energy was also illustrative of the vagaries of policy implementation under high levels of politicization in the energy sector, short-termism in policy-making, disregard for investment needs in infrastructure and frequent policy change. Romania's promising energy future is still hampered by its energy past.

Cross-References

▶ Energy Governance in Hungary
▶ Energy Governance in Lithuania
▶ Energy Governance in Russia: From a Fossil to a Green Giant?
▶ Energy Governance in the Czech Republic
▶ Energy Governance in the Republic of Poland

▶ Energy Policies in the EU: A Fiscal Federalism Perspective
▶ Energy Poverty
▶ Monitoring Energy Policy
▶ Transition of Energy Systems: Patterns of Stability and Change

References

Balmaceda, M. (2013). *The politics of energy dependency: Ukraine, Belarus, and Lithuania between domestic oligarchs and Russian pressure*. Toronto: University of Toronto Press.

Balmaceda, M. (2017). The fall of the Soviet Union and the legacies of energy dependencies in Eastern Europe. In J. Perović (Ed.), *Cold war energy: A transnational history of soviet oil and gas* (pp. 401–420). Cham: Springer.

Ban, C. (2019). Dependent development at a crossroads? Romanian capitalism and its contradictions. *West European Politics, 42*(5), 1041–1068.

Braun, M. (2014a). EU climate norms in east-Central Europe. *Journal of Common Market Studies, 52*(3), 445–460.

Braun, M. (2014b). *Europeanization of environmental policy in the new Europe: Beyond conditionality*. Ashgate Publishing, Ltd.

Budusan, I. (2011). De ce a esuat industria de biocombustibili in Romania, *Manager*. Accessed on 22 Apr 2014 at http://www.manager.ro/articole/analize/analiza-de-ce-a-esuat-industria-de-biocombustibili-in-romania-11761.html

Buzogány, A. (2011). Rumänien: Verbände zwischen Transformation und Europäisierung. In W. Reutter (Ed.), *Verbände in Europa*. VS Verlag.

Buzogány, A. (2015). Building governance on fragile grounds: Lessons from Romania. *Environment and Planning C: Government and Policy, 33*(5), 901–918.

Buzogány, A. (2021). Beyond Balkan exceptionalism. Assessing compliance with EU law in Bulgaria and Romania. *European. Politics and Society, 22*(2), 185–202.

Buzogány, A., & Ćetković, S. (2021). Fractionalized but ambitious? Voting on energy and climate policy in the European Parliament. *Journal of European Public Policy, 28*(7), 1038–1056.

Capital. (2007). Contre la nivel înalt pentru Turceni, Rovinari şi Craiova. Retrieved from http://www.capital.ro/detalii-articole/stiri/contre-la-nivel-icircnalt-pentru-turceni-rovinari-x15fi-craiova-102055.html

Ćetković, S., & Buzogány, A. (2016). Varieties of capitalism and clean energy transitions in the European Union: When renewable energy hits different economic logics. *Climate Policy, 16*(5), 642–657.

Ćetković, S., & Buzogány, A. (2019). The political economy of EU climate and energy policies in central and Eastern Europe revisited: Shifting coalitions and prospects for clean energy transitions. *Politics and Governance, 7*(1), 124–138.

Ćetković, S., & Hagemann, C. (2020). Changing climate for populists? Examining the influence of radical-right political parties on low-carbon energy transitions in Western Europe. *Energy Research & Social Science, 66*, 101571.

Chiriac, M., & Vasilache, A. (2006). Biocarburantii – o tinta ratata momentan de Romania. *HotNews*. Accessed on 10 Nov 2013 at http://www.hotnews.ro/stiri-arhiva-1151709-biocarburantii-tinta-ratata-momentan-romania.htm

Cîrstea, Ş. D., Martiş, C. S., Cîrstea, A., Constantinescu-Dobra, A., & Fülöp, M. T. (2018). Current situation and future perspectives of the Romanian renewable energy. *Energies, 11*(12), 3289.

Consiliul Concurenţei, Societatea Academică din România, & CEROPE. (2010). *The challenges of the single market and the competition in sensitive sectors*. Bucharest.

Constantinescu, J. (2013). Reforma in energia electrica: Ce s-a vrut, ce-a iesit si cum ar trebui sa arate. Accessed on 20 May 2014 at http://cursdeguvernare.ro/despre-reforma-in-energia-electrica-ce-s-a-vrut-si-ce-a-iesit-i-cum-ar-trebui-sa-arate-o-reforma-prietenoasa-pentru-economie-si-consumator.html

Costea, G., Pusch, M. T., Bănăduc, D., Cosmoiu, D., & Curtean-Bănăduc, A. (2021). A review of hydropower plants in Romania: Distribution, current knowledge, and their effects on fish in headwater streams. *Renewable and Sustainable Energy Reviews, 111003*.

Craig, J., Gerali, F., MacAulay, F., & Sorkhabi, R. (2018). The history of the European oil and gas industry (1600s–2000s). *Geological Society, London, Special Publications, 465*(1), 1–24.

Crețan, R., & Vesalon, L. (2017). The political economy of hydropower in the communist space: Iron gates revisited. *Tijdschrift voor Economische en Sociale Geografie, 108*(5), 688–701.

DANCEE. (2003). *Romania's road to the accession: The need for an environmental focus.* Copenhagen: Danish Environmental Assistance to Eastern Europe (DANCEE).

Davidescu, S. (2017). The Europeanization of renewable energy policy in Romania. In *A guide to EU renewable energy policy*. Edward Elgar Publishing.

Davidescu, S. (2018). Environmental policy in times of crisis: Romania's troubled transition. In C. Burns, P. Tobin, & S. Sewerin (Eds.), *The impact of the economic crisis on European environmental policy*. Oxford University Press.

Davidescu, S. (2021). Great expectations: The green economy discourse and practice in Romania. In Fairbrass & Vasilakos (Eds.), *Emerging governance of a green economy. Cases of European implementation*. Cambridge University Press.

Davidescu, S., & Buzogány, A. (2021). Cutting deals: Transnational advocacy networks and the European Union timber regulation at the eastern border. *The International Spectator.* https://doi.org/10.1080/03932729.2021.1935680

Davidescu, S., Hiteva, R., & Maltby, T. (2018). Two steps forward, one step back: Renewable energy transitions in Bulgaria and Romania. *Public Administration, 96*(3), 611–625.

Diaconu, O., Oprescu, G., & Pittman, R. (2009). Electricity reform in Romania. *Utilities Policy, 17*(1), 114–124.

Dragomirescu, S., Muica, C., & Turnock, D. (1998). Environmental action during Romania's early transition years. *Environmental Politics, 7*(1), 162–182.

Dudău, R. (2019). 'Three stereotypes of the Romanian energy establishment', Energy Policy Group, Bucharest. https://www.enpg.ro/three-stereotypes-of-the-romanian-energy-establishment/

Dunai, M. (2021). 'Romania's political logjam deepens crises over pandemic and energy', *Financial Times,* 02 November 2021, Bucharest. https://www.ft.com/content/b8598fff-a222-40b6-86c0-1fbc60df0b6f

Energy Ministry. (2018). 'Strategia Energetica a Romaniei 2019-2030, cu perspectiva anului 2050' [Romania's energy strategy 2019–2030 with a perspective on 2050], Romanian Government, Bucharest. www.energie.gov.ro

European Commission. (2020). 'Commission staff working document. Assessment of the final national energy and climate plan of Romania', Brussels, 14.10.2020. https://ec.europa.eu/energy/sites/default/files/documents/staff_working_document_assessment_necp_romania_en.pdf

European Commission. (2021). 'Next Generation EU: European Commission endorses Romania's Euro 29.2 billion recovery and resilience plan', Press Release, 27 September 2021, Brussels. https://ec.europa.eu/commission/presscorner/detail/en/ip_21_4876

Eurostat. (2020). Energy dependence (publication no. https://ec.europa.eu/eurostat/databrowser/view/t2020_rd320/default/table?lang=en), https://ec.europa.eu/eurostat/databrowser/view/t2020_rd320/default/table?lang=en

Fairlie, I. (2007). Cernavoda 3 and 4. Environmental Impact Analysis. Report for Greenpeace, London. https://www.banktrack.org/download/cernavoda_3_and_4_environment_impact_analysis_report_for_greenpeace/200709_cernavoda_report_for_gp_central_europe_final.pdf

Financiarul. (2008). 'Băsescu și Tăriceanu, mulțumiți de rezultatele Consiliului European de iarnă'. Accessed on 10 Dec 2012 at http://www.financiarul.ro/2008/12/12/basescu-si-tariceanu-multumiti-de-rezultatele-consiliului-european-de-iarna/

Gerali, F., & Gregory, J. (2017). Understanding and finding oil over the centuries: The case of the Wallachian petroleum company in Romania. *Earth Sciences History, 36*(1), 41–62.

Gheorghe, E. (2013). Atomic maverick: Romania's negotiations for nuclear technology, 1964–1970. *Cold War History, 13*(3), 373–392.

Gheorghe, E. (2014). Building détente in Europe? East–West trade and the beginnings of Romania's nuclear programme, 1964–70. *European Review of History: Revue européenne d'histoire, 21*(2), 235–253.

Gledhill, J. (2005). States of contention: State-led political violence in post-socialist Romania. *East European Politics and Societies, 19*(01), 76–104.

Greenpeace. (2020). 'Greenpeace and WWF Romania – Joint Position Letter on Romania's Energy Strategy 2020–2030, with a 2050 perspective', version from August 2020. Available at https://www.greenpeace.org/romania/articol/4648/greenpeace-romania-si-wwf-romania-scrisoare-comuna-de-pozitie-privind-strategia-energetica-a-romaniei-2020-2030-cu-perspectiva-anului-2050-versiunea-august-2020/

Haar, L. N., & Marinescu, N. (2011). Energy policy and European utilities' strategy: Lessons from the liberalisation and privatisation of the energy sector in Romania. *Energy Policy, 39*(5), 2245–2255.

Hidroelectrica. (2020). 'Istoric Hidroelectrica', 06 February 2020, Romania. https://www.hidroelectrica.ro/article/15

Ilovan, O.-R., Bagoly-Simó, P., & Herbstritt, G. (2018). Visual discourse in Romanian geography textbooks during socialism (1948-1989). *Romanian Review of Geographical Education, 7*(2), 59–70.

Ivanov, K. (2008). Legitimate conditionality? The European Union and nuclear power safety in Central and Eastern Europe. *International Politics, 45*, 146–167.

Jasanoff, S., & Kim, S.-H. (2013). Sociotechnical imaginaries and national energy policies. *Science as Culture, 22*(2), 189–196.

Kideckel, D. (2004). Miners and wives in Romania's Jiu Valley: Perspectives on Postsocialist class, gender, and social change. *Identities, 11*(1), 39–63.

Kideckel, D. (2019). The decline of coal, structural power, memory, and future choices in the Jiu Valley and central Appalachia. *Bulletin of the Transilvania University of Brașov, Series IV: Philology & Cultural Studies, 12*, 9–24.

Kornai, J. (1992). *The socialist system. The political economy of communism*. Princeton: Princeton University Press.

Leal-Arcas, R., Filis, A., & Nalule, V. (2020). Energy decentralization and decarbonization: The case of Romania and Malta. *Nature Resources Journal, 60*, 117–152.

Manoleli, D., Georgescu, L. P., Platon, V., Prisecaru, P., & Stanescu, R. (2002). Impactul acquis-ului European de mediu asupra unor sectoare industriale în Romania.

Maris, G., & Flouros, F. (2021). The Green Deal, national energy and climate plans in Europe: Member states' compliance and strategies. *Administrative Sciences, 11*(3), 75.

Matei, C. (2014). 'Strategia energetică a României 2014–2035, finalizată în toamna acestui an, estimează Karoly Borbely', *Agerpres*, 10 May. Accessed on 10 Oct 2014 at http://www.agerpres.ro/externe/2014/06/10/strategia-energetica-a-romaniei-2014-2035-finalizata-in-toamna-acestui-an-estimeaza-karoly-borbely-15-01-29

Michalache, A.-E. (2018). Romania. In W. Ostrowski & E. Butler (Eds.), *Understanding energy security in central and Eastern Europe: Russia, transition and National Interest* (pp. 93–115). Abdingdon: Routledge.

Ministry of Economy. (2010). 'Master Plan Biomasa pentru Romania', drafted with NL Agency, Netherlands and ENERO Romania. Accessed on 15 Apr 2007 at http://www.minind.ro/biomasa/Plan_de_Actiune_pentru_Biomasa.pdf

Ministry of Energy. (2016). 'The Energy Strategy of Romania for 2016–2030, with the perspective of 2050', 19 December 2016, Romania, Bucharest. available at: http://energie.gov.ro/wp-content/uploads/2016/12/Strategia-Energetica-a-Romaniei-2016-2030_FINAL_19-decembrie-2.pdf. Accessed on 05 Mar 2017.

Miron, R. (2014). The socioeconomic impacts of local energy programmes: A case study of Avrig, Romania. *Management of Environmental Quality: An International Journal, 25*(3), 352–360.

Mulas-Granados, C., Koranchelian, T., & Segura-Ubiergo, A. (2008). *Reforming government subsidies in the new member states of the European Union*. International Monetary Fund, Fiscal Affairs Dept.

Năstase, G., Şerban, A., Dragomir, G., Brezeanu, A. I., & Bucur, I. (2018). Photovoltaic development in Romania. Reviewing what has been done. *Renewable and Sustainable Energy Reviews, 94*, 523–535.

Năstase, G., Şerban, A., Năstase, A. F., Dragomir, G., Brezeanu, A. I., & Iordan, N. F. (2017). Hydropower development in Romania. A review from its beginnings to the present. *Renewable and Sustainable Energy Reviews, 80*, 297–312.

Neagu, B. (2021). 'Romania will start extracting gas from Black Sea in 2026, minister says', *Euractiv Romania*, 17 December 2021, Bucharest. https://www.euractiv.com/section/energy/news/romania-will-start-extracting-gas-from-black-sea-in-2026-minister-says/

Nosko, A., & Mišík, M. (2017). No united front: The political economy of energy in central and Eastern Europe. In S. Andersen, A. Goldthau, & N. Sitter (Eds.), *Energy Union* (International political economy series). London: Palgrave Macmillan. https://doi.org/10.1057/978-1-137-59104-3_12.

Ostrowski, W. (2018). Poland. In W. Ostrowski & E. Butler (Eds.), *Understanding energy security in central and Eastern Europe: Russia, transition and National Interest* (pp. 116–137). Abingdon: Routledge.

Pencea, D. (1993). Renewable energy development in Romania. *Renewable Energy, 3*(2–3), 137–139.

Pilat, N. M. (2007). Towards the Europeanisation of trade unions in post-communist Romania. *SEER-South-East Europe Review for Labour and Social Affairs, 2*, 95–107.

Pirvoiu, C. (2010). Contractele cu baietii destepti din energie: De ce unii cumpara mai ieftin, iar altii mai scump, si de ce nu este vanduta energia de la Hidroelectrica pe bursa. Retrieved from http://economie.hotnews.ro/stiri-energie-7970922-contractele-baietii-destepti-din-energie-cumpara-unii-mai-ieftin-iar-altii-mai-scump-nu-este-vanduta-energia-hidroelectrica-bursa.htm

Pirvoiu, C. (2013). 'Daniela Lulache made it as nuclear electrica's director general' [Daniela Lulache a ajuns director general la Nuclearelectrica], 14 Mai 2013, Hotnews, Bucharest.

Pirvoiu, C. (2020). 'Dupa patru ani de discutii, Guvernul vrea sa adopte de urgenta Strategia Energetica' [After four years of debate, the Government wants to adopt the Energy Strategy by emergency legislation], 19 November 2020, Hotnews, Bucharest.

Pirvoiu, C. (2021). 'Dezbatere: Cat este de pregatita Romania pentru tranzitia energetica?' [Debate: How well prepared is Romania for the energy transition?], Guest speakers Razvan Nicolescu and Dumitru Chisalita, Hotnews, 23 May 2021, https://www.hotnews.ro/stiri-romania_in_europa-24814854-dezbatere-cat-este-pregatita-romania-pentru-tranzitia-energetica-razvan-nicolescu-dumitru-chisalita-interviurile-hotnews-live-luni-11-45.htm

Popescu, C., & Gavriş, A. (2020). "And they lived (un) happily ever after". State institutions, public enterprises in the energy sector and the value of environment in Romania. *Eurasian Geography and Economics*, 1–27.

Popescu, L., & Brinza, A. (2018). Romania-China relations. Political and economic challenges in the BRI era. *Romanian Journal of European Affairs, 18*, 2.

Raileanu, M. (2015). Campanii de mediu vs. sceptici/grupuri lobby. România pe harta schimbărilor climatice (Environmental campaigns versus Skeptical/Lobbysts. Romania on climate changes map). *România pe harta schimbărilor climatice (Environmental Campaigns versus Skeptical/Lobbysts. Romania on Climate Changes Map)(March 31, 2015). Impactul transformărilor socio-economice şi tehnologice la nivel national, european si mondial* (1).

Roberts, C., Geels, F. W., Lockwood, M., Newell, P., Schmitz, H., Turnheim, B., & Jordan, A. (2018). The politics of accelerating low-carbon transitions: Towards a new research agenda. *Energy Research & Social Science, 44*, 304–311.

Romanian Government. (2021). *The National Commission for the control of nuclear activities*, Bucharest. http://www.cncan.ro/despre-noi/istoric-2/

Șerban, S. (2020). Techno-nationalizing the levees on the Danube: Romania and Bulgaria after world war II. *Nationalities Papers, 48*(2), 373–387.

Simon, F., & Taylor, K. (2022) Leak: EU drafts plan to label gas and nuclear investments as green, *Euractiv,* 01 January 2022, Brussels. https://www.euractiv.com/section/energy-environment/news/leak-eu-drafts-plan-to-label-gas-and-nuclear-investments-as-green/

Sinea, A. (2020). *Romania as an energy actor in the EU: Cooperation in European energy policy.* London: Routledge.

Štanzel, A. (2017). *Wasserträume und Wasserräume im Staatssozialismus: Ein umwelthistorischer Vergleich anhand der tschechoslowakischen und rumänischen Wasserwirtschaft 1948–1989.* Göttingen: Vandenhoeck & Ruprecht.

Szeman, I., & Boyer, D. (2017). *Energy humanities: An anthology.* Baltimore: Johns Hopkins University Press.

The Diplomat. (2017). *Future challenges for Romania's energy industry.* Retrieved from http://www.thediplomat.ro/articol.php?id=7900

Tudorache, B. (2016). The green energy blockade: 2016 starts with more bankruptcies, losses of billions of Euro and investments at a standstill, *The Diploma.* http://www.thediplomat.ro/articol.php?id=6863, Bucharest.

Tudoroiu, T. (2008). From spheres of influence to energy wars: Russian influence in post-communist Romania. *Journal of Communist Studies and Transition Politics, 24*(3), 386–414.

Tulucan, A. D., Soveja-Iacob, L.-E., & Krezsek, C. (2018). History of the oil and gas industry in Romania. *Geological Society, London, Special Publications, 465*(1), 191–200.

Turnock, D. (1970). The pattern of industrialization in Romania. *Annals of the Association of American Geographers, 60*(3), 540–559.

Turnock, D. (2007). *Aspects of independent Romania's economic history with particular reference to transition for EU accession.* Aldershot/Burlington: Ashgate.

Volintiru, C., Bârgăoanu, A., Ștefan, G., & Durach, F. (2021). East-west divide in the European Union: Legacy or developmental failure? *Romanian Journal of European Affairs, 21*(1).

Vulpe, S. N. (2020). Cooling down the future. A discourse analysis of climate change skepticism. *The Social Science Journal,* 1–17. https://doi.org/10.1080/03623319.2020.1848294.

World Nuclear Association. (2021). *Nuclear power in Romania.* https://world-nuclear.org/information-library/country-profiles/countries-o-s/romania.aspx

World Nuclear News. (2013). *Romania signals intent with China', World Nuclear News,* 26 November 2013, Bucharest. https://www.world-nuclear-news.org/Articles/Romania-signals-intent-with-China

World Nuclear News. (2016). *Romania expresses support for China's role at Cernavoda,* 25 January 2016, Bucharest. https://www.world-nuclear-news.org/Articles/Romania-expresses-support-for-China-s-role-at-Cern

World Nuclear News. (2020). *Romania and USA agree to cooperate in nuclear projects,* 12 October 2020, Bucharest. https://www.world-nuclear-news.org/Articles/Romania-and-USA-agree-to-cooperate-in-nuclear-proj

World Nuclear News. (2021). *Romanian energy policy would see nuclear double,* 10 May 2021, Bucharest. https://www.world-nuclear-news.org/Articles/Romanian-energy-policy-will-see-nuclear-double

WWF. (2015). *EC starts an infringement procedure against Romania on small hydropower,* 11 June 2015. https://wwf.panda.org/wwf_news/?248033/EC-starts-an-infringement-procedure-against-Romania-on-small-hydropower

Zamfir, A., Colesca, S. E., & Corbos, R.-A. (2016). Public policies to support the development of renewable energy in Romania: A review. *Renewable and Sustainable Energy Reviews, 58,* 87–106.

Energy Governance in Russia: From a Fossil to a Green Giant?

Veli-Pekka Tynkkynen

Contents

Introduction	1020
General Conditions of Energy Governance in Russia	1021
Path Dependencies	1021
Composition of the "Energy Mix"	1022
Discourse on Energy Issues	1023
Political Institutions and Actors	1024
Coordination, Instruments, and Issues of the Russian Energy Transition	1026
Drivers of Energy Transition	1026
Strategies and Instruments of Energy Transition	1029
Coordination Mechanisms and Multilevel Governance	1030
Multilevel Energy Governance: Gas vs. Bioenergy	1032
Outcomes: Challenges and Prospects of Energy Governance	1033
Monitoring and Surveillance	1033
Sector Integration and Conflicts	1033
Cross-References	1034
References	1035

Abstract

Russia is an energy giant in terms of both nonrenewable and renewable energy. Furthermore, Russia has large resources and the technologically relatively well-developed society and economy needed to foster an energy transition towards renewables and a low-carbon economy. Russia has a large bioenergy potential via its forest resources, but its vast territory also gives it the potential to develop wind, small-scale hydro, and solar and geothermal power in an economically viable way. Despite this promising starting point, high dependence on the extraction of natural resources – which defines the Russian economy and politics – is a factor

---

V.-P. Tynkkynen (✉)
Aleksanteri Institute, University of Helsinki, Helsinki, Finland
e-mail: veli-pekka.tynkkynen@helsinki.fi

© Springer Nature Switzerland AG 2022
M. Knodt, J. Kemmerzell (eds.), *Handbook of Energy Governance in Europe*,
https://doi.org/10.1007/978-3-030-43250-8_25

delimiting the transition towards carbon neutrality and renewable energy. In particular, the central role played by oil and gas industries in the Russian economy and the strong linkages between political power and the fossil energy sector seem to be at odds with the energy transition objectives that have also been set in Russian official strategies since the early 2000s. The energy sector covers roughly a quarter of national GDP, and export of oil and gas alone accounts for one third to half of Russian state budget revenues. In this situation, defined by the realities of Russia's political economy, it is difficult to set a fair playing ground for those industries and actors that make it possible to pave the way for an energy transition towards a low-carbon society. Despite this challenging political and institutional situation, Russia has officially promoted the use of renewables and an increase in its energy efficiency.

Keywords

Russia · Renewable energy · Path dependency · Hydrocarbon culture · Gazprom · Rosneft · Rosatom

Introduction

Russia is an energy giant – and this applies to fossil and nonrenewable energy as well as renewable energy sources (RES). Furthermore, Russia has the large resources and technologically relatively developed society and economy needed to foster an energy transition towards renewables and low-carbon economy. Russia has a large bioenergy potential via its forest resources, which are the biggest in the world, but its vast territory also gives it the potential to develop wind, small-scale hydro, and solar and geothermal power in an economically viable way. Despite this promising starting point, a second glance reveals that high dependence on extraction of natural resources, which defines the Russian economy and politics, is a factor delimiting the transition towards carbon neutrality and renewable energy. Thus, the central role played by oil and gas industries in the Russian economy and the strong linkages between political power and the fossil energy sector seem to be, at least so far, at odds with the energy transition objectives that have also been set in Russian official strategies since the early 2000s. The energy sector covers roughly a quarter of national GDP, and export of oil and gas alone adds from one third to one half, depending on the year and thus on the price of oil, to Russian state budget revenues. In this situation, defined by the realities of Russia's political economy, it is difficult to set a fair playing ground for those industries and actors that make it possible to pave the way for an energy transition towards a low-carbon society.

Despite this challenging political and institutional situation, Russia has officially promoted the use of renewables and increase of its energy efficiency. All the energy strategies that Russia has approved during the 2000s – in 2003, 2009, and 2017 – underline the necessity to increase energy efficiency in the Russian economy, from households to the public sector and industry. This plea for higher efficiency is in line with the economic rationale to benefit from the barrels and cubic meters of hydrocarbons used less in the Russian economy and allow these volumes to be sold on the international energy markets with a better premium than domestically. Moreover, energy efficiency aims to promote, at least on the discursive level, the deployment of RES, as renewables are also seen as a substitute – especially for oil and coal – in the domestic energy mix. However, this aim seems to be very difficult to meet even though the normative base for investing in renewable energy projects has been laid during the last couple of years, and there are even a few examples of successful RES projects carried out recently. Russia has all the resources needed to become a *Green Giant*, but at the moment, it is severely lagging behind all other major energy power centers of the world – EU, China, and the USA – in RES deployment. Finally, the proportional increases in RES utilization may encourage the idea that a major shift is already taking place in Russia, but this is only due to the extremely low starting point of RES utilized in Russia.

General Conditions of Energy Governance in Russia

Path Dependencies

The most crucial factor defining energy governance in Russia is the fact that its territory is endowed with large deposits of fossil and nonrenewable energy: oil, gas, coal, and uranium. Russia is also rich in renewable energy resources. The plethora of the latter resources range from hydropower – especially in the Siberian peripheries – to bioenergy (a quarter of global forests), solar, wind, and geothermal. However, the potential of these low-carbon and renewable energy resources has not been unleashed, with the exception of hydropower in the European part of Russia. The reason for this lies at the heart of Russia's political economy: the political elite has grown highly dependent on the fossil and nonrenewable energy sectors, i.e., rents derived from oil, gas, coal, and uranium industries are a primary cause for the centrality of these sectors in defining the direction of Russia's energy, environmental, and climate policies. For example, energy efficiency, which is a vast problem due to its low level in energy production, transport, and consumption in Russia, can be regarded as a potential yet poorly managed energy resource because of the centrality of the fossil energy industries in the country (IFC 2014).

Historical path dependencies are the biggest factor dictating today's approach to energy, resources, and the environment in Russia. An important factor is the centrality of resource extractive industries in the Russian economy during the previous centuries (from furs, coal, and ore to oil and gas), which has produced economic and environmental practices resembling those of colonial contexts in Africa, Asia, and the Americas. This legacy plays an important role, especially in the Siberian part of Russia, but it also has an impact on the rationalities and practices of the political and economic elites of the country. Thus, the Soviet-era industrialization, with its dependence on unchecked utilization of natural resources and an emphasis on heavy industries, has led to institutional settings and interdependencies in the

Russian society where energy flows and infrastructures, and rents derived via them, have produced a strong inertia against endogenous political agendas wishing to challenge these trajectories (Rogers 2015; Wengle 2015; Tynkkynen 2016a).

Energy and resource abundance coupled with historical trajectories have created massive industries in all nonrenewable energy sectors in Russia. However, the vast size of the industries and companies in the natural resource sector is the result not only of political history and large resources per se but also of specific resource geographies: the globally important deposits of oil, gas, coal, and uranium are not evenly distributed in the Russian Eurasian space but concentrated in specific regions and territories, mostly far away from the population centers of Russia. Therefore, the fossil energy and uranium industries have required significant infrastructural investments in order to develop resources found mainly in the periphery. The fact that gas giant Gazprom manages 40,000 km of gas pipelines is thus due to the history of political economy in Russia, as well as the specific population and resource geographies of the country, which have the tendency to "stretch" these infrastructures. This factor then amplifies the energy-society loop: the more Russia has been compelled to invest in the energy infrastructures (e.g., in gas and oil pipelines, ports, etc.) to maintain production volumes that allow a certain level of rents, the more its political choices have been narrowed down concerning the energy transition from a carbon-based to a carbon-free energy system.

Composition of the "Energy Mix"

Russia is a major energy exporter, and rents derived via exports of oil, gas, coal, uranium, and nuclear technologies constitute about half of Russia's budget revenues, in addition to which the energy sector produces circa a quarter of Russia's GDP. Approximately half of the energy produced in Russia is internally consumed, i.e., 730 million tons of oil equivalent (toe) out of 1370 toe total. Since the last decades of the Soviet era – from the 1970s onward – the share of natural gas has increased significantly in the energy mix, constituting half of the overall energy consumption in today's Russia. Oil covers just over one fifth of Russia's energy demand, coal a little less than 20%, and nuclear 6%. Both hydropower and renewables cover between 1% and 2% of the overall energy demand, yet hydropower together with nuclear power constitutes one third of electricity production in Russia, 15% each. Gas dominates electricity production with a production share of almost 50%, yet its role has diminished during the last decade, whereas nuclear, coal, and hydropower each constitute about one sixth of electricity produced in Russia (Table 1 below).

The switch from heavy oil and coal to gas in heat and power generation is a major systemic change in the energy sector of Russia. This change is highly important not only due to its positive local and global environmental impacts – gas consumption releases far less pollutants affecting human health and ecosystems on a local (SO_2, NO_X, soot, etc.) as well as global (CO_2) level than oil and coal – but also in relation to the role of actors in the field of energy markets and policy. The gas sector is therefore central in all energy policy fields in Russia: gas covers half of overall

Table 1 TPES in Russia (IEA 2018)

Key data (2016)
Total energy production: 1373.7 Mtoe (natural gas 39.2%, oil 40.0%, coal 15.2%, nuclear 3.8%, hydro 1.2%, biofuels and waste 0.6%), +29.5% since 2002
TPES: 732.4 Mtoe (natural gas 50.7%, oil 23.7%, coal 15.5%, nuclear 7.0%, hydro 2.2%, biofuels and waste 1.1%), +18.4% since 2002
TPES per capita: 5.2 toe, +21.4% since 2002
TPES per real GDP: 0.34 toe/USD 1000 GDP PPP, −23.6% since 2002
Electricity generation: 1088.9 TWh (natural gas 47.9%, nuclear 18.1%, coal 15.7%, hydro 17.0%, oil 1.0%, biofuels and waste 0.2%, geothermal 0.1%), +21.6% since 2002
Heat generation per capita: 10,370 kWh, electricity generation per capita: 7560 kWh

energy consumption, as well as electricity production; households are highly dependent on gas indirectly via district heating and directly due to the fact that gas is widely used in cooking. Furthermore, although to a lesser degree, gas is even used in transport.

However, there are major regional differences in the energy mix. The European part of Russia, excluding the high North, relies on gas, nuclear, and hydropower, whereas Siberian Russia, especially the Far East, is still dependent on coal as the primary energy source. On the other hand, major Siberian industrial centers have evolved around gigantic hydropower plants that function as the primary source of energy for the heavy industries in these cities (Novosibirsk, Krasnoyarsk, Irkutsk, etc.). High dependence on coal, particularly in the Russian Far East, is a factor that affects regional and even foreign policy considerations in the Kremlin. The national gas distribution program, Gazifikatsiya Rossii, is therefore carried out not only to increase gas coverage in the peripheral parts of European Russia and combat the high level of energy poverty in these locations but also to connect Siberian and Far Eastern regions and cities to "mainland" Russia. This connectivity is important both in maintaining the center's control over these faraway regions and in that way deterring Chinese influence in this region, which Moscow sees as a geopolitical matter: a potentially separatist region (Wengle 2015, 10).

Discourse on Energy Issues

Approaching energy policies and choices from the discursive angle, one can state that two main narratives define the Russian discussion on energy: security of demand and security of supply. First, security of demand refers mainly to the Russia-EU energy trade and the long-lasting fear in Russia that the EU will diversify away from Russian energy to an extent that makes Russia's investments into new energy projects and infrastructures in the upstream overscaled and subsequently unprofitable (Gromov and Kurichev 2014). This hydrocarbon lock-in, caused by the fact that Russia has to offer hydrocarbons to global markets on a massive scale, also diverts new investments within the energy sector predominantly to oil and gas projects. In this discursive environment, it is challenging to promote RES even if energy efficiency goals concerning oil and gas, e.g., flaring less associated petroleum gas in Russian oil fields, would in principle also promote the onset of RES utilization. Second, the security of supply narrative refers once again to the partly dysfunctional domestic energy markets and especially the low level of energy equity between and within the regions of Russia (Tynkkynen 2016a). The social contract derived from the requirements people ask of the state – low fees on energy for the people of an energy giant – causes path dependencies impacting the deployment of RES, as renewables cannot compete with the subsidized prices of coal, gas, and oil and thus of electricity and heat. Therefore, the Russian government has agreed on this social contract by promising to eradicate energy poverty in the country, and this is predominantly done by switching from wood, coal, and heavy oil to gas.

Energy poverty is therefore an issue with regional, energy, and even security political ramifications, as it includes key critique towards Putin's regime. People claim that 200 km away from (a luxurious) Moscow, people do not even have access to gas (Tynkkynen 2016a). Extending gas distribution infrastructure to new regions and in the peripheries of urbanized European Russia is the Russian political solution to increasing energy equity. Alongside energy infrastructure construction, the image of a responsible gas company, Gazprom, in an energy-rich state is promoted by discursive means. This is done by using different information channels to produce a positive attitude to fossil energy among the Russian population, high reliance on energy exports in the economy, and the ability to increase Russia's political strength in foreign affairs via energy (Tynkkynen 2016b). All in all, it is a specific "hydrocarbon culture" that impacts Russia's choices in the fields of economy and energy, a state-led construction of identity where a positive view of fossil energy is intertwined with great power ambitions of the state and a sceptic and even denialist position on human-induced climate change (Tynkkynen and Tynkkynen 2018). In this situation, there is very little room to develop the renewables sector.

Political Institutions and Actors

The official bodies responsible for energy issues within the Russian state administration are the Ministry of Energy and the Ministry of Natural Resources and the Environment. The former is responsible for outlining and planning the energy policy of Russia, such as the Energy Strategy of Russia (Ministry of the Energy RF 2009, 2017), whereas the latter has the authority to issue licenses on new energy developments, for example, granting rights concerning which companies can access which energy sources and deposits. The president and the presidential administration (en.kremlin.ru/structure/administration) do not have a separate body to address energy issues and policy, yet the president has legislative powers via decrees (*ukaz*) that also affect the energy sector. However, the president has direct influence on the decision-making of the three state-owned energy companies, Gazprom, Rosneft, and Rosatom, all of which are pivotal actors in defining energy policies in Russia. Gazprom is an open joint-stock company (OAO) in which 50% plus one stock has belonged to the Russian state since 2005. It is the successor to the Soviet

Ministry of Gas Industry and currently employs more than 450,000 workers, produces 70% of Russia's gas, and also includes finance and media in its portfolio. Despite the fact that, in a legal sense, Gazprom is a commercial enterprise and not a state corporation, one can define it as a parastatal company. Designating it as a parastatal company implies that the Russian state and President Putin's regime exercise authority over the decisions of the company more than its position as a commercial enterprise would allow. Naturally, not all the decisions of the company are politically motivated, as business rationale is the main motivation for operational decisions taken by the company. Moreover, Gazprom is a large company that has dozens of regional subsidiaries with objectives and political voices stemming from the realities of the Russian regions. That said, all strategic moves, especially concerning overseas operations and major infrastructure decisions, are made by Putin's entourage. Therefore, as the company is steered by Russia's political elite, it has more privileges but also more state-defined societal tasks than any other company in Russia. In the 2010s, Gazprom lost its monopoly over gas exports and had to provide other companies, primarily Novatek, Rosneft, and Lukoil, with access to the domestic gas pipeline system. However, a de facto monopoly still prevails despite the fact that more competition is now allowed. This position provides the possibility to diminish competitors' opportunities to increase their market share in regional energy mixes or the national gas market. That makes Gazprom's position in the Russian domestic energy sector an exceptional one: it has the power to sideline both renewable energy and coal producers who have prospects to increase demand for their products in the Russian regions and to block oil companies trying to feed associated petroleum gas to the national pipeline system.

Rosneft, another state champion focusing primarily on oil production and the world's largest listed oil company by output with 250,000 employees, comes close to Gazprom in terms of its role and maneuvering space in the Russian economy and society. With its 50% state ownership, Rosneft can be defined as a parastatal company in a similar manner despite significant private and foreign ownership (e.g., BP and unknown offshore owners each have a 19% share in the company). The national oil company, also known as the heir to Mikhail Khodorkovsky's Yukos oil company and was taken over by the state in the early 2000s, is increasingly challenging Gazprom's monopoly in the gas sector, along with the second largest gas producer Novatek, which is privately owned yet still controlled by people close to the president. Rosneft plays a pivotal role in the energy efficiency of oil production in Russia, which is a major contributor to the country's GHG emissions as well as other environmental problems. This is linked to the fact that Rosneft produces two thirds of Russia's oil, while simultaneously having the lowest energy efficiency in the oil sector. This is most evident when looking at the issue of burning of associated petroleum gas on the site of production, i.e., APG flaring (see discussion below).

The third major energy player in Russia is Rosatom, a state corporation (Gosudarstvennaya Korporatsiya) functioning in the nuclear energy business and also producing nuclear weapons. Unlike Gazprom and Rosneft, Russian legislation does not require Rosatom to produce an economic surplus. The nuclear giant is therefore better equipped and positioned to promote energy and other policy objectives set by the state domestically and internationally. In Russia, nuclear power is prioritized vis-à-vis renewable energy and coal, and internationally Rosatom is able to compete and increase Russian influence via very attractive nuclear power plant and uranium provision offers (Aalto et al. 2017; Tynkkynen 2016c). For example, Rosatom has managed to secure nuclear power plant deals in Turkey, India, and Finland.

Coordination, Instruments, and Issues of the Russian Energy Transition

Drivers of Energy Transition

The centrality of energy efficiency policies, which have been listed among the primary objectives in Russia's energy strategies since the 1990s, stems from the fact that due to Soviet legacies, the economy is underperforming in terms of energy consumption per capita (5.2 toe/a) versus produced GDP (0.34 toe/1000 USD) (IEA 2014). Furthermore, energy efficiency is central, as the cubic meters of gas and oil barrels saved in domestic consumption release these volumes to be traded on international markets – a business covering 35–50% of Russia's budget revenues yearly.

Socio-technical evolution of the global energy sector, and particularly the European scene, represents an important external influence on the Russian energy sector and the objectives set in the official energy policies. The European and Russian energy sectors are interlinked via many material and social networks, pipelines, and joint ventures. European energy development and the deployment of RES is the primary benchmark for Russian actors, and it has at least a twofold influence on Russia's choices. First, Russia copies many legal and governance approaches when facilitating and promoting RES deployment. This particularly affects the official energy policy choices. However, in Russia's authoritarian and fossil energy-dependent society, informal practices and politics play a far more important role than the official, particularly when it comes to the energy sector itself. Therefore, the legal and governance setting for RES deployment is de jure in place (Boute 2011, 2012a, b), but de facto this scheme has been very difficult to promote (Pristupa and Mol 2015). For example, the capacity market conditions and feed-in tariffs for solar and wind power in Russia are very competitive (Kozlova 2015), but construction of new capacity has still been very moderate. Global comparison shows that Russia lags far behind other major energy producer and consumer countries: Russia's wind power capacity, including capacity that is installed and under construction, is about 150 times less than the installed wind power capacity of China and about 80 less than that of the USA (Frangoul 2018). This might not seem like such a bad figure, as Russia is typically classified in the category of other fossil energy giants, such as Saudi Arabia and Iran. However, Russia's vast territory – 17 million square kilometers – sets the potential wind power capacity at thousands of terawatts (IRENA 2017, 33), and in this context, the negligible 110 MWs of installed wind capacity and still low 2000 MWs under construction (IRENA 2017, 12) reveals the vast mismatch between potential and current deployment.

Another external driver framing Russia's energy policies and RES deployment is global climate policies and governance. Historically, Russia has oscillated between opposition to the mainstream understanding of anthropogenic climate change and its endorsement. Pivotal in understanding this dualism is the Cold War era science battle between Soviet natural science based on empirical research and Western-led climate science, which relied on modeling and the large computational capacities that were lacking in the Soviet bloc (Doose and Oldfield 2019). Thus, the current climate denialist tones being circulated in Russian society by the political and economic elites, which are unfortunately growing stronger as Putin's entourage takes a tighter grip on power (Tynkkynen and Tynkkynen 2018), can in part be explained by the positions affected by nationalism and great power perceptions: international climate science must be opposed in order to block the hegemony of Western science and Western political and military power. However, this dualist situation has recently fractured into several climate change and governance positions. Trump's climate denial is fully compatible to that of Putin's, but due to the soft power gains, Russia is playing along with the US Democrat, EU, and also Chinese sentiments that climate change must be mitigated. The crucial take-home point is that if Russia is able to promote mitigation in real life, the triggers are fully economic and (geo)political. However, Russia's international soft-power choices, which in this respect reflect China's climate leadership, may lead to more ambitious climate mitigation policies domestically, even though the entanglement of the political and energy elite and the rent-seeking practices related to fossil energy temper very ambitious climate mitigation policies in Russia.

There are also several internal drivers for RES deployment in Russia. On a discursive level, the resource wealth of Russia in terms of renewables potential in all categories – wind, solar, bio, small hydro, geothermal, and tidal – and the potential economic gains derived via a domestic energy transition from fossil to renewable energy, including the diversion of fossil energy from domestic consumption to export and capitalizing on increased energy efficiency during the transition, are the two most prominent themes utilized in the domestic discussion (Smeets 2017). The choice to emphasize resource wealth fits conveniently into the overall discursive frame, where wealth in natural resources and energy play a pivotal role in defining Russian economic and political potential. In other words, highlighting the resource potential in renewables allows continuation of the same grand strategy that has characterized Russia's practical economic choices and reflects the realities of political economy in the country. Thus, a domestic energy transition to renewables enhances Russia's position as a potential exporter of RES and electricity produced with RES in Russia. On the one hand, this "discursive fit" promotes the energy transition in a difficult institutional and political setting dominated by the fossil energy sector, as it is well-suited to the centuries-old extensive economic model in Russia, which is based on the export of raw materials and commodities with a low extent of value added. On the other hand, it can be seen as counterproductive in the framework of Russian modernization aims: seeing RES as a new Eldorado for Russia dwarfs the efforts to diversify the Russian economy from its overall economic dependence on energy.

One of the most potential areas to develop and deploy RES in Russia is the off-grid territories, i.e., regions, cities, and towns that are outside the national electricity and gas grids. Russia's energy strategies also underline this fact and urge these areas to be at the forefront of RES deployment by designating them as pilot areas for promoting RES in Russia. These areas, mainly in the Russian Far North and East Siberia, have traditionally relied on Northern Delivery (*severnyi zavos*) to maintain exclave's electricity and heating systems. Thus, the communities in these areas rely on imported heavy oil and coal from Russia's energy production centers, thousands of kilometers away, despite the fact that many Northern communities have renewable (bioenergy, wind, wave, micro-hydro, solar) energy resources available that could be utilized cost-efficiently. The fact that this Northern Delivery, which dates back to the Soviet times, is an expensive and inefficient system makes local and regional renewable energy solutions more appealing. Piloting of RES in these communities has been the cornerstone of Russia's renewables policies, yet the results have been less than promising mainly due to the vested interests of traditional energy sectors, gas, coal, oil, and the rent-seeking networks that have evolved around the Northern Delivery system (e.g., Salonen 2018: 74). Therefore, a constraining factor for deploying local RES is the Northern Delivery system itself: the people, the companies, and the official and unofficial institutions that are intertwined in this system, where rent-seeking inevitably takes place, make it hard to switch to a new system based on local and regional RES despite the direct economic gains for the regional economy.

Furthermore, many regions and cities within the national electricity and gas grids would enjoy similar economic benefits by switching to local and regional RES. The regional policies in many regions of Russia include plans to enhance energy self-sufficiency, in other words, to rely on the region's own energy potential instead of producing electricity and heat by burning energy commodities (coal, oil, gas) hauled in from other regions (Tynkkynen 2014). However, these plans have run into obstacles as the regional aims are at odds with national objectives, such as those of the national gas distribution program run by Gazprom (Tynkkynen 2016b).

One peculiar but very positive feature in Russian goal-setting concerning an energy transition towards carbon neutrality is the fact that, on the discursive as well as normative levels, promotion of energy efficiency is elementarily tied to renewable energy deployment. The discourse that emphasizes the role of renewable energies in pushing energy efficiencies is made normative via the government resolution "On The Main Areas of Government Policy to Raise the Energy Efficiency of Electric Power from Renewable Energy Sources for the Period to 2020" (Government of Russia 2009). This stems from the objective stated in all Russia's energy strategies during the 2000s: renewables and nuclear power are the means to promote energy efficiency in Russia, as replacing hydrocarbons with renewables inside Russia releases oil and gas to be exported. And, as it is more economically viable to export hydrocarbons than consume them at home, energy efficiencies in oil and gas production and consumption will be enhanced.

Strategies and Instruments of Energy Transition

The regulatory framework for deploying renewables in Russia, targeting wind power and bioenergy in particular, was initiated in the early 2000s and has recently been elaborated by the Russian Government via several new regulations concerning both wholesale and retail electricity markets (Gsänger and Denisov 2017, Appendix 2.). Two pivotal governmental strategies set the scene. The first is the Government Decree "On the mechanism of promoting the use of renewable energies in the wholesale electricity market and power" (No. 449) passed in May 2013, which introduces mechanisms for deploying renewable energy projects within the wholesale electricity market. This decree has been elaborated several times with amendments and executive orders since its onset. The second is the Government Decree "The scheme of the territorial planning of the Russian Federation in the field of energy" (No.1634-r) issued in 2016, which sets a goal to build more than a dozen wind farms of over 100 MW with the objective of gaining a total wind power capacity of 4.5 GW by 2030.

With regard to wind power, the issued legal framework is relatively generous in terms of the guaranteed return on investments. If they meet the capacity supply contract criteria with respect to efficiency and utilized capacity, investments in wind power capacity have a 12% guaranteed return on capital. Despite this alluring official setting, deployment of wind power has been very slow in Russia: the ongoing wind installation projects constitute less than 2000 MW. However, the finalization of these projects will provide a 100-fold increase in Russia's wind power capacity. Most of the future capacity will be contributed by big players, such as Rosatom. However, some relatively large-scale projects are also being developed by newcomers, such as Wind Power Generation Company (2019) and Alten (2019), i.e., actors outside the traditional energy sectors (IRENA 2017, 12). Gsänger and Denisov (2017) list several obstacles hindering the deployment of wind power in Russia. First, investments in the sector are few in number, because the remuneration scheme is non-transparent. Second, the institutional setting does not favor the wind power sector, as the actors are scattered and lack the scale needed to push policies through on the national level. This weakness is further amplified by the very small market volume of the wind power business in Russia. Third, despite the fact that a legal framework exists, it is considered weak especially with regard to technical standards and land use issues. For example, the standards are very hard to follow, as there are complicated regulations concerning the requirements for domestic production and procurement of technical appliances and parts. Finally, grid connection is challenging for small-volume wind generator companies, as powerful energy sector players in the thermal and nuclear power and hydropower areas dominate the scene.

The potential for growth in the bioenergy sector is more geographically confined than in the wind power sector. Northwest Russia, South Central Siberia, and the Far East are prominent areas in Russia for deploying bioenergy, as there is a solid resource base and commercial and institutional actors – the forest industry – capable of promoting the branch. The regulatory framework for bioenergy deployment is partially laid out in the same governmental strategies and regulations that apply to the wind power sector.

Table 2 Central governmental decisions to enhance the energy transition in Russia

Governmental documents on the energy transition	Year of issue	Scope and aim
Resolution of the Russian Government "On the main areas of Government policy to raise the energy efficiency of electric power from renewable energy sources for the period to 2020" (No. 1-r)	2009	Piloting of RES projects deploying wind and solar power installations, power and heat plants running on bioenergy
The Government Decree "On the mechanism of promoting the use of renewable energies in the wholesale electricity market and power" (No. 449)	2013	Introducing mechanisms for deploying renewable energy projects within the wholesale electricity market
The Government Decree "The scheme of the territorial planning of the Russian Federation in the field of energy" (No.1634-r)	2016	Aiming to build several wind farms bigger than 100 MW with the objective of gaining a total wind power capacity of 4.5 GW by 2030

One specific geographical area in Russia would benefit the most from RES deployment: the off-grid territories of Northwest Russia and the Russian Far North. In energy policy terms, this area is defined as exceptional: its security of supply is based on the Northern Delivery system, described briefly above. These areas have been designated in governmental documents (Government of Russia 2009) for piloting of RES projects deploying mainly wind and solar power installations and for power and heat plants running on bioenergy. The renewable energy projects carried out in this area should set the scene for successful RES deployment in other parts of Russia (Table 2).

Coordination Mechanisms and Multilevel Governance

Officially, Russia's energy policy is drawn up by the experts within the collective of the Ministry of Energy (Ministry of Energy RF 2009, 2017). The same ministry is also responsible for implementing the strategy, i.e., ensuring that legal and administrative norms are pushed forward in the spirit of the strategy. The strategy itself is not a binding document but a "document for documents" (Gromov and Kurichev 2014: 17). Thus, the Ministry of Energy is coordinating the projects promoted under the strategic umbrella with other ministries and governmental bodies, as well as monitoring its implementation. The Ministry of Natural Resources and the Environment is also a central body responsible for setting the policy field concerning development and tapping of new energy resources and therefore also in promoting energy efficiency and RES deployment objectives. Despite being criticized for excessive optimism, especially concerning energy efficiency goals and increasing the use of renewable energy, which are central objectives in the strategies, (Tynkkynen and Aalto 2012: 107; Tynkkynen 2014), the three strategies that have been elaborated during the 2000s – in 2003, 2009, and 2017 – all reflect the political goals set for the energy sector by the political elite. The strategies thus tell something about the direction in which official Russia would like to see its energy policies shift and aim to convince the rest of the world that Russia is a modern state with modern goals but lacks the tools to operationalize these somewhat lofty objectives. The overly optimistic character of the strategies is particularly evident when looking at how the issue of RES deployment has been discussed, what kind of goals are set, and how these objectives have been met during the last decade. The 2009 strategy, aiming at 2030, states that the share of renewables in the Russian energy mix should cover 14% of the total energy demand by 2030 and the share of electricity produced via RES should reach 4.5% (Ministry of the Energy RF 2009). At the time of writing in summer 2018, Russia's energy mix contains only 1% so-called new renewables, and the goal set for electricity produced by renewables will be extremely difficult to attain.

The factual power houses within the Russian energy policy formation, as discussed above in the section on Political Institutions and Actors, are the parastatal energy companies: Gazprom, Rosneft, and Rosatom. The decisions within these companies are mainly dictated by economic rationale. However, in terms of central sociopolitical issues in Russia – the social contract between the state and its people in which energy and the social are intrinsically intertwined – the objectives of the state and Putin's regime play a pivotal role. Therefore, as Russians have become accustomed to cheap electricity, gas, and heating (Collier 2011; Tynkkynen 2014), it is difficult to change this "fatal" relationship of hydrocarbons and the social, as renewables and energy efficiency would entail a more market-based system in which people pay real prices for the energy they consume.

Private energy companies, such as Surgutneftegas and Lukoil, do play a role in influencing, if not framing, energy policies in those regions where they operate: Western Siberia for the former and the Perm region and Komi Republic for the latter (Rogers 2015). In the coal industry-dominated Southern part of Central Siberia, the Kuzbass coal region, and the Russian Far East, energy policies are mainly dictated by these industrial interests (Wengle 2015). Thus, it has been difficult to replace the use of coal with renewables or even gas in these areas because regional business interests have been able to resist the national gas champion, Gazprom.

The presidential administration and President Vladimir Putin himself are naturally pivotal players in defining the main directions of Russia's energy policy (Tynkkynen and Aalto 2012) and therefore also the fate of energy efficiency and deployment of RES. During the Medvedev presidency in 2008–2012, modernization of the Russian society and economy were emphasized much more than during Putin 2.0, i.e., after he returned to office in 2012. Putin and his entourage are underlining the role of the energy sector in modernizing the country (Gustafson 2012). Therefore, one qualitative difference from the Medvedev years is the fact that modernization as diversification away from fossil energy dependence is less and less mentioned and the emphasis has been shifted to economic, rather than societal or political, modernization via the hydrocarbon sector. This choice, which keeps the unofficial networks of the energy and political elite intact, is naturally an antidote for policies and practices that strive to promote renewables in Russia.

This shift towards more conservative values, both economic and political, is not good news for promotion of a low-carbon transition in Russia. However, energy efficiency was on the political agenda even before the Medvedev presidency, so Putin's entourage understands its economic value. For example, associated petroleum gas (APG) flaring reduction policies were established already in 2007 but fully operationalized only in 2014. The positive tendency of oil companies to utilize the associated gas in electricity production for their own needs or to increase the pressure in oil wells by injecting it back to the deposit has decreased APG flaring in the Russian oil industry by approximately half: from a devastating 50 bcm per year in 2007 to some 20 bcm in 2016 (Korppoo 2018). One could argue that this change would have happened without deliberate state policies on APG, as the economic realities set by the Russian electricity market rules have been the primary cause for flaring reductions that started to take effect long before the official APG policies were implemented. Moreover, the successes in this area have taken place in the West Siberian brownfield areas, i.e., old production regions which have a dense network of hydrocarbon infrastructures and oil *and* gas pipelines. However, there are severe difficulties in meeting the set norms in the new Arctic and East Siberian greenfield locations, which are sparsely populated with energy and other infrastructures. This indicates that prevailing unofficial practices make it possible to circumvent official APG reduction norms in greenfield oil deposits, which are in need of high capital investments and pivotal to maintaining the high oil production levels that are politically and economically crucial for Putin's Russia. Thus, implementing uniform energy efficiency policies, and providing a uniform playing field for renewables promotion, is going to be a very demanding task in Russia. It is not clear whether this is even possible, as the oil industry is so pivotal to the power and success of Putin's regime. The same applies to increasing prices and reducing subsidies for household gas, which is an even more central factor in enhancing renewables. The social contract between Russian people and the regime concerning subsidized gas and heat, carried out by Gazprom, is thus a political and even cultural barrier for RES enhancement in Russia (Tynkkynen 2016a, b), as explained below in a more nuanced analysis of the role of gas in the Russia energy transition.

Multilevel Energy Governance: Gas vs. Bioenergy

Gazprom does not only transport gas via its pipelines; its numerous projects and programs are firmly tied to the nationwide gas program Gazifikatsiia Rossii. On the grounds of enhancing energy security and promoting economic growth, regional investment, and environmental protection, Gazprom asserts the importance of extending the country's gas distribution network to its peripheries. The Republic of Karelia, bordering on Finland and the EU, is one such region. Gazprom (2012) extended its domestic gas infrastructure investment program in 2011, enabling it to further consolidate its role in the domestic market. A social infrastructure component is tied to all pipeline projects and power plants built by Gazprom. In the case of Karelia, this has been significant. As Gazprom cannot evade certain philanthropic obligations set by the state, the company prioritizes charity that can maximize gains for the company.

The Republic of Karelia imports 70% of its energy, including electricity from outside the region and oil and coal for heating purposes. This region has a long history of local forestry, and the forest industry supplies the remaining 30% of energy consumed. Because of its rich forest resource base, Karelia made several plans and agreements in 2001–2003 to decrease energy import dependency by constructing new power plants running on woodchips and peat (Pravitelstvo 2001). However, in 2004, Gazprom moved in with negotiations to expand its gas distribution pipelines in Karelia and construct heat power plants running on gas. This resulted in an agreement between Gazprom and the Republic of Karelia in 2006 on "Gasification of the Republic." However, the gas investment program was not simply sold to Karelian decision-makers on the basis of economic and energy security arguments but with promises of social infrastructure construction in the form of sport halls. Such projects provided links to national objectives that were considered positive (a great sport nation, Gazprom as the sponsor of Russian and international sports, etc.), making gas look more appealing than local energy sources and energy self-sufficiency. Thus, the broader societal context makes it difficult to deploy renewables even in localities where there is great economic potential for it.

Outcomes: Challenges and Prospects of Energy Governance

Monitoring and Surveillance

The legal basis for RES promotion has been laid in Russia during the last 10 years. Despite the lucrative feed-in tariffs introduced recently, development in the sector has been slow. The ambitious goals set for RES deployment included in all Russia's energy strategies published during the 2000s have not been fulfilled, and Russia lags far behind all major energy markets in terms of building energy capacities based on RES. Monitoring of achievements within the sector is only evolving now as new, wind and solar power parks are being constructed and even piloted. The lack of a proper monitoring system to follow and encourage RES deployment in the country is partly due to the declarative nature of energy strategies ("document of documents"): Russia lacks genuine normative policy-making to promote RES. The lack of monitoring and surveillance of achievements is partially related to the power of the traditional hydrocarbon sector in Russian society and economy and its central role in defining politics and policies. Therefore, the low institutional capacity and power of actors within the renewables sector is at the heart of the problem.

Sector Integration and Conflicts

Despite this rather gloomy outlook for RES deployment in Russia, a few positive features have to be mentioned, and one of these is linked to sector integration within the energy sector. As noted above, the actors within the renewables sector have thus far been weak in defining the energy policy field and promoting RES in the fossil energy-dominated context. However, the latest solar and wind power projects, e.g., wind power parks with a capacity of up to 700 MW, have been initiated by traditional energy companies like the Russian nuclear operator Rosatom (2018). Players in the Russian power and heat sector that are dependent on gas and coal, such as Fortum, have also invested in major wind parks. Thus, it seems that major energy players must take the first steps in order to establish the renewables sector institutionally in Russia. It may well be that this centralized and state-centered approach to RES deployment is defining the way in which RES will be promoted in Russia for years to come. Furthermore, this may even be the only way to promote RES in Russia in light of the present political realities. However, bioenergy differs from wind and solar in profound ways, as the potential actors promoting bioenergy are bigger and thus more economically and politically powerful, at least on a regional scale. The forest industry in Northwest Russia, South Central Siberia, and the Far East is an actor that enables growth in deployment of bioenergy. Bioenergy may not be the central RES that Russia will develop in the future, but it will certainly play a pivotal role in the taiga (coniferous) zone of Russia, where bioenergy can replace the use of coal, oil, and gas (e.g., Salonen 2018).

However, deploying RES in those localities and regions where it would seem to be the most prominent option both economically and environmentally is difficult because of the centrality of gas and the fact that gas links Russia's energy and regional and social policies closely together. The Gazifikatsiia Rossii gas distribution program and its policies, practices, and discourses, which are carried out by the parastatal Gazprom (2012), send the following message to the Russian people: regions that do not choose and invite Gazprom and its gas will not develop. The narrative is that prosperous settlements choose gas, while backward ones choose other sources of energy and are thus doomed to scarcity. Moreover, a city or town that chooses to join Gazprom's network becomes part of "Putin's enterprise," whose gas pipelines extend from production sites to consumers. This expansive network is viewed by the company as the material manifestation of Russia's new role as an energy superpower (Tynkkynen 2016a). This kind of hydrocarbon-based social contract adds to the difficulty of officially governing the energy transition away from fossil energy in Russia. In this kind of a societal, political, and even cultural setting, it is a very demanding task to promote renewables and foster the energy transition towards a low-carbon society. Therefore, in this context, it seems that the transformation towards renewables will only happen after the major energy players of Russia – Gazprom, Rosneft, and Rosatom – start the process. The latter of these giants is already in the renewables business, so an otherwise gloomy outlook for the possibilities of RES in Russia does not seem so hopeless after all.

Cross-References

▶ Energy Poverty
▶ Energy Relations in the EU Eastern Partnership
▶ EU-Russia Energy Relations
▶ The EU in Global Energy Governance

References

Aalto, P., Nyyssönen, H., Kojo, M., & Pal, P. (2017). Russian nuclear energy diplomacy in Finland and Hungary. *Eurasian Geography and Economics, 58*(4), 386–417.

Alten. (2019). http://www.alten.ru/en/. Accessed 22 May 2019.

Boute, A. (2011). A comparative analysis of the European and Russian support schemes for renewable energy: Return on EU experience for Russia. *The Journal of World Energy Law & Business, 4*(2), 1–24.

Boute, A. (2012a). Modernizing the Russian district heating sector: Financing energy efficiency and renewable energy investments under the New Federal Heat Law. *Pace Environmental Law Review, 29*(1), 746–810.

Boute, A. (2012b). Promoting renewable energy through capacity markets: An analysis of the Russian support scheme. *Energy Policy, 46*(1), 68–77.

Collier, S. (2011). *Post-soviet social. Neoliberalism, social modernity, biopolitics*. Princeton: Princeton University Press.

Doose, K., & Oldfield, J. (2019). Natural and anthropogenic climate change understanding in the Soviet Union, 1960s – 1980s. In M. Poberezhskaya & T. Ashe (Eds.), *Climate change discourse in Russia. Past and present* (pp. 17–31). New York: Routledge.

Frangoul, A. (2018). From China to Brazil, these are the world titans of wind power. *CNBC*. https://www.cnbc.com/2018/06/04/from-china-to-brazil-these-are-the-world-titans-of-wind-power.html. Accessed 4 Dec 2018.

Gazprom. (2012). *Gazifikatsiia* [Gas infrastructure expansion]. www.gazprom.ru/about/production/gasification. Accessed 24 Jan 2016.

Government of Russia. (2009). Ob osnovnykh napravleniyakh gosudarstvennoi politiki v sfere povysheniya energeticheskoi effektivnosti elektroenergetiki na osnove ispol'zovaniya vozobnovlyaemykh istochnikov energii [On the main areas of government policy to raise the energy efficiency of electric power from renewable energy sources for the period to 2020], approved by Resolution of the Russian Government No. 1-r 8 January.

Gromov, A., & Kurichev, N. (2014). The energy strategy of Russia for period up to 2030. Risks and opportunities. In S. Oxenstierna & V.-P. Tynkkynen (Eds.), *Russian energy and security up to 2030* (pp. 16–40). Abingdon: Routledge.

Gsänger, S. & Denisov, R. (2017). *Perspectives of the wind energy market in Russia*. Friedrich Ebert Stiftung and World Wind Energy Association. http://library.fes.de/pdf-files/bueros/moskau/13474.pdf. Accessed 23 Apr 2018.

Gustafson, T. (2012). *Wheel of fortune. The battle for oil and power in Russia*. Cambridge, MA: Belknap Press of Harvard University Press.

IEA, International Energy Agency (2014). Russia 2014. Energy Policies Beyond IEA Countries. Available at: http://www.iea.org/publications/freepublications/publication/Russia_2014.pdf, last accessed 11th May 2018.

IEA, International Energy Agency. (2018). *World energy balances*. https://www.oecd-ilibrary.org/docserver/world_energy_bal-2018-en.pdf?expires=1543574142&id=id&accname=ocid194948&checksum=109CED77D3909776200230304BD18B61. Accessed 30 Nov 2018.

IFC, International Finance Corporation. (2014). *Energy efficiency in Russia: Untapped reserves*. https://www.ifc.org/wps/wcm/connect/de1e58804aababd79797d79e0dc67fc6/IFC+EE+in+Russia+Untapped+Potential.pdf?MOD=AJPERES. Accessed 30 Nov 2018.

IRENA. (2017). *REmap 2030. Renewable energy prospects for the Russian Federation. April 2017. Working paper*. http://www.irena.org/DocumentDownloads/Publications/IRENA_REmap_Russia_paper_2017.pdf. Accessed 30 Nov 2018.

Korppoo, A. (2018). Russian associated petroleum gas flaring limits: Interplay of formal and informal institutions. *Energy Policy, 116*, 232–241.

Kozlova, M. (2015). *Analyzing the effects of the new renewable energy policy in Russia on investments into wind, solar and small hydro power* (Master's Thesis). Lappeenranta University of Technology.

Ministry of the Energy RF. (2009). *Energeticheskaya strategiya Rossii do 2030 goda [Energy strategy of Russia up to 2030]*. Adopted by the government 13 November, Ministry of Energy RF. Online. https://minenergo.gov.ru/node/1026. Accessed 25 Apr 2018.

Ministry of the Energy RF. (2017). *Energeticheskaya strategiya Rossii do 2035 goda [Energy strategy of Russia up to 2035]*. Adopted by the government 1 February, Ministry of Energy RF. Online. https://minenergo.gov.ru/node/1920. Accessed 25 Apr 2018.

Pravitelstvo, R.K. (2001). *Pazporyazhenie ot 22 Oktyabrya 2001 Goda N 241r-P [Decree From the 22nd of October 2001 No. N241r-P]*. http://kodeks.karelia.ru/api/show/919308348. Accessed 25 June 2015.

Pristupa, A., & Mol, A. (2015). Renewable energy in Russia: The take off in solid bioenergy? *Renewable and Sustainable Energy Reviews, 50*, 315–324.

Rogers, D. (2015). *The depths of Russia. Oil, power, and culture after socialism*. Ithaca: Cornell University Press.

Rosatom. (2018). *Wind energy*. http://www.rosatom.ru/en/rosatom-group/wind-energy/. Accessed 11 May 2018.

Salonen, H. (2018). Public justification analysis of Russian renewable energy strategies. *Polar Geography, 41*(2), 75–86.

Smeets, N. (2017). *The Green Menace: Unraveling Russia's elite discourse on enabling and constraining factors of renewable energy policies*. Working Paper prepared for the first Ghent Russia colloquium "EU-Russia Relations: How to get out of the 'midlife' crisis?", 22 Sep 2017.

Tynkkynen, V.-P. (2014). Russian bioenergy and the EU's renewable energy goals: Perspectives of security. In S. Oxenstierna & V.-P. Tynkkynen (Eds.), *Russian energy and security up to 2030* (pp. 95–113). Abingdon: Routledge.

Tynkkynen, V.-P. (2016a). Energy as power—Gazprom, gas infrastructure, and geo-governmentality in Putin's Russia. *Slavic Review, 75*(2), 374–395.

Tynkkynen, V.-P. (2016b). Sports fields and corporate governmentality: Gazprom's all-Russian gas program as energopower. In N. Koch (Ed.), *Critical geographies of sport. Space, power and sport in global perspective* (pp. 75–90). London: Routledge.

Tynkkynen, V.-P. (2016c). Russia's nuclear power and Finland's foreign policy. *Russian Analytical Digest, 193*, 2–5. http://www.css.ethz.ch/content/dam/ethz/special-interest/gess/cis/center-for-securities-studies/pdfs/RAD193.pdf. Accessed 5 Dec 2018.

Tynkkynen, N., & Aalto, P. (2012). Environmental sustainability of Russia's energy policies. In P. Aalto (Ed.), *Russia's energy policies. National, interregional and global levels* (pp. 92–114). Cheltenham: Edward Elgar.

Tynkkynen, V.-P., & Tynkkynen, N. (2018). Climate denial revisited: (re)contextualising Russian public discourse on climate change during Putin 2.0. *Europe-Asia Studies, 70*(7), 1103–1120.

Wengle, S. (2015). *Post-soviet power. State led development and Russia's marketization*. New York: Cambridge University Press.

Wind Power Generation Company. (2019). http://www.wind-pgc.com/en/. Accessed 22 May 2019.

Energy Governance in Serbia

41

Stefan Ćetković

Contents

Introduction	1038
General Conditions of Energy Governance in Serbia: Legacies from the Past	1039
Energy Mix and Path Dependence: Relying on Coal and Large Hydropower	1039
War Legacy and the Lack of Regional Energy Cooperation	1040
Energy Narratives	1042
Political Institutions and Actors	1042
Coordination, Instruments, and Issues of Energy Transitions within a Multilevel Context	1044
Drivers of Energy Transition	1044
Strategies and Instruments of Energy Transition	1046
Coordination Mechanisms and Multi-Level Governance	1048
Outcomes, Challenges, and Prospects of Energy Governance	1050
Cross-References	1051
References	1051

Abstract

This chapter discusses the historical origins and current issues and challenges of energy governance in Serbia. On one hand, Serbia is still a transitioning economy endowed with considerable domestic coal and hydropower resources and with a legacy of top-down and nontransparent energy policy making. On the other hand, Serbia is an EU candidate country, which has increasingly taken efforts to meet the ever-expanding EU rules and standards aimed at fostering liberalization and sustainability of the energy system. In light of these inherent contradictions and ongoing disturbances in the energy regime, this chapter outlines the dynamic processes, actors, ideas, and institutions behind the current energy governance in Serbia and sheds more light on the key factors, which affect the stability and change of Serbia's energy development path.

S. Ćetković (✉)
Bavarian School of Public Policy, Technical University of Munich, Munich, Germany
e-mail: stefan.cetkovic@hfp.tum.de

© Springer Nature Switzerland AG 2022
M. Knodt, J. Kemmerzell (eds.), *Handbook of Energy Governance in Europe*,
https://doi.org/10.1007/978-3-030-43250-8_26

Keywords

Serbia · Energy governance · Energy transition · Energy efficiency · Renewable energy

Introduction

Energy governance in Serbia has traditionally been based on centralized policy-making, closed policy and epistemic communities, and hierarchically structured and politically controlled energy companies. The operation of the latter has been primarily driven by geostrategic and socioeconomic concerns rather than environmental soundness, competitiveness, and economic efficiency. Such energy system has produced the patterns of subsidized energy prices, high energy, and carbon intensity in the industry and households, indebted public energy utilities, and the declining efficiency of the energy infrastructure. These factors, together with the persistently low economic growth in the country and the significant domestic reserves of lignite, have made it difficult for alternative ideas and technologies to challenge the established energy regime. Recently, however, the growing awareness about climate change and the efforts towards decarbonization of the energy sector at the international and particularly EU level have placed the long-lasting energy policy consensus in Serbia under increasing pressure.

Although a comparatively small and landlocked country, Serbia has a considerable potential in virtually all renewable energy sources. One portion of that potential has already been utilized in in the form of wood for heating in households and the large hydropower plants that were built during the industrialization period of former Yugoslavia in the 1960s and 1970s. This use of hydropower in large hydropower plants has for a long time served to support the narrative that Serbia is already ahead of many countries in the use of renewable energy sources and that further efforts in that regard are neither necessary nor economically rational. Apart from hydropower, by far the most important energy source in the electricity mix is domestically exploited lignite which supplies two thirds of electricity consumption and which is controlled by *Elektroprivreda Srbije (EPS),* the state-owned electric power utility. As EU candidate country, Serbia has obliged itself to increase the share of renewable energy sources in the overall energy mix, from 21.2% in 2009 to 27% until 2020 (Ministry of Mining and Energy 2019a). This ambitious goal, together with other EU regulations and standards in the areas of energy efficiency, market liberalization, climate change mitigation, and environmental protection, has been increasingly difficult to reconcile with the long-entrenched interests, ideas, and norms surrounding the energy governance in Serbia.

The increase in energy efficiency and utilization of renewable energy sources have generally been slow but with some important differences across sectors both in terms of the actors involved and outcomes achieved. Whereas the developments in the power sector have seen the emerging role of few new domestic and foreign investors in the technologies such as wind power, small hydropower, and biogas, the energy transition efforts in the heating sector have mostly targeted the established actors: local energy suppliers and households. The least progress has been made in the transportation sector where little institutional and behavioral change has occurred. This chapter seeks to outline the dynamic processes and institutions behind the current energy governance in Serbia and to shed more light on the key factors, which affect stability and change in Serbia's energy development.

General Conditions of Energy Governance in Serbia: Legacies from the Past

Energy Mix and Path Dependence: Relying on Coal and Large Hydropower

One of the dominant traits of the Serbian energy system is its high dependency on domestically exploited coal for electricity supply. Serbia has large reserves of coal. Around 97% of coal reserves are in lignite, the least efficient and the most polluting type of coal (Ministry of Mining and Energy 2016a). Out of 8.88 billion tons of coal lignite reserves, 4.5 billion are located in Kosovo (Ministry of Mining and Energy 2016a), the former province of Serbia which self-declared independency in 2008 but has not been recognized by the Serbian authorities. Since 1999 and the ending of the military conflicts in Kosovo, Serbia has effectively lost the access and control over coal reserves in Kosovo (EPS n.d.). Still, even the remaining reserves of coal lignite on the Serbian territory are described in the Energy Development Strategy of Serbia as significant and as a "realistic basis for further long-term development of the energy sector in general and particularly for the electricity generation" (Ministry of Mining and Energy 2016b). Approximately two thirds of electricity generation capacities in Serbia are based on coal. In 2017, for instance, 73% of electricity production in Serbia was generated in coal power plants (see Fig. 1). The abundance of coal lignite as a relatively cheap domestic energy source combined with the strong state involvement in the production and use of coal have established the coal sector as the cornerstone of the national energy security and economic growth. Next to coal, the second main source of electricity is hydropower, mostly utilized in large hydropower plants. Overall, the electricity production in Serbia is remarkably concentrated in few large power production facilities. Out of 4,390 megawatt (MW) of the installed electric power in coal power plants, 2,817 MW is produced in the blocks A and B of the coal power plant *Nikola Tesla* while 913 MW is generated in two blocks of the coal power plant *Kostolac*. In addition, from 2,936 MW of the total capacity in hydropower, slightly less than a half (1,369 MW) is produced in the hydropower plants *Djerdap* 1 and 2 (EPS n.d.). The high concentration of energy production illustrates the magnitude of the challenge for the system to embrace more locally based and decentralized renewable energy systems. The extraction of coal and the operation of coal and hydro power plants is managed by the vertically structured state-owned electric power utility EPS. Both the hydropower and coal sectors are deeply embedded within the "socio-technical regime" (Geels 2004) populated by the

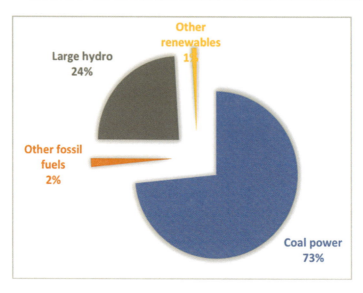

Fig. 1 Electricity production in Serbia by source in 2017. (Source: Based on Ministry of Energy and Mining 2016a)

established actors and their relations and beliefs spanning across the fields of policy, industry, science, labor, and consumers. An important feature of the regime is the regulated below-market electricity prices. Serbia has electricity prices which are far below the EU average and which rates are lower than in all EU members and candidates, except for Kosovo (Eurostat 2016).

The heating system is largely based on natural gas in the district heating systems and wooden biomass in households, which are not connected to the district heating systems. Although Serbia has some limited domestic production of natural gas, the largest share of natural gas is imported from Russia. Overall, Serbia imports 31% of energy to meet its energy needs, which indicates a modest energy dependency. Fifty-nine percent of the imported energy is oil and oil derivatives, natural gas 34%, and coal 10%. The structure of the domestic energy production, which is heavily based on fossil fuels, particularly coal, is provided in Fig. 2.

War Legacy and the Lack of Regional Energy Cooperation

The legacy of civil war, which followed the dissolution of Yugoslavia in the 1990s, continues to burden the regional cooperation in the Western Balkans. This has important implications for the cooperation in the area of energy infrastructure and trading. Cross-border policy coordination is crucial for developing a diversified and sustainable energy supply in the region. Optimal utilization of significant renewable energy potential in the region is particularly reliant on cross-border cooperation. Renewable power generation is often volatile and thus, cross-border

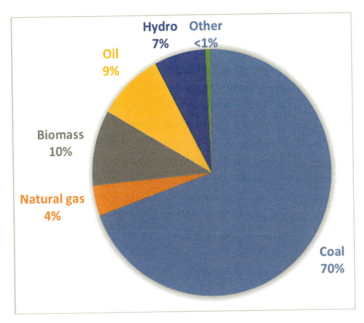

Fig. 2 Total energy production in Serbia in 2017. (Source: Based on Ministry of Energy and Mining 2016a)

inter-connectivity that can help balance renewable energy inputs into the grid are important. As hydropower potential is in several cases also located on the border between two countries, as in the case with the Drina River between Bosnia and Serbia, cooperation on infrastructure development and energy sharing and distribution are needed. A coordinated regional approach is not only important for achieving the energy goals of the Southern and Eastern European countries but also for the EU energy union as a whole. The legacy of conflicts and the damaged mutual trust have prompted national governments in the region to emphasize national energy security over regional cooperation. While the necessity of a coordinated regional response to energy challenges has been long acknowledged by major actors in the region and has been facilitate through the EU integration process, the concrete results have so far been mixed.

A particularly tensed relationship recently emerged between the Serbian power transmission system operator and its counter-apart in Kosovo (Energy Community Secretariat 2018a). Kosovo self-declared independence from Serbia in 2004 but the Serbian authorities have not recognized Kosovo as an independent state. Kosovo and Serbia are both members of the Energy Community that provides the framework for transposing the EU energy rules and standards into national legislation of the official EU candidates and neighboring countries. Serbia and Kosovo have failed to stabilize mutual relations in many areas including energy. The electricity systems in Kosovo and Serbia are deeply interlinked and there has been a long-standing dispute over production and distribution of electricity in Kosovo, particularly in the northern part, which has a majority of ethnic Serbian population. Due to the inability to find an agreement over the mutual responsibilities for supplying electricity and balancing the system, the Kosovo transmission system (KOSTT) has not been able to become a full member of the European Network of Transmission System Operators for Electricity (ENTSO-E). In its recent report, the Energy Community Secretariat has highlighted the dispute between Kosovo and Serbia as the main obstacle to the regional electricity cooperation (Energy Community Secretariat 2018b).

Energy Narratives

The current energy system in Serbia was largely built during the period of former Yugoslavia where large-scale energy projects and energy affordability were key to economic development, technological modernization, and industrialization of the country. Although Yugoslavia in its form ceased to exist in the beginning of the 1990s, the prevailing view among Serbian energy decision-makers which favors energy security and affordable energy prices in the form of large-scale centrally planned projects has hardly changed. In contrast to the past times of Yugoslavia when large and technologically advanced energy projects were expending to keep up with the rising economic growth, the government of Serbia confronted with the legacy of civil war and slow economic recovery has struggled to maintain the existing energy infrastructure, let alone to build new larger power capacities. Still, the dominant policy narrative stressing the importance of the existing domestic energy industry, energy security, and short-term affordability has survived. The EU integration process and the EU energy policy requirements have ensured that Serbian energy actors increasingly embrace the principles and narratives of environmental sustainability and market liberalization. Rather than causing a more paradigmatic change, however, the goals of environmental sustainability and renewable energy development have been added as a new "layer" (Howlett and Rayner 2007) to the existing energy policy approach. Serbian authorities have thus embraced the idea of renewable energy utilization in the official discourse while continuing to commit to the further use of domestic lignite. The narrative of civic participation and decentralization of the energy system by small-scale low-carbon energy technologies has remained absent from the mainstream political and public discourse on energy issues.

Political Institutions and Actors

The primary power and responsibility for energy policy lies within the Ministry of Energy and Mining. In 2008, the organizational unit for renewable energy sources was established as part of the energy department. The main task of this unit is to support the drafting and execution of renewable energy legislation. The renewable energy unit has little political weight and influence as all major decisions on renewable energy promotion are made at the level of the heads of the ministry

(Ćetković 2015a). Until 2012, there was operating an Energy Efficiency Agency of Serbia (EEAS). It performed an important role in implementing third-party funded projects and promoting energy efficiency and renewable energy initiatives at the local level. With the abolishment of the EEAS and its incorporation into the energy ministry, as part of the rationalization of the public administration, an important actor and a potential policy entrepreneur disappeared (Ćetković 2015a). The Energy Agency of Serbia is an important independent regulatory body which serves to secure a transparent functioning of the energy market. Although the Energy Agency has contributed to strengthening the enforcement of legal rules in the energy market, its work has also been influenced by domestic political pressures (Energy Community Secretariat 2018a).

Next to the national government and public sector authorities, state-owned energy utilities play a crucial role in the energy regime. The power sector is largely managed by the state-owned utility EPS. Although the electricity market is liberalized, 95% of it is still controlled by EPS due to the regulated low electricity prices. EPS suffers from poor economic and organizational management due to political and party influence. This influence negatively affects the professional standards of the staff recruitment and forces EPS to provide below-market electricity prices and tolerate non-payment of bills by some households and public utilities (Fiscal Council 2017a). The rationalization of EPS is a pressing issue often raised by international financial organizations, but it has been politically difficult to implement. The report of the Fiscal Council of Serbia for 2017 notes that EPS has been avoiding the overdue reform which hampers the productivity of the company and the overall economic trends in the country (Fiscal Council 2017a). As part of the market liberalization process, the transmission power system has been formally unbundled from electricity supply and is now operated by the separate but still fully state-owned company *Elektromreza Srbije* (EMS). The gas sector is managed by the state-owned utility *Srbijagas* which is also confronted with poor management and high financial losses mainly due to the inability to collect payments from public enterprises (Fiscal Council 2017a). In the oil sector, Serbia privatized the major oil company *Oil Industry of Serbia* (NIS) in 2008 by selling 51% shares of the company to the Russian gas giant *Gazprom*. A number of other public utilities, such as those in the areas of water and forest management, are also worthwhile mentioning due to their role in assessing the application and issuing permits for renewable energy projects, which use public waters or forest.

The experience of several countries highlights the important role of subnational governments as agents of change in the process of energy transition (Beermann and Tews 2015). Serbia is a unitary state but with the trend to delegate more political and economic power to local governments. In the area of energy policy, the powers of local governments are still limited and mostly confined to executing the administrative procedures and drafting local energy and spatial plans. Whereas in the electricity sector local governments exercise little influence, the Energy Law adopted in 2014 provides the opportunity to local governments to establish incentives schemes for local heating projects based on renewable energy sources and highly efficient co-generation (Serbian Parliament 2014). Local governments play an important role in establishing energy management capacities for the efficient use of energy and ensuring the implementation of energy efficiency measures, particularly in the building sector. Overall, the institutional space for local governments to shape energy development and induce a change by supporting alternative energy ideas and technologies is significantly constrained. This is not least because of the large financial problems, accumulated debts, and budgetary deficits, which are characteristic of many local governments in Serbia (Fiscal Council 2017b).

In a transitioning economy of Serbia, civil society has been increasingly vibrant but still weak to exercise pressure and contribute to formulating alternative energy policies. The actions of civil society groups have been most visible in the forms of protests against some local hydropower projects stressing their negative social and environmental effects. This has often caused the projects to be delayed or fully abandoned (Balkan Insight 2018).

Beyond the national boundaries, the EU institutions and policies have decisively shaped energy policy and planning in Serbia. The EU's influence has been mainly reflected in the set of regulations in the broader area of energy policy which Serbia has been obliged to adopt. Alongside the "stick" of conditionality in transposing EU laws, the EU institutions have also worked continuously with the Serbian authorities to provide financial and technical support in fulfilling the EU requirements and institutionalizing policy change (European Commission 2017). Next to the EU, other major foreign actors have also influenced energy developments in Serbia with a particularly important role of Russia and China. Russia has mainly been involved in the oil and gas sector in Serbia. Russia privatized the Oil Industry of Serbia in 2008 and continuous to be the dominant supplier of natural gas in Serbia. The Chinese interest in financing infrastructure projects in Serbia as part of its "Belt and Road" strategy has been of a more recent origin. In 2017, the construction of a new production unit of 350 MW in the largest lignite power plant in Serbia *Kostolac* was launched. The financing for the project is provided by the Chinese Export-Import Bank and the Chinese companies are also tasked with the project implementation. The Chinese investments in the state-controlled coal power sector in Serbia have been welcomed by the Serbian officials but have faced criticism given their environmental and climate change impact (Reuters 2017).

Coordination, Instruments, and Issues of Energy Transitions within a Multilevel Context

Drivers of Energy Transition

Despite the strong policy dependence and fossil-fuel technological "lock-in," there are multiple drivers of energy transition in Serbia. These drivers can be conceptualized following the classical multilevel perspective which differentiates among three main levels affecting sociotechnical systems: landscape, regime, and niche (Geels 2004). On the landscape level, the driving force of energy transition in Serbia has clearly been the EU and its climate and energy policies. The integration into the EU system has been one of the central strategic goals of all Serbian governments ever since the democratic change which took place in the country in 2000. In 2006, Serbia joined the Vienna-based Energy Community, which serves as a framework to enhance the creation of a common regional energy market and ensure the transposition of EU energy and climate policy into national legislation of the EU candidates and some neighboring countries. EU policies on energy market liberalization, regional energy cooperation, energy efficiency, renewable energy, and environmental sustainability had to gradually be incorporated into national laws and policy practice if Serbia was to progress in the EU accession process. It is thus no coincidence that Serbia and Montenegro, the two countries in the region which have made the largest progress in EU accession have also invested greatest efforts to formally comply with EU energy and climate policy (Energy Community Secretariat 2018a). The EU Renewable Energy Directive from 2009 has been particularly instrumental in facilitating the institutional capacity building and the creation of the policy framework in Serbia for fostering renewable energy utilization (Ćetković 2015a). Broader international climate agreements have also contributed to raising awareness and promoting a less carbon-intensive energy development in Serbia. Moreover, the declining costs of new renewable energy technologies will likely support the case for implementing new renewable energy projects in Serbia for pure economic reasons. On the other hand, other landscape-related factors such as sluggish economic growth, high public debt, and insufficient national governing capacities have contributed to delaying the necessary reforms towards the modernization and decarbonization of the energy system.

On the regime level, the inherited tensions and contradictions have become increasingly apparent. While coal and hydropower are likely to continue to play the dominant role in the future electricity mix, both energy technologies carry important challenges and opportunities for change. The extensive environmental pollution tied to the production and use of coal is becoming widely acknowledged among the decision-makers in Serbia and the costs of modernizing the existing coal power plants and building more efficient new coal plants are remarkable. The required investments in modernization of the existing large coal power plants are estimated to 634.5 million EUR in order to bring these facilities in line with the environmental requirements stipulated in the EU Directive on Large Combustion Plants (Ministry of Mining and Energy 2016b). This makes the financial calculation about the competitiveness of coal power production in Serbia increasingly complex and uncertain. The other key electricity source, hydropower, is highly dependent on weather conditions, which at times forces Serbia to resort to emergent electricity imports when rainfalls are scarce. Although Serbia's energy dependency is not dramatic, the country almost fully relies on the costly imports of oil and gas in the heating and transport sectors. This all signifies the importance of diversifying energy supply and possibly shifting the priority towards increasingly competitive and domestic renewable energy sources. Furthermore, the reversible hydropower plants in Serbia could technically provide a good match as a "battery" for expanding and balancing the electricity produced from intermittent renewable energy sources, particularly solar power and wind power.

On the niche level, little experimentation with new energy technologies can be noted. Some scientific capacities have been developed in the form of regional energy efficiency centers located at major technical universities across Serbia. This has strengthened the link between local energy planning and scientific and technical know-how (Ćetković 2014). However, as the general domestic industrial and innovation base is low and civil society weak, there is little domestic capacity and efforts for developing and adopting new low-carbon energy technologies and practices.

Strategies and Instruments of Energy Transition

The objectives of the Serbian energy policy are outlined in the Law on Energy and further specified in the documents such as national energy strategy and the program for its implementation. The Law on Energy adopted in late 2014 points out a range of long-term energy policy objectives including the security and reliability of the energy supply, liberalization of the electricity market, diversification of the electricity supply, and the promotion of renewable energy sources (Serbian Parliament 2014). In fact, the Law explicitly states in Article 65 that the utilization of renewable energy sources is in the interest of the country (Serbian Parliament 2014). It is interesting to note that the draft of the energy strategy through 2025 for the first time introduces the concept of "transition towards sustainable energy" as one of the key goals of the energy policy, next to the energy security and the introduction of market mechanisms into the energy system. Furthermore, the transition towards sustainable energy, according to the document, will be based on the domestic renewable energy sources and the implementation of "clean coal" technologies (Ministry of Mining and Energy 2016b). The emphasis on "clean coal" is related to the established domestic industries and considerable coal lignite reserves. The policy-makers in Serbia have thus adopted a strategic position to accommodate the demands for increasing the share of renewable energy sources while maintaining and even further expanding the use of coal. The Energy Development Strategy foresees that several below-300 MW coal power plants will be decommissioned by 2024 due to their age and low-efficiency. To replace these capacities, the Strategy envisages the construction of several new large coal power plants together with new large and small hydropower installations. The modest expansion of other new renewable energy facilities beyond the already accepted commitments for 2020 is also planned by the document. Although the Strategy operates with two different scenarios of the energy consumption growth, it is very likely that the construction of all suggested projects would lead to overcapacity with little room to export electricity in the already saturated regional market. This may cause higher competition among different technologies and the necessity for decision-makers to make strategic choices, particularly between renewable energy and coal.

In terms of regulatory policy instruments for steering energy development and supporting energy transition, Serbia has mainly relied on incorporating EU rules and standards such as the regulations on fuel quality, energy efficiency of buildings or environmental standards of large combustion plants. The formal transposition and compliance with these measures have been mixed. In the transportation sector, the regulatory instruments for fuel quality and sustainability criteria for biofuels have been either poorly enforced or not adopted. In energy efficiency, Serbia has actively drafted and transposed the EU regulations such as Energy Efficiency Directive and Energy Performance of Buildings Directive, although some level of noncompliance is still present (Energy Community Secretariat 2018a).

The economic incentives have been primarily used to foster the realization of renewable energy projects in the electricity sector. To that end, the Serbian government adopted the Feed-in Tariff (FiT) scheme in 2009 based on the provisions in the Energy Law from 2004. The FiT offers support to all renewable energy technologies at the guaranteed technology-specific price for the duration of 12 years. The implementation of FiT was difficult in the first years due to the lack of all supporting legislation leading to low investment security. In 2014, the new Law on Energy introduced important improvements for renewable energy investments. For instance, the status of *temporary privileged producer* was made available for all renewable energy technologies, not only for wind and solar as under the previous regulation (Serbian Parliament 2014). Another important novelty is that alongside legal entities also natural persons are able to acquire the status of renewable energy producer for the installed capacity of up to 30 KW (Serbian Parliament 2014). The FiT scheme from 2009 established the cap on wind and solar power projects eligible for support, to 450 MW and 5 MW, respectively. The revised support scheme in 2013 decreased the cap for wind energy to 350 MW by 2015 with an envisaged increase to 500 MW by 2020. The cap for solar was set to as little as 10 MW until 2020. The government clearly prioritized the established technologies such as hydropower and biomass at the expense of solar and wind which were perceived as expensive imported technologies (Ćetković 2015a). The FiT scheme so far had limited effects as only smaller projects in hydropower, solar and biogas have been realized. In 2016, a set of amendments to the FiT scheme was enacted to provide further regulatory certainty, particularly when it comes to larger wind power projects. With the approaching deadline for meeting the 2020 renewable energy targets and the slow progress achieved, the government has turned to the already in pipeline large wind energy investments for helping fulfil the target. The National Renewable Energy Action Plan has envisaged the construction of 1092 MW in renewable electricity capacities as the national target by 2020. By the end of 2018, only 1108 MW were installed under the existing FiT scheme (Ministry of Mining and Energy 2019a). During 2019, in efforts to narrow the gap to the 2020 target, Serbian authorities facilitated the completion of three large wind parks with the total installed capacity of 305 MW (Ministry of Mining and Energy 2019b). The Energy Community has criticized the FiT scheme in Serbia as inefficient and not aligned with the EU state aid guidelines, which requires EU members to shift their renewable energy support schemes towards market-based auctioning systems (Energy Community Secretariat 2018a).

In the heating sector, no national financial incentive for renewable energy sources has been established and the responsibility for decarbonizing the heating system has largely been left to local governments, energy utilities, and international development aid and financial institutions. An example of such efforts is the project for the development of the biomass market in Serbia which has been supported by the German government and German Development Bank (KfW) and which offers technical and financial assistance for converting local district heating systems from fossil-fuels to biomass (Bioenergy-Serbia 2014). The progress in meeting the sectoral renewable energy target for the heating sector has been behind the established interim targets (Ministry of Mining and Energy 2019a).

The Serbian government has made use of some soft governance instruments to facilitate the implementation of sustainable energy policies mostly supported by international organizations. An example is the set of guides for renewable energy investors published to increase awareness of the necessary administrative steps for realizing renewable energy projects (Ministry of Mining and Energy 2016c). The activities of foreign development agencies have also been directed towards awareness-raising and dissemination of knowledge and best practices on sustainable energy policies and technologies. The instruments aimed specifically at internalizing environmental costs have not yet been practiced in Serbia but this is set to change as the country gets more closely integrated into the EU system and the EU Emission Trading Scheme. However, Serbia, as an EU candidate country, still does not participate in the European Emission Trading Scheme (ETS) and so the energy production utilities in Serbia are not directly exposed to the emission limits and rising carbon prices under the ETS.

The polluter pays principle has been enshrined in the regulatory framework of Serbia but environmental taxes have been either poorly enforced or have been imposed for the sole purpose of revenue raising. Serbia has the highest shares of revenues from environmental taxes in the overall government revenues from taxes and social contributions among the EU members and candidate countries amounting to 11.7%. Out of all environmental taxes, energy taxes account for 84.8% in Serbia, the highest rate among the EU members and candidates (Eurostat 2018). This signifies the importance of the energy sector for the public budget in Serbia. At the same time, the revenues from the taxes on pollution and resource use account for only 4.9% and 1.7% of total revenues from environmental taxes, respectively (Statistical Office of the Republic of Serbia 2018).

Coordination Mechanisms and Multi-Level Governance

The coordination of increasingly complex energy governance in Serbia has proven to be a difficult task given the considerable misfit (Börzel and Risse 2003) between the rising external expectations and demands, on the one hand, and the available governing capacity, on the other. In terms of horizontal coordination, energy policy-making is highly centralized and concentrated in the Ministry of Energy and Infrastructure. The concentration of decision-making does not imply policy coherence and effective policy implementation given the cross-sectoral character of most energy policy measures. Unlike the case in many countries where energy departments have increasingly been institutionally linked to the departments of economy, environment, or climate, the institutional structure of the Serbian Energy and Mining

Ministry depicts the prevailing approach to energy as a technical and infrastructural issue of extraction and exploitation. The governing capacity of the energy ministry is hampered by frequent personal changes at the head of the ministry. In the past decade (2007–2017), the head of the ministry changed on five occasions. The coordination is also negatively affected by the practice of arranging some large bi-lateral energy projects at the government level with little involvement of the energy ministry. The example is the agreement from 2011 with the Italian government to construct hydropower plants in Serbia for the purpose of exporting renewable electricity to Italy. This agreement was drafted without the necessary participation of the energy ministry and renewable energy unit (Ćetković 2015a). The Serbian government cabinet is rather fragmented and the Ministry of Environment and Spatial Planning and other relevant ministries have not been significantly involved in energy policy planning (Ćetković 2015a).

Vertically, the governance structure is even more complex comprising different governance levels, including the EU, central government, and regional and local authorities. Each level is populated by multiple and often only loosely coordinated actors. The EU-level institutions, particularly the European Commission and the Energy Community, have played a major role in shaping Serbian energy governance priorities, providing policy guidelines and monitoring the policy implementation. This has not been a one-way street; however, as the Serbian government secured the right to filter to some extent the external impulses and so influence the actual character and pace of policy change. For instance, Serbia was free to decide on the preferred policy instrument for promoting renewable energy sources and the specific renewable energy technologies it plans to support. The decision on whether to rely on large-scale renewable energy projects or community-owned bottom-up initiatives in fulfilling national renewable energy targets was also left to the national government. Serbia authorities have prioritized the established technologies such as hydropower, at the expense of other technologies such as solar energy. Furthermore, the domestic and foreign investors with closer ties to the government, as illustrated for instance in wind energy projects (Ćetković 2015b), have gained the upper hand in benefiting from the government support. The efforts of the high-level EU institutions have been accompanied by more concrete supporting programs in the area of capacity building and financing, implemented by EU-related institutions such as the European Bank for Development and Reconstruction, and development agencies from EU member states. These activities have targeted both national and particularly local government actors. The public utilities in the energy sector, water, and forest management and their regional and local branches have been very important in the process of issuing necessary permits for the development of renewable energy projects in particular. Given the lack of coordination capacity and even political will, the administrative procedures for new energy projects have typically been long and insufficiently transparent. This created the situation where renewable energy projects could be easily blocked or substantially delayed at different stages of project development (Ćetković 2015a; Energy Community Secretariat 2018a). The coordination between central and local government has also been insufficient causing the problems in implementation and local-ownership of the policy measures designed at the national level. The lack of human resources and know how at the local level has slowed-down the development and realization of many energy policy measures, particularly in enhancing energy efficiency of buildings (Serbian Government 2016).

Outcomes, Challenges, and Prospects of Energy Governance

The governance towards more sustainable energy development in Serbia has evolved into a dynamic and complex process involving an increasing number of actors and institutions. The old energy regime has not been disturbed but the newly added layers of policies, goals, and institutions planting the seed of potential mid- and long-term change. Driven by the obligations from the EU accession process, Serbia has invested efforts to transpose the EU energy and climate policy packages into national legislation. This has empowered new actors and ideas but more substantial policy shifts have been constrained by the closed policy-making structure in the energy field, lack of administrative capacity, and the unfavorable broader political economic factors. As a result, the progress in developing renewable energy sources has been slow and the emphasis has been placed on hydropower where the state-owned power utility EPS has expertise as well as on large wind power plants. In 2018, Serbia was not on track to meet its 27% renewable energy target by 2020, although several wind power projects have been granted political support recently to narrow the gap (European Commission 2018; Balkan Green Energy News 2018). In the transport sector, the share of biofuels has been virtually zero and Serbia is likely to miss the adopted target of reaching the share of 10% of biofuels in the transportation sector by 2020 (Ministry of Mining and Energy 2019a). The improvements in energy efficiency have been made but the vast potential in this area has remained largely untapped and the achievement of the national target of energy savings of 9% by 2018 compared to 2008 is uncertain (Serbian Government 2016; European Commission 2018).

The dependent-market features (Nölke and Vliegenhart 2009) of the Serbian economy such as high-dependence on foreign capital and investors, clientelism, and general lack of state capacity to steer economic processes, cheap labor, weak civil society, and poor domestic industrial and innovation base offer key explanatory factors for the evolving energy transition pathway. The demands for more sustainable energy policy planning have clashed with the economic growth model based on cheap production inputs (energy, labor), foreign direct investments, and the lack of governing capacity to involve and coordinate actors from industry, finance, science, and civil society. Dolata (2009) identifies several facilitating factors that make the sociotechnological regimes adaptable to new technologies including: high intensity of innovation and market competition, transformation-supporting industry structures, horizontally structured and collaboratively embedded focal actors, and institutionalized mechanisms of transfer between academia and industry. None of these factors have been sufficiently present in the Serbian energy system and the broader political-economic environment. In consequence, the energy transition pressures have been resisted to the highest possible extent as a threat to the economic model and established interests. Where the change was difficult to avoid, such as in meeting national renewable electricity targets, the process evolved along the established power structures to benefit the influential domestic and foreign actors with little involvement of domestic knowledge and bottom-up initiatives from the society.

The main challenge in the energy sector in Serbia remains to overcome the dysfunctional elements in the sectoral and national political-economic context. This should be necessary to accelerate the transition towards a more sustainable system of energy production and consumption, while at the same time ensuring a high level of domestic ownership in this process in terms of value creation, technological modernization, and civic participation (Ćetković 2015b). This is primarily the question of adequate governance design but also of supportive factors, which should facilitate the emergence of more effective and just governance arrangements. The insufficient power of subnational governments as niches for the experimentation with new low-carbon energy technologies, lack of a strong Green Party in the parliament, and the fact that the Serbian political environment has been burdened by the Kosovo conflict and more recently the austerity measures, do not provide a favorable environment for sustainable energy governance. On the other hand, with the expanding EU energy and climate policies causing a reduction in the costs of renewable energy technologies and an increase in CO_2 prices, the decarbonization and liberalization of the energy sector in Serbia appear to be only a matter of time. The exact scope and pace of energy transformation in Serbia will be conditioned on a number of factors, including those discussed in this chapter.

Cross-References

► Energy Governance in Europe: Introduction
► European Union Energy Policy: A Discourse Perspective
► Transition of Energy Systems: Patterns of Stability and Change

References

Balkan Green Energy News. (2018). Prve aukcije za vetroparkove i solarne elektrane u drugoj polovini 2019. godine (First auctions for wind parks and solar plants in the second half of 2019). Retrieved from: https://balkangreenenergynews.com/rs/prve-aukcije-za-vetroparkove-i-solarne-elektrane-u-drugoj-polovini-2019-godine/. Accessed 1 Oct 2018.

Balkan Insight. (2018). Serbia's greens mobilize against threat to mountain rivers. Retrieved from: http://www.balkaninsight.com/en/article/serbia-s-greens-mobilise-against-threat-to-mountain-rivers-09-17-2018. Accessed 1 Oct 2018.

Beermann, J., & Tews, K. (2015). *Preserving decentralised laboratories for experimentation under adverse framework conditions – Why local initiatives as a driving force for Germany's renewable energy expansion must reinvent themselves*. Berlin: Forschungszentrum für Umweltpolitik.

Bioenergy-Serbia. (2014). About the programme. Retreived from: http://www.bioenergy-serbia.rs/index.php/en/about-us

Börzel, T. A., & Risse, T. (2003). Conceptualising the domestic impact of Europe. In K. Featherstone & C. Radaelli (Eds.), *The politics of Europeanisation*. Oxford: Oxford University Press.

Ćetković, S. (2014). *Governing the green economy in Serbia: Promises and pitfalls in the renewable electricity and organic farming sectors*. Doctoral dissertation, FU Berlin, Berlin.

Ćetković, S. (2015a). Policy capacity for promoting green sectors reconsidered: Lessons from the renewable electricity and organic farming sectors in Serbia. *Journal of Environmental Policy & Planning, 17*(1), 65–83.

Ćetković, S. (2015b). The challenge of promoting green sectors in Serbia: Between international demands, national controversies and sectoral struggles. In N. Papakostas & N. Passamitros (Eds.), *An agenda for the Western Balkans: From elite politics to social sustainability* (pp. 71–95). Stuttgart: Ibidem Verlag.

Dolata, U. (2009). Technological innovations and sectoral change transformative capacity, adaptability, patterns of change: An analytical framework. *Research Policy, 38*(6), 1066–1076.

Energy Community Secretariat. (2018a). *Annual implementation report*. Vienna: Energy Community.

Energy Community Secretariat. (2018b). WB6 electricity monitoring report. Retrieved from: https://www.energy-community.org/dam/jcr:b88fc717-9a34-43e2-be0d-b6a19456194c/ECS_WB6_EL_062018.pdf. Accessed 1 Oct 2018. b6a19456194c/ECS_WB6_EL_062018.pdf

EPS. (n.d.). *Production capacity*. Retrieved from: http://www.eps.rs/en/poslovanje-ee/Pages/Kapaciteti-ElEn.aspx. Accessed 1 Oct 2018.

European Commission. (2017). Serbia: EU support to the energy sector. Retrieved from: https://ec.europa.eu/neighbourhood-enlargement/sites/near/files/2017-040500.06-eu_support_to_the_energy_sector.pdf. Accessed 1 Oct 2018.

European Commission. (2018). Serbia 2018 Report. Retrieved from: https://ec.europa.eu/neighbourhood-enlargement/sites/near/files/20180417-serbia-report.pdf. Accessed 1 Oct 2018.

Eurostat. (2016). Electricity prices for household consumers, second half 2015. Retrieved from http://ec.europa.eu/eurostat/statistics-explained/index.php/File:Electricity_prices_for_household_consumers,_second_half_2015_(^{1})_(EUR_per_kWh)_YB16.png. Accessed 1 Oct 2018.

Eurostat. (2018). Environmental tax statistics. Retrieved from: https://ec.europa.eu/eurostat/statistics-explained/index.php/Environmental_tax_statistics. Accessed 1 Oct 2018.

Fiscal Council. (2017a). Fiscal trends in 2017 and recommendations for 2018. Retrieved from http://www.fiskalnisavet.rs/doc/eng/Summary%202017.pdf. Accessed 1 Oct 2018.

Fiscal Council. (2017b). Local public finances: Issues, risks and recommendaitons. Retrieved from: http://www.fiskalnisavet.rs/doc/eng/Summary_%20Local%20public%20finances%20-%20problems%20risks%20and%20reccomendations%20(2017).pdf. Accessed 1 Oct 2018.

Geels, F. W. (2004). From sectoral systems of innovation to socio-technical systems – Insights about dynamics and change from sociology and institutional theory. *Research Policy, 33*(6–7), 897–920.

Howlett and Rayner. (2007). Design principles for policy mixes: Cohesion and coherence in 'new governance arrangements'. *Policy and Society, 26*(4), 1–18.

Ministry of Energy and Mining. (2016a). *Energy balance of Serbia for 2017*. Retrieved from: http://www.mre.gov.rs/doc/efikasnost-izvori/EN%20BILANS%20ZA%202017%2012.12.2016.pdf. Accessed 1 Oct 2018.

Ministry of Mining and Energy. (2016b). E*nergy development strategy of Serbia until 2025 with the view to 2030*. Retrieved from: http://www.mre.gov.rs/doc/efikasnost-izvori/23.06.02016%20ENERGY%20SECTOR%20DEVELOPMENT%20STRATEGY%20OF%20THE%20REPUBLIC%20OF%20SERBIA.pdf. Accessed 1 Oct 2018.

Ministry of Mining and Energy. (2016c). Investors' guide for projects relating to renewable energy sources: Retrieved from: https://www.mre.gov.rs/doc/efikasnost-izvori/Guide%20RES%202016%20A4.pdf. Accessed 1 Oct 2018.

Ministry of Mining and Energy. (2019a). *Renewable energy action plan implementation progress*. Retrieved from: https://author.energy-community.org/enc-author-prd/dam/jcr:dbbb73d5-93b3-4c0a-bad2-dafa49b0e861/RS_Progress_RE_2017.pdf. Accessed 29 Nov 2019.

Ministry of Mining and Energy. (2019b). Renewable energy registry. Retrieved from: https://www.mre.gov.rs/doc/registar-291119.html. Accessed 29 Nov 2019.

Nölke, A., & Vliegenthart, A. (2009). Enlarging the varieties of capitalism: The emergence of dependent market economies in east Central Europe. *World Politics, 61*(4), 670–702.

Reuters. (2017). Balkan push for new coal-fired plants raises environmental concerns. Retreived from: https://www.reuters.com/article/us-serbia-energy-coal/balkan-push-for-new-coal-fired-plants-raises-environmental-concerns-idUSKBN1572G7. Accessed 1 Oct 2018.

Serbian Government. (2016). Third National Energy Efficiency Action Plan for the Period until 2018. Retrieved from http://www.mre.gov.rs/doc/efikasnost-izvori/efikasnost/Treci_akcioni_plan_za_energetsku_efikasnost_Republike_Srbije_za_period_do_2018_godine.pdf. Accessed 1 Oct 2018.

Serbian Parliament. (2014). *Law on energy.* Retrieved from: https://www.aers.rs/FILES/Zakoni/Eng/Zakon%20o%20energetici_57-11.pdf. Accessed 1 Oct 2018.

Statistical Office of the Republic of Serbia. (2018). Environmental taxes 2016. Retrieved from: http://www.stat.gov.rs/en-us/vesti/20181009-porezi-u-oblasti-životne-sredine-2016/. Accessed 1 Oct 2018.

Energy Governance in Slovakia

42

Matúš Mišík and Veronika Oravcová

Contents

Introduction	1056
General Conditions of Energy Governance in Slovakia	1057
Past Legacies	1057
Composition of the Energy Mix	1061
Discourse on Energy Issues	1062
Coordination, Instruments, and Issues of Slovak Energy Transition	1064
Drivers of Energy Transition	1064
Nuclear Decommissioning	1064
Renewable Sources of Energy	1065
Coal Phase-Out	1066
Energy Efficiency	1069
Electromobility	1070
Political Actors and Policy Coordination	1071
Outcomes, Challenges, and Prospects for Energy Governance	1076
Cross-References	1078
References	1079

Abstract

This chapter examines the governance of energy policy in the Slovak Republic, focusing on nuclear energy and renewables as the main domestic energy sources in a country dependent on fossil fuels import. Slovak energy policy experienced a significant change towards energy security prioritization after the 2009 gas crisis, which left the country without natural gas supplies for over 2 weeks. The chapter argues that external factors, especially the crisis and EU membership, have had the main impact on Slovak energy policy governance, although support for nuclear energy is rooted in domestic energy policy preferences connected to energy security, which still creates the backbone of energy policy discourse.

M. Mišík (✉) · V. Oravcová
Department of Political Science, Comenius University in Bratislava, Bratislava, Slovakia
e-mail: matus.misik@uniba.sk; veronika.oravcova@uniba.sk

© Springer Nature Switzerland AG 2022
M. Knodt, J. Kemmerzell (eds.), *Handbook of Energy Governance in Europe*,
https://doi.org/10.1007/978-3-030-43250-8_27

The Slovak government considers nuclear energy to be a significant part of energy transition due to its low carbon footprint, while domestic coal is currently being phased-out due to concerns related to climate issues.

Keywords

Energy security · Nuclear energy · Coal phase-out · Nuclear decommissioning · Feed-in tariffs

Introduction

This chapter examines the governance of energy policy in the Slovak Republic, its main characteristics, and challenges. The country's membership in the European Union (EU) and its high energy import dependency (the country has almost no domestic fossil fuels) are the main factors influencing its energy policy and governance. As one of the countries most severely hit by the 2009 natural gas crisis (Feklyunina 2012), energy security is foremost among the Slovak government's priorities despite the significant improvements made in this area during the last decade (Mišík 2019). Route diversification has been considered the best way to prevent similar crisis and the post-2009 activities in this area resulted in the development of reverse flows with Austria and the Czech Republic, as well as the building of new interconnectors with Hungary (already being upgraded) and Poland (currently under construction). EU support in the form of access to funds – specifically, the European Energy Programme for Recovery and later the Connecting Europe Facility (via the Projects of Common Interest list) – has contributed to the materialization of all of these projects. EU funds have played a crucial role in improving the Slovak energy infrastructure, as well as the energy networks of other Central and Eastern European countries (Oravcová and Mišík 2018).

Nuclear energy holds a crucial position within Slovak energy policy and the government is very supportive of its further development. There are currently four reactors within two nuclear power plants (NPP) that generate more than half of all electricity produced in the country (see Table 1). Two more reactors are currently being finalized (Mochovce 3 and 4) and the government has been flip-flopping on the idea of developing (up to two) new sites for nuclear facilities. In contrast, renewable energy sources enjoy much less support: the recent decrease of their share in the energy mix has brought Slovakia's ability to reach its 2020 goal of 14% renewables share in the mix set within the 2009 Renewable Directive into question. While domestic coal is still supported for energy security reasons, the 2019 decision to stop subsidizing electricity generation from domestic low-quality lignite after 2023 will have a positive impact on Slovak climate policy.

The Slovak energy governance is closely interconnected with EU policies, and there are only very few areas that are not guided by the Community rules; the nuclear sector (on which there is no unity within the EU) is a prime example. The state does not have a dominant position within the energy market since the main companies

Table 1 Nuclear reactors in Slovakia

Name	Type	Installed capacity (MWe)	In operation since	Shut down
Bohunice A1	HWGCR	110	1972	1979
Bohunice V1-1	VVER 440/230	440	1978	2006
Bohunice V1-2	VVER 440/230	440	1980	2008
Bohunice V2-1	VVER 440/213	505	1984	2044[a]
Bohunice V2-2	VVER 440/213	505	1985	2045[a]
Mochovce 1	VVER 440/213	470	1998	2058[a]
Mochovce 2	VVER 440/213	470	1999	2060[a]
Mochovce 3	VVER 440/213	440	2020[b]	N/A
Mochovce 4	VVER 440/213	440	2021[b]	N/A

Source: IAEA (2020)
Note: [a]Estimated
[b]Planned date of commencement

were (at least partially) privatized during the 1990s and 2000s. The government gained back full control over the dominant gas company Slovenský plynárenský priemysel, a.s. (SPP), in 2014. However, this translates into only limited control over a liberalized and unbundled market, although governmental interventions into the company's price policy have been repeatedly criticized by the other market players. The energy market regulator (Regulatory Office for Network Industries) was also accused of not being independent and following governmental policies (Szalai 2019), although the government created after 2020 general elections aims to improve the Office's independence.

General Conditions of Energy Governance in Slovakia

Past Legacies

After a peaceful dissolution of the federal Czechoslovak state during the so-called "velvet divorce," Slovakia became an independent state on 1 January 1993 (Hilde 1999). With the exception of the Second World War period (1938–1945), the common Czechoslovak state lasted since 1918, with the Slovak energy policy (and infrastructure) being developed as part of the common state's energy policy. During the Communist regime (1948–1989), Czechoslovakia was one of the satellite states of the Soviet Union and both its politics and individual policies were thus closely monitored (and guided) by Moscow. This period left many legacies in the energy policy area as the Soviet Union was not only the sole supplier of natural gas and oil but also the provider of nuclear technology. These legacies are visible especially in the case of nuclear technology, as even the two units at the Mochovce nuclear power plant (Units 3 and 4) which are currently being finalized are based on upgraded Russian technology (VVER 440 reactors), similar to the rest of the existing reactors in Slovakia. The Slovak transmission system was also developed during the Communist period when the Soviet Union built magistral natural gas and oil pipelines (Brotherhood and Druzhba) running through Czechoslovakia to western European countries, including Austria, Germany, and Italy (Högselius 2013). Czechoslovakia was chosen because of the possibility to develop the transmission network by scaling up the existing transit infrastructure and the closeness of Austrian natural gas infrastructure to Slovak borders (Perović 2017). Although Slovakia still imports most of the natural gas and oil from the Russian Federation, a diversification process took place, focusing on enabling access to alternative supplies during flow interruptions. This agenda was triggered by the gas crisis of January 2009 which highlighted the nonexistent route diversification of natural gas supply and the reliance of the Slovak natural gas market on a single external supplier (Gazprom).

Therefore, the gas crisis is, together with the EU membership, one on the main factors shaping the current Slovak energy policy and governance. Slovakia became an EU member state in 2004, after catching up with the rest of the candidates from Central and Eastern Europe in the accession negotiations at the end of the 1990s, and concluding membership negotiations in record time (Pridham 2008). Energy policy became one of the main issues during the accession negotiation as the EU requested Slovakia to shut down its two oldest reactors: Units 1 and 2 at Jaslovské Bohunice (the so-called V1) NPP. These reactors – type VVER 400, model 230 – were based on Soviet technology. A similar requirement also concerned Bulgarian and Lithuanian NPPs (Kozloduy and Ignalina), the latter of which has a different type of reactor (similar to the one used in Chernobyl NPP). Although these reactors underwent modernization during the second half of 1990s, the international community and the EU considered them non-upgradeable to western security standards. This fact was often mentioned by those who criticized the then incumbent Slovak government led by Mikuláš Dzurinda, which in 1999 adopted the decision (Government of the Slovak Republic 1999) to shut down the two reactors at the end of 2006 and 2008, thus fulfilling the Commission's requirement (Ivanov 2008).

This decision impacted the country's electricity production as nuclear has been responsible for more than half of all electricity production and a positive Slovak electricity balance already since the 1990s (when the first and second reactors at Mochovce NPP were commenced; see Fig. 1). As a result, the country was no longer self-sufficient in electricity production after 2006, a situation perceived as an energy security problem (Ministry of Economy 2008). Following the shutdown, the V1 NPP entered the decommissioning phase. This created significant costs that have been covered primarily from the funds pledged by the EU and its member states during the accession negotiation (JAVYS 2018).

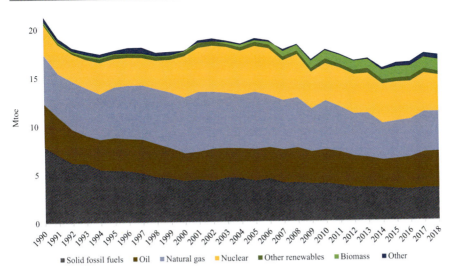

Fig. 1 Gross energy consumption. (Source: Eurostat 2020)

Nuclear also became a significant issue for the country during the 2009 gas crisis, when the Slovak government considered restarting the then recently shutdown second reactor at Jaslovské Bohunice V1 NPP. The government claimed that the changes in electricity generation caused by the closure of the reactor, coupled with the unavailability of natural gas for electricity generation, could cause problems with electricity grid balancing, which, in turn, could only be prevented by restarting the reactor (Sme 2009). The Commission assumed a very negative position towards the proposed step and the reactor was ultimately not restarted (Euractiv 2009). At the very beginning of 2009, Slovakia did not have access to any gas supplies for more than 2 weeks; this was the result of the cut-off of Russian gas transit via the Brotherhood pipeline, which, at the time, was the only external source of natural gas for the import-dependent country (Mišík 2019). Minimal domestic production, underground storage designed for supporting transit rather than providing emergency services, and the one-directional transit pipeline design (from east to west) were not able to replace the missing supplies from Russia and were responsible for the harsh impact of the event on the Slovak economy. Consequently, Slovakia was (together with Bulgaria) one of the countries most severely hit by the crisis, an experience which led to energy security taking precedence among national priorities in the following period.

Slovakia has a tradition of fossil fuel extraction. In addition to brown coal (lignite) extraction, the country has developed a natural gas and oil industry; however, it is fairly small and accounts for only a minimal share of domestic consumption (see the following section). The coal industry underwent an important shift during the three decades following the fall of Communism in 1989. The industry shrank significantly, its main center remaining in the Horná Nitra region, approximately 150 km north of Bratislava, the country' capital. Following mergers and a series of mine closures, Hornonitrianske bane Prievidza, a.s. (HBP), became the only functioning mining company in Slovakia and sole producer of coal (lignite) in 2016. A mine in the southern part of the country near the city of Veľký Krtíš named Baňa Dolina, a.s., stopped operating in 2015, while another mine, Baňa Čáry, a.s., was bought by HBP in 2016. This development corresponded with a significant decrease in coal production. While lignite production in Slovakia at the beginning of the 1990s was 1,397 ktoe per year, it was only 366 ktoe in 2018 (IEA 2019). Domestically produced coal was utilized in both electricity production and heating. However, strengthening the emission limits in connection with increased environmental awareness, the wide introduction of natural gas at the beginning of the 1990s (Slovakia has one of the densest natural gas distribution networks in Europe) and low gas prices during this period led to the decrease in the use of coal for electricity generation purposes, and a shift from coal to natural gas in residential and district heating. Domestically produced coal has never covered all the needs of Slovak economy since only lignite is extracted, while the country's industry – especially steel manufacturing – also necessitates hard coal. A large share of coal is therefore supplied from abroad. More than two-thirds of coal used in Slovakia is imported, with the Russian Federation, the Czech Republic, Poland, and the USA being the four main current suppliers.

Renewable sources of energy have traditionally been represented by hydropower, which has been developed on the longest Slovak River Váh as a way to power the nascent heavy industry (arms industry and metallurgy) since the 1950s. In 1977, a bilateral agreement was signed with Hungary to develop a system of two huge, mutually interconnected dams on the River Danube. These were supposed to not only provide further generation capacity, but also regulate the Danube, known at the time for its spring flooding. While Slovakia constructed its part (Gabčíkovo hydropower plant), Hungary did not build the dam on its territory (at Nagymaros); this led to a lawsuit taken to the International Court of Justice in Hague in 1997. Although the ruling stated that the Hungarian side had to build the dam to honor its obligations defined by the bilateral agreement, the project was not constructed. However, the incident left a mark on Slovak-Hungarian relations, already plagued by nationalism during the 1990s. Other types of renewables had only had a minimal share in the Slovak energy mix until the country became an EU member co-responsible for the Union's climate and energy goals, including the 2020 and 2030 targets. However, the support schemes established in the 2009 law on renewables in the form of feed-in tariffs (FiT) were set too high and did not reflect the situation in the photovoltaic industry. A very high level of subsidies and high anticipated returns on investment also attracted actors from non-energy sectors, some of them with questionable backgrounds (Krajanová 2018). This led to a sharp turn in the country's renewable policy and abandonment of the FiT support scheme already in 2011. It was not until 2018 that the decision to scale up the support for renewables was made, although with a different type of subsidies in the form of a feed-in premium option (Ministry of Economy 2020).

Composition of the Energy Mix

The structure of the Slovak energy mix has changed over time with nuclear energy gaining dominant position during the late 1990s and early 2000s, when altogether six reactors in two NPPs were active (between 1999 and 2006; see Table 1). At the same time, the share of coal declined, although the sharp decline in domestic production (of lignite) was replaced by import. The role of natural gas was most dominant during the 1990s, when its position in heating was strengthened thanks to a significant improvement of the distribution network and subsequent increase in the share of gas in heating; the subsidized price of natural gas also contributed to its popularity within this sector. Since the mid-2000s, the share of natural gas has been declining. The role of oil stayed almost the same since the early 1990s, while the share of renewables (especially biomass) has been on the increase since mid-2000s (see Fig. 1).

Two key characteristics of the Slovak energy mix are high supply dependency and a very high share of nuclear in electricity production (the second highest share of nuclear in the electricity mix in the world after France). The total primary energy supply in 2017 was 17.0 million of ton equivalent (Mtoe), which is a decline of 4.8% in comparison to 2007. Nuclear had the biggest share in the primary energy supply (23.6%), followed by different types of fossil fuels (natural gas 22.9%, oil 21.8%, and coal 19.6%). Renewable energy sources (together with waste) amounted for 10.6% of the total primary energy supply, while electricity imports were responsible for 1.5% of the total primary energy supply (IEA 2018). Energy production in Slovakia amounted to only 6.7 Mtoe in 2017, which required an import of 10.3 Mtoe of energy from abroad. There is a small domestic production of oil and natural gas, but it only accounts for approximately 2% of the total supply, so the country relies on supplies from abroad. The Russian Federation is the main source for both types of fossil fuels, as well as the biggest external supplier of coal.

The main domestic source of energy is nuclear, which supplied 60.1% of energy produced in Slovakia in 2017 (IEA 2018). Slovak nuclear power plants were responsible for 15.1 TWh out of 26.4 TWh of electricity produced in Slovakia in 2017. This means that nuclear energy accounted for 57% of the overall electricity generation within the country (IEA 2018). Two new reactors in Mochovce (Units 3 and 4) that are close to completion will increase the production by another approximately 7 TWh a year what will make Slovakia the world leader in the share of nuclear in electricity production. The Units were supposed to be finalized – after almost a decade of delays – in 2020 and 2021 respectively, however, in June 2020, when this text was finalized, it was already clear that the Covid-19 pandemic will have – at that time unknown – impact on these deadlines.

Renewables – including waste (biofuels, hydropower, and solar energy) – provided 27% of domestic electricity production in 2017. There is almost no wind energy in the country: there are only two sites (in operation since 2003 and 2004) with five turbines in the western part, with total installed capacity of less than 3 MW

(Greenenergy Slovakia 2020). Greater potential lies in geothermal energy, particularly for the heating sector. Together with oil and natural gas, coal (especially hard coal which is not mined in Slovakia) is imported in large qualities from abroad to fuel predominantly (steel) industry, as well as the thermal coal-fired power plant in eastern Slovakia (Elektrárne Vojany).

Discourse on Energy Issues

Ever since the 2009 natural gas crisis left the country without natural gas supplies for more than 2 weeks, energy security dominated the Slovak energy policy discourse (Mišík 2019). The previous energy policy discourse was much less intensive, with issues other than energy policy dominating the country's political discourse. Considering the nature of the pre-1989 Communist regime, we cannot talk about a real political discourse during the second half of twentieth century. Consequently, the Slovak energy discourse can only be traced back to the beginning of 1990s, when the discourse concerned mainly the construction of the Gabčíkovo hydropower plant and Mochovce NPP (Units 1 and 2). The construction of the latter was interrupted at the beginning of 1990s, after the fall of the Communist regime and the consequent political and economic changes. This was followed by a discussion on building two additional nuclear units at the same location (Mochovce NPP Units 3 and 4) during the 2000s. However, these discussions had an important political dimension and were thus more connected to the incumbent government's ideological stances and political issues (preference for nuclear) than to the examination of the different energy policy options and priorities. Moreover, neither of these two discourses were as widely spread and complex as the one on energy security that emerged after the gas crisis. Energy security was given precedence by the Slovak government in the early 2009, in the aftermath of the biggest natural gas supply crisis the country has ever faced (Mišík 2015). Most of the activities in the energy policy area were connected to security, a dimension that had repeatedly been used as an argument for supporting particular policy choices. The energy security discourse in Slovakia encompasses several aspects connected to energy transit (especially natural gas), nuclear power, and (until recently) coal.

Nuclear power is part of the Slovak energy security discourse as it is considered to be a domestic source of energy that improves the country's energy security, in spite of the fact that all nuclear fuel is imported from the same provider as all other types of energy – Russia. Examining the Slovak media discourse since the 2009 gas crisis, Kratochvíl and Mišík (2020) argue that it is characterized by a perceived unreliability of the external environment and presents nuclear energy as the most appropriate response to energy security challenges. In addition to being a domestic source of energy, nuclear is discursively constructed as "green" energy which contributes to the country's climate goals. For example, when Prime Minister Peter Pellegrini confirmed Slovakia's commitment to becoming a carbon-neutral economy by 2050, he stressed the importance of nuclear as a carbon-free source of energy (Government of the Slovak Republic 2019b). Interestingly enough, wide discussions among decision-makers and society on deep geological repository of spent nuclear waste have not yet taken place.

Slovakia is an important transit country for Russian natural gas and oil as two of Russia's main pipelines – Brotherhood and Druzhba – run via Slovak territory further to the west. The natural gas transit system is especially well-developed, with the capacity of the Brotherhood pipeline of up to 100 billion cubic meters (bcm) a year. Although its utilization is currently much smaller (64 bcm in 2017; Eustream 2019), the 2019 agreement between the Russian Gazprom and the Ukrainian Naftogaz secured transit via the pipeline for another 5 years (Soldatkin and Zinets 2019). The Slovak government considers transit to be a safeguard of energy security, which is why the negotiations leading to the aforementioned transit agreement were followed very closely. This argument is based on the assumption that the country is not only a business partner but also a transit one, and that playing both these roles protects Slovakia from a cut-off of supplies as it improves its position vis-à-vis the supplier (i.e., the Russian Federation). Moreover, the Slovak government used a similar line of argumentation to back up the Eastring pipeline project, which was developed as an alternative to the current transit situation, although a critical analysis claims that the project's main purpose is to keep the gas transit volumes – and thus also revenues – as high as possible (Mišík and Nosko 2017).

Domestic coal has also been presented as an energy source that decreases dependency on energy supplies from abroad and thus improves the country's energy security. The Slovak government has repeatedly used this argument to support the extraction of domestic, low-quality, and economically unviable lignite – predominantly used for electricity generation purposes (see below) – in the Horná Nitra region. Another argument repeatedly used to support the domestic coal industry is connected to social policy, as maintaining employment in the coal industry was considered to be crucial for the Horná Nitra region. This is also the home region of the former Slovak Prime Minister Robert Fico, who was a strong supporter of the mining industry and miners (Dargaj 2018), and was among the few public figures who signed a petition calling for the preservation of coal mining in the region (SITA 2018). The third argument supporting domestic coal mining is linked to the strategic position of the local thermal power plant for electricity grid balancing and stability.

Recent years have seen slight changes in the energy discourse, with the political elite adopting a rhetoric connected to decarbonization and climate issues, although energy security issues have not fully disappeared from the national discourse. The trend of climate-related discourse is especially notable within the presidential office. Elected in March 2019, the current President Zuzana Čaputová has become one of the political leaders who draw attention to climate changes (Vasilko 2019). This trend is expected to continue since energy-related topics connected to climate change (energy efficiency measures, increase of renewable sources, or cleaner mobility) were part of the campaign prior to the February 2020 parliamentary elections (Oravcová et al. 2020). These topics have made it into the 2020 government memorandum that can be considered to be very green as it focuses on climate issues and decarbonization (Government of the Slovak Republic 2020). Moreover, Slovakia nominated Maroš Šefčovič for the position of Vice President for the Energy

Union in the Jean-Claude Juncker Commission (2014–2019) who was actively engaged not only in debates on the diversification in Central and Eastern Europe but also the decarbonization of the energy sector and economy.

Coordination, Instruments, and Issues of Slovak Energy Transition

Drivers of Energy Transition

Energy transition in Slovakia has mostly been influenced by EU policies and can therefore be considered to be driven by external actors. Slovak energy policy is directly connected to the energy and climate policy of the EU via its strategic document, Energy Policy of the Slovak Republic, which "is based on the fundamental European goals for energy outlined in the Europe 2020 strategy" (Ministry of Economy 2014, p. 4). As a result, the four strategic pillars of the country's energy policy reflect those of the EU: energy security, energy efficiency, competitiveness, and sustainability. Within the 2020 energy and climate package, Slovakia committed to a goal of a 14% share of renewable sources within the country's gross final energy consumption by 2020; however, by 2017, it reached only a 11.5% share which does not inspire a lot of confidence that the 2020 goal will be reached (Eurostat 2019b). The other two goals outlined in the 2020 energy and climate package have been already reached: namely, by 2016, non-ETS (Emission Trading System) emissions have fallen by 14% compared to 1990 (the goal was 13% more compared to the 2005 level), while the nonbinding energy efficiency goal of decreasing total energy consumption to the level of 16.4 Mtoe was met in 2011 (Eurostat 2019a). This section identifies several main drivers of energy transition in Slovakia, including nuclear energy, renewables, coal phase-out, energy efficiency, and electromobility. It also examines the actors involved in energy transition.

Nuclear Decommissioning

Nuclear energy is a strategic energy source for Slovakia which has enjoyed long-term governmental support as a secure and climate-friendly energy source (see section "Discourse on Energy Issues"). Nuclear energy is part of Slovakia's answer to the question how to decarbonize the economy; however, the country's energy transition also needs to deal with the technology's back cycle – nuclear fuel management and especially decommissioning the two shut down NPPs (see Table 1). Construction of the very first NPP in the former Czechoslovakia, called A1, began in 1958 in Jaslovské Bohunice, Slovakia. The rather small reactor with the capacity of 110 MW entered the commercial phase in 1972, but was already phased off in 1979, following two accidents in 1976 and 1977 (Božik and Galbička 2015). The decommissioning itself started in 1999, after all the spent nuclear fuel was shipped to the Russian Federation, which significantly decreased the level of highly radioactive materials at the site. Slovakia faced a difficult situation when deciding on the termination of the two reactors at V1 NPP in Jaslovské Bohunice in the late 1990s, as there were no specialized domestic financial sources for this purpose. The decommissioning fund – the National Nuclear Fund – was established only in 2006 by Act. 238/2006 Coll. and is currently responsible for financing the decommissioning of both A1 and V1 NPPs in Jaslovské Bohunice. Its budget consists of fees coming from the operator of both NPPs – Slovenské elektrárne, a.s. – and the electricity distribution system operators that charge the end consumers in form of surcharges. Slovenské elektrárne, a.s., are partially owned by the Slovak government, which holds 34% of shares, and the private Slovak Power Holding BV. The rest of Slovenské elektrárne, a.s., used to be fully owned by Enel (66%). Enel created the Slovak Power Holding, transferred all its shares to this new company, and sold 50% of the company to Energetický a průmyslový holding (EPH) in 2015. The rest of the shares shall be sold after Units 3 and 4 in Mochovce NPP will be commenced.

Electricity generation from nuclear fuel is governed by the Nuclear Regulatory Authority (NRA) and the main agency responsible for decommissioning the Slovak NPPs is the Nuclear and Decommissioning Company. The decommissioning of Jaslovské Bohunice V1 began in 2011 and is financed by the National Nuclear Fund, the EU, and other donors through the Bohunice International Decommissioning Support Fund (BIDSF), which was designed as a compensation for the phasing off of the V1 NPP Jaslovské Bohunice. Its original budget was 90 million EUR for the period 2004–2006 and 423 million EUR for the period 2007–2013 (Council of the EU 2007). Along with contributions from other donors, the Slovak Republic received 624 million EUR in support for decommissioning the V1 NPP until the end of 2013 (Government of the Slovak Republic 2018b). Council Regulation (Euratom) No. 1368/2013 from December 2013 (Council of the EU 2013) provided another 225 million EUR for decommissioning the V1 NPP for the period 2014–2020. The proposal for the newest regulation that would provide financing for the period 2021–2027 suggests additional support for the decommissioning of the V1 NPP in the amount of 55 million EUR (Council of the EU 2018). Until mid-2018, more than 650 million EUR provided by BIDSF were used to decommission the V1 NPP in Jaslovské Bohunice (EBRD 2019), with additional funds coming from other sources.

Renewable Sources of Energy

The paths towards energy transition within the EU are country specific and in the Slovak case are more closely connected to nuclear than renewable sources of energy. As the previous section on Slovak energy discourse showed, nuclear power plays an important role in the discussion on decarbonization and the Slovak government has repeatedly supported the idea of nuclear energy being part of the solution for developing a post-carbon economy. In its National Energy and Climate Plan, the Slovak government set its 2030 renewable goal rather low (19.2% share of energy in gross final consumption), even though the Commission recommended 24%

(Ministry of Economy 2019). The position towards renewables is much less positive due to (among other factors) the development connected to the application of FiT at the end of 2000s. The tariffs were considered to be an important incentive for market players to invest into renewables, which still had a very low share in the energy mix in the mid-2000s. The share of renewables in the gross final energy consumption was only 6.7% in 2005, with hydropower plants responsible for almost the whole production (as well as the installed capacity). Out of the 4,653 GWh produced by different renewables sources in Slovakia in 2005, 4,638 GWh were produced in hydropower plants (Government of the Slovak Republic 2007).

A huge increase in the installed capacity of renewables, especially photovoltaic (PV) capacity, followed the introduction of Act No. 309/2009 Coll. on the Promotion of Renewable Energy Sources and High-Efficiency Co-generation. New rules provided FiT for select types of renewables sources for 15 years, as well as other types of support including preferential grid access, which guaranteed the purchase of all generated energy by the system operators. The support scheme was aimed at helping Slovakia reach its national renewables target of 14% by 2020. Following the introduction of the Act, the total installed capacity of photovoltaic power plants skyrocketed from 19 MW in 2009 to 496 MW in 2011. This proved to be a financial challenge as the generous subsidies increased the price of electricity for the end consumers (including households) by almost 5%, while, according to the government, the poorly integrated intermitted renewables also had also a destabilizing effect on the electricity grid (Ministry of Economy 2011). While the overall subsidies for the installations commenced under the 2009 Act amounted to 375 million EUR in 2016 (IEA 2018), the support for the 2011–2018 period was more than 3 billion EUR (SITA 2019a).

In order to deal with this situation, the support scheme was revised in 2011 and further changed in 2013. An additional small increase in photovoltaic installations was recorded between 2011 and 2013 (to 533 MW); however, after that, the increase was almost fully halted due to changes in the FiT framework. The maximum size for supported installations was scaled down from 125 MW to 100 kW and the FiT were significantly lowered in 2011. An amendment to the abovementioned Act 309/2009 on renewables support adopted in 2013 further limited the subsidies for PV to only rooftop installations of max. 30 kW capacity. The discussion on large-scale PV power plants was restarted in 2018, when the proposition to employ a feed-in premium system of support, so-called auctions (Ministry of Economy 2020), was made. The first round of the call for auctions was published at the beginning of 2020; however, due to the outbreak of the Covid-19 pandemic, it was cancelled in April 2020.

Coal Phase-Out

The domestic production of coal (lignite) and its utilization in electricity generation has been considered an energy security issue since the mid-2000s, although energy security as such had not dominated the Slovak energy policy discourse until 2009. Already the 2005 Act on energy policy suggested support for domestic coal as a way to improve the country's energy security (National Council of the Slovak Republic 2004). A similar argument was also used in the 2012 amendment of the Act. In practical terms, the government supports domestic coal production by ordering a certain amount of electricity to be generated within the so-called "general economic interest" by the coal-fired thermal plant Elektrárne Nováky (ENO) in the Horná Nitra region. This power plant receives its coal from the only Slovak coal mining company HBP, a.s., of which ENO is an almost exclusive partner as it buys almost all of its production. Out of the total 1,934,000 (metric) tons of coal produced in HBP in 2016, 1,821,407 tons (94.2%) were delivered to ENO, while only 112,593 tons were delivered to households and other companies (HBP 2017). In practice, this support scheme introduces a preferential dispatch for ENO and a guaranteed price for electricity generated from coal. The government set the amounts of supported production for each year, with the production peaking in 2011 with 1,755 GWh of electricity supplied from ENO. Although the amount of supplied electricity has decreased since then, the financial support paradoxically increased, rising from 34 million EUR in 2007 to almost 93 million EUR in 2014 (the 100 million EUR benchmark is used by the Slovak Ministry of Environment to describe the total costs of the support scheme; Ministry of Environment 2017b). According to the International Energy Agency, this support amounts to around 14,000 EUR per employee in coal mining and supporting services (IEA 2018). The difference between the wholesale price of electricity and the guaranteed price for which ENO produces electricity from coal is paid by the Regulatory Office for Network Industries, which adds it to the end customers' final bill in the form of surcharge, which amounts to approximately 4.5 EUR/MWh of retail electricity (IEA 2018).

The *Slovak Energy Policy*, the government's strategic document in the energy policy area, claims that domestic coal "increases the security of electricity supply and lowers Slovakia's energy dependence" (Ministry of Economy 2014, p. 46). However, the operator of the ENO power plant is not willing to maintain the installation without support as the aging plant requires steady investments due to the low-grade lignite coming from domestic production that is being burned in the power plant. In fact, the only reason some of the power plant's sections were able to operate was that they were exempt from EU emissions rules. Even more importantly, Slovak lignite is not competitive in comparison to imported coal, while the production of electricity from it is not competitive at all. This is the conclusion of a 2012 study by the Slovak government, according to which electricity production from domestic coal is viable only thanks to support schemes (Government of the Slovak Republic 2012). The government's decision No. 381/2013 (Government of the Slovak Republic 2013), which revisited the amount of coal produced in HBP mines and burned in the ENO power plant for electricity generation purposes, only addressed the technical changes in the coal mines and the power plant but did not aim to change the existing policies in any way.

The Decision of the Ministry of Economy No. 23/2015 set the levels of electricity required to be produced from domestic coal to 1,350 GWh of supplied electricity, expecting this support to last at least until 2030 (Ministry of Economy 2015). Energy security and the "general economic interest" were cited as reasons for supporting electricity generation in coal-fired power plants. With the Slovak government adopting these decisions, there was no indication of any policy changes in this area. Despite the rather strong opposition from domestic and international environmental groups against coal mining in Slovakia, as well as the fact that the Ministry of Environment also recommended that the mines be gradually closed down, the position of domestic coal in electricity production seemed to still be firm in 2015.

In its report, the Ministry of Environment (2017b) recommended a gradual shutting down of coal mining in Slovakia as a way to improve living conditions for the miners themselves, as well as the environment in the Horná Nitra region and the whole country. The Ministry estimated that shutting down ENO would bring 500 million EUR in health benefits, as ENO produces up to 72% of all sulfur dioxide and 8% of all particle matters produced in the country. In 2015, the power plant was the second biggest emitter of sulfur dioxide in Europe (Mertanová and Szalai 2017). Moreover, the OECD's last two economic surveys on Slovakia (2014 and 2017) recommended a gradual phasing out of coal subsidies (OECD 2017).

Lately, the priorities of the Slovak government have shifted towards a just transition of the mining region (Horná Nitra), which emphasizes its sustainable development and the phasing out of domestic coal from the electricity mix. The Slovak government is currently launching a process of coal industry transformation with the ultimate goal of phasing out coal from the country's energy mix by 2023. Following the July 2019 governmental decision, electricity production based on domestic coal will no longer be supported after 2023. This will mark the end of domestic coal production as almost all domestically produced coal is being utilized in the ENO power plant. It will also spell the end of the coal plant itself, which will not be profitable without governmental subsidies. This process began in December 2017, when the Minister of Environment announced at the One Planet Summit in Paris that Slovakia will phase-out coal from its electricity generation (Blondeel et al. 2020). Since then, this commitment has repeatedly been confirmed by different representatives of the Slovak government and the process of transforming the Horná Nitra region has already started (Government of the Slovak Republic 2018b). It was also confirmed by both Prime Minister Peter Pellegrini and President Zuzana Čaputová in a joint statement in June 2019.

The mining region of Horná Nitra has been included among the 14 pilot regions to undergo transition towards a post-coal economy within the Platform for Coal Regions in Transition launched by the Commission in December 2017 (JRC 2018). Initial support for the Horná Nitra region came from the Structural Reform Support Programme 2017–2020, for which the Ministry of Economy applied in October 2017. Based on this, the Commission provided support in the amount of 350,000 EUR (Government of the Slovak Republic 2018a). The main outcome of this technical assistance (Greece received similar assistance), primarily aimed at assisting countries with developing a long-term transition strategy, was "The Action Plan for the Transformation of the Horná Nitra Region" published in June 2019. March 2018 saw the institutionalization of the Horná Nitra region transformation process, when the Working Group for Preparation and Implementation of the Transformation Action Plan for the Upper [Horná] Nitra Region was set up within the Slovak government (Ibid.). Moreover, in 2019, the Platform for Coal Regions in Transition Secretariat was established at the EU level to aid the transformation of these regions.

Energy Efficiency

Energy efficiency has been an important energy transition issue for the Slovak government, which introduced several particular policies and financial incentives to support energy savings. The biggest progress in decreasing energy intensity in Slovakia occurred between 2002 and 2012, when the overall energy intensity decreased by 45% (Ministry of Economy 2014). Success factors included the restructuralization of the national industry, and the introduction of energy efficiency measures in industry and household sectors. Even though Slovakia's energy intensity has dropped, it still remains above the EU average (IEA 2018) due to the structure of the economy dominated by industry. The most energy intensive sector is industry, followed by residential and commercial sectors, and transport.

Slovakia adopted the Energy Efficiency Act No. 321/2014 Coll. setting a legal framework for energy efficiency policies and measures, in particular the guidelines for energy audit, design of energy efficiency action plans, and establishing the framework for energy service. The first strategy on energy efficiency was approved already in 2007 and implemented by the first Action plan on energy efficiency for 2008–2010. The Action plan was further updated in 2011, 2014, and 2017 (as per EU requirements) by setting targets for total energy savings and savings across individual sectors, including policies, to meet these targets. The action plans are based on EU directives 2006/32/EC on energy end-use efficiency and energy services, and directive 2012/27/EU, which extends the obligations to submit action plans and their scope. Slovakia set its 2030 energy efficiency target at 30.3%, which is slightly below the overall EU target of 32.5% (Ministry of Economy 2019). The Ministry of Economy, together with the Slovak Innovation and Energy Agency (implementation agency), has managed to improve the process of collecting data through the Energy Efficiency Monitoring System that monitors energy consumption across sectors and serves as the basis for developing related policies (SIEA 2014).

Slovakia managed to significantly decrease its energy intensity, largely thanks to improved thermal insulation in the building sector, which contributed to the decreasing of heat consumption. By the end of 2018, more than 60% of apartment buildings and 50% of family houses were refitted, with the expectation that, at the current pace of renovation, all apartment buildings will be renovated by the end of 2030 and all family houses by the end of 2043 (Ministry of Economy 2019). The current pace of renovation of apartment buildings and family houses is around 3% and 2.5% per year, respectively, while the country is lagging behind in renovation of public buildings, where the figure is only around 1% per year (Buildings for future 2017). However, the rate of improvement of energy efficiency measures in this sector declined in recent years, as many improvements have already been made (IEA 2018). Several policy measures and funding support programs for energy savings have been introduced, many of which are managed by the State Housing Development Fund (the Fund) under the Ministry for Transport and Construction. Together with EU funds, the Fund is a key financial instrument for supporting energy efficiency measures in the residential sector. The Fund was established by Act No. 124/1996 Coll., which was repealed in 2003 and is currently governed by Act

No. 150/2013 Coll. on the State Fund for Housing Development. One of its main aims is to support building renovation and improve the thermal performance of buildings via retrofitting and insulation.

Another energy efficiency support scheme is the Slovak Sustainable Energy Financing Facility (SlovSEFF), developed by the European Bank for Reconstruction and Development (EBRD) in cooperation with the Slovak Ministry of Environment. The program is based on incentive payments funded through carbon credit transaction between Slovakia and Spain. The program provides loans and grants for energy efficiency projects in the residential area and industry, and facilitates renewables investment plans. Additional funding for incentive payments and technical assistance is also provided by the BIDSF. Within the total budget of approximately 90 million EUR, more than 60% of investments were directed towards residential energy efficiency projects leading to average energy savings of 33% (SlovSEFF 2020). In terms of energy efficiency, the building sector is most important, which is expected to remain crucial for meeting Slovak energy efficiency targets even after 2020.

Electromobility

Given the fact that the automotive industry is a vital pillar of the Slovak economy, the decarbonization of the transport sector will have a decisive impact on the future of the country's industry, as well as the country as such. There are four car producers in Slovakia (Volkswagen, KIA, PSA Peugeot Citroën, and Jaguar Land Rover), making it the world's leading car manufacturer in per capita terms (Sme 2020). The transport sector is the second largest source of greenhouse gases emissions and belongs among the main climate concerns. However, while the share of cars in individual transport has been on the increase, the share of electric cars remains very low and the development of electromobility is only at its inception stage. Slovakia has a relatively old vehicle fleet, which significantly impacts air quality.

The main step forward was made in March 2019, when the government adopted the Action plan for the development of electromobility in Slovakia, which sets long-term goals in this area. The Action plan updates the existing strategy from 2015 and contains 15 key measures that support the development of electromobility, including research and the development of batteries, creating low-emission zones, facilitating the building of charging infrastructure, and the introduction of different colors for vehicle registration plates (Government of the Slovak Republic 2019a). The Action plan estimates there will be around 35,000 electric vehicles in Slovakia by 2030; this goal should be achieved with the help of financial subsidies and the development of charging stations in cooperation with municipalities. However, considering that about 110,000 cars are registered annually (with an expected growth), the number of planned electric vehicles is rather low and far from ambitious.

The first subsidy program was launched by the Ministry of Economy in cooperation with the Automotive Industry Association of the Slovak Republic in November 2016, with the overall budget of 5.2 million EUR. Customers who bought an electric vehicle were able to apply for a subsidy in the amount of 5,000 EUR in the case of battery electric cars and 3,000 EUR in the case of plug-in hybrid cars. Due to high costs of electric vehicles and the lack of charging infrastructure, the budget was not spent and the remaining one million EUR was used by municipalities in the second round of the program in 2018 to purchase electric cars with 5% co-financing (Supreme Audit Office of the Slovak Republic 2019b). While only 183 and 422 new electric and hybrid vehicles were registered in 2015 and 2016 respectively, the number increased sharply after the launch of the subsidy program at the end of 2016, with 2,145 and 2,727 new electric vehicle registrations in 2017 and 2018, respectively (Energoklub 2020). The number of newly registered electric or hybrid cars has increased every year thanks to the subsidies; however, as a consequence, 2019 saw a sharp decrease in registration as buyers postponed their purchases in expectation of a new subsidy scheme at the end of that year. The second subsidy scheme published by the Ministry of Economy and the Slovak Innovation and Energy Agency (implementation agency for this call) had the total budget of 6 million EUR (8,000 EUR for battery electric cars and 5,000 EUR for plug-in hybrid cars) that were distributed among the applicants in the form of vouchers in less than 4 minutes (Kálmán 2019). The Ministry of Economy suspended the program at the beginning of April 2020 due to the Covid-19 pandemic; however, it restarted the scheme already the following month.

Political Actors and Policy Coordination

Slovakia is party to the United Nations Framework Convention on Climate Change (UNFCCC). The government ratified the Kyoto Protocol in 2002 and the Paris Agreement in 2016. Slovakia's energy and climate governance is guided by EU policies, as the country transposes Community's energy and climate legislation. While this chapter argues that external factors influence Slovakia's energy governance to a significant degree, domestic actors still have day-to-day impact on energy governance. Responsibility for policies within the energy sector is divided between three ministries. The Ministry of Economy, responsible for setting the legal framework and developing strategic documents, including the integrated National Energy and Climate Plan, assumes a crucial role. Other main actors include the Ministry of Environment, responsible for environmental and climate protection policies, including the National Adaptation Plan which outlines a crisis scenario within the energy sector, and the Ministry of Transport and Construction, which focuses on energy efficiency in the transport and building sector. Moreover, two other ministries also influence developments in the energy sector: the national funding of research, including innovations, and research and development (R&D) within energy sector falls within the auspices of the Ministry of Education, Science, Research, and Sport, while the Ministry of Agriculture and Rural Development develops and implements renewable energy policy and the use of biomass.

Several strategic documents developed by the Slovak government have been prepared in cooperation between different ministries (for instruments, see Table 2).

Table 2 The most important instruments of energy transition

	Key policies and strategies	Key decisions	Key tools/ implementation/ monitoring	Key financing program	Desired results
Electricity sector	Units 3 and 4 at Mochovce NPP	Agreement between government and Enel	Nuclear Regulatory Authority of the SR	Funded by Slovenské elektrárne	Decarbonization of electricity sector
	Transformation Action Plan for the Upper Nitra Coal Region	Resolution of the Government No. 336/2019	The platform for coal regions in transition	EU funds	Phase-out of domestic coal by 2023 and transformation of the mining region
Heat sector	Subsidies for the replacement of furnaces	Resolution of the Government No. 193/2019	Slovak Innovation and Energy Agency	EU funds	Replacement of 10,000 furnaces for solid fuels
Transport sector	Slovak Strategic Transport Development Plan until 2030	Resolution of the Government No. 13/2017	Modernization of public transport fleet; development of integrated transport systems	EU funds	Increase share of passengers in public transport (especially rail)
	Action plan for the development of electromobility	Resolution of the Government No. 110/2019	Slovak Innovation and Energy Agency	Ministry of Economy	Electromobility development
	National Policy Frameworks for the development of the market as regards alternative fuels	Resolution of the Government No. 504/2016	Biofuels blending obligation	Not applicable	The biofuels target is 8.2% for the period 2022–2030
	National policy for the implementation of infrastructure for alternative fuels	Resolution of the Government No. 505/2016			

Energy efficiency	Energy Efficiency Action Plan 2017–2019 with an outlook up to 2020	Resolution of the Government No. 200/2017	Improvement of the thermal performance in buildings; energy efficiency monitoring system	State Housing Development Fund; SlovSEFF; Environmental Fund; EU Funds; Modernisation Fund	Further energy efficiency improvement (20% of primary energy consumption by 2020 compared to 2007 levels)
	National Action Plans for greening public procurement for 2016–2020	Resolution of the Government No. 590/2016; Resolution of the Government No. 478/2019	Strategy for development and implementation of green public procurement in Slovakia	Not applicable	Achieve 50% of all state contracts through "green" public procurement (further increased to 70%)
Renewable energy sources	National Renewable Energy Action Plan	Resolution of the Government No. 677/2010	Green Households programme through Slovak Innovation and Energy Agency	SlovSEFF programme; EU funds	15.3% share of RES in the gross final energy consumption by 2020 (later decreased to 14%)
	Promotion of Renewable Energy Sources and High-Efficiency Co-generation	Act No. 309/2009 Coll.	Feed-in tariff; feed-in premium	End-users (surcharge to electricity price)	Construction and upgrade of heat distribution systems and high-efficiency co-generation plants
General – climate-related strategies	Strategy of the Environmental Policy of the Slovak Republic until 2030	Resolution of the Government No. 87/2019	"Polluter pays" principle	EU funds; State funds	Circular economy; environment improvement; biodiversity protection
	National Adaptation Strategy to Climate Change	Resolution of the Government No. 478/2018	Establishment of an institutional framework and coordination mechanism	EU funds; State funds	Ensure effective implementation of adaptation measures

(continued)

Table 2 (continued)

Key policies and strategies	Key decisions	Key tools/implementation/monitoring	Key financing program	Desired results
Low-carbon strategy of Slovakia until 2030	Resolution of the Government No. 104/2020	Proposed measures in energy sector, industry, transport, agriculture, land use, and waste sector	Modernisation fund; Environmental fund; EU funds; State and local funds	Carbon neutrality up to 2050
Strategy on air protection until 2030	Act No. 137/2010 Coll. on air protection	National Programme for Emission Decrease (Resolution of the Government No. 103/2020)	EU funds	Air pollution decrease; emissions decrease

Source: Authors

For example, the long-term low-carbon strategy, a cross-sectoral strategic document adopted in 2019, which shifts Slovakia's focus to decarbonization, was prepared in cooperation with the World Bank. One of the guiding strategies developed by the Ministry of Environment, entitled Strategy of the Environmental Policy of the Slovak Republic until 2030 (also called "Greener Slovakia"), defines improving environmental quality as the main objective for 2030 and aims to develop a sustainable circular economy. Given the Slovak government high priority on energy security, it is rather surprising that the main strategic document governing this area is outdated and actually pre-dates the 2009 gas crisis. The Energy Security Strategy (Ministry of Economy 2008) was adopted by the Slovak government back in 2008 and can therefore be seen as failing to reflect on the main developments in this area in the last decade. Approved in 2017, the National Adaptation Plan identifies only those examples of best practices for energy infrastructure protection that could be used to prevent crisis scenarios connected to climate change (Ministry of Environment 2017a).

The ministries implement energy and climate policies through several agencies. The Slovak Innovation and Energy Agency (SIEA) is an implementation agency under the Ministry of Economy, responsible for support schemes aimed at developing innovation activities with a special focus on energy efficiency and renewable energy. One of its largest funding programs, called "Green Households," focuses on renewable energy support for individual households, such as small PV installations, heat pumps, or ecological furnaces. The Agency also monitors energy efficiency measures and the quality of their implementation. The Slovak Hydrometeorological Institute (SHMÚ) provides hydrological and meteorological services but also develops and maintains a National Emission Inventory System and publishes smog alerts (as well as weather alerts). It is a state-subsidized organization operating under the Ministry of Environment.

The principal authority responsible for regulating the gas and electricity sectors is the Regulatory Office for Network Industries (ÚRSO), established by the Act No. 276/2001 Coll. The Office is responsible for price regulation and nontariff decisions, such as issuing licenses to carry out regulated activities. It regulates prices for households and small businesses based on EU regulation rules and creates a regulatory framework for a 5-year regulatory period based on the price cap method. Currently, the Office follows the 2017–2021 regulatory framework; the new regulatory period will begin in 2022. The regulated sectors include electricity, natural gas, thermal energy (heat for district heating), and water management. The Office is supposed to be a public authority which is independent from the government and acts in a transparent and nondiscriminatory manner. However, its independency and transparency of price setting are often questioned, and the government has been repeatedly accused of interfering with the activities of the Office (Kollárová 2017). For example, the government has an exclusive right to appoint the chairperson of the Office. "Stable energy prices" was one of the main slogans of the then incumbent governmental party Smer-Sociálna demokracia (Direction-Social Democracy) during its 2016–2020 coalition government, when the current regulatory framework was developed (Poracký 2016). The Office implements the government policy on regulating (capping) end-user prices for electricity and natural gas (as well as heat and water management) for the so-called vulnerable customers, i.e., all households and small businesses with the annual consumption no more than 100,000 kWh for the previous year. Electricity prices for households and small and medium-sized companies are capped under price regulation, which, according to the International Energy Agency (2018), limits retail market competition, and discourages energy-efficient behavior and investment in the electricity sector at large. It has therefore been recommended that the Office develops a more transparent price-setting framework in order to eliminate this system of regulated end-user prices of electricity and natural gas (IEA 2018). The Office has been undergoing modification since May 2020 when the then new government led by Igor Matovič decided to foster the Office's independence and transparency.

Even though most of the policies are decided at the national or the EU level, several nongovernmental actors have also become active in recent years. This is especially due to the fact that energy policy has gained attention through the discussion on climate change. One of the most visible organizations in this respect is the Slovak Climate Initiative (SKI), which brings the topics of energy and climate into the public discourse. While its main goal is to gather support among political leaders for energy efficiency solutions, renewable sources of energy, or fossil fuel phase-out, the Initiative also focuses on the issue of energy poverty and tries to shape the public debate on this topic. Its founding members include the following nongovernmental organizations dealing with issues connected to energy transition: Buildings for Future, Friends of Earth – CEPA, the Slovak Association of Photovoltaic Industry and RES (SAPI), and the Prognostics Centre of Slovak Academy of Sciences. SAPI also contributes to the discussion on renewable energy legislation and helps shape the public discussion on this policy, as well as the barriers to renewables implementation. Various international organizations such as Greenpeace have also been active in the process of coal phase-out planning; however, their influence on policy is rather limited. Organizations which have had more success with policy shaping in the field of transport include the Automotive Industry Association of the Slovak Republic and the Slovak Electric Vehicle Association. While most energy actors currently operate on the national level, this could change in the future, as Slovakia plans to develop local energy centers tasked with monitoring energy consumption in public buildings, improving energy efficiency, supporting the development of renewables, and supporting the preparation of regional energy action plans (Ministry of Economy 2019). However, the development and competences of these local energy centers are not yet clear.

Outcomes, Challenges, and Prospects for Energy Governance

Slovakia opts for a low-ambition approach, its future developments in the energy sector being strongly tied to its past legacies. So far, energy governance has largely been shaped through the prism of energy security, as the 2009 natural gas crisis found the country unprepared in terms of infrastructure and storage capacities. That is why the country placed the diversification of routes among its top priorities and started to build new or strengthen existing capacities in the electricity, gas, and oil sectors (Mišík 2019). Even though the 2009 scenario is not likely to be repeated due to new energy infrastructure and storage capacities, diversification remains an important issue on the political agenda in the energy sector. A good example is the proposed Eastring gas pipeline, providing access to the Black Sea (Ministry of Economy 2019). Domestic sources of energy – especially nuclear – are considered to be an important dimension of energy security. Moreover, nuclear is considered to be a carbon-free electricity source that is key for achieving a carbon-neutral economy. However, Units 3 and 4 at Mochovce NPP, which should have been operational since 2012 and 2013, respectively, are still not finished. The postponement was caused by several factors, including increased safety demands following the 2011 Fukushima disaster, as well as several corruption scandals connected to overpriced supplies (Kováč 2020). Although there are plans for developing new reactors in Jaslovské Bohunice, it is questionable whether the government would be able to find an investor to build new NPPs or find domestic sources. International funds play a key role in the decommissioning of the two reactors at V1 NPP in Jaslovské Bohunice, which is estimated to cost 1.237 billion EUR in total (TASR 2019). Furthermore, international support is dedicated to the decommissioning of the much older and smaller A1 NPP. However, the question of a deep geological repository of spent nuclear fuel has not yet entered the public discourse.

While energy security has been an important issue in the last decade, other challenges connected to energy transition and climate change lie ahead. Consequently, the priorities of the energy governance have slowly been refocusing on decarbonization. Energy governance in Slovakia is highly centralized, with the primary responsibility resting with the Ministry of Economy, along with the Regulatory Office for Network Industries. Climate change mitigation and adaptation will present a challenge to the cooperation among the ministries at the national level, as the responsibility for emission decrease is divided among various sectors, such as transport, buildings, and agriculture. Decarbonization of the energy sector will be especially challenging in the future, as the government argues that this sector is already dominated by low-carbon technologies: nuclear energy in electricity and natural gas in the heating sector. Future measures should therefore focus on energy efficiency, higher deployment of renewables, and the transport sector (Ministry of Economy 2019).

Further development of nuclear energy and higher penetration of renewables will put pressure on the stability of the electric grid. This is why the government plans to dedicate research and innovation funds into research on electricity grid stability, smart grids architecture, nuclear energy, and renewables (Ministry of Economy 2019). The government plans to further decarbonize the energy sector by means of higher deployment of renewables. However, it is struggling to meet the 14% renewables target by 2020. Hydropower plants, which generate the majority of renewable electricity, are often criticized for not being built efficiently and causing serious damage to the impacted ecosystems (Derka 2019). Moreover, hydropower plants represent a potential problem for the future, as their maintenance has been neglected over the past years. Built in the 1950s and 1960s, most Slovak dams are in critical conditions and their safe functioning is at risk (Supreme Audit Office of the Slovak Republic 2019a).

While Slovakia was able to decrease its emissions during the 1990s, mainly thanks to the closing of heavy industry, further decrease will require strict measures. The country's economy remains energy intensive, which means the introduction of new energy efficiency measures will require large investment, especially in the industry sector. This will be the case with U.S. Steel Košice, the largest integrated steel producer in Central Europe and one of the largest employers in Slovakia, as well as the biggest air polluter in the country (SHMÚ 2018). Similarly, the problem of air pollution is connected to the rise of individual road transport. However, decarbonization efforts in the transport sector require not only the deployment of electromobility on a larger scale (especially developing the charging infrastructure), but also and especially substantial changes in public transport, which, in turn, demands massive infrastructure investments and efficient spatial planning.

Coal phase-out was already agreed on at the national level, as electricity generation based on domestic coal (lignite) will no longer be supported by 2023. However, the end of subsidies does not mean the end of coal use. Within the government's decarbonization efforts, the residential heating sector represents a particular challenge and concerns over local air pollution from solid fuels combustion should be addressed. Significant air pollutants are especially prominent in locations where residential heating by solid fuels is widespread. The Ministry of Environment estimates there are approximately 350,000 households with solid fuel furnaces, with 120,000 of them more than 30 years old. The Ministry made the first step by announcing subsidies for replacing domestic furnaces with gas-fired furnaces and allocating 35 million EUR for this program (SITA 2019b). The problem of solid fuel utilization in households is also connected to the issue of energy poverty (SHMÚ 2018), which has not been adequately addressed in the country.

It is difficult to predict the consequences the Covid-19 pandemic will have on Slovak as well as EU energy transition. Although there have been calls for the post-pandemic economic recovery to be a green one, at the same time, the industry in general and the automotive industry in particular are calling for a relaxation of the existing (not only emissions) requirements.

Cross-References

- ▶ Energy Governance in Austria
- ▶ Energy Governance in France
- ▶ Energy Governance in Hungary
- ▶ Energy Governance in Lithuania
- ▶ Energy Governance in Russia: From a Fossil to a Green Giant?
- ▶ Energy Governance in the Czech Republic
- ▶ Energy Governance in the Republic of Poland

- Energy Policies in the EU: A Fiscal Federalism Perspective
- Energy Poverty
- Monitoring Energy Policy
- Transition of Energy Systems: Patterns of Stability and Change

Acknowledgments This work was supported by the Slovak Research and Development Agency Grant No. APVV-16-0062 (Priorities of the Central and Eastern European countries in the context of the Energy Union). The authors would like to thank Nada Kujundžić for the language editing.

References

Blondeel, M., Van de Graaf, T., & Haesebrouck, T. (2020). Moving beyond coal: Exploring and explaining the powering past coal alliance. *Energy Research & Social Science, 59*, 101304. https://doi.org/10.1016/j.erss.2019.101304.

Božik, M., & Galbička, I. (2015). História prevádzky a vyraďovania jadrového zariadenia A1. https://www.javys.sk/data/web/dokumenty/Publikacie/a1/a1-ukoncenie-prevadzky.pdf. Accessed 4 Jan 2020.

Buildings for Future. (2017). Program budovy 2050. https://bpb.sk/wp-content/uploads/2018/10/Program-Budovy-2050.pdf. Accessed 28 Feb 2020.

Council of the EU. (2007). Council Regulation (EURATOM) No 549/2007. https://eur-lex.europa.eu/legal-content/EN/TXT/PDF/?uri=CELEX:32007R0549&from=GA. Accessed 4 Jan 2020.

Council of the EU. (2013). Council Regulation (Euratom) No. 1368/2013 of 13 December 2013 on Union support for the nuclear decommissioning assistance programmes in Bulgaria and Slovakia. https://eur-lex.europa.eu/legal-content/EN/TXT/PDF/?uri=CELEX:32013R1368&from=EN. Accessed 4 Jan 2020.

Council of the EU. (2018). Proposal for a Council Regulation establishing a dedicated financial programme for decommissioning of nuclear facilities and management of radioactive waste. https://eur-lex.europa.eu/resource.html?uri=cellar:b2c29440-6ef1-11e8-9483-01aa75ed71a1.0002.03/DOC_1&format=PDF. Accessed 4 Jan 2020.

Dargaj, M. (2018). Fico absolútne odmieta zatváranie baní na Hornej Nitre. SITA. https://www.webnoviny.sk/venergetike/fico-absolutne-odmieta-zatvaranie-bani-na-hornej-nitre/. Accessed 20 Febr 2020.

Derka, T. (2019, March 20). Malé vodné elektrárne sú horšie ako veľké, dôkazov je dosť. Euractiv. https://euractiv.sk/section/voda/opinion/male-vodne-elektrarne-su-horsie-ako-velke-dokazov-je-dost/. Accessed 26 Feb 2020.

EBRD. (2019). Bohunice International Decommissioning Support Fund. https://www.ebrd.com/what-we-do/sectors/nuclear-safety/bohunice.html. Accessed 4 Jan 2020.

Energoklub. (2020, January 24). Počet registrácií elektromobilov sa medziročne prepadol o vyše 40%. https://energoklub.sk/sk/clanky/pocet-registracii-elektromobilov-sa-medzirocne-prepadol-o-vyse-40/. Accessed 25 Feb 2020.

Euractiv. (2009, January 12). Gas crisis gives Slovakia excuse to restart nuclear unit. https://www.euractiv.com/section/med-south/news/gas-crisis-gives-slovakia-excuse-to-restart-nuclear-unit/. Accessed 26 Feb 2020.

Eurostat. (2019a). Europe 2020 indicators – Slovakia. https://ec.europa.eu/eurostat/statistics-explained/index.php?title=Europe_2020_indicators_-_Slovakia. Accessed 4 Jan 2020.

Eurostat. (2019b). Europe 2020 targets: Statistics and indicators for Slovakia. https://ec.europa.eu/info/business-economy-euro/economic-and-fiscal-policy-coordination/eu-economic-governance-monitoring-prevention-correction/european-semester/european-semester-your-country/slovakia/europe-2020-targets-statistics-and-indicators-slovakia_en. Accessed 4 Jan 2020.

Eurostat. (2020). Energy datasheets: EU countries. https://ec.europa.eu/energy/sites/ener/files/energy_statistical_countrydatasheets.xlsx. Accessed 17 June 2020.

Eustream. (2019). Annual report: 1 January 2018 – 31 July 2018. https://www.eustream.sk/en_download-file/annual-report-1-january-2018%2D%2D-31-july-2018/a89d20893991ba5ef00f1376a762de4f. Accessed 12 Jan 2020.

Feklyunina, V. (2012). Russia's international images and its energy policy. An unreliable supplier? *Europe-Asia Studies, 64*(3), 449–469. https://doi.org/10.1080/09668136.2012.661923.

Government of the Slovak Republic. (1999). Decision no. 801/1999 of the Government of the SR on early shutdown. https://www.government.gov.sk//uznesenia/1999/0914/uz_0801_1999.html. Accessed 28 Feb 2020.

Government of the Slovak Republic. (2007). Návrh Stratégie vyššieho využitia obnoviteľných zdrojov energie v SR – nové znenie. https://rokovania.gov.sk/RVL/Material/19293/1. Accessed 6 Jan 2020.

Government of the Slovak Republic. (2012). Aktualizácia analýzy fungovania štátnej podpory baníctva. https://rokovania.gov.sk/RVL/Material/8900/1. Accessed 6 Jan 2020.

Government of the Slovak Republic. (2013). Decision no. 381/2013 of the Government of the SR on employment creation in Horná Nitra region. https://rokovania.gov.sk/RVL/Resolution/7019. Accessed 28 Feb 2020.

Government of the Slovak Republic. (2018a). Proposal for an Integrated National Energy and Climate Plan. https://ec.europa.eu/energy/sites/ener/files/documents/ec_courtesy_translation_sk_necp.pdf.Accessed 26 March 2020.

Government of the Slovak Republic. (2018b). Správa o činnosti Medzinárodného podporného fondu na odstavenie Jadrovej elektrárne V1 v Jaslovských Bohuniciach. https://rokovania.gov.sk/download.dat?id=651FEF15B6C24492AD21A0196EC359E1-7614E5F84A87269FEAAD24D36BF88E16. Accessed 4 Jan 2020.

Government of the Slovak Republic. (2019a). Návrh Akčného plánu rozvoja elektromobility v Slovenskej republike. https://rokovania.gov.sk/RVL/Material/23601/1. Accessed 20 Feb 2020.

Government of the Slovak Republic. (2019b). Pellegrini potvrdil dohodu krajín EÚ na uhlíkovej neutralite. https://www.vlada.gov.sk//pellegrini-potvrdil-dohodu-krajin-eu-na-uhlikovej-neutralite/. Accessed 20 Feb 2020.

Government of the Slovak Republic. (2020). Programové vyhlásenie vlády Slovenskej republiky na obdobie rokov 2020–2024. https://www.mpsr.sk/download.php?fID=18769. Accessed 18 June 2020.

Greenenergy Slovakia. (2020). Veterné elektrárne. http://greenenergy.sk/sk/veterna-energia/. Accessed 28 Feb 2020.

HBP. (2017). Výročná správa za rok 2017. http://www.registeruz.sk/cruz-public/domain/financialreport/attachment/5664028. Accessed 7 Jan 2020.

Hilde, P. S. (1999). Slovak nationalism and the break-up of Czechoslovakia. *Europe-Asia Studies, 51*(4), 647–665. https://doi.org/10.1080/09668139998831.

Högselius, P. (2013). *Red gas*. London: Palgrave.

IAEA. (2020). Country nuclear power profiles. Slovakia. https://cnpp.iaea.org/countryprofiles/Slovakia/Slovakia.htm. Accessed 28 Feb 2020.

IEA. (2018). *Slovak Republic. 2018 review*. Paris: International Energy Agency.

IEA. (2019). Statistics. https://www.iea.org/statistics/. Accessed 6 Jan 2020.

Ivanov, K. (2008). Legitimate conditionality? The European union and nuclear power safety in Central and Eastern Europe. *International Politics, 45*(2), 146–167. https://doi.org/10.1057/palgrave.ip.8800224.

JAVYS. (2018). Výročná správa 2018. https://www.javys.sk/data/web/dokumenty/vyrocne-spravy/vs-javys-2018-sk.pdf. Accessed 4 Jan 2020.

JRC. (2018). EU coal regions: Opportunities and challenges ahead. http://publications.jrc.ec.europa.eu/repository/bitstream/JRC112593/kjna29292enn.pdf. Accessed 27 Mar 2020.

Kálmán, J. (2019, December 16). Dotácie na elektromobily sa rozdali za pár minút. Sme. https://auto.sme.sk/c/22284781/dotacie-na-elektromobily-sa-minuli-za-par-minut.html. Accessed 20 Feb 2020.

Kollárová, Z. (2017, February 1). Chaos v energiách: V každej civilizovanej krajine by prišlo nezávislé vyšetrovanie. Trend. https://www.etrend.sk/ekonomika/chaos-v-energiach-v-kazdej-civilizovanej-krajine-by-nasledovalo-nezavisle-vysetrovanie.html. Accessed 24 Feb 2020.

Kováč, J. (2020, March 3). Stovka policajtov pátrala po chybných rúrach. NAKA sa vrátila do Mochoviec. Denník N. https://e.dennikn.sk/1783043/stovka-policajtov-patrala-po-chybnych-rurach-naka-sa-vratila-do-mochoviec/. Accessed 24 Mar 2020.

Krajanová, D. (2018, March 11). Slnečné elektrárne, ktoré štartoval Vadala za vlády Smeru, dostávajú od štátu ročne 10 miliónov. DenníkN. https://e.dennikn.sk/1058286/slnecne-elektrarne-ktore-startoval-vadala-za-vlady-smeru-dostavaju-od-statu-rocne-10-milionov/. Accessed 24 Feb 2020.

Kratochvíl, P., & Mišík, M. (2020). Bad external actors and good nuclear energy: Media discourse on energy supplies in the Czech Republic and Slovakia. *Energy Policy, 136*, 111058. https://doi.org/10.1016/j.enpol.2019.111058.

Mertanová, K. & Szalai, P. (2017, July 20). Slovenská elektráreň patrí medzi troch najväčších znečisťovateľov. Euractiv. https://euractiv.sk/section/energetika/infographic/slovenska-elektraren-patri-medzi-troch-najvacsich-znecistovatelov-infografika/. Accessed 7 Jan 2020.

Ministry of Economy. (2008). Návrh stratégie energetickej bezpečnosti SR - upravené nové znenie. https://rokovania.gov.sk/RVL/Material/4819/1. Accessed 28 Feb 2020.

Ministry of Economy. (2011). Analýza systému podpory obnoviteľných zdrojov energie a návrh na jeho prehodnotenie. https://www.economy.gov.sk/uploads/files/W58vMbYo.pdf. Accessed 4 Jan 2020.

Ministry of Economy. (2014). Energy policy of the Slovak Republic. https://www.mhsr.sk/uploads/files/47NgRIPQ.pdf. Accessed 4 Jan 2020.

Ministry of Economy. (2015). Rozhodnutie č.23/2015 Ministerstva hospodárstva SR. https://www.mhsr.sk/uploads/files/hDYurwt5.pdf. Accessed 4 Jan 2020.

Ministry of Economy. (2019). Integrovaný národný energetický a klimatický plán na roky 2021–2030. https://www.economy.gov.sk/uploads/files/IjkPMQAc.pdf. Accessed 25 Feb 2020.

Ministry of Economy. (2020). MH SR spúšťa historicky prvú aukciu na výrobu zelenej energie. https://www.mhsr.sk/aktuality/mh-sr-spusta-historicky-prvu-aukciu-na-vyrobu-zelenej-energie-1. Accessed 20 Feb 2020.

Ministry of Environment. (2017a). Stratégia adaptácie Slovenskej republiky na nepriaznivé dôsledky zmeny klímy. https://www.minzp.sk/files/odbor-politiky-zmeny-klimy/strategia-adaptacie-sr-nepriaznive-dosledky-zmeny-klimy-aktualizacia.pdf. Accesed 26 Mar 2020.

Ministry of Environment. (2017b). Revízia výdavkov na životné prostredie. Záverečná správa. https://www.minzp.sk/files/iep/zaverecna_sprava_zivotne_prostredie.pdf. Accesed 26 Mar 2020.

Mišík, M. (2015). The influence of perception on the preferences of the new member states of the European Union: The case of energy policy. *Comparative European Politics, 13*(2), 198–221. https://doi.org/10.1057/cep.2013.9.

Mišík, M. (2019). *External energy security in the European Union. Small member states' perspective*. London: Routledge.

Mišík, M., & Nosko, A. (2017). Eastring gas pipeline in the context of Central and Eastern European gas supply challenge. *Nature Energy, 2*(11), 844–848. https://doi.org/10.1038/s41560-017-0019-6.

National Council of the Slovak Republic. (2004). Dôvodová správa. https://www.nrsr.sk/web/Dynamic/DocumentPreview.aspx?DocID=188823. Accessed 7 Jan 2020.

OECD. (2017). OECD economic survey: Slovak Republic. https://read.oecd-ilibrary.org/economics/oecd-economic-surveys-slovak-republic-2017_eco_surveys-svk-2017-en#page1. Accessed 7 Jan 2020.

Oravcová, V., & Mišík, M. (2018). EU funds and limited cooperation: Energy infrastructure development in the Visegrad Group. *International Issues & Slovak Foreign Policy Affairs, 27*(3–4), 11–26.

Oravcová, V., Hajko, J., & Kováč, P. (2020). Postoje politických strán k energetickým a klimatickým témam. SFPA. http://www.sfpa.sk/publication/postoje-politickych-stran-k-energetickym-a-klimatickym-temam/. Accessed 20 Mar 2020.

Perović, J. (2017). *Cold war energy. A transnational history of soviet oil and gas*. London: Palgrave.

Poracký, M. (2016, December 1). Domácnosti vraj ušetria na elektrine. Neplatí to pre všetky. Sme. https://ekonomika.sme.sk/c/20398321/domacnosti-vraj-usetria-na-elektrine-neplati-to-pre-vsetky.html. Accessed 26 Mar 2020.

Pridham, G. (2008). The EU's political conditionality and post-accession tendencies: Comparisons from Slovakia and Latvia. *Journal of Common Market Studies, 46*(2), 365–387. https://doi.org/10.1111/j.1468-5965.2007.00780.x.

SHMÚ. (2018). Správa o kvalite ovzdušia v Slovenskej republike. http://www.shmu.sk/File/oko/rocenky/SHMU_Sprava_o_kvalite_ovzdusia_SR_2018_v3.pdf. Accessed 25 Feb 2020.

SIEA. (2014). Monitorovací systém energetickej efektívnosti. https://www.siea.sk/monitorovaci-system/. Accessed 25 Feb 2020.

SITA. (2018, May 10). Ľudia musia mať svoju prácu, vyhlásil Fico a podpísal petíciu baníkov z Hornej Nitry. https://www.webnoviny.sk/video-ludia-musia-mat-svoju-pracu-vyhlasil-fico-podpisal-peticiu-banikov-z-hornej-nitry/. Accessed 28 Feb 2020.

SITA. (2019a, October 29). Vyše tri miliardy eur. Toľko nás zatiaľ stála podpora zelenej elektriny. Websnoviny. https://www.webnoviny.sk/venergetike/tri-miliardy-eur-tolko-nas-zatial-stala-podpora-zelenej-elektriny/. Accessed 27 Mar 2020.

SITA. (2019b, October 1). Ministerstvo chce zlepšiť ovzdušie, domácnostiam rozdá na nové kotly 35 miliónov. Sme. https://ekonomika.sme.sk/c/22225882/ministerstvo-chce-zlepsit-ovzdusie-domacnostiam-rozda-na-kotly-35-milionov.html. Accessed 26 Feb 2020.

SlovSEFF. (2020). SLOVSEFF I & II. http://www.slovseff.eu/index.php/sk/slovseff-iii-sk/slovseff-i-ii-sk. Accessed 25 Feb 2020.

Sme. (2009, January 10). Jaslovské Bohunice znova zapnú, rozhodla vláda. https://ekonomika.sme.sk/c/4256833/jaslovske-bohunice-znova-zapnu-rozhodla-vlada.html. Accessed 4 Jan 2020.

Sme. (2020, January 10). Rekordné číslo. Slovensko ostáva lídrom vo výrobe áut na obyvateľa. https://ekonomika.sme.sk/c/22299052/slovensko-ostava-lidrom-v-produkcii-automobilov-na-obyvatela.html. Accessed 20 Feb 2020.

Soldatkin, V., & Zinets, N. (2019, December 30). Russia, Ukraine clinch final gas deal on gas transit to Europe. Reuters. https://www.reuters.com/article/us-ukraine-russia-gas-deal/russia-ukraine-clinch-final-gas-deal-on-gas-transit-to-europe-idUSKBN1YY1FY. Accessed 12 Jan 2020.

Supreme Audit Office of the Slovak Republic. (2019a). Záverečná správa: Kontrola Slovenského vodohospodárskeho podniku, š.p. a zakladateľskej pôsobnosti Ministerstva životného prostredia SR. https://www.nku.gov.sk/documents/10157/1407476/Zaverecna_sprava_SVP.pdf/7456a6ce-9999-4e58-b690-6477f599aaee. Accessed 26 Feb 2020.

Supreme Audit Office of the Slovak Republic. (2019b). Záverečná správa: Podpora vo vybraných oblastiach klimaticko-energetickej politiky s dôrazom na zachovanie dlhodobej udržateľnosti verejných príjmov. https://www.nku.gov.sk/documents/10157/1407476/Z%C3%A1vere%C4%8Dn%C3%A1+spr%C3%A1va_KA-014_2018_1030_1100_na+publikovanie.pdf/a31a534f-18aa-4536-9e5f-84fb0a7fa0b2. Accessed 25 Feb 2020.

Szalai, P. (2019, February 6). Regulácia slovenských cien elektriny nebola nezávislá. Komisia situáciu "sleduje". Euractiv. https://euractiv.sk/section/energetika/news/regulacia-slovenskych-cien-elektriny-nebola-nezavisla-komisia-situaciu-na-sleduje/. Accessed 20 Feb 2020.

TASR. (2019, December 18). Náklady na vyradenie elektrárne V1 v Mochovciach budú 1.237 mld. eur. https://www.teraz.sk/ekonomika/naklady-na-vyradenie-elektrarne-v1-v-m/436508-clanok.html. Accessed 20 Feb 2020.

Vasilko, T. (2019, September 23). Čaputová vystúpila na klimatickom samite OSN: Máme dlh voči planéte a musíme zmeniť životný štýl. Dennik N. https://dennikn.sk/1594139/caputova-vystupila-na-klimatickom-samite-mame-dlh-voci-planete-povedala/. Accessed 20 Feb 2020.

Energy Governance in Slovenia

Danijel Crnčec

Contents

Introduction	1084
General Conditions of Energy Governance in Slovenia	1085
Legacies	1085
Composition of the Energy Mix	1088
Discourse on Energy Issues	1090
Coordination, Instruments, and Issues of The Slovenian Energy Transition	1093
Strategic and Legal Framework of Slovenian Energy Governance	1093
Political Actors and Policy Coordination	1094
Key Drivers and Issues of Energy Transition	1102
Outcomes, Challenges, and Prospects of Energy Governance	1113
Cross-References	1115
References	1115

Abstract

This chapter examines the governance of energy policy in Slovenia, focusing on renewable energy, nuclear energy, and the coal phaseout as the main issues in a country that considers itself one of the leading green countries in the EU, and also aspires to become climate neutral by 2050. Slovenia represents a relatively small energy system with specific challenges on the path to climate neutrality, the most prominent being transport, spatial planning for renewables, the dilemma of the long-term use of nuclear energy, and the coal phaseout. This chapter argues that despite its self-perceived "greenness," EU membership has had a significant impact on the country. Slovenia needs to overcome a significant gap in strategic policy planning for the period 2010–2020, as well as in implementation, especially in the deployment of renewable energy, to become de facto one of green leaders in the EU. Energy efficiency, nuclear energy, and renewables are

D. Crnčec (✉)
Faculty of Social Sciences, University of Ljubljana, Ljubljana, Slovenia
e-mail: danijel.crncec@fdv.uni-lj.si

© Springer Nature Switzerland AG 2022
M. Knodt, J. Kemmerzell (eds.), *Handbook of Energy Governance in Europe*,
https://doi.org/10.1007/978-3-030-43250-8_28

traditionally anchored in national energy policy preferences and are expected to remain the backbone of Slovenia's energy policy while the country decides on its coal-phaseout ambitions.

Keywords

Slovenia · Energy governance · Energy transition · Nuclear energy · Coal phaseout · Renewable energy · Climate neutrality

Introduction

Slovenia is a Central European and Mediterranean country located in the heart of the Alpine, Adriatic, and Danube regions. It has a diversified energy mix for electricity generation and competitive and fully developed wholesale and retail energy markets. It is well interconnected with its neighboring countries, except Hungary, with which it plans to build gas and electricity interconnectors soon. Despite its full dependence on imports of natural gas and petroleum products, energy import dependence has declined over the last decade and remains below the EU average. Slovenia stands out for its strong performance in energy security. The country supported the transition to climate neutrality by 2050, which must lead to significant changes in the Slovenian energy system and society as a whole.

On the way to an affordable, reliable, and climate-neutral energy system, Slovenia faces several challenges. One of them is energy consumption in the transport sector, the largest energy-consuming sector in Slovenia, which has increased in recent years mainly due to road transport. Public acceptance for further deployment of renewable energy sources (RES), especially hydropower plants (HPPs) and wind power plants (WPPs), was relatively low and represented one of the crucial challenges to achieve a higher share of RES in final energy consumption. Lengthy spatial planning procedures were another key challenge for investment in the RES. In 2021, the country was expected to decide on the coal phaseout, while the issue of future long-term use of nuclear energy remained likely. Coal and nuclear energy each accounted for about one-third of the country's electricity production and contributed significantly to a high level of energy security.

The aim of this chapter is to analyze energy governance in Slovenia at a time of profound change driven by technological progress and environmental and climate concerns. It argues that external factors, in particular the development of the EU Energy Union and Climate Action, have had a significant impact on energy governance in Slovenia following its accession to the EU in 2004. However, as the country represents a relatively small energy system with specific national circumstances, these need to be taken into account not only at the national but also at the EU level if the energy transition toward a climate-neutral society is to be successful. In addition to the specific challenges, various incumbent players strongly influence the day-to-day energy discourse in the country, represent significant inertia, and exhibit an extensive technological lock-in related to the long-term use of nuclear energy and coal phaseout.

The next section discusses the general conditions of energy governance in Slovenia focusing on legacies, the composition of the energy mix, and issues of the energy discourse. The third section begins with the analysis of the strategic energy framework, political actors, and policy coordination. The section continues with the analysis of the main drivers and issues of the energy transition focusing on the long-term use of nuclear energy, the phaseout of coal, the further deployment of RES, transport, and electromobility. The chapter concludes with a brief discussion on the outcomes, challenges, and prospects of energy governance in Slovenia.

General Conditions of Energy Governance in Slovenia

Legacies

The first power plant in Slovenia was built in 1883 when the country was under Austro-Hungarian rule. The introduction of the three-phase transmission system in the 1890s enabled the social and economic development of the country (Hrovatin 2008). In 1915, the first large HPP was built in the Gorenjska region, soon followed by a large HPP on the Drava River in 1918. However, the process of electrification after World War I, when Slovenia became part of the Kingdom of Serbs, Croats, and Slovenes, renamed the Kingdom of Yugoslavia in 1929, lagged behind developed European countries. Between the two world wars, mainly small TPPs were built, as their costs were lower than those of HPPs. After World War II, the Socialist Federal Republic of Yugoslavia was established, and extensive and systematic electrification was initiated, along with intensive construction of large HPPs and thermal power plants (TPPs) (Mravlje 2004). During the Yugoslav period, which lasted until June 25, 1991, when Slovenia proclaimed its independence, several long-lasting legacies in the field of energy policy were established.

Hydropower has traditionally been a part of Slovenia's energy mix. Since 1883, many large and small HPPs have been built on Slovenian rivers. Large HPPs were located on three major rivers: the Sava, the Drava, and the Soča. The first large HPP on the Drava (s.a.) was followed by the construction of 7 large HPPs (between 1944 and 1978). In 2021, the Drava was the most exploited river accounting for as much as 68% of the total hydropower, i.e., almost a quarter of the total electricity generated in Slovenia (DEM n.d.).

In parallel, three large HPPs were built on the upper course of the Sava between 1952 and 1986, and one in 1993 on the lower course. The latter was to be the first in a chain of 6 large HPPs. The construction of the remaining five large HPPs started in 2002, and by 2020 four of them were built, while the last one (Mokrice HPP) was pending due to the complaint of nongovernmental organizations (NGOs) at the Administrative Court. In 1979, a concept of energy use of the Sava River in its middle course was drafted, but it was never realized.

Small HPPs were built on the Soča River even before World War I. After Italy gained control over the Primorska region with the Treaty of Rapallo in 1920, ten large HPPs were planned and construction of the first two (Doblar & Plave) started in

1936. When the Primorska region was regained after World War II, only three large HPPs were planned, one of which was built (Solkan in 1984), while plans for the other two (Trnovo & Kobarid) in the upper course of the Soča River had to be abandoned due to opposition from the local population (Soške elektrarne 2007). Two more HPPs (Plave II & Doblar II) were built in 2002 next to already existing HPPs, and in 2009, the only pump HPP (Avče) in Slovenia.

Hydropower, which accounted for about 30% of electricity generation in Slovenia, is perceived as one of the pillars of security of supply. However, plans for further deployment of small and large HPPs, especially on the middle course of the Sava and Mura rivers, provoked opposition by the local population and NGOs.

After Slovenia acceded to the EU in 2004, further deployment of RES (apart from hydro) gradually came to the forefront of energy governance. To promote electricity generation from RES, a state aid scheme was introduced in 2009 to support RES and combined heat and power (CHP) plants. In 2014, support for solar power plants was reduced and the scheme lost its attractiveness. The National Renewable Energy Action Plan 2010–2020 also envisaged the installation of 106 MW of wind power (2010, p. 128). By 2020, only 5 MW had been installed. Spatial planning and siting of wind farms has emerged as a major challenge in implementation.

Slovenia has also a long tradition of using coal. As early as 1689, a well-known Slovenian historian, Janez Vajkard Valvasor, wrote about "black earth," which was sold by pharmacists as "dragon's blood" to treat cattle. In 1766, the Austrian government issued a decree that anyone could search for coal. Soon it was discovered that three bays of the ancient Pannonian Sea extended into what is now Slovenia, which formed brown coal basins and, together with the later lignite in the Šaleški basin, a raw material base for the development of TPPs in Slovenia (in Šoštanj, Trbovlje, Ljubljana, and Brestanica) (Hrovatin et al. 2007, p. 141). The beginnings of coal mining were connected with the introduction of steam engines, and the first coal mines (of brown coal in Zagorje, Trbovlje, and Hrastnik) were established in the mid-eighteenth and early nineteenth centuries. The construction of the railway Trieste-Vienna in the 1860s and the process of industrialization led to a strong development of coal mining. In the Savinjsko-Šaleška region, the exploitation of coal (lignite) began in 1875 and intensified after World War II with the construction of the Šoštanj TPP. Coal production in Slovenia peaked in 1985 with almost seven million tonnes of coal (75% lignite and 25% brown coal) (Tomašič 2014). The coal extracted in Savinjsko-Šaleška region has a calorific value of approx. 10 MJ/kg and is referred to as lignite. The coal extracted in Zasavje region has a calorific value of approx. 11 MJ/kg and is referred to as brown coal.

The construction of TPPs in Slovenia was connected with the discoveries of coal, the development of electrical engineering, and three-phase current (1893). From 1883, when the first steam TPP in Maribor was built (5 kW), the installed capacity of TPPs increased significantly (1115 kW in 1900, 1152 MW in 2000). Before the end of World War I, many TPPs were built, the largest of which was in Trbovlje. During World War II, a TPP was built by the Germans in Brestanica (Rajhenburg), while their plan for building a TPP in Velenje was not realized. Similarly, Yugoslav planned to build a TPP with Czech equipment in the late 1940s which failed due to the dispute between Yugoslav leader Broz and Stalin, followed by the economic blockade of Yugoslavia by the Eastern Bloc. Finally, in the 1950s, a new TPP was built in the region (Šoštanj I) with Swiss equipment. Units 3, 4, and 5 followed in the 1960s and 1970s due to increased energy demand (Hrovatin et al. 2007, pp. 144–166). Together with the TPP in Trbovlje (TET) and the coal-fired CHP plant in Ljubljana (TE-TOL), the use of coal (mostly domestic lignite and brown coal) became one of the three pillars of secure electricity supply in Slovenia. Before the construction of the Krško nuclear power plant (NPP), it accounted for more than half of the total electricity generation, and after the commissioning of the Krško NPP in 1983, the use of coal accounted for about one-third of the total domestic electricity generation.

Coal mining peaked in the 1980s, and by 2000 smallest and most economically unviable coal mined had closed. In 1999, a referendum was held on the construction of Unit 3 at the Trbovlje TPP. After its rejection, the decision on the closure of the coal mine Trbovlje Hrastnik (RTH) in the period 2000–2015 was taken. The process of closure was extended twice – once until 2018 and then until 2021 (Ministry of Infrastructure 2019a). The only active coal mine remained in Velenje, whose lignite was used in the nearby Šoštanj TPP, where the highly controversial unit 6 was commissioned in 2014. In 2018, unit 4 at TPP Šoštanj was shut down, leaving unit 5 (345 MW) and unit 6 (545 MW) in operation.

One of the legacies, which not only had a significant impact on energy discourse and governance in Slovenia but has also been burdening bilateral relations with Croatia, was the issue of nuclear energy. The Krško NPP was built in 1974–1981 as a joint venture between Slovenia and Croatia, two former socialist republics of Yugoslavia, and their energy utilities. It is located in Vrbina in the municipality of Krško, near the border with Croatia and about 50 km from its capital Zagreb. The NPP went into commercial operation on 1 January 1983. It is a Westinghouse 2-loop-pressurized water reactor with an original net capacity of 632 MWe, which was upgraded to 727/696 MWe (gross electrical power/net electrical power) in 2000. The operating company, Nuklearna elektrarna Krško (NEK), was co-owned (50:50) by the Slovenian state-owned energy company GEN energija and the Croatian state-owned energy company Hrvatska elektroprivreda (HEP). The electricity generated by the Krško NPP was shared equally between the two countries (ARAO and Fund NPP 2019, p. 2–3).

The contractual framework for the construction and operation of the Krško NPP was outlined by four governing agreements establishing the parity principle (ICSID Case No. ARB/05/24, para 90). The original plan to build two NPPs, one in each republic, was abandoned in the 1980s due to the unstable political situation and the Chernobyl accident. In the 1990s, after the disintegration of Yugoslavia, disagreements arose over the operation and status of the Krško NPP and the application of the governing agreements. Negotiations on a new agreement started in March 1994, but many controversies led to the suspension of electricity supplies to Croatia in July 1998 (ICSID Case No. ARB/05/24, paras 104–138). In June 2001, there was a breakthrough in the negotiations, and in December 2001 *Agreement between the Government of the Republic of Slovenia and the Government of the Republic of*

Croatia on the Regulation of the Status and Other Legal Relations Regarding the Investment, Exploitation, and Decommissioning of the Krško NPP (the NEK Agreement) was signed. It established equal ownership of the Krško NPP, joint responsibility for nuclear waste, and the settlement of mutual claims. The Interstate Commission was also established to monitor the implementation in accordance with the NEK Agreement (Art. 18).

Croatia ratified the NEK agreement in July 2002, while Slovenia did so only in February 2003, after a constitutional challenge to the agreement was unsuccessful. As the resumption of electricity deliveries to Croatia did not take place until April 2003, ICSID arbitration proceedings were initiated by the Croatian HEP against Slovenia. The final ICSID award in 2015 ended the long-running arbitration in favor of the Croatian HEP and awarded it more than €40 million in damages, interest, and legal fees (ICSID Case No. ARB /05/24).

In 2012, the owners and the Slovenian regulatory body, Slovenian Nuclear Safety Administration, approved a lifetime extension of the Krško NPP for another 20 years, until 2043, subject to the successful completion of periodic safety reviews in 2023 and 2033 (ARAO and Fund NPP 2019, p. 3). The extension became an important issue of energy discourse, as NGOs demanded that an environmental impact assessment should be conducted. After 2000, also the idea of building a new NPP in Krško was launched, which was presented as both a driver and an obstacle to the energy transition. It became one of the most divisive issues of energy governance.

Composition of the Energy Mix

In 2019, Slovenia's total primary energy supply was 6.6 Mtoe (278 PJ). The share of petroleum products predominated (32.4%), followed by nuclear energy (22.7%), RES (including hydro) (17.9%), coal (15.9%), and natural gas (11.1%) (see Fig. 1 below). Compared to the EU-27, Slovenia had a higher share of nuclear energy and RES, but a significantly lower share of natural gas.

The structure of the Slovenian energy mix has been rather stable since the late 1990s, except RES that has been gradually increasing (mainly hydro), while the role of solid fuels has been decreasing (see Fig. 2).

Slovenia's energy import dependence has been gradually increasing since 2000, peaking in 2008 at almost 55% of all energy imports. However, with the breakout of the financial and economic crisis, energy import dependence, along with the GDP, decreased (47% in 2009). Since then, it has remained at around 50%, slightly below the EU average. Slovenia is fully dependent on imports of petroleum products. The only refinery in Slovenia, in Lendava, was shut down in 2000. Since then, Slovenia has been importing only refined petroleum products and no crude oil. All petroleum products came from the world market. Slovenia was also almost entirely dependent on imports of natural gas. The country had no underground natural gas storage facilities or liquefied natural gas terminals and could import natural gas via neighboring Austria, Italy, and Croatia.

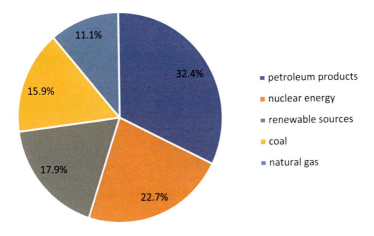

Fig. 1 Energy Supply, Slovenia, 2019. (Source: SORS 2020a)

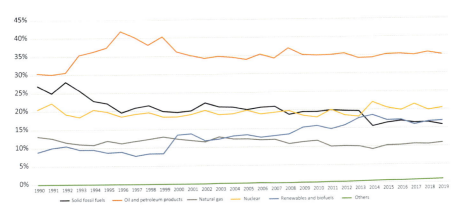

Fig. 2 Energy Mix (%), Slovenia, 1990–2019. (Source: Eurostat, 2021)

Slovenia's gas imports are not very diversified. In 2019, 88% of the total imported natural gas was imported from Austria, the rest was imported from Russia. Only 0.23% of (Algerian) natural gas was imported from Italy in 2019. The volume of long-term contracts traditionally concluded directly with Russian gas producers was significantly reduced due to market liberalization and replaced by short-term contracts concluded at gas hubs, exchanges, and other points within the EU. In 2019, 81.7% of natural gas was procured through short-term contracts with a duration of less than 1 year, which could impact security of supply in the event of a gas shortage (Energy Agency 2020, p. 187). Slovenia imported only limited quantities of hard coal. Uranium ore was purchased and chemically processed overseas, and the nuclear fuel elements for the Krško NPP were manufactured by Westinghouse in the USA.

Electricity in Slovenia is generated mainly from fossil fuels, nuclear fuel, and RES. Large HPPs, TPPs, and the NPP were connected to the Slovenian transmission system and contributed to more than 90% of domestic production. Electricity produced in HPPs was price competitive and depended mainly on hydrology in a given period. The utilization factor in the Krško NPP was generally very high and constant in time, while the level of production in fossil power plants was highly dependent on the daily consumption curve (energy demand) and some other market factors. In 2019, production in the transmission system from hydro accounted for 35% of total domestic production, while production from thermal accounted for 33% and from nuclear for 23% (i.e., 50% share from Krško NPP). Electricity production amounted to approximately 12 GWh, while total electricity consumption was 14.3 GWh. Thus, domestic production covered 83.5% of total consumption, while the rest was imported (Agency Energy 2020, pp. 25–26).

Discourse on Energy Issues

Slovenian energy policy discourse revolved around past legacies. It focused on security of energy supply, with a clear emphasis on energy efficiency, followed by environmental sustainability and competitiveness of energy supply. Initially, security of supply was dominant in the energy discourse. However, with Slovenia's accession to the EU in 2004, environmental sustainability gradually came to the fore with a focus on a "clean" energy supply based on low-carbon sources. Key persisting issues within the energy discourse were primarily the use of nuclear energy, as well as the use of coal and the deployment of RES.

Nuclear energy in Slovenia involved several interdependent aspects. First, the 2012 decision to extend the operation of the existing Krško NPP by another 20 years (until 2043) was met with opposition from part of the NGOs (Focus 2017). The Administrative Court overturned the decision that an environmental impact assessment was not required, and in 2020 it was decided that an environmental permit for the extension of the operation of the Krško NPP until 2043 had to be obtained (ARSO 2020). The procedure will involve transboundary consultations with neighboring countries, with strong opposition expected from Austria, which has opposed the Krško NPP for decades (Tavčar and Malovrh 2020).

Second, the issue of radioactive waste from the Krško NPP and its decommissioning was important not only in the energy discourse in Slovenia but also in bilateral relations with Croatia. The NEK Agreement stipulates that the countries should provide an effective joint solution regarding radioactive waste disposal (Article 10, para 1 and 2). After unsuccessful talks in 2018 and 2019, Slovenia and Croatia will build separate disposals for low and intermediate-level radioactive waste from the Krško NPP. In parallel, the Slovenian Court of Audit has assessed that the Slovenian Government has not provided for control over the management of funds for financing the decommissioning of the Krško NPP and the disposal of radioactive waste (Court of Audit 2017).

Third, the most prominent and divisive, as well as future-determining, issue of energy governance and discourse was the long-term use of nuclear energy and the construction of a new NPP. Initially, it was framed in the context of energy security, but eventually, its proponents began to emphasize carbon-free power generation and its contribution to decarbonization. The company GEN energija, which operated the Krško NPP, was vocal in its support for the long-term use of nuclear energy in combination with RES as the only sustainable option for electricity generation in Slovenia. They insisted that a new NPP should be built in Krško, presenting it as a domestic energy source that would reduce Slovenia's energy dependence and ensure a predictable and stable electricity price. As a low-carbon energy source, it should ensure the reduction of CO_2 emissions at the national level (GEN energija 2021).

The issue was highly controversial and contested, polarizing experts and the general public. On the one hand, the nuclear community (GEN energija and nuclear experts) strongly advocated the long-term use of nuclear energy and the construction of a new NPP as a necessary element and driver of the transition to a climate-neutral society (Kosmač 2019). On the other hand, opponents of nuclear energy claimed that it was a twentieth-century technology with serious safety risks and negative externalities related to uranium mining and nuclear waste disposal. Moreover, it represented a specific and significant risk for Slovenia as a small country, which could severely hinder other energy investments (especially in RES), urgently needed for the energy transition, due to the large scale of the required financial investment (Huš 2020). It also involved the technological split over whether to build a reactor similar to Westinghouse's existing one or opt for small modular reactors. While the company GEN energija called for a quick decision on the second nuclear power unit and advocated the commercially available technologies (EPosavje 2020), some nuclear experts stressed that Slovenia could or should wait to decide to see if small nuclear reactor technology becomes commercially viable (Vorkapić 2020; Novak 2021).

The long-term use of nuclear energy also became an important agenda item in bilateral relations with the United States. During the visit of the US Secretary of Energy Rick Perry in 2019 in the framework of the Three Seas Initiative and the US Secretary of State Mike Pompeo in 2020, the development of small modular reactors and cooperation in the civil use of nuclear energy were discussed. Since the existing Krško NPP used Westinghouse technology, the issue of nuclear energy was perceived by Slovenian politicians as an important opportunity for improving energy cooperation and political and economic relations with the United States. Indeed, in December 2020, the countries signed the Memorandum on Civilian Nuclear Cooperation (Government of Slovenia 2020a).

Another important aspect of the energy discourse was the use of domestic coal for electricity generation. For many years, coal was considered an important element of domestic energy supply (ReNEP Proposal 2011, pp. 27–28). Moreover, the environmental dimension was also emphasized with respect to Unit 6 at the Šoštanj TPP as its purpose was to gradually replace the technologically obsolete four oldest units with the best available technology. By consuming 30% less coal, the Unit 6 would significantly reduce CO_2 emissions and the level of pollution (TEŠ 2021). However, the construction of Unit 6 in Šoštanj was highly controversial, as there was no clear consensus among decision-makers or in the energy community. When the initial price of €600 million increased to €1.4 billion, the project came under the scrutiny of anticorruption authorities of Slovenia and the EU, and many national and international institutions expressed suspicions of corruption. Indeed, in March 2021, HSE and General Electric (the legal successor to Alstom, which had built Unit 6) signed an arbitration settlement worth €261 million. In parallel, criminal proceedings against 16 people were underway in national courts (Kos and Eržen 2021).

In 2021, the Šoštanj TPP and its Unit 6 again came to the forefront of energy policy discourse due to the proposed coal phaseout in 2033, i.e., the closure of Unit 6 at the Šoštanj TPP (which was to operate until 2054) and the Velenje coal mine. The proposed date was strongly contested by the local municipality and coal and energy unions, who argued for a much later coal phaseout (even until 2046). They supported the domestic coal industry by repeatedly claiming that enough time was needed for economic restructuring to minimize the negative social consequences of the coal phaseout (Strniša 2021). Some other stakeholders emphasized the positive environmental and climate impacts of the coal phaseout, as well as the rising prices of emission allowances in the EU ETS and the unsustainable economics of using coal for electricity generation (Tavčar 2021). In addition, NGOs have called for the closure of the Šoštanj TPP and the Velenje coal mine well before 2030. The decision on coal phaseout should be made by summer 2021.

Similarly, the deployment of RES was one of the most important issues of energy discourse in Slovenia. After Slovenia's accession to the EU, it has been framed mainly in the context of decarbonization and climate change mitigation. Under the Renewable Energy Directive 2009/28/ ES, the target for Slovenia was set at 25% (in the reference year 2005, it was 16.2%). The country was likely to miss it, as it was lagging in the electricity and transport sectors in 2019. In the electricity sector, one of the main problems was spatial planning of large energy infrastructure (especially hydro and wind). On the one hand, large WPPs and HPPs (on the Mura and Sava rivers) have been met with increasing opposition from the local population and some environmental NGOs. On the other hand, in April 2019, 65% of respondents in Slovenia considered it very important and 28% important that the government set ambitious targets to increase the share of RES such as wind or solar energy by 2030 (Eurobarometer 2019).

In 2018, the center-left government announced its decision to protect the Mura River (Coalition Agreement 2018–2022, 2018), and in 2019 all further activities related to the proposed HPP Hrastje-Mota on the Mura River were halted due to its environmental unacceptability. Despite the opposition from the part of environmental NGOs, the political elite was quite consensual regarding further deployment of hydro energy on the Sava River. Both the center-left (2018–2020) and center-right (2020–2022) governments announced that they would complete the construction of the last remaining large hydropower plant on the lower Sava River and enhance spatial planning processes for large HPPs on the middle Sava River (Coalition Agreement 2018–2022, 2018; Coalition Agreement 2020–2022, 2020). However, the proposed HPPs on the middle Sava River had to be excluded from the Integrated

National Energy and Climate Plan (NECP) due to their assessed negative impacts on surface waters quality, biodiversity protection, and natural areas (Environmental Report (draft) 2019, p. xix). Despite that, in October 2020, the government and the company HSE Group signed the concession agreement for the use of water for electricity production on the middle Sava River (Government of Slovenia 2020b). In December 2020, the government adopted the (first-ever) decision on the overriding public interest of energy over public interest of nature conservation in Slovenia in the case of the last remaining HPP on the lower Sava River (Mokrice) (Government of Slovenia 2020c). The decision was challenged by NGOs and was pending in 2021 in Administrative Court. Hydropower was perceived as one of the cornerstones of the future energy mix of Slovenia, but contestation and tensions between different stakeholders regarding its deployment were significant.

In the past, some other issues have also shaped the energy discourse in Slovenia, but sporadically and for a limited period of time. One of the most prominent was the South Stream project, which became an important and promising political and economic issue in the relations with Russia. The intergovernmental agreement between Slovenia and Russia on the operation of South Stream pipeline in Slovenia, which should be a bridge between Hungary and Italy, was signed in November 2009. However, following Putin's announcement in December 2014 that the South Stream project had been canceled, all further activities were suspended.

Coordination, Instruments, and Issues of The Slovenian Energy Transition

Strategic and Legal Framework of Slovenian Energy Governance

The 1996 Resolution on the Strategy of Energy Use and Supply of Slovenia focused on the efficient use of energy and energy supply. It stressed energy efficiency as the long-term strategic guideline on all fields of energy use, sufficient and reliable energy supply, and achieving of faster growth of gross domestic product compared to growth of final and primary energy and growth of energy dependence (Resolution on the Strategy of Energy Use and Supply of Slovenia 1996). The 1999 Energy Act introduced the obligation to adopt a National Energy Program to set, among other things, long-term goals and orientations for energy systems and supply, investments in public infrastructure, incentives for investments in renewable energy sources, and efficient energy use (Energy Act 1999, Art. 13). The National Energy Program adopted in 2004 grouped the objectives of Slovenian energy policy into three pillars of sustainable development: security of energy supply, competitiveness, and environmental impact. The National Energy Program should have been updated at least every 5 years, but its 2011 proposal, with completed strategic environmental assessment (and cross-border consultations with neighboring countries), was not approved. It emphasized that all three energy policy objectives were equally important and proposed operational targets, among which energy efficiency and renewable energy were prioritized.

In 2014, a new Energy Act came into force, replacing the previous one from 1999. It aimed to "ensure a competitive, secure, reliable and affordable supply of energy and energy services while respecting the principles of sustainable development" (Energy Act 2014, Art. 2). It also stipulated that the Energy Concept of Slovenia should be adopted every 5 years as a basic long-term development program (constituting a national energy program) for the next 20 years (with a 40-year outlook) (Energy Act 2014, Art. 23). After 4 years of preparation, the proposal was adopted by the government in 2018 and submitted to National Assembly but was not approved. The "curse" of not being able to adopt a comprehensive strategic energy policy document since 2004 was finally overcome with the adoption of the NECP in February 2020, which set national energy and climate goals for 2030 (with an outlook to 2040).

The structure and wording of the adopted and proposed strategic documents show that the focus has gradually shifted from energy security and efficient energy use (1996) to the three pillars of energy policy in 2011 and 2018 (security of supply, environmental/climate sustainability, and competitiveness). The NECP (its structure was established by the Governance Regulation (EU) 2018/1999) further emphasized that improving energy and resource efficiency in all sectors (and thus reducing the consumption of energy and other resources) was the first and most important tool for the transition to a climate-neutral society (see Table 1 below).

The adoption of the EU legislative package "Clean Energy for all Europeans" was followed by a comprehensive update of the energy legislation in Slovenia. The existing Energy Act was divided into a general energy act and several specific acts regulating individual energy sectors. By joining the European Commission initiative, Slovenia also started the preparation of its coal phaseout strategy (expected to be adopted in 2021) and two territorial plans for just transition in two coal regions, while the Long-Term Strategy for Renovation of Buildings to 2050 was adopted in March 2021. In July 2021, the Long-Term Climate Strategy of Slovenia to 2050 was finally adopted, outlining two scenarios for attaining climate neutrality and setting key climate and energy objectives, policies, and measures to 2050 (with intermediate milestones for 2030 and 2040). It was prepared using the same expert bases and energy balances as of the NECP. Following its adoption, the Ministry of Infrastrucure proposed to abandon the preparation of the Energy Concept of Slovenia. The existing relevant strategic and legal energy policy framework is shown in Fig. 3.

Political Actors and Policy Coordination

While this chapter argues that external drivers and actors significantly shaped strategic energy governance in Slovenia, domestic actors still had an important influence on the specifics of energy discourse and governance. Since 2014, the Ministry of Infrastructure has been responsible for energy policy. It has had the responsibility to prepare the strategic, political, and legal energy framework, as well as to guide and implement energy policy. It successfully prepared and coordinated

43 Energy Governance in Slovenia

Table 1 Strategic energy policy framework and overview of key policies and targets (1996–2021)

Document	Year of adoption	Key Policies and Targets				
		Long-term strategic directions	Security of supply	Renewable energy	Efficient use of energy	Reduction of GHGs
Resolution on the Strategy of Energy Use and Supply of Slovenia	1996	Energy efficiency in all areas of energy use A significant increase in the share of RES in primary energy balance Abandoning the existing production of electricity based on nuclear energy Acceptable volume of electricity generation at existing and planned new TPPs and CHP Increasing the utilization of hydropower	Sufficient and reliable energy supply: utilization of all technical capacities for efficient use of energy and for the use of domestic and RES gradual reduction of the use of fossil energy sources No new nuclear units planned, while creating conditions for nuclear phaseout (the decision should be adopted at least 10 years in advance)	RES as the most important source of primary energy in Slovenia and one of its strategic energy reserves Enhancing the use of hydropower, biomass, geothermal, and solar energy, as well as the use of waste heat	Improving energy efficiency Reducing energy consumption Providing quality energy services	For all energy plans, environmental impact assessments should be done No policy or targets on GHG emission reductions
Resolution on National Energy Program	2004	Energy efficiency in all areas of energy use as a long-term strategic guideline	Reliable and high-quality electricity supply Balanced diversification of the use of primary energy sources Economically	Increase from 8.8% in 2001 to 12% share of RES in primary energy by 2010: from 22% to 25% in heat supply from 32% to 33.6% in electricity	Improving energy efficiency by 2010 (compared to 2004): in industry and service sector by 10% in buildings by 10% in the public	Reduction of GHG emissions by 8% in 2008–2012 (Kyoto I period) compared to 1986

(continued)

Table 1 (continued)

Document	Year of adoption	Key Policies and Targets					
		Long-term strategic directions	Security of supply	Renewable energy	Efficient use of energy	Reduction of GHGs
			justified use of RES and promoting of CHP Competitive electricity supply from domestic energy sources, of at least 75% of current consumption Operation of the Krško NPP until the end of its regular lifetime (2023)	2% of biofuels Construction of five large HPPs on the lower Sava river Construction of WPPs	sector by 15% in transport by 10% Double the share of electricity from CHP	
(Proposed) National energy program to 2030	*2011 proposal, not approved*	*Energy efficiency, the use of RES, and the development of active electricity distribution networks as priority areas to ensure gradual transition to a low-carbon society*	*Reduction of import dependence to at least 45% by 2030 and diversification of energy supply sources*	25% share of RES in gross final energy consumption by 2020 30% share of RES by 2030	20% improvement by 2020 27% improvement by 2030 Reduction of energy intensity by 29% by 2020 and by 46% by 2030 100% share of near-zero energy buildings between new and refurbished buildings by 2020 and in the public sector by 2018	*9.5% reduction in GHG emissions from fuel combustion by 2020* *18% reduction by 2030*

(Proposed) Resolution on Energy Concept of Slovenia	2018 proposal, not adopted	Reliable, secure, and competitive energy supply in a sustainable way for the transition to a low-carbon society	- Sufficient supply of energy sources, sufficient capacity and diversification of supply routes Efficient and regularly maintained networks Adequate cross-border connections Reliable and efficient cooperation of energy systems, electricity sources, and energy storage facilities	25% share of RES in gross final energy consumption by 2020 (no targets to 2030 and 2050)	Improve energy efficiency by 20% by 2020 (no targets to 2030 and 2050)	Meeting GHG emission targets in non-ETS sectors by 2020 (no targets to 2030 and 2050)
Integrated National Energy and Climate Plan	2020	Improving energy and material efficiency in all sectors as the first and key instrument for the transition to a climate-neutral society	High level of electricity connection with neighboring countries (no interconnectivity target; in 2017: 83,6%) At least 75% of electricity supply from sources in Slovenia	At least 27% share of RES by 2030: 43% in RES-E 41% in RES-H&C 21% in RES-T (biofuels content at least 11%)	Improve energy efficiency by at least 35% to 2030 (compared to 2007 reference scenario) Use 20% less energy in buildings and reduce GHG emissions by −70% by 2030 compared to 2005	GHG reduction by at least 20% to 2030 in non-ETS sectors (compared to 2005) Indicative targets: transport (+12%), agriculture (−1%), widespread use (−76%) of which buildings (−70%), non-ETS industry

(continued)

Table 1 (continued)

| Document | Year of adoption | Key Policies and Targets |||||
		Long-term strategic directions	Security of supply	Renewable energy	Efficient use of energy	Reduction of GHGs
			Reduce use of fossil fuels and import dependency (−30% coal by 2030; ban of sale and installation of new oil boilers until 2023) Increase the share of the underground medium voltage network from 35% to at least 50% Hydrogen and synthetic methane demonstration projects Energy poverty to be mitigated and reduced			(−43%), waste management (−65%), and non-ETS energy (−34%) No net emissions in LULUCF by 2030

Resolution on the Long-term climate strategy of Slovenia to 2050	2021	Priority to energy efficiency measures over the construction of new energy supply capacities Immediate implementation of already adopted policies and instruments End of implementation and adoption of policies and instruments that run counter to GHG emission reductions	Two scenarios of the development of large electricity generation facilities after 2030: (a) continued use of nuclear energy with the construction of a new unit (b) construction of larger gas-steam units [PPE] in combination with the use of natural or synthetic gas Slovenia confirmed that it plans long-term use of nuclear energy, and to carry out the necessary administrative procedures and prepare documentation for investment decision-making Share of electricity in final energy consumption to increase to 50% by 2050	The total share of RES of at least 60%, and indicatively: at least 80% share in gross final consumption of electricity at least 50% share in heating and cooling At least 65% share in transport Decarbonization of electricity generation by phasing out fossil fuel use by 2050 at the latest	Reduction of final energy consumption by almost 30% (compared to 2017), i.e., final energy consumption below 40 TWh (In 2040: final energy consumption below 47 TWh, primary energy consumption below 65 TWh)	Climate neutrality, i.e., net zero emissions by 2050: reduce GHG emissions by 80-90% improve sinks (at least 2,500 kt CO_2 annually) Strategic goal for 2040: reduction of GHG emissions by 55–66%

Source: author

Fig. 3 Relevant national strategic and legal energy policy framework. (Source: author)

the adoption of the NECP in 2019 and 2020. However, it was less successful with the proposal of the Energy Concept of Slovenia, which was in preparation between 2014 and 2018 but was not adopted. In 2021, the Ministry of Infrastructure was preparing the national coal phaseout strategy.

In addition to the Ministry of Infrastructure, the Ministry of Environment and Spatial Planning also played an important role in energy governance: first, at the strategic level, through the development of national long-term climate policy and the conduct of strategic environmental assessments of strategic energy documents; and second, at the implementation level through spatial planning of energy infrastructure. To a lesser extent, some other ministries also influenced developments in the energy sector, e.g., the Ministry of Economic Development and Technology was responsible for the formulation of Slovenia's industrial policy (covering also energy-intensive industries), the Ministry of Education, Science and Sport was responsible for national funding of research and development (including in the energy sector), and the Ministry of Labour, Family, Social Affairs and Equal Opportunities was responsible for the policy on (energy) poverty.

Energy and climate policies were implemented through various national agencies and institutions. The Energy Agency was established after Slovenia joined the EU. It constituted the national energy regulator and was responsible for creating a level-playing field for all energy market participants. The Agency also managed the state aid scheme promoting electricity generation through RES and CHP. Once it granted support, the beneficiary could enter the support scheme, which was administered by Borzen, the Slovenian electricity market operator. Borzen also provided an impetus for environmental policy and promoted public awareness. An important role in the implementation of energy efficiency and renewable energy measures was played by Slovenian Environmental Fund (the Eco Fund) by offering financial incentives such as soft loans and grants for various environmental investment projects. The Environment

Agency, which was an agency of the Ministry of Environment and Spatial Planning, performed technical, analytical, regulatory, and administrative functions related to the environment at the national level. It issued a variety of environmental permits and kept records of emissions, regulated and monitored remediation programs, and paid special attention to raising awareness of the environment and related issues.

In 2019, nine companies operated large-scale plants with an installed capacity of more than 10 MW. They were organized in two wholesale, fully state-owned, energy pillars and significantly influenced not only the specifics of energy discourse but also energy policy strategic planning and governance. The Holding Slovenske elektrarne (HSE) group represented the first energy pillar of the Slovenian wholesale market and included the company Dravske elektrarne Maribor (DEM) with eight HPPs on the Drava River, the company Soške elektrarne Nova Gorica (SENG) with 5 HPPs on the Soča River and one pump storage HPP, HSE Energetska družba Trbovlje (HSE ED Trbovlje), a successor of the closed TPP Trbovlje, and the lignite-fired TPP Šoštanj. The GEN energija group represented the second energy pillar and owned the company Savske elekarne Ljubljana (SEL) with 5 HPPs on the Sava River, Brestanica TPP, and 50% of the NPP Krško. The company Hidroelektrarne na Spodnji Savi (HESS) with 4 HPPs on the lower Sava River was co-owned by the HSE group (51%) and GEN energija (49%). In 2019, the HSE Group accounted for 57% of total electricity production, while the GEN Group accounted for 29% of all electricity production (Energy Agency 2020, p. 21–22).

The energy sector was actively involved in the national strategic planning of energy and climate policies, in particular the HSE group and GEN energija. During the preparation of the NECP, the HSE group advocated an ambitious national RES target, the deployment of decentralized RES, and the construction of large HPPs (on the Sava and Mura rivers) together with instruments that would allow easier and faster spatial planning of HPPs and other energy infrastructure. GEN energija strongly supported a combination of nuclear and RES as the only sustainable option for future electricity generation and supported a second NPP in Krško. In contrast to the HSE group, GEN energija was more conservative in its ambition to use RES. Both supported the establishment of a special government body to make decisions on "priority projects of national importance" (Ministry of Infrastructure 2019b).

Environmental NGOs in Slovenia are well developed and active in larger European NGO networks. On the one hand, they were very active in energy strategic planning and strategic environmental assessments, with some NGOs strongly advocating high national climate and energy targets. Their influence on energy strategic planning was limited, but they were able to gain a lot of media attention and successfully publicly name and shame the government for not setting more ambitious energy and climate targets and policies (Focus 2019). On the other hand, some environmental NGOs actively participated in spatial planning processes for large energy infrastructure and their environmental impact assessments, strongly advocating for nature conservation and opposing any further construction of large energy infrastructure, especially HPPs and WPPs. A vivid example of the collision between energy and nature conservation goals was the construction of the Mokrice HPP, the last HPP on the lower Sava River, which was pending in Administrative Court.

The lack of human resources at all levels – from ministries to energy companies and energy end users – constitutes a major challenge related to energy (and climate) governance and policy implementation in all sectors (NECP 2020, p. 218). It was assessed that Slovenia faced a systemic lack of human resources in all institutions involved in climate policy implementation, especially in the Ministry of Environment and Spatial Planning (Petelin Visočnik et al. 2020, p. 42). Therefore, a government service should be established to provide organizational, technical, and other support to the government on climate policy and to coordinate the work of ministries in this regard (ibid.). In July 2021, the National Assembly adopted the Resolution on the Long-Term Climate Strategy of Slovenia to 2050, which emphasized that the goal of climate neutrality by 2050 can only be achieved with the effective, successful, and coordinated implementation of long-term climate policy, and provided for the establishment of a government service responsible for the coordination of Slovenia's climate policy (Resolucija o Dolgoročni podnebni strategiji do leta 2050 (ReDPSS50)). Interestingly, Slovenia already had a Government Office for Climate Change in the past (June 2009–March 2012), which was abolished when the current Prime Minister Janša took office for the second time. In the past, visible members of his (ruling) political party publicly denied anthropogenic climate change and the need to act (Zgonik 2019).

Finally, political actors, especially the ruling political parties, have in the past either neglected energy policy governance or failed to demonstrate leadership and a clear vision. Slovenia lacked a long-term strategic energy framework – the last long-term strategic energy document was adopted in 2004 and should have been updated within 5 years. The adoption of proposed energy strategic documents in 2011 and 2018 failed. In 2014, a highly controversial Unit 6 of the TPP Šoštanj was put into operation, also due to, according to the findings of the parliamentary inquiry on TEŠ 6, "irresponsible or at least negligent governments in the period 2004-2012, imputed to the TPP Šoštanj company" (National Assembly 2018, pp. 445–446).

Nonetheless, the adoption of the NECP in February 2020 and of the more ambitious non-ETS target by 2030, as well as of the of the Long-Term Climate Strategy and the preparation of the National Strategy on the Coal Phaseout, indicated a more determined and coherent approach. However, all three documents were prepared and adopted primarily as a result of obligations stemming from EU energy and climate legislation and conditionality arising from access to EU funds.

Key Drivers and Issues of Energy Transition

A comprehensive analysis of the drivers and challenges of the energy transition in Slovenia from a multilevel perspective (Crnčec, Sučić and Merše 2021) has shown that the energy transition was influenced both by internal and mainly external drivers. First, the NGO sector and the epistemic community in Slovenia were well developed and represented a strong proponent of energy transition as a response to climate change. They were joined by a youth climate movement, and together they called on governments to declare a climate crisis, close the Šoštanj TPP before 2030, and stressed the need for a transition to a carbon-neutral Slovenia by 2040 (Podnebnakriza.si 2019; Government of Slovenia 2019; Youth for Climate Justice 2019). Second, there was strong support in public opinion regarding the energy transition. More than three-quarters of respondents in the 2019 Eurobarometer survey in Slovenia considered climate change to be a "very serious" problem (76%), and almost four out of five respondents (79%) had already taken personal action to combat climate change. Slovenians generally felt it was important for their national government to support improving energy efficiency by 2030 and to set ambitious targets for increasing the use of renewable energy by 2030. They strongly supported (92%) the goal of a climate-neutral EU by 2050 (Eurobarometer 2019). And third, since Slovenia's accession to the EU, EU climate and energy policy have been the main driver of the energy transition in Slovenia. The drafting and adoption of strategic energy documents chronologically followed developments in EU energy and climate policy and often (solely) reflected targets set at the EU level. An important external actor promoting the development of Slovenian energy and climate policy and its ambitions was to some extent also the European Commission, especially in the iterative process of NECP preparation (Crnčec, Sučić, and Merše 2021).

Slovenia did not stand out as an innovation leader in the EU. The Eco-Innovation Index showed Slovenia as an average eco-innovation performer, slightly above the EU average (Crnčec 2020). In addition, Slovenia was also significantly behind the Barcelona target of achieving total public and private investment of at least 3% of GDP in R&D by 2020. In 2019, government R&D expenditure as a share of GDP was only 0.3% (the 2020 target was 1%), while gross domestic expenditure on R&D was 2% (the 2020 target was 3%) (SORS 2021a, b). Nevertheless, some research institutions showed research excellence and successfully participated in innovation activities under Horizon 2020. In addition, Slovenia showed some niche knowledge and research initiatives also in the integration of RES and advanced consumers, regulation of electricity systems, and ensuring the stability of the transmission grid. The leading actor was ELES, the Slovenian electricity transmission system operator, which successfully and actively cooperates with leading European institutions and companies (Crnčec, Sučić, and Merše 2021).

In the following subsections, some key issues of the energy transition in Slovenia are identified and analyzed, including nuclear energy, coal phaseout, further deployment of RES, energy efficiency, and transport and electric mobility.

Nuclear Energy: From the Extension of the Operation of the Existing Unit to the Construction of a New Nuclear Unit?

In 1970, the decision to build the NPP in Krško was made due to electricity shortages, and after the NPP started commercial operation in 1983, it became one of the three pillars of secure energy supply in Slovenia (along with coal and hydro). The use of nuclear energy involved several different but interdependent aspects, and the governance of nuclear energy policy has been anything but predictable since its early beginnings.

The Krško NPP was built on the premise that another NPP would be built in neighboring Croatia. After the disintegration of Yugoslavia, this idea was abandoned, and in the 1990s Slovenia even decided on the long-term strategic direction of abandoning existing nuclear power generation. It decided not to plan any new nuclear power plants, while the continued operation and gradual creation of conditions for the safe decommissioning of the Krško NPP were to be determined by the National Energy Program (Resolution on the Strategy of Energy Use and Supply of Slovenia, 1996). In contrast, National Energy Program (2004) stated that the possibility of extending the operation of the Krško NPP should be considered. While the decision to extend the operation for another 20 years (until 2043) was made in 2012, it was only in 2020 that it was clarified that an environmental impact assessment had to be carried out. The extension of the operation of the Krško NPP was widely supported by Slovenian politicians; however, the implementation of the environmental impact assessment proved to be a demanding and lengthy procedure. If not completed by 2023 or negative, the Krško NPP would have to be (temporarily) shut down (Hreščak 2020). This would severely affect Slovenian (and Croatian) security of electricity supply, as no alternative source existed. It would increase import dependence and electricity prices (Tavčar in Malovrh 2020).

An important aspect of (nuclear) energy governance was also the issue of radioactive waste from the Krško NPP, which was temporarily stored on the premises of the Krško NPP, and its decommissioning. The NEK Agreement (Article 10, para 1 and 2) stipulates that the management of radioactive waste and spent nuclear fuel is a joint obligation of both countries. However, Slovenia and Croatia were unable to agree on joint radioactive waste management. Slovenia decided to build a repository for low and intermediate-level radioactive waste at the Vrbina site, near the Krško NPP. In 2018 and 2019, discussions were held with Croatia on its possible participation, but the Interstate Commission was unable to resolve the issues of Croatian institutional nuclear waste and the amount of compensation to be paid to the local community. In addition, the latter opposed the proposal that Croatia would store its other nuclear waste in Krško. Countries will thus build separate repositories for low and intermediate-level radioactive waste from their joint NPP, and they will independently bear their own costs, which will be higher compared to a joint solution. While the low and intermediate-level radioactive waste from the Krško NPP must be removed no later than two years after the end of regular operation (i.e., by 2025) (NEK Agreement, Art. 10(7)), the spent nuclear fuel will remain at the NPP site until the end of operation (2043) (RTV Slovenia 2018; RTV Slovenia 2019a; Government of Slovenia 2020d).

Similarly, the issue of decommissioning of the existing NPP has been hardly well managed. Two decommissioning programs were prepared and adopted in 1996 and 2004. The second revision in 2010 and 2011 was not approved, and only in 2020 the third revision was approved, estimating that Slovenia would have to allocate €1.09 billion and Croatia €1.03 billion for the management of low and intermediate level waste, spent fuel, and decommissioning (ARAO and Fund NPP 2020, pp. 259–260). However, by the end of 2019, the Slovenian NPP fund accumulated (only) about €207 million (Sklad NEK 2020, p. 56), as the level of payments was unchanged since 2004, when it was established by the Act on the Fund. That was contrary to the NEK Agreement, which stipulates (Art. 10 and 11) that payments are determined by the decommissioning program, which is approved by Interstate Commission and reviewed at least every five years. Moreover, the existing Act on the Fund did not provide for control over the management of the funds (Court of Audit 2017). The Government proposed its update in 2017 and again in 2020, but unsuccessfully. Only in July 2020, the Government succeeded to increase the payments of the Krško NPP to the Slovenian NPP Fund from approximately €eight million to approximately €13 million annually (Government of Slovenia 2020e).

Strategic planning regarding a new NPP in Slovenia was unclear, unpredictable, and controversial (see also the section on energy governance). While Slovenia decided in the 1990s not to plan any new NPP (Resolution on the Strategy of Energy Use and Supply of Slovenia 1996), it approved in 2004 that it would support a joint construction of Croatian territory by 2015 (ReNEP 2004). In contrast, in 2006 the government included a new NPP in Krško in its *Resolution on the national development projects 2007–2013* (2006, p. 69) (PWR technology, 1000 MW, to be in operation by 2017). In 2011, the construction of a new NPP in Krško (1000–1600 MW) was analyzed in the update of the national energy program (ReNEP Proposal 2011, p. 27), which was not adopted. Eventually, the 2010 application of GEN energija for an energy permit for the second unit of the Krško NPP was not approved, and the procedure was finally terminated in 2014 with the adoption of the new Energy Act (Court of Audit 2019, p. 5). Still, in 2015, GEN energija was named as the provider of the planned investment in the new NPP. Before the final decision on the investment, all necessary economic and other expert analyses should be carried out and a consultative referendum should be organized (Ordinance on State Assets Management Strategy 2015, p. 58). Since then, all governments avoided the issue by tacitly or even publicly supporting the idea of a new NPP but without adopting a clear and final strategic decision.

In 2019, the Court of Audit concluded that governments were not effective between 2006 and 2016 in their strategic planning regarding the long-term use of nuclear energy for electricity generation (Court of Audit 2019). Despite that, the proposed Resolution on the Energy Concept of Slovenia, which should determine the "objectives of a secure, sustainable and competitive energy supply for the next 20 years and approximately 40 years" (Energy Act 2014, Art. 23), prepared in 2018 but not adopted, only mentioned (2018, para 86) the need to provide a solution for disposal of low- and intermediate-level nuclear waste, as well as a permanent solution for the management of high-level radioactive waste in the period 2020–2030, or before a possible decision on the construction of a new NPP can be taken. In 2019, the then Prime Minister Šarec unexpectedly publicly supported the construction of a second NPP, which led to strong internal reactions from national NGOs and external ones from Austria (RTV Slovenia 2019b). Nevertheless, the majority of other (parliamentary) political parties remained cautious, often emphasizing that before deciding on the construction of the second NPP, the issues of radioactive storage and decommissioning, as well as the lifetime extension of the existing plant, must be fully resolved. Some political parties also advocated that a referendum would be necessary (Pušnik 2019).

For the preparation of the NECP and the Long-Term Climate Strategy 2050, two long-term scenarios for 2050 were developed. One with a larger share of electricity generation from CO_2-neutral synthetic gas and the other that includes the construction of a new NPP (Urbančič et al. 2020). The NECP adopted in February 2020, referring only to the period 2021–2030, stated that expertise must be provided to decide on a possible new NPP by 2027 (NECP 2020, p. 55), which would correspond to the time window in which small modular reactors could be available on the market.

However, the following government of Prime Minister Janša included the project of a new NPP in Krško on the list of priority investments in the Covid-19 intervention law and foresaw a possible start of construction by the end of 2027 (Government of Slovenia 2020f). Considering the length of spatial planning and decision-making procedures, the stated start of construction in 2027 seems highly unrealistic and could be seen as an attempt to bring the issue to the fore. Indeed, in April 2021 the government adopted the Proposal of the Resolution on Long-Term Climate Strategy to 2050 and send it to the National Assembly for approval. Surprisingly, the National Assembly, in contrast to the version in public consultation, adopted an amended resolution stating (p. 36) that "Slovenia plans the long-term use of nuclear energy and will for this purpose conduct administrative procedures and prepare documentation for investment decision-making."

Finally, in 2020, the company GEN energija submitted a new application for the energy permit for a new NPP. One week after the adoption of the Long-Term Climate Strategy in July 2021, the Ministry of Infrastructure issued the energy permit for the second NPP (Ministry of Infrastructure, 2021), raising strong objections by Austria and NGOs, that there was no public consultation and environmental assessment (Focus, 2021). It is expected that the NGOs will oppose it also by going to the court.

Coal Phaseout

Since the beginnings of the country's electrification, domestic coal (brown coal in Zasavje and lignite in Savinjsko Šaleška region) has become one of the pillars of the Slovenian energy system and the secure supply of electricity. With Slovenia's accession to the EU and the development of the common environmental and climate policy, the environmentally harmful dimension of coal extraction and its use for electricity generation has become important.

After the referendum on Trbovlje TPP (Unit 3) in 1999, the government decided to close the coal mine in Zasavje region (RTH), and in 2014 the last remaining unit of Trbovlje TPP (125 MW) was shut down. After 2014, only the lignite mine in Velenje remained in operation, which was expected to supply the new Unit 6 at the Šoštanj TPP by 2054. In 2019, Slovenia joined the European Commission initiative "Coal Regions in Transition" in 2019 with two regions (Zasavje and Savinjsko-Šaleška region).

The NECP, adopted in February 2020, on the one hand, confirmed the objectives of reliable and competitive energy supply and at least 75% of electricity generation from domestic sources, which should continue to be based largely on the use of a mix of primary domestic sources, in particular RES, nuclear, and lignite (NECP 2020, pp. 56 & 59). On the other hand, it also decided that electricity generation should be decarbonized. By 2030, at least 30% less coal would be used by shutting down Unit 5 at the Šoštanj TPP and abandoning the use of imported coal for electricity generation at the Ljubljana power plant (TE-TOL). A decision on the complete coal phaseout, including the date of closure of the Velenje coal mine and Unit 6 at the Šoštanj TPP, should be taken in 2021 (NECP 2020, p. 34).

In April 2021, the draft coal phaseout strategy was in public consultation, proposing the most ambitious coal phaseout scenario by 2033. The Strategic Environmental Assessment showed that phasing out coal by 2033 would have the most positive impacts on the environment, nature, and human health compared to the alternative coal phaseout scenarios by 2038 and 2042. In addition, it was found that the use of coal beyond 2035 would require mitigation measures due to exceeding the allowed estimated carbon budget (Environmental Report (draft) 2021). The Ministry of Infrastructure and the Slovenian Transmission System Operator (TSO) also emphasized the deteriorating economics of using coal for electricity generation. They estimated that the Šoštanj TPP could generate up to €150 million in losses due to rising ETS prices as early as 2022 (Bahun 2021). While the coal and energy unions, and the Velenje municipality, which were joined by Ministry of Economic Development and Technology, opposed to an early coal phaseout, the HSE Group, which operates TPP Šoštanj, stressed that state aid will be necessary to operate the Šoštanj TPP until 2033 (Dernovšek 2021).

An important issue was the substitution of coal in domestic electricity production in line with the objective of ensuring at least 75% of electricity production with domestic energy sources. The draft strategy on the coal phaseout only stated that the energy site in Šoštanj would be maintained, while the decision on the alternative to coal in electricity generation would be adopted by the NECP update in 2023/2024. As the economic and social transition from coal in Zasavje region was incomplete and only partially successful, the draft strategy emphasized the principles of just transition and set economic, energy, and environmental as well as comprehensive social goals for both coal regions. Based on the (draft) strategy, two territorial plans, one for each coal region, were under preparation, as a basis for drawing the EU funds from the Just Transition Mechanism. However, by midsummer 2021, the prospects for the adoption of strategy and early coal phaseout became blurred.

Further Deployment of Renewable Energy

With the beginning of electrification in the late nineteenth century, many small and large HPPs have been built on Slovenian rivers, and in 2020, hydro accounted for about one-third of domestic electricity generation. Besides hydro, Slovenia has been able to deploy other RES (e.g., solar and wind) only to a small extent. The first National Energy Program (ReNEP 2004) emphasized that the use of domestic sources including RES should be one of the starting points of energy supply. The long-term strategic direction at that time was to increase the use of Slovenian hydro potential and to increase its share in the primary balance, strictly respecting the limitations arising from nature protection. Following Directive 2009/28/ES, Slovenia's target was set at 25% share of energy from RES in gross final consumption by 2020, and the National Renewable Energy Action Plan 2010–2020 set the shares for individual sectors, i.e., 39.3% for electricity, 30.8% for heating and cooling, and 10.5% for transport. Its update, prepared in 2017, was not adopted due to complaints from environmental NGOs, which were followed by a case at Administrative Court.

The National Energy Program (proposal 2011) proposed a target of 30% share of RES by 2030. Since it was not adopted, as well as the proposed Energy Concept of Slovenia in 2018, the first strategic energy document to set targets for 2030 was the NECP, adopted in February 2020. In contrast to National Energy Program (proposal 2011), it proposed (only) a target of 27% share of RES in gross final consumption by 2030. Although a potential to achieve 29.2% by 2030 was indicated, provided that all instruments are fully implemented, this still fell well short of the 37% target recommended by the European Commission (European Commission 2020, p. 9).

The revised statistical data in 2021 confirmed that Slovenia was able to make very limited progress in RES deployment in the last decade, which merely compensated for the growth in final energy consumption. Indeed, in the period 2010–2019, the share of RES increased by less than 1 percentage point. Except for the heating and cooling sector, the country was unlikely to be able to meet its 2020 targets in the electricity and transport sectors (Table 2 and Fig. 4).

After 2000, the deployment of hydro in Slovenia received an important impetus by the decision to build a chain of five large HPPs on the lower Sava River. The construction of the first HPP (Boštanj) started in 2003 (commissioned in 2006). In the following years (2010–2017), three new HPPs were built. The national spatial

Table 2 RES in gross final consumption in the period 2004–2019 (%)

Year (%)	2004	2006	2008	2010	2012	2014	2016	2018	2019	2020 (target)	2030 (target)
RES-H&C	22,82	24,35	27,52	29,54	33,14	34,64	35,56	32,34	32,16	30,8	41
RES-E	29,27	28,23	29,96	32,20	31,63	33,94	32,06	32,31	32,63	39,3	43
RES-T	0,85	1,06	1,77	3,12	3,25	2,88	1,60	5,48	7,98	10,5	21
RES overall	18,40	18,42	18,65	21,08	21,55	22,46	21,98	21,38	21,97	**25,0**	**27**

Source: SORS 2021

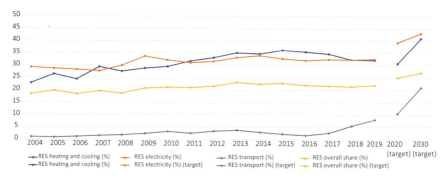

Fig. 4 Renewable energy in gross final consumption in the period 2004–2019 (%) (Source: SORS 2021a, b)

plan for the last remaining HPP (Mokrice) was approved in 2013, but its construction did not start due to opposition from several NGOs. When fully completed, the chain of these new five HPPs on the lower Sava River would contribute 187 MW of installed capacity and 720 GWh annually (Hrovatin et al. 2007, p. 124).

A state aid scheme to support electricity generation from RES and in CHP plants in the form of guaranteed prices or operating subsidies was introduced in 2009. It constituted one of the most important energy policy instruments. Before 2014, all producers or investors who installed RES and CHP production units were eligible for state aid. Thus, from 2010 to 2014, 3479 RES generation units (of which 3319 were solar) were included in the support scheme. After 2014, only generation units preselected in a competitive procedure with public calls run by the Energy Agency could enter the support scheme, which led to a significant decrease in the attractiveness of the scheme. Only 12 new generation units were included by 2019. A large part of the available funds remained unallocated due to fewer applications because of the significantly higher reference market price for electricity (especially for larger solar power plants), which meant that the difference between the market price and the cost of generating electricity was almost zero (Energy Agency 2020, pp. 35–38).

The state aid scheme also revealed major challenges to the deployment of wind energy in Slovenia. Before the building permit became a mandatory application component in 2019, investors in wind energy had shown great interest, and among the selected projects WPPs were strongly predominating (with 214 MW out of 263 MW). The deadline by which most wind projects must be completed to receive support is 2023. Given the past experience that spatial planning and siting processes for wind farms are very time-consuming, the Energy Agency questions their timely completion. In 2019, the share of electricity generated from RES under the support scheme accounted for 4.8% of total electricity generation in Slovenia (Energy Agency 2020, p. 38).

At the end of 2015, the Decree on self-supply of electricity from RES was adopted, which enabled an increasing number of self-supply devices to be connected to the distribution network between 2016 (135 devices with a total installed capacity of 1.1 MW) and 2019 (almost 2500 devices with a total installed capacity of 31 MW); 99.5% of them were solar power plants. The rising number can be linked to the increasing use of electricity to heat buildings with heat pumps and to charge electric vehicles at home. The Energy Agency estimates (2020, pp. 44–46) that by the end of 2023 there will be nearly 23,000 customers with a total self-supply capacity of nearly 278 MW.

In addition to the state aid scheme and self-supply, the deployment of solar energy has also been supported under the Cohesion Policy for the period 2019–2022. Furthermore, the deployment of RES (self-supply and RES communities, synthetic gas and methane entering the state aid scheme, more effective spatial planning and administrative procedures for RES, RES in transport, etc.) will be comprehensively addressed and supported with the upcoming Renewable Energy Promotion Act.

Slovenia highlighted in its NECP some relevant national circumstances that have been affecting the deployment of RES and had to be taken into account when adopting the national RES target by 2030. First, as mentioned above, the construction of HPPs and WPPs was often subject to environmental and other constraints. Namely, almost 38% of Slovenia's territory was covered by Natura 2000 sites, a large part of which were also areas most suitable for wind and hydropower deployment. Further deployment of wind and hydropower was therefore only possible if appropriate environmental solutions were found within the spatial planning processes. For example, in the draft NECP, three large HPPs on the middle Sava River were foreseen but had to be omitted due to their negative environmental impact assessment. Moreover, it was estimated that already for reaching the target of 27% share of RES by 2030, successful procedures of overriding public interest in energy over nature conservation will be indispensable. By 2021, only one such procedure had been carried out for the HPP Mokrice on the lower Sava River. At the time of writing this chapter, it was pending due to the complaint of NGOs on the Administrative Court. In addition, further deployment of wind and hydro energy was opposed by many local communities or some environmental NGOs, emphasizing either nonacceptance of large energy infrastructure, or collision of energy goals with environmental goals and restrictions related to protected and endangered areas (Natura 2000). In the case of WPPs, the majority of potential sites were located either in Natura 2000 areas or (too) close to human settlements.

Second, the successful increase in energy efficiency in the heating and cooling sector reduced the consumption of RES (biomass) in this sector and reduced the overall share of RES. Third, almost two-thirds (62%) of final energy in the industry was consumed by four energy-intensive sectors where commercially available technologies do not (yet) allow for greater use of RES. And fourth, a very high share of energy consumption in the transport sector hampered progress in the deployment of RES, taking into account that biofuels could only be deployed to a limited extent due to different standards (especially first generation) (NECP 2020, pp. 47–50).

Energy Efficiency

The issue of energy efficiency was prominent in Slovenia's energy governance. Already in the 1996 Resolution on the Strategy of Energy Use and Supply of Slovenia, energy efficiency was listed as one of the long-term strategic guidelines, which was confirmed and reinforced in all subsequent strategic documents (National Energy Program 2004 and the proposed update in 2011). In the adopted NECP 2020, the instrument of improving energy and material efficiency in all sectors (and thus reducing the consumption of energy and other natural resources) was reaffirmed as the first and key instrument for the transition to a climate-neutral society. Slovenia managed to reduce its energy intensity by 30% in the period 2004–2019 (from 228 to 159 kgoe/1000 euro). However, compared to the average energy intensity of the EU-27, it was still significantly behind, by 33% in 2019 (Eurostat 2021).

The first National Energy Efficiency Action Plan (NEEAP) was adopted in January 2008 for the period 2008–2016 in accordance with Article 14 of Directive 2006/32/EC to achieve 9% final energy savings over 9 years (NEEAP 2008). Updated Energy Efficiency Action Plans followed in 2011, 2014, and 2017, the latter two adopted under Directive 2012/27/EC with a target to achieve 20% energy efficiency improvement by 2020 (NEEAP 2015, 2017). During the period 2000–2009, primary and final

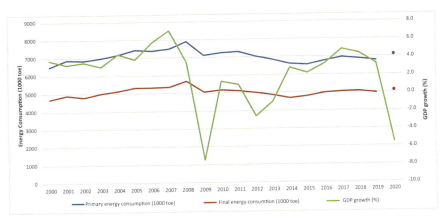

Fig. 5 Primary and Final Energy Consumption, GDP growth, Slovenia, 2000–2020. (Source: SORS 2021a, b)

energy consumption increased in line with GDP growth. However, with the financial and economic crisis and the significant GDP decline, energy consumption also declined, and only after 2015, it started to increase again until 2018 (Fig. 5). In 2019, primary and final energy consumption were below the 2020 target, and with the economic collapse due to the Covid-19 pandemic, it was expected that Slovenia would meet its energy efficiency target (Urbančič et al. 2021, pp. 14–15).

Final energy consumption was dependent on energy consumption in specific sectors. In 2018, the largest consumer was the transport sector (40%), followed by industry (almost 28%), households (21%), and services (11%). The transport sector had a particularly large impact on total final energy consumption, as its share in total final energy consumption increased in 2018 compared to 2000 by 12 percentage points, while the shares of the other sectors decreased. Despite the assessment that the transport sector would remain below its 2020 indicative target, this sector remained critical due to its large share in total final energy consumption and the fact that the impact of energy efficiency instruments was very limited.

In the NECP, Slovenia adopted a target to improve energy efficiency by 35% in 2030 compared to the projections of the PRIMES 2007 scenario. It built on existing instruments and essentially combined financial and fiscal incentives as well as regulatory and other support instruments, mainly targeting the buildings and transport sectors. In the latter, financial incentives aimed to support modal shift, modernization of the railway network, and the use of more efficient vehicles, combined with regulatory measures and green driving. Regarding energy efficiency in buildings, Slovenia aimed to reduce final energy consumption by 20% and greenhouse gas (GHG) emissions from buildings by at least 70% by 2030 compared to 2005. The final energy savings should have been achieved through the implementation of energy services and instruments put in place by energy suppliers, and with the support of the Eco Fund and fiscal mechanisms. Even though the Slovenian target was well above the EU headline target of 32.5% and well above the aggregate ambition of the final NECPs, i.e., 29.7% for primary energy consumption and 29.4% for final energy consumption, the European Commission assessed the Slovenian ambition as modest for primary energy consumption and low for final energy consumption (NECP 2020; European Commission 2020, p. 10).

Transport and Electromobility

Until recently, the transport sector was not seen as a challenge to the energy transition. However, in 2019, the transport sector was the largest consumer of final energy consumption in Slovenia (39%), followed by manufacturing and construction (30%), households (21%), and other uses and agriculture (10%) (SORS 2020b). In addition, the transport sector was the largest emitter of GHG emissions in the non-ETS sector. In 2018, it accounted for 53% of all non-ETS emissions, followed by agriculture (15%), widespread use (11%), and industry (10%). The transport sector was also the only non-ETS sector where GHG emissions increased between 2005–2018 (almost +32%, while the 2020 target was +27%) (Urbančič et al. 2021, pp. 7–8). These figures clearly showed that the transport sector has become key to the energy transition in Slovenia.

Slovenia has supported e-mobility since 2004 through the Eco Fund with low-cost loans and since 2011 with subsidies (i.e., grants) for the purchase of electric and hybrid cars. Initially, these instruments met with strong public reservations. In 2011, for example, only three buyers received a grant. However, public acceptance of sustainable transport solutions gradually increased and, in parallel, so did the number of grants. A grant per electric car was up to 7500€ and per hybrid car up to 4500€ until 2019. However, in 2020, grants for hybrid cars were removed and grants for electric cars were reduced to up to €4500. The justification for this was that the prices for electric cars have fallen, while the amount of the subsidies has doubled every year (RTV Slovenia 2020).

At the end of 2019, almost 1,608,000 road vehicles were registered in Slovenia, out of which over 1,165,000 were passenger cars (75%) (SORS 2020c). Slovenia ranked 11th in the EU with 549 passenger cars per 1000 inhabitants (Eurostat 2021). 50% of registered passenger cars were using diesel and 49% petrol. Compared to 2018, the number of hybrid passenger cars increased by 48% and exceeded 6800, whereas the number of electric passenger cars increased by 53% and reached almost 2000 vehicles. The number of first registrations of new electric passenger cars increased in 1 year by 33% (SORS 2020c).

The Alternative Fuels Strategy for Transport (2017) envisaged a rapid increase in electric and hybrid vehicles under the Optimal Scenario. By 2030, there would be at least 17% of electric and hybrid vehicles (about 200,000) and 12% of electric light goods vehicles (11,000). Due to the projected rapid increase in electric vehicles by 2030, it would be necessary to increase the number of charging stations. In 2019, the Action Plan was adopted for 3 years in line with the Strategy and the indicative GHG emission target by 2030 (18%) (Action Plan on Alternative Fuels Infrastructure 2019). However, with the adoption of the NECP in 2020, the indicative GHG emissions target for the transport sector for 2030 was increased to 12%. The transport sector was the only non-ETS sector expected to increase its GHG emissions over the period 2005–2030, especially due to freight transport (NECP 2020, p. 152).

Due to the continued growth of passenger and freight transport, it would be crucial for Slovenia, on the one hand, to strengthen rail transport and implement sustainable mobility instruments. This would reduce the carbon footprint in the transport sector and relieve heavy traffic, which is no longer sustainable, inter alia, by upgrading the railway infrastructure, developing integrated public transport, encouraging less use of the private car, shifting freight transit to rail, and supporting the introduction of alternative fuels for freight (e.g., LNG) and passenger transport (CNG, hydrogen, etc.). On the other hand, Slovenia also wants to strongly support the shift to low-emission vehicles (NECP 2020, pp. 33–34). Thus, the Slovenian NECP identified a wide range of support instruments, including those that contribute to a more efficient organization of the transport system and to improved energy efficiency and reduced emissions, as well as a wide range of instruments to promote electromobility (European Commission 2020, p. 8). Slovenia also focuses on the development, production, and use of advanced sustainable biofuels. It adopted a sectoral target for the share of RES in transport of 20% in 2030, which was a significant increase compared to the draft plan and the pace of biofuel deployment in 2010–2020.

Outcomes, Challenges, and Prospects of Energy Governance

It is promising that Slovenia was on track to meet its 2020 GHG emission reduction target in the non-ETS sector. In the period 2005–2018, the country managed to reduce its GHG emissions by 5.9%, while the target for the period 2005–2020 was +4% (Urbančič et al. 2021, p. 7). Nevertheless, emissions in the transport and industry sectors were well above the indicative sectoral targets. The instruments and their implementation in these two sectors, which cumulatively accounted for almost 64% of all GHG emissions in the non-ETS sectors, would need to be strengthened to ensure long-term GHG emission reductions, especially in view of the increased 2030 targets at EU level.

In the EU ETS sector, GHG emissions decreased significantly more in the period 2005–2018 (−25.8%) than in the non-ETS sector (−5.9%), while in the LULUCF sector emissions increased for the first time in 2018 due to natural disasters and subsequent sanitary logging (Urbančič et al. 2021, p. 9). Slovenia has also been successful in improving its energy efficiency. In 2018, primary energy consumption was 4.4% and final energy consumption 2.8% below the 2020 target. Taking into account the decrease in final and primary energy consumption due to the Covid-19 pandemic, the country was expected to overachieve its 2020 target. However, to reach the 2030 target, it would be crucial for Slovenia to successfully manage final energy consumption, especially in the transport sector (which accounted for 40% of total final energy consumption), as well as in industry and households (Urbančič et al. 2021, pp. 14–19).

Slovenia was less successful in deployment of RES between 2010 and 2020. In 2019, it was 3 percentage points below its 2020 target. In the electricity sector, the country lagged significantly (by almost 7 percentage points in 2019). The situation improved in the transport sector, where the share of RES increased from 1.6% to almost 8% in 2016–2019, but it was still below its sectoral target (10.5%).

For 2030, Slovenia adopted a more ambitious GHG emission reduction target for the non-ETS sector compared to Effort Sharing Regulation (−20% and − 15%, respectively). The country also adopted a target to improve energy efficiency by at least 35%, which was higher than the EU headline target (32.5%), while Slovenian RES target for 2030 (27%) was significantly lower than the European Commission recommendation (37%). Since the country was likely to miss its 2020 RES target, it would have to buy statistical transfers or contribute to the EU's Renewable Energy Financing Mechanism, resulting in some financial burden. Although modeling suggested that it could exceed a 29% share by 2030, provided all instruments were fully implemented, Slovenia was reluctant to adopt a more ambitious target than 27%.

Energy governance and discourse were heavily influenced by the past legacies in the energy sector. In the 1990s, energy governance was shaped primarily through the prism of energy security. After Slovenia's EU-accession in 2004, the three-pillar structure (energy security, affordability, and environmental sustainability) came to the fore. During the last decade, with the development of the EU Energy Union and Climate Action, environmental sustainability of energy supply penetrated energy governance and discourse. Consequently, the period 2010–2020 revealed four significant challenges for Slovenian energy governance and transition.

First, the coal phaseout decision was expected in 2021. While by midsummer 2021, there was no clear consensus on the proposed (most) ambitious coal phaseout scenario by 2033 at the latest, the uncertainty and risk of potential (earlier) shutdown of the Šoštanj TPP due to economic reasons was increasing, thereby endangering the security of energy supply. Second, the extension of the operation of the existing Krško NPP until 2043 was subject to successful environmental impact assessment (by 2023 at latest), whereas the positions on the potential new NPP remained strongly divided. Third, further deployment of renewables in the electricity sector was largely dependent on finding appropriate solutions to the collision between environmental and energy goals, and acceptance of large energy infrastructure (especially hydro and wind) by civil society in spatial planning procedures. And fourth, management of final energy consumption in the transport sector, its electrification, and the use of (sustainable) biofuels, as well as its integration with other sectors, remain key for a successful energy transition to a climate-neutral society.

All these issues raised another significant and equally demanding challenge, namely the lack of human resources at all levels of energy governance, and comprehensive and effective policy coordination. Slovenia experienced difficulties in adopting long-term energy strategic documents and in bridging a gap between adopted targets and their implementation (especially in the deployment of RES) between 2010 and 2020. Although some 2020 targets were expected to be met (GHG emissions and energy efficiency), it would be naïve to conclude that energy governance had comprehensively and successfully taken into account developments in all sectors. In contrast, external developments contributed significantly to the achievement of national targets (notably economic downturns that followed the economic and financial crisis and the Covid-19 pandemic). However, the NECP and the proposed Long-term Climate Strategy 2050 stated that a new government body should be established to coordinate the implementation of the adopted measures to ensure the achievement of the energy and climate targets by 2030 and 2050 and the transition to a climate-neutral society.

Finally, the Covid-19 pandemic led to a significant decline in economic activity and final energy consumption, which should help to reduce GHG emissions and energy consumption in the short term. The EU Recovery Plan and the largest economic stimulus package, designed to boost economic recovery, are supposed to represent an opportunity for a significant step toward an energy (and digital) transition. However, this was not reflected in the preparation of the Slovenian draft Recovery and Resilience Plan. The latter has been widely criticized for not involving civil society and the public, and for containing instruments that were unlikely to contribute positively to the green transition. Whether a gap between adopted strategic directions and day-to-day policies could be overcome, thus, remains unclear.

Cross-References

- Energy Governance in Austria
- Energy Governance in Croatia
- Energy Governance in Hungary
- Energy Governance in Italy
- Energy Governance in Russia: From a Fossil to a Green Giant?
- Energy Poverty
- Monitoring Energy Policy
- Transition of Energy Systems: Patterns of Stability and Change

Acknowledgments This research was financially supported by the Slovenian Research Agency (Project code: ID J5-2562). The author would like to sincerely thank Dr. Boris Sučić (»Jožef Stefan« Institute, Energy Efficiency Centre) for his valuable comments and suggestions.

References

Action Plan on Alternative Fuels Infrastructure. (2019). https://www.gov.si/assets/ministrstva/MzI/Dokumenti/Akcijski-program-za-alternativna-goriva-v-prometu.doc. Accessed 15 Apr 2021.

Agreement between the Government of the Republic of Slovenia and the Government of the Republic of Croatia on the Regulation of the Status and Other Legal Relations Regarding the Investment, Exploitation and Decommissioning of the Krško NPP. https://www.uradni-list.si/glasilo-uradni-list-rs/vsebina?urlmpid=200312. Accessed 15 Apr 2021.

ARAO and Fund NPP. (2019). Third Revision of the Krško NPP Radioactive Waste and Spent Fuel Disposal Program. (2019). https://www.energetika-portal.si/fileadmin/dokumenti/novice/nek/program_odlag_rao_rev3_sep2019-web.pdf. Accessed 15 Apr 2021.

ARSO. (2020). Sklep Za nameravani poseg: Podaljšanje obratovalne dobe Nuklearne elektrarne Krško s 40 na 60 let do leta 2043. https://www.arso.gov.si/novice/datoteke/043411-NEK.pdf. Accessed 15 Apr 2021.

Bahun, P. (2021). Izhod iz premoga je neizbežen, 30 March. Naš Stik. https://www.nas-stik.si/1/Novice/Clanki/tabid/208/ID/10152/Izhod-iz-premoga-je-neizbezen.aspx. Accessed 15 Apr 2021.

Coalition Agreement 2018–2022. (2018). https://www.strankalms.si/wp-content/uploads/2018/08/Koalicijski-sporazum-o-sodelovanju-v-Vladi-Republike-Slovenije-za-mandatno-obdobje-2018%E2%80%932022.pdf. Accessed 15 Apr 2021.

Coalition Agreement 2020-2022. (2020). https://www.gov.si/assets/vlada/Vlada_predstavitev_dokumenti/Koalicijska-pogodba-2020-2022.pdf. Accessed 15 Apr 2021.

Court of Audit. (2017). Porevizijsko poročilo Popravljalni ukrepi pri reviziji zagotavljanja sredstev za razgradnjo Nuklearne elektrarne Krško in za odlaganje radioaktivnih odpadkov iz Nuklearne elektrarne Krško. https://www.rs-rs.si/fileadmin/user_upload/revizija/14/SkladNek_SP10-14_porev.pdf. Accessed 15 Apr 2021.

Court of Audit. (2019). REVIZIJSKO POROČILO Učinkovitost strateškega načrtovanja dolgoročnega izkoriščanja jedrske energije za proizvodnjo električne energije in načrtovanja proizvodnje električne energije v jedrskih elektrarnah. https://www.rs-rs.si/fileadmin/user_upload/Datoteke/Revizije/2019/DrugiBlok_NEK/DrugiBlokNEK_SP06-16.pdf. Accessed 15 Apr 2021.

Crnčec, D. (2020). Eco-Innovation in Slovenia. EIO Country Profile 2018–2019. https://ec.europa.eu/environment/ecoap/sites/default/files/field/field-country-files/eio_country_profile_2018-2019_slovenia.pdf. Accessed 15 Apr 2021.

Crnčec, D., Sučić, B., & Merše, S. (2021). Slovenia: drivers and challenges of energy transition to climate neutrality. In M. Mišík & V. Oravcová (Eds.), *p* (pp. 247–282). Palgrave Macmillan.

DEM. (n.d.). Ideja o združitvi tedanjih elektrarn na reki Dravi v enotno podjetje se je prvič pojavila leta 1950. https://www.dem.si/sl/o-druzbi/zgodovina/. Accessed 15 Apr 2021.

Dernovšek, G. (2021). GZS: Premog mora ostati vsaj do leta 2036. Dnevnik. https://www.dnevnik.si/1042952163/posel/novice/premog-se-do-2036-ali-2038. Accessed 15 Apr 2021.

Energy Act. Official Gazette of the Republic of Slovenia, No. 60/19. https://www.uradni-list.si/_pdf/2019/Ur/u2019060.pdf. Accessed 15 Apr 2021.

Energy Agency. (2020). Report on the energy sector in Slovenia. https://www.agen-rs.si/documents/54870/68629/Report-on-the-energy-sector-in-Slovenia-for-2019/ce1c3cd8-489a-401d-9a1a-502a7c5715e4. Accessed 15 Apr 2021.

Environmental Report (draft). National Strategy on the Coal Phase-Out (draft February 2021). (2021). https://www.energetika-portal.si/fileadmin/dokumenti/publikacije/premog_izhod/cpvo-feb2021.pdf. Accessed 15 Apr 2021.

Environmental Report (draft). NECP. (2019). https://www.energetika-portal.si/fileadmin/dokumenti/publikacije/nepn/cpvo/op_nepn_osnutek_nov2019.pdf. Accessed 15 Apr 2021.

EPosavje. (2020). Gen: "Potrebujemo čim hitrejšo odločitev za izgradnjo JEK2", 17 January. https://www.eposavje.com/gospodarstvo/potrebujemo-cim-hitrejso-odlocitev-za-izgradnjo-jek2. Accessed 15 Apr 2021.

Eurobarometer. (2019). Special Eurobarometer 490. Climate Change. Slovenia. https://ec.europa.eu/clima/sites/clima/files/support/docs/si_climate_2019_en.pdf. Accessed 15 Apr 2021.

European Commission. (2013). Long term infrastructure vision for Europe and beyond. http://eur-lex.europa.eu/legal-content/EN/TXT/DOC/?uri=CELEX:52013DC0711&from=EN. Accessed 15 Apr 2021.

European Commission. (2020). Assessment of the final national energy and climate plan of Slovenia. https://ec.europa.eu/energy/sites/default/files/documents/staff_working_document_assessment_necp_slovenia_en.pdf. Accessed 15 Apr 2021.

Eurostat. (2021). Energy datasheets: EU countries. https://ec.europa.eu/energy/sites/ener/files/energy_statistical_countrydatasheets.xlsx. Accessed 15 Apr 2021.

Focus. (2017). Nevladne organizacije zahtevajo presojo vplivov na okolje glede podaljšanja delovanja NEK. https://focus.si/nevladne-organizacije-zahtevajo-presojo-vplivov-na-okolje-glede-podaljsanja-delovanja-nek/. Accessed 15 Apr 2021.

Focus. (2019). Slovenija v Bruselj poslala najslabši osnutek energetsko-podnebnega načrta. https://focus.si/slovenija-v-bruselj-poslala-najslabsi-osnutek-energetsko-podnebnega-nacrta/. Accessed 15 Apr 2021.

Focus. (2021). Energetsko dovoljenje za gradnjo 2. bloka NEK izdano v nasprotju z evropskim pravom – brez javne razprave in brez presoje vplivov na okolje in varnost. https://focus.si/

energetsko-dovoljenje-za-gradnjo-2-bloka-nek-izdano-v-nasprotju-z-evropskim-pravom-brez-javne-razprave-in-brez-presoje-vplivov-na-okolje-in-varnost/. Accessed 27 Aug 2021.

GEN energija. (n.d.). Projekt JEK 2. https://www.gen-energija.si/investiramo-in-razvijamo/jek-2. Accessed 15 Apr 2021.

Government of Slovenia. (2019). Predlog stališča Vlade Republike Slovenije do "Zahteve za določitev in izvedbo ukrepov za prehod v ogljično nevtralno Slovenijo do 2040 "nevladnih organizacij". http://84.39.218.201/MANDAT18/VLADNAGRADIVA.NSF/277bdf36cd5b7373c1256efa00399a6b/42afd131b35a1a19c125847700305f70/$FILE/VG_razogljicenje_P.pdf. Accessed 15 Apr 2021.

Government of Slovenia. (2020a). Minister Vrtovec na delovnem obisku v ZDA za nadgradnjo dobrih odnosov med državama na področju energetike. https://www.gov.si/novice/2020-12-07-minister-vrtovec-na-delovnem-obisku-v-zda-za-nadgradnjo-dobrih-odnosov-med-drzavama-na-podrocju-energetike/. Accessed 15 Apr 2021.

Government of Slovenia. (2020b). Opuščamo premog, preklapljamo na obnovljive vire energije. https://www.gov.si/novice/2020-10-02-opuscamo-premog-preklapljamo-na-obnovljive-vire-energije/. Accessed 15 Apr 2021.

Government of Slovenia. (2020c). 43. redna seja Vlade Republike Slovenije. https://www.gov.si/assets/vlada/Seja-vlade-SZJ/2020/12-2020/SPsev143.docx. Accessed 15 Apr 2021.

Government of Slovenia. (2020d). Odločitve 26. redne seje Vlade Republike Slovenije s področja Ministrstva za okolje in prostor. https://www.gov.si/novice/2020-07-16-odlocitve-26-redne-seje-vlade-republike-slovenije-s-podrocja-ministrstva-za-okolje-in-prostor/. Accessed 15 Apr 2021.

Government of Slovenia. (2020e). Določitev višine vplačila sredstev v Sklad za financiranje razgradnje Nuklearne elekrarne Krško in odlaganja radioaktivnih odpadkov iz Nuklearne elekrarne Krško – predlog za obravnavo. http://84.39.218.201/MANDAT20/VLADNAGRADIVA.NSF/18a6b9887c33a0bdc12570e50034eb54/900b4e6d4c53bbf7c12585a7004f1243/$FILE/vg_sklad.pdf. Accessed 15 Apr 2021.

Government of Slovenia. (2020f). Pospešena izvedba pomembnih investicij za zagon gospodarstva po epidemiji. https://www.gov.si/teme/pospesena-izvedba-pomembnih-investicij-za-zagon-gospodarstva-po-epidemiji/. Accessed 15 Apr 2021.

Hreščak, A. (2020). Sloveniji čez slaba tri leta grozi električni mrk, 5 October. Dnevnik. https://www.dnevnik.si/1042940441/posel/novice/sloveniji-cez-slaba-tri-leta-grozi-elektricni-mrk. Accessed 15 Apr 2021.

Hrovatin, J. (2008). Izbrane značilnosti slovenskega elektrogospodarstva. *Electrotechnical Review*, 75(1), 7–11. https://ev.fe.uni-lj.si/1-2-2008/Hrovatin.pdf. Accessed 15 Apr 2021.

Hrovatin, J., et al. (2007). *Zgodovina slovenskega elektrogospodarstva*. Ljubljana.

Huš. K. (2020). Veter in sonce ali tabletke uranovega dioksida, 5 September. Delo. https://www.delo.si/sobotna-priloga/veter-in-sonce-ali-tabletke-uranovega-dioksida/. Accessed 15 Apr 2021.

I U 2135/2018-17. (2018). https://a9g3u8k4.stackpathcdn.com/wp-content/uploads/2020/02/sodba-o-NEK-feb2020.pdf. Accessed 15 Apr 2021.

ICSID Case No. ARB/05/24. (2015). https://www.italaw.com/sites/default/files/case-documents/ITA%20LAW%207012.pdf. Accessed 15 Apr 2021.

Kos, S. and B. Eržen. (2021). Kakšni so prvi odzivi na poravnavo, 10 March. Delo. https://www.delo.si/novice/slovenija/kaksni-so-prvi-odzivi-na-poravnavo/. Accessed 15 Apr 2021.

Kosmač, G. (2019). Iztok Tiselj: Za NEK 2 bi morali najprej na referendum. https://www.rtvslo.si/znanost-in-tehnologija/iztok-tiselj-za-nek-2-bi-morali-najprej-na-referendum/500659. Accessed 15 Apr 2021.

Ministry of Infrastructure. (2019a). Vlada sprejela program zapiranja rudnika Trbovlje-Hrastnik. https://www.energetika-portal.si/nc/novica/n/vlada-sprejela-program-zapiranja-rudnika-trbovlje-hrastnik-4212/. Accessed 15 Apr 2021.

Ministry of Infrastructure. (2019b). NEPN–Predhodno posvetovanje. https://www.energetika-portal.si/fileadmin/dokumenti/publikacije/nepn/predhodno_posvetovanje/nepn_predhodno_posvetovanje_final_web_11.4.2019.xlsx. Accessed 15 Apr 2021.

Ministry of Infrastructure. (2021). Izdano energetsko dovoljenje za JEK2. https://www.energetika-portal.si/nc/novica/n/izdano-energetsko-dovoljenje-za-projekt-jek2-4578/. Accessed 27 August 2021.

Mravlje, S. (2004). Liberalizacija trga električne energije na ozemlju nekdanje SFRJ. http://www.cek.ef.uni-lj.si/u_diplome/mravlje1633.pdf. Accessed 15 Apr 2021.

Nacionalna strategija za izstop iz premoga in prestrukturiranje premogovnih regij v skladu z načeli pravičnega prehoda (osnutek za javno obravnavo). (2021). https://www.energetika-portal.si/fileadmin/dokumenti/publikacije/premog_izhod/strategija_premog_v2_jo_mar2021.pdf. Accessed 15 Apr 2021.

National Assembly. (2018). Final report on the TEŠ 6 investment. https://imss.dz-rs.si/IMiS/ImisAdmin.nsf/ImisnetAgent?OpenAgent&2&DZ-MSS-01/ec2b6f77d62fbb1f20722a702990ab6f6122ff685d377eac368046f9e41e35b3. Accessed 15 Apr 2021.

National Energy Efficiency Action Plan for 2014-2020. (2015). https://www.energetika-portal.si/fileadmin/dokumenti/publikacije/an_ure/neeap_slo_2014-2020_eng.pdf. Accessed 15 Apr 2021.

National Energy Efficiency Action Plan until 2020. (2017). https://www.energetika-portal.si/fileadmin/dokumenti/publikacije/an_ure/an_ure_2017-2020_final.pdf. Accessed 15 Apr 2021.

National Energy Program to 2030 (proposal). (2011). https://www.energetika-portal.si/fileadmin/dokumenti/publikacije/nep/nep_2030_jun_2011.pdf. Accessed 15 Apr 2021.

National Renewable Energy Action Plan 2010-2020. (2010). https://www.energetika-portal.si/fileadmin/dokumenti/publikacije/an_ove/an-ove_eng.pdf. Accessed 15 Apr 2021.

NECP (Integrated National Energy & Climate Plan of the Republic of Slovenia). (2020). https://www.energetika-portal.si/dokumenti/strateski-razvojni-dokumenti/nacionalni-energetski-in-podnebni-nacrt/. Accessed 15 Apr 2021.

NEEAP (National Energy Efficiency Action Plan for 2008-2016). (2008). https://www.energetika-portal.si/fileadmin/dokumenti/publikacije/an_ure/an_ure1.pdf. Accessed 15 Apr 2021.

NEK sklad (Sklad za financiranje razgradnje NEL in za odlaganje radioaktivnih odpadkov iz NEK). (2020). Letno poročilo za leto 2019. https://www.sklad-nek.si/datoteke/katalogKategorija/letno-porocilo-2019.pdf. Accessed 15 Apr 2021.

Novak, P. (2021). Jedrska energija je vse prej kot mrtva. Le hitro umira na obroke, 10 April. Delo. https://www.delo.si/sobotna-priloga/jedrska-energija-je-vse-prej-kot-mrtva-le-hitro-umira-na-obroke/. Accessed 15 Apr 2021.

Ordinance on State Assets Management Strategy. (2015). https://www.sdh.si/Data/Documents/asset-management/State%20Assets%20Management%20Strategy.pdf. Accessed 15 Apr 2021.

Petelin Visočnik, B. (2020). Podnebno ogledalo 2020 Povzetek za odločanje. https://www.podnebnapot2050.si/wp-content/uploads/2021/01/PO2020_Zvezek0_Povzetek_Koncen_2021-01-21.pdf. Accessed 15 Apr 2021.

Podnebnakriza.si. (2019). Nujni poziv Vladi Republike Slovenije. https://drive.google.com/file/d/1-CBlCXeWNFqVfJH4IlokMk47_KyBagEs/view. Accessed 15 Apr 2021.

Pušnik, N. (2019). 'Glede uporabe jedrske energije imam mešane občutke, toda bolj naklonjene kot ne', 26 July. https://www.24ur.com/novice/slovenija/prihodnost-jedrske-energije-v-oceh-politike.html. Accessed 15 Apr 2021.

ReNEP (Resolution on the National Energy Program). (2004). http://www.pisrs.si/Pis.web/pregledPredpisa?id=NACP45. Accessed 15 Apr 2021.

ReNEP Proposal (Resolution on the National Energy Program). (2011). https://www.energetika-portal.si/fileadmin/dokumenti/publikacije/nep/nep_2030_jun_2011.pdf. Accessed 15 Apr 2021.

Resolucija o Dolgoročni podnebni strategiji do leta 2050 (ReDPSS50). (2021). Official Gazette, 119/2021. https://www.uradni-list.si/glasilo-uradni-list-rs/vsebina/2021-01-2552/resolucija-o-dolgorocni-podnebni-strategiji-slovenije-do-leta-2050-redps50. Accessed 27 Aug 2021.

Resolution on the Energy Concept of Slovenia (proposal). (2018). https://www.energetika-portal.si/fileadmin/dokumenti/publikacije/eks/resolucija_eks/resol_eks_final.pdf Accessed 15 Apr 2021.

Resolution on the national development projects 2007-2013. (2008). http://www.slovenijajutri.gov.si/fileadmin/urednik/publikacije/061127_resolucija.pdf. Accessed 15 Apr 2021.

Resolution on the Strategy of Energy Use and Supply of Slovenia. (1996). Official Gazette, 9/1996. https://www.uradni-list.si/glasilo-uradni-list-rs/vsebina/1996-01-0418/resolucija-o-strategiji-rabe-in-oskrbe-slovenije-z-energijo-resroe. Accessed 15 Apr 2021.

RTV Slovenia. (2018). Hrvaška in Slovenija sta se dogovorili o skladiščenju radioaktivnih odpadkov. https://www.rtvslo.si/okolje/hrvaska-in-slovenija-sta-se-dogovorili-o-skladiscenju-radioaktivnih-odpadkov/472366. Accessed 15 Apr 2021.

RTV Slovenia. (2019a). Slovenija bo odlagališče za jedrske odpadke v Vrbini gradila brez Hrvatov. https://www.rtvslo.si/okolje/novice/slovenija-bo-odlagalisce-za-jedrske-odpadke-v-vrbini-gradila-brez-hrvatov/500932. Accessed 15 Apr 2021.

RTV Slovenia. (2019b). Šarec s podporo drugemu bloku NEK-a razburil Avstrijce. https://www.rtvslo.si/okolje/sarec-s-podporo-drugemu-bloku-nek-a-razburil-avstrijce/497660. Accessed 15 Apr 2021.

RTV Slovenia. (2020). Subvencije za električne avtomobile po novem nižje. https://www.rtvslo.si/zabava-in-slog/avtomobilnost/subvencije-za-elektricne-avtomobile-po-novem-nizje/545582. Accessed 15 Apr 2021.

Sklad NEK. (2020). Letno poročilo 2019. https://www.sklad-nek.si/datoteke/katalogKategorija/letno-porocilo-2019.pdf. Accessed 15 Apr 2021.

SORS. (2020a). Energy dependency of Slovenia in 2019 was at 48%. https://www.stat.si/StatWeb/en/News/Index/8524. Accessed 15 Apr 2021.

SORS. (2020b). In 2019, final energy consumption in Slovenia was almost 208,000 TJ. https://www.stat.si/StatWeb/en/News/Index/9109. Accessed 15 Apr 2021.

SORS. (2020c). Over 1,165,000 passenger cars registered in Slovenia in 2019. https://www.stat.si/StatWeb/en/News/Index/8827. Accessed 15 Apr 2021.

SORS. (2021a). Final data on research and development activity (R&D) in Slovenia for 2019 are here. https://www.stat.si/StatWeb/en/News/Index/9400. Accessed 15 Apr 2021.

SORS. (2021b). Energy Indicators. https://pxweb.stat.si/SiStatData/pxweb/en/Data/-/1817902S.px/. Accessed 15 Apr 2021.

Soške elektrarne. (2007). Zgodba o luči. https://www.seng.si/mma/zbornik-60-letpdf/2018030611000073/. Accessed 15 Apr 2021.

Strniša, E. (2021). Ministrstvo predlaga opustitev premoga do leta 2033. https://www.rtvslo.si/okolje/ministrstvo-predlaga-opustitev-premoga-do-leta-2033/573053. Accessed 15 Apr 2021.

Tavčar, B. (2021). Najprej program razvoja, šele nato zaprtje, 30 March. Delo. https://www.delo.si/novice/okolje/najprej-program-razvoja-sele-nato-zaprtje/. Accessed 15 Apr 2021.

Tavčar, B. and P. Malovrh. (2020). Arso mora v okoljsko presojo nuklearke, 19 February. Delo. https://www.delo.si/gospodarstvo/novice/arso-mora-v-okoljsko-presojo-nuklearke/. Accessed 15 Apr 2021.

TEŠ. (2021). O podjetju. https://www.te-sostanj.si/podjetje/o-podjetju/. Accessed 15 Apr 2021.

The Alternative Fuels Strategy for Transport (Strategija na področju razvoja trga za vzpostavitev ustrezne infrastrukture v zvezi z alternativnimi gorivi v prometnem sektorju v Republiki Sloveniji). (2017). https://www.energetika-portal.si/fileadmin/dokumenti/publikacije/alternativna_goriva/strategija_alternativna_goriva_final.pdf. Accessed 15 Apr 2021.

Tomašič, T. (2014). Zaloge, proizvodnja in poraba premoga v Sloveniji. https://core.ac.uk/download/pdf/67554161.pdf. Accessed 15 Apr 2021.

Urbančič, A. et al. (2020). Povzetek analize scenarijev za odločanje o Dolgoročni podnebni strategiji Slovenije do leta 2050. https://www.energetika-portal.si/fileadmin/dokumenti/publikacije/nepn/dokumenti/life_climatepath2050_strokovne_podlage_nepn_dpss.pdf. Accessed 15 Apr 2021.

Urbančič, A. et al. (2021). Podnebno ogledalo 2020. Ocena doseganja ciljev. https://www.podnebnapot2050.si/wp-content/uploads/2021/01/PO2020_Zvezek1_Cilji_Dopolnitev_Koncen_2021-01-21.pdf. Accessed 15 Apr 2021.

Vorkapić, M. (2020). Kaj prinaša memorandum o civilnem jedrskem sodelovanju z ZDA?, 6 December. https://www.24ur.com/novice/slovenija/memorandum-o-civilnem-jedrskem-sodelovanju-z-zda-ni-podlaga-za-konkreten-posel.html. Accessed 15 Apr 2021.

Youth for Climate Justice. (2019). Zahteve gibanja. https://drive.google.com/file/d/1rIiFxXgWiJ7MxfKGY8e-qk6A6vrVdojR/view. Accessed 15 Apr 2021.

Zgonik, S. (2019). Levičarska zarota. Mladina. https://www.mladina.si/191913/levicarska-zarota/. Accessed 15 Apr 2021.

Energy Governance in Spain

44

Jose M. Campos-Martín, Laura Crespo, and Rosa M. Fernandez

Contents

Introduction	1122
General conditions of Energy Governance in Spain	1124
Legacies of the Energy System	1125
Multilevel Governance	1132
Institutions for Energy Governance in Spain	1134
Actors for Energy Governance in Spain	1135
Coordination, Instruments and Issues of the Spanish Energy Transition	1139
External Constraints of the Energy Transition	1142
Internal Constraints of the Energy Transition	1144
Outcomes, Challenges and Prospects of the Energy Transition in Spain	1146
Energy Efficiency in Spain. Trends by Sector	1146
Sources of Energy in the Productive Sectors	1148
Demand for Petroleum Products	1148
Cross-References	1149
References	1149

Abstract

Spain is lagging behind in the transition to a sustainable energy system compared to other EU member states. Its unique position as an energy island, coupled with errors in energy planning inherited from previous government regimes, constitute

J. M. Campos-Martín (✉)
Instituto de Catálisis y Petroleoquímica, CSIC, Madrid, Spain
e-mail: jm.campos@csic.es

L. Crespo
Centro de Estudios y Experimentación de Obras Públicas, CEDEX, Madrid, Spain
e-mail: Laura.Crespo@cedex.es

R. M. Fernandez
Department of Social and Political Science, University of Chester, Chester, UK
e-mail: r.fernandez@chester.ac.uk

© Springer Nature Switzerland AG 2022
M. Knodt, J. Kemmerzell (eds.), *Handbook of Energy Governance in Europe*,
https://doi.org/10.1007/978-3-030-43250-8_29

a legacy that makes changes in the system difficult to achieve. Current political instability adds to the difficulties, under a governance framework characterised by lack of coordination and supremacy of the central government in the decision making process, in an environment where traditional energy companies still exert lobby power. The continuous changes in the regulatory framework of the energy sector have hindered investments in low carbon sources of energy due to perceived uncertainty. Small changes in the right direction are being observed though, with a more prominent role expected from the local levels of government. But many measures still originate on requirements linked to EU commitments and more initiatives at the national level need to be seen.

Keywords

Spain · Energy dependency · Energy island · Energy transition · Multi-level governance · Energy planning

Introduction

Spain is a territory with scarce energy resources (Eurostat 2018). Using the Eurostat methodology to measure the level of Spain's energy dependence, Spain improved in 2016 over the previous year with 71.9% dependence on external energy sources (Eurostat 2018). Other sources, such as Comillas University's reports on sustainability, are not so positive about Spain's progression, indicating an energy dependency of 86% (almost 87%), not showing improvement between 2014 and 2016 (Bellver et al. 2016, 2018). This makes the country particularly vulnerable and dependent on other countries because energy is a fundamental piece in the development of a society and its citizens' welfare (Bellver et al. 2016). In addition, because of its geography, Spain is an energy island, being an appendage on the fringes of Europe. The Pyrenees are a geographic obstacle to Spain's connection with the European electricity grid, while it is connected with Africa through a sub-Mediterranean cable to Morocco (REE 2018a).

Planning to meet energy needs is driven by energy supply, which results in the development of energy supply infrastructures that lack the necessary previous planning. The State conducts only indicatory planning, due to a liberalized marketplace with "light" state intervention, thus respecting the European legislative framework (BOE 2015). In some cases, this has led to certain imbalances, creating a system heavily concentrated on certain sources of energy, such as too many combined-cycle power plants: they represent 22% of the power installed, while generating 11.17% of the energy, according to the energy balance of 2017 (REE 2018a). This has hindered the sustainable progress of the system. An example of the necessary change of approach is the deployment of smart meters and the use of digitization in this sector so that the consumer can have a more active role in energy demand, which will facilitate a more sustainable management of energy needs. The main electricity distributors have the responsibility to install smart meters in dwellings with a contracted power less than or equal to 15 kW, with a deadline of December 31, 2019 (Ledo 2018).

The energy system is in the middle of a transition phase – a technological, regulatory and environmental transition – with financial stability challenges. Energy prices and consumer participation in energy markets will play important roles in the competitiveness of the economy, the development of the country and the vulnerability of households suffering from energy poverty. By energy poverty, we mean the inability of a household to obtain the minimum amount of energy services to cover basic domestic needs such as home heating and cooling, cooking, cleaning or communications (Tirado Herrero et al. 2018).

Political groups are working to protect the most vulnerable consumers by proposing a new social welfare regulation based on European frameworks. Data from the Living Conditions Survey reflect that in 2016 there were 6.8 million people in Spain, the equivalent of 15% of the population, suffering from inadequate housing temperatures or delay in the payment of bills (Tirado Herrero et al. 2018). To fulfill environmental protection objectives and in the context of climate change, the latest National Renewable Energy Action Plan proposes an electric power generation capability with 40% coming from renewable energy sources, constituting 17.3% of total primary energy supply, to comply with the European objectives to be achieved by 2020. A more difficult challenge is to comply with the energy efficiency commitment to be achieved by 2020 – Improvement of 20% (IDAE 2010). The repeal of the Directive was delayed more than it should have been, which led to the initiation of a sanctioning process by the European Commission (EC) (EC 2018a, b).

Spain is progressing very slowly in the area of European interconnection, currently at 2.8%, which is far from the 10% European commitment (EC 2017; Inelfe 2011; REE 2019a) and the 15% that it should aspire to by 2030 (REE 2019b; RTVE.es 2018).

In 2012, the national energy policy priority was to address the tariff deficit in the electricity system, a 30 billion euro debt, which must be absorbed by a system whose prices are among the highest in Europe. The instrument used to address this tariff deficit was fiscal reform (Law on Fiscal Measures for Energy Sustainability of December 27, 2012 –BOE 2012), which imposed various taxes on power generation companies and natural gas for industrial use and power cogeneration. This law aimed to collect taxes to compensate for the growing deficit. It resulted in an increased rate to be paid by consumers and a certain redistribution of benefits among the different technologies, which affected, in particular, cogeneration, photovoltaic and power generation from residual biomass.

With this measure and the Royal Decree (RD) on renewables approved in June 2014 (BOE 2014a), Spain has shifted from a world leader in solar and wind power to almost nonexistent growth in installed renewable power capability. This is the result of the government's decision to suspend incentives for renewables as per the rules established by the Royal Decree, foretold by the 'electricity reform' package in 2013. The reform was the culmination of well-known regulatory errors that have been translated in increasing payment obligations for electricity.

Another notable event in the national energy field is the regulation of self-consumption of renewable energy, approved by Royal Decree RD 900/2015 (BOE

2015) on self-consumption, in which the so-called 'sun tax' was introduced, cutting off all possibility of home-based renewable energy generation by taxing the energy produced with solar panels and consumed on-site. This mechanism discourages any saving initiatives in the system, when the consumer is already paying an electricity rate for the energy used and for the cost of the system itself. Said cost includes subsidies for clean energy to mitigate climate change, for domestic coal, for social tariffs and for energy efficiency, together with payments for regulatory or planning errors made in preceding years. These are the so-called stranded costs of the transition to a competitive system (CTC-'Costes de Transición a la Competencia') (Calero Pérez 2000). With the "sun tax," as it was first known, a backup rate is charged for consumption, which is a tax for access to the electricity grid to use it as backup energy source because the total amount of electricity billed in Spain does not cover all the fixed costs of the system. As such, a flat *complementary* rate was created for those self-consumers (prosumers) who wish to be connected to the grid. Recently, the new socialist party government published the Royal Decree-law 15/2018 (BOE 2018a), which among other changes in the regulation of the energy market, finally repealed the 'sun tax'.

In the field of environmental taxation, the European Environmental Agency study on 'Environmental Taxation and EU Environmental Policies' (EEA 2016), reports that the income obtained by Spain through environmental fiscal policies is among the lowest in the European Union. After Lithuania and Slovakia, Spain has the third-lowest percentage of tax revenue from environmental taxes in the EU, accounting for only 1.85% of GDP compared to an average of 2.46% for the European Union as a whole.

The report states that Spain has "a clear opportunity to review environmental taxes, mainly in the transportation and energy sectors, but also in the areas of pollution and the use of natural resources" (EEA 2016). More specifically, it criticizes Spain by saying it "still subsidizes fossil fuels, domestic coal, company cars and diesel more than gasoline, when its political objectives could be achieved in a manner less harmful to the environment" (EEA 2016). The price of fuels used on roads – gasoline and diesel – is the lowest in the EU because of lower taxes than other countries in its area (EC 2018c). This encourages unsustainable behavior from an environmental perspective: transporting passengers and goods by road is chosen instead of the electric railroad, which pays taxes for CO_2 emissions because electricity generation is included in the Emissions Trading System (ETS).

The picture described in the previous paragraphs does not show an environment conductive to a sustainable energy transition in Spain, but in order to assess the depth of the problem it is necessary to look back at all the factors influencing the current situation.

General conditions of Energy Governance in Spain

The Spanish economy reveals a profile of high energy consumption, addicted to fossil fuels and very dependent on foreign sources. This makes the Spanish energy model prone to cause negative impacts on development (Fernandez 2018a).

In addition, the historical development of energy policy has led to a series of legacies that complicate the governance of energy policy in Spain, with a wide variety of pressure groups, particularly energy companies (Solorio and Fernandez 2017), that impedes a clear strategy and gives rise to changing and even contradictory situations.

Historically, energy policy was characterized by the legacies of the Franco dictatorship, which was founded on self-sufficiency (De la Escosura and Sanz 1996) and led to the creation of some of today's energy companies (Castán Broto 2015). During this period, there was no energy planning, which led to the supply problems of the initial oil crises. These supply problems subsequently led to the first energy policy planning attempts, which had a series of planning errors that resulted in a system with some oversized sectors, limited competition and prices higher than the European average.

Legacies of the Energy System

(a) **High domestic energy consumption**: Spanish energy consumption did not stop increasing between 1990 and 2007 (Fig. 1), with only a significant pause during the recession caused by the financial crisis (2008 to date) and the collapse of the construction sector, a traditional energy consumer (Ministry of Energy 2017). Aside from this crisis period, energy consumption almost doubled from 1990 to 2007, despite a population that did not grow proportionally. From 1980 to 2008, the year-on-year energy consumption increase rate was close to 2.5%. This occurred despite the availability of more efficient energy technology.

(b) **Energy efficiency and intensity that can be improved**: The modernization of the Spanish economy has managed to reduce by a few percentage points the energy needed to produce one unit of gross domestic product. Energy intensity is close to the average of the EU27 (Ministry of Energy 2017), but that can be attributed to the importance of the services sector in Spain's GDP, a traditionally non-energy consuming one. Nevertheless, the energy intensity of the manufacturing sector is far from that of the most efficient countries (Fig. 2).

(c) **High energy dependence**: Spain has dangerously high energy dependence given the previous energy mix (Fig. 1) and the scarce availability of fossil fuels in the territory. Therefore, Spain's dependence on other countries for oil, gas and uranium is close to 100%, as well as for most of its coal (EC, 2015a). Almost half of the energy consumed in Spain is for fuel oil combustion. Therefore, external dependence on this fuel is the most vulnerable aspect of the Spanish system, from the point of view of internal energy security defined in conventional terms, although refinement and distribution of petroleum products are quite unregulated and Spain is an exporter of these products. In the case of Spain, almost 100% of vehicle fleets use oil derivatives. Therefore, transportation has an almost complete dependence on external sources except in the electric railway system. Taxes on hydrocarbons for road transportation are among the lowest in the EU, which has enabled the movement of goods and passengers by road (Fig. 3) (EC 2018c).

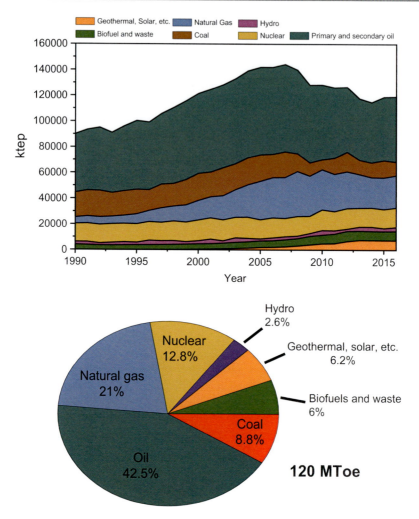

Fig. 1 Primary energy consumption and distribution profile, historical and for 2016 (International Energy Agency 2017)

The second highest area of energy dependence for Spain is natural gas (EC 2015a). In this regard, Law 34/1998, for the hydrocarbons sector (BOE 1998), specified the maximum allowable percentage of gas imports from a single country, regulated the right of third-parties to access gas and oil distribution and storage networks, and established that the Company for Hydrocarbon Logistics (*Compañia Logística de Hidrocarburos – CLH*) would be responsible for a logistics system that is open to all operators.

This high energy dependence is an important factor in the external trade balance, as it is responsible for an energy trade deficit, which is close to 2% of GDP, almost 20 billion euros per year in 2017 (Maqueda 2018).

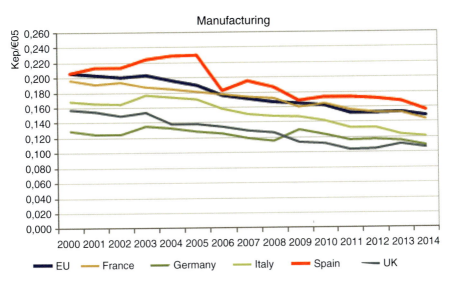

Fig. 2 Changes in energy intensity in the manufacturing sector (Ministry of Energy 2017)

(d) **Installed capacity, overcapacity**: One of the factors that shaped the current Spanish energy regime is errors in demand planning. The first such planning exercise was the creation of the National Energy Plan (*Plan Energético Nacional – PEN*) in 1975 corrected in the National Energy Plan in 1978 (Mir 1999). Both PEN-75 and PEN-78 focused on the promotion of nuclear energy. These plans assumed a 6% GDP growth rate and, based on this, outlined what was described as the most ambitious nuclear power plant construction program in the world. Later on, it was found that the GDP growth expectations in the plan did not align with reality, which led to a serious debt problem (World Bank 2019). At the beginning of the 1980s, the election victory of the socialist party coinciding with a new increase in oil prices linked to the second oil crisis (1979), plus a growth in domestic energy demand, originated a change in the National Energy Plan in 1983 (Delgado-Iribarren Garcia-Campero 1984; Mir 1999). PEN-83 proposed an energy diversification to guarantee supply through massive contribution of energy sources such as coal and hydroelectric, and slowly, natural gas. Starting in 1998, the Spanish model had shifted from national planning of the entire energy system to national planning of infrastructure. The second major expansion of installed electric power generation began in the late 1990s with the deployment of a large number of combined cycle natural gas installations, an expansion of the Spanish economy, and the expectation of energy consumption growth. While energy consumption growth indeed took place, it was lower than expected because of the use of more efficient technologies. The installed overcapacity is evident if one compares capacity and historical peak consumption data (Mir 1999; REE 2018b). The maximum consumption in 2016 reached 40,144 MWh while installed capacity was 100,053 MWh. Even if installed capacity from wind and solar (thermal and photovoltaic) is subtracted, there is still significant installed capacity (REE 2018a) (Fig. 4).

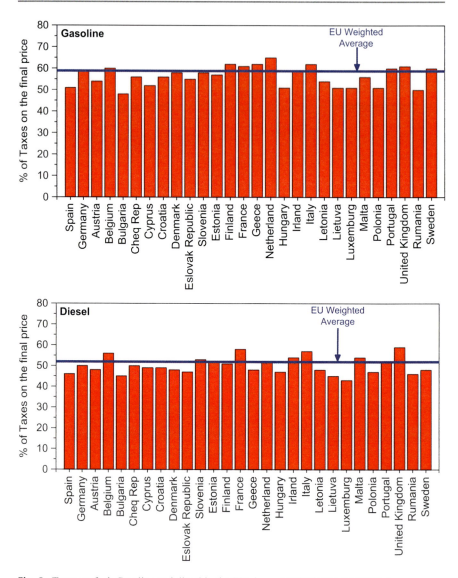

Fig. 3 Taxes on fuel: Gasoline and diesel in the EU share at 15/10/2018 (EC 2018c)

(e) **Unstable legal framework**. The generation of electricity has an interesting renewable energy component, but the change in energy policy favours greater penetration by fossil and nuclear fuels, mostly coming from abroad. The contribution of renewable energies to the electricity generation mix has two very different origins. There is a hydroelectric generation capability developed mostly through Franco's dictatorship (1939–1975), during which a large number of hydroelectric power plants were built (Castán Broto 2015). The second expansion of renewable energies occurred at the beginning of the 21st century, with

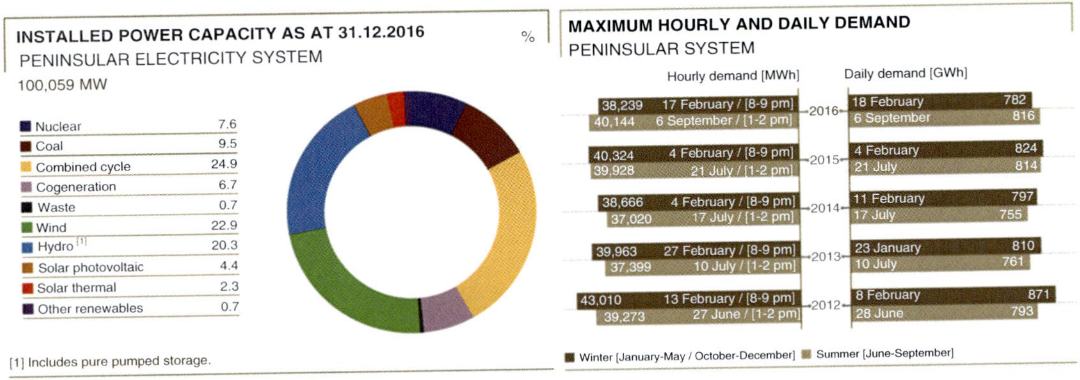

Fig. 4 Total installed electric power capacity and historical maximum consumption (REE 2018b)

the help of a feed-in tariff system since 1997 (Held et al. 2007). A quantitative increase in the installation of renewable energy took place during the first mandate of President Zapatero's socialist government, although the technology was not very mature. Additionally, the granting of rewards or incentives (Royal Decree 661/2007 – BOE 2007) produced a very notable increase in the production of electricity from renewable sources (Fernandez 2016). This positioned Spain as a frontrunner, becoming one of the most advanced countries in the world for renewable energy production (IDAE 2017). However, during the second mandate of Zapatero as Prime Minister, and with more intensity since the 2008 economic crisis, legislative changes have caused a halt in renewable energy investment, which remains at minimal levels (IDAE 2017) (Fig. 5).

Electric power generation has a high percentage of penetration by renewable energy. The process of deregulation of the Spanish energy sector was initiated with two EU directives: Directive EC/92/96 for the electricity market and Directive EC/30/98 for the natural gas market. The application of these directives in Spain established the foundation for the development of a new energy model, which went from a state-regulated system that considered energy supply to be a public service to a mixed system of unregulated activities by market participants. As such, the current situation is that power generation and sale are considered unregulated activities, while transportation and gas and electricity distribution are activities undertaken by private companies but regulated by law. The deregulation of the Spanish energy sector was formalized by Law 54/1997 (BOE 1997), for the Electricity Sector, and by Law 34/1998 (BOE 1998), for the Hydrocarbons Sector.

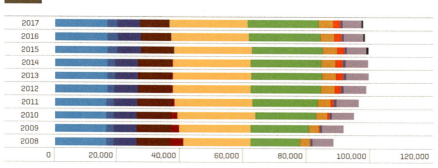

Fig. 5 Evolution of installed power capacity in the Spanish peninsula electricity system (REE 2018b)

This regulation has been revised and reformed on countless occasions, with the most notable of them being:
- Royal Decree-Law 6/2000, on measures to stimulate competition in the markets for goods and services;
- Royal Decree-Law 1/2012, with a moratorium on the system of incentives for new installations of the special generation regime (cogeneration, sources of renewable energies and residual biomass), except for those already pre-registered. The latter are those unbuilt installations that are already authorized to collect their incentive payment. This was a blow to the renewable energy sector, as effectively it eliminated any incentive to increase the generation capacity through renewable sources; and the already mentioned
- Law of Fiscal Measures for Energy Sustainability (BOE 2012), which imposed a 7% tax on power generation companies disregarding the source of the power generated.

More recent reforms, enacted in the second half of 2013 and beginning of 2014, came in the form of a package including numerous royal decrees, administrative orders, a legal resolution and a proposed law, all preceded by a Royal Decree-Law. It is no surprise that many investors negatively affected by all the regulatory changes have challenged them in court. Their legitimacy has also been questioned (Fernandez 2018b) due to the extensive use of the Royal Decree-Law, an instrument that is thought for emergency cases only, and that does not require prior parliamentary approval.

This package became particularly controversial because, as indicated by different camps (experts-[Mendoza 2015], regulatory agencies, civil society organizations, and even the European Commission-[Williams 2012]), it imposed all sorts of obstacles to the development of the renewables sector and outlined as first priority the elimination of the tariff deficit. However, said priority cannot be achieved if its causes are not addressed. Effectively the regulation favored conventional energy sources by incentivizing the increase in capacity of combined cycled plants, ending retroactively the support for renewables and making self-consumption (prosumption) economically unviable.

This does not mean that the incentives system was perfect. It had a series of defects that could jeopardize the financial health of the electricity system overall, due to the very generous incentives granted to certain technologies, namely solar photovoltaic (Held et al. 2010).

The unstable landscape was translated into a halt to renewable energy investment, which has remained at minimal levels due to legal uncertainty (Chen 2014). The negative consequences that these legislative changes brought for investors have been repeatedly challenged in court. We are currently seeing the first decisions issued against Spain by the international arbitration court, for damages to international investors. Paradoxically, international investors are being compensated for the change in remuneration of the feed-in tariff system, while domestic investors are not, as they are subject to decisions by Spanish courts (La información 2017).

(f) **Energy poverty**. Electricity and energy prices in general are very high, causing many households to lack sufficient resources to meet the most basic needs (Tirado Herrero et al. 2018). This has forced the government to provide assistance known as the electricity tariff subsidy (*bono social*), in place since 2009. It has undergone certain modifications on the right to access to be applied in 2019, including the prohibition to stop the electricity supply due to lack of payment to those households were minors under 16 live (Tarifaluzhora 2019).

Multilevel Governance

Spain has a territorial coverage of 504,645 km^2 and a population of 46,698,569 inhabitants (01/01/2018) (INE 2018). The country is governed under a parliamentary monarchy (BOE 1978) with a high level of decentralization and devolution to the regional governments of the 17 regions (Autonomous Communities) and the municipalities, which were established through the end of the 1970s and the beginning of the 1980s. In less than a quarter of a century, the country has evolved from being one of the most centralized states in Europe to being characterized by many of the features of a federal state (Calvo 2018; Rius and Martin Zamorano 2014). There are four levels of government: the Central Government, the autonomous communities, the provinces and the municipalities. The Constitution guarantees the autonomy of the last three levels, but such autonomy differs in nature. On the one hand, provinces and municipalities are local tiers of government with administrative autonomy, which means that they are responsible for the development of secondary legislation and the management of urban public services. On the other hand, autonomous communities have real political autonomy, with legislative power on a relevant number of issues guaranteed by the Constitution (BOE 1978).

Competencies in energy policy are distributed in a multilevel manner between the central government, the European Commission (Gouardères 2018) and sub-national administrations (Fernandez 2018a). Although there is a certain dialogue between central governments and Brussels and to a lesser extent with the autonomous communities, the central government imperatives prevail in energy matters.

The European Commission regulates internal competition in the electricity market and thus tries to avoid the national cartelization of markets and other forces that hinder a free internal market. It also attempts to guarantee the overall energy security of the European Union through the physical integration of a still fragmented energy system, by means such as high voltage interconnections and gas and oil pipelines (Gouardères 2018).

The European Commission is also responsible for defining and financing a large part of the mega-infrastructures for the supply and storage of energy, both inside and outside the EU, which it calls 'projects of common interest' (EC n.d.). An example of such projects in Spain is the Castor Project – the offshore gas storage facility along the coasts of Catalonia and Valencia (EC 2013). This European financing is provided mostly by the European Investment Bank (EIB) (EC 2013) and the European Bank for Reconstruction and Development (EBRD), although financing from regional development banks is also sought. The participation of European institutions in the planning of energy infrastructures is not a guarantee of success. The aforementioned Castor Project was a failure and had to be stopped due to the tremors caused in the area, with the government and the participant companies in court trying to determine who and how deserves compensation, while consumers have started paying higher gas bills in its account (The Corner 2017).

Energy is one policy area particularly characterized by multi-level governance (Eberlein and Kerwer 2004). At the highest hierarchical level, the European Union, through the Commission, negotiates as a bloc on certain issues related to the regulation of other markets with the objective, among others, of opening them to the investments of European energy companies (Boromisa 2014). At the same time, different lobby groups try to influence EU policy outcomes, and in the energy area such activity is fierce (Cerulus and Panichi 2015). It is not surprising then to find difficulties in representing the cacophonous and sometimes contradictory diversity of geostrategic interests of the member countries, their lobby groups, and even third countries. Despite the preferred approach of soft governance in energy matters (Ringel and Knodt 2018), the European Commission has often approved environmental/climate change related directives that member states must incorporate into their respective state regulations and that affect the execution of energy projects, with environmental impact assessment procedures, integrated environmental authorization and the emissions trading system (ETS), among others.

However, a significant part of energy governance is exercised by central governments who do not want to give up sovereignty in a recognized strategic policy (Grubliauskas and Rühle 2018) and whose control gives access to great economic benefit for related interest groups (Kang 2016). In this manner, the Spanish state controls policy for energy security, competition and sustainability, using the leeway provided by the domestic application of European Union directives, which often allow some discretion and are not always complied with. In this sense, it is worth noting that Spain is particularly bad in the transposition of directives related to environment (Mullerat 2010).

Finally, regional administrations, particularly the autonomous communities, hold territorial competencies on issues such as the organization of infrastructures and their security, competencies that are granted by the Spanish Constitution (BOE 1978) and the Statutes of Autonomy of each territory. Despite an apparent lack of competencies in energy matters by the lowest level of government, local governments are taking the lead in the energy transition. It is under their wing that the Network of Cities for Climate has been created (FEMP 2017). In this network, the initiatives of the adhered town councils are grouped, and training actions are carried out for the local authorities. In addition, some municipalities are taking an even more proactive position, making energy purchases only from renewable sources (Costantini 2018; Navarro Castelló 2018; Velez 2017) and favoring self-consumption facilities for companies or individuals within their municipality with a tax reduction (Ayuntamiento de Madrid 2018; Peña 2018).

Institutions for Energy Governance in Spain

If the transition towards more sustainable energy systems is to be measured by the integration of environmental concerns with energy matters, it is worth noting that in Spain, energy has never been part of the competencies of any Environment Ministry, falling traditionally under the remit of the Ministry of Industry or Economy (Fernandez 2018b). This has recently changed, however, with the creation of a Ministry for Ecological Transition (Royal Decree 355/2018 – BOE 2018b) by the new socialist government established after the no-confidence vote in the conservative prime minister, in June 2018 (Torres 2018). The new government has been short lived, and a snap election was called for April 2019 after the failure to get the national budget approved (Hall 2019). This comes to show the fragile and unstable political environment of the country, which poses questions about the continuation of any incumbent project for a sustainable energy transition.

In the meantime, the Ministry for Ecological Transition is responsible for the overarching energy related functions that correspond to the central government (the State). Within this Ministry, the new Secretary of State for Energy (Royal Decree 864/2018 – BOE 2018c), has been created, in charge, among others, of the following functions:

(a) The development of energy and mining policy;
(b) The elaboration and, where appropriate, application of measures for ensuring the supply of energy;
(c) The preparation of proposals on regulation and, where appropriate, approval of tariffs, prices of energy products and tolls, fees, and charges as well as remuneration for activities conducted within the energy sector framework in accordance with current legislation;
(d) The processing of carbon subsidies in accordance with European Union regulations, in collaboration with the General Technical Secretariat, and participation in working groups and other activities related to the coal industry, through the Institute for the Restructuring of Coal Mining and Alternative Development of Mining Regions.
(e) The economic and financial analysis and monitoring of energy markets.
(f) Regulation, monitoring and analysis of gas and electricity auctions. The settlement of costs and revenues of the energy sectors.
(g) The management of the system of certification of consumption and sale of biofuels.
(h) The exercise of powers of control, inspection and sanction in energy matters, when it is the responsibility of the General State Administration, in accordance with the provisions of current legislation.
(i) Knowledge of the acquisition of shares in the electricity and hydrocarbon sectors.
(j) The preparation, coordination and analysis of energy studies and statistics, in coordination with the Technical General Secretariat.

The division of functions does not finish with the Secretary of State, and the bulk of actions (proposals, asset management, permissions) is the responsibility of the next institutional layer, the General Directorate for Energy Policy (BOE 2018c).

The Ministry for Ecological Transition acts as an umbrella for a series of institutions with very relevant roles in the energy transition, and in general the management of energy matters within the country. Through the Secretary of State, it oversees the Public-Corporate Entity for the Management of Radioactive Waste (ENRESA) (BOE 2018c), and also the Corporation for Strategic Reserves of Petroleum Products (CORES), an organization responsible for managing and maintaining minimum levels of oil and petroleum product stocks for energy security. This in itself is not special, since it responds to the EU Directive on minimum reserves of crude oil or petroleum products (OJEU 2009). However, one of the most important institutions is the Institute for Energy Diversification and Saving (IDAE), born in 1974 as Centre for the Studies of Energy (IDAE n.d.-a). Its functions are the promotion of energy efficiency and renewable energies, and it is the responsible for the elaboration of the National Plans for the Promotion of Renewable Energies, some of which already mentioned in this chapter.

Other institutions, out of the remit of the Ministry for Ecological Transition, undertake fundamental work for the transition to more sustainable energy systems. The most relevant one is probably the Center for Energy, Environmental and Technological Research (CIEMAT). It is a public research body assigned to the Ministry of Science, Innovation and Universities, which replaced the Nuclear Energy Board, an institution with origins in the dictatorship, in charge or nuclear fission control since 1951 (CIEMAT n.d.). Its functions are the research and development of new energy technologies as well as participation in international programs in this field.

The National Commission for Markets and Competition (CNMC) has supervisory and control functions to ensure the correct functioning of the electricity and natural gas markets, with energy in general being one of their main areas of activity. This is the body in charge of transparency in the operation of energy system for the protection of consumers and other agents (CNMC n.d.). Last but not least, the Nuclear Safety Council (CSN), an independent agency of the Administration, has functions related to nuclear safety and radiation protection (CSN n.d.). Bearing in mind the all important and related functions these institutions perform, it is remarkable that with the exception of a few joint initiatives between IDAE and CIEMAT (CIEMAT 2017; Energías Renovables 2004), there is no overarching strategy to coordinate their activities nor to ensure that their respective plans do not contradict each other.

Actors for Energy Governance in Spain

The energy sector is deregulated but has a series of restrictions to ensure supply. The producers and distributors are private equity entities, but the state plays an important role in electricity transmission through the Spanish Electricity Network (*Red Eléctrica Española, REE*) (BOE 1997), and through the infrastructure of gas pipelines (ENAGAS) (BOE 1998). The electricity and natural gas markets are dominated by large private equity companies such as: *IBERDROLA, Gas Natural/*

Fenosa, *ENDESA*, *Viesgo*, *Hidrocantabrico Energia* and *Naturgas* (Table 1) along with some other smaller operators. Large companies have a 65% market share in generation and an 83% market share in sales (CNMC 2017).

The petroleum products market is dominated by three companies with in-country refineries (REPSOL, CEPSA, and BP) (Table 1), representing 50% of sales, while the market penetration of other wholesalers is much lower. In addition, the Hydrocarbons Logistics Company (CLH) is a private company that operates under state regulation (Article 41.1 of Law 34/1998 of the Hydrocarbons Sector – BOE 1998). It facilitates the distribution of any company's petroleum products by allowing the use of its storage and transportation facilities (Fig. 6) without discrimination and with competitive, public prices in order to promote open competition. Finally, the non-for-profit public corporation CORES contributes to guaranteeing the security of Spain's hydrocarbons supply by maintaining petroleum product reserves and controlling the industry's petroleum product, liquid petroleum gas (LPG) and natural gas stocks. It also has been a source of information on the hydrocarbons sector since its creation in 1995 (CORES n.d.).

There are several conclusions that can be extracted from Table 1. On one side, the number of energy companies operating is Spain is quite reduced, which defines de

Table 1 Main companies in Spain's energy sector. (Source: AELEC (n.d.), AOP (n.d.), CNMV (n.d.) and Corporate websites)

Company name	Ownership
IBERDROLA	8.5% Qatar Investment Authority, 5.1% Capital Research and Management Company, 3% Blackrock, Inc., 83.4% other shareholders
Gas Natural/Fenosa	24.44% Criteria Caixa, S.A.U., 20% Gip III Canary 1, S.A.R.L, 20% Repsol S.A., 3.85% Sonatrach, 31.71% other shareholders
ENDESA	70.10% ENEL SPA, 29.90% other shareholders
Viesgo	60% Macquarie European Investment Fund (MEIF) IV, 40% Kuwait Investment Authority (KIA)
Hidrocantabrico Energía	100% EDP (Electricidad de Portugal)
Naturgas	100% EDP (Electricidad de Portugal)
REE	20% SEPI (Spanish State), 80% other shareholders
ENAGAS S. A.	5% SEPI (Spanish State), 95% other shareholders
REPSOL S. A.	9.6% Caixabank, 8.0% Sacyr, 4.3% Temasek. 78.1% other shareholders
Compañía Española de Petróleos S.A.U. (CEPSA)	100% Mubadala Investment Company
BP España, S.A.U.	100% BP
CLH	25% Servet Shareholdings, S.L. 24.77% Borealis Spain Parent B.V., 20% MEIF 5 Rey Holdings, S.L., 10% Marthilores 3, S.L., 10% Vaugirard Infra S.L., 5% Stichting Depositary APG Infrastructure Pool 2017 II, 5% Simcoe Titán, S.L., 0.32% other shareholders
CORES	100% state-owned (Spain)

Fig. 6 Hydrocarbon storage and transportation facilities. (Source: CLH 2018)

market as an oligopoly (The Economist 2009). On the other side, it becomes apparent that the market is open to the participation of foreign owners, which is a remarkable shift, bearing in mind that the privatization process that began in the 1980s intended to preserve ownership in national hands due to the strategic nature of the sector (Arocena 2004). In any case, big energy companies have a prominent role in the governance of the energy system in Spain, with a visible concomitance between them and the political power (government) (Solorio and Fernandez 2017), which 'raises concern about the viability of a higher level of energy sovereignty and the achievement of international commitments regarding climate change' (Gabaldón-Estevan et al. 2018). It is worth noting that this concomitance occurs at the national level, with the local level following the opposite approach. It is not unusual to find examples in which the national government approves energy measures against the opinion of the local government affected (AFP 2015). It has also become common to find the big energy companies taking the local governments to court for replacing them by renewable energy providers (Costantini 2018). Private energy companies are highly organized, not only to lobby individually, but also as members of different associations specifically established to defend their interests. Some of the most prominent are (Club Español de la Energía n.d.):

- **Electric companies**: the Spanish Electricity Industry Association (UNESA) (large companies) and the Electric Company Association (ASEME) (medium and small companies);

- **Renewable Energy**: Association of Renewable Energy Companies (APPA), Aeolic Energy Business Association (AEE), Spanish Photovoltaic Union (UNEF), National Association of Photovoltaic Energy Producers (Anpier), Association of the Solar Thermal Energy Industry (ASIT), Spanish Association of the Solar Thermoelectric Energy Industry (Protermosolar), and Spanish Association for the Promotion of Biomass Energy (Avebiom);
- **Cogeneration companies**: ACOGEN; and
- **Petroleum products**: Spanish Association of Petroleum Product Operators (AOP) and Spanish Association of Hydrocarbon Research, Exploration and Production Companies (ACIEP)

In general, associations of this type in Spain are not tightly knit, companies may be members of several associations at the same time, and they can even be members of bigger lobby groups at European level. It is not a surprise then, that debate in Spanish society about the energy model is rather lacking, as it appears dominated by the big companies and their lobby groups. This may well be partly due to the fact that traditionally environment has not been a priority for Spanish citizens (Chaques and Palau 2011).

Other Actors

Political parties: In general, the conservative parties have not favored changes toward a new energy model based on renewable energies. The so called progressist parties are in theory more supportive (El periódico de la energía 2017; PSOE 2017), but we must bear in mind that political interests have dominated their decisions in this area (Fernandez 2018a), and in all cases, they feel obligated by the European Union's commitments. There is no 'green party' in Spain with political representation at the national level.

Trade unions: The unions do not have a clear position. While in theory they are supporters of an energy transition, their main membership comes from traditional industry and coal mining constituents. Their discourse has focused on a 'just transition' (Stevis and Felli 2015) in order to avoid more negative effects over employment, in a country where the crisis damaged employment levels profoundly. Spain has seen how employment in the mining sector has decreased from 45,000 miners to less than 2000 in 28 years (Martin Murillo 2018), but mitigated by a generous subsidies system that would be unthinkable for any other sector of the economy. Pressures to the system came from the EU, to end with coal production that was not economically viable. The socialist government created after the vote of no confidence in 2018, committed to follow Brussels guidelines to close 26 uncompetitive mines by the end of the year, or they would have to return the aid they had received (Tamma 2018). At the same time, the country had to present its national energy and climate plan to achieve the 2030 targets, and mines burning other fuels would have until 2020 to comply with the new Industrial Emissions Directive (Tamma 2018). Unions have been fighting, in the mining regions, for new extensions in the original closure plans, but ultimately applauded the agreement thanks to the €250 million committed to regenerate mining sites and protect the affected communities (Industriall 2018).

Environmentalists: Environmental organizations (Greenpeace, Friends of the Earth, and Ecologists in Action) have a relatively small presence in Spain, but have managed to mobilize citizens in critical areas for the energy transition, such as the protests against the 'sun tax' (Planelles 2015), or the defense of energy self-consumption (prosumption) (Ecologistas en accion 2019). They lobby for changes in the energy model towards the use of clean energies, arguing the potential of the country to reach a 100% of electricity generation through renewables (Greenpeace 2019), but also lobby for a change in the governance of the energy system, with local communities exerting 'energy sovereignty', by participating in the management of energy resources, following the examples of countries such as Germany or Denmark (Amigos de la tierra n.d.).

Consumer organizations: Consumer organizations are in favor of a transition toward a cleaner energy model in particular if it can bring cost savings for their energy bills. This is the reason why their focus has been the defense of self-consumption and protests against the 'sun tax' (Energías Renovables 2017).

Most of the social agents above mentioned have created specific alliances and produced joint manifestos in favor of the energy transition. An example of this is the Alliance for Self-consumption, with more than 40 associations of environmentalists, companies, social organisations and unions (Ecologistas en Accion 2019).

Coordination, Instruments and Issues of the Spanish Energy Transition

Energy policy in Spain is proposed as a state policy, and it is a state function to make policy through forward-looking planning that is subsequently implemented through the IDAE (Institute of Energy Diversification and Saving) and the Energy Councils of the Autonomous Communities (CCAA). In turn, these use local government entities to provide the financial instruments needed to channel funds that promote changes in the energy model at the local level. The coordination of these instruments is based on the distribution of functions defined in the Spanish Constitution (BOE 1978), but it is fair to say that there is not so much coordination, and overlaps and conflicts happen sometimes (Smith and Heywood 2000). The Spanish state has assumed all the energy and climate change policies of the European Union and as such is immersed in the new, future commitments defined in what is known as the "Winter Package" (Hancher and Winters 2017). This sets forth a long-term vision in the Integrated Plan for Energy and Climate (EC 2017) that is formalized as regulation, including one for the Governance of the Energy Union (EC 2016a). The Winter Package clarifies the European Union's commitment to a more sustainable and decarbonized energy model, through improved energy savings and efficiency and a more informed consumer. This, in turn, should facilitate energy management based on demand-driven political action, supported by modern, knowledge-based technologies.

In Spain, one of the problems facing the energy transition is the oversized electrical generation capacity, as it has been previously outlined. which has tripled the needs for backup power provided by combined cycle generation (Del Rio and Janeiro 2016). This has justified a prolonged halt in renewable investment so that investments made in combined cycle backup technologies could be redeemed. The initial purpose of said investments was to supply power to the electrical system for longer hours, matching the supply and demand prices of the electricity market.

Connected with prices, another problem arises related to the political action undertaken on electricity tariffs. The Spanish state recognized debt to electricity companies for payment of various obligations (Johannesson Linden et al. 2014). The growth of the debt overtime has been used as justification to modify and subsequently eliminate the incentives system in support of renewable energies (BOE 2012), which in turn has hindered Spanish progress towards its commitments under European Directives (European Renewable Energy Council 2013).

Another source of issues for Spain's energy transition is electric transport, which is very expensive and poses physical and technological barriers for the transport of goods (Palacios 2018). Electric transportation of people requires cars with greater autonomy than that provided by current technology so that citizens invest in that type of car as feasible alternative to traditional ones. Progress on development of high-cost public and private vehicle charging facilities has also been very limited in the country, with perhaps a need to modify the regulatory framework. At present, only big companies can manage both regulations and costs of charging points (Palacios 2018).

Transportation of goods occurs mainly by highway (road), amounting to 40% of final energy consumption in Spain (De Arriba Segurado and Garcia Barquero 2017). Spain is the EU member state with the lowest use of railways for the transport of goods. The reasons for this are historical – railway track widths that do not conform to European standards, its orography and peninsular geography – making Spain an appendix within Europe (Jordan, nd). These factors have not contributed to improve the conditions for the transport of goods by rail. Spain's Mediterranean corridor may provide the right conditions if there is a suitable connection with France through the Pyrenees. The situation has recently improved, to a limited extent, due to greater comfort and faster travel times for passenger transportation by rail, which has surpassed air travel in corridors with high-speed rail (Madrid-Seville and Madrid-Barcelona) (Fortea 2015). There are areas of the country where the investments in these infrastructures is lacking, and passengers experience, including delays, cancellations and accidents, has originated complaints from the regional authorities to the central government, in charge of the allocation of funding for these projects.

In other areas such as climate change, more progress has been achieved. Since 2005, the National Climate Council (CNC) and the Climate Change Policy Coordination Commission (CCPCC) have been working on climate change policies. The latter was conceived to facilitate coordination and collaboration between the central State Administration and the autonomous communities for the implementation of the emission permits trading scheme and the fulfillment of its information-related international and European Union obligations (Ministry for Ecological Transition n.d.). In 2017, Spain's president announced the urgent release of a Law on Climate Change and Energy Transition to be debated by different social agents and experts (Fundacion para la Eficiencia Energetica y el Medioambiente 2017). The Council of Ministers approved the creation of an expert committee to prepare a report on different energy transition scenarios and analyze possible energy policy alternatives, taking into consideration environmental and economic impacts while allowing the achievement of the established targets in the most efficient way possible. The Council of Ministers gave the go ahead to the parliamentary process (RETEMA 2019). After the snap election, a few modifications have been added to the project, but its main lines remain unchanged (El periódico de la energía 2019). Once the Law is approved, it will be communicated and operationalized through the Autonomous Communities and City Councils.

At the municipal level, as it has been already mentioned, the Network of Cities for Climate is part of the Spanish Federation of Municipalities and Provinces (FEMP), dedicated to fight against climate change and its side effects. The rationale was to deal with the possible risks of increasing vulnerability for towns and cities, which could directly affect local populations and territorial heritage (FEMP 2017). The goal of the Network of Cities for Climate was to promote sustainability policies in Spanish cities, particularly those related to the reduction of greenhouse gas emissions.

The agreement between FEMP and the Ministry aims to promote institutional collaboration to develop pollution and climate change prevention initiatives with local sustainability as the general context. The agreement is also focused on the implementation of the Local Agenda 21, based on coordination and inter-administrative cooperation, and other activities of joint interest (FEMP n.d.). In this sense, the FEMP is signatory of the Covenant of Mayors, an initiative of the European Commission, with the commitment of achieving sustainable energy for urban areas.

With the same purpose of working to reduce emissions, the IDAE issues calls for subsidies co-financed with FEDER funds within the low-carbon economy, aimed at improving outdoor lighting, programs to aid modal shifts and modes of transport, efficiency energy in the railway sector and energy rehabilitation of buildings (IDAE 2018).

These actions are shared with the regional administration with energy-related functions. IDAE subsidizes activities for improving the energy efficiency of buildings and the Ministry of Energy promotes concrete actions for private apartments (IDAE 2018). IDAE maintains direct participation in these investments through the Energy Efficiency Fund.

To coordinate these activities, the REBECA Network was created (IDAE 2018). From 2014 to 2020, the Low Carbon Economic Network (*Red de Economía Baja en Carbono – REBECA*) has and will act as a mechanism to coordinate, promote and support the management and evaluation of activities in the low carbon economy co-financed by structural funds. It is also a necessary instrument for sharing good practices and disseminating the results of energy efficiency projects, renewable energy networks and receiving European funding. The Low Carbon Economic Network comprises the following (IDAE 2018):

- Entities responsible for the General State Administration's community funds;
- Entities responsible for low-carbon economic policies of the General State Administration (IDAE, Spanish Office of Climate Change, Secretary of State for Energy, General Directorate of Architecture, Housing and Land);

- Entities responsible for the community funds of the Autonomous Communities;
- Entities responsible for the low carbon economic policies of the Autonomous Communities;
- Representatives of local entities (FEMP);
- Representatives of other sectoral networks (the Network of Environmental Authorities, the Urban Initiatives Network, the Research, Development and Innovation Network and the Equality Network);
- Representatives from other funds (EAFRD, ESF and FEMP); and
- European Commission (DG REGIO and DG ENER).

As it can be observed, Spain counts on what should be the necessary institutions and coordination mechanisms for a sustainable energy transition, but the unsettled political environment acts as a distraction for the progress on this area.

External Constraints of the Energy Transition

European Climate Policy and Security of Supply Policy

Spain has taken on the climate change objectives set by the EU related to energy saving, energy efficiency and indigenous power generation using renewable energies. These all reinforce energy security of supply in a continent that depends on external energy sources, making it vulnerable to the ups and downs of geopolitical interests. At the moment, between 30% and 40% of electricity in Spain is generated by renewable sources, which represents 17.3% of primary energy (EC 2015a). The goal is to achieve 20% by 2020 (IDAE 2010). As it has been previously mentioned, the regulatory changes that suspended the support for renewables compromised the achievement of this target, but there seems to be a governmental shift in this regard (among other reasons due to the adverse court decisions against said regulations). The government has recently assigned through auction the installation of additional 3000 MW of renewable energy capacity, mostly wind (Ministry for Ecological Transition 2018), in order to make progress towards the 2020 target, but most importantly, with a longer term view of 100% renewables penetration by 2050.

With regard to energy efficiency, there is a commitment to achieve energy efficiency savings of 20% by 2020, which will be difficult for Spain due once more to the paralysis created by the regulatory changes of 2012 and 2013. The latest attempt to correct the situation involves the creation of a National Energy Efficiency Fund (BOE 2014b), financed through the IDAE. The purpose of said Fund is to finance economic and technical assistance, training, information or other measures to increase energy efficiency in the different energy consuming sectors. Its aim is to do this in a way that contributes to achieving the national energy saving objective established by the National System of Energy Efficiency Obligations published in article 7 of Directive 2012/27/EU (BOE 2014b). This is an indication that the measures adopted are not part of the country's own initiative, but forced by the commitments made as requirement of EU membership.

As part of the National Energy Efficiency Fund, there are specific aid programs designed to improve the situation in particular sectors or activities, which contribute to interaction between different actors in the energy governance system. Examples of said programs are: Aid program for energy efficiency activities in small and medium enterprises, and large companies in the industrial sector (IDAE n.d.-b) – This program aims to facilitate the implementation of energy saving and efficiency measures as a result of energy audits in facilities, replacement of equipment and implementation of energy management systems.

Aid program for municipal lighting (IDAE n.d.-b) – The purpose of this program is the renovation of municipal outdoor lighting installations establishing a line of credit for local entities. There is also an aid program for energy efficiency in the railway sector, and another program is being designed for the hospitality industry, which is expected to have a great impact because Spain receives a large number of tourists and the sector is one of the main sources of income for the country.

There seems to be some competition between IDAE's activities financed with FEDER funds and those of the Energy Efficiency Fund, so coordination mechanisms are required to avoid duplicities. What has become apparent is that the Institute for Energy Diversification and Saving (IDAE) is by far the most relevant institution in the governance of the energy system in Spain.

Given Spain's energy dependency, the interconnections with other member states are expected to play an important role in the transition to a more sustainable energy system. FEDER funds are used for electrical interconnections of peninsular and insular Spain. Interconnection with the EU has risen from 1.4% to 2.8%, through France. But this is still far from the 10% commitment in Europe and the 15% target for the year 2030 (EC 2015b). These connections facilitate the exchange of energy with the continent and could meet the renewable energy penetration objective in the electricity mix. However the progress with the interconnection with France have been slowed by France reticence, particularly with regard to gas pipelines. An agreement between France, Spain and Portugal has been reached to improve the electricity links (Gotev 2018). Progress with gas is conditional to the continuation of demand, as it has been assessed that existing projects elsewhere in Europe are not operating at full capacity (Fig. 7).

State of the Technology for Electricity Generation from Renewable Sources, the Internet of Things and the EU's Winter Package

The energy transition is driven by two powerful forces: the already described global commitment to the fight against climate change embodied in the Paris Agreement; and technological development, with renewable energies becoming increasingly competitive compared to traditional technologies, better lighting and air conditioning systems, more efficient combustion engines, and more advanced batteries and electric vehicles.

The Winter Package approved by the European Commission in November 2016 (EC 2016b) grants the electricity consumer the right to consume, generate and sell electricity, and moves towards the presence of distributed and decentralized energy resources, generators, batteries, electric cars, and flexible demand. This is all

Fig. 7 Electricity interconnections. Spanish Electricity Network (*Red Eléctrica de España. REE*) (INELFE 2017)

converging to convert the consumer into an active agent and transformer of energy, supported by the Internet of Things. In theory, this will enable governments, including the Spanish one, to redirect behaviors arising from past commitments with electricity companies that could hamper this evolution, by reimbursing agreed exploitation costs in other electricity generation frameworks, which are very far from the current state of technology.

Internal Constraints of the Energy Transition

The Iberian Peninsula Behaves Like an Island in Energy Matters and in the Transportation of Goods by Rail

Peninsular and island Spain become de facto energy islands with regard to electricity supply, with natural borders that limit exchanges with their neighboring countries: Portugal and Morocco, and the aforementioned France. This energy island effect also extends to freight transportation by rail, characterized by the mountainous terrain (Jordan n.d.) that complicates railway routes and increases operating costs and timeframes. Additional complicating factors are the three different railway gauges used in Spain and the geographical location of the peninsula in the global traffic of goods (Observatorio del Transporte y la Logística en España – OTLE 2018).

The mountainous topography of the Iberian Peninsula and the geographic location of the Peninsula in the European continent has constrained the transportation of goods from Spain, which are primarily moved by roadway. These constraints prevent the electric system from becoming the basic energy vector of the productive sectors of the low carbon economy and also result in a situation where freight transport via highway is the dominant mode of transportation, being 100% dependent on fossil fuels and thus, not the best exponent of a sustainable transition.

Electric Energy Pricing Policy
The electricity tariff paid by the consumer has three components – the price of energy in the electricity market, transmission network costs and the various regulatory charges included in the electricity tariff. Essentially, the tariff has two parts – a charge corresponding to the contracted power and another one proportional to the energy consumed (Bellver et al. 2018). The charge for the contracted power includes the contracted regulatory commitments and payment for the use of the transmission and distribution network. These costs are 50% of the electricity tariff (Bellver et al. 2018). With such a system, it would make sense that when consumers generate electricity in their homes, they should at least partially avoid paying regulatory charges and some of the transmission network costs. But the regulation approved in the middle of the last economic crisis did exactly the opposite. It obliged the owner of the installation to pay for the energy generated, creating the famous 'sun tax'. So during the last few years, Spain has seen how self-production/consumption was inhibited and any energy-saving incentive disappeared (Mendoza 2015).

Electricity in Spain is expensive in comparison with other countries in its area (Stücklin 2016). These energy prices are not positive factors for the stability of industrial sectors such as the steel industry, which are very dependent on electricity. The regulation that attempted to finish with the tariff deficit, despite the already high prices of energy, influenced the behavior of the industrial sector. Effectively, the regulation (BOE 2013), limited the paid cogeneration hours that are fed into the electricity system. This practice had the effect of mobilizing resources in the industrial sector to promote energy saving, by recovering residual heat from production processes to produce heat and electricity. The Royal Decree – Law 9/2013 (BOE 2013), later modified by Royal Decree 413/2014 (BOE 2014a), regulating electricity production from renewable energy sources, cogeneration and waste, was further modified by Ministerial Order 1045/2014 (BOE 2014c), approving retribution parameters applicable to some of the installations that produce electricity from renewable energy sources, cogeneration and waste. The same Ministerial Order also identifies the remuneration for operating costs and investments during the first half of the 2016 regulatory period for all the defined types. This myriad of regulatory changes have contributed to the increase in the price of electricity for consumers, uncertainty for producers and investors, and distrust in the system. More stability is required, which is not guaranteed with a new election on its way.

Outcomes, Challenges and Prospects of the Energy Transition in Spain

One of the determining factors for Spain's progress in its energy transition is its population. Currently, Spain's population is 47 million inhabitants, according to 2015 data, and it is expected to decline to 46 million by 2030 (CEPSA 2017). The working-age population will decrease from 32% in 2015 to 31% in 2030. This will happen because Spain, like many other OECD countries, faces a population decline due to the failure to address the causes of a sharp decline in the birth rate (CEPSA 2017). Lack of job stability for working couples, at times reinforced by insecure employment type, has been a constant of the Spanish development model, with higher unemployment rates than its European counterparts even in times of prosperity (Fernandez 2018a). It is forecasted that the Spanish economy will return to a stable growth path, enjoying moderate growth along with its neighboring countries. An initial growth rate of 3% in 2017 is expected, with moderation in the progression but positive growth averaging more than 2% per year up to 2020 (OECD 2018). It is possible that growth trend will be moderated in the future by the declining population but the fact that it will also be an aging population will have an influence on higher services consumption, which can still lead to an increase in energy consumption. The expectation is, however, that consumption growth will be offset by an increase in energy efficiency (CEPSA 2017) and by 2030 demand for energy should return to 2015 levels, thus meeting the objectives of reducing the EU's energy demand, through savings and energy efficiency in the productive sectors (CEPSA 2017).

Energy Efficiency in Spain. Trends by Sector

Efficiency will improve in all sectors and particularly in transportation. The forecast for Spain is the reduction of energy consumption due to improvements in energy efficiency and the combined effects of population decline and moderate growth in the transportation sector coupled with economic activity improvements (CORES 2018)

The transportation sector, an end-use energy sector, reached its peak demand in 2009, a level that will not be reached again. Changes in the population's transportation and mobility habits, accentuated by the characteristics of an aging population, will reach their highest levels before 2020.

Growth of energy consumption in the residential sector will also be moderate as will be growth in the number of households. Any expansion will occur in the services, buildings and tourism sectors (CORES 2018). The transportation sector will still account for most of the energy demand in 2030 – one-third of total demand. The transportation of people will continue to account for two-thirds of energy consumption in the sector as a whole, a proportion similar to the current one. However, the transportation vehicles for people – cars and airplanes – will be approximately 25–30% more efficient than current vehicles, with the caveat that the rate of renewal of automobiles will be much higher than that of aircraft, which have a longer useful life (CORES 2018). It is also expected that freight transportation efficiency will improve by 15% in terms of energy intensity, by increasing the transportation of goods with higher Gross Value Added (GVA) and improving logistics (CORES 2018).

The industrial sector follows the transportation sector in energy consumption despite the strong contraction in demand experienced in 2009 due to the European economic crisis. This affected industrial activities linked to construction: cement and non-metallic minerals (aggregates and siliceous sands). In terms of energy consumption, this sector increased efficiency from 2004 to 2005 in the most energy intensive sectors by improving production processes (more efficient technology changes), while facing the inclusion of more productive and energy-intensive subsectors in the emissions trading system (ETS) (CORES 2018). In general, there has been a shift in energy consumption from industry to the service sector and from speculative, construction-related industrial production to other productive activities: chemicals, agri-food, beverages and tobacco, equipment components and non-metallic minerals associated with daily life (animal beds, detergent support, etc.). Energy improvements have come from the use of measures for horizontal technology, process technology and technology for new processes (CORES 2018).

Still lacking is a firm decision to push for the renovation of building envelopes, windows and building orientation (bioclimatic buildings). These investments today are already included in FEDER funding for the low carbon economy. It is expected that the services sector (offices, tourism and shopping centers) will have a greater presence as the industrial sector loses significance and tourism explores the as-yet unexploited potential to attract high-quality tourism such as cultural and eco-tourism (CORES 2018).

It is not a good prospect though, that regarding energy sources, petroleum products will still dominate Spain's energy mix in 2030, although in lower proportion than today. Natural gas, biomass and electricity will be the most used sources in the energy mix, to the detriment of petroleum products and coal. Petroleum derivatives will continue to dominate Spanish transportation in 2030. Petroleum derivatives will constitute half of all final energy in 2030 (currently, they represent 51%), although their presence in primary energy will decline due to a higher volume of renewable energy (CORES 2018).

Natural gas is expected to have a slowly increasing presence in the energy mix, particularly as it substitutes petroleum products for heat in the residential and commercial sectors. Biofuels will be increasingly used for road transportation to meet the 8.5% objective of the EU. The increased use of renewable energy sources for power generation and the possible increased use of fuel mixtures on roadways will help Spain fulfill the objectives of the Renewable Energy Plan 2011–2020 (IDAE 2010), which includes as one of its measures the introduction of biofuels for transportation.

Power generation in the energy mix Power from wind and solar energy will need to more than double in 2030 to meet the targets for renewable energy. The expectation is that in 2030, electricity demand will exceed 60% of final energy consumption (CEPSA 2017), which will make it easier to meet renewable energy targets. The electricity generated by wind and solar power will account for more than 50% of total power, while it currently stands at 27% (CORES 2018). This would require the installation of 50 GW of new wind and solar power, compared to the 30 GW currently installed. Wind energy will constitute two-thirds of the energy mix, while the remained will be solar. Auctions will be the mechanism used to install new capacity, with an annual ratio of 3 GW per year until attaining the 2030 requirements.

Combined cycle capacity will be maintained at current levels, but their utilization ratios will drop due to the greater presence of renewable power in the energy mix. Hydroelectric power capacity will remain at current levels, while nuclear capacity will be reduced significantly (Spain will have to articulate its plans on the closure of nuclear power plants) (Morgan 2018).

Sources of Energy in the Productive Sectors

It is expected that natural gas generation will decline in light of the increase in renewables, representing by 2030 just 7–8% of all the electricity generated in Spain. Natural gas will be the main source of energy in cogeneration plants used to produce heat and electricity for industry, with the cogeneration plants maintaining natural gas consumption levels similar to 2015 (CORES 2018). With all this, a slight increase will be seen in the proportion of natural gas in the energy mix. Demand will increase by 5% (final energy), rising from 17% to 22%, or a fifth of all final energy.

The gas pipelines of North Africa will consolidate their position to supply the demand for natural gas. LNG will have a less dominant position as a supply source, although it will evolve into being the first source of gas. The LNG will be transported with methane tankers, and the gas pipelines will supply the rest; this supply is not expected to change.

Demand for Petroleum Products

After a few years of recovery in Spain's consumption demand for oil products, consumption will drop after 2020 (CEPSA 2017). The recovery in demand for petroleum products has been increasing since 2015, growth that will continue until the years 2019–2020 (CEPSA 2017). From this point forward, demand is expected to slow down because of energy efficiency impacts and, to a lesser extent, the availability of oil substitutes.

In accordance with other indicators, the energy intensity of fuel in Spain, defined as the fuel consumption needed to generate one million in economic activity, began to decline before the peak energy demand was reached in 2005 (IDAE n.d.-c). This is the result of promoting efficiency and improvements to energy sources (more efficient fuels and technology improvements). The economic crisis of 2009 caused a drop in energy intensity, due to the decline of sectors with more intensive energy consumption. From 2008 to 2015, demand for petroleum products dropped by 25%, while the efficiency of processes improved and the use of more efficient fuels pushed demand for primary energy down to 1995 levels (CORES 2018).

It is still expected that economic growth will boost demand for oil in the near future, due to increases in automobile sales and tourism that will boost demand for energy consumption related to road and air travel, so Spain will still have problems to decouple energy consumption from economic growth. However, after 2020, economic growth will be fed by more efficient vehicle technology, better fuels, higher occupancy of vehicles and the growing use of electric vehicles, which will result in lower consumption of petroleum products from 2020 to 2030 (Moselle et al. 2010).

The scenario presented here complies with the commitments made to the EU to enable a moderate transition to a low carbon economy, but these objectives can be achieved by opting for a closed national model with an energy system based on distributed generation or another electricity supply model that uses renewable energy generated in other countries with powerful distribution networks, storage systems and management.

In a networked Europe, the geographical position of the Iberian Peninsula and its natural barriers are obstacles to supply Spain with renewable electricity from the European Union countries and other neighbors with energy supply potential. All this underscores the need for electrical interconnections but also for gas and a single market for energy. In the different renewable penetration scenarios, an interconnected system and natural gas backup power is required (although this may slowly disappear). In these hybrid scenarios, interconnections are key for supplying and balancing different types of electricity systems (wind and solar) and obtaining adequate storage capacity. Better coordination between all the actors and institutions that comprise the governance system for the energy transition, and above all, political stability that guarantees a continuation of the path recently initiated and security of the regulatory framework, will be all key factors for the uncertain future of Spain's energy system.

Cross-References

▶ Cities in European Energy and Climate Governance
▶ Energy Governance in France
▶ Energy Governance in the Netherlands
▶ Energy Poverty

References

AELEC. (n.d.). Nuestros asociados. Asociación de empresas de energía eléctrica. https://www.aelec.es/asociados. Accessed 27 Feb 2019.

AFP. (2015, January 19). Repsol scraps controversial oil exploration off Canary Islands. *The Guardian*. https://www.theguardian.com/environment/2015/jan/19/repsol-scraps-controversial-oil-exploration-off-canary-islands. Accessed 27 Feb 2018.

Amigos de la Tierra. (n.d.). Clima y energía. https://www.tierra.org/02clima-y-energia/03proponemos-cambio-climatico/. Accessed 27 Feb 2019.

AOP. (n.d.). Asociados. Asociacion Española de Operadores de Productos Petroliferos. http://www.aop.es/quienes-somos/asociados/. Accessed 27 Feb 2019.

Arocena, P. (2004). Privatisation Policy in Spain: Stuck between liberalisation and the protection of Nationals' Interests. *CESifo,* Working paper no. 1187. Category 9: Industrial Organisation. May 2004.

Ayuntamiento de Madrid. (2018). Impuesto Bienes Inmuebles (IBI). Bonificación instalación sistemas aprovechamiento energía solar. https://sede.madrid.es/portal/site/tramites/menuitem.62876cb64 654a55e2dbd7003a8a409a0/?vgnextoid=2dcb67713959f010VgnVCM1000000b205a0aRCRD &vgnextchannel=69cca38813180210VgnVCM100000c90da8c0RCRD&vgnextfmt=pda#. Accessed 25 Sep 2018.

Bellver, J., Conchado, A., Cossent, R., Linares, P., Pérez-Arriaga, I., & Romero, J. C. (2016). *Informe sobre Energía y Sostenibilidad en España 2015.* Madrid, Spain: Cátedra BP de Energía y Sostenibilidad, Universidad Pontificia Comillas.

Bellver, J., Conchado, A., Cossent, R., Linares, P., Pérez-Arriaga, I., & Romero, J. C. (2018). *Informe sobre Energía y Sostenibilidad en España 2016.* Madrid, Spain: Cátedra BP de Energía y Sostenibilidad, Universidad Pontificia Comillas.

BOE. (1978). Constitución Española. BOE-A-1978-31229.

BOE. (1997). Ley 54/1997, de 27 de noviembre, del Sector Eléctrico. BOE-A-1997-25340.

BOE. (1998). Ley 34/1998, de 7 de octubre, del sector de hidrocarburos. BOE-A-1998-23284.

BOE. (2007). Real Decreto 661/2007, de 25 de mayo, por el que se regula la actividad de producción de energía eléctrica en régimen especial. BOE-A-2007-10556.

BOE. (2012). Ley 15/2012, de 27 de diciembre, de medidas fiscales para la sostenibilidad energética. BOE-A-2012-15649.

BOE. (2013). Real Decreto-ley 9/2013, de 12 de julio, por el que se adoptan medidas urgentes para garantizar la estabilidad financiera del sistema eléctrico. BOE-A-2013-7705.

BOE. (2014a). Real Decreto 413/2014, de 6 de junio, por el que se regula la actividad de producción de energía eléctrica a partir de fuentes de energía renovables, cogeneración y residuos.

BOE. (2014b). Ley 18/2014, de 15 de octubre, de aprobación de medidas urgentes para el crecimiento, la competitividad y la eficiencia. BOE-A-2014-10517.

BOE. (2014c). Orden IET/1045/2014, de 16 de junio, por la que se aprueban los parámetros retributivos de las instalaciones tipo aplicables a determinadas instalaciones de producción de energía eléctrica a partir de fuentes de energía renovables, cogeneración y residuos. BOE-A-2014-6495.

BOE. (2015). Orden IET/2209/2015, de 21 de octubre, por la que se publica el Acuerdo del Consejo de Ministros de 16 de octubre de 2015, por el que se aprueba el documento de Planificación Energética. Plan de Desarrollo de la Red de Transporte de Energía Eléctrica 2015–2020.

BOE. (2018a). Real Decreto-ley 15/2018, de 5 de octubre, de medidas urgentes para la transición energética y la protección de los consumidores.

BOE. (2018b). Real Decreto 355/2018, de 6 de junio, por el que se reestructuran los departamentos ministeriales. BOE-A-2018-7575.

BOE. (2018c). Real Decreto 864/2018, de 13 de julio, por el que se desarrolla la estructura orgánica básica del Ministerio para la Transición Ecológica. BOE-A-2018-9859.

Boromisa, A.-M. (2014). Will outsiders apply EU rules, and why? In C. Cambini & A. Rubino (Eds.), *Regional energy initiatives. MedReg and the eenrgy community* (pp. 63–83). Abingdon: Routledge.

Calero Pérez, P. (2000). La aparición de los costes de transición a la competencia en la reestructuración de los sistemas eléctricos: el caso español. *Boletín Económico de ICE, 2662,* 21–34.

Calvo, S. (2018). ¿Es España un Estado descentralizado? *Instituto Juan de Mariana.* https://www.juandemariana.org/ijm-actualidad/analisis-diario/es-espana-un-estado-descentralizado. Accessed 27 Feb 2019.

Castán Broto, V. (2015). Innovation territories and energy transitions: Energy, water and modernity in Spain, 1939–1975. *Journal of Environmental Policy and Planning.* https://doi.org/10.1080/1523908X.2015.1075195.

CEPSA. (2017). CEPSA energy outlook 2030. 2017 Edition. Available at https://www.cepsa.com/en/the%E2%80%93company/strategy/cepsa%E2%80%932030.

Cerulus, L., & Panichi, J. (2015, October 13). The new EU power source: Energy-efficient lobbying. *Politico*. https://www.politico.eu/article/lobbyingnet-web-of-influence-brussels-lobbying-energy-commission-transparency/. Accessed 27 Feb 2019.

Chaques, L., & Palau, A. M. (2011). Assessing the responsiveness of Spanish policymakers to the priorities of their citizens. *West European Politics, 34*(4), 706–730.

Chen, C.-C. (2014). An examination on the feed-in tariff policy for renewable electricity: Taiwan's case example. *International journal of Environmental Science and Technology, 2011*(11), 1223–1236. https://doi.org/10.1007/s13762-013-0297-x.

CIEMAT. (2017, August 1). Etiquetado para consumidores de aerogeneradores de pequeña potencia. *Ciemat*. http://www.ciemat.es/cargarAplicacionNoticias.do;jsessionid=F9BE2C6052ACE7A1BA661173C1444EE6?idArea=-1&identificador=1365. Accessed 15 Mar 2019.

CIEMAT. (n.d.). Presentation. http://www.ciemat.es/portal.do?IDM=283&NM=2. Accessed 14 Mar 2019.

CLH. (2018). Map of infrastructure. http://www.clh.es/section.cfm?id=2&side=134&lang=en. Accessed 27 Feb 2019.

Club Español de la Energía. (n.d.). Junta Directiva. https://www.enerclub.es/extfrontenerclub/img/File/indexed/enerclub/Junta_Directiva.pdf. Accessed 15 Mar 2019.

CNMC. (2017). Informe de supervisión del mercado minorista de electricidad. Comisión Nacional de los Mercados y la Competencia.

CNMC. (n.d.). Energy. https://www.cnmc.es/en/ambitos-de-actuacion/energia. Accessed 15 Mar 2019.

CNMV. (n.d.). Participaciones significativas y autocartera en sociedades cotizadas. Comisión Nacional del Mercado de Valores. http://www.cnmv.es/portal/consultas/busqueda.aspx?id=7. Accessed 27 Feb 2019.

CORES. (2018). Informe Estadistico Anual 2017. Corporacion the Reservas Estrategicas de Productos Petroliferos de Espana. Madrid.

CORES. (n.d.). About us. https://www.cores.es/en/cores/quienes-somos. Accessed 25 Sep 2018.

Costantini, L. (2018, May 18). Dos compañías de renovables darán luz al Ayuntamiento de Madrid por 82 millones. *El País*. https://elpais.com/ccaa/2018/05/18/madrid/1526635734_767657.html

CSN. (n.d.). Strategic plan. https://www.csn.es/en/plan-estrategico-del-csn. Accessed 15 Mar 2019.

De Arriba Segurado, P., & Garcia Barquero, C. (2017) Opportunity of DAFI to ensure a more efficient and sustainable transport in the EU. The Spanish case. ODYSSEE-MURE Policy Brief. June 2017.

De la Escosura, L., & Sanz, J. (1996). Growth and macroeconomic performance in Spain, 1939–93. In N. Crafts & G. Toniolo (Eds.), *Economic growth in Europe since 1945* (pp. 355–387). Cambridge: Cambridge University Press. https://doi.org/10.1017/CBO9780511758683.013.

Del Rio, P., & Janeiro, L. (2016). Overcapacity as a barrier to renewable energy deployment: The Spanish case. *Journal of Energy*, Hindawi Publishing Corporation. https://doi.org/10.1155/2016/8510527.

Delgado-Iribarren Garcia-Campero, M. (1984). El Plan Energético Nacoinal (PEN) 1983. *Revista de Administración Pública, 104*, 449–461.

Eberlein, B., & Kerwer, D. (2004). New Governance in the European Union: A theoretical perspective. *Journal of Common Market Studies, 42*(1), 121–142.

Ecologistas en Accion. (2019). Alegaciones para un autoconsumo compartido y de proximidad real y efectivo. https://www.ecologistasenaccion.org/?p=114788. Accessed 18 Mar 2019.

EEA. (2016). *Environmental taxation and EU environmental policies*. EEA report no. 17/2016. Luxembourg: EEA

El periódico de la energía. (2017, October 20). El Congreso votará la propuesta energética de Unidos Podemos para 2030: 45% de renovables y 40% de eficiencia. *El Periódico de la energía*. https://elperiodicodelaenergia.com/el-congreso-votara-la-propuesta-energetica-de-unidos-podemos-para-2030-45-de-renovables-y-40-de-eficiencia-vinculantes/. Accessed 27 Feb 2019.

El periódico de la energía. (2019, June 24). El Gobierno modifica el Anteproyecto de Ley de Cambio Climático y Transición Energética: estos son los principales cambios. *El periódico de la energía*.

https://elperiodicodelaenergia.com/el-gobierno-modifica-el-anteproyecto-de-ley-de-cambio-climatico-y-transicion-energetica-estos-son-los-principales-cambios/. Accessed 24 July 2019.

Energías Renovables. (2004, June 17). IDAE, CIEMAT y Greenpeace, juntos por la energía solar termoeléctrica. *Energías Renovables*. https://www.energias-renovables.com/solar-termica/idae-ciemat-y-greenpeace-juntos-por-la. Accessed 15 Mar 2019.

Energías Renovables. (2017, January 17). Una veintena de asociaciones acusa al ministro de Energía de perseguir el autoconsumo. *Energías Renovables*. https://www.energias-renovables.com/fotovoltaica/una-veintena-de-asociaciones-acusa-al-ministro-20170117. Accessed 27 Feb 2019.

European Commission. (2013). European Investment Bank welcomes first successful use of project bond credit enhancement and provides EUR 500m for Castor energy storage project in Spain. Press Release BEI/13/117, 30 July 2013.

European Commission. (2015a). Commission Staff Working Document. Country Factsheet Spain, Accompanying the document: Communication from the Commission to the European Parliament, the Council, the European Economic and Social Committee, the Committee of the Regions and the European Investment Bank: State of the Energy Union. SWD(2015) 239 final. Brussels, 18 Nov 2015.

European Commission. (2015b). Energy Union Package. Communication from the Commission to the European Parliament and the Council. Achieving the 10% electricity interconnection target. Making Europe's electricity grid fit for 2020. COM (2015) 82 final. Brussels, 25 Feb 2015.

European Commission. (2016a). Proposal for a Regulation of the European Parliament and of the Council on the Governance of the Energy Union, amending Directive 94/22/EC, Directive 98/70/EC, Directive 2009/31/EC, Regulation (EC) No 663/2009, Regulation (EC) No 715/2009, Directive 2009/73/EC, Council Directive 2009/119/EC, Directive 2010/31/EU, Directive 2012/27/EU, Directive 2013/30/EU and Council Directive (EU) 2015/652 and repealing Regulation (EU) No 525/2013. COM (2016) 759 final. Brussels, 30 Nov 2016.

European Commission. (2016b). Communication from the Commission to the European Parliament, the Councial, the European Economic and Social Committee, the Committee of the Regions and the European Investment Bank. Clean Energy For All Europeans. COM (2016) 860 final. Brussels, 30 Nov 2016.

European Commission. (2017). The EU and energy union and climate action. Part of THE EU AND series. https://doi.org/10.2775/980053.

European Commission. (2018a). *March infringements package: Key decisions*. Press Release. http://europa.eu/rapid/press-release_MEMO-18-1444_EN.htm. Accessed 15 Feb 2019.

European Commission. (2018b). *November infringements package: Key decisions*. Press Release. http://europa.eu/rapid/press-release_MEMO-18-6247_EN.htm. Accessed 15 Feb 2019.

European Commission. (2018c). *Latest taxation share in the consumer price of Euro-Super 95 and diesel oil*. https://ec.europa.eu/energy/maps/maps_weekly_oil_bulletin/latest_taxation_oil_prices.pdf. Accessed 23 Oct 2018.

European Commission. (n.d.). Funding for projects of common interest. https://ec.europa.eu/energy/en/topics/infrastructure/projects-common-interest/funding-projects-common-interest. Accessed 27 Feb 2019.

European Renewable Energy Council. (2013). EU tracking roadmap 2013. Keeping track of renewable energy targets towards 2020. Brussels, Belgium.

Eurostat. (2018). Energy balance sheets, 2016 data. In *Statistical books*. Luxembourg: Eurostat.

FEMP. (2017). Red de Ciudades por el Clima [Online]. http://www.redciudadesclima.es/. Accessed 25 Sep 2018.

FEMP. (n.d.). Area Tematica: Medio Ambiente. http://femp.femp.es/Portal/Front/Atencion_al_asociado/Comision_Detalle/_Gy7fWupkSJCxh3Gu8nNimkXA1gGmPf8-TGdP8k5NtSrmGpnyv2WkOKPXN5-cpd1NUx6Z9ARpX1KR9_0fuRhC3e-mSbsV9uqrbFX78cBSL4lTNKuT%2D%2DWKYbhIu4Ru8beNhoUvpB4OioIMRfj6gi6DpMLE2KcoiDEZIxCIBE1EQf4R_rhD8HJ4G-GXbxhkydpsgAWA9xv_38IjwmE_Uy16KQeQJe944Gk3RTHYQ7YYB3OUWkWGe-MScdNwxhPYLNP9. Accessed 28 Feb 2019.

Fernandez, M. (2016, November 22). Auge y caída de las energías renovables. *El Boletin*. https://www.elboletin.com/economia/142322/auge-caida-energias-renovables.html. Accessed 15 Feb 2019.

Fernandez, R. M. (2018a). Interaction of regional and national environmental policies: The case of Spain. *Cogent Economics & Finance, 2018*(6). https://doi.org/10.1080/23322039.2018.1442092.

Fernandez, R. M. (2018b). The effects of the international economic crisis on Spain's environmental policy. In C. Burns, P. Tobin, & S. Sewerin (Eds.), *The impact of the economic crisis on European environmental policy* (pp. 152–174). Oxford, UK: Oxford University Press.

Fortea, P. (2015). The Spanish railway industry: A benchmark worldwide. https://www.globalrailwayreview.com/article/24885/the-spanish-railway-industry-a-benchmark-worldwide/. Accessed 19 Mar 2019.

Fundacion para la Eficiencia Energetica y el Medioambiente. (2017). La Ley de Cambio Climático y Transición Energética, a debate en el Mapama. http://www.f2e.es/es/ley-de-cambio-climatico-y-transicion-energetica-a-debate-en-mapama. Accessed 18 Mar 2019.

Gabaldón-Estevan, D., Peñalvo-López, E., & Alfonso Solar, D. (2018). The Spanish turn against renewable energy development. *Sustainability, 10*, 1208. https://doi.org/10.3390/su10041208.

Gotev, G. (2018, July 30). France, Spain, Portugal up energy links. *Euractiv.* https://www.euractiv.com/section/energy/news/france-spain-portugal-up-energy-links/. Accessed 19 Mar 2019.

Gouardères, F. (2018). Energy policy: General principles. *Fact Sheets on the European Union – 2019.* European Parliament. 10/2018.

Greenpeace. (2019). Energias renovables. https://es.greenpeace.org/es/trabajamos-en/cambio-climatico/energias-renovables/. Accessed 27 Feb 2019.

Grubliauskas, J., & Rühle, M. (2018, July 26). Energy security: A critical concern for Allies and partners. *NATO Review.* https://www.nato.int/docu/review/2018/Also-in-2018/energy-security-a-critical-concern-for-allies-and-partners/EN/index.htm. Accessed 14 Mar 2019.

Hall, B. (2019, February 13). New elections loom as Spain is stuck in a cycle of instability. *Financial Times.* https://www.ft.com/content/ac7b2074-2fb0-11e9-ba00-0251022932c8. Accessed 15 Mar 2019.

Hancher, L., & Winters, B. M. (2017). *The EU winter package. Briefing oaper.* Amsterdam, The Netherlands: Allen & Overy LLP.

Held, A., Ragwitz, M., Huber, C., Resch, G., Faber, T., & Vertin, K. (2007). *Feed-In systems in Germany, Spain and Slovenia – A comparison.* Karlsruhe, Germany: Fraunhofer Institute Systems and Innovation Research.

Held, A., Regwitz, M., Resch, G., Nemac, F., & Vertin, K. (2010). Feed-In Systems in Germany, Spain and Slovenia – A comparison, Fraunhofer Institute, Energy Restructuring Agency and Energy Economics Group. December 2010.

IDAE. (2010). *Spain's National Renewable Energy Action Plan 2011–2020.* Ministry of Industry, Commerce and Tourism. Madrid, Spain, 30 June 2010.

IDAE. (2017). *Informe Estadistico Energías Renovables.* https://informeestadistico.idae.es/t5.htm. Accessed 15 Feb 2019.

IDAE. (2018). REBECA. Red de Economía Baja en Carbono. https://www.idae.es/ayudas-y-financiacion/fondos-feder/rebeca-red-de-economia-baja-en-carbono. Accessed 25 Sep 2018.

IDAE. (n.d.-a). Our history. Public commitment to energy efficiency and renewable energies. https://www.idae.es/en/conozcanos/quienes-somos/our-history. Accessed 14 Dec 2018.

IDAE. (n.d.-b). Fondo Nacional de Eficiencia Energética. https://www.idae.es/ayudas-y-financiacion/fondo-nacional-de-eficiencia-energetica. Accessed 19 Mar 2019.

IDAE. (n.d.-c). Consumo de energia final. http://sieeweb.idae.es/consumofinal/. Accessed 28 Feb 2019.

Industriall. (2018). Spanish coal unions win landmark Just Transition deal. http://www.industriall-union.org/spanish-coal-unions-win-landmark-just-transition-deal. Accessed 15 Mar 2019.

INE. (2018). *Población inscrita en el padrón a 01/01/2018.* https://ine.es/dyngs/INEbase/en/operacion.htm?c=Estadistica_C&cid=1254736177012&menu=ultiDatos&idp=1254734710990. Accessed 25 Sep 2018.

Inelfe. (2011). Interconexión eléctrica por los Pirineos catalanes. https://www.ree.es/sites/default/files/monograficoinelfe.pdf. Accessed 15 Feb 2019.

INELFE. (2017). Spain-France electricity interconnection across the Bay of Biscay. Red Electrica de Espana.

International Energy Agency. (2017). Energy statistics 2017. http://data.iea.org/. Accessed 22 Feb 2019.

Johannesson Linden, A.; Kalantzis, F.; Maincent, E., & Pienkowski, J. (2014) *Electricity tariff deficit: Temporary or permanent problem in the EU?* (Economic papers 534). European Economy. European Commission – Economic and Financial Affairs. Brussels, Belgium.

Jordan, S. (n.d.). A history of Spanish railways. http://www.gaugemaster.com/articles/guides/history-of-spanish-railways.html. Accessed 18 Mar 2019.

Kang, K. (2016). Policy influence and private returns from lobbying in the energy sector. *Review of Economic Studies, 83*, 269–305.

La información. (2017). España pierde el primer arbitraje por los recortes a las renovables. https://www.lainformacion.com/medio-ambiente/energia-alternativa/Espana-arbitraje-internacional-Ciadi-renovables_0_1023497920.html. Accessed 15 Jan 2019.

Ledo, S. (2018, October 21). España ya mide la luz con contadores inteligentes. *El Periodico*. https://www.elperiodico.com/es/economia/20181021/espana-mide-luz-contadores-inteligentes-7098751. Accessed 15 Feb 2019.

Maqueda, A. (2018, February 20). Las importaciones españolas cerraron 2017 con un récord histórico. *El País*. https://elpais.com/economia/2018/02/20/actualidad/1519125373_507496.html. Accessed 18 Oct 2018.

Martin Murillo, L. (2018, January 24). La transición del carbón en España. ¿Qué es y qué no es una transición justa? *Revista Contexto*. No. 153.

Mendoza, A. I. (2015). *El real decreto de autoconsumo eléctrico o la paradoja de pagar por generar energía. Análisis Gómez Acebo & Pombo* (November). Available at https://www.ga-p.com/publicaciones/el-real-decreto-de-autoconsumo-electrico-o-la-paradoja-de-pagar-por-generar-energia/.

Ministry for Ecological Transition. (2018, August 10). El Ministerio para la Transición Ecológica ha resuelto favorablemente 86 solicitudes para construcción de nuevas instalaciones de energías renovables. *Press Release*. https://www.miteco.gob.es/es/prensa/180810notadeprensasubastarenovables_tcm30-478359.pdf. Accessed 19 Mar 2019.

Ministry for Ecological Transition. (n.d.). La Comisión de Coordinación de Políticas de Cambio Climático (CCPCC). https://www.miteco.gob.es/es/cambio-climatico/temas/organismos-e-instituciones-implicados-en-la-lucha-contra-el-cambio-climatico-a-nivel-nacional/la-comision-de-coordinacion-de-politicas-de-cambio-climatico/. Accessed 18 Mar 2019.

Ministry of Energy. (2017). *2017–2020 National energy efficiency action plan*. (Spain). 23 May 2017. Available at https://ec.europa.eu/energy/sites/ener/files/documents/es_neeap_2017_en.pdf.

Mir, M. C. (1999). Evaluación de los Planes Energéticos Nacionales en España (1975–1998). *Revista de Historia Industrial, 15*, 161.

Morgan, S. (2018, November 15). Spain to nix nuclear and coal power by 2030. *Euractiv*. https://www.euractiv.com/section/energy/news/spain-to-nix-nuclear-and-coal-power-by-2030/. Accessed 19 Mar 2019.

Moselle, B., Padilla, J., & Schmalensee, R. (Eds.). (2010). *Electricidad verde: Energias renovables y Sistema eléctrico*. Madrid: Marcial Pons.

Mullerat, R. (2010). *How Spain Implements European Law* (Jean Monnet/Robert Schuman paper series) (Vol. 10, No. 2). University of Miami – Florida European Union Center. Miami, United States.

Navarro Castelló, C. (2018, May 17). Energía 100% renovable para las dependencias municipales de València. *Eldiario.es*. https://www.eldiario.es/cv/Toda-consumida-municipales-Valencia-renovable_0_772373650.html

OECD. (2018). *OECD economic outlook. Economic forecast summary – Spain*. Available at http://www.oecd.org/economy/spain-economic-snapshot/.

Official Journal of the European Union (OJEU). (2009). Council Directive 2009/119/EC of 14 September 2009 imposing an obligation on Member States to maintain minimum stocks of crude oil and/or petroleum products. 9 Oct 2009 (L265).

OTLE. (2018). Informe annual 2017. Marzo 2018. Ministerio de Fomento. Available at http://observator iotransporte.fomento.es/NR/rdonlyres/EE4D9E3E-74A9-4C1F-A5FC-284D30BBAFFA/148831/INFORMEOTLE2017.pdf

Palacios, J. (2018, October 4). Electric vehicles tough sell in Spain. *Wardsauto*. https://www.wardsauto.com/alternative-propulsion/electric-vehicles-tough-sell-spain. Accessed 18 Mar 2019.

Peña, J. C. (2018, October 24). Madrid baja impuestos a las empresas que instalen paneles solares para autoconsumo. *El Confidencial*. https://www.elconfidencial.com/economia/2018-10-24/carmena-baja-impuestos-empresas-isntalacion-paneles-solares-autoconsumo_1634719/

Planelles, M. (2015, October 29). Environmentalists appeal to Spanish parties ahead of December elections. *The Guardian*. Climate Publishers Network. https://www.theguardian.com/environment/2015/oct/29/environmentalists-appeal-to-spanish-parties-ahead-of-december-elections. Accessed 18 Mar 2019.

PSOE. (2017). Proposición no de Ley sobre el fomento del uso de energía procedente de fuentes renovables. http://www.psoe.es/congreso/nuestra-actividad/iniciativas/proposiciones-no-de-ley/fomento-del-uso-de-energia-procedente-de-fuentes-renovables/. Accessed 27 Feb 2019.

REE. (2018a). *The Spanish electricity system 2017 report summary*. Red Eléctrica Española https://www.ree.es/sites/default/files/11_PUBLICACIONES/Documentos/InformesSistemaElectrico/2017/spanish_electricity_system_2017_summary.pdf. Accessed 18 Oct 2018.

REE. (2018b). *The Spanish electricity system 2017 report 2017*. Red Eléctrica Española. https://www.ree.es/sites/default/files/11_PUBLICACIONES/Documentos/InformesSistemaElectrico/2017/spanish-electricity-system-2017.pdf. Accessed 18 Oct 2018.

REE. (2019a). *Spain-France underground interconnection* [Online]. https://www.ree.es/en/activities/unique-projects/new-interconnection-with-france. Accessed 15 Feb 2019.

REE. (2019b). *Spain-France submarine interconnection* [Online]. https://ree.es/en/activities/unique-projects/submarine-interconnection-with-france. Accessed 15 Feb 2019.

RETEMA. (2019). Luz verde al anteproyecto de Ley de Cambio Climático y Transición Energética. https://www.retema.es/noticia/luz-verde-anteproyecto-de-ley-de-cambio-climatico-y-transicion-energetica-4gl9o. Accessed 19 Mar 2019.

Ringel, M., & Knodt, M. (2018). The governance of the European energy union: Efficiency, effectiveness and acceptance of the winter package 2016. *Energy Policy, 112*, 209–220.

Rius, J., & Martin Zamorano, M. (2014). ¿Es España un Estado casi-federal en política cultural? Articulación y conflicto entre la política cultural del Estado central y la del gobierno de Cataluña. *Revista d'Estudis Autonomics i Federals, 19*, 274–309.

RTVE.es. (2018). *La UE destina 578 millones de euros a financiar la interconexión eléctrica entre España y Francia* [Online]. Spain. http://www.rtve.es/noticias/20180125/ue-destina-578-millones-euros-financiar-interconexion-electrica-entre-espana-francia/1666321.shtml. Accessed 15 Feb 2019.

Smith, A., & Heywood, P. (2000). *Regional government in France & Spain*. Supported by Joseph Rowntree Foundation. August 2000.

Solorio, I., & Fernandez, R. M. (2017). Spain and renewable energy promotion: Europeanization upside down. In I. Solorio & H. Jörgens (Eds.), *A guide to EU renewable energy policy. Comparing europeanization and domestic policy change in EU Member States*. Cheltenham: Edward Elgar.

Stevis, D., & Felli, R. (2015). Global labour unions and just transition to a green economy. *International Environmental Agreements, 15*, 29–43.

Stücklin, M. (2016). Cost of electricity in Spain high by EU standards. https://www.spanishpropertyinsight.com/2016/06/06/cost-electricity-spain-high-eu-standards/. Accessed 19 Mar 2019.

Tamma, P. (2018, July 13). Spanish Socialists face a coal vs. climate dilemma. *Politico*. https://www.politico.eu/article/spain-pedro-sanchez-coal-hspanish-socialists-face-climate-dilemma/. Accessed 15 Mar 2019.

Tarifaluzhora. (2019). Bono social de luz 2019. https://tarifaluzhora.es/info/bono-social-electricidad. Accessed 26 Feb 2019.

The Corner. (2017, December 29). The castor project; Spaniards are paying for the failure of this gas storage installation. *The Corner*. http://thecorner.eu/spain-economy/the-castor-project-spaniards-are-paying-for-the-failure-of-this-gas-storage-installation/69669/. Accessed 4 Mar 2019.

The Economist. (2009, February 26). Power games – European energy. *The Economist*. https://www.economist.com/business/2009/02/26/power-games. Accessed 14 Mar 2019.

Tirado Herrero, S., Jiménez Meneses, L., Lopez Fernández, J. L., Perero Van Hove, E., & Irigoyen Hidalgo, V. M. (2018). *Pobreza Energética en España. Hacia un sistema de indicadores y una estrategia de actuación estatal*. Madrid: Asociación de Ciencias Ambientales.

Torres, D. (2018, June 1). Spain's Rajoy ousted in no-confidence vote. *Politico*. https://www.politico.eu/article/spains-rajoy-ousted-in-no-confidence-vote/. Accessed 14 Mar 2019.

Velez, A. M. (2017, January 13). El 100% de la electricidad consumida por el Ayuntamiento de Barcelona será renovable. *Eldiario.es*. https://www.eldiario.es/catalunya/barcelona/Ayuntamiento-Barcelona-exigira-electricidad-renovable_0_601240188.html

Williams, D. (2012, January 31). EU commission criticises Spain for stopping renewable energy subsidies. *Power Engineering International*. http://www.powerengineeringint.com/articles/2012/01/-uropean-commission-critical-of-spanish-halt-to-renewable-energy-subsidies.html. Accessed 26 Feb 2019.

World Bank. (2019). *World Bank national accounts data, and OECD National Accounts data files* [Online]. The World Bank. https://data.worldbank.org/indicator/NY.GDP.MKTP.KD.ZG?locations=ES. Accessed 15 Feb 2019.

Energy Governance in Sweden

45

Bengt Johansson

Contents

Introduction	1158
The General State of Energy Governance in Sweden	1160
Legacies of Swedish Energy Governance	1160
Composition of the Energy Mix	1161
Discourse on Energy Issues	1164
Political Institutions and Actors	1167
Coordination, Instruments, and Drivers of the Swedish Energy Transition	1169
Drivers of the Energy Transition	1169
Strategies, Instruments, and Coordinating Mechanisms	1170
Swedish National Energy Governance and EU	1177
Outcomes, Challenges, and Prospects	1178
Developments Toward European and National Targets	1178
Toward a Power Sector Based on Renewable Energy	1178
The Future Role of Bioenergy	1179
The Main Challenges of Energy Transition in Energy-Intensive Industries and the Transport Sector	1179
Concluding Remarks	1180
Cross-References	1181
References	1181

Abstract

Sweden is a sparsely populated country with significant hydro, bioenergy, and wind resources. Renewable energy sources currently account for more than 50% of total Swedish use and both electricity production and residential heating are virtually fossil-free. Swedish energy policy can be characterized by the perceived conflict between an ambitious climate policy and the competitiveness of the energy-intensive industries. Related to this, the future of nuclear power has

B. Johansson (✉)
Environmental and Energy Systems Studies, Lund University, Lund, Sweden
e-mail: Bengt.Johansson@miljo.lth.se

© Springer Nature Switzerland AG 2022
M. Knodt, J. Kemmerzell (eds.), *Handbook of Energy Governance in Europe*,
https://doi.org/10.1007/978-3-030-43250-8_30

played a key role in the Swedish energy discourse over the last 40 years. Energy governance through market solutions is widely embraced in Sweden and includes the use of economic policy instruments such as carbon and energy taxes, the EU Emissions Trading System, and renewable electricity certificates. Fully decarbonized electricity and heating sectors would appear to be within reach in the coming decade, although technical and institutional adaptations will be necessary to manage the expected continued expansion of variable electricity production. However, major challenges remain for decarbonization of the transport and industrial sectors in Sweden. In both sectors, electrification and the continued role of bioenergy are regarded as key options for the future.

Keywords

Sweden · Decarbonization · Renewable energy · Nuclear power · Market liberalization · Economic policy instruments

Introduction

Sweden's energy system has the highest share (55%) of renewable energy in the EU (European Commission 2020). Sweden is characterized by an almost *fossil-free electricity* system, and most fossil fuels used for domestic heating have been replaced by biomass, electricity, and district heating. The broad diffusion of *renewable energy* reflects both the favorable geographic conditions and the implementation of policy initiatives. Sweden is a sparsely populated country with large renewable resources such as bioenergy (forests cover approximately 70% of the country), rivers that lend themselves to hydropower production, and vast areas of land that are suitable for wind energy exploitation.

The expansion of district heating, a large forest industry, and the early introduction (1991) of carbon taxation have supported the increased use of biomass in the energy system. The forest industry accounts for approximately one-third of industrial energy demand and a significant part of this is covered by biofuels. Unlike many other European countries, both coal and natural gas play only a minor role in the Swedish energy mix and there are no domestic fossil-fuel resources. Currently, coal is primarily used in the steel industry, while natural gas is used regionally in southwestern Sweden. Petroleum products are still significantly used, although mainly in the transport sector (Swedish Energy Agency 2020b).

The *nuclear power* issue has dominated the Swedish *energy discourse* for the last 40 years and Vedung (2001) states that "nuclear power, not oil is the hub around which Swedish energy policy conflicts move." Consequently, energy policy has largely been regarded as being equivalent to electricity policy. After a rapid nuclear expansion during the 1970s, driven by expectations of growing electricity demand and a desire to reduce oil dependence, following a referendum in 1980, the Swedish parliament decided to halt the expansion after already commissioned plants had been built. It was then decided that a step-by-step decommissioning of nuclear power plants should be conducted with an end date in 2010. Since this time, this decision has regularly been challenged and, in 2018, nuclear power still accounted for approximately 40% (Swedish Energy Agency 2020b) of the electricity supply. There is currently no end date and some political parties support building new nuclear plants while the owners of some of the plants have decided to shut them down because of reduced profitability.

Sweden has largely embraced the market paradigm and pursued opening up the electricity and gas markets, even though the state has continued to own one of the major power companies, Vattenfall AB, a company that has also been active outside Sweden with acquisitions in Germany, Poland, and The Netherlands. The Swedish electricity market is closely integrated with the other Nordic countries through the power marketplace, Nordpool, and is also interconnected with other neighboring countries.

There is a general acceptance of the government's role in directing the energy system in an environmentally benign way. In Sweden, there is an overarching *governance* principle of "steering by environmental objectives" (Hildingsson and Johansson 2016), although the markets play a significant role in achieving these objectives. Cost efficiency plays a prominent role in defining how policies should be designed (Hildingsson 2014), and Swedish policy largely relies on economic policy instruments such as carbon taxes, *Renewable Electricity Certificates* (REC), and the European Emission Trading System (EU ETS).

Sweden is regarded as being at the forefront of climate ambitions (Sarasini 2009; Zannakis 2015) and has implemented several ambitious policies and set a national target for becoming a country with no net GHG emissions by 2045. Within the EU, Sweden belongs to a group of countries that have argued for more ambitious *climate policies*, while being less concerned about issues such as energy dependence. Also, Sweden has usually readily implemented new EU regulations (Nilsson 2011). However, one area of conflict relates to bioenergy, in which Sweden and Finland have a more positive attitude towards the opportunity to combine the utilization of biomass with sustainable forestry than many other countries have (Baylan and Tiilikainen 2018).

For competitive reasons, the industrial sector has been protected from the most stringent climate policies through, for example, substantial tax deductions. Although taxation levels for road transport are significant and there are other support schemes as well, these initiatives have not been enough to ensure sufficient reductions in greenhouse gases (GHG) in this sector, as efficiency improvements have been partially counterbalanced by increased demand for road transport. For the future, industry and transport are arguably the most challenging sectors concerning energy-related greenhouse gas reductions.

This chapter aims to provide an overview of Swedish energy governance with a focus on how it contributes to a low carbon transition. The chapter starts with a brief description of the historic development of the energy system and the current energy mix. The main energy policy discourses and actors are presented. Key Swedish policy objectives and instruments are then described followed by an analysis of the current and projected outcomes and the challenges of achieving a low carbon energy system.

The General State of Energy Governance in Sweden

Legacies of Swedish Energy Governance

From its early days, the Swedish electricity system was characterized by the huge significance of *hydropower*. Interest in nuclear power started in the 1950s when the country was also considering developing nuclear weapons for its armed forces. The decision to invest in nuclear energy was based on the conviction that it would be in the interests of the nation to use the assets of natural uranium, advanced reactor technology, and the expertise on nuclear physics that the country had at its disposal (Anshelm 2009). Increased electricity demand and opposition to the continued exploitation of rivers for hydropower by the end of the 1960s required new sources of electricity to be found. During the 1970s, as *oil replacement* was high on the agenda, nuclear power appeared to be the most natural replacement for oil in the electricity system. At the end of the 1960s, criticism of nuclear power started to emerge. This intensified during the 1970s and contributed to a change of government in 1976 (Hakkarainen and Fjaestad 2012). A referendum in 1980 following the Three Mile Island accident led to a parliamentary decision to decommission nuclear power plants, although nuclear power continued to expand with the last reactor taken in operation in 1985. The combination of a nuclear share of electricity production that was close to 50%, existing decommission plans, and high climate ambitions have created a policy nexus around which much Swedish energy policy has revolved.

The development of *district heating*, starting in the 1950s, has also been an important structuring factor for the Swedish energy system. The district heating infrastructure was initially developed by municipalities to produce combined heat and power (CHP). Interest in CHP diminished with the expansion of nuclear power and low electricity prices but re-emerged during the 1990s following new support schemes (Di Lucia and Ericsson 2014; Higa et al. 2020). Other forms of motivation for district heating were to reduce oil dependence in individual buildings and local air pollution (Ericsson and Werner 2016). In the early stages, district heating was dominated by fossil fuels, but from 1990, an expansion in biomass made district heating systems an integral part of the Swedish bioenergy system. In 2018, approximately 60% of heat demand for residential buildings and offices was supplied by district heating (Swedish Energy Agency 2020b).

Before fossil fuels started to dominate the energy system, traditional energy sources such as wood fuel dominated the Swedish energy supply (Kander and Stern 2014). Following the oil crisis in 1973, a renewed interest in this "domestic and renewable" resource emerged. This interest grew even stronger in the 1990s as a part of increasing climate policy ambitions. The forest industry infrastructure and district heating systems facilitated a rapid replacement of fossil fuels with biomass and related emission reductions (Ericsson et al. 2004).

The state and *energy-intensive industries* have enjoyed a special relationship and the perception of these industries' key role in Sweden is expressed in the often-used term "basic industry" (Hildingsson et al. 2019; Johansson et al. 2017). The need to prioritize this industry has been pursued in the form of a perceived common interest between industrial owners and trade unions. The connection between trade unions and the long-governing Social Democratic Party has strengthened this view and has gained importance through the corporative governance traditions that are present in at least some of the areas of Swedish policy (Kronsell et al. 2019). This has led to a strong prioritization of *competitiveness* in these sectors and has allowed them to resist stringent climate policies (Hildingsson and Khan 2015; Hildingsson et al. 2019). However, there are now indications that this is changing, with greater commitment to transition from the energy-intensive industries in recent years (Hildingsson et al. 2019).

Energy policy emerged as a policy field in its own right after the oil crisis 1973 when Swedish dependence on imported oil became apparent to most people (Kaijser 2001). In order to increase energy security, Sweden has pursued a *diversification* strand with regard to both energy balance and choice of supplier and has also highlighted policies for energy conservation (Kaijser and Högselius 2019). The acceptance of governmental policies in the environmental field and the use of environmental taxes as a policy instrument are also relatively high. However, since the 1980s there has been a general trend toward deregulation and privatization in Sweden that has also been reflected in developments in the Swedish electricity and district heating markets.

Composition of the Energy Mix

Final energy use in Sweden has been relatively stable between 1970 and 2020 (Fig. 1). However, total energy use has increased significantly, and this is mainly attributable to energy losses in nuclear power plants. The composition of the energy

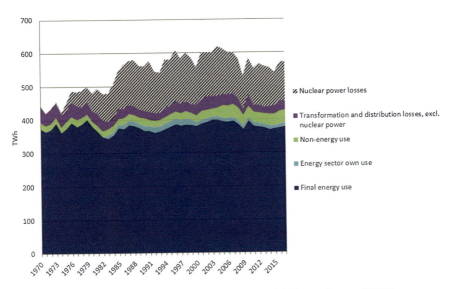

Fig. 1 Total energy use, by final energy, losses, etc. (Swedish Energy Agency 2019a)

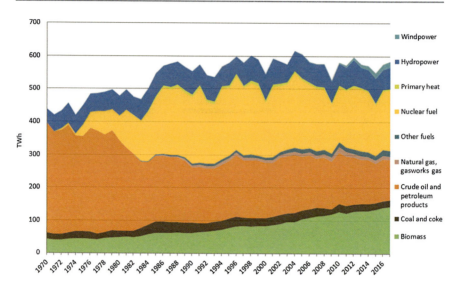

Fig. 2 Total energy supply by commodity (Swedish Energy Agency 2019a)

mix has also changed significantly (Fig. 2). Oil consumption has more than halved and is now almost exclusively used in the transport sector. The share of *renewable energy* has increased significantly and in 2018 accounted for around 55% of Swedish energy use (Swedish Energy Agency 2020a). Also, the role of nuclear power has increased since its introduction in the mid-1970s. Coal/coke and natural gas account for only 4% and 2%, respectively (Swedish Energy Agency 2020b).

Both electricity demand and production have remained relatively stable since the mid-1980s and have long been dominated by hydro and nuclear power complemented by electricity from CHP produced in district heating systems and the industrial sector, Fig. 3. In 2018, nuclear power accounted for 41% of Sweden's electricity production. The production of fuel-based electricity in condensing plants is virtually nonexistent, except for backup purposes. The last decade has seen significant growth in wind power largely due to the existing REC system. The increase in renewable electricity production combined with a rather stable demand has led to an annual electricity surplus of 10–15% that enables the net export of electricity to neighboring countries (on an hourly basis, Sweden is sometimes a net importer and sometimes net exporter depending on the actual supply and demand conditions). The residential and service sectors use more than 50% of electricity, followed by the industrial sector, which accounts for almost 35% of electricity. A significant share of electricity demand (14%) is used for domestic heating (Swedish Energy Agency 2020b). This is largely a legacy of the surplus electricity in the 1980s due to the rapid expansion of nuclear power plants and dedicated oil replacement policies at the time.

Oil products still dominate energy use in the transport sector, although *biofuels* have grown significantly in recent decades. In 2018, renewable energy (biofuels and

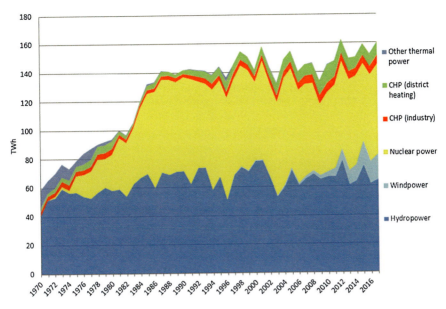

Fig. 3 Electricity production by source. Source: Swedish Energy Agency (2019a)

electricity) accounted for 23% of the energy demand for domestic transport (Swedish Energy Agency 2020a). If calculated in accordance with the Renewable Energy Directive in which fuels from certain types of residues are multiplied by two and electricity from renewable energy used for rail transport and road transport is multiplied by factors of 2.5 and 5, respectively, the share is nearly 30%. The biofuels mainly comprise FAME (fatty acid methyl esters), HVO (hydrogenated vegetable oils), ethanol, and biogas. Most of these biofuels are currently produced abroad or are based on non-domestic feedstocks (Swedish Energy Agency 2020b) from around the world, despite there being vast bioresources in Sweden. This is primarily due to higher domestic production costs and a lack of production facilities to meet the rapid increase in demand.

Industrial final energy use has remained relatively stable for decades and is dominated by three energy-intensive sectors: paper and pulp (51% of total energy use), iron, steel and metalworks (16%), and the chemical industry (9%) (Swedish Energy Agency 2020b). Industrial energy is dominated by biomass (39%) and electricity (35%) while the remaining use of coal in Sweden is in the iron and steel industry, a sector that currently accounts for more than 10% of Sweden's GHG emissions. Oil, previously a dominating energy source in the sector, currently accounts for around 7% of industrial energy supply.

Energy use in the residential and service sectors has decreased by approximately 10% since 1970, despite the significant expansion of heated areas (Swedish Energy Agency 2020b). This has largely been a result of targeted energy efficiency initiatives that started with the oil crisis in the 1970s. (Since 1995, specific energy use (MJ/m2) has been reduced by approximately 20% (Swedish Energy Agency

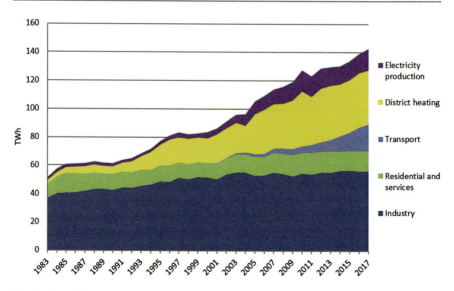

Fig. 4 Use of biomass per sector. Source: Swedish Energy Agency (2019a)

2020b).) During this period, district heating almost quadrupled, and combined with the expansion of electricity (including electric heat pumps) and modern small-scale biomass heating, the direct use of fossil fuels for heating purposes has virtually ceased.

This is underscored by developments in district heating systems in which fossil fuels have been largely replaced. Currently, the district heating supply is dominated by wood fuels, municipal waste incineration, electric heat pumps, and industrial waste heat. The fossil content in waste accounts for more than one-half of the remaining GHG emission in Swedish district heating systems and approximately 5% of total Swedish GHG emissions.

Swedish *biomass* use has more than doubled since 1990, see Fig. 4. The biomass used in stationary applications is currently dominated by industrial by-products (mainly pulping liquors and other industrial by-products), although a minor proportion of logs is also used for small-scale heating. As previously mentioned, there is significant use of liquid biofuels in the transport sector.

Discourse on Energy Issues

Sweden's discourse on energy issues has largely been characterized by the tension between a rather broadly rooted high environmental ambition and the concerns about industrial competitiveness with the associated need to provide the industrial sector with low energy prices.

The issue of *nuclear power* has dominated the Swedish *energy discourse* over the last 45 years. In the discussion associated with the previously mentioned nuclear referendum of 1980, the risks of nuclear power were contrasted to a lack of confidence in the capacity of renewable energy to supply the required electricity. In the referendum, the voters had three options that all stated that nuclear power should be phased out. However, two options were regarded as being pro-nuclear as they accepted that the already commissioned new reactors could be used, while one option was more obviously against nuclear power and required the rapid decommissioning of nuclear power plants (Edberg and Tarasova 2016; Hakkarainen and Fjaestad 2012). Even though after the referendum the Swedish parliament decided that nuclear power plants should be decommissioned by 2010, very little happened. The start of the phase-out was conditional upon a reduction in nuclear power being fully compensated by energy conservation and new renewable capacity and it was not until 1999 that the first reactor was shut down. In 2010 the existing regulations prohibiting nuclear power were removed, but with decreasing electricity prices and fierce market competition the economic prerequisites for new nuclear power were simply not there. The most recent comprehensive parliamentary energy decision from 2018 (Swedish Government 2018) is ambiguous in terms of the decommissioning of nuclear power plants. It states that the electricity system should be 100% renewable by 2045 while simultaneously arguing that this should not be seen as an end date for nuclear power (Swedish Government 2018). This ambiguous approach is probably explained by the fact that the decision was based on a compromise including both governmental and oppositional parties. This compromise has already been challenged. While the power companies have decided to shut down several reactors in 2020 and 2021, industrial lobby groups and pro-nuclear political parties (the Liberal party, the Christian Democrats, the conservative Moderate party and the right-wing populist Sweden Democrats) argue that nuclear power is needed in a system that has increasing amounts of variable renewable electricity production and expected growth in electricity demand due to the electrification of industry and transport.

High *climate ambitions* have broad support in most political parties. However, there are significant differences concerning the timing, exact mitigation levels, and methods of achieving the targets, for example, the role that the markets should play compared to public spending schemes and the level of focus on domestic mitigation measures compared to Swedish investments in mitigation abroad. Hildingsson (2014) has identified a discursive struggle between a dominating neoliberal *climate policy narrative* and a competing decarbonization narrative that provides an alternative notion of low carbon transitions. The neoliberal narrative primarily focuses on emission reductions and identifies market failures as being the main problem, which could be addressed by the internalization of external costs using market mechanisms. The decarbonization narrative sees the need for broader energy system transformations and the need to remove multiple barriers and implementation deficits. In order to achieve this, a broad portfolio of policies is regarded as being necessary.

Swedish *low-carbon transition* policies have often been motivated by the desire to lead by example to act as a role model in the international arena. The transition has also been motivated by using concepts such as ecological modernization and the existence of win-win combinations (Sarasini 2009). Zannakis (2015) similarly noted that motivations for Sweden to be an early mover were based on two storylines in which the first storyline highlighted the competitive advantage of early action and the second storyline, emphasizing ecological justice as a more altruistic motivation. However, these positive storylines have regularly been challenged by a storyline that highlights the fact that early mitigation means unnecessary sacrifice, arguing that Sweden should not commit to more than necessary.

A recent example reflects some of the disputes above. These emerged in connection with an application from the petroleum company Preem for a license to expand the capacity of one of its refineries. Those actors who were against granting the company a license argued that new fossil fuel capacity should be prohibited to meet the 1.5 °C aspirational target of the Paris Agreement. Those who were in favor argued that prohibiting the expansion would only lead to production elsewhere in less efficient production plants and that prohibition would be unnecessary as refineries were already regulated by the EU ETS. Before the government managed to take a final stand on the issue, in September 2020, Preem withdrew its application on commercial grounds.

The increasing role of markets in the energy sector is widely embraced in Sweden. This was reflected in the relatively early *deregulation* of the electricity market. This process started in the 1980s and led to new legislation in 1996 for a more deregulated electricity market. According to Högselius and Kaijser (2010), the point of departure was the new ideological climate that has been present in Sweden since the early 1980s, which emphasized *competition* as being a positive force for economic efficiency in providing infrastructure service and in the public sector in general. Although the benefits for the various market actors were not evident, they regarded the change as inevitable and, in different ways, prepared themselves for the change. According to Nilsson (2011), the market reform and the framing of the electricity sector as a deregulated market in Sweden have now become deeply institutionalized.

The concern for *energy security* was the main reason why energy policy emerged as a separate policy field in the 1970s, although it was later absent from the key energy discourse for an extended period because the national energy system was regarded as being robust and the external supply of petroleum was thought to be secured through relatively stable international markets. However, security of supply has grown in importance in recent years following the expansion of variable electricity production and concern is being expressed that the closure of nuclear power and CHP plants due to lack of profitability will increase the risk of capacity shortages in parts of Sweden and negative impact on other electric qualities such as frequency stability and reactive power. The discussion regarding whether renewable energy can supply power as inexpensively as nuclear power is also still ongoing. Recently, the lack of local production and *distribution capacity* has emerged as a central issue in the energy discourse, in which it is argued that this prevents regional development if expanding industries are not given access to the grid or that the *electrification* of transport is hindered. (A collection of debate articles that provide a good picture of this discourse can be found at Sydsvenskan (2020) and Svenska Dagbladet (2020).)

Wind power development was rather slow until the introduction of the REC system (see below). The expansion sparked a debate about the potential tension between the desire for more renewable energy, driven by high climate ambitions, and local environmental protection and other interests, for example, from the armed forces (see Liljenfeldt 2015; Söderholm et al. 2007; Lindgren et al. 2013). Partially as a consequence of this, much of the production has been established in Northern Sweden in which there are fewer conflicting interests due to the less dense population, even though protection of the landscape and reindeer herding still cause conflict.

Swedish energy policy has been dominated by a strong belief in technological solutions and the role of *innovation* in solving energy challenges. Several nongovernmental organizations (NGOs) and political parties have argued that this is not enough and that more significant societal changes, including behavioral changes, are necessary. For example, many politicians, researchers, and industry actors are now convinced that the electrification of transport will be the solution to mitigating the climate impact of transportation, whereas other actors argue that transport planning that takes reduced demand into account is necessary to manage the challenges.

Political Institutions and Actors

The Swedish administrative model is characterized by relatively small ministries and large governmental agencies that have a relatively high degree of autonomy in relation to the government (Hall 2016). Over the years, energy as a policy field has been assigned to different ministries such as the Ministry of Industry, the Ministry of Environment and Energy, the Ministry of Enterprise, and now, the Ministry of Infrastructure. Regardless of ministerial location, energy policy is also heavily influenced by the interests of the Ministry of Finance. The sector is affected by several forms of legislation such as the Electricity Act, the Environmental Code, the Energy Taxation Law, and the Planning and Building Act.

The Swedish Energy Agency is broadly responsible for monitoring and *developing energy policies*, as well as for statistics, advice, and research funding. It also administers policy instruments such as the REC system and various other support schemes. The Swedish Energy Markets Inspectorate (EMI) is the main *regulator* of the electricity and gas markets in Sweden and monitors the functioning of these markets and supervises price setting for monopolistic distribution services. The Swedish Radiation Safety Authority is responsible for nuclear safety and has the mandate to stop reactors if threats to reactor safety and security are identified. Finally, Svenska Kraftnät is the authority responsible for the Swedish transmission system. It is the system operator for Sweden with overall responsibility for keeping the balance between supply and demand. This includes developing new transmission infrastructure and ensuring a reserve production capacity when the market is unable to do so. In addition to these direct energy-related agencies, energy policy is influenced by other agencies such as the Swedish Environmental Protection Agency and the Swedish National Board of Housing, Building, and Planning.

Typical for the Swedish political system is the use of *commissions of inquiries* to develop policy proposals in different fields and to anchor policy proposals in different segments of society (Petersson 2016). This could be in the form of either individual investigators or broad parliamentary commissions regarding the more strategic decisions. The commissions often use experts and special advisors who represent ministries and public agencies with the relevant responsibilities and different stakeholders representing, for example, enterprises or NGOs. The proposals from the committees undergo a mandatory *referral procedure* in which different societal actors have the opportunity to submit their comments before the government sends the bill to parliament for decision. The works of both the parliamentary Energy Commission (2017) and the Cross-Party Committee on Environmental Objectives (2016) have been influential in identifying important policy goals and compromises for Swedish energy policy.

A new type of actor with potential impact on energy policy is the *Climate Policy Council*, comprising a group of senior scientists tasked with scrutinizing government policy and verifying whether such policy is in line with the Swedish Climate Act, which has been in force in Sweden since 2017 (Swedish Code of Statutes 2017). The introduction of this organization into the Swedish policy arena was clearly inspired by the Committee on Climate Change in the UK (cf. ► Chap. 5, "Monitoring Energy Policy").

Local authorities (municipalities) in Sweden have a considerable degree of autonomy including taxation rights but also broad responsibilities that are determined through national legislation (Feltenius 2016). Their impact on energy systems is manifold. First, they are important end-users through their ownership of a large stock of buildings used for schools, elderly care, etc. Many municipalities also own housing companies. Second, some municipalities own energy companies that are responsible for district heating and electricity production and distribution. Third, the authorities have a so-called local planning monopoly and can decide on the proper use of land including the location of businesses, residential, and shopping areas, with a major impact on transportation demand and the development opportunities for public transport. Their influence on the location of wind power plants has also been a decisive factor through their comprehensive planning and their right to veto new wind power plants, although this right to veto is currently (2020) under scrutiny (Lauf et al. 2020; Liljenfeldt 2015). Many national subsidy programs also target municipalities and fund local energy projects (Baker and Eckerberg 2007; Lundqvist and Kasa 2017).

Self-governing authorities on the regional level (Regions) are responsible for public transport, and important actors for driving the decarbonization in this field (Aldenius 2018; Aldenius and Khan 2017). In parallel, regional administrations of the central government (County Administrative Boards) also play a role in regional planning and are responsible for coordinating and managing regional initiatives in the field of crisis management, and in developing and implementing regional energy and climate strategies.

The interaction between public and private actors is partially through legislation but there is also *institutionalized collaboration* through participation in public committees, remitting procedures, and in various collaborative groups. For several decades, dialogue and collaboration have characterized the relationship between state and industry in Sweden (Hildingsson et al. 2019; Söderholm and Söderholm 2020). The inclusion of stakeholders in two public inquiries by the Energy Commission and the Cross-Party Committee on Environmental Objectives (CCEO) is an example of a more formal form of collaboration. In their interview study, Kronsell et al. (2019) noted that the CCEO was referred to as a good example of a policy deliberation that established the joint view that decarbonization was possible without compromising the economic viability of the industrial sector. However, the authors note that environmental and social movements have been given a marginal role in these examples of policy deliberation (Kronsell et al. 2019). In addition to controlled formal and organized consultations, there are increasingly more ad hoc, spontaneous, and informal forms of interaction in policy processes in which ideas are exchanged and input is given to the policy process (Kronsell et al. 2019).

Coordination, Instruments, and Drivers of the Swedish Energy Transition

Drivers of the Energy Transition

The most important driver of the ongoing transitions in Sweden is the high *climate ambitions* both nationally and within the EU. Many policymakers and researchers regard Sweden as being a frontrunner in environmental policy, although this role has also been challenged by others (Hysing 2014). However, the general level of support for a stringent climate policy has been quite broad and stable and, consequently, Sweden has often set more stringent targets than required by international obligations, implemented a broad range of policy instruments (see below) and been an advocate for strict international commitments.

In Sweden, technological *research and development* has been seen as an engine of change in Swedish energy policy (Bergquist and Söderholm 2015). Technology improvements and cost reduction in wind and solar power, mainly resulting from global developments, have accelerated the transition to more renewable electricity. Also, green groups and wind power lobby groups have driven the government to increase its ambition for renewable electricity expansion, and it has consequently adapted its policy instruments. For example, the targets for the Electricity Certificate System (see below) have step by step become more ambitious since its introduction in 2003, most recently in 2017 (Swedish Government 2017).

The interest in *bioenergy* has been supported by the existence of an important forest industry, modern forestry, and district heating systems. They have collectively provided the infrastructure, logistics, and expertise that made it possible to react to the implemented policy instruments, particularly the carbon taxation (Ericsson et al. 2004). However, support has not been without challenges as there were previous concerns that an increased bioenergy demand would increase the competition for bioresources traditionally used for pulp and paper (Higa et al. 2020), as well as concerns about its compatibility with the preservation of biodiversity.

Strategies, Instruments, and Coordinating Mechanisms

Swedish energy policy, just like EU policy (▶ Chap. 7, "European Union Energy Policy: A Discourse Perspective"), aims to combine ecological sustainability, competitiveness, and security of supply (Swedish Government 2018). The strategy for a low-carbon energy transition has been reframed several times since the first *climate target* was introduced in 1988, with continuously increasing ambitions. In recent years, a perspective that focuses on identifying the most efficient areas for mitigation has turned to a broader decarbonization narrative that recognizes that all sectors must achieve near-zero emissions. However, the primacy of cost efficiency in much of the policy discourse has meant that sectoral targets have been avoided, except for a specific focus on a fossil-free transport sector. Parallel to dedicated climate strategies, strategies on infrastructure, a circular economy, and bio-economy have also been introduced with direct and indirect implications for energy. In 2017, the Swedish parliament decided on a new institutional setting for the energy transition through a Climate Act that established a framework for future climate policies that regulate the government and its agencies and introduced an independent evaluation body (cf. above).

The climate restrictions for the energy system are based on both EU and *national targets*, see Table 1. The Swedish Climate Act has a fixed target for achieving net-zero emissions by 2045 that cover all sectors of society. On its way to achieving

Table 1 National climate targets and EU obligations for Sweden (Swedish Climate Policy Council 2020; European Union 2018)

	Swedish national climate targets. Changes in GHG emissions compared to 1990, if not otherwise stated	Swedish obligations according to the EU's effort-sharing obligations. GHG emissions in sectors outside the EU ETS compared to 2005 levels
2020	Sectors outside EU ETS −40% compared to 1990. A maximum of 13 percentage points of the reductions through flexible mechanisms	−17%
2030	Sectors outside the EU ETS −63%. A maximum of 8 percentage points of the reductions through additional measures Domestic transport − 70% compared to 2010	−40%
2040	Sectors outside the EU ETS −75%. A maximum of 2 percentage points of the reductions through additional measures	
2045	Net-zero emissions (including the EU ETS). A minimum of 85% domestic reductions. The remainder can be achieved through additional measures	

Additional measures include net sequestration in forests, verified emission reductions through Swedish investments abroad, and carbon capture and storage from the combustion of biomass (bio-CCS)

this target, there are regulated milestones for sectors outside the EU ETS. In addition, there is a sectoral target for transportation for 2030, which requires a 70% reduction in GHG emissions compared to 2010. The EU has also determined legally binding targets for sectors that are not covered by the EU ETS through its Effort Sharing Regulation (ESR) (European Union 2018).

The most recent broad energy policy decision (primarily dealing with electricity) state that the electricity system should be based on 100% renewable energy by 2045. In addition, the energy policy decision set a target for a 50% increase of energy efficiency by 2030 compared to 2005, measured as energy supply in relation to GNP. A national target has been set for the share of renewable energy in 2020 (50%) but no national target for renewable energy for the entire energy system has been set for later years.

A number of policy instruments are used to reach these targets, and a selection of the most prominent ones is presented in Table 2 and further discussed below.

Cross-Sectoral Policy Instruments

General economic policy instruments have been a key part of Swedish energy and climate policy for several decades. *Fuel taxes* were introduced as early as 1924 for transportation fuels and during the 1950s for energy used for other purposes. However, it was primarily from 1991, when the carbon and sulfur taxes, as well as nitrogen oxide charges, were introduced as part of a major tax reform (Skovgaard et al. 2019; Sterner 1994), that they came to be more clearly regarded as a policy instrument rather than a source of financial revenue.

The standard level of *carbon taxation* has more than quadrupled since its introduction and is currently the highest in the world. However, for a fair cross-national comparison, it is necessary to study how the carbon tax interacts with other taxes. For example, the taxation on transportation fuels is not higher in Sweden than in many other European countries, although the part specifically called carbon tax is higher. In 2019, the level was equivalent to approximately 120 EUR/ton CO_2 (SEK 1.18/kg) (Swedish Government 2020b). Energy tax levels vary among the different fossil fuels with the highest levels applied to transportation fuels. However, these standard levels only apply to a fraction of energy use (heating, transport, and certain parts of the industrial sector), and several exemptions and deductions are in place, see Table 3. For example, no carbon tax is paid for fossil fuels used in metallurgical processes, electricity production, aviation, or industrial facilities in the EU ETS. Previously, agriculture and industry outside the EU ETS had reduced carbon tax levels but these *tax deductions* have been removed on a stepwise basis (Skoovgaard et al. 2019). There are currently proposals to also abolish the energy tax deductions for these sectors as part of a tax reform switching the tax burden from labor to environment (Swedish Ministry of Finance 2020).

The general tax level on electricity consumption is relatively high but there are minor tax deductions for consumers in certain rural areas and major tax deductions for energy-intensive industries (these lower levels are set by the EU's minimum tax levels and are less than 2% of the general levels). Recently, data centers have been granted the same low tax levels. The tax loss relating to this measure was

Table 2 A selection of key energy and climate policy instruments in Sweden, following the typology of this handbook. As described in text, the policy instruments do not apply to all the actors in the respective sector in the same way due to specific design features

	Regulative instruments	Incentive-based instruments	Internalizing instruments	Soft governance
Cross-sectoral instruments	Environmental code Planning and building act	Cross sectoral funding schemes (LIP, KLIMP, climate stride)	Energy and carbon taxes EU ETS	RD&D Regional planning
Electricity supply	Electricity market directive Electricity act	Renewable electricity certificates Investment grants for solar electricity Tax deductions for small-scale electricity production	Waste incineration tax	Fossil free Sweden public-private collaboration
Industry		"Industrial stride"-funding scheme		Fossil free Sweden public-private collaboration
Transportation	Emission requirements for new vehicles Emissions reduction obligations for diesel and petrol Biofuel supply obligations for major filling stations	Support schemes for vehicles with environmental technology	CO_2 differentiated vehicle tax Tax on air travel	Urban environment agreements Infrastructure planning Public procurement
Household and service sector	Building regulation EU eco design directive			Energy and climate advisory services Voluntary agreements Energy declarations Public procurement

compensated by higher electricity taxes on households and services. In addition to energy and carbon taxes, VAT is applied to energy. In 2019, taxes (incl. VAT) contributed to approximately 60% of the consumer price of petrol and 40% of the electricity costs for domestic electricity consumers with electricity use of 20,000 kWh/year (Swedish Energy Agency 2020a; Swedish Energy Markets Inspectorate 2020b). Several studies have identified carbon taxes as being important for

Table 3 Carbon and energy tax deductions for various operations. The information reflects the levels in November 2020

	Carbon tax deduction Percentage reductions from standard levels	Deductions on fuel energy taxes Percentage reductions from standard levels
Fuels used for other purposes than motor fuel or heat production.	100	100
Fuels used in industry within the EU ETS	100	70
Fuels used in industry outside the EU ETS	0	70
Heat produced in CHP within the EU ETS	9	0
Fuels used for aviation, shipping and rail transport	100	100

both fuel replacement (particularly the expansion of biomass) and energy efficiency in Sweden (see, e.g., Johansson 2000; Nilsson et al. 2004).

Since 2005, Sweden has participated in the *EU ETS* and the emissions regulated by the system were equivalent to slightly less than 40% of Swedish domestic GHG emissions (Swedish Environmental Protection Agency 2018). As the introduction of the EU ETS has been accompanied by significant exemptions from carbon taxes in many sectors, it has provided few additional incentives for emission reductions. Since heating plants that use biomass have been allocated emission allowances without having to report their emissions, the total allocation of emissions allowances to Swedish installations has been approximately 10% higher than the reported emissions (Swedish Environmental Protection Agency 2019).

In recent decades, broad economic *subsidies* directed at municipalities and other actors have been implemented, including the Local Investment Programme (LIP) 1998–2002, the Climate Investment Programmes (KLIMP) 2003–2012, and, since, 2015, the Climate Stride (Klimatklivet). The Climate Stride supports fuel conversion projects, public systems for EV charging, filling stations for alternative fuels, biogas plants, etc. (Swedish Environmental Protection Agency 2020). The goal of these programs has been to generate initiatives and engagement in municipalities and industries, and they have often included parallel goals such as sustainable development and job creation (Baker and Eckerberg 2007). There have also been several more subsidy programs directed at specific technologies, fuels, or sectors, some of which will be described below in detail.

Over the years, support for energy *RD&D* has also been regarded as an important policy instrument. The Swedish Energy Research Programme has changed its direction and focus multiple times since it was established in 1975, following changes in national policy priorities (Haegermark 2001). Energy research existed before 1975 and both government and industry research made important contributions to power transmission and hydro and nuclear power technologies. Many forms of collaboration between government and private industry have evolved during the program.

Haegermark (2001) noted that although the main objective of the program has always been energy policy, support for Swedish energy and environment-related industries has been a significant secondary goal. This has not changed over the last two decades. The most recent government bill on energy research (Swedish Government 2016) identified five key areas to which research should contribute: i) an energy system that is fully based on renewable energy, ii) a flexible and robust energy system, iii) a resource-efficient society, iv) innovation for job creation and climate mitigation, and v) integration of different parts of the energy system (Swedish Government 2016). Between 2017 and 2020, approximately SEK 1,600 million/year (160 MEUR/year) (Swedish Government 2020b) was directed toward energy research.

Electricity and heat production units, refineries, and large energy users, including industrial facilities, are all regulated by the *environmental code* as "environmentally hazardous activities." They require permits that regulate both pollution and resource conservation. However, under the EU directive (European Union 2010), it is not permitted to regulate GHG emission levels or the volumes of fossil fuels used for plants within the EU ETS regarding GHGs.

Electricity

The electricity sector in Sweden is regulated in accordance with the EU *electricity market* directive with a separation between energy producers and distributors and a free choice of electricity suppliers combined with local and regional distribution monopolies. The Swedish Electricity Act (Swedish Code of Statutes 1997) includes regulated fees that distributors must pay consumers if disruptions to the power supply last longer than 12 h. In addition, the price that distributors can charge consumers is regulated and monitored by the Swedish Energy Markets Inspectorate. On several occasions, the Swedish EMI has limited the prices set by the distribution companies, although this has been successfully legally challenged by many utility companies (Swedish Energy Markets Inspectorate 2016).

The development of the *transmission system* is governed by the Swedish TSO (Transmission System Operator), Svenska Kraftnät, which is permitted to cover its costs through transmission charges. According to government directives to Svenska Kraftnät, investments in new transmission infrastructure should be based on socio-economic cost-benefit assessments (Swedish Code of Statutes 2007). However, this approach has been criticized for leading to underinvestment in infrastructure compared to what is needed for the future.

The expansion of renewable electricity is primarily driven by the *REC system* that was introduced in 2003. It replaced previous subsidy systems such as investment grants and production subsidies. It comprises a *quota obligation* for electricity suppliers who must procure electricity certificates corresponding to a certain percentage (in 2020 it was 26.5%) of their electricity supplies. Supplies to energy-intensive industries are exempted. Since 2012, there has been a joint REC system for Sweden and Norway, although the quota obligations differ between the countries, depending on policy ambitions.

In principle, all types of renewable electricity are eligible for certificates, except for large-scale hydropower plants (1500 kW) built before 2002. Also, peat, which is not classified as renewable energy, was included in the system as a result of intense lobbying on the part of the peat industry. A renewable power plant can receive certificates for 15 years of operation. In the last decade, the total costs for onshore wind power production have fallen rapidly, making them competitive at current electricity price levels. This has driven down the certificate price to a very low level and the set targets have been achieved ahead of the schedule. In November 2020, a decision was made by the Swedish parliament to phase out the system (Swedish Government 2020a). With a few exceptions, further expansion of renewable electricity will mainly rely on market forces and the price-driving effects of the EU ETS.

One of the motivations for the *REC system* was cost-effectiveness in the sense that it would lead to the prioritization of renewable electricity options with the lowest costs. At the start, this primarily referred to biomass-based electricity and, more recently, onshore wind power plants. Other options, such as solar and offshore wind power, cannot compete without additional support. Some researchers and policymakers have regarded this as a general problem for REC systems as it would hinder technological development, see, for example, Bergek and Jacobsson (2010). To allow for more costly options such as offshore wind power and solar energy, over the years, different Swedish governments have complemented the REC system with different forms of investment grants. Apart from that, small-scale plants received indirect subsidies as electricity tax is not applied to electricity produced for self-consumption, and through tax deductions when small-scale producers sell electricity to the grid. Overall, these initiatives have led to a rapid expansion of small-scale solar electricity production in recent years, albeit from low initial levels.

Transportation
Achieving a low carbon transport system requires a combination of new and improved technologies and measures that affect means of transport and transport demand, per se. A broad range of policy instruments has been applied to this sector. High *fuel taxes* have been an important driver for limiting energy use in the transport sector in Sweden, affecting both transport demand and vehicle energy efficiency. In addition, vehicle efficiency improvements driven by EU directives regulate the average energy efficiency on an EU level (European Union 2009).

Other drivers for more low-polluting vehicles in Sweden have been vehicle taxes differentiated according to their level of CO_2 emissions. Since 2018, a *bonus-malus system* has been in place that combines higher taxation for high-emission vehicles (malus) and financial support for "environmental vehicles" (bonus). This system applies to vehicles that are newer than 3 years. After this time, car owners pay a *vehicle tax* that is differentiated depending on the estimated CO_2 emissions. The bonus-malus system is expected to balance taxes and subsidies whereas the vehicle tax provides revenues to the state budget. Preferential taxes for company cars have also been adopted to support environmentally friendly vehicles. There have also been subsidies for electric buses (Swedish Code of Statutes 2016) and a system for subsidies for improved urban environments (Swedish Code of Statutes 2015).

The share of *biofuels* in the transport sector has increased largely due to tax exemptions. These exemptions have regularly been scrutinized by the EU to verify whether they comply with state aid rules. This has made the system less predictable. In order to partially avoid this problem, a new system of *emission reduction obligations* has been introduced. These obligations mandate reduced emissions from fossil transport fuels. This is achieved through blending with renewable fuels. Current obligations are equivalent to an emission reduction of 4.2% for petrol and 21% for diesel. In autumn 2020, the government proposed increasing reduction levels reaching an equivalent to a 28% reduction for petrol and a 66% reduction for diesel by 2030 (Swedish Government 2020c). The government has also proposed the introduction of a reduction obligation for aviation fuels (Swedish Government 2020d). Single or high blend fuels such as biogas and E85 continue to receive tax exemptions. In order to make biofuels more widely available, a requirement for large filling stations to provide at least one type of renewable fuel was implemented in 2009. The ambition to develop a fossil-free transport sector is also reflected in the government inquiry that was appointed in 2020 and tasked with proposing a date for when fossil transport fuels would be phased out and analyzing the conditions for prohibiting the sale of new fossil-fuel vehicles (Swedish Government 2019).

In 2018 a tax on flights was introduced following a broad political discussion. It was regarded as a second-best option as the preferred option of a fuel tax was not deemed compatible with the IATA's (International Air Transport Association) agreements (Aviation Tax Inquiry 2016). Thus, the tax has received a certain amount of criticism for not targeting GHG emissions accurately enough, thereby rendering it inefficient. It would also, according to the critique, risk driving international flights from Sweden to neighboring countries where similar taxes do not exist. However, proponents of the reform argued that there was a need for air travel to be treated in the same way as other transport options and even argued for significantly higher tax levels. Thus far, there has been no long-term evaluation of the effect of this taxation.

Industry

The industrial sector has in different ways been protected against policy instruments that could threaten its competitiveness. As previously mentioned, taxes on fuels and electricity for the industrial sector have generally been significantly lower than for other consumers and some uses (e.g., industrial processes) have been totally tax free. Similarly, the allocation rules in the EU ETS have protected sectors that are vulnerable to international competition. In addition, the obligation to procure REC has not applied for electricity supplied to energy-intensive industries. For the industrial sector, the REC system has been beneficial so far as it has driven electricity prices down (Åhman et al. 2020) while some industries, such as the pulp and paper industry, have been able to increase their production of renewable electricity, receiving support through the REC system (Ericsson et al. 2011).

The Swedish government has also chosen to prioritize various *voluntary agreements* and collaborative approaches (Stenqvist and Nilsson 2012). Most recently, a public-private initiative for developing *low-carbon road maps* has received significant attention (Fossil Free Sweden 2020). The road maps were developed through roundtable discussions between different stakeholders in order to resolve conflicts, find constructive ways forward, and common ground for policy propositions. In the road maps, designated responsibilities have been distributed to the industrial sectors and the government, respectively.

Future-looking technologies have been supported through different schemes, most recently the so-called Industrial Stride program. An often-highlighted example is HYBRIT, a collaboration between the state-owned mining company LKAB, the state-owned electricity utility Vattenfall and the main steel producer SSAB, aimed at developing a process for carbon-free steel. A pilot plant recently opened and was supported by significant state funding (approximately 50 MEUR (Swedish Energy Agency 2018)).

Having said that, the industrial sector is and has been historically driven toward achieving lower environmental impact through environmental regulations that require the use of the *best available technology* (BAT) and resource conservation. This system, which in its modern form has been in place since 1969, has been particularly successful in mitigating local and regional pollutants without excessive mitigation costs. Söderholm et al. (2019) argue that important factors for this are firm flexibility in terms of compliance measures, industry-wide R&D cooperation, knowledge transfer between public R&D support, and technology adoption choices at the company level, as well as the use of extended compliance periods for permit experimentation and high regulatory expertise.

Buildings

The residential sector has long been the focus of emission reduction strategies. As early as the oil crisis of the 1970s, robust initiatives for energy conservation were introduced and several instruments for energy efficiency improvements were used with a focus on *building codes*, subsidies, and information activities (Kiss et al. 2010). CO_2 taxes have also contributed to more efficient energy use and have influenced the choice of heating systems. Other instruments such as networking initiatives, technology procurement, and voluntary standards have also been used (Kiss et al. 2010).

For several years, the expansion of district heating systems was supported by local and national policies, including various investment grants (Di Lucia and Ericsson 2014). Carbon and energy taxes have supported the expansion of non-fossil fuels both in district heating systems and in individual boilers. The expansion of heat pumps also accelerated in the early 2000s (Nilsson et al. 2005). The expansion of small-scale biomass combustion driven by increased oil prices created concern regarding the risk of local pollution from individual wood boilers. This concern has led to regulations on small-scale bioenergy requiring the use of state-of-the-art technology, which also provided incentives for increased use of wood pellets instead of wood logs.

Swedish National Energy Governance and EU

Sweden has a generally positive approach to *multilateral institutions* and free trade. Sweden plays an active role in UNFCCC and is a strong proponent of ambitious policies. Swedish activities within the UNFCCC are, however, strongly coordinated with the EU's priorities. Much of Swedish Energy Policy is determined by common EU rules. Sweden joined the EU in 1995 and belongs to the Northern/Western Group in EU energy policy that values sustainability relatively higher than security of supply compared to the Southern/Eastern countries (▶ Chap. 7, "European Union Energy Policy: A Discourse Perspective"). Sweden has been swift and compliant to align domestic policies with EU requirements and, even before it joined the EU, was relatively coordinated with European energy policy (Nilsson 2011). However, the country is a strong defender of independence regarding financial policy and has therefore been reluctant to adopt a common taxation system and earmark incomes from the EU ETS. However, this independence is somewhat restricted as the use of different forms of national tax exemption, support schemes, and investment grants must be aligned with competition and state aid rules.

Outcomes, Challenges, and Prospects

Developments Toward European and National Targets

Swedish domestic GHG emissions decreased by 27% between 1990 and 2018. The emissions in the sectors outside the EU ETS are in line with both the domestic and the EU targets for 2020 (Swedish Climate Policy Council 2020). The expansion of renewable energy has been significant in recent decades and the EU target for 2020 of 49%, as well as the domestic target of 50% renewable energy, has been met by a considerable margin. The EU target for renewable transportation fuels of 10% by 2020 will also be exceeded.

Forecasts for 2030 indicate further increases in the renewable share of both total and transport energy demand (Swedish Government 2020b). Compared to the long-term *climate targets*, the forecasts are less positive and the Swedish Climate Policy Council (2020) has concluded that neither the overall Swedish targets nor the target for the Swedish transport sector will be met without major additional policy initiatives.

Toward a Power Sector Based on Renewable Energy

The ongoing development toward a *carbon-free power sector* is expected to continue and the forecasts show only minor contributions of fossil carbon from the combustion of waste gases from steel production, the fossil carbon fraction in waste incineration, and production in reserve plants. However, there are challenges regarding the expected increase in electricity demand due to the *electrification* of the industrial and transport sectors and transport (e.g., producing fossil-free steel through electrification would require electricity equivalent to more than 10% of current Swedish electricity demand (Kushnir et al. 2020)), new data centers, etc. In recent "high electrification" scenarios from the Swedish Energy Agency, electricity demand could increase by as much as 40% by 2050 compared to current levels

(Swedish Energy Agency 2019b). This could be compared with various reference scenarios that have seen increases of less than 10% over the same period.

Another issue that has been one of the main priorities in recent years is the need to improve the *capacity* of both the transmission and the distribution grid. Thus far, tardy and complicated planning and permitting processes have slowed down the process of expanding this capacity (SWECO 2019). The need to identify solutions to these problems has become even more urgent due to the new production patterns resulting from the closure of nuclear power plants and the expansion of wind power plants, primarily in Northern Sweden (Svenska Kraftnät 2017). Overall, this has created a new discussion regarding the need for new institutional settings and new and more efficient planning approaches that would provide incentives for *grid expansion, flexible demand solutions,* as well as balancing technologies such as gas turbines, batteries, and hydrogen (SWECO 2019; Swedish Energy Markets Inspectorate 2020a; Svenska Kraftnät 2017).

The Future Role of Bioenergy

Bioenergy's key role and long tradition in the Swedish energy system are grounds for assuming that it could contribute even more to climate-neutral solutions for both energy and materials in the future. This expectation has led to questions regarding the degree to which the resources will suffice for all these demands and, if not, regarding where they could be used most efficiently. The potential conflict between biomass utilization and nature conservation and *biodiversity* is also an important issue. Swedish research has a long tradition of studying the interaction between bioenergy use and other environmental impacts and has identified methods that minimize negative side effects of bioenergy use and has also identified important synergies in which biomass, particularly from agricultural land, could contribute to improved environmental conditions (Cintas et al. 2016; de Jong et al. 2017; Englund et al. 2020). Recent estimates indicate that biomass supply from Swedish agriculture and forest land could increase significantly in the future (Börjesson 2016) but the domestic demand will depend on the degree of electrification and energy efficiency improvements in the industrial and transport sectors (Börjesson et al. 2017). The current situation in which most of the biomass used for transportation fuels is imported also illustrates that domestic demand is not necessarily covered by domestic supply but depends on different market conditions and policies implemented both domestically and abroad.

The Main Challenges of Energy Transition in Energy-Intensive Industries and the Transport Sector

Swedish industrial GHG emissions have been reduced by approximately 20% since 1990. Good examples of emission mitigation can be found, for example, in the paper and pulp industry, which has managed to reduce CO_2 emissions by 85% from 1973 to 2011 (Söderholm and Söderholm 2020). In this respect, the sector has significantly benefited from the availability of internal renewable energy that could be used to replace oil (Bergquist and Söderholm 2015). In other sectors, similar opportunities have been lacking and the *decarbonization* of the industrial sector has long been regarded as a challenge. This applies to the steel sector, which is responsible for around 10% of Swedish emissions, but also to the cement and chemical industries. Since the mid-2010s, the perspective of the respective industries has changed from a defensive approach in which the industry must be protected to the understanding that in a zero-emission future, all sectors must contribute to decarbonization (Fossil Free Sweden 2020; Hildingsson et al. 2019). However, although domestic initiatives are important for initiating technological change, to achieve a full transition, the Swedish industrial sector is heavily dependent on developments on both an EU and a global level.

While the implementation of high *carbon prices* appears to be difficult as long as multiple competitors are active in countries that have less ambitious climate policies, EU state aid regulations are regarded as an obstacle to direct support for mitigation measures and technological development (Johansson et al. 2018; Åhman et al. 2016), even though state support for R&D projects such as the previously mentioned HYBRIT has proved to be in line with these regulations. In addition, *carbon border adjustments* on the EU level, which is part of an on-going discussion, as well as a more consumption-driven demand for low carbon materials, can influence the creation of the necessary conditions for technological change.

A broad range of policy instruments have been implemented in the transport sector and have affected vehicle efficiency, fuel choices, and transport demand positively. However, as economic resources have grown over time, they have partially been used on bigger and heavier vehicles, partially counteracted efficiency gains, and enabled an increase in national passenger and freight transport and rapid growth in international aviation. Freight transport and aviation have been less strictly regulated than domestic passenger transport (in terms of internalizing external costs) out of consideration for the competitiveness of Swedish businesses and lax international aviation regulations. Although a future challenge will be to plan for a more *transport-efficient society*, there is much optimism for the *electrification* of transport, both passenger and freight vehicles, even though this electrification would require significant investments in infrastructure.

Concluding Remarks

Since the 1970s, Sweden's energy policies have developed from a strong focus on oil replacement to an ambition to meet stringent climate objectives. Swedish energy policies are also heavily integrated with policy developments in the EU, which Sweden joined in 1995. Swedish policies have largely been successful regarding the decarbonization of electricity and heating systems and expansion of the use of renewable energy. However, major challenges remain in the industrial and transport sectors. In these sectors, the technological solutions have been less obvious and concern about retaining the competitiveness in the industrial sector has restricted the implementation of sufficiently strong policy instruments. For transportation, several policy instruments have existed simultaneously. However, increasing transport demands have largely mitigated the effects of more efficient vehicles, and there will be a need for renewable transportation fuels and broader transport policy initiatives. Both sectors show high expectations for *electrification* based on the continued expansion of renewable energy. The role of *nuclear power* remains high on the policy agenda, regardless of the parliamentary decision made 40 years ago that nuclear power should be phased out and private operators decided to shut down several reactors due to low profitability. This, together with the rapid expansion of variable electricity production and the expectation of the broad electrification of society, has placed security of supply high on the policy agenda, with a number of actors expressing concern that deficiencies in the electricity system's supply, distribution, and balancing capacities will prevent both decarbonization and economic development.

Cross-References

► Energy Governance in Finland
► Energy Governance in Norway
► Energy Governance in the United Kingdom
► European Union Energy Policy: A Discourse Perspective
► Monitoring Energy Policy

Acknowledgments This author thanks the Swedish Energy Agency for financial support. This text has been written within the research projects "The politics of economic policy instruments- between idea and practice" and "The political dimensions of electricity distribution in a future electrified and climate neutral energy system." The author is also grateful for valuable comments on previous versions of this chapter from Jamil Khan, Karin Ericsson, Roger Hildingsson, Jens Portinson Hylander, Andre Månberger, Lars J Nilsson, Hannes Sonnsjö, and Per Svenningsson.

References

Åhman, M., Nilsson, L. J., & Johansson, B. (2016). Global climate policy and deep decarbonization of energy-intensive industries. *Climate Policy, 17*(5), 634–649. https://doi.org/10.1080/14693062.2016.1167009.

Åhman, M., Wiertzema, H., & Arens, M. (2020). Industrial electrification and access to electricity at competitive prices. In *Review of climate and energy policy influence on electricity prices for industry and future implications for industrial electrification, EEES report 115*. Lund: Environmental and Energy Systems Studies, Lund University.

Aldenius, M. (2018). Influence of public bus transport organisation on the introduction of renewable fuel. *Research in Transportation Economics, 69*, 106–115. https://doi.org/10.1016/j.retrec.2018.07.004.

Aldenius, M., & Khan, J. (2017). Strategic use of green public procurement in the bus sector: Challenges and opportunities. *Journal of Cleaner Production, 164*, 250–257. https://doi.org/10.1016/j.jclepro.2017.06.196.

Anshelm, J. (2009). Among demons and wizards: The nuclear energy discourse in Sweden and the re-enchantment of the world. *Bulletin of Science, Technology & Society, 30*(1), 43–53. https://doi.org/10.1177/0270467609355054.

Aviation Tax Inquiry. (2016). *En svensk flygskatt.* SOU 2016:83. Stockholm.

Baker, S., & Eckerberg, K. (2007). Governance for sustainable development in Sweden: The experience of the local investment programme. *Local Environment, 12*(4), 325–342. https://doi.org/10.1080/13549830701412455.

Baylan, I., & Tiilikainen, K. (2018). *Letter to the European Parliament 10 January 2018.* Retrieved from https://www.regeringen.se/pressmeddelanden/2018/01/sverige-och-finland-uppmanar-eu-parlamentariker-att-rosta-for-en-framtid-med-bioenergi/

Bergek, A., & Jacobsson, S. (2010). Are tradable green certificates a cost-efficient policy driving technical change or a rent-generating machine? Lessons from Sweden 2003–2008. *Energy Policy, 38*(3), 1255–1271. https://doi.org/10.1016/j.enpol.2009.11.001.

Bergquist, A.-K., & Söderholm, K. (2015). Sustainable energy transition: The case of the Swedish pulp and paper industry 1973–1990. *Energy Efficiency, 9*(5), 1179–1192. https://doi.org/10.1007/s12053-015-9416-5.

Börjesson, P. (2016). *Potential för ökad produktion och avsättning av inhemsk biomassa i en växande svensk bioekonomi IMES Rapport 97.* Lund: Environmental and Energy Systems Studies, Lund University.

Börjesson, P., Hansson, J., & Berndes, G. (2017). Future demand for forest-based biomass for energy purposes in Sweden. *Forest Ecology and Management, 383*, 17–26. https://doi.org/10.1016/j.foreco.2016.09.018.

Cintas, O., Berndes, G., Cowie, A. L., Egnell, G., Holmström, H., & Ågren, G. I. (2016). The climate effect of increased forest bioenergy use in Sweden: Evaluation at different spatial and temporal scales. *WIREs Energy and Environment, 5*(3), 351–369. https://doi.org/10.1002/wene.178.

de Jong, J., Akselsson, C., Egnell, G., Löfgren, S., & Olsson, B. A. (2017). Realizing the energy potential of forest biomass in Sweden – How much is environmentally sustainable? *Forest Ecology and Management, 383*, 3–16. https://doi.org/10.1016/j.foreco.2016.06.028.

Di Lucia, L., & Ericsson, K. (2014). Low-carbon district heating in Sweden – Examining a successful energy transition. *Energy Research & Social Science, 4*, 10–20. https://doi.org/10.1016/j.erss.2014.08.005.

Edberg, K., & Tarasova, E. (2016). Phasing out or phasing in: Framing the role of nuclear power in the Swedish energy transition. *Energy Research & Social Science, 13*, 170–179. https://doi.org/10.1016/j.erss.2015.12.008.

Energy Commission. (2017). *Kraftsamling för framtidens energi* Vol. SOU 2017:2, Stockholm.

Englund, O., Börjesson, P., Berndes, G., Scarlat, N., Dallemand, J.-F., Grizzetti, B., Dimitriou, I., Mola-Yudego, B., Fahl, F. (2020). Beneficial land use change: Strategic expansion of new biomass plantations can reduce environmental impacts from EU agriculture. Global Environmental Change, 60, 101990. https://doi.org/10.1016/j.gloenvcha.2019.101990

Ericsson, K., & Werner, S. (2016). The introduction and expansion of biomass use in Swedish district heating systems. *Biomass and Bioenergy, 94*, 57–65. https://doi.org/10.1016/j.biombioe.2016.08.011.

Ericsson, K., Huttunen, S., Nilsson, L. J., & Svenningsson, P. (2004). Bioenergy policy and market development in Finland and Sweden. *Energy Policy, 32*(15), 1707–1721. https://doi.org/10.1016/S0301-4215(03)00161-7.

Ericsson, K., Nilsson, L. J., & Nilsson, M. (2011). New energy strategies in the Swedish pulp and paper industry – The role of national and EU climate and energy policies. *Energy Policy, 39*(3), 1439–1449. https://doi.org/10.1016/j.enpol.2010.12.016.

European Commission. (2020). *EU energy in figures. Statistical pocketbook 2020.* Luxembourg: Publications Office of the European Union.

European Union. (2009). *Directive 2009/33/EC of the European Parliament and of the Council of 23 April 2009 on the promotion of clean and energy-efficient road transport vehicles.*

European Union. (2010). *Directive 2010/75/EU of the European Parliament and of the Council of 24 November 2010 on industrial emissions (integrated pollution prevention and control)*.

European Union. (2018). *Regulation (EU) 2018/842 of the European Parliament and of the Council of 30 May 2018 on binding annual greenhouse gas emission reductions by Member States from 2021 to 2030 contributing to climate action to meet commitments under the Paris Agreement and amending Regulation (EU) No 525/2013*.

Feltenius, D. (2016). Subnational government in a multilevel perspective. In J. Pierre (Ed.), *The Oxford handbook of Swedish politics*. Oxford: Oxford University Press.

Fossil Free Sweden. (2020). *Roadmap for fossil free competitivness – Summary report*. Retrieved from http://fossilfritt-sverige.se/wp-content/uploads/2018/02/roadmap_for_fossil_free_competitiveness_klar.pdf

Haegermark, H. (2001). Priorities of energy research in Sweden. In S. Silveira (Ed.), *Building sustainable energy systems. Swedish experiences* (pp. 163–195). Stockholm: Svensk Byggtjänst, Swedish National Energy Administration.

Hakkarainen, P., & Fjaestad, M. (2012). Diverging nuclear energy paths: Swedish and Finnish reactions to the German Energiewende. *Renewable Energy Law and Policy Review, 3*(4), 232–242.

Hall, P. (2016). The Swedish administrative model. In J. Pierre (Ed.), *The Oxford handbook of Swedish politics*. Oxford: Oxford University Press.

Higa, C., Cunha, M., & Silveira, S. (2020). Coalitions towards the carbon tax in the Swedish heating sector. *Sustainability, 12*(20). https://doi.org/10.3390/su12208530.

Hildingsson, R. (2014). Too many targets or too few measures? Discourses on decarbonisation in Swedish climate policy-making. In R. Hildingsson (Ed.), *Governing decarbonisation: The state and the new politics of climate change* (Vol. Lund political studies 172). Lund: Lund University.

Hildingsson, R., & Johansson, B. (2016). Governing low-carbon energy transitions in sustainable ways: Potential synergies and conflicts between climate and environmental policy objectives. *Energy Policy, 88*, 245–252. https://doi.org/10.1016/j.enpol.2015.10.029.

Hildingsson, R., & Khan, J. (2015). Towards a decarbonized green state? The politics of low-carbon governance in Sweden. In K. Bäckstrand & A. Kronsell (Eds.), *Rethinking the green state. Environmental governance towards climate and sustainability transitions* (pp. 156–173). Abingdon, Oxon; New York: Routledge.

Hildingsson, R., Kronsell, A., & Khan, J. (2019). The green state and industrial decarbonisation. *Environmental Politics, 28*(5), 909–928. https://doi.org/10.1080/09644016.2018.1488484.

Högselius, P., & Kaijser, A. (2010). The politics of electricity deregulation in Sweden: The art of acting on multiple arenas. *Energy Policy, 38*(5), 2245–2254. https://doi.org/10.1016/j.enpol.2009.12.012.

Hysing, E. (2014). A green star fading? A critical assessment of Swedish environmental policy change. *Environmental Policy and Governance, 24*(4), 262–274. https://doi.org/10.1002/eet.1645.

Johansson, B. (2000). *Economic instruments in practice 1: Carbon tax in Sweden*. Paper presented at the workshop on innovation and the environment, Paris.

Johansson, B., Nilsson, L. J., Andersson, F. N. G., Coenen, L., Ericsson, K., Hansen, T., Hildingsson, T., Khan, J., Kronsell, A., Svensson, O., & Åhman, M. (2017). *Nollutsläpp i basindustrin-förutsättningar för en ny industripolitik*. Lund: Lund Unviersity.

Johansson, B., Nilsson, L. J., & Åhman, M. (2018). *Towards zero carbon emissions – Climate policy instruments for energy intensive industries, materials and products*. Paper presented at the ECEEE industrial efficiency, Berlin.

Kaijser, A. (2001). From tile stoves to nuclear plants – The history of Swedish energy systems. In S. Silveira (Ed.), *Building sustainable energy systems. Swedish experiences* (pp. 57–93). Stockholm: Svensk Byggtjänst, Swedish National Energy Administration.

Kaijser, A., & Högselius, P. (2019). Under the Damocles sword: Managing Swedish energy dependence in the twentieth century. *Energy Policy, 126*, 157–164. https://doi.org/10.1016/j.enpol.2018.11.023.

Kander, A., & Stern, D. I. (2014). Economic growth and the transition from traditional to modern energy in Sweden. *Energy Economics, 46,* 56–65. https://doi.org/10.1016/j.eneco.2014.08.025.

Kiss, B., McCormick, K., Neij, L., & Mundaca, L. (2010). *Policy instruments for energy efficiency in buildings: Experiences and lessons from nordic countries.* Paper presented at the counting on energy programs: It's why evaluation matters, Paris.

Kronsell, A., Khan, J., & Hildingsson, R. (2019). Actor relations in climate policymaking: Governing decarbonisation in a corporatist green state. *Environmental Policy and Governance, 29*(6), 399–408. https://doi.org/10.1002/eet.1867.

Kushnir, D., Hansen, T., Vogl, V., & Åhman, M. (2020). Adopting hydrogen direct reduction for the Swedish steel industry: A technological innovation system (TIS) study. *Journal of Cleaner Production, 242,* 118185. https://doi.org/10.1016/j.jclepro.2019.118185.

Lauf, T., Ek, K., Gawel, E., Lehmann, P., & Söderholm, P. (2020). The regional heterogeneity of wind power deployment: An empirical investigation of land-use policies in Germany and Sweden. *Journal of Environmental Planning and Management, 63*(4), 751–778. https://doi.org/10.1080/09640568.2019.1613221.

Liljenfeldt, J. (2015). Legitimacy and efficiency in planning processes – (How) does wind power change the situation? *European Planning Studies, 23*(4), 811–827. https://doi.org/10.1080/09654313.2014.979766.

Lindgren, F., Johansson, B., Malmlof, T., & Lindvall, F. (2013). Siting conflicts between wind power and military aviation-problems and potential solutions. *Land Use Policy, 34,* 104–111. https://doi.org/10.1016/j.landusepol.2013.02.006.

Lundqvist, L. J., & Kasa, S. (2017). Between national soft regulations and strong economic incentives: Local climate and energy strategies in Sweden. *Journal of Environmental Planning and Management, 60*(6), 1092–1111. https://doi.org/10.1080/09640568.2016.1197827.

Nilsson, M. (2011). Changing the decision space: European policy influences on energy policy and systems change in Sweden. *Public Administration, 89*(4), 1509–1525. https://doi.org/10.1111/j.1467-9299.2011.01946.x.

Nilsson, L. J., Johansson, B., Neij, L., Åstrand, K., Ericsson, K., Svenningsson, P., & Börjesson, P. (2004). Seeing the wood for the trees: 25 years of renewable energy policy in Sweden. *Energy for Sustainable Development, 8*(1), 67–81.

Nilsson, L. J., Åhman, M., & Nordqvist, J. (2005). *Cygnet or ugly duckling – what makes the difference? A tale of heat-pump market developments in Sweden.* Paper presented at the ECEEE, Mandelieu.

Petersson, O. (2016). Rational politics: Commissions of inquiry and the referral system in Sweden. In J. Pierre (Ed.), *The Oxford handbook of Swedish politics.* Oxford: Oxford University Press.

Sarasini, S. (2009). Constituting leadership via policy: Sweden as a pioneer of climate change mitigation. *Mitigation and Adaptation Strategies for Global Change, 14*(7), 635–653. https://doi.org/10.1007/s11027-009-9188-3.

Skoovgaard, J., Hildingsson, R., & Johanssson, B. (2019). Environmental policy and the economic crisis: The Swedish and Danish cases. In C. Burns, P. Tobin, & S. Sewerin (Eds.), *The impact of the economic crisis on European environmental policy* (pp. 112–132). Oxford: Oxford University Press.

Skovgaard, J., Ferrari, S. S., & Knaggård, Å. (2019). Mapping and clustering the adoption of carbon pricing policies: What polities price carbon and why? *Climate Policy, 19*(9), 1173–1185. https://doi.org/10.1080/14693062.2019.1641460.

Söderholm, K., & Söderholm, P. (2020). Industrial energy transitions and the dynamics of innovation systems: The Swedish pulp and paper industry, 1970–2010. *Environments, 7*(9), 70. Retrieved from https://www.mdpi.com/2076-3298/7/9/70.

Söderholm, P., Ek, K., & Pettersson, M. (2007). Wind power development in Sweden: Global policies and local obstacles. *Renewable and Sustainable Energy Reviews, 11*(3), 365–400. https://doi.org/10.1016/j.rser.2005.03.001.

Söderholm, P., Bergquist, A.-K., & Söderholm, K. (2019). Environmental regulation in the pulp and paper industry: Impacts and challenges. *Current Forestry Reports, 5*(4), 185–198. https://doi.org/10.1007/s40725-019-00097-0.

Stenqvist, C., & Nilsson, L. J. (2012). Energy efficiency in energy-intensive industries – An evaluation of the Swedish voluntary agreement PFE. *Energy Efficiency, 5*(2), 225–241. https://doi.org/10.1007/s12053-011-9131-9.

Sterner, T. (1994). Environmental tax reform: The Swedish experience. *European Environment, 4*(6), 20–25. https://doi.org/10.1002/eet.3320040606.

Svenska Dagbladet. (2020). Sveriges elförsörning. https://www.svd.se/om/sveriges-elforsorjning. Retrieved 3 Dec 2020.

Svenska Kraftnät. (2017). System development plan 2018–2027. Towards a flexible power system in a changing world. Sundbyberg.

SWECO. (2019). *Elnätsutmaningen. En rapport till Svenskt Näringsliv 2019-12-11.* Retrieved from Stockholm: https://www.svensktnaringsliv.se/fragor/elforsorjning/elnatsutmaningen_1139046.html

Swedish Climate Policy Council. (2020). *Klimatpolitiska rådets rapport 2020.* Stockholm.

Swedish Code of Statutes. (1997). *Ellag (1997:857).*

Swedish Code of Statutes. (2007). *Förordning (2007:1119) med instruktion för Affärsverket svenska kraftnät.*

Swedish Code of Statutes. (2015). *Förordning (2015:579) om stöd för att främja hållbara stadsmiljöer.*

Swedish Code of Statutes. (2016). *Förordning (2016:836) om elbusspremie.*

Swedish Code of Statutes (2019). *Klimatlag (2017:720)*

Swedish Energy Agency. (2018). Storsatsning på världsunik anläggning för fossilfritt stål. http://www.energimyndigheten.se/nyhetsarkiv/2018/storsatsning-pa-varldsunik-anlaggning-for-fossilfritt-stal/. Retrieved 3 Dec 2020.

Swedish Energy Agency. (2019a). Energy in Sweden. Facts and figures 2019. https://www.energimyndigheten.se/statistik/energilaget/?currentTab=1#mainheading

Swedish Energy Agency. (2019b). *Scenarier över Sveriges energisystem 2018.* Eskilstuna.

Swedish Energy Agency. (2020a). *Energiindikatorer 2020. Uppföljning av Sveriges energipolitiska mål.* Eskilstuna.

Swedish Energy Agency. (2020b). *Energiläget 2020*, Eskilstuna.

Swedish Energy Markets Inspectorate. (2016, February 26). Domstolsprocesser kring intäktsramar. Retrieved from https://www.ei.se/sv/for-energiforetag/el/Elnat-och-natprisreglering/domstolsprocesser-kring-intaktsramar/

Swedish Energy Markets Inspectorate. (2020a). *Kapacitetsutmaningen i elnätet* (Ei R2020:06). Retrieved from Eskilstuna.

Swedish Energy Markets Inspectorate. (2020b). *Sveriges el- och naturgasmarknad* (Ei R2020:5). Retrieved from Eskilstuna.

Swedish Environmental Protection Agency. (2018). *Fördjupad analys av svensk klimatstatistik* Rapport 6848. Stockholm.

Swedish Environmental Protection Agency. (2019). *Fakta-PM om EU:s utsläppshandel 2019.* Stockholm.

Swedish Environmental Protection Agency. (2020). *Lägesbeskrivning för klimatklivet.* Retrieved from Stockholm: http://www.naturvardsverket.se/upload/stod-i-miljoarbetet/bidrag-och-ersattning/bidrag/klimatklivet/lagesbeskrivning-klimatklivet-2020.pdf

Swedish Government. (2016). *Forskning och innovation på energiområdet för ekologisk hållbarhet, konkurrenskraft och försörjningstrygghet,* Prop 2016/17:66. Stockholm.

Swedish Government. (2017). *Nytt mål för förnybar el och kontrollstation för elcertifikatssystemet 2017.* Prop. 2016/17:179.

Swedish Government. (2018). *Energipolitikens inriktning.* Prop 2017/18:228.

Swedish Government. (2019). *Utfasning av fossila drivmedel och förbud mot försäljning av nya bensin-och dieseldrivna bilar,* Dir 2019:106.

Swedish Government. (2020a). *Elcertifikat – stoppregel och kontrollstation 2019,* Prop 2020/21:16.

Swedish Government. (2020b). *Sweden's integrated national energy and climate plan.* Stockholm: Ministry of Infrastructure.

Swedish Government. (2020c). *Reduktionsplikt för bensin och diesel-kontrollstation. Promemoria.*
Swedish Government. (2020d). *Reduktionsplikt för flygfotogen. Lagrådsremiss.*
Swedish Ministry of Finance. (2020). *Slopad nedsättning av energiskatt på bränslen i vissa sektorer* (Fi2020/04247).
Sydsvenskan. (2020). Elbrist i Skåne. https://www.sydsvenskan.se/story/elbrist-i-skane. Retrieved 3 Dec 2020.
Vedung, E. (2001). The politics of Swedish energy policies. In S. Silveira (Ed.), *Building sustainable energy systems. Swedish experiences* (pp. 95–130). Stockholm: Svensk Byggtjänst, Swedish National Energy Administration.
Zannakis, M. (2015). The blending of discourses in Sweden's 'urge to go ahead' in climate politics. *International Environmental Agreements: Politics, Law & Economics, 15*(2), 217–236. https://doi.org/10.1007/s10784-013-9235-0.

Energy Governance in Switzerland

46

Andreas Balthasar

Contents

Introduction	1188
General Conditions of Energy Governance in Switzerland	1190
Energy Policy Framework Conditions	1190
Natural Framework Conditions	1192
Energy and Climate Debate	1193
Liberalization of the Swiss Electricity Market	1194
Nuclear Energy Debate	1196
Climate Policy	1196
Institutions and Stakeholders	1197
State Institutions and Stakeholders	1197
Interest Groups	1199
The People	1200
Issues, Instruments, and Coordination of the Swiss Energy Transition	1201
Issues of Energy Transitions	1201
Instruments of Energy Transitions	1202
Coordination	1209
Outcomes, Challenges, and Prospects	1210
Outcomes	1210
Challenges	1210
Prospects	1211
Cross-References	1211
References	1212

Abstract

The Fukushima nuclear disaster in 2011 had a massive impact on Swiss energy policy. At the Paris Climate Summit held at the end of 2015, Switzerland also committed to an ambitious reduction in its greenhouse gas emissions by 2030. In 2017, the people of Switzerland approved the first package of measures under

A. Balthasar (✉)
University of Lucerne, Lucerne, Switzerland
e-mail: andreas.balthasar@unilu.ch

© Springer Nature Switzerland AG 2022
M. Knodt, J. Kemmerzell (eds.), *Handbook of Energy Governance in Europe*,
https://doi.org/10.1007/978-3-030-43250-8_31

Energy Strategy 2050. Since this time, Swiss energy policy has been focused on the phasing out of nuclear energy and the goal of abandoning fossil fuels. The technical and economic requirements for transforming the energy supply in a climate-neutral and socially acceptable manner, while at the same time ensuring supply security, are in place. However, the institutional framework that shapes Swiss politics poses major challenges to the implementation of these policy goals. On the one hand, Switzerland's distinct federal system makes it difficult to implement the necessary political measures in a quick and uniform fashion. The Swiss cantons not only have the authority to define and enforce energy policy measures for new buildings and renovation projects but rather also make decisions for the location of hydropower plants and wind farms as well as geothermal plants. They are also responsible for the specification and payment of subsidies provided by the federal government for the promotion of energy efficiency and renewable energies. On the other hand, the instruments of direct democracy available to the Swiss people often influence the realization of energy policy goals. In the direct democratic context of Switzerland, finding a majority view is a particular hurdle to overcome for the introduction of effective measures. Legal measures, as well as decisions concerning the expansion of hydropower, the location of wind farms or the implementation of solar plants, must, as a rule, be approved by the population in referendums. This not only applies to national projects but rather also to projects at a cantonal and municipal level. This means that social acceptance at all federal levels will be the key element for ensuring the success of Switzerland's Energy Strategy 2050.

Keywords

Swiss politics · Energy policy · Climate policy · Heating · Electricity · Mobility · Electricity surplus · Hydropower · Federalism · Net zero emissions · Decarbonization

Introduction

Switzerland is one of the world's successful industrialized nations. To achieve and consolidate this position, the country has been and remains dependent on access to sufficient and cheap energy. This may well explain why Switzerland started to develop hydropower at an early stage, with large reservoirs now characterizing many parts of the Swiss Alps. Today, approximately 60% of Switzerland's electricity comes from hydropower. Other renewable energies, on the other hand, are not very widespread. Despite great progress in recent years, photovoltaics and geothermal energy still only account for around 0.5% of final energy consumption (BFE 2020c). At present, in addition to hydropower, Switzerland's energy supply is therefore chiefly covered by nuclear energy. In contrast, heating requirements and mobility still heavily rely on the combustion of fossil fuels, particularly crude oil. All uranium, crude oil, and natural gas in Switzerland has to be imported.

From a historical perspective, Swiss energy policy was therefore largely its electricity policy until towards the end of the twentieth century. It was not until 1990 that the people of Switzerland approved an Energy Article in the Federal Constitution. Under this article, the federal government is primarily responsible for nuclear energy as well as for the formulation of principles and subsidies. The cantons can formulate requirements for new buildings and renovations and take decisions for the location of hydropower plants and wind farms as well as geothermal plants. Switzerland's federal basic principles shape the country's energy policy.

Since 2000, energy policy has become more dynamic. The first decisive factor in this change was the liberalization of the electricity market within the European Union. While Switzerland is not a member of the EU, it has at least followed this development in part. This is because Switzerland is very closely linked to the European electricity market due to its location and historical development (Jegen 2009). The lack of a framework agreement with the EU means that this relationship is clouded, however.

The second factor was the Fukushima nuclear disaster in 2011. While Swiss politicians had wanted to keep the option of nuclear energy open until this point, the decision was taken to phase out nuclear energy with Energy Strategy 2050. At the same time, climate change, which has been a driving force behind energy policy in recent years, has moved into the public consciousness as a third factor. In 2017, the people of Switzerland approved a first package of measures under Energy Strategy 2050 (Bundesrat 2012b). In 2021, a vote was held on the CO_2 Act, which provides for an incentive tax on fuels, among other things. However, the Swiss electorate rejected this Act in June with a majority of 51.6%. This means that objective of phasing out nuclear energy while at the same time abandoning fossil fuels by 2050 remains highly ambitious. The technical and economic issues are less challenging. Difficulties primarily occur on a societal level. Switzerland's system of direct democracy means that both fundamental political decisions and decisions relating to the expansion of infrastructures are regularly subject to national as well as cantonal and municipal referendums. As a result, the transition of the energy system in Switzerland will only succeed if the majority of the electorate is convinced of the necessity of each step (Balthasar et al. 2019).

The following discussion initially describes the main features of the Swiss political system that significantly determine energy policy. After this, the most important stages in the development of this policy field and the key stakeholders are addressed. This information forms the basis for describing the content, instruments, and coordination efforts of Swiss energy policy. The closing section discusses the successes achieved to date and the remaining challenges to be overcome on the way to phasing out nuclear energy and abandoning fossil fuels.

This chapter is primarily based on official documents from the responsible federal and cantonal agencies as well as research work that has been conducted within the framework of the National Research Programme "Energy" of the Swiss National Science Foundation (SNF 2021a) as well as at the Swiss Competence Centers for Energy Research SCCER (Innosuisse 2021).

General Conditions of Energy Governance in Switzerland

Energy Policy Framework Conditions

Federalism, direct democracy, and concordance are key institutional framework conditions of the Swiss political system. They also play a significant role in shaping the country's energy policy (Kammermann and Freiburghaus 2019).

Federalism

Federalism refers to the division of tasks between the Swiss federal state, the 26 cantons and the municipalities, which currently total around 2200. Switzerland maintains a marked degree of federalism (Vatter 2016). The basis is formed by the principle of subsidiarity, which is enshrined in the Swiss Constitution. According to this principle, the higher state level is only responsible for those tasks that the subordinate level cannot handle alone (Widmer and Strebel 2011, p. 39). The principle of subsidiarity has the advantage that those responsible can implement solutions considering specific regional circumstances (Balthasar et al. 2020). The principle can, however, give rise to very different regulations in the cantons. Not only can this be costly, but it can also lead to the unequal treatment of citizens living in different cantons.

The first consequence of the country's federal basic principles is that in the area of energy policy, as is the case in most other policy areas in Switzerland, responsibilities are shared between the federal government and the cantons. The Energy Article of the Federal Constitution stipulates that the national authorities are primarily responsible for defining principles for the use of domestic and renewable energies as well as principles for the economical and rational use of energy. They can also issue regulations on energy consumption by plants, vehicles, and devices as well as promote the development of energy technologies, in particular in the areas of energy saving and renewable energies. Finally, the federal government is responsible for embedding Swiss energy policy in the international context. For most other issues, the responsibility lies with the cantons. This includes regulations concerning the renovation of old buildings and the construction of new buildings. The current federal division of labor means that there are no uniform regulations in place in Switzerland's construction sector. Instead, each canton defines and controls its own specifications. The cantons are likewise responsible for decisions regarding the location of hydropower plants, wind farms, and geothermal plants.

The second consequence of the Swiss federal model is that the cantons are not only responsible for the implementation of their legal regulations but also the implementation of federal policy. This so-called *cooperative federalism* represents a defining structural model in the realm of Swiss politics (Balthasar 2021). In the area of energy policy, for example, this means that the cantons are responsible for the specification and payment of a large part of the subsidies that the federal government has earmarked for the promotion of energy efficiency and renewable energies. The system of cooperative federalism also leads to differences that impact the effect of federal policy. Legislative, financing, and implementation powers of the cantons are of great significance for Swiss energy policy (Kammermann and Freiburghaus 2019). The cantons play a considerable role in shaping national energy policy.

In addition to the cantons, the approximately 2200 Swiss municipalities should also not be forgotten as part of the institutional energy policy framework. They have room for maneuver, for example, as the responsible bodies for the issuing of building permits, owners of power utilities, and due to their responsibility for urban public transport.

Direct Democracy

Direct democracy allows Swiss citizens as well as interest groups and political parties to actively participate in energy policy decisions. In no other country does the population have so many and such direct opportunities for participation as in Switzerland (Vatter 2016, p. 359). Popular initiatives, optional referendums, and mandatory referendums form the heart of direct democracy (see Table 1).

The antinuclear movement has made extensive use of direct democratic instruments (see Table 2). The most recent example is the CO_2 Act, which was approved in September 2020 by the Swiss parliament. However, a referendum against the decision was subsequently called for by two sides. On the one hand, organizations from the automobile and crude oil sectors have collected signatures as they want to prevent the imposition of higher taxes. On the other, activists from the climate movement feel that the current act does not go far enough. The legislative referendum option not only influences legislation by providing opportunities for the rejection of a bill. Just as important is the indirect effect that this has on the legislative process in both the pre-parliamentary and parliamentary phases. Organizations that may be able to collect enough signatures for a referendum and get the majority of votes behind them can effectively influence the legislative process by threatening the prospect of a referendum. The example of the CO_2 Act also points to the problem of *unholy alliances* that can likewise bring down proposed legislation.

Table 1 Direct democratic instruments in Switzerland

Designation	Explanation
Popular initiative	Popular initiatives give citizens the right to propose an amendment or addition to the Federal Constitution. For such an initiative to come about, the signatures of 100,000 voters who support the proposal must be collected within 18 months. The authorities sometimes respond to an initiative with a direct counterproposal in the hope that a majority of the people support that instead.
Optional referendum	Optional referendums allow people to demand that any bill approved by the Federal Assembly be put to a nationwide vote. To bring about a national referendum, 50,000 valid signatures must be collected within 100 days of publication of the new legislation.
Mandatory referendum	All constitutional amendments approved by parliament are subject to a mandatory referendum, i.e., they must be put to a nationwide popular vote. The electorate is also required to approve Swiss membership of specific international organizations.

Source: FDFA (2021)

What is meant here is the accumulation of resistance from forces who feel that the change is too progressive and those who reject the change as being overly conservative.

Direct democratic instruments are not only found at a federal level. At a cantonal and municipal level, these instruments are even more developed in some cases (Vatter 2016, p. 368). This means that laws concerning the promotion of renewable energies (e.g., the selection of sites for new infrastructure) or energy efficiency (e.g., building standards) must also be regularly submitted to the population to be decided upon at a cantonal or municipal level. It has proven that more conservative cantons from German-speaking Switzerland are often opposed to environmentally motivated bills (Rohm and Wurster 2016). Urban regions are committed to a faster rate of change, while rural areas tend to be more reluctant (Thaler et al. 2019). Generally speaking, however, it can be said that the cantons are united in backing the general focus of Energy Strategy 2050. However, some of them are setting very different priorities when it comes to energy sources, steering instruments and the rate of change (Stadelmann-Steffen et al. 2018).

System of Concordance

The third defining element of the Swiss political system is concordance. This means that in everyday political life, solutions always have to be sought that are agreed to by a broad majority of political forces. Concordance is a direct consequence of the codetermination rights of the Swiss people held under the system of direct democracy. The instruments of direct democracy provide interest groups with a wide range of opportunities to exert influence on the development of energy policy. For this reason, the positions of these groups have to be incorporated into solutions as far as possible. A direct consequence of concordance is also the fact that legislative processes in Switzerland are very time intensive (Kammermann and Freiburghaus 2019). However, the time-consuming negotiation processes also contribute to the identification of viable political solutions that are then usually also quickly implemented.

Natural Framework Conditions

Switzerland is heavily dependent on importing primary energy from abroad: all of the country's crude oil, natural gas, coal, and uranium have to be imported. At present, only 25% of primary energy consumption can be covered by domestic energy sources. Specifically, these sources chiefly comprise hydropower as well as solar, wood, and biomass energy and environmental heat. The growth in Swiss primary energy consumption since the Second World War has, as has been the case in other European countries, been greatly dependent on crude oil products and nuclear energy. However, Switzerland's situation differs from that found in other countries due to the low importance of gas and coal as well as the high share of nuclear energy and hydropower (IEA 2018).

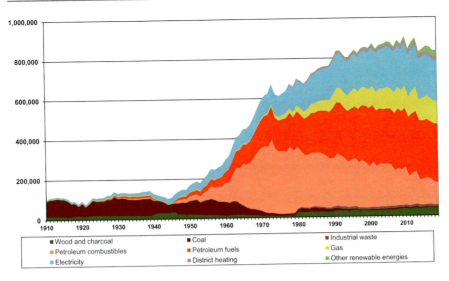

Fig. 1 Source: BFE 2020c

Figure 1 indicates that Switzerland has succeeded in stabilizing its energy consumption and even reducing it in recent years.

Average per capita energy consumption has fallen since 1990. The reason for this lies, in particular, in the rational use of energy through the use of efficient electrical appliances, heating systems, production plants, machinery, and motors (Bundesrat 2017). In 2016, per capita energy consumption in Switzerland is in the same range as the European average of 38,000 kWh (BFE 2019; data does not take account of grey energy). In 2019, around 834,000 terajoules of energy were consumed in Switzerland. Households and services together accounted for 43% of this total energy consumption, followed by transport with 38%. The industrial sector was responsible for 18%.

Energy and Climate Debate

Swiss energy policy started with electrification at the start of the twentieth century (Kupper and Pallua 2016, p. 40). At this time, the tasks of the federal government were limited to supervising the safety of electrical installations. The political absence of the federal government in energy policy throughout almost the entire twentieth century provided the electricity sector and cantons with great room for maneuver (Sager 2017, p. 733). The federal government's sphere of responsibility was not expanded until 1959 when the Atomic Energy Act assigned powers in the nuclear sector to the federal government. For a long time, Swiss politicians placed great hopes in nuclear energy, as they wanted to free themselves from dependence on imported crude oil. The 1973 oil crisis only served to reinforce this conviction. The nuclear accidents on Three Mile Island (1979) and in Chernobyl (1986) dampened this hope and strengthened the antinuclear movement that had emerged in the preceding years. In 1979, the people of Switzerland narrowly rejected an initial antinuclear initiative. This initiative wanted to establish a regime under which the affected population had to have a vote on the construction of nuclear power plants. Between 1979 and 2003, Swiss energy policy was greatly influenced by the conflict between the supporters and opponents of nuclear power (Table 2).

Table 2 shows that the subject of nuclear energy has dominated debate in the area of energy policy since the end of the 1970s. Triggered by this debate, efforts have been made since the beginning of the 1980s to govern the relevant responsibilities in the realm of energy policy at a constitutional level. In 1990, the people of Switzerland approved a constitutional article with a clear majority. In the same year, a popular initiative was adopted that established a 10-year stop to the construction of new nuclear power plants. At the same time, however, the phasing out of nuclear energy was rejected by the population.

The approval by constitutional referendum in 1990 provided the foundation for legislation under which the federal government was required to "contribute to ensuring a secure, sufficient, efficient, diversified and environmentally compatible energy supply" (Bundesrat 1988, p. 534) through the promotion of economical and rational energy use. Based on this law, the Federal Council created the first national energy policy program under the name "Energy 2000" (Balthasar 2000). Energy 2000 was underpinned exclusively by voluntary measures and focused on issues for which there was a social consensus. These included, in particular, the expansion of renewable energies and the promotion of energy efficiency. The debate on nuclear energy was left out.

Between 2000 and 2020, Swiss energy policy was dominated by three issues: the liberalization of the electricity market, the phasing out of nuclear energy, and the climate debate.

Liberalization of the Swiss Electricity Market

The liberalization of the Swiss electricity market was triggered by developments at a European level during the 1990s. While Switzerland is not a member of the European Union, the Swiss electricity market is very closely intertwined with that of the EU. Around 10% of electricity exchange within the EU flows through Switzerland (VSE 2021). It is for this reason that the Swiss electricity industry was also early pushed for the liberalization of the Swiss market. An initial proposal for a corresponding law failed in 2002, however, due to opposition from trade unions and parties on the right of the political spectrum. It was not until 2009 that a modified bill, namely the Electricity Supply Act, was accepted. This act provided the basis for the liberalization of the market for large-scale consumers. It also stipulates that small

Table 2 Selection of national votes on energy issues between 1979 and 2021

Subject of the vote and year	Direct democratic instrument	Result of the vote
Antinuclear initiative (1979)	Popular initiative	Rejected (49% yes)
Federal Decree on the Atomic Energy Act (1979)	Optional referendum	Approved (69% yes)
Federal Decree on the Energy Article in the Federal Constitution (1983)	Mandatory referendum	Rejected (49% yes)
Popular initiative for a future without nuclear power plants (1984)	Popular initiative	Rejected (45% yes)
Energy initiative (1984)	Popular initiative	Rejected (46% yes)
Popular initiative to phase out nuclear energy (1990)	Popular initiative	Rejected (47% yes)
Constitutional article on energy (1990)	Mandatory referendum	Approved (71% yes)
Moratorium initiative (1990)	Popular initiative	Approved (55% yes)
Popular initiative for a solar centime (solar initiative) (2000)	Popular initiative	Rejected (33% yes)
Constitutional article on a subsidy tax for renewable energies (counter-draft to the popular initiative for a solar centime) (2000)	Mandatory referendum	Rejected (48% yes)
Constitutional article on an energy steering tax for the environment (2000)	Mandatory referendum	Rejected (45% yes)
"Tax energy instead of work" initiative (2001)	Popular initiative	Rejected (23% yes)
Electricity Market Act (2002)	Optional referendum	Rejected (47% yes)
Popular initiative "Electricity without nuclear power – for an energy transition and the gradual decommissioning of nuclear power plants" (2003)	Popular initiative	Rejected (34% yes)
Popular initiative for the extension of the nuclear power plant construction freeze (2003)	Popular initiative	Rejected (42% yes)
Popular initiative "Energy instead of VAT" (2015)	Popular initiative	Rejected (8% yes)
Popular initiative "Green economy" (2016)	Popular initiative	Rejected (14% yes)
Initiative for the orderly phase out of nuclear energy (2016)	Popular initiative	Rejected (36% yes)
Energy Strategy 2050 – Energy Act (2017)	Optional referendum	Approved (58% yes)
CO_2 Act (2021)	Optional referendum	Rejected (48% yes)

Key: The direct democratic instruments are explained in Sect. 1. Source: https://swissvotes.ch/vote/

companies and households should likewise have access to the free market after 5 years. However, this step is still yet to be taken. It is opposed, in particular, by left-wing parties and environmental organizations. They believe that electricity supply falls under the public service remit and that access should not be opened up any further, especially for foreign providers. A further important point of discussion in connection with the electricity market is the renewal of the electricity agreement with the EU. This is considered to be of great importance for the country's supply security. While such an agreement is said to be ready for signature, the European Union predicates its completion on the conclusion of a framework agreement between Switzerland and the European Union. Nevertheless, in May 2021, the Swiss government ceased negotiations with the EU on such a framework agreement.

Nuclear Energy Debate

Table 2 refers to the significance of the nuclear energy debate in Swiss energy policy. Whereas until the Fukushima nuclear disaster in 2011 the political majority was in favor of nuclear energy, the Federal Council already moved to present Energy Strategy 2050 around two and a half months after the event. This strategy provides for a gradual phasing out of nuclear energy. The decisive factor in this shift was primarily a change in how the associated risks were assessed by the parties in the political center. A further factor may also have been the perception that a nuclear power plant cannot be built and operated economically in Switzerland today. Accordingly, representatives of the nuclear energy sector have lost a great deal of influence in recent years (Markard et al. 2016; Brändli et al. 2020).

Energy Strategy 2050 is the most important energy policy bill of recent years. At the same time, it aims to bring about the phasing out of nuclear energy and the abandonment of fossil fuels. This is tantamount to a radical restructuring of the Swiss energy system. On 21 May 2017, the first package of measures under Energy Strategy 2050 was approved by 58% of voters in a referendum. The act fundamentally contains three measures. Firstly, the phasing out of nuclear energy is codified, however, without setting a deadline for the decommissioning of the nuclear power plants. General licenses for the construction of new nuclear power plants will no longer be issued. Secondly, the production of renewable energies is to be expanded. And thirdly, measures have been defined to increase the energy efficiency of buildings, mobility, industry, and appliances. A steering tax on fuels is not included in this package (Bundesrat 2012b).

Climate Policy

Since the late 1980s, climate policy has become increasingly important in Switzerland. In the Kyoto Protocol, governments undertook to reduce greenhouse gas emissions in 1997. With the CO_2 Act, Switzerland took an initial step in this direction in 2000. While a reduction target is set under the act, a CO_2 tax was not introduced. However, a procedure was established that allowed for the introduction of such a tax if the climate targets were not met. This procedure was applied after it became apparent in 2004 that the set climate targets would not be achieved. Nevertheless, the CO_2 tax introduced in 2008 is limited to combustibles. The automobile associations successfully resisted the introduction of the tax for fuels.

At the Paris Climate Summit held at the end of 2015, Switzerland not only undertook to reduce its greenhouse gas emissions by 50% by 2030 compared to 1990 but rather also announced a total reduction of 70–85% by 2050 (BAFU 2015). This climate policy decision necessitates the accelerated phasing out of fossil fuels. In 2017, the Federal Council proposed a total revision of the CO_2 Act to parliament. However, the proposal only gained a majority in the Swiss parliament following the 2019 elections. The climate movement, which had also reached Switzerland, played a key role in this. Those representing environmental concerns emerged stronger from the parliamentary elections, helping the bill to gain a breakthrough in parliament. The total revision of the CO_2 Act, which was approved by parliament at the end of 2020, set an end to the installation of new oil heating systems, an increase in the CO_2 tax on combustibles and a CO_2 tax on petrol and diesel as well. In addition, it was planned to impose a levy on airline tickets. Yet the population rejected the revision of the CO_2 Act in June 2021.

Institutions and Stakeholders

State Institutions and Stakeholders

National Level
The most important national stakeholder is the Swiss Federal Office of Energy (SFOE). It is responsible for the preparation and enforcement of energy policy laws and programs. Furthermore, it is the licensing authority for nuclear power. The federal government's central information and advisory platform in the area of energy efficiency and renewable energies, "SwissEnergy," is also based at the SFOE. Unlike most other federal offices, the SFOE has extensive funds of its own to promote application-oriented research as well as pilot and demonstration plants. The SFOE also ensures that Swiss researchers have access to the research programs of the International Energy Agency (IEA).

Responsibility for Swiss climate policy is assumed by the Federal Office for the Environment (FOEN). This office develops climate-policy strategies and objectives for Switzerland supports the government in fleshing out climate policy, provides information to the public on climate policy measures, and participates in international climate policy committees.

In the case of energy issues relating to mobility, responsibility is assumed by the Federal Roads Office (FEDRO), the Federal Office of Transport (FOT), and the Federal Office of Civil Aviation (FOCA). In addition, the Federal Office for Spatial Development (ARE) is responsible for issues regarding overall transport developments. FEDRO is primarily concerned with road traffic. The FOT is chiefly responsible for public transport. The FOCA deals will aviation development and monitoring. FEDRO is committed to promoting e-mobility with – among other efforts – a research program. The FOT has launched the "Energy Strategy for Public Transport 2050" program and is supporting projects within the sector that aim to ensure the rational use of energy and the utilization of renewable energies. In comparison to the SFOE, these federal offices are of secondary importance for energy policy.

Various regulatory and supervisory authorities working in the energy sector are also located at the federal level (Gilardi et al. 2013). These include, in particular, the Federal Electricity Commission (ElCom) and the Swiss Federal Nuclear Safety Inspectorate (ENSI). ElCom is the sector-specific regulator (Hettich and Rechsteiner 2014). This commission is chiefly responsible for ensuring supply security in the electricity sector. It also regulates issues concerning international electricity transportation and trade. ENSI is the Swiss supervisory authority for nuclear safety. Both bodies are appointed by the Federal Council and act independently of the administration.

A special role is assigned to the national grid company Swissgrid, which was founded in 2006 in the wake of the liberalization of the Swiss electricity market. The company owns the transmission grid, while cantons and municipalities hold majority shares of Swissgrid. The task of Swissgrid is to "ensure the permanent, non-discriminatory, reliable and efficient operation of the transmission grid" (Hettich and Rechsteiner 2014, p. 728).

Finally, the National Cooperative for the Disposal of Radioactive Waste (Nagra) should be mentioned. Nagra is a cooperative with the participation of the Swiss Confederation. It is responsible for the safe final disposal of radioactive waste (Kupper and Pallua 2016, p. 80).

Cantonal Level

Given the great importance bestowed on the cantons in the area of energy policy, it stands to reason that all cantons have ministers and administrative units that take on responsibility for energy issues (Widmer and Strebel 2011). Depending on the size of the canton and its administration, as well as the political majorities, the cantons have already developed very different energy policies over the years, setting greatly diverging priorities in the process (Delley and Mader 1986). The construction sector, in particular, has suffered from this, as it has been confronted with a wide range of regulations concerning building envelopes and building technologies in different areas, some of which are extremely detailed. As far back as the 1990s, the Conference of Cantonal Energy Directors endeavored to bring about the harmonization of cantonal regulations and procedures (see section "Heating"). The ministerial conference is supported by the Conference of Cantonal Energy Directors, the conference of senior officers from the 26 cantons.

Municipal Level

Municipalities are also important public stakeholders in the area of energy policy. First, because they play a decisive role in the approval of construction projects. Secondly, as building owners, they can take concrete measures and act as role models. Thirdly, larger municipalities and cities, in particular, are often responsible for public transport, which can significantly influence the mobility behavior of the population and their energy consumption. And fourthly, they often have considerable stakes in energy supply companies and thus in the expansion of production capacities for renewable energy sources. Like the cantons, the municipalities also have associations that serve to exchange information among themselves and represent their common interests in dealing with politicians. The "Association of Swiss Municipalities" represents the interests of all municipalities, while the "Association of Swiss Cities" represents those of the cities and urban municipalities. Both organizations cover all political issues and also regularly comment on energy themes. A more influential player in the area of energy policy is "Swisspower," a strategic alliance primarily made up of municipal energy suppliers.

Interest Groups

Energy Sector

The energy sector has interest groups that not only enjoy strong representation in the national parliament but also in the cantonal parliaments. This primarily applies to the Association of Swiss Electricity Companies (VSE). The electricity suppliers that are members of the VSE produce around 90% of Swiss electricity. The interests of the importers of liquid combustibles and fuels are represented by Avenergy Suisse. The efforts of this organization are often supported by the automobile associations, which count more than 1.5 million members. The Water Industry Association, which works together closely with the mountain cantons, also has a considerable influence on energy policy. Studies have shown that the water industry exhibits great assertiveness in the area of energy policy. The position it adopts is often decisive in reaching compromises (Brändli et al. 2020, p. 27). The Swiss Landlords Association should also be mentioned. This association not only has a large number of members but is rather also very well represented in the national and cantonal parliaments. It frequently opposes regulations that seek to promote energy efficiency and renewable energy in buildings.

economiesuisse, the Swiss economy's largest umbrella organization, also has a strong influence on the shaping of energy policy. The members of economiesuisse include around 100 industry associations, 20 cantonal business associations, and numerous individual companies. AEE Suisse, the economic sector's umbrella organization for renewable energies and energy efficiency, is a relatively young interest group. It represents the interests of companies and utilities from the areas of renewable energy and energy efficiency. The "Swisscleantech" association has a similar focus. It is an association of around 250 Swiss companies that are committed to a CO_2-neutral Switzerland. The surveys of Brändli et al. (2020, p. 27) point out that a transformation has taken place in the energy sector over recent years. Ever broader sections of the business community are convinced that the progress of energy technologies, as well as energy and climate legislation, will lead to interesting market developments.

Environmental and Climate Organizations

In addition to the energy sector, Swiss energy policy is also influenced by environmental and climate organizations. Several of these organizations emerged during the 1970s in connection with opposition to nuclear power plants or new reservoirs. One such example is the Swiss Energy Foundation, which has been involved in all antinuclear initiatives. There are also other environmental stakeholders, including the Swiss Foundation for Landscape Protection and Pro Natura, which regularly put forward their interests in energy policy debates. During such debates, these organizations often receive support from associations that advocate nonmotorized transport or sustainable development in general. In recent years, these have been joined by numerous climate youth initiatives.

The business and environmental associations make use of various means to exert influence on energy policy. In particular, they get involved in the pre-parliamentary consultation process, participate in parliamentary debates through their members, or organize referendum campaigns. These traditional channels are supplemented by extra-parliamentary activities in the form of demonstrations or the climate strike. Environmental associations make particularly frequent use of their rights under Switzerland's system of direct democracy, as Table 2 made clear. While they have enjoyed limited direct success to date, at an indirect level, the popular initiatives have contributed to the continuous tightening of safety regulations for nuclear power plants. Furthermore, environmental organizations often successfully use their right of action to force local project managers to make adjustments to their plans. At the end of 2020, for example, the Federal Supreme Court upheld the objection of nature conservation organizations to the heightening of a dam. According to the Federal Supreme Court, the canton responsible for approval had failed to comprehensively weigh up the interests of protecting the surrounding nature and those of the economy (Bundesgericht 2020).

The People

The people as the third stakeholder group influence energy policy, on the one hand, in their role as energy consumers for heating, hot water, cooking, washing, lighting, communication, and mobility. On the other hand, the population plays a decisive role in determining the direction taken by energy policy thanks to its far-reaching rights of codetermination. For decades, the party-political divides in the area of energy policy largely centered around the position taken on nuclear energy: the right-wing Swiss People's Party (SVP), the Liberal Party (FDP), and the former Christian Democratic People's Party of Switzerland, which found itself at the center of the political spectrum, supported nuclear energy (Jegen 2003; Rieder 1998). Parties on the left, i.e., the Social Democratic Party and the Greens, were closely aligned with the antinuclear movement. This weighting of views changed with the Fukushima disaster in 2011 (Kammermann and Strotz 2014). Those parties in the center and the FDP, in particular, who until this point had been opposed to a phasing out of nuclear energy, changed their minds. Except for the

SVP, all major political parties are now behind the expansion of renewable energies. And since the elections of 2019, the FDP has been actively committed to combating climate change.

Within the direct-democratic context of Switzerland, the knowledge of the population plays a more important role than in other countries, where primarily the government and parliament decide on energy policy. In Switzerland, even small steps towards achieving the ultimate goal require the support of broad sections of the population. Current research findings suggest that there are, in some cases, considerable gaps in knowledge among the Swiss population in this regard (Stadelmann-Steffen et al. 2018). This manifests itself in, among other things, a surprisingly high proportion of 20% of the population who do not believe that global warming is taking place (SNF 2021b). Furthermore, energy and environmental issues are not at the top of the list of priorities of the majority of people in Switzerland. Instead, emphasis is placed on issues that are related to the personal quality of life, such as health, well-being, convenience, and security (Sahakian and Bertho 2018).

Issues, Instruments, and Coordination of the Swiss Energy Transition

Issues of Energy Transitions

The discussion surrounding energy policy in Switzerland can be assigned to the heating, electricity, and mobility sectors, with the situation being similar to that in other European countries. Schaffer and Levis (2021) have shown that the transparency of energy policy decisions is enhanced if the debates in different areas are analyzed separately.

The Swiss *heating supply* is primarily based on mineral oil and, to a lesser extent, natural gas. In Switzerland, a CO_2 tax is payable on crude oil and natural gas. The heating supply is rarely the subject of national policy. This is because most competencies in this regard lie with the cantons, as they are responsible for the building sector. Below, it is shown how the cantons are attempting to increase the energy efficiency of buildings and broaden the use of renewable energies.

Approximately 60% of the Swiss *electricity supply* is based on hydropower, with 32% being accounted for by nuclear energy and 8% by renewable energies. Electricity is therefore only responsible for a negligible part of Swiss greenhouse gas emissions. However, as the phasing out of nuclear energy is a declared goal of Energy Strategy 2050 and greenhouse gas emissions are to be significantly reduced at the same time, Switzerland has to significantly reduce its electricity consumption through efficiency measures, while also massively expanding the share of renewable energies in the area of electricity generation.

For a long time, *mobility* was not the focus of energy policy. Nevertheless, private road transport is responsible for around 20% of total energy demand. This transport is today based almost entirely on fossil fuels. E-mobility is still not very widespread in Switzerland.

Instruments of Energy Transitions

The field of political science primarily distinguishes between regulatory, financial, and persuasive steering instruments (Bemelmans-Videc et al. 1998). Table 3 makes clear that Swiss energy and climate policy utilizes a combination of these instruments.

Switzerland's federal assignment of responsibilities means that there are different responsibilities within the three sectors. The instruments of Swiss energy and climate policy are described in detail below.

Heating

In the heating sector, regulatory instruments, such as regulations in the building sector, are supplemented by subsidies as well as information and advisory services.

Table 3 Selection of Swiss energy policy instruments

	Regulatory steering (commands and prohibitions)	Financial steering (subsidies, taxes, etc.)	Persuasive steering (information, advice, etc.)
Heating	Legal requirements in the building sector (model provisions of the cantons in the energy sector – MuKEn)	Financial support for new buildings and renovations (national building program and cantonal funding programs) CO_2 tax on combustibles	Target agreements with the industrial sector Building energy certificate Information and advice Research and development
Electricity	Electricity market regulation	Compensatory feed-in remuneration – KEV (until 2022) Competitive tendering processes Subsidization of renewable energies	Target agreements with the industrial sector Energy label for appliances Information and advice Research and development
Mobility	CO_2 emission regulations for new vehicles Target agreements with car importers Compensation obligation for mineral oil companies	CO_2 tax on fuels Fuel-related motor-vehicle taxes Promotion of public transport	Energy label for vehicles Information and advice Research and development

Source: Table based on Balthasar and Walker (2015)

As already mentioned, responsibility for improving energy efficiency and disseminating renewable energies in new buildings and as part of renovation projects lies with the cantons. For more than 30 years, the Conference of Cantonal Energy Directors (EnDK) has been striving to standardize and step up the activities of the cantons in this regard. This purpose is primarily served by the "model provisions of the cantons in the energy sector" (MuKEn). These are energy law requirements applied to new buildings and the renovation of old buildings. Generally speaking, these requirements are developed by the Swiss Association of Engineers and Architects (SIA) based on the cutting edge of technological developments. In addition, the cantons are also making efforts to standardize financial support. To this end, the conference adopted a "harmonised funding model" for the first time in 2003 and recommended it to the cantons for implementation. Since 2003, the federal government has co-financed cantonal programs that provide financial support to measures aimed at increasing energy efficiency and the use of renewable energies as part of renovation projects and in new buildings. The "harmonised funding model" of the cantons defines a list of measures in the building sector for which financial support can be made available by the federal government. It also makes recommendations on how a funding program should be structured to ensure it is as effective as possible (Sigrist and Kessler 2016).

All cantons have adopted the "harmonised funding model," albeit with some differences in content. The standardization of cantonal regulations in the building sector is progressing much less quickly, however. In 2008, the EnDK adopted a first package under the MuKEn. The conference recommended that the cantons adopt and implement this package. However, the cantons are free to decide whether to follow the conference's recommendation. The will of the people also plays a role here. This is expressed, for example, in referendums against energy-motivated revisions to building legislation. Today, the requirements formulated in 2008 are implemented in almost all cantons. The more stringent package of 2014, however, has yet to be widely implemented. In a detailed analysis of the diffusion process, Widmer and Strebel (2011, p. 11) point out that the model provisions have had a significant effect. On the one hand, they have influenced the legal bases in the cantons. On the other, they have succeeded in harmonizing cantonal legislation, for example, through the standardization of terminology and indicators.

The federal government has attempted to quantify the impact of the model cantonal provisions with respect to the reduction in energy consumption and CO_2 emissions (BAFU and BFE 2018). The results reflect the influence of the above-average energy-efficiency requirements placed on buildings in the cantons of Basel-Landschaft, Basel-Stadt, and Geneva. More difficult to interpret are rising CO_2 emissions in cantons particularly active in climate policy. The authors attribute this observation to the cantons' different starting points. For example, certain cantons have an above-average share of electric heating systems. Over recent years, these have been replaced by fossil-fuel heating systems due to energy policy requirements. The calculations show that this has led to an increase in CO_2 emissions (BAFU and BFE 2018, p. 24).

Federal government is supporting the cantons' energy-policy efforts in the building sector with subsidies. Within the framework of the so-called "building programme," it made CHF 265 million available to the cantons in 2019 in the form of global subsidies. These are financed through funds from the CO_2 tax on combustibles. Most cantons supplement these federal funds with cantonal funds. They determine individually which measures they wish to support and under what conditions. In doing so, they are guided by the "harmonised funding model" described above. The cantons also support the implementation of the legislation and the funding programs with various persuasive measures. These include information events for authorities as well as enforcement officers and planners and the provision of information and advice to building owners. Almost all of the cantons also have one or more information centers that are available to the general public. The federal government's center of expertise for energy efficiency in buildings, which is part of "SwissEnergy," also supports the activities of the cantons with awareness-raising campaigns, education and training, and quality assurance measures.

Certain parts of the industrial sector are burdened by the CO_2 tax on combustibles. To protect their competitiveness, CO_2-levies are reimbursed if taxable enterprises undertake actions to reduce their emissions and demonstrate this reduction in a monitoring report. The operators of large plants are integrated within the emission trading system and also receive a reimbursement of the CO_2 tax. Furthermore, the federal government and cantons are striving to reach target agreements with the economy to increase the sector's energy efficiency and reduce CO_2 emissions.

Electricity

In the electricity sector, the challenge lies in taking account of the three overriding goals of "efficiency," "environmental compatibility," and "supply security" at all times. The Swiss electricity market has been partially liberalized since 2007 when a structural separation between the providers and owners of the transport grid took place. A further revision of the legal basis of the electricity market is currently being prepared. In particular, this will seek the full opening of the market. Decentralized electricity production should also be facilitated. This serves, in particular, to integrate renewable energies into the electricity market (ElCom 2018).

In addition to the regulation of market organization, subsidization is also of great importance in the area of electricity policy. It is useful to consider the energy sources separately.

Some 60% of Swiss electricity is generated by *hydropower*. The country's topography and its considerable average precipitation mean that Switzerland has ideal conditions for the use of hydropower (Balthasar and Schalcher 2020). However, spatial options for the further expansion of hydropower are limited. Furthermore, the expansion of hydropower is often caught between exploitation interests and environmental protection. The federal government as well as the cantons and municipalities pursue specific interests with respect to the further development of hydropower, complicating the implementation of energy policy objectives in the electricity sector. The federal government promotes hydropower, for example, with feed-in remuneration and a market premium for large-scale hydropower. It also supports hydropower by setting maximum rates for the compensation that power plant operators are required to pay the cantons or municipalities for the use of water resources. However, should the federal government now wish to promote hydropower by reducing this compensation, the cantons and municipalities will oppose this move as they fear a loss of revenue (Thaler et al. 2019, p. 6). The stakeholders at different government levels also don't always follow the same goals when it comes to the expansion of reservoirs. Against the backdrop of this initial situation, the area of energy research has turned its attention away from expansion in recent years and focused more on the optimized use of existing hydropower plants. It has been shown, for example, that reliable hydrometeorological forecasts can allow for operational optimizations with a production increase of up to 6% per year (Balthasar and Schalcher 2020).

In 2009, compensatory feed-in remuneration (KEV) was introduced for electricity produced from renewable energies. The aim was to protect producers of renewable energy in the liberalized market (Rieder et al. 2012). The KEV was financed by the grid surcharge paid by electricity consumers. For small-scale hydropower, photovoltaics, wind energy, geothermal energy, and biomass energy, compensation was provided for the difference between production costs and the market price. In 2017, around CHF 577 million was paid out (KEV Foundation 2018). In 2018, the federal government replaced the KEV with a modified feed-in remuneration system. While remuneration continues to be paid, the rentability of the investment is no longer guaranteed. This system is also time limited. It will expire at the end of 2022 and is set to be replaced by one-off payments.

Despite considerable financial support, photovoltaics is today responsible for around just 3% of Swiss electricity production (BFE 2020c). Energy Strategy 2050 envisages a significant expansion. By 2050, around 20% of electricity demand should be covered by photovoltaics. In addition to systems on roofs, building-integrated photovoltaics also represents an option. While roof-based systems can already largely be operated on a profitable basis, solar facades are likely to remain a niche product for some time to come.

Under Energy Strategy 2050, around 7% of electricity demand is to be covered by *wind energy* in 2050. At present, however, this figure in Switzerland stands at just 0.2%. This shows that the realization of wind farms in Switzerland is only progressing slowly. An explanation for this may lie in the topographical conditions. At least equally as important is a lack of acceptance within society (Geissmann 2015). This is much higher in other countries, as is clearly illustrated in Fig. 2 below, which compares the prevalence of wind energy in Switzerland and Austria.

Research results show that the acceptance of wind turbines and other energy infrastructures is greatly dependent on the landscape type and the already existing use of the landscape. In lowland areas with settlements and Alpine landscapes with tourist infrastructure, such as ski lifts or mountain railways, solar and wind energy infrastructures are more likely to be accepted than is the case in largely untouched landscapes (Salak et al. 2019). It has also become clear that projects with participation opportunities for residents or with a local fund that is fed by revenues from the respective wind power project are viewed much more positively than projects that exclusively benefit individuals (Walter 2012).

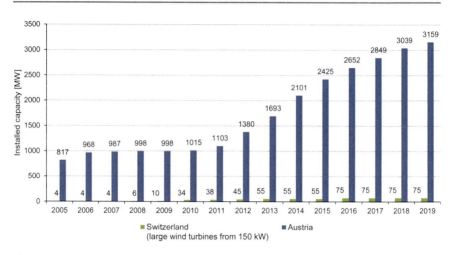

Fig. 2 Source: suisse éole 2021

Energy Strategy 2050 has also defined national targets for *geothermal energy*. By 2050, this technology is expected to cover around a quarter of the heating requirements. At present, this share stands at around 4%. Near-to-surface geothermal energy with heat pumps is already widespread in Switzerland. In the energy system of the future, deep geothermal energy should also play an important role (Guidati and Giardini 2019). Focus is placed on the supply of heat for buildings and industrial processes. Geothermal electricity production still finds itself in the development phase. In French-speaking Switzerland, the first such plant recently went into operation and is used to generate electricity for around 900 households, while also supplying a thermal bath. This application is based on deep drilling (2300–3000 m). In principle, the population and environmental organizations have a positive stance towards geothermal energy as an alternative to fossil energy sources and nuclear power plants (Stadelmann-Steffen and Dermont 2016). However, deep drilling as part of pilot projects has led to widely noticed earthquakes in urban areas, unsettling both politicians and the population (Ejderyan et al. 2019).

At present, the Swiss energy grid is considered to have a very high level of supply reliability. An average Swiss end consumer only has to do without electricity for about 20 min a year, while residents of France and Italy generally have to go without for between 1 h and 90 min (VSE 2021). The planned expansion of solar and wind energy will, however, lead to an increase in the load on the grid. This may negatively impact supply reliability. For this reason, the federal government developed the "Electricity Grid Strategy" in 2013 as part of Energy Strategy 2050 (Bundesrat 2013). The strategy contains guidelines that have to be taken into account in the further development of the electricity grid. These guidelines concern, among other things, the integration of decentralized electricity producers, the connection to the European grid, overarching spatial coordination, the national importance of electricity grids, and the consideration of new technologies. Assigning the quality of "national importance" facilitates the construction of infrastructure facilities by giving energy supply concerns precedence over those of nature and landscape conservation. Digitalization towards the establishment of a smart grid is also part of the grid development process (Balthasar and Schalcher 2020). The legal basis stipulates that 80% of all measuring devices must meet the digital requirements by 2027. In 2019, this figure was just short of 17% (BFE 2020a, p. 26).

In addition to market organization, the electricity policy instruments presented so far primarily relate to the promotion of renewable energies. There are also numerous efforts to increase energy efficiency at both a cantonal and local level. The federal government's energy label, which declares energy consumption, as well as the information and advice services of "SwissEnergy," are important in this context. The federal government is also trying to reduce energy consumption in industry and services through competitive tendering processes as well as in households through the provision of financial support for electricity efficiency measures. Support is given to projects and programs that save as much electricity as possible for each franc of funding. Companies can also conclude target agreements in the electricity sector regarding efficiency measures and, for example, apply for the refunding of the grid surcharge.

Mobility

In the area of mobility, the federal government commands regulatory, financial, and persuasive measures. At a regulatory level, CO_2 emission regulations for new vehicles are established. While Switzerland is orienting itself toward the applicable EU requirements in this regard, it still allows for higher pollutant emissions at present. Energy Strategy 2050 makes clear that the required reduction in CO_2 emissions can only be achieved through a significantly higher share of electric vehicles. Based on the specified target values, each importer's fleet must meet a target. The federal government also specifies compensation obligations for mineral oil companies. In 2021, importers of fossil fuels will have to provide compensation for 12% of CO_2 emissions caused by their use of fuels in the form of climate protection projects in Switzerland.

Financial steering is primarily achieved through the heavy vehicle charge, the exempting of electric vehicles from import and mineral oil taxes, and the promotion of public transport. The performance-related heavy vehicle charge, which was introduced in 2001, applies to all Swiss roads and not only motorways. This has helped to shift heavy goods traffic to rail, which also contributes to reducing CO_2 (Rüefli and Schenkel 2009, p. 124). Furthermore, the federal government's Coordination Office for Sustainable Mobility (COMO) can support future-oriented mobility solutions with financial contributions (Hammer et al. 2019). However, a CO_2 tax on fuels is still pending. Most cantons support electric cars through lower tax rates. In some cases, this tax is waived altogether.

In the mobility sector, the energy label for vehicles has a persuasive effect. This label provides information on fuel consumption, CO_2 emissions, and energy efficiency. The information on the energy label must be published in both advertising and on price lists. In addition, "SwissEnergy" not only offers information and advice upon the purchase of energy-efficient passenger vehicles but rather also when selecting efficient forms of mobility and with a view to an efficient driving style. Financial support can also be provided to innovative projects from the mobility sector.

Despite this promotion, the share of electric vehicles in Switzerland's road traffic remains very low. At present, only around 6% of newly registered passenger vehicles are powered by electricity. This share is expected to rise to over 40% by 2050 (Source: http://www.swiss-emobility.ch).

Research

Public spending on energy research has increased greatly in recent years (Fig. 3). During the 1960s and 1970s, Swiss energy research was practically synonymous with nuclear energy research. Focus is now placed on renewable energies and energy efficiency.

Together with Energy Strategy 2050, the federal government also adopted an "Action Plan for a Coordinated Swiss Energy Research" in 2012 and stepped up activities in this area (Bundesrat 2012a). In particular, it initiated the creation of eight interinstitutional Swiss Competence Centers for Energy Research (SCCER) with which personnel capacities were built up in selected research areas between 2013 and 2020. Since the start of 2021, the SWEET program has been helping to align these capacities with Energy Strategy 2050. In addition, target-oriented project funding was expanded with two temporary national research programs on the topic of energy. One of these focuses on social science energy research (Balthasar et al. 2019). This program made a significant contribution to, for example, sociological, psychological, and political science aspects receiving more attention in the area of Swiss energy research. This is reflected in the current Federal Energy Research Concept 2021–2024 (CORE 2020). Here, the development of energy management fundamentals, which also include the field of social science energy research, form a focus area of increasing importance. This points to the significance of social aspects for the transformation of the energy system.

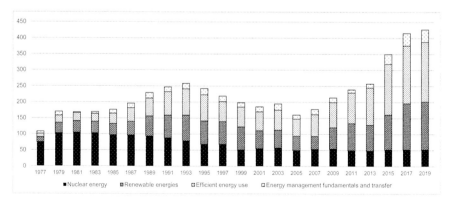

Fig. 3 Source: BFE 2020c

Coordination

Swiss energy and climate policy face a wide range of coordination tasks.

The first affects *coordination with the EU* in the electricity sector. As already mentioned, the Swiss electricity grid has traditionally been very closely linked to that of the EU (Hettich and Kachi 2021). In the past, Switzerland was therefore influential in the further development of the European grid and its standards. Due to the progress seen in the integration of the European energy markets, however, and the simultaneous deterioration in relations between Switzerland and the EU, Switzerland has seen its influence on the European market diminish in recent decades. With the liberalization and harmonization of its energy markets, the EU has also formalized the role of various organizations so that they are now under European jurisdiction. Switzerland is becoming increasingly marginalized (Hettich and Rechsteiner 2014; Maggetti and Gilardi 2011). This is already having an impact on electricity trading with the EU. While in the past Swiss hydropower plants were able to make profitable use of their flexible pumping capacities to exploit international price differences, they have been increasingly restricted in this respect in recent years (Dierks 2019).

The second coordination task concerns *energy policy cooperation within Switzerland's federal system*. Given the division of responsibilities, both vertical (e.g., federal and cantonal support for renewable energies) and horizontal coordination (e.g., harmonization of regulations between the cantons) are essential for an effective energy policy in Switzerland (Thaler et al. 2019). The federal government and cantons are currently working to this end in various committees as well as with, above all, the "harmonised funding model" and "model provisions of the cantons in the energy sector." However, the use of these aids is voluntary and coordination is only progressing at a slow pace.

Thirdly, the coordination of various *public policy areas* that are of relevance for energy and climate policy represents a challenge. This is especially evident in the mobility sector. Not only are energy, climate, transport, spatial, and regional planning affected here, but rather also tax and financial policy. The problem not only arises in the area of energy policy but also the realm of climate policy. To improve coordination of federal policies, the interdepartmental committee on the climate (IDA Klima) was established. There is currently no comparable body in the mobility sector.

Finally, it is vital to consider the need for coordination between the *different sectors* of the energy system (electricity, heating, mobility) (Andersson 2019). The topic of *energy storage* is also related to this. The linking of the different energy sources is of great importance as a future storage strategy (Schalcher 2019). This can be used, for example, to convert electric energy into energy forms that are easier to store when needed. This will be necessary, as the spread of solar and wind energy will increase the need for seasonal storage capacities. Furthermore, the deterioration of Switzerland's relations with the EU in the electricity market will necessitate an expansion of domestic storage capacities. Switzerland's ability to store heat and electricity will be decisive for the implementation of Energy Strategy 2050 (Balthasar and Schalcher 2020).

Outcomes, Challenges, and Prospects

What has Swiss energy policy achieved in recent years? Where does it stand on the road to phasing out nuclear energy and abandoning fossil fuels? And what are the upcoming challenges and prospects?

Outcomes

The dramatic events in Fukushima in 2011 led to a considerable change in Swiss energy policy. While up until this point a narrow political majority had continued to place its faith in nuclear energy, the decision was taken to phase out this technology with Energy Strategy 2050. At the same time, the goal of abandoning fossil fuels was enshrined in law.

The federal government has thus assumed a leading role in Swiss energy policy. For the important topic of heating, which especially affects the building sector, responsibility continues to lie with the cantons. It is only in recent years that mobility has been viewed as part of energy policy.

Modelling initiated by the federal government shows that Switzerland can convert its energy supply to be carbon-neutral by 2050 without jeopardizing the provision of an adequate energy supply (BFE 2020b). In order to continuously check whether Switzerland is on track to achieve this goal, the federal government undertakes annual monitoring (BFE 2020a). This reveals that Switzerland is on course in this respect.

Challenges

Over the long term, however, major challenges will have to be overcome if the objectives set out in Energy Strategy 2050 are to be achieved. In particular, the targeted rapid expansion of photovoltaics, the implementation of production goals in the area of geothermal energy and energy capacities in winter are critical. In recent years, the spread of photovoltaics has been greatly slowed by environmental, landscape, and townscape protection concerns. And the expansion of hydropower is faced with conflicting goals between energy policy and environmental protection (Thaler et al. 2019).

Direct democracy is thus addressed as the key challenge for the energy transition. The National Research Programme "Energy" has summarized the current situation to the effect that a socially acceptable transformation of the energy system is technically possible and financially feasible. The particular challenge will, however, lie in gaining social acceptance (Balthasar and Schalcher 2020). Generally speaking, this means that the political implementation of Energy Strategy 2050 will depend on the success of creating majorities for corresponding measures and projects. In the direct democratic context of Switzerland, finding a majority view is a particular hurdle to overcome for the introduction of effective measures. This is indicated not least by the – repeatedly successful – referendums against national and cantonal energy laws.

The participation of citizens, interest groups, and other stakeholders in the process of developing energy infrastructure projects is one of the key elements for achieving the politically necessary acceptance (Balthasar et al. 2019). Research results indicate that dialogue between investors and authorities with the local population is especially worthwhile if it starts early and when communication is open and transparent at all times (Balthasar and Strotz 2017). In this context, it is important to note that the people of Switzerland are more likely to approve projects for the expansion of renewable energy if they are supported by local Swiss companies. Concerns of public companies and cooperatives with citizen participation meet with particular favor (Rivas et al. 2018; Schmid and Seidl 2018). "Swissness" is a key criterion for the acceptance of infrastructure projects (Balthasar et al. 2019).

Prospects

Many Swiss stakeholders are asking themselves where the country's electricity will come from if its nuclear power plants are decommissioned. There is also uncertainty as to whether it will be possible to abandon the use of fossil fuels and electrify transport (Brändli et al. 2020, p. 31). While the energy prospects drawn up by the federal government provide answers, not all stakeholders have faith in the feasibility of the proposed solutions. It is undisputed, however, that the goal of ensuring supply security can only be achieved in close cooperation with neighboring countries. Nevertheless, whether and how the relationship with the EU will be regulated is the subject of fundamental national policy debates that affect Switzerland's self-image as an independent and neutral state.

Switzerland's future energy system will be more complex than at present. The number of involved parties will increase, energy will be provided on an irregular basis, and system responsibility will lie with an increasing number of stakeholders. This complexity requires politicians to adopt a coordinated approach between the different federal levels, policy areas, and technological sectors (Balthasar and Schalcher 2020). This needs to be supported by a broad majority of the population if it is to have any chance of success in Switzerland's direct democratic system.

Cross-References

▶ Energy Governance in Austria
▶ Energy Governance in Europe: Country Comparison and Conclusion
▶ Energy Governance in Germany
▶ Transition of Energy Systems: Patterns of Stability and Change

Acknowledgments I have most benefited from feedback provided by Dr. Rolf Schmitz, Research Director at the Swiss Federal Office of Energy, and his team as well as by Dr. Stefan Husi,

Programme Manager of the Swiss National Science Foundation. The Swiss National Science Foundation provided financial support for the preparation of this chapter. I would like to sincerely thank everyone involved for their support.

References

Andersson, G. (2019). *Thematische Synthese "Energienetze" des NFP "Energie"* (Eds.: Leitungsgruppen der Nationalen Forschungsprogramme "Energiewende" (NFP 70) & "Steuerung des Energieverbrauchs" (NFP 71)). Bern: Schweizerischer Nationalfonds. https://nfp-energie.ch/de/key-themes/196/synthese/impressum. Accessed 31 May 2021.

Balthasar, A. (2000). *Energie 2000: Programmwirkungen und Folgerungen aus der Evaluation.* Chur/Zürich: Rüegger.

Balthasar, A. (2021). Der Vollzug und die Wirkungen öffentlicher Politiken. In Y. Papadopoulos, P. Sciarini, A. Vatter, S. Häusermann, P. Emmenegger, & F. Fossati (Eds.), *Handbuch der Schweizer Politik = Manuel de la politique suisse* (7th ed., pp. xy–zz). Zürich: NZZ Libro.

Balthasar, A., & Schalcher, H.-R. (2020). *Forschung für die Schweizer Energiezukunft: Resümee des Nationalen Forschungsprogramms "Energie"* (Eds: Leitungsgruppen der Nationalen Forschungsprogramme "Energiewende" NFP 70 & "Steuerung des Energieverbrauchs" NFP 71). Bern: Schweizerischer Nationalfonds zur Förderung der wissenschaftlichen Forschung SNF.

Balthasar, A., & Strotz, C. (2017). Akzeptanz von erneuerbaren Energien: Erfolgsfaktoren für Infrastrukturprojekte. *bulletin.ch* (by VSE – Verband Schweizerischer Elektrizitätsunternehmen, Aarau), No. 10/2017, 20–23.

Balthasar, A., & Walker, D. (2015). Lenkungsabgaben alleine genügen nicht. *Die Volkswirtschaft, 88*(6), 44–47.

Balthasar, A., Varone, F., & Meierhans, D. (2019). *Thematische Synthese "Akzeptanz" des NFP Energie* (Eds.: Leitungsgruppen der Nationalen Forschungsprogramme "Energiewende" (NFP 70) & "Steuerung des Energieverbrauchs" (NFP 71)). Bern: Schweizerischer Nationalfonds. https://nfp-energie.ch/de/key-themes/195/synthese/impressum?_=1622457223686&open=true. Accessed 31 May 2021.

Balthasar, A., Schreurs, M. A., & Varone, F. (2020). Energy transition in Europe and the United States: Policy entrepreneurs and veto players in federalist systems. *Journal of Environment & Development, 29*(1), 3–25.

Bemelmans-Videc, M.-L., Rist, R. C., & Vedung, E. (Eds.). (1998). *Carrots, sticks & sermons: Policy instruments & their evaluation.* New Brunswick: Transaction Publishers.

Brändli, D., Schäpper, C., Schoch, M., & Wüthrich, J. (2020). *Politikfeldanalyse Strompolitik in der Schweiz.* Abschlussbericht (Capstone-Kurs September 2019 – Juni 2020). Zürich: Institut für Politikwissenschaft, Universität.

Bundesamt für Energie (BFE). (2019). *Energieverbrauch weltweit und in der Schweiz, Fakten zur Energie,* Nr. 4. Bern. https://pubdb.bfe.admin.ch/bfe/de/7976-Factsheet4_Energieverbrauch-DE-1.pdf. Accessed 29 May 2021.

Bundesamt für Energie (BFE). (2020a). *Energiestrategie 2050. Monitoringbericht 2020. Kurzfassung.* Bern. https://www.bfe.admin.ch/bfe/de/home/versorgung/statistik-und-geodaten/monitoring-energiestrategie-2050.html. Accessed 29 May 2021.

Bundesamt für Energie (BFE). (2020b). *Energieperspektiven 2050+. Kurzbericht.* Bern. https://www.bfe.admin.ch/bfe/de/home/politik/energieperspektiven-2050-plus.html. Accessed 29 May 2021.

Bundesamt für Energie (BFE). (2020c). *Schweizerische Gesamtenergiestatistik 2019.* Bern. https://www.bfe.admin.ch/bfe/de/home/versorgung/statistik-und-geodaten/energiestatistiken/gesamtenergiestatistik.html. Accessed 29 May 2021.

Bundesamt für Umwelt & Bundesamt für Energie (BAFU & BFE) (Ed.). (2018). *Wirkung der Klima- und Energiepolitik in den Kantonen: 2016, Sektor Gebäude.* Bern: BAFU & BFE.

Bundesamt für Umwelt (BAFU). (2015). *Switzerland's intended nationally determined contribution (INDC) and clarifying information.* https://www.newsd.admin.ch/newsd/message/attachments/38514.pdf. Accessed 27 May 2021.

Bundesgericht. (2020). Urteil vom 4. November 2020 (1C_356/2019). *Ausbau Grimselstausee: Beschwerde von Naturschutzorganisationen gutgeheissen* (Medienmitteilung des Bundesgerichts vom 26. November 2020). https://www.bger.ch/files/live/sites/bger/files/pdf/de/1c_0356_2019_2020_11_26_T_d_14_44_39.pdf. Accessed 30 May 2021.

Bundesrat. (1988). *Botschaft betreffend den Bundesbeschluss über eine sparsame und rationelle Energieverwendung (Energienutzungsbeschluss)* vom 21. Dezember 1988. Bern.

Bundesrat. (2012a). *Botschaft zum Aktionsplan "Koordinierte Energieforschung Schweiz" – Massnahmen in den Jahren 2013–2016.* Bern.

Bundesrat. (2012b). *Erläuternder Bericht zur Energiestrategie 2050* (Vernehmlassungsvorlage). Bern.

Bundesrat. (2013). *Strategie Stromnetze; Detailkonzept im Rahmen der Energiestrategie 2050.* Bern.

Bundesrat. (2017). *Ursachen der Stromverbrauchsentwicklung der Schweiz*: Bericht des Bundesrates in Erfüllung des Postulates 15.3583, Nordmann, 17.06.2015. Bern.

CORE – Eidgenössische Energieforschungskommission. (2020). *Konzept der Energieforschung des Bundes 2021–2024.* Bern: CORE.

Delley, J.-D., & Mader, L. (1986). *L'Etat face au défi énergétique: étude de mise en œuvre des mesures fédérales et cantonales en matière d'économie d'énergie.* Lausanne: Payot.

Dierks, S. (2019). Schweizer Netz stand kurz vor dem Blackout. *energate messenger.ch* (publ. 27 May 2019). https://www.energate-messenger.ch/news/192046/schweizer-netz-stand-kurz-vor-dem-blackout. Accessed 30 May 2021.

Eidgenössische Elektrizitätskommission (ElCom). (2018). *Aktuelle Ergebnisse zur Versorgungssicherheit 2025.* https://www.admin.ch/gov/de/start/dokumentation/medienmitteilungen.msg-id-70953.html. Accessed 30 May 2021.

Ejderyan, O., Ruef, F., & Stauffacher, M. (2019). Entanglement of top-down and bottom-up: Sociotechnical innovation pathways of geothermal energy in Switzerland. *The Journal of Environment & Development, 29*(1), 99–122. https://doi.org/10.1177/1070496519886008.

Federal Department of Foreign Affairs (FDFA). (2021). *Direct Democracy.* https://www.eda.admin.ch/aboutswitzerland/en/home/politik/uebersicht/direkte-demokratie.html. Accessed 27 May 2021.

Geissmann, M. (Ed.). (2015). Social acceptance of wind energy projects: Winning hearts and minds. State-of-the-art Report. Country Report for Switzerland. IEA Wind Task 28. http://www.socialacceptance.ch/images/State-of-the-Art_Acceptance_Wind_Energy_Switzerland.pdf. Accessed 30 May 2021.

Gilardi, F., Maggetti, M., & Servalli, F. (2013). Regulierungsbehörden in der Schweiz, Chapter 11. In A. Ladner, J.-L. Chappelet, Y. Emery, P. Knoepfel, L. Mader, N. Soguel, & F. Varone (Eds.), *Handbuch der öffentlichen Verwaltung in der Schweiz* (pp. 199–217). Zürich: Verlag Neue Zürcher Zeitung.

Guidati, G., & Giardini, D. (2019). *Verbundsynthese "Geothermie" des NFP "Energie"* (Eds. Leitungsgruppen der Nationalen Forschungsprogramme "Energiewende" (NFP 70) & "Steuerung des Energieverbrauchs" (NFP 71)). Bern: Schweizerischer Nationalfonds. https://nfp-energie.ch/de/dossiers/192/impressum. Accessed 31 May 2021.

Hammer, S., Petry, C., & Schmidt, M. (2019). *Evaluation der von KOMO/DZM geförderten Mobilitätsprojekte: Schlussbericht.* Zürich: Infras.

Hettich, P., & Kachi, A. (Eds.). (2021). *Swiss energy governance.* New York: Springer.

Hettich, P., & Rechsteiner, S. (2014). Energie. In H. M. Tschudi, B. Schindler, A. Ruch, E. Jakob, & M. Friesecke (Eds.), *Die grenzüberschreitende Zusammenarbeit der Schweiz : juristisches Handbuch zur grenzüberschreitenden Zusammenarbeit von Bund und Kantonen* (pp. 707–730). Zürich: Dike.

Innosuisse – Swiss Innovation Agency. (2021). *Energy funding programme 2013–2020: final report and evaluation.* https://www.innosuisse.ch/inno/en/home/promotion-initiatives/energy-funding-programme-SCCER.html. Accessed 22 Nov 2021.

International Energy Agency (IEA). (2018). *World energy balances: Overview.* Complete energy balances for over 180 countries and regions. https://www.iea.org/reports/world-energy-balances-overview. Accessed 31 May 2021.

Jegen, M. (2003). *Energiepolitische Vernetzung in der Schweiz: Analyse der Kooperationsnetzwerke und Ideensysteme der energiepolitischen Entscheidungsträger.* Basel: Helbing & Lichtenhahn.

Jegen, M. (2009). Swiss energy policy and the challenge of European governance. *Swiss Political Science Review, 15*(4), 577–602. https://doi.org/10.1002/j.1662-6370.2009.tb00146.x.

Kammermann, L., & Freiburghaus, R. (2019). Konsensdemokratie und die Transformation der schweizerischen Energiepolitik. *Rdms – der moderne staat – Zeitschrift für Public Policy Recht und Management, 12*(2), 329–346. https://doi.org/10.3224/dms.v12i2.09.

Kammermann, L., & Strotz, C. (2014). *Akteure und Koalitionen in der Schweizer Energiepolitik nach Fukushima.* Bern: Institut für Politikwissenschaft, Universität. https://doi.org/10.13140/RG.2.2.15550.

KEV Foundation – Stiftung Kostendeckende Einspeisevergütung. (2018). *Geschäftsbericht 2017.* Frick: KEV.

Kupper, P., & Pallua, I. (2016). *Energieregime in der Schweiz seit 1800.* Bern: Bundesamt für Energie BFE.

Maggetti, M., & Gilardi, F. (2011). The policy-making structure of European regulatory networks and the domestic adoption of standards. *Journal of European Public Policy, 18*(6), 830–847. https://doi.org/10.1080/13501763.2011.593311.

Markard, J., Suter, M., & Ingold, K. (2016). Socio-technical transitions and policy change – Advocacy coalitions in Swiss energy policy. *Environmental Innovation and Societal Transitions, 18,* 215–237. https://doi.org/10.1016/j.eist.2015.05.003.

Rieder, S. (1998). *Regieren und Reagieren in der Energiepolitik: die Strategien Dänemarks, Schleswig-Holsteins und der Schweiz im Vergleich (Berner Studien zur Politikwissenschaft)* (Vol. 5). Bern/Stuttgart/Wien: P. Haupt.

Rieder, S., Bernath, K., Walker, D., Fussen, D., Varone, F., Marx, L., & Bader, C. (2012). *Evaluation der kostendeckenden Einspeisevergütung (KEV).* Bern: Bundesamt für Energie BFE.

Rivas, J., Schmid, B., & Seidl, I. (2018). *Energiegenossenschaften in der Schweiz: Ergebnisse einer Befragung (WSL Berichte, 71).* Birmensdorf: Eidgenössische Forschungsanstalt für Wald, Schnee und Landschaft WSL.

Rohm, C., & Wurster, S. (2016). Volk oder Parlament: Wer entscheidet nachhaltiger? Eine vergleichende Untersuchung von Nachhaltigkeitsabstimmungen in der Schweiz. *Swiss Political Science Review, 22*(2), 185–212.

Rüefli, C., & Schenkel, W. (2009). *Evaluation Verlagerungspolitik/Güterverkehr: Schlussbericht an die Begleitgruppe.* Bern: Büro Vatter Politikforschung & -beratung/synergo.

Sager, F. (2017). Infrastrukturpolitik: Verkehr, Energie und Telekommunikation. In P. Knoepfel, Y. Papadopoulos, P. Sciarini, A. Vatter, & S. Häusermann (Eds.), *Handbuch der Schweizer Politik = Manuel de la politique suisse* (6th ed., pp. 721–748). Zürich: Verlag Neue Zürcher Zeitung.

Sahakian, M., & Bertho, B. (2018). Exploring emotions and norms around Swiss household energy usage: When methods inform understandings of the social. *Energy Research & Social Science, 45,* 81–90.

Salak, B., Kienast, F., Olschewski, R., Spielhofer, R., Wissen, U., Grêt-Regamey, A., & Hunziker, M. (2019). steuerBAR? Wo wollen wir "Energielandschaften" und wo nicht? In A. B. Gurung (Ed.), *Schweiz erneuerbar! (WSL Berichte)* (Vol. 84, pp. 15–22). Birmensdorf: Eidgenössische Forschungsanstalt für Wald, Schnee und Landschaft WSL.

Schaffer, L. M., & Levis, A. (2021). Public discourses on (sectoral) energy policy in Switzerland: Insights from structural topic models. In P. Hettich & A. Kachi (Eds.), *Swiss energy governance: Political, economic and legal challenges and opportunities in the energy transition.* Cham: Springer Nature.

Schalcher, H.-R. (2019). *Thematische Synthese "Gebäude und Siedlungen" des NFP "Energie"* (Eds.: Leitungsgruppen der Nationalen Forschungsprogramme "Energiewende" (NFP 70) & "Steuerung des Energieverbrauchs" (NFP 71)). Bern: Schweizerischer Nationalfonds. https://nfp-energie.ch/de/key-themes/197/synthese/impressum. Accessed 31 May 2021.

Schmid, B., & Seidl, I. (2018). Zivilgesellschaftliches Engagement und Rahmenbedingungen für erneuerbare Energie in der Schweiz. In L. Holstenkamp & J. Radtke (Eds.), *Handbuch Energiewende und Partizipation* (pp. 1093–1106). Wiesbaden: Springer VS.

Schweizerischer Nationalfonds zur Förderung der wissenschaftlichen Forschung (SNF). (Ed.). (2021a). NFP Energie: Nationale Forschungsprogramme 70 und 71. https://nfp-energie.ch. Accessed 22 Nov 2021.

Schweizerischer Nationalfonds zur Förderung der wissenschaftlichen Forschung (SNF). (Ed.). (2021b). Wissen ist von grundlegender Bedeutung. https://nfp-energie.ch/de/key-themes/195/synthese/3/cards/27. Accessed 20 Nov 2021.

Sigrist, D., & Kessler, S. (2016). *Harmonisiertes Fördermodell der Kantone (HFM 2015). Schlussbericht. Revidierte Fassung vom September 2016*. Bern: Bundesamt für Energie BFE & Konferenz Kantonaler Energiefachstellen EnFK.

Stadelmann-Steffen, I., & Dermont, C. (2016). *Energie-Enquete 2016 – erste Einblicke*. Bern: Institut für Politikwissenschaft, Universität. https://ipwenergy.shinyapps.io/preferences/. Accessed 30 May 2021.

Stadelmann-Steffen, I., Ingold, K., Rieder, S., Dermont, C., Kammermann, L., & Strotz, C. (2018). *Akzeptanz erneuerbarer Energie (= Nationales Forschungsprogramm 71: Steuerung des Energieverbrauchs)*. Bern/Luzern/Dübendorf: Universität Bern/Interface Politikstudien Forschung Beratung/EAWAG.

suisse éole. (2021). *Statistik (CH/International)*. https://www.suisse-eole.ch/de/windenergie/statistik/. Accessed 02 Feb 2021.

Thaler, P., Hofmann, B., Abegg, A., Bornemann, B., Braunreiter, L., Burger, P., Dörig, L., Ejderyan, O., Heselhaus, S., Opitz, C., Petrovich, B., Rinscheid, A., Schillig, I., Schreiber, M., & Sohre, A. (2019). *Schweizer Energiepolitik zwischen Bund, Kantonen und Gemeinden: zentralisieren, dezentralisieren oder koordinieren?* SCCER CREST White Paper 7. https://www.sccer-crest.ch/fileadmin/user_upload/White_Paper_7_Energiepolitik_FINAL.pdf. Accessed 30 May 2021.

Vatter, A. (2016). *Das politische System der Schweiz* (2nd act. ed.). Baden-Baden: Nomos.

Verband Schweizerischer Elektrizitätsunternehmen (VSE). (2021). Energiewissen. https://www.strom.ch/de/energiewissen. Accessed 22 Nov 2021.

Walter, G. (2012). *Sozialpsychologische Akzeptanz von Windkraftprojekten an potentiellen Standorten: eine quasiexperimentelle Untersuchung*. Bern: Bundesamt für Energie BFE.

Widmer, T., & Strebel, F. (2011). *Determinanten des Vollzugs energiepolitischer Massnahmen auf kantonaler Ebene: Schlussbericht*. Bern: Bundesamt für Energie BFE.

Energy Governance in Turkey

47

Emre İşeri and Tuğçe Uygurtürk

Contents

Introduction	1218
General Conditions of Energy Governance	1218
Legacies/Path Dependencies	1218
Composition of the Energy Mix	1220
Discourses/Narratives on Turkey's Energy Policy	1223
Political Institutions and Actors	1227
Instruments and Coordination of the Turkish Energy Transition	1228
Drivers of Energy Transition	1228
Strategies and Instruments of Energy Transitions	1232
Coordination Mechanisms and Issues of Multilevel Governance	1244
Outcomes, Challenges, and Prospects of Energy Governance	1247
Cross-References	1249
References	1249

Abstract

Energy governance has been widely prescribed to address the energy trilemma (i.e., energy security, energy equity, and environmental sustainability) at global, regional, and national levels. This is a particularly daunting task for those net energy importer developing countries with growing energy consumption levels to fuel their growth. Drawing on primary documents and statistics along with the relevant academic literature and reports, the chapter scrutinizes energy governance in Turkey with a particular emphasis on the neoliberal developmentalist model of its carbon-intense economy with ambitious regional energy diplomacy (i.e., pipeline politics). Albeit its generous renewable energy resource endowment

E. İşeri (✉)
Department of International Relations, Yaşar University, İzmir, Turkey
e-mail: emre.iseri@yasar.edu.tr

T. Uygurtürk
Deparment of Economics, Yaşar University, İzmir, Turkey
e-mail: tugce.uygurturk@yasar.edu.tr

© Springer Nature Switzerland AG 2022
M. Knodt, J. Kemmerzell (eds.), *Handbook of Energy Governance in Europe*,
https://doi.org/10.1007/978-3-030-43250-8_32

and renewable energy support mechanisms/initiatives, energy governance deficits with limited norm diffusion/policy transfer/convergence prospects from the EU slowdown energy transition of the country. The chapter concludes that the new normal of the post-COVID-19 provides a significant opportunity not only for the revitalization of its economy based on the renewable energy sector and energy-efficient technologies but also harnesses the energy transition of Turkey towards a green economy.

Keywords

Turkey · Energy governance · Energy transition · Energy diplomacy

Introduction

As one of the top 25 countries in energy consumption, with a population of 82 million, Turkey is an upper-middle income-developing country with a rising current account deficit. The incumbent Justice and Development Party's (*Adalet ve Kalkınma Partisi*- Ak Party) political Vision for 2023 (2012), the 100th anniversary of the foundation of the Republic, set the target for the country to become among the ten largest economies, up from the 18th largest economy as of 2019 (IMF 2019). This ambitious goal has prompted the Ak Party through its neoliberal developmentalist model to exploit domestic resources including nuclear energy at the expense of environmental governance (Erensü 2018; Adaman et al. 2019; Şahin 2019) and energy market liberalization (i.e., electricity and natural gas) with mixed results (Akkemik and Oğuz 2011; Karahan and Toptas 2013; Demir 2020). Acknowledging that domestic resources would not suffice to fuel its carbon-intensive economy, Turkey relies heavily on energy-diplomacy (i.e., pipeline politics) in its gas sector to extract sources from conflict-prone geography bestowed with 70–75% proven hydrocarbons of the world (İşeri 2015; Raszewki 2018; Erşen and Çelikpala 2019). Notwithstanding its plentiful renewable energy-resource endowment and generous renewable energy support mechanisms/initiatives, energy governance deficits (e.g., clientelism, patronage, and dependent regulatory agencies) (TEPAV 2016, pp. 19–23) and ambitious energy diplomacy undermine the energy policy of Turkey's prospects for norm diffusion and policy transfer from the regional energy governance of the EU as the primary external driver of its energy transition.

General Conditions of Energy Governance

Legacies/Path Dependencies

As geopolitics, military decision-making, and energy security prompted the energy transition from coal to oil before the First World War (Ediger and Bowlus 2019), the heir of the Ottoman Empire, modern Turkey, had been forced to abrogate its claims over untapped Mesopotamian oil basins to the British Mandate of Iraq with the Frontier Treaty of 1926 (Uluğbay 2008, pp. 225–388). This obliged Turkey to fully exploit those resources endowed by geology, typology, and geographical location with a typical Mediterranean climate, namely large mineral reserves (primarily lignite as fossil fuel) (Ediger et al. 2014) and renewable energy potential such as hydro (Bilgili et al. 2018) and geothermal (Erdoğdu 2007; Melikoglu 2017).

To reduce dependency and thus to ensure energy security, exploration of domestic resources is of significant importance. Located in the East Mediterranean, Turkey is advantageous in terms of reaching large gas potential. Yet, several factors ranging from technical requirements to political conflicts have affected the position of Turkey among the others. Since both dynamic political relations and geopolitical factors have constantly prompted the emergence of new alignments, setting a long-term energy agenda could be a formidable task in the region. Turkey, in this sense, has been positioned separately (Karbuz 2018).

Before elaborating on contemporary energy trends in Turkey, we shall emphasize historical landmarks of three primary energy resources (oil, liquefied petroleum gas (LPG), and natural gas) (Hepbasli and Özgener 2004, p. 962): (1) The first productive oil well was drilled in the Raman in 1940; (2) Liquefied Petroleum Gas (LPG) began to be used as an alternative to city gas and kerosene in Turkey since the beginning of the 1960s; and (3) Natural gas consumption had started in 1976 with the usage of limited indigenous natural gas production in a few fields, and those resources began penetrating the Turkish energy market in the late 1980s.

Against the backdrop of those energy landmarks, it would be plausible to examine the historical trends of Turkey's energy profile. Classified as a "medium-class" energy consumer with a 0.77% share of total primary energy consumption (TPEC) in 1999 (Ediger 2003, pp. 2993–2996), Turkey's success in harnessing energy transition hinges on its adoption and implementation of sustainable energy policy. This entails addressing the following three most important problems of its energy system: dependence on imported resources (i.e., oil and natural gas), fossil fuel-weighted consumption, and lower-energy efficiency in comparison to other countries. Historical energy consumption of Turkey between 1950 and 2006 reveals that the share of oil increased from 7.6% in 1950 to 55.7% in 1977 at its peak, and then decreased continuously to 30–35% today. Coal consumption fluctuated around 30%, except for the 19.8% drop between 1967 and 1984. Natural gas has been steadily increasing since 1976, cutting the coal curve around 27% in 2005. On the other hand, hydro generally ranges around 34%, and modern renewables range around 12%. This clearly shows that in the Turkish energy system for the last 20 years, oil and traditional renewables had been replaced by natural gas at the expense of the country's increasing dependence on this imported resource. Despite the high demand increase in energy demand (minimum 6.3% in 2001 and maximum 11.59% in 1972) in overall energy resources, Turkish primary energy production increased in the same period only by 2.7%. The growing dependence on energy imports represents one of the most important challenges of the economy in a way that endangers the country's transition to a sustainable energy system (Ediger 2009; Oksay and Iseri 2011).

Composition of the Energy Mix

In Turkey, the developing economy accompanying with a considerable increase in population has induced a remarkable rise in energy demand. A rapid increase in energy demand could result in a considerable rise in total primary energy supply (TPES). TPES was 145.887 million tons of oil equivalent (Mtoe) in 2018, which is 48% higher than the one recorded as 98.419 Mtoe in 2008 (IEA). Along with the high level of energy dependency rates, a relatively low-domestic production could be problematic while there is a stable rise in energy demand. The currently available data suggest that domestic production could only meet 28% of TPES. Natural gas, among the other energy sources, has seen the most remarkable increase in TPES. Since 1990, which corresponds to the starting of intense depletion of natural gas, noteworthy increases such as 343%, 148%, and 31% have been recorded for every 10 years. These rates have made Turkey vulnerable to natural gas supply. To quantify the already obvious vulnerability, Berk and Ediger (2018) developed an index to quantify natural gas vulnerability in Turkey. Contrary to general expectations, they found that the effect of natural gas import resources is negligible. The principal factors that affect the vulnerability are the natural gas share in consumption and import as well. Additionally, coal and oil have similar shares (30%, 29%, respectively). In other words, fossil fuels have constituted almost 87% of TPES. Based on the fossil fuels share in TPES, Turkey ranks top ten among International Energy Agency (IEA) member countries.

As to final energy consumption, the data should be disaggregated as much as possible. Otherwise, double-counting particularly arising from the energy sector may lead to a misleading interpretation of data. For this purpose, the gross energy consumption of Turkey has been mostly driven by fossil fuels, a large part of which is used to generate electricity (Fig. 1). The recent data propose that coal ranks first in electricity generation. The share of coal enormously increased (by 96% between 2008 and 2018) and reached 113.249 GWh in 2018. Together with coal, natural gas (31%) and hydro (20%) are the sources that dominate electricity generation by almost 90% in total. The energy sector, industry, and transport are the

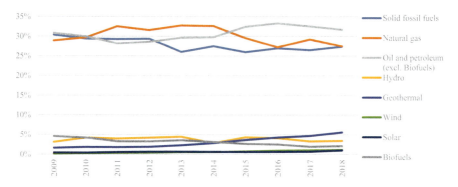

Fig. 1 Gross energy consumption by product. (Source: EUROSTAT)

sectors that consume the largest share of the energy (Fig. 2). For the former one, the use of natural gas has remarkably risen by 222% since 2008. As for the latter one, the oil products have also experienced a noteworthy increase (83%) in the same period. In recent years, particularly since 2015, the share of coal has risen dramatically (coal used in electricity generation increased by 49% between 2015 and 2018). High import rates on natural gas along with the depreciation of the Turkish lira against the US Dollar have triggered such an increase in coal share. This could be attributable to ensuring energy security considerations in the sense that coal is used as a domestic resource.

Due to its limited hydrocarbon production levels and Liquefied Natural Gas (LNG) facilities, Turkey is heavily dependent on natural gas imports through pipelines (Map 1). Contrary to the general trend of an increasing number of short-term contracts with various competing natural gas suppliers in the USA and Western Europe, Turkey made long-haul take-or-pay contracts with its primary natural gas

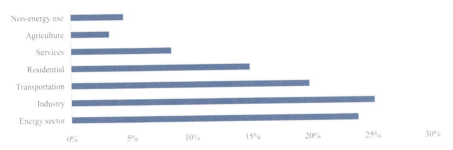

Fig. 2 Gross energy consumption by sector. (Source: Directorate General of Energy Affairs)

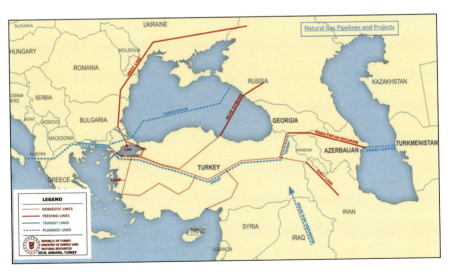

Map 1 Natural gas pipelines and projects through Turkey. (Source: Turkish Ministry of Energy and Natural Resources)

supplier Russia (Özdemir 2017a) (Tables 1 and 2). The dependency of imported oil and natural gas with high figures could be risky while considering the figures demonstrated in Fig. 3.

As to energy production, fossil fuels have been heavily used for electricity generation. Coal and natural gas with almost 38% and 30% (TEİAŞ) share,

Table 1 Gas imports on a resource-basis origin

	2010 (%)	2018 (%)
Russia	46.20%	47%
Iran	20.40%	16%
Azerbaijan	11.90%	15%
LNG (Algeria + Nigeria + Spot)	21.50%	22%

Source: PETFORM (2020)

Table 2 Gas import agreements

Contracts	Signature date	operational date	Year	Volume (Plato – billion cubic meters/year)	End date
Nigeria (LNG)	1995	1999	22	1.2	2021
Iran	1996	2001	25	10	2026
Algeria	1988	1994	27	4	2021
Russia (Blue Stream)	1997	2003	25	16	2028
Russia	1998	1998	23	8	2021
Russia	1998	1998	23	4	2021
Russia	2013	2013	23	1	2036
Russia	2013	2013	30	5	2043
Turkmenistan	1999	------	30	16	---
Azerbaijan	2001	2007	15	6.6	2022

Source: PETFORM

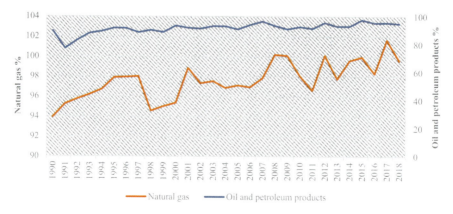

Fig. 3 Energy import dependency. (Source: EUROSTAT)

respectively, have been the major sources. Although renewable energy support mechanisms have been employed in recent years, their share in electricity generation has stood limited as demonstrated in Fig. 4. Only hydro could make a considerable contribution (59.755 GWh in 2018). Yet, solar PV (7.477 GWh) and wind power (19.882 GWh) together could not reach even half of the hydro. Another important issue of renewable energy is the transfer process. The distance between the location of renewable sources and consumption centers poses a problem. Particularly, hydro sources are mostly located in the eastern regions of Turkey. Within this scope, the electricity network should be improved and be prioritized. By this means, it is likely to meet volatile and prompt demand for electricity.

However, it should be noted that considering energy sources without their impacts could result in other problems. Coal, with high carbon emissions, could have impacts to a larger extent than other energy sources, such as hydro. Put it in another way, the concept of energy security should be evaluated within a multidimensional framework. One of the integral dimensions of energy security is climate change concern.

The extensive use of fossil fuels has inevitably led to climate change concerns, which pose a challenge against the backdrop of sustainable energy policies. Although Turkey's contribution to global CO_2 emissions stayed about 1%, it has started to increase dramatically since the beginning of the 2000s. The levels have surged dramatically compared to the average level recorded in many EU countries. The main reason for the striking rise is the domination of fossil fuel use while generating electricity. As shown in Fig. 5, the electricity sector originates the largest share of CO_2 emissions (at almost 40% as of 2018), because of the extensive use of coal. Nearly 43% of the total CO_2 emissions come from coal. Although the emissions led by coal depletion account for almost half of the total, the current energy policies continue to encourage coal use through subsidies. Actually, it is not an easy task to determine the real value of coal subsidies in Turkey mostly because it excludes social cost and the existence of indirect incentives as well. The total subsidy to the coal sector (including direct and indirect subsidies) was estimated at $730 million in 2013 (Acar et al. 2015). Following coal, oil products account for 31%, and the rest arises from natural gas use.

Discourses/Narratives on Turkey's Energy Policy

Historically, the idea of "catching up" with the West has been central to Turkish politics prompting "growth fetishism" as a magical formula to solve the country's socioeconomic problems (Arsel et al. 2015, p.376). This outlook has long paved the way for Turkish policy-makers to come up with energy policy preferences prioritizing affordable and uninterrupted supply. These energy preferences have been translated into allegedly complementary energy policy outputs: Full exploitation of domestic resources (e.g., coal and hydro) along with homegrown nuclear at the domestic level, reliance on energy diplomacy (i.e., pipeline politics) at an ever-changing regional geopolitical context. Against this backdrop, this section will examine contending discourses on Turkey's energy policy under two broad categories: energy security/competitiveness and ecologic sustainability/energy equity.

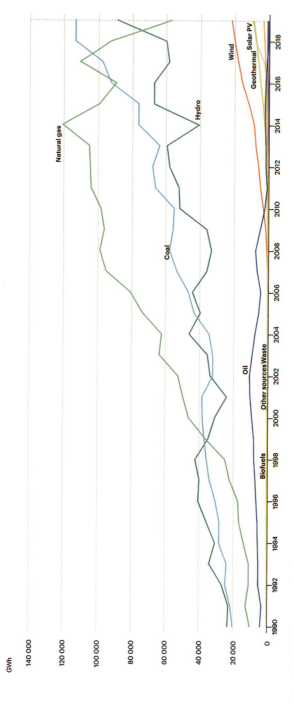

Fig. 4 Electricity generation by source. (Source: IEA)

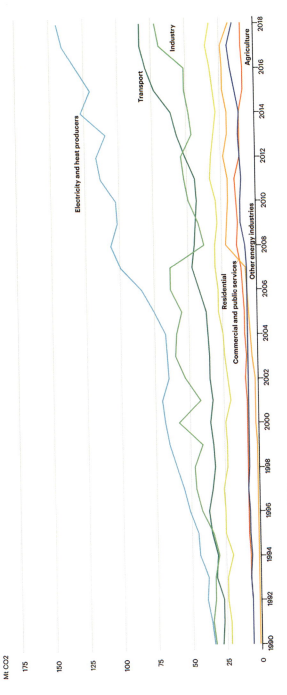

Fig. 5 CO2 emissions by sector. (Source: IEA)

Energy Security and Competitiveness

In 2017, then Turkish Energy Minister Berat Albayrak has launched the "National Energy and Mining Policy" (*Milli Enerji ve Maden Politikası*) (NEMP) (MENR 2017; Bayraktar 2018) to ensure "strong economy and national security" for Turkey. This policy has three pillars: security of supply, localization, and predictability in the markets. About supply security and localization, the NEMP has reiterated the pledge to exploit all types of its national resources (lignite coal, hydro, and renewables) along with controversial nuclear plants. Notwithstanding the presence of contending perspectives on Turkey's nuclear program (İşeri et al. 2018; Aydın 2020), Balkan-Şahin (2018, p. 457) elaborates how the Turkish government manages to create a hegemonic discourse around nuclear: "...the AKP [Ak Party] government has framed nuclear energy as the only alternative for Turkey to *diversify energy resources*, trigger *economic growth* and *boost the competitiveness* of the country" [emphasized by the authors of this chapter].

By the same token, the Energy Strategic Plan for 2019–2023 (MENR 2019) emphasized those two pillars (security of supply and localization) in its preamble with this motto: "more national, more renewable" (*daha çok yerli, daha çok yenilenebilir*) by determining seven targets. Among those targets, "ensuring sustainable energy supply security" states increasing supply from national resources including nuclear, "prioritization and increasing energy efficiency" emphasize efficient governance of the demand side, "technological advancements and localization" delineates initiatives to promote national production of energy equipment and systems. Acknowledging that those aforementioned targets would not suffice to close the growing gap between consumption and production in energy, the strategy document has a separate target of "increasing regional and global trade in energy and natural sources."

Under this target, there are two goals. The first goal pertains continuing pledge to transform the country's transit country status into an energy hub through the materialization of the Southern Gas Corridor (SGC) (İşeri and Almaz 2013) and various pipelines in both north and south axes (e.g., TANAP, the Turkish Stream) (Özdemir 2017b; Yılmaz-Bozkus 2019) (Map 1). The second goal is about enhancing cooperation and investment opportunities with target countries. Fulfilling those two goals necessitates delicate (energy) diplomacy in an ever-changing geopolitical environment of the Middle East (Özdemir and Raszewski 2016), Eurasia (Erşen and Çelikpala 2019), and the Eastern Mediterranean (Karbuz 2018; İşeri 2019; İşeri and Bartan 2019) without tensing relations with the EU (Tsakiris et al. 2018).

Ecological Sustainability/Energy Equity

Rapid growth-oriented top-down modernization and developmentalism have been the main pillars of the Turkish policy-makers to attain social consent to legitimize their rule. This pattern has taken a new form under the Ak Party with its peculiar "crony neoliberalism," appearing in the relationship between energy and construction as locomotives of Turkish carbon-intense economic growth by transforming rural and urban space. Unsurprisingly, the Ak Party-led neoliberal developmentalism has prompted its discontent among various fractions of civil society around the country (Adaman et al. 2017). Those civil discontents galvanized into uprisings around the Gezi Park in 2013 along with numerous sporadic smaller protests against coal mining, nuclear, and hydro in the rural areas seldom remaining purely issue-based calling for environmental justice (Knudsen 2015; Arsel et al. 2015; Erensü 2017; Adaman et al. 2019; Sayan and Kibaroğlu 2020).

Indeed, academic literature on Turkish public attitudes toward energy and the environment has also revealed public discontent with the AK Party-led Turkey's energy policies. Among those studies, Ertör-Akyazı et al. (2012) found that the majority of the 2422 respondents in urban space objected to coal (82.9%) and nuclear (62.5%) mainly due to environmental considerations. Drawing on the PEW Research Center Global Attitudes Survey (2015), İşeri and Günay (2017) highlight that 35% of Turkish respondents rank climate change as the top global concern contradicting with Turkey's "politics of special circumstances" to refrain from binding carbon emission commitments (Turhan et al. 2016). Parallel to this, Ediger et al. (2018, pp. 497–498) reveal that the Turkish public perceives energy (78.9%) as a major contributor to global warming and prefers the installation of renewables – wind (86.2%) and solar (86.0%) – over coal and nuclear plants in their neighborhood. Differently put, the Turkish public adopts a relatively ecological stance toward the AK Party government's energy policies, despite poor (environmental) journalism quality in the country's "press-party parallelism" dominant "polarized media system" (Şahin and Uzelgun 2016; Günay et al. 2019; Ersoy and İşeri 2020).

Political Institutions and Actors

Establishing an institutional structure to manage the abovementioned intense energy agenda is not an easy task. The interconnection between institutions sometimes has been reorganized to get more efficiency. Figure 6 summarizes the current scheme. As a main actor in the energy market, the Ministry of Energy and Natural Resources (MENR) retains all actions with the collaboration of several institutions related to the economic, environmental, and physical security of energy supply. The management of energy supply from the physical security side is summarized in the graph shown above. The leading institution MENR has been interrelated with several regulatory authorities such as EMRA, NRA, BOREN, and newly established NATEN. While EMRA has shaped the legal framework of energy markets (electricity, natural gas, and petroleum) and all transactions, other institutions have been mostly based on research for exploration and improvement of the current technologies. Under the MENR, specialized public institutions for each type of energy have been established. For electricity generation, EÜAŞ is the one having no privatized generation plants and works with other operational complementary institutions (TETAŞ, TEDAŞ, and TEİAŞ). As to coal, TTK and TKİ are two significant institutions whose primary task is to supply coal to electricity generation. BOTAŞ is responsible for trade and pipeline operations of natural gas which dominates the energy demand. As an oil-dependent country, Turkey has allocated immense funds for upstream. TPAO, the only national state-owned oil company, has carried out both production and exploration for more than half a century. Moreover, each process from electricity generation to distribution requires the ability of technical equipment construction. All steps for the construction of electricity generation plants (including manufacturing, installation, operation, and supply of technical equipment as well) are conducted by TEMSAN.

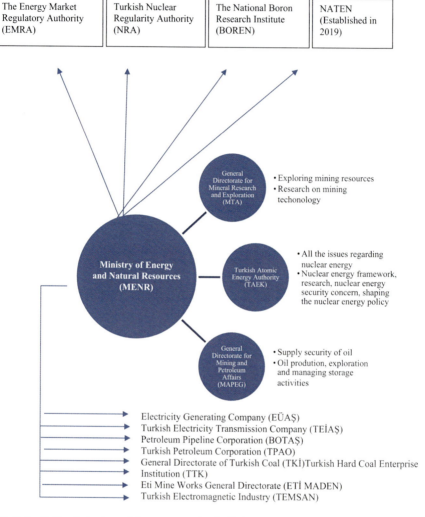

Fig. 6 Institutional structure of the energy market in Turkey

Instruments and Coordination of the Turkish Energy Transition

Drivers of Energy Transition

Internal Driver

MENR and the Energy Market Regulation Authority (EMRA) are the two main institutions supervising Turkey's energy sector. On the one hand, MENR is the key body preparing energy policies and setting strategy; on the other hand, "independent" regulatory body EMRA's role is providing supervision and insights. Due to politicians' tendencies to meddle in the corporate governance of state-led organizations (e.g., Petroleum Pipeline Corporation – BOTAŞ-dominating nominally open Turkish gas market) and in the decision-making of EMRA, the country's energy governance has various deficits such as clientelism, patronage, and regulatory dependence (TEPAV 2016, pp. 19–23).

The Directorate of Climate Change, which is the subdivision of the Ministry of Environment and Urbanization (MoEU), leads Turkey's energy transition. Besides the MENR as the principal body for energy-related mitigation policies, various ministries have contributed to this endeavor. While the Ministry of Foreign Affairs (MFA) gives diplomatic support in international platforms, the Ministry of Development (MOD) delivers economic analysis, the Ministry of Forestry and Water Affairs harnesses adaptation efforts, and the Ministry of Food, Agriculture, and Livestock harnesses mitigation and adaptation efforts in agriculture. Despite the role of the MOEU as the principal body of climate governance, the MOD and the MENR have been vocal in their reservations. While the former is critical on mitigation and low-carbon policies, the latter puts obstacles on climate action contradicting with the country's energy strategy based on hydrocarbons. The economy bureaucracy (e.g., The Treasury, the Ministry of Economy, and the MOD) is the principal body by having the authority to allocate the climate budget (Turhan et al. 2016).

Despite Turkey's progress on climate policy, it largely remained limited to several nonobligatory plans and policy frameworks, measures to ensure a coordinated policy among national agencies, and deliver soft guidance to the local governments. At a turtle pace, cities have been engaged in climate policies. Thanks to their membership in several transnational municipal networks and due to their proactive staff, those pioneering cities (Gaziantep and Bursa) accompanied by Antalya, İstanbul, İzmir, and Kocaeli's metropolitan municipalities have adopted climate action plans. However, those local actors' achievement has remained limited to small-scale initiatives and projects on climate change mitigation (Balaban 2019).

Various environmental civil society organizations (CSOs) or nongovernmental organizations (NGOs) (e.g., Doğa Association, Greenpeace Mediterranean, the Turkish Foundation for Combating Soil Erosion, for Reforestation and the Protection of Natural Habitats, and World Wildlife Fund – Turkey) participate in policy processes in Turkey. Nonetheless, their effectiveness has remained limited. The Turkish state obsessed with economic growth has continued to adopt legislation causing environmental degradation (e.g., coal mining, hydro, and nuclear). The inability of those CSOs to influence the legal agenda stems from political (e.g., absence of a participatory framework for collaborations with the often arbitrary state) and economic constraints (i.e., raising funds) in their antagonistic relations with the Turkish state and (neoliberal) economic actors (Paker et al. 2013). Adding insult to injury, polarized political setting along with secular and Islamist partisan cleavages, narrows the environmental sphere (Özler and Obach 2018), and de-Europeanization couples with growing skepticism toward pro-EU environmental organizations in Turkey (Boşnak 2016).

External Drivers

A variety of external drivers (e.g., IMF, UNFCCC, UNDP, and REC Turkey) have influenced Turkey's energy/environmental governance, which had been subject to several reforms based on the post-Washington consensus principles in the 2000s. During the "golden age of Europeanization" (2002–2005), through its conditionality mechanisms, the EU was successful in pressuring Turkey to adopt reforms (Öniş and Yılmaz 2009). As Sirin and Ege (2012, p. 4924) put, "most of the economic, political and social reforms in Turkey in recent years are mostly made because of EU accession negotiations to align Turkish legal framework in line with *acquis communautaire*, and the same is true for energy legislation notably regarding liberalization, energy efficiency, and renewable energy." Simultaneously, Turkey has accomplished significant progress in the liberalization and restructuring of the electricity market in alignment with the EU *acquis* as discussed below. Since 2006, however, Turkey-EU relations have entered into a period of stalled negotiations in which the EU blocked several chapters including the Energy Chapter – mainly due to Cyprus' veto – accompanied by the gradual decline of Turkey's progress in reforms. In the absence of a visible external political stimulus (i.e., EU membership), it seems that Turkey's primary orientation is intensifying cooperation with the EU in those areas where its energy priorities and interests are met (Colantoni et al. 2017a). In this context, they have accomplished various mutual interests including procurement diversification in natural gas import (i.e., the SGC), Turkey's electricity market synchronization of the European Network of Transmission System Operators Electricity (ENTSO-E), and other European initiatives aiming at the integration of the two polities' energy markets. From the perspective of the EU, the mutual relation in the energy field is of vital importance as Turkey plays a key role in enhancing EU energy security. Thus, negotiations on the Energy Chapter have continued to evolve such as the new negotiation "A High-Level Energy Dialogue," which was initiated in 2015. The European Commission's Turkey Report (EC 2019) stresses the following: clarifying nuclear energy regulation, deepening gas market reform, and implementing the national energy efficiency action plan (NEEAP). Differently put, the Commission focuses on those policy areas that would harness Turkey's transition to the de-carbonized energy mix. Indeed, energy transition could serve as a robust framework for enhanced Turkey-EU dialogue on energy and climate change in the future (Colantoni et al. 2017b). At the current stage, the EU's effect on the domestic transformation of Turkey decreased; nonetheless, it has been continuing in a restricted manner through social learning, discursive resource, and persuasion processes (e.g., EU-funded projects/programs, policy networks) (Günay and İşeri 2017; Savaşan 2019).

Indeed, Turkey's energy transition has been largely financed by EU funds. One of the biggest funds, Instrument for pre-Accession Assistance (IPA), has been implemented in two stages (IPA 1, IPA 2) since 2007. For both of these, three areas have been prioritized. The first is related to the improvement of energy market infrastructure and its integration into the European energy market. Energy efficiency and renewable energy rank second to carry out an integrated energy policy, which also considers climate change concerns. The last one focuses on nuclear energy.

For the first period of IPA (2007–2013), 34 projects have been completed worth a total of €133 million. A certain part of this amount has been collaboratively managed by other international funds such as the World Bank (WB), European Bank for Reconstruction and Development (EBRD), and European Investment Bank (EIB). Each of these has been supporting many projects focusing on sustainable energy policy. For example, 13% of EBRD's current energy sector portfolio has been allocated to Turkey. Furthermore, a considerable amount of EBRD's total energy sector investment (amount of €16.698 million) has been received by Turkey since its operations launched in 2009. Within this framework, the role of EBRD in supporting sustainable energy use is of crucial importance. One of the prominent programs developed by EBRD is *Turkey Sustainable Energy Financing Facility* (TurSEFF), which has provided €645 million for sustainable energy projects for both public and private sectors since 2010. Major players in the Turkish energy market have been provided with a large amount of loan recently ($100 million to both Enerjisa and İçtaş A.Ş., $330 million to Zorlu Energy, $120 million to Akfen Energy, and $60 million to Efeler Energy). Likewise, the World Bank has provided loans for energy efficiency, renewable energy use, and improvement of distribution and storage activities as well. Recently, substantial loan support (TRY 1 billion) has been received by the MoEU from the WB. The goal is to increase energy efficiency in public buildings. The WB has lately approved an additional loan (€289.5 million) whose first phase started in 2014 with an initial loan amount of €217 million to TEİAŞ. On the other hand, the private sector has also been supported by loans ($182.4 million) provided to small and medium-sized enterprises for energy efficiency projects. In addition to these, EIB is one of the leading financial institutions which has been operating for a long time in Turkey. The funds provided by EIB date back to 1959. Most of the early energy projects financed by EIB have been based on infrastructure improvement. Considering the funds provided to fundamental actors of energy market such as BOTAŞ and TEDAŞ (for BOTAŞ infrastructure €80 million in 1996, for improvement of TEDAŞ total €325 million in 2006, 2008, and 2009), its contribution should be appreciated. On the other hand, the recent projects have been principally focusing on projects regarding climate change issues in parallel with EU policies. To date, total financed projects amount to nearly €2.8 billion since 1959.

Turning to the second phase of IPA, covering the period 2014–2020, it is seen that, different from the first period, universities and municipalities have been included among the institutions to be financed. A budget project of almost €4.5 million is provided by IPA II, which aims at increasing renewable energy use and energy efficiency. At this point, it is important to distinguish renewable energy and energy efficiency projects significantly. While renewable energy has started to gain considerable space in the energy agenda because of both cost reductions and increasing concerns about climate change, inadequate attention was paid to energy efficiency. Although Turkey has immense potential in terms of energy efficiency, it is not very successful in turning the potential into practice. Considering a multi-dimensional structure of energy efficiency, such a transformation could only be achieved within a harmonized system. Regulation, market-based policy mechanisms, business models, financing mechanisms, and system efficiency are the categories that should be encompassed in this system. The investment required to fully implement this potential is estimated at $30 billion for the next 10 years (SHURA 2020). As a result of the investments, not only could the energy transformation be completed, but also new expansion could be experienced in the fields of employment, finance, and technology development.

In line with global patterns, Turkey has tried to employ carbon-pricing tools. Emissions trading scheme (ETS), as the instrument of the carbon pricing which internalizes negative externalities of GHG emissions, has been planned to be established in Turkey. For this purpose, Turkey has received a World Bank grant under the program called Partnership for Market Readiness (PMR) since 2013. PMR Turkey, with the collaboration of MoEU, has conducted several analyses that resulted in roadmap reports for the establishment of market-based GHG-emission-reduction policies. The first step of the PMR project in Turkey is the implementation of the Monitoring, Report, and Verification (MRV) system for tracking GHG emission levels. The main objective of MRV is to enhance transparency while measuring emission levels in the sense that it makes an international comparison in terms of mitigation targets possible.

However, the implementation of ETS should be considered in conjunction with the existing energy policies, i.e., energy efficiency targets, current renewable energy policies, and voluntary emission reduction projects. Moreover, it should be underlined that if the balance between energy efficiency policies and ETS is not set well, the ultimate output could not be cost-effective. Namely, energy efficiency targets implemented in specific sectors for encouraging emissions mitigation are not likely to fit in ETS applications. Another important priority of the current energy policies, renewable energy, should be taken into account while performing the ETS. As the largest share of CO_2 emissions in Turkey arises from the power sector, it is not easy to introduce an ETS. Because the power sector is likely to be included in the ETS, reaching the cost-effective output could be an ambitious challenge while setting energy policy goals. In light of this, improving a holistic (renewable energy & ETS) energy policy appears to be the most convenient way (IEA 2016). The last point that should be addressed is the Voluntary Carbon Market (VCM) (or Voluntary Emission Reduction Offset Market) which has been in force since 2005. VCM, with an achievement of 25 million tonnes of emission reduction, could be seen as a preliminary attempt for the carbon market in future.

Strategies and Instruments of Energy Transitions

Electricity Market Liberalization

Besides those targets comprising supply security and localization pillars of Turkish energy policy, the strategy document (MENR 2019) set the target of "increasing predictability in [energy] market" indicating various measures to improve efficiency, transparency, and predictability. Regulation of the Turkish energy sector (in particular electricity) and markets has set the agenda of the country's developing economy since its transition from import-substitution to an export-oriented neoliberal model in post-1980. Due to their differing economic principles, the neoliberal transition of Turkey can be divided into two subperiods: The first phase, 1980–2000, was principally shaped by the Washington Consensus principles (i.e., gradual opening of the economy with the ultimate aim to full integration with the world commodity and financial markets). The second phase of Turkey's neoliberal transition covers the post-2001 period. In line with the principles of the post-Washington consensus (i.e., good governance through strong market-regulating institution, consumer protection, and competition regulation), the country's electricity market has been re-restructured (Kızıl Voyvoda and Voyvoda 2019).

Actually, devastating economic consequences (e.g., severe energy and food shortages) of the global oil crisis in 1973 provided the ground for a neoliberal turn in Turkey (Erensü 2018, p.150). Drawing on the "24 January decisions" in 1980 proposing neoliberal prescription (e.g., fiscal austerity measures, foreign trade liberalization, and the privatization of stated led enterprises (SOEs)) in response to an economic crisis, Turgut Özal led post-coup government adopted the neoliberal shock therapy in the 1980s (Yalman 2009; Öniş 2004). In this process, the electricity sector topped the neoliberal structuring agenda, and the Law no. 3096 entitled "Authorization of Enterprises other than the Turkish Electricity Administration to Produce, Transmit, Distribute and Trade Electricity" was enacted in 1984. It became the first legal measure to incentivize the private sector to invest in the energy sector through the BOT (build, operate, and transfer) and the TOOR (transfer of operating rights) schemes. After this first attempt in the neoliberal era, in 1993, the Ministerial Cabinet decided to separate the vertically integrated structure of the Turkish Electricity Institution (*Türkiye Elektrik Kurumu* – TEK): the Turkish Electricity Generation and Transmission Corporation (*Türkiye Elektrik Üretim ve İletim Anonim Şirketi* – TEAŞ) and the Turkish Electricity Distribution Corporation (*Türkiye Elektrik Dağıtım Anonim Şirketi* – TEDAŞ). This organizational restructuring in the electricity sector was accompanied by the enactment of Law no. 3996 expanding the scope of the BOT model of Law no. 3096 to include those infrastructure projects that would bring advanced technology and generate significant wealth. In 1997, Law no. 4283 was enacted proposing the BOO (build, own, and operate) scheme for thermal power plants and regulating those plants' electricity sales.

The post-2011 period heralds the second phase of the neoliberal restructuring of the Turkish economy based on the principles of "the post-Washington consensus." This "new" era has precipitated a new legal framework for the energy sector and market with the Electricity Market Law no. 4628 in February 2001, which founded the Electricity Market Regulatory Authority as the independent supervisory agency in the electricity market. With the approval of Electricity Market Law No. 6446 in 2013, the agency's name altered to the Energy Market Regulatory Authority (EMRA).

Under this new regime, TEAŞ split into three independent entities: Electricity Generation Company *Elektrik Üretim A.Ş.* – EÜAŞ for the generation, Turkish Electricity Trading and Contracting Company for wholesale trade, and Turkish Electricity Transmission Company (*Türkiye Elektrik İletim A.Ş.* – TEİAŞ) for transmission activities. In March 2004, therefore, the High Planning Council (*Yüksek Planlama Kurulu* – YPK) proposed its plan for restructuring and privatizing the electricity sector to begin in mid-2006 and to be completed by 2010. In the 2000s, those legal arrangements and planning in the energy sector served as an important tool for the (re)transformation of the state-market relationship, which was shaped by the goals of "ensuring the smooth functioning of the markets" and "accepting competition rules within the legal system." However, the process is far from continuous, regular, and smooth processing. Aiming to ensure the establishment of a financially sound, stable, and transparent electricity market operating in a competitive environment, Law No. 6446 came into force in March 2013. However, it has been continuously revised for different reasons and purposes since the relevant date. The last of these changes were made within the framework of the restructuring of institutions with the transition to the presidential system as of 2018 (Kızıl Voyvoda and Voyvoda 2019).

In November 2007, the Turkish Parliament passed a new law (no.5710) on the Construction and Operation of Nuclear Power Plants and Energy Sale (of their electricity) that was subsequently approved by the then President. It promulgated the Turkish Atomic Energy Authority (TAEK) to set the criteria for building and operating the plants and the Turkish Electricity Trade & Contract Corporation (TETAS) to buy all the power under 15-year contracts. This process culminated with nuclear bids from foreign companies. The Russian stated-owned Atomstroyexport received the approval to construct the country's first nuclear power plant in Akkuyu on the BOT basis, which is expected to be commissioned in 2023. Construction dates for planned nuclear power plants in Sinop and Igneada are uncertain (WNA February 2020).

Despite ever-changing regulations in different periods on their scope and forms in the post-2001 era, nonstate enterprises have significantly increased their share in Turkey's electricity sector. With the implementation of the privatization programs for electricity distribution in this period, the share of the private sector, which was around 25% at the beginning of the period, was recorded as approximately 80% in 2015 (Kızıl Voyvoda and Voyvoda 2019, p. 148) Due to various cancelations and delays, it was not until 2013 that privatization of electricity distributions was completed. Under the shadow of various cancellations and ongoing discussions about adopted methods and welfare implications, the privatization process of electricity production has been going on (Kızıl Voyvoda and Voyvoda 2019, p. 152). Briefly, Turkey has reduced the state's role in electricity generation and energy trading through privatization acts and adopted market methods to improve transparency in the post-2001 era. However, the Ak Party-led government still holds 25% of the total installed power supply and offers a price below market prices, creating a ceiling that sets a price below market levels.

Despite the abovementioned efforts put by the government to lower electricity prices in Turkey, it is still above the European average concerning purchasing power standards. The electricity price is determined by EMRA by updating every quarter of the year. Considering the purchasing power standard as a currency, Turkey ranks first among the European countries (including all taxes and levies). It should also be addressed that an increase in electricity price particularly for the last 2 years has been quite remarkable as depicted in Fig. 7. In 2018 and 2019, 34% and 20% increases, respectively, point out that the following period might be challenging.

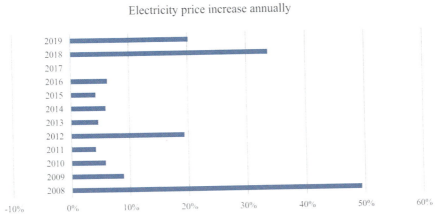

Fig. 7 Electricity price increase (in national currency). (Source: EUROSTAT)

Another important point is the tax portion of electricity prices that is not that high as general public perception suggests. As of 2019, the tax rate in electricity price is 19% (EUROSTAT). This is rather low compared to some other European countries (Germany 54%, Denmark 65%, Spain 45%, and Italy 39%). Electricity generation accounts for the largest share of electricity prices because the generation depends to a large extent on imported natural gas.

As a result of the liberalization process, consumers have gained the right to choose their suppliers whether consumption is above the specified level. Consumers in the electricity market are classified as "eligible" or "non-eligible." The distinction between these two depends on their electricity consumption level. The eligible consumers have the right to choose their suppliers if their annual consumption exceeds the amount determined by EMRA. By 2020, the limit has been decreased by 12.5% compared to 2019, and those consuming 1400 kWh or above could be eligible. This scheme has also led to an increase in the number of licenses gained by the private sector (Table 3).

Another milestone regarding the liberalization process is fully privatized distribution service in the electricity market. All electricity distribution activities were privatized to set a competitive environment for the electricity sector (Law No. 2004/22 enacted by the High Board of Privatization). Following the privatization process of electricity distribution, 21 regions (electricity distribution regions) were established. These are determined concerning energy demand, geographical distance, and common economic and technical similarities as well.

Despite these improvements in the electricity market operations, the production structure could not make progress. The share of domestic resources in electricity generation has declined even though renewable energy use has been gradually encouraged (Fig. 8).

Figure 9 demonstrates that both renewable energy and coal (hard coal and lignite) use have markedly increased throughout the last two decades. Yet, their share in total electricity production decreased as total production had risen by 143% at the same time.

Table 3 Electricity licenses of private and public sector

License type	Public sector	Private sector
Production	4	969
Supply	0	150
Distribution	0	21
Organized industry production	0	1
Conduction-transmission	1	0

Source: EPİAŞ, https://rapor.epias.com.tr/rapor/xhtml/dgpKatilimciSayisi.xhtml

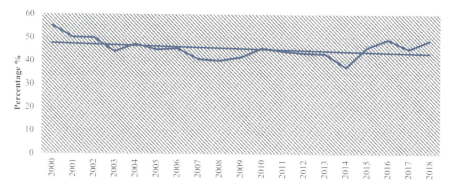

Fig. 8 Domestic resource share in electricity production. (Source: TEIAŞ. 2020)

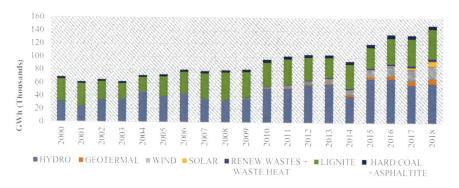

Fig. 9 Domestic resources based on electricity generation. (Source: TEİAŞ)

To cope with the electricity demand in the market, several new tools have been introduced. The capacity mechanism, one of the most important instruments, was set to hold electric power plants at disposal in case of urgency. Considering the high-energy dependency rates of Turkey, such a supporting system also could help to enhance energy supply security.

The last step that completes the liberalization process of the electricity market is the opening of EPİAŞ. Balancing Power Market (BPM) and the Day-ahead market were

47 Energy Governance in Turkey

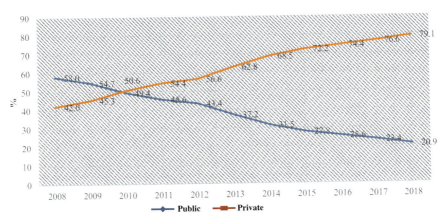

Fig. 10 Share of the public and private sector in installed capacity. (Source: TEİAŞ. 2020)

Table 4 Share of the public and private sector in hydropower plants

			HPP by DSI, 1956–2018			HPP by private sector, 1924–2018		
Nbr of HPP	Installed power (MW)	Average energy production (GWh/Year)	Nbr of HPP	Installed power (MW)	Average energy production (GWh/Year)	Nbr of HPP	Installed power (MW)	Average energy production (GWh/Year)
659	28,431.02	98,332.33	67	12,559.31	44,574.38	592	15,871.71	53,757.95

Source: State Hydraulic Works (Devlet Su İşleri-DSİ 2020)

performing together with the name of Market Financial Settlement Center "PMUM" until EPİAŞ was established in 2015. Since then, the day-ahead market and intraday market have been operating under the control of EPİAŞ. BPM separately serves under TEİAŞ. The new mechanism has constituted a basis for compliance to the European Network of Transmission System Operators for Electricity (ENTSO-E) which aims at setting an ambitious EU energy market with further liberalization.

Consequently, it should be addressed that the liberalization process of the electricity market has directly changed the participation of the public and private sectors as seen in Fig. 10. Another striking figure related to the participation of the private sector is given in Table 4. The number of hydroelectric power plants constructed by the private sector is almost nine times higher than the ones set by State Hydraulic Works. The government has gained about $10 billion from the ongoing privatization of thermal power plants in the first half of the last decade. In the second half, this amount has been reported as $6.2 billion (Directorate of Privatization Administration).

Renewable Energy

Turkey, with a high energy security concern, has tried to diversify energy sources to reduce the adverse effects of supply shocks. IEA highlights the critical issues that Turkey should employ for a sustainable energy policy. Special attention should be paid to energy efficiency and renewable sources. As it is endowed with rich renewable energy sources, Turkey could have an advantage for a powerful energy transition. Renewables have a significant role in the energy transition process. The study conducted by Karbuz (2014) also sets forth the contribution of renewable energy in Turkey with a quantitative approach. Based on the two scenarios, conservative (based on the discreet policies in terms of implementing new resources) and proactive (based on encouraging diversification of energy supply), the obtained results reveal that the share of electricity generation from fossil fuels is likely to decrease more in the latter between 2012 and 2030. The difference in terms of reduction will be due to a large proportion of wind and the contribution of hydro and solar, respectively. Energy security through diversifying energy resources, increasing energy efficiency, liberalizing the electricity and gas market, and employing renewable energy has paved the way for setting sustainable energy governance.

Based on the installed capacity, hydropower ranks first with almost 63,9% of the total in 2019 (Fig. 11). In terms of geothermal and hydropower potential, Turkey has been listed in the top ten around the world; geothermal and hydropower rank fourth and eighth, respectively (IRENA 2020), and geothermal energy is not as attractive as hydropower. It is the same in the failure of solar power to attract investment compared to wind energy. This is mostly related to legal barriers set up for each type of renewable source. Related renewable energy legislation is compiled in Fig. 12.

The limited share of solar power could be related to higher export rates for solar power equipment. While the share of the high technology import of solar energy equipment is 48%, the export share is only 4%. This could inevitably lead to a

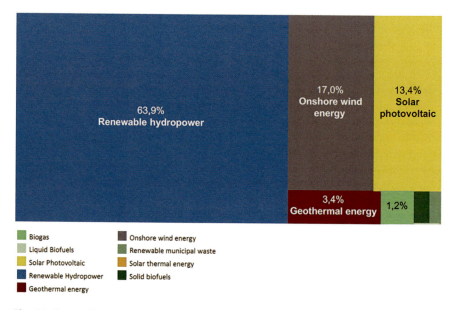

Fig. 11 Renewable energy technology based on installed capacity. (Source: IRENA)

Renewable Energy Legislation in Turkey

Law			Regulation	
1. The Law No. 6446	2. The Law No. 5346	3. The Law No. 5686	Technical analysis of renewable energy sources for electricity	Support electricity production process
The law defines electricity energy market in which production, transfer, sale and export/import are conducted within the scope of competition rule.	The policies for encouraging renewable energy and the base for constructing domestic manufacturing industry for renewable enegry equipments.	The main aim of the law is to put forth principles about exploration, production and protection of geothermal and natural mineral water resources	-Electricity Market License Regulation -Technical Analysis of Solar, Wind Power Applications for electricity generation	-Support for using domestic equipment while producing electricity -Support for research and development projects

Fig. 12 Renewable energy legislation

technology gap. Thus, renewable energy policy should be pursued with technology-supporting R&D activities. Rather than increasing the capacity of renewable energy, it is more important to invest in renewable energy technology, because each additional capacity increase in renewable energy could lead to an increase in the trade deficit in both solar and wind energy (Shura 2019). A rise in renewable energy technology levels would also raise opportunities for the manufacturing of renewable energy equipment (Fig. 13). Renewable energy investments are likely to stimulate business opportunities and ensures a qualified workforce that the sector needs. Considering that hydro power dominates the majority of renewable energy employment (Fig. 13), the necessity of development in the other fields is emerging for a more comprehensive renewable energy policy. Thus, renewable energy transmission could provide a new branch for the domestic manufacturing sector behind low carbon economy transmission. Figure 14 reveals that R&D studies in Turkey in terms of the number of patents have mainly focused on improving solar power. Although the number of patents is not satisfactory, its increasing share in total could be promising for the progress of solar power.

An increasing level of renewable energy in Turkey's final energy consumption could be seen as an opportunity for the domestic-energy-manufacturing sector. Renewable Energy Resources Zones (RE-ZONE), which are allocated for renewable energy projects, serve this purpose. Within the scope of RE-ZONE, wind and solar power plants must provide a certain domestic production rate in equipment used. It is obligatory to have a certain amount of domestic employment in the R&D centers of these plants as well. The main aim is to reduce technology imports and improve domestic production skills. Considering the positive externalities in terms of new opportunities for employment and trade, RE-ZONE is significant. With spillover effects of RE-ZONE and the geopolitical importance as well, Turkey could also be a

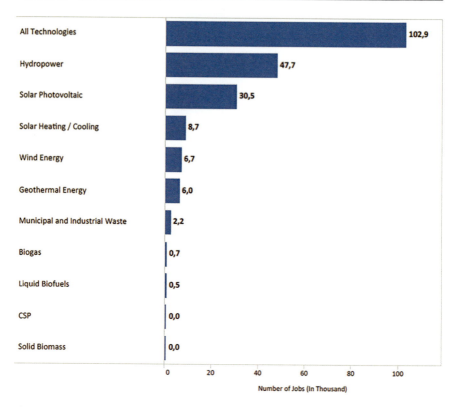

Fig. 13 Renewable energy employment by technology. (Source: IRENA)

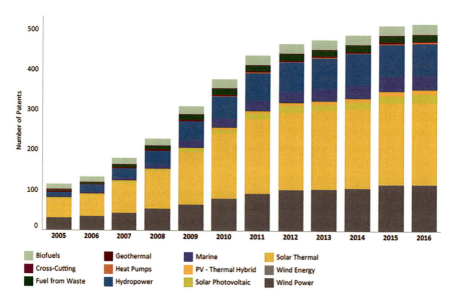

Fig. 14 Renewable energy patents evolution – Turkey. (Source: IRENA)

candidate for renewable energy hub. For this purpose, subsidies for the construction of renewable energy facilities should not be reached only by large shareholders but also by microscale ones. If all available information on renewable energy (technical details regarding power plant construction, technological improvements in terms of tools and techniques, etc.) could be shared with all stakeholders, the process would work much more beneficially (TMMOB 2019).

At this point, it is also essential to emphasize the importance of foreign direct investment (FDI) in the renewable energy sector, also called Green Foreign Direct Investment (GFDI). As GFDI offers job opportunities and makes the transfer of technology and knowledge easier, it could be considered as a promising development policy for an environmentally friendly growth strategy. Thus, to increase FDI flow in the renewable energy sector, related legislation should be amended under the current conditions. Turkey, in this context, has proposed several investment models to establish a lucrative investment environment. The aim is to increase the share of the energy sector FDI in the total (As of 2018, the energy sector FDI in the total is almost 9%).

As demonstrated in Fig. 15, FDI flow has experienced a rise until 2011 and hit the highest level at 4293 million USD. After a sharp decrease following a peak, it has continued to fall steadily. And the recent level of flow (2019) is below 98% of the highest record. New policy tools should be introduced to revive the investment climate. Fiscal measures such as tax incentives, feed-in tariffs, and carbon taxation tools are proved to be the most efficient ones to attract FDI (Wall et al. 2019). Similarly, tax exemption and avoidance of double taxation as they reduce investment costs are also effective for driving FDI inflows (Mahbub and Jongwanish 2019). Keeley and Matsumoto (2018), on the other hand, underline the recent FDI inflow dynamics that are found to be more important than the traditional ones. Recently, the competitive environment and opportunities offered by local legislation have been decisive for investors. Besides, the depth of incentives is one of the key instruments to determine the direction of FDI inflows.

As we discussed above, energy investments may result in huge losses. Arguably, lack of storage and the difficulty of foreseeing electricity demand could be the main reasons. Excess demand for electricity could disrupt financing of the sector, as the vast majority of its debt is in foreign currency, which is quite volatile against the Turkish lira. Turkey's renewable energy sector has tried to cope with the emerging

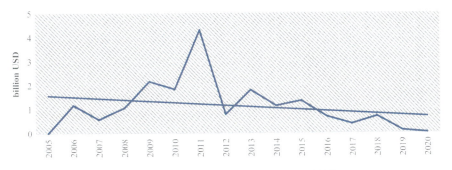

Fig. 15 Inward FDI to electricity and natural gas. (Source: TCMB 2020)

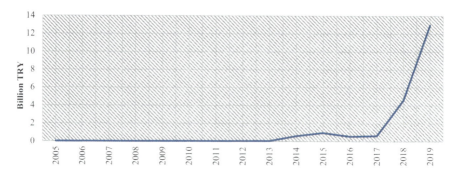

Fig. 16 Nonperforming loan volume in renewable energy. (Source: Banking Regulation and Supervision Agency 2020)

investment debt crisis. According to the current data released by Banking Regulation and Supervision Agency, nonperforming loan has strikingly increased since 2017 (Fig. 16). In 2018, an increase in the nonperforming loan was recorded by 633% compared to the previous year.

This could be highly linked to the fall in Turkish currency against the dollar. As players in the energy sector borrow in foreign currency, depreciation of TL has led to a considerable burden on them. As a result, some of the foreign investors have pulled out of the Turkish energy market such as German EWE and Austria OMV (Sözcü 2018a, b). As a precaution against rising nonperforming loan volume, the Banks Association of Turkey structured the Renewable Energy Venture Capital Fund. The debt volume reaching to almost $13 billion has made such a formation mandatory. Overall, the current debt crisis is likely to result in not only financial consequences but also difficulties for improving the technological level of the renewable energy; manufacturing sector as a foreign direct investment makes technology transfer easier.

Renewable Energy Incentive Mechanism

To promote the use of renewable energy sources, an incentive mechanism called the Renewable Energy Sources Support (RES Support) has been introduced in 2010. The main aim is to provide an attractive market for renewable energy investors. Both licensed and unlicensed facilities could benefit from the incentives within the scope of RES Support. Feed-in tariffs, for a maximum of 10 years, could be the most remarkable tool of the support mechanism among the others: land acquisition (permissions for the areas under the disposal of state), domestic equipment support (for licensed facilities), and regionally differentiated supports. The number of RES Support projects has increased by almost 40-fold since 2011. As Fig. 17 illustrates, RES Support incentives have continued to rise at a rapid rate. RES Support will expire by the end of 2020. However, it is highly expected that there will be regulations ensuring the continuation of the incentive mechanism. Yet, throughout the time, the cost of funding RES Support projects has been noticeably increased due to both electricity price and exchange rate effect. The cost per unit of energy for RES Support is 139.531 TRY as of March 2020 (EPİAŞ). The other obstacles to better functioning of the incentive system

47 Energy Governance in Turkey

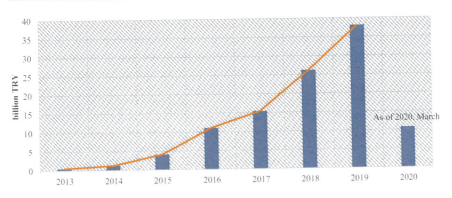

Fig. 17 RES Support incentives. (Source: EPİAŞ)

could be uncertainty in electricity prices, exchange rate volatility, and long-term finance requirement for investments (IEA 2016). Under these circumstances, such support mechanisms due to the abovementioned difficulties are vital to accelerating the renewable energy transition.

Natural Gas Market Liberalization

The natural gas market, on the other hand, has remained largely under state control (i.e., BOTAŞ), and this has prevented the energy market from further development. Contrary to growing demand, notably low production level in natural gas brings up supply security to the current energy agenda. There has been a close link between natural gas market liberalization and supply security (PwC 2014).

It is widely accepted that the liberalization process of the natural gas market is not able to reach the level that the electricity market has attained. Considering the natural gas share in electricity generation and impact on the electricity market, this gap is likely to seem quite complicated. The most visible reason could be the failure of the continuation of the unbundling process. Although requirements regarding the separation of trading, transmission, and storage activities of natural gas have been enacted by EMRA with current regulations (published in No. 30024 Official Gazette on 31 March 2017), the distribution of natural gas is the only service no longer dominated by BOTAŞ.

Moreover, both retail and wholesale markets should be competitive to complete the unbundling process. The retail market has improved by fostering a competitive environment. Customers with consumption above 75,000 cm have obtained a concession to choose their suppliers since 2013. Moreover, the liberalization of the natural gas market is of vital importance in the sense that it contributes to Turkey's pledge to become a regional natural gas hub. Turkey has a geographical advantage, as it is located at the center of natural gas trade from the world's richest gas reserves of Europe and Asia. This has offered a favorable opportunity; however, Turkey is unlikely to progress due to a noticeable dominance of state-owned entities (i.e., BOTAŞ) and lack of legal framework. Acknowledging that Russian gas dominates half of the natural gas market with a higher price tag than the European average, Özdemir (2017b, 111) puts that Turkey has turned into "a gas corridor especially for producers [primarily Russia] rather than consumers." Actually, creating comprehensive and well-organized legislation on this issue could be a virtual tool for the energy chapter of EU negotiations. The main EU legislation regarding the natural gas market (EU Gas Directive 2009/73/EC, Gas Regulation No. 715/2009) requires full separation of trade, transmission, and storage activities, and transparency of the wholesale market.

Coordination Mechanisms and Issues of Multilevel Governance

Turkey with rapidly increasing CO_2 emissions should set a well-designed climate change adaptation and mitigation policy. Republic of Turkey Climate Change Strategy 2010–2020 set the objective to "integrate policies and measures for mitigating and adapting to climate change into national development plans" (p. 11). As mentioned in the drivers of the energy transition section, the Climate Change Coordination Committee (CCCC) was established in 2001. This committee was reconstituted as the Climate Change and Air Management Coordination Committee encompassing several members ranging from related Ministries (Ministry of Environment and Urbanization, Energy and Natural Resources, Industry and Technology, Interior, Foreign Affairs, Health) to Unions of Business Associations (TOBB, TÜSİAD, MÜSİAD) in 2013. One should note that the committee has neither environmental NGOs nor academics among its members (IEA 2016).

In line with the global efforts for climate change concern, Turkey became a party to UNFCCC in 2004 and signed the Kyoto Protocol in 2009. Throughout the first period of the Kyoto Protocol until 2012, Turkey was not expected to commit any quantitative emission mitigation targets since it was not a member of Annex-B countries. Since then, efforts to conduct a legal framework of climate change policies have accelerated. The first official document released by the Ministry of Environment and Urbanization (MoEU) is "Climate Change Strategy 2010-2023." One of the striking targets mentioned in the document is to increase the share of renewable energy to 30% in electricity generation by 2023. Turkey has been able to achieve 28.6% of the target as of 2018. Another important long-term aim set in the Climate Change Strategy by 2020 is a decrease in energy intensity compared to the 2004 level. However, the current data demonstrate that there has been no remarkable decline in the energy intensity per unit of GDP (energy intensity decreased from 3.3 to 3.0 MJ/USD from 2004 to 2016). As required by the Climate Change Strategy, "Turkey's National Climate Change Adaptation Strategy and Action Plan" was introduced in 2012. The plan lists the actions that should be taken to ensure climate change adaptation. Water resources and forestry management, agriculture security, natural disaster risk analysis, and health management are the headings within the scope of the actions. Nonetheless, the aims are mostly based on identifying the possible effects of climate change rather than setting quantitative targets to mitigate.

Besides the abovementioned plan and actions, climate change concern has taken place in the Development Plans as it is one of the most critical dimensions of sustainability. The term climate change together with greenhouse gas emissions first appears in the VIII. Development Plan (2001–2005). The only intention set forth is the necessity of the "Action Plan" to be prepared. However, both the IX. and X. Development Plans lack concrete measures against climate change. Moreover, even the recent one (XI. Development Plan, 2019–2023) has contained no quantitative targets in terms of greenhouse gas mitigation. As underlined by Acar and Yeldan (2018), sectoral emission reduction targets should be taken into account while implementing efficient climate change policies.

Undoubtedly, it is also crucial to employ appropriate fiscal tools while constructing a comprehensive climate change policy. From the point of view of tax policy, the environmental tax has been applied to internalize environmental costs. However, the scope of the environmental tax could not be defined well. For just "environment cleaning," residents and commercial buildings are liable for paying the tax to the municipality. As it is charged by a fixed amount determined by the municipality, the efficiency of the tax policy has remained controversial. It is considered that the environmental tax is just a tool for municipalities' revenue rather than the one which internalizes environmental damage. However, environmental tax within this context is far away from setting a cost to polluters. Despite "environmental tax" (also known as "environmental cleaning tax"), which is the only direct tax levied on consumers, there are other types of taxes such as motor vehicle tax, special consumption tax to indirectly internalize negative externalities of environmental damage. These indirect taxes have been published by EUROSTAT under the same category as "environmental tax" to make a meaningful comparison in terms of the cost of pollution. EUROSTAT has split the environmental tax into three subcomponents: energy taxes, transport taxes, and taxes on pollution and resources. While energy taxes include energy products for both transport and stationary purposes and greenhouse gases, transport taxes consist of the taxes appearing in each type of transportation transaction (annual motor vehicle tax, flight tickets, congestion charges, and city tools). Also, taxes on pollution and resources cover extracting and harvesting of natural resources and polluting activities shown in Figs. 18 and 19; Turkey has experienced a striking decrease since 2016, contrary to a stable increasing trend for taxes in the EU.

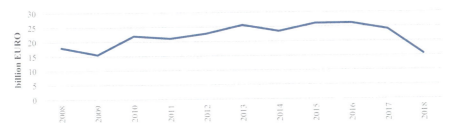

Fig. 18 Environmental tax revenues – Turkey. (Source: EUROSTAT)

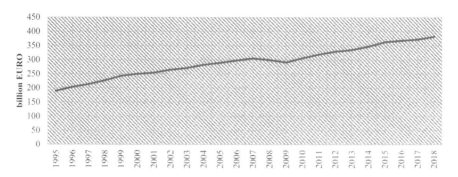

Fig. 19 Environmental tax revenues – EU. (Source: EUROSTAT)

Oil Storage Activities

High oil import rates along with the rising share of oil products in total consumption have made it essential to deliberate on measures for a secure supply of oil. The oil crises in the 1970s could be seen as a driving force for taking such precautions as the period had led to huge supply shortages. As a result, an oil-stockholding process, the Strategic Petroleum Reserve (SPR), has been employed by many countries. The level of the SPR that countries are liable to hold is determined proportionally to their import levels. The higher level of the SPR, by this means, could mitigate the adverse consequences of a lack of prompt supply.

In line with the international stockholding standards, 40% of SPR must be processed and 60% must be composed of crude oil. The management of SPR should not be steered by the state. Private agencies could also take part in it. The well-known independent agencies conducting stockholding are in Germany (EBV), Belgium (APETRA), Netherland (COVA), Hungary (HUSA), and Swiss (CARBURA) as well.

In Turkey, the Directorate General of Mining has carried out stockholding operations and Petroleum affiliated to MENR since 2018. Under Article 6 of the Petroleum Market Law No. 5015, the industry is obliged to keep stock. The total liability is 10.5 million tons. After a steady trend from the end of the 1990s to 2010, oil stock has exhibited an increase. Along with the SPR sites determined by the government, refineries and distributors are also responsible for holding SPR.

Turkish Petroleum Refineries Corporation (TUPRAS) conducts all refinery activities. There are main four refineries İzmir, İzmit, Batman, and Kırıkkale encompassed by the TUPRAS. Of these four refineries, İzmit and İzmir have equal processing capacity with an amount of 11 million tonnes. Kırıkkale and Batman rank third and last with the processing capacity of 5 and 1.1 million tonnes, respectively.

Additionally, as a part of the obligatory national petrol stock requirement, the coupon system was introduced in 2017. Within the scope of the coupon system, distributor companies and refineries are supposed to reserve 20 times of their daily circulation as stock. The coupon system is also very important in terms of leakage and losses tracking as it provides online monitoring of oil stock.

Natural Gas Storage

Increasing natural gas consumption has reached to nearly 50 billion m3 per year. At certain times of the year, particularly winter, this hits the highest figures being the most preferred type of energy for residential heating. Natural gas supply that is insufficient to meet increasing demand has been prominently featured in media as well. Both threats of closing down gas taps and insufficient gas storage levels have been the headlines of the last years. To overcome the problem arising from the inadequate gas supply which also threatens energy security to a great extent, Turkey has made significant investments. In this regard, the construction of gas storage facilities has been becoming more critical to ensure supply security.

Each storage type, namely underground and liquefied natural gas (LNG), has been employed to reduce vulnerability to the natural gas supply shortage (Berk and Ediger 2018). Lake Tuz Natural Gas Storage starting to operate in Aksaray Province with a salt dome structure is one of the largest underground facilities. With a capacity of 1.2 billion cubic meters, it takes second place after Silivri Underground Natural Gas Facility with a capacity of 2.8 billion cubic meters. For expansion in Silivri and Lake Tuz Storage facilities' capacity, a $1.2 billion loan has been provided after an agreement signed between BOTAŞ and the Industrial and Commercial Bank of China (ICBC) in 2018. Lake Tuz Storage expansion project has also received an additional loan of $600 million jointly provided by the World Bank and the Asian Infrastructure Investment Bank. Thus, 20% of total consumption is planned to be stored by 2023. Additionally, the storage capacity of Tuz Lake will increase from 1.2 billion m3 to 5.4 billion m3 to become the largest natural gas storage facility (salt dome formation) in the world. The other two storage facilities, operating since 2014, are located in Mersin.

LNG storage has been employed particularly since 2010. LNG makes both storage and transportation easier as converting natural gas to LNG can decrease the volume up to 600 times. In Turkey, there are four LNG storage facilities located in Hatay, İzmir, and Tekirdağ Provinces. Among these facilities, Hatay Dörtyol and İzmir Aliağa have Floating Storage Regasification Units (FSRU) which can regasify stored LNG. Moreover, FSRUs could reduce dependence on pipeline imports and provide a supply source which can be easily accessible. So, energy security could also be enhanced.

Outcomes, Challenges, and Prospects of Energy Governance

A growing literature has been discussing the utility of energy governance to address the energy trilemma and harness energy transition. It is a challenging task for emerging economies with rapidly growing populations to prioritize accessing uninterrupted affordable energy supplies to fuel the growth of their carbon-intense economies. As an upper-middle-income developing country, through its neoliberal developmentalist model, Turkey has embarked on ensuring its energy security in three ways: (1) exploiting domestic resources (coal, hydro, and renewables), nuclear power generation, and increasing energy efficiency; (2) energy market liberalization; and (3) energy diplomacy (i.e., pipeline politics) with an ambitious vision to become a regional energy hub. Those policies have prompted mixed unless contradictory, interrelated outcomes for the country's energy governance.

First, Turkey's energy governance has not managed to decrease the energy intensity level of its carbon-based economy, which is still one of the highest among OECD countries. However, it does not have a concrete plan for energy-intensity improvement, and its intended nationally determined contributions (INDCs) in the Paris Conference (COP 21) are far from expectations. The country still struggles to improve its energy efficiency in the overall economy and divert away from carbon-intense sectors (e.g., iron-steel and cement). Second, the rate of renewable energy (excluding hydro) utilization has not commensurated with growing energy consumption. Despite their dramatic increase in generating electricity, the rate of renewable energy (excluding hydro) contribution has remained relatively low (Fig. 1). Third, the ratio of domestic energy production to consumption has declined and reached today's levels of 25–30%. This means that Turkey has become more dependent on imported energy (e.g., oil, natural gas, and coal) (Fig. 3). Due to regionalized characteristics of natural gas markets and its insufficient storage/LNG facilities, Turkey has been procuring its natural gas primarily through pipelines from few suppliers, mainly from Russia. Fourth, Turkey's ambitious energy diplomacy for procurement diversification and elevating its transit role to a regional energy hub caused mixed results. On the one hand, the materialization of the SGC has not only supplied additional Azeri gas to its energy portfolio but also contributed Turkey's pledge to become the fourth arbitrary of the European natural gas market, unless regional energy hub. On the other hand, Turkey's coercive energy diplomacy in the Eastern Mediterranean has further strained its relations with the EU. Fifth, Turkey has completed the electricity market liberalization. The process is at standstill in the natural gas sector in which the state-led BOTAŞ's dominance has been continuing.

Those outcomes of Turkey's energy governance come with various challenges for the country's energy transition. First, Turkey's neoliberal developmentalist model and ambitious (coercive) energy diplomacy provide limited prospects for policy diffusion and policy transfer from the EU's energy governance. Regardless of their mutual success in the materialization of the SGC, this has not served as a catalyzer to converge Turkey's energy governance to the EU's standards. Adding insult to injury, the energy chapter is still closed. Second, Turkey's failure to liberalize the natural gas sector, the dependency of regulatory agency (i.e., EMRA) on the state, and uncertainties in initiatives/licensing yield additional risk for investors. Third, more than 40 billion USD worth of sunk credit in the electricity sector cast doubt on its governance. Fourth, long-term take or pay contracts with a changing price tag over the European average set the legal framework for Turkey's natural gas trade with Russia. Fifth, Turkey is highly dependent on Russia not only in natural gas supplies but also in import infrastructure (i.e., pipelines). Sixth, the country has limited gas storage capacity (5% of its annual consumption) and LNG capacity (15% of its annual consumption). Seventh, there is neither investment in the storage of renewable energy nor in new electricity transmission lines. Finally, the Turkish government will likely cut the budget of renewable energy resources supports mechanisms by shifting priorities away from energy transition amid COVID-19.

Despite those challenges, there are numerous prospects for energy transition. First, post-COVID 19 provides a significant opportunity for Turkey to revitalize the economy through the renewables energy sector and energy-efficient technologies. Second, Turkey has significant idle renewable energy, particularly solar and wind. Third, the EU and the World Bank provide generous funding for Turkey's energy transition projects. Fourth, the shrinking costs of renewable energy technologies will increase the feasibility of utilizing its idle resources. Fifth, Turkey's generous Renewable Energy Resources Support Mechanism will likely be updated. Sixth, EPİAŞ's transparency platform could contribute to the improvement of energy governance. Seventh, numerous local governments' plans and/or initiatives are supposed to back carbon emission reductions. Eighth, the presence of environmental organizations with international networks is posed to inform public debates and increase public awareness, and public broadcasts and campaigns may raise public awareness. Those informational factors could count on the already existing sensibility of environmental risks and uncertainties in the Turkish public. Ninth, contract renewable dates for long-term take or pay contracts in natural gas are approaching. Last but not least, Turkey's natural gas discoveries of the Turkish Black Sea coast could import energy dependence, thereby, cut the country's energy bills.

Cross-References

▶ Energy Democracy and Participation in Energy Transitions
▶ Energy Governance in Azerbaijan
▶ Energy Governance in Europe: Introduction
▶ Energy Governance in Russia: From a Fossil to a Green Giant?
▶ Monitoring Energy Policy
▶ The EU in Global Energy Governance

References

Acar, S., & Yeldan, A. E. (2018). Investigating patterns of carbon convergence in an uneven economy: The case of Turkey. *Structural Change and Economic Dynamics, 46*, 96–106. https://doi.org/10.1016/j.strueco.2018.04.006.

Acar, S., Kitson, L., & Bridle, R. (2015). *Subsidies to coal and renewable energy in Turkey.* International Institute for Sustainable Development (IISD), Global Subsidies Initiative Report.

Adaman, F., Akbulut, B., & Arsel, M. (2017). Introduction neoliberal developmentalism in turkey: Continuity, rupture, consolidation. In F. Adaman, B. Akbulut, & M. Arsel (Eds.), *Neoliberal Turkey and its discontents: Economic policy and the environment under Erdogan* (pp. 1–17). London/New York: I.B. Tauris.

Adaman, F., Arsel, M., & Akbulut, B. (2019). Neoliberal developmentalism, authoritarian populism, and extractivism in the countryside: The Soma mining disaster in Turkey. *The Journal of Peasant Studies, 46*(3), 514–536. https://doi.org/10.1080/03066150.2018.1515737.

AK Parti. (2012). *2023 Siyasi Vizyonu: Siyaset, Toplum, Dünya (Political Vision 2023: Politics, Society, World)*. Ankara: AK Parti Genel Merkezi. https://www.akparti.org.tr/site/akparti/2023-siyasi-vizyon. Accessed 13 May 2020.

Akkemik, K. A., & Oğuz, F. (2011). Regulation, efficiency and equilibrium: A general equilibrium analysis of liberalization in the Turkish electricity market. *Energy, 36*(5), 3282–3292. https://doi.org/10.1016/j.energy.2011.03.024.

Arsel, M., Akbulut, B., & Adaman, F. (2015). Environmentalism of the malcontent: Anatomy of an anti-coal power struggle in Turkey. *The Journal of Peasant Studies, 42*(2), 371–395. https://doi.org/10.1080/03066150.2014.971766.

Aydın, C. İ. (2020). Nuclear energy debate in Turkey: Stakeholders, policy alternatives, and governance issues. *Energy Policy, 136*, 1–17. https://doi.org/10.1016/j.enpol.2019.111041.

Balaban, O. (2019). Challenges to Turkey's transition to a low-carbon urban development: A roadmap for an effective climate change policy. In Ö. B. Ö. Sarı, S. S. Özdemir, & N. Uzun (Eds.), *Urban and regional planning in Turkey* (pp. 261–279). Cham: Springer.

Balkan-Şahin, S. (2018). Nuclear energy as a hegemonic discourse in Turkey. *Journal of Balkan and Near Eastern Studies, 21*(4), 443–461. https://doi.org/10.1080/19448953.2018.1506282.

Bayraktar, A. (2018). Energy transition in Turkey. *Turkish Policy Quarterly, 17*(3), 19–26.

BDDK. (2020). *Monthly banking sector data*. Available at: https://www.bddk.org.tr/BultenAylik/en.

Berk, İ., & Ediger, V. Ş. (2018). A historical assessment of Turkey's natural gas import vulnerability. *Energy, 145*, 540–547. https://doi.org/10.1016/j.energy.2018.01.022.

Bilgili, M., Bilirgen, H., Ozbek, A., Ekinci, F., & Demirdelen, T. (2018). The role of hydropower installations for sustainable energy development in Turkey and the world. *Renewable Energy, 126*, 755–764.

Boşnak, B. (2016). Europeanisation and de-Europeanisation dynamics in Turkey: The case of environmental organisations. *South European Society and Politics, 21*(1), 75–90. https://doi.org/10.1080/13608746.2016.1151476.

Colantoni, L., Kormaz, D., Sartori, N., Schröder M., Sever, S. D., & Yilmaz, S. (2017a, March). *Energy and climate strategies, interests and priorities of the EU and Turkey*. FEUTURE Online Paper No. 2. Available at: https://feuture.uni-koeln.de/sites/feuture/user_upload/FEUTURE_5.2_Energy_and_Climate_Strategies.pdf. Accessed 1 May 2020.

Colantoni, L., Sever, S. D., & Yilmaz, S. (2017b, September). *Energy and climate security priorities and challenges in the changing global energy order*. FEUTURE Online Paper No. 6, Available at: https://feuture.uni-koeln.de/sites/feuture/pdf/FEUTURE_Online_Paper_5.4.pdf. Accessed on 13 May 2020.

Demir, O. (2020). Turkey's natural gas market liberalisation in the context of the EU. In O. Demir (Ed.), *Liberalisation of natural gas markets: Potential and challenges of integrating Turkey into the EU market* (pp. 161–229). Singapore: Palgrave Macmillan.

Directorate General of Energy Affairs. (2020). *Energy balance tables*. Available at: https://enerji.gov.tr/enerji-isleri-genel-mudurlugu-denge-tablolari-en.

DSI. (2020). *Official statistics*. Available at: http://www.dsi.gov.tr/dsi-resmi-istatistikler/resmi-istatistikler-2018/2018-y%C4%B1l%C4%B1-verileri.

EC. (2019). *Turkey report*. Available at: https://www.ab.gov.tr/siteimages/resimler/20190529-turkey-report(1).pdf. Accessed on 13 May 2020.

Ediger, V. Ş. (2003). Classification and performance analysis of primary energy consumers during 1980–1999. *Energy Conversion and Management, 44*, 2991–3000. https://doi.org/10.1016/S0196-8904(03)00102-X.

Ediger, V. Ş. (2009). Türkiye'nin sürdürülebilir enerji gelişimi [Turkey's sustainable energy development]. *TÜBA Günce, 39*, 18–25.

Ediger, V. Ş., & Bowlus, J. V. (2019). A Farewell to King Coal: Geopolitics, energy security, and the transition to oil, 1898–1917. *The Historical Journal, 62*(2), 427–449. https://doi.org/10.1017/S0018246X18000109.

Ediger, V. Ş., Berk, İ., & Kösebalaban, A. (2014). Lignite resources of Turkey: Geology, reserves, and exploration history. *International Journal of Coal Geology, 132*, 13–22. https://doi.org/10.1016/j.coal.2014.06.008.

Ediger, V. Ş., Kirkil, G., Çelebi, E., Ucal, M., & Kentmen-Çin, Ç. (2018). Turkish public preferences for energy. *Energy Policy, 120*, 492–502. https://doi.org/10.1016/j.enpol.2018.05.043.

EPİAŞ. (2020). *EPIAS transparency platform*. Available at: https://seffaflik.epias.com.tr/transparency/index.xhtml.

Erdoğdu, E. (2007). Nuclear power in open energy markets: A case study of Turkey. Energy Policy, 35, 3061-307.

Erensü, S. (2017). Turkey's hydopower renaissance: Nature, neoliberalism and development in the cracks of infrastructure. In F. Adaman, B. Akbulut, & M. Arsel (Eds.), *Neoliberal Turkey and its discontents: Economic policy and the environment under Erdogan* (pp. 120–146). London/New York: I.B. Tauris.

Erensü, S. (2018). Powering neoliberalization: Energy and politics in the making of a new Turkey. *Energy Research and Social Science, 41*, 148–157. https://doi.org/10.1016/j.erss.2018.04.037.

Erşen, E., & Çelikpala, M. (2019). Turkey and the changing energy geopolitics of Eurasia. *Energy Policy, 128*, 584–592. https://doi.org/10.1016/j.enpol.2019.01.036.

Ersoy, M., & İşeri, E. (2020). Framing environmental debates over nuclear energy in Turkey's polarized media system. *Turkish Studies*. https://doi.org/10.1080/14683849.2020.1746908.

Ertör-Akyazı, P., Adaman, F., Özkaynak, B., & Zenginobuz, Ü. (2012). Citizens' preferences on nuclear and renewable energy sources: Evidence from Turkey. *Energy Policy, 47*, 309–320. https://doi.org/10.1016/j.enpol.2012.04.072.

EUROSTAT. (2020). *Database*. Available at: https://ec.europa.eu/eurostat/data/database. Accessed on 15 April 2020.

Günay, D., & İşeri, E. (2017). Unexpected persistence amidst enlargement stasis: Usages of Europe in Turkey's nuclear energy debate. *South European Society and Politics, 22*(1), 101–119. https://doi.org/10.1080/13608746.2016.1151128.

Günay, D., İşeri, E., & Ersoy, M. (2018). Alternative media and the securitization of climate change in Turkey. *Alternatives, 43*(2), 96–114. https://doi.org/10.1177/0304375418820384.

Günay, D., İşeri, E., & Ersoy, M. (2019). Alternative Media and the Securitization of Climate Change in Turkey. *Alternatives: Global, Local, Political, 43*(2), 96–114. https://doi.org/10.1177/0304375418820384.

Hepbasli, A., & Özgener, Ö. (2004). Turkey's renewable energy sources: Part 1. Historical development. *Energy Sources, 26*(10), 961–969. https://doi.org/10.1080/00908310490473183.

IEA. (2020). *Data&Statistics*. Available at: https://www.iea.org/data-and-statistics/data-tables?country=WORLD.

IEA (International Energy Agency). (2016). *Energy policies of IEA countries: Turkey, 2016 review*. Paris, France: OECD/IEA. Available at: https://webstore.iea.org/energy-policies-of-iea-countries-turkey-2016-review. Accessed on 5 Apr 2020.

IMF. (October 2019). *World economic outlook database*. Available at: https://www.imf.org/external/pubs/ft/weo/2019/02/weodata/index.aspx. Accessed on 19 May 2020.

IRENA. (2020). *Data&Statistics*. Available at: https://www.irena.org/Statistics/View-Data-by-Topic/Capacity-and-Generation/Country-Rankings.

İşeri, E. (2015). Addressing the pipeline security regime of the prospective regional energy hub Turkey. *Security Journal, 28*(1), 1–15. https://doi.org/10.1057/sj.2012.38.

İşeri, E. (2019). Turkey's entangled (energy) security concerns and the Cyprus question in the Eastern Mediterranean. In A. Heraclides & G. A. Çakmak (Eds.), *Greece and Turkey in conflict and cooperation: From Europeanization to De-Europeanization* (pp. 257–270). London: Routledge.

İşeri, E., & Almaz, A. (2013). Turkey's Energy Strategy and the Southern Gas Corridor. *Caspian Report, 5*, 84–95.

İşeri, E., & Günay, D. (2017). Assessing Turkey's climate change commitments: The case of Turkey's energy policy. *Perceptions, 12*(2-3), 107–130.

İşeri, E., & Bartan, A. Ç. (2019). Turkey's geostrategic vision and energy concerns in the Eastern Mediterranean security architecture: A view from Ankara. In Z. Tziarras (Ed.), *The new geopolitics of the Eastern Mediterranean: Trilateral partnerships and regional security* (pp. 111–124). Nicosia: PRIO Cyprus Centre.

İşeri, E., Günay, D., & Almaz, A. (2018). Contending narratives on the sustainability of nuclear energy in Turkey. *Environment and Planning C: Politics and Space, 36*(1), 160–177. https://doi.org/10.1177/2399654417704199.

Karahan, H., & Toptas, M. (2013). The effect of power distribution privatization on electricity prices in Turkey: Has liberalization served the purpose? *Energy Policy, 63*, 614–621. https://doi.org/10.1016/j.enpol.2013.08.090.

Karbuz, S. (2014). Turkey's energy future. A quantitative assessment. *European Energy Journal, 4*(1), 67–70.

Karbuz, S. (2018). Geostrategic importance of East Mediterranean gas resources. In A. Dorsman, V. Ediger, & M. Karan (Eds.), *Energy economy, finance and geostrategy*. Cham: Springer. https://doi.org/10.1007/978-3-319-76867-0_12.

Keeley, A. R., & Matsumoto, K. (2018). Investors' perspective on determinants of foreign direct investment in wind and solar energy in developing economies-Review and expert opinions. *Journal Cleaner Production, 179*, 132–142.

Kızıl Voyvoda, Ö., & Voyvoda, E. (2019). Türkiye'de Enerji Sektörünün Yeniden Yapılandırılması Sürecinde Hukuk Düzenlemeleri – Elektrik Sektörü [Legal regulations in the process of restructuring of the energy sector in Turkey – Electricity sector]. *Çalışma Toplum, 60*(1), 127–154.

Knudsen, S. (2015). Protests against energy projects in Turkey: Environmental activism above politics? *British Journal of Middle Eastern Studies, 43*(3), 302–323. https://doi.org/10.1080/13530194.2015.1102707.

Mahbub, T., & Jongwanish, J. (2019). Determinants of Foreign Direct Investment (FDI) in the power sector: A case study of Bangladesh. *Energy Strategy Reviews, 24*, 178–192.

Melikoglu, M. (2017). Geothermal energy in Turkey and around the World: A review of the literature and an analysis based on Turkey's Vision 2023 energy targets. *Renewable and Sustainable Energy Reviews, 76*, 485–492. https://doi.org/10.1016/j.rser.2017.03.082.

MENR (2010). Republic of Turkey Climate Change Strategy 2010–2020 at: http://www.dsi.gov.tr/docs/iklim-degisikligi/ulusal_iklim_de%C4%9Fi%C5%9Fikli%C4%9Fi_strateji_belgesi_eng.pdf?sfvrsn=0. Accessed 17 Oct 2020.

MENR (2015). Republic of Turkey Ministry of Energy and Natural Resources. *2015–2019 Stratejik Planı* [Strategic plan of 2015–2019]. Available at: https://www.enerji.gov.tr/File/?path=ROOT%2F1%2FDocuments%2FStratejik+Plan%2FETKB+2015-2019+Stratejik+Plani.pdf. Accessed 1 May 2020.

MENR (2019). Republic of Turkey Ministry of Energy and Natural Resources. *2019–2023 Stratejik Planı* [Strategic plan of 2019–2023]. Available at: http://www.sp.gov.tr/upload/xSPStratejikPlan/files/LBigi+ENERJI_VE_TABII_KAYNAKLAR_BAKANLIGI_2019-2023_STRATEJIK_PLANI.pdf. Accessed 1 May 2020.

MENR (2017). Republic of Turkey Ministry of Energy and Natural Resources. *Milli Enerji ve Maden Politikası* [National Energy and Mineral Politics]. Available at: https://www.enerji.gov.tr/tr-tr/bakanlik-haberleri/milli-enerji-ve-maden-politikasi-tanitim-programi. Accessed 1 May 2020.

Oksay, S., & Iseri, E. (2011). A new energy paradigm for Turkey: A political risk-inclusive cost analysis for sustainable energy. *Energy Policy, 39*(5), 2386–2395. https://doi.org/10.1016/j.enpol.2011.01.061.

Öniş, Z. (2004). Turgut Özal and his economic legacy: Turkish neo-liberalism in critical perspective. *Middle Eastern Studies, 40*(4), 113–134. https://doi.org/10.1080/0026320041000170038.

Öniş, Z., & Yılmaz, Ş. (2009). Between Europeanization and Euro-Asianism: Foreign policy activism in Turkey during the AKP era. *Turkish Studies, 10*(1), 7–24. https://doi.org/10.1080/14683840802648562.

Özdemir, V. (2017a). *Doğal Gaz Piyasaları: Türkiye Enerji Güvenliği Üzerine Tezler* [Natural gas markets: Theses on Turkey's energy security]. İstanbul: Kaynak Yayınları.

Özdemir, V. (2017b). The political economy of the Turkey's gas geopolitics. In M. Schröder, M. O. Bettzüge, & W. Wessels (Eds.), *Turkey as an energy hub?* (pp. 109–122)., https://www.nomos-elibrary.de/10.5771/9783845282190-109/the-political-economy-of-the-turkey-s-gas-geopolitics. Accessed 1 May 2020.

Özdemir, V., & Raszewski, S. (2016). State and substate oil trade: The Turkey-KRG deal. *Middle East Policy, 23*(1), 125–135. https://doi.org/10.1111/mepo.12178.

Özler, Ş. İ., & Obach, B. (2018). Polarization and the environmental movement in Turkey. *Journal of Civil Society, 14*(4), 311–327. https://doi.org/10.1080/17448689.2018.1518773.

Paker, H., Adaman, F., Kadirbeyoğlu, Z., & Özkaynak, B. (2013). Environmental organisations in Turkey: Engaging the state and capital. *Environmental Politics, 22*(5), 760–778.

PETFORM (Petroleum and Natural Gas Platform Association). (2020). *Natural gas market in Turkey.* Available at: https://www.petform.org.tr/en/dogal-gaz-piyasasi/turkiye-dogal-gaz-piyasasi/.

Presidency of the Republic of Turkey Presidency of Strategy and Budget. (2019). *The Eleventh Development Plan* (2019–2023).

PwC. (2014). *Liberalizing natural gas in Turkey.* Available at: https://www.pwc.com.tr/tr/publications/industrial/energy/assets/dogal-gaz-piyasasi-raporu.pdf. Accessed 1 May 2020.

Raszewki, S. (2018). Emerging economies and energy: The case of Turkey. In A. Goldthau, M. F. Keating, & C. Kuzemko (Eds.), *Handbook of the international political economy of energy and natural resources* (pp. 263–280). Edward Elgar Publishing: Cheltenham.

Republic of Turkey Prime Ministry State Planning Organization. (2000). *Long term strategy and eight five-year development plan* (2001–2005).

Republic of Turkey Prime Ministry State Planning Organization. (2006). *Ninth development plan* (2007–2013).

Şahin, Ü. (2019). The politics of environment and climate change. In A. Özerdem & M. Whiting (Eds.), *The Routledge handbook of Turkish politics* (pp. 177–189). Oxon: Routledge.

Şahin, Ü., & Uzelgun, A. M. (2016). *İklim Değişikliği ve Medya* (Climate change and media) İstanbul Politikalar Merkezi. Available at: https://www.researchgate.net/profile/Uemit_Sahin3/publication/312070898_Iklim_Degisikligi_ve_Medya/links/586e28ff08ae8fce491b65f6/Iklim-Degisikligi-ve-Medya.pdf. Accessed 1 May 2020.

Savaşan, Z. (2019). Climate governance in Turkey: A forward-looking perspective. *Turkish Studies, 20*(4), 541–571. https://doi.org/10.1080/14683849.2019.1613895.

Sayan, R. C., & Kibaroğlu, A. (2020). Exploring environmental justice: Meaningful participation and Turkey's small-scale hydroelectricity power plants practices. In Z. Savaşan & V. Sümer (Eds.), *Environmental law and policies in Turkey* (pp. 141–158). Cham: Springer.

SHURA Energy Transition Centre. (2019). *Energy pricing and non-market flows in Turkey's Energy Sector, Istanbul.* Available at: https://www.shura.org.tr/wp-content/uploads/2020/05/raporweb_ENG-.pdf. Accessed 20 Apr 2020.

SHURA Energy Transition Centre. (2020). *The most economical solution for Turkey's Power System: Energy efficiency and business models, Istanbul.* Available at: https://www.shura.org.tr/executive-summary-the-most-economical-solution-for-turkeys-power-system-energy-efficiency-and-business-models/.

Sirin, S. M., & Ege, A. (2012). Overcoming problems in Turkey's renewable energy policy: How can EU contribute? *Renewable and Sustainable Energy Reviews, 16*(7), 4917–4926. https://doi.org/10.1016/j.rser.2012.03.067.

Sözcü. (2018a, March 30). *Alman EWE Türkiye'den Çıkıyor* [German EWE is existing from Turkey]. Retrieved from https://www.sozcu.com.tr/2018/ekonomi/alman-ewe-turkiyeden-cikiyor-2319563/. Accessed 28 May 2020.

Sözcü. (2018b, March 30). *OVM Türkiye'de Enerji Üretiminden Çıktı* [OVM existed from energy production in Turkey]. Retrieved from https://www.sozcu.com.tr/2018/ekonomi/ovm-turkiyede-enerji-uretiminden-cikti-2439682/. Accessed 28 May 2020.

TCMB. (2020). *Balance of payment statistics.* Available at: https://www.tcmb.gov.tr/wps/wcm/connect/TR/TCMB+TR/Main+Menu/Istatistikler/Odemeler+Dengesi+ve+Ilgili+Istatistikler/Odemeler+Dengesi+Istatistikleri/.

TEIAŞ. (2020). *Electricity statistics.* Available at: https://www.teias.gov.tr/tr-TR/turkiye-elektrik-uretim-iletim-istatistikleri.

TEPAV. (2016). Ensuring effective cooperation between EU and Turkey to foster energy security. *Policy Brief.* https://www.tepav.org.tr/upload/files/1502095519-7.Policy_Brief_July__2016_

Ensuring_Effective_Cooperation_Between_EU_and_Turkey_to_Foster_Energy_Security.pdf. Accessed 13 May 2020.

TMMOB Makina Mühendisleri Odası Enerji Çalışma Grubu (2019). *Türkiye Enerji Görünümü* [Turkey's Energy Profile] 2019.

Tsakiris, T., Ulgen, S., & Han, A. K. (2018). *Gas developments in the Eastern Mediterranean: Trigger or obstacle for EU-Turkey Cooperation*. FEUTURE Online Paper No. 22, Trans European Policy Studies Association. https://feuture.uni-koeln.de/sites/feuture/user_upload/Online_Paper_No.22_D5.6_final_upload1.pdf. Accessed 29 Apr 2020.

Turhan, E., Mazlum, C. S., Şorman, H. A., & Gündoğan, A. C. (2016). Beyond special circumstances: Climate change policy in Turkey 1992–2015. *WIREs Climate Change, 7*, 448–460. https://doi.org/10.1002/wcc.390.

Uluğbay, H. (2008). *İmparatorluk'tan Cumhuriyet'e Petropolitik* [Petropolitics from the Empire to the Republic]. Ankara: Farklı Yayıncılık.

Wall, R., Grafakos, S., Gianoli, A., & Stavropoulos, S. (2019). Which policy instruments attract foreign direct investment in renewable energy? *Climate Policy, 19*(1), 59–72.

WNA (World Nuclear Association). (2020, February). *Nuclear power in Turkey*. https://www.world-nuclear.org/information-library/country-profiles/countries-t-z/turkey.aspx. Accessed 28 May 2020.

Yalman, G. L. (2009). *Transition to Neoliberalism: The case of Turkey in the 1980s*. İstanbul: İstanbul Bilgi Üniversitesi Yayınları.

Yılmaz-Bozkus, Y. (2019). Analysis of Turkey's role as a possible energy hub. *Geo Journal, 84*, 1353–1364. https://link.springer.com/article/10.1007/s10708-018-9928-6.

Energy Governance in the United Kingdom

48

Matthew Lockwood, Catherine Mitchell, and Richard Hoggett

Contents

Introduction	1256
General Conditions of Energy Governance in the UK	1257
Legacies	1257
Composition of the Energy Mix	1259
Discourse on Energy Issues	1260
Political Institutions and Actors	1262
Coordination, Instruments, and Issues of the UK Energy Transition	1264
Drivers of Energy Transition	1264
Strategies and Instruments of Energy Transitions	1266
Coordination Mechanisms and Multilevel Governance	1274
Outcomes, Challenges, and Prospects of Energy Governance	1275
Cross-References	1279
References	1280

Abstract

The UK's energy transition path has been shaped by a legacy of fossil fuel use across electricity generation, transport and heat, but also by the institutions and ideas that make up the governance of energy. Some important elements, such as a market-led policy paradigm and the delegation of regulation to arm's-length bodies, are the result of privatization in the 1980s. Others, such as a heavily centralized, supply-led power sector and a resilient nuclear lobby, are

M. Lockwood (✉)
Science Policy Research Unit, University of Sussex, Brighton, UK
e-mail: m.lockwood@sussex.ac.uk

C. Mitchell · R. Hoggett
Energy Policy Group, University of Exeter, Penryn, UK
e-mail: Catherine.Mitchell@exeter.ac.uk; r.d.hoggett@exeter.ac.uk

© Springer Nature Switzerland AG 2022
M. Knodt, J. Kemmerzell (eds.), *Handbook of Energy Governance in Europe*,
https://doi.org/10.1007/978-3-030-43250-8_34

continuities from an earlier period. This governance system, strongly concentrated within central government, was challenged in a major way in the 2000s by a wave of concern about climate change. This driver has meant that the UK energy transition has been primarily about emissions reduction, rather than specific technologies such as renewable energy, whose expansion in the UK has largely been the result of European-level policy. With a preference for incentive-based and internalizing instruments over direct regulation arising from the market-led paradigm, the UK has managed to bring about a major decline in power sector emissions and some increase in renewable energy, especially in electricity generation, while at the same time trying to support a program of new nuclear build. However, as the country now enters the next phase of transition, involving integration of intermittent renewables into electricity sector systems and institutions, and of transport and heat into electricity, the coherence of policy, clarity of direction, and coordination of regulatory change are all open to question.

Keywords

Energy policy · Climate policy · Electricity · Governance · Transition · Policy paradigm · Lobby · Integration

Introduction

As it entered the era of energy transformation, the UK brought with it the legacy of a system with significant use of fossil fuels, especially coal in power generation, natural gas in heating, and petroleum products in transport. The response to this situation, especially since the 2000s, when climate change rose up the political agenda, has been shaped by a number of important aspects of the UK energy governance system.

The evolution of UK energy governance over the last 25 years can be seen as the product of a series of "critical junctures" (Capoccia and Kelemen 2007), interspersed with more gradual processes of institutional change, especially the layering of new policies on older ones (Mahoney and Thelen 2010), giving rise to an overall pattern of "punctuated evolution." The nature of energy policy over the last 30 years was fundamentally set by the privatization and liberalization reforms of the 1980s. These institutional changes were accompanied by a powerful market-led policy paradigm, which has evolved over time but remains deeply entrenched. This paradigm has driven a strong preference for internalizing and incentive-based instruments in energy policy and an aversion to direct regulation and administrative price setting. Privatization also created a powerful group of large incumbent energy utilities which have used their considerable influence over policy making to slow and shape (but not necessarily to stop) transition to a low-carbon system. Over a longer period, the UK has also had a resilient and persistent nuclear technology lobby. Another key continuity, especially within the electricity sector, is a centralized model of power generation, transmission, and distribution that has shaped policy thinking since the 1950s.

Energy governance has also been framed by the wider political economy. The UK has a highly centralized system of political administration, with little devolution of powers in energy policy, but with considerable delegation to arm's-length bodies, meaning that the key coordination challenges are within central government and between government and those bodies, rather than with nations, regions, and cities within the UK. The UK also has a large low-wage economy, which has produced a political reluctance to taxing energy use by households visibly and directly.

The resulting strategy for energy transition, which has thus far mainly focused on electricity as the lead sector, has been to use carbon pricing and incentive-based instruments to try to promote large-scale low-carbon technologies, notably new nuclear power and carbon capture and storage technologies. This strategy has been partially successful, especially through use of a carbon price floor to dramatically reduce coal-fired power generation, but it is in fact renewable electricity which has emerged as the main low-carbon alternative, despite resistance on the part of the government. This development shows the importance of the role of the European Union (EU) and raises questions about the direction the UK will take once it leaves.

The growth of renewable electricity generation places issues of intermittency and integration on the agenda. However, an equally profound challenge for the energy governance system arises from the rapid growth and development of distributed energy resources (DER) in the UK, including not only smaller-scale renewables but also demand-side response and storage (including batteries in electric vehicles). While much uncertainty remains, these developments point to the need for but also the possibility of a smart, flexible energy system that integrates electricity, heat, and transport in a hybrid system incorporating both large-scale generation and DER while also providing new solutions to the intermittency issue. They promise the possibility of deep decarbonization through a transformation of the system. But realizing this promise will depend upon whether UK energy governance and its institutions are adequate for the rapidity and scale of change. We argue that a new set of principles will be needed, including a focus on the needs of energy consumers, new governance frameworks for the local level, the fair and open use of data, and more legitimate and effective direction setting for and coordination of policy and regulatory change to support the transition.

General Conditions of Energy Governance in the UK

Legacies

The evolution of the UK energy system has been heavily influenced by its domestic natural resources, initially of coal, latterly of oil and gas, and now of wind. Coal played a key role in the Industrial Revolution, and it remained central to the economy until the middle of the twentieth century. From this point onward, however, a mix of foreign competition and action on pollution in the 1956 Clean Air Act drove its decline, which was further hastened by the 1984–1985 miners' strike (Turnheim and Geels 2012). Nevertheless, coal (largely imported) has continued to play an important role in power generation until very recently. Oil and gas from the North Sea became an important resource after the 1973 oil crisis. Gas in particular became the main energy source for domestic heating after the construction of the largest gas distribution network in Europe in the 1970s. In the 1990s gas also became an important fuel for electricity generation. However, North Sea oil and gas production peaked in the 1990s, and by the mid-2000s, the UK had become a net importer of both. In total the country now has a net import dependency of over a third of total energy used (BEIS 2017a). Thus while domestic natural energy resources themselves have now been seriously depleted, they have left a legacy of fossil fuel use across the energy system, in electricity, heat, and transport.

The pathway to decarbonization in the UK has also been shaped by its political and institutional legacies. Perhaps most important was the "critical juncture" of Thatcherism in the 1980s and the adoption of a neoliberal approach to wider economic policy. There was a dramatic shift in the paradigm for energy policy, from state ownership and planning to the market, and the creation of large privately owned energy companies (Helm 2004). At the same time, the UK economy more widely moved away from neo-corporatism toward deregulated labor markets, weak unions, and a large low-wage sector (Hall and Soskice 2001). These developments have produced a strong hostility to taxes among key sections of the electorate, meaning that successive governments have had an aversion to using financial incentives for energy and climate policy in the household sector. They have also led to an aversion to the notion of industrial policy.

However, there have also been some important continuities from the earlier postwar period. One is the highly centralized nature of the British state, with few veto players (Tsebelis 2002). While the 1990s saw a degree of devolution of policy to the newly created national assemblies in Scotland and Wales, the transfer of energy policy powers was limited, especially for the latter. Instead, Westminster-based governments have tended to delegate powers, especially to the energy regulator and, in some cases, to the energy industry itself. These deep-seated institutional arrangements have meant that the main challenge to the energy policy choices of the central state has come, externally, from the EU. They have also meant that contradictions have often opened up between high-level policy and detailed regulation in ways that have sometimes slowed the transition process.

A second continuity is the centralized, flexible supply nature of the socio-technical systems (Geels 2004) for energy. The dominant model for electricity since the 1940s has been generation by large-scale power plants and one-way transport via national and regional networks to consumers. There is a similar model for gas. The model for road transport energy is somewhat less centralized but still involves large-scale actors in production and refining and national distribution systems to fueling stations. In all cases, systems have been designed so that the supply of energy is flexible and meets whatever changes in demand there are. These characteristics of energy systems have had a considerable influence on the approach to governing the transition in the UK, especially in electricity.

A final legacy arises out of the UK's status as a nuclear state since the early 1950s. Johnstone et al. (2017) argue that the military use of nuclear technology has produced a civil nuclear energy lobby as a spillover from innovation policy and industrial systems linked to the former. Certainly, this lobby has been a deep-seated, persistent, and resilient feature of UK energy policy, through both state-led and market-led phases (Mitchell 2008: 96–120).

Composition of the Energy Mix

As noted above, up until the 1980s, coal dominated as a fuel for both in the wider economy and in power generation, along with some nuclear plants (Figs. 1 and 2). The large scale and capital risk of coal-fired and nuclear power plants was well suited to state ownership (Jaccard 1995). Transport energy was provided by petroleum products, sourced in part through the state-owned British Petroleum and increasingly from domestic production in the North Sea from the late 1960s.

Over the subsequent 45 years, this energy mix has changed in several ways. The first has been a long-term shift away from coal as an energy source, first to natural gas and then more recently renewable energy, especially wind power. A first wave of the adoption of natural gas came in the 1970s and 1980s in domestic heating. A subsequent wave came in the 1990s with the "dash for gas" in electricity generation. The latter can be seen particularly clearly in Fig. 2. Coal use for power fell sharply from 1990 to 2000 as natural gas replaced it. Coal is now fairly marginal to electricity generation and will be phased out completely by 2025 (BEIS 2018).

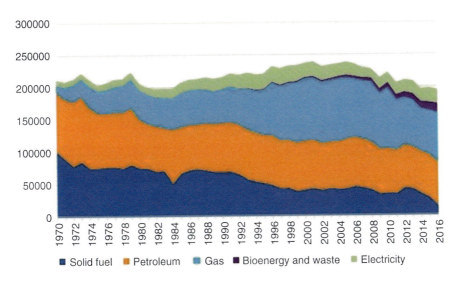

Fig. 1 Final energy consumption by fuel type 1970–2016, primary energy equivalents. (Source: Energy Consumption UK, https://www.gov.uk/government/statistics/energy-consumption-in-the-uk. Note: Primary energy equivalents are the amount of fossil fuels and other natural resources required to produce the final energy consumed)

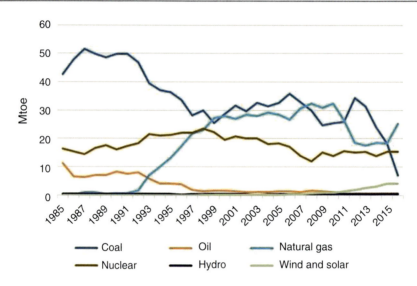

Fig. 2 Fuels used in electricity generation 1985–2016, Mtoe. (Source: https://www.gov.uk/government/statistical-data-sets/historical-electricity-data-1920-to-2011)

Some of the UK's now aging nuclear power plants are starting to be retired, but unlike with coal, a new generation of nuclear is being planned.

Renewable sources, especially wind and to a degree bioenergy, have come to play a major role in electricity generation only recently. For many years, the UK lagged behind countries such as Denmark, Spain, and Germany in the development of renewables, and it is only since the late 2000s that the pace of investment has picked up, with renewables now providing around a quarter of total generation (Fig. 3), slightly less than neighboring Ireland (▶ Energy Governance in Ireland). After initial growth, expansion of onshore wind has now been halted, but offshore wind has begun to develop quickly and is expected to play a major role in the future. By contrast, renewable sources of heat in the UK remain more marginal.

Discourse on Energy Issues

The election of Margaret Thatcher in 1979 saw the start of a decisive move in the paradigm for economic policy in the UK, from state intervention to free markets (Hall 1993; Oliver and Pemberton 2004). In the energy sector, the new paradigm was most famously signaled in 1982 by the then Energy Secretary Nigel Lawson, who stated that the task of government was not to plan energy but: "rather to set a framework which will ensure that the market operates with a minimum of distortion and energy is produced and consumed efficiently" (Lawson 1982, quoted in Fudge et al. 2011: 295–296). This approach involved the privatization and liberalization of energy production and supply in all sectors and was the earliest and most thorough in Europe (Helm 2004; Pearson and Watson 2012).

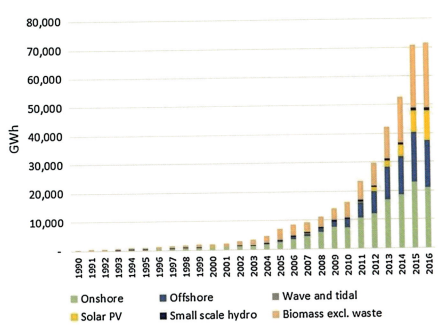

Fig. 3 Electricity generated from renewable sources, GWh. (Source: https://www.gov.uk/government/statistics/renewable-sources-of-energy-chapter-6-digest-of-united-kingdom-energy-statistics-dukes)

The introduction of what Rutledge (2010) calls "market fundamentalism" appeared to spell the end of energy policy. However, even before the process of liberalization was complete, new problems emerged which led to the return of government intervention. First, despite the supposed benefits from privatization and liberalization in terms of efficient pricing, many low-income households struggled with energy bills, and the eradication of "fuel poverty" was introduced as a policy goal in 2001. A second issue was the need to decarbonize the energy system, a movement which gained political momentum especially as climate change became more salient in the early 2000s (see section "Drivers of Energy Transition" below). Third, because of the trend toward oil and gas import dependency, energy security rose rapidly back up the political agenda, especially with the two Russia-Ukraine gas disputes in the second half of the decade (Kuzemko 2013). Thus by the late 2000s, a "trilemma" of energy policy goals, often framed as affordability, security, and low carbon, had become acknowledged by both government and industry.

There is some debate as to whether this means that a new paradigm for energy policy has emerged (Helm 2005; Fudge et al. 2011; Kern et al. 2014a). On the one hand, new objectives have been adopted, and since the late 1990s, an increasing number of interventions have been made in all energy markets. In electricity generation, for example, a series of interventions over the last 25 years means that virtually no form of power generation is now without some framework of government support (except, ironically, onshore wind). On the other hand, the idea that markets are the best route for solving the trilemma has remained very powerful among UK policy makers (Helm 2005: 16; Kern et al. 2014a: 10). Where policy makers have intervened, the preferred design of policy has almost always been "market friendly," with a claim to technological neutrality. For example, in support of renewable energy (see section "Electricity Generation"), there has been a strong preference for quantity-based measures or auctions. The use of regulation has been sparing and administrative price setting even more so. However, in many cases these interventions themselves have not worked well and have needed adjustments, or further policies layered on top, and unanticipated interactions have multiplied. The result is a messy compromise, with inconsistencies that exercise many observers and lead to calls for a return to pure markets (Keay et al. 2012; Bird 2015; Helm 2013; Porter 2014).

Political Institutions and Actors

While the ideational paradigm has changed radically since the 1980s, the centralized nature of the British state has not (in which it is similar to the Republic of Ireland (▶ Energy Governance in Ireland)). Despite the creation of devolved administrations in the nations within the UK (i.e., Scotland, Wales, and Northern Ireland) in 1997, energy policy remains largely within the ambit of Westminster-based central government, which has retained "control of key constitutional-legal, hierarchical and financial resources of the energy sphere" (Cowell et al. (2017: 172)).

The exception is Northern Ireland, which is in several ways a special case. Since 2007, Northern Ireland has also effectively been part of an all-Ireland Single Electricity Market together with the Republic of Ireland, with increasingly integrated networks. It also has a separate energy regulator from the rest of Britain. At the other end of the spectrum, Wales has few devolved powers. Scotland (the largest of the devolved nations) is in an intermediate position, having a degree of control over policy which it has used to mark out a somewhat distinctive position. The Scottish Government has rejected hydraulic fracturing ("fracking") for shale oil and gas and the siting of any new nuclear plants in Scotland. It has also had some control over its own renewable policy, and greater political support for wind power has led to its more extensive deployment and the greater involvement of community groups in wind farm ownership (Cowell et al. 2017). Nevertheless, Scotland remains within an overall energy policy and regulatory framework set in London.

When it comes to local government, including within England, the main area of influence is over planning. Its role in blocking or allowing consent for wind power projects under 50 megawatts (MW), and all onshore wind since 2016, has been important (Toke 2005). City governments have been proactive advocates for decarbonization and have done what they can within the limits (policy-related and financial) they face. Recently, as the agenda has turned to the role of distributed energy resources, they are beginning to see new opportunities. Some cities (e.g., Bristol and Nottingham) have set up their own energy supply companies. London government has long pursued the agenda of trying to establish more low-carbon electricity generation within the city and has used its additional strategic planning powers over large developments to require developers to consider combined heat and power. Nevertheless, the powers and resources of these actors remain limited (Eckersley 2018).

Within central government, the status and location of energy policy has changed over time. The Department of Energy was first established in the early 1970s at the time of the oil crisis. Following the privatization revolution and the "end" of energy policy, this department was abolished, and responsibility for energy was handed to the Department for Trade and Industry. In 2008, at the time the Climate Change Act was passed, a new Department for Energy and Climate Change (DECC) was created, which became a champion of energy transition within the bureaucracy. DECC's first step was the development of a Low Carbon Transition Plan in 2009. However, in 2016, shortly after the Brexit referendum, DECC was dissolved and energy policy was moved back to the business ministry.

Privatization involved the creation of independent arm's-length regulators for gas and electricity, subsequently merged into the Office of Gas and Electricity Markets (Ofgem) in 2000. The formal remit of the energy regulators initially focused narrowly on efficiency and competition, but as new issues entered the government's own agenda, the remit expanded, with a number of changes to its duties and objectives over the period from the 1980s to the 2010s including in the area of sustainability (DECC 2010). As a result, Ofgem has acquired an increasing degree of discretion.

Beyond formal decision-makers, certain groups in civil society have had important influences on energy policy. The first is the environmentalist movement. The UK's majoritarian electoral rules mean that small parties, including the Green Party, are largely absent from parliament, so the environmentalist concerns of voters have been channelled through a relatively large and active nongovernmental organization (NGO) movement. This movement has played an important role in pushing for more ambition on renewable energy and in opposing the use of fossil fuels. Key policy changes in which these groups have played a major role include the banning of new coal-fired power stations in 2008, the introduction of a fixed feed-in tariff for small-scale renewables in 2010, and the adoption of the carbon price floor in 2011. The "Big Ask" campaign, coordinated by Friends of the Earth, also provided the initial impetus for the 2008 Climate Change Act (Lorenzoni and Benson 2014). By contrast, parts of the print media have been influential both in opposing some renewables, especially onshore wind, and in funnelling political pressure onto the government at times of high energy prices.

Finally, there are the large incumbent energy firms. Despite liberalization through the 1990s, UK energy markets have been prone to oligopoly and since the early 2000s have effectively been dominated by six large retail companies – known as the "Big Six" – which are vertically integrated in electricity (e.g., Roques et al. 2005). These actors invest significantly in lobbying to shape policy (Mitchell 2008; Geels 2014) and also have direct influence in some parts of regulation through the governance of industry codes (Lockwood et al. 2017). National Grid, the major transmission networks owner and system operator in electricity and gas, is also an influential corporate actor.

Overall, the influence of civil society groups and incumbents has arguably been amplified by the UK's centralized state, in the sense that lobbying focused on only a relatively small number of high-level officials and ministers can have a large impact.

Coordination, Instruments, and Issues of the UK Energy Transition

Drivers of Energy Transition

Up until the mid-2000s, there were few internal "landscape" drivers (e.g., Geels 2010; Geels and Schot 2007) for energy transition in the UK. The pressure to decarbonize the energy system was initially external, in the form of the Kyoto Protocol. Policies in the 1990s and early 2000s were largely ineffective (Carter and Ockwell 2007; Lorenzoni et al. 2008). Decarbonization in the power sector, seen as the priority area for action, had been achieved coincidentally through the "dash for gas" rather than by any targeted policies, and some of these gains were subsequently reversed (Fig. 4).

However, this picture changed significantly over the course of the 2000s. From 2004 onward, domestic awareness and concern about climate change rose sharply in a classic issue-attention cycle (Lockwood 2013). Campaign groups channelled public pressure into the demand for a Climate Change Bill, a demand that was taken up by both major political parties seeking to compete on the issue (Carter 2009) with the result that a Climate Change Act was passed at the end of 2008 (see Box 1).

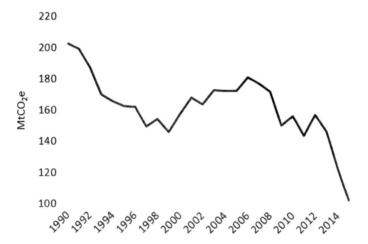

Fig. 4 Power sector carbon emissions, MtCO$_2$e. (Source: https://www.gov.uk/government/statistics/final-uk-greenhouse-gas-emissions-national-statistics-1990-2015)

> **Box 1 The 2008 Climate Change Act**
> The 2008 Climate Change Act set a target of reducing UK greenhouse gas emissions by 80% by 2050 from a 1990 baseline. The Act also created a Committee on Climate Change (CCC), which was tasked with recommending five-yearly carbon budgets that the government must meet to comply with the law. This is a relatively technocratic approach, delegating key high-level objectives to an independent, arm's-length body (although the CCC has only a limited power, able to recommend but not set budgets and can comment on but cannot direct policy making). It contrasts with the exercises in societal consensus-building seen in the Netherlands (▶ "Energy Governance in the Netherlands") or Denmark. However, so far the approach has been successful in terms of emissions reductions, with the first two carbon budgets easily met, although this is partly due to the effects of economic depression as well as policy.

There were also few early domestic drivers for renewable energy policy (compared with Denmark and Germany) where the government and industry incumbents were unenthusiastic. Because of the UK's centralized policy, there was only a weak challenge to this approach domestically (mainly from the Scottish Government, which wanted better support for onshore wind power), and it was the EU that forced the UK to adopt a specific support mechanism and later on targets for the growth of renewables. Through the 2000s, despite growing pressure from the environmentalist movement, the government remained fairly resistant, with renewable support seen as both expensive and (in line with the market-led paradigm) an inappropriately technology-specific intervention. The UK government actively lobbied against the adoption of the target of 20% renewable energy in the EU 2020 Climate and Energy Package in the late 2000s.

In part due to policy design (see section "Electricity Generation" below), renewable energy in the UK has also suffered from a more challenging political dynamic than in Germany and Denmark, as the ownership of renewables has been concentrated in the hands of the Big Six and other large commercial developers rather than communities. While this is not the only factor in local opposition to wind farms, there is evidence that it has contributed to that opposition (Szarka 2006; Toke et al. 2008; Toke 2010). Local resistance led ultimately to the withdrawal of all forms of support for new onshore wind in 2015. The wider market-led economic policy paradigm has also meant a fairly passive approach to industrial policy until recently, and successive governments did not seek to develop a "home market" for a domestic renewable supply chain. As a result the UK has historically had a relatively weak domestic onshore wind and solar photovoltaic (PV) manufacturing and supply chain base, and consequently the powerful industrial lobby for renewables seen elsewhere, such as Germany (Jacobsson and Lauber 2006), has been lacking.

However, because of the scaling up of deployment and manufacturing of wind and solar technologies elsewhere in the world, rapidly falling costs did lead to an acceleration of investment in the UK in the early 2010s. The political challenges facing onshore wind led to an increasing focus on offshore wind, which is also the renewable technology closest to the large-scale centralized generation model. Cost reduction has exceeded expectations, and it remains a projected growth area into the 2020s (HM Government 2017). Offshore wind growth is also the first area where the UK has stimulated significant domestic supply chain activity, including turbine manufacture, developing a supportive political constituency especially in North East England and Scotland (Kern et al. 2014b).

It is also worth considering the role of energy industry lobbies in the politics of the transition. Partly because of policy design, unlike as in Germany, the main utilities did not seek to completely block the emergence of renewables, but also unlike as in Spain, they did not strategically embrace them (Stenzel and Frenzel 2008). Rather, they have sought to influence the pace of change (Mitchell 2008) and have adopted a hedging strategy, adding renewables to their portfolio – in 2010, the Big Six owned about half the renewable electricity capacity in the UK (BNEF 2012) – while retaining their existing high-carbon assets. By contrast, there has been a strong technology lobby for nuclear power, which came to play a major role in the government's transition strategy in the late 2000s. There has also been a lobby for the development of fracking for gas in the UK, to which the government has been receptive, although there has been no commercial extraction to date, and there is a lack of consensus about the actual potential of the resource as well as strong local opposition at drilling sites (Keeler 2016).

Finally, concerns about the political consequences of transition policy costs, which are passed through to energy consumers (CEER 2015), have driven caution in governance. As noted above, these concerns were always particularly salient in the UK's economy, with a polarized labor market and the prevalence of low wages (Goos and Manning 2007). The 2000s saw not only stagnation in real wages for lower-skilled workers but also a rapid rise in underlying energy costs. This was followed by recession after the 2008–2009 financial crisis and a fall in the median real wage (Gregg et al. 2014). By the early 2010s, energy costs were a highly sensitive issue; for example, in October 2012, a source in the prime minister's office was quoted as saying: "This is very big. Energy prices is one of the biggest issues on the doorstep and we are determined to do something" (Wintour and Carrington 2012). Politicians began calling for caps on prices, which were eventually introduced in 2017.

Strategies and Instruments of Energy Transitions

Electricity Generation

Thus far, the strategy of the UK energy transition to date has been led and is still largely been confined to electricity generation. With government and incumbents until very recently working within a shared centralized generation model, the strategy has been first to decarbonize by fuel-switching from coal to gas within the existing system and second to develop new large-scale low-carbon technologies that fitted into the model, i.e., carbon capture and storage (CCS) and new nuclear power.

However, the initial strategy has been problematic because the main policy instruments have in many cases struggled to deliver the desired outcomes. Table 1

Table 1 Key UK energy transition policy instruments by sector and type

	Regulatory	Incentive based	Internalizing	Soft governance
Electricity supply	Large Combustion Plant Directive (2001) Ban on new unabated coal-fired power stations (2009) Industrial Emissions Directive (2010) Phaseout of coal-fired power generation by 2025 (2017)	NFFO/SRO (1990–2001) Renewables Obligation (2001–2017) Small-scale feed-in tariff (2010) CfD FiT (2015) Capacity Market (2014) CCS competitions (2007–2011, 2012–2015)	EU ETS (2005) Carbon Price Support (2011)	
Heat supply		Renewable Heat Incentive (2011)		
Household energy efficiency	Supplier obligations (1994 onward) Building regulations ongoing Zero Carbon Homes (2006–2015)	Green Deal (2013–2015)		Voluntary incandescent lighting phaseout (2007) Energy Savings Trust
Fuel poverty	Cold Weather Payments (1986) Winter Fuel Payments (1997) Warm Front (2000–2013) Supplier obligation targeting (from 2002)			
Industrial and commercial energy efficiency			Climate Change Levy (2001) Carbon Reduction Commitment (2008–2016)	Carbon Trust Climate Change Agreements (2001) Labelling (EPBD 2002, 2010)
Transport	Phaseout of new petrol and diesel cars by 2030 (2017)	Vehicle Excise Duty banding (2005) Plug-in grant program (2011) Congestion charge (London) (2003)	Fuel Duty Accelerator (1997, frozen since 1999)	Integrated transport planning (London, Manchester)

shows the main policy instruments used in the UK energy transition, organized by type and sector. We follow the categorization of policy types adopted in the Introduction to this handbook, distinguishing four types: direct regulation, internalizing instruments (e.g., carbon pricing), incentive-based instruments (e.g., subsidies for low-carbon energy production), and soft governance (e.g., information schemes and voluntary agreements). The choice of instruments has been heavily driven by the market-led policy paradigm (Pearson and Watson 2012; Fudge et al. 2011), with a preference for internalizing and incentive-based instruments and an aversion to direct regulation. The government (particularly the Treasury) has long been keen on carbon pricing as an internalizing instrument for decarbonization in the power sector and was an enthusiastic early supporter of the EU Emissions Trading Scheme (ETS) (e.g., HM Government 2006, 2009). It took a number of years for the government to accept that the ETS was not going to produce a significant and stable carbon price. Also driven by a desire to raise revenue to cut the deficit, a carbon floor price for electricity generators was introduced (HM Treasury 2010), which has played a part in driving fuel-switching from coal to gas and caused a sharp fall in power sector carbon emissions in the UK (Fig. 4).

Coal-fired power generation has also come under pressure via direct regulations. However, these were not the choice of the UK government and were driven rather by other actors. In two cases, regulation was imposed by EU Directives relating to sulfur and nitrogen oxide emissions (the Large Combustion Plant Directive of 2001 and Industrial Emissions Directive of 2010, respectively). In a third case, the UK government banned new coal-fired power generation not covered by CCS in 2009, but only after an extended high-profile campaign by environmental NGOs.

To drive investment in new low-carbon power generation, incentive-based instruments have been used, with a strong preference for "market-compatible" or auction designs. Since the mid-2000s, the government had signalled that it wanted new nuclear energy (HM Government 2006), but while incumbent energy companies showed interest, it was clear they would not invest without major state backing. At this time there was a support scheme for renewables (see below) but none for new nuclear, so in 2010 a major Electricity Market Reform (EMR) was launched that created a new incentive-based support policy for a more widely defined "low-carbon" electricity that also included new nuclear (DECC 2011).

The new support instrument – a Contract for Difference Feed-in Tariff (CfD FiT) – was supposed to set a fixed price competitively through reverse auctions, but in practice, the first contract for new nuclear was actually set through a bilateral negotiation with the company EdF, as all the other new build consortia had collapsed. The wider policy cannot be seen as a success; the first plant will be expensive, scraped through the State Aid process only after a highly politicized negotiation with other member states, it is not scheduled to be delivered before 2025, and there are considerable uncertainties about any further plants.

The development of CCS has been a complete failure (Kern et al. 2016), despite the UK having many of the potential elements of success, including skills and storage locations in the North Sea. Despite the complexity and scale of innovation required, there was no strong coordinating intervention, but rather (again linked to the market-led paradigm) an incentive-based instrument in the form of competitive bids. As with new nuclear, the scale and risk of the project, and in this case the lack of drivers for the companies involved, meant that consortia dropped out. Most environmental campaign groups were also opposed to or did not actively support CCS. Two rounds of competitions were launched and subsequently cancelled between 2007 and 2016 (NAO 2017).

By contrast with its pursuit of new nuclear power and CCS, the UK government was initially unenthusiastic about renewable technologies. In the 1990s, renewables were folded into a scheme designed to support nuclear power (Mitchell and Connor 2004). However, the 2001 EU Renewables Directive required the introduction of a dedicated incentive instrument. The model of fixed feed-in tariffs widespread on the continent at the time was rejected, since the administrative setting of subsidies and targeting of specific technologies was seen as "picking winners" and against market principles (Woodman and Mitchell 2011). Instead, the new policy, the Renewables Obligation (RO), was set up as a tradeable quota system, with the idea that a price would emerge through a market. However, in practice the RO was relatively expensive and ineffective (Ragwitz et al. 2007; Butler and Neuhoff 2008). It favored the one technology nearest maturity (i.e., onshore wind) and also involved considerable price and volume risk (Mitchell et al. 2006). These factors deterred the small-scale community and cooperative investors seen in other European countries, with investment dominated by the incumbent energy companies and other large developers. In 2014, only 60 MW or around 0.3% of generation capacity in the UK was community owned (DECC 2014). This left the policy politically exposed (see section "Drivers of Energy Transition").

The policy was reformed multiple times over the 2000s (Woodman and Mitchell 2011), and with cost reductions in wind and solar PV due to successful niche development and deployment elsewhere in the world, investment in the UK did begin to grow rapidly at the end of the decade. In 2010, under campaigning pressure from environmentalists, a fixed feed-in tariff scheme for small-scale renewables (<5 MW) was introduced which also drove expansion. By this point, however, the decision to expand support mechanisms to include new nuclear had been made, so the RO had been phased out and renewable support transferred to the CfD FiT. As discussed above, the government is most enthusiastic about offshore wind, and it is in this area that the UK has now come closest to establishing its own successful socio-technical niche (Kern et al. 2015).

The success of renewables brought the issues of suppressed wholesale prices and how to manage intermittency onto the agenda (e.g., Pöyry 2009). The responses were again shaped by the centralized model. One was to start to plan for more interconnection with the rest of Europe, although this strategy is now facing uncertainty with Brexit (Froggatt et al. 2017). The other was to create a Capacity Market (DECC 2011), whose reverse auction design was again influenced by the market-led paradigm, even though this meant providing support for some high-carbon plants that would otherwise probably have been retired.

The government's expectation was that the Capacity Market would incentivize new large-scale gas plants to provide backup generation. However, by the time that the policy started to be implemented, it was becoming clear that the future of the electricity system would be far more distributed, with costs falling rapidly in storage, i.e., batteries (again due to niches mostly elsewhere in the world) and the realization that smart technology would allow greater flexibility in demand (see section "Outcomes, Challenges, and Prospects of Energy Governance"). This direction has been reinforced by the investment of the major car manufacturers in electric vehicles. Policy and regulation is struggling to keep up with the pace of change in distributed energy, which is now the frontier in UK energy system change.

Heat Production

Compared with electricity supply, attempts at decarbonizing heat in the UK are still in their infancy. Domestic and commercial space and water heating are dominated by natural gas, a legacy of the discovery and development of North Sea gas and the rapid expansion of a national gas grid in the 1970s. Around 90% of households are heated by gas boilers (Palmer and Cooper 2013), an unusually high proportion in Europe with the exception of the Netherlands (▶ Energy Governance in the Netherlands). The UK largely lacks the district heating networks found in the cities of other northern European countries (DECC 2013). District heat networks remain underdeveloped because the approach does not fit well with the liberalized approach in retail markets (Toke and Fragaki 2008) and also because of the marginalization of municipal government in the centralized political system (Hawkey et al. 2013).

The main instrument for heat supply decarbonization to date has been an incentive-based measure for low-carbon heat technologies that are new to the UK market, including biomass boilers and heat pumps (Table 1). This scheme, the Renewable Heat Incentive (RHI), is unusual in providing fixed price support, probably driven by the desire to avoid high transactions costs (Connor et al. 2015). It was introduced for commercial organizations in 2011 and for domestic households in 2014. The vast majority of support under the RHI has gone to biomass boilers. However, it remains a small scheme relative to overall heat demand. Total *cumulative* heat production under the RHI between 2011 and September 2017 is estimated at 17.6 TWh (most of which is in the commercial sector), but *annual* domestic heat consumption alone is of the order of 400 TWh (Douglas 2015).

Debates are only just beginning about the direction of long-run strategies for heat supply decarbonization (e.g., DECC 2013; ETI 2016; NIC 2017). There is some consensus that a range of technology options will be needed in order to serve the needs of demand in different contexts, e.g., rural vs densely settled urban (Chaudry et al. 2015). A key area of controversy (and where are significant incumbent interests) is over the potential role of the existing gas network in decarbonizing heat using low- or lower-carbon forms of gas such as biogas or hydrogen (Dodds and McDowall 2013). The current government position is simply to continue to develop various technologies and keep options open (e.g., HM Government 2017).

Energy Efficiency

Beyond the changes in electricity, the other important element in the UK energy transition to date has been the reduction in energy demand by households since 2007 and a longer-term trend of declining energy use in manufacturing. A relatively small part of the fall in manufacturing energy use has been due to fuel-switching, restructuring, and relocation to other countries; the majority of the decline is due to a decrease in energy intensity (Hammond and Norman 2012). However, the overall rate of decline has been less, and the role of structural changes greater, in the energy-intensive industries.

Unlike as in electricity generation, successive governments have generally shied away from using incentive-based instruments, especially taxes, for greater household action on efficiency (Table 1). There is no explicit carbon tax on the end use of gas or electricity in homes, and energy used by households has been subject to a lower rate of value-added tax (VAT) than other goods and services since 1997. Instead, a combination of "soft" governance measures has been used, such as information and market transformation approaches and regulations placed mostly not on households themselves but rather on suppliers, housebuilders, and manufacturers. This latter approach has been reinforced in recent years by EU Directives on energy labelling (2010) and on eco-design (2009).

The most important intervention has been an obligation placed on energy supply companies to deliver efficiency measures. This approach was originally introduced in 1994, with successive schemes increased in ambition almost 80-fold up to the end of the 2000s (Rosenow 2012). From 2001 onward, these programs were also used to try to address fuel poverty through targeting poorer households, alongside direct transfers such as Cold Weather Payments and bespoke energy-saving programs for vulnerable households such as Warm Front.

However, the cost of delivering these measures was passed through to consumers in general, and with concerns about increasing energy bills, a new center-right government in 2010 slashed the level of ambition by about four-fifths (Rosenow and Eyre 2013). Instead, a new "Green Deal" approach was launched, aimed at overcoming upfront cost barriers by setting up a dedicated source of financing for energy efficiency that was intended to catalyze the emergence of a new market for energy efficiency by better off households. This idea was in part inspired by the role of the KfW in Germany (Rosenow et al. 2013; Kuzemko et al. 2017), but again reflected the UK market-led paradigm by charging commercial rates of interest, far higher than in the case of the KfW. The scheme also failed to address other potential barriers to energy efficiency investments and ran for little more than 2 years before it was closed in 2015 (BEIS 2017b).

Beyond the obligation on suppliers, various other instruments have also played a role in household energy efficiency policy. Among the most important of these has been the use of regulations to improve gas boiler efficiency. The Netherlands led the development and deployment of condensing boilers through a coordinated market transformation program in the 1990s (Weber et al. 2002). In line with the market-led paradigm, the UK government hoped that a similar transformation could be led voluntarily by the gas fitting industry, but a lack of incentives and training meant that this approach failed, and in 2005 the government fell back on a regulatory instrument working through the boiler fitting industry (Mallaburn and Eyre 2014). Before this change, only 7% of households had high-efficiency condensing boilers, but by 2011 over half did (Palmer and Cooper 2013) and around 70% today (CCC 2017).

Other instruments were "soft" governance measures, including information and advice campaigns and labelling schemes for appliances (reinforced by the EU Energy Efficiency Directive). A voluntary phaseout of low-efficiency incandescent lighting in 2007 (ahead of the EU phaseout announced in 2009) has encouraged a widespread shift to light-emitting diode (LED) lighting.

By contrast with the politically sensitive household sector, the government has been more willing to use externalizing and incentive-based instruments to drive industrial, commercial, and public sector energy efficiency (Table 1). First, a number of large industrial facilities are covered by the EU ETS, which effectively taxes fuel consumption. Second, a tax on fuels and electricity used by all businesses and public sector organizations, the Climate Change Levy (CCL), was introduced in 2001. After lobbying, it was agreed that energy-intensive users could obtain an exemption of up to 90% of the levy if they signed a climate change agreement under which they pledged to undertake certain efficiency measures. However, these agreements have been less effective than the price-based instrument (Martin et al. 2009).

For larger commercial and public sector organizations not covered by the EU ETS, the government also introduced a tradeable permit scheme in 2008 called the Carbon Reduction Commitment (CRC). Again, the instrument showed the government's enthusiasm for externalizing instruments and a market design. However, the CRC was subsequently criticized for its complexity, and it was withdrawn in 2016.

As in other areas, where energy use in commercial and public sector organizations was subject to regulatory instruments, these were mainly driven by European legislation rather than domestic policy choice, e.g., the Energy Performance of Buildings Directive. Soft governance instruments for the business sector were also to be found in the UK. Using revenues from the CCL, the government set up an agency, the Carbon Trust, to help organizations identify energy and carbon savings in 2001, although its funding was cut back significantly in 2011.

Transport

The governance of transport energy in the UK has historically been quite separate from that of electricity and gas, both institutionally and in terms of the policy networks active in these areas. However, this is now beginning to change, as an integration of sectors through a revolution in electric vehicle (EV) use is widely anticipated.

Unlike as in electricity decarbonization, where the dominance of a few large commercial actors has given the government more predictable policy levers to work with, decarbonizing transport involves influencing the decisions of millions of households and enterprises. However, governments have been more willing to use externalizing and incentive-based instruments to try to drive the transition to lower emissions, in part because these instruments already existed. Predating any climate change concerns, transport fuels in the UK were taxed quite heavily via fuel duty (Leicester 2006). In 1993, in response to concerns about rising congestion and environmental damage, a fuel duty "escalator" was introduced, raising duty every year at 3% above inflation. By 1997 the escalator rate was raised to 6% above inflation. However, with underlying road fuel prices starting to rise, so did opposition, and the level of fuel duty was frozen from 1999 (Dresner et al. 2006). More recently, attempts to reintroduce increases in duty in 2011 and 2012 were swiftly reversed under pressure from the media. Thus internalizing instruments for decarbonizing transport face real political limits in the UK.

The government has also attempted to use an incentive-based approach through the banding of Vehicle Excise Duty (VED), an annual tax to keep a vehicle on the road. In 2001, the government introduced banding of VED by carbon emissions, with very low-carbon vehicles, including EVs, attracting a zero rate. The banding scheme has been revised twice since.

Incentives in the form of subsidies for the purchase of electric or plug-in hybrid electric vehicles were started in 2011, offering a reduction of up to 25% of the cost of purchase, capped at £5000. However, the scale of grants was subsequently reduced. Sales of "ultra-low emission vehicles" (including both EVs and PHEVs) started to rise sharply from 2014 onward from a very low base (DfT 2017), but this is likely to reflect reductions in battery costs and the appearance of new models as much as the subsidy program itself. Other instruments include the EU-wide voluntary agreement between manufacturers to reduce average emissions in new cars and a long-term target to end new sales of petrol and diesel cars by 2030.

These measures have driven a move to more efficient and lower emission vehicles, but emissions from transport have not decreased at all and were virtually the same in 2015 as they were in 1990 (Fig. 5). This is because the number of vehicles and the distance driven have both increased. The government has done far less in seeking to achieve a modal shift away from car use or to limit mobility more

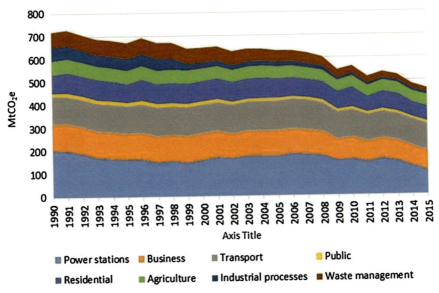

Fig. 5 Carbon emissions by source 1990–2015, MtCO$_2$e. (Source: https://www.gov.uk/government/statistics/final-uk-greenhouse-gas-emissions-national-statistics-1990-2015)

widely. Bus services were deregulated in the 1980s and train services privatized in the 1990s. The government has supported rail financially, with a substantial subsidy of £4.8 billion in 2015–2016, and train travel has more than doubled since privatization. However, despite some evidence of "peak car" use in the UK (as elsewhere in the developed world), this does not represent a secular shift from road to rail but rather a general increase in mobility over the last 25 years. There are also limited powers and resources in most cities and towns in the UK with which to plan integrated transport. There is a relatively small subsidy to bus service operators to run unprofitable routes (£200 million in 2015–2026), but powers to regulate and coordinate transport within cities were taken away from all municipal authorities, with the exception of London (and very recently, Manchester).

Coordination Mechanisms and Multilevel Governance

The concentration of energy policy powers in the UK means that central government remains the key coordinating actor for transition. Probably the most important exception has been onshore wind in Scotland, where the Scottish Government has used its relative autonomy over renewable policy to drive greater deployment than elsewhere in the UK (Scotland has about ten times the amount of installed onshore wind capacity per person than England does and more than double than that in Northern Ireland and Wales). Within central government, a major problem for energy transition had historically been the separation of responsibility for energy, located in the ministry for business and trade, and responsibility for climate policy, located in the environment ministry. In 2008, following frustrations about getting action on energy efficiency policies, the prime minister's office intervened and set up an Office of Climate Change to improve coordination. This was followed shortly afterward by the creation of a new Department of Energy and Climate Change. This move allowed far greater coordination of wider policy for decarbonization, especially in the power sector. The reabsorption of energy into the business department in 2016 raised fears that the climate change agenda would be weakened and transition slowed. This danger remains a possibility, but at present it appears that the reverse is the case, and decarbonization is becoming a core part of the business department's industrial strategy (HM Government 2017).

Throughout these changes, other government departments have continued to play important roles in relation to energy transition. For example, building regulations, which are important for household energy efficiency, are overseen by the Department for Communities and Local Government. With the focus moving to the electrification of transport, the Department for Transport (DfT) will become an increasingly important actor. Since 2009, the DfT has housed an Office for Low Emission Vehicles (OLEV) to coordinate with other ministries. Above all, the Treasury has always been a powerful player and has acted to initiate, veto, or limit policy (e.g., the Electricity Market Reform process) in overall levels of support for renewable energy (Lockwood 2016).

While central government has devolved few powers to other levels of political authority, it has delegated considerable powers to arm's-length institutions which have national scope. This is the other key set of coordination relationships. In formal terms, at the apex of the coordination of the energy transition within the UK is the independent Committee on Climate Change (CCC), created by the 2008 CCA (see Box 1). The CCC sets carbon budgets, which have fundamental implications for the energy sector, and under the act the government is required to publish a plan for policies to meet the budgets. In practice, the connection between budgets, plans, and specific policies and regulations remains weak. In part this is because elements of de facto delivery have been delegated to the energy regulator, Ofgem. In theory, Ofgem is an economic regulator which does not make policy. However, the body has taken on more and more objectives over the years (see section "Political Institutions and Actors"), which means it has to negotiate trade-offs between policy goals in the way that it handles regulation, and in practice often makes decisions which affect the shape and pace of transition. Indeed, Ofgem is now taking a leading role alongside government in recent moves toward a smarter and more flexible electricity system (BEIS/Ofgem 2016).

Ofgem in turn delegates a significant degree of control over industry codes, detailed technical and commercial rules for electricity and gas markets and networks, to the energy industry itself (Lockwood et al. 2017). These codes are living documents, under continual modification, but the process lacks objectives relating to sustainability and is governed by panels on which the incumbents, including network companies, have a dominant position. The result is that there is frequently a gap between high-level policy and practice on the ground.

Outcomes, Challenges, and Prospects of Energy Governance

At present, the decarbonization of the UK energy system appears to be a success story. Greenhouse gas emissions in 2016, measured on a production basis, were down 42% from the 1990 baseline, and the country will comfortably meet the second carbon budget (CCC 2017). The UK is also on track and projected to meet its 2020 EU non-traded greenhouse gas reduction target of 16% from 2005 levels under the effort-sharing decision framework (EEA 2017). The UK is currently decarbonizing faster than any other G20 country. A large part of this reduction has come from the energy sector, especially electricity generation; three-quarters of emissions reductions in the period 2012 to 2016 were due to falling coal-fired power generation alone.

However, the picture elsewhere is not quite so successful. Despite the increased targeting of energy efficiency programs on poor households, rising energy prices have meant that the proportion of households in fuel poverty has not been seriously reduced. In 2012 a target of eradicating fuel poverty by 2016 was abandoned and replaced with a weaker set of goals for the period 2020–2030. Progress in renewable energy has also been mixed, and there are real risks that the UK will not reach its target of 15% of energy from renewable sources as its contribution to meeting the EU 20-20-20 targets. The challenging areas have been transport and particularly heat. By contrast, after a slow start, renewable electricity has now expanded significantly in the UK, providing around one-quarter of generation in 2016 (Fig. 3), and is expected to continue to grow further.

In the longer run, the wider governance of energy transition in the UK has been problematic. Despite efforts to coordinate the policy mix (Kivimaa and Kern 2016), it has not followed a simple, planned pathway. Rather, governance has been an evolving process of setting off in particular directions and then having to change course, of following and then retreating from blind alleys, and of reacting to surprises in costs and political responses. While there have been some examples of policy learning, for example, in the evolution of renewable policy design from the initial Renewables Obligation through to a sophisticated feed-in tariff design with auctioning, there is no general pattern, with plenty of examples where mistakes have simply been repeated, for example, on CCS competitions. There has also been a layering of policies (Mahoney and Thelen 2010) in a way that has led to complex interactions, incoherence, and unanticipated consequences (e.g., Sorrell and Sijm 2005; Keay et al. 2012; Bird 2015). Periodically there is an attempt at rationalization through a major reset, such as the Electricity Market Reform in 2010–2013, but the complexity of such exercises generally means that they also generate further unintended consequences of their own.

The market-led policy paradigm has meant that the government has sometimes been slow to intervene, and when it has done so, policy design has often been driven by doctrine rather than by effectiveness – for example, in early renewable support mechanisms. At the same time, the paradigm has had its limits. One limit can be seen in a strong political aversion to levy energy and carbon taxes directly and visibly on households. This aversion, along with a degree of skepticism among the Treasury's economists, has produced weak energy efficiency policy that has shied away from creating strong incentives for improvements in the energy performance of housing. There are other aspects of the politics of energy transition that have also proven difficult, including local opposition to onshore wind.

As the energy transition approaches a phase in which relatively incremental change, mainly consisting of growing renewable electricity generation, is giving way to radical system transformation, the governance debate is increasingly about the need for a different, more coherent, and more directed approach. The UK is currently experiencing a fast-moving revolution occurring in the decentralization of power generation. Historically, power stations were connected to the transmission system, and distribution networks were passive one-way systems carrying electricity to loads. This is now changing, with an estimated 28 gigawatts (GW) of generation capacity (including 12 GW of solar PV) connected to distribution networks in 2016 and a lot more contracted (BEIS/Ofgem 2016) – to put this in context, peak demand in GB in 2016 was 52.3 GW. This development represents a challenge to distribution grid operators, as their networks were not designed for managing generation, but it also represents an opportunity for the active management of power flows through smart grid techniques and a transformation of their role to local system operators (e.g., WPD 2017).

More widely, the distinctions between producers and consumers of electricity are beginning to break down, and this change is expected to accelerate (Mitchell et al. 2016; Energy UK 2016; Howard and Bengerbi 2016; IET/Energy Systems Catapult 2017; Sandys et al. 2017). A number of experiments in local markets and peer-to-peer trading are already underway in various parts of Britain (Ofgem 2017). These involve a range of technologies and practices, including small-scale renewables, demand-side response, and storage. The costs of battery storage are falling rapidly. There is currently almost 500 MW of large-scale battery storage in the UK, offering services mainly to the Capacity Market and the national system operator (Regen 2017), but a much larger amount has secured accepted connection offers from network operators. Forecasts for grid-scale storage by 2030 range from 8 GW up to 15 GW. With growing uptake of electric vehicles (see section "Transport") and the trialling of vehicle-to-grid technologies, the role of total battery storage in the flexible balancing of the system is potentially very large. The potential benefits of more flexibility are also significant; one estimate is that a smart, flexible energy system could achieve savings of up to £8 billion a year (Pöyry/Imperial College 2017).

These developments both require and are made possible by ICTs embedded in networks and in the form of smart meters, which are expected to be fully rolled out in Britain by the early 2020s. With the increasing embedding of ICTs into the system and the use of the much larger amounts of data that are then generated, new opportunities for flexible energy demand will arise. Demand-side response (DSR) has historically been confined to a handful of large industrial users contracted to the system operator for frequency control services. However, with the digitization of the electricity system, there is increasingly the potential for a much larger number of actors, including households, to provide DSR services in a range of relationships ranging from system operators at both the national and distribution level down to local platforms. The capacity of households to offer DSR will also increase significantly with the adoption of EVs and possible electrification of heat. These developments will require new data handling techniques, including block chain approaches, and new business models. They also suggest a central role for consumers and raise questions of control and trust in relation to data (Ofgem 2016; Sandys et al. 2017; Hoggett 2017).

The emergence of distributed energy resources (DERs) has occurred in spite of UK energy governance and is already disruptive, especially for large energy utilities and network companies (Sandys et al. 2017). The DER revolution is a major challenge to the centralized model of the electricity system. It is unlikely that the future UK energy system will be fully decentralized, as large-scale technologies such as offshore wind will play an important role and an increasing amount of interconnection capacity to the rest of Europe is being built. But it is already moving toward a hybrid model containing both centralized and decentralized elements.

These challenges raise the question of how major system change occurring at a rapid pace can be directed, managed, and coordinated. While past UK governance arrangements and coordination mechanisms may have been appropriate for a situation of technological stability or incremental change, they seem increasingly unable to cope with the approaching system transformation. The challenge is compounded by the uncertainties surrounding the future of the energy relationship between the

UK and the EU post-Brexit (see Box 2), especially in areas such as electricity interconnection.

> **Box 2 Brexit and UK energy governance**
> The UK has become increasingly integrated with the rest of the European Union in energy terms over the last 25 years through a series of policy packages that have created the Internal Energy Market (IEM). Many of the reforms have focused on the liberalization of energy markets, a shift both based on and encouraged by the UK's own experience. As a result, the main effect of EU policy on the UK has so far been mainly in the area of renewable support rather than major institutional change. The effects of Brexit on UK energy governance will depend on the final terms of the Brexit deal, which at the time of writing were still undecided. The UK could potentially remain within the IEM, but it would lose its current ability to participate in the shaping of the policy and regulation. Some trade of electricity and gas between the UK and the EU27 is likely to continue, with virtually no tariffs even under WTO rules. However, some of the main issues are likely to be:
>
> - The future of UK involvement in electricity market coupling and shared balancing services, which is likely to become increasingly important as the share of intermittent renewables rises
> - Increased investment costs for the UK in the short term due to uncertainty, currency movements, and skill shortages
> - As a result of the previous two factors, uncertainty about the amount of future electricity interconnection between the UK, Ireland, and the continent
> - The future of the Irish Single Electricity Market (SEM), which currently integrates Northern Ireland and the Republic of Ireland
>
> Based on Froggatt et al. (2017)

Regulation and policy are currently lagging activity on the ground. Even in basic areas, such as how to facilitate half-hourly settlement for households and small businesses, policy and regulation is struggling to keep up with the pace of change. In some areas, such as regulations covering batteries, the government and Ofgem are focusing on removing barriers and uncertainties (HMG/Ofgem 2017). However, there are also entirely new areas of activity, such a local electricity trading platforms, for which the current system simply has no framework. Active participants, who will also in theory become involved in the industry codes processes, will expand from a relatively small number of companies to hundreds of thousands or even millions of people (IET 2013).

Mitchell et al. (2016) argue that a new set of governance principles is needed. One principle is that governance must be centered on the needs of end users of energy rather than the interests of networks or suppliers (see also Sandys et al. 2017 and Hoggett 2017). In the emerging digitized, data-driven energy system, governance frameworks must be able to engender trust and engagement in households, which will involve offering the right mix of safeguards and removal of barriers to their participation.

A second principle is that new governance frameworks are needed at the local and distribution levels, since it is here that most change will happen. Mitchell et al. (2016) explore the approach taken in New York state where distribution companies take a lead role in coordinating local platforms, but there is a range of possible different models and initiatives around the world, and an active debate about which will work best in the UK context (see also Sandys et al. 2017 and HMG/Ofgem 2017). Whichever model is chosen, it is clear that open and transparent access to data will be a key governance element because of the centrality of data in a distributed energy system. Mitchell et al. (2016) argue for a dedicated body to oversee the fair and open use of data.

There is also debate about the need for more coordination and direction setting during the process of transformation. This is potentially needed at several different levels, not only within electricity systems (e.g., between transmission and distribution levels or between network power flows and energy balancing) but also between traditionally separate vectors (e.g., heat, transport, and electricity) with their own distinct governance systems. There are some irreversible decisions with large and long-lasting consequences. What to do with the gas network is one such example.

A range of actors have called for some type of body or process to provide leadership and coordination during the transition, whether this is a "system architect" (IET 2013; Energy UK 2016; Taylor and Walker 2017), an "energy commission" (ETI 2016), or an "enabling framework process" (IET/Catapult Energy Systems 2017). Mitchell et al. (2016) argue that a body or forum is needed that cannot only set a direction of change but must also provide transparency and legitimacy to underpin the political consensus that will be needed to provide stability for investment in the new system. They also argue that delivery of new policy and regulation should be coordinated through a fully independent system operator and integrated across gas and electricity and across transmission and distribution levels (see also ETI 2016). However, the government has so far been resistant to calls for greater coordination and direction setting. Still working fundamentally within a market-led paradigm – a rejection of planning and a fear of the risks of creating stranded assets – the government and Ofgem are expecting much of the direction of change to be set by the industry itself (BEIS/Ofgem 2016: 77).

Cross-References

- Energy Governance in Germany
- Energy Governance in Ireland
- Energy Governance in the Netherlands
- Transition of Energy Systems: Patterns of Stability and Change

Acknowledgments The authors would like to thank Richard Lowes and Jessica Britton for comments and help with information and to Jörg Kemmerzell, Michèle Knodt, and participants at a workshop in Darmstadt in November 2017 for useful feedback and suggestions. The analysis presented here draws in part on research on governance and innovation in the UK energy system supported by the Engineering and Physical Sciences Research Council [EP/N014170/1].

References

Bird J. (2015). Let's get it right: A suggested framework for improving Government low carbon interventions. Sustainability first. http://www.sustainabilityfirst.org.uk/images/publications/other/Sustainability%20First%20-%20Lets%20Get%20It%20Right%20-%20A%20Suggested%20Framework%20for%20Low%20Carbon%20Interventions%20-%20Discussion%20Document%20-%20June%202015%20-%20Final%20Revise.pdf. Accessed 13 Oct 2017.

Bloomberg New Energy Finance (BNEF). (2012). UK Big 6 utility investment trends: A report for Greenpeace UK on the generation investments of the Big 6 utilities. https://about.bnef.com/blog/uk-big-6-utility-investment-trends-for-greenpeace-uk-the-generation-investments-of-the-big-6/. Accessed 25 Sept 2017.

Business, Energy and Industrial Strategy Department (BEIS). (2017a). Digest of UK energy statistics 2017. https://assets.publishing.service.gov.uk/government/uploads/system/uploads/attachment_data/file/643414/DUKES_2017.pdf. Accessed 16 May 2018.

Business, Energy and Industrial Strategy Department (BEIS). (2017b). A call for evidence on the reform of the Green Deal Framework. https://www.gov.uk/government/uploads/system/uploads/attachment_data/file/651304/Green_Deal_Framework_-_Call_for_Evidence_-_final.pdf. Accessed 3 Nov 2017.

Business, Energy and Industrial Strategy Department (BEIS). (2018). Implementing the end of unabated coal by 2025. https://assets.publishing.service.gov.uk/government/uploads/system/uploads/attachment_data/file/672137/Government_Response_to_unabated_coal_consultation_and_statement_of_policy.pdf. Accessed 18 May 2018.

Business, Energy and Industrial Strategy Department (BEIS)/Ofgem. (2016). A smart flexible energy system: A call for evidence. https://www.ofgem.gov.uk/system/files/docs/2016/12/smart_flexible_energy_system_a_call_for_evidence.pdf. Accessed 10 Oct 2017.

Butler, L., & Neuhoff, K. (2008). Comparison of feed-in tariff, quota and auction mechanisms to support wind power development. *Renewable Energy, 33*(8), 1854–1867.

Capoccia, G., & Kelemen, R. D. (2007). The study of critical junctures: Theory, narrative and counterfactuals in historical institutionalism. *World Politics, 59*, 341–369.

Carter, N. (2009). Vote blue, go green? Cameron's conservatives and the environment. *Political Quarterly, 80*(2), 233–242.

Carter, N., & Ockwell, D. (2007). New labour, new environment? An analysis of the labour Government's policy on climate change and biodiversity loss. Report to friends of the Earth. http://celp.org.uk/projects/foe/docs/fullreportfinal.pdf. Accessed 29 Sept 2017.

Chaudry, M., Abeysekera, M., Hosseini, S. H. R., Jenkins, N., & Wu, J. (2015). Uncertainties in decarbonising heat in the UK. *Energy Policy, 87*, 623–640.

Committee on Climate Change (CCC). (2017). Meeting carbon budgets: closing the policy gap – 2017 Report to Parliament. https://www.theccc.org.uk/wp-content/uploads/2017/06/2017-Report-to-Parliament-Meeting-Carbon-Budgets-Closing-the-policy-gap.pdf. Accessed 28 Sept 2017.

Connor, P. M., Xie, L., Lowes, R., Britton, J., & Richardson, T. (2015). The development of renewable heating policy in the United Kingdom. *Renewable Energy, 75*, 733–744.

Council of European Energy Regulators (CEER). (2015). Status review of renewable and energy efficiency support schemes in Europe in 2012 and 2013. https://www.ceer.eu/documents/104400/-/-/8b86f561-fa0b-0908-4a57-436bffceeb30. Accessed 2 Oct 2017.

Cowell, R., Ellis, G., Sherry-Brennan, F., Strachan, P. A., & Toke, D. (2017). Energy transitions, sub-national government and regime flexibility: How has devolution in the United Kingdom affected renewable energy development? *Energy Research and Social Science, 23*, 169–181.

Department for Transport (DfT). (2017). Vehicle licensing statistics: Annual 2016. https://www.gov.uk/government/uploads/system/uploads/attachment_data/file/608374/vehicle-licensing-statistics-2016.pdf. Accessed 6 Oct 2017.

Department of Energy and Climate Change (DECC). (2010). Ofgem review: Final report. https://www.gov.uk/government/uploads/system/uploads/attachment_data/file/48134/2151-ofgem-review-final-report.pdf. Accessed 20 Sept 2017.

Department of Energy and Climate Change (DECC). (2011). Planning our electric future: A White Paper for secure, affordable and low carbon electricity. https://www.gov.uk/government/uploads/system/uploads/attachment_data/file/48129/2176-emr-white-paper.pdf. Accessed 19 Sept 2017.

Department of Energy and Climate Change (DECC). (2013). The future of heating: Meeting the challenge. https://www.gov.uk/government/uploads/system/uploads/attachment_data/file/190149/16_04-DECC-The_Future_of_Heating_Accessible-10.pdf. Accessed 3 Oct 2017.

Department of Energy and Climate Change (DECC). (2014). Community energy strategy. https://www.gov.uk/government/uploads/system/uploads/attachment_data/file/275163/20140126Community_Energy_Strategy.pdf. Accessed 4 Oct 2017.

Dodds, P. E., & McDowall, W. (2013). The future of the UK gas network. *Energy Policy, 60*, 305–316.

Douglas, J. (2015). Decarbonising heat for UK homes, Energy Technologies Institute. https://s3-eu-west-1.amazonaws.com/assets.eti.co.uk/legacyUploads/2015/05/ETI-Smart-Systems-and-Heat-for-Energy-Institute-19-May-2015-Final.pdf. Accessed 5 Oct 2017.

Dresner, S., Jackson, T., & Gilbert, N. (2006). History and social responses to environmental tax reform in the United Kingdom. *Energy Policy, 34*(8), 930–939.

Eckersley, P. (2018). Who shapes local climate policy? Unpicking governance arrangements in English and German cities. *Environmental Politics, 27*(1), 139–160.

Energy UK (2016). Pathways for the GB electricity sector to 2030. https://www.energy-uk.org.uk/publication.html?task=file.download&id=5722. Accessed 4 Nov 2017.

Energy Technologies Institute (ETI). (2016). Enabling efficient networks for low-carbon futures: Options for Governance and Regulation. https://d2umxnkyjne36n.cloudfront.net/insightReports/3594-ETI---EEN-Report---V6-LINKS.pdf?mtime=20161004120524. Accessed 3 Oct 2017.

European Environment Agency (EEA). (2017). Trends and projections in Europe 2017: Tracking progress towards Europe's climate and energy targets. EEA Report No. 17/2017. https://www.eea.europa.eu/themes/climate/trends-and-projections-in-europe/trends-and-projections-in-europe-2017/index. Accessed 16 May 2018.

Froggatt, A., Wright, G., & Lockwood, M. (2017). Staying connected: Key elements for UK-EU27 energy cooperation after Brexit. https://www.chathamhouse.org/sites/files/chathamhouse/publications/research/2017-05-10-staying-connected-energy-cooperation-brexit-froggatt-wright-lockwood.pdf. Accessed 16 May 2018.

Fudge, S., Peters, M., Mulugetta, Y., & Jackson, T. (2011). Paradigms, policy and governance: The politics of energy regulation in the UK post-2000. *Environmental Policy and Governance, 21*, 291–302.

Geels, F. W. (2004). From sectoral systems of innovation to socio-technical systems: Insights about dynamics and change from sociology and institutional theory. *Research Policy, 33*(6–7), 897–920.

Geels, F. W. (2010). Ontologies, socio-technical transitions (to sustainability), and the multi-level perspective. *Research Policy, 39*, 495–510.

Geels, F. W. (2014). Regime resistance against low-carbon transitions: Introducing politics and power into the multi-level perspective. *Theory, Culture and Society, 31*(5), 21–40.

Geels, F., & Schot, J. (2007). Typology of sociotechnical transition pathways. *Research Policy, 36*, 399–417.

Goos, M., & Manning, A. (2007). Lousy and lovely jobs: The rising polarization of work in Britain. *Review of Economics and Statistics, 89*(1), 118–133.

Gregg, P., Machin, S., & Fernández-Salgado, K. (2014). Real wages and unemployment in the big squeeze. *Economic Journal, 124*(576), 408–432.

H.M. Government. (2006). The Energy challenge – Energy review. https://assets.publishing.service.gov.uk/government/uploads/system/uploads/attachment_data/file/272376/6887.pdf. Accessed 20 Oct 2017.

H.M. Government. (2009). The UK low carbon transition plan: National strategy for climate and energy. https://assets.publishing.service.gov.uk/government/uploads/system/uploads/attachment_data/file/228752/9780108508394.pdf. Accessed 20 Oct 2017.

H.M. Government. (2017). Clean growth strategy. https://www.gov.uk/government/uploads/system/uploads/attachment_data/file/651916/BEIS_The_Clean_Growth_online_12.10.17.pdf. Accessed 3 Nov 2017.

H.M. Government/Ofgem. (2017). *Upgrading our energy system: Smart systems and flexibility plan*. London: HMG/Ofgem. https://www.gov.uk/government/uploads/system/uploads/attachment_data/file/633442/upgrading-our-energy-system-july-2017.pdf. Accessed 29 Sept 2017.

H.M. Treasury. (2010). Carbon price floor: Support and certainty for low-carbon investment. https://assets.publishing.service.gov.uk/government/uploads/system/uploads/attachment_data/file/81273/consult_carbon_price_support_condoc.pdf. Accessed 17 Oct 2017.

Hall, P. (1993). Policy paradigms, social learning, and the state: The case of economic policymaking in Britain. *Comparative Politics, 25*(3), 275–296.

Hall, P. A., & Soskice, D. (2001). An introduction to varieties of capitalism. In P. A. Hall & D. Soskice (Eds.), *Varieties of capitalism: The institutional foundations of comparative advantage* (pp. 1–68). Oxford: Oxford University Press.

Hammond, G. P., & Norman, J. B. (2012). Decomposition analysis of energy-related carbon emissions from UK manufacturing. *Energy, 41*, 220–227.

Hawkey, D., Webb, J., & Winksel, M. (2013). Organization and governance of urban energy systems: District heating and cooling in the UK. *Journal of Cleaner Production, 50*(1), 22–31.

Helm, D. (2004). *Energy, the state and the market: British energy policy since 1979*. Oxford: Oxford University Press.

Helm, D. (2005). The assessment: The new energy paradigm. *Oxford Review of Economic Policy, 21*(1), 1–18.

Helm, D. (2013). British infrastructure policy and the gradual return of the state. *Oxford Review of Economic Policy, 29*, 287–306.

Hoggett, R. (2017). People, demand and governance in future energy systems. Working paper 1701, Energy Policy Group, University of Exeter. http://projects.exeter.ac.uk/igov/wp-content/uploads/2017/02/People-Demand-and-Governance-in-Future-Energy-Systems.pdf. Accessed 3 Nov 2017.

Howard, R., & Bengherbi, Z. (2016). Power 2.0: Building a smarter, greener, cheaper electricity system. https://policyexchange.org.uk/wp-content/uploads/2016/11/POWER-2.0.pdf. Accessed 2 Nov 2017.

Institution of Engineering and Technology (IET). (2013). Electricity networks: Handling a shock to the system. https://www.theiet.org/factfiles/energy/pnjv-page.cfm. Accessed 2 Nov 2017.

Institution of Engineering and Technology (IET)/Energy Catapult Systems. (2017). Future power systems architecture 2: Synthesis report. https://www.theiet.org/sectors/energy/resources/fpsa/fpsa-future-system-challenges.cfm. Accessed 2 Nov 2017.

Jaccard, M. (1995). The changing rationale for government intervention in the electricity industry. *Energy Policy, 23*(7), 579–592.

Jacobsson, S., & Lauber, V. (2006). The politics and policy of energy system transformation – Explaining the German diffusion of renewable energy technology. *Energy Policy, 34*(3), 256–276.

Johnstone, P., Stirling, A., & Sovacool, B. (2017). Policy mixes for incumbency: Exploring the destructive recreation of renewable energy, shale gas 'fracking,' and nuclear power in the United Kingdom. *Energy Research and Social Science, 33*, 147–162.

Keay, M., Rhys, J., & Robinson, D. (2012). Decarbonization of the electricity industry – Is there still a place for markets? Working paper EL9, Oxford Institute for Energy Studies. https://www.oxfordenergy.org/wpcms/wp-content/uploads/2012/11/EL-9.pdf. Accessed 2 Oct 2017.

Keeler, J. T. S. (2016). The politics of shale gas and anti-fracking movements in France and the UK. In Y. Wang & W. E. Hefley (Eds.), *The global impact of unconventional shale gas development*. Basel: Springer.

Kern, F., Kuzemko, C., & Mitchell, C. (2014a). Measuring and explaining policy paradigm change: The case of UK energy policy. *Policy and Politics, 42*(4), 513–530.

Kern, F., Smith, A., Shaw, C., et al. (2014b). From laggard to leader: Explaining offshore wind developments in the UK. *Energy Policy, 69*, 635–646.

Kern, F., Verhees, B., Raven, R., & Smith, A. (2015). Empowering sustainable niches: Comparing UK and Dutch offshore wind developments. *Technological Forecasting and Social Change, 100*, 344–355.

Kern, F., Gaede, J., Meadowcroft, J., & Watson, J. (2016). The political economy of carbon capture and storage: An analysis of two demonstration projects. *Technological Forecasting and Social Change, 102*, 250–260.

Kivimaa, P., & Kern, F. (2016). Creative destruction or mere niche support? Innovation policy mixes for sustainability transitions. *Research Policy, 45*(1), 205–217.

Kuzemko, C. (2013). *The energy security-climate nexus: Institutional change in the UK and beyond*. Basingstoke/New York: Palgrave Macmillan.

Kuzemko, C., Mitchell, C., Lockwood, M., & Hoggett, R. (2017). Policies, politics and demand side innovations: The untold story of Germany's energy transition. *Energy Research and Social Science, 28*, 58–67.

Leicester, A. (2006). *The UK tax system and the environment*. London: The Institute for Fiscal Studies.

Lockwood, M. (2013). The political sustainability of climate policy: The case of the UK climate change act. *Global Environmental Change, 23*(5), 1339–1348.

Lockwood, M. (2016). The UK's levy control framework: Effects and significance. *Energy Policy, 97*, 193–201.

Lockwood, M., Mitchell, C., Hoggett, R., & Kuzmeko, C. (2017). The governance of industry rules and energy system innovation: The case of codes in Great Britain. *Utilities Policy, 47*, 41–49.

Lorenzoni, I., & Benson, D. (2014). Radical institutional change in environmental governance: Explaining the origins of the UK Climate Change Act 2008 through discursive and streams perspectives. *Global Environmental Change, 29*, 10–21.

Lorenzoni, I., O'Riordan, T., & Pidgeon, N. (2008). Hot air and cold feet: The UK response to climate change. In H. Compston & I. Bailey (Eds.), *Turning down the heat: The politics of climate policy in affluent democracies* (pp. 104–124). Basingstoke/New York: Palgrave Macmillan.

Mahoney, J., & Thelen, K. (2010). A theory of gradual institutional change. In J. Mahoney & K. Thelen (Eds.), *Explaining institutional change: Ambiguity, agency and power* (pp. 1–37). Cambridge: Cambridge University Press.

Mallaburn, P. S., & Eyre, N. (2014). Lessons from energy efficiency policy and programmes in the UK from 1973 to 2013. *Energy Efficiency, 7*, 23–41.

Martin, R., de Preux, L. B., & Wagner, U. J. (2009). The impacts of the climate change levy on business: Evidence from micro-data. Discussion Paper 6, Centre for Economic Performance, London School of Economics. http://eprints.lse.ac.uk/28592/1/dp0917.pdf. Accessed 17 Oct 2017.

Mitchell, C. (2008). *The political economy of sustainable energy*. Basingstoke/New York: Palgrave.

Mitchell, C., & Connor, P. (2004). Renewable energy policy in the UK 1990–2003. *Energy Policy, 32*(17), 1935–1947.

Mitchell, C., Bauknecht, D., & Conor, P. (2006). Effectiveness through risk reduction: A comparison of the renewable obligation in England and Wales and the feed-in system in Germany. *Energy Policy, 34*(3), 297–305.

Mitchell, C., Lockwood, M., Hoggett, R., & Kuzemko, C. (2016). Governing for innovation, sustainability and affordability: An institutional framework. Energy policy group, University of Exeter. http://projects.exeter.ac.uk/igov/wp-content/uploads/2016/11/Final-Framework-Paper.pdf. Accessed 5 Nov 2017.

National Audit Office (NAO). (2017). Carbon capture and storage: The second competition for government support. Report by the Comptroller and Auditor General. https://www.nao.org.uk/

wp-content/uploads/2017/01/Carbon-Capture-and-Storage-the-second-competition-for-government-support.pdf. Accessed 22 Oct 2017.

National Infrastructure Commission (NIC). (2017). Congestion, capacity, carbon: Priorities for National Infrastructure. https://www.nic.org.uk/wp-content/uploads/Congestion-Capacity-Carbon_-Priorities-for-national-infrastructure.pdf. Accessed 4 Oct.

Ofgem. (2016). Overview paper – Future insights. https://www.ofgem.gov.uk/system/files/docs/2016/10/future_insights_overview_paper.pdf. Accessed 30 Oct 2017.

Ofgem. (2017). Local energy in a transforming energy system. Future Insights Series https://www.ofgem.gov.uk/system/files/docs/2017/01/ofgem_future_insights_series_3_local_energy_final_300117.pdf. Accessed 3 Nov 2017.

Oliver, M. J., & Pemberton, H. (2004). Learning and change in 20th century British economic policy. *Governance, 17*(3), 415–441.

Palmer, J., & Cooper, I. (2013). Household energy fact file 2013, Department of Energy and Climate Change. https://www.gov.uk/government/uploads/system/uploads/attachment_data/file/345141/uk_housing_fact_file_2013.pdf. Accessed 13 Oct.

Pearson, P., & Watson, J. (2012). *UK energy policy 1980–2010: A history and lessons to be learnt*. London: Parliamentary Group for Energy Studies. http://sro.sussex.ac.uk/38852/1/uk-energy-policy.pdf. Accessed 23 Sept 2017.

Porter, D. (2014). *Electricity supply: The British experiment*. Cirencester: Mereo Books.

Pöyry. (2009). Impact of intermittency: How wind variability could change the shape of the British and Irish electricity markets. http://www.poyry.co.uk/sites/www.poyry.co.uk/files/media/related_material/impact-of-intermittency.pdf. Accessed 27 Oct 2017.

Pöyry/Imperial College. (2017). Roadmap for flexibility services to 2030: A report to the committee on climate change. https://www.theccc.org.uk/wp-content/uploads/2017/06/Roadmap-for-flexibility-services-to-2030-Poyry-and-Imperial-College-London.pdf. Accessed 23 Oct 2017.

Ragwitz, M., Held, A., Resch, G., et al. (2007). Assessment and optimization of renewable energy support schemes in the European electricity market – Final report. OPTRES, Intelligent Energy for Europe. https://ec.europa.eu/energy/sites/ener/files/documents/2007_02_optres.pdf. Accessed 11 Oct 2017.

Regen. (2017). Energy storage: The next wave – Growth prospects and market outlook for energy storage. https://www.regensw.co.uk/Handlers/Download.ashx?IDMF=9d010979-7cc4-4515-b900-a65a4a4765b7. Accessed 17 May 2018.

Roques, F., Newberry, D., & Nuttall, W. (2005). Investment incentives and electricity market design: The British experience. *Review of Network Economics, 4*(2), 93–127.

Rosenow, J. (2012). Energy savings obligations in the UK – A history of change. *Energy Policy, 49*, 373–382.

Rosenow, J., & Eyre, N. (2013). The green deal and the energy company obligation. *Proceedings of the Institution of Civil Engineers, Energy, 166*(EN3), 127–136.

Rosenow, J., Eyre, N., Bürger, V., & Rohde, C. (2013). Overcoming the upfront investment barrier – Comparing the German CO_2 building rehabilitation programme and the British green deal. *Energy and Environment, 24*(1–2), 83–103.

Rutledge, I. (2010). UK energy policy and market fundamentalism: A historical overview. In I. Rutledge & P. Wright (Eds.), *UK Energy policy and the end of market fundamentalism* (pp. 1–35). Oxford: Oxford University Press.

Sandys, L., Hardy, J., & Green R. (2017). ReShaping regulation: Powering from the future. https://www.imperial.ac.uk/media/imperial-college/grantham-institute/public/publications/collaborative-publications/Reshaping-Regulation-Powering-from-the-future.pdf. Accessed 1 Nov 2017

Sorrell, S., & Sijm, J. (2005). Carbon trading in the policy mix. In D. Helm (Ed.), *Climate-change policy* (pp. 194–217). Oxford: Oxford University Press.

Stenzel, T., & Frenzel, A. (2008). Regulating technological change – The strategic reactions of utility companies towards subsidy policies in the German, Spanish and UK electricity markets. *Energy Policy, 36*, 2645–2657.

Szarka, J. (2006). Wind power, policy learning and paradigm change. *Energy Policy, 34*, 3041–3048.

Taylor, P., & Walker, S. (2017) The role of the system architect. National Centre for Energy Systems Integration, University of Newcastle. https://blogs.ncl.ac.uk/cesi/files/2017/09/The-Role-of-the-System-Architect-CESI-Publications-CESI-TF-0006-02.pdf. Accessed 3 Nov 2017.

Toke, D. (2005). Explaining wind power planning outcomes: Some findings from a study in England and Wales. *Energy Policy, 33*(12), 1527–1539.

Toke, D. (2010). Wind power in UK and Denmark: Can rational choice help explain different outcomes? *Environmental Politics, 11*(4), 83–100.

Toke, D., & Fragaki, A. (2008). Do liberalised electricity markets help or hinder CHP and district heating? The case of the UK. *Energy Policy, 36*(4), 1448–1456.

Toke, D., Wolsink, M., & Breukers, S. (2008). Wind power deployment outcomes: How can we account for the differences? *Renewable and Sustainable Energy Reviews, 12*(4), 1129–1147.

Tsebelis, G. (2002). *Veto players: How political institutions work*. Princeton: Princeton University Press.

Turnheim, B., & Geels, F. W. (2012). Regime destabilization as the flipside of energy transitions: Lessons from the history of the British coal industry (1913–1997). *Energy Policy, 50*, 35–49.

Weber, C., Gebhardt, B., & Fahl, U. (2002). Market transformation for energy efficient technologies – Success factors and empirical evidence for gas condensing boilers. *Energy, 27*(3), 287–315.

Western Power Distribution (WPD). (2017). DSO transition strategy: December 2017 update. https://www.westernpower.co.uk/docs/About-us/Our-business/Our-network/Strategic-network-investment/DSO-Strategy/DSO-Transition-Strategy.aspx. 15 May 2018.

Wintour, P., & Carrington, D. (2012, 19 October). Fuel price row: Cameron tries to firm up energy tariff plan, The Guardian. https://www.theguardian.com/money/2012/oct/18/david-cameron-energy-bill-tariff-plan. Accessed 13 Oct 2017.

Woodman, B., & Mitchell, C. (2011). Learning from experience? The development of the renewables obligation in England and Wales. *Energy Policy, 39*(7), 3914–3921.

Part V

Comparison and Conclusion

Energy Governance in Europe: Country Comparison and Conclusion

49

Jörg Kemmerzell, Nils Bruch, and Michèle Knodt

Contents

Introduction	1290
Long-Term Development of the European Energy Mix	1291
Solid Fossil Fuels	1294
Oil, Petroleum, and Natural Gas	1297
Nuclear Energy	1299
Renewable Energy	1302
Governance and Policy Instruments of Transition	1305
Transition Outcomes	1308
Conclusion: An Energy Mix and Energy Governance for Climate Neutrality?	1313
Cross-References	1314
References	1315

Abstract

The final chapter draws on the findings from this handbook, particularly the country studies. We present energy policy in Europe by examining statistical data on the development of the European energy system and examples from individual countries. We first assess the long-term development of Europe's energy mix and then continue with a closer look at the developments of the main energy sources, governance structures, and policy instruments. To assess the overall results of the energy transition in Europe, we introduce a scoring system that takes into account both transition successes and greenhouse gas emission reductions. This scoring system is then applied to the EU-27 and the UK to compare the results of the different countries and to take stock of the development over the last 20 years. Finally, we give an outlook on the European challenges and perspectives on the way to climate neutrality by 2050.

J. Kemmerzell (✉) · N. Bruch · M. Knodt
Institute of Political Science, Technical University of Darmstadt, Darmstadt, Germany
e-mail: kemmerzell@pg.tu-darmstadt.de; nils.bruch@tu-darmstadt.de; knodt@pg.tu-darmstadt.de

© Springer Nature Switzerland AG 2022
M. Knodt, J. Kemmerzell (eds.), *Handbook of Energy Governance in Europe*,
https://doi.org/10.1007/978-3-030-43250-8_1

Keywords

Energy Transition · Comparison · Europe · European Union · Renewable Energy · Nuclear · Coal · Fossil Fuels · Energy Governance · Energy Policy

Introduction

This concluding chapter draws on the findings of this handbook, particularly on the country studies. It concentrates on the EU member states (including the United Kingdom which definitively left the EU in 2020), but takes, as seems appropriate, a sideways glance at non-EU countries. The chapter particularly draws on the contributions to national energy governance published in this handbook. At the time this chapter was finished, the impacts of the 2022 Russian invasion of Ukraine on the European energy policy were not yet predictable and will only be mentioned briefly in the text. However, it is expected that the war will have severe short and long-term consequences concerning all dimensions of energy policy.

Energy transitions are nothing new in the development of humankind, as major transitions from the use of traditional biomass to coal and other fossil fuels as our primary energy sources can be observed in the past. The European energy systems as we know them today are heavily shaped by the *third energy transition.* According to the environmental historian Vaclav Smil, the first energy transition came with the ability to make a fire by burning plants. The invention of farming established the second transition, which converted solar energy into food resources and replaced the sustenance economy. The third transition came along with industrialization and the rise of fossil fuels, (coal, mineral oil, and natural gas), and energy supply became the domain of machines, such as coal-fired power plants (Smil 2015, 2021). However, industrialization took different national path developments, since energy systems depend on geographic conditions as well as on a country's particular economic development and crucial political decisions (e.g., to phase in or refrain from energy supply by nuclear power). These path developments constitute powerful legacies and inertia even for the course of the *fourth energy transition*, which unlike the first three, aspires to climb back down the power density ladder, from highly concentrated fossil fuels to more dispersed renewable sources (Smil 2015).

It comes as no surprise that this fourth energy transition while displaying more or less an overall trend, at least in Europe, took different path developments with various policy instruments resulting in a variety of governance regimes. Even European policies spur differentiation rather than unification, as a recent analysis of renewable energy policies, has shown (Boasson et al. 2021). Therefore, the current European energy and climate goals (climate-neutrality by 2050) and policies (such as the *National Energy and Climate Plans* or the *EU Taxonomy for Sustainable Activities*) will probably lead to diverging and sometimes competing answers when it comes to implementation by national governance.

In this chapter, we portray energy governance in Europe by examining statistical data on the development of the European energy system and drawing on examples from individual countries. We first assess the long-term evolution of Europe's energy mix. Then we take a closer look at the developments of the main energy sources, governance structures, and policy instruments. To assess the overall results of the energy transition in Europe, we develop a scoring system that takes into account both transition successes and greenhouse gas reductions. This scoring system is then applied to the EU-27 and the UK to compare the results of the different countries and to take stock of the development over the last 20 years. Finally, we give an outlook on the European challenges and perspectives on the way to climate neutrality by 2050.

Long-Term Development of the European Energy Mix

Looking at long-term developments of the European energy mix grants important insights into which achievements have been made by the energy policies of the European Union in the member states and how other political, economic, and social developments influence the energy sector over time.

Figure 1 shows the energy mix in the European Union from 2000 to 2019. This time frame can be separated into three phases to outline major developments that ultimately led to the present energy mix. The first phase (2000–2007) is characterized by a high consistency in the composition of the energy mix, with no disruptive changes and only minor fluctuations. Although the objective of a comprehensive European energy transition was already discussed, not enough political and societal momentum has built up yet to initiate developments that would have a significant influence on the total European energy mix. The immediate effects and aftermath of the global economic crisis, which started in 2008 and led to a worldwide recession, shape the second phase (2008–2014). The macroeconomic development caused a drop in activity in all economic sectors of the European Union and led to a significant reduction in energy consumption. Greece is a prime example where the crisis hit the economy exceptionally hard and in turn, led to a significant decrease in energy consumption (▶ Chap. 29, "Energy Governance in Greece"). Similarly, the steady increase of energy consumption in Spain came to a halt when the high energy-consuming construction sector collapsed under the pressure of the economic crisis (▶ Chap. 44, "Energy Governance in Spain"). In the recent phase (2015–2019), the European ambitions for a sustainable energy transition came further into fruition, as renewable energy sources surpassed nuclear energy and solid fossil fuels, which dropped to an all-time low of 10.69% in 2019. Yet, liquid fossil fuels (oil and petroleum) experienced a renaissance in Europe during the recovery from the economic crisis, primarily because of a surge of fuel consumption in transport, and remain the most important energy sources in the European Union (Thomas and Rosenow 2020). Over the last two decades, the energy mix composition changed only slowly, illustrating the inertia inherent in the development of the European energy sector.

Going into more detail of the particular sources in the energy mix, the most evident observation of the long-term development is the dominance of oil and petroleum products, accounting for 34.6% to 38.3% of gross inland consumption during the time between 2000 and 2019. One of the main factors contributing to this

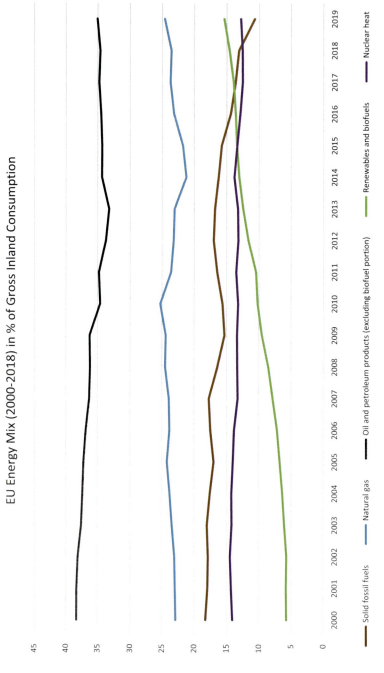

Fig. 1 Long-term development of the energy mix in the European Union, share of gross inland consumption 2000–2019 (Eurostat 2021a)

dominance is the transport sector, where oil and petroleum products are omnipresent as fuels for combustion engines in cars, trucks, ships, and airplanes. The transition from conventional combustion technologies to sustainable alternatives is facing major challenges (Tagliapietra et al. 2019; Dominković et al. 2018), so the slow developments in the transport sector are upholding oil and petroleum products as the most important energy source in the European Union. Furthermore, particularly in Southern Europe, oil had (Italy, Spain, or Portugal), or still has (Cyprus and Greece), made up a significant share in electricity generation.

The second most important energy source is natural gas accounting for 21% to 25% of gross inland consumption in the last two decades and used primarily for heating, industry and electricity production. As the combustion of natural gas emits less CO_2 than oil and has a far better greenhouse gas balance compared to solid fossil fuels, discussions about the use of natural gas as a bridge technology for the energy transition are ongoing (Szabo 2021; Mac Kinnon et al. 2018). However, the role of natural gas as a vital part of the energy transition is contested, as the controversial debates about the integration of gas infrastructure projects on the list of Projects of Common Interests of the EU have shown (CAN Europe 2021). These discussions showcase not only the relevancy but also the divisiveness between actors, of the future role of natural gas in the energy mix (Levoyannis 2021).

Becoming more unpopular in light of recent developments in energy and climate policy, solid fossil fuels such as hard coal and lignite have been on a downward trend since 2015, from 15% down to 10% of gross inland consumption in the European Union. To advance their energy transitions and reduce CO_2 emissions, most EU countries announced a coal phase-out and so contributed to the decline of solid fossil fuels (Rentier et al. 2019). However, a few EU members, such as Poland or Romania, are still heavily invested in solid fossil fuels, as they have large domestic resources of coal and lignite that can be used for cheap electricity production, and secure jobs in local economies (▶ Chaps. 37, "Energy Governance in the Republic of Poland," and ▶ 39, "Energy Governance in Romania").

Serving as an energy source mainly for the electricity baseload, the share of nuclear energy stayed at almost the same level throughout the last two decades. Still, a slow decline from 14% to 12.8% can be observed, resulting from several nuclear phase-outs, for example, in Germany (Jahn and Korolczuk 2012), Lithuania (Gaigalis et al. 2013), and Italy (▶ Chap. 32, "Energy Governance in Italy") due to domestic concerns about safety in the aftermath of the 2011 Fukushima Daiichi nuclear disaster and issues regarding nuclear waste disposal.

Lastly, the development of renewables can be characterized as a constant increase: from being the least important energy source that only accounted for 5.7% of gross inland consumption, to overtaking nuclear heat in 2015 and solid fossil fuels in 2017, to become the third most important energy source in the European energy mix with 15.3% of gross inland consumption. Progress in renewable energy technology, raising concerns about climate change followed by measures to decarbonize the energy sector, as well as energy and climate policy developments at international and European levels, supported the scaling-up of renewables during the last decade (Kanellakis et al. 2013; Sen and Ganguly 2017;

Pacesila et al. 2016). As a consequence, renewables are the energy source with the most drastic upturn over the time frame, substituting significant shares of other energy sources such as solid fossil fuels.

The long-term development of the energy mix in Europe is influenced by economic, political, and social developments that impact national and European energy policies. Yet, changes in the overall composition of the energy mix tend to be slow due to the inertia of sectoral supply and transport infrastructures that usually have amortization periods of many decades. However, change takes place, as the rising share of renewable energy shows. While the main developments of the energy sources were already briefly outlined, the next sections will go more deeply into the details and contextual factors that contributed to the distinct developments of each energy source.

Solid Fossil Fuels

The exploitation of coal, which accounts for the vast majority of solid fossil fuels, was central to the development of the European economic model, as coal combustion was a key driver of industrialization (Brüggemeier 2018). Thus the third energy transition, starting in the early nineteenth century, was based on an increase in *power density* (Smil 2015). Coal is used to generate heat for industrial processes, in iron and steel production, in power plants to generate electricity, and in cogeneration of heat and power. After all, coal was the most important energy source for heat generation in private households in Western Europe until the 1960s, (and still is today to some extent in parts of Eastern Europe), but since has been gradually replaced by natural gas, oil, district heating, or direct electricity use.

The importance of coal becomes visible in the European Coal and Steel Community (ECSC), which was the origin of the European Union. It was founded after World War II to regulate the coal and steel industries. Formally established in 1951 by the Treaty of Paris and signed by Belgium, France, Italy, Luxembourg, the Netherlands, and the Federal Republic of Germany, the ECSC was the first European organization based on the principle of supranationalism. The Treaty founded a common market for coal and steel among its member states and curtailed external coal trade (▶ Chap. 7, "European Union Energy Policy: A Discourse Perspective").

When talking about coal, a rough distinction must be made between lignite and hard coal. Large lignite deposits are found in Central Europe, among other places, with Germany being the largest producing country worldwide in 2018, closely followed by China and Turkey. Germany, Poland, and the Czech Republic are the most important producers and users of lignite within the European Union. Due to its low calorific value and high water content, lignite is hardly ever transported over long distances but is combusted in power plants close to the mines. The relatively low cost of opencast lignite mining has a positive effect on its economic competitiveness. Its spatial concentration has led to the emergence of typical coal regions, for example in Lusatia and the western Lower Rhine region (Germany), in northern Bohemia (Czech Republic), or Silesia (Poland). Of all the common fossil fuels, lignite has the worst greenhouse gas balance. Depending on the quality of the coal, about 0.4 kilograms of carbon dioxide are emitted per kWh of electricity generated. Hard coal has a significantly higher calorific value and a somewhat more favorable greenhouse gas balance. Global hard coal reserves are more than twice as high as lignite reserves. Due to its physical properties, there is a global trading market for hard coal; more than half of the hard coal consumed in the EU today comes from imports (Eurostat 2021a). Hard coal is used both in power generation and, as coking coal, as a basic material in iron and steel production. The major share of hard coal is imported, in particular from Russia, Colombia, and the United States. In the European Union, Poland is now the only country with significant hard coal production; all other traditional hard coal producing countries, such as Germany, the United Kingdom, France, Belgium, or the Czech Republic, have ceased or significantly reduced hard coal mining (Kemmerzell and Knodt 2021).

However, while the share of solid fossil fuels in domestic primary energy supply within the European Union decreased by 72% from 1990 to 2019, its share in gross energy consumption decreased by only 60%. This indicates that the decline in production was at least partly substituted by imports (Fig. 2).

The importance of coal varies greatly from one European country to another. Germany, Poland, the Czech Republic, Bulgaria, and Slovakia belong to the coal heartland (Osička et al. 2020a), where coal mining and combustion continue to play an important role and the coal industry remains an important employer. These countries are characterized by the fact that coal currently accounts for more than 20% of primary energy supply and gross energy consumption. In absolute terms, Poland is the largest producer with a production volume of 47 million tons, while Germany is the largest consumer within the European Union with 69 million tons. In Romania and Hungary, coal production plays a constant but less important role than in the aforementioned countries. Estonia is a special case, covering about 75% of its gross energy consumption by oil shale combustion. Like coal, oil shale is a solid fossil fuel, but it has an even worse carbon footprint. As a result, the Estonian economy is considered the most carbon dioxide intensive in the European Union (OECD 2017).

Former major coal-producing countries in which coal production has declined significantly or even ceased are the United Kingdom, Spain, Belgium, and France. In these countries, coal consumption has also declined rapidly, albeit to varying degrees. Coal particularly declined in the UK, where it accounted for 26% of primary energy supply and 30% of gross energy consumption in 1990, whereas in 2018, these figures had fallen to 1.3% and 4.3% respectively. This sharp decline has been explained by the *liberal* character of British economic governance. While coordinated market economies tend to be more reluctant to phase-out policies without consensual agreement, in liberal market economies the use of coal depends more strongly upon its market price, which could more easily be affected by carbon pricing: in the British case the *Carbon Floor Price* (Rentier et al. 2019; ▶ Chap. 48, "Energy Governance in the United Kingdom").

There has also been a significant decline in coal consumption in countries that have only small coal reserves of their own, but where coal has accounted for a significant share of the energy mix. This group of countries includes Austria, Italy, Denmark, Luxemburg, and the Netherlands. Denmark has been steadily replacing coal with renewables since the 1990s, particularly wind power for electricity and biomass for

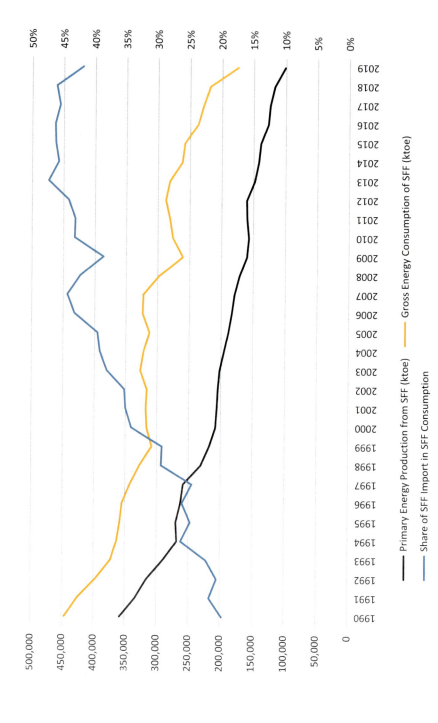

Fig. 2 Solid Fossil Fuel (SFF) production and consumption in the European Union, import share of SFF (Eurostat 2021a)

Table 1 Coal phase-out in the EU (Europe Beyond Coal 2022)

Coal phase-out	Countries
Completed	Austria (2020), Belgium (2016), Portugal (2021), Sweden (2020)
Announced	Bulgaria (2040), Czech Republic (2033), Croatia (2033), Denmark (2028), Finland (2029, 2025 if possible), France (2022), Germany (2035/38, 2030 if possible) Greece (2025), Hungary (2025), Ireland (2025), Italy (2025), Netherlands (2029), Romania (2032), Slovakia (2030), Slovenia (2033), Spain (2030), United Kingdom (2024)
Under discussion	Poland (2049)
No coal in power generation	Cyprus, Latvia, Lithuania, Luxemburg, Malta; Estonia as special case due to oil shale combustion

heating. The share of coal in gross energy consumption has fallen from 34% in 1990 to less than 10% in 2019. The Netherlands has met an important part of its energy needs through natural gas since the discovery of the Groningen gas field in 1959 but maintained a constant coal share in the energy mix of about 10%. However, the Dutch government has decided to stop gas production maybe already by 2022 due to dwindling gas reserves and increasing geological problems.

Finally, a group of particularly small countries neither produce coal nor have a significant share of coal in their energy mix. These include Lithuania, the Republic of Latvia, and Cyprus. Croatia has two smaller coal-fired power plants, but they contribute only about 4% to the national energy supply. Due to their age, however, their operation could be discontinued if modernization measures are not carried out because of non-compliance with pollutant limits.

In all countries of the European Union, coal is in massive retreat, albeit to varying degrees. The majority of EU members have even opted for a phase-out of coal (before the long-term European goal of climate-neutrality in 2050) or have already done so. Four groups of countries can be distinguished: Countries that have completed the coal phase-out; countries that have set a fixed phase-out date, countries with coal phase-out under discussion, and countries without coal in power generation (Table 1).

Outside the EU, however, the situation is different. In highly developed countries, such as Norway and Switzerland, coal lost importance already in the last millennium, whereas in the poorer countries of the Western Balkans a phase-out of coal is not yet being discussed. In Ukraine and Turkey, which are among the most important coal-dependent countries, there are no signals of a coal phase-out; on the contrary, Turkey is planning a considerable expansion of its power plant capacities (Kemmerzell and Knodt 2021, p. 69).

Oil, Petroleum, and Natural Gas

Oil and natural gas have always been vital elements in the energy system of Europe. Oil and petroleum products are primarily consumed as gasoline, diesel, kerosene, or heavy fuel oil in the transport sector which includes road transport, aviation, and water transport. Furthermore, oil is used in the production of non-energy products, such as lubricants, plastics, or bitumen used for road construction (Eurostat 2021d). The most important European crude oil producers are Norway and the United Kingdom which possess exploitable offshore reserves within their maritime boundaries. However, production in both these countries peaked around the turn of the century. Top crude oil producers of the European Union are Denmark, Italy, and Romania which have only a small production volume in comparison to Norway and the UK (Eurostat 2021d). The structure of natural gas consumption differs in multiple ways from that of oil and petroleum because it only plays a marginal role in transport and is used primarily in the household sector for heating. The share of natural gas in electricity production has also increased steadily over the past decade (Eurostat 2021a). Production of natural gas in the European Union is led by the Netherlands which has access to large offshore gas fields. However, gas production in the Netherlands will significantly decrease over the coming years due to a phase-out of onshore gas production in the Groningen gas field (the largest gas field in Europe), as the extraction is causing earthquakes in the region. In comparison, the second and third most important producers, Romania and Germany, only produce marginal amounts (Eurostat 2021c).

Even if crude oil and natural gas can be exploited and produced in Europe, the bulk has to be imported to satisfy the demand of European countries, as the high import dependency rates in European countries illustrate (Eurostat 2021d). In Greece, oil and petroleum products are the most important energy source in the energy mix, of which 98% have to be imported, making the country highly dependent on their suppliers, with little political efforts to change this situation. Oil is mainly used in transport, where the introduction of alternatives for diesel and gasoline vehicles in the market has not been successful and is lagging in comparison with other European states (▶ Chap. 29, "Energy Governance in Greece"). In contrast, the reduction of oil dependency has been a priority of the Swedish energy policy since the 1970s, enabling the replacement of oil-based energy technologies with nuclear and renewable energy, especially in the electricity and heating sectors (▶ Chap. 45, "Energy Governance in Sweden"). The remaining share of oil is mostly used in transport, but measures were introduced to decrease oil dependency in this sector too, one of which being the use of biofuels as a surrogate for petroleum products. The share of biofuels increased steadily so that in 2018, 23% of energy demand in transport was met by non-fossil fuels. However, most of the biofuels are imported because of high domestic production costs (▶ Chap. 45, "Energy Governance in Sweden").

In contrast to oil and petroleum products, natural gas is mostly used in heating, industry and electricity production instead of the transport sector. Natural gas plays a particularly important role in Hungary, where energy policy was strongly influenced by the cheap supply of natural gas by the Soviet Union (▶ Chap. 30, "Energy Governance in Hungary"). Even after its collapse, Hungary could rely on cheap supply from the former Soviet Union which enabled a national energy policy focused strongly on the affordability of natural gas. The role of gas increased further when decarbonization became a more prominent aspect of the energy policy in light of rising carbon prices of coal-based electricity production. Even if Hungary plans to reduce its share of natural gas and substitute the demand with renewable sources, natural gas still plays a major role in the energy mix, with favorable relations to

Russia reinforcing the existing energy supply structure (▶ Chap. 30, "Energy Governance in Hungary"). Contrary to Hungary, natural gas only plays a minor role in Finland. The energy policy discourse in the Nordic country is centered on security of supply and the reduction of import dependency. Byproducts of their large domestic forestry industry have been successfully utilized for different energy products and the extensive use of nuclear energy further secured energy supply and contributed to the political goal of reducing the dependence on Russian energy (▶ Chap. 26, "Energy Governance in Finland"). The comparison of the role of natural gas in Hungary and Finland shows that historical path dependencies, national energy priorities, and external factors, such as bilateral relations with energy-exporting countries, influence the utilization of natural gas in the domestic energy systems.

Besides country-specific factors, debates about natural gas as a bridge technology for the energy transition will also decide the future of natural gas in the European energy system (Szabo 2021). The substitution of coal with natural gas is seen by one side as a crucial step for the rapid decarbonization of the energy sector, complementing renewable energy development (Safari et al. 2019). Others describe the use of natural gas in the context of decarbonization as greenwashing of fossil fuels and predict technological lock-ins contradicting effective energy transitions (Stephenson et al. 2012; Zhang et al. 2016) and negligible mitigation effects (Gürsan and de Gooyert 2021; Levi 2013). This controversial debate before the war in Ukraine suggested, that natural gas would continue to play an important role in the national energy systems and the European energy transition. This development was disrupted with the invasion of Ukraine by Russia and the sanctions against Russia that followed. Oil and petroleum products are not seen as bridge technologies in the European Union, yet the transition of the transport sector away from oil is a major challenge, even if different technologies exist to achieve decarbonization. Electrification is seen as a solution with high potential for a large-scale transition of the European car fleet (Dominković et al. 2018), while the decarbonization of maritime transport and aviation might be achieved by other technologies such as hydrogen or E-fuels. Despite the very strong efforts needed and the major challenges to be faced, it is expected that the role of oil will diminish in the coming decades (Cherif et al. 2021).

Nuclear Energy

Nuclear energy is a constant factor as a baseload energy source in Europe. Thermal nuclear power plants display a high level of power density and constant energy supply under ordinary operation. After the Second World War, the civil use of nuclear energy became a compelling socio-technical future vision. Europe did not abstain from adopting the promises of the nuclear age, so in 1957 EURATOM became, alongside the ECSC and the European Economic Community (EEC), one of the foundations of European integration. EURATOM was intended to provide a European legal framework for the development of the nuclear industry and is still active. Even though EURATOM comprises all EU member countries, it remained outside the legal framework of the European Union (Fischer 2011). EURATOM, despite the membership of countries critical of nuclear energy, is in its own right a member of the international consortia for the development of Generation IV reactors and the fusion reactor ITER. Furthermore, it is active in energy partnerships with external partners such as Ukraine, where it is operative in the upgrading of nuclear power plants (NPP) (World Nuclear Association 2022).

While the overall development in Europe with respect to fossil fuels generally points in a similar direction, we observe a sharp divide in nuclear energy (Table 2). Nearly half of the European Union member countries (13 of 27) operate 103 nuclear power plants, while 14 countries do not operate NPPs. Additionally, 69 reactors are operational in five non-EU countries (World Nuclear Association 2022). When it comes to prospects of nuclear power, we can distinguish countries that propose or are already constructing new reactors and countries that abstain from planning new NPPs.

The first group comprises countries that already have NPPs and plan to keep nuclear power in their energy portfolios and those that intend to phase in. The most important operator of NPPs is France which recently announced the modernization of its reactor fleet. But the example of their most well-known project, the reactor of *Flamanville*, was supposed to go online in 2012 and cost € 3.3bn but meanwhile was postponed to 2023 and costs raised to nearly €13 bn. A country to look out for is Poland, which has no nuclear power capacities to date but has proposed the commission of six reactors in the 2030s to compensate for ceasing coal capacities. This seems remarkable, as to date all NPP projects seem strongly subjected to the "iron law of megaprojects," "over time, over budget, under benefits, over and over again" (Flyvbjerg 2017, p. 1). In addition to *Flamanville*, the Finnish NPP *Olkiluoto* can serve as a further example here. The commissioning of the third unit of the NPP has been postponed several times. While originally grid-access was envisioned in 2011, the reactor did not reach criticality until December 2021. Likewise, costs crowded out in a significant way from € 3bn to about € 11bn (Schneider and Froggatt 2019, p. 66).

Among the latter are countries that phase-out existing NPPs without building new ones and countries that neither have, nor intend to construct, NPPs. A special case among the countries that aspire to a nuclear phase-out is Germany which decided to close down NPPs before they reached their standard service life of at least 40 years. Sweden and Belgium pursued a similar policy until the 2000s but returned to operating NPPs as long as their service life permitted, resulting in a prolonged operational life of 50 years in Belgium. Outside the EU, Switzerland shows a similar picture, abandoning preliminary plans for an accelerated phase-out and allowing operation until the end of

Table 2 Nuclear Power Plants (NPPs) in EU member countries (World Nuclear Association 2022, own compilation)

	NPPs operational in 2021	No NPPs operational in 2021
New NPPs proposed	Bulgaria, Czech Republic, Croatia, Finland, France, Hungary, Romania, Slovakia, Slovenia	Lithuania, Poland
No new NPPs proposed	Belgium, Germany, Netherlands, Spain, Sweden	Austria, Cyprus, Denmark, Estonia, Greece, Ireland, Italy, Latvia, Luxemburg, Malta, Portugal

the 50-year service life. The last Swiss NPP will therefore go offline in 2034. Italy and Lithuania are remarkable cases, as they have already phased out nuclear energy. In Italy, a referendum held in 1987 decided for an immediate decommission of the then three operating NPPs. Subsequently, the government implemented the referendum result and shut down the last NPP in 1990. Lithuania decommissioned the *Ignalina* NPP in 2009, as agreed in the accession negotiations to the EU, but probably aspires to build a new NPP in the long-term.

While countries differ significantly in their attitudes toward the use of nuclear energy, its share in energy supply and consumption has remained highly stable over the past 30 years. This is due to the nature of nuclear infrastructures, which indicate high upfront costs and require long-term investments in NPPs with very long service life. After a smooth increase since 1990, the share of nuclear power in primary energy production reached its peak of 28.7% in 2006 and has remained stable at around 28% since then (Fig. 3).

While on the one hand, it might seem that nuclear power and renewables, which are characterized by constant growth, will form the future foundation of the electricity supply, on the other hand, there are fundamental systemic conflicts between the two energy sources. Nuclear power plants deliver a constant output independent of external influences but are sluggish and hardly adjustable. Renewables, on the other hand, are flexible, easily regulated, but (at least in the case of photovoltaics and onshore wind energy) highly dependent on external influences. Both forms of energy, therefore, require different grid architectures and provoke system conflicts when feeding them into the grid (Verbruggen 2008).

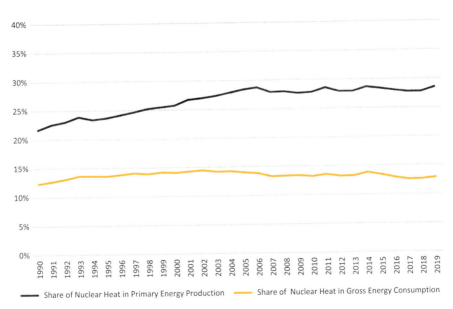

Fig. 3 Nuclear heat production and consumption in the European Union (Eurostat 2021a)

Consequently, both the nuclear and the renewable lobbies raise the issue of compatibility of NPPs and renewable energy. For example, the World Nuclear Association complains about the "preferential access to the grid by subsidized renewable sources," which undermines the "load factors for incumbent base-load providers" (World Nuclear Association 2022). Furthermore, in the integrated European electricity market, this effect does not stop at the national borders, but leads to severe interconnection problems, as intermittent renewable surplus electricity is dumped on transmission systems of neighboring countries (World Nuclear Association 2022). Similarly, the German think tank Agora Energiewende which strongly promotes the expansion of renewables, emphasizes that in an electricity system dominated by renewables, NPPs are a somewhat foreign element as they lack the required flexibility (Fraunhofer IWES 2015).

Within EU energy policy, notwithstanding the fundamental sovereignty of the member states over their energy mix, nuclear power remains one of the most controversial issues. Particularly the proposal of the EU Commission to categorize nuclear power (as well as natural gas) as *green* in the *EU Taxonomy for Sustainable Activities* raised a heated debate (Simon 2022). While two EU members, Austria and Luxembourg, have announced a lawsuit against the Commission, the countries that openly support nuclear power seem to be ahead of the game, particularly as the majority of member states apparently are unwilling to commit political capital to this dispute. The strength of the pro-nuclear faction is expressed, for example, in a joint article by ministers from ten EU countries, including France and all four *Visegrád countries*, which was published in eight leading European dailies such as La Republicca, El País, and Die Welt. They emphasize that modern nuclear power plants must be an indispensable part of a climate-neutral energy supply because they alone combine climate friendliness and high security of supply (Le Maire 2021).

Renewable Energy

Renewable energy is defined as "energy obtained from naturally repetitive and persistent flows of energy occurring in the local environment" and comprises water, wind, and solar power, as well as biomass and other sources (Twidell and Weir 2015). The use of renewable energy is the foundation of the energy transition as it is necessary to decarbonize the energy system. The share of renewable energy increased steadily over the last 20 years. In 2019, the European Union, plus the United Kingdom, achieved a total share of 19% renewables in gross energy consumption. But the availability and production of renewable energy sources differ significantly among European countries. Renewable energy systems require technical transformations to handle a higher degree of decentralization and volatile energy production. Besides technical elements, political, social, and economic factors are affecting renewable energy development on the national scale, leading to major differences between European countries (Fig. 4).

These differences concern the total share of renewable energy in the national energy mix, the major renewable energy sources, and the sectors where renewable energy is consumed (Table 3).

49 Energy Governance in Europe: Country Comparison and Conclusion

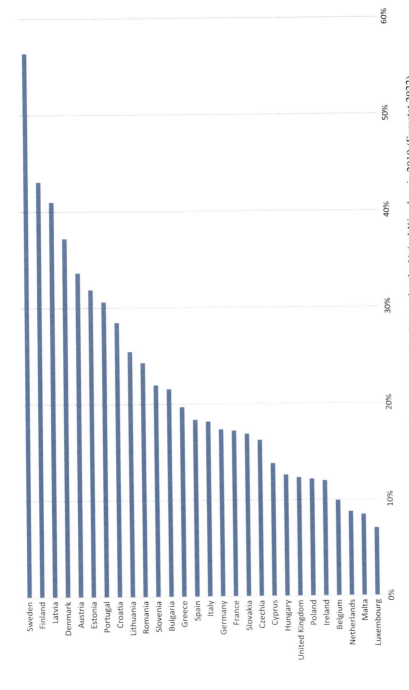

Fig. 4 Share of renewable energy in gross energy consumption of EU Member States plus the United Kingdom in 2019 (Eurostat 2022)

Table 3 Sectoral share of renewable energy in 2019 (Eurostat 2022)

Country	Electricity (%)	Transport (%)	Heating/Cooling (%)	Total share (%)
Belgium	20.83	6.81	8.31	9.92
Bulgaria	23.51	7.89	35.51	21.56
Czechia	14.05	7.83	22.65	16.24
Denmark	65.35	7.17	48.02	37.20
Germany	40.82	7.68	14.55	17.35
Estonia	22.00	5.15	52.28	31.89
Ireland	36.49	8.93	6.32	11.98
Greece	31.30	4.05	30.19	19.68
Spain	36.93	7.61	18.86	18.36
France	22.38	9.25	22.46	17.22
Croatia	49.78	5.85	36.79	28.47
Italy	34.97	9.05	19.70	18.18
Cyprus	9.76	3.32	35.10	13.80
Latvia	53.42	5.11	57.76	40.97
Lithuania	18.79	4.05	47.36	25.46
Luxembourg	10.86	7.65	8.71	7.05
Hungary	9.99	8.03	18.12	12.61
Malta	8.04	8.69	25.69	8.49
Netherlands	18.22	12.51	7.08	8.77
Austria	75.14	9.77	33.80	33.63
Poland	14.35	6.12	15.98	12.16
Portugal	53.77	9.09	41.65	30.62
Romania	41.71	7.85	25.74	24.29
Slovenia	32.63	7.98	32.16	21.97
Slovakia	21.94	8.31	19.70	16.89
Finland	38.07	21.29	57.49	43.08
Sweden	71.19	30.31	66.12	56.39
United Kingdom	34.77	8.86	7.84	12.34
EU-28	34.17	8.89	20.55	18.88

The country with the highest renewable energy share in the European Union is Sweden. As already described in the section on oil and natural gas, the energy policy of Sweden has been aimed at a reduction of import dependency since the 1970s and introduced renewable energy early on to address this issue, making the country a frontrunner in renewable energy development. Almost two-thirds of renewable energy is produced by using hydro power, followed by wind. In total 71.19% of electricity is powered by renewable energy. This is only topped among EU members by Austria, with 75.14% of electricity from renewable sources, mainly from large hydropower plants (▶ Chap. 20, "Energy Governance in Austria"). With a large lead over other European countries, Sweden is the leader in renewable energy consumption in the transport sector with a share of 31.3%. This can be attributed to the use of biofuels and increasing numbers of electric vehicles powered by renewable electricity, as well as electrified rail transport. In the heating sector, Sweden is also the number one in

Europe after transforming residential heating systems from fossil fuel-based technology to biomass-based district heating and electric heat pumps, powered by renewable electricity (▶ Chap. 45, "Energy Governance in Sweden").

But what about the other end of the scale? Here, we find that the Netherlands has one of the lowest shares of renewable energy in the European Union, with only 8.77% in 2019. A significant factor responsible for the small share is that the natural gas reserves of the Netherlands can secure energy supply until at least 2030. Even if renewable energy policies have been part of the Dutch energy policy since the early 1990s, the abundance of fossil resources has damped high political ambitions in renewable energy development until climate change became more salient on the political agenda (▶ Chap. 35, "Energy Governance in the Netherlands"). Renewables accounted for 18.79% of electricity in the year 2019, of which almost half was generated by wind turbines. Due to its geographical location at the North Sea, the Netherlands has a lot of potential for offshore wind parks and the development of the renewable energy industry. Wind power, therefore, has been identified as a priority area for the energy strategy of the Dutch government. In the transport sector, 12.51% of energy consumption is covered by renewable energy and so the Netherlands is above the European average of 8.8% in this sector. The largest deficit can be found in the heating sector, with a renewable share of only 7.08%. The heating sector is dominated by natural gas, for example, in the form of gas-fired combined heat and power plants, which also receive governmental support via tax exemptions (▶ Chap. 35, "Energy Governance in the Netherlands"). Around 90% of Dutch households are connected to the natural gas grid, supplied by domestic reserves and therefore major transformative efforts are needed to increase the share of renewable energy in the heating sector (Jansma et al. 2020). The comparison of the Netherlands and Sweden shows that contextual factors impact the development of renewable energy on a national scale. While Sweden was able to increase its renewable energy share through political ambitions to reduce import dependency on fossil fuels, the Netherlands has abundant natural gas reserves, triggering lock-in effects that hindered large-scale development of renewables, as natural gas was affordable and could be supplied without depending on imports.

Despite the national differences in the energy mixes, renewable energy is continuously on the rise in Europe. But a further intensive increase is necessary to achieve the goal of the European Union to become climate-neutral by 2050. The decarbonization of electricity production, transport, heating, and industry by direct and indirect electrification requires a vast expansion of renewable energy production in every Member State to supply the necessary electricity. Even with renewable energy on the rise in Europe, many technical, economic, political, and social challenges in the context of renewable energy development remain, ranging from the international to the local scale.

Governance and Policy Instruments of Transition

Governance arrangements and policy instruments for energy transitions are multifaceted, as every national energy system is embedded in unique institutional structures, political dynamics, and historical path dependencies. Every country developed an individual policy mix of incentive-based instruments, regulatory policies, internalizing instruments, and soft governance as a response to their peculiar challenges and objectives. In the following, concepts and examples of the different policy instruments used in the governance of energy transitions are presented.

By offering benefits to participating actors, incentive-based instruments stimulate voluntary behavioral change by providing subsidies, grants, loans, tax expenditures, and more (Bemelmans-Videc et al. 1998). The most common incentive-based instruments used in energy transitions are support schemes for renewable energy, which are either based on price (e.g., feed-in-tariffs) or quantity (e.g., auction and tendering schemes). Feed-in-tariffs (FITs) are implemented and managed by national authorities and guarantee renewable energy producers access to the electricity grid and the right to sell their generated electricity at a fixed price (Goldemberg 2012). Auctions are also organized by national authorities by a call for tenders for a specific capacity of renewable energy. Developers can submit a bid for the construction and management of a renewable energy project. In the auction, the government will grant the project to the bid with the lowest price, ensuring public funding is used in the most effective way (Ferroukhi et al. 2015). In Europe, both types of incentive-based instruments are used to foster renewable energy development. In Germany, a FIT was already introduced in the 1990s to support renewable energy development, which at the time was a niche technology and not competitive in the electricity market. Through the FIT, a crucial increase and cost-reduction of renewable energy production could be realized and the technology became economically competitive in the market (▶ Chap. 28, "Energy Governance in Germany"). Many countries combine different incentive-based instruments for renewable energy development. Spain has a FIT in force but also used auction schemes to manage large-scale projects to speed up the increase of the renewable energy share to reach their target of the Renewable Energy Directive in time (▶ Chap. 44, "Energy Governance in Spain"). Similarly, tender schemes are used to develop offshore wind parks in Denmark, while onshore wind energy is managed solely through FITs (▶ Chap. 25, "Energy Governance in Denmark"). After introducing a rather ineffective and unsuccessful Renewables Obligation in the United Kingdom, a system based on FITs in combination with Contracts for Differences was implemented for renewable energy (▶ Chap. 48, "Energy Governance in the United Kingdom"). Furthermore, the change from an obligatory scheme to a contract for difference feed-in-tariff in the United Kingdom is a prime example of how incentive-based instruments are changed and adapted to new contexts and challenges.

Another type of policy instrument for the governance of energy transitions is regulatory policy-making. This type of instrument is characterized by the implementation via hierarchical government interventions to set standards or prohibit certain technologies. For example, Italy defined minimum energy performance standards for buildings to achieve their national energy efficiency targets, set out in the European Energy Efficiency Directive (▶ Chap. 32, "Energy Governance in Italy"). Regulatory instruments to prohibit technologies include the phasing-out of coal and nuclear power. The first Member State to phase out coal was Belgium, which closed the last coal-fired power plant in 2016 (▶ Chap. 22, "Energy

Governance in Belgium"), followed by Sweden and Austria in 2020. Other countries such as Germany, Finland, and Slovakia will follow in the future and have already laid out the legislative foundations for the phase-out. An example of a regulatory policy in the transport sector is the mandatory share of biofuels implemented in Finland to reduce emissions and introduce renewable forms of fuels (▶ Chap. 26, "Energy Governance in Finland"). Regulatory policy-making also supplements incentive-based instruments, for example, by requiring utility companies operating the electricity grid to feed in the electricity from renewable energy producers, as is the case in Finland (▶ Chap. 26, "Energy Governance in Finland") and many other European countries. Additionally, regulations can be used to facilitate and accelerate authorization procedures for renewable energy projects, such as the so-called Single Authorization in Italy (▶ Chap. 32, "Energy Governance in Italy"). Additionally, regulatory policies emerge from the European level and then have to be implemented in the member states. For example, the Renewable Energy Directive from 2009 set out legally binding targets for the national share of renewable energy to be accomplished by the year 2020. But target setting can only be considered a regulatory measure if non-compliance with the target is sanctionable. When non-compliance has no direct consequences, it is considered a soft governance measure.

Soft governance describes measures such as information sharing, benchmarking, guidelines, and recommendations that are non-binding in nature, meaning that non-compliance is not sanctionable (Knodt et al. 2020). Soft governance is ubiquitous in energy governance and comes in a variety of forms. In the Netherlands, the government and its leading advisory council organized public consultations to integrate citizens' opinions on the future of the national energy policy (▶ Chap. 35, "Energy Governance in the Netherlands"). In the Czech Republic, the government established Energy Consultation and Information Centers that inform the public about investment opportunities in renewable energy, energy efficiency measures, and alternative heat supply (▶ Chap. 24, "Energy Governance in the Czech Republic"). In Ireland, education programs were developed to achieve behavioral change in transport, informing about sustainable ways of traveling (▶ Chap. 31, "Energy Governance in Ireland"). While soft governance might not lead to immediate or grand scale change due to its non-binding nature, these measures can be a first step toward later regulations.

Internalizing instruments incorporate external costs that carbon emissions cause in the future and aim to foster immediate emission reductions through market mechanisms. The most prominent type of internalizing instruments are cap-and-trade schemes, such as the Emissions Trading Scheme of the European Union (EU ETS). In the EU ETS, the amount of emissions that can be emitted by companies is limited by a cap. The EU allocates a fixed number of allowances to companies that can be used to permit greenhouse gas emissions or can be sold to other participants of the scheme that need more allowances than they received. After a determined time frame, more allowances are removed from the market, increasing the price of emitting greenhouse gases (Ellerman et al. 2010). Carbon taxes are another form of internalizing instrument, typically levied on the use of specific energy carriers, such as coal, oil, and natural gas. In contrast to emission trading schemes, where the price of emitting is determined by market forces, carbon taxes are fixed (Goldemberg 2012). Quite a few member states of the EU are levying carbon taxes, for example, Sweden has a carbon tax on transportation fuels, agriculture, and industries outside of the EU ETS (▶ Chap. 45, "Energy Governance in Sweden"). Similarly, in Ireland, the purchase of solid fossil fuels, natural gas, oil and petroleum products, and peat is taxed on basis of carbon emissions. Industries that are already part of the EU ETS are exempt from these taxes to avoid a double burden for affected companies (▶ Chap. 31, "Energy Governance in Ireland"). National carbon taxes, therefore, mostly complement the EU ETS by internalizing the carbon emissions costs of actors outside of the European system.

Energy transition governance is a dynamic and erratic learning process, which manifests itself in experiments and combinations of different policy instruments, as no blueprint for a successful transition exists. Therefore, what all European countries included in this handbook have in common, is the constant adjustment, adaptation, and rearrangement of their instrument mix, sometimes with positive, sometimes with negative effects on the energy transition.

Transition Outcomes

To take stock of the transition outcomes, a scoring system has been developed to compare the achievements made by the EU member states since 2000. The scoring summarizes how member states performed in achieving the objectives of the energy transition. The objectives are to transform the energy system from the use of fossil fuels to sustainable energy sources. This, in turn, should reduce greenhouse gas emissions to mitigate the effects of climate change. These two intertwined objectives are therefore operationalized to assess the outcomes of the energy transition.

After observing the data of the long-term energy mix development of the member states since 2000, four distinct development paths toward a sustainable energy system were identified. The first path, the advanced transition path, includes member states where renewable energy is competing with fossil fuels for the lead in the energy mix. Renewables are on the brink of becoming the most important energy source across all sectors of the energy system. In the European Union, this path can be observed in Denmark and Latvia. Another variation of this path can be observed in Finland and Sweden, where renewables are backed by nuclear power in substituting fossil fuels as the dominant energy source.

The second path describes member states with an emerging transition, where a significant increase in the share of renewable energy occurred in the time frame from 2000 to 2019, and started to substitute fossil fuels in the energy mix. Yet, fossil fuels are still the dominant energy source and major additional developments are needed to transform the energy system. This path can be observed in Austria, Croatia, Italy, and Portugal. A variation of this path exists in Germany and Lithuania. In these two countries, a significant increase of the renewable energy share occurred in parallel to a decline of nuclear power in the context of national phase-outs. Therefore, renewable energy substituted nuclear power instead of fossil fuels.

The third path includes countries with a restrained transition. A restrained transition is characterized by a slight increase, but overall low level, of renewable energy that substitutes a minor amount of fossil fuels that are still by far the most dominant energy source. The transition process is slow-paced and major developments are needed to transform the energy system. This path can be observed in Estonia, Greece, and Ireland. Besides the original path, two other variations can be identified. In Bulgaria, Czech Republic, Hungary, Slovakia, Slovenia, Spain, and Romania, nuclear power plays an important role in the energy system, alongside fossil fuels and a low but increasing share of renewable energy. In a variation of the third path, the share of nuclear power is steadily declining. This is the case in Belgium and in the United Kingdom, where the decline of nuclear power is substituted by a slow increase of renewable energy and stabilized by the use of fossil fuels.

The fourth path describes countries that have difficulties in the transition process and experience stagnation. In these member states, fossil fuels are the most dominant energy source and only marginal developments of renewable energy without significant impact on the energy mix can be observed. These states are Cyprus, Luxembourg, Malta, Netherlands, and Poland.

While the long-term development of the energy mix is an important factor, additional evidence is needed to assess the progress of the energy transition. The ultimate goal is the reduction of greenhouse gas (GHG) emissions; therefore this aspect has to be considered when evaluating the transition outcomes of European states. To assess the impact of the developments in the energy systems, data of the GHG emissions per capita is used instead of the total emissions to allow a fair comparison between countries with different populations. In 2019, the average emissions of the EU-27 plus the United Kingdom was 8.2 tons of CO2-equivalents per capita (tCO_2eq), ranging from 20.3 tCO_2eq in Luxembourg to 5.2 tCO_2eq in Sweden. These numbers represent the most recent picture of the emissions of European countries and show which countries are the biggest GHG emitters. But it is also important to look at the long-term developments of national emissions, to assess the outcomes of the energy transition. Comparing the annual national GHG emissions in 2000 and 2019 sheds light on reductions achieved by the transition of the energy system. Out of the 28 observed countries, 23 have reduced annual GHG emissions, four have recorded an increase and one country has the same annual GHG emissions in 2019 as in 2000. The reductions range from 5.7 tCO_2eq per capita in Denmark (from 13.8 tCO_2eq/capita in 2000 to 8.1 tCO_2eq/capita in 2019) to lower reductions of 0.5 tCO_2eq per capita in Hungary and Romania. The highest increase in annual GHG emissions is shown by Lithuania which emitted 1.8 tCO_2eq per capita more in 2019 than in 2000 (Fig. 5).

To summarize, three aspects constituting the transition outcome were established: the transition path based on the long-term development of the energy mix, the most recent GHG emissions per capita, and the reduction of GHG emissions per capita over the last two decades. These aspects are transferred into a scoring system providing a ranking of European countries based on their transition outcomes (Table 4). The scores range from 6 points, indicating an advanced transition with significant impacts on GHG reductions, to 1 point, indicating a stagnant transition with no significant impacts on GHG emissions. The transition pathway was

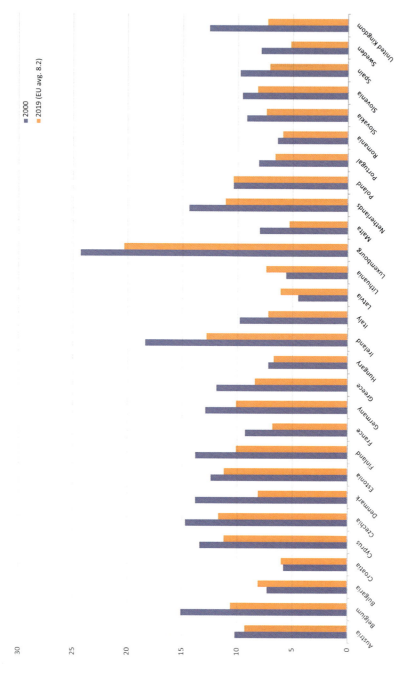

Fig. 5 Annual greenhouse gas emissions per capita of the EU Member States plus the United Kingdom in 2000 and 2019 (Eurostat 2021b)

Table 4 Scoring system for the transition outcomes

Transition pathway	CO_2 per capita (2019)	Annual reduction of GHG-emissions
Advanced (4P)	Below Average or Average (1P)	Yes (1P)
Emerging (3P)		
Restrained (2P)	Above Average (0P)	No (0P)
Stagnant (1P)		

emphasized in the scoring system. This gives more weight to the development of the countries' energy mixes toward a sustainable energy system, which is the focal point of the comparison.

If the scoring system is applied to the EU member states and the United Kingdom, an overview of the transition outcomes is generated and a comparison of the observed countries is possible (Table 5). Denmark and Sweden have the highest possible score and are therefore the countries with the most advanced transition, including significant impacts on GHG emissions. Most countries achieved a score in the midrange between 3 and 4, indicating that the majority of European countries have made progress, but major additional efforts are needed to advance the transition of the energy system and ultimately reduce more GHG emissions. Only four countries have achieved a low score of 1 or 2, indicating major challenges in transforming the energy system and a lack of progress in reducing GHG emissions.

It is not surprising that countries characterized by an advanced transition path also perform well in reducing their GHG-emission, as the transition path implies an energy system development toward energy sources with a low carbon footprint, such as renewables, but also nuclear energy. Yet the results show that reduction of GHG emissions and a lower level of emissions per capita are not exclusively determined by the defined transition paths. Countries such as Hungary, Romania, Slovakia, Spain, the UK, and Malta have all reduced their GHG emissions over the past 20 years and are emitting less CO_2 per capita than average. This can be attributed to less intensive economic activity and a focus on natural gas in their energy systems, which is less CO_2-intensive than coal. While these attributes can lead to significant reductions in GHG emissions, natural gas is still considered a bridge fuel, meaning it should be used for an interim stage before renewable energy (or nuclear) becomes the major component of the energy mix. As the threat of technological lock-in effects is still pending over the use of natural gas, the ranking of these countries on the lower ranks is justified, as the course for deep decarbonization is not finally set.

As for the method of this analysis, there are downsides to the approach used in the evaluation of the transition outcomes. For example, renewable energy projects that are in the planning or building process are not included in the transition pathways. This information could give more context about the immediate future of the energy mix development, but a lack of standardized data and uncertainties as to which projects will be finalized led to the decision to use only the official data on the energy mix composition. Additionally, the use of the average CO_2 emission per capita as a threshold to decide on the transition outcome can be discussed. While the long-term goal of decarbonization would be to achieve GHG emissions of near-zero tons CO_2-

Table 5 Transition outcome ranking of the EU member states and the United Kingdom

Member state	Score	Type of transition	Reduction of total GHG-emissions since 2000 (in tCO2-eq per capita)	CO_2 per capita (Avg.: 8.2 tCO2-eq)
Denmark	6	Advanced Transition	Yes(−5.7)	Below Average (8.1)
Sweden	6	Advanced Transition	Yes(−2.7)	Below Average (5.2)
Latvia	5	Advanced Transition	No (+1.6)	Below Average (6.1)
Finland	5	Advanced Transition	Yes(−3.7)	Above Average (10.1)
Italy	5	Emerging Transition	Yes(−2.6)	Below Average (7.2)
Portugal	5	Emerging Transition	Yes(−1.5)	Below Average (6.6)
France	5	Emerging Transition	Yes(−2.5)	Below Average (6.8)
Austria	4	Emerging Transition	Yes(−0.9)	Above Average (9.3)
Croatia	4	Emerging Transition	No (+0.2)	Below Average (6.0)
Lithuania	4	Emerging Transition	No (+1.8)	Below Average (7.4)
Germany	4	Emerging Transition	Yes(−2.8)	Above Average (10.1)
Hungary	4	Restrained Transition	Yes(−0.5)	Below Average (6.7)
Romania	4	Restrained Transition	Yes(−0.5)	Below Average (5.9)
Slovakia	4	Restrained Transition	Yes(−1.8)	Below Average (7.4)
Slovenia	4	Restrained Transition	Yes(−1.4)	Average (8.2)
Spain	4	Restrained Transition	Yes(−2.7)	Below Average (7.1)
United Kingdom	4	Restrained Transition	Yes(−5.3)	Below Average (7.3)
Greece	3	Restrained Transition	Yes(−3.5)	Above Average (8.4)
Malta	3	Stagnant Transition	Yes(−2.7)	Below Average (5.3)
Ireland	3	Restrained Transition	Yes(−5.6)	Above Average (12.8)
Czech Republic	3	Restrained Transition	Yes(−3.0)	Above Average (11.7)
Bulgaria	3	Restrained Transition	No (+0.8)	Below Average (8.1)

(continued)

Table 5 (continued)

Member state	Score	Type of transition	Reduction of total GHG-emissions since 2000 (in tCO2-eq per capita)	CO_2 per capita (Avg.: 8.2 tCO2-eq)
Belgium	3	Restrained Transition	Yes(−4.5)	Above Average (10.6)
Estonia	3	Restrained Transition	Yes(−1.2)	Above Average (11.2)
Cyprus	2	Stagnant Transition	Yes(−2.2)	Above Average (11.2)
Luxembourg	2	Stagnant Transition	Yes(−4.0)	Above Average (20.3)
Netherlands	2	Stagnant Transition	Yes(−3.3)	Above Average (11.1)
Poland	1	Stagnant Transition	No (0.0)	Above Average (10.4)

equivalents per capita, there is no definite number deemed necessary to be achieved by 2020. The approach of using the EU average circumvents this problem and allows quantification of a high and low quantity of CO_2 emissions that can be used to evaluate and compare the European countries, based on their overall achievements. Overall, the comparison of the national transition outcomes is a complicated task, as every single country has a distinct energy policy, historical path dependencies, and geographic and economic opportunities. In using broader categories and comparable numbers, the comparative approach is used to deal with the uniqueness of the national energy systems and to provide results showing an overall picture of the European energy transition that summarizes the findings of the country chapters in this handbook.

Conclusion: An Energy Mix and Energy Governance for Climate Neutrality?

European energy systems are in a continuous process of change. The share of renewable energy has increased rapidly in the last 20 years, underlining the growing importance of carbon-neutral energy sources. But to achieve a climate-neutral energy system, a massive expansion of renewables is necessary, which poses major technological, economic, social, and political challenges. While the utilization of renewables in the electricity sector is far advanced, they also have to be used to decarbonize sectors and applications that cannot be electrified directly. This indirect electrification will require even more renewable energy capacities, for example, to produce renewable hydrogen and synthetic fuels for industry and transport sector use. For some member states, nuclear power is another option to decarbonize the energy system, e.g., in Romania and Slovakia (▶ Chaps. 39, "Energy Governance in Romania," and ▶ 42, "Energy Governance in Slovakia"), where energy discourses explicitly frame nuclear energy as a technology of the energy transition. Nuclear power has provided a constant baseload of electricity throughout the last 20 years. However, due to security and environmental risks, the energy source is politically and socially contested, leading to a divide between members states that want to expand or phase-in nuclear power and member states that reject the use of nuclear power or want to phase out the technology. By contrast, European states widely consent on the topic of reducing and ultimately phasing-out fossil fuels. Looking at solid fossil fuels, hard coal and lignite, there is a significant retreat in the EU member states' energy mix and a majority of states with completed or announced phase-outs, due to the negative climate impact of the energy source (IEA 2021). In contrast, oil still plays a crucial role in the European energy system and has the highest share of all sources in the energy mix, due to its dominance in the transport sector. Natural gas will also remain an important element of the energy system and its relevance could even increase as it is discussed as being a necessary part of the energy transition by using it as a bridge fuel. While the share of fossil fuels is declining, its significance in the energy system is still exceptionally high and major efforts in renewable energy and end-use technology development are needed to substitute solid fossil fuels, oil and petroleum, and natural gas.

On the EU level, the overlap of two jurisdictions characterizes energy governance. While climate policy is basically supranational, energy policy largely remains a domain of the member states. As long as energy policy is a national competence, there will be a plurality of governance instruments. However, the common goal of climate neutrality and the supranational character of climate policy could strengthen the importance of climate mitigation instruments, i.e., the European ETS and the proposed ETS 2. That would not come without conflicts and disadvantages, as a concentration on CO_2 pricing yields issues of distributive fairness and incentives. Particularly when it comes to asset-specific investments, e.g., in infrastructures, price-signals to private investors might be insufficient or misleading as governance instruments. Following the raising of European targets to achieve climate neutrality in 2050, it is clear that these cannot be achieved through emissions trading alone, not even by extending trading to the transport and heat sectors. Achieving the targets requires a massive expansion of renewable energies as well as an increase in energy efficiency. Here, the EU is trying to enrich the soft governance in the energy sector with harder elements of governance in the *Fit for 55 package* (▶ Chap. 7, "European Union Energy Policy: A Discourse Perspective"). The achievement of the goals will depend on the achievement of tougher governance in the EU's energy legislation, as well as on the further development of emissions trading. Furthermore, the impacts of the recent Russian invasion in Ukraine cannot yet be assessed, but it is safe to say that it will change the European energy policy development and will have significant impacts on the way energy policy is approached in the coming years.

Cross-References

- Energy Governance in Austria
- Energy Governance in Belgium
- Energy Governance in Denmark

- ▶ Energy Governance in Finland
- ▶ Energy Governance in Germany
- ▶ Energy Governance in Greece
- ▶ Energy Governance in Hungary
- ▶ Energy Governance in Ireland
- ▶ Energy Governance in Italy
- ▶ Energy Governance in Romania
- ▶ Energy Governance in Slovakia
- ▶ Energy Governance in Spain
- ▶ Energy Governance in Sweden
- ▶ Energy Governance in the Czech Republic
- ▶ Energy Governance in the Netherlands
- ▶ Energy Governance in the Republic of Poland
- ▶ Energy Governance in the United Kingdom
- ▶ European Union Energy Policy: A Discourse Perspective

References

Bemelmans-Videc, M.-L., Rist, R. C., & Vedung, E. (1998). Policy instruments: Typologies and theories. In M.-L. Bemelmans-Videc, C. R. Ray, & E. Vedung (Eds.), *Carrots, sticks & sermons: Policy instruments & their evaluation* (pp. 21–58). Routledge.

Boasson, E. L., Leiren, M. D., & Wettestad, J. (2021). Comparative assessments and conclusions. In E. L. Boasson, M. D. Leiren, & J. Wettestad (Eds.), *Comparative renewables policy: Political, organizational and European fields* (pp. 219–239). Abingdon/New York: Routledge.

Brüggemeier, F.-J. (2018). *Grubengold: Das Zeitalter der Kohle von 1750 bis heute* (1st ed.). München: C.H. Beck.

CAN Europe. (2021). Candidate projects for the 5th PCI list: a final push for fossil gas? – CAN Europe. https://caneurope.org/candidate-projects-5th-pci-list-briefing-push-fossil-gas/. Accessed 12 May 2021.

Cherif, R., Hasanov, F., & Pande, A. (2021). Riding the energy transition: Oil beyond 2040. *Asian Economic Policy Review, 16*, 117–137. https://doi.org/10.1111/aepr.12317.

Dominković, D. F., Bačeković, I., Pedersen, A. S., & Krajačić, G. (2018). The future of transportation in sustainable energy systems: Opportunities and barriers in a clean energy transition. *Renewable and Sustainable Energy Reviews, 82*, 1823–1838. https://doi.org/10.1016/j.rser.2017.06.117.

Ellerman, A. D., Convery, F. J., & de Perthuis, C. (2010). *Pricing carbon: The European Union emissions trading scheme* (1st ed.). Cambridge: Cambridge Univ. Press.

Eurostat. (2021a). Complete Energy Balances (nrg_bal_c). https://appsso.eurostat.ec.europa.eu/nui/show.do?dataset=nrg_bal_c. Accessed 4 Nov 2021.

Eurostat. (2021b). Greenhouse gas emissions per capita. https://ec.europa.eu/eurostat/databrowser/view/t2020_rd300/default/table?lang=en. Accessed 12 Jan 2022.

Eurostat. (2021c). Natural gas supply statistics. https://ec.europa.eu/eurostat/statistics-explained/index.php?title=Natural_gas_supply_statistics#Consumption_trends. Accessed 4 Nov 2021.

Eurostat. (2021d). Oil and petroleum products - a statistical overview. https://ec.europa.eu/eurostat/statistics-explained/index.php?title=Oil_and_petroleum_products_-_a_statistical_overview#Production_of_crude_oil. Accessed 3 Nov 2021.

Eurostat. (2022). SHARES (Renewables) – Energy – Eurostat. Eurostat. https://ec.europa.eu/eurostat/web/energy/data/shares. Accessed 23 Mar 2022.

Ferroukhi, R., Hawila, D., Vinci, S., & Nagpal, D. (2015). Renewable energy auctions: A guide to design. https://www.irena.org/-/media/Files/IRENA/Agency/Publication/2015/Jun/IRENA_Renewable_Energy_Auctions_A_Guide_to_Design_2015.pdf

Fischer, S. (2011). *EURATOM und die Energiewende: Szenarien für die Zukunft des europäischen Atomvertrags*. Arbeitspapier Forschungsgruppe EU-Integration (Arbeitspapier der FG 1, 2011/ Nr. 03). Berlin.

Flyvbjerg, B. (2017). Introduction: The iron law of megaproject management. In *The Oxford handbook of megaproject management* (pp. 1–18).

Fraunhofer IWES. (2015). The European power system in 2030: Flexibility challenges and integration benefits: An analysis with a focus on the pentalateral energy forum region. *Analysis on behalf of Agora Energiewende*. Analysis. Berlin. https://www.agora-energiewende.de/fileadmin/Projekte/2014/Ein-flexibler-Strommarkt-2030/Agora_European_Flexibility_Challenges_Integration_Benefits_WEB_Rev1.pdf

Gaigalis, V., Markevicius, A., Katinas, V., Skema, R., & Tumosa, A. (2013). Analysis of energy transition possibilities after the decommission of a nuclear power plant in Ignalina region in Lithuania. *Renewable and Sustainable Energy Reviews, 24*, 45–56. https://doi.org/10.1016/j.rser.2013.03.028.

Goldemberg, J. (2012). *Energy: What everyone needs to know* (What everyone needs to know). Oxford: Oxford University Press USA.

Gürsan, C., & de Gooyert, V. (2021). The systemic impact of a transition fuel: Does natural gas help or hinder the energy transition? *Renewable and Sustainable Energy Reviews, 138*, 110552. https://doi.org/10.1016/j.rser.2020.110552.

Jahn, D., & Korolczuk, S. (2012). German exceptionalism: The end of nuclear energy in Germany! *Environmental Politics, 21*, 159–164. https://doi.org/10.1080/09644016.2011.643374.

Jansma, S. R., Gosselt, J. F., & de Jong, M. D. (2020). Kissing natural gas goodbye? Homeowner versus tenant perceptions of the transition towards sustainable heat in the Netherlands. *Energy Research & Social Science, 69*, 101694. https://doi.org/10.1016/j.erss.2020.101694.

Kanellakis, M., Martinopoulos, G., & Zachariadis, T. (2013). European energy policy – A review. *Energy Policy, 62*, 1020–1030. https://doi.org/10.1016/j.enpol.2013.08.008.

Kemmerzell, J., & Knodt, M. (2021). Dekarbonisierung der Energieversorgung: Der deutsche Kohleausstieg im europäischen Kontext. In Bundeszentrale für politische Bildung (Ed.), *Abschied von der Kohle: Struktur- und Kulturwandel im Ruhrgebiet und in der Lausitz* (pp. 58–73). Bundeszentrale für politische Bildung: Bonn.

Knodt, M., Ringel, M., & Müller, R. (2020). 'Harder' soft governance in the European Energy Union. *Journal of Environmental Policy & Planning, 22*, 787–800. https://doi.org/10.1080/1523908X.2020.1781604.

Le Maire, B. (2021, October 10). Aufruf von EU-Ministern: Warum Europa Kernenergie braucht. WELT. https://www.welt.de/debatte/kommentare/article234330374/Aufruf-von-EU-Ministern-Warum-Europa-Kernenergie-braucht.html. Accessed 15 Feb 2022.

Levi, M. (2013). Climate consequences of natural gas as a bridge fuel. *Climatic Change, 118*, 609–623. https://doi.org/10.1007/s10584-012-0658-3.

Levoyannis, C. (2021). The EU green deal and the impact on the future of gas and gas infrastructure in the European Union. In M. Mathioulakis (Ed.), *Aspects of the Energy Union: Application and effects of European energy policies in SE Europe and Eastern Mediterranean* (Energy, Climate and the Environment) (1st ed., pp. 201–224). Cham: Springer International Publishing; Imprint: Palgrave Macmillan.

Mac Kinnon, M. A., Brouwer, J., & Samuelsen, S. (2018). The role of natural gas and its infrastructure in mitigating greenhouse gas emissions, improving regional air quality, and renewable resource integration. *Progress in Energy and Combustion Science, 64*, 62–92. https://doi.org/10.1016/j.pecs.2017.10.002.

OECD. (2017). *OECD Environmental Performance Reviews: Estonia 2017* (OECD Environmental Performance Reviews). Paris. https://doi.org/10.1787/9789264268241-en.

Osička, J., Kemmerzell, J., Zoll, M., Lehotský, L., Černoch, F., & Knodt, M. (2020a). What's next for the European coal heartland? Exploring the future of coal as presented in German, Polish and Czech press. *Energy Research & Social Science, 61*, 101316. https://doi.org/10.1016/j.erss.2019.101316.

Pacesila, M., Burcea, S. G., & Colesca, S. E. (2016). Analysis of renewable energies in European Union. *Renewable and Sustainable Energy Reviews, 56*, 156–170. https://doi.org/10.1016/j.rser.2015.10.152.

Rentier, G., Lelieveldt, H., & Kramer, G. J. (2019). Varieties of coal-fired power phase-out across Europe. *Energy Policy, 132*, 620–632. https://doi.org/10.1016/j.enpol.2019.05.042.

Safari, A., Das, N., Langhelle, O., Roy, J., & Assadi, M. (2019). Natural gas: A transition fuel for sustainable energy system transformation? *Energy Science & Engineering, 7*, 1075–1094. https://doi.org/10.1002/ese3.380.

Schneider, M., & Froggatt, A. (2019). *The world nuclear industry status report 2019*. Paris/Budapest.

Sen, S., & Ganguly, S. (2017). Opportunities, barriers and issues with renewable energy development – A discussion. *Renewable and Sustainable Energy Reviews, 69*, 1170–1181. https://doi.org/10.1016/j.rser.2016.09.137.

Simon, F. (2022, February 2). EU puts green label for nuclear and gas officially on the table. EURACTIV.com. https://www.euractiv.com/section/energy-environment/news/eu-puts-green-label-for-nuclear-and-gas-officially-on-the-table/. Accessed 15 Feb 2022.

Smil, V. (2015). *Power density: A key to understanding energy sources and uses*. MIT Press.

Smil, V. (2021). *Grand transitions: How the modern world was made*. Oxford University Press.

Stephenson, E., Doukas, A., & Shaw, K. (2012). Greenwashing gas: Might a 'transition fuel' label legitimize carbon-intensive natural gas development? *Energy Policy, 46*, 452–459. https://doi.org/10.1016/j.enpol.2012.04.010.

Szabo, J. (2021). Natural gas' changing discourse in European decarbonisation. In M. Mišík & N. Kujundžić (Eds.), *Energy humanities. Current state and future directions* (1st ed., pp. 67–88). Cham: Springer International Publishing.

Tagliapietra, S., Zachmann, G., Edenhofer, O., Glachant, J.-M., Linares, P., & Loeschel, A. (2019). The European Union energy transition: Key priorities for the next five years. *Energy Policy, 132*, 950–954. https://doi.org/10.1016/j.enpol.2019.06.060.

Thomas, S., & Rosenow, J. (2020). Drivers of increasing energy consumption in Europe and policy implications. *Energy Policy, 137*, 111108. https://doi.org/10.1016/j.enpol.2019.111108.

Twidell, J., & Weir, A. D. (2015). *Renewable energy resources*. Abingdon: Routledge.

Verbruggen, A. (2008). Renewable and nuclear power: A common future? *Energy Policy, 36*, 4036–4047. https://doi.org/10.1016/j.enpol.2008.06.024.

World Nuclear Association. (2022). *Nuclear power in the European Union*. World Nuclear Association. https://www.world-nuclear.org/information-library/country-profiles/others/european-union.aspx

Zhang, X., Myhrvold, N. P., Hausfather, Z., & Caldeira, K. (2016). Climate benefits of natural gas as a bridge fuel and potential delay of near-zero energy systems. *Applied Energy, 167*, 317–322. https://doi.org/10.1016/j.apenergy.2015.10.016.

Index

A
AB Litgrid, 858
Accelerated capital allowance (ACA) scheme, 783
Acceptance, 1205
Action Plan, 299
Actor, 22, 42
Adalet ve Kalkınma Partisi- Ak Party, 1218, 1226
Additionality, 110, 112
Administrative interest-intermediation, 886
Advisory body, 864
Advocacy organization, 639
Affordability, 113, 542, 544–546
Agency for Electric Energy (ANEEL), 197
Agency for Legal Transactions and Real Estate (APN), 553
Agency for Oil, Gas and Biofuels (ANP), 197
Agency theory, 82
Agricultural sector, 726
Agriculture, 292
Air pollution, 1078
Algeria, 514, 1222
Alternative and renewable energy, 485, 491, 493, 495–497, 499, 500, 502–504
  resources, 494–496
  sector, 497, 501
Alternative energy requirement (AER) program, 780
Alternative fuels strategy, 1112
Amber Grid, 852, 853
Anti-nuclear movement, 28, 29, 41, 1191, 1194
Antwerp, 512
APG flaring, 1025, 1032
Armenia, 291–294
  conditions of energy governance in, 434–441
  drivers of energy transition, 441–442
  energy efficiency, 448–450
  hydropower energy, 446–448
  outcomes, challenges and prospects for energy governance, 450–451
  renewable energy, 442–443
  solar energy, 445–446
  wind energy, 443–444
Artificial federalism, 462
Asymmetrical interdependence, 928
Atomic bombs, 515
Atomic Energy Act, 1193
Authoritarian, 739
Authority for Energy, Networks and the Environment (ARERA), 809
Authority for Nuclear Safety, 653
Automotive industry, 1070
Azerbaijan, 294–296, 1222
Azeri gas, 1248

B
Baltic Energy Market Interconnection Plan, 829, 844
Baltic Nuclear Power Plant, 850
Baltic Pipe, 612
Baltic (Russian Federation) 849–850
Baltic States, 824, 844, 846, 854, 857
Bargaining power, 179
Baseload power, 754
Belarus, 296–298, 828
Belgium
  energy governance in, 513–521, 529
  industrialization, 513
  location, 512
  phased out coal, 517
Belt and Road Initiative (BRI), 362
Best available technology (BAT), 1177
Better energy communities scheme, 782
Better energy warmer homes scheme, 782
Bilateral Investment Treaty (BITs), 358

Bilateral relations, 193
Biodiversity, 1179
Bioenergy, 621, 626–630, 637, 830, 1020, 1021, 1028–1030, 1032–1033, 1034, 1169
Biofuel(s), 196, 620, 631, 637, 640, 756, 912, 963, 1047, 1162, 1175
  obligation scheme, 782
  and waste, 827
Biogas, 929, 930, 1038
Biomass, 600, 672, 676, 925, 929, 930, 946, 949, 1047, 1061
  consumption, 744
  Swedish, 1164
Bio-methane, 806
Biorefineries, 640
Blockade of Azerbaijan and Turkey, 450
Bohunice International Decommissioning Support Fund (BIDSF), 1065
Bonus-malus system, 1175
BOTAȘ, 1227, 1229, 1231, 1243, 1247, 1248
Brazil, 85, 194
  energy dialogue, 194–203
BRELL, 857
Brexit, 774, 1263, 1269, 1278
BRICSalization, 201
Brotherhood, 1058
Bryansk Oblast, 851
Build, operate, and transfer (BOT), 1233
Build, own, and operate (BOO) scheme, 1233
Building codes, subsidies, 1177
Building sector, 724
Būtingė terminal, 851
Būtingės nafta company, 851

C

Cacophony, 371
Calls for tenders, 659
Canada, 270–272, 278–281, 283
Cantons, 1190, 1198
Capability approach, 74
Capacity, 22, 30, 31
Capital cost subsidy, 800
Čaputová, Zuzana, 1063
Carbon border adjustments, 1180
Carbon capture and storage (CCS), 881, 901, 913, 915
Carbon-free power sector, 1178
Carbon-intense economy, 1226, 1247
Carbon intensity, 1038
Carbon leakage rules, 904
Carbon lock-in, 770
Carbon-neutral, 1210
  economy, 982

Carbon neutrality, 628, 629, 635, 637, 639, 641
  target, 910
Carbon prices, 1180
Carbon pricing, 1232
Carbon tax, 658, 659, 780
Carbon taxation, 910, 1171
Cases, 85–92
Caspian region, 269
Ceaușescu, N., 996
Center for Monitoring the Energy Sector and Investments, 553
Central and Eastern European (CEE), 738
Central government, 551
Centralization, 145, 146, 154, 155, 650, 686, 691, 697–699
Centralized governance, 463, 486, 493, 801
Centralized model, 1256, 1269, 1277
Cernavodă nuclear plant, 1008
Challenger, 23, 30, 33, 38–40
Chernobyl disaster, 522
Chernobyl NPP, 1058
Chernobyl nuclear accident, 871
China, 85, 210
  energy dialogue, 210–220
Chooz, 522
Circular economy, 629
Cities, 414–420
Citizen dialogue, 59, 60
Citizen participation, 775
  community energy, 55–56
  policy making, 59–60
  spatial planning, 57–59
Citizens Assembly, 775
Citizen's Climate Convention, 658
Civic participation, 961
'Civilian power' Europe, 372
Civil society organizations (CSOs), 1229
CJSC Electric Networks of Armenia, 436
Clean Energy for All Europeans Package, 550
Cleantech, 629
Clientelistic structures, 489
Climate Act, 625–627, 633, 634, 640
Climate action and Low Carbon Development Act, 777
Climate Action Plan, 107
Climate ambitions, 1165, 1169
Climate change, 20, 24, 39, 41, 256, 269, 348, 350, 356, 358, 361, 412, 414, 416–418, 441, 655, 660, 668, 670, 676, 699, 700, 751, 924, 925, 933, 949, 966, 1001, 1011, 1189, 1223, 1229, 1261, 1263, 1265, 1272, 1274, 1305, 1308
Climate Change Act, 91
Climate Change Advisory Council, 771

Climate Change Agreement, 865
Climate change consensus, 595, 601, 605, 612
Climate change performance index, 785
Climate change plan, 629, 636
Climate change policies, 877
Climate clubs, 181
Climate Council, 604
Climate law, 878
Climate leadership, 661
Climate movement, 1197
Climate-neutral energy system, 1313
Climate neutrality, 668, 669, 677, 701, 1314
Climate policy, 412, 417, 420, 424, 742, 831, 903–906, 925, 931, 933, 934, 938, 945, 949, 1159, 1196–1197, 1258, 1274
  narrative, 1165
Climate Policy Council, 1168
Climate protection policies, 873
Climate settlement, 907
Climate skepticism, 564
Climate target, 1170, 1178
Club of Rome, 870
CO_2 Act, 1191
CO_2 emissions, 221, 865, 1203, 1223, 1244
  regulations, 1207
  tax, 550
CO_2 prices, 1051
CO2 tax, 903, 910, 1204
Coal, 20, 30, 38, 266, 276, 460, 464, 600, 668–673, 675, 677, 680, 681, 684–688, 690, 698, 962, 1021–1026, 1028, 1031, 1033, 1034, 1086, 1192, 1219, 1221, 1223, 1293, 1294–1297, 1314
  extraction, 513
  mines, 1010
  production, decrease in, 1060
Coal Commission, 670, 680, 686, 687, 700, 701
Coal-fired power plants, 866
Coal-fired power stations, 866
Coal phase-out, 1066, 1293
  strategy, 1107
Co-benefits, 105
Cohesion and structural funds, 806
Cold War, 265
Collapse of the Soviet Union, 434
Combined Cycle Gas Turbine (CCGT), 517
Combined heat and power (CHP), 31, 40, 41
  applications, 109
Commission, 399
Commission for Railway Regulation, 779
Commission for Regulation of Utilities (CRU), 777
Commission for the Regulation of Electricity and Gas (CREG), 521

Commissions of inquiries, 1168
Commission Wallonne pour l'Energie (CWaPE), 521
Committee on Climate Change, 91
Community energy, 55–56
Community engagement, 786
Comparison of natural gas
  in Hungary and Finland, 1299
  Netherlands and Sweden, 1305
  Norway and the UK, 1298
Compensation obligations, 1207
Competition, 653, 1166
  authority, 804
Competitiveness, 6, 9, 203, 374, 654, 1294
  prioritization of, 1161
Comprehensive and Enhanced Partnership Agreement (CEPA), 290
Comprehensive Economic and Trade Agreement (CETA), 278, 280
Computer-aided content analysis (CATA), 388
Concordance, 1192
Confederation of British industry, 785
Conflict regulation, 57
Congo, 514
Connecting Europe Facility, 1056
Connectivity, 378, 380
Consensus, 867
Conservative Party, 851
Consociational and corporatist patterns, 867
Consumption tariffs, 972
Conto Energia, 810
Control Committee for Electricity, 521
Convergence, 145, 148, 156
Conversion, 34
Cooperative(s), 608
  federalism, 1190
  initiatives, 880
  policy-making, 874
Coordination, 679, 681, 691
  mechanisms, 633–636, 760
  tasks, 1209
COP15, 598
COP21, 513
Corporate governance, 556
Corporatism, 697, 700
Correlations analysis, 391
Corruption, 547, 995, 1009
Cost efficiency, 901
Council of Europe, 850
Council of European Municipalities and Regions (CEMR), 417
Council of the European Union, 171, 357

Country strategy paper (CSP), 292
Coupling, 104, 107
Court of Justice of the EU (CJEU), 358
Covenant of Mayors (CoM), 816
Covenant of Mayors for Climate & Energy, 420, 551
  foundation and instruments of, 420–421
  governance achievements and shortcomings of, 423–424
  membership patterns of, 421–423
Covenants, 880
Croatia, 534, 1087
  affordability, 544, 545
  discourse on energy issues, 542–547
  energy mix, composition of, 539–542
  final energy consumption, 543
  general reform framework and specific developments, 536
  installed capacity and produced electric power, 542
  insufficient institutional capacity, 546
  legacies, 535–538
  outcomes, challenges and prospects of energy governance, 555–558
  political will, 546
  primary energy production, 540, 542
  security of supply, 543, 544
  sustainability, 544, 545
  total electricity consumption, 540
Croatian Energy Regulatory Agency (HERA), 553
Croatian energy transition
  coordination mechanisms and multilevel governance, 551–555
  Croatian energy efficiency policy, 550
  European integration, 548
  long-term investments, 548
  privatization, 548
  strategies and instruments, 549–551
Crony neoliberalism, 1226
Crude oil, 1192
Cut offs, 72

D

Danish District Heating Association, 607
Danish Emission Trading System, 603
Danish Energy Agency, 610
Danish energy policy, 602
2012 Danish EU presidency, 610
Danish green energy agenda, 604
DCFTA, 299
Debt, 72

Decarbonization, 109, 534, 775, 777, 778, 785, 786, 816, 1051, 1075, 1165, 1168–1170, 1180
Decarbonizing the energy system, 105
Decentralization, 145, 147, 155, 653, 660, 800
  governance, 463, 801
  renewable energy sources, 656
  technologies, 50
Decision-making system
  horizontally fragmented, 748, 757
  vertically integrated, 748, 757
Decommissioning, 663, 1064
  programs, 1104
Deep geological repository, spent nuclear waste, 1063
De-Europeanization, 1229
Delegation, 886
Delegation of the European Union to Brazil (DelBRA), 199
Deliberative assembly, 658
Deliberative democracy, 52, 54, 58
Demand-side efficiency, 111
Demand side management, 639
Democratic decision-making, 51, 53, 60
Democratic legitimacy, 58
Democratic procedure, 50, 52
De-monopolization and reform, 435
Denmark, 1235
Denmark, energy governance
  discourse on energy issues, 601–602
  electricity sector, 607–608
  energy conflicts, 612–613
  energy efficiency, 609–610
  energy mix, 599–601
  energy transitions, 604–610
  heating sector, 606–607
  monitoring of climate goals and sector integration, 610–612
  multilevel governance, 613–614
  policy legacies, 596–599
  political institutions, 602–604
  renewable energies, support for, 608–609
Department of Communications, Climate Action and Environment (DCCAE), 776
Department of Energy (DE), 222
Department of Environment, Food and Rural Affairs (DEFRA), 91
Department of Statistics of the Republic of Lithuania, 846
Department of Transport, Tourism and Sport (DTTAS), 779
Dependence, 829
Dependency, 24, 36

Index

Deprivation, 71
Deregulation, 534, 1166
Desertec, 326
DG Development and Cooperation (DevCo), 199
DG Energy, 172, 199
Digitalization process, 818
Direct democracy, 1191–1192
Discourse, 932–933, 933, 948, 950
Displacement, 34, 38
Dispute settlement, 348, 352, 355, 359, 360
Distributed energy, 1257, 1262, 1270, 1277, 1279
Distributed generation, 802
Distribution capacity, 1166
District heating, 826, 1160
Distrigaz, 514
Diversification, 354, 829, 1161
Doğa Association, 1229
Domestic coal, 1063
Drift, 34, 38
Druzhba, 1058
Druzhba Adria project, 546
"Druzhba" pipeline, 851
Dzurinda, Mikuláš, 1058

E

Eandis, 514
Eastern Europe Energy Efficiency and Environment Partnership (E5P), 292
Eastern Mediterranean, 1226
Eastern Partnership, 288
    Armenia, 291–294
    Azerbaijan, 294–296
    Belarus, 296–298
    energy relations between EU and, 291–307
    and European Neighbourhood policy, 289–291
    Georgia, 298–300
    Republic of Moldova, 300–303
    Ukraine, 303–307
Eastring pipeline project, 1063
Ecologically problematic, 826
Ecological sustainability, 1226–1227
Economic competitiveness, 179–181
Economic crisis, 723, 836
Economic Europe, 372
Economic policy instruments, 1159, 1171
Economic subsidies, 1173
Economies of scale, 146, 148, 153
Economies of scope, 153
Eco-tourism, 1147

EDP, 969, 971
EEA Agreement, 917
Efficiency first, 111
Efficiency obligation scheme, 782
Effort sharing decision (ESD), 945
EirGrid, 778
Electrabel, 523
Electricity, 928, 930–932, 935, 939, 940, 947, 948, 1204–1207, 1266–1270
    consumption, 495–497
    export, 914
    liberalization, 603, 607
    mix, 652, 1143
    prices, 899, 903
    production, 496
    sector, 435
    storage systems, 882
    surplus, 899
    trade, 626
Electricity Act 1999, 773
Electricity generation, 795, 1224, 1235
    coal, 1220
    fossil fuels, 1222
Electricity market, 866, 1194, 1204
    directive, 1174
    liberalization, 1232–1237
    reform, 91
Electricity Supply Board (ESB), 778
Electric transport, 1140
Electric vehicles (EVs), 756, 818, 901, 904, 905, 912, 914, 917, 975, 1207
Electrification, 612, 622, 975, 1166, 1178, 1180, 1181
Electro mobility, 1070
Electro-Mobility Development Plan, 931
Electronuclear program, 651
Electro Power System Operator CJSC (EPSO), 440
Elektrárne Nováky (ENO), 1067
Emerging powers, 190, 194
Emission(s), 377
    reduction obligations, 1176
Emissions of 2.07 tCO2eq, 441
Emissions trading scheme (ETS), 1232
Emission trading system (ETS), 609, 610
E-mobility, 1201
ENELX group, 819
Energieakkoord, 864
Energiewende, 92, 668, 671, 673, 676, 677, 679, 681–683, 686, 688, 692–694, 697, 701
Energiewende project, 569
Energijos Tiekimas, 853

Energy, 1038
  2000, 1194
  actorness, 165, 169
  agency, 831
  Agreement, 864
  and climate diplomacy, 747
  and climate issues, 747
  and climate policy, 462
  and climate strategies, 620, 624, 625, 627, 629, 633, 636, 640, 641
  Article, 1190
  auditing scheme, 782
  certification, 912
  citizen, 775
  coalition, 652
  community, 174, 178, 305, 354, 718, 1041
  companies, 1125
  conservation, 111
  cooperation, 174
  costs, 775, 877, 973, 979
  dependence, 441, 451
  diplomacy, 169, 171, 265, 266, 268, 269, 272, 273, 278, 1218, 1223, 1248
  Directives, 354, 357
  discourse, 463–464, 1158, 1164
  efficiency policy, 89
  elite, 621, 625
  equity, 175, 1226–1227
  hub, 1226, 1248
  import dependency, 963
  incumbents, 640
  independence, 832
  industry, 565, 566, 573
  infrastructure, 377, 496, 504
  investment, 377
  island, 825
  justice, 75
  label, 1207
  Law, 436
  Ministry, 1006
  mix, 489, 622–623, 651, 864, 930–932, 997–998, 1147
  monopolies, 653
  partnership, 178, 274
  planning, 1125
  price, 620, 624
  RD&D, 1173
  regime, 24, 35–41, 1038
  research, 1208
  resources, 485, 487, 494, 500
  sovereignty, 584, 1139
  statistics, 87
  storage, 881, 1209
  strategies, Russia, 1020
  supply, 484, 490
  system structure, 866
  tax, 879
  technologies, 602
  trade, 282
  transit, 1062
  transmission network, 878
  transport network, 880
  trilemma, 175
  Union, 88, 144, 243, 244, 264, 265, 274, 844, 924, 928, 937
  weapon, 240
Energy Charter Treaty (ECT), 180, 269, 324, 348, 350–352
  gas transit disputes and decoupling of legal orders, 353–355
  international trends and theoretical/practical debates, 349
  modernisation and IEC, 355–357
  politicization of ISDS and climate change, 358–361
Energy consumption, 211, 744, 816, 964, 1193
  per capita, 620
Energy democracy, 50, 583
  and participatory governance, 52–54
Energy dependency, 740, 1045
  rates, 927
Energy Dialogue, 193, 878, 884
  EU-BICS bilateral, 193–194
  EU-Brazil, 194–203
  EU-China, 210–220
  EU-India, 203–210
  EU-South Africa, 220–228
Energy efficiency, 106, 110, 111, 211, 292, 298, 377, 384, 385, 392, 401, 439, 440, 448–450, 494, 495, 498, 502, 504, 594, 596–599, 602, 604, 605, 609–610, 621, 624, 627, 630, 631, 633, 662, 678, 680–683, 693, 694, 697, 699, 757, 793, 837, 864, 877, 925, 945, 974, 1038, 1110, 1197, 1207, 1230
  agriculture, 725–726
  industrial sector, 1147
  industry, 726
  railway sector, 1143
  regulatory changes, 1142
  small and medium enterprises, 1143
  transport sector, 724–725
Energy Efficiency Directive, 385, 392
Energy Efficiency Security Plan, 449

Index

Energy governance, 4, 136, 191, 199, 205, 209, 214, 216, 224, 412, 413, 1290, 1307, 1313–1314
  composition of energy mix, 1220–1225
  discourse, 932–934
  discourses/narratives on Turkey's energy policy, 1223–1227
  energy mix, 930–932
  energy transitions, 937–945
  of European countries (*see* European energy governance)
  legacies/path dependencies, 1218–1219
  legacies, 925–930
  monitoring and surveillance, 945–946
  in Netherlands, 865–867
  nexus quality, 5
  political institutions and actors, 934–937, 1227
  prospects, 948–950
  sector integration, 946–948
  in Spain (*see* Spain)
Energy governance, Czech Republic
  coordination mechanisms and multilevel governance, 581–583
  energy mix, 567
  energy transition and long-term strategies, 572–575
  institutions and actors, 570–572
  outlook, challenges and prospects for, 583–585
  strategies and instruments of energy transition, 575–581
Energy governance, in Austria
  coordination, instruments and issues of energy transition, 464–476
  distribution of electricity, 470–472
  drivers of energy transition, 465
  electricity supply, 467–469
  energy discourse, 463–464
  energy efficiency and consumption, 472–476
  energy mix composition, 459–461
  general conditions of, 457–464
  legacies, 457–459
  outcome, challenges and prospects, 476–478
  political institutions and actors, 461–463
  strategies and instruments of energy transition, 465–467
Energy governance, in Finland
  coordination mechanisms and multilevel governance, 633–636
  discourses on energy, 624–625
  drivers of energy transition, 626–629
  energy mix, 622–623
  forestry problem, 637–638
  monitoring and surveillance, 640–641
  overall energy transitions, 638–640
  patterns of energy consumption, 621–622
  political institutions, 625–626
  strategies and instruments of energy transitions, 629–633
Energy governance, in Greece, *see* Greece
Energy governance, in Italy, *see* Italy
Energy governance, in Portugal
  administrative actors, 967
  challenges, 980–981
  discourse on energy issues, 966–967
  energy generation and retailing companies, 969
  energy mix, 963–965
  feed-in tariffs, 975–976
  Government, 967
  Green parties and environmental movement, 968
  legacies, 961–963
  liberalization, 970–972
  outcomes, 979–980
  renewable energy auctions, 977–978
  renewable energy policy, 972–973
  transmission and distribution companies, 969
Energy governance, in Russia
  coordination mechanisms and multilevel governance, 1030–1032
  energy mix, 1022–1023
  gas *vs.* bioenergy, 1032–1033
  Gazprom, 1024
  global climate policies and governance, 1027
  hydrocarbon culture, 1024
  Lukoil, 1025
  Ministry of Energy, 1024
  Ministry of Natural Resources and the Environment, 1024
  monitoring and surveillance, 1033
  Novatek, 1025
  path dependencies, 1021–1022
  RES, 1027
  Rosatom, 1024, 1025
  Rosneft, 1024, 1025
  sector integration and conflicts, 1033–1034
  security of demand, 1023
  security of supply, 1023
  strategies, of energy transition, 1029–1030
  wind power, 1026

Energy Industry Act under Section 1 EnWG, 111
Energy intensity, 620, 621, 626, 1069, 1125
  economies, 620
Energy-intensive industries, 1160
Energy market, 484, 503, 504, 553
  in Azerbaijan, 484
  liberalisation of, 497, 503
Energy market liberalization, 653
Energy Markets Inspectorate (EMI), 1167
Energy Performance in Buildings Directive (EPBD), 135
Energy policy, 6–7, 14, 190, 570, 621, 624–628, 636, 640, 797, 831, 924, 931, 933–935, 938, 943, 1189–1194, 1196–1204, 1209, 1210, 1257, 1261, 1263, 1298, 1304, 1305, 1314
  in Belgium, 513
  competences for, 520
  developing, 1167
  dominant frame in, 518
  EU, 903
  European, 573–574
  framework 2007–2020, 775
  German, 574–575
  governance, 377
  legislative innovation, 522
  Norwegian, 902
  and politics, 906
Energy poverty, 545, 726, 926, 939, 949, 981, 1132
  access, 68
  affordability, 68
  drivers, 70–71
  income, 71–72
  measures, 68–70
  policy instruments and effectiveness, 73–74
  social rights, 74, 75
Energy saving, 498, 502, 624, 634, 871, 877
  potentials, 838
Energy sector, 484, 485, 488, 492, 493, 496–498, 500, 504
  governance in, 484
  liberalization of, 490, 502
Energy security, 6, 9, 176–178, 268–270, 275, 594, 596, 597, 599, 601, 602, 605, 607, 608, 612, 613, 620, 624, 627, 752, 762, 775, 830, 833–835, 837, 838, 915, 925, 928–930, 934, 937, 1056, 1058, 1062, 1166, 1218, 1221, 1226
  discourse, 1062
Energy Security Action Plan for 2014-2020, 443

Energy Services Regulatory Authority (ERSE), 968
Energy Strategy 2050, 1196, 1205
Energy System Integration, 106
Energy transformation
  citizen participation in, 54–60
  goals, 52
  sustainable, 50
Energy transition, 4, 6, 8, 9, 31, 35, 105, 176, 178, 181, 182, 273, 417, 494, 497, 499, 504, 534, 535, 539, 546, 548–550, 552, 554–558, 621, 626–633, 634, 638–640, 648, 669, 676–678, 681–684, 686, 695–698, 752, 924, 961, 994, 1039, 1218, 1290, 1291, 1294, 1305, 1309
  building sector, 724
  coal phase-out, 1293
  coordination mechanisms and multi-level governance, 943–945
  Denmark, 40–41
  drivers, 938–940
  economic crisis, 719
  electricity market liberalization, 1232–1237
  energy poverty, 726
  European, 1291
  external drivers, 1230–1232
  Germany, 38–39
  governance, 1306, 1308
  historical, 37
  internal driver, 1228–1229
  narrative, 656
  natural gas, 1293, 1299
  policies, 864
  privatization, 719
  renewable energy, 1302
  renewable energy sector, 721–724
  scenarios, 1141
  strategies and instruments, 720–721, 940–943
  tourism, 720
  in transport, 724–725
  variants of, 36
Energy Transition Council, 551
Energy transitions instrument
  energy efficiency, 810
  fiscal regulation mechanisms, 811
  long-term strategies, 808
  regulatory instruments, 808–809
  renewable energy sources support, 809
  soft governance, 811
  white certificates, 810
Ente Nazionale Energia Elettrica (ENEL), 794, 804

Ente Nazionale Idrocarburi (ENI), 794, 805
Environmental Assessment Agency, 874
Environmental Audit Committee, 91
Environmental code, 1174
Environmental impact assessment, 806
Environmental non-governmental organizations (ENGOs), 966
Environmental Project Management Agency, 856
Environmental sustainability, 544, 545
Environmental taxation, 1124, 1245
Environmental think tanks, 603
Environment worth the money, 595, 598, 599
EPSO-G, 852
Equinor, 908
Equity, 9
ESCOs, 810
ESKOM, 224
Esso, 514
Estonia 854, 857
Ethanol, 195
Ethical Europe, 372
EU-Canada relations, 280
EU-Canada summit, 279, 280
EU 2030 Climate and Energy Framework, 844
EU climate goals, 752
EU Commission, 151, 857
EU commitments, 534
EU common energy policy, 842
EU conditionality, 548
EU delegations, 172
EU Directive on Electricity Production from Renewable Energy Sources 2001/77/EC, 522
EU Emissions Trading System (EU ETS), 84, 550, 738, 876, 903
EU energy efficiency directive, 610
EU energy market, 859
EU energy policy 843, 844, 851
EU energy policy agenda, 843
EU energy union, 608
EU external perceptions, 370
EU-imposed climate targets, 762
EU LNG and Storage Strategy, 854
EU-mandated climate
 centrally controlled, 762
 contradictions, 762
 moderately paced, 762
Eurasia, 1226
Eurasian Economic Union (EEU), 440
EU regulative model, 843
Euro-Mediterranean Partnership (EMP), 320
European Atomic Energy Commission (EURATOM), 264, 267, 271, 279

European Atomic Energy Community (EURATOM), 125
European Bank for Reconstruction and Development (EBRD), 448, 1070, 1231
European Coal and Steel Community (ECSC), 125, 264, 266, 267
European Commission, 83, 171, 243–245, 248, 250–252, 350–352, 354, 357, 361, 384, 385, 392, 400, 609, 676, 680, 682, 699, 854
European Commission's Energy Green Paper, 844
European Commission under the Connecting Europe Facility (CEF) 858
European Council, 169
European Court of Justice (ECJ), 926
European Economic Agreement (EEA), 898
European Economic Community (EEC), 125–126, 267
European Emission Trading System (EU ETS), 1159, 1173
European energy governance, 6–8
 coordination mechanisms and multilevel governance, 12–13
 drivers of energy transitions, 11
 instruments, 11–12
 structural conditions and legacies, 8–9
 transition of socio-technical regime, 10–11
European Energy Governance System, 844
European Energy Programme for Recovery, 1056
European Environment Agency (EEA), 88
European environmental policy, 728
European External Action Service (EEAS), 172, 265
European Green Deal (EGD), 7, 138, 164, 181, 368, 370, 373, 380, 391, 399
European integration, 832
European Investment Bank (EIB), 1231
Europeanization, 994, 1230
European Neighborhood Instrument, 322–323
European Neighborhood Policy (ENP), 288–290, 299, 321, 354
European Network of Transmission System Operators Electricity (ENTSO-E), 1230, 1237
European Parliament, 89, 173
European part of Russia, 1021, 1023
European Pressurized Reactor (EPR), 656, 663
European Regional Development Fund (ERDF), 815
European Semester, 555
European states 842, 855

European Union (EU), 11, 215, 316, 412, 413, 655, 661, 663, 680, 682, 699, 701, 751, 994, 1189, 1299
  aims, 164
  air pollution standards, 997
  Algeria, 335
  bilateral cooperation, 320–323
  challenges to external energy, 181–182
  competences on external energy policies, 166–168
  economic competitiveness, 179–181
  Egypt, 336
  energy mix in, 1291
  energy security, 176–178
  energy supply, 317
  environmental sustainability, 178–179
  Euro-Mediterranean Partnership, 324
  external energy instruments, 173–174
  fossil fuels oil and gas, 329–331
  global energy governance landscape, 174–182
  institutional set-up, 170
  Israel, 337
  Jordan, 336
  large combustion plants, 997
  Morocco, 336
  multilateral cooperation, 320
  nuclear energy, 338–340, 1299–1302
  Poland, 1295
  renewables, 332–338
  role of energy in partnership with southern neighborhood, 323–340
  role of institutions external energy policy, 169–170
  solid fossil fuels, 1294–1297
  and southern neighborhood, 319–323
  Sweden, 1304
  Tunisia, 336
European Union energy policy, 122
  cleavage between Northern and Western and (Middle) Eastern member states, 133–135
  competitiveness, 123
  discourses and frames, 123–124
  ECSC treaty, 125
  emergence of sustainability frame, 127–130
  EURATOM Treaty, 125
  European Economic Community, 125
  international energy threats and framing of security, 126–127
  security of supply, 123
  solidarity nexus and security of supply, 130–133
  sustainability, 123

European Union oil, petroleum and natural gas, 1297–1299
European Union's Renewable Energy Directive (RED II), 112
European Union (EU)-Russia energy relations, 238
  developments in gas trade, 245–246
  in historical perspective, 241–242
  Nord Stream 2 controversy, 247–250
  nuclear power, 254–255
  renewable energy, 255–256
  research and debates, 239–241
  trade and Ukraine crisis, 242–245
  TurkStream project, 247
  Ukraine's gas transit role, 250–252
  WTO cases, 253
EUROSTAT, 1245
EU's climate and energy governance, 753
EU strategic narrative, 369–370
  content and levels, 371–373
  narrators, 370–371
  receivers, 371
  Sustainable Energy Europe, 373–378
EU Sustainable Energy Week (EUSEW), 369, 375
2020 and 2030 EU targets, 753
EU-US Energy Council, 277
EU-US energy relations, 276
EU-US Summit, 276, 278
EWE, 1242
Exclusion, 70
Exnovation, 29, 43
Expert institution, 874
Exports, 297, 305
External Action Service (EEAS), 199
External energy policies, European Union
  competences, 166–169
  institutions' role, 169–170
Externalities, 155
External relations, 289
Extreme weather events, 775

F
Far East, 1023, 1029, 1031, 1034
Federal Climate Protection Act, 107
Federal Electricity Commission, 1198
Federalism, 462, 697, 699, 1190–1191
Federal Ministry for Economic Affairs, 92
Federal Office for the Environment, 1197
Federal Office of Civil Aviation, 1197
Federal Office of Transport, 1197
Federal Roads Office, 1197

Federal state, 520
  See also Belgium
Feed-in premium, 578
Feed-in-tariff (FIT), 56, 524, 551, 578, 655, 659, 802, 975–976, 1047, 1060
Final energy consumption, 1111
Financial crisis, 961
Financial independence, 944
Finland, 854
Fiscal federalism, 146–153, 154
Fiscal incentives, 812
Fiscal regulation mechanisms, 811
Flexibility, 106, 110
Flexible demand solutions, 1179
Fluvius, 514
Fluxys, 514
Force for good Europe, 372
Foreign direct investment (FDI), 1241
Foreign investment, 350, 355, 362, 995
Foreign investors, 489, 999
Forerunner, 594, 597, 604, 611, 613, 628, 638
Forest-based bioeconomy, 628
Forest-based industry, 620
Forests, 621, 628, 629, 636–638, 640
Forms of control and ownership, 51
Formulation, 376
Fortum, 1034
Fossil-free electricity system, 1158
Fossil fuel(s), 535, 539, 540, 623–625, 628, 632, 637, 640, 668–673, 677, 687, 694, 701
  subsidies, 86
Fossil resources, 488, 489, 494
Fracking, 929
Fragmentation of global governance, 182
Frame, 378, 380
Framework Agreement, 271, 280
French energy governance
  energy transition narrative, 655–657
  French energy mix, 651–652
  historical legacies, 649–651
  horizontal and vertical coordination, 660–662
  incumbent resilience and evolutions, 652–654
  outcomes, challenges and prospects, 662–664
  from state modernization to climate leadership, 654–655
  strategies, 657–659
French energy policy, 650
French energy transition, 655–662
Fuel oil combustion, 1125

Fuel Quality Directive, 279
Fuel taxes, 1171, 1175
Fukushima, 655, 656, 1200
Fukushima nuclear disaster, 1189
Fund for Environmental Protection and Energy Efficiency (EPEEF), 552

G
G20, 180
G7, 180
Gabčíkovo hydro power plant, 1060
GALP, 969
Gap-filler mechanism, 136
Gas, 38, 239, 242, 329–332, 673, 675, 677–679, 701, 702, 927–929, 933–935, 949
  crises, 349, 355
  developments in gas trade, 245–246
  EU-Russia gas trade, 242–245
  extraction, 864
  prices, 353, 355
  TurkStream project, 247
  Ukraine's transit role, 250–252
2009 gas crisis, 1059
Gas Directive, 249
Gas-power plants, 904
Gasum Oy, 852
Gazifikatsiya Rossii, 1023
Gazprom, 242–248, 250, 252, 354, 361, 612, 825, 854, 1022, 1024, 1025, 1028, 1031–1034, 1063
GDP, 859
General economic interest, 1067
Generational change, 569
Georgia, 298–300
Geothermal energy, 1206
German Energy Industry Act (EnWG), 110, 113
German energy transition, 52
German Federal Network Agency (BNetzA), 110
German government's climate protection plan, 107
Germany, 92, 242, 247–249, 254, 1235
Gestore dei Sistemi Energetici (GSE), 804
Global climate policies and governance, 1027
Global cost-efficiency approach, 898, 901, 903, 905–907, 909, 917
Global energy governance
  economic competitiveness, 176–179
  ECT (*see* Energy Charter Treaty (ECT))
  energy security, 176–178
  environmental sustainability, 178–179

Global energy politics, 164
Global Europe, 372
Global warming, 966
Good sector coupling, 103, 108–114
Governance, 535, 797, 865
　principle, 1159
Governance, energy
　composition of energy mix, 1259–1261
　discourse on energy issues, 1260–1262
　legacies, 1257–1259
　political institutions and actors, 1262–1264
Governmental actors, 935, 936
Government platform, 907
Government Program, 624, 625, 633, 634, 636
Greece
　bureaucracy, 723
　economic crisis, 711, 719
　economic recession, 720
　energy communities, 727
　energy discourses, 713–716
　energy market, 718
　energy mix, 712–713
　energy policy, 727
　energy poverty, 726
　energy reform, 710
　energy sector, 717
　energy security, 720
　energy transition, 719
　lignite, 710, 711
　local and regional authorities, 727
　path dependencies, 711–712
　post lignite era, 716
　public power corporation, 713–716
　transport sector, 724
Green battery, 914
Green certificates, 911, 914, 915
Green certificate scheme, 812
Green coalition, 653–656
Green Deal, 278, 384, 385, 387, 388, 391, 394, 397, 398, 400–401, 412, 680, 879
Green electricity, 469
Green energy technology, 605, 855–856
Green Europe, 368, 372
Green foreign direct investment (GFDI), 1241
Green growth, 595, 872
Greenhouse emissions, 300
Greenhouse gas (GHG), 20, 24, 925, 945
　emissions, 107, 112, 868, 1201, 1232
Green hydrogen, 103, 669
Green party(ies), 654, 655, 968
Greenpeace, 1076
　Mediterranean, 1229
Green polder model, 874

Green School Travel Programme, 783
Green transition, 917
Grid connection, 974
Grid expansion, 57, 1179
Grid tariffs, 914
Groningen gas field, 873
GROWIAN project, 56

H

Hard coal, 925, 926, 930, 931, 938
Heating, 1202–1204
Heavy industry, 621, 636
Heavy vehicle charge, 1207
Hedegaard, Connie, 598
Hidroelectrica, 1003
Hierarchical federalism, 462
High-Level Energy Dialogue, 281
High-Level Group on the Baltic Energy Market Interconnection Plan (BEMIP) 859
Hinkley Point, 90
Historical legacies, 649–651
Historical lock-ins, 761
Hitachi Europe Limited, 847
Höegh LNG 852, 853
Holding Slovenske elektrarne (HSE), 1101
Horizontal coordination, 660
Horizontal governance, 417–419
　integration of, 419–420
Hrazdan River, 447
Human security Europe, 372
Hungarian energy sector
　challenges, 763
　cooking, 745
　energy consumption, 743
　energy transition policy instruments, 758
　space heating, 745
　water heating, 745
Hybrid cars, 1071
Hybrid regime, 739
Hydrocarbon culture, 1024
Hydroelectricity, 652
Hydrogen, 103, 677, 680, 982
Hydropower, 196, 437, 457, 460, 461, 464, 465, 825–829, 831, 832, 838, 962, 996, 1002–1004, 1021–1023, 1038, 1085, 1160, 1188–1190, 1192, 1201, 1204, 1205, 1209, 1210, 1238
　energy, 446–448
　producers, 447
　production, 899, 903
Hydropower plants (HPPs), 1084
Hyundai Heavy Industries, 853

Index

I

ICSID arbitration, 1088
Identity narrative, 373
Ignalina, 1058
Ignalina Nuclear Power Plant 845, 846, 852, 855
Illiberal democracy, 739
Illiberal energy governance, 760
IMF, 1230
Implementation, 662
Implicit powers, 166
Import-dependent hydrocarbon-based energy system, 742
Imports, 305
Import terminal in Būtingė, 851
Incentive(s), 630, 631, 633
  system, 801
Incentive-based instruments, 12
Income poverty, 70, 71, 71–72
Incumbent, 21, 23, 30, 32
Independent regulatory authority, 653
India, 203
  energy dialogue, 203–210
Indicators, 81
Industrial policy, 638, 639, 753
Inefficient, 826
Information and communication technologies (ICTs), 551
Information system for energy management, 553
Infrastructure, 108, 535
  policy-making, 57
Infrax, 514
Innovation, 22, 28, 30, 33, 41, 626, 631
  in solving energy challenges, 1167
Institution, 21, 24, 26, 30, 34
Institutional adaptations, 865
Institutional capacity, 456, 457, 535
Institutional change, 33–35, 42
Institutional instability, 486–487, 493, 503
Institutionalized collaboration, 1168
Institutional "lock-ins", 663
Institutional reforms, 493, 498
Institutional transition, 34
Instrument(s), 627, 629, 629–633, 636, 640
  mix, 632
Instrument for pre-Accession Assistance (IPA), 1230
Integrated energy system, 106
Integrated National Energy and Climate Plans (iNECPs), 136, 151
Integration, 104, 1257, 1272
  of renewable energy, 109

Intended nationally determined contributions (INDCs), 1248
Intercommunales, 521
Interconnection gas pipeline, 543
Interdependence, 239, 241, 242
Interest groups, 571
Interference with nature, 838
Intergovernmental logic, 169
Intergovernmental Panel on Climate Change (IPCC), 85
Intermittent energy, 626
  production, 639
Internal Energy Market, 126, 349, 350, 353, 354, 357
International Atomic Energy Agency (IAEA), 281
International Civil Aviation Organization (ICAO), 86
International Energy Agency (IEA), 176, 268, 270, 272, 281, 282, 350, 362, 1220
International Energy Charter (IEC), 348, 349, 356, 357, 361, 362
International Energy Forum (IEF), 177, 282
International investment, 484, 488
International investors, 997
International Marine Organization (IMO), 86
International Maritime Organization, 82
International Monetary Fund, 772
International Renewable Energy Agency (IRENA), 179, 281, 282, 362, 930
Inter-sectoral energy flow, 108
Intraclass correlation (ICC) coefficients, 393
Investment, 550, 556, 761
Investor State Dispute Settlement (ISDS), 349, 358–360
IPS/UPS (Integrated Power System/Unified Power System) 857
Iran, 1222
Ireland
  agencification, 776
  Bord na Móna, 774
  challenges, 785–786
  Climate Action and Low Carbon Development Act, 777
  Climate Change Advisory Council, 771
  Commission for Regulation of Utilities, 777
  Corrib gas field, 774
  delegation, 776
  Department of Communications, Climate Action and Environment, 776
  economic crisis, 771
  electricity generation, 780–781
  electricity interconnectors, 773

Ireland (*cont.*)
  Electricity Supply Board, 778
  electric vehicle, 778
  on energy, 775
  energy policy, 775–776
  energy transition (*see* Irish energy transition)
  2015 Energy White Paper, 770
  gross energy consumption, 772–773
  heating, 781–782
  Kinsale Head gas field, 774
  nuclear power, 773
  peat supply, 774
  per capita emissions, 785
  pharmaceutical industry, 772
  population density, 772
  single electricity market, 777
  Sustainable Energy Authority of Ireland, 778
  transport, 782–784
  veto players, 770
Irish energy transition
  carbon tax, 780
  electricity generation, 780–781
  EU 2020 climate and energy package, 779
  heating, 781–782
  national adaptation framework, 780
  national planning framework, 780
  transport, 782–784
  UK Climate Change Act, 779
Island of Krk, 548
Italian Commission for Nuclear Energy (CNEN), 798
Italian energy transition
  drivers, 806–808
  instruments, 808–813
Italy, 1235
  centralized governance, 801
  competitiveness, 799–800
  coordination mechanisms, 814
  decarbonization framework, 818
  decentralized governance, 801
  discourse, 797
  distributed generation, 802
  district heating and cooling, 804, 812
  electric utilities, 798
  energy balance, 795
  energy independence, 813
  energy policy, 797
  energy transition (*see* Italian energy transition)
  Europeanization, 808
  incumbents matter, 794
  issues, 797–802
  liberalization, 799–800
  lock-ins energy system, 794
  multi-level governance, 814–816
  nuclear discourse, 797
  path dependence, 793–795
  political institutions and actor, 802–805
  renewable energy sources sector, 801
  security of supply, 797–799
  societal debate, 797
  streamline permission, 806
  sustainable energy paths, 801

J

Jaslovské Bohunice V1 NPP, 1059
Jean-Claude Juncker Commission, 1064
Jens Stoltenberg, 907
Jukos, 1025

K

Kaliningrad Oblast of the Russian Federation, 857
Klaipėda LNG terminal, 853
Klaipėda Port, 854
Klaipėdos Nafta, 852
Klimaatakkoord, 865
Kozloduy, 1058
Krško Nuclear Power Plant, 553, 1087, 1103
Kruskal-Wallis test, 390, 395
Kyoto Protocol, 270, 282, 539, 868, 909, 1196, 1244

L

Laboratory federalism, 147, 154
Landscape, 22, 23, 31, 39, 41, 42, 1044
Land Use, Land Use Change and Forestry (LULUCF) Regulation, 621, 629, 637, 638, 1113
Large industry energy network, 782
Latvenergo, 831
Latvia, 824, 846, 854, 855, 857
  coordination mechanisms and multilevel governance, 836–837
  discourse on energy issues, 829–830
  diversification, 829
  energy efficiency, 830
  energy independence, 832
  energy mix, composition of, 826–829
  energy regulation goals, 832
  European integration, 832

Index

general conditions of energy governance, 824–832
lack of natural resources, 830
legacies/path dependencies, 824–826
outcomes, challenges and prospects of energy governance, 838
political institutions, 830–832
social surveys, 833
strategies and instruments of energy transition, 834–836
Latvijas Gāze, 831
Layering, 34, 42
Leadership, 662
Lebanon, 337
LESTO, 853
Liberalization, 594, 603, 607, 608, 653, 867, 970–972, 1189, 1194
 of energy market, 534, 978
Liberal Party, 598
Lietuvos Dujos 846, 852, 853
Lietuvos Dujų Tiekimas, 853
Lietuvos Energija 852, 853
Life-cycle greenhouse gas emissions, 114
Lifestyle change, 835
Liga, 853
Lignite, 668–670, 673, 675, 687, 688, 925, 926, 928–931, 939, 944, 1038
 extraction, 714
 plant construction, 716
 production, 713
 public power corporation, 711
Liquefied natural gas (LNG), 277, 279, 1221, 1247
Liquefied petroleum gas (LPG), 1219
Lisbon Treaty, 82, 123, 166, 264, 973
Lithuania
 Baltic (Russian Federation) 849–850
 challenges 858–860
 composition of energy mix, 845
 energy policy 843–844
 Green energy 855–856
 issues of the Lithuanian energy transition 850–851
 LNG terminal 853–854
 Nord Stream 2 854–855
 nuclear power 845–847
 oil and gas infrastructure 851–853
 Ostrovets Nuclear Power Plant 849–850
 outcomes 858–860
 Republic of Belarus 849–850
 synchronization of electricity network with EU networks, 857
 threats 847–848

Lithuania 2030 Strategy, 851
Lithuanian economy, 842
Lithuanian energy, 858
Lithuanian energy governance, 843
Lithuanian energy policy 849, 858, 860
Lithuanian energy sector 844, 850, 859
Lithuanian gas sector, 853
Lithuanian Ministry of Energy, 859
Lithuanian National Energy Independence Strategy, 844
Lithuanian National Energy Strategy, 855
Lithuanian national security, 849
LNG terminal, 540, 543, 853–854
Lobby, 1256, 1259, 1264–1266
Lobbying, 582
Local authorities, 661
Local governments, 551
Lock-in, 21, 22, 752
Long-Term Development Strategy for 2014-2025, 443
Loop flows, 569
Low carbon, 1141
 economy, 1147
 road maps, 1176
Low-carbon energy, 535
 transition, 546, 761
Low-carbon transition, 512
 policies, 1165
Low emissions vehicles, 611
Low income/high cost indicator (LIHC), 68
Low-income households, 72
Lukoil, 1025, 1031

M

Majority, 1210
Manhattan Project, 515
Mann-Whitney-U test, 391, 397
Market design, 568
Market economy, 484, 548
Market integration, 567
Market liberalization, 974
Market power Europe, 372
Maroš Šefčovič, 1063
Marshall Plan, 265, 266
Mažeikiai nafta group, 851
Mažeikiai Refinery, 851
Medgrid, 326
Media discourse, 966
Median energy bill, 69
Median income, 69
Mediterranean Solar Plan (MSP), 325
Medium-term climate plan, 626, 629, 640

Medvedev, 1031
Medzamor, 433
Meliti II, 716
Metaphors, 377
Methodological framework, 191
Mátra Power Plant, 744
'Metrosexual power' Europe, 372
Mexico, 85
MIBEL, 971
Micro-hydro power, 1010
Micro-producers, 975
Middle East, 1226
Middle East and North Africa (MENA) countries, 322, 339
Miners, 997, 999
Mineworkers, 518
Mini-contracting, 73
Minister of Foreign Affairs, 855
Ministry of Coal (MoC), 205
Ministry of Commerce, 212
Ministry of Commerce of China (MOFCOM), 211
Ministry of Economy, 830
Ministry of Economy and Sustainable Development (MESD), 552
Ministry of Energy, 7, 850, 1024, 1030
Ministry of Energy and Natural Resources (MENR), 1227
Ministry of Energy of Lithuania, 852
Ministry of Environment and Urbanization (MoEU), 1229
Ministry of External Relations (MRE), 197
Ministry of Finance of Lithuania, 852
Ministry of Foreign Affairs (MFA), 212
Ministry of Mines and Energy (MME), 197
Ministry of Natural Resources and the Environment, 1024, 1030
Ministry of New and Renewable Energies (MNRE), 205
Ministry of Petroleum and Natural Gas (MoPNG), 205
Ministry of Power (MoP), 205
Mixed economy, 669
Mobility, 679, 681–683, 693–695, 697, 702, 1188, 1196, 1197, 1199–1202, 1207–1208
Modernization process of energy efficiency, 451
Moldova, 300–303
Mongstad, 913
Monitoring commission, 875
Monitoring cost, 84
Monitoring mechanism, 88, 89

Monitoring, reporting and verification (MRV), 82
Monitoring, review and verification (MRV), 84
Monopolist, 484
Motor tax, 783
Movement, 29, 41
Multi-energy system, 106
Multilateral institutions, 1177
Multilateralism, 369
Multilevel energy governance, 281–283
Multi-level governance, 412, 415, 416, 613–614, 800, 807, 924, 937, 943–945, 1132–1133
  municipal level, 816
  national level, 814
  regional level, 815–816
  supranational level, 814
Multi-level-perspective (MLP), 23, 33, 36, 39, 604, 1044
Multi-party system, 906
Multipolar world, 190
Municipal actors, 979
Municipalities, 603, 606, 625, 627, 636, 934, 938, 939, 944, 948, 949, 1190, 1198
Mutual self-commitment, 886

N
Nabucco pipeline project, 132
Naftogaz, 1063
Nagorno-Karabakh conflict, 434
Narratives, 30, 649
Narrators, 370, 379
National Action Plan (NAP), 808
National adaptation framework, 780
National Adaptation Plan 2021-2030, 442
National and Energy Climate Plan, 1002
National Audit Office, 90
National consultation, 655
National Control Commission for Prices and Energy, 856
National Development and Reform Commission (NDRC), 212
National Dialogue on Climate Action, 776
Nationale Klimainitiative, 92
National Energy Administration (NEA), 211, 212
National Energy and Climate Plan (NECP), 7, 549, 744, 754, 834, 1071, 1093, 1094, 1100, 1138
National energy efficiency action plan (NEEAP), 448, 1230
National Energy Program, 1093

Index

National Energy Regulatory Council (NERC) 858
National Energy Strategy (NES), 792, 808, 846
National Integrated Energy and Climate Action Plans, 844
Nationalizations, 650, 741, 750
National Low Carbon Strategy, 658
National mitigation plan (NMP), 777
National Nuclear Energy Agency (CNEN), 797
National Plan for Recovery and Resilience, 1012
National planning framework, 780
National Policies and Measures System (SPeM), 979
National Renewable Energy Laboratory, 444
National renewables target, 915, 1066
National Roads Authority, 779
National security, 937
National stakeholders, 979
National Strategy for Energetic Independence, 859
National Strategy for the Development of Renewable Energy Sources, 856
National targets, 1170
National Transport Authority (NTA), 779
NATO, 268–270, 272, 275, 280, 282
Natural gas, 306, 433, 437, 460, 1022, 1126, 1148, 1192, 1219–1221, 1290, 1297–1299, 1305
  storage, 1247
  systems, 799
Nearly zero energy buildings, 781
Negotiation democracy, 865, 867, 886, 887
Neighborhood Investment Facility (NIF), 322
Neo-corporatist pattern, 867
Neoliberal developmentalist model, 1218, 1247
Neoliberal structuring agenda, 1233
Netherlands, 864
  Energy Governance in, 865–867
  energy transitions issues, 875–885
Network(s), 418
  analysis, 192
  of cities for climate, 1141
Neutrality targets, 901
New Arctic and East Siberian greenfield locations, 1032
New policy instruments, 659
Niche, 22, 28, 30, 33, 37, 39–41, 1044
Nigeria, 1222
Non-ETS sectors, 611, 903
Non-for-profit principle, 594, 603, 607

Non-governmental organizations (NGOs), 86, 1001, 1007, 1085, 1086, 1090, 1101, 1229
Nonstate actors, 978
Nord Pool, 607, 608
Nord Stream 1, 304–305, 612
Nord Stream 2, 247–250, 306, 613, 854–855
Nord Stream 2 AG v. European Union, 359, 361
Nord Stream, 928
Normative Power Europe, 372
Norm diffusion and policy transfer, 1218
Northern Delivery, 1028, 1030
North Sea oil, 594, 596, 599
Northwest Russia, 1029, 1034
Norwegian Politics, 906, 907, 917
Novatek, 1025
Nuclear, 306, 338–340, 928, 930, 931, 946, 1022, 1023, 1025, 1028, 1029, 1034
  decommissioning, 1064
  disaster, 1196
  phase-out, 512, 515, 522, 529, 530, 1293
  reactor, 515
Nuclear energy, 457, 460, 465, 566, 623, 624, 628, 639, 648, 650–652, 654–656, 663, 670, 674, 675, 677, 681, 685, 1056, 1061, 1064, 1065, 1077, 1090, 1103, 1193, 1230, 1299–1302, 1311
  regime, 35
Nuclear power, 24, 28, 36, 40, 254–255, 795, 962, 1007, 1062, 1260, 1266
  closure of, 1179
  criticism of, 1160
  electricity from CHP, 1162
  expansion of, 1160
  interest in, 1160
  issue of, 1164
  losses in, 1161
  role of, 1162, 1181
  Sweden, 1158
Nuclear Power Law of the Republic of Lithuania, 846
Nuclear power plants (NPP), 451, 797, 1056

O

OECD Oil Committee, 268
Offsetting, 909
Offshore wind parks, 608
Off-shore wind projects, 525
Oil, 241, 242, 245, 298, 329–331, 457, 458, 460, 465, 963, 1020–1023, 1025, 1028, 1032–1034, 1219, 1297–1299
  crises, 87, 866, 870
  and gas sector, 484, 494, 496

Oil (*cont.*)
   and natural gas, domestic production of, 1061
   price crisis, 519
   prices, 491, 494, 495
   production, 487, 491, 494
   replacement, 1160
   revenues, 489, 494, 495
   storage activities, 1246
1973 oil crisis, 650
1973 Oil price crisis, 268
Ombla Hydro Power Project, 546
OMV, 1242
One Planet Summit in Paris, 1068
Onshore wind power, 973
"On the main areas of Government policy to raise the energy efficiency of electric power from renewable energy sources for the period to 2020", 1028, 1030
"On the mechanism of promoting the use of renewable energies in the wholesale electricity market and power", 1029, 1030
OPAL pipeline, 253
Open method of coordination (OMC), 150
Orbán, Viktor (Prime Minister), 738
Orchestration, 420, 423, 424
Organization for Economic Co-operation and Development (OECD), 78, 267, 270, 272, 282, 1068
Organization for European Economic Co-operation (OEEC), 268, 272, 282
Organization of Petroleum Exporting Countries (OPEC), 350
Organization of the Petroleum Exporting Countries (OPEC), 177, 268, 281, 282
OSCE, 850
Ostrovets Nuclear Power Plant 849–850
Ostrovets Power Plant, 850
Ottoman Empire, 1218

P

Paks Nuclear Power Plant, 744, 749
Paldiski LNG, 854
Palestine, 337
Paradigm, 1260, 1269
   shift, 605, 613
Paradiplomacy, 274
Paris Agreement, 85, 93, 270, 273, 278, 282, 361, 441, 661, 869, 924, 931, 937
Paris Climate Summit, 1197
Paris Conference (COP 21), 1248
Paris Rulebook, 94

Parliament, 625, 627, 633, 640
Participation, 663, 1191, 1211
Participatory governance, 51, 52–54, 865
Participatory innovations, 54
Parties, 1200
Partnership for market readiness (PMR), 1232
Path dependency, 8, 22, 26–27, 697, 865, 887, 1021–1022, 1305, 1313
Patrimonial patterns, 503
Peat, 623–625, 628, 632, 634, 635
People-Animals-Nature (PAN), 968
Petoro, 909
PETROBRAS, 200
Petrofina, 514
Petroleum policy, 907
Petrom, 1006
Photovoltaic(s), 20, 24, 39, 672, 676, 691, 701, 1205
   technology, 445
Photovoltaic systems (PV), 795
Pioneership, 602
Planning, 658, 661
Platform for Coal Regions in Transition, 1068
Poland, 238, 241, 248, 857
Polder model, 867
Policy entrepreneurship, 912
Policy evaluation, 83
Policy instrument, 659, 879
Policy integration, 660
Policy learning, 632, 640
Policy-making, 648, 650, 657, 659, 966
Policy monitoring, 78
   administrative task,, 81–84
   future research, 93–94
   Germany, 91–92
   United Kingdom, 90–91
Policy narrative, 655
Policy network, 650
Policy paradigm, 1256, 1265, 1268, 1276
Polish energy companies, 937
Polish Prime Minister Mateusz Morawiecki, 855
Political conflict, 84
Political institutions, 491–494
Political parties, 967
Political regulation, 58, 59
Political will, 542, 546, 548
Politicization, 1008
Polluter pays principle, 1048
Polyphony, 371
Poor housing, 70
Popular initiatives, 1191
Portuguese Energy Association (APE), 970

Index

Portuguese Environmental Agency (APA), 968
Portuguese renewable energy plan, 973
Post-Washington consensus, 1233
Power, 20, 24–26, 30, 31, 38, 40
Power plants, 488, 492, 496–498
Primary energy consumption, 490
Primary energy production, 489, 900
Primary energy resources, 485, 487, 489
Principles, 108, 110
Privatization, 491, 492, 495, 496, 501, 534, 539, 545, 548, 653, 741, 1237
Procedural fairness, 54
Production subsidies, 630, 633
Productivist, 650
Projection, 375, 376–377
Projects of Common Interest, 1056
Proportional representation, 906
Ptolemaida V, 716
Public acceptance, 51, 57, 62
Public consultation, 657
Public debate, 657
Public participation, 657
Public Power Corporation (PPC)
 economic crisis, 714
 lignite, 714
 privatization, 710, 714, 718
Public protest, 50, 57
Public service, 650, 654
Public service obligations (PSO), 609
Public Services Regulatory Commission (PSRC), 439
Public transport, 1207
Public utilities, 650
Putin, Valdimir, 1024, 1025, 1027, 1031

Q
Quota obligation, 1174

R
Railway Procurement Agency, 779
RA Law on Energy, 439
RAPL, 514
Reception, 375, 377–378
REC system, 1174, 1175
REC Turkey, 1230
Reduction target, 834
Referendum, 799, 1191
Referral procedure, 1168
REFIT 1, 780
REFIT 2, 781
REFIT 3, 781
Regime, 22

Regional authorities, 979
Regional Baltic LNG Terminal, 853
Regional Economic Integration Organisation (REIO), 354, 356, 357
Regional Gas Market Coordination Group (RGMCG) 858
Regional governments, 551, 800
Regulator, electricity, 1167
Regulatory authority, 803
Relevant national circumstances, 1109
Reliable data, 557
Renewable(s), 298, 460, 464, 466, 467–469, 540, 542, 549, 551, 555, 557, 652, 662, 754, 924, 925, 929, 933, 938–940, 944–946, 948, 949
 and alternative energy, 485
 hydrogen, 1313
 support scheme, 899
Renewable electricity support scheme (RESS), 781
Renewable energy(ies), 9, 11–14, 20, 24, 28, 30, 36, 39, 51, 89, 195, 255–256, 292, 360, 384, 385, 390, 392, 400, 401, 414, 433, 442–443, 497, 498, 500, 597, 601, 605, 607–609, 611, 620, 625, 626, 628, 629, 633–635, 637, 639, 663, 668, 669, 672, 673, 676, 681, 682, 688, 690, 692, 693, 697–699, 960, 1207, 1230, 1238, 1302–1305
 auctions, 977–978
 broad diffusion of, 1158
 capacity of, 1165
 directive, 384, 392, 396, 400, 783
 domestic transport, 1163
 employment, 1240
 expansion of, 1178
 investment, 1130
 legislation, 1239
 penetration, 1143
 policy, 806
 power sector based on, 1178
 promotion of, 1046
 sector, 718, 721–724, 1241
 share of, 1162
 support schemes, 961
 system goals, 58
 target, 540
 technologies, 50, 51, 54, 56
 technology, 1238
 transformations, 50
 transitions, 60
 in Turkey, 1239
 use of, 1180

Renewable Energy Certificates (REC), 1159
Renewable energy communities (REC), 550, 817
Renewable Energy Resources Zones (RE-ZONE), 1239
Renewable energy sources (RES), 324–326, 792, 795, 925, 929, 940, 944, 948, 1020, 1021, 1023, 1026–1028, 1030–1034, 1038, 1084
Renewable energy sources support (RES support), 1242
Rent-seeking, 566
Representative democracy, 53, 57, 58
Republic of Belarus 847, 849–850, 857
Republic of Karelia, 1032, 1033
Republic of Poland, 924
Research and development (R&D), 794, 1169
  activities, 1239
Resource, 23, 25, 27, 30, 36
Reticent attitude, 838
Retro-fitting, 73, 74
Revolving door phenomena, 582
Ribbon development, 514
Right of First Refusal (ROFR), 353
Right to energy, 74, 75
Rising powers, 190
Romania
  challenges for energy governance, 1010–1012
  conditions of energy governance, 995–1001
  drivers of energy transition, 1001–1002
  energy discourses, 999–1001
  energy mix, 997–998
  hydro power, 1002–1004
  nuclear sector, 1007–1010
  past legacies, 995–997
  renewables, 1004–1007
Rome Euro-Mediterranean Energy Platform (REMEP), 325
Rosatom, 1024, 1025, 1029, 1031, 1034
Rosneft, 354, 1024, 1025, 1031, 1034
Rotterdam, 514
Route diversification, 1056
Rulebook, 85, 86
Rule export, 174
Russia, 237, 297, 739, 760, 824–826, 828–830, 832, 837, 846, 855, 857, 1000, 1222, 1248
  energy governance in (see Energy governance, in Russia)
Russia-centric geopolitical relations, 762
Russia-friendly element, 750
Russian Far North, 1028, 1030

Russian Federation, 857
Russian gas, 1243
Russian geopolitical interests, 850
Russian State Atomic Energy Corporation (Rosatom), 254–255
Russia-policy, 748
Russia-Ukraine conflict, 304

S

Salience, 385, 387, 389–391, 393, 398–399, 401–402
Sanctions, 297
Savinjsko Šaleška region, 1106
Science and Technology Studies (STS), 21
Science-policy interaction, 871
SDE+ scheme, 879
Sector(s), 107
  integration, 557
Sector coupling, 102–106, 113, 114, 668, 673, 678, 683, 694
  of future, 112
Security, 349, 350, 361, 362
  of demand, 1023
  of energy supply, 654
  of supply, 113, 202, 374, 539, 542, 544, 546, 549, 1023, 1024, 1030
Self-sufficiency, 566
Self-sufficient, 600
Sentiments, 377
Seven Sisters, 267, 268
Shadow of hierarchy, 886
Shale revolution, 270, 275–277
Shared competencies, 273
Shell, 514
Shock therapy, 925
Siberian part of Russia, 1021
Single authorization, 809
Single electricity market (SEM), 777
Single European Act (SEA), 166, 972
Sinks, 629, 637, 638
Slovakia, 1066
Slovenia, 1084, 1086, 1087, 1089, 1092, 1102, 1105, 1107
  challenges, 1114
  coal-phase out, 1092, 1106, 1107
  Covid-19, 1115
  diversified energy mix, 1084
  electromobility, 1112, 1113
  energy concept, 1094
  energy efficiency, 1110, 1111
  energy mix, 1088, 1090
  energy policy, 1103

Index   1339

energy policy discourse, 1090
EU ETS, 1113
external drivers, 1102
human resources, 1114
legacies, 1085–1088
legal framework, 1093, 1094
multi-level perspective, 1102
NECP, 1094
NGOs, 1101
non-ETS sector, 1113
nuclear energy, 1090, 1103–1106
policy coordination, 1101, 1102
political actors, 1094, 1100
public opinion, 1103
radioactive waste, 1104
renewable energy, 1107–1109
RES, 1092
self-supply, 1109
transport, 1112
Slovenský plynárenský priemysel (SPP), 1057
Smarter Travel Areas Pilot Programme, 783
Smarter Travel Campus Programme, 783
Smarter Travel Workplaces Programme, 783
Social and Economic Council, 864
Social Democratic Party, 601
Social dimensions of energy system, 50
Social Europe, 372
Social inequality, 70, 75
Socialist Federative Republic Yugoslavia (SFRY), 534, 535
Social media, 369, 375, 376
Social movement, 21, 27, 29
Social rights, 74, 75
Social science energy research, 1208
Social security, 72, 74
Social surveys, 833
Société Générale de Belgique, 513
Socio-technical regime, 21–23, 25, 1039
Socio-technical transition, 23, 638
Soft governance, 811
Solar auctions, 982
Solar energy, 445–446, 998
Solar photovoltaics, 753
Solar power, 964, 1045
Solar PV systems, 756
Solar sources, 445
Solid fossil fuels, 1294–1297
SONI, 778
Šoštanj TPP, 1106
South Africa, 220
    energy dialogue, 220–228
Southern Gas Corridor (SGC), 1226, 1230, 1248

South-South cooperation, 201
South Stream, 354
Sovereign Wealth Funds (SWFs), 362
Soviet government, 492
Soviet legacy, 485
Soviet times, 491
Soviet Union, 241, 293, 740, 824, 855, 996
Spain, 1235
    climate change, 1123
    competition, 1133
    consumption demand, 1148
    costs, 1134
    electricity links, 1143
    energy dependency, 1122
    energy efficiency, 1142
    energy imbalances, 1122
    energy island, 1122
    energy policy, 1139
    energy supply potential, 1149
    energy transition (*see* Spanish energy transition)
    environmental organizations, 1139
    governance of energy policy, 1125
    infrastructure, 1135
    interconnection, 1123
    interest groups, 1133
    local governments, 1137
    market, 1137
    multilevel governance, 1132–1133
    nuclear safety, 1135
    Paris agreement, 1143
    regulation, 1134
    renewable energy investment, 1130
    self-consumption, 1139
    single market for energy, 1149
    solar, 1138
    sustainability, 1122
    sustainability policies, 1141
    sustainable energy transition, 1124
    technological development, 1143
    transparency, 1135
Spanish energy system
    consumption, 1125
    demand, 1148
    demand planning, 1127
    energy consumption, 1127
    energy intensity, 1125
    energy poverty, 1132
    financing, 1132
    high energy dependence, 1125
    integration, 1134
    investors, 1131
    legacies, 1125

Spanish energy system (*cont.*)
  legitimacy, 1131
  lobby groups, 1133
  political power, 1137
  strategic of sector, 1137
  subsidies, 1124
  sun tax, 1124
  tariff deficit, 1123
  transition, 1123
  unregulated activities, 1130
  vulnerable, 1125
Spanish energy transition
  combined cycle, 1139
  electric transport, 1140
  funding, 1141
  generation capacity, 1139
  institutional collaboration, 1141
  interconnections, 1143
  local entities, 1142
  long-term, 1139
  mountainous topography, 1145
  population, 1146
  regional administration, 1141
  services consumption, 1146
  snap election, 1141
  tourism sectors, 1146
  unions, 1138
  unstable political environment, 1134
  Winter Package, 1139
Spatial planning, 57–59
Stability, 25–32
Stakeholder(s), 385, 387, 388, 390, 393, 872, 1197, 1198, 1200, 1205, 1211
Standardization of monitoring procedures, 83
State-aid regulations, 915
State aid scheme, 1109
State Energy Regulation Service, 853
State-led governance, 935, 937, 943
State-owned companies, 491–493, 496, 501, 502
State-owned enterprises (SOEs), 206, 362
State support, 753
Statism, 742
Statkraft, 905
Statoil, 908
Steering instruments, 1202
Strategic action fields (SAF), 23, 33, 38–40, 42
Strategic communication, 373
Strategic narratives, EU, 369–370
  content and levels, 371–373
  narrators, 370–371
  receivers, 371
  Sustainable Energy Europe, 373–378

Strategic Partners, 193
Strategic Partnership, 190, 193, 194, 203, 220, 229
Strategic Partnership Agreement, 280
Strategic Petroleum Reserve (SPR), 1246
Strategic planning system, 557
Strategic urbanism, 419
Strategy, 658
Subsidiarity, 1190
Subsidies, 974, 1190
Subsidization, 761, 1204
Subsidizing prices, 749
Suburbanization, 514
Suez, 513
Suez Crisis, 267
Sun tax, 1124
Supply reliability, 1206
Supply security, 750, 1196
Support scheme(s), 755
  for renewable heat, 782
Survey, 192
Sustainability, 4, 7, 9, 20, 28, 43, 113, 178–179, 203, 368, 371–379, 414, 416, 542, 544–546, 915
Sustainable, 628, 634, 637–639
  development, 377
  energy development, 832
  energy paths, 801
  energy systems, 1134
  energy transformations, 50
Sustainable Development Goals, 361
Sustainable Energy Act 2002, 778
Sustainable Energy Action Plans (SEAP), 816, 938
Sustainable Energy and Climate Action Plans (SECAP), 421
Sustainable Energy Authority of Ireland (SEAI), 778
Sustainable Energy Europe, issue-specific narrative
  formulation, 376
  life-cycle of narratives, 375–378
  projection, 376–377
  reception, 377–378
  structure, 373–375
Sustainable Europe, strategic narrative, 369–370
  content and levels, 371–373
  narrators, 370–371
  receivers, 371
  Sustainable Energy Europe, 373–378
Sweden, 846
  climate ambitions, 1159

Index

discourse on energy issues, 1164
electricity production, 1162
fossil-free electricity system, 1158
governance principle, 1159
local authorities, 1168
state and industry in, 1169
Swiss Federal Nuclear Safety Inspectorate, 1198
Swiss Federal Office of Energy (SFOE), 1197
Swiss political system, 1190
Switzerland, energy governance
  cantonal level, 1198
  climate policy, 1196–1197
  coordination, 1209
  direct democracy, 1191–1192
  electricity, 1204–1207
  energy sector, 1199
  energy transition, 1201–1209
  environmental and climate organizations, 1200
  federalism, 1190–1191
  heating, 1202–1204
  interest groups, 1199–1200
  liberalization of the Swiss electricity market, 1194–1196
  mobility, 1207–1208
  municipal level, 1198–1199
  national level, 1197–1198
  natural framework conditions, 1192–1193
  nuclear energy debate, 1196
  research, 1208
  state institutions and stakeholders, 1197–1199
  system of concordance, 1192
System, 22, 31, 37, 40, 43
  narrative, 373
Systemic governance risk, 182

T
Take-or-pay contracts, 1221
Tallinn LNG, 854
TANAP, 1226
TATENA, 850
2030 targets, 550
Targets, 658, 661
20-20-20 targets, 876
Tariff policy, 502
Taxation, 630–632, 634
Tax deductions, 879, 1171
Tax policy, 1245
Tax subsidies, 632

Technical Assistance to the Commonwealth of Independent States (TACIS) programme, 289, 291
Technocratic elites, 650
Technological innovations, 866
Technological 'lock-in, 1044
Technological neutral policy, 605
Technological solutions, 835
Technology-neutrality, 113
Technology-neutral scheme, 911
Technology standards, 905
TEDAŞ, 1231
Territorialization, 664
Texaco, 514
The Energy Law, 445
The post-Washington consensus, 1233
Thermal account, 809
Thermal efficiency, 71, 74
Thermal insulation, 72
  in building sector, 1069
Thermoelectric generation, 795
"The scheme of the territorial planning of the Russian Federation in the field of energy", 1029, 1030
Third Energy Package 851, 852
Third Gas Directive, 357
Third Party Access (TPA), 351, 353
Top-down approach, 760
Total energy consumption, 620, 641
Total primary energy supply, 541
Town gas, 514
TPAO, 1227
Tractebel, 521
Tradable green certificate (TGC) system, 524
Transatlantic energy relations, 273–275
  Canada, 278–281
  United States, 275–278
Transatlantic Marketplace, 280
Transatlantic Trade and Investment Partnership (TTIP), 350, 359
Trans-European networks, 122
Transfer of operating rights (TOOR) schemes, 1233
Transformation, 33, 35, 43, 869, 880
Transformative Europe, 372
Transformer of energy, 1144
Transit dispute settlement, 355
Transition, 22, 23, 32–35, 621, 626–633, 634, 638, 639, 641, 1267
  management, 864
  narrative, 649, 658, 662
  path, 792, 872
Transit Protocol, 349, 353–356

Trans-local action space, 419
Transmission grid, 908
Transmission system, 1174
Transnational municipal networks, 417
Transnuklear scandal, 519
Transparency, 82, 91
Transport, 527, 620, 630–632, 634, 640
  policy, 83, 915
Transportation sector, 981
Transport-efficient society, 1180
Treaty of Lisbon, 374
Treaty of Rome, 87, 267
Treaty on the Functioning of the European Union, 82
Turkey
  coordination mechanisms and issues of multilevel governance, 1244–1247
  discourses/narratives on energy policy, 1223–1227
  drivers of energy transition, 1228–1232
  ecological sustainability/energy equity, 1226–1227
  energy security and competitiveness, 1226
  natural gas pipelines and projects, 1221
  natural gas storage, 1247
  oil storage activities, 1246
  strategies and instruments of energy transitions, 1232–1244
Turkey Sustainable Energy Financing Facility (TurSEFF), 1231
Turkish Foundation for Combating Soil Erosion, 1229
Turkish Petroleum Refineries Corporation (TUPRAS), 1246
Turkish Stream, 1226
Turkmenistan, 1222
TurkStream project, 247
Twitter, 369, 373, 375–379

U

UK Climate Change Act, 779
Ukraine, 303–307, 829
  crisis, 242–245
  gas transit role, 250–252
Unbundling, 353, 357, 534, 653
  energy companies, 876
  of monopolies, 800
UNCITRAL, 355
Unconventional oil, 279
Underinvestment, 995
UNDP, 1230
Unecha junction, 851

Union for the Co-ordination of Transmission for Electricity (UCTE), 539
Union for the Mediterranean (UfM), 318, 320, 324, 326
Union Minière, 514
United Nations Framework Convention on Climate Change (UNFCCC), 80, 85–87, 178, 844, 1071, 1230, 1244
United States, 266–270, 275–278, 283
Uranium, 271
Urbanization, 377
Urban planning, 514
Urgenda Climate Case, 887
U.S. Agency for International Development, 449
USD, 1241
US Dollar, 1221
U.S. Steel Košice, 1078
Utility prices, 748
  reductions, 750

V

Value conflicts, 58
Varieties of capitalism approach, 943
Vehicle registration tax (VRT), 783
Vehicle tax, 1175
Velenje coal mine, 1107
Ventspils Oil Terminal, 851
Vertical coordination, 660
Vertical governance, 415–416
  integration of, 419–420
Virtual power plants, 982
Vlaamse Regulator voor Elektriciteit en Gas (VREG), 521
Vojany, Elektrárne, 1062
Volatile renewable energy, 105
Voluntary agreements, 1176
Von der Leyen, Ursula, 368
Vulnerable consumers, 72–74

W

Washington Consensus, 1233
Water management, 865
Weakness of public administration, 555
Weapons of mass destruction (WMD), 338
Western Balkans, 1040
Westinghouse, 518
White certificates (WhCs), 811
Wind, 929, 930, 939, 940, 946, 998
  energy, 51, 57, 443–444, 594, 659, 962, 1047, 1205
  farms, 835
Windmills, 604

Index

Wind power, 28, 39, 40, 444, 668, 672, 677, 681, 688, 690, 691, 701, 1026, 1029, 1034, 1038
   development, 1167
   employment, 885
   plant, 755, 1084
Winter fuel payments, 73, 74
Winter mortality, 70
Winter Package, 1139, 1143
World Bank, 448, 1231, 1232, 1249
World Trade Organization (WTO), 180, 272, 275, 276, 348
World Wildlife Fund-Turkey, 1229
WWF, 909

Y

Yamal LNG, 246, 247
Yellow vests, 658, 660
Yugoslavia, 1040
Yukos, 355

Z

Zasavje, 1106
Zeebrugge, 512
Zero energy buildings, 810